Encyclopedia of World Cultures

Volume IX

Africa and the Middle East

Encyclopedia of World Cultures

David Levinson
Editor in Chief

North America
Oceania
South Asia
Europe (Central, Western, and Southeastern Europe)
East and Southeast Asia
Russia and Eurasia / China
South America
Middle America and the Caribbean
Africa and the Middle East
Index

The *Encyclopedia of World Cultures* was prepared under the auspices and with the support of the Human Relations Area Files at Yale University. HRAF, the foremost international research organization in the field of cultural anthropology, is a not-for-profit consortium of twenty-three sponsoring members and 300 participating member institutions in twenty-five countries. The HRAF archive, established in 1949, contains nearly one million pages of information on the cultures of the world.

Encyclopedia of World Cultures

Volume IX

AFRICA AND THE MIDDLE EAST

John Middleton and Amal Rassam
Volume Editors

Candice Bradley and Laurel L. Rose
Associate Volume Editors

G.K. Hall & Co.
Boston, Massachusetts

MEASUREMENT CONVERSIONS

When You Know	Multiply By	To Find
LENGTH		
inches	2.54	centimeters
feet	30	centimeters
yards	0.9	meters
miles	1.6	kilometers
millimeters	0.04	inches
centimeters	0.4	inches
meters	3.3	feet
meters	1.1	yards
kilometers	0.6	miles
AREA		
square feet	0.09	square meters
square yards	0.8	square meters
square miles	2.6	square kilometers
acres	0.4	hectares
hectares	2.5	acres
square meters	1.2	square yards
square kilometers	0.4	square miles

TEMPERATURE
°C = (°F − 32) ÷ 1.8
°F = (°C × 1.8) + 32

First published 1995
by G.K. Hall & Co., an imprint of Macmillan Inc.
866 Third Avenue
New York, NY 10022

10 9 8 7 6 5 4 3 2 1

Library of Congress Cataloging-in-Publication Data
(Revised for volume 9)

Encyclopedia of world cultures.

Includes bibliographical references, filmographies, and indexes.
Contents: v. 1. North America / Timothy J. O'Leary, David Levinson, volume editors — [etc] — v. 9 Africa and the Middle East / John Middleton and Amal Rassam, volume editors.
1. Ethnology—Encyclopedias. I. Levinson, David, 1947-
GN307.E53 1991 306'.097 90-49123
ISBN 0-8161-1840-X (set : alk. paper)
ISBN 0-8161-1808-6 (v. 1 : alk. paper)

Library of Congress Cataloging-in-Publication Data
ISBN 0-8161-1815-9 (v. 9 : alk. paper)

The paper used in this publication meets the minimum requirements of American National Standard for Information Sciences—Permanence of Paper for Printed Library Materials. ANSI Z39.48-1984. ∞™
MANUFACTURED IN THE UNITED STATES OF AMERICA

Contents

Project Staff

Research
Patricia D. Andreucci
Bonnie Dyer-Bennet
Ronald Johnson

Editorial and Production
Victoria Crocco
Elly Dickason
Abraham Maramba
Ara Salibian
L. C. Salibian
Christine Wright

Cartography
Robert Sullivan
Rhode Island College

Editorial Board

Contributors

J. Abbink
Institut voor Culturele en Sociale Antropologie
Katholieke Universiteit
Nijmegen
The Netherlands
Falasha; Suri

Ray G. Abrahams
Department of Social Anthropology
Cambridge University
Cambridge
United Kingdom
Nyamwezi and Sukuma

Ifi Amadiume
Department of Religion
Dartmouth College
Hanover, New Hampshire
United States
Ibibio; Igbo

Nawal H. Ammar
Department of Criminal Justice
Kent State University
Kent, Ohio
United States
Nubians

Ronald R. Atkinson
Department of History.
University of South Carolina
Columbia, South Carolina
United States
Acholi

Kevin Avruch
Department of Sociology and Anthropology
George Mason University
Fairfax, Virginia
United States
Jews of Israel

Joëlle Bahloul
Department of Anthropology
Indiana University
Bloomington, Indiana
United States
Jews of Algeria

Sandra T. Barnes
Department of Anthropology
University of Pennsylvania
Philadelphia, Pennsylvania
United States
Yoruba

Alan A. Bartholomew
Library
Albertus Magnus College
New Haven, Connecticut
United States

Turks

Daniel G. Bates
Department of Anthropology
Hunter College of the City University of New York
New York, New York
United States

Yörük

Dan F. Bauer
Department of Anthropology and Sociology
Lafayette College
Easton, Pennsylvania
United States

Tigray

Lois Beck
Department of Anthropology
Washington University
St. Louis, Missouri
United States

Qashqa'i

John M. Beierle
Human Relations Area Files
New Haven, Connecticut
United States

Dogon

Paula Girshick Ben-Amos
Department of Anthropology
Indiana University
Bloomington, Indiana
United States

Edo

Barbara A. Bianco
Social Science Research Council
New York, New York
United States

Pokot

Paul Bohannan
Three Rivers, California
United States

Tiv

Emile Boonzaier
Department of Social Anthropology
University of Cape Town
Rondebosch Cape
South Africa

Khoi

M. F. C. Bourdillon
Department of Sociology
University of Zimbabwe
Mount Pleasant, Harare
Zimbabwe

Shona

Candice Bradley
Lawrence University
Appleton, Wisconsin
United States

Luyia

John W. Burton
Department of Anthropology
Connecticut College
New London, Connecticut
United States

Anuak; Dinka; Nuer; Shilluk

Annette Busby
San Rafael, California
United States ***Kurds***

Peter Carstens
University College
University of Toronto
Toronto
Canada ***Cape Coloureds***

Dawn Chatty
The Sultanate of Oman ***Bedouin***

Sumi Colligan
Department of Sociology, Anthropology, and Social Work
North Adams State College
North Adams, Massachusetts
United States ***Karaites***

Elizabeth Colson
Department of Anthropology
University of California, Berkeley
Berkeley, California
United States ***Tonga***

Richard T. Curley
Department of Anthropology
University of California, Davis
Davis, California
United States ***Lango***

Michael M. Donovan
Brooklyn, New York
United States ***Kipsigis***

Vernon R. Dorjahn
Department of Anthropology
University of Oregon
Eugene, Oregon
United States ***Temne***

Susan Drucker-Brown
Department of Social Anthropology
Cambridge University
Cambridge
United Kingdom ***Mamprusi***

Gerald M. Erchak
Department of Anthropology, Sociology, and Social Work
Skidmore College
Saratoga Springs, New York
United States ***Kpelle***

Caesar E. Farah
Department of History
University of Minnesota
Minneapolis, Minnesota
United States ***Chaldeans; Jacobites; Maronites; Nestorians; Syriacs***

Pamela Feldman-Savelsberg
Department of Sociology and Anthropology
Carleton College
Northfield, Minnesota
United States ***Bamiléké***

Gregory A. Finnegan
Tozzer Library
Harvard University
Cambridge, Massachusetts
United States

Mossi

Jean-Gabriel Gauthier
Laboratoire de l'Anthropologie
Université de Bordeaux I
Talence
France

Fali

Michelle Gilbert
Guilford, Connecticut
United States

Akan

Eva Gillies
Lewes, Sussex
United Kingdom

Zande

Jack Glazier
Department of Anthropology
Oberlin College
Oberlin, Ohio
United States

Mbeere

Jack Goody
St. Johns College
Cambridge University
Cambridge
United Kingdom

Lobi-Dagarti Peoples

N. Thomas Hakansson
Department of Anthropology
University of Kentucky
Lexington, Kentucky
United States

Gusii

C. R. Hallpike
Department of Anthropology
McMaster University
Hamilton, Ontario
Canada

Konso

Rosemary Harris
Department of Anthropology
University College London
London
United Kingdom

Yakö

David M. Hart
Garrucha (Almería)
Spain

Berbers of Morocco

Bernhard Helander
Department of Cultural Anthropology
University of Uppsala
Uppsala
Sweden

Somalis

Barry S. Hewlett
Department of Anthropology
Washington State University
Pullman, Washington
United States

Tropical-Forest Foragers

Deborah James
Department of Social Anthropology
University of Witwatersrand
Witwatersrand
South Africa

Pedi

Ronald Johnson
Human Relations Area Files
New Haven, Connecticut
United States

Afrikaners; Arabs; Asians of Africa; Assyrians; Basseri; Karamojong; Lozi; Lur; Mangbetu; Mongo; Persians

Ivan Karp
Department of Anthropology
National Museum of Natural History
Smithsonian Institution
Washington, D.C.
United States

Iteso

Michael G. Kenny
Department of Sociology and Anthropology
Simon Fraser University
Burnaby, British Columbia
Canada

Nyakyusa and Ngonde

Igor Kopytoff
Department of Anthropology
University of Pennsylvania
Philadelphia, Pennsylvania
United States

Suku

Conrad P. Kottak
Department of Anthropology
University of Michigan
Ann Arbor, Michigan
United States

Betsileo

Corinne A. Kratz
Institute of African Studies
Emory University
Atlanta, Georgia
United States

Okiek

Robert O. Lagacé
Hamden, Connecticut
United States

Wolof

Robert Launay
Department of Anthropology
Northwestern University
Evanston, Illinois
United States

Dyula

Herbert S. Lewis
Department of Anthropology
University of Wisconsin
Madison, Wisconsin
United States

Jews of Yemen

Laurence D. Loeb
Department of Anthropology
University of Utah
Salt Lake City, Utah
United States

Jews of Iran

J. Terrence McCabe
Department of Anthropology
University of Colorado at Boulder
Boulder, Colorado
United States

Turkana

Wyatt MacGaffey
Haverford College
Haverford, Pennsylvania
United States

Kongo

Simon D. Messing
Hamden, Connecticut
United States

Amhara

Barbara J. Michael
Department of Anthropology
University of Alabama—Birmingham
Birmingham, Alabama
United States

Baggara

John Middleton
Department of Anthropology
Yale University
New Haven, Connecticut
United States

Lugbara; Swahili

Karen Middleton
Oxford University
Oxford
United Kingdom

Tandroy

S. G. Mjema
Tampere
Finland

Zaramo

Sally Falk Moore
Department of Anthropology
Harvard University
Cambridge, Massachusetts
United States

Chagga

Jean-Claude Muller
Department of Anthropology
University of Montreal
Montreal, Quebec
Canada

Rukuba

Regina Smith Oboler
Ursinus College
Collegeville, Pennsylvania
United States

Nandi and Other Kalenjin Peoples

Thomas M. Painter
Atlanta, Georgia
United States

Zarma

Deborah Pellow
Department of Anthropology
Syracuse University
Syracuse, New York
United States

Hausa

Pierre Petit
Institut de Sociologie
Université Libre de Bruxelles
Brussels
Belgium

Luba of Shaba

James Anthony Pritchett
African Study Center
Boston University
Boston, Massachusetts
United States

Lunda

Aparna Rao
Institut für Völkerkunde
Universität zu Köln
Cologne
Germany

Ghorbat; Peripatetics of Afghanistan, Iran, and Turkey; Peripatetics of Iraq, Syria, Lebanon, Jordan, Israel, Egypt, Sudan, and Yemen; Peripatetics of the Maghreb; Sleb

Susan J. Rasmussen
Department of Anthropology
University of Houston
Houston, Texas
United States

Tuareg

S. P. Reyna
Department of Anthropology
University of New Hampshire
Durham, New Hampshire
United States

Bagirmi; Sara

Laurel L. Rose
Pittsburgh, Pennsylvania
United States

Swazi

Judy Rosenthal
Department of Anthropology
University of Michigan—Flint
Flint, Michigan
United States

Ewe and Fon

Yona Sabar
Near Eastern Languages and Cultures
University of California, Los Angeles
Los Angeles, California
United States

Jews of Kurdistan

Frank A. Salamone
Iona College
New Rochelle, New York
United States

Fulani

Sabina Shahrokhizadeh
Chicago, Illinois
United States

Zoroastrians

Seteney Shami
Institute of Archaeology and Anthropology
Yarmouk University
Irbid
Jordan

Circassians

Lesley A. Sharp
Department of Anthropology
Barnard College
Columbia University
New York, New York
United States

Sakalava

Katherine A. Snyder
Tryon, North Carolina
United States

Iraqw

Jacqueline S. Solway
Comparative Development Studies
Trent University
Peterborough, Ontario
Canada

Tswana

Léon de Sousberghe
Namur
Belgium

Pende

Aidan Southall
Tocane-St.-Apre
France

Alur

Paul Spencer
School of Oriental and African Studies
University of London
London
United Kingdom

Maasai

Paul Stoller
Department of Anthropology and Sociology
West Chester University
West Chester, Pennsylvania
United States

Songhay

Ghada Hashem Talhami
Department of Politics
Lake Forest College
Lake Forest, Illinois
United States

Palestinians

Richard Tapper
School of Oriental and African Studies
University of London
London
United Kingdom

Shahsevan

Edith L. B. Turner
Department of Anthropology
University of Virginia
Charlottesville, Virginia
United States

Ndembu

Chris J. Van Vuuren
University of South Africa
Pretoria, Gauteng
South Africa

Ndebele

Frank Robert Vivelo
Wharton County Junior College
Wharton, Texas
United States

Herero

Delores M. Walters
Department of Anthropology and Sociology
Lake Forest College
Lake Forest, Illinois
United States

Yemenis

Roy G. Willis
Department of Social Anthropology
University of Edinburgh
Edinburgh
Scotland

Fipa

Edwin N. Wilmsen
African Studies Center
Boston University
Boston, Massachusetts
United States

San-Speaking Peoples

Peter J. Wilson
Department of Anthropology
University of Otago
Dunedin
New Zealand

Tsimihety

Walter P. Zenner
Department of Anthropology
State University of New York at Albany
Albany, New York
United States

Jews, Arabic-Speaking; Jews of the Middle East

Preface

This project began in 1987 with the goal of assembling a basic reference source that provides accurate, clear, and concise descriptions of the cultures of the world. We wanted to be as comprehensive and authoritative as possible: comprehensive, by providing descriptions of all the cultures of each region of the world or by describing a representative sample of cultures for regions where full coverage is impossible, and authoritative by providing accurate descriptions of the cultures for both the past and the present.

The publication of the *Encyclopedia of World Cultures* in the last decade of the twentieth century is especially timely. The political, economic, and social changes of the past fifty years have produced a world more complex and fluid than at any time in human history. Three sweeping transformations of the worldwide cultural landscape are especially significant.

First is what some social scientists are calling the "New Diaspora"—the dispersal of cultural groups to new locations across the world. This dispersal affects all nations and takes a wide variety of forms: in East African nations, the formation of new towns inhabited by people from dozens of different ethnic groups; in Micronesia and Polynesia, the movement of islanders to cities in New Zealand and the United States; in North America, the replacement by Asians and Latin Americans of Europeans as the most numerous immigrants; in Europe, the increased reliance on workers from the Middle East and North Africa; and so on.

Second, and related to this dispersal, is the internal division of what were once single, unified cultural groups into two or more relatively distinct groups. This pattern of internal division is most dramatic among indigenous or third or fourth world cultures whose traditional ways of life have been altered by contact with the outside world. Underlying this division are both the population dispersion mentioned above and sustained contact with the economically developed world. The result is that groups who at one time saw themselves and were seen by others as single cultural groups have been transformed into two or more distinct groups. Thus, in many cultural groups, we find deep and probably permanent divisions between those who live in the country and those who live in cities, those who follow the traditional religion and those who have converted to Christianity, those who live inland and those who live on the seacoast, and those who live by means of a subsistence economy and those now enmeshed in a cash economy.

The third important transformation of the worldwide cultural landscape is the revival of ethnic nationalism, with many peoples claiming and fighting for political freedom and territorial integrity on the basis of ethnic solidarity and ethnic-based claims to their traditional homeland. Although most attention has focused recently on ethnic nationalism in Eastern Europe and the former Soviet Union, the trend is nonetheless a worldwide phenomenon involving, for example, American Indian cultures in North and South America, the Basques in Spain and France, the Tamil and Sinhalese in Sri Lanka, and the Tutsi and Hutu in Burundi, among others.

To be informed citizens of our rapidly changing multicultural world we must understand the ways of life of people from cultures different from our own. "We" is used here in the broadest sense, to include not just scholars who study the cultures of the world and businesspeople and government officials who work in the world community but also the average citizen who reads or hears about multicultural events in the news every day and young people who are growing up in this complex cultural world. For all of these people—which means all of us—there is a pressing need for information on the cultures of the world. This encyclopedia provides this information in two ways. First, its descriptions of the traditional ways of life of the world's cultures can serve as a baseline against which cultural change can be measured and understood. Second, it acquaints the reader with the contemporary ways of life throughout the world.

We are able to provide this information largely through the efforts of the volume editors and the nearly one thousand contributors who wrote the cultural summaries that are the heart of the book. The contributors are social scientists (anthropologists, sociologists, historians, and geographers) as well as educators, government officials, and missionaries who usually have firsthand research-based knowledge of the cultures they write about. In many cases they are the major expert or one of the leading experts on the culture, and some are themselves members of the cultures. As experts, they are able to provide accurate, up-to-date information. This is crucial for many parts of the world where indigenous cultures may be overlooked by official information seekers such as government census takers. These experts have often lived among the people they write about, conducting participant-observations with them and speaking their language. Thus they are able to provide integrated, holistic descriptions of the cultures, not just a list of facts. Their portraits of the cultures leave the reader with a real sense of what it means to be a "Taos" or a "Rom" or a "Sicilian."

Those summaries not written by an expert on the culture have usually been written by a researcher at the Human Relations Area Files, Inc., working from primary source materials.

The Human Relations Area Files, an international educational and research institute, is recognized by professionals in the social and behavioral sciences, humanities, and medical sciences as a major source of information on the cultures of the world.

Uses of the Encyclopedia

This encyclopedia is meant to be used by a variety of people for a variety of purposes. It can be used both to gain a general understanding of a culture and to find a specific piece of information by looking it up under the relevant subheading in a summary. It can also be used to learn about a particular region or subregion of the world and the social, economic, and political forces that have shaped the cultures in that region. The encyclopedia is also a resource guide that leads readers who want a deeper understanding of particular cultures to additional sources of information. Resource guides in the encyclopedia include ethnonyms listed in each summary, which can be used as entry points into the social science literature where the culture may sometimes be identified by a different name; a bibliography at the end of each summary, which lists books and articles about the culture; and a filmography at the end of each volume, which lists films and videos on many of the cultures.

Beyond being a basic reference resource, the encyclopedia also serves readers with more focused needs. For researchers interested in comparing cultures, the encyclopedia serves as the most complete and up-to-date sampling frame from which to select cultures for further study. For those interested in international studies, the encyclopedia leads one quickly into the relevant social science literature as well as providing a state-of-the-art assessment of our knowledge of the cultures of a particular region. For curriculum developers and teachers seeking to internationalize their curriculum, the encyclopedia is itself a basic reference and educational resource as well as a directory to other materials. For government officials, it is a repository of information not likely to be available in any other single publication or, in some cases, not available at all. For students, from high school through graduate school, it provides background and bibliographic information for term papers and class projects. And for travelers, it provides an introduction into the ways of life of the indigenous peoples in the area of the world they will be visiting.

Format of the Encyclopedia

The encyclopedia comprises ten volumes, ordered by geographical regions of the world. The order of publication is not meant to represent any sort of priority. Volumes 1 through 9 contain a total of about fifteen hundred summaries along with maps, glossaries, and indexes of alternate names for the cultural groups. The tenth and final volume contains cumulative lists of the cultures of the world, their alternate names, and a bibliography of selected publications pertaining to those groups.

North America covers the cultures of Canada, Greenland, and the United States of America.

Oceania covers the cultures of Australia, New Zealand, Melanesia, Micronesia, and Polynesia.

South Asia covers the cultures of Bangladesh, India, Pakistan, Sri Lanka and other South Asian islands and the Himalayan states.

Europe covers the cultures of Europe.

East and Southeast Asia covers the cultures of Japan, Korea, mainland and insular Southeast Asia, and Taiwan.

Russia and Eurasia / China covers the cultures of Mongolia, the People's Republic of China, and the former Union of Soviet Socialist Republics.

South America covers the cultures of South America.

Middle America and the Caribbean covers the cultures of Central America, Mexico, and the Caribbean islands.

Africa and the Middle East covers the cultures of Madagascar and sub-Saharan Africa, North Africa, the Middle East, and south-central Asia.

Format of the Volumes

Each volume contains this preface, an introductory essay by the volume editor, the cultural summaries ranging from a few lines to several pages each, maps pinpointing the location of the cultures, a filmography, an ethnonym index of alternate names for the cultures, and a glossary of scientific and technical terms. All entries are listed in alphabetical order and are extensively cross-referenced.

Cultures Covered

A central issue in selecting cultures for coverage in the encyclopedia has been how to define what we mean by a cultural group. The questions of what a culture is and what criteria can be used to classify a particular social group (such as a religious group, ethnic group, nationality, or territorial group) as a cultural group have long perplexed social scientists and have yet to be answered to everyone's satisfaction. Two realities account for why the questions cannot be answered definitively. First, a wide variety of different types of cultures exists around the world. Among common types are national cultures, regional cultures, ethnic groups, indigenous societies, religious groups, and unassimilated immigrant groups. No single criterion or marker of cultural uniqueness can consistently distinguish among the hundreds of cultures that fit into these general types. Second, as noted above, single cultures or what were at one time identified as single cultures can and do vary internally over time and place. Thus a marker that may identify a specific group as a culture in one location or at one time may not work for that culture in another place or at another time. For example, use of the Yiddish language would have been a marker of Jewish cultural identity in Eastern Europe in the nineteenth century, but it would not serve as a marker for Jews in twentieth-century United States, where most speak English. Similarly, residence on one of the Cook Islands in Polynesia would have been a marker of Cook Islander identity in eighteenth century, but not in the twentieth century when two-thirds of Cook Islanders live in New Zealand and elsewhere.

Given these considerations, no attempt has been made to develop and use a single definition of a cultural unit or to develop and use a fixed list of criteria for identifying cultural units. Instead, the task of selecting cultures was left to the volume editors, and the criteria and procedures they used are discussed in their introductory essays. In general, however, six criteria were used, sometimes alone and sometimes in combination to classify social groups as cultural groups: (1) geographical localization, (2) identification in the social science literature as a distinct group, (3) distinct language, (4) shared traditions, religion, folklore, or values, (5) maintenance of group identity in the face of strong assimilative pressures, and (6) previous listing in an inventory of the world's cultures such as *Ethnographic Atlas* (Murdock 1967) or the *Outline of World Cultures* (Murdock 1983).

In general, we have been "lumpers" rather than "splitters" in writing the summaries. That is, if there is some question about whether a particular group is really one culture or two related cultures, we have more often than not treated it as a single culture, with internal differences noted in the summary. Similarly, we have sometimes chosen to describe a number of very similar cultures in a single summary rather than in a series of summaries that would be mostly redundant. There is, however, some variation from one region to another in this approach, and the rationale for each region is discussed in the volume editor's essay.

Two categories of cultures are usually not covered in the encyclopedia. First, extinct cultures, especially those that have not existed as distinct cultural units for some time, are usually not described. Cultural extinction is often, though certainly not always, indicated by the disappearance of the culture's language. So, for example, the Aztec are not covered, although living descendants of the Aztec, the Nahuatl-speakers of central Mexico, are described.

Second, the ways of life of immigrant groups are usually not described in much detail, unless there is a long history of resistance to assimilation and the group has maintained its distinct identity, as have the Amish in North America. These cultures are, however, described in the location where they traditionally lived and, for the most part, continue to live, and migration patterns are noted. For example, the Hmong in Laos are described in the Southeast Asia volume, but the refugee communities in the United States and Canada are covered only in the general summaries on Southeast Asians in those two countries in the North America volume. Although it would be ideal to provide descriptions of all the immigrant cultures or communities of the world, that is an undertaking well beyond the scope of this encyclopedia, for there are probably more than five thousand such communities in the world.

Finally, it should be noted that not all nationalities are covered, only those that are also distinct cultures as well as political entities. For example, the Vietnamese and Burmese are included but Indians (citizens of the Republic of India) are not, because the latter is a political entity made up of a great mix of cultural groups. In the case of nations whose populations include a number of different, relatively unassimilated groups or cultural regions, each of the groups is described separately. For example, there is no summary for Italians as such in the Europe volume, but there are summaries for the regional cultures of Italy, such as the Tuscans, Sicilians, and Tirolians, and other cultures such as the Sinti Piemontese.

Cultural Summaries

The heart of this encyclopedia is the descriptive summaries of the cultures, which range from a few lines to five or six pages in length. They provide a mix of demographic, historical, social, economic, political, and religious information on the cultures. Their emphasis or flavor is cultural; that is, they focus on the ways of life of the people—both past and present—and the factors that have caused the culture to change over time and place.

A key issue has been how to decide which cultures should be described by longer summaries and which by shorter ones. This decision was made by the volume editors, who had to balance a number of intellectual and practical considerations. Again, the rationale for these decisions is discussed in their essays. But among the factors that were considered by all the editors were the total number of cultures in their region, the availability of experts to write summaries, the availability of information on the cultures, the degree of similarity between cultures, and the importance of a culture in a scientific or political sense.

The summary authors followed a standardized outline so that each summary provides information on a core list of topics. The authors, however, had some leeway in deciding how much attention was to be given each topic and whether additional information should be included. Summaries usually provide information on the following topics:

CULTURE NAME: The name used most often in the social science literature to refer to the culture or the name the group uses for itself.

ETHNONYMS: Alternate names for the culture including names used by outsiders, the self-name, and alternate spellings, within reasonable limits.

ORIENTATION

Identification. Location of the culture and the derivation of its name and ethnonyms.

Location. Where the culture is located and a description of the physical environment.

Demography. Population history and the most recent reliable population figures or estimates.

Linguistic Affiliation. The name of the language spoken and/or written by the culture, its place in an international language classification system, and internal variation in language use.

HISTORY AND CULTURAL RELATIONS: A tracing of the origins and history of the culture and the past and current nature of relationships with other groups.

SETTLEMENTS: The location of settlements, types of settlements, types of structures, housing design, and materials.

ECONOMY

Subsistence and Commercial Activities. The primary methods of obtaining, consuming, and distributing money, food, and other necessities.

Industrial Arts. Implements and objects produced by the culture either for its own use or for sale or trade.

Trade. Products traded and patterns of trade with other groups.

Division of Labor. How basic economic tasks are assigned by age, sex, ability, occupational specialization, or status.

Land Tenure. Rules and practices concerning the allocation of land and land-use rights to members of the culture and to outsiders.

KINSHIP

Kin Groups and Descent. Rules and practices concerning kin-based features of social organization such as lineages and clans and alliances between these groups.

Kinship Terminology. Classification of the kinship terminological system on the basis of either cousin terms or generation, and information about any unique aspects of kinship terminology.

MARRIAGE AND FAMILY

Marriage. Rules and practices concerning reasons for marriage, types of marriage, economic aspects of marriage, postmarital residence, divorce, and remarriage.

Domestic Unit. Description of the basic household unit including type, size, and composition.

Inheritance. Rules and practices concerning the inheritance of property.

Socialization. Rules and practices concerning child rearing including caretakers, values inculcated, child-rearing methods, initiation rites, and education.

SOCIOPOLITICAL ORGANIZATION

Social Organization. Rules and practices concerning the internal organization of the culture, including social status, primary and secondary groups, and social stratification.

Political Organization. Rules and practices concerning leadership, politics, governmental organizations, and decision making.

Social Control. The sources of conflict within the culture and informal and formal social control mechanisms.

Conflict. The sources of conflict with other groups and informal and formal means of resolving conflicts.

RELIGION AND EXPRESSIVE CULTURE

Religious Beliefs. The nature of religious beliefs including beliefs in supernatural entities, traditional beliefs, and the effects of major religions.

Religious Practitioners. The types, sources of power, and activities of religious specialists such as shamans and priests.

Ceremonies. The nature, type, and frequency of religious and other ceremonies and rites.

Arts. The nature, types, and characteristics of artistic activities including literature, music, dance, carving, and so on.

Medicine. The nature of traditional medical beliefs and practices and the influence of scientific medicine.

Death and Afterlife. The nature of beliefs and practices concerning death, the deceased, funerals, and the afterlife.

BIBLIOGRAPHY: A selected list of publications about the culture. The list usually includes publications that describe both the traditional and the contemporary culture.

AUTHOR'S NAME: The name of the summary author.

Maps

Each regional volume contains maps pinpointing the current location of the cultures described in that volume. The first map in each volume is usually an overview, showing the countries in that region. The other maps provide more detail by marking the locations of the cultures in four or five subregions.

Filmography

Each volume contains a list of films and videos about cultures covered in that volume. This list is provided as a service and in no way indicates an endorsement by the editor, the volume editor, or the summary authors. Addresses of distributors are provided so that information about availability and prices can be readily obtained.

Ethnonym Index

Each volume contains an ethnonym index for the cultures covered in that volume. As mentioned above, ethnonyms are alternative names for the culture—that is, names different from those used here as the summary headings. Ethnonyms may be alternative spellings of the culture name, a totally different name used by outsiders, a name used in the past but no longer used, or the name in another language. It is not unusual that some ethnonyms are considered degrading and insulting by the people to whom they refer. These names may nevertheless be included here because they do identify the group and may help some users locate the summary or additional information on the culture in other sources. Ethnonyms are cross-referenced to the culture name in the index.

Glossary

Each volume contains a glossary of technical and scientific terms found in the summaries. Both general social science terms and region-specific terms are included.

Special Considerations

In a project of this magnitude, decisions had to be made about the handling of some information that cannot easily be standardized for all areas of the world. The two most troublesome matters concerned population figures and units of measure.

Population Figures

We have tried to be as up-to-date and as accurate as possible in reporting population figures. This is no easy task, as some groups are not counted in official government censuses, some groups are very likely undercounted, and in some cases the definition of a cultural group used by the census takers differs from the definition we have used. In general, we have relied on population figures supplied by the summary authors. When other population data sources have been used in a volume, they are so noted by the volume editor. If the reported figure is from an earlier date—say, the 1970s—it is usually because it is the most accurate figure that could be found.

Units of Measure

In an international encyclopedia, editors encounter the problem of how to report distances, units of space, and temperature. In much of the world, the metric system is used, but scientists prefer the International System of Units (similar to the metric system), and in Great Britain and North America the English system is usually used. We decided to use English measures in the North America volume and metric measures in the other volumes. Each volume contains a conversion table.

Acknowledgments

In a project of this size, there are many people to acknowledge and thank for their contributions. In its planning stages, members of the research staff of the Human Relations Area Files provided many useful ideas. These included Timothy J. O'Leary, Marlene Martin, John Beierle, Gerald Reid, Delores Walters, Richard Wagner, and Christopher Latham. The advisory editors, of course, also played a major role in planning the project, and not just for their own volumes but also for the project as a whole. Timothy O'Leary, Terence Hays, and Paul Hockings deserve special thanks for their comments on this preface and the glossary, as does Melvin Ember, president of the Human Relations Area Files. Members of the office and technical staff also must be thanked for so quickly and carefully attending to the many tasks a project of this size inevitably generates. They are Erlinda Maramba, Abraham Maramba, Victoria Crocco, Nancy Gratton, and Douglas Black. At Macmillan and G.K. Hall, the encyclopedia has benefited from the wise and careful editorial management of Elly Dickason, Elizabeth Kubik, and Elizabeth Holthaus, and the editorial and production management of Ara Salibian.

Finally, I would like to thank Melvin Ember and the board of directors of the Human Relations Area Files for their administrative and intellectual support for this project.

DAVID LEVINSON

References

Murdock, George Peter (1967). *Ethnographic Atlas*. Pittsburgh: University of Pittsburgh Press.

Murdock, George Peter (1983). *Outline of World Cultures*. 6th rev. ed. New Haven: Human Relations Area Files.

Introduction to Africa

This introduction provides some basic information as background for the detailed accounts of the particular cultures that follow. The cultures have been selected to represent Africa, in the sense that they include the larger and better-known cultures or clusters of cultures out of the more than two thousand cultures that compose the complex entity that we call "African civilization."

The Peoples and Their Classification

The peoples of Africa may be classified according to several criteria, probably the oldest of which is race. Africa is occupied by members of the Negroid race, the most numerous; then by members of the Caucasoid race, mainly in northern and southern Africa; the Mongoloid race (in Madagascar); and by the so-called Bushmanoid and Pygmoid races or subraces. Previous work in this field has shown the difficulties and contradictions that result from using the concept of "race," and it is clear that this criterion does not contribute to an understanding of the cultures and identities of African societies.

Most attempts at physical or racial classification refer back to earlier efforts to understand the origins and development of humans in various parts of Africa. Paleontological search for the origins of humankind in Africa has a long history, over the course of which it has become virtually certain that the first humans originated in Africa. Paleontologists have discovered skeletal remains (often the merest fragments) of ever-earlier apes and hominids. Remains of various types of apes date back to about 25 million years ago, mainly in southern and eastern Africa, where the limestone deposits are ideal sites for preservation of this material. A primate in the hominid line of descent, known as Ramapithecus, has been found in eastern Africa dating back perhaps 14 million years, and even earlier types are being discovered in Ethiopia. Toolmaking species of hominids have been found in South Africa and at Olduvai Gorge in Tanzania that date back about 5 million years. One of these, a slender form, has been named Australopithecus africanus; the other, a larger and later form, is called Australopithecus robustus (a variant species from Olduvai is known as Zinjanthropus). The more modern types, Homo habilis and Homo erectus, developed in East Africa by about a million years ago, by which time the Australopithecus types had become extinct. Neanderthal forms in northeastern Africa evolved about 60,000 years ago. Many other modern forms that developed since then have been found, merging into modern hominids. About 35,000 years ago, the African Middle Stone Age marked the spread of modern humans throughout Africa.

Despite efforts to portray the hunting and gathering Bushmen of southwestern Africa as the living representatives of earlier types, little direct evidence has been derived from tracing of Bushmanoid ancestors. It had been assumed that the contemporary Bushman economy is the same as that of prehistory, but these rather simplistic and at times racist evolutionist views have little foundation. It is reasonable to suppose that there must have been some kind of ancestral linkages, both in physical development over countless generations and also in cultural development. However, the immensely long periods of slow human development—during which variations in climate and the availability of resources occurred, resulting in continual migrations of people throughout the continent—imply so many changes that any direct descendance can hardly be proved.

A more meaningful classification is based on language. During the eighteenth and nineteenth centuries, it was surmised that African languages, of which some knowledge had been percolating to Europe since at least the sixteenth century, were among the most "primitive," an expectation that was never supported by evidence. Philologists were the first Europeans to try to classify African peoples by "tribe" (or similar terms), which they defined as a "territorially limited language group."

Most of the linguistic hypotheses were based not only on language but also on the kind of diffusionist hypotheses that confused language affiliation, economy, and forms of government. The most influential was the so-called Hamitic Theory, according to which there was a link between pastoralism, divine or sacred kingship, and the Hamitic languages. The "tribes" that had all three were thought to to be of common ancient-Egyptian ancestry. Similar diffusionist theories are continually being presented, the most influential today being that associated with a Senegalese scholar, Cheikh Anta Diop, who claims that ancient-Egyptian civilization was "Black" African and that it was the source of Mediterranean and Greek civilization. There is no supporting evidence for these suggestions.

After many increasingly sophisticated attempts to classify African languages had been made, Joseph H. Greenberg (1963) offered a classification that, with a few minor revisions, has generally been accepted. This classification is based solely on linguistic criteria and comprises the following groups:

Niger-Kordofanian, which is divided into Niger-Congo and Kordofanian. The Niger-Congo languages (comprising the largest African language cluster) are spoken from Senegal to the Congo region and throughout central, eastern, and southern Africa, dispersed through the Bantu languages. They include, from west to east, the subgroups known as West Atlantic, Mande, Voltaic, Kwa, Benue-Congo, and Adamawa-Eastern. Kordofanian comprises fifteen languages that are spoken only in a small area of southwestern Sudan.

Nilo-Saharan, stretching along the savannas from the Middle Niger to the Nile. These languages include several that are spoken in the Upper Niger–Lake Chad region.

Hamito-Semitic, or Afro-Asiatic, including Ancient Egyptian, Berber, Chadic, the Hamitic languages of northern and Saharan Africa, and the Semitic and Cushitic languages of northeastern Africa.

Khoisan, or Click, spoken by the Bushmen and Khoi of southwestern Africa and by a few peoples in East Africa proper. They are known as "Click" languages because of their extensive use of clicks as gutturals.

Malayo-Polynesian, represented by the languages of Madagascar.

Some 2,500 languages and dialects have been recorded throughout Africa. It has been customary to use them as indicators of distinct cultures and social systems, and, in general, this criterion has been a useful one. Care must be taken, however, not to rigidify any such correlation: languages and dialects, like other elements of culture, can be learned, adopted, and then forgotten. Today the persistence of many of the less widely spoken languages is threatened by governmental educational policies as well as by the near-extinction of many groups and their cultures.

Various pidgin and creole languages are spoken in the areas that have had long histories of trade with European colonial enterprises. Most are found along the western African coast, especially in Sierra Leone, Liberia, and Guinea-Bissau (known as Krio); in the Niger Delta (known as pidgin); and on outlying islands such as Cape Verde, Mauritius, and the Seychelles. Many languages, in particular Hausa in Nigeria and Swahili in eastern Africa, have become both trade languages and modern lingua francas over wide areas: they remain, however, distinct languages in their own rights, with their own native speakers. In addition, the former colonial languages (especially English, French, and Portuguese) are spoken widely by people in government, commerce, education, and popular culture. In South Africa, a minority of the population has for centuries spoken a form of Dutch (Afrikaans).

Almost all African languages have been committed to writing within the past hundred years, usually through Christian missionary endeavors, using Roman script. The Semitic and some of the Hamitic languages, however, have for centuries been written: examples include Ancient Egyptian, Arabic, Amharic (Ge'ez), and other related languages. Still others—languages of Muslim peoples, such as Hausa and Swahili—have long been written in Arabic script, although in recent years Roman script has proved to be more useful. A few African languages have been written in their own indigenous scripts, such as Berber and Tuareg of the Sahara, Vai of Sierra Leone, and Bamum of Cameroon. The latter two (and some others) were invented by local nineteenth-century scholars.

It should be emphasized that the fact that a language belongs to a particular language group does not necessarily mean that it and its fellows in that group are mutually intelligible, although they will usually share certain characteristics, such as the use (or nonuse) of semantic tones, grammatical rules, and word roots. All African languages include regional dialects, and these may often be mutually intelligible over small localities. The pattern of historical dispersal of a set of related languages—such as the Bantu languages that are today spoken over most of eastern, central, and southern Africa—may be ascertained through glottochronology, the study of the differences in variation from a surmised original language form.

Social Groups and Culture Areas

Languages and their dialects are crucial elements in determining identity. The boundaries between languages and dialects should not be drawn too rigidly: each shades into others within a local area, and probably most Africans can speak those of their neighbors as well as their own. Nonetheless, linguistic boundaries are recognized and have meanings for those who live within them. They are essential between the social and cultural groups that have conventionally been called "tribes," a word that is today often considered derogatory. The existence of "tribes" is therefore often denied, and at times the concept claimed to have been "invented" by Europeans. The problem is not whether or not tribes exist—for in fact they do. They have names, and Africans use those names, and they hold great significance for their members, to whom they give a firm identity. The problem concerns exactly how they may be defined and how they came into existence. A tribe is now often referred to by a term such as "ethnic group," "society," or "culture." The first two terms are almost meaningless in this context, and the third refers not to a group of living people but to their conventional patterns of behavior. Perhaps the term that best conveys both their distinctiveness and the absence of rigid boundaries between them is simply "people."

How may a people be defined? The obvious criteria include occupying a common territory; speaking a single language or dialect; having a single social organization; having a sense of identity, cohesion, and history; sharing a common religion; and having a single set of customs and behavioral rules (as in marriage, clothing, diet, taboos, and so on). One problem is that any or all of these criteria can change at any time, so that a map of the peoples who live in Africa can soon grow out of date.

Two commonly used words deserve comment. These are "indigenous" and "traditional." Both are often used with the implication of being unchanging or static, but properly they do not have this connotation.

"Indigenous" is conventionally used not as meaning autochthonous or primordial, but rather in the sense of having priority of settlement; it is also used to distinguish Africans from non-African incomers. The word "native," although properly having that same meaning, is today rarely used.

"Traditional" refers to the customs, beliefs, and practices that the local people of any area consider to have been theirs in the past and not to have changed today from what they were in that past. It is a notion that is held by the people themselves, and not by outside observers. In this sense, a traditional society is one whose members see their lives and the future lives of their children as being essentially the same as those of their forebears, in spite of whatever changes may in fact have been made in the underlying structure of their society. All African societies change continually, but the people themselves may be unaware of this fact or may choose to ignore it as unimportant.

In addition to the classifications that are based upon race and language, various attempts have been made to classify the peoples of Africa by "culture area," a concept based on early American Indian ethnology. The most widely accepted classifications for Africa are those made by Melville Herskovits (1924) and George Peter Murdock (1959). These two classifications are useful because they give a comprehensive view of African societies and cultures and bring a degree of order into an often confusing overall situation. The simpler system is that of Herskovits, who developed the following seven categories: Khoisan, in southwestern Africa, comprising the Bushmen and Khoi only; East African Cattle Complex, stretching northward from southeastern Africa (a category is too much of a ragbag to be of much use, given that it is based on close relationships between humans and their cattle but ignores other important differences); Eastern Sudan, from the Nile westward to Lake Chad (a category based on geographical region rather than on more significant criteria); Congo, comprising the Congo (or Zaire) Basin and surrounding areas, all of whom speak Bantu languages; Guinea Coast, stretching from the Bight of Biafra to Senegal, a densely populated region, the inhabitants of which speak Niger-Congo languages and occupy mainly forested areas; Western Sudan, which is occupied by many peoples who share the occupation of the sub-Saharan savannas; and East African Horn (northern Ethiopia and Somalia), another cluster that is defined geographically.

This classification scheme, which excludes northern Africa, is based essentially on geography and basic economies. Murdock's classification is far more sophisticated and complete, and it includes northern Africa and Madagascar. Although also basically geographical, it rests to a greater extent upon criteria of social organization, language, and history. It consists of forty-five main clusters, each subdivided into constituent groups. It lists a total of some 2,700 peoples, of whom about 2,300 live in sub-Saharan Africa (about 700 main groups and 1,600 subgroups), with about 360 in northern Africa, and 40 in Madagascar and on the smaller islands. Although questions can be raised about the identities of many of the subgroups, the general picture is one of an immense number of distinct peoples, each with its own identity, language, and culture. The complexity is overwhelming.

It may be useful here to present some of the principal features of the main geographical regions of the continent, so as to give an idea of their general social, cultural, and historical places within the complexity of African cultures. Each of these wide regions includes a great variety of traditional economies, forms of government, familial organizations, and religious systems, all of which are discussed in more detail later in this introduction.

Western Africa stretches from Senegal in the west to Cameroon in the east. It includes the two main zones of the Saharan borderland savannas—known generally as the Sahel—and that of the forested belt along the coast. It holds a third of the total population of the continent. Whereas communication is difficult and slow from east to west in the forest zone, it is relatively easy along the savanna belt. Located in the savanna zones are Senegal, Gambia, Mauritania, Mali, Burkina Faso, and Niger, as well as the northern parts of the forest-zone countries of Guinea-Bissau, Liberia, Sierra Leone, Guinea, Ivory Coast, Ghana, Togo, Benin, Nigeria, and Cameroon.

The main crops of the savanna zone are grains: millets, sorghums, maize, and, in the west, rice. Savanna trees, oil plants (mainly sesame), and spices are also grown in most of this zone. The forest belt grows mainly root and tree crops: yams; cocoyams; oil, raffia, and other palms; spices; kola; and cocoa—all crops that are important both for domestic use and for export. Livestock are kept throughout the savanna: cattle of several varieties, horses, sheep, goats, fowl, and pigs are all valuable. Cattle and horses cannot survive in the forests to the south, however, because of the tsetse fly. Minerals—gold, bauxite, diamonds—are important products of the forest zone. Houses are mainly of mud in the savanna zone (including immense and long-lasting adobe structures such as palaces and mosques), but are of less durable materials in the forests, where precipitation is heavy. The region is world famous for its wood carvings, pottery, metal casting, and textile weaving. Trade, both at local markets and through long-distance merchants, has always been and remains of central economic and social importance, from both west and east and also from the forest zone to northern Africa, across the Sahara Desert. In the savanna zone, Islam is perhaps the principal religion; most societies in the forest zone have traditionally had their own local religions and today have added Christianity.

Western Africa contains both large, permanent towns and cities and large, powerful kingdoms, some of which have endured since the Middle Ages. The latter include the forest states of Benin (in Nigeria, not in the modern state that has taken the same name); the cluster of Yoruba states in southwestern Nigeria; Dahomey, in the modern Benin; Asante and the other Akan kingdoms of Ghana and Ivory Coast. In the savanna zone are the Muslim emirates of the Hausa in northern Nigeria and Niger (Sokoto, Zaria, Kano, and others), which were established by conquest by the Fulani in the early nineteenth century; the kingdom of Nupe in central Nigeria; and the Mossi kingdoms of Burkina Faso, among others. There are also several noncentralized societies in both the savanna and the forest zones, which vary politically and organizationally but which recognize either clans or lineages as the basis for governing many kinds of associations: age groups; village associations (as among the Igbo of southeastern Nigeria); and, in the west, the so-called secret societies of the Mende and Temne, in Sierra Leone.

Central Africa may also be divided into two main parts. One is the easterly extension of western Africa, with the Nile as its eastern boundary, that includes the savanna-zone countries of Cameroon, Chad, the Central African Republic, and the southwestern part of Sudan. The other part stretches southward through the present-day countries of Congo, Gabon, Zaire, Angola, and Equatorial Africa, much of which territory is forested and is occupied by peoples with differing economies and cultures. The central region is ethnically mixed, with Baggara and other Arabs in the north, Bantu-speaking farmers throughout most of both the savanna and forest, and the Pygmies in parts of the forest. Kingdoms are found throughout the region: in the north, that of the Bamiléké and those of several others in Cameroon, and, further east, those of the Mangbetu and the Azande. The forest areas include the kingdoms of the Kongo, Kuba, Luba, Lunda, and many others.

Eastern Africa stretches from Ethiopia southward to the Zambezi, and from the Indian Ocean westward to the Great Lakes. It covers the present-day nations of Sudan, Ethiopia, Eritrea, Somalia, Kenya, Tanzania, Rwanda, and Burundi.

Various forms of savanna economies of mixed farming are found throughout this region, with basic dependence on pastoralism in the southern Sudan (by the Nuer and the Dinka), in the Rift Valley of Kenya and Tanzania (by the Maasai), and in Somalia (by the Somalis). The Ethiopian, Kenyan, and Great Lakes highlands support large and dense populations, including those of the great kingdom of the Amhara in Ethiopia, the Nile state of Shilluk in the Sudan, and the Interlacustrine Bantu kingdoms of Ganda, Nyoro, Rwanda, Burundi, Toro, and others. Noncentralized peoples include the Nuer and the Dinka of southern Sudan; the Somalis of Somalia; the Kikuyu, Luyia, and Luo of Kenya; the numerous small societies in Tanzania and Zambia; and the Shona and Ndebele of Zimbabwe.

Southern Africa—which includes the present-day nations of South Africa, Botswana, Namibia, Mozambique, Angola, Malawi, Zambia, Zimbabwe, Lesotho, and Swaziland—is characterized by savannas, occasional coastal forests, and the arid areas of the Kalahari Desert. Bushmen and Khoi live in the Kalahari region; the remainder of the region is occupied by Bantu-speaking peoples, the better known of whom include the kingdoms of Zulu, Swazi, Suto, Xhosa, Lozi, Bemba, and Ndebele. In the southwestern tip live the Cape Coloureds, as well as the Afrikaners. Except for the Bushmen and the Khoi, their traditional economies have been those of mixed farming and livestock keeping. Today this region—in which the large modern cities of Johannesburg, Cape Town, and Durban are located—is the most highly industrialized in all of Africa.

Northern Africa comprises the narrow coastal strip from Egypt to Morocco, together with the Sahara Desert to its south. This strip was at one time inhabited mainly by Berber peoples but today has been taken over by Arab immigrants from Arabia, who have subjugated the Berbers and driven many of them into the Sahara itself.

Off the eastern coast of Africa lies Madagascar, inhabited by immigrants from what is now Indonesia, who arrived on the island probably in the first half of the first millennium. Despite some admixture from the mainland, Madagascar's economies, societies, and cultures are noticeably different from those of the rest of Africa.

History

There is quite a gap between the paleontological history of the early physical development of humans in Africa and the more recent history of African societies and civilizations. The former deals with human bodies; the latter is concerned with the social and imaginative constructs that have been made by peoples of many different appearances and periods. We can dig up traces of the former, but traces of the latter are far harder to find and to interpret. Until very recently, "African history" was mainly the study of colonial history from colonial records and was imbued with many of the underlying assumptions about the "Dark Continent" that had been held by some of the earliest writers. The development of social anthropology led to the contextual study of local tradition and myth. Many historians naively continued to accept mythical tradition as historical record, but others sided with anthropologists in recognizing that, although traditions revealed much about the past, they also portrayed African views of the past only as they are interpreted today. Archaeologists, too, have for many years offered valuable information on past societies, and modern archaeology—devoid of the implicit racism of some earlier work—is uncovering new and reliable data about both the material and the nonmaterial conditions of previous periods of history.

We may divide the history of modern Africa into three main phases: that of the precolonial past, that of the colonial period, and that of the postcolonial present. These are merely the convenient phases that have been constructed by historians: the chronologies for one part of the continent vary greatly from those that apply to others; and the length, the nature, and the depth of consequences of colonial rule have varied from one region and country to another. Evaluative historiography tends to simplify complex historical trends and developments and often to substitute myth for "objective" history, however problematic the latter may in fact be.

The earliest African civilization of which we have reliable knowledge is that of Egypt, which linked Africa and western Asia. By about 5000 B.C., settled Neolithic communities had come into existence, based on the domestication of plants and animals, the making of pottery, and the smelting of metals. Lower and Upper Egypt were united into a single kingdom, which had knowledge of writing, by 3000 B.C., and, by 2700 B.C., Egypt's civilization was at its height. Its mercantile and cultural influence went as far south as Nubia and Ethiopia. By about 2000 B.C., Egypt's power was in decline, and the center moved southward to the Nubian state of Kush. Still later, the rise and spread of ironworking (to replace bronze) led to the growing importance of Meroë, which flourished for some 600 years and was probably the main center for the knowledge of ironworking that spread out through the remainder of Africa, with far-reaching social and cultural consequences. Meroë was eclipsed by the Ethiopian state of Aksum in the fourth century A.D., and by several Christian successor states in present-day southwestern Sudan.

Although archaeologists are providing more and more information about the internal organizations and cultures of these various places and their peoples, the earliest historically known post-Egyptian societies of which we possess considerable knowledge are the "medieval" empires of the southern Saharan borderland: Ghana (not to be confused with modern Ghana), Mali, Songhay, Kanem, and others that flourished at various times after the eighth century. They were trading states, based on the exchange of gold from the south, salt from the north, and many other items between the forest region of western Africa and the northern Sahara and Mediterranean regions. The height of mercantile power in the area was from the twelfth until the sixteenth centuries. These early states were militarily powerful empires, the rulers of which accepted Islam and, therefore, literacy, as part of their mercantile roles. As middlemen in the Saharan trade, they ensured the safety of caravan routes across the desert and of markets in the western African savanna and forest zones, in return for taxes and tribute from Saharan and Mediterranean merchants. Ghana and Mali were eventually subdued by attacks from the Berbers from northwestern Africa, but the Hausa and Kanem states to the east have continued to exist until the present day, even though weakened by the raids and "holy wars" of Muslim Fulani and other groups. The "medieval" empires have otherwise long vanished, but their old traditions and myths persist and still play important parts in the construction and retention of ethnic ideologies throughout much of western Africa.

Elsewhere in Africa, most of the early "medieval" societies of which we have knowledge became prominent somewhat later. All were based upon trade, both long-distance trade within Africa and, increasingly, trade with Asia and Europe. Aksum and, later, the Swahili towns of the eastern African coast were, from the first part of the first millennium, engaged in trade with Arabia and countries to the east across the Indian Ocean, a commerce that in the Swahili case lasted until the twentieth century. Slaves, ivory, and gold were the most important items exported, in immense quantities, over almost 2,000 years. In southern Africa lay the gold-producing empire of Monomatapa, with its citadel of Zimbabwe, which exported its gold through the southern Swahili ports. In the region of the great lakes were the powerful states of Nyoro, Ganda, and Rwanda, among others; farther south, the several trading states of the Angola-Congo region, as well as the kingdom of Kongo, which was early Christianized by the Portuguese. In western Africa, the domination of the Saharan borderland states was supplanted by the rise of successor states along the forest belt: Asante, Benin, the Yoruba states of Nigeria and Dahomey, and others. Although these states flourished during the colonial period as providers of ivory, slaves, gold, palm oil, and other commodities to Europeans, they had been established much earlier. They were not mere petty and short-lived kingdoms, but large, powerful, and long-lasting trading states whose commerce linked most of the lesser societies of the continent into a single mercantile network, one that was destroyed only by the advent of European colonial powers.

Every part of Africa has at one time or another come under the imperialist and colonialist overrule of Asia and the West (even Liberia was long a de facto colony of the United States). Today every part of the continent except for one or two small and remote islands has become politically, even if not in all cases economically, independent. The brutality of colonial rule may have been exaggerated and mythologized, but there is no doubt that the colonial period had deep-seated consequences for the development of the African peoples. Even if in the long run it may be seen as merely an interlude in "la longue durée" of African history, the colonial rule of Europe and Asia served to "underdevelop" Africa, leading to the continent's relatively long economic and political stagnation.

Apart from the early colonial incursions by Rome along the coast of northern Africa and those by Arabian states in the Horn and along the eastern African coast, the first colonial rulers were the Portuguese, who, from the twelfth century onward, set up small colonial trading settlements southward down the western African coastline from present-day Senegal, the Cape Verde Islands, and Guinea-Bissau (which had 500 years of Portuguese presence), to Benin, Kongo, and Angola. At the end of the fifteenth century, they rounded the Cape and reached eastern Africa. Other countries—Holland, France, Britain, Brandenberg, Denmark, Sweden, Oman, Belgium, Germany—sent colonial expeditions to Africa in the wake of the Portuguese. All established trading outposts and then moved inland to take over the remainder of the continent. They could rarely take over internal kingdoms and other societies without force, however, and during the eighteenth and nineteenth centuries Africa was the scene of continual warfare and economic exploitation. The most obvious series of events was that involving the trade in slaves to the Americas from western and south-central Africa (figures vary from 30 million to 100 million) and from eastern Africa to Arabia, Persia, and India (figures certainly run into many millions). Slaves were captured by indigenous African rulers themselves and sold to Europeans and Arabs. That trade was conducted alongside commerce in ivory, gold, and other items, the collection of which required people to be diverted from farming and their settled peasant livelihoods.

The third phase of African history is the contemporary era—a period of some thirty years in the middle of the twentieth century during which political independence was taken by, and in some cases rather grudgingly given to, the present African nation-states. It is still too early to evaluate the post-colonial history of Africa, which has been characterized by a series of attempts to construct new democracies that have in most cases failed (or at least been uncertain), combined with a few examples of destructive dictatorship. In addition, this period has been marked by the process of neocolonialism and "development," of the continued exploitation of Africa by the outside world—not in the form of the taking of human beings but of the taking of material resources in return for manufactures. The African elites have flourished, but the lot of most of the ordinary people has been impoverishment.

Ecology, Economies, and Technologies

A wide range of economic systems can be identified in Africa, all of which are dependent on ecological as well as on demographic, political, and cultural factors. The indigenous preindustrial economies have conventionally been classified into three main types: hunter-gatherer, pastoral, and agricultural. Few if any economies can be defined as being totally of one or another of these three types, which are remnants of long-outmoded evolutionist theories. Nonetheless, they make a useful starting point for description.

In the traditional past, most arid areas have supported various forms of hunting and gathering, as have parts of the denser forest areas of the Congo region: the Bushmen of the Kalahari and the foragers of the rain forests are the prime examples. Hunting-and-gathering societies necessarily have a low population density, but it must be remembered that none of these societies is based solely on this type of economy. They have also occasionally practiced agriculture and always some trade; they have not been isolated communities, but have been in contact with and usually exploited by their neighbors who live in more fertile areas.

Pastoralism (livestock keeping) is widespread throughout the continent. Domesticated animals include cattle (both the long-horned Mediterranean type and the Indian humped zebu cattle), sheep, goats, camels, donkeys, pigs, fowl, and the ubiquitous dogs and cats. Strict dependence on pastoralism, however, is limited to a few regions, chiefly the northern and southern Saharan fringes, the upper Nile Valley, and the East African plains and semideserts. None of these areas support peoples who depend solely on livestock. There has always been some complementary farming and, wherever possible, fishing. Complete dependence on pastoralism is found only among certain portions of the population, such as the warriors of the Maasai, and then for only limited periods of time (e.g., they subsist solely on milk and blood drawn from the cattle's necks, and they do not kill the beasts for meat). Trade in livestock includes long-distance exchanges of the animals themselves as well as of their hides and skins. The societies that are largely dependent on livestock use them also for sacrificial and other ritual purposes, and the cattle are given great symbolic and emotive value.

The benefits of pastoralism are unfortunately overlooked by African governments, members of which often despise pastoralists as "primitive." Raising livestock remains the only form of production that flourishes in semiarid lands, which are quickly eroded by farming. Pastoralists require large areas of land for grazing and transhumance (there are no "nomads" in Africa). They must therefore maintain low population density. Widespread expropriation of grazing lands for use by agriculturists, on the other hand, has led invariably to desertification, especially along the southern Saharan borderline.

The traditional economy of some 90 percent of the African populations has been one or another form of agriculture. The number of species and varieties of cultivated plants is enormous. Food plants grown in Africa today include not only those that have come from within the continent but also some that have been introduced into it at various times throughout history. Indigenous African crops have also been taken to other world regions. The principal cultivated plants that originate in Africa itself include millets and sorghums, several legumes, cotton, the oil palm, false plantains, sesame, castor, okra, gourds, tamarind, coffee, kola, and khat (Arabic: *qāt*). From Asia have come wheat and barley, additional legumes, onions, date palms, rice, yams, taro (cocoyams), eggplants, bananas, coconut palms, sugarcane, mangoes, flax, and various fruits and spices. From the Americas have come maize, manioc (cassava), groundnuts, sweet potatoes, tomatoes, cacao, pepper, tobacco, and still more fruits and spices.

Very few of these plants can be grown in every part of the continent. In the savanna regions, the staples are grains, including millets, sorghums, and maize; in the more densely forested regions, they are mainly root crops, such as yams, cocoyams, and sweet potatoes. In some areas, manioc, rice, plantains, and false plantains (*Ensete*) provide the staples. Groundnuts and many kinds of bean, pea, and cucurbit are almost universal. The chief oil plants include sesame, castors, and oil palm; and coconut and other palms are grown on suitable soils. Spices and condiments include peppers, coffee, cocoa, tea, tobacco, sugarcane, qāt, and kola, all widely grown wherever the climate permits. Wild plants, palms, and trees of many kinds are grown wherever possible. A certain amount of livestock keeping, hunting, and fishing is typically found as part of the total local economy.

African farming techniques are small in scale but are highly productive within the ecological limitations of the continent. The traditional technologies are, however, limited in efficiency. Seed is generally of low yield, and methods of storage, transport, and weed and pest control are simple, although everywhere as efficient as can be managed in stringent climatic conditions. In general, African soils are not capable of continual cropping, and various forms of fallowing and shifting agriculture are practiced. Manuring is widely practiced, as are various forms of irrigation wherever feasible; many elaborate irrigation-terracing works have lasted for centuries, mainly in eastern Africa. Fertility is almost everywhere enhanced by burning trees and grass while clearing fields, thus adding nitrogen as well as destroying pests. Traditionally, mixed cropping has been widespread, in an effort to control soil erosion thereby being controlled. However, with the universal growing of cash crops, many of which are grown in pure stands and cannot be fitted into the traditional mixed plantings and crop rotations, and with the widespread land shortage and subsequent lengthening of crop cycles, soil erosion has become everywhere a serious problem. The overcutting of timber for export, charcoal, and fuel has also caused widespread deforestation and soil erosion.

Many culturally determined forms of division of labor are recognized—between men and women, between old and young, and between people of different occupations and ranks. The general principle has been that men are responsible for the heavier tasks of farming and production, and also for warfare, ritual, and government; women are responsible for lighter farm work, for domestic tasks related to household maintenance and child rearing, and for giving personal and informal advice in everyday family and political matters. There are great variations in the apportionment of such work as cattle milking and care, divination, craft production, and local trade. Women are traditionally disadvantaged legally (for example, they may rarely initiate divorce). But much of the description of African gender roles has been based on non-African viewpoints and requires more ethnographic research and understanding. With modern changes in everyday life, these traditionally complementary roles are frequently being redefined and resanctioned. In many areas, labor has always been scarce, and traditional forms of slavery, peonage, and other forms of nonpaid labor have been imposed. Nonpaid labor has been an essential aspect of most of the elaborate and powerful kingdoms, the rulers of which have been able to command a large labor supply for both productive and military purposes. Until the late twentieth century, wage labor seems to have been unknown.

Until about the mid-twentieth century, production had been largely for subsistence, with little surplus. Exchange of kin and gifts has been practiced. Exchange by redistribution of foodstuffs and other items was also widespread, in the forms of tribute to local rulers and in the latters' reciprocal hospitality and protection. The items that were given to rulers included both subsistence items and also those with symbolic value (such as elephant tusks and eagle feathers, both of which symbolize royal power), as well as labor and military service. Local exchange by barter has been almost universal, owing largely to lack of traditional forms of money, except in places—mainly in coastal areas—where there had been early trade with Europeans and Asians.

Where there was exchange by money, it was of various kinds. The most typical involved forms of money that were of limited use and rather than being intended for universal exchange, such as metal bars called "manillas." Markets are found in most areas of the continent, and are typically held periodically. In most of them, even today, some items are exchanged without money. Long-distance trade has always been far more widespread than was reported by early European travelers. Items traded have been animal products, such as ivory, hides, and skins; slaves; salt; gold, copper, and iron; and craft goods of many kinds. Most of the long-distance trade routes were ultimately linked to the extra-African ocean trade at ports along the coasts.

The present economy of Africa is one of rapid change and considerable variation in types of production and distribution. The continent is, to a greater extent than ever before, part of a single world economy, but its role in that economy remains essentially that of a region that is being exploited.

Since the late nineteenth century, in particular, the impact of colonial rule by European powers has greatly affected the traditional economies, in addition to the consequences of several centuries of slave trading by European and Asian slavers. Whereas previously the exploitation of metals had been in most areas a marginal form of production, the extraction of gold, copper, bauxite, and diamonds has become paramount. Other factors that have deeply marked twentieth-century African life include the establishment of large-scale plantation enterprises (for such products as cocoa, coffee, tea, palm oil, cotton, hemp, rubber, and sugar); the introduction of modern consumer goods and the establishment of forms of taxation by cash that can be obtained only by ever-increasing labor migration from poorer regions to magnet areas; the increasing inequality between the elite and the poor; the growth of industrial centers and the construction of long-distance road and rail transport facilities; the introduction of widely available forms of money and the lessening of interpersonal forms of exchange; and the appearance of more populous urban centers, that attract impoverished proletariats. The pace of these changes has been more and more rapid: greater and deeper changes have occurred in the years since World War II than had occurred throughout the nineteenth century.

Patterns of Settlement

Africa has always been and remains even now a region of small rural settlements, with urban centers of several kinds interspersed among them. Settlement patterns vary regionally, depending on differences in ecology, economy, and routes of communication and on the distribution of natural resources and of trading centers. With the general poverty of production in most parts of Africa, the most efficient pattern of settlement has been that of many small villages, each generally self-sufficient and not dependent on transport or trade, except for specialty items. In most of Africa, short-lasting materials have generally been used for building houses, which, therefore, have only rarely been permanent. The dwellings built of adobe or stone last longer than those of mud and wood, and, in many areas—especially the western African savanna—they have been architecturally quite elaborate. But with a general pattern of shifting farming and pastoralism, coupled with a lack of means for the accumulation of wealth by inheritance, the almost universal pattern of settlements that last for only a few years, certainly for less than a generation, has been highly efficient.

Nonetheless, Africa has also been, and is increasingly, a continent on which urbanism and urbanization have flourished. We may distinguish three main types of urban centers. One is that of the traditional precolonial town, built of long-lasting materials and typically occupied by people who are engaged in craft production and commerce. The greatest of these centers are in northern Africa—in Egypt, Morocco, Algeria, and Tunisia. Others are in western Africa, in particular in both northern and southern Nigeria—cities such as Ibadan and Kano, each of which numbered many thousands in population even before the advent of colonial rule. There are also the ancient towns of Ethiopia and the Sudan and the stone-built trading towns along the eastern African coast that have been on the same sites for many centuries (e.g., Mombasa, in Kenya). Ancient (often ruined) towns also exist elsewhere along the southern Saharan fringes (e.g., the medieval town of Djenné, in Mali) and in other places (e.g., the ruins of the stone fortresses of ancient Zimbabwe). Most of these traditional towns and cities have had ethnically homogeneous populations, ruled by indigenous kings, and their residents' main occupations have beeen both trade and farming, with farmers living in the towns and commuting out to their farms.

A second type of town comprises those built by the colonial powers, usually as new industrial centers associated with extractive industries (gold, diamonds, copper). These towns were often sited in areas of low population density, and they have needed a continuous influx of labor, as was the case in Johannesburg and the towns of the Zambian and Zairean Copperbelt. Other colonial towns, such as Nairobi, in Kenya, were established as communication centers. Most of these modern cities have also become administrative and business centers. They have heterogeneous populations, drawing as they do on immigrants from wide areas, and typically they have a sexual imbalance, given that most immigrants are men whose wives stay behind to farm in the rural areas.

In the third category of town are the many small "townships" that were established during the colonial period as local administrative and trading centers. They remain important everywhere as markets, and they provide links between the rural areas and the more modern cities.

One factor of crucial importance to African urbanization is that of labor migration, especially in the newly established cities that need large numbers of unskilled laborers. Because the African continent is generally impoverished, the cities act as magnet areas, as places where men (and some women) can make the money that is unobtainable in the rural areas. The general process (since around the mid-twentieth century) has been that the cities attract men from the country, who work in them until they grow old and return to their rural homes. Meanwhile, the rural areas have a surplus of women, on whose shoulders fall all the tasks of farming. In some areas, especially in southern Africa, this imbalance has led to serious land crowding, underproduction, and social collapse in the countryside and to a violent and predatory life in the large cities, where the men are never more than temporary sojourners. Furthermore, such cities are the seats of modern elites, attracted by the money and power that are available there, who are skilled enough to benefit from the new opportunities offered by modern industry and commerce. During the twentieth century, a new class structure has been emerging, which closely resembles those found in the countries of the modern industrialized world outside Africa. Within this upper elite are both wealthy merchants and modern political leaders, whose interests are more likely to coincide with those of fellow members of the elite elsewhere than with members of the local communities from which they have come.

Family, Kinship, and Domestic Groupings

The family is a universal group throughout Africa, with many different forms and functions. Everywhere the basic family unit is the elementary or nuclear family, a small domestic group made up of a husband, his wife, and their children; frequently, attached kin are included as well. This group is formed by a marriage and ends either with the death of one of the spouses or with divorce. Where polygyny is permitted, a husband and his wives form a compound family. Elementary and compound families in most parts of the continent traditionally have also been units of wider and longer-lasting families, known as joint or extended families. In these families, there are typically two or more generations, either a group of brothers and sons and their wives and children (a patrilineal joint family) or, in some places, a group of sisters and their husbands and children (a matrilineal joint family). This kind of family is long-lasting, and indeed self-perpetuating; a death makes no difference to its overall structure, and thus it can last over several generations, with a membership of up to a hundred people and more. As a general rule, joint and extended families are found in rural rather than in urban settlements, the latter more usually being occupied by many elementary families, each in isolation from the others. But here are many exceptions (e.g., the Yoruba of the traditional southern Nigerian cities, who maintain extended families even today).

The basis of kinship, in Africa as elsewhere, is descent from an ancestor. The most widespread descent group is known as the clan, which can be either patrilineal or matrilineal. The members of the former type of clan comprise all those who are born from a single founding ancestor through the male line only; those of the latter comprise all those born from a single founding ancestor or ancestress through the female line only. Patriliny is far more common in Africa than matriliny, which is limited mainly to parts of Zambia and Malawi, in central Africa, and to Ghana and Ivory Coast, in western Africa. Regardless of the means of descent, authority in the family and elsewhere is always formally held by men; therefore, men have domestic authority in both patrilineal and matrilineal families (formal matriarchy is unknown in Africa). Clans, which are rarely corporate units in Africa, are clusters of kin who claim a single common ancestry but can rarely, if ever, trace the actual links of descent. Usually clans are exogamous units and may recognize various ritual prohibitions, such as taboos on certain foods, that give them a sense of unity and of distinctiveness from others.

Clans are typically segmented into constituent groups, with each group recognizing a founding ancestor more recent than the clan founder; these are known in the literature as lineages, one of the criteria for a lineage being that its members—patrilineal or matrilineal—can trace actual kinship links between themselves. Lineages may themselves be segmented into smaller units, the smallest typically being the group around which a domestic family is established. Such a family (if patrilineal) includes the husband and his children, all members of the small lineage, and his wife, who by the rule of exogamy must come from another clan.

Other forms of descent are recognized, the most common of which is cognatic descent, whereby local kin groups are composed of members who recognize their common descent through both men and women. A few societies recognize both patrilineal and matrilineal descent simultaneously. Some societies in Africa do not formally recognize these forms of descent at all, but they are not typical and usually consist of long-settled urban dwellers.

Almost every African society has some form of descent group, however transitory, as the basis of its social organization. The recognition of these variations of ancestral descent is an effective way of constructing local groups that can last for several—often for many—generations and in which the close-knit ties of kinship provide powerful links through the notion of common "blood." By claiming exclusive ancestry, such a group can claim exclusive rights to clan and lineage property. Marriages between their members, by the rule of exogamy, cement them into larger communities and societies, each possessing its own sense of common ethnic and cultural "belonging." Although these traditional forms of family and kinship are lessening in importance, with the continuing need for urban and industrialized labor and the consequent increase in labor migration, the strength of kin groups remains great. They are well suited to traditional forms of production and exchange where these are found (which is still the case among the majority of African peoples), and they provide a sense of personal identity and security that is of high emotive value.

Marriage

In most of Africa, marriage is more a of union between two lineages or families than it is a union between the individual husband and wife. Marriage is undertaken for many reasons, but the primary ones are to provide legitimate successors to status and inheritors of property rights and to form alliances and ties between clans and other units, in order to knit them into a single society.

Incest within certain degrees of kinship is everywhere forbidden. Exogamy, the prohibition of marriage within certain descent groups, is typically practiced with regard to clan and other basic social units, such as those of the tribe and settlement. Endogamy is found in some societies, those in which there are political or mercantile elites that prefer to retain power and wealth within their own hands through marriages among themselves.

A crucial factor in any marriage arrangement is whether patrilineal, matrilineal, or cognatic groups form the basic social structure. In patrilineal systems, marriage is typically sealed by the transfer of property, known as bride-wealth, usually in the form of cattle. The husband's group transfers property to that of the wife, in return for the transfer to them of rights of procreation and sexuality on the part of the wife from those who have been her guardians (e.g., her father or her brothers). Usually, if divorce later occurs, the bride-wealth must be returned, less a proportion for each child who remains with the husband's group. There are many variations, but this simple principle generally holds true. In matrilineal societies, bride-wealth is not transferred because the children belong to the wife's clan or lineage and will inherit from that group; the husband's heirs are his sisters' children, and his own children inherit from his wife's brothers, their maternal uncles. There is no need for bride-wealth, as rights in a woman's children are not transferred, although small gifts are always presented, and the husband may have to work for his wife's parents for some time.

Residence after marriage is linked to several factors. In patrilineal systems, it is nearly always virilocal, with the wife living in her husband's natal settlement and being regarded as a "stranger" until she has borne children to his group. In matrilineal systems, residence may be virilocal, or it may be uxorilocal, in which case the husband goes to live with his wife's relatives and remains a "stranger" in that settlement. With uxorilocal residence in particular, the husband's position is often ambivalent, and divorce is more frequent. In many places, however, especially in urban centers, residence after marriage is increasingly becoming neolocal: the husband and wife establish their own home, away from those of either set of parents.

Polygyny has traditionally been the ideal. It is rare, however, for more than a quarter of the men in a community to have more than one wife, and a man's later wives are frequently those inherited from a senior deceased kinsman (by the institution of the levirate or by widow inheritance). In many societies, women marry at puberty, but men marry in their thirties or even later. This makes polygyny possible because by then there are fewer marriageable men, as many will have died from natural causes or from warfare.

Government and Politics

African societies today have two levels of government: the indigenous organization, which pertains to local groups, and the national government of the independent nation-states. The relationship between the two levels is complex and has led to serious incompatibilities and conflicts.

It has become usual to classify the multitude of indigenous forms of African government into three main categories, conventionally known as bands, tribes, and kingdoms. Bands are relatively few and are limited to the societies with economies based on hunting and gathering, especially those of the Bushmen of the Kalahari and the foragers of the central African forests. Their economies require a low density of population and, therefore, its wide distribution over large areas, which inhibits permanent or large settlements. These bands are not found in total isolation but are interspersed with culturally different groups with distinct and complementary economies. Essentially, the bands are large kinship groups under the authority of family elders and shamanic ritual leaders.

"Tribes," a word less often used today than it was formerly because it is held to imply "primitiveness," form the numerically largest political category. Tribes are larger and more settled than bands, but they still lack any overall form of centralized political authority. They have no kings and, in the past, usually had no formally appointed chiefs, although there have always been ritual leaders with some degree of political authority. Most of these societies are based upon a structure of clans, which are segmented into subclans and lineages, often with three or four levels of segmentation. A clan or lineage is the basic unit of such a tribal organization, in which the tribe resembles a series of small, equal, and quasi-autonomous groups. The traditional sanctions for social order are ritual, feud, and warfare. Other tribal systems place emphasis on age rather than on descent, and everyday government is in the hands of councils based on the recruitment of men (and women) of similar age. Initiation at puberty is extremely important, in order that ties between age-mates (whether young warriors or legislative elders) overcome those of birth and descent. These societies are found especially in eastern Africa among pastoralists, such as the Maasai. In yet other tribal societies, mostly in western Africa, government is by some form of association (including the so-called "secret societies") of men and women of equal age and standing.

In the third type of indigenous political structure—that of the kingdom or state—political authority is centered on the office of a king (sometimes a queen), who is chosen from a royal clan and given sacred attributes by his or her subjects. Kingdoms range in population from a few thousand people to several million, and their rulers vary from being little more than ritual figureheads (as among the Shilluk of the southern Sudan, the prototype of James G. Frazer's "divine" king) to military despots with powers of life and death. These kingdoms may have arisen by conquest (as those of the Zulu or Swazi of southern Africa) or by combining into a federation of culturally related states (as those of the Asante or Ghana). The ruler may be regarded as a senior kinsman to his subjects, as a member of a socially senior royal clan, or as a member of an ethnically distinct autocracy (as in the former Rwanda and Burundi kingdoms). In all of the kingdoms, however powerful their rulers, there have always been institutionalized means by which the people controlled royal power. Such axioms as "the king is a slave" are accepted in many African kingdoms. In addition, it has been almost universal for there to be periodic rituals of purification of both the king as an individual and the kingship as an office or institution in its own right, independent of the temporary incumbent (well-known examples are those held in the kingdoms of the Swazi, Zulu, and Akan).

All of these different kinds of political units exist today, although the traditional powers of kings were invariably limited and weakened during colonial rule. In some colonial systems, in particular that of the British, the indigenous rulers were permitted to reign without the power of inflicting death or waging war, under the policy of "indirect rule"; in other systems, especially in the French colonies, it was more usual for indigenous rulers to become little more than figureheads—or even to be abolished.

Above the level of indigenous forms of polity is that of the modern nation-state. There are today almost sixty such nations in Africa, their boundaries remaining those established by the colonial powers that divided Africa at the end of the nineteenth century, with scant regard for the interests of the Africans themselves. It is little wonder that there have been perennial boundary disputes, which have almost all been settled by the Organization of African Unity.

The leaders of these new states have been faced with the problem trying to construct and retain notions of national identity, and to this aim have they tended to reduce still further the powers of traditional rulers and of the local councils and courts, which are based on association or descent. The indigenous local political units may retain the loyalties of their members, but this loyalty has typically been condemned as "tribalism" and (usually mistakenly) considered to be antithetical to "nationalism." The indigenous ruling elites have been weakened and have been replaced by modern elites, whose memberships are based on wealth and commerce rather than on traditional affiliations. The clashes between the two principles of organization—class and descent—have led to gross conflicts of interest and often to armed struggles within military and one-party governments, which have suppressed protestations and expressions of democratic dissent as "tribalism."

Religion

African traditional religions were at one time (and still today to some extent) considered by outsiders to be "primitive," filled with "jujus" and witchcraft, or else to be based on emotional display beyond the comprehension of non-Africans. Both are racist views: the reality is quite different.

African traditional religions all recognize the existence of a Supreme Divinity or Creator God, usually otiose and beyond personal contact by ordinary people. Each indigenous society has its own divinity in this sense. Between the people and the divinity there are believed to be both mystical and living intermediaries. The former include various spirits and ancestors, to whom sacrifice and prayer are typically offered in response to ill health, lack of success, or uncertainty of role. Contact is also made between the living and these mystical agents through possession. Living intermediaries include priests, diviners, and prophets, all of whom are thought to have divine knowledge. Priests are rarely specialists; they are more often the heads of lineages and families, although some, such as rainmakers, play more specialized roles. Diviners (and oracle operators) are thought to have the power to explain the meanings of the past and present and to foretell the future. Prophets are the messengers or emissaries of the divinity. They come to communities that experience disasters and troubles (natural, medical, or political) beyond their comprehension and control, bringing advice and messages from the divinity. They exercise charismatic authority over their followers, and, if successful, may establish new forms of social organization that may, in time, take on political and other functions, in addition to the primarily religious ones.

Beliefs in evildoers, especially witches and sorcerers, are widespread. These evildoers bring harm to their rivals by mystical means, an expression of the traditionally small-scale, personal organization of local societies: harm comes from kin and neighbors who are in disagreement or are having a dispute, rather than from distant impersonal forces.

Both Christianity and Islam have long histories in Africa. Christianity was introduced to Ethiopia as early as the fourth century, but in most of the continent, it was spread by European evangelization, beginning with the Portuguese on the western African coast and in the kingdom of Kongo in the fifteenth and sixteenth centuries, and also along the eastern African coast. Missionary enterprise did not reach its peak until after the eighteenth century. During the twentieth century, most conversion has been by African Christian prophets and other local leaders. Islam was taken to the northern and eastern African coasts in the seventh and tenth centuries, respectively, and was carried southward into the Sudan and throughout the western African savanna zone after the eleventh century, largely by Islamic traders and brotherhoods and occasionally through a jihad, or "holy war."

Africa today has a higher rate of conversion to Christianity than does any other continent; Islam is also widespread. One cause of this high rate of conversion is the steadily widening gap, throughout the continent, between the most wealthy and the most impoverished, with a concomitant decline in the importance of local deities and mystical forces. Education is another important factor, especially where vernacular translations of the Bible have been made available. Anti-European sentiment has undoubtedly fed Africans' wishes to form purely African religious congregations, with their own local leaders, ut it would be a mistake to suggest that local people see the various religions that are open to them in strictly either-or terms. Most people, in Africa as elsewhere, may assent to more than one religion and turn to whichever one would appear to be the more likely to bring good health, success, certainty, and happiness in any specific situation.

Conclusion

African societies, with their strong recognition of cultural traditions, face the deep problems that characterize a modern society, most of which are neither of their making nor even of their wishing. African societies and their cultures have undergone continual change as far back as history and prehistory can illumine, and their experience of several centuries of the overwhelming economic, military, social, and cultural power of colonial overrule has led to both changes and stagnation. Postcolonial "development" strategies, well-intentioned or not, have in many respects continued the effects of colonialism, through economic exploitation and financial indebtedness. In addition, Africa has been used by outside powers, especially during the cold war, as a surrogate battleground between these powers. Most postcolonial "economic development" has failed, owing to its being controlled by "experts" who have assumed that African societies are the same as those of industrialized nations and who are ignorant of the minute details of African cultures, social organization, and problems of local identity and purpose that lie below the level of the nation-state. Sadly, little progress has been made since the end of colonialism toward any real improvement in the lives of the ordinary people: instead, change has been at the level of the elites, who have taken charge of "modernization" and benefited from it. Nevertheless, African cultural traditions remain strong, and they are still capable of absorbing external influences and transforming them into their own.

Bibliography

GENERAL

Bohannan, Paul, and Philip Curtin (1988). *Africa and Africans*. 3rd ed. Prospect Heights, Ill.: Waveland Press.

Davidson, Basil (1969). *The African Genius*. Boston: Little, Brown & Co.

Forde, C. Daryll, ed. (1950–). *The Ethnographic Survey of Africa*. London: International African Institute.

Gibbs, James (1965). *The Peoples of Africa*. New York: Holt, Rinehart & Winston.

Martin, Phyllis, and Patrick O'Meara (1977). *Africa*. Bloomington: Indiana University Press.

Middleton, John (1970). *Black Africa: Its People and Their Cultures Today*. New York: Macmillan.

Murdock, George P. (1959). *Africa: Its People and Their Culture History*. New York: McGraw-Hill.

Oliver, Roland, and Michael Crowder, eds. (1981). *The Cambridge Encyclopedia of Africa*. Cambridge: Cambridge University Press.

Ottenberg, Simon, and Phoebe Ottenberg (n.d.). *Cultures and Societies of Africa*. New York: Random House.

HISTORY AND PREHISTORY

Clark, J. Desmond (1970). *The Prehistory of Africa*. N.p.

Coquery-Vidrovich, Catherine (1988). *Africa*. Berkeley and Los Angeles: University of California Press.

Curtin, Philip, Leonard Thompson, Steven Feierman, and Jan Vansina, eds. (1978). *African History*. Boston: Little, Brown & Co.

Davidson, Basil (1986). *Africa in History*. New York: Macmillan.

Davidson, Basil (1992). *The Black Man's Burden*. New York: Times Books.

Hiernaux, Jean (1974). *The People of Africa*. New York: Charles Scribner's Sons.

Newman, James L. (1994). *The Peopling of Africa*. New Haven: Yale University Press.

Oliver, Roland A. (1961). *The Dawn of African History*. London: Oxford University Press.

Oliver, Roland A. (1967). *The Middle Age of African History*. London: Oxford University Press.

Oliver, Rowland A., and John Fage (1962). *A Short History of Africa*. Harmondsworth: Penguin Books.

Vansina, Jan (1966). *Kingdoms of the Savanna*. Madison: University of Wisconsin Press.

Vansina, Jan (1978). *The Children of Woot: A History of the Kuba People*. Madison: University of Wisconsin Press.

Wilks, Ivor (1975). *Asante in the Nineteenth Century*. Cambridge: Cambridge University Press.

SOCIAL, ECONOMIC, AND POLITICAL SYSTEMS

Balandier, Georges (1970). *Political Anthropology*. Harmondsworth: Penguin Books.

Bohannan, Paul, and George Dalton, eds. (1962). *Markets in Africa*. Evanston, Ill.: Northwestern University Press.

Colson, E., and Max Gluckman, eds. (1951). *Seven Tribes of British Central Africa*. London: Oxford University Press.

Deng, Francis (1971). *Tradition and Modernization*. New Haven: Yale University Press.

Evans-Pritchard, E. E. (1940). *The Nuer*. Oxford: Clarendon Press.

Fallers, L. A. (1956). *A Bantu Bureaucracy*. Cambridge: Heffer.

Fallers, L. A. (1964). *The King's Men*. London: Oxford University Press.

Fortes, Meyer, and E. E. Evans-Pritchard, eds. (1940). *African Political Systems*. London: Oxford University Press.

Gluckman, Max (1963). *Order and Rebellion in Tribal Africa*. London: Cohen & West.

Kuper, Hilda (1947). *An African Aristocracy*. London: Oxford University Press (Swazi).

Mair, Lucy (1962). *Primitive Government*. Harmondsworth: Penguin Books.

Mair, Lucy (1974). *African Societies*. Cambridge: Cambridge University Press.

Mair, Lucy (1977). *African Kingdoms*. Oxford: Clarendon Press.

Nadel, S. F. (1942). *A Black Byzantium*. London: Oxford University Press.

Radcliffe-Brown, A. R., and D. Forde, eds. (1950). *African Systems of Kinship and Marriage*. London: Oxford University Press.

Richards, A. I. (1939). *Land, Labor, and Diet among the Bemba*. London: Oxford University Press.

Smith, Michael G. (1960). *Government in Zazzau*. London: Oxford University Press.

Southall, A. W. (1956). *Alur Society*. Cambridge: Heffer.

Winter, Edward H. (1956). *Bwamba*. Cambridge: Heffer.

RELIGION, PHILOSOPHY, AND SYMBOLISM

Arens, W., and I. Karp, eds. (1989). *Creativity of Power: Cosmology and Action in African Societies*. Washington, D.C.: Smithsonian Institution Press.

Beattie, John, and John Middleton, eds. (1969). *Spirit Mediumship and Society in Africa*. London: Routledge & Kegan Paul.

Biebuyck, Daniel, and K. Mateene (1969). *The Mwindo Epic*. Berkeley and Los Angeles: University of California Press.

Bloch, Maurice (1971). *Placing the Dead: Tombs, Ancestral Villages, and Kinship Organization on Madagascar*. New York: Seminar Press.

Boddy, Janice (1989). *Wombs and Alien Spirits*. Madison: University of Wisconsin Press.

Drewal, Henry, and John Pemberton (1989). *Yoruba: Nine Centuries of African Art and Thought*. New York: Abrams.

Evans-Pritchard, E. E. (1937). *Nuer Religion*. Oxford: Clarendon Press.

Evans-Pritchard, E. E. (1937). *Witchcraft, Oracles, and Magic among the Azande*. Oxford: Clarendon Press.

Forde, Daryll, ed. (1954). *African Worlds*. London: Oxford University Press.

Fortes, Meyer, and Germaine Dieterlen, eds. (1965). *African Systems of Thought*. London: Oxford University Press.

Greenberg, Joseph H. (1963). *The Languages of Africa*. Indiana University Research Center in Anthropology, Folklore, and Linguistics, Publication no. 25. The Hague: Mouton.

Horton, Robin (1993). *Patterns of Thought in Africa and the West*. Cambridge: Cambridge University Press.

Karp, Ivan, and C. Bird, eds. (1980). *Explorations in African Thought*. Bloomington: Indiana University Press.

Lan, David (1986). *Guns and Rain*. Manchester: Manchester University Press.

Lewis, Ioan M. (1971). *Ecstatic Religion*. Harmondsworth: Penguin Books.

Lewis, Ioan M., ed. (1966). *Islam in Tropical Africa*. London: Oxford University Press.

Lienhardt, R. G. (1961). *Divinity and Experience: The Religion of the Dinka*. Oxford: Clarendon Press.

MacGaffey, Wyatt (1986). *Religion and Society in Central Africa: The BaKongo of Lower Zaire*. Chicago: University of Chicago Press.

Mbiti, John S. (1969). *African Religions and Philosophy*. London: Heinemann.

Middleton, John (1960). *Lugbara Religion*. London: Oxford University Press.

Middleton, John, and E. H. Winter, eds. (1963). *Witchcraft and Sorcery in East Africa*. London: Routledge & Kegan Paul.

Mudimbe, V. Y. (1988). *The Invention of Africa*. Bloomington: Indiana University Press.

Mudimbe, V. Y. (1994). *The Idea of Africa*. Bloomington: Indiana University Press.

Parrinder, E. G. (1954). *African Traditional Religion*. London: Sheldon Press.

Peel, J. D. Y. (1968). *Aladura*. London: Oxford University Press.

Taylor, John V. (1963). *The Primal Vision*. London: SMC Press.

Tempels, Placide (1949). *La philosophie bantoue*. Paris: Présence Africaine. Translated into English as *Bantu Philosophy*, 1959.

Trimingham, John S. (1968). *The Influence of Islam upon Africa*. London: Longmans.

Turner, V. W. (1967). *The Forest of Symbols*. Ithaca, N.Y.: Cornell University Press.

Turner, V. W. (1968). *The Drums of Affliction*. Oxford: Clarendon Press.

Willett, Frank (1971). *African Art*. London: Thames & Hudson.

JOHN MIDDLETON

Introduction to the Middle East

The term "Middle East" is generally recognized today to refer to a region that stretches from the Atlantic Ocean in the west to Afghanistan in the east, a distance of approximately 5,600 kilometers. It has a total population of around 300 million people and encompasses the countries of Morocco, Algeria, Tunisia, Libya, Egypt, Israel, Lebanon, Syria, Jordan, Saudi Arabia, Kuwait, Bahrain, Qatar, the United Arab Emirates, Oman, Yemen, Iraq, Turkey, and Iran. The African countries of Mauritania and Sudan are also considered to be within the "Middle East."

This usage of the term "Middle East" has increasingly come to supplant the more conventional usage, which divided the area into two regions, the Middle East and North Africa. The term "North Africa" referred to the Arab countries of Morocco, Algeria, Tunisia, and Libya; "the Middle East," on the other hand, referred to Egypt (which is geographically located in North Africa) as well as the rest of the Arab countries to the east plus Israel, Turkey, and Iran. French scholars, in general, continue to refer to France's former North African colonies of Morocco, Algeria, and Tunisia by the Arabic term "Maghreb" and to Egypt and the rest of the Arab countries as the "Near East." The term "Maghreb" derives from the Arabic designation *bilād al-Maghreb*, meaning "the countries of the west" or, more literally, "the land where the sun sets." The term was traditionally used by Arabs to distinguish this part of the Arab world from the more eastern parts, which were referred to as *bilād al-Mashreq*, the "countries of the east" or "the land where the sun rises."

Today, however, the terms "Middle Eastern" and "Middle East" have been adopted by the people of the entire region to refer to themselves and to their part of the world, in much the same way as such terms as "Europe," "Central Asia," and "Southeast Asia" are used to broadly identify highly complex and culturally diversified regions of the world.

The Middle East, as defined above, encompasses four distinct culture areas: Arab, Turkish, Iranian, and the newly evolved Israeli culture. The Arab, Turkish, and Iranian cultures are heirs to great Islamic empires that had their centers in the region and represent three distinct variations within the global Islamic civilization. The most recent and most enduring of these, the Ottoman Empire, ruled over most of the Middle East, as well as parts of eastern Europe, for almost 500 years, until its demise and dismemberment at the end of World War I. Out of its ashes arose the modern state of Turkey, as well as the majority of the contemprary Arab nation-states.

From the historical perspective, the Middle East is known as the "cradle of civilizations." Its two major river systems, the Nile Valley in Egypt, and the Tigris-Euphrates in Iraq (ancient Mesopotamia) were the sites of the world's earliest civilizations (e.g., Egyptian, Sumerian, Babylonian, and Assyrian). This is where urban life and centralized forms of political organization arose; it is also the birthplace of the world's three major monotheistic religions, Judaism, Christianity, and Islam.

These three distinct yet related religions were forged in the context of the Middle East, and all three continue today to find expression in and give meaning to the lives of the people of the region.

Archaeologists working in the area have uncovered evidence of the prehistoric domestication of plants and animals and the beginning of settled life as far back back in time as the Neolithic or New Stone Age. From sites scattered along the hilly flanks of the mountain ranges in Iraq, Iran, and Israel, archaeologists are reconstructing the cultural evolution that transformed our human ancestors from nomadic hunters and gatherers into settled villagers who cultivated domesticated varieties of wheat and barley and kept domesticated sheep and goats. This major epoch in human history, which can be dated back to 8000 B.C., has been referred to as the "Agricultural Revolution" to underscore its significance in the development of our cultural history.

The transition from an adaptation based on hunting and gathering to one based on food production and settled community life was the prelude to the next phase in human cultural evolution, the beginning of civilization, which in the Middle East goes back to about 5000 B.C. The culture complex we refer to as "civilization" includes urbanism, a writing system, monumental architecture, long-distance trade, a complex social order, and a centralized state system, often focused on a divine king. This transformation is fully illustrated in the archaeological records of the different civilizations that succeeded each other in the region: Sumer, Egypt, Akkad, Babylon, and Assyria. The history of dynastic Egypt is perhaps the most complete; it has been traced back to 3100 B.C., when Menes, the king of Upper Egypt, successfully conquered Lower Egypt and ruled the newly united kingdom of Egypt from his capital in Thebes. Despite a series of invasions—Roman, Arab, Ottoman, and British—Egypt has always remained a united country with a very strong sense of its unique identity.

Iran, or Persia, as it was formerly known, is a country with a long and illustrious history. The Iranians, who speak an Indo-European language, Farsi, are also heirs to a great civilization and an imperial past. Prior to its conquest by the Muslim Arabs in the seventh century, Iran was the center of the

Sāssānid Empire, a Persian dynasty that had adopted Zoroastrianism as the state religion. Zoroastrianism is considered by some scholars to be one of the first "ethical" religions and a precursor to early Judaism. The prophet Zoroaster declared the coexistence of Good and Evil in the world and called on humans to uphold the Good by combatting Evil. Although the overwhelming majority of Zoroastrians were converted following the Muslim invasion, a small community of them remains today in Iran.

Physical and Human Geography

To best appreciate the ethnic complexity and cultural history of the Middle East, it is necessary to know a little about the physical and human geography of the region. Population patterns, modes of subsistence, and cultural systems have their basis in the early adaptation of the human population to its natural environment and its constraints. In the Middle East, the natural environment is best described as semiarid. In fact, more than 80 percent of the region is desert that receives less than 25 centimeters of rainfall a year. A few areas, such as the coastal zones of North Africa, Turkey, and the Eastern Mediterranean, receive adequate rainfall to support agriculture. The rainfall pattern in the interior of the region tends to be highly unpredictable from one year to the next; consequently, rain-dependent agriculture is a risky venture. Peasants traditionally combine extensive cultivation with animal husbandry to minimize risk and ensure their subsistence.

From antiquity, the people of the Middle East have developed elaborate means of water control and management. Irrigation systems developed along the river valleys of Egypt and Mesopotamia are, in large part, credited with providing the basis for the development of the ancient civilizations. Today, massive hydraulic projects like the Aswan Dam of Egypt and the Kur River plan of south-central Iran testify to the continued need to conserve water and extend its distribution for agriculture. On a more modest scale, traditional systems of underwater canals were constructed to carry water from the seasonally formed underwater mountain streams to the fields nearby.

Topography is another determining factor in human settlement and adaptation. The Middle East landscape alternates between high rugged mountains and plateaus and dry lowland areas, where the line between the desert and even marginally cultivatable land is sharply drawn. Egypt, which has been called "the gift of the Nile," is essentially a narrow ribbon of densely settled valley carved out of the desert. It is estimated that over 95 percent of Egypt's population is concentrated on 5 percent of its territory.

The mountains in the Middle East include the Atlas chain in Morocco, the Aurès in Algeria, the Lebanons, the Taurus and Pontic ranges in Turkey, and the Zagros and Elburz in Iran; the highest peak, Damāvand in the Elburz Mountains, has an elevation of 5,738 meters. The mountains in Turkey and Iran enclose two high plateaus, punctuated by brackish lakes (Van in Turkey and Urmia in Iran), that consist of large tracts of salt flats and deserts.

Apart from oil, the region is generally poor in mineral resources. The mountains of North Africa, Turkey, and Iran contain limited amounts of iron ore, copper, coal, and some gold. Important phosphate deposits are found in Morocco and in adjacent Western Sahara; in fact Morocco is the world's third-largest producer of phosphates, after the United States and Russia.

The Middle East is rich in petroleum. The proven oil reserves of Saudi Arabia alone are known to be 25 percent of the world's total; those of Iraq, Iran, and Kuwait constitute another 25 percent. Overall, it is estimated that more than 62 percent of all proven oil reserves are found in the Middle East and North Africa. Furthermore, Middle Eastern oil is both cheap to produce and of high quality.

The climate regime throughout the region is generally Mediterranean, characterized by hot dry summers and cool wet winters. Along the Gulf region, however, as in some other parts of the region, summer temperatures can peak at 49° C. At the same time, in the winter, mountain villagers in Morocco, Iraq, Turkey, and Iran experience freezing temperatures and heavy snows.

Patterns of Living

In response to the challenges posed by the climate, topography, and limited water supply, the people of the Middle East have from the beginning of recorded history pursued three different but related living patterns: urban, rural, and nomadic. The juxtaposition of the city, the village, and the nomad's camp is a distinctive feature of the Middle East as a culture area.

The region boasts some of the oldest cities in the world, such as Damascus and İstanbul. Middle Eastern cities have been and remain the center of political, religious, economic, and intellectual life; they dominate and overshadow the rural countryside where, until fairly recently, the majority of the population lived as peasants, working on land owned or controlled by absentee urban landlords. In 1900 it was estimated that no more than 10 percent of the region's population was urban dwelling; by 1970, the proportion had grown to 40 percent. Although there is no agreement concerning the definition of a "city" or "urban settlement," scholars agree that, on the whole, slightly over half the inhabitants of the Middle East today live in centers of more than 20,000 people. The projection for the year 2000 is that more than 70 percent of the inhabitants will be urban dwellers. The largest city in the region, Cairo, has more than 12 million inhabitants and there are now thirty cities with populations exceeding half a million. As is the case with other parts of the third world, this accelerated urban growth, which is largely the result of rural-urban migration, has generated severe problems in housing, employment, schooling, and services. Given that the majority of the region's population is below 20 years of age, it is not surprising that cities and towns, with their burgeoning shanty towns, are hotbeds of political dissent and activism.

In contrast with the urban and rural populations, nomadic pastoralists have always constituted a small minority of the total population of the region (and in the late twentieth century, no more than an estimated 1 percent). Although conditions affecting nomads vary from one country to the next, overall, nomadic pastoralism has been on the decline since the turn of the twentieth century. In Iraq, for example, nomads were estimated to make up about 35 to 40 percent of the population in 1900; by the 1970s, their proportion had declined to 2.8 percent. In Saudi Arabia, nomads constituted approximately 40 percent of the population, a figure that had declined to about 11 percent by 1970. Likewise, Libya's population was 25 percent nomadic in 1960; in the mid-1990s nomads constitute only 3.5 percent of the total.

This decline was vastly accelerated in the 1950s with the establishment of the modern nation-states and the influx of oil wealth into the region; nomadic pastoralists have been increasingly brought under the authority of central governments. In Saudi Arabia, the once proudly independent "noble" camel-herding Bedouin are now members of the Saudi Reserve National Guard or laborers in the oil fields. In Iraq, Syria, Iran, and Egypt, land-reform measures, changing patterns of land use, and the availability of wages have combined to undermine the nomads' traditional way of life by hastening their integration into the national culture.

As an economic strategy, pastoral nomadism is an adaptation to the general semiaridity of the region. Where true desert conditions obtain, such as in the Sudanic belt of northern Africa and in the Arabian Peninsula, camel breeding dominates. In other, less arid areas, including the high plateaus and mountains of the region, nomads concentrate on sheep and goats.

Nomadic pastoralists, who account for a small part of food production in the region (when compared with peasants), have a historical and cultural significance that far outweighs their number and economic contribution. This is generally true for all tribally organized nomadic populations, be they Arab, Berber, Turkish, Kurdish, or Persian speakers. Historically, armed and mounted tribally organized Arab-speaking nomads played an important role in the early Islamic conquests of the Byzantine and Sāssānid empires. Likewise, Berber-speaking nomadic and seminomadic tribes were instrumental in the Muslim conquest of Spain. On the local level, nomadic pastoralists have traditionally posed a challenge to the political authority of their respective states as they struggled to maintain their political autonomy and their distinct cultural traditions.

Despite certain shared elements of economic and sociopolitical organization, it is important to keep in mind that nomadic pastoralists do not represent a homogeneous segment of Middle Eastern population. They differ in language, sectarian affiliation, and cultural traditions. Even within one country, pastoralists may vary widely. In southeastern Turkey, for example, Turkish-, Arabic-, and Kurdish-speaking groups share a common territory. Likewise, in southwestern Iran, the powerful Khamseh Confederacy is made up of Arabic, Persian, and Turkish tribes. The large majority of Kurdish pastoralists are Sunni Muslims, but some groups profess Shia Islam. In Mauritania, Morocco, and Algeria, Arab- and Berber-speaking tribes commingle.

The Ethnic Mosaic

The ethnic and cultural diversity exhibited by nomadic pastoralists is of course reflected in the larger "ethnic mosaic" of the Middle East. It should be noted that Western scholars have, on the whole, overemphasized the sectarian and cultural differentiation in the Middle East, thereby projecting a picture of a highly fragmented society torn apart by opposed primordial loyalties and ancient animosities. The fact is that, when compared with other parts of the world such as Russia, Eastern Europe, and Southeast Asia, the Middle East exhibits remarkable coherence as a culture area.

Various factors account for this coherence. First, Turkey and Iran aside, the overwhelming majority of the inhabitants of the region are Arabic speakers, who, despite national and regional variations in dialect, share a single standard written version of Arabic, the language taught in school and used over the radio and in the newspapers. Second, the region is predominantly Muslim and has been so for over a millennium. From Morocco to Iraq and into Turkey, the overwhelming majority of the population profess Sunni Islam; the Iranians, by contrast, are on the whole Shia Muslims. Third, the tripartite division of the population into urban, rural, and nomadic segments is a universal feature throughout the area defined here as the Middle East.

To claim a relative cultural coherence to the region is not to deny the cultural diversity that exists; in fact, each country in the area contains groups or minorities that are distinct from the larger population in terms of some cultural "marker" that is recognized by themselves and others as the hallmark of their identity. These ethnic or communal markers include religious affiliation, language, tribal membership, racial variation, and local customs. Of these, the two most important markers of ethnic and cultural identity in the Middle East are language and religion.

It is important to note that the recognition and acceptance of ethnic and communal differences have traditionally been a fundamental principle of social organization in the Middle East. This is especially the case for communities defined by religion. Until the demise of the Ottoman Empire and the rise of modern nationalism in the region, social interaction was structured in terms of the individual's membership in a given confessional or "tribal" grouping. This tendency persists today; nationalist movements and secular ideologies have failed to completely erode the more narrowly defined identities based on kinship (i.e., tribe), religion, or language.

The four major language families in the region are Indo-European, Semitic, Altaic or Turkic, and Afro-Asiatic. Persian (Farsi), Kurdish, Luri, Baluchi, and Armenian are Indo-European languages. Arabic and Hebrew belong to the Semitic Family. Turkic languages include the modern standard Turkish, Azeri, and Turkmen. Hebrew, Persian, and Turkish are the national languages of Israel, Iran, and Turkey, respectively. Arabic is the national language of all the other countries in the region. Persian is written in Arabic characters and its vocabulary includes a large number of Arabic words. Under the Ottomans, Turkish was also written in Arabic characters; following the defeat of the Ottomans in World War I, and as part of the effort to modernize Turkey, a state edict in 1928 replaced Arabic with Roman characters.

In northwestern Africa (especially in the mountainous regions of Morocco and Algeria) and in parts of the Sahara Desert, several dialects of Berber are spoken. Berber is an Afro-Asiatic language spoken by the indigenous inhabitants of North Africa and parts of the Sahara.

The Kurds, who number an estimated twenty million people, constitute the largest linguistically differentiated "ethnic" group in the Middle East. The large majority of the Kurds are Sunni Muslims, many of whom also subscribe to a Sufi brotherhood, or *tariqa;* a minority of the Kurds adhere to an extreme form of Shia Islam. The Kurds speak several dialects of Kurdish, an Indo-European language, and inhabit a mountainous area that straddles the national frontiers of Turkey, Iran, Iraq, the former Soviet Union, and Syria. In all of these countries, the Kurds constitute a significant "minority." The dismemberment of the Kurdish homeland and dispersion of the Kurdish people among a number of different countries was a legacy of the European colonial powers (England and France in particular), the policies and rivalries of whom were instrumental in giving shape to the political map of the Middle East as we know it today.

The Kurds have a long and complicated history of political activism; going back to the 1920s, secular and religious leaders have led movements aimed at achieving national independence or, in some cases, regional autonomy. The relative success or failure of these movements, whether in Iran, Iraq, or Turkey, has varied with the nature of the ruling regime and the geopolitical interests of the world powers.

The Berber-speaking groups of Morocco and Algeria, who are mostly rural dwellers living in mountain villages and desert encampments, are Sunni Muslims, like their Arabic-speaking compatriots. Berbers have a strong sense of their own distinct cultural identity, based on their separate language and on their claim to be the indigenous inhabitants of the region, predating the Arab-Muslim invasions of the seventh century. This "ethnic consciousness," however, remains at the cultural level and does not imply political cleavage. During the many years of French-colonial domination of the region, French policy was to encourage the notion that "Berber" identity and "culture" were distinct from and opposed to that of the urban "Arab" and "Muslim" Moroccan. This attempt to "divide and rule" was not a success, however; in fact, Berbers were in the forefront of the movements for national independence in Morocco and in Algeria.

Religion

Religion is perhaps the single most important marker of communal identity in the region. Islam, the religion of the overwhelming majority of the population, originated in northern Arabia when the Prophet Mohammed (A.D. 570–632) succeeded in converting the animist and pagan tribes of the Arabian Peninsula to the new religion. Following the death of the prophet Mohammed, Arab-Muslim armies swept out of Arabia in a series of military expeditions that pitched the Muslims against the Christian Byzantines and the Sāssānians, who were Zoroastrians. Defeated by the Muslims, the Byzantines were forced to withdraw their armies from Jerusalem and Damascus into the heartland of Anatolia, closer to their capital of Constantinople. The Sāssānians were routed out of Iraq and Persia, which became provinces of the newly formed Arab-Muslim state, based first in Damascus and later in Baghdad. Within a hundred years after the Prophet's death, the borders of the Muslim Empire had reached the Pyrenees in the west and Afghanistan in the east. The conquest of this vast and heterogenous territory was accompanied by mass conversions to Islam.

During his lifetime, the prophet Mohammed had recognized the Jews and Christians as "People of the Book," recipients of a valid but incomplete revelation. As such and unlike the pagan Arabs, the small Jewish and Christian communities in northern Arabia were not forced to convert to Islam; they were tolerated and given a special status within the larger Muslim community, or *umma*, as "protected" people.

This policy was followed by all the Muslim successor states; the Jews and the various Christian sects were allowed to practice their faith and retain their institutions and customs. They were, however, required to pay a special poll tax and were not allowed to serve in the army. This policy was later adopted by the Ottomans and extended to a large number of non-Muslim communities, including the Armenians and the Druze. Known as the *millet* system, it formed a basic principle of Ottoman administration; at the turn of the twentieth century, seventeen different communities were recognized. This practice was, to a large extent, responsible for the encapsulation and the survival of religious communities as inherent components of Middle Eastern social structure. Concomitantly, it served to reinforce the social and political significance of sectarian identity.

The Christians of the Middle East have a long and complex history. Besides the Greek Orthodox Church (which was the official church of the Byzantine Empire), other indigenous Christian churches have their origin in one or another of the many schismatic movements of the fifth and sixth centuries. The two largest Christian communities in the Middle East, those of the Copts of Egypt and the Maronites of Lebanon, originated in religious controversies of the fifth century.

Another Christian minority that dates back to the same era is the Assyrian Nestorian community of Iraq. The Nestorian church was formed as a result of a schism within the Byzantine church at the Council of Chalcedon in 451 A.D. The Assyrians, who speak an Aramaic dialect, were originally located in several villages scattered in the mountains that divide northern Iraq from Turkey. Like other minorities in the region, the Assyrians were caught in the web of colonial politics; with Britain's encouragement, a group of Assyrians sought to secede from the newly independent state of Iraq and establish their own nation-state in the north. This misguided attempt led to tragedy when, in an attempt to flee Iraq into French-held Syria in 1933, several thousand of them were massacred by the Iraqi army.

The Copts constitute the single largest Christian community in the Middle East, as well as 5 to 7 percent of the Egyptian population of about 56 million people. The Copts speak Egyptian Arabic and are, generally speaking, hard to distinguish culturally from the rest of the Egyptians. The Coptic church is a national church, limited to Egypt; it has its own liturgy (in Coptic), ceremonial calendar, and clerical hierarchy headed by a patriarch.

The Maronite church is the largest of the Uniate churches of the Middle East and is limited mainly to Lebanon. The term "Uniate" refers to a number of Middle Eastern churches that chose to abandon the Eastern Orthodox rites, recognize the authority of the pope, and adopt Latin rites. Another Uniate church is that of the Chaldeans, who lived predominantly in Iraq (with a small group in Syria and Iran) and were prominent in the hotel and restaurant business there. Following World War II, a large number of Chaldeans emigrated to the United States and Canada.

When the Republic of Lebanon was proclaimed in 1926, the different sectarian groups, all of whom speak Arabic, were formally recognized as corporate political communities, each of which was allotted a number of representatives in the national parliament. Furthermore, it was also decreed that the president of the country had to be a Maronite, the prime minister a Sunni Muslim, and the speaker of the house a Shia Muslim. The system failed to work as anticipated, and, by the mid-1970s, inherent strains and foreign pressures exploded in a civil war that has plagued Lebanon into the late twentieth century. It is difficult at this juncture to predict the future shape of the Lebanese polity and the role that sectarianism will play in the political domain.

Prior to the establishment of the state of Israel in 1948 and the collapse of the European colonial regimes in the region, large Jewish communities had existed in most countries of the Middle East and North Africa, with the exception of Saudi Arabia and the Gulf states. The Jews generally spoke the national language of their respective countries (i.e., Arabic, Persian, or Turkish) and, with a few notable exceptions, tended to concentrate in urban areas. In northern Iraq, there used to be a small Jewish community scattered in a number of villages in an area dominated by Kurdish tribal chiefs. These so-called "Kurdish Jews" spoke a dialect of Hebrew known as *targum*. Similarly, throughout the mountainous areas of Morocco, Jewish communities were established among the rural Berber-speaking population. As might be expected, Jewish communities of the Middle East varied greatly among themselves, as they tended to reflect the life-style and cultural traditions of the specific country or region that they inhabited. Ranging from wealthy bankers and merchants to humble artisans and poor shopkeepers, community members were widely differentiated in terms of wealth, education, and influence.

Since the massive emigration of Jews to Israel, the United States, Canada, France, and other countries in the 1950s, only a few thousand Jews remain today in Turkey, the Arab countries, and Iran. In Israel, immigrants from such countries as Iraq, Morocco, Yemen, Tunisia, and Libya are referred to as "Oriental Jews," or "Mizrashim." Despite their numerical advantage (they make up about half of the population of Israel), they tend to lag behind the European Jews in terms of political power and social status.

Besides the Christian and Jewish communities, there exist a number of distinctive religiously defined minorities in the region. These minorities had their origin in intra-Muslim religio-political disputes; most of them represent schismatic offshoots from Shiism. This is the case with the Druze who inhabit the mountain zones of Syria, Lebanon, and Israel; the Alawi of Syria and Turkey; the Zaidi of the Yemen highlands; and the Yazidi of northern Iraq. These groups share a history of political dissidence, defeat, and persecution, as a result of which they are found in marginal areas far from the direct reach of the dynasty in power. Despite the differences in their religious beliefs and practices and their cultural styles, these communities tend to be tightly organized under the leadership of an oligarchy of religious elders; they also tend to be highly endogamous, secretive, and inaccessible to outsiders.

Lastly, a community may have its own distinctive cultural identity which is not based on language, religion, or life-style. The Circassians, who are Sunni Muslims and speak Arabic, form such a group; they are found in Turkey, Jordan, Syria, and Iraq. Some of the Circassians came to the Middle East as refugees after having fled their homeland in the Caucasus during the nineteenth century; others were brought in by the Ottomans and resettled as buffer groups in hard-to-administer Arab areas of the Ottoman Empire. Small in number and divided as they are among several nation-states, the Circassians have preserved their sense of cultural identity through the collective memory of a shared historical past and a common place of origin.

Contemporary Political Considerations

The vast oil wealth of the region, coupled with the volatile and seemingly intractable Israeli-Palestinian conflict, has increasingly drawn the Middle East into the forefront of world politics and economics. More recently, the rise of Islamic-fundamentalist movements in the political arena has introduced a new dimension to political life in the region. It has once again opened the debate on one of the most fundamental questions in the history of the Muslim civilization: what is the proper relationship between Islam and the state? Furthermore, what status would non-Muslims have in a "Muslim state?" The problem is also posed in the case of Israel, which was founded as an exclusively "Jewish" state.

Bibliography

Bates, D., and A. Rassam (1983). *Peoples and Cultures of the Middle East*. Englewood Cliffs, N.J.: Prentice-Hall.

Carelton, Coon (1961). *Caravan: The Story of the Middle East*. New York: Holt, Rinehart & Winston.

Eickelman, Dale (1981). *The Middle East: An Anthropological Approach*. Englewood Cliffs, N.J.: Prentice-Hall.

Richard, A., and J. Waterbury (1990). *A Political Economy of the Middle East: State, Class, and Economic Development*. Boulder, Colo.: Westview Press.

AMAL RASSAM

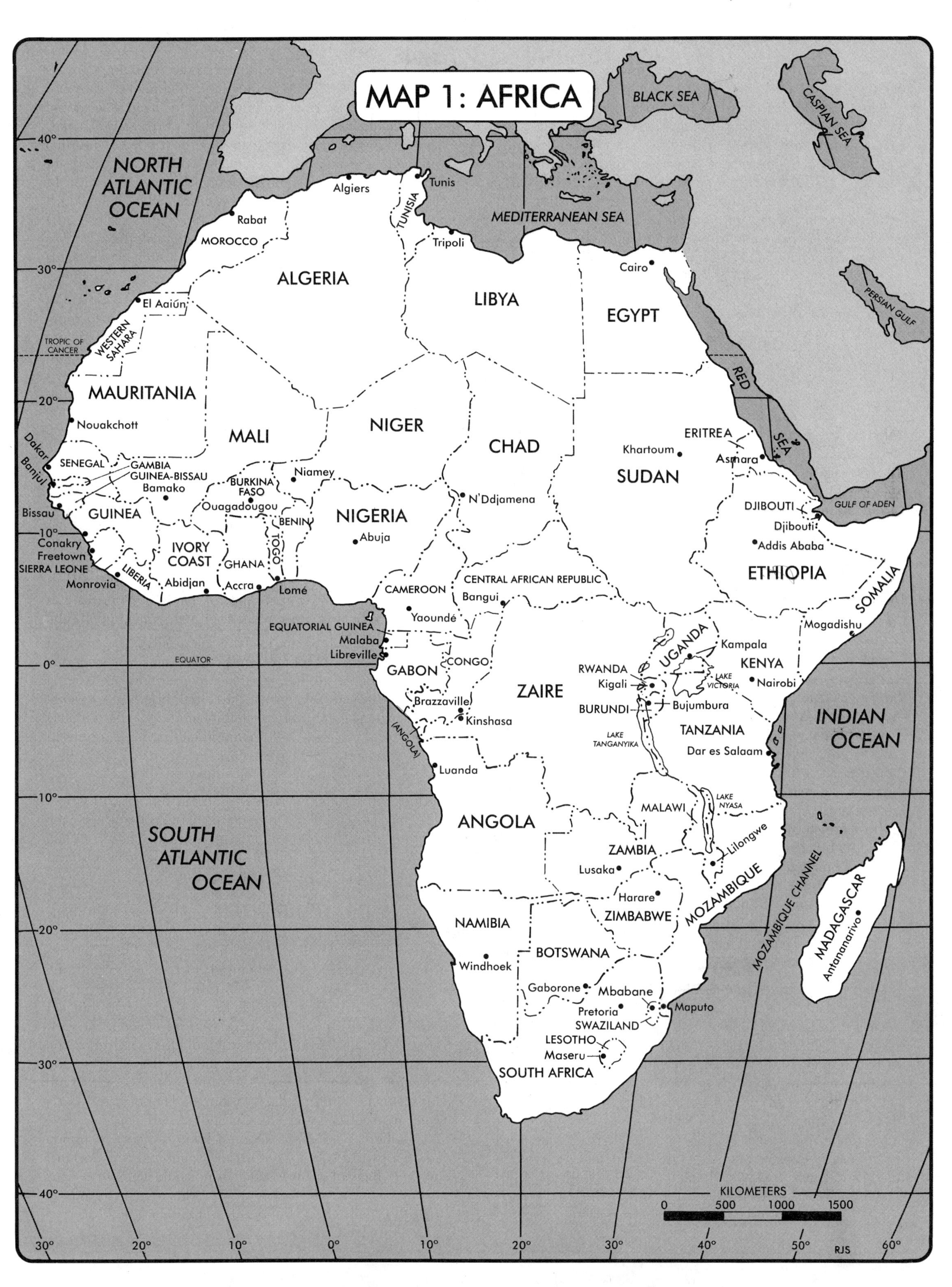
MAP 1: AFRICA
NORTH ATLANTIC OCEAN
SOUTH ATLANTIC OCEAN
INDIAN OCEAN
MEDITERRANEAN SEA
BLACK SEA
CASPIAN SEA
PERSIAN GULF
RED SEA
GULF OF ADEN
MOZAMBIQUE CHANNEL
TROPIC OF CANCER
EQUATOR
LAKE VICTORIA
LAKE TANGANYIKA
LAKE NYASA
MOROCCO
Rabat
ALGERIA
Algiers
TUNISIA
Tunis
LIBYA
Tripoli
EGYPT
Cairo
WESTERN SAHARA
El Aaiún
MAURITANIA
Nouakchott
MALI
Bamako
NIGER
Niamey
CHAD
N'Ddjamena
SUDAN
Khartoum
ERITREA
Asmara
DJIBOUTI
Djibouti
ETHIOPIA
Addis Ababa
SOMALIA
Mogadishu
SENEGAL
Dakar
GAMBIA
Banjul
GUINEA-BISSAU
Bissau
GUINEA
Conakry
SIERRA LEONE
Freetown
LIBERIA
Monrovia
IVORY COAST
Abidjan
BURKINA FASO
Ouagadougou
GHANA
Accra
TOGO
Lomé
BENIN
NIGERIA
Abuja
CAMEROON
Yaoundé
CENTRAL AFRICAN REPUBLIC
Bangui
EQUATORIAL GUINEA
Malabo
Libreville
GABON
CONGO
Brazzaville
ZAIRE
Kinshasa
(ANGOLA)
UGANDA
Kampala
KENYA
Nairobi
RWANDA
Kigali
BURUNDI
Bujumbura
TANZANIA
Dar es Salaam
ANGOLA
Luanda
MALAWI
Lilongwe
ZAMBIA
Lusaka
ZIMBABWE
Harare
MOZAMBIQUE
Maputo
MADAGASCAR
Antananarivo
NAMIBIA
Windhoek
BOTSWANA
Gaborone
Mbabane
SWAZILAND
Pretoria
LESOTHO
Maseru
SOUTH AFRICA
40°
30°
20°
10°
0°
10°
20°
30°
40°
30°
20°
10°
0°
10°
20°
30°
40°
50°
60°
KILOMETERS
0
500
1000
1500
RJS

MAP 2 LEGEND: CULTURES OF AFRICA

1. ACHOLI
2. AFAR
3. AKAN
4. ALUR
5. AMHARA
6. ANUAK
7. TANDROY
8. ARABS
9. BAGGARA
10. BAGIRMI
11. BAMILEKE
12. BEDOUIN
13. BEMBA
14. BERBERS
15. BETSILEO
16. CHAGGA
17. DINKA
18. DOGON
19. DYULA
20. EDO
21. EWE
22. FALI

23a. FIPA

23. FON
24. FULANI
25. GANDA
26. GUSII
27. HAUSA
28. HERERO
29. IBIBIO
30. IGBO
31. IRAQW
32. ITESO
33. KANURI
34. KARAMOJONG
35. KHOI
36. KIKUYU
37. KIPSIGIS
38. KONGO
39. KONSO
40. KPELLE
41. LANGO
42. LOBI-DAGARTI
43. LOZI
44. LUBA
45. LUGBARA
46. LUNDA
47. LUO
48. LUYIA
49. MAASAI
50. MAMPRUSI
51. MANDE
52. MANGBETU
53. MBEERE
54. MENDE
55. MIJIKENDA
56. MONGO
57. MOSSI
58. NANDI AND OTHER KALENJIN
59. NDEBELE
60. NDEMBU
61. NUBIANS
62. NUER
63. NYAKYUSA
64. NYAMWEZI
65. OKIEK
66. PENDE
67. POKOT
68. RUKUBA
69. SAKALAVA
70. SAN-SPEAKING PEOPLES
71. SARA
72. SHILLUK
73. SHONA
74. SOMALIS
75. SONGHAY
76. SUKU
77. SUKUMA
78. SURI
79. SWAHILI
80. SWAZI
81. TEDA
82. TEMNE
83. TIGRAY
84. TIV
85. TONGA
86. TROPICAL-FOREST FORAGERS
87. TSIMIHETY
88. TSWANA
89. TUAREG
90. TURKANA
91. WOLOF
92. XHOSA
93. YAKO
94. YORUBA
95. ZANDE
96. ZARAMO
97. ZARMA
98. ZULU

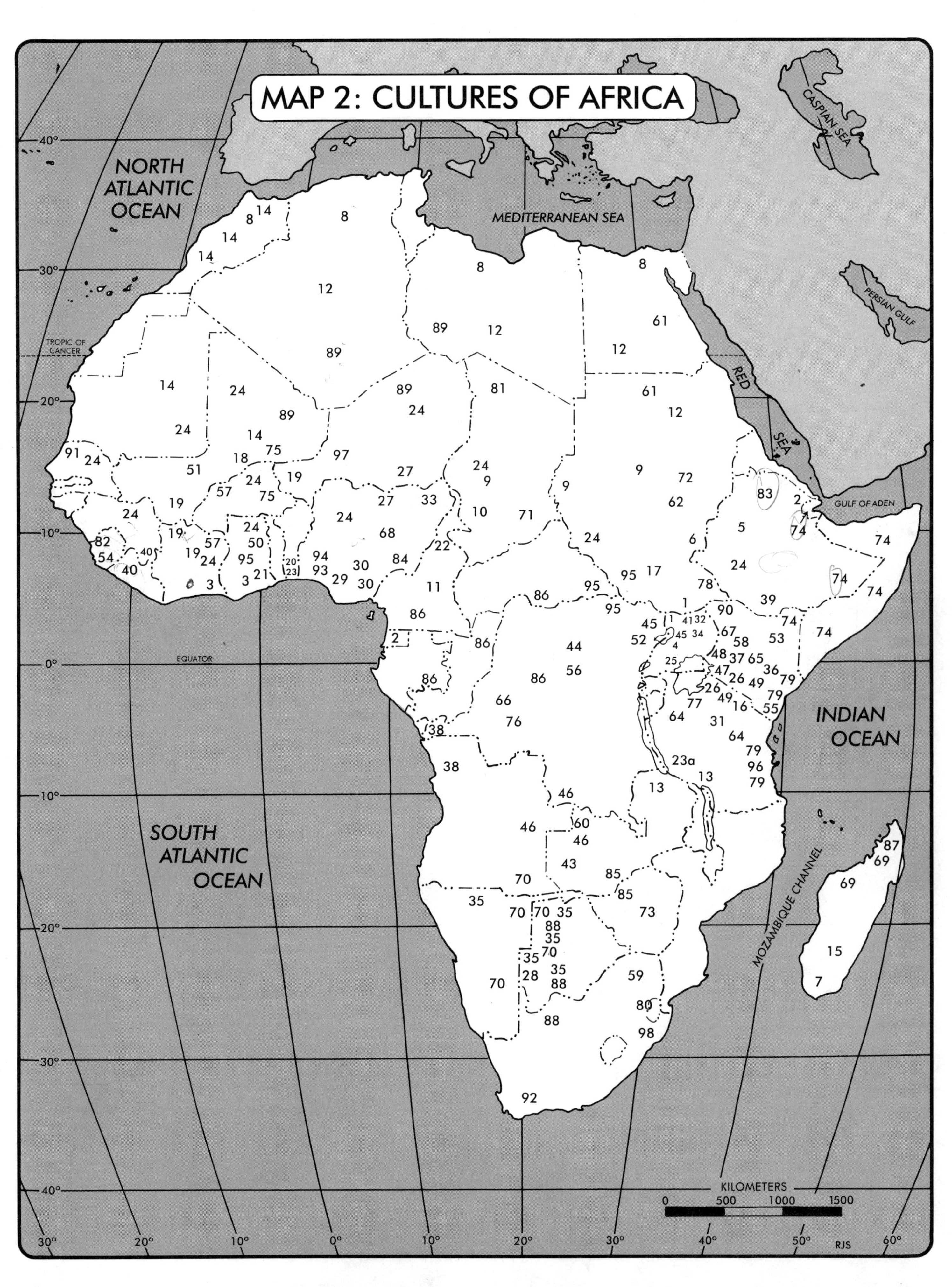

MAP 2: CULTURES OF AFRICA
NORTH ATLANTIC OCEAN
MEDITERRANEAN SEA
CASPIAN SEA
PERSIAN GULF
RED SEA
GULF OF ADEN
TROPIC OF CANCER
EQUATOR
INDIAN OCEAN
SOUTH ATLANTIC OCEAN
MOZAMBIQUE CHANNEL
KILOMETERS
0
500
1000
1500
RJS

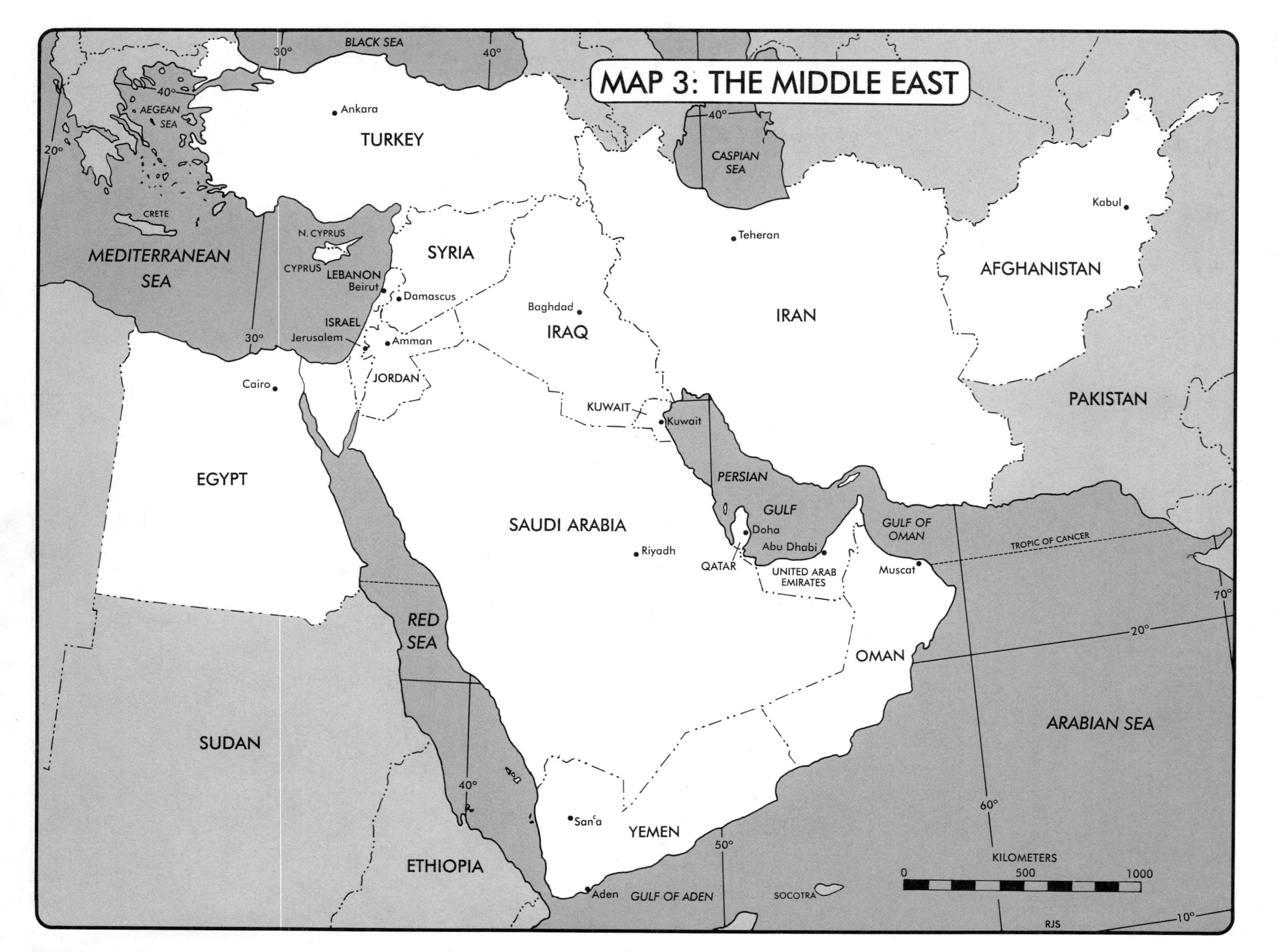
MAP 3: THE MIDDLE EAST
BLACK SEA
30°
40°
AEGEAN SEA
20°
Ankara
TURKEY
CRETE
MEDITERRANEAN SEA
N. CYPRUS
CYPRUS
LEBANON
Beirut
Damascus
SYRIA
ISRAEL
Jerusalem
Amman
JORDAN
Cairo
EGYPT
CASPIAN SEA
Teheran
IRAN
Kabul
AFGHANISTAN
PAKISTAN
Baghdad
IRAQ
KUWAIT
Kuwait
PERSIAN GULF
Doha
Abu Dhabi
QATAR
UNITED ARAB EMIRATES
GULF OF OMAN
Muscat
TROPIC OF CANCER
SAUDI ARABIA
Riyadh
OMAN
RED SEA
SUDAN
ETHIOPIA
San'a
YEMEN
Aden
GULF OF ADEN
SOCOTRA
ARABIAN SEA
50°
60°
70°
10°
KILOMETERS
0
500
1000
RJS

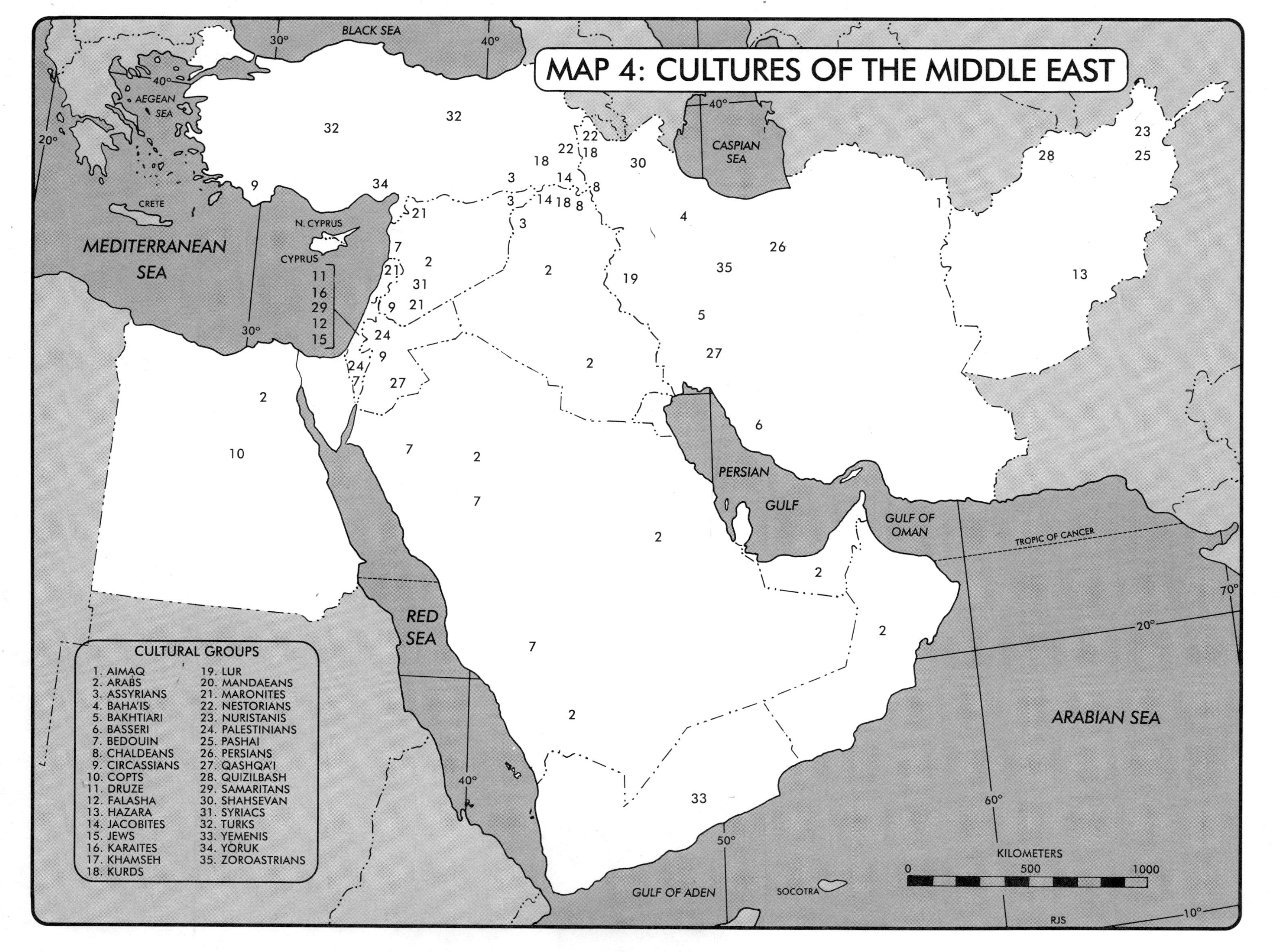

MAP 4: CULTURES OF THE MIDDLE EAST
BLACK SEA
AEGEAN SEA
CRETE
MEDITERRANEAN SEA
N. CYPRUS
CYPRUS
CASPIAN SEA
PERSIAN GULF
GULF OF OMAN
TROPIC OF CANCER
RED SEA
GULF OF ADEN
SOCOTRA
ARABIAN SEA
KILOMETERS
0
500
1000
RJS
CULTURAL GROUPS
1. AIMAQ
2. ARABS
3. ASSYRIANS
4. BAHA'IS
5. BAKHTIARI
6. BASSERI
7. BEDOUIN
8. CHALDEANS
9. CIRCASSIANS
10. COPTS
11. DRUZE
12. FALASHA
13. HAZARA
14. JACOBITES
15. JEWS
16. KARAITES
17. KHAMSEH
18. KURDS
19. LUR
20. MANDAEANS
21. MARONITES
22. NESTORIANS
23. NURISTANIS
24. PALESTINIANS
25. PASHAI
26. PERSIANS
27. QASHQA'I
28. QUIZILBASH
29. SAMARITANS
30. SHAHSEVAN
31. SYRIACS
32. TURKS
33. YEMENIS
34. YORUK
35. ZOROASTRIANS

Encyclopedia of World Cultures

Volume IX

AFRICA AND THE MIDDLE EAST

Acholi

ETHNONYMS: Acoli, Acooli; historically: Gani, Lango, Lo-Gang, Shuuli

Orientation

Identification. The name "Acholi" is used for peoples living in the former Acholi District of northern Uganda (now divided into the Gulu and Kitgum districts) and the adjoining area of the southern Sudan. The term is derived from "Shuuli," first used by nineteenth-century ivory and slave traders who noted the similarity of Acholi Luo to the language of the previously encountered Shilluk or "Collo" of the southern Sudan (Crazzolara 1938, vii-viii). Despite their common language and ethnic designation, the Acholi of Uganda and the southern Sudan have distinct origins and developed along different historical trajectories; the remainder of this cultural summary will focus on the more populous Uganda Acholi.

Location. The Acholi occupy a 39,000-square-kilometer area, three-fourths of which lies within Uganda, extending roughly from 2°15′ to 4°15′9 N and 31°25′ to 33°45′ E. Their neighbors include the Luo-speaking Lango, Paluo, and Alur to the south and southwest, the Central Sudanic-speaking Madi to the west, and the Eastern Nilotic Jie and Karamojong to the east. Situated 1,025 to 1,350 meters above sea level, the Acholi landscape is typical East African game country—rolling grasslands with scattered trees, streams, and rock outcrops. A single rainy season, from April-May to October-November, produces a reliable annual rainfall nine years of every ten, ranging from 102 centimeters in the central and western portions of Acholi to only 51 centimeters in much of the north and east. The dry season is long and hot, with temperatures that can reach more than 35° C.

Demography. The 1980 population of the Uganda Acholi was approximately 580,000 (Kasozi 1994, ii), up from some 465,000 in 1969 (Langlands 1971), perhaps 125,000 in 1900 and about 100,000 at the end of the eighteenth century (Atkinson 1994, 275–281). These figures represent population densities of 20.4 persons per square kilometer in 1980, 16.5 per square kilometer in 1969, and about one-fourth and one-fifth the 1969 densities during the earlier two periods. Twentieth-century densities have been consistently the second lowest in all of Uganda (after Karamoja).

Linguistic Affiliation. The primary language of Acholi today is Luo, a Western Nilotic language spoken by groups scattered across East Africa from the southern Sudan to Tanzania; many also speak English and/or Kiswahili.

History and Cultural Relations

Archaeological and linguistic evidence suggests that from early in the Christian era, Acholi was settled mainly by Central Sudanic (or "proto-Central Sudanic") speakers in the west and Eastern Nilotic ("proto-Eastern Nilotic") speakers in the east. Before the late seventeenth century, Luo speakers were limited to only a few peripheral areas of Acholi. All of these early inhabitants were ironworking mixed farmers, organized into localized patrilineal lineages or, in some cases, into temporary groupings of two to four such lineages.

A new sociopolitical order—and the basis of an Acholi identity—was established when chiefly institutions and ideology were introduced into Acholi by Luo-speaking Paluo from the neighboring kingdom of Bunyoro-Kitara. Central to the new order were a set of notions about political leadership in which chiefs (*rwodi;* sing. *rwot*) shared power and decision making with the heads of chiefdoms' constituent lineages; a system of redistributive tribute within each polity, with the chief at the center; and royal, often rainmaking, drums as symbols of sovereignty and authority. Over the late seventeenth and eighteenth centuries, some seventy chiefdoms were founded throughout the area that became Acholi, leading to the development of a new social order and political culture, the spread of a new language (Luo), and the evolution of a new society and collective identity. This complex process was helped along by two major droughts, probably during the 1720s and c. 1790, which promoted larger-scale political leadership that held the promise of greater stability and security, and by the formation of neighboring identities against which members of an emergent Acholi could compete, compare, and define themselves.

Over the second half of the nineteenth century, Acholi was incorporated into international trade networks through the activities of northern, Arabic-speaking ivory and slave traders. This trade brought new wealth into Acholi that was unevenly accumulated, with rwodi and interpreters (and eventually their sons and other kinsmen) the major beneficiaries. The northerners also contributed to the further evolution of an Acholi identity, not only by introducing the name "Shuuli," which eventually became "Acholi," but by acting in ways that promoted Acholi as a meaningful ethnic and geographic entity.

When Britain established its rule during the early twentieth century, both ideological predisposition and practical utility prompted the colonizers to consider the Acholi a "tribe" and to administer the area as a "tribal" unit. From the beginning, the Acholi were marginal compared to Britain's concern with Buganda, at the core of the colony. Acholi's role in the colonial economy was confined mainly to the peasant production of cotton as a cash crop and the provision of recruits for the colonial army or police and migrant labor for the more "developed" Buganda. Both Protestant and Catholic missionaries were active in Acholi from early colonial rule, providing written Luo religious, educational, and historical texts and producing a local educated elite, all of which fostered the further development of an Acholi identity within the colonial context of "tribal" culture, consciousness, and politics.

With independence, the Acholi remained marginal within the framework of Uganda as a whole, with one crucial exception: their disproportionate numbers in the police and army. Comprising less than 5 percent of the country's population, during the early years of independence the Acholi constituted more than 15 percent of the police force and fully a third of the army. This special access to Uganda's security forces has alternately presented opportunity and danger as a succession of regimes replaced one another in a cycle of political violence often played out in ethnic (or "tribal") terms. In the most recent phase of the cycle, beginning in the mid-1980s, Acholi has largely been on the receiving end of the violence. Uganda's current army, various local rebel groups (some headed by apocalyptic "prophets" such as Alice Lakwena), and heavily armed Karamojong raiders have all raped, looted, killed, and destroyed, making any kind of normal life in Acholi impossible.

Settlements

Acholi chiefdoms ranged in population from under 1,000 to as many as 20,000 people and consisted of a number of fenced villages, each with recognized land rights vested in the patrilineal lineage (*kaka*) at its core. Lineage heads, assisted by lineage elders, organized both production (based on cooperative village-lineage labor) and reproduction (through the control of the material means and ideological rules of marriage). They also oversaw village-lineage ritual and chiefdomwide ritual, were the main advisors to their rwot, and were responsible for most of the social control exercised in Acholi. Over the twentieth century, chiefdoms in Acholi have become vestigial institutions, and the fences that once enclosed villages have disappeared. Most Acholi, however, continue to live in neighborhoods (parishes) that not only consist predominantly of patrilineal kinsmen and their wives, but often carry the old lineage names. Most Acholi also continue to live in thatched, round mud houses, although wealthier Acholi and those who live in town or near major roads have square houses of mud or block, with iron or tile roofs.

Economy

Subsistence and Commercial Activities. When not disrupted or dispossessed by the violence endemic since the mid-1980s, most Acholi remain primarily mixed farmers. The old staples of eleusine (finger) millet, sorghum, sesame, and various peas, beans, and leafy green vegetables continue to be grown, along with twentieth-century crops such as cassava, maize, peanuts (groundnuts), fruits, and cotton. As they have for centuries, Acholi farmers rely mainly on iron hoes and other hand tools. The most common domestic animals are (and have long been) chickens and goats, with some cattle, especially in the dryer portions of Acholi. Large, dry-season hunts were an important part of the precolonial economy; these gradually decreased in significance as the varied roster of both large and small game animals dwindled over the twentieth century.

Industrial Arts. Ironworking, mainly but not entirely confined to certain lineages, appears to be almost as ancient as agriculture, going back perhaps to the first millennium B.C. Pottery and basket making were widespread and relatively nonspecialized arts, carried out by both men and women. In most chiefdoms, only members of designated lineages could make or repair royal drums.

Trade. Precolonial trade, both within Acholi and throughout the region, focused mainly on obtaining iron ore and finished iron products in exchange for baskets or products of the farm, herd, or hunt. Significantly, iron-ore deposits were located mainly at or just beyond the western, northeastern, southeastern, and southern boundaries of what became Acholi, and trade for this iron created networks of movement and interaction that helped determine a collective identity within these boundaries. During the later nineteenth century, the emergent Acholi became involved in the international trade in ivory and slaves, which were exchanged mainly for cattle, beads, blankets, cotton cloth, and firearms. Colonial rule brought the penetration of a money economy into Acholi, along with the establishment of numerous rural and small-town trading centers and the two major urban centers of Gulu and Kitgum, where a range of local and imported goods are available.

Division of Labor. In the precolonial era, warfare, herding, and hunting were the domain of men. Men have also traditionally played a significant role in agriculture, especially for such time-limited, labor-intensive tasks as clearing, planting, and harvesting (often as part of lineage-based cooperative labor teams). Women also provide major labor in the fields, as well as being responsible for most child rearing and all cooking and other food-preparation tasks. The building of houses and granaries has historically involved both men and women, with each performing specified functions. Boys and girls are typically socialized into distinct gender roles, and do household and other chores accordingly. Since the entrenchment of colonial rule, an average of 10 to 20 percent of adult Acholi males at any one time have been involved in migrant labor or employment in the police or army that has taken them from their home and families. Relatively small numbers of Acholi have filled middle-level or senior civil-service positions in independent Uganda.

Land Tenure. Traditionally, land rights were vested in localized patrilineal lineages, under the control and guidance of lineage heads and elders. This included both agricultural and hunting land. An individual had personal claim to land that he and his wife (or wives) had under cultivation or that had been cultivated but was lying fallow, and such rights passed from father to son. Given the low population densities and minimal land pressure, almost anyone who was willing to clear and work unused land has been welcomed by lineage heads responsible for such land and, while they functioned, by the rwodi of chiefdoms within whose domains the land lay. Girling (1960) notes that as late as 1950 there was still no system of individual land tenure in Acholi; however, such tenure has become increasingly common since independence.

Kinship

Kin Groups and Descent. Localized patrilineal lineages, some of which have "brother" lineages of the same or different name in other parts of Acholi, have long been the fundamental social and economic units in Acholi. Numbering between 400 and 500 by the turn of the twentieth century, these exogamous groups claim descent from a common ancestor (although means exist to incorporate many types of "outsiders" as well) and have special lineage shrines, ritual ceremonies, praise-calls, and totems.

Kinship Terminology. The Acholi have a modified Iroquois kinship-terminology system, reflecting Acholi's patrilineal and patrilocal ideology. All lineage males, for example, are called "grandfather," "father," "brother," or "son," and all (likely resident) females "sister" or "daughter," depending upon their generational relationship to the speaker. All affines, meanwhile, are known as "mother." The relationship between (real) brother and sister is often very close, especially when one acts as the *lapidi* (nurse-child) to the other, as are the bonds between the children of sisters. After his own father, however, a man's strongest kinship ties are typically with his mother's brother.

Marriage and Family

Marriage. Traditionally, a young man was dependent upon his lineage head and elders both for permission to marry and for the material goods required for bride-wealth; elders of the woman's lineage were also much involved in the discussions and negotiations surrounding the marriage. Bride-wealth has varied over time but has usually included iron objects, domestic animals, and, in the twentieth century, money. Marriage has been typically patrilocal and patriarchal, with the husband and father as the undisputed head of the household. Although polygyny has often been presented as an ideal, limited means have always made it rare in practice. Children are highly prized, and historically a couple did not set up their own household until the birth of their first child, living until then in the household of the husband's mother. Childlessness is one of the most serious misfortunes imaginable; women are typically blamed, and the marriage often ends or the husband takes a second wife. Divorce, which can occur for numerous reasons, is not uncommon and may or may not involve return of the bride-wealth; children, as members of the father's lineage, usually either stay with the father or return to him later. Even bride-wealth marriages are now often mainly nuclear-family affairs, and other alternatives to traditional marriage are common. These include Christian marriage (with or without bride-wealth), elopement, and single parenthood.

Domestic Unit. A typical household consists of a nuclear family (husband, wife, and unmarried children), although aged parents, unmarried siblings, offspring of deceased siblings, or others are often household members as well. All members of the household acknowledge the authority of its head, the husband; each wife or other adult female in the household has traditionally had her own fields, granaries, and kitchen or cooking hut.

Inheritance. Inheritance has been, and largely remains, patrilineal. Apart from land, the rights to which were passed on equally to all sons, the eldest son was traditionally the designated heir of the father's property, although he was supposed to provide for the needs of his younger brothers.

Socialization. Mothers are responsible for the initial care of their children and for much of their socialization. After weaning and up to the age of 5 or 6, however, much of the day-to-day caretaking of a child has customarily been done by an opposite-sex sibling or other preadolescent (often a member of the father's lineage), called lapidi (nurse-child). From early on, girls and boys learn gender-appropriate behaviors and activities, and these are reflected in both their play and their chores and other responsibilities. Sons have traditionally learned about farming, hunting, herding, and lineage and chiefdom traditions from their fathers and other lineage males; girls learn farming and domestic duties from their mothers. Since independence, formal schooling has provided a strong socializing influence from outside the home for more and more Acholi, especially those attending secondary school. Army membership has also supplied a distinct, if largely negative, socializing influence on many Acholi young men. Some Acholi mothers exclaim that they do not know their sons after they have been away in the army.

Sociopolitical Organization

Social Organization. Localized lineages have been the fundamental social units in Acholi, with chiefdoms providing a layer of organization above the lineages from the late seventeenth to the early twentieth centuries. While rwodi, members of royal lineages, and lineage heads all seem to have been somewhat better off than others before the latter part of the nineteenth century, social stratification appears limited, owing primarily to both limited wealth in the society and redistribution. Certain rwodi and interpreters began to accumulate some of the new wealth brought into Acholi by international trade, and descendants of some of these men used their inherited wealth to build up prominent twentieth-century families. Since independence, a relatively few Acholi army officers have managed to accumulate substantial fortunes, as have a few traders. More commonly, almost any salaried job in the public or private sector represents an income that averages several times that of a member of the majority peasant population.

Political Organization. During the colonial period, political leadership in Acholi was contested among those with traditional leadership qualifications and others who benefited from the new dispensation, including collaborators with the British and those who managed to obtain Western education. Administrative divisions within Acholi, however, both during colonial rule and since independence, have often reflected preexisting sociopolitical units: lineages at the parish level; chiefdoms at the subcounty level; and larger zones of the most intensive (and peaceful) interpolity interactions at the county level.

Social Control. In precolonial Acholi, lineage heads and elders were most responsible for social control, though one of the attractions that assisted the development of chiefdoms seems to have been the ability of rwodi to help settle disputes that involved more than one lineage. With colonial rule came a new hierarchy of chiefs, clerks, and policemen, all under the authority of a district commissioner. Much of that hierarchy continued into the independence era. The essential lawlessness of the Idi Amin and second Milton Obote regimes, however, as well as of the various rebel groups, the Ugandan army, and Karamojong raiders (who have been active in Acholi since the mid-1980s) have led to a breakdown of any meaningful social control in the area.

Conflict. The available evidence suggests that conflict in Acholi before the end of the nineteenth century, both among Acholi chiefdoms and with neighboring peoples, was neither rare nor endemic. When conflict did occur, however, it was usually limited in scope, with relatively few deaths. Recognized compensation and reconciliation procedures seem to have often limited or prevented serious conflict, especially among neighboring chiefdoms within the same zone. With the coming of the ivory and slave trades, and the firearms that accompanied them, conflict became more frequent, more deadly, and more widely spread. A rebellion in 1911 in response to the British confiscation of Acholi guns was the last large-scale conflict in Acholi until Amin came to power in 1971. During Obote's first term as president, and especially during his second term, Acholi soldiers played key roles in the massive conflict in other parts of Uganda, where hundreds of thousands of people—many of them innocent civilians—lost their lives; from the mid-1980s into the 1990s, Acholi was the scene of similar levels of conflict.

Religion and Expressive Culture

Religious Beliefs. Once chiefdoms were established, Acholi religious beliefs focused on three types of spirits (*jogi;* sing. *jok*). There were the spirits of known relatives, especially lineage ancestors; a second type was the nonancestral jok of the chiefdom as a whole. Spirits of both of these types were generally beneficent. They were approached in regard to such general concerns as good health, fertility, and appeals or thanks for good harvests in ceremonies that usually emphasized the consciousness, cohesiveness, and continuation of their respective groups as functioning corporate entities. The third group of spirits were those of unknown persons and dangerous beasts; these were hostile, personified as ghosts, believed to cause sickness and other misfortunes, and dealt with by means of spirit possession.

Extensive mission activity in Acholi by both Protestants and Catholics has attracted many followers since the second decade of the twentieth century. Traditional beliefs, however, still persist, often meshed with Christian doctrine in complex ways. One illustration of this is the various spirit-possession-based millennial (and military) movements that have been prominent in Acholi during the extremely difficult period of the late 1980s and early 1990s, most famously the Holy Spirit Movement of Alice Lakwena.

Religious Practitioners. Traditionally, lineage heads and elders were the most knowledgeable about—and involved with—the lineage and chiefdom jogi, although rwodi also had a role to play in ceremonies involving the latter. In addition there were priest- or priestess-diviners, private practitioners who worked for the well-being of their clients, and witches, who worked in private for evil or destructive purposes. Contemporary versions or amalgams of these practitioners continue to function in Acholi.

Ceremonies. Each type of spirit had numerous ceremonies associated with it; many ceremonies included small offerings of food and drink. Historically, the most important public ceremonies were probably those associated with birth, planting, harvesting, and the killing of a large animal or another human being. Dances and other activities surrounding spirit possession seem to have been originally introduced from Bunyoro in the early nineteenth century and then became more widespread during the tumultuous years of the latter part of that century.

Arts. The major art forms of the Acholi have been drumming, singing, and dancing.

Medicine. In the past, medical problems were addressed through approaches to various spirits, by visits to diviners, and by the use of herbs, roots, and other folk medicines. Many contemporary Acholi continue to use these treatments, although nearly all with access to clinics and hospitals rely on these as well, whenever they can.

Death and Afterlife. Acholi conceive of death as an inevitable, personal defeat and tragedy, against which there is no ultimate defense. The personal and group loss resulting from death is acknowledged as real and permanent. Traditionally, a grave is dug as soon as a person has died, following which a small and brief ceremony is held in the deceased's house prior to burial. All procedures are conducted with care, to attempt to ensure that the spirit of the departed does not become angry. Further tidying up and smoothing over the grave take place within the week. Then a final dance and feast takes place at a time chosen to make possible the maximum attendance by relatives and other interested people. The size and nature of this occasion depend on the age and status of the deceased, with the most lavish and festive celebrations taking place when the person who died was both aged and important. In terms of the afterlife, although spirits of the dead are believed to continue to exist and manifest themselves, there is no belief in a heaven to reward the virtuous or a hell to punish the sinful.

Bibliography

Apoko, Anna (1967). "At Home in the Village: Growing Up in Acholi." In *East African Childhood: Three Versions*, edited by L. K. Fox, 43–75. Nairobi: Oxford University Press.

Atkinson, Ronald R. (1989). "The Evolution of Ethnicity among the Acholi of Uganda: The Pre-colonial Phase." *Ethnohistory* 36(1): 19–43.

Atkinson, Ronald R. (1994). *The Roots of Ethnicity: The Origins of the Acholi of Uganda before 1800*. Philadelphia: University of Pennsylvania Press.

Behrend, Heike (1991). "Is Alice Lakwena a Witch? The Holy Spirit Movement and Its Fight against Evil in the North." In *Changing Uganda: The Dilemmas of Structural Adjustment and Revolutionary Change*, edited by Holger B. Hansen and Michael Twaddle, 162–177. London: James Currey.

Crazzolara, J. P. (1938). *A Study of the Acooli Language: Grammar and Vocabulary*. London: Oxford University Press.

Crazzolara, J. P. (1950–1954). *The Lwoo*. 3 vols. Verona: Editrice Nigrizia.

Dwyer, John O. (1972). *The Acholi of Uganda: Adjustment to Imperialism*. Ann Arbor: University Microfilms International.

Girling, F. K. (1960). *The Acholi of Uganda*. London: Her Majesty's Stationery Office.

Hansen, Holger B., and Michael Twaddle, eds. (1988). *Uganda Now: Between Decay and Development*. London: James Currey.

Hansen, Holger B., and Michael Twaddle, eds. (1991). *Changing Uganda: The Dilemmas of Structural Adjustment and Revolutionary Change*. London: James Currey.

Kasozi, A. B. K. (1994). *The Social Origins of Violence in Uganda, 1964–1985*. Montreal and Kingston: McGill-Queen's University Press.

Langlands, B. W. (1971). *The Population Geography of Acholi District*. Occasional Paper no. 30. Makerere University (Kampala), Department of Geography.

Malandra, Alfred (1939). "The Ancestral Shrine of the Acholi." *Uganda Journal* 7(1): 27–43.

Ocheng, D. O. (1955). "Land Tenure in Acholi." *Uganda Journal* 19(1): 57–61.

Odongo, J. M. Onyango-ku-, and J. B. Webster, eds. (1976). *The Central Lwo during the Aconya*. Nairobi: East African Literature Bureau.

Okeny, Kenneth (1982). "State Formation in Acholi: The Emergence of Obbo, Pajok, and Panyikwara States c. 1679–1914." M.A. thesis, University of Nairobi.

Okot p'Bitek (1963). "The Concept of Jok among the Acholi and Lango." *Uganda Journal* 27(1): 15–30.

Okot p'Bitek (1971). *Religion of the Central Luo*. Nairobi: East African Literature Bureau.

Uma, F. K. (1971). "Acholi-Arab Nubian Relations in the Nineteenth Century." B.A. Graduating Essay, Department of History, Makerere University (Kampala).

Wright, A. C. A. (1936). "Some Notes on Acholi Religious Ceremonies." *Uganda Journal* 3(3): 175-202.

RONALD R. ATKINSON

Afar

ETHNONYMS: Adal, Danakil

The Afar occupy a 143,000-square-kilometer area of Djibouti and northeastern Ethiopia, sometimes called the Afar Triangle. The eastern point of the triangle lies at the intersection of the Red Sea and the Indian Ocean. Their neighbors include the Esa Somali, Ittu, and Enia Galla to the south; the Wallo, Yaju, and Raya Galla to the west; and the Saho to the northwest. There is a long history of hostility between the Afar and the surrounding groups, and, as a result, the Afar are often considered fierce and warlike.

The Afar claim descent from Arabs, and the name "Danakil" first appeared in the writings of thirteenth-century Arab geographers. The name may be derived from the Ankala tribe, which is centered on the Buri Peninsula. They speak an eastern Cushitic language, and remnants of Cushitic animistic cults persist in contemporary Afar culture. They numbered about 143,000 in Djibouti in 1988 and 400,000 in Ethiopia in 1987 (Grimes 1988).

The land inhabited by the Afar is extremely arid and barren, consisting of stone and sand desert interspersed with salt lakes and lava streams. The Danakil Depression, which lies within this area, is 91 meters below sea level and may be the hottest place on earth. There is only one fertile area, which is along the Awash River, where some cultivation is possible. Conditions are also less harsh in the Mabra Mountains, the Horma highlands, and around Mount Biru.

Nomadic pastoralism is the traditional form of subsistence for the Afar, although some coastal Afar are fishers. Livestock consists of goats, sheep, and camels where the terrain is suitable, and some cattle in a few places. The Afar subsist mostly on meat, both domestic and wild, and dairy products, along with agricultural products that are sometimes stolen and sometimes obtained in trade with villagers in the Rift Valley or in the highlands. Until about 1930, the Afar were involved in the trans–Red Sea slave trade, which may have added substantially to their subsistence base. More recently, the Afar have engaged in trade with Christian farmers on the Abyssinian plateau to the west, exchanging butter, hides, livestock, and rope for agricultural goods.

The pastoralism of the Afar is actually closer to transhumance than to full nomadism. Transhumance is a patterned movement of people among several regularly visited locations, at least one of which is permanently occupied by a part of the population, or is improved by some structure, such as a house, corral, or storage bin. The encampments established during the seasonal migrations often consist of no more than grass lean-tos. The migrating unit has a more permanent homestead somewhere else, with larger dwelling structures surrounded by thorn-and-brush fences. Often, it is only the younger members of the group who go on the seasonal migrations; they take the more highly valued camels and cattle to higher pastures, leaving the sheep and goats in the care of the older folk at the more permanent location.

Traditionally, the Afar were divided into two classes, the Asaimara ("the red ones") or nobles, and the Adoimara ("the white ones") or commoners. Sometimes Asaimara and Adoimara clans existed as separate territorial groups, but for the most part tribal groups contained a mixture of both, and the Asaimara/Adoimara distinction cut across the whole of Afar society. Adoimara groups living among Asaimara formerly paid tribute, but there were also independent Adoimara tribes and Adoimara tribes that later obtained independent status. In the mixed Asaimara/Adoimara groups, the chiefs and heads of kin groups in whom territorial rights were vested were Asaimara, whereas the client Adoimara had their own herds of livestock with grazing rights on their patrons' land. Today the two classes are territorially intermingled and do not seem to have any distinguishing behavioral characteristics.

The Afar territorial, political, and fighting unit is called a *mela*, which is usually translated as "tribe." Historically, there has been a great deal of hostility between different tribes. Feuds are common both within and between tribes. Within tribal units, feuds were caused by the death of one or more parties in a dispute, and could be settled with the payment of blood compensation. Disputes between tribes usually resulted in warfare. Today the Ethiopian government takes a more involved role in the resolution of disputes.

Tribes are divided into clans, which have an agnatic lineage structure. Tribal endogamy is the general rule, and there is a preference for cross-cousin marriage. Girls are eligible for marriage after their tenth year, whereas a man is traditionally not supposed to marry until after he has killed someone in battle. Like most Muslim groups, the Afar are patriarchal; leadership roles are assigned to men. Residence can be either matrilocal or patrilocal but is predominantly patrilocal. Women are assigned the tasks of building the nomadic hut, collecting wood and water, milking, preparing food, and weaving mats. Some Afar tribes have age sets in which men of similar age are grouped under a common chief and are initiated together.

The Afar were formerly divided into four paramount sultanates, each of which was divided into smaller confederate territories. Today the Afar are increasingly under the control of national governments. Even so, most Afar are still on the fringes of state control and retain a relatively high degree of political, social, and economic independence.

Islam is the predominant religion of the Afar, who follow the practices of the Sufi sect. The practice of Islam is rather unorthodox, particularly among pastoral Afar, in comparison to other groups (e.g., the Somali). There are still traces of the Cushitic religion, which can be seen in shrines erected on mountain tops to offer sacrifices to the sky/god Zar/Wak. Zar/Wak, the father of the universe, perhaps provided an easy transition to Allah and Islam. *Jenile*, or oracle dancing, is also connected to the Cushitic religion, and aspects of the dance may have been incorporated into Sufi Islamic ceremonies.

Bibliography

Englebert, Victor (1970). "The Danakil: Nomads of Ethiopia's Wasteland." *National Geographic Magazine* 147(2): 186–212.

Grimes, Barbara F., ed. (1988). *Ethnologue: Languages of the World*. Dallas: Summer Institute of Linguistics.

Lewis, Ioan Myrddin, ed. (1955). *Peoples of the Horn: Somali, Afar, and Saho*. London: International African Institute.

Pastner, Stephen (1984). "Afar." In *Muslim Peoples: A World Ethnographic Survey*, edited by Richard V. Weekes, 10–14. Westport, Conn.: Greenwood Press.

Pastner, Stephen (1979). "Lords of the Desert Border: Frontier Feudalism in Southern Baluchistan and Eastern Ethiopia." *International Journal of Middle East Studies* 10:93–106.

Weissleder, Wolfgang. "The Promotion of Suzerainty between Sedentary and Nomadic Populations in East Ethiopia." In *Nomadic Alternative*, edited by Wolfgang Weissleder. World Anthropology Series. The Hague: Mouton.

Afrikaners

ETHNONYM: Trekkers

Orientation

The Afrikaners are descendants, to a great extent, of Dutch, German, and French Huguenot settlers, and, to a lesser extent, of English, Scottish, Irish, and other settlers of South Africa. The Dutch that was the language of the first White settlers, who arrived in 1652, evolved into Afrikaans, which retained much of the structure and grammar of the original Dutch. In 1986 there were 5,800,000 speakers of Afrikaans in South Africa, of which 3,000,000 were classified as "Whites" and 2,800,000 were classified as "Coloureds" (Grimes 1988). Afrikaners are members of an ethnic group who are predominantly White, speakers of Afrikaans, of Western European descent, politically aligned with the National party, belong to the Dutch Reformed church (NGK), and share a distinctive history with other Afrikaners. The extent to which members share all of these characteristics is variable, but it is widely believed, because of the central importance of language, that speaking Afrikaans is probably the most salient indicator of group membership. Furthermore, because loyalty has been a highly regarded value, political-party affiliation is another category that is frequently used to define the in-group and to challenge potential dissidents.

History and Cultural Relations

Besides language, one of the defining characteristics of Afrikaners is their history. Many of the earlier settlers moved away from Cape Town, in part because of their resistance to Dutch and British rule, but also because of their attraction to their new environment. Their relations with the indigenous populations were mixed. They had generally good relations with the Khoi-khoi (Hottentots) and the San, but there was a mutual distrust and fear between the "trekkers," as the inland settlers came to be called, and the Xhosa. Based on these experiences, as well as a strong Christian (Calvinist) faith, Afrikaners came to believe that the only possible relationship between Blacks and Whites was master to slave or enemy to enemy.

A pivotal event, or series of events, in Afrikaner history was the northeasterly migration of the trekkers, or Voortrekkers (the pioneers). Precipitated by a number of conditions, including the annexation of Cape Town by the British, unpopular British regulations, and the emancipation of slaves, this "Great Trek" began in 1835. The Voortrekkers founded the republics of the Transvaal and the Orange Free State, establishing constitutions that disallowed racial equality in church or state. Along the way, the Voortrekkers defeated the powerful Zulu nation, after its leader, Dingane, killed Pieter Retief and his party while they were his guests. Their deaths were avenged on 16 December 1838 at the Battle of Blood River; the date is now celebrated as a national holiday.

Another important event in Afrikaner history was the Anglo-Boer War (1899–1902), which was precipitated by conflicts between British gold seekers and Afrikaner farmers. Although the British won this war, it had the effect of creating an Afrikaner nation by providing a reason for Afrikaners of the Cape Colony to unite with Afrikaners who lived inland. The British soon restored self-rule to the two republics and convened a convention to plan the Union of South Africa. There were no Black representatives at the convention, and only White voters were allowed to vote on the ratification of the new constitution of South Africa. The Commonwealth country that was created established a color bar that literally prohibited Blacks or Coloureds from participating as equal members in the society. Britain sanctioned this policy by approving the formation of the Union of South Africa in the British Parliament.

The founding of the National party in 1914 is an important event in Afrikaner history, because that party played a major role in the policy that became known as "apartheid." When General Hertzog, the founder of the party (although later rejected by it), was elected prime minister in 1924, a number of policies were initiated that divided the Afrikaans-speaking people from the English-speaking people, as well as from all other people in the country. Afrikaans superseded Dutch as one of the two official languages. The separation of children by color in the schools became more absolute, and Afrikaners began to predominate in many official organizations, such as the South African Police and the civil service. The most powerful of all Afrikaner bodies at this time was the secret Broederbond (League of Brothers), consisting of the elite, the thinkers, and the philosophers of Afrikanerdom. They planned and worked for radical changes in South African society, which they were able to accomplish when, for the first time, they were able to bring to power one of their own, in 1948. In that year the first candidate, Dr. Daniel François Malan, who had the overwhelming support of the National party, was elected prime minister. His government was dedicated to achieving sovereign independence and the preservation of Afrikanerdom and the White race through apartheid. He began what many believe was a total restructuring of South African society, including the political, social, educational, and cultural separation of races. He carried out this transformation through a series of acts, including the Mixed Marriages Act, which prohibited marriages between the races, the Immorality Act, which prohibited sexual relations between the races, the Group Areas Act, which defined where people of different races could live, and the Population Registration Act, which determined the racial category of every person in the country.

Religion

The first settlers of South Africa brought with them a fundamentalist form of Calvinism, which, in the frontier, remained unrefined. Events in African history have acquired a religious significance when the leaders of Afrikaner nationalism used them as evidence of a divine calling for the Afrikaner people. When neo-Calvinists suggested that God reveals himself in nature and in history, Afrikaner revisionists jumped to the conclusions that God must be recognized in all things, and that the will of God was apparent in all things. The existence and development of the Afrikaner people, therefore, is an act of God, and, because God created the nation, the nation must continue. A similar argument often heard in the past was that God had willed that there should be separate nations and races.

Many early Afrikaners identified with the Israelites of the Old Testament and saw a parallel between their history and that of the Jews. Like the Jews, they believed and fought for their right to nationhood and, perhaps to a large extent, believed that they were, like God's chosen people, forbidden to mix with others not of their blood.

The Dutch Reformed church, clearly the dominant one among Afrikaners, is distinct from other Protestant churches in that its theology is Calvinist in principle; more important, it supports political policies of the National party. By the time the Afrikaner government came to power in 1948, the NGK had lost contact with the original teachings of Calvin and, in so doing, conveniently provided the theological foundation for apartheid. The National party's policies led to the elevation of apartheid to a civil religion in which the secular notions of *volk,* culture, and politics became prominent features, and the NGK became a virtual puppet of the National party government, often providing scriptural support for apartheid.

The events that occurred in the late 1980s and in the 1990s, which were primarily of a political nature—the freeing of Nelson Mandela from prison, his election as president, and the dismantling of apartheid—will provide a challenge to the survival of the Afrikaners as an ethnic group in the years to come. Because Afrikaners are fiercely loyal and they have expressed their loyalty to the National party, which supported apartheid policies, how they will respond as a group to the dismantling of apartheid will perhaps be a key factor in their survival as an ethnic group. If they cling to a minority view and make that view a necessary part of their identity, as they have in the past, Afrikaners may dissolve into nothing more than a political party. If, on the other hand, they can remain an endogamous group while accepting antiapartheid or non–National party views, their survival as an ethnic group will be more likely.

Bibliography

Adam, Heribert, ed. (1983). *South Africa: The Limits of Reform Politics*. Leiden: E. J. Brill.

Adam, Heribert, and Hermann Giliomee (1979). *Ethnic Power Mobilized: Can South Africa Change?* New Haven: Yale University Press.

February, Vernon (1991). *The Afrikaners of South Africa*. London: Kegan Paul International.

Giliomee, Hermann (1989). "Beginnings of Afrikaner Ethnic Consciousness, 1850–1915." In *Creation of Tribalism in Southern Africa*. Berkeley and Los Angeles: University of California Press.

Grimes, Barbara F. (1988). *Ethnologue: Languages of the World*. Dallas: Summer Institute of Linguistics.

Harrison, David (1982). *The White Tribe of Africa: South Africa in Perspective*. London: British Broadcasting Corporation.

Kaplan, Irving, and Harold D. Nelson (1980). "Religious Life." In *South Africa: A Country Study*. Washington, D.C.: Department of the Army.

Leach, Graham (1989). *The Afrikaners: Their Last Great Trek*. London: Macmillan.

Louw-Potgieter, Joha (1988). *Afrikaner Dissidents: A Social Psychological Study of Identity and Dissent.* Clevedon, Eng.: Multilingual Matters.

Munger, Edwin S., ed. (1979). *The Afrikaners*. Cape Town: Tafelberg.

Perry, John, and Cassandra Perry (1985). "Tinkering with Tradition: Apartheid and Change in South Africa." *Canberra Anthropology* 8(1–2): 4–31.

RONALD JOHNSON

Aimaq

ETHNONYMS: Barbari, Berberi, Chahar (or Char) Aimaq

In western Afghanistan and far eastern Iran, "Aimaq" means "tribal people," which distinguishes the Aimaq from the nontribal population in the area, the Persians (Fariswan) and Tajiks. Most of the population of 800,000 (1980) live in Afghanistan. In 1984, 120,000 Aimaq lived in Iran. They are considered to be Hanafi Sunni Muslims.

Linguistically, the Aimaq differ little from the majority of Persians surrounding them. The local dialects of the Aimaq tribes are very close either to eastern Khorasan Farsi or to Dari, the Herati dialect of Farsi.

The Char Aimaq (*chahar*, four), an administrative grouping of four seminomadic tribes, is the largest of twenty Aimaq groups. There are six other seminomadic or nomadic Aimaq groups in western Afghanistan, including the Timuri, Tahiri, Zuri, Maleki, and Mishmast. Other sedentary groups that may be considered Aimaq are the Kipchak, Chenghizi, Chagatai, Mobari, Ghuri, Kakeri, Damanrigi, and Khamidi. Geographically, the Char Aimaq live within an area stretching from the central hills of Bādghis north and northeast of Herāt to the mountains of Ghor in the west of central Afghanistan.

The four tribes of the Char Aimaq are the Jamshidi, the Aimaq-Hazara, the Firuzkuhi, and the Taimani. The tribes of Char Aimaq date to the sixteenth and seventeenth centuries, when the groups were unified by chiefs coming from outside the area. Descendants of these founders are still influential in tribal affairs, although they have lost their traditional power.

During the second half of the nineteenth century and early in the twentieth century, the Jamshidi were forced to lead a nomadic life. All of the tribe or greater parts of it had been exiled in Persia, in Khiva, and in northeastern Afghanistan. Thousands of Taimani and Tajiks of Ghor were forcibly transplanted to the north of Herāt, and the largest of the other Aimaq tribes, the Timuri, was nearly exterminated.

Tribalism is strong among all Aimaq groups. For example, feuds tend to be settled by tribal rather than by government authorities. The traditional concept of honor and shame, which is very important in tribal law, is still stronger than Islamic or state law.

The Aimaq, in sharp contrast with other societies in rural Afghanistan, accord women high status: women participate in group discussions, even when outsiders are present, and a girl may reject a groom chosen by her father. Bride-service is sometimes practiced; a groom lives in the compound of his future bride's parents and serves for a specific period of time (usually two years or more). After his bride-service is completed, the wedding takes place, and husband and wife begin their lives together. Where the influence of the orthodox Muslim clergy is stronger, however, as in the vicinity of Herāt, such traditional practices are much less common.

Agriculture and animal husbandry form the basis of the Char Aimaq economy. Bādghis is one of the most fertile areas of Afghanistan. Water is plentiful and is used for irrigating fields of rice, cotton, and grapes. Wheat and melons are also grown. Herding is a primary subsistence activity. Fat-tailed sheep, including karakuls, graze year round. Herds, which graze on pastures near the villages, are cared for by one of several brothers in an extended family during the spring and summer. Shepherds take the flocks to the lower steppes along the former Soviet border in the autumn and winter. In most years, surplus agricultural products can be sold at markets in Herāt or Qala Nau. Carpet weaving is another activity that earns cash.

There is less rainfall outside Bādghis, and yields from farming are much lower. In addition, cattle must be kept in stables during the severe winters, which limits the number of animals that can be herded. Groups outside of Bādghis are thus less densely populated and more economically restricted than is the population of Bādghis.

The Timuri were the most powerful and most numerous of the other Aimaq groups. Their original homeland is western Bādghis, where they adjoin the Jamshidi. In this area, high-quality Herāt Baluch rugs are woven by women of some of the Timuri subtribes.

Many of the Timuri have moved to what is now Iranian Khorāsān, where thay have joined with various small groups of Jamshidi, Zuri, and other Aimaq. There are a few Jamshidi and Aimaq-Hazara living in the vicinity of Mashhad who have preserved traditional customs. The Timuri in Iran and some of those near Bādghis tend to be nomadic, whereas those near the oases of Herāt tend to be settled.

There have been few reports on the Aimaq since the invasion of Afghanistan by the former Soviet Union in 1979.

Bibliography

Aslanov, A. G., et al. (1969). "Ethnography of Afghanistan." In *Afghanistan: Some New Approaches*, edited by George Grassmuch and Ludwig W. Adamac. Ann Arbor: University of Michigan Press.

Grimes, Barbara F., ed. (1988). *Ethnologue: Languages of the World*. Dallas: Summer Institute of Linguistics.

Janata, Alfred (1984). "Aimaq." In *Muslim Peoples: A World Ethnographic Survey*, edited by Richard V. Weekes, 14–18. Westport, Conn.: Greenwood Press.

Singer, Andre F. V. (1976). "A Study of the Impact of Social and Cultural Change upon Ethnic Identity in Eastern Iran." Ph.D. dissertation, Exeter College, Oxford.

Akan

ETHNONYMS: none

Orientation

The Akan comprise a cluster of peoples living in southern and central Ghana and in southeastern Ivory Coast. They form a series of distinct kingdoms and share a common language, known as Twi, which has many dialects. Twi is a tonal language and, since missionary work during the eighteenth and nineteenth centuries, has been written in Roman script.

The total Akan population numbers some five or six million. The main constituent kingdoms include Akyem, Akwamu, Akuapem, and Kwahu; the Anyi cluster of some fifteen kingdoms; Asante (with Ahanta and Wasa); the Attie cluster of four kingdoms; the Baule cluster of some seven kingdoms; Brong; and the several Fante states.

History

The long, complex history of the Akan peoples is one of internecine conflicts and, since the eighteenth century, of opposition to the encroachment of various colonial powers: the Dutch, Portuguese, Danish, French, and English. In addition, there have been continual threats from the Islamic peoples of the southern Saharan fringe. Essentially all these conflicts have been over monopolies in trade, first across the Sahara with northern Africa and, in later centuries, across the Atlantic with the countries of Europe and the Americas.

It appears certain that there were early cultural and commercial links with the empires of the southern Sahara, the latter consisting mainly of the exchange of gold from the Akan region for salt and other commodities from the Sahara. Many of the cultural traits of the Akan indicate that their kingdoms may, in many cases, be considered successor-states to ancient Ghana and Mali. Also evident are many cultural similarities with forest peoples to their east, such as the Fon, Yoruba, and Edo, although these must have developed many centuries ago.

Economy and Settlement

The Akan are almost all forest dwellers; the exceptions are a few outlying groups northward in the savanna and eastward in the hills and valley of the Volta River.

The basic crops are forest root plants (including yams, cocoyams, sweet potatoes, plantains) and trees (including oil-palm, many other palms, and cocoa). In many areas, minerals—especially gold and bauxite—have been and remain important. Some Akan kingdoms have lacked gold sources, their political weakness reflecting the lack of this valuable trade commodity. Livestock have never been of great importance, but in some areas hunting has been so until the late twentieth century. For most of the Akan kingdoms, trade—mainly in gold—has been a crucial resource. Weaving in cotton and silk is of a technically and aesthetically high order, and much commerce is built around it. Wood carvings have also become a valuable commodity, especially with the rise of the tourist trade in the late twentieth century.

The basic Akan pattern of settlement is extremely variable but, in the main, is one of towns each centered on the palace of its chief. Attached to these towns, but away from them in less densely inhabited land, are villages and farms, some large and long-lasting and others little more than clusters of the houses of single small families. The houses in the larger towns, constructed of materials that can last for several years before they crumble, are set along permanent roads. The dwellings in the villages are made of less durable materials and are typically arranged with no plan and no clearly marked center, being merely clusters of the houses of kin.

Men and women share in labor, but both may own farms and houses and both may provide the labor for them. In former times, until the end of the nineteenth century, much or most farm labor was supplied by various forms of servile persons: slaves, pawns, and many categories of "servant." Today different types of sharecropping and labor hired for cash are the most prevalent, although domestic peonage is still common.

Kinship, Family, and Marriage

All Akan groups recognize matrilineal descent. The basic group is the clan, of which there are eight; they are dispersed among the many kingdoms. Members of a subclan tend to occupy a single town or village. The clan is an exogamous group. It is comprised of constituent groups that may be referred to as lineages, but these do not form any kind of segmentary lineage system, lineages being attached to others by propinquity and the power and wealth of the host lineage. Although there has been much confusion in accounts of the Akan peoples between matriliny and matriarchy, authority within clans and lineages is held firmly by men, succession being from a man to his brother or to his closest sister's son.

Marriage is expected to be exogamous, and is extremely simple. There is no bride-wealth, the union being effected by the transfer of rum or other drink and some money from the groom to the bride's immediate family. Divorce is extremely easy and may be initiated by either men or women. The most usual causes are adultery and the barrenness of wives.

Legitimacy is important both for inheritance and to define a person as having, or not having, slave ancestry. It demands not only a proper marriage, however short-lasting, but also a recognized pater: he gives the child his own spiritual identity and his or her name; he admits his responsibility for the child's education, and he has the expectation that the child will carry out the father's funerary rites.

A child inherits his or her blood from the mother, and character or temperament from the father. Maternal blood ensures the child's membership in the *abusua* (clan or lineage); paternity bestows membership in one of nine other groups or categories. Although some accounts claim the Akan descent system is one of double descent, this view appears to be based on a misreading of the actual roles of the two lines of descent.

Despite being jurally matrilineal, inheritance is to some extent divided between sister's children and a man's own children. The basic principle is that lineage-inherited property goes to sisters' children, and property acquired with the help of a man's wife and children is distributed among the latter at his death.

The Akan practiced slavery, obtaining slaves from northern slave dealers, usually Muslims. War captives, criminals, persons who opposed local chiefs, and many local ritual leaders were also enslaved. Slaves were used for domestic and field labor, for sale to traders across the Sahara and across the Atlantic, and as sacrifices to royal and other ancestors. In the middle of the nineteenth century, slaves amounted to half of the population in many towns.

Political Organization

The several Akan peoples each consist of a single kingdom ruled by a king, *omanhene* (lit., "state-chief"). The king comes from whatever clan provides the royal line in a particular kingdom, and is chosen in rotation from one of this clan's kingly lineages (there are often other, nonkingly, lineages within a royal clan). He is elected by various officials, of which the most important is the *ohemmaa* (or similar terms; lit. "woman-chief" and usually translated in the literature as "queen-mother") although she is typically not the actual mother but a senior woman of the clan, who "knows" genealogy and may have her own court and be assisted by various officials. Criteria for the selection of a king include assumed competence, general personality, and the fact that kingly lines usually rotate in providing the king. Once selected, the king is "enstooled"—that is, seated upon the stool of kingship. His former status is annulled symbolically, his debts and lawsuits are settled, his clothing and personal possessions stored; he is then symbolically reborn and given the identity of one of his forebears. He assumes the royal name and title borne by that previous ruler.

A king has his palace, in which work members of his court. Details vary considerably, but, in general, the royal officials comprise several categories: those from the royal clan itself; those representing the remainder of the people; and ritual officials, drummers, and others who were considered the "children" of the king, being recruited from many sources, including royal slaves, and often observing patrilineal descent.

The king is a sacred person. He may not be observed eating or drinking and may not be heard to speak nor be spoken to publicly (speaking only through a spokesman or "linguist," *okyeame*). He is covered from the sky by a royal umbrella, avoids contact with the earth by wearing royal sandals, and wears insignia of gold and elaborate and beautiful cloth of royal design. In the past, an Akan king held power over the life and death of his subjects and slaves. These powers were eroded during colonial rule, but today an Akan king remains extremely powerful, representing his people both politically and ritually and acting as a focus for the identity of his kingdom. By far the most powerful is the king of Asante, who has the largest of all the Akan kingdoms, the Asantehene at Kumasi.

Warfare has historically been a central institution, a means of extending of territory and controlling external trade. An Akan state is typically divided into five or six military formations or "wings," each under the authority of a wing chief. Beneath the wing chiefs, who are chosen by the king, are the chiefs of the main towns of a kingdom. The latter are from the town's ruling line.

Religion

Indigenous Akan religion is based upon the worship of a High God, various spirits or deities, and ancestors. The High God—known as Onyame, Onyankopon, and by other names—is the Creator, now otiose; he is accompanied by Asase Yaa, the goddess of the earth. The ancestors live in the land of the dead and may demand offerings, in the past including those of slaves. The royal ancestors are at the heart of the ritual protection of a kingdom. They are "fed" at shrines in the form of blackened stools of wood and kept in the "stool rooms" in palaces and houses. Traditionally, the stools were anointed with human blood, gunpowder, and spider webs, and given alcoholic drink; human sacrifices are no longer made. Spirits or deities are many, and the living can communicate with them through prayer, sacrifice, and possession. Each has its own *osofo*, or priest; an *okomfo* is a living spirit medium who interprets the words of a spirit who is consulted to remove sickness and human disasters. Each kingdom and town has, or had in past years, an annual purification ritual, known as *odwira*, in which the king, the office of kingship, the kingdom, and the town are purified of the pollution of the preceding year; this is often known in the literature as a "yam festival."

The Akan have largely been Christian since the nineteenth century, except for most kings, who have had to retain their indigenous religious status and practices. European Christian missions were highly successful, bringing not only Christianity but also education, and most Akan have been literate for a long time. Islam has a long history among the Akan, having been introduced by early traders from the north. Royalty made use of Muslim scribes for court duties. The Akan have a long history of "prophets" of many kinds—Christian, Muslim, and "heathen"—and of separatist Christian movements. All these various forms of religious belief and activity exist side by side, and most people have recourse to all of them, according to their particular needs and wishes.

Bibliography

Busia, K. A. (1951). *The Position of the Chief in the Modern Political System of Ashanti*. London: Oxford University Press, for the International African Institute.

McCaskie, T. C. (1995). *State and Society in Pre-Colonial Asante*. Cambridge and New York: Cambridge University Press.

McLeod, M. D. (1981). *Asante*. London: British Museum Publications, for the Trustees of the British Museum.

Rattray, R. S. (1923). *Ashanti*. Oxford: Clarendon Press.

Rattray, R. S. (1927). *Religion and Art in Ashanti*. Oxford: Clarendon Press.

Rattray, R. S. (1929). *Ashanti Law and Constitution*. Oxford: Clarendon Press.

Wilks, Ivor (1975). *Assante in the Nineteenth Century*. London and New York: Cambridge University Press.

MICHELLE GILBERT

Alur

ETHNONYMS: none

Orientation

Identification. The Alur speak DhuAlur, a Western Nilotic language of the Lwo Group. They live in northwestern Uganda and in the neighboring parts of northeastern Zaire. The total Alur population at the time of the 1948 census was approximately 300,000. In censuses taken since then, the Alur have not been counted as a separate ethnic group, but their population can now be conservatively estimated at around half a million. Some two-fifths of the Alur live in Uganda and three-fifths in Zaire.

Location. Alur territory occupies the northwestern shores of Lake Albert and of the Albert Nile, which runs out of it. The lacustrine and riverine areas have an elevation of about 600 meters, and the land rises from the lake at a steep escarpment. Farther north, it rises more gradually to hilly plateaus, which average from 1,500 to 1,800 meters and which have the most rainfall (100 to 200 centimeters), the most fertile soil, and the densest population, as well as the coolest climate in the region. In contrast, the shore areas are very hot and humid. In Uganda, the density ranges from 25 persons per square kilometer in the lowlands to 43 in the highlands.

Economy

Subsistence and Commercial Activities. Finger millet, the staple food, has been partially displaced by cassava, which colonial authorities compelled the Alur to plant as a reserve against famine; flour from both crops is usually mixed in cooking. Maize has been extensively grown during the twentieth century, a great part of it used for brewing. Beans, *simsim* (sesame), spinach (both wild and cultivated), and, at lower elevations, shea butternuts are important elements of the diet. In addition to cattle, the Alur raise chickens, goats, and some sheep. Edible ants and seasonal swarms of grasshoppers are further supplements. Elephants, antelopes, buffalo, rhinoceroses, hippopotamuses, crocodiles, edible rats, rabbits, and porcupines were once hunted, but government regulations, population growth, and sparsity of game have brought almost to an end the hunting of these animals, except for the last three.

The highland areas consist mainly of grassland cleared from primeval forest, the lowland areas of savanna bush. Everywhere, cattle are kept to some extent, but they flourish best in the highlands, which have also been more favorable than the lowlands to the increase of human population. Cotton is grown mainly in the midland areas, and, since the 1960s, arabica coffee has been planted extensively in the highlands, superseding cattle as the main source of cash. The Alur of the lowlands fish in the lake and river, trading smoke-dried fish to the highlands and neighboring parts of Uganda and Zaire. Mineral salt is obtained from a few localities, and vegetable salt is made by filtering the ash of suitable grasses.

Industrial Arts. The Okeodo, an ethnic subgroup of the Alur, formerly melted iron and forged tools and weapons. Skins, leaves, fibers, and bark cloth were worn as clothing until after World War II, when imported cotton came to be universally adopted.

Houses, utensils, and musical instruments are still made domestically, by individuals who have developed special skills, from local materials that are accessible to all. The houses are now usually roofed with imported iron corrugated sheets instead of local thatch, however, and the availibility of imported utensils and musical instruments has caused local production to dwindle.

Trade. There has always been some exchange of salt, iron goods, fish, livestock, and foodstuffs, but regular markets did not develop until after World War II; retail shops and and administrative centers can be found at a few crossroads. Some non-Africans, especially Arabs, and African Muslims were prominent in the early development of these retail and administrative centers, but the Indo-Pakistani retailers, pervasive throughout Uganda, were confined to the district headquarters town of Arua, which lay outside Alur territory.

Land Tenure. All Alur had free access to land through kinship and descent. Most people lived in territory that was under the control of a corporate descent group to which people belonged by agnatic descent, but some might also live in another territory, to which they were linked through a mother's brother or other close cognatic relative.

Division of Labor. Traditionally, there was a fairly clear division of labor by sex among the Alur. Women were responsible for the domestic economy—preparing, cooking, and serving food, including brewing beer (and, for some of them, distilling spirits), collecting fuel, and maintaining the walls and floors of houses. Men cleared the land and hoed the fields, women weeded and harvested. The division of labor has become more diversified: both men and women work as teachers, shopkeepers, and medical staff (e.g., orderlies, nurses). Many women pursue careers away from home, especially around Kampala.

Kinship, Marriage, and Family

The family is polygynous, patrilineal, and patrilocal, based economically on the house-property complex. A man with more than one wife is required to provide each woman with her own house, granaries, and fields. The elementary cell of the compound family is thus an independent inheritance group. Its land is inheritable by its male members; its female members inherit nothing except possibly a few ornaments, articles of dress, and household utensils from their mother. Most of the animals that are received at a daughter's marriage become the property of the elementary family, consisting of her father, mother, and brothers. The head of the compound family is the trustee of the property of each of its component elementary families. The compound family is a self-contained property-holding unit. Bride-wealth received within it does not go outside it, except for special debts, and only its members share in the inheritance at the death of its head. The eldest son of the first wife usually succeeds as chief heir, although any son of any wife can do so if he is considered better qualified; however, such a succession may cause a split in the lineage. The son who inherits is the formal guardian of any young children left by his father. He has the first choice in the leviratic inheritance of widows (other than his own mother), but if there is more than one, he does not inherit both, but probably allows one to go to a younger brother who is not yet married.

Neighborhood groups are usually composed of exogamous lineages, lineage segments, or composite clan sections, with possibly a few other individuals and families linked to them cognatically. A man has special ties and privileges toward his mother's brother's clan as a whole, although such ties and privileges are usually exercised only toward the mother's brother's own corporate lineage. The man's relationship to his father's sister is equally important, but, as sisters marry into different lineages, that relationship is usually centered on a particular father's sister, always involving her husband and his fellow agnates, all of whom refer to the man as "son of our brother-in-law." Of course, the new affinal relations created in one generation always become the cognatic relations of the next.

Because marriage is a lengthy process of contract between two lineages, the Alur try to avoid divorce, which involves costly and disruptive rearrangements of property. Barrenness of women, sterility of men (rarely admitted), witchcraft on the part of either, and gross failure in domestic marital obligations are all grounds for divorce. Most of the bride-wealth must be repaid in case of divorce, with deductions made for any children born of the marriage.

The Alur familial authority system, in relation to the individual, is essentially continuous, collective, and generalized. Within the permanent and pervasive groups, which are mutually interdependent, children are taught to assume generalized roles that impose their inevitable limitations of habit and whose pattern is easily extended to cover like groups. The individual's first experience of authority comes in the form of parental discipline, but training and discipline also come from a fairly wide group of senior paternal and maternal kin. Authority rests on a noticeably collective basis, and the parental role is much less marked than in Western family systems. Alur children go through a process of learning that begins with toilet training and feeding themselves and ranges to respecting persons and property, running errands, and generally emulating older persons of their own sex. Some aspects of this process invite comparison with those of the wider political system. The Alur describe their system of discipline as stern and rigid, yet observation of their daily life conveys the opposite impression. It must be that the stern enforcement of minimum rules of conduct on rare and exemplary occasions during maturation is sufficient to fix observance of these minimum requirements by the majority without any further reminders and with infrequent need for punishment. The tempo of their life is slow, their physical stamina is great, and they endure spells of exhaustingly hard work, but the greater part of life among the Alur consists of tasks that are monotonous but not exacting, which enables the young to have great freedom and yet to be inducted into adult life without any striking period of tension or ritualized initiation. Legitimate authority, both in the family and in the political system, cannot be directly challenged, but it can be evaded. In family life, the escape from authority, although usually more or less temporary, is also an integral part of the system and brings into play various categories of kinship without challenging the legitimacy of familial authority as such. The introduction of spheres of activity beyond the direct control of Alur society, such as schooling, migrant labor, and professional careers outside Alur territory, constitutes a much graver threat to the integrity of the Alur system of socialization.

Sociopolitical Organization

At one time, the Alur had begun to develop specialized political institutions, but they remained embedded in the extended kin-based structure of segmentary lineages through which political processes also were expressed. The ruling lines of Lwo descent reached their present territory some three or four centuries ago, as part of a larger Nilotic migration from what is now Sudan. They gradually established dominance over small groups from other ethnic groups (Okebo, Madi, Lendu) and incorporated them into a new society. This dominance seems to have been established with little or no actual warfare, by employing peaceful methods that provided a somewhat larger scale of organization, by instituting more effective methods of dispute settlement, and, above all, by supplying the nonmaterial means of production in the mystical form of rainmaking, which attracted the support and allegiance of all. Such mystical powers are held in exclusive possession by the hereditary heads of the principal Lwo lineages, which reached different parts of the country by various routes. With the passage of time and demographic growth, the major lineages themselves segmented, and the mystical services of rainmaking and sacred kingship proliferated and expanded to cover an ever larger territory.

Two chief mechanisms led to this proliferation and expansion. The king would send an unruly, troublesome son out to live among as yet unincorporated groups of non-Alur. The son would go with followers and cattle, providing feasts and receiving gifts in return, setting up a new cycle of economic and marital exchange and redistribution, mediating and arbitrating disputes, and providing a channel of privileged access to the rainmaking powers of the king, his father, which eventually became powers exercised by himself and his heirs in their own right. Alur lineages and clan sections sometimes petitioned the king to send them one of his sons to be their local ruler, making them more highly respected by neighboring groups, who might also have done the same, and providing them with the same mystical, political, and economic services. These rulers did not endeavor to eliminate interpersonal violence altogether. Compensation for offenses, including homicide, could be sought by the men of the lineage concerned, and lineages could even fight if they failed to agree. To continue fighting was an offense against the king's stool (i.e., his mystical authority), however, and had to be resolved by payment of a fine. If a group refused to pay, the king's only ultimate recourse was to call other groups to join with him in plundering the offenders. This was a rare but feared deterrent.

In sum, the segmentary state was characterized by an elementary political sovereignty that was restricted to a small, central-core domain, but a general ritual suzerainty spread out more widely. This relationship of sovereignty and suzerainty at the center was repeated on a smaller scale at the peripheral centers that were derived from it, creating a pyramidal structure.

Religion and Expressive Culture

The central religious concept of the tradional Alur was *jok*, which could be perceived either as a pervasive unity or as a composite entity of innumerable particular entities that were associated with prominent or extraordinary manifestations of nature, rocks, trees, wells, and streams and also with the ancestral spirits of the lineages. Every family head built one shrine for his patrilineal ancestors and another for the spirits of female and cognatic kin. The shrine that was built by a lineage head was more important, and the shrine of the ruler, although also dedicated to his ancestors, virtually amounted to a shrine for the polity as a whole and received the largest attendance for seasonal sacrifice and celebration. The diviner (*ajuoga*) and the witch (*jajok*) or sorcerer (not terminologically distinguished) were thus linguistically linked to jok and were manifestations of the same power. There were various methods of divination, whereby the ajuoga diagnosed the nature and discerned the cure of a patient's afflictions and ascertained the cause of a death. Accused witches were subjected to ordeals in which poison was administered to chickens, which were watched to see which suspect they pointed to in their death throes. Witches convicted in this way formerly were put to death, and they still may be forced to move to another community. Many afflictions emerge in the form of possession by spirits, which are also various manifestations of jok. Possession is dealt with by having the appropriate diviner exhort the patient with drumming and by dancing on the part of those who have previously been cured, in order to accept and welcome the spirit, allow it to come out, and "dance" in its honor. This is called *idho jok*, "to climb jok."

Cuts were made in certain parts of the body for the insertion of medicine, and foreign bodies implanted in the body by sorcery were said to be extracted by sucking them out through horns. Curative bloodletting was also practiced.

The death of prominent people is marked by a mourning "dance" (*ywak*), which allows the free expression of grief and also of aggressive hostility toward death and its presumed human mystical instrument. The real dance (*myel*) of the Alur is a joyous celebration that brings together people of many neighboring corporate groups in a mystically enforced truce, secured by ritual, that provides an opportunity for young people to become attracted to each other and proceed to courtship and marriage.

Alur artistic expression is evinced in singing; dancing; playing drums, harps, and horns; and making aesthetically pleasing objects of practical use. Herbal medicine is part of the practice of diviners. The Lendu who have been incorporated into Alur society have contributed a rich body of herbal lore. Cicatrizations were made by girls on the forehead and belly, and by the young men of some areas, in patterns that varied regionally. Because the latter tended to spend long periods away from home under foreign influence, they discontinued this practice long before girls did.

Death is marked by sacrifice, feasting, beer drinking, and inquisition into the causes of death, involving an extensive rehearsal and a sifting of all the accumulated tensions, disputes, and witchcraft episodes that have marred the harmony of the local community.

Bibliography

Crazzolara, J. P. (1950, 1951, 1954). *The Lwoo.* Part 1, 59–66; Part 2, 179–222; Part 3, 401–447. Verona: Editrice Nigrizia.

Quix, J. P. (1939). "Au pays de Mahagi." *Congo* 1(3): 276–294; 1(4): 387–411.

Southall, Aidan (1954). "Alur Tradition and Its Historical Significance." *Uganda Journal* 18(2): 137–165.

Southall, Aidan (1956). *Alur Society: A Study in Processes and Types of Domination.* Cambridge: Heffer. Reprint. 1972. Nairobi: Oxford University Press.

Southall, Aidan (1958). "Oedipus in Alur Folklore." *Uganda Journal* 22(2): 167–169. Reprinted in *Oedipus: A Folklore Casebook,* edited by Lowell Edmunds and Alan Dundes, 35–39. New York: Garland.

Southall, Aidan (1960). "Alur Homicide and Suicide." In *African Homicide and Suicide,* edited by Paul Bohannan, 214–229. Princeton, N.J.: Princeton University Press.

Southall, Aidan (1969). "Spirit Mediumship Cults among the Alur." In *Spirit Mediumship and Society in Africa,* edited by John Beattie and John Middleton, 232–272. London: Routledge & Kegan Paul.

Southall, Aidan (1970). "Incorporation among the Alur." In *From Tribe to Nation in Africa,* edited by John Middleton and Ronald Cohen, 71–92. Scranton, Pa.: Chandler Publishing Co.

Southall, Aidan (1985). "The Partition of the Alur." In *Partitioned Africans,* edited by A. I. Asiwaju, 87–103. Lagos: University of Lagos Press.

Vanneste, M. (1949). "Legenden, Geschiedenis en Gebruiken van een Nilotisch Volk." *Institut Royal Colonial Belge, Mémoires* 18, fasc. 1.

Vanneste, M. (1953). "Sprookjes van een Nilotisch Volk, Alur-Teksten (Mahagi, Belgisch Congo)." *Institut Royal Colonial Belge, Mémoires* 254, fasc. 3.

AIDAN SOUTHALL

Amhara

ETHNONYM: Amara

Orientation

Identification. The term "Amhara" is derived from *amari*, meaning "one who is pleasing, agreeable, beautiful, and gracious." Amhara culture is often identified with Abyssinian culture, which is regarded as the heir to the cultural blending of ancient Semitic and Cushitic (African) patterns; other heirs are the Tigre-speaking people of Eritrea, and the Tegreñña speakers of northern Ethiopia. The name "Ethiopia" is derived from an ancient Greek term meaning "people with sunburned faces" and has been revived to designate the present-day state, which also includes non-Abyssinians. The Amhara themselves often use the term "Amhara" synonymously with "Ethiopian Orthodox (Monophysite) Christian," although their own, more precise expression for this religion is

"Towahedo" (Orthodox). In the past, books on Ethiopia have often referred to this religion as "Coptic," derived from the Greek term for Egyptian. Until Haile Selassie was crowned emperor in 1930, the Coptic metropolitan of Alexandria, Egypt, had also been the head of this Ethiopian church and had appointed Ethiopian archbishops.

Location. Ethiopia is located in the northeastern part of Africa, roughly between 5° and 16° N and 33° and 43° E. It is mountainous, separated from the Red Sea by hot lowland deserts; a steep escarpment in the west borders the hot lowland in Sudan. The mountain-fortress type of landscape has frequently enabled the plateau people to retain their independence against would-be invaders. Begemder, Gojam, and Welo are Amharic speaking, as are parts of Shewa since Amhara expansion under emperor Menilek II in the 1880s.

Demography. According to the 1984 census, the population of Ethiopia was estimated as 42 million. Of these, 28 percent referred to themselves as "Amhara," and 32 percent stated that they spoke Amharic at home. Hence, about 14 million could be identified as Amhara, subject to qualification by the effects of Amharization during the rule of Emperor Haile Selassie (1930–1974) and the political strife against Amhara domination since then. Ethiopia is essentially a rural country. Apart from the capital, Addis Ababa, few towns have a permanent population in excess of 10,000: Gonder, the old caravan town on the way from the highlands to the Sudan; Harer, the coffee city; and Dire Dawa, the railroad junction to the coast. The many small towns are essentially marketplaces, serving the farming hinterland.

Linguistic Affiliation. There are three major linguistic families in Ethiopia: Cushitic, Semitic, and Nilo-Saharan. Cushitic and Semitic are two families of the Afro-Asian Phylum. Nilo-Sarahan languages of the Sudanic Phylum predominate along the northern and western escarpment. Cushitic includes Oromo (formerly called Galla), Sidamo, Somali, and Agau. Semitic languages, spoken mainly in the northern half of the country, are related to the Ge'ez language, which was spoken there from about the first half of the first millennium B.C. and had a writing system from which the present Amharic writing is derived. Ge'ez ceased to be spoken before the fourteenth century A.D., but it survives in the Orthodox liturgy to this day. It has been the language of religious and historical documents almost until the present, and linguists have referred to it as "Ethiopic." Amharic is related to Ge'ez but contains strong influences from Cushitic. It has been important since the fourteenth century A.D., when the earliest Amharic document, "Songs of the Kings," was written. Amharic, which is the predominant language on the plateau of northwest-central Ethiopia, is now the official national language of Ethiopia.

History and Cultural Relations

There is a paucity of reliable data about the prehistory of Ethiopia because archaeological excavation was long prohibited. Three procedures can be followed, however: interpretation of surface archaeological sites, tracing ancient trade routes, and linguistic analysis. Rock paintings resemble those of Libya; others depict cattle without humps, suggesting an early population of cattle breeders prior to the entry from Yemen of breeders of humped cattle (which are predominant today), via the Bab al-Mandab. The elaborate obelisks at Aksum, 27 to 30 meters tall, with false doors and windows (which have counterparts in ancient Yemen), appear to fall into the Semitic period of about 500 B.C. to A.D. 300.

Certain basic trade routes—for instance, the iron route—have scarcely changed in thousands of years. Salt must still be brought in from the coast of the Red Sea. Ivory, gold, and slaves were brought from the south to pay for imports. Wild coffee was brought from the south of Ethiopia to Yemen, perhaps to pay for humped *sebu* cattle. *Mashella* (guinea corn) may have originated on the western Ethiopian plateau and spread westward from there. Foreign trade was given great impetus when the camel was introduced to those Ethiopian regions too dry for donkeys, about A.D. 100. There is a record of hunting expeditions by the Ptolemean rulers of Egypt in Ethiopia. Ptolemy III (245–222 B.C.) placed at the port of Adulis (near present-day Mesewa) a Greek inscription recording that he captured elephants, and an inscribed block of stones with magical hieroglyphs. At the same port about A.D. 60, a Greek merchant named Periplus recorded the importation of iron and the production of spears for hunting elephants, and in A.D. 350 Aeizana, king of Aksum, defeated the Nubians and carried off iron and bronze from Meroë.

The Abyssinian tradition of the Solomonic dynasty, as told in the Ge'ez-language book *Kebra Nagast* (Honor of the Kings) refers to the rule of Menilek I, about 975–950 B.C. It relates that he was the son of Makeda, conceived from King Solomon during her visit to Jerusalem. Interrupted in A.D. 927 by sovereigns of a Zagwe line, the Solomonic line was restored in 1260 and claimed continuity until Emperor Haile Selassie was deposed in 1974. Abyssinian churches are still built on the principle of Solomon's temple of Jerusalem, with a Holy of Holies section in the interior. Christianity came to Aksum in the fourth century A.D., when Greek-speaking Syrians converted the royal family. This strain of Christianity retained a number of Old Testament rules, some of which are observed to this day: the consumption of pork is forbidden; circumcision of boys takes place about a week after birth; upper-level priests consider Saturday a day of rest, second only to Sunday; weddings preferably take place on Sunday, so that the presumed deflowering, after nightfall, is considered to have taken place on the eve of Monday. Ecclesiastic rule over Abyssinia was administered early on by the archbishop of Alexandria, detached only after World War II. At the Council of Chalcedon in A.D. 451, the theological Monophysites of Alexandria, including the Abyssinians, had broken away from the European church; hence the designation "Coptic."

The spread of Islam to regions surrounding it produced relative isolation in Ethiopia from the seventh to the sixteenth centuries. During this period, the Solomonic dynasty was restored in 1260 in the province of Shewa by King Yekuno Amlak, who extended his realm from Abyssinia to some Cuchitic-speaking lands south and east. Amharic developed out of this linguistic blend. From time to time, Europeans heard rumors of a Prester John, a Christian king on the other side of the Muslim world. Using a vast number of serfs on feudal church territories, Abuna (archbishop) Tekle Haymanot built churches and monasteries, often on easily defensible hilltops, such as Debra Libanos monastery in Shewa, which is still the most important in Ethiopia.

With the Muslim conquest of Somali land in 1430, the ring around Abyssinia was complete, and recently Islamicized Oromo (Galla) seminomadic tribes from the south invaded through the Rift Valley, burning churches and monasteries. Some manuscripts and church paintings had to be hidden on islands on Lake Tana. When a second wave of invaders came, equipped with Turkish firearms, the Shewan king Lebna Dengel sent a young Armenian to Portugal to solicit aid. Before it could arrive, the Oromo leader Mohammed Grañ ("the left-handed") attacked with the aid of Arabs from Yemen, Somalis, and Danakils and proceeded as far north as Aksum, which he razed, killing the king in battle in 1540. His children and the clergy took refuge on and north of Lake Tana. One year later, Som Christofo Da Gama landed at Mesewa with 450 Portuguese musketeers; the slain king's son, Galaudeos (Claudius), fought on until he died in battle. The tide turned, however, and in 1543 Mohammed Grañ fell in battle.

Shewa nevertheless remained settled by Oromo, who learned the agriculture of the region. The royal family had only a tent city in what became the town of Gonder. There the Portuguese built bridges and castles, and Jesuits began to convert the royal family to Roman Christianity. King Za Dengel was the first royal convert, but the Monophysite clergy organized a rebellion that led to his removal. His successor, King Susneos, had also been converted but was careful not to urge his people to convert; shortly before his death in 1632, he proclaimed religious liberty for all his subjects.

The new king, Fasilidas (1632–1667), expelled the Portuguese and restored the privileges of the Monophysite clergy. He—and later his son and grandson—employed workmen trained by the Portuguese to build the castles that stand to this day. Special walled paths shielded the royal family from common sight, but the king, while sitting under a fig tree, judged cases brought before him. A stone-lined water pool was constructed under his balcony, and a mausoleum entombed his favorite horse. All these structures still exist. But the skills of stonemasonry later fell into disuse; warfare required mobility, which necessitated the formation of military tent cities. Portuguese viticulture was also lost (though the name of the middle elevation remains "Woyna Dega"), and the clergy had to import raisins to produce sacramental wine.

Gonder had been abandoned by the Solomonic line when a usurping commoner chieftain, Kassa, chose it as the location to have himself crowned King Theodore in 1855. He defeated the king of Shewa and held the dynastic heir, the boy Menilek II, hostage at his court. Theodore realized the urgency of uniting the many ethnic groups of the country into a nation, to prevent Ethiopia from losing its independence to European colonial powers. Thinking that all Europeans knew how to manufacture cannons, Theodore invited foreign technicians and, at first, even welcomed foreign missionaries. But when the latter proved unable to cast cannons for him and even criticized his often violent behavior, he jailed and chained British missionaries. This led to the Lord Napier expedition, which was welcomed and assisted by the population of Tigray Province. When the fort of Magdalla fell, Theodore committed suicide. A conservative Tigray chief, Yohannes, was crowned at Aksum.

In 1889 the Muslim mahdi took advantage of the disarray in Ethiopia; he razed Gonder and devastated the subprovince of Dembeya, causing a severe and prolonged famine. Meanwhile, the Shewan dynastic heir, Menilek II, had grown to manhood and realized that Ethiopia could no longer isolate itself if it were to retain independence. He proceeded, with patient persistence, to unify the country. As an Amhara from Shewa, he understood his Oromo neighbors and won their loyalty with land grants and military alliances. He negotiated a settlement with the Tigray. He equipped his forces with firearms from whatever source, some even from the Italians (in exchange for granting them territory in Eritrea).

His policies were so successful that he managed to defeat the Italian invasion at Adwa, in 1896, an event that placed Ethiopia on the international map diplomatically. Empress Taitu liked the hot mineral springs of a district in Shewa, even though it was in an Oromo region, and the emperor therefore agreed to build his capital there, naming it "Addis Ababa" (new flower). When expanding Addis Ababa threatened to exhaust the local fuel supply, Menilek ordered the importation of eucalyptus trees from Australia, which grew rapidly during each three-month rainy season.

Menilek II died in 1913, and his daughter Zauditu became nominal head; a second cousin, Ras Tafari Makonnen, became regent and was crowned King of Kings Haile Selassie I in 1930. He made it possible for Ethiopia to join the League of Nations in 1923, by outlawing the slave trade. One of his first acts as emperor was to grant his subjects a written constitution. He allied himself by marriage to the Oromo king of Welo Province. When Mussolini invaded Ethiopia in 1935, Emperor Haile Selassie appeared in Geneva to plead his case before the League, warning that his country would not be the last victim of aggression. The Italian occupation ended in 1941 with surrender to the British and return of the emperor. During succeeding decades, the emperor promoted an educated elite and sought assistance from the United States, rather than the British, in various fields. Beginning in about 1960, a young, educated generation of Ethiopians grew increasingly impatient with the slowness of development, especially in the political sphere. At the same time, the aging emperor, who was suffering memory loss, was losing his ability to maintain control. In 1974 he was deposed, and he died a year later. The revolutionary committees, claiming to follow a Marxist ideology, formed military dictatorships that deported villagers under conditions of great suffering and executed students and each other without legal trials. Dictator Mengistu Haile Mariam fled Ethiopia in May 1991 as Eritrean and Tigrayan rebel armies approached from the north. The country remains largely rural; traditional culture patterns and means of survival are the norm.

Settlements

The typical rural settlement is the hamlet, *ṭis*, called *mender* if several are linked on one large hill. The hamlet may consist of two to a dozen huts. Thus, the hamlet is often little more than an isolated or semi-isolated farmstead, and another hamlet may be close by if their plowed fields are near. Four factors appear to determine where a hamlet is likely to be situated: ecological considerations, such as water within a woman's walking distance, or available pasturage for the flock; kinship considerations—persons within a hamlet are nearly always related and form a family economic community; administrative considerations, such as inherited family ownership of land, tenancy of land belonging to a feudal lord of former times, or continuing agreement with the nearby church that had held the land as a fief up to 1975 and continues to receive part of the crop in exchange for its services; and ethnic considerations. A hamlet may be entirely inhabited by Falasha blacksmiths and pottery makers or Faqi tanners. Most of the Falasha have now left Ethiopia.

To avoid being flooded during the rainy season, settlements are typically built on or near hilltops. There is usually a valley in between, where brooks or irrigation canals form the border for planted fields. The hillsides, if not terrace farmed, serve as pasturage for all hamlets on the hill. Not only sheep and goats, but also cows, climb over fairly steep, bushy hillsides to feed. Carrying water and branches for fuel is still considered a woman's job, and she may have to climb for several hours from the nearest year-round water supply. The hamlet is usually patrilocal and patrilineal. When marriage occurs, usually early in life, a son may receive use of part of his father's rented (or owned) field and build his hut nearby. If no land is available owing to fragmentation, the son may reluctantly be compelled to establish himself at the bride's hamlet. When warfare has killed off the adult males in a hamlet, in-laws may also be able to move in. Some hamlets are fenced in by thorn bushes against night-roving hyenas and to corral cattle. Calves and the family mule may be taken into the living hut at night. There is usually at least one fierce reddish-brown dog in each hamlet.

Economy

Much Amhara ingenuity has long been invested in the direct exploitation of natural resources. An Amhara would rather spend as much time as necessary searching for suitably shaped hard or soft saplings for a walking cane than perform carpentry, which is traditionally largely limited to constructing the master bed (*alga*), wooden saddles, and simple musical instruments. Soap is obtained by crushing the fruit of the *endod* (*Pircunia abyssinica*) bush. Tannin for depilation of hides and curing is obtained from the yellow fruit of the *embway* bush. Butter is preserved and perfumed by boiling it with the leaves of the *ades* (myrtle) bush. In times of crop failure, edible oil is obtained by gathering and crushing wild-growing sunflower seeds (*Carthamus tinctorus*). If necessary, leaves of the *lola* bush can be split by women to bake the festive bread *dabbo*. The honey of a small, tiny-stingered bee (*Apis dorsata*) is gathered to produce alcoholic mead, *ṭej*, whereas the honey of the wild bee *ṭazemma* (*Apis Africans miaia*) is gathered to treat colds and heart ailments. Fishing is mostly limited to the three-month rainy season, when rivers are full and the water is muddy from runoff so that the fish cannot see the fishers. Hunting elephants used to be a sport of young feudal nobles, but hunting for ivory took place largely in non-Amhara regions. Since rifles became available in Amhara farming regions, Ethiopian duikers and guinea fowl have nearly disappeared.

Subsistence farming provides the main economy for most rural Amhara. The traditional method required much land to lie fallow because no fertilization was applied. Cattle manure is formed into flat cakes, sun dried, and used as fuel for cooking. New land, if available, is cleared by the slash-and-burn method. A wooden scratch plow with a pointed iron tip, pulled by oxen, is the main farming tool. Insecurity of land tenure has long been a major factor in discouraging Amhara farmers from producing more than the amount required for subsistence. The sharecropping peasant (*gabbar*) was little more than a serf who feared the (often absentee) feudal landlord or military quartering that would absorb any surplus. The revolutionary government (1975–1991) added additional fears by its villagization program, moving peasants at command to facilitate state control and deporting peasants to the south of Ethiopia, where many perished owing to poor government planning and support.

The preferred crop of the Amhara is *ṭyeff* (*Eragrostis abyssinica; Poa abyssinica*), the small seeds of which are rich in iron. At lower or drier elevations, several sorghums (durras) are grown: *mashella* (*Andropogon sorghum*), often mixed with the costlier ṭyeff flower to bake the flapjack bread *injera; zengada* (*Eleusina multiforma*), grown as crop insurance; and *dagussa* (*Eleusine coracana*, or *tocusso*), used as an ingredient in beer together with barley. Wheat (*Triticum* spp.), *sendē*, is grown in higher elevations and is considered a luxury. Barley (*Hordeum* spp.), *gebs*, is a year-round crop, used primarily for brewing *talla*, a mild beer, or to pop a parched grain, *gebs qolo*, a ready snack kept available for guests. Maize, *bahēr mashella*, is recognized as a foreign-introduced crop.

The most important vegetable oil derives from *nug* (*Guizotia abyssinica*), the black Niger seed, and from *talba* (*Linum usitatissimum*), flax seed. Cabbage (*gomen*) is regarded as a poor food. Chick-peas are appreciated as a staple that is not expected to fail even in war and famine; they are consumed during the Lenten season, as are peas. Onions and garlic are grown as ingredients for *woṭ*, the spicy stew that also contains beans, may include chicken, and always features spicy red peppers—unless ill heath prevents their consumption. Lentils substitute for meat during fasting periods. The raising of livestock is traditionally not directly related to available pasture, but to agriculture and the desire for prestige. Oxen are needed to pull the plow, but traditionally there was no breeding to obtain good milkers. Coffee may grow wild, but the beans are usually bought at a market and crushed and boiled in front of guests; salt—but not sugar—may be added.

Division of Labor. Although much needed, the castelike skilled occupations like blacksmithing, pottery making, and tanning are held in low esteem and, in rural regions, are usually associated with a socially excluded ethnic grouping. Moreover, ethnic workmanship is suspected of having been acquired by dealings with evil spirits that enable the artisans to turn themselves into hyenas at night to consume corpses, cause diseases by staring, and turn humans into donkeys to utilize their labor. Such false accusations can be very serious. On the other hand, the magic power accredited to these workers is believed to make their products strong, whereas those manufactured by an outsider who might have learned the trade would soon break. The trade of weaving is not afflicted by such suspicions, although it is sometimes associated with Muslims or migrants from the south.

Land Tenure. Land tenure among traditional rural Amhara resembled that of medieval Europe more than that found elsewhere in Africa. Feudal institutions required the gabbar to perform labor (*hudād*) for his lord and allocated land use in exchange for military service, *gult*. In a system resembling the European entail, inheritable land, *rest*, was subject to taxation (which could be passed on to the sharecroppers) and to expropriation in case of rebellion against the king. Over the centuries, endowed land was added to fief-holding church land, *and debber ager*. Royal household lands were classified as *mādbet*, and *melkenya* land was granted to tax collectors. Emperor Haile Selassie attempted to change the feudal system early in his administration. He defeated feudal armies, but was stymied in abrogating feudalistic land tenure, especially in the Amhara region, by feudal lords such as Ras Kassa. The parliament that he had called into existence had no real power. All remaining feudal land tenure was abrogated during the revolutionary dictatorship (1975–1991), but feudalistic attitudes practiced by rural officials, such as *shum shir* (frequently moving lower officials to other positions to maintain control), appear to have persisted.

Kinship

The extended patrilocal, patrilineal, patriarchal family is particularly strong among holders of rest land tenure, but is found, in principle, even on the hamlet level of sharecroppers. There are several levels of kin, *zemed,* which also include those by affinity, *amachenet*. In view of the emphasis on seeking security in kinship relations, there are also several formal methods of establishing fictive kinship, *zemed hone*, provided the person to be adopted is *aṭṭenṭam* ("of good bones," i.e., not of Shanqalla slave ancestry). Full adoption provides a breast father (*yeṭuṭ abbat*) or a breast mother (*yeṭuṭ ennat*). The traditional public ceremony included coating the nipples with honey and simulating breast-feeding, even if the child was already in adolescence.

Marriage and Family

Marriage. There are three predominant types of marriage in Amhara tradition. Only a minority—the priesthood, some older persons, and nobility—engage in eucharistic church marriage (*qurban*). No divorce is possible. Widows and widowers may remarry, except for priests, who are instead expected to become monks.

Kin-negotiated civil marriage (*semanya;* lit., "eighty") is most common. (Violation of the oath of marriage used to be penalized by a fine of 80 Maria Theresa thalers.) No church ceremony is involved, but a priest may be present at the wedding to bless the couple. Divorce, which involves the division of property and determination of custody of children, can be negotiated. Temporary marriage (*damoz*) obliges the husband to pay housekeeper's wages for a period stated in advance. This was felt to be an essential arrangement in an economy where restaurant and hotel services were not available. The term is a contraction of *demewez,* "blood and sweat" (compensation). The contract, although oral, was before witnesses and was therefore enforceable by court order. The wife had no right of inheritance, but if children were conceived during the contract period, they could make a claim for part of the father's property, should he die. Damoz rights were even recognized in modern law during the rule of Emperor Haile Selassie.

Socialization in the domestic unit begins with the naming of the baby (giving him or her the "world name"), a privilege that usually belongs to the mother. She may base it on her predominant emotion at the time (e.g., Desta [joy] or Almaz [diamond]), on a significant event occurring at the time, or on a special wish she may have for the personality or future of her baby (Seyum, "to be appointed to dignity").

Socialization. Breast-feeding may last two years, during which the nursling is never out of touch with the body of the mother or another woman. Until they are weaned, at about age 7, children are treated with permissiveness, in contrast to the authoritarian training that is to follow. The state of reason and incipient discipline begins gradually at about age 5 for girls and 7 for boys. The former assist their mothers in watching babies and fetching wood; boys take sheep and cows to pasture and, with slingshots, guard crops against birds and baboons. Both can be questioned in court to express preferences concerning guardianship in case of their parents' divorce. Neglect of duty is punished by immediate scolding and beating.

Formal education in the traditional rural church school rarely began before age 11 for boys. Hazing patterns to test courage are common among boys as they grow up, both physically and verbally. Girls are enculturated to appear shy, but may play house with boys prior to adolescence. Adolescence is the beginning of stricter obedience for both sexes, compensated by pride in being assigned greater responsibilities. Young men are addressed as *ashker* and do most of the plowing; by age 18 they may be addressed as *gobez,* signifying (strong, handsome) young warrior. On the Ṭemqet (baptism of Jesus) festival, the young men encounter each other in teams to compete in the game of *guks,* a tournament fought on horseback with blunt, wooden lances, in which injuries are avoided by ducking or protecting oneself with leather shields. At Christmas, a hockeylike game called *genna* is played and celebrated by boasting (*fukkara*). Female adolescents are addressed as *qonjo* (beautiful), no longer as *leja-gered* (servant maid), unless criticized. Singing loudly in groups while gathering firewood attracts groups of young men, away from parental supervision. Young men and women also meet following the guks and genna games, wearing new clothes and traditional makeup and hairstyles. Outdoor flirting reaches a peak on Easter (Fassika), at the end of the dry season.

Domestic Unit. The traditional age of a girl at first marriage may be as young as 14, to protect her virginity, and to enable the groom to tame her more easily. A groom three to five years older than the bride is preferred. To protect the bride against excessive violence, she is assigned two best men, who wait behind a curtain as the marriage is consummated; later, she may call on them in case of batter.

The term *shemagelyē* signifies an elder and connotes seriousness, wisdom, and command of human relations within the residential kin group or beyond. He may be 40 years of age and already a grandfather. There is no automatic equivalency for elder women, but they can take the *qob* of a nun and continue to live at home while working in the churchyard, baking bread and brewing beer for the priests. Only women past menopause, usually widows, are accepted as nuns by the Monophysite Aybssinian church. Younger women are not considered sufficiently serious to be able to deny their sex drives.

Inheritance. When death is approaching, elder kin of the dying person bring the confessor, and the last will concerning inheritance is pronounced. Fields are given to patrilineal descendants, cattle to all offspring. Personal belongings, such as oxhide mats and a *shamma* (toga), may be given to the confessor, who administers last rites and assigns a burial place in the churchyard. Endowments to the church are handled by the *qes gobez*.

Sociopolitical Organization

Social organization is linked to land tenure of kinfolk, feudalistic traditions and the church, ethnic division of labor, gender, and age status. The peasant class is divided between landowning farmers, who, even though they have no formal political power, can thwart distant government power by their rural remoteness, poor roads, and weight of numbers, and the sharecroppers, who have no such power against local landlords. Fear of a person who engages in a skilled occupation, *ṭebib* (lit., "the knowing one," to whom supernatural secrets are revealed), enters into class stratification, especially for blacksmiths, pottery makers, and tanners. They are despised as members of a lower caste, but their products are needed, and therefore they are tolerated. Below them on the social scale are the descendants of slaves who used to be imported from the negroid Shanqalla of the Sudanese border, or the Nilotic Barya, so that both terms became synonymous with "slave."

Social control is traditionally maintained, and conflict situations are resolved, in accordance with the power hierarchy. Judges interpret laws subjectively and make no sharp distinction between civil and criminal procedures. In addition to written Abyssinian and church laws, there are unwritten codes, such as the payment of blood money to the kin of a murder victim. An aggrieved person could appeal to a higher authority by lying prostrate in his path and shouting "*abyet*" (hear me). Contracts did not have to be written, provided there were reliable witnesses. To obtain a loan or a job, a personal guarantor (*wās*) is necessary, and the wās can also act as bondsman to keep an accused out of jail. The drama of litigation, to talk well in court, is much appreciated. Even children enact it with the proper body language of pointing a toga at the judge to emphasize the speech.

Religion and Expressive Culture

The religious belief of most Amhara is Monophysite—that is, Tewahedo (Orthodox) Christianity, to such an extent that the term "Amhara" is used synonymously with "Abyssinian Christian." Christian Amhara wear a blue neck cord (*meteb*), to distinguish themselves from Muslims. In rural regions, the rules of the church have the de facto force of law, and many people are consecrated to church functions: priests, boy deacons and church students, chorister-scribes, monks, and nuns. Besides the ecclesiastical function of the *qes* (parish priest), the chorister-scribe—who is not ordained—fulfills many services. He translates the liturgy from Ge'ez to Amharic, chants and sometimes composes devotional poetry (*qēnē*), and writes amulets. The latter may be unofficial and discouraged by the priests, but ailing persons believe strongly in them and may use them to prevent disease. Prior to examinations, church students often chew and swallow a *Datura* weed called *astenager* (lit., "to stimulate talk") to enhance memory of biblical quotations and other details learned by rote and to aid correct pronunciation of the liturgy.

Ceremonies. Ceremonies often mark the annual cycle for the public, despite the sacredotal emphasis of the religion. The calendar of Abyssinia is Julian, but the year begins on 11 September, following ancient Egyptian usage, and is called *amete mehrāt* (year of grace). Thus, the Abyssinian year 1948 A.M. corresponds roughly with the Gregorian (Western) A.D. 1956. The new year begins with the month of Meskerem, which follows the rainy season and is named after the first religious holy day of the year, Mesqel-abeba, celebrating the Feast of the Cross. On the seventeenth day, huge poles are stacked up for the bonfire in the evening, with much public parading, dancing, and feasting. By contrast, Christmas (Ledet) has little social significance except for the genna game of the young men. Far more important is Epiphany (Ṭemqet), on the eleventh day of Ṭer. Ceremonial parades escort the priests who carry the *tabot*, symbolic of the holy ark, on their heads, to a water pool. There are all-night services, public feasting, and prayers for plentiful rains.

This is the end of the genna season and the beginning of the guks tournaments fought on horseback by the young men. The long Lenten season is approaching, and clergy as well as the public look forward to the feasting at Easter (Fassika), on the seventeenth day of Miyazya. Children receive new clothes and collect gifts, chanting house to house. Even the voluntary fraternal association *mehabber* is said to have originated from the practice of private communion. Members take turns as hosts at monthly meetings, drinking barley beer together with the confessor-priest, who intones prayers. Members are expected to act as a mutual aid society, raising regular contributions, extending loans, even paying for the *tazkar* (formal memorial service) forty days after a member's death, if his family cannot afford it.

Arts. Verbal arts—such as *bedanya fit* (speaking well before a judge)—are highly esteemed in general Amhara culture, but there is a pronounced class distinction between the speech of the rustic peasant, *balager* (hence *belegē*, unpolished, sometimes even vulgar), and *chowa lij*, upper-class speech. A further differentiation within the latter is the speech of those whose traditional education has included *sewassow* (Ge'ez: grammar; lit., "ladder," "uplifting"), which is fully mastered mainly by church scholars; the speeches of former emperor Haile Selassie, who had also mastered sewassow, impressed the average layperson as esoteric and hard to understand, and therefore all the more to be respected. In the arts of politeness, veiled mockery, puns with double meanings, such as *semmena-worq* (wax and gold), even partial knowledge of grammar is an advantage. The draping of the toga (shamma) is used at court and other occasions to emphasize spoken words, or to communicate even without speech. It is draped differently to express social status in deference to a person of high status, on different occasions, and even to express moods ranging from outgoing and expansive to calm sobriety, to sadness, reserve, pride, social distance, desperate pleading, religious devotion, and so on. Artistic expression in the fine arts had long been linked to the church, as in paintings, and sponsorship by feudal lords who could afford it, especially when giving feasts celebrated with a variety of musical instruments.

Medicine. The basic concepts and practices of Amhara medicine can be traced to ancient Egypt and the ancient Near East and can also be attributed to regional ecological links within Ethiopia. Often no sharp distinctions are made between bodily and spiritual ailments, but there are special occupations: the *woggesha* (surgeon-herbologist) is a pragmatist in practice; the *debtera* (scribe) invokes the spirit world. The latter is officially or unofficially linked to the church, but the *zar* cult is apart and may even be female dominated. Its spirit healing has a complex cosmology; it involves the social status of the patient and includes group therapy. The chief zar doctor is often a matriarch who entered the profession when she herself was possessed by a spirit; she has managed to control some powerful spirits that she can then employ in her battles to overcome the spirits that possess her patients. No cure is expected, only control through negotiation and appeasement of the offended spirit, in the hope of turning it into a *weqabi* (protective spirit).

Many men consider the zar cult effeminate and consult its doctors by stealth only, at night. Husbands may resent the financial outlays if their wives are patients, but fear the wives' relapse into hysterical or catatonic states. Women, whose participation in the Abyssinian church is severely limited, find expression in the zar cult. The zar doctors at Gonder hold their annual convention on the twenty-third night of the month of Yekatit, just before the beginning of the Monophysite Christian Lent (Kudade; lit., "suffering"). There is much chanting, dancing, drumming, and consumption of various drinks at the love feasts of the zars. Poor patients who are unable to pay with money or commodities can work off their debts in labor service to the cult—waitressing, weaving baskets, fetching water and fuel, brewing barley beer, and so forth. They are generally analyzed by the zar doctor as being possessed by a low-status zar spirit.

By contrast, possession by an evil spirit (*buda*) is considered more serious and less manageable than possession by a zar, and there is no cult. An effort is made to prevent it by wearing amulets and avoiding ṭebib persons, who are skilled in trades like blacksmithing and pottery making. Since these spirits are believed to strike beautiful or successful persons, such individuals—especially if they are children—must not be praised out loud. If a person sickens and wastes away, an exorcism by the church may be attempted, or a *tanqway* (diviner-sorcerer) may be consulted; however, the latter recourse is considered risky and shameful.

Death and Afterlife. When an elder is near death, other elders from his kin group bring the confessor and say to him, "Confess yourself." Then they ask him for his last will—what to leave to his children and what for his soul (the church). The confessor gives last rites and, after death, assigns a burial place in the churchyard. The corpse is washed, wrapped in a shamma, carried to church for the mass, and buried, traditionally without a marker except for a circle of rocks. Women express grief with loud keening and wailing. This is repeated when kinfolk arrive to console. A memorial feast (tazkar) is held forty days after the death of a man or a woman, when the soul has the earliest opportunity to be freed from purgatory. Preparations for this feast begin at the time of the funeral: money is provided for the priest to recite the *fetet*, the prayer for absolution, and materials, food, and drink are accumulated. It is often the greatest single economic expenditure of an individual's lifetime and, hence, a major social event. For the feasting, a large, rectangular shelter (*dass*) is erected, and even distant kin are expected to participate and consume as much talla and woṭ as available.

Bibliography

Hoben, Alan (1973). *Land Tenure among the Amhara of Ethiopia: The Dynamics of Cognatic Descent*. Chicago: University of Chicago Press.

Levine, Donald M. (1965). *Wax and Gold: Tradition and Innovation in Ethiopian Culture*. Chicago: University of Chicago Press.

Messing, Simon D. (1985). *Highland Plateau Amhara of Ethiopia*. Edited by Lionel M. Bender. 3 vols. New Haven: HRAFlex Books, Human Relations Area Files.

Molvar, R. K. (1980). *Tradition and Change in Ethiopia: Social and Cultural Life as Reflected in Amharic Fictional Literature ca. 1930–1974*. Leiden: E. J. Brill.

Young, Alan L. (1975). "Magic as a Quasi-Profession: The Organization of Magic and Magical Healing among Amhara." *Ethnology* 14:245–265.

SIMON D. MESSING

Anuak

ETHNONYM: Lwo

Orientation

The Anuak live in a region straddling the border of the southern Sudan and Ethiopia, between 10° and 5° N and 34° to 38° E. The Anuak language is most closely related to Shilluk. Together, the two languages comprise a subfamily within the larger classification of Nilotic. Although an accurate census has not been carried out since the late 1950s, the Anuak are estimated to number between 35,000 and 50,000 individuals. Anuak live in small isolated compounds or hamlets that vary in size from 30 to 500 individuals.

History and Cultural Relations

Anuak traditions suggest that they migrated into their present country from the northwest, beginning some four hundred years ago. It has been suggested by a number of authorities that the ecological variation that exists within the territory they came to settle has had a significant impact on the course of intracultural variation among different Anuak settlements. In the northwestern regions of their country, the land is low and flat and is thus subject to seasonal flooding from the Pibor and Sobat rivers, which feed the White Nile. Settlements in this part of Anuak country tend to be dispersed and isolated, particularly during the season of rains and floods (April to September). Farther to the south and east, however, the elevation of the countryside increases. Here, hamlets are typically in closer proximity, and communication between different settlements is more frequent throughout the year. The population densities of hamlets in the southeastern part of the country are notably higher than in the northwest. Villages are often surrounded by wooden enclosures.

Economy

Subsistence activities are centered around the cultivation of maize, millet, beans, sesame, and a number of additional crops that supplement the staple grain diet. Gardens are dependent upon natural rainfall, and the use of draft animals was unknown in aboriginal times. The horticultural diet is supplemented by the meat and milk of domesticated sheep and goats. Additional animal protein is gained through the exploitation of riverine resources. Anuak also hunt the larger game animals that are found locally, such as giraffes, elephants, and a variety of antelope. Although the Anuak are a settled, horticultural society, their language includes a wide variety of terms relating to cattle raising, suggesting that before they began to settle in their present country, domesticated cattle may have been the primary focus of their economic life and culture.

Sociopolitical Organization

Among the northwestern Anuak, residents of isolated hamlets claim kinship links with a single "core" patrilineal descent group, which is spoken of collectively as the "owners of the land." Living members of this core lineage are imagined to be descendants of the long-deceased ancestors who originally established or settled each hamlet. In each hamlet, one finds a "headman" who is able to trace especially close links with the founding ancestor. Only sons of former headmen can ever inherit this office as adults. Because of his direct link with deceased ancestors, the headman has a quasi-sacred authority, and with this elevated status he carries the authority to settle disputes and regulate certain rituals. On a day-to-day basis, his most important obligation is to provide feasts for the hamlet's residents. Given the character of Anuak system of descent, the headman of any single hamlet is also patrilineally related to headmen in other hamlets. The headman governs with his charisma and authority, rather than through secular power. When a headman becomes "stingy" in the eyes of hamlet residents, he is deposed in favor of another member of the core lineage, often a younger man whose father was previously a headman. Research has shown that most headmen remain in office for a relatively short time, two to three years being the norm.

The sociopolitical organization of hamlets in southeastern Anuak country tends toward a more fixed hierarchical form. Here there exists a single patrilineal clan. The founder of this noble clan is said to have emerged from a river, long ago. He was then abducted by residents of one hamlet in order to replace the then-reigning headman. It has been observed that the Anuak noble clan may be regarded as a single lineage of potential ruling headmen scattered throughout Anuak country.

Religion

No detailed study of Anuak cosmology has yet been published. In general, Anuak explanations and interpretations of personal misfortune call attention to a variety of spiritual agents who are thought to bring illness and ultimately death to human beings. Anuak are especially concerned with the capability of ghosts of the recently deceased to seek vengeance among the living. Only a small number of Anuak have professed Islam or Christianity in favor of their traditional religious customs and tenets. The Anuak were last visited by a professional anthropologist in the early 1950s. As a result, it is difficult to provide an authoritative depiction of their present society and culture.

Bibliography

Crazzolara, J. P. (1950). *The Lwoo*. Verona: Missioi Africane.

Evans-Pritchard, E. E. (1940). *The Political System of the Anuak*. London: Lund & Humphries.

Evans-Pritchard, E. E. (1947). "Further Observations of the Political System of the Anuak." *Sudan Notes and Records* 26:62–97.

Lienhardt, R. G. (1957–1958). "Anuak Village Headman." *Africa* 27:341–355; 28:23–36.

Wall, L. (1976). "Anuak Politics, Ecology, and the Origins of Shilluk Kingship." *Ethnology* 15:151–162.

JOHN W. BURTON

Arabs

ETHNONYMS: none

Orientation

The Arab world is usually considered to be comprised of the following nineteen countries: Mauritania, Morocco, Algeria, Tunisia, Libya, Chad, Lebanon, Egypt, Sudan, Jordan, Syria, Iraq, Kuwait, Bahrain, Qatar, United Arab Emirates, Saudi Arabia, Oman, and Yemen. There are also significant Arab populations in Iran, Turkey, East Africa, South America, Europe, and Southeast Asia. The total population of Arabs in the world is roughly 160 million (Eickelman 1987), or about 3 percent of the world's population. This large ethnic group has a very heterogeneous population, but there are a number of characteristics that a majority of Arabs share.

Religion

Perhaps the most common Arab characteristic is adherence to the Islamic faith. Muslim Arabs comprize about 93 percent of the Arab population and belong to several different sects including Shia (Ithna Ashari and Ismaili), Alawi, Zaidi, and Sunni, which is the largest. The other 7 percent of Arabs are largely Christian or Druze.

The link between Arabs and Islam has deep historical roots. It was among Arabs early in the seventh century that Mohammed preached the tenets of Islam. Mohammed's successors quickly spread the word of Allah into Southwest Asia, across North Africa and into Spain, into Persia, Afghanistan, and Central Asia, and to the east coast of Africa. Wherever Muslims went, they left elements of Arab culture along with their religion. The cultures of the assimilated territories, which included Christian, Jewish, and Zoroastrian populations, were not only influenced by the Arab invaders and their religion, but, in turn, substantially influenced the nature of Arab culture.

The conquered populations were subjugated politically, but their administrative skills, crafts, arts, and worldviews gradually transformed their conquerors. This transformation of Arab identity and tradition has been a continuing process for over 1,300 years. Pre-Islamic poetry indicates that in the year 600 "Arab" referred to the Semitic-speaking tribes of the Arabian Peninsula. Quranic usage and other Arabian sources suggest that the word referred primarily to the pastoral Bedouin tribes of the region. Even though camel-herding pastoral nomads were only a minority during Mohammed's lifetime, it seems clear that Arabs were an important social and political force. Their rich oral literature, especially their poetry, and their rejection of authoritarian political forms presented a powerful cultural ideal. Nevertheless, townspeople and others often used the term "Arab" in a pejorative sense. Southern Arabians, both farmers and urban residents, probably did not at first regard themselves as Arab. They probably only adopted this identity when there were political and economic advantages to doing so after the adoption of Islam.

The early Islamic period was a time when Arab identity meant that one belonged to an all-encompassing patrilineal descent system. Membership in an Arab descent group brought recognition, honor, and certain privileges, such as exemption from some taxes. The significance attributed to one's genealogical ties has not prevented Arab societies from assimilating non-Arabs into Arab society, a practice that has remained important throughout Arab history. In the first years after the Arab conquest, it was common to convert to Islam and become an Arab at the same time by forming a relationship with an Arab tribe. Later, converting to Islam and acquiring Arab identity became separate processes. Islamization continued, but it was no longer tied to Arabization.

Muslim Arab leaders created great empires that lasted hundreds of years. Following Mohammed, the Umayyid dynasty was established in Damascus in 661 and lasted until 750. Religious and ethnic minorities were given a large measure of self-rule under Umayyid domination. The succeeding ʿAbbāsid dynasty ruled the Muslim world from Baghdad, its capital, for nearly 500 years, of which the first 200 (750–950) are called the Golden Age of Arab civilization.

Arab rulers brought intellectual Jews, Christians, Greeks, Persians, and Indians to Baghdad and other centers of learning during the ʿAbbāsid dynasty. These foreign intellectuals contributed elements from their own cultures to the development of Arab culture. The works of Plato and Aristotle were translated from Greek into Arabic before they were translated into other European languages. Indian scientists brought the concept of "zero" to the Arabs, who combined it with Arabic numerals and transmitted the mathematical systems of algebra, geometry, and trigonometry to Europe. There are also many other important scientific discoveries that can be traced to the ʿAbbāsid dynasty. ʿAbbāsid scientists disproved Euclid's theory that the eye emanates rays, ʿAbbāsid chemists introduced such concepts as "alkali" and "alcohol," and ʿAbbāsid medical scholars compiled the world's first medical encyclopedia. What was happening throughout the world at that time was being recorded and passed on to later civilizations by Arab historians.

The ʿAbbāsid Empire was declining by the thirteenth century. Largely because of European colonization of North and South America, European trade with the Arab world virtually stopped and did not resume until the opening of the Suez Canal in 1869. The outlying provinces of the empire were the first to break away. Then, the Arabs were pushed out of Spain. Invading Turks and Mongols from the north destroyed not only the cities and towns in their path, but also irrigation systems. The Arab economy never recovered from the destruction. By the sixteenth century, Seljuk and Ottoman Turkish invaders conquered the remaining Arab territories; they ruled until World War I, when the Turkish Empire in turn disintegrated.

Language

Another important and unifying characteristic of Arabs is a common language. Arabic, like Hebrew, is a Semitic language of the Afro-Asiatic Family. Evidence of its first use appears in accounts of wars in 853 B.C. Arabic became a high-status language in the early Islamic centuries. It also became widely used in trade and commerce. Over the centuries, it became the predominant religious language of the world's Muslims. Even though most Muslims cannot speak Arabic today, it is revered as the language that God chose to reveal the Quran, and, because of this, it has profoundly influenced the language and thought of all Muslims.

Arabic has developed into at least two distinct forms. Classical Arabic is the religious and literary language. It is spoken and written throughout the Arab world and serves as a bond among all literate Muslims. Colloquial Arabic, an informal spoken language, varies by dialect from region to region, and is not always mutually intelligible. Both forms of the language are in use today and provide an important force for Arab cohesion.

Politics

Although unified by language and some cultural attributes, Arabs have been politically divided since the first Islamic centuries. With the rise of the Ottoman Empire in the sixteenth century, most of the Arabic-speaking regions of the Middle East and North Africa were turned into Ottoman provinces. There were relatively few economic, political, or intellectual achievements that were inherently Arab during Ottoman rule. During the latter half of the nineteenth century, however, there were some attempts to emulate the perceived achievements of European civilization. It was at this time that the idea of Arabism, perhaps as a counterpart to European nationalist movements, began to emerge. It was not until after World War II, however, that Arabs once again ruled their own lands, and by then the imported system of political nationalism had divided the Arabs into separate states, which undermined the political unity (i.e., the Arabism), of the ethnic group as a whole.

Arab culture developed in the desert among the peoples of the Arabian Peninsula, who lived either as tribal nomads or town folk. Town folk were strongly influenced by Bedouin values and practices. Mohammed was a townsman, but his tribe, the Quraysh, included many Bedouin, and Mohammed and his followers adhered to many pre-Islamic tribal traditions. These traditions, arising within the harsh environment of the desert, included strict codes of proper economic and social behavior, which were legitimized by Islam and became part of Arab culture.

Traditionally, Bedouin moved often, living in tents and earning their living as stock breeders, transporters, or traders.

They produced the livestock for much of the sedentary Arab world, raising camels, horses, and donkeys as beasts of burden and sheep and goats for food, clothing, and manure. As transporters, they moved products from the countryside to towns and between settlements not connected by roads. As traders, they provided a link between villages and towns, bringing to the villagers manufactured utensils and products that were not available locally. Their relationships with settled people were based on reciprocity and followed carefully defined rules of protocol.

A completely different facet of Arab culture developed along the Mediterranean shore, where Arabs had direct contact with the cultures of Europe. Compromise replaced rigidity, and religious fundamentalism gave way to accommodation and the acceptance of new ideas. There were thriving economies in the cities of Beirut, Cairo, Alexandria, Tunis, Algiers, and Casablanca, which offered the traditional Arab the possibility of entering new professions. Attending universities became an option for a changing population. European-styled nationalism replaced tribal allegiance and European imperialism.

Urban Life

About half of Muslim Arabs live in cities and towns. They have a greater variety of occupations, weaker family ties, greater freedom for women to leave the home, fewer arranged marriages, and fewer social pressures to conform to religious practices than do nonurban Arabs. The social structure of the urban Muslim Arab is considerably more complex than that of his desert or village counterpart.

Arabs who live in towns are also experiencing changes in their traditional patterns of living, but to a lesser degree than the city dwellers. Nomads, villagers, and urban traders meet in the *suq* (marketplace) to exchange goods and products. Representatives of government agencies (e.g., tax collectors, army conscriptors, police, and irrigation officers) make contacts with most of the population in the towns.

The townspeople are disdainful of the villagers. Town residents are more religiously conservative and more intimately involved in their kin network than urban dwellers are. The ideal values of the nomad are not so strong in the town. There is less concern with hospitality and defiance and more concern with symbols of economic prosperity—property, wealth, and education. Family honor remains important, however, and women continue to live a secluded life under the watchful eyes of husbands, brothers, and fathers.

Rural Life

Most Arabs are farmers who live between the two extremes of the desert on the one hand, with its conservative rigidity, and the cities and towns on the other hand, with their changing traditions and practices. The Arab village is usually composed of walled, mud-floored homes built of mud bricks. These homes hide the villagers' insecurities from strangers and provide an intimate environment in which strong family ties are nurtured.

Arab villagers grow only what they need to eat or trade—cereal grains, vegetables, livestock, and cotton. They are often in debt, and seldom have enough money to pay off their debts or to save for investments. Villagers live by tradition and lack the incentives, knowledge, or security to make changes. Change is seen as disruptive and threatening to the harmonious relationship that Arabs have established with their environment and their fellow villagers. Village values stem from the ideal values of the nomad. Unlike the Bedouin, villagers will relate to nonkin, but loyalty to the group is as strong as it is among the tribesmen. As among the Bedouin, village segments may also feud with each other. Similarly, standards of hospitality are high among villagers, as is awareness of family honor. The villager lives in an extended family in which family life is tightly controlled. Each family member has a defined role, and there is little individual deviation. Like the Bedouin, the villager finds security in the family during times of economic hardship and in old age. Changes in individual roles, such as when a son goes off to work in a town, often weaken the family socioeconomic system.

Children are a family's greatest asset, providing the parents with a work force and social security. The patrilineal system is reflected by Islamic rules of inheritance, which give more to boys than to girls, particularly in terms of real estate. A girl's value is linked to her function of tying one family to another through marriage, and to her primary role as a mother. Births are celebrated, particularly those of boys. Births are often accompanied by non-Islamic rituals such as burying the placenta to protect the mother and baby from enemy spirits or dressing boys as girls to decieve evil spirits. A child's first possession is often an amulet to ward off malevolence, and the first word a baby hears is "Allah."

Boys are circumcised at age 7, a ritual event that formally brings the boy into the religious community. Animistic rituals may also accompany this ceremony. Circumcisions, or clitoridectomies of girls, if they are performed, are not accompanied by any public ceremonies.

Arab boys and girls are treated very differently. Boys are given great affection and are pampered by their mothers. Girls are also given affection, but are weaned much earlier than boys and are not pampered. A mother is viewed as a symbol of warmth and love throughout a child's life. A father is viewed as a stern disciplinarian who administers corporal punishment and instills a degree of fear within his children. Boys are especially taught—often harshly—to obey and respect older males.

Children are given adult responsibilities and sex-specific socialization early in life. Boys work in the fields, and girls help their mothers cook and care for siblings. Adolescents have no contact with the opposite sex outside the family, and girls are watched closely to protect their chastity. A girl's primary protector is her older brother, who continues to watch over his sister even after she is married.

Marriages are arranged by parents. Girls marry between the ages of 14 and 19, whereas boys are usually somewhat older. Marriages establish important ties within one's own kin group or with other lineages that have economic or status advantages. Marriage is endogamous within one's kin group. The preferred match is between brothers' children. Bride and groom often meet for the first time on the day of the wedding, when the bride-wealth (*mahr*) is determined and a marriage contract is signed.

The lives of Arab village men and women are very distinct. Men work in the fields, women in the home. For social contact, men go to coffee houses, but women visit neighbors and relatives or receive such visits in their own homes. Men and women often eat separately, and they always pray separately.

Arab villagers follow a mixture of Islamic folk beliefs and rituals. Religion provides explanation for many unknown and uncontrollable events in their lives. God's will dictates the direction of life and provides divine authority for action. Religion confirms changes in social status, for example, at circumcision and marriage. It provides hope for a better life after death. Religious festivals, such as ʿId al-Adhha, ʿId al-Fitr and, for Shia Arabs, Muharram, break the monotony of village life. Men worship at a mosque. Women, often not allowed in mosques, attend ceremonies conducted in a home by female religious leaders.

Cultural Change

Change is occurring at a rapid pace throughout the Arab world. The Bedouin have had to deal with the many changes arising from oil-based economies—oil fields, trucks, and other forms of transportation, for example. Road building has also decreased the degree of isolation of thousands of villages and increased the number of contacts between villagers and the outside world. Radios bring new ideas to Bedouin and villager alike. Land reform has brought new systems of landownership, agricultural credit, and new farming technology. Overcrowding and diminishing economic opportunities in the village have prompted many villagers to migrate to the towns and cities. Migration from poorer Arab countries to oil-rich states has also become an economic opportunity and an important source of revenue for millions of Arabs.

See also Bedouin; Copts; Druze; Jacobites; Mandeans; Nestorians; Palestinians; Syriacs

Bibliography

Atiyeh, George N., ed. (1977). *Arab and American Cultures*. Washington, D.C.: American Enterprise Institute for Public Policy Research.

Bacharach, Jere L. (1984). *A Middle East Studies Handbook*. Seattle: University of Washington Press.

Bates, Daniel C., and Amal Rassam (1983). *Peoples and Cultures of the Middle East*. Englewood Cliffs, N.J.: Prentice Hall.

Beck, Lois, and Nikki Keddie, eds. (1978). *Women in the Muslim World*. Cambridge: Harvard University Press.

Carmichael, Joel (1977). *Arabs Today*. Garden City, N.Y.: Anchor Press.

Eickelman, Dale F. (1987). "Arab Society: Tradition and the Present." In *The Middle East*, edited by Michael Adams. Handbooks to the Modern World. New York: Facts on File.

Eickelman, Dale F. (1989). *The Middle East: An Anthropological Approach*. Englewood Cliffs, N.J.: Prentice Hall.

Faris, Nabih Amin, ed. (1963). *The Arab Heritage*. New York: Russell & Russell.

Friedlander, Jonathan, ed. (1981). *The Middle East: The Image and the Reality*. Berkeley and Los Angeles: University of California Press.

Gulick, John, ed. (1965). "Dimensions of Cultural Change in the Middle East." *Human Organization* 24 (Special Issue).

Hopkins, Nicholas, and Saad Eddin Ibrahim, eds. (1985). *Arab Society: Social Science Perspectives*. New York: Columbia University Press.

Hourani, Albert (1991). *A History of the Arab Peoples*. Cambridge: Harvard University Press, Belknap Press. Reprint. 1992. New York: Warner Books.

Knapp, Wilfred (1977). *North-West Africa: A Political and Economic Survey*. 3rd ed. Oxford: Oxford University Press.

Lutifiyya, Abdulla M., and Charles W. Churchill, eds. (1970). *Readings in Arab Middle Eastern Societies and Cultures*. The Hague: Mouton.

Mansfield, Peter (1980). *The Middle East: A Political and Economic Survey*. 5th ed. Oxford: Oxford University Press.

Mostyn, Trevor, and Albert Hourani, eds. (1988). *The Cambridge Encyclopedia of the Middle East and North Africa*. Cambridge: Cambridge University Press.

Nydell, Margaret K. (1987). *Understanding Arabs: A Guide for Westerners*. Yarmouth, Me.: Intercultural Press.

Raban, Jonathan (1979). *Arabia: A Journey through the Labyrinth*. New York: Simon & Schuster.

Sweet, Louise E. (1971). *The Central Middle East*. New Haven: HRAF Press.

Weekes, Richard V. (1984). "Arabs." In *Muslim Peoples: A World Ethnographic Survey*, edited by Richard V. Weekes, 35–45. Westport, Conn.: Greenwood Press.

RONALD JOHNSON

Asians of Africa

The Asian population of Africa is a small but significant minority. Whereas there have been Asians, primarily merchants, who lived on the east coast of Africa for hundreds, if not thousands, of years, a great influx of Asians came to Africa during the British colonial period. Asians in Africa are primarily from the Indian subcontinent, although there is a small proportion, perhaps 2 percent, who are from China.

A combination of famines in India and plentiful opportunities for work in Africa prompted thousands of Indians to immigrate to east, central, and southern Africa before the end of the nineteenth century. It was the British colonial interests that provided the opportunities for Indian immigration, particularly the building of the Uganda Railway. Local African labor was considered unreliable, so the British government brought in about 32,000 indentured laborers from India. The majority either died from diseases such as blackwater fever or returned to India, but 7,000 settled in East Africa. During the construction of the railway, some Indians began to come in as merchants and to establish *dukas* (shops), which initially catered to fellow Indians. After the end of the railway construction, merchant immigration from India continued until the 1920s, by which time the entire retail trade of East Africa was monopolized by Indians.

During the colonial period, Asians (Indians) in East and Central Africa came to occupy the middle rung of a three-tiered hierarchial system. Europeans, particularly the British, occupied the top level of the social, political, and economic pyramid, and Africans occupied the bottom level. Social apartheid in some countries, such as Kenya, was nearly as rigid as it was in South Africa. Although some Asians were able to compete with Europeans in the professions, by far the greatest numbers were retail traders who had shops in small towns, or were artisans, clerks, or bureaucrats on limited salaries. They couldn't compete seriously with Europeans, but in African eyes, Indians always seemed to occupy all the positions to which ambitious Africans with a little education might aspire.

The Asians were a very visible minority. Their skin color, in the mid-range of the colonial scale of color prejudice, set them off from both Europeans and Africans. Likewise, their distinctive style of dress, the smell of their cooking, the sound of their language and music, the architecture of their churches—and, generally speaking, their entire culture—were very distinct from both African and European cultures.

Rural Indian shopkeepers became somewhat Africanized and urban Indians became somewhat Anglicized, but, for the most part, Indians lived among themselves and felt culturally superior to Africans. The Indians as a group were fairly homogeneous; they came mostly from Gujarat and the Punjab, but they represented a microcosm of the diverse Indian culture, with its multiple religious, linguistic, and caste divisions. These internal differences, particularly religious and caste distinctions, tended to divide the Indian minority. The same caste or religious group maintained closer ties with their small group in other parts of Africa, or back in India, than they did with their Indian neighbors from different castes or religions.

Political independence for the countries where Indians were living brought new problems for the Indians. First, Asians were pushed out of rural areas, then, more gradually, out of the urban areas. Their exodus from the cities was slower because Asians occupied 30 to 40 percent of all key managerial, clerical, technical, professional, and skilled manual jobs. They were not easily replaceable, but there was clear political pressure, created by years of resentment against Asians, to force them out of trade and middle-echelon jobs.

In Kenya and Tanzania, to avoid economic disruptions, Asians were forced out gradually; in Uganda, however, they were expelled more quickly and dramatically. When Idi Amin took over Uganda in 1971, he simply ordered all Asians out of the country, forcing 80,000 of them to leave without their assets. In 1968 there were 345,000 Asians residents in Kenya, Tanzania, Zambia, Malawi, and Uganda. By 1984, according to the Minority Rights Group (1990), their numbers had fallen to about 85,000, which included 40,000 in Kenya, 20,000 in Tanzania, 3,000 in Zambia, 1,000 in Malawi, and 1,000 in Uganda. Although these numbers may be overestimates (Grimes 1988; Thobani 1984), it seems clear that many Asians left East and Central African countries after those countries achieved political independence.

The situation of Asians in South Africa was in many ways very similar that of Asians in East and Central Africa, with some important distinctions, primarily the government-sanctioned policy of apartheid, which subsumed Asians in a category like "Coloureds." Unlike the East and Central African Asians, the South African Asians are primarily (90 percent) descendants of indentured laborers, who are now fifth- and sixth-generation South Africans. Like East and Central African Asians, traders followed the indentured Indians to South Africa, established businesses, and attracted other merchant Indians. Also, in a similar way, South African Asians found themselves in the middle of a basically three-tiered hierarchy, with Whites (Europeans) at the top and Blacks (Africans) at the bottom.

Today about 90 percent of Indians are urban, and 85 percent live in Natal. Regional, religious, and caste distinctions have not had a great significance among South African Indians, and as a group they are more cohesive than East and Central African Indians. In the past, distinctions based on mode of entry (indentured versus merchant or passenger Indians) were very divisive, but today the main obstacles to Indian solidarity are variations in wealth. A small number are very wealthy, a larger number are well-off (upper-middle class), and the greatest portion have incomes derived from small-scale trading, low-level clerical occupations, or blue-collar work.

There were about 800,000 Asians in South Africa in 1980 (including about 10,000 Chinese). Despite the stresses of apartheid, South African Indians have not left South Africa in large numbers. With the late twentieth-century dismantling of apartheid, it remains to be seen whether or not they will be squeezed out of their relatively higher economic positions by the predominant African population.

Bibliography

Bharati, Agehananda (1972). *The Asians in East Africa: Jayhind and Uhuru*. Chicago: Nelson-Hall.

Chattopadhyaya, Haraprasad (1970). *Indians in Africa: A Socio-Economic Study*. Calcutta: Bookland Private.

Ghai, Dharam P., ed. (1965). *Portrait of a Minority: Asians in East Africa*. London: Oxford University Press.

Ghai, Yash, and Dharam P. Ghai (1983). *The Asian Minorities of East and Central Africa (up to 1971)*. Minority Rights Group Report no. 4. Originally published 1971.

Ginwala, Frene (1979). *Indian South Africans*. Minority Rights Group Report no. 34. Originally published 1977.

Grimes, Barbara F. (1988). *Ethnologue: Languages of the World*. Dallas: Summer Institute of Linguistics.

Minority Rights Group, ed. (1990). "Asians of East and Central Africa." In *World Directory of Minorities*, 222–225. Chicago: St. James Press.

Ridd, Rosemary E. (1984). "South Africans." In *Muslim Peoples: A World Ethnographic Survey*, edited by Richard V. Weekes, 718–723. Westport, Conn.: Greenwood Press.

Salvadori, Cynthia (1989). *Through Open Doors: A View of Asian Cultures in Kenya*. Nairobi: Kenway Publications.

Tandon, Yash, and Arnold Raphael (1978). *The New Position of East Africa's Asians: Problems of a Displaced Minority*. Minority Rights Group Report no. 16. Originally published 1973.

Thobani, Akbarali H. (1984). "Asians of East Africa." In *Muslim Peoples: A World Ethnographic Survey*, edited by Richard V. Weekes, 54–58. Westport, Conn.: Greenwood Press.

Twaddle, Michael (1975). *Expulsion of a Minority: Essays on Ugandan Asians*. London: Athlone Press.

RONALD JOHNSON

Assyrians

ETHNONYMS: Chaldeans, Nestorians, Surayi

Ancient Assyrians were inhabitants of one the world's earliest civilizations, Mesopotamia, which began to emerge around 3500 B.C. The Assyrians invented the world's first written language and the 360-degree circle, established Hammurabi's code of law, and are credited with many other military, artistic, and architectural achievements. For 300 years Assyrians controlled the entire Fertile Crescent, from the Persian Gulf to Egypt. In 612 B.C., however, Assyria's capital, Nineveh, was besieged and destroyed by a coalition of Medes, Scythians, and Chaldeans, decimating the previously powerful Assyrian Empire.

Modern Assyrians claim descent from the inhabitants of the ancient Assyrian Empire, and linguistic evidence seems to support that contention. Different dialects have developed from ancient Aramaic, a language used within the Assyrian Empire. The modern language is sometimes called Assyrian, but some scholars reserve the terms "Assyrian" and "Babylonian" for the cuneiform writing of the ancient empire. The modern language, then, is generally referred to as "neo-Aramaic," "Chaldean," or "Syriac" and is considered to be 75 percent pure (i.e., ancient) Aramaic. The ancient and modern Assyrian languages belong to the Semitic Language Family. The survival of Syriac as a spoken language is an important indication that the Assyrians have been a cohesive, endogamous group for more than two thousand years.

Religion is an important factor in the identification and description of both ancient and modern Assyrians. Modern Assyrians refer to themselves as "Surayi," which can be translated as either "Assyrian" or "Syrian." Assyrians may be further divided into Assyrian Nestorians and Assyrian Jacobites, some of whom prefer to be called Syrian Aramaeans. In their homelands, the Nestorians are considered the easterners and the Jacobites the westerners. The distinctions between the two are based primarily on religious differences. The term "Nestorian" derives from Nestorius, who was the patriarch of Constantinople from A.D. 428 to 431. Nestorius was condemned for heresy; he and his followers fled from Syria to Persia, where they practiced their distinctive religion for fifteen centuries. The Jacobites are named for Jacobus Baradeus, who was also considered heretical at the Council of Chalcedon in A.D. 451; his followers have kept their faith for as long as the Nestorians.

The ancient split between the Church of the East (Nestorians) and the Church of Antioch (Jacobites), and between these two and the rest of Christianity, has continued to the present. The picture was further complicated when, beginning in the sixteenth century, Christian missionaries from various denominations made their way to the Middle East to convert the indigenous Christians. Their limited success led to a variety of Christian denominations and patriarchs in the Middle East. Some Nestorians have continued to support the Church of the East; others, known as "Chaldeans," converted to Roman Catholicism. Most Jacobites remained with the Church of Antioch, but those who converted to Catholicism are called Syrian Catholics. All four of these groups support a church hierarchy or patriarchy in the homeland.

Geography has also played an important role in the history and culture of the Assyrians, especially Nestorian Assyrians. The geographic heart of Assyria was traditionally located in the north Tigris highlands, north of Babylon and south of Armenia. In classical times, Persia and Byzantium boxed in the mountain Assyrians. Later, they found themselves between Turks and Persians, Kurds and Arabs. After the rise of Islam, the Assyrians were the target of converging Sunni forces from the south and the north and Shiite forces from the east. For security and collective well-being, they took refuge in the rocky Hakkâri Mountains, which served as a natural military fortress.

The Assyrians, or their Nestorian descendants, lived in small villages along the Great Zab River and in the Sapna Valley of northern Iraq, as well as near the shore of Lake Urmia in western Iran until the twentieth century. They survived as a group in this compact, relatively contiguous area for more than 1,500 years. Unfortunately, this area had the great disadvantage of lying within the boundaries of three different states—Turkey, Iraq, and Iran.

Within this environment, the Nestorian Assyrians' subsistence stemmed from irrigation agriculture. Crops included wheat, barley, millet, melons, lentils, and other vegetables. A few sheep, goats, donkeys, and water buffalo were also raised. The staple foods consisted of cereals, vegetables, and milk products. Meat was rarely eaten.

The extended patriarchal family was the primary social and ecomomic unit of the Nestorian Assyrians. Tribal formations sometimes led to internal conflicts, but the constant threat of outside attacks led to internal cohesion and group solidarity. Nestorian Assyrians did not intermarry with other Christians, and intermarriage with Muslims was, generally speaking, not even an option.

Women in ancient Assyria may have received greater status or dignity than their counterparts in other Middle Eastern cultures have since then. In the mid-twentieth century Nestorian women were treated almost as equals with men. For example, most women were considered companions to their husbands and, as such, participated in social gatherings. In Iraq, Assyrian Christian women were often more literate than

Muslim men. The patriarchal tradition, however, assured that male predominance in husband-wife relations was the norm.

Because of many factors, including the massacres of 1918 (by Turks and Kurds) and 1933 (by Iraqi Arabs and Kurds), constant battles with the Kurds, forced migrations, forced participation in Iraqi wars, assimilation and "Arabization" into majority cultures, and emigration out of their traditional homeland, the population of the Assyrians in their traditional homeland has dwindled considerably. Additionally, confusion over the terms "Assyrian," "Chaldean," "Nestorian," and "Jacobite"—as well as a lack of consensus over which groups of people they designate—makes counting the Assyrians even more difficult. One estimate of the number of Chaldean Catholic Assyrians in Iraq is 750,000, or 4 percent of the population (1991). From available census counts, there are about 10,000 Assyrians in Syria (interpolated from Grimes 1988), 77,375 in Iraq (1986), 40,000 in Iran (1982), 25,000 in Turkey (1981), and 15,000 in the former Soviet Union (1979). It is estimated that there are also 150,000 Assyrians in the United States (Ishaya and Naby 1980); some Assyrian leaders believe there are about one million Assyrians scattered throughout the world.

In Iraq, the extent to which Assyrians are surviving or accommodating to Arabization attempts is not clear. Outside the Middle East, particularly in the United States, Assyrian group life continues to reflect ancient religious as well as relatively new political divisions. For example, the Syrian Aramaeans of New Jersey are Jacobites, but they prefer to call themselves Syrian rather than Assyrian in order to avoid political implications with which they disagree. Further, some Assyrians are in favor of the establishment of an Assyrian homeland, and some are not.

Within the United States, there may be a collective revitalization taking place. There are two major Assyrian centers in the United States—one in Chicago, the other in California. Preserving ethnic ties and cultivating social relations have become important goals for these Assyrian communities. There is a concerted effort by Assyrians outside of Iraq to maintain their self-determination, and some Assyrians still hope for their own territory.

Bibliography

Bynum, Joyce (1991). "Oral History and Modern Identity: A Case Study." *Et Cetera* 48:220–227.

Grimes, Barbara F., ed. (1988). *Ethnologue: Languages of the World*, 406, 411, 418–419. Dallas: Summer Institute of Linguistics.

Ishaya, Arian, and Eden Naby (1980). "Assyrians." In *Harvard Encyclopedia of American Ethnic Groups*, edited by Stephan Thernstrom, 160–163. Cambridge: Harvard University Press, Belknap Press.

Nisan, Mordechai (1991). *Minorities in the Middle East: A History of Struggle and Self-Expression*. Jefferson, N.C.: McFarland & Co.

Severy, Merle (1991). "Iraq: Crucible of Civilization." *National Geographic* 179(5): 102–115.

RONALD JOHNSON

Baggara

ETHNONYM: Baqqara

Orientation

Identification. The Baggara derive their name from the Arabic word for cow, *bagar* (pl. *bagarat*), and are known, therefore, as the "cattle people." "Baggara" as a term refers to a group of tribes that share certain cultural characteristics and claim kinship to each other and to a tribe in the Hejaz (southern Arabian Peninsula). The five main tribes of Baggara are the Messiriya, Humr, Hawazma, Reizegat, and Habbania. Other groups include the Beni Selim, Oulad Hamayd, Ta'aisha, Beni Helba, Beni Khuzam, Beni Husayn, and Salamat.

Location. The Baggara occupy an area of savanna in what are now the Sudanese provinces of Darfur and North and South Kordofan, at a latitude south of the thirteenth parallel and in a belt from the White Nile to Lake Chad. Moving east to west, the Baggara groups can be located geographically as follows: the Beni Selim on the banks of the White Nile; the Oulad Hamayd, south of Um Ruaba, Kordofan; the Habbania, around Takali; the Hawazma, in the vicinity of Al-Ubayyid, Dilling, and Talodi, South Kordofan; the Messiriya, south of Abu Zabad, South Kordofan; the Humr, between El Odaya and the Bahr al-Arab, South Kordofan; the Reizegat, Habbania, Ta'aisha, Beni Helba, and Beni Khuzam, in southern Darfur; the Messiriya and Beni Husayn, in Darfur; and the Beni Helba, Beni Khuzam, and Salamat, in the area of the former sultanates of Ouadaï, Bornu, and Bagirmi, in Darfur.

Baggara territories are better adapted to cattle than to camels. These zones range from sparse scrubland in the northern areas, through arid and semiarid bushlands, to wooded savannas. Although the Nuba Mountains are found in central South Kordofan, most of the area is flat savanna. The zone is characterized by a hot, semiarid climate. Temperature means range from 30° to 32° C (March, April) to 25° to 27° C (December, January). Annual rainfall varies from about 10 centimeters in the northern areas to about 80 centimeters in the southern areas. Rains occur in a single season, primarily from June to September. Soil types, extending in west-to-east bands (which are important factors in vegetation and cattle movement) range from sandy (*qoz*), in the north; to noncracking clay (*gardud*), in the central areas; to cracking clay (*tiin*), in the southern Baggara areas. The vegetation consists primarily of several varieties of savanna grasses and several varieties of acacia trees and other scrubby, thorny brush. Except for a few small animals (primates, foxes, snakes) and large numbers of birds, most indigenous species have been decimated. Cunnison (1958) reported that Humr were hunting giraffes and that there were formerly elephants, large cats, ostriches, and gazelles in the area.

Demography. Statistics from the 1955–1956 census give the Rural Nomad population of Kordofan Province as 393,519. Statistics from the 1973 census give the Rural Nomad population of Kordofan as 406,710 and that of Darfur as 411,580. These figures are not broken down into tribal divisions; for comparison, Cunnison (1966) gives the 1955 Humr population as 54,997. Camping-unit composition and size vary seasonally, but generally range from 8 to 20 households, with a total camp population of 40 to 100 persons. The number of people who can camp together depends partly on factors such as the size of cattle herds and the availability of grazing and water.

Linguistic Affiliation. The Baggara speak a dialect of Arabic that is distinct from classical Arabic and from the Sudanese dialect, although the dialects are mutually intelligible.

History and Cultural Relations

Baggara genealogies claim that their origins go back centuries to connect with the Juhayna in the Hejaz before the days of the Prophet Mohammed. It is unclear how the Baggara reached their present areas. One theory suggests that after the Arab invasion of Egypt (A.D. 1100–1200) the groups that became Baggara continued across North Africa to Tunisia, then came south across the desert into western Sudan. According to another theory, they were part of an invasion up the Nile Valley into Ouadaï and Bornu in the late fourteenth century. Throughout the centuries, there has been movement east and west. The Baggara, on the southern fringes of the sultanates of Darfur, Ouadaï, and Bagirmi in the west, and Al-Fung to the east, between the two Niles, moved east and west along the line of the sultanates according to their political fortunes. The Baggara retained access to goods and booty while avoiding payment of tribute. New tribes were added to the Baggara between the fifteenth and eighteenth centuries—for example, the Beni Khuzam and the Beni Helba. By the eighteenth century, the Baggara were concentrated to the east of Lake Chad, and north of Lake Chad in Darfur and Dar Ouadaï. At this period, some of the groups began moving eastward; first the Reizegat (into eastern Darfur), followed by the Messiriya, the Humr, and the Messiriya Zuruq, and the Hawazma. Cunnison (1966, 3) says that the Humr probably moved eastward from Ouadaï about 1775, and that by 1795 there were references to the Messiriya in the southwestern corner of what is now Kordofan. Baggara groups have become widely scattered, as a result of their lateral movement over the centuries. Although different groups tend to be concentrated in particular areas, territories are not as discrete as might be expected. There is some overlap and concurrent use of many areas. For example, the Hawazma and the Messiriya traverse much of the same territory, and they may, in the rainy season particularly, be found in adjacent camps. Kordofan and Darfur are characterized by great ethnic diversity and interdigitation; no group is wholly isolated or bounded from other groups. In the various regions, Baggara have close associations with camel nomads (Hamar, Shenabla), settled agriculturists (Nuba, Daju, Tungur, Bedayria, Gima'a, Zaghawa, Dar Hamid), and camel and sheep nomads (Ma'alia). Symbiotic relationships between herders and farmers are typical wherever pastoralists are found. In Kordofan, the relationship between the Hawazma and the Nuba is particularly significant. Traditionally, the Nuba were concentrated on and around the hills of the Nuba Mountains, rather than on the plains. Some Nuba groups claim to have always lived on the hills, whereas others moved up into the inaccessible areas as protection from Baggara raids and Mahdist troops. Whatever the case, the Hawazma and the Nuba represent an important example of symbiotic use of the same savanna ecozone. The Nuba are settled farmers who grow sorghum. They provide the Hawazma with some manufactured goods and with labor for both cropping and herding. For their part, the Hawazma provide animal products, milk, hides, and manure to the Nuba.

Settlements

Pastoral Baggara live in camping units called *furgan* (sing. *fariq*). Residents in a camp typically belong to one or more patrilines of a lineage. Houses are arranged on the perimeter of a circle. Cattle are brought into the center of the camp at night, to mill loosely about, near the household of their owners. Adult, married women own the houses and their housekeeping contents. Dry-season houses are generally larger than rainy-season houses—3.6 to 4.5 meters in diameter, as compared to 3 meters in diameter, and 3 meters in center height, as compared to 1.8 to 2.4 meters. Houses are spherical, built by placing saplings in holes around the perimeter, then bending them over and tying them to form a dome. Smaller branches, tied onto the frame horizontally, support the structure, which is then covered with thatch in the dry season or with mats and tarpaulins in the rainy season. A bed for a woman and her young children is built first, and the house frame is then built around it. Men and older boys sleep on cots in the center of the camp, near the cattle. Another important component of a camp is the men's tree—or a sun shelter constructed instead—where men gather to eat, talk, or nap and to receive male visitors. The men's tree is usually in the center of the camp or just outside the camp circle. Sedentary Baggara live in agricultural settlements or towns, often in compounds grouped according to lineages. The houses of the settled Baggara are built of mud brick and have thatched roofs, which is typical of other sedentary Sudanese. Corrals are built of thorny trees and shrubs to contain young animals. No fences are built around the camp itself or the houses in the dry-season camps, which are located in the people's home territory, or *dar*, but fences are built around houses in the rainy-season camps.

Economy

Subsistence and Commercial Activities. The Baggara are cattle pastoralists. Herds are comprised primarily of cattle, although Baggara also herd sheep and goats. Camels are kept for riding and as pack animals, and oxen are also specially trained for riding and carrying loads. Many households also have donkeys. Most pastoral Baggara have fields of sorghum in their dar, which they plant at the beginning of the rainy season, before leaving on their annual trek. Some households also plant sesame and beans. Usually crops are left unattended; therefore yields are low. Few households grow sufficient grain to provision them for the entire year. Baggara women milk the cows, allocating appropriate quantities for household use and for sale. Women earn considerable amounts by selling raw milk to seasonal cheese factories during the rainy season, when yields are higher. Women also sell processed milk in the form of a sort of liquid yogurt and clarified butter. In the dry season, they sell small quantities of milk door-to-door in the towns near their camps. The Baggara seem to be unusual in the sense that women not only provide productive labor but also maintain control of their efforts, keeping any cash income they earn to be used for household expenses or goods for themselves. Men sell small numbers of cattle for such expenses as buying sorghum or paying school fees. Small stock are also sold. Hawazma Baggara have significant links between the men's and the women's productive activities, as well as between pastoral and agricultural households. Baggara men frequently have more than one wife—one may reside in a pastoral camp and another in an agricultural village or a town, for example. Some products and labor are exchanged between the two types of households. Because men and women have autonomous cash resources and Baggara women earn substantial amounts, Baggara men may go away for international wage labor for one or two years at a time. Women largely manage to support their households; accordingly, men save their earnings to purchase more cattle upon their return.

Industrial Arts. Women make mats (which are used both for house coverings and for seating), gourd containers, and a variety of leather goods (including containers and bags). Men make cots and a variety of equipment that is used in animal husbandry, including hobbles, chicken coops, and braided-grass bull saddles. Pottery, metal items, and clothing are purchased.

Trade. Some Baggara men are experts in marketing animals, both large and small stock. These men may act for themselves and also as agents for their relatives. Baggara women frequently sell milk products in the "women's market." They may also sell chickens and, occasionally, the goats that they own. Men do all the trading in larger animals in a separate market. Once in a while, Baggara have enough sesame or sesame cake (used as a supplementary animal feed) to sell, but they also purchase these items. Baggara men frequently purchase veterinary medicines and either administer them themselves or hire veterinarians to do so.

Division of Labor. Men's and women's roles are generally strictly separated. Women do the household work and the work associated with milking, including churning and marketing. Men may assist with milking, but they turn over all of the milk to the women. Women fetch water, sometimes walking for forty-five minutes in each direction to carry four gallons. Men have primary care of herds: management, herding, marketing, and health care. Men plant, tend, and harvest whatever crops are grown. Women may help with threshing, but usually they go to the distant fields only to cook for their menfolk during the harvest. Young boys may herd calves and small stock, whereas older youths and men herd the cattle. House building is done by women, the only exception being the building of the wedding house, a task in which all members of the community join. Women build kitchen structures and any other structure associated with the house. Women gather all the materials used for house building. Men build the sun shelters that are used by all the men of the camp for meals or as places to entertain male guests. Women are responsible for the everyday cooking, although men may cook meat for communal feasts. Men slaughter cattle, sheep, goats, and sometimes chickens. Women may also slaughter chickens. Men butcher cattle; either men or women may butcher other animals—always working, however, in gender-segregated groups. All members of the household, including men and children, do their own laundry. Young boys and girls begin early to help with household or herding tasks.

Land Tenure. The Baggara have communal grazing and water rights, but they own cropping land as individuals. Members of an extended family often cultivate close to one another, and they regard the area as their dar, or home territory. Because the soil fertility is low, fields may be moved every five years or so. Most groups have several blocks of land in which their members have fields. Land is passed from father to son.

Kinship

Kin Groups and Descent. The Baggara are patrilineal. They are normatively endogamous, and the preferred marriage partner is one of the close cousins, either a patrilateral or matrilateral, or a parallel or cross cousin. The preferred close-cousin marriage pattern creates bilateral, multiplex kinship links, which serve to strengthen group cohesiveness. Genealogies are reckoned to a depth of five or six generations. Kinship relationships move outward to define units in a segmentary lineage system. The first segment is the *iyal rajul* (sons of a man), a minimal lineage of about three generations' depth. A minimal lineage forms the basis of a camping unit. A major lineage segment, known as the *khashm beit* ("mouth of the house"), is composed of a number of minimal lineages.

Kinship Terminology. Baggara kinship terminology distinguishes between agnatic (patrilineal) and uterine (matrilineal) kin. This descriptive system allows a person to single out specific kin and state precisely what relationship exists. Another system that is used is classificatory: it allows a person to include large numbers of people among his or her close relatives, even when close genealogical relationships do not exist. Thus, all members of one's own generation are addressed as brother or sister, and so on.

Marriage and Family

Marriage. Marriages are traditionally endogamous and are frequently polygynous. Bride-wealth, in cattle and other goods, is provided by the prospective husband, with help from his near relatives. Part of the bride-wealth is used to buy household furnishings; some of it may also be used to buy food for the marriage celebration, which takes place in the bride's camp. After the marriage, the new couple lives near the bride's mother's house, just outside the camp circle, for about ten days. Then the new couple moves ceremoniously a residence the husband has chosen, an occasion that involves another feast, this one provided by the husband's family. In polygynous marriages, each wife owns her own house, which she operates independently. Co-wives may share meals, but not any differently than they might with other women in the camp. A divorced woman is looked after by her brother, unless she has a son older than about age 14 who can do so.

Domestic Unit. The primary domestic unit is a woman and her young children, with a male protector. A man may be the protector of more than one household, either through polygynous marriages or through assigned responsibility for a divorced or widowed woman or for the wife of an absent husband (usually his brother). Residence may change several times over the course of a person's life, with movement from camp to camp or from camp to town. Residence changes may be related to a person's marriage status; a woman's pregnancy; a change in emphasis of a man's economic mode (pastoral, agricultural, or wage labor); or the location of a woman's male protector.

Inheritance. Inheritance is patrilineal. Women inherit household goods and perhaps some small stock from their mothers. They may also inherit cattle, although their brothers usually retain control over such animals, so that they can be used to maintain the women should they be divorced or widowed.

Socialization. Mothers are the primary caretakers of young children. Fathers also show a great deal of attention to their infants and young children. Siblings often help with child care. Any adult may discipline a child or provide care, particularly when a child's mother has gone out of the camp. More and more Baggara children—particularly boys—are now attending at least some years of school; however, the eldest son may remain at home so that he can be well trained in animal husbandry. Boys may attend school through the secondary level, whereas girls rarely pass beyond six years of schooling. A small number of boys may gain some sort of postsecondary training.

Sociopolitical Organization

Political Organization. Traditionally, each Baggara camp is led by a *shaykh* (pl. *shuyukh*). Although sons tend to inherit the position from their fathers, adult male members of a camp must agree on a man to fill the position. The shaykh's power is essentially limited to his being a spokesperson for the consensus decision of the male members of the camp, although he may wield considerable influence, owing to his wisdom and economic status. In 1911, during Turkish rule in Sudan, two additional political positions were introducted: nazir (pl. *nuzara*) and ʿomda (pl. *umad*). Nuzara were placed as the leaders of main tribal sections. Within each main tribal section, further divisions (*khushum beyut;* sing. *khashm beyt*) are headed by umad.

Social Control. One administrative role of a shaykh is to assist in tax collection. Nuzara have courts at which suits are heard from their own sections. Umad are arbitrators in disputes within their *omodiyat* (sing. *omodiya*). If the ʿomda fails to arbitrate to the satisfaction of both parties, the suit goes to one of the courts. The most serious disputes heard by the ʿomda are those involving homicide, in which settlement may involve negotiation and payment of a blood debt. Less serious disputes within a camp are handled by persuasive discussion by the shaykh, the elders, and the other senior men. Sometimes disputes arise between herders and farmers, particularly when cattle destroy crops. In such cases, the injured farmer has the right to impound the cattle in question. Then, he and the owners meet, perhaps under the men's tree, to negotiate a suitable fine. Once the fine has been paid, the cattle are released.

Conflict. In former times, the Baggara were participants in cattle and slave raids and in various military alliances with the sultanates. Today several of the Baggara tribes are involved in the ongoing Sudanese civil war, particularly in South Kordofan, and often find themselves caught between government and rebel forces.

Religion and Expressive Culture

Religious Beliefs. The Baggara are Muslims, and they observe the Five Pillars of Islam: the declaration of faith, the five daily prayers, almsgiving, fasting, and the pilgrimage to Mecca. Many Baggara men, and some women, manage to make the pilgrimage to Mecca. Since the mid-1980s, men have used the pilgrimage to Mecca as an opportunity to seek wage labor, often staying a year or two beyond the pilgrimage to work before returning home.

Ceremonies. In conjunction with or in addition to religious celebrations, Baggara celebrate life-stage transitions. Marriage and the various stages toward it are the occasions for important celebrations for both men and women. The various marriage celebrations (betrothal, marriage, moving residence) all include feasting and dancing, which provide courting opportunities for young people. Circumcision is important for both boys and girls. Giving birth is also cause for celebration. Many occasions are found for communal feasting, such as unexpected good fortune, the arrival of a visitor, the return of someone from a trip, or the condolence visitations after a death.

Arts. Baggara decorative arts are integral with the making of various practical items. Some of the mats they make, for example, may be plain, but others are quite colorful, with geometric designs woven into the fabric. Leather bags may have decorative stitching, and many containers, whether of basketry or gourds, have long leather fringe as decoration. Older Baggara women have decorative facial scarification, whereas younger women sometimes have tattoos, particularly on their lips. Women's hair braiding can also be most elaborate. Baggara are traditionally known for their poetry and songs, which are composed by both men and women to celebrate or narrate events. Baggara men participate in wrestling matches and often spend a great deal of time decorating their costumes and their bodies for the events.

Medicine. Today Baggara people seek medical care in a variety of settings, including clinics run by nurse practitioners, doctors' clinics, and hospitals. Because many of them frequently live long distances from such clinics, traditional medicine is also still important. Some men are well known as bonesetters; older women serve as midwives. A few Baggara women have been trained in Traditional Birth Attendant programs so that they can incorporate modern techniques into their midwifery practices. The use of modern medicine is also important to Baggara animal husbandry. Men often seek the services of government veterinarians, or they may purchase and administer various veterinary medications themselves. These practices are important in the prevention of animal diseases such as bovine pleuropneumonia.

Death and Afterlife. Funerary practices accord to the Islamic stipulation that burial take place within twenty-four hours of death. An elder man or woman prepares the body for burial. After burial, many people come to visit the bereaved, and there is often a night-long vigil on the night of the death. Women mourners greet the bereaved with ritualized wailing, which includes a praise litany about the deceased. A forty-day mourning period is observed by both the men and the women who are close relatives of the deceased. This period may be more restrictive for a man, however, who may stay—with little activity and without shaving—under the men's sun shelter, where he receives visitors. The end of the forty-day mourning period is celebrated with a feast.

Bibliography

Abdel-Rahim, Abdel-Hamid Mohamed Osman (1986). "The Hawazma Baggara: Some Issues and Problems in Pastoral Adaptations." Master's thesis, University of Bergen.

Carlisle, Roxanne Connick (1973). "Women Singers in Darfur, Sudan Republic." *Anthropos* 68, fasc. 516:785–814.

Cunnison, Ian (1958). "Giraffe Hunting among the Humr Tribe." *Sudan Notes and Records* 39:49–60.

Cunnison, Ian (1960a). "The Omda." In *In the Company of Man*, edited by Joseph B. Casagrande, 309–331. New York: Harper.

Cunnison, Ian (1960b). "The Social Role of Cattle." *Sudan Journal of Veterinary Science and Animal Husbandry* 1(1): 1–18.

Cunnison, Ian (1962). "Some Social Aspects of Nomadism in a Baggara Tribe." *Philosophical Society of the Sudan. Proceedings of the Tenth Annual Conference*. Khartoum.

Cunnison, Ian (1963a). "The Position of Women among the Humr." *Sudan Society* 2:24–34.

Cunnison, Ian (1963b). "Subsidiary Nomadic Movements of the Humr." *Geographical Magazine* (University of Khartoum) 1:25–30.

Cunnison, Ian (1966). *The Baggara Arabs: Power and Lineage in a Sudanese Nomad Tribe*. Oxford: Clarendon Press.

Demeny, Paul (1968). "The Demography of the Sudan: An Analysis of the 1955/56 Census." In *The Demography of Tropical Africa*, edited by William Brass et al. Princeton, N.J.: Princeton University Press.

Michael, Barbara J. (1985). *Production and Consumption by Gender and Role among Transhumants in Western Sudan: The Baggara (Hawazma) of Kordofan*. Western Sudan Agricultural Research Project, Publication no. 52. Khartoum and Pullman: Washington State University.

Michael, Barbara J. (1987a). *Cows, Bulls, and Gender Roles: Pastoral Strategies for Survival and Continuity in Western Sudan*. Ann Arbor: University Microfilms International.

Michael, Barbara J. (1987b). "Milk Production and Sales by the Hawazma (Baggara) of the Sudan: Implications for Gender Roles." *Research in Economic Anthropology* 9:105–141.

Michael, Barbara J. (1991). "The Impact of International Wage Labor Migration on Baggara Nomadism." *Nomadic Peoples* 28:56–70.

Michael, Barbara J. (1995). "Female Heads of Patriarchal Households." Manuscript.

Michael, Barbara J. (Forthcoming 1996). "Baggara Women as Market Strategists." In *Middle Eastern Women in the "Invisible" Economy*, edited by Richard Lobban. Gainesville: University of Florida Press.

Michael, Barbara J., with Anne M. Kocherhans (1994). *Nomads on the Savanna*. 3/4" video, 30 min. University Park: Pennsylvania State Audio-Visual Services.

Sudan. H.Q. Council of Ministers. Department of Statistics (1962). *First Population Census of Sudan. 1955/56*. Final Report, vol. 3. Khartoum.

Sudan. Ministry of Finance, Planning, and National Economy. Department of Statistics (1977). *Second Population Census. 1973*. Vol. 7, *Kordofan Province*. Khartoum.

Sudan. Ministry of Finance, Planning, and National Economy. Department of Statistics (1977). *Second Population Census, 1973*. Vol. 3, *Characteristics of Nomadic Population*. Khartoum.

BARBARA J. MICHAEL

Bagirmi

ETHNONYM: Dar Massenya

Orientation

Identification. The term "Bagirmi" refers to a multiethnic society organized as an archaic state. Major populations in the Bagirmi region were the Barma, who formed and dominated the state; Arabs, who were its most numerous inhabitants; and the Fulani, who were significant in its religious life. "Bagirmi" derives from Arabic (*bagar*, cattle; *mia*, one hundred) and, according to one tradition, indicates the amount of tribute that the Arabs and the Fulani were obliged to pay to their first ruler.

Location. The core of Bagirmi was located in the Republic of Chad along the Chari and Bahr Erguig rivers, roughly from N'Djamena in the north to Bousso in the south. This core was surrounded by tributaries. Bagirmi was situated between two competing kingdoms: Bornu to the northwest and Wadai to the northeast.

Demography. In 1954 there were about 25,000 Barma, 78,000 Arabs, and 25,000 Fulani in the area that roughly corresponds to the core and tributary zones of nineteenth-century Bagirmi. There is evidence of emigration from Bagirmi beginning in late precolonial times and continuing through the present. Relatively low fertility is reported for Bagirmi.

Linguistic Affiliation. The Barma speak Tar Barma, which belongs to the Central Sudanic Branch of Nilo-Saharan languages and is closely related to languages spoken by the Sara, Kenga, and Bulala peoples in Chad.

History and Cultural Relations

Bagirmi's precolonial history centered around the affairs of its ruler (the *mbang*) and his court. There were four periods: formative, offensive, counteroffensive, and final.

The formative period (c. 1522–1608) roughly corresponds to the rule of the first four sovereigns. Tradition suggests that Dala Birni, the first of these, led followers from Kenga territory around 1522. This band was believed to have stopped under a tamarind tree (Tar Barma: *mas*), where there was a young Fulani milkmaid named Enya. Later, a settlement was built around this tree, which, to commemorate both the tree and the milkmaid, became known as "Massenya," and it became Bagirmi's capital. Dala Birni is supposed to have protected the people in this area, and in return they paid tribute, the amount of which became the name of the kingdom (see "Identification"). Nothing is known about the second and third sovereigns. The fourth sovereign is remembered for imposing Islam upon Bagirmi, greatly expanding the state, and creating much of its governmental structure. With his death, traditionally set at about 1608, Bagirmi entered a more offensive phase.

During the period from about 1608 to 1806, Bagirmi may well have enjoyed a rough hegemony in east-central Sudan. According to its traditions, this pugnacious polity created tributaries to the north among the Medogo, the Bulala, the Kuka, and the Babelyia; to the west among the Kotoko; to the south among the Sarua, the Somrai, the Niellim, the N'Dam, and the Bua; and to the east among the Kenga and the Sokoro. The town of Bidiri was a center of Islamic learning, and its merchants were active throughout the region. This period ended at the close of the eighteenth century, when Wadai attacked. Wadaian aggression resulted from the conviction that Gaurang, Bagirmi's ruler, had committed incest by marrying a sister. Gaurang's defeat, in about 1806, initiated a period lasting until the arrival of the French, during which Bagirmi, seeking to regain its lost preeminence, mounted counteroffensives against both Wadai and Bornu. These actions were generally unsuccessful; however, there was expansion to the south.

At the end of the nineteenth century, France had decided to incorporate the central Sudan into its empire. The interval (1897–1912) prior to formal French colonization constituted the final period. Bagirmi signed a treaty with France in 1897, hoping thereby to gain support in conflicts with Wadai. Officials of Bagirmi also went behind the backs of the French and conspired with Wadai. After a final struggle with the French that ended in 1912, Bagirmi became a *circonscription* under the direct administration of a French *chef de circonscription*. Thus, during the subsequent colonial period (1912–1960) and, after 1960, as part of Chad, Bagirmi was no longer independent.

Settlements

Towns and rural settlements in the form of villages and camps were the two major precolonial settlement patterns. Many Barma lived in permanent towns located on or near streams and swamps. Towns, which could have thousands of inhabitants, were often walled; they had various wards and large, open markets, around which might be found mosques and official residences. A major postcolonial change in settlement pattern, however, has been a reduction in the size of the Barma towns. The Arabs and the Fulani were semisedentary: they lived in villages and camps. Villages were small, often housing fewer than 100 persons, and tended to be located in northern and eastern Bagirmi. They were places of farming and herding during the rains (June to September); when precipitation diminished, many persons migrated with their animals in a southwesterly direction. Camps—small groups of 10 to 30 living in impermanent residences—were the settlement type adopted by those in transhumance.

Economy

Subsistence and Commercial Activities. Subsistence production seems little changed from precolonial times. The Barma still cultivate cereals and vegetables using swidden and flood-recession (i.e., planting as the flood recedes) techniques. The staples are sorghums and millets; peanuts, cotton, and okra are also grown. Barma who reside by streams fish. Arabs and Fulani are primarily livestock breeders: they raise cattle, sheep, and goats on open range. They also grow some cereals, generally by slash-and-burn techniques. All foodstuffs are increasingly grown as cash crops as well as for subsistence. French attempts to make cotton an important cash crop failed during the colonial period. Cutting wood to sell in urban areas is common.

Industrial Arts. Bagirmi had a reputation for fine craftsmanship in precolonial times. Its textiles and leatherwork were especially appreciated, but these have both largely disappeared.

Trade. There was trans-Saharan, interregional, and local trade in precolonial Bagirmi. Trans-Saharan commerce involved the exchange of slaves, captured to the south of Bagirmi, for sumptuary goods and weapons produced in the circum-Mediterranean area. Interregional commerce involved the exchange of commodities produced in different West African ecological zones. Kola from the forest might be exchanged in Bagirmi for salt from the desert. Local trade involved the exchange of subsistence and craft goods produced in particular localities, and especially included the barter of dairy products for cereal products. Trans-Saharan slaving was conducted by Bagirmi officials and professional slave traders, who normally were not Bagirmi. The interregional trade tended to be in the hands of professional merchants, many of whom were not Bagirmi. Local trade was conducted by the producers themselves. These commercial patterns were greatly altered in the twentieth century. One major change was the suppression of the trans-Saharan trade and its replacement by one dominated by European trading houses.

Division of Labor. In the 1970s Barma men had large fields on which they produced cereals, whereas women had smaller plots on which vegetables were cultivated. Men fish, trade, and build houses; women do the vast bulk of the domestic chores, produce crafts, and are the primary marketers of foodstuffs.

Land Tenure. The precolonial system of land tenure facilitated, rather than restricted, access to land. Membership in social groups guaranteed access to land, which could neither be bought nor sold. Today there are coexisting tenure systems: the traditional ones—the specifics of which tend to vary with region and ethnic group—and modern land law, based upon European conceptions of tenure. Powerful individuals can use the latter system to acquire freehold land privately.

Kinship

The Barma lacked descent groups; however, strong adherence to patrilocality in the 1970s resulted in neighborhoods in which the men of households tended to be agnatically related. The Arabs and the Fulani each had differing systems of patrilineal descent. Barma kinship terminology was Iroquoian.

Marriage and Family

Marriage. The Barma traditionally preferred marriage with either cross cousin; in the 1970s, however, most of their marriages were to nonkin. Bride-price was paid in the vast majority of marriages. Levirate and sororate were not practiced. Polygny occurred most frequently among middle-aged men of political, economic, or religious distinction. Divorce was easy and frequent.

Domestic Unit. Although the Barma are ideally patrilocal and have large, extended families, only about one-third of the households in the 1970s were characterized by such features. Most households had some form of the nuclear family.

Inheritance. The Barma appear to be increasingly influenced by Islamic inheritance rules.

Socialization. Barma children are raised in a moderately permissive fashion. Flouting of cultural rules is not tolerated, and, when necessary, offenders are verbally reprimanded or spanked. Some adolescent males attend Quranic schools, but very few children receive any other type of formal education.

Sociopolitical Organization

Social Organization. Precolonial Bagirmi society was a collection of tribal groups organized on the basis of class. Class position, however, depended upon control over political—not economic—resources. The upper class consisted of officials organized in an elaborate hierarchy around the sovereign at Massenya. The two lower classes—slave and free—were food producers. Most officials were Barma. Barma, Arabs, and Fulani were free food producers; slaves usually came from tribes in southern Chad, such as the Sara. A revenue system allowed officials to extract resources from food producers. Because there were very few relations between officials and food producers, other than those involving revenues, tribal systems continued within the class structure, organizing reproductive, enculturative, economic, and religious activities.

Political Organization. There were three levels in the official hierarchy of the precolonial state: those of the sovereign, the court, and the estate officials. The ruler had responsibilities extending throughout the polity, whereas court officials had duties within their estates, which were a collection of villages, ethnic groups, tributaries, and, occasionally, places such as markets. Estate officials, who might be heads of tributaries, villages, or the like, administered a portion of a court official's estate. The sovereign and his court resided at Massenya, and estate officials were distributed throughout the core and tributary areas. Court officials might be of royal, free, or slave origin; those with major military responsibilities tended to be slaves, whose office depended upon the will of the ruler.

Social Control. Gossip, ostracism, sorcery, and witchcraft were and continue to be important forms of social control. Traditional Islamic specialists and courts settle disputes according to Malekite law. Today the most serious crimes are likely to be adjudicated within the nation-state's legal system.

Conflict. Precolonial Bagirmi experienced police actions, raids, warfare, and rebellion. Violence was a state monopoly, with officials serving as mounted cavalry. Officials usually directed police actions against food producers in the core, often because of unpaid taxes. Raids were mounted by officials, usually against non-Muslim, acephalous populations, to acquire slaves. Officials both conducted wars against external states and contested among themselves for control of the Bagirmi state. Since Chad gained independence in 1960, Bagirmi, like many other areas of the country, has experienced civil war that has resulted from attempts to control the nation-state.

Religion and Expressive Culture

Religious Beliefs. Precolonial religious notions were syncretic and, at least in part, varied with class. Officials tended to be Muslims, who at the same time affirmed the divinity of their king. Many food producers appear to have been unaware of the finer points of either Islam or the Bagirmi conception of divine kingship. Islam appeared to be expanding during the 1970s; especially popular was the Tidjaniya Brotherhood.

Precolonial Bagirmi appear often to have held conflicting religious ideas. For example, officials professed that there was one Supreme Being, Allah, while at the same time they insisted that their ruler was the earthly incarnation of the two forces *mao* and *karkata*, which animated all things in the universe. Food producers, for their part, appear to have believed that *shetani* (devils) were responsible for many of their afflictions. They also believed that Allah was responsible for all things, including afflictions.

The Barma, it will be recalled, are linguistically related to the Kenga and traditionally trace the origin of Bagirmi to a migration from Kenga territory. Kenga religion is dominated by beliefs in *margai* (genies of places). There is a report that some Bagirmi also believe in margai.

Religious Practitioners. Two types of officials conducted rituals, which officials were likely to attend. Islamic specialists, whom the Barma called *mallams*, performed Muslim ceremonials, and officials themselves performed the rituals associated with the sovereign's divinity. Food producers tended to be served by mallams, but they were also served by a variety of non-Islamic practitioners, about whom little is known.

Ceremonies. Two sorts of ceremonials tended to dominate the religious life of officials in the precolonial state. There were the normal Islamic rituals, such as Id al-Kabir or Id el-Fitr, as well as those that pertained to divine kingship. The latter included the ruler's installation, his observance of the sunset, and his funeral. Next to nothing is known about the precolonial, non-Islamic rituals of food producers.

Arts. Traditional music and dance celebrated the ruler in precolonial times. Visual arts were weakly developed; there was no painting, and sculpting was restricted to designs on wooden implements.

Medicine. There is scant knowledge of precolonial Bagirmi medical practices. During the 1970s, much illness, both physical and mental, appears to have been attributed to sorcery and to the actions of shetani.

Death and Afterlife. Very little is known about precolonial, non-Muslim ideas of death and afterlife. Devils and sorcerers were believed to cause some deaths in the 1970s. Conventional Islamic attitudes toward death and afterlife were gaining in currency in the 1970s.

Bibliography

Nachtigal, Gustav (1987). *Sahara and Sudan; The Chad Basin and Bagirmi*. London: C. Hurst & Co.

Pacques, Viviana (1977). *Le roi pêcheur et le roi chasseur*. Travaux de l'Institut d'Anthropologie de Strasbourg. Strasbourg.

Reyna, S. P. (1990). *Wars without End*. Hanover, N.H.: University Press of New England.

S. P. REYNA

Baha'is

ETHNONYMS: none

The Baha'i faith originated from one of the sects within the Shiite Muslim religion in Iran. The nature of the religion has changed dramatically since its beginning in the middle of the nineteenth century. The Baha'i religion developed directly from the Babis, an extremely militant sect willing to die to convert the people of the world to their faith. Because of this zeal, the Babis were condemned and persecuted; their leader, the Bab, was executed in 1850. The search for the Bab's successor and some important changes in beliefs and methods, in turn, led to the formation of the Baha'i religion. The Bab's successor, who came to be known as Baha'ulla, and his followers transformed militant Babism into the more peaceful Baha'i sect.

There are about five and a half million people who count themselves as Baha'is today. The largest groups of Baha'is are in India and Malaysia, each of which has approximately one million members. In Iran, where they originated and where they still face persecution, they are a small minority of 150,000 to 300,000.

Baha'is believe that God is completely transcendent and unknowable. They disagree with the Jewish, Christian, and Muslim belief that knowledge of and union with God are attainable. To the Baha'i, divine manifestations occur in the form of prophets or messengers who mirror God's reflection. They believe that the first prophet was Adam, followed by Judaic prophets such as Abraham and Moses, followed by Jesus, then Mohammed. Unlike Muslims, they also recognize Buddha, Zoroaster, Confucius, and the Bab.

Among the major tenets of Bahaism are that all religions originate from the same basic beliefs and are therefore equally valid; that the holy prophets of all religions are manifestations or messengers of the same deities; and that the faithful are required to gather communally every nineteen days. Egalitarianism is stressed—differences in wealth are ignored, and there is equality between the sexes.

In Iran, Baha'is have been persecuted, in part because of their origin as Babis. Memories of militant Babis still influence the stereotypes of present-day Baha'is. A greater problem is that Bahaism is not considered a religion by Iranian Shiite Muslim officials, and Baha'is are therefore not classified as a religious minority. The belief that Mohammed, although an important prophet, was not the last, is considered heretical by Muslims. This helps to explain why Iranians have little sympathy for Baha'is, even though the Baha'is have pledged loyalty to the government.

Bibliography

Cooper, Roger (1982). "The Baha'is of Iran." Minority Rights Group Report no. 51. London.

Esslemont, J. E. (1923). *Baha'u'llah and the New Era*. New York.

Levinson, David (1994). *Ethnic Relations*. Santa Barbara, Calif.: ABC-Clio.

Bakhtiari

ETHNONYMNS: none

The term "Bakhtiari" refers to a group of people and to the area they occupy. The Bakhtiari inhabit about 156,000 square kilometers in and near the central Zagros Mountains of Iran. The most recent estimates place their population at about 700,000 in the 1980s. The Bakhtiari are traditionally nomadic pastoralists who make their winter encampments in the low hills along the narrow fringe of the northeast Khūzestān plain and their summer pastures in the intermontane valleys. Some also find summer pastures at the western edge of the central plateau, which is also the permanent habitat for a sedentary village population. Other Bakhtiari live in permanent agricultural settlements throughout the larger area, except at the highest elevations.

Sheep and goats are the basis of the Bakhtiari economy, and Bakhtiari nomadism arises from the search for pastures. Sheep and goat products are used for subsistence and for economic exchange with the sedentary population.

The family is the basic unit of production and of flock- and landownership, as well as of political and social organization. Families cooperate in the sharing of pastures. At successive levels of segmentation, families regroup and redefine themselves under different political and kin headings. The smallest political/kin unit is the *rish safid,* and successively higher units include *kalantars* (headmen), khans (chiefs), and an *ilkhani* (paramount chief of the entire confederation).

The confederation, Il-i-Bakhtiari (*il,* tribe) is the unit that includes all those who live in the territory, speak a subdialect of the Luri dialect of Persian, and acknowledge the leadership of the khans and the ilkhani. Historically, the Bakhtiari have been divided into two major sections, the Haft Lang and the Chahar Lang, but in contemporary times the most important division has been Ilkhani and Hajji Ilkhani (two moieties from which the ilkhani were chosen).

Migration, competition for scarce resources, and the need for exchange with sedentary groups create a potential for much conflict in Bakhtiari society. Add to that the pressures of external conflict with other tribes, including defending tribal territory, and the demands of the central government, and it becomes clear that there is a need for khans as mediators and intermediaries. Traditionally, the power of the khans and ilkhani comes from personal abilities as well as the inherent power of the position. It is based on the benefits they can provide, the respect they attain through birth, their coercive capabilities within the tribe, and the support given to them by the central government or by outside sources of power.

The Bakhtiari political system has been described as a hierarchy of khans, but it is similar to a segmentary lineage in that there are segmented levels that function in balanced opposition, with certain activities and responsibilities associated with each segment. The tribes and subtribes of the Bakhtiari use force against each other, their khans, and their ilkhani. Therefore, as in a segmentary lineage, intergroup and intragroup relations are based on a balance of power at each level. Tribes that fight each other at one time may unite to fight a third tribe at another.

The Bakhtiari confederation was once much more powerful than it is today. Reza Shah considered the Bakhtiari a direct threat to his sovereignty and, in the 1920s, took military, economic, and administrative actions to subjugate them. His policy of forced sedentarization, intended to break the tribal economy and prevent tribal identification, destroyed the political power of the ruling khans but was less successful in forcing the Bakhtiari to settle in one place.

The Bakhtiari now appear to be choosing sedentarism as a way of life much more than in the past. Formerly, only the richest and poorest lived a sedentary life-stlye; today many Bakhtiari not only settle in agricultural villages, they also work in the oil fields or urban centers. Although there is little reliable information on the Bakhtiari in post-Pahlavi Iran, it appears that changes are taking place. Along with increased sedentarism has come improved communications, and many government activities may be effectively transferring loyalty and identification from the tribe to the nation-state.

Bibliography

Case, Paul E. (1947). "I Became a Bakhtiari." *National Geographic Magazine* 91(3): 325–358.

Garthwaite, Gene R. (1983). *Khans and Shahs: A Documentary Analysis of the Bakhtiyari in Iran*. Cambridge: Cambridge University Press.

Garthwaite, Gene R. (1984). "Bakhtiari." In *Muslim Peoples: A World Ethnographic Survey,* edited by Richard V. Weekes, 81–84. Westport, Conn.: Greenwood Press.

Grimes, Barbara F., ed. (1988). *Ethnologue: Languages of the World.* Dallas: Summer Institute of Linguistics.

Johnson, Douglas L. (1969) *The Nature of Nomadism: A Comparative Study of Pastoral Migrations in Southwestern Asia and Northern Africa*. Chicago: University of Chicago, Department of Geography.

Bamiléké

ETHNONYMS: Aghem, Babadjou, Bafang, Bafou, Bafoussam, Bagam, Baloum, Bamaha, Bamdendjina, Bamendjou, Bamenkoumbit, Bamenyam, Bana, Bandjoun, Bangangté, Bangoua, Bangwa, Bangwa-Fontem, Bapi, Batcham, Batchingou, Bati, Batié, Dschang, Fe'e Fe'e, Fomopea, Fongondeng, Foto, Fotouni, Mbouda

Orientation

Identification. Bamiléké is a collective term referring to a loose agglomeration of some 100 kingdoms or chiefdoms of the eastern Grassfields in the Western Province of Cameroon. These kingdoms are of varying size but have similar cosmology and social and political structures; they speak distinct, although related, languages. "Bamiléké" derives from the German mispronunciation of a Bali (western Grassfields) interpreter's designation, "Mba Lekeo," or "the people down there," which has been associated with this region since at least 1910, possibly since the 1890s. Currently, Bamiléké people most often refer to themselves as "Bamiléké" when speaking with non-Bamiléké, and as members of their specific kingdoms and villages when speaking with other Bamiléké.

Location. The 6,196-square-kilometer Bamiléké region extends roughly from 5° to 6° N and 10° to 11° E. It is bounded by the Bamboutos Mountains on the northwest and by the Noun River on the southeast. With the Bamoun area it constitutes the southeastern half of the Grassfields, a mountainous plateau spanning the Western and Northwestern provinces of the Republic of Cameroon. The Bamiléké region is made up of five administrative divisions within the Western Province: Bamboutos, Haut-Nkam, Mifi, Menoua, and Ndé. The region is characterized by its irregular, hilly relief and great differences in soil quality. Valleys, which have the richer soils, are mixed savanna and forest. Basalt and other volcanic rocks are common. The high-altitude prairie, for which the Grassfields are named, consists of noncultivated land at an average elevation of 1,400 meters. Temperatures range from 13° C to 23° C, and rainfall amounts to more than 160 centimeters per year. The dry season lasts from mid-November to mid-February, with a fluctuating rainy season occurring during the remaining months.

Demography. No census data exist on the Bamiléké as a people, but scholars estimate that they constitute about 25 percent of Cameroon's diverse population. The overall population of the Bamiléké in the late 1980s was approximately 2 million, 1 million of whom resided on the Bamiléké plateau. Average population density is 125 persons per square kilometer but ranges from 15 to over 400 inhabitants per square kilometer. The Bamiléké region represents a pocket of relatively high fertility within the central African "infertility belt." The birthrate is 49 per thousand, and completed fertility is 6.3. Infant mortality is 158 per thousand; life expectancy is 39.9 at birth, increasing to 49.2 at age 5.

The Bamiléké area has served as a labor reserve since the early colonial period. Emigration, beginning at the turn of the twentieth century and intensifying in the 1930s, has greatly influenced Bamiléké demography and social life. The order, intensity, and scale of emigration have varied over time. Most immigrants were Bana during German colonization; Bafang, Bafoussam, Bangangté, and Dschang in the 1940s; and Bangangté in the late 1950s and 1960s. In urban centers and peripheral regions of agricultural colonization, Bangangté continue to provide the largest numbers of emigrés. This predominantly male migration continues, as youths search for jobs to earn cash for consumer goods, bride-wealth, and to gain titles. Kingdom-specific voluntary associations play an important role in the social life of urban emigrés and help link them socially, politically, and economically to their place of origin. Many Bamiléké maintain land in their home areas ("a foot in the land of the ancestors"), and movement back and forth between urban centers and rural villages is common.

Linguistic Affiliation. Bamiléké languages, which are tonal, belong to the Grasslands Bantu Group of Broad Bantu languages. While Voegelin (1977) lists twenty-four Bamiléké languages, nearly every kingdom names its own dialect as a separate language. Bamiléké languages are not always mutually intelligible. Bordering kingdoms may speak languages that differ only slightly, but, because of intense migration over the past three hundred years, geographic proximity is not always a predictor of mutual intelligibility. Many contemporary Bamiléké also speak French, and quite a few speak Wes Cos Pidgin and/or English.

History and Cultural Relations

The earliest Bamiléké kingdoms were formed during the sixteenth century, a result of a complex dynamic of conquest, ruse, and shifting allegiance when population movements in Adamoua pushed the "pre-Tikar" Ndobo into the Bamiléké plateau. Succession disputes, the search for new hunting grounds, and demographic pressure led to the emergence of new kingdoms from the first core polities. The number, size, and shape of Bamiléké kingdoms continued to change until European colonization, when interkingdom warfare was curtailed and the limits of territories were frozen at borders partly determined by the colonizers. This history of shifting borders, alliances, and the influx of refugees from neighboring kingdoms makes each Bamiléké kingdom a political composite of diverse peoples owing allegiance to the king and to established royal institutions.

During the precolonial era, the Bamiléké fought wars among their constituent kingdoms as well as with the neighboring Nso and Bamoun. Relations among kingdoms included economic exchange and cooperation as well as territorial belligerence. German expeditions into Bamiléké territory in 1902 and 1904 found a rich and cultivated territory, maintaining multiple commercial relations, as evinced by paths and markers.

The colonial era began on 12 July 1884, when coastal Duala chiefs signed a treaty with the German Empire. Colonial German penetration into the Bamiléké highlands began in the 1890s and became increasingly important over the next decade. Between 1914 and 1916, Cameroon was conquered by French and British forces. Nearly all Bamiléké kingdoms were subsequently governed by France under League of Nations mandate and, following World War II, under United Nations Trusteeship. Independence was achieved in 1960. Political steps toward independence, especially the outlawing of the trade union-based Union des Populations Camerounaises (UPC), led to civil war in the Bamiléké region from 1958 through 1972. Bamiléké refer to this as a time of troubles; others refer to it as the Bamiléké rebellion. Both personal and political scars remain. The region continues under a nominal state of emergency. Popular discourse surrounding more recent political and economic turmoil in Cameroon makes reference to this history of civil and interethnic strife.

Settlements

Bamiléké kingdoms are divided into quarters, villages, compounds, and houses. The "quarter" is a territorial unit of traditional kingdom government. Both "quarter" and "village" are units of Cameroonian state administration. Family compounds may be monogamous (consisting of a conjugal house, a kitchen, and an outhouse) or polygynous (consisting of the husband's house surrounded by either a single semicircle or two rectangular "quarters" of his wives' kitchen-houses. All Bamiléké royal compounds are built on slopes and follow a prescribed layout. Below an entry gate made of spines of the raffia palm ("bamboo") and either thatch or corrugated iron, a wide path (the "foot" of the compound) divides the two wives' quarters, each quarter ruled by titled queens. A second gate leads to the king's palace, a variety of meeting houses of secret societies, a traditional court building, and a sacred water source used only for the king's meals. The area above the second gate is considered dry and infertile; the area below it is regarded as moist, rich, fertile, and spiritually complicated.

Each wife in a polygynous compound lives in her kitchen-house with her children. Both boys and girls live in their mother's compound until they go away to school or get married. Child fosterage is common. Most kitchen-houses have one room, with a hearth in the middle and a granary of raffia bamboo above the hearth; usually they are built of mud bricks and roofed with thatch or tin. Previously, houses were square, constructed of raffia bamboo, with sliding doors and thatched, conical roofs. Rural compounds were surrounded by fences or hedges during the precolonial and early colonial periods, but now rarely are.

Before the UPC-related civil war, settlements were dispersed, and compounds were built near cultivated land. During the time of troubles, the French authorities resettled Bamiléké in villages along roads.

Economy

Subsistence and Commercial Activities. Rural Bamiléké are primarily farmers; they also keep pygmy goats and sheep. The staples are maize (the preferred food) and plantains, supplemented by beans and peanuts. Cassava is used primarily to bridge the hungry time between harvests. Tomatoes, onions, pumpkins, and condiments are grown on the ends of rows. Farms are tilled with iron hoes. The major cash crop is coffee. Some Bamiléké in lower elevations grow cocoa, and in higher elevations European vegetables such as potatoes, eggplants, and leeks for local and urban markets. A few have experimented with growing strawberries.

French agricultural policy from 1920 to 1950 favored production of food crops, and many Bamiléké kings, fearing a loss of control over the fortunes of their subjects, discouraged the production of coffee. This confluence of colonial and indigenous agricultural policy encouraged the small-scale commercialization of women's food crops, starting in the 1930s, as well as male labor migration.

Trade. Trade, which has always been important for both women and men, is conducted in local markets organized around an eight-day weekly cycle, as well as in long-distance interethnic exchange. Bamiléké traded agricultural goods, game, and small livestock for salt, palm oil, and iron hoes. Weekly local and regional market centers grew during the colonial and postcolonial eras. In these centers, both local and European goods were bought or bartered. One of these market centers, Bafoussam, has grown into a bustling city of over 120,000 inhabitants. Bamiléké emigrés are known as aggressive entrepreneurs. They are active in many sectors and often dominate the taxi and transportation industries of the urban centers.

Division of Labor. Since precolonial times, women have been the primary producers of food crops (maize, beans, and peanuts). Men have been responsible for tree crops, clearing women's fields, and building fences. Men's cash-crop cultivation of coffee and cocoa, shopkeeping, and taxi and truck driving have replaced precolonial involvement in animal husbandry and war. Hunting, once the subject of heroic tales of the founders of dynasties, is now practiced only occasionally; hunters work mostly at night and must seek the local king's permission.

Land Tenure. Within each Bamiléké kingdom, the king (called *fo, fon,* or *mfen* in various Bamiléké languages) is the titular owner of all land. Quarter chiefs distribute usufruct rights to male heads of patrilineages. These lineage heads then distribute plots of land to their wives, their noninheriting brothers, and their sisters. Inheritance of usufruct rights is impartible; only one son is heir, often leaving his siblings to seek their fortune in urban centers. With increasing population pressure and increasing privatization of landownership, lineage heads now often fail to award plots of land to their sisters.

Kinship

Kin Groups and Descent. Bamiléké practice a system of dual descent, in some kingdoms accompanied by institutionalized relations among a diffuse uterine group (*pam nto'* in Bangangté, *atsen'ndia* among the Bangwa-Fontem). Most anthropologists studying various Bamiléké groups have emphasized agnatic relations. At the center of descent groups are lines of heirs and heiresses who inherit the property, titles, and skull custodianship of their ascendants. Each lineage head chooses a single heir or heiress, who "becomes" that person in terms of titles in customary associations, as well as rights and duties toward all dependents. Patrilineal descent determines village membership and the inheritance of titles, land, compound, and wives. For nonheirs, the obligation to sacrifice to patrilineal skulls ceases after two generations. Matrilineal descent determines inheritance of titles, movable property, and moral and legal obligation to lineage members. In theory, the obligation to sacrifice to matrilineal skulls does not diminish with structural distance; in practice, facing misfortune often motivates people to renew their obligations to matrilineal ancestresses. Bamiléké have no clans.

Kinship Terminology. Bamiléké refer to their father and his heir by the same term (*ta*), and to their mother and her heiress by the same term (*ma*). Cousins are addressed by sibling terms, but both they and half-siblings are distinguished in everyday conversation. Special sibling terms indicate birth order (e.g., firstborn) and relation to twins (e.g., born following a set of twins). A complex system of praise names, indicating the village of origin of a person's mother or father, with variations in alternating generations, are important terms of address in the Bamiléké kingdoms of Ndé Division. Joking relations of fictive, namesake kin are sometimes generated from the use of these praise names. Skill in using praise names is an important marker of cultural competence. Distinctions between "deracinated" urban dwellers and "traditional" rural relatives are becoming increasingly important.

Marriage and Family

Marriage. Marriage is exogamous, preventing individuals with patrilineal links up to the fourth generation from marrying, and preventing marriage with any matrilineal kin. Two forms of exchange govern relations between wife givers and wife receivers. In bride-price marriage, the groom gains reproductive, sexual, and domestic rights by giving gifts of palm oil, goats, blankets, firewood, and money to the family of his bride. In *ta nkap* marriage, no bride-price is exchanged between the bride's father and the groom. The bride's father retains rights over the marriage and patrilineal identity of his granddaughters, thus becoming their ta nkap ("father by money"). These rights of ta nkap can be inherited, and are a way of capitalizing on matrimonial rights. Although outlawed by the French in 1927 and 1928, the practice continues. In addition to these two traditional marriage options, contemporary Bamiléké may choose Christian marriage with or without bride-wealth, marriage by a justice of the peace, elopement, and single parenthood.

Traditional Bamiléké marriage is virilocal, and sons attempt to settle near their father if there is enough land. Polygyny is a goal that is increasingly difficult to achieve, especially on a grand scale, because of the inflation of bride-price and changing ideas about conjugal relations. The amount of bride-price, although higher for women with more education, seems primarily dependent upon the groom's ability to pay. The term for marriage is "to cook inside," condensing the symbolism of the married woman's confinement to her kitchen, where she literally cooks her husband's meals and figuratively "cooks" (procreates) children.

Domestic Unit. A married man is the de jure head of a household consisting of his wife or wives and their children. In polygynous compounds, co-wives have separate dwellings (see "Settlements"). Although sometimes contentious and competitive, relations among co-wives can be warm and companionable. In royal compounds, older co-wives are assigned to younger co-wives as foster mothers. Full siblings feel strong ties of solidarity, whereas half-siblings are often in competition with each other for attention and inheritance.

Inheritance. Land and real estate are inherited patrilineally and impartibly. Titles are inherited according to both matrilineal and patrilineal rule of descent (see "Land Tenure" and "Kin Groups and Descent").

Socialization. Social roles are learned through example and through stories told around the mother's hearth at mealtimes. Bamiléké report particularly warm relations among full siblings, and refer to hearthside commensality and storytelling as the source of this solidarity. Although mothers play a primary role in child rearing, small children may be left with older siblings or co-wives while their mothers do other work. After age 6, Bamiléké consider child fosterage an appropriate strategy to deal with scarce resources and to help the child learn to interact with a variety of personalities. There are no formal group-initiation ceremonies at puberty. Boys are now usually circumcised soon after birth. In the past, girls whose families could afford it spent up to six months in seclusion (*nja*), eating fattening foods and learning about marriage and sexuality from female kin. Elderly Bamiléké say that school has now replaced this custom.

Sociopolitical Organization

Social Organization. Bamiléké kingdoms are highly stratified, with kings and queen mothers at the apex, followed by various levels of title-holding nobility, royal retainers, commoners, and (prior to colonization) slaves. This system of social stratification exists alongside differences in wealth and power based upon commercial and educational success and participation in national party politics. Differences in wealth, formal education, and religious affiliation have become increasingly important.

Political Organization. In the precolonial era, Bamiléké kings had control over the life and death of their subjects. They were aided by the nobility, especially the *nkam be'e* (the council of nine highest nobles), royal retainers, and members of secret societies. Young men were organized into warrior associations such as *mandjo*. In postcolonial Cameroon, Bamiléké kings are still counseled by the nkam be'e and other societies of nobles. They have jurisdiction over civil but not criminal court cases in rural areas. They have official duties and receive salaries as justices of the peace, maintaining vital records of their rural subjects. There is no overarching Bamiléké political organization, neither traditionally nor in terms of contemporary party politics. As in the past, Bamiléké practice active interkingdom diplomacy.

Social Control. Disputes, depending upon their seriousness, were originally resolved by the lineage head, the quarter chief, or the king, each in consultation with other elders or notables. Oracles who made use of chickens, earth spiders, or poison ordeals were often consulted. Most of these forms of dispute resolution now exist alongside the Cameroonian court system, which in the Bamiléké region is fashioned after French statutory law.

Conflict. Bamiléké kingdoms raided and warred against each other and against their non-Bamiléké neighbors. This activity nearly stopped owing to a pax Germanica by 1905, but full cessation of armed hostilities was only achieved in the early 1930s. New conflicts arose during the struggle for independence. More recent conflicts are associated with a struggle for multiparty democracy following the end of the cold war, and extend beyond the Bamiléké area.

Religion and Expressive Culture

Religious Beliefs. Prior to missionization, Bamiléké believed in a creator God, Nsi. Some groups believed in local deities relating to natural features (streams, groves of trees, rocks) and personal spirits. All Bamiléké believed in the power of ancestors, through the metonym of the ancestral skull (*tu*), to cause good or bad fortune for their descendants. Matrilineal ancestresses were believed to be especially prone to anger. Although these beliefs persist, many Bamiléké are now members of Christian churches. The dominance of two major denominations, Catholic and the Église Evangélique du Cameroun (of French Calvinist origin), varies by locale. The Baptist, Jehovah's Witness, and Adventist churches are active in the Bamiléké area, but to a lesser degree.

Religious Practitioners. Religion and politics are not easily distinguished. The Bamiléké king is considered divine and responsible for the health and well-being of his subjects. He is aided in his religious duties by the *bandansi* (the men of the house of god), a secret society. Three other groups are also important in religious practice. Lineage heads, as custodians of ancestral skulls, control access to propitiary rites. Diviners and spirit mediums are active in determining the need for ceremonies and in healing. Healers and witches use the same supernatural power, *ka*, but to good or bad ends.

Ceremonies. Life-cycle ceremonies include burying the placenta and umbilical cord by the mother's kitchen at birth, circumcision for boys and prepuberty seclusion for girls (both termed nja), burial, and death celebrations performed approximately one year after death. Death celebrations (*funerailles*) are public diplays of wealth, of the value of the deceased, and of the new heir. They mark the end of a period of mourning, when the deceased has completed the transition to ancestorhood.

Royal rituals enact the transformation of a new king from a mere mortal to a divine being, the embodiment of the office of kingship. These rituals include capturing the new king, and enclosing him and two of his queens in a special temporary structure (*la' kwa*) for nine weeks. During this time they are fed medicines and taught their new duties. A ritual—complete with the symbolism of birth and feeding—marks the emergence of the king from la' kwa. He fully becomes king only after he has sired at least one male and one female child.

Arts. Bamiléké are famous for their wooden sculpture, masks, and stools (often ornamented with beads and cowries), and carved house posts. Motifs include human figures (ancestors and, occasionally, witches) and animals (representing such qualities as royalty, wisdom, or fertility), as well as geometric designs. Baskets, mats, and bags, woven of raffia-palm fibers, are common and beautifully executed household items. The Bamiléké blue and white royal display cloth is distinctive. Bamiléké artisans import cotton cloth woven in the north of Cameroon, sew a pattern of raffia fibers as a resist, and send the cloth back north to be dyed in indigo vats. Although some centers of tourist art exist, these are most developed in neighboring Bamoun and in the western Grassfields. Music played by Bamiléké secret societies utilizes drums, balofons, and whistles. This music has been incorporated into the repertoires of some contemporary Cameroonian pop musicians.

Medicine. Bamiléké traditional medical practitioners include herbalists, diviners, spirit mediums, and religious specialists. Many healers combine divination with herbal medicine. In the past, diviners, spirit mediums, and religious specialists had higher status than herbalists. This relation is now reversing, along with a trend toward more individual and fee-for-service treatment. Contemporary Bamiléké seek medical assistance from both private and public hospitals and clinics as well as from their rich array of traditional practitioners (see "Religious Practitioners").

Death and Afterlife. Death may be attributed to natural causes, but in most cases Bamiléké use divination to answer the questions why this person, why now, and who did it? Varying forms of witchcraft figure prominently in causes of death, and public autopsies are performed in some Bamiléké kingdoms as part of the search for cause. Immediately following death, female kin wail, announcing the death to the neighborhood. Burial generally occurs within twenty-four hours, during a one-week period of public mourning (French: *deuil;* Pidgin: *cry-die*). Close relatives of the deceased shave their heads and don blue or black clothes of mourning. Approximately one year later, lavish death celebrations are performed (see "Ceremonies"). Widows can resume sexual relations following the death celebration. Some time after this celebration the heir or heiress will exhume and care for ancestral skulls in clay pots or in small houselike tombs. Bamiléké believe that improper care of ancestral skulls leads to ancestral wrath, illness, infertility, and even death.

Bibliography

Brain, Robert. (1972). *Bangwa Kinship and Marriage*. Cambridge: Cambridge University Press.

DeLancey, Mark W. (1978). "Health and Disease on the Plantations of Cameroon, 1884–1939." In *Disease in African History,* edited by G. W. Hartwig and K. D. Patterson, 153–179. Durham, N.C.: Duke University Press.

den Ouden, Jan H. B. (1980). "Incorporation and Changes in the Composite Household: The Effects of Coffee Introduction and Food Crop Commercialization in Two Bamiléké Chiefdoms, Cameroon. In *The Household, Women, and Agricultural Development,* edited by C. Presvelou and S. Spijkers-Zwart, 41–67. Wageningen: H. Veenman and Zonen, B.V.

den Ouden, Jan H. B. (1987). "In Search of Personal Mobility: Changing Interpersonal Relations in Two Bamiléké Chiefdoms, Cameroon." *Africa* 57(1): 3–27.

Dongmo, J.-L. (1981). *Le dynamisme bamiléké (Cameroun)*. Vol. 1, *La maîtrise de l'espace agraire*. Yaoundé: Université de Yaoundé.

Feldman-Savelsberg, Pamela (1990). "'Then We Were Many': Bangangté Women's Conceptions of Health, Fertility, and Social Change in a Bamiléké Chiefdom, Cameroon." Ph.D. dissertation, Johns Hopkins University.

Feldman-Savelsberg, Pamela (1995). "Cooking Inside: Kinship and Gender in Bangangté Metaphors of Marriage and Procreation." *American Ethnologist* 22(3): 20–37.

Ghomsi, Emmanuel (1971). "La naissance des chefferies bamiléké et les relations entre divers groupements avant la conquête allemande." *Revue Camerounaise d'Histoire* 1:94–121.

Hirsch, Klaus (1987). *Bamiléké: Die Menschen aus den Schluchten*. Berlin: Express Edition.

Hurault, Jean (1962). *La structure sociale des bamiléké*. Paris: Mouton.

Joseph, Richard A. (1977). *Radical Nationalism in Cameroun: Social Origins of the UPC (Union des Populations du Cameroun) Rebellion*. Oxford: Clarendon Press.

Kuczynski, R. R. (1939). The *Cameroons and Togoland: A Demographic Study*. London: Oxford University Press.

Nkwi, Paul N., and Flavien Tiokou Ndonko (1989). "Epilepsy among the Bamiléké of Maham in the Ndé Division, West Province of Cameroon." *Culture, Medicine, and Psychiatry* 13:437–448.

Notué, Jean P., and Louis Perrois (1984). *Contribution à l'étude des sociétés secrètes chez les bamiléké (ouest Cameroun)*. Yaoundé: ISH; ORSTOM.

Pradelles de Latour, Charles-Henry (1994). "Marriage Payments, Debt, and Fatherhood among the Bangoua: A Lacanian Analysis of a Kinship System." *Africa* 64:21–33.

Rohde, Eckart (1990). *Chefferie Bamiléké: Traditionelle Herrschaft und Kolonialsystem*. Münster: Lit Verlag.

Rowlands, Michael, and Jean-Pierre Warnier (1988). "Sorcery, Power, and the Modern State in Cameroon." *Man* n.s. 23:118–132.

Soen, D., and P. de Comarmon (1969–1970). "The Secret Societies and Age Groups of the Bamiléké and Their Potential Adaptability to Cooperative Organization." *Wiener Völkerkundliche Mitteilungen* 11–12:71–88.

Tardits, Claude (1960). *Contribution à l'étude des populations bamiléké de l'ouest de Cameroun*. Paris: Éditions Berger-Levrault.

Voegelin, Charles F., and F. M. Voegelin (1977). *Classification and Index of the World's Languages*. New York: Elsevier.

World Fertility Survey (1983). *Enquête nationale sur la fécondité du Cameroun, 1978*. Yaoundé: MINEP.

PAMELA FELDMAN-SAVELSBERG

Basseri

ETHNONYMS: none

Orientation

The Basseri are traditional pastoral nomads who inhabit the Iranian province of Fārs and migrate along the steppes and mountains near the town of Shīrāz. The Basseri are a clearly delineated group, defined—as are most groups in the area—by political rather than by ethnic or geographical criteria. In the late 1950s there were an estimated 16,000 Basseri living in Iran. More recent estimates of the Basseri population have not been widely published. This article focuses on the traditional Basseri culture, which still existed in the late 1950s. Owing to political circumstances in the region, the current situation is not reliably known.

The Basseri speak a dialect of Farsi. The majority know only the Basseri dialect, but a few also speak Turkish or Arabic. Most of the groups with which the Basseri come in contact speak Farsi, Turkish, or Arabic. Some of these groups claim a common or collateral ancestral link with the Basseri. Many people among the settled populations in southern Iran claim to have Basseri origins. There are also other nomadic groups—namely the Yazd-e-Khast, the Bugard-Basseri, and the Basseri near Semnan east of Tehran—who are believed to be genetically connected with the Basseri of Fārs.

The Basseri were part of the Khamseh confederacy, which formed in the mid-nineteenth century. At the outset, they were not predominant within this organization, and, later, when the Basseri grew in importance within the confederacy, the confederacy lost its importance as a political and social unit.

The habitat of the Basseri derives from the hot and arid climate of the Persian Gulf. The approximately 18,000 to 21,000 square kilometers that they traditionally inhabit spans a large ecological range. In the southern section there are deserts at elevations of 600 to 900 meters, and in the north there are high mountains, preeminent among which is 4,000-meter Kuh-i-Bul. Annual precipitation totals about 25 centimeters a year, which falls mainly in the higher regions in the form of snow. Much of this is conserved for the shorter growing season in that area. Mountain precipitation also provides support for considerable vegetation, and even some forests, in the higher elevations. In the southern lowland, however, rapid runoff and summer droughts limit vegetation to hardy desert scrubs and temporary grass cover in the rainy season of winter and early spring.

Economy

Extensive pastures are an essential part of the pastoral economy of the Basseri, but these pastures cannot support flocks continuously over the course of a year. Along the migratory routes of the Basseri, pastures are utilized by different Basseri groups in succession. While snow covers the pastures in the mountains in the north, extensive though rather poor pastures are available in the south. In spring, good pastures are plentiful in the low and middle altitudes, but, beginning in early March in the far south, they progressively dry up. Usable pastures are available in the summer in areas above 6,000 feet, but the grasses dry up in the latter part of the summer. In the fall, when pastures are generally poor, the remains of harvested fields become available for pasturage.

All of the major tribes of Fārs have traditional routes that they travel in their seasonal migrations. They also have a traditional schedule of pasture occupations at different locations. The combined route and schedule, which describes the locations of a group at different times in the yearly cycle, constitutes their *il-rah*. An il-rah is regarded by tribesmen as the property of their tribe. Implicit within the concept of il-rah are rights to pass on roads and over uncultivated lands, to draw water everywhere except from private wells, and to pasture flocks outside cultivated fields. These rights are recognized by the local populations and authorities.

Although the Basseri keep a variety of domesticated animals, sheep and goats have the greatest economic importance. Other domesticated animals include donkeys for transport and riding (mainly by women and children), horses for riding only (predominantly by men), camels for heavy transport and wool, and dogs for keeping watch in camp. Poultry are sometimes kept as a source of meat, but not for eggs. Cattle are not herded because of the long migrations and the rocky terrain.

Sheep and goats provide milk, meat, wool, and hides. Camels provide only wool. These products are consumed immediately, stored for later consumption, or traded.

Kinship and Sociopolitical Organization

One of the primary social units of Basseri society is the group of people who share a tent. The Basseri keep a count of their numbers and describe their camp groups in terms of tents (sing. *khune*, "house"). Each tent is occupied by an independent household, typically consisting of a nuclear family. Tents are units of production and consumption; each is represented by its male head. Tent residents hold rights over all movable property including flocks, and they can act as independent units for political purposes. For purposes of more efficient herding, these households combine in small herding units, the composition of which depends on expediency rather than kinship or other basic principles of organization.

In winter, groups of two to five tents associated in herding units make up local camps separated by 3 or 4 kilometers from the next group. At all other times of the year, camps are larger—usually numbering ten to forty tents. These camps are in a very real sense the primary communities of nomadic Basseri society. The members of a camp are a very clearly bounded social group. Their relations to each other as continuing neighbors are relatively constant, whereas all other contacts are passing, ephemeral, and governed by chance.

The maintenance of a camp as a social unit requires daily unanimous agreement on questions of migration, the selection of campsites, and all other economically vital considerations. Such agreement may be achieved in various ways, ranging from coercion by a powerful leader to mutual consent through compromise by all concerned. The compositon of a camp will thus indirectly be determined by shifting circumstances in the formation of a consensus whereby the movements of economically independent households can be controlled and coordinated. The unity of a camp is enhanced by the existence of a recognized leader, who represents the group for political and administrative purposes. Leaders of different camps may be of two kinds: headmen (sing. *katkhoda*), who are formally recognized by the Basseri chief, and, where no headman resides in camp, informal leaders (sing. *riz safid;* lit., "white beard"). The latter, by common consent, are recognized to represent their camp in the same way as a headman does but without the formal recognition of the Basseri chief. Technically, therefore, the riz safid is under a headman in a different camp.

The Basseri chief is the head of a very strongly centralized political system and has immense authority over all members of the Basseri tribe. The chief, in his dealing with the headmen, draws on their power and influence but does not delegate any of his own power back to them. Some material goods—mostly gifts of some economic and prestige value, such as riding horses and weapons—flow from the chief to the headmen. A headman is in a politically convenient position: he can communicate much more freely with the chief than can ordinary tribesmen, and thus can bring up cases that are to his own advantage and, to some extent, block or delay the discussion of matters detrimental to his own interests. Nonetheless, the political power that a headman derives from the chief is very limited.

The authority of headmen is derived from agnatic kinship in a ramifying descent system, as well as from matrilateral and affinal relations. As is commonly the case in the Middle East, the agnatic lines of the Basseri are predominant in matters of succession. The son of a Basseri is regarded as Basseri even though his mother may be from another tribe or village. On the other hand, when a Basseri woman marries outside the tribe she transmits no rights in the tribe to her offspring. Although patrilineal kinship unites larger kin-based groups, bonds of solidarity also tie matrikin together. For example, the relation between a mother's brother and a sister's child is an indulgent one among the Basseri. Affinal relations are also regarded as relations of solidarity and kinship. They appear to be most effective in establishing political bonds between tents.

A marriage is a transaction between kin groups constituting whole households, and not merely between contracting spouses. The head of a household, or tent, holds the authority to make marriage contracts for the members of his household. A married man may arrange subsequent marriages for himself, whereas all women and unmarried boys are subject to the authority of a marriage guardian, who is the head of their household. The marriage contract is often drawn up and written by a nontribal ritual specialist, or holy man. It stipulates certain bride-payments for the girl and the domestic equipment she is expected to bring, and the divorce or widow's insurance, which is a prearranged share of the husband's estate, payable upon divorce or in the event of his death.

When a household was established by marriage, the groom's father gave the new household an "anticipatory inheritance"—the groom received from his father's herd the arithmetic fraction that he would receive as an heir if his father were to die at that moment. From then on, the new household was on its own. If its herds failed, it received no second inheritance, nor was it lent animals to help it maintain itself.

Religion

The Basseri are Shia Muslims who accept the prescriptions and prohibitions of Islam to the extent that they are familiar with them. The Basseri, however, seem not to be very familiar with Muslim beliefs, customs, and ceremonies. There is some confusion among the Basseri with respect to the divisions and events of the Muslim year, even though they are continually reminded of them through their contacts with sedentary villages. Even when they are aware of specific customs, they are not consistent in observing them. Islamic feast days are rarely celebrated. Even the fast of Ramadan and the feast of Moharram, which are of central importance to the surrounding Muslims, are observed by only a few Basseri. Rituals are more often connected with the life cycle—birth, marriage, death—than with Islamic traditions.

Bibliography

Barth, Fredrik (1961). *Nomads of South Persia*. Boston: Little, Brown & Co.

Barth, Fredrick (1964). "Capital, Investment, and the Social Structure of a Pastoral Nomad Group in South Persia." In *Capital, Saving, and Credit in Peasant Societies*, edited by R. Firth and B.S. Yamey, 69–81. Chicago: Aldine.

Beck, Lois (1986). *The Qashqa'i of Iran*. New Haven: Yale University Press.

Bradburd, Daniel (1989). "Producing Their Fates: Why Poor Basseri Settled but Poor Komachi and Yomut Did Not." *American Ethnologist* 16:502–517.

Magee, Lt. G. F. (1945). *The Tribes of Fars*. Government of India, Political and Secret Records: Persia: Internal. India Office Records Library, London.

Tapper, Richard, ed. (1983). *The Conflict of Tribe and State in Iran and Afghanistan*. New York: St. Martin's Press.

RONALD JOHNSON

Bedouin

ETHNONYMS: Aʿraab, Bedu (sing. Bedawi)

Orientation

Identification. The term "Bedouin" is the anglicization of the Arabic "*bedu*." The term is used to differentiate between those populations whose livelihood is based on the raising of livestock by mainly natural graze and browse and those populations who have an agricultural or urban base (*hadar*). Given that the opposition of bedu to hadar is a specifically Arab cultural tradition, it is arguable whether non-Arab-speaking pastoralists in the region should be termed "Bedouin." Most of these societies prefer expressions such as "ʿArab ar-Rashaayida" (the Rashaayda Arabs), or "qabiilat Fedʿaan" (the Fedʿaan tribe), rather than the term "Bedouin." Among sedentary Arabs, another common term is "Aʿraab" which, since the beginning of Islam, has been synonymous with "nomad."

Location. Bedouin societies are found in the arid steppe regions of Arabia and North Africa and along the margins of rain-fed cultivation. In some areas rainfall is very unpredictable and measures less than 5 centimeters per year. Bedouin living in such areas tend to move camp irregularly, as dictated by the availability of green pasture and seasonal occult precipitation (heavy morning dew). Often they have access to small date gardens for short periods of the year. In areas where winter rainfall is less unpredictable (in the Arabian Badia and the Nejd and in parts of Sudan, Egypt, southern Tunisia, and Libya), Bedouin groups move their animals to areas where pasture is regularly found. Often these societies plant grain along their migration routes, which they harvest on their return to their winter camping areas. In areas where winter rain falls predictably on mountain plateaus (Morocco), the Bedouin practice transhumance, planting their crops near their permanent homes in the valleys at the onset of the rains and then moving their livestock to the highland pastures.

Linguistic Affiliation. Like other Arabs, Bedouin speak various dialects of Arabic, which belongs to the Semitic Language Group. Other living languages of this group are Modern Hebrew, Amharic and other spoken languages of Ethiopia (Harari, Tigre), Aramaic dialects (current in parts of Syria, Lebanon, and Iraq), and Maltese.

History and Cultural Relations

Agriculturists and pastoralists have inhabited the southern edge of the arid Syrian Steppe since 6000 B.C. (Fagan 1986, 234). By about 850 B.C., a complex of oasis settlements and pastoral camps was established by a people known as "Aʿraab." These Semitic speakers were the latest in a succession of farming and stock-breeding societies. They were distinguished from their Assyrian neighbors to the north, however, by their Arabic language and by their use of domesticated camels for trade and warfare. These Aʿraab were the cultural forerunners of the modern-day Arabs. They carried out a caravan trade with their camels between southern Arabia and the large city-states of Syria. By the first century B.C., they had moved westward into Jordan and the Sinai Peninsula and southwestward along the coast of the Red Sea. The creation of a powerful Islamic state in western Arabia in the middle of the seventh century A.D. gave a dramatic impetus to Arab expansion. Thousands of Arab Muslims—many of them Bedouin—left the Arabian Peninsula to settle in the newly conquered lands around it. As a result, the bedu/hadar distinction was reproduced in those Arabized territories where such a regional division of labor was ecologically and geographically practicable.

Bedouin societies are always linked to other nonpastoral societies by economic, social, and political relations. In the local context, a "Bedouin" is a regional specialist in livestock breeding whose closest social and political ties are with his pastoral kinsmen. The sedentary Arab, by contrast, places less emphasis on relations with genealogically distant kin. During periods when premodern states were weak and large-scale irrigated agriculture declined, some settled cultivators increased their reliance on breeding of small stock and moved into Bedouin social circles. In modern times, strong centralized authority and the monetarization of the rural economy have prompted some Bedouin to seek wage labor in cities and become sedentary. Regardless of their occupation and residence patterns, however, they remain culturally Bedouin as long as they maintain close social ties with pastoralist kin and retain the local linguistic and cultural markers that identify them as Bedouin.

Settlements

Bedouin societies traditionally eschew permanent settlement, preferring portable shelters that allow them the flexibility that their pastoral nomadic way of life requires. Kin-related domestic units or households generally migrate together during the spring and summer months and tend to converge with other households of near kin during the winter months. In the past, Bedouin residence units were composed exclusively of tents (*buyuut;* sing. *bayt*). Depending upon the season of the year and, more specifically, the quality of surrounding pastureland, as few as three buyuut, and sometimes as many as fifteen, formed a camping unit. Among some Bedouin groups that spend the winter months in the same place year after year, stone houses (*buyuut hajar*) are also common. In many cases, these winter encampments are only partially deserted during the spring and summer—the very young and the very old are left behind to benefit from government efforts to extend health care and schooling facilities to these settlements. In certain areas of North Africa where transhumance is practiced, the seasonality of movement is somewhat different, although the principle is the same. Structurally, the tent and stone dwellings are alike. Both are rectangular in shape and consist of two—or occasionally three—sections. One section is the women's domain, kitchen, and storeroom. The other section is almost exclusively the domain of men and visitors—where hospitality is extended to guests, clients, and kinsmen alike. Sometimes the Bedouin home includes a third section, where sick or very young animals are given care.

Economy

Subsistence and Commercial Activities. The primary economic activity of the Bedouin is animal husbandry by natural graze and browse of sheep, goats, and camels. This way of life, called pastoral nomadism, has been in existence for at least three millennia. At the core of pastoral nomadism is migration, the pattern of which is determined by a combination of seasonal and areal variability in the location of pasture and water. Because water and grass can be in short supply in a particular area at the same time that it is abundant elsewhere, survival of both herds and herders makes movement from deficit to surplus areas both logical and necessary. Pasture and water are seldom found randomly scattered about in a given region, but generally are distributed in a regular fashion in accordance with a particular seasonal pattern of climate. Since the 1960s, trucks and other motor vehicles have come to replace camels as beasts of burden; today a truck often serves to bring feed and water to the herds in the desert.

Industrial Arts. The pastoral adaptation to the ecological environment presupposes the presence of sedentary communities and access to their products. None of the essentials of metal or cured leather are produced by pastoralists. They are dependent on persons outside their own group for practically all specialized work. In some regions, roving Gypsy tinkers and traders provide specialized services and goods to Bedouin households.

Trade. There are several traditional means utilized by Bedouin to guarantee themselves access to grain and other sedentary produce. A household may, if its tribal land is close enough to rain-fed cultivation, sow and harvest crops. More commonly, rent from oasis or agricultural land owned by the group is collected in kind. At one time, *khuwa* (tribute) was exacted from sedentary farmers in return for protection from raids by tribes in the region. This tribute/raid relationship was a simple business proposition whereby the pastoralists received a needed product (grain) and the farmer acquired a scarce commodity (security). In principle, it was not very different from the most widespread relationship today whereby animal products are exchanged for dates and grain.

Division of Labor. As with most pastoral societies, the division of labor among Bedouin is determined by the type of animals that are herded. When both large and small domesticated animals are kept, the larger animals—camels and, in a few cases, cattle—are the responsibility of the men. Women are often barred from close contact with these animals. It is generally the responsibility of the women and older girls to herd, feed, and milk the smaller animals (i.e., goats and sheep). When only sheep and goats are kept, men tend to be the herders, and women help with the feeding and milking of the flock.

Land Tenure. Each Bedouin group seeks to control a land area that contains sufficient resources to sustain communal life. Each has a definite zone with well-understood, though often variable, limits and has certain rights of usufruct denied to other Bedouin groups. Only in an emergency does a pastoral unit attempt to graze its herds outside of its traditional area, and this eventuality is often preceded by negotiations at a higher political level. Governments throughout the Middle East and North Africa no longer recognize Bedouin collective territory. These areas are now considered "state-owned" land.

Kinship

Kin Groups and Descent. Like all Arabs, the Bedouin are patrilineal. Names consist of a personal name, the father's name, and at least the agnatic grandfather's name. Women retain their father's family name unchanged even after marriage. The smallest residential unit (bayt) is named after its senior male resident. Unlike settled peoples, however, most Bedouin are also members of larger patrilineal descent groups (buyuut), which are linked by agnation to form even larger lineages (*afkhaadh;* sing. *fakhadh;* lit., "thigh"), tribes (*qabaaʿil;* sing. *qabila*), and sometimes even tribal confederations (such as the ʿAnayza and the Shammar of northwestern Arabia). Bedouin frequently name more than five generations of patrilineal ancestors and conceptualize relations among descent groups in terms of a segmentary genealogical model. This model of nested patrilineal groups, each unit included in a larger one and itself including smaller units that are internally divided, provides the main framework for discussing marital alliances and for resolving legal disputes and violent conflicts.

Kinship Terminology. There are distinctive terms for kin on the mother's side and kin on the father's side in Ego's generation and the first ascending generation. All terms indicate the sex of the person designated.

Marriage and Family

Marriage. Marriage is normally contracted within the minimal lineage (bayt). The ideal marriage is to the closest relative permitted by the Quran (surah 4:23). This is between a man and his father's brother's daughter. Not only is marriage to the *bint ʿamm* (female parallel cousin) or the *ibn ʿamm* (male parallel cousin) preferred, but, in addition, the father's brother's son has a customary right to his cousin. Although the female cousin may refuse to marry her father's brother's son, she may not marry anyone else without his consent first. Although parallel-cousin marriage is actively favored, in many of these marriages the term "first cousin" is only a classificatory one. In many cases, the bint ʿamm or ibn ʿamm is actually a second or third cousin. Nevertheless, these cousin marriages are seen as reinforcing the unity and authority of the minimal lineage. Although plural marriage is permitted, the incidence of polygyny is not particularly high. It is generally limited to those older men who are wealthy enough to maintain separate households for each wife. Divorce is frequent and can be initiated by either the husband or the wife. In either case, the wife will return to her father's home for protection and support until her marital crisis has been resolved.

Domestic Unit. The three-generation extended family is the ideal domestic unit. Although this group, averaging between nine and eleven persons, may sleep under more than one tent or shelter, its meals are generally taken together. The newly formed nuclear family of husband and wife tends to remain with the larger domestic unit until it has sufficient manpower and a large enough herd to survive on its own. On occasion, a combination of brothers or patrilineal cousins will join forces to form a single domestic unit.

Inheritance. Property is divided in accordance to Quranic precepts: among surviving children, a son receives half, a daughter a quarter, and other near kin the percentage specified (surah 4:12). Among some Bedouin groups the division of the animal holdings of the deceased is complicated by the fact that women may not look after the larger domesticated animals. Thus, if a woman receives an inheritance of a number of camels, these must be put in trust for her and are generally incorporated into a brother's or cousin's herd.

Socialization. Children and infants are raised by the extended family unit. Parents, older siblings, grandparents, aunts, uncles, and cousins all take part in the rearing of the young. By the age of 6 or 7, the child begins to take on simple household tasks and soon thereafter becomes a full working member of the family. Adolescence is hardly recognized; by the early teens, the individual is accepted as a full working member of Bedouin society.

Sociopolitical Organization

In a sense, the Bedouin form a number of "nations." That is, groups of families are united by common ancestry and by shared territorial allegiance. The exploitation and defense of their common territorial area is effected through a universally accepted system of leadership. For centuries, these "nations" of Bedouin tribes and their leaders operated in the ecologically and politically shifting landscapes of the Middle East and North Africa. Only in the course of the twentieth century has their traditional flexibility and mobility been checked. Factors foreign to their universe have damaged the territorial mainstay of their societies, necessitating the adoption of new bases of identification with their "nations" and its leaders.

Social Organization. Bedouin society is organized on the basis of a series of real and fictive overlapping kin groups. The smallest unit is generally agreed to be the bayt (minimal lineage). Numerous buyuut, claiming descent from a common ancestor, form a fakhadh (maximal lineage). Theoretically, each male household head in a bayt or the larger fakhadh is the equal of all the other adult males. In practice, age, religious piety, and personal characteristics such as generosity and hospitality set some men above others in the organization of the group.

Political Organization. The buyuut are the basic social and economic units of Bedouin society, but the leaders of these units generally form a council of elders, directed by the head of the tribe. In some larger tribes with more centralization, the fakhadh head is linked to a subtribe (*ˁashiira*) leader, who comes immediately under the direction of the head (*shaykh*; pl. *shuyukh*) of the tribe (qabiila). Thus, traditional chains of command link the individual groups ultimately to the shaykh. He traditionally exercises authority over the allocation of pasture and the arbitration of disputes. His position is usually derived from his own astute reading of the majority opinion. He generally has no power to enforce a decision and therefore has to rely on his moral authority and the concurrence of the community with his point of view.

Social Control. In the small-scale, exclusive communities that constitute Bedouin society, face-to-face (as opposed to anonymous) relations are of paramount importance. The concepts of honor and shame are thus a constant preoccupation and, to a large extent, serve to control the social behavior of individuals. *Sharaf* (honor), which is inherited from the family, has to be constantly asserted or vindicated. A man's share of honor is largely determined by his own behavior and that of his near agnatic kin. Sharaf can be subject to increase or decrease, to development or deterioration, according to the conduct of the person and his kin. There is an exclusive term, *ird*, for the honor of the women of a kin group. This is used only in connection with female chastity. Ird differs from sharaf in that sharaf can be acquired or augmented through right behavior and achievement, whereas ird can only be lost by the "misconduct" of the woman; once lost, it cannot be regained. At the community level, the threat of *jalaaˁ* (expulsion) as punishment for a grave social offense tends to be regarded with great seriousness.

Conflict. In the past, most tribal conflicts revolved about the rights to scarce pasture and water resources. Numerous tribal campaigns were once fought to acquire or defend pastures and watering holes. Since the middle of the twentieth century, however, the centralized political authority of the modern nation-states in the region has successfully pacified the Bedouin tribes.

Religion and Expressive Culture

Religious Beliefs. Although a few Bedouin societies in Jordan have remained Christian since the early Islamic period, the vast majority of Bedouin are Sunni Muslims. The Five Pillars of Islam are the declaration of faith, the five daily ritual prayers, almsgiving, fasting, and the pilgrimage to Mecca. Most Bedouin societies observe the fast of Ramadan, perform the obligatory prayers, and celebrate the two major Islamic holidays—ˁIid al-Fitr and ˁIid al-Adhha. Some groups endeavor to make the hajj (the pilgrimage to Mecca) more than once in a lifetime, and individual piety is sometimes reflected in the number of pilgrimages an individual manages to undertake. The Bedouin societies throughout the region variously believe in the presence of spirits (jinn), some playful and others malevolent, that interfere in the life of humans. The "envious eye" is also very real to the Bedouin, and children are believed to be particularly vulnerable. For this reason, they often have protective amulets attached to their clothing or hung around their necks. Some Bedouin groups postulate the existence ogresses and of monstrous supernaturals (*ahl al-ard*, "people of the earth"), who are sometimes met by lone travelers in the desert.

Religious Practitioners. There is no formal clergy in Islam and no center of "priests." Bedouin societies have no formal religious specialists. Bedouin groups traditionally arrange for religious specialists from adjacent settled regions to spend several months a year with them to teach the young to read the Quran. These specialists are often called "shuyukh" (sing. shaykh). Other rural or settled religious specialists that Bedouin seek out for curative and preventative measures are variously called *kaatibiin* (sing. *katib*), *shaatirin* (sing. *shatir*), and *mutawwiˁiin* (sing. *mutawi*).

Ceremonies and Rituals. In addition to the religious observances discussed under "Religious Beliefs," Bedouin ceremonies and rituals include elaborate celebrations of weddings, ritual namings of newborn infants, and the circumcision of children (boys universally, girls frequently). Those Bedouin who are influenced by Sufism (Islamic mysticism)—for example, the Bedouin of southern Sinai and Libya—also celebrate the Prophet's birthday and carry out pilgrimages to the tombs of saints. Hospitality is extensively ritualized. Whenever an animal is slaughtered for a guest, men ritually sacrifice it in accordance with Islamic law. Guests are ritually incorporated into their hosts' households; in case of armed conflict, guests must be protected as if they were family members. Other rituals contribute to the definition of household membership and household space. For instance, a newborn child is made a household member through rites of seclusion and purification, which new mothers observe for between seven and forty days after childbirth.

Arts. Simple tattooing of the face (and in some cases the hand) is practiced. Drawing on sand is sometimes engaged in, particularly among children. Women weave sheep's wool—and occasionally goats' hair—into tent strips, rugs, blankets, saddlebags, and camel and horse trappings. Important artistic expression in design, color, and pattern is incorporated into these handicrafts. Most aesthetic expression, however, focuses on the recitation of poetry, some memorized and some composed for the occasion. Both men and women engage in contests of oral skills among their peer groups. Traditional musical instruments are mostly limited to the single-stringed instrument, various types of drums, and, in places, a type of recorder or wind instrument.

Medicine. Illness is attributed to a number of causes: imbalance of elements in the body and spirit possession, as well as germ invasion. Traditional preventative and curative measures include locally prepared herbal remedies, branding, the wearing of amulets, and the carrying of Quranic inscriptions. Western medical treatment is also sought out, particularly when traditional efforts fail.

Death and Afterlife. Islamic tradition dictates the practices associated with death. The body is buried as soon as possible and always within twenty-four hours. Among some Bedouin groups, an effort is made to bury the dead in one place (sometimes called the *bilaad*), although often it is impossible to reach it within the strict time limit imposed by Islamic practices. Funeral rites are very simple, and graves tend to be either unmarked or undifferentiated.

Bibliography

Abu-Lughod, Lila (1986). *Veiled Sentiments: Honor and Poetry in a Bedouin Society*. Berkeley and Los Angeles: University of California Press.

Asad, Talal (1970). *The Kababish Arabs: Power, Authority, and Consent in a Nomadic Tribe*. London: C. Hurst & Co.

"Badw" (1979). In *Encyclopedia of Islam*. Vol. 1, A–B, 872–882. New ed. Leiden: E. J. Brill.

Behnke, Roy (1980). *The Herders of Cyrenaica: Ecology, Economy, and Kinship among the Bedouin of Eastern Libya*. Urbana: University of Illinois Press.

Chatty, Dawn (1986). *From Camel to Truck: The Bedouin in the Modern World*. New York: Vantage Press.

Cole, Donald (1975). *Nomads of the Nomads: The Al Murrah of the Empty Quarter*. Chicago: Aldine Publishing Co.

Fagan, Brian (1986). *Peoples of the Earth: An Introduction to World Prehistory*. Boston: Little, Brown & Co.

Lancaster, William (1981). *The Rwala Bedouin Today*. Cambridge: Cambridge University Press.

Marx, Emanuel (1967). *Bedouin of the Negev*. Manchester: Manchester University Press.

Peters, Emrys (1968). "The Tied and the Free: An Account of a Type of Patron-Client Relationship among the Bedouin Pastoralists of Cyrenaica." In *Contributions to Mediterranean Sociology*, edited by J. G. Peristiany. The Hague: Mouton & Co.

DAWN CHATTY AND WILLIAM YOUNG

Bemba

ETHNONYMS: Babemba, Chibemba, Chiwemba, Ichibemba, Wemba

The Bemba are the largest ethnic group in the Northern Province of Zambia, where they occupy the high plateau land between 9° and 12° S and between 29° and 32° E, covering the whole district of Kasama and much of Mpika, Chinsali, Luwingu, and Mporokoso districts. The 1986 Zambian census placed the Bemba population at approximately 1,700,000 in Zambia, with another 150,000 in neighboring countries.

Some seventeen or eighteen ethnic groups in this general area of Zambia comprise the Bemba-speaking peoples, and they form with the Bemba a closely related culture cluster. All of these peoples are predominantly agricultural and have a matrilineal-matrilocal emphasis. They practice shifting cultivation, growing finger millet (*Eleusine corocana*), which is the staple crop in the eastern part of the area, including among the Bemba, and manioc among the western groups. There is a general absence of cattle because this area is within the tsetse belt, but the Bemba do have a few sheep and goats. The Bemba-speaking peoples, together with several other ethnic clusters, are generally considered to comprise a broader cultural-linguistic category known as the Central Bantu.

The Bemba recognize the following distinctive marks of societal membership: a common name, Babemba; a common language, Cibemba, which in their eyes forms a distinct dialect; distinctive scarification, a vertical cut on each temple behind the eyes, almost one inch long; common historical traditions; and allegiance to a common paramount chief, the *citimukulu*, whose rule of the Bemba territory is unquestioned.

Descent, sib affiliation, and succession to office follow the matrilineal line, and marital residence is matrilocal. Each individual belongs to a matrilineal lineage, which determines his succession to different offices and his status in the community. He also belongs to an exogamous, matrilineal sib (*mukoa*), which is important for certain hereditary offices. There are about thirty sibs among the Bemba, and they are ranked according to status based on their relations with the royal crocodile sib. Inheritance is relatively unimportant, since there are few forms of inheritable wealth.

Despite this matrilineal orientation, the Bemba kinship system in some ways is bilateral in nature. The kin group to which a person constantly refers in everyday affairs is the *lupwa*, a bilateral group of near relatives on both sides of his family (i.e., a kindred), who join in religious ceremonies, matrimonial transactions, mortuary ritual, and inheritance. This group may be more important to a Bemba than his matrilineal sib. In addition, a patrilineal emphasis has been increasing in the late twentieth century, including a broadening of the father's authority within the family.

Superimposed upon this kinship base is a highly centralized, hierarchical, and authoritarian political system consisting of three main levels of organization: the state, the district, and the village. As previously noted, the state is ruled by a paramount chief (citimukulu), whose office is hereditary within a royal sib. His authority is nearly absolute, and he is believed to have supernatural powers. The citimukulu is assisted by a council consisting of thirty to forty hereditary officials (the *bakabilo*), many of royal descent, and each responsible for some special ritual duty kept secret from the ordinary members of the society.

The Bemba state is divided into political districts (*ifyalo;* sing. *icalo*), usually five or more in number. Each icalo is a geographical unit with a more or less fixed boundary and name, and it is also a ritual unit. A hereditary, territorial chief (*mfumu*) rules over each icalo. These chieftainships are arranged in order of precedence, according to their nearness to the center of the country and the antiquity of their offices. To the most important of these chiefdoms the citimukulu appoints his nearest relatives. In 1933 there were three major districts: the citimukulu's personal district (called Lubemba—the center of the country), comprised of 160 villages; the Ituna district, with 69 villages; and Icinga district, with 76 villages. Each territorial chief also has his own councillors.

Each territorial chief has under him a number of subchiefs, who might rule over very small tracts of country, or rather, over a few villages. A district or territorial chief is also chief of his own village (*musumba*), and there is a significant difference in size between a chief's village and a village with a commoner as headman. The average Bemba village is rather small in size, with 30 to 50 huts and a population range of about 60 to 160. In contrast, chief's villages are very much larger in size. In the old days, a chief's village might have had thousands of inhabitants; in 1934, the villages of important chiefs had 400 to 600 huts. They were divided into quarters, ruled over by loyal supporters of the chief. The nucleus of a commoner Bemba village consists of the headman's matrilocal extended family. In older villages, such as Kasaka, there may be three or four related matrilocal family groups. The heads of these family groups are the most influential members of the community; they are known as the "great ones of the village" (*bakalamba*). It can be seen that rank is a marked feature of Bemba society. It is based ultimately on kinship—real or fictive—with the paramount chief and, derivatively, with the territorial chiefs.

The religious beliefs and practices of the Bemba are related to their social organization, particularly the matrilineal basis of the society. Traditionally the Bemba-speaking people adhered to a house religion, in which the married woman was in charge of all the domestic ritual and had access to the divine through the intercession of her forebears. She was the one who led the veneration of the recently dead at the small house shrine. She also led the public remembrance services to the ancient guardians of the land. Furthermore, the knowledge of the community's religious heritage and the guidelines for worshiping the transcendent were passed on by the women during the ceremonies of initiation.

The original house religion of the Bemba was radically altered during the centralization of chiefly authority and the imposition of Bemba paramountcy, which occurred around 1700. The chiefs manipulated Bemba religion to enhance their own power. The worship of the spirits (*imipashi*) of dead chiefs—both paramount and territorial chiefs—has since become an essential element of Bemba religion. The focus shifted from the traditional house shrine, attended by the housewife, to the court cult, where the royal relics were venerated along with other magical objects. This cult had slowly acquired more power and authority than the ritual of the house shrine, in spite of the insistence on service to the immediate family spirits and to the guardians of the land by women.

The first Christian missionaries arrived toward the end of the nineteenth century, when chiefly power was being used in particularly cruel ways. The common people regarded these missionaries as liberators, who by their medical and social work seemed to have preferential regard for the poor and for those who suffered. Women accepted them as allies in their struggle to restore the house cult, the family spirits, and the guardians of the land. The Western missionaries were seen as the messengers of God pointing the way to a better future, and as such their teaching was incorporated into the already existing worldview of the people.

From the 1920s to the 1950s, women experienced increasing difficulties with the further demands of what was called the "new way." By then, their sacred position had come under severe attack. At that time a Western style of education, with its emphasis on modernity, was strongly emphasized within Bemba society. The Protestants and the Catholics competed for the allegiance of boys and young men. Both groups saw the religious role of women as reactionary and dangerous. Their teaching was considered pagan and was discouraged as much as possible.

Women found redress only by turning to prophets who pushed for a return to older customs and traditions. For example, Emilio Mulolani, a fervent lay preacher, was in favor of the restoration of the house cult, and taught that men and women were equal, especially in the act of procreation, which was sacred. Many women were influenced by these ideas and expressed the need to have the Christian message expressed in the religious concepts of the domestic cult.

By 1964, however, with Zambian independence, it was still apparent that women were not equal partners in religious matters. Widespread spirit possession within Bemba society, which has become incorporated into Bemba Christianity, may be a cultural response to the reduction of the woman's role in the religious sphere.

Bibliography

Hinfelaar, Hugo F. (1994). *Bemba-Speaking Women of Zambia in a Century of Religious Change (1892–1992)*. Leiden: E. J. Brill.

Labrecque, Éd. (1931). "Le marriage chez les babemba." *Africa* 4:209–221.

Richards, Audrey I. (1940). "The Political System of the Bemba Tribe—North-Eastern Rhodesia." In *African Political Systems*, edited by Meyer Fortes and E. E. Evans-Pritchard, 83–120. London: International African Institute.

Richards, Audrey I. (1956). *Chisungu: A Girl's Initiation Ceremony among the Bemba of Northern Rhodesia*. London: Faber & Faber.

Slaski, J. (1950). "Peoples of the Lower Luapula Valley." In *Bemba and Related Peoples of Northern Rhodesia*, by Wilfred Whitely, 77–100. Ethnographic Survey of Africa: East Central Africa: Part 2. London: International African Institute.

Whiteley, Wilfred (1950). *Bemba and Related Peoples of Northern Rhodesia*, 1–32, 70–76. Ethnographic Survey of Africa: East Central Africa, Part 2. London: International African Institute.

Berbers of Morocco

ETHNONYMS: "Imazighen" (sing. Amazigh) since 1980 has come to refer to all North African Berbers, whereas distinct names refer to regional subgroups, almost all territorially discontinuous from each other: Irifiyen (sing. Arifi) refers to the Rifians of northeastern Morocco; Imazighen, again and in its original meaning, to the Berbers of central and southeast-central Morocco; Ishilhayen (sing. Ashilhay), to the Shluh or Swasa (sing. Susi) of southwestern Morocco; Iqbaʾiliyen (sing. Aqbaʾili), to the Kabyles of the Algerian Jurjura; Ishawiyen (sing. Ashawi), to the Shawiya of the Algerian Aurès; Imzabiyen (sing. Amzabi), to the oasis dwellers of the Algerian Mzab; and Imajeghen (sing. Amajegh), to the Ahaggar Tuareg of the southern Algerian Sahara, with similar names for other Tuareg groups in Mali and Niger. In this article, only the three Moroccan regional subgroups will be discussed.

Orientation

Identification. "Berber" refers to any native speaker of a dialect of the Berber language, although many—if not most—Arabic speakers in North Africa are also Berber by descent, even if they have lost the language. Especially in Morocco, "Imazighen" is today the preferred vernacular name for the three main regional subgroups of Berbers themselves, and its feminine form, "Tamazight," refers to their language. In the northern Moroccan Rif, encompassing the provinces of El Hoceima and Nador and part of Taza, major tribal groups include the Aith Waryaghar, Ibuqquyen, Aith ʿAmmarth, Igzinnayen, Thimsaman, Axt Tuzin, Aith Saʿid, Aith Wurishik, and Iqarʿayen. In the larger and properly Imazighen region embracing the Middle Atlas and Central High Atlas chains, the Saghro (pronounced "Saghru") massif, and the Presaharan oasis regions and encompassing parts of Kenitra, Meknes, Fès, and Taza provinces and all of Khenifra, Azilal, Ouarzazate, and Rachidia provinces, major tribal groups include the Zimmur, Ait Ndhir, Ait Yusi, Ait Warayin, Iziyyan, Ait Imyill, Ait Mhand, Ait Massad, Ait Sukhman, Ihansalen, Ait Siddrat, Ait ʿAtta, Ait Murghad, Ait Hadiddu, Ait Izdig, Ait ʿAyyash, and Ait Saghrushshn. In the Ishilhayen region embracing the Western High Atlas, the Sus Valley, and the Anti-Atlas and parts of the Essaouira, Marrakech, and Ouarzazate provinces and all of Agadir, Taroudant, and Tiznit provinces, important tribal groups include the Ihahan, Imtuggan, Iseksawen, Idemsiren, Igundafen, Igedmiwen, Imsfiwen, Iglawn, Ait Wawzgit, Id aw-Zaddagh, Ind aw-Zal, Id aw Zkri, Id aw Zkri, Isaffen, Id aw-Kansus, Isuktan, Id aw-Tanan, Ashtuken, Illalen, Id aw-Ltit, Ammeln, Ait ʿAli, Mjjat, l-Akhsas, Ait Ba ʿAmran, and Ait n-Nuss.

Location. Of the three major Moroccan Berber-speaking areas, the northern Rif runs from roughly 34°30′ to 35°20′ N and from 2°30′ to 4°30′ W; the central region from roughly 29°30′ to 34°00′ N and from 3°30′ to 6°30′ W; and the southwestern region from roughly from 29°30′ to 31°30′ N and from 7°00′ to 10°30′ W. In Morocco, too, all three Berber-speaking areas are essentially mountainous. The highest peak in the Rif chain (actually just west of the Rif proper) is Adrar n-Tidighin, at 2,458 meters. The two highest in the Central and Eastern Atlas are Adrar Mgun and Adrar n-l-ʿAyyashi, at 4,071 meters and 3,737 meters, respectively. The highest peak in the Western Atlas and highest in the country is Adrar n-Tubkal, at 4,165 meters. The Atlas chain forms the backbone of Moroccan geography and orography. The higher mountains are always snow-covered in winter and during the rainy season. Precipitation is irregular, however, and only the higher areas receive more than 100 days' rainfall per year, generally much less. Morocco and Algeria are semiarid countries, and, even in the mountains, summers are hot, with temperatures often reaching more than 30° C. The western part of the Rif chain, inhabited by Arabic-speaking Jbala and not by Rifians, is one of the few parts of the country to receive more than 200 centimeters of rainfall per year. The eastern part—the Rif proper—is much drier and badly deforested. Overpopulation and the infertility of the soil have brought about a long-standing Rifian labor migration. The same is largely true of the Anti-Atlas, another area of strong Berber labor migration. Only the Middle Atlas has considerable agricultural and stock-raising potential. Since Moroccan independence from France in 1956, many Berbers have become urban dwellers as well. Tangier, Tétouan, and Fès have long been urban centers for Rifians, and since 1936 Casablanca has become a major center for the Ishilhayen or Swasa.

Demography. Morocco has never had a census taken along ethnolinguistic lines—and neither has Algeria. At the beginning of the colonial period in 1912, when France annexed Morocco and leased its northern tier, the Rif chain, and the Ifni enclave on the southwest coast to Spain, the population was an estimated 4.5 million, of which an estimated 40 percent was Berber speaking. The remainder speak Arabic, the official language in both countries. As of 1960, Morocco's population was 11.2 million, and by 1972, 15.7 million. By 1993, it had risen to 27 million, as had that of Algeria. Berber was only given nominal recognition as a second language by the authorities in both countries in 1994 and censuses of Berber speakers have pointedly not been taken. In-depth figures can be provided only for the 1960 Moroccan census, which, entirely by interpolation, yielded roughly 903,000 Rifians, 1,573,000 Imazighen, and 1,724,000 Ishilhayen/Swasa, amounting to a total of 4.2 million—or 37.5 percent.

Linguistic Affiliation. "Berber" is primarily a linguistic term and designation; the Berber or Tamazight language belongs to the Hamitic or African Branch of the Hamito-Semitic or Afro-Asiatic Family. Dialects of Berber are spoken here and there all over North Africa, from Morocco to the Siwa oasis in western Egypt and from the Algerian Jurjura to Mali and Niger, but in no case is Berber the national language of any country in which it is spoken. The various dialects (Tharifith or Rifian, Tamazight "Proper" or Central Atlas Highland, and Tashilhit or Southwestern Atlas Highland in Morocco; Taqbaʾilit, Tashawit, and Tamahaq or Ahaggar Tuareg in Algeria; other Tuareg dialects in Burkina Faso, Mali, and Niger; and various oasis dialects from Algeria to western Egypt) are all closely related from grammatical and syntactical standpoints but in no case to the point of total mutual comprehensibility. Many contemporary Berber speakers also know colloquial Arabic, and some even know literary Arabic, French, and Spanish.

History and Cultural Relations

The Berbers are the autochthonous inhabitants of North Africa. The sedentary agricultural tribes are largely old and long established, and certain important tribal names in the Rif may go back almost to the beginnings of Islam in Morocco in the late eighth century. Berber identification with Islam thus goes back itself to the initial Arab conquests in the late seventh century, barring initial resistance and certain resultant heresies. The sedentary Ishilhayen tribes of the Western Atlas are probably also long established, although there is little Arabic documentation on them prior to the early fifteenth century. The transhumant Imazighen tribes of Central Morocco are more recent, although the great northwest passage of Imazighen from the Saghro massif across the Atlas in search of grass for their sheep began about 1550 and was still unfinished when the Franco-Spanish protectorate was established in 1912. Primary resistance to colonial penetration was heaviest in the Berber-speaking areas. In the Rif, it was led by Muhammad bin ʿAbd al-Krim al-Khattabi of the Aith Waryaghar in a major two-front war—first against Spain in 1921, then against both Spain and France in 1925-1926. In the Atlas, although the French won over to their side the three major *quyad* (sing. *qaʾid*), the tribal leaders of the Imtuggan, the Igundafen, and the Iglawn, resistance nonetheless began in 1913 and continued piecemeal, on a tribe-by-tribe basis for the most part, until the Ait ʿAtta of the Saghro and the Ait Murghad and Ait Hadiddu of the eastern Central Atlas were "pacified" in 1933, and the Anti-Atlas was fully occupied the following year.

During this period, the French made the mistake of promulgating the "Berber Dahir," or decree of 1930, which placed all Berber tribes in their zone (although not those of the Spanish-held Rif) under the jural aegis of customary-law tribunals. In effect, this subtracted them from the jurisdiction of the Sharia, of Muslim law as enjoined by the Quran. At Moroccan independence in 1956, the Berber Dahir was rescinded, and normal Muslim law courts under *qudat* (sing. *qadi*) were installed in the Berber-speaking areas. Since about 1986, customary law appears to be coming back in small and low-key ways, but not to the extent of resuscitating collective oaths (see "Social Control").

Settlements

Precolonial settlements varied according to region. In the Rif, local communities (*dshur;* sing. *dshar*) consisted of highly dispersed individual homesteads, one-floored, flat-roofed structures of mud and stone, with rooms formed around a central courtyard. Each was at least 300 meters from the next and housed either a large nuclear family or an extended one of father and married sons or of brothers and their wives and children. Since the 1970s, however, owing to unprecedented labor migration to Western Europe, the Rif has become "urbanized," with apartment-type buildings now studding the countryside. In the Central Atlas, local communities (*timizar;* sing. *tamazirt*) consisted of three or four fortlike structures called *qsur* (Arabic; sing. *qsar*) or *igharman* (Tamazight; sing. *igharm*). Made of adobe and stone, these structures stood three or four stories high. Each had a central courtyard and internal staircases leading to individual rooms of the various nuclear families (*tashat;* pl. *tashatin*) comprising the several patrilineages (*ighsan;* sing. *ighs;* lit., "bone") that constituted the tribal section (*taqbilt;* pl. *tiqbilin*). The igharman were generally named after one of the sections, and these names were usually replicated in other localities. Imazighen who take their sheep on transhumance up into the Atlas in spring live in black goat-hair tents while pasturing them during the summer in special reserves called *igudlan* (sing. *agudal*), which have rigid opening and closing dates and which are usually owned exclusively by the group in question. The Imazighen return to their permanent igharman in the fall for agricultural operations. The villages (*l-mwadaʿ;* sing. *l-mudaʿ*) of the Ishilhayen show features combining the Central Atlas igharman with Rifian-type homesteads in the lower areas and compact Kabyle-type villages in the higher ones. Collective storehouses (*agadir;* pl. *igudar,* but also igharm), still to be found in the Central Atlas, also existed in this area but were abandoned during the colonial period.

Economy

Subsistence and Commercial Activities. Except for the transhumant Imazighen tribes of central Morocco, Berber groups traditionally consisted of sedentary subsistence agriculturalists, although a limited transhumance has been reported for parts of the Western Atlas. In the Rif, a wide variety of crops was grown, albeit on a much lesser scale: in particular, barley and wheat, plus maize and broad beans, supplemented by fig, olive, almond, and walnut trees. *Kif* (*Cannabis sativa*) became a semilegal cash crop on the western fringe of the area only after independence. Almost every family has a cow, a few goats and chickens, and a mule or donkey, as well as the ubiquitous guard dog. Being transhumants, all the Imazighen tribes have sheep, and the southern ones also have camels for transport. For plowing, two cows or a cow and a mule or donkey may be yoked together; lending of individual animals by one farmer to another for plowing or threshing is the norm. Crops grown by the Imazighen and Ishilhayen differ somewhat, but wheat and barley are still staples. Turnips are common in the higher mountains, and, in some areas, apples and potatoes have, since the mid-1980s, become cash crops, which are trucked to Marrakech and elsewhere. Since 1970, however, traditional agriculture, in the Rif in particular, has been disappearing as Moroccans and Algerians have continued to swell the ranks of industrial workers in Europe.

Industrial Arts. In the Rif, important traditional crafts were blacksmithing, pottery, basketry, and utilitarian woodwork such as plow handles and yokes. Blacksmithing was done by members of a totally endogamous, low-status occupational group from one tribe, the Axt Tuzin, which also provided low-status musicians who doubled as mule and donkey breeders. Women made pottery by hand in the Rif, but low-status, endogamous Black men used the pottery wheel in the Atlas (the same group that provided the blacksmiths of southern Morocco). There is strikingly little economic specialization in the region at large, however, and local men do craft work as needed. Only blacksmithing and, in the Imazighen and Ishilhayen areas, pottery making carry occupational stigmata. Silversmithing and packsaddle making, occupations formerly practiced by rural Jews, did as well, but all the latter migrated to Israel shortly after independence.

Trade. All trade in rural North Africa is carried out in the *suq* (market), found in almost every tribal territory of sufficient size and named both for the day of the week on which it is held and for the tribe in whose land it is located. Large tribes, like the Aith Waryaghar of the Rif (who are unique in North Africa for having special women's markets, without economic value, which are forbidden to men), may have several markets held on different days and in different tribal sections, whereas in the Imazighen region markets are often located not in the centers of tribal territories but on their fringes, as among the Ait ʿAtta. Local and European goods could be bought or sold at most markets during the colonial period, when markets also became effective centers of tribal control by the colonial power. Since the postindependence upsurge of labor migration to Europe, however, many Rifian markets have now become full-fledged urban centers where, even in the 1960s, such items as transistor radios were readily available, since replaced by color televisions.

Division of Labor. In precolonial times, feuding and warfare were everywhere male occupations, as is true today of agriculture, driving animals, and, very occasionally, hunting. Women do all the housework (except for making tea for guests, a male occupation) and perform two agricultural tasks: helping the men with the harvest and taking newly cut grain in baskets to the threshing floor. Men build the houses but women whitewash the walls and blacken and smooth the floors, bring in manure to the collective manure pile, milk the animals, and fetch water and firewood. Poultry and rabbits are also exclusively female concerns. Marketing was traditionally a man's job, but, even in colonial times, poorer and older women could be seen vending at market stalls, and today women are as numerous in the markets as are men. Smaller boys and girls both herded goats on the slopes, and girls tended younger children. At home the sex division of labor has remained much as it was traditionally, but both sexes have become exposed to more varied occupational opportunities. Greater emphasis on schooling has made small boys especially less available for household chores.

Land Tenure. Agricultural land is traditionally inherited patrilaterally throughout Morocco, but whether or not it is divided up among sons on their father's death or remains in indivision is a question that, in most cases, must be resolved on the spot. As land in the Rif is a scarce resource, Rifians tend always to divide it; conflicts and feuds over landownership were inherent in their social structure, whereas transhumant Imazighen were more inclined to remain in indivision. Land closest to settlements is, in all areas, generally used for agricultural purposes, with or without irrigation; land farther away is used for grazing and tends to be held by the community in indivision. In addition, a very few communities in the Rif, and probably in the Anti-Atlas, have some *habus* land, donated by individuals to the local mosque or pious foundation for religious or charitable purposes, although this last is much more an urban than a rural phenomenon.

Kinship

Kin Groups and Descent. Everywhere in North Africa except among some of the Tuareg groups of the Central Sahara, descent is patrilineal, and residence is patrilocal. The fundamental unit of Berber social organization is the patrilineage (*dharfiqth* [pl. *dharfiqin*]; in the Rif, ighs among the Imazighen and *afus* [lit. "hand"; pl. *ifassen*] among the Ishilhayen), which is seldom more than four to six generations in depth in the Rif and only four in the Atlas, where, however, it is corporate in character, unlike the Rifian lineage (see "Conflict"). Exogamy or endogamy is a matter of choice and circumstance: Rifians favor the former and Imazighen the latter, where possible.

Kinship Terminology. Both Arabic and most Berber kinship terminologies (those of the Tuareg apart) are, as they stand, "Sudanese," in Murdock's terminology; however, Rifians, Ishilhayen, and Algerian Kabyles all have the classificatory term *ayyaw* (fem. *dhayyawxth*), meaning variously "father's sister's child," "sister's child," "daughter's child," and, asymmetrically, "son's child," and its existence thus turns these kinship systems from "Normal Sudanese" into "Modified Omaha." As for terms of address, all close kin, whether patrilateral or matrilateral, are addressed either by the appropriate kin term or by name, or, especially if in an ascending generation, by the kin term plus the name. The same holds generally true for known elders of any sort in terms of their kinship distance from the speaker.

Marriage and Family

Marriage. In the Rif, unlike the practice in certain other Berber-speaking areas, parallel-cousin marriage with the father's brother's daughter was permitted, although not highly regarded. These marriages accounted for 12 percent of a total of 1,625 marriages recorded between 1953 and 1955 among the Aith Waryaghar (3 percent true father's brother's daughter marriages and 9 percent classificatory—that is, not with true father's brother's daughter, but within the lineage). By far the most common form was local-lineage exogamy—marriages between lineages within the same tribal section—at 54 percent, whereas marriages between spouses of different sections accounted for 22 percent, and marriages with spouses of other tribes (both male and female) amounted again to 12 percent. Polygynous marriages accounted for 11 percent of the total (with each co-wife having her separate dwelling or household), secondary or successive marriages for 5 percent, and 3 percent of marriages terminated in divorce. There was a high rate of widow inheritance (as opposed to levirate) at 5 percent, but sororate, although permitted, accounted for only 0.8 percent. Marriage by exchange of sisters accounted for 2.5 percent, as did two brothers marrying two sisters; 20 percent of all marriages—whether endogamous or exogamous—were between individuals of different generations, even though they may have been of nearly equivalent ages (Hart 1976, 217–229).

Among the Imazighen of south-central Morocco, parallel-cousin marriage with the father's brother's daughter is strongly favored, but among the Ait ʿAtta of Usikis on the south-central slope of the Atlas, it accounted for only 17 percent of 313 marriages recorded between 1961 and 1962 (of which only 3 percent were with true father's brother's daughter and 14 percent were with the classificatory father's brother's daughter, within the lineage). Lineage exogamy within the section accounted for 42 percent, intersectional marriages within the community of Usikis for 39 percent, and extracommunity or extratribal marriages for only 2 percent. Plural marriages accounted for 9 percent of the total, secondary or successive ones for 4 percent. Three percent of marriages ended in divorce; the rate of widow inheritance was 3 percent and that of the sororate only 1 percent. Of all marriages, endogamous or exogamous, 10 percent were cross-generational (Hart 1981, 148–151, 251–253).

Bride-wealth or bride-price is heavy in the Rif but minimal in the Imazighen region. Normally only a husband can initiate divorce (except in cases of impotency). Bride-wealth is generally returned in such cases, but children remain with their fathers. Childlessness is a normal cause for divorce.

Domestic Unit. The nuclear family (Rifian: *nubth* [lit., "turn"; pl. *nubath*]; Tharifith: *tashat* [lit., "hearth"]) of father, mother, and unmarried children constitutes the domestic unit, all of whose members eat together when guests are not present, but—owing to the prevalence of male labor migration to Europe—women are now often de facto heads of rural households.

Inheritance. Land is inherited patrilaterally (see "Land Tenure"). Although the Sharia stipulates that, for purposes of inheritance, one son equals two daughters, with one-eighth subtracted at a man's death for his widow, in areas like the Imazighen region, where customary law prevailed until independence, daughters generally got nothing and tended rather to be inherited by their fathers' brothers, in order to be married off to the latters' sons.

Socialization. Under maternal and grandparental supervision, all Berber communities are characterized by a high degree of sibling caretaking, with elder siblings taking care of younger ones while their mothers do household work. Grandparents and grandchildren are close, but sex segregation begins when boys and girls reach 6 or 7 years of age and start to herd goats. By the time they reach puberty, which traditionally is not long before the age to marry, it is fully ingrained.

Sociopolitical Organization

Social Organization. The agnatic lineage or patrilineage (Rifian: dharfiqth; Imazighen: ighs; Ishilhayen: afus) was, until after Moroccan independence from France and Spain in 1956, the basic social unit, with a depth of four to six generations in the Rif and of only four among the Imazighen (see "Kin Groups and Descent"). Among the latter, however, it was corporate in character, which was not, or not always, the case in the Rif. In the latter half of the twentieth century and particularly since the 1970s as a result of labor migration, the patrilineage has been overshadowed in importance by the nuclear family. Above the patrilineage is the local community, and above this the tribal section (Rifian: *rbaʿ or khums*, Imazighen/Ishilhayen: taqbilt), and finally the tribe itself. Within certain Moroccan tribes in precolonial times, sections were grouped together to form five primary units or "fifths" (*khamsa khmas*)—as among the Aith Waryaghar of the Rif and the Ait ʿAtta of the Saghro and Central Atlas—which might differ widely from each other in terms of function; however, except in southern Morocco and the Presaharan oases, there is no formal hierarchy, and indeed among Berber lay tribesmen everywhere there has always been a fierce egalitarianism. In the south, holy lineages descended from the Prophet Mohammed (very numerous in Morocco, even among Berbers) form a top stratum. The mass of lay and illiterate White Berber tribespeople form the middle stratum, and the many residential clusters (or qsur) of *haratin*—sedentary Black date-palm cultivators, some of whom stand traditionally in a clientage relationship to specific Berber tribal sections—form the bottom one. This precolonial social stratification, however, is today turning into a class system based mainly on wealth and economic considerations.

Political Organization. In the precolonial Rif, the highest unit of political integration was the tribe (*dhaqbitsh*, which like "taqbilt" is derived from Arabic *qabila*), although as a unit it was invoked far less often than the section (rbaʿ or khums). A three-tiered system of representative councils (*aitharbiʿin*, *agraw*), for the community, the section, and the tribe, respectively, was convoked as needed and generally met in the suq in any case. The councillors (Rifian: *imgharen;* sing. *amghar*) were always tribal notables. As of the late nineteenth century, the choice of top tribal quyad, although generally ratified by sultanic decree, tended to confirm local strongmen in their positions. Among the Imazighen tribes, annual elections for chiefs at the tribal, sectional, and community levels were held in spring through rotation and complementarity of participant sections. Each year, it was the turn of one of the sections to provide the chief; its members sat apart, and members of the other sections selected the chief from among them. The chief's badge of office was a blade of grass that the electors placed in his turban. Among the Ait ʿAtta, this procedure took place, until final "pacification" by the French in 1933, at the tribal capital and supreme court seat of Igharm Amazdar, in the Saghro. Given the egalitarian ideology, the top chief, or *amghar n-ufilla,* like the lesser chiefs, had little power and could be removed from office before his year was up if he were deemed unfit in any way, or if the year in question had been a bad or calamitous one. Conversely, if he were an able leader during war and if under his term of office the harvest had been good and the sheep had grown fat, he was likely to stay on for another year, or even longer. Today tribes have been nominally eradicated administratively, and the tribal sections have given way to the rural commune, but the communal councils are still elected and representative bodies that meet every week in the markets to deliberate on local issues.

Social Control. In the Rif and elsewhere, the sectional council was competent to handle most misdemeanors, such as theft or land disputes, but woundings and murders generally fell under the competence of the tribal council (*aitharbiʿin n-tqbitsh*). Prohibitively heavy fines (*haqq;* lit., "truth, right") were imposed by the council members on anyone who committed a murder in the market or on any path leading to or from it on market day, the day before it, and the day after it. In all Berber areas, especially among the Imazighen, the most effective and drastic form of sociopolitical control was the collective oath (Tamazight: *tagallit*), in which a man accused of any crime had to attest his innocence backed up by his agnates. One did this in front of a saint's shrine, with the number of agnates, as his cojurors, varying with the gravity of the offense. Supernatural sanctions of death or blindness in the event of perjury acted as a powerful incentive against swearing falsely. Although bin ʿAbd al-Krim decollectivized Rifian oaths in 1922, they persisted in the Atlas until the end of the colonial period, with the rescinding of the Berber Dahir. By colonial times (after the Rifians were defeated in 1926), vengeance killings became far less common than they had been prior to 1921; these cases were handled by the courts of the protecting power. The qaʾid's tribunal heard lesser cases and the qudat were concerned with torts. Since about 1986, customary law, now under the aegis of local specialists, has been reintroduced in embryonic form in most Moroccan Berber tribal areas, and this development is evidently looked upon with favor by the tribes in question.

Conflict. In the precolonial Rif in particular, both blood feuds (between lineage groups) and vendettas (within lineages, and generally between brothers and their sons) were endemic. Among the Aith Waryaghar, the latter outnumbered the former by about two to one: of the 193 conflicts recorded by Hart (1994) for the period from approximately 1880 to 1921, 122 were vendettas as opposed to only 71 feuds, indicating the lack of a corporate base in the Rifian lineage. Alliance networks, called *lfuf* (sing. *liff*), conceived as equal in size but usually not so in fact, either embraced whole tribal sections or cleaved them in two, but essentially they did not extend beyond individual tribal borders. However, given the emphasis on corporate lineages in the Imazighen, and possibly the Ishilhayen regions as well, the emphasis here was on feud. Feuding was partially responsible for a degree of dispersal of individuals, given the fact that it was customary for a murderer, with or without his coresponsible agnatic kinsmen, to flee from home and seek exile in another tribe. In all regions, however, the resolution of conflicts between groups was the work of *imrabdhen* (sing. *amrabit*) or *igurramen* (sing. *agurram*), members of holy and generally charismatic lineages descended from the Prophet; conflict mediation between lay tribesmen was part of their stock-in-trade.

Religion and Expressive Culture

Religious Beliefs. All Moroccans, whether Berbers or Arabs, are Sunni (i.e., orthodox and mainstream) Muslims of the Maliki rite, which predominates in North Africa. Their beliefs are exactly the same as those of Sunni Muslims elsewhere. It should be noted, however, that Islam in rural North Africa has traditionally placed a strong emphasis on *baraka* (lit., "blessing"), the charisma and miracle-working abilities of *shurfa*ʾ (sing. *sharif*), descendants of the Prophet, whose shrines dot the countryside and whose living representatives have traditionally been mediators of conflicts between lineages or sections of lay Berber tribesmen.

Religious Practitioners. In Islam, there is, in theory, no intermediary between man and God, but every Moroccan rural community, whether Berber or Arab, has its *fqih* or schoolmaster, who teaches the boys to recite the Quran. The fqih, who is contracted by the community on an annual basis, leads the prayers in the mosque and gives the Friday sermon. He also writes charms (from Quranic verses) with a view to curing diseases, although any elements of witchcraft and sorcery that do not involve the use of (Arabic) writing are generally the preserve of women.

Ceremonies. The major ceremonies in the individual life cycle are birth, marriage, and death, with the first haircut and circumcision as additional rites for small boys. Circumcision, although not specifically mentioned in the Quran, is nonetheless practiced by all Muslims. Rifians perform it when boys reach 2 years of age, whereas the Imazighen tend to wait until boys are 5 or 6—they are told by their elders to bear it bravely. There is no female circumcision. The marriage ceremony is the most important, lengthy, and elaborate ritual for both sexes. In addition, everyone observes the normal Muslim religious festivals of the lunar year. During the first ten days of the first month, the ʿAshura is celebrated; in Morocco, children are invariably given toys and other presents at this time of year. The month-long fast of Ramadan, in the ninth month, is followed immediately by the ʿAyd al-Saghir or Small Feast to break the fast. The ʿAyd al-Kabir or Great Feast, when every householder must sacrifice a sheep, occurs in the last month of the year and coincides with the hajj, the pilgrimage to Mecca.

Arts. The only specialized arts among Berbers are performed by women and consist, among Rifians, of pottery decoration and, among Imazighen in the Middle Atlas, of rug weaving.

Medicine. Traditional healers continue to flourish, but today hospitals and clinics are also much in use.

Death and Afterlife. Death may be attributed either to natural or supernatural causes, and every community has its cemetery. If the deceased is a man, his body is washed and enshrouded by the fqih, and if a woman, by another woman. Anyone who dies in the morning is buried the same afternoon and anyone who dies at night is buried the following morning, in a hole that must be only a spread handspan plus an extra half-thumb length in width. Of overriding importance in the orientation of an Islamic grave is the *qibla,* the direction of Mecca. In Morocco, the body is therefore placed in the grave more or less on its right side, with its face turned toward Mecca, while the fqih intones an appropriate chapter of the Quran. Only men attend funerals, and among the Imazighen the kinsmen of the deceased give a feast seven days after the death for those who mourned at the burial. In the Rif, a widow gives a feast forty days after her husband's death, which theoretically marks the end of the mourning period. Ideally, it should also correspond to the obligatory ʿ*idda,* or three-month period between widowhood, or divorce, and remarriage, in order to determine paternity in case of pregnancy. Anyone who dies during Ramadan will go to paradise immediately, far faster than at any other time of year. The Quran is quite specific on the subject both of paradise, *ajinna,* and of hell, *jahannama;* it also teaches that two invisible recording angels sit on everyone's shoulders, one recording good deeds, the other bad ones.

Bibliography

Bourdieu, Pierre (1962). *The Algerians*. Translated by Alan C. M. Ross. Boston: Beacon Press.

Bousquet, Georges-Henri (1961). *Les berbères*. Que Sais-Je? no. 718. Paris: Presses Universitaires de France. Originally published in 1957.

Chiapuris, John (1979). *The Ait Ayash of the High Moulouya Plain: Rural Social Organization in Morocco*. University of Michigan Museum of Anthropology, Anthropological Papers, no. 69. Ann Arbor: University of Michigan Press.

Gellner, Ernest (1969). *Saints of the Atlas*. London: Weidenfeld & Nicholson.

Gellner, Ernest, and Charles Micaud, eds. (1973). *Arabs and Berbers: From Tribe to Nation in North Africa*. London: Duckworth.

Hart, David M. (1976). *The Aith Waryaghar of the Moroccan Rif: An Ethnography and History*. Viking Fund Publications in Anthropology, no. 55. Tucson: University of Arizona Press.

Hart, David M. (1981). *Dadda ʿAtta and His Forty Grandsons: The Socio-Political Organisation of the Ait ʿAtta of Southern Morocco*. Wisbech, Cambridgeshire: MENAS Press.

Hart, David M. (1984a). *The Ait 'Atta of Southern Morocco: Daily Life and Recent History*. Wisbech, Cambridgeshire: MENAS Press.

Hart, David M. (1984b). "Segmentary Systems and the Role of 'Five Fifths' in Tribal Morocco." In *Islam in Tribal Societies: From the Atlas to the Indus*, edited by Akbar S. Ahmed and David M. Hart, 66–105. London: Routledge & Kegan Paul. Originally published in 1967.

Hart, David M. (1989). "Rejoinder to Henry Munson, Jr.: 'On the Irrelevance of the Segmentary Model in the Moroccan Rif.'" *American Anthropologist* 91:765–769.

Hart, David M. (1992). "Tradicion, continuidad y modernidad en el derecho consuetudinario islamico: Ejemplos del marruecos bereber y de las agencias tribales pujtunes de Pakistan." In *Amazigh-Tamazight: Debate Abierto*, edited by Vicente Moga Romero, 133–150. Aldaba, no. 19. Melilla: Universidad Nacional de Educacion a Distancia (UNED).

Hart, David M. (1993). "Four Centuries of History on the Hoof: The Northwest Passage of Berber Sheep Transhumants across the Moroccan Atlas, 1550–1912." *Morocco: Journal of the Society for Moroccan Studies* 3:21–55.

Hart, David M. (1994). "Conflits extérieurs et vendettas dans le Djurdjura algérien et le Rif marocain." *Awal: Cahiers d'Études Berbères* 11:95–122.

Hart, David M. (1995). *Traditional Society and the Feud in the Moroccan Rif*. Wisbech, Cambridgeshire: MENAS Press; Rabat: Faculté des Lettres et des Sciences Humaines, Université Mohammed V. In press.

Hart, David M., ed. and trans. (1975). *Emilio Blanco Izaga: Colonel in the Rif*. 2 vols. Ethnography Series, HRAFlex Books, MX3–001. New Haven: Human Relations Area Files.

Kraus, Wolfgang (1991). *Die Ayt Hdiddu: Wirtschaft und Gesellschaft im zentralen Hohen Atlas*. Oesterreichische Akademie der Wissenschaften, Philosophisch-Historische Klasse, Sitzungsberichte, 574. Band, Veroeffentlichungen der ethnologischen Kommission, Bd. 7. Vienna: Verlag der oesterreichischen Akademie der Wissenschaften.

Montagne, Robert (1930). *Les berbères et le Makhzen dans le sud du Maroc: Essai sur la transformation politique des Berbères sedentaires (groupe Chleuh)*. Paris: Félix Alcan.

Montagne, Robert (1973). *The Berbers: Their Social and Political Organisation*. Translated by David Seddon. London: Frank Cass. Originally published in French in 1931.

Murdock, George Peter (1960). *Social Structure*. New York: Macmillan. Originally published in 1949.

Neumann, Wolfgang (1987). *Die Berber: Vielfalt und Einheit einer alten nordafrikanischen Kultur*. Cologne: DuMont Verlag. Originally published in 1983.

Raha Ahmed, Rachid, ed. (1994). *Imazighen del Magreb entre Occidente y Oriente: Introduccion a los bereberes*. Granada: Copisteria La Gioconda.

Royaume du Maroc, Ministère de l'Économie Nationale, Division de la Coordination Économique et du Plan (1962). *Population rurale du Maroc: Recensement démographique (juin 1960)*. Rabat: Service Central des Statistiques.

Vinogradov, Amal Rassam (1974). *The Ait Ndhir of Morocco: A Study of the Social Transformation of a Berber Tribe*. University of Michigan Museum of Anthropology, Anthropological Papers, no. 55. Ann Arbor: University of Michigan Press.

Waterbury, John (1972). *North for the Trade: The Life and Times of a Berber Merchant*. Berkeley, Los Angeles, and London: University of California Press.

DAVID M. HART

Betsileo

ETHNONYMS: The main political units in what is now Betsileo territory, prior to its conquest in 1830 by the Merina, northern neighbors of the Betsileo, were Lalangina (east), Isandra (west), and the various statelets and chiefdoms of Arindrano (south). The ethnic label "Betsileo" is a product of Merina conquest; it does not appear on a list of Malagasy societies published by Étienne de Flacourt in 1661. The term "Arindrano" (Eringdranes) was in use by the mid-seventeenth century, according to French explorers.

Orientation

Identification. The Betsileo (Bts) are one of approximately twenty "ethnies," or ethnic units, into which Madagascar divides its population. The Betsileo began to use that term for themselves after their conquest by the Merina in the nineteenth century. Around 1830, their ancestors were incorporated as Betsileo Province, the sixth major subdivision of the Merina Empire, which conquered much of Madagascar. Before that date, several statelets and chiefdoms administered what is now the Betsileo homeland. The most prominent of those polities were Lalangina in the east and Isandra in the west.

Like other Malagasy, the Betsileo routinely use the words *fomba* (culture, customs) and *fomban-drazana* (ancestral ways of doing things) in discussing their culture and indicating its traditional nature and distinctiveness. "Tanin-drazana" (the land of the ancestors) is the word for "homeland."

Location. The most elevated part of Madagascar's central highlands (sometimes called the "high plateau"), comprising the homelands of the Merina (Imerina) and the Betsileo, extends some 600 kilometers from north to south (roughly between 18° and 22° S), with a maximum width of 200 kilometers. The Betsileo homeland spans approximately 40,000 square kilometers of the southern half of that area. One officially leaves southern Imerina and enters Betsileo country by crossing the Mania River, located at 20° S. The Betsileo capital is the city of Fianarantsoa. Besides the Merina to the north, the Betsileo's immediate neighbors are the Tanala to the east, the Bara to the south and southwest, and the Sakalava to the west and northwest.

Demography. The Betsileo population—408,000 in 1900 and 737,000 in 1964—stands around 1.5 million in the mid-1990s. Supported by a productive rice-based economy and a diversified diet, the Betsileo rate of population increase, well above 3 percent per year, is one of the highest in Madagascar. As population has increased, Betsileo have migrated widely to other parts of Madagascar, including the extreme north.

Linguistic Affiliation. The Betsileo share with other Malagasy a linguistic and cultural descent from the Proto-Malagasy, a mixed African-Indonesian population that began to settle the island between 2,000 and 1,500 years ago. The Proto-Malagasy were most probably an oceangoing population who participated in a vast Indian Ocean trade network that tied Indonesia to points east and west. To the west, the Proto-Malagasy traveled along the Indian, Arabian, and East African shorelines, eventually reaching Madagascar, where the most ancient settlements have been found in the north, dating to around A.D. 500. A hybrid gene pool has been enriched over the centuries as Malagasy populations, especially on the coasts, have remained in an exchange system linking them to East Africa and even Arabia. This has led to the tremendous diversity in physical types observed among present-day Malagasy, including the Betsileo.

Malagasy languages and dialects are more closely interrelated than are the Romance languages derived from Latin. All of the former descend from Proto-Malagasy, a member of the Western Indonesian Subgroup of the Malayo-Polynesian Language Family. The closest linguistic relatives of the Malagasy languages are spoken in southeastern Borneo; they include Maanyan and other languages and dialects in the Barito area.

The Proto-Malagasy soon differentiated into three groups, one in the north, one in the west and south, and the third—which includes the Betsileo—in the eastern and central parts of the island. There was a later split between east and central (Betsileo, Merina, Bezanozano, Sihanaka) subgroups. Merina (also known as Malagasy, the national language) is the closest linguistic relative of the Betsileo dialect; northern Betsileo is as closely related to Merina speech as it is to southern Betsileo speech.

Settlements

The Betsileo live in hamlets, which surround villages. From north to south, the major administrative centers are Ambositra (northern Betsileo), Ambohimahasoa and Fianarantsoa (central Betsileo), and Ambalavao (southern Betsileo). Smaller towns, also with administrative and market functions, stand between these small cities and the village level. There is no standard size for Betsileo villages, which range from seventy-five to several hundred inhabitants. The usual rural settlement pattern is one of villages and hamlets located on high ground above valleys where rice is cultivated. Streams and rivers flow through these valleys, providing water and alluvial soils from rainy-season flooding, and, once canals have been constructed, water for irrigation of many of the rice fields. There is often a striking visual contrast between the bareness of a village, the houses and red ground of which stand out in the absence of trees, and the vivid colors of the vegetation below—the rice in the valleys and terraces and the secondary crops growing between the village and the rice fields. More rarely, settlements are located high in the hills above or below elaborate spring-fed rice terraces. Even more mountainous sites, atop massive granitic outcrops, were occupied in the past for purposes of defense.

Economy

Subsistence and Commercial Activities. The Betsileo are peasants—agriculturists in a state-organized society. They grow rice, their preferred and staple food, on permanent plots that are cultivated with a single annual rice crop from year to year. Some fields are irrigated; others are rainfall-dependent. The irrigated fields may be transplanted in October; the others depend on the advent of November rains. Humped zebu cattle are essential to agriculture as most Betsileo practice it. Their dung, collected in stone semisubterranean corrals, is used as fertilizer. The cattle are attached to carts and used to pull plows and harrows, as well as to trample flooded fields after they have been plowed and tilled. There has been a historic shift from cattle (pastoralism) toward rice (intensive agriculture) throughout the Betsileo homeland, a trend that is most evident in the north and east. In the south and west especially, some Betsileo still breed and raise cattle, but most buy them in markets. Cattle are used to store wealth, as a means of production in the rice economy, and for ceremonial slaughter.

The Betsileo supplement a diet of rice and beef with other livestock (pigs, chickens, ducks, geese, guinea fowl, turkeys; formerly goats and sheep) and many secondary crops: sweet manioc, sweet potatoes, white potatoes, taro, beans, cape peas, peanuts, maize, greens, tomatoes, onions, and bananas. Tobacco is grown as a cash crop. The Betsileo grow their own coffee and have many fruit trees, both tropical (e.g., mango, guava, passion fruit) and temperate (orange, lime, peach, plum, apricot). Occasional fishing is done in streams and rivers; eels are prized.

Industrial Arts. Houses are made of varied materials, including wattle and daub, bricks, and wood. The best houses are painted or whitewashed and have two or three stories, four to six rooms, tile roofs, and at least some brick or wood. The poorest houses have a single story with one or two rooms; their frames are wattle and daub and their roofs are composed of long grass collected on hillsides near the village. Works in stone dot the Betsileo landscape. These include monoliths raised to commemorate particular events, memorials of people who have died outside their homeland, and family tombs. The most common tomb is a rectangular semisubterranean structure rising about a meter above ground level. The Betsileo hire Merina masons to build their tombs. Modern tombs are of cement; more traditional structures are of small stones, like those used in the cattle corral. Along two or three walls inside the tomb are the beds (between six and nine) where the ancestors are deposited.

Trade. Coastal and interior Malagasy, including the Betsileo, have been linked for centuries through trade (including the slave trade), migration, raiding, and other kinds of contact and exchange. During the seventeenth century, southern highlanders were gradually exposed to various effects of the presence of European traders on the coasts. The emergence of the Sakalava as west coast subsidiaries of the Europeans eventually affected the highlands, as the Sakalava and other western-southern groups sought booty for trade through raiding. Europeans appear to have begun to exchange firearms with coastal Malagasy around 1660 to 1670 (Kent 1970); several decades were to elapse before firearms, exchanged for slaves, reached the Betsileo heartland. During the eighteenth century, muskets, bullets, and gunpowder became standard exchange items for cattle and slaves.

Market towns have a long tradition in central Madagascar, dating at least from the nineteenth century. Today varied products and produce, including beef and bread, are sold at weekly markets held throughout Betsileo country. Market towns hold market on the same day each week, and a given village usually has access to at least two such market towns. Ambalavao, in southern Betsileo country, has one of Madagascar's largest cattle markets. Cattle are taken there from the pastoral south and west (often by members of other ethnic groups, such as Bara and Antandroy) and are bought and taken as far north as Imerina.

Division of Labor. On average, the Betsileo expend about 1,700 hours of human labor annually to farm one hectare of rice land, and about 1,400 hours for the average household rice holding. A division of labor by age and gender is marked in the cultivation and preparation of rice. Before transplanting, an activity performed by women, takes place, fields are flooded. Young men drive cattle through the flooded field and excite them to a frenzy, and, as the cattle trample the field, they produce a mud of even consistency in which rice seedlings are transplanted. Armed with the characteristic *angady,* a long-handled spade (used also in bund cleaning and the maintenance of irrigation ditches), older men then arrive to break up clumps of earth the cattle have missed. At harvest time, men cut the rice, which women carry to the threshing floor, where they stack it. Older men and women stand on the stacked paddy stalks, stomping so as to compact the pile. After the paddy has dried, younger men thresh, against rocks, and older men use a stick to beat the paddy stalks to remove the remaining grain. All household members work together at winnowing and transport to the granary (as they do in weeding, the most arduous task in rice cultivation). Each day, women use mortars and pestles to pound the rice to remove the husks, and they cook and serve meals. Young boys and old men are the usual cattle guardians. Women tend other animals, especially fowl. The Betsileo lack pronounced gender stratification. Both men and women have been rulers. The Betsileo mention both in their genealogies and ancestral rites. Men and women of various ages sell produce in the marketplace and keep the cash they receive.

Land Tenure. Associated with localized corporate descent groups are estates consisting of tombs, houses, rice fields, water rights, woods (sometimes), and land used to graze cattle and cultivate secondary crops. The original settlers of an area are considered the owners or caretakers of the land. Later immigrants have obtained land through purchase, grants, and government distribution programs. Land may be sold and registered in an individual's name, but in areas where corporate descent remains strong, individuals are discouraged from selling land to nonrelatives. Legal disputes over access to land are common. Status differences are evident in landownership and house type. Older men, who control land, labor, and other strategic resources, also have the most elaborate homes.

Kinship

Kin Groups and Descent. Betsileo kinship and descent is ambilineal (optative, nonexclusive), with a strong patrilineal bias. Most marriages are (patri)virilocal. A Betsileo is simultaneously a member of several descent groups. One is the local descent group, with whom a man resides and cultivates his main rice field, usually from his father's or father's father's estate, although fields may also be inherited through the mother. After marriage, a woman retains membership in the local descent group of her origin. When she dies, a delegation from her village will ask that she be buried in her ancestral tomb there. Such a request is usually denied, and she is buried in her husband's family tomb.

Aside from one's primary membership in a mostly patrilineal local descent group, a Betsileo (man or woman) also belongs to several totally ambilineal tomb-focused descent groups. People have the right to be buried in any tomb in which they have an ancestor. This can (in theory, but rarely in practice) extend back to eight great-grandparents. Betsileo maintain their membership in tomb groups by contributing to their construction costs and upkeep. Despite ambilineal rights, the social organization of the dead people in the tombs is patrilineally skewed because most people are buried in the tomb of their local descent group.

Descent groups are named; many are supralocal, with branches in several villages. The more prominent ones span regions and ancient political divisions. Some villages have a single named descent group; others have two or more. Each local descent group has its own tomb. Sometimes the coresidence of multiple descent groups in the same village is a continuation of phratry organization of the past, when three to five local descent groups banded together for defense or were united in the same political division (perhaps as an advisory council for a chief). In some villages (especially among recent migrants or descendants of slaves) descent is unimportant as an organizing principle.

In a 1966–1967 survey, 998 named descent groups were identified in the Betsileo homeland, spanning 1,300 settlements (Kottak 1980). About half of them existed only as local descent groups, confined to a single village. Another 154 spanned just two villages, whereas 244 were present in between 3 and 9 villages. Only 83 (less than 10 percent of the total) appeared as local descent groups in 10 or more villages. Just 16 named descent groups spanned 50 or more of the villages in the sample, with the largest and most geographically dispersed located in 183 villages. The larger and more expansive groups are those that have played major historic roles, as nobles and senior commoners (see "Social Organization"). The smaller groups include junior commoners, migrants, and descendants of slaves.

The Betsileo use fictive kinship rituals (e.g., that establishing blood siblinghood, *vaki-ra*) to convert nonkin (including people from other ethnic groups, such as the Bara) into structural analogues of blood relatives. Fosterage (usually of relatives) is common; adoption (of nonrelatives) is allowed but rare.

Kinship Terminology. The Betsileo use generational terminology for the parental generation and Hawaiian terminology for Ego's generation. Siblings' children and own children are called by the same term (*zanaka*), as are children of the grandchild generation (*zafy*). Kin terms recognize age differences among siblings, distinguishing between older (*zoky*) and younger (*zandry*). The cross-parallel distinction, which does not show up in cousin terminology, is, however, implicit in the terms that brothers and sisters use for their siblings of the same and other gender. *Raha-* means "same," and *ana-* denotes "difference"; *lahy* means "male" and *vavy*, "female." Thus men refer to their brothers as *rahalahy* (same, male), and women refer to their sisters as *rahavavy* (same, female). Men's sisters are *anabavy* (different, female) and women's brothers are *anadahy* (different, male).

The Betsileo use teknonymy. Many parents change their name when a child (usually the first) is born. The terms for father and mother are *ray* and *reny*. If the child is named "Talata" (born on Tuesday), the father and mother will become "Rainitalata" (Tuesday's father) and "Renitalata" (Tuesday's mother), respectively.

Marriage and Family

Marriage. When Betsileo marry, a steer (*vodiondry;* lit., sheep's rump) is traditionally given by the family of the groom to the family of the bride. Preferentially and usually, postmarital residence is patrivirilocal, but the couple may reside in the wife's village if land is more abundant or if men are scarce. Since French conquest, marriages have been registered with the government. In the past, polygyny was associated with wealth and political status. Wives usually resided in different settlements; men with multiple rice fields often maintained wives and family households in each location. Marriages are arranged and may be with cousins, except that marriage is tabooed for the children of sisters. There are few first-cousin marriages, which the Betsileo believe lead to impaired fertility and hereditary maladies. Marriage is permitted between members of different local branches of the same named descent group. Older women play a key role in arranging marriages. There are cases of infant betrothal; husbands are usually a few years older than their wives. Trial marriages are common, and couples may begin living together as teenagers. Frequently, a marriage is formalized only after the woman becomes pregnant. By custom, the first child is supposed to be born in its mother's village, where the husband does brief bride-service. The marriage is formalized when a party from the husband's village goes to the wife's village to bring her and the child back to his village, where they reside virilocally. Divorce is permitted, but uncommon. Status considerations are important in arranging a good marriage, and there is a tendency toward stratum endogamy (see "Social Organization").

Domestic Unit. There is no standard or ideal Betsileo household. Nuclear families occupy, on average, 40 to 45 percent of the households in a village. Expanded-family households are common in wealthier villages. Older people, who tend to head such households, control the larger fields and can support more people, including adult children, grandchildren, and foster children. Single-person and couple households tend to be found more often in poorer villages. Households go through a developmental cycle; those that begin with nuclear families often become expanded or couple households, depending on wealth and kin networks. Ultimogeniture governs the inheritance of houses. The youngest child tends to remain in the parental household longest and stay on after the death of one or both parents.

Inheritance. Most men eventually inherit (part of) their father's estate, but Betsileo may also cultivate fields inherited through the mother. The disposition of land and other resources is subject to national law, but most estates are cultivated and passed on in accordance with tradition. When an old man dies, his oldest son customarily allocates the estate among himself and his brothers, usually taking the most productive field for himself. Because a women is expected to have the benefits of her husband's estate, she generally receives no rice fields of her own; however, husbands and sons of such a woman are sometimes allowed to cultivate her ancestral estate (and reside with or join her local descent group) if need is great, or if her father has few male heirs, or none. The inheritance rights transmitted through women are guaranteed in national law and can be enforced legally when kin become enmeshed in a legal dispute.

Socialization. Enculturation is an informal process that goes on in the community rather than principally in the parental household. Besides parents, grandparents, aunts, uncles, and siblings are important socializing agents. It is common for a child to be fostered by an aunt, uncle, or grandparent for several years. Discipline of children is neither marked nor severe. For generations, education has been highly valued, and most boys and girls study through primary school. Under the French, and continuing for several years after independence, many Betsileo children learned both French and Malagasy languages. As a result of nationalization programs of the 1970s and 1980s, French instruction lagged. It is not unusual today for high school graduates to speak only Malagasy.

Sociopolitical Organization

Social Organization. The Betsileo have a complex system of social stratification. Social distinctions dating back a century or more continue to have salience. Indigenous rulers, nobles, and their descendants are called *hova Betsileo;* commoners are known as *olompotsy*, and slave descendants may be called *hovavao*. Domestic slavery was widespread in Madagascar until the French declared its end in 1895. People were enslaved as prisoners of war and for certain crimes. Eventually, slaves were sold in markets; slave status was inherited. Like other Malagasy with a history of slavery, the Betsileo avoid (as they must, by law) the highly stigmatized term *andevo*, but slave ancestry remains a cause for shame and discrimination. Within the commoner stratum, there is an important distinction between junior and senior commoners. The latter were important advisors to—and checks on—the power of Betsileo chiefs and rulers. Today there is little or no evident wealth contrast between descendants of nobles and those of senior commoners. The tendency toward stratum endogamy is most marked for slave descendants.

Political Organization. For about three centuries, the Betsileo have lived in state-organized societies, first under their own rulers (sing. *mpanjaka*—the general Malagasy term for chief, king, or queen), after 1830 under Merina administrators, and subsequently, following its annexation of Madagascar in 1896, under the rule of France. The Malagasy Republic gained independence in 1960. There has been a marked deterioration of state control since the 1970s.

The main political units in the southern highlands before Merina conquest were Lalangina (east), Isandra (west), and the various statelets and chiefdoms of Arindrano (south). The largest of the southern highlands polities were Isandra and Lalangina. The process of state formation had advanced furthest in the latter. South of these were the six formerly independent polities that the Merina overlords eventually designated collectively as Arindrano: northern and southern Vohibato, Tsienimparihy, Manambolo, Lalanindro, and Homatrazo. In the eighteenth century, the commitment to agriculture was greatest in Lalangina and northern Vohibato, although wet-rice cultivation was spreading south and west.

Social Control. In addition to formal political organization (rulers, chiefs, their agents, and those of modern government) social control is a feature of the kinship system. Men are obliged to work for their fathers and older brothers. The oldest son is said to replace the father. Modern village chiefs, who fill formal government positions, have limited authority; often they are mere "errand boys," young men chosen by the elders to deal with external authorities. Real local authority is vested in the village elders, male and female, who have regular meetings to hear cases, discuss issues, and make decisions.

Conflict. Among the chiefdoms and petty states of the eighteenth and nineteenth centuries, war and raids were endemic, as fortified sites attest. The more effective Betsileo polities (especially Lalangina) maintained internal security, which was extended under the Merina, French, and early Malagasy Republic regimes. At present, with the collapse of state control, cattle rustling and banditry pose a serious threat to law and order in Betsileo territory. Legal disputes, especially over land, are common; they are usually resolved—often after protracted litigation—in formal courts in administrative towns.

Religion and Expressive Culture

Religious Beliefs and Practices. Christian missionaries have been active in Madagascar since the nineteenth century, and most Betsileo are either Catholics or Protestants. The Betsileo also continue to observe many aspects of their pre-Christian religion. Their supernatural realm includes beings, powers, and forces. Among the beings are deities, souls, ancestral spirits, ghosts of evildoers and legendary beings, and spirits of nature and water. The pre-Christian Betsileo recognized a creator god (still invoked to initiate ceremonies), Andriananahary or Zanahary, but he had little to do with human affairs. Christian missionaries chose another Malagasy deity, Andriamanitra, the sweet lord or fragrant prince, as equivalent to the Christian God. The Betsileo also recognize a mana-like efficacious force called *hasina*—a sacred essence that flows from the land through ancestors to living people and into the sociopolitical order.

An exuberant ceremonial season spans July and, especially, August, the agricultural off-season. The largest ceremonies center on ancestral tombs. Besides funerals, which occur throughout the year, the most important ceremonial event is a *famadihana*—an occasion to enter tombs, remove, and rewrap corpses. Among the Betsileo, the most lavish famadihana occur when a new tomb is inaugurated, and mortal remains are carried to it from one or more old tombs. When large groups of people assemble for funerals and ceremonies, cattle are slaughtered, and meat is distributed.

Religious Practitioners. The knowledge that diviners, curers, and witches have of words, techniques, paraphernalia, and persons is dependent, in part, on their manipulation of hasina. Witches may cause illness and death from a distance by manipulating occult powers; sorcerers use actual poisons. Hasina has a malicious aspect, called *hery*, which can be used to attack people and the social order. The dualism of the concept permits its use in explaining both illness and curing and both the quality that makes something taboo (*fady*) and the force that punishes taboo violations.

Specialists among the Betsileo include curers and diviners (see "Medicine"), as well as astrologers, who calculate "day and destiny." For a newborn child, an astrologer routinely determines—on the basis of the day, date, time of birth, and zodiac sign—that child's lifetime horoscope (*vintana*). Astrologers suggest ways of combating dangerous or unfortunate destinies. Astrology is also used to set dates of ceremonies and to schedule and coordinate agricultural activities.

Arts. The major traditional Betsileo art was the weaving of raw silk coverings called *lamba;* these served as colorful mantles for the living and funerary shrouds for the dead. Through the early twentieth century, there was an active husbandry of silkworms in southern Betsileo country. In Tsienimparihy, one of the Arindrano statelets, the ruler collected silk as tribute and oversaw the manufacture and distribution of *lamba landy*, the most magnificent shrouds, due individuals of high status on burial. Factory manufacture has by and large supplanted the local weaving of lamba. As noted, Merina masons have taken over Betsileo tomb manufacture; Merina musicians also play at Betsileo funerals and ceremonies. The Betsileo have abandoned their traditional tattooing (Dubois 1938), but women still coif elaborate hairdos.

Medicine. Betsileo cosmology recognizes no conditions or events that lack cause, and causes are often personalistic. Diviners determine causes by examining patterns of seeds and beans as they fall in a gridlike setting. Diviners function as diagnosticians and curers; they are paid for their work. Causes of illness, sterility, diminished prosperity, or other misfortune include malicious use of occult powers by living people, ancestral displeasure, infringement of taboos, spirit possession, loss of soul, and action by ghosts. Once a diagnosis is made, the diviner suggests a course of action designed to effect a cure. This usually requires sacrificing an ox. Medical specialists also prepare, dispense, and prescribe concoctions made from native roots, barks, leaves, and pieces of wood, sometimes obtained from colleagues in the Tanala forest. A variety of these remedies is available in local markets.

Death and Afterlife. Upon death, at least two spirits leave the body. One goes to Ambondrombe, a mountain in Tanala country to the southeast, or nowadays to heaven or hell, and has no more to do with the living. The other (*ambiroa*) stays nearby, wandering the hills, occasionally invading homes and dreams. Ambiroa are summoned to receive offerings from the living at the start of any tomb-centered ceremony, the focus of Betsileo religion.

Bibliography

Dubois, H-M. (1938). *Monographie des betsileo*. Paris: Institut d'Ethnologie.

Flacourt, Étienne de (1661). "Histoire de la grande île de Madagascar." In *Collections des ouvrages anciens concernant Madagascar,* edited by A. Grandidier, 9:1–426. Paris: Union Coloniale.

Kent, R. (1970). *Early Kingdoms in Madagascar (1500–1700).* New York: Holt, Rinehart & Winston.

Kottak, Conrad P. (1971a). "Cultural Adaptation, Kinship, and Descent in Madagascar." *Southwestern Journal of Anthropology* 27(2): 129–147.

Kottak, Conrad P. (1971b). "Social Groups and Kinship Calculation among the Southern Betsileo." *American Anthropologist* 73:178–193.

Kottak, Conrad P. (1972). "A Cultural Adaptive Approach to Malagasy Political Organization." In *Social Exchange and Interaction,* edited by Edwin N. Wilmsen, 107–128. University of Michigan, Anthropological Papers of the Museum of Anthropology, no. 46.

Kottak, Conrad P. (1977). "The Process of State Formation in Madagascar." *American Ethnologist* 4:136–155.

Kottak, Conrad P. (1980). *The Past in the Present: History, Ecology and Cultural Variation in Highland Madagascar.* Ann Arbor: University of Michigan Press.

Kottak, Conrad P., J-A. Rakotoarisoa, Aidan Southall, and P. Vérin (1986). *Madagascar: Society and History.* Durham, N.C.: Carolina Academic Press.

Vérin, P., Conrad P. Kottak, and P. Gorlin (1970). "The Glottochronology of Malagasy Speech Communities." *Oceanic Linguistics* 8(1): 26–83.

CONRAD P. KOTTAK

Cape Coloureds

ETHNONYMS: Basters (mixed), Bruinmense (brown people), Cape Coloured People, Coloureds

Orientation

Identification. The term "Cape Coloureds" generally refers to those South Africans of mixed cultural and racial stock whose ancestors include Europeans, Khoi and other indigenous African people, and Asians. The Coloureds were complexly and artificially defined for political convenience by the South African state in the Population Registration Act No. 30 of 1950 (as amended) on the premise that they occupied a middle political estate between Whites and indigenous Blacks, a designation that entrenched still further that structural position and the varying attendant feelings of marginality among individuals. The legal definition distinguished seven subcategories, only one of which was designated the "Cape Coloured group." The remaining six were listed as "Malay," "Griqua," "Chinese" (*sic*), "Indian," "other Asiatic," and "other Coloured."

Location. Historically, the ethnonym "Cape Coloureds" alluded specifically to their origin in and around what is now the city of Cape Town and, more generally, in the Cape Colony (Province). Today their descendants are found throughout South Africa, Namibia, Botswana, Lesotho, Swaziland, and Zimbabwe, and the term "Coloured" is often used indiscriminately for all people of mixed racial origin.

Demography. In 1988 the total Coloured population in South Africa, excluding Asians, was 3,127,000, representing about 8.7 percent of the total population of that country. Roughly 75 percent of the Coloured population live in urban areas. In neighboring Namibia, 42,241 people were classified as Coloureds in 1981. The 25,181 Rehoboth Basters, who physically resemble the Namibian Coloured people, regard themselves as a separate "nation" because of their historical and political position in that country. The various Baster groups in South Africa tend to maintain a similar ethnic aloofness.

Linguistic Affiliation. By and large, Coloured people speak either or both of the official state languages, Afrikaans and English. In 1980, 83.3 percent claimed Afrikaans as their home language, as opposed to the 10.3 percent who spoke English. Only 4.5 percent of all Coloured families reported that they were bilingual. Various dialects of both English and Afrikaans are also spoken, especially in Cape Town. Some families in rural areas speak Khoe or a Bantu language (nearly 2 percent in 1980).

History and Cultural Relations

The history of the Coloured people is coemergent with the first permanent European settlement on the Cape Peninsula, which was established in 1652. Intermarriage and cohabitation between settlers and Khoi was common and, at that time, often encouraged by all parties. When slaves were introduced from East Africa, India, Ceylon, and Malaysia, the process was repeated. The heterogeneity of the Coloured people intensified with the continuing arrival of diverse immigrant populations throughout the history of South Africa. In 1950 Parliament enacted two laws designed to prevent both intermarriage and miscegenation; this legislation was repealed thirty-five years later, having proved unenforceable. The history of the Coloureds has thus always been inextricably bound up with both Whites and people of color. Many Whites resemble Coloureds and vice versa, a reality that inspired the South African state to enforce a rigid color bar through the Population Registration Act.

The culture of the Coloured frontiersmen of the northwestern Cape and Namibia, known as the Basters, is similar to that of their White counterparts in other parts of southern Africa. It is often impossible to distinguish between the institutions of the White and Brown Voortrekkers. The special place of the Cape Malays (who are Muslims) in the culture of the urban Cape Coloureds must also be noted.

Settlements

In both rural and urban areas, few differences between Coloured and White settlements exist, other than those imposed by the government policies of racial segregation. Thus, the large number of Coloureds living in shantytowns and low-cost housing schemes in South African cities and small towns is essentially a reflection of the wider stratified society, not one of choice or the product of culture. Similarly, Coloured people living on reserves and on European farms must be seen against the background of their sociopolitical and economic referents. The architecture of many attractive rural cottages built by Cape Coloureds exhibits Dutch and Malaysian influence. It is only in the district of Namaqualand that traditional Khoi mat houses are found; many White people in the area chose to build in similar architectural designs.

Economy

One could speculate that had it not been for the growth of race prejudice, the Coloured population would scarcely differ from South African Whites in terms of their occupational profiles. In practice, although there are Coloured physicians, professors, teachers, entrepreneurs, civil servants, and skilled artisans, the majority are semiskilled and unskilled workers and laborers. Coloureds living on reserves and mission stations rarely make ends meet as farmers, and most domestic families are involved in the migratory labor force in one way or another. The success of the White farmers in Western Cape Province has, over the years, largely been made possible by the employment of poorly paid Coloured labor. Many members of the Cape Malay population enjoy a high economic status, related in part to their historical position as skilled artisans, professional fishers, and petty commodity producers.

Kinship, Marriage, and Family

The generally heterogeneous nature of Coloured culture is also reflected in patterns of family life, kinship, and marriage. Thus, on the Namaqualand reserves, a number of families follow practices regarding descent, generation, age, and sex that are recognizably Nama Khoi, whereas most middle-class families in the major urban areas hardly differ from Western middle-class families generally. Meaningful analysis of kinship and marriage can therefore be carried out only within a particular community or a specific regional context. It is quite erroneous to suggest that where matricentric families are found, evidence of pre-Emancipation slave culture is still evident.

An important aspect of Coloured kinship and marriage lies in people's preoccupation with class, status, and color, reflecting the extent to which Coloured people are enmeshed in the structure of South African society and their preoccupation with White values in particular. In the reserve communities of the district of Namaqualand, people distinguish four lineage categories. Marriages within and between these categories are guided by various preferential rules of status endogamy based on such criteria as skin color, hair form, ethnic origin, and so forth. Similar patterns are found in urban areas, where the emphasis on biological characteristics and ethnicity is complicated by indexes of association, educational achievement, political and religious affiliation, occupation, and the like. Some light-skinned Coloured individuals were able to change their official race classification to White. The process was a complex one and could only be undertaken successfully by higher-status people with established social networks among people in the White estate.

Sociopolitical Organization

Like other non-White people in South Africa prior to 1994, the Coloured population has never enjoyed equal political rights with those regarded as White. With the advent of the Union of South Africa in 1909, for example, the franchise was given to Coloured males in the Cape Province only, subject to specified property and income qualifications. In 1951 those rights were removed, and voters were placed on a separate Coloured roll. In 1984 the government introduced a tricameral parliamentary system that made provision for the election of representatives to be responsible for the administration of so-called Coloured affairs. In the pre-1951 system, White political parties hoped to lure Coloured voters, and in certain urban areas the more liberal parties considered the Coloured vote crucial to their success. One of the reasons for removing the Coloureds from the voter roll was to reduce their political power as the number of qualified voters increased.

Coloured involvement in political protest in White-dominated South Africa changed radically after 1951, and, by the mid-1970s, many Coloureds began to identify themselves with national struggles against apartheid, reflecting their disillusionment with White liberalism.

Various segments of those people who came to be known as the Basters formed, with the assistance of missionaries, largely autonomous political communities and cultivated their marginal ethnic identity. These included the Grigua, the various Baster groups of Little Namaqualand, and the Rehoboth Basters, who established a republic in what is now Namibia in 1870. All these Baster nations developed formal written constitutions after they had lived for a period under customary law during their seminomadic pastoral stage, as did the White Voortrekkers. The constitutions of the Basters resembled very closely those of their White counterparts (cf. the thirty-three articles of the constitution of the South African Republic of 1844 with the sixty-four articles of that of the Rehoboth Baster nation of 1874).

The Coloured reserves of Little Namaqualand have similar histories to that of the Rehoboth nation of Namibia, although the former never enjoyed full political autonomy.

Religion

Apart from the Muslim Cape Malays (6.7 percent), the Coloured people are by and large nominal Christians (26 percent Dutch Reformed, 10.7 percent Anglican, 5.7 percent

Methodist, 7 percent Congregationalist, 10 percent Catholic), a pattern very similar to that of Whites. Compared with the Bantu-speaking peoples, the Coloureds have engaged in relatively few minor schismatic movements in reaction to White domination in religion.

On the Coloured reserves and mission stations, the churches and the Christian religion stand at the core of communal and political life. Some residents have retained aspects of traditional Khoi religion, magic, and sorcery, and they hold these beliefs together with their articulation of Christianity. In urban areas, varieties of magico-medical traditions persist. Many of these, notably divination and the prescription of "home remedies" for illness, are often associated with people of Cape Malay background.

Bibliography

Carstens, Peter (1966). *The Social Structure of Cape Coloured Reserve*. Cape Town and New York: Oxford University Press.

Carstens, Peter (1983–1984). "Opting Out of Colonial Rule: The Brown Voortrekkers of South Africa and Their Constitutions." *African Studies* 42(2): 135–152; 43(1): 19–30.

Goldin, Ian (1987). *Making Race: The Politics and Economics of Coloured Identity in South Africa*. London and New York: Longman.

Marais, J. S. (1939). *The Cape Coloured People, 1652–1937*. Johannesburg: Witwatersrand University Press.

Patterson, Sheila (1953). *Colour and Culture in South Africa*. London: Routledge & Kegan Paul.

Van der Ross, R. E. (1979). *Myths and Attitudes: An Inside Look at the Coloured People*. Cape Town: Tafelberg Publishers.

Venter, Al J. (1974). *Coloured: A Profile of Two Million South Africans*. Cape Town: Human & Rousseau.

PETER CARSTENS

Chagga

ETHNONYMS: Chaga, Dschagga, Jagga, Wa-caga, Waschagga (sing., Mchagga; contemporary self-designation)

Orientation

Identification and Location. In the nineteenth century the Kichagga-speaking people on Mount Kilimanjaro were divided into many small, autonomous chiefdoms. Early accounts frequently identify the inhabitants of each chiefdom as a separate "tribe." Although the Chagga are principally located on Mount Kilimanjaro in northern Tanzania, numerous families have migrated elsewhere over the course of the twentieth century.

Demography. Around the beginning of the twentieth century, the German colonial government estimated that there were about 28,000 households on Kilimanjaro. The 1988 Tanzanian census counted 744,271 individuals. (With very few exceptions, only Chagga live on Kilimanjaro.) Obviously, the mountain population has increased at a rapid rate during the twentieth century, and the high rate of increase seems to be continuing.

Linguistic Affiliation. Kichagga is a Bantu language. There are significant dialectal differences in the Kichagga spoken in the easterly, central, and westerly divisions of Kilimanjaro. The inhabitants of Ugweno, which was once the northernmost chiefdom of the Pare Mountains, speak a language related to Kichagga.

History and Cultural Relations

Bantu peoples came to Kilimanjaro in a succession of migrations that started at least five or six hundred years ago. It is likely that there were other peoples on the mountain for hundreds of years before they arrived. Reliable written historical accounts of the Chagga date from the nineteenth century. The first European to reach the mountain was a missionary, Johannes Rebmann, who arrived there in 1848. At that time, Rebmann found that Kilimanjaro was so actively involved in far-reaching trading connections that a chief whose court he visited had a coastal Swahili resident in his entourage. Chagga chiefdoms traded with each other, with the peoples of the regions immediately surrounding the mountain (such as the Kamba, the Maasai, and the Pare), and also with coastal caravans. Some of this trading was hand to hand, some of it at markets, which were a general feature of the area. Many chiefdoms had several produce markets largely run by women, just as they are today.

As far back into local history as the accounts go, Chagga chiefdoms were chronically at war with one another and with nearby peoples. Various alliances and consolidations were achieved through conquest, others through diplomacy, but the resulting political units were not always durable. Alignments changed and were reorganized with the ebb and flow of the fortunes of war and trade. Presumably, the fighting between the chiefdoms was over control of trade routes, over monopolies on the provisioning of caravans, over ivory, slaves, cattle, iron, and other booty of war, and over the right to exact tribute. Outlines of the process are known from the eighteenth century onward. As large as some of the blocs of allies became, at no time in the precolonial period did any one chiefdom rule all the others. That unitary consolidation was not achieved until the German colonial government imposed it.

Initially (i.e., before the German conquest), various Chagga chiefdoms welcomed missionaries, travelers, and foreign representatives as they did traders; in the 1880s, however, when the Chagga gradually lost their autonomy, they became more hostile. In 1886 Germany and Britain divided their spheres of influence in East Africa; Kilimanjaro was allocated to the Germans. Some Chagga chiefs became German allies and helped the Germans to defeat old rivals in other Chagga chiefdoms. Sudanese and Zulu troops were also brought in when some strong chiefly resistance to German control manifested itself. By the 1890s, all the Chagga had been subjugated.

Chagga society experienced a radical change. Taxes in cash were imposed to force Africans to work for Europeans from whom they could receive wages. A native system of corvée was expanded for the benefit of the colonial government. A handful of armed Germans successfully ruled a hundred thousand Chagga by controlling them through their chiefs. The chiefs who cooperated were rewarded with more power than they had ever known. The resisting chiefs were deposed or hanged, and more malleable substitutes were appointed in their stead.

Warfare came to an end and, with it, Chagga military organization, which had been a system of male age grades. Christianity spread, and, eventually, most Chagga became, at least nominally, Christians. The churches, Catholic and Lutheran, were allocated religious control over different parts of Kilimanjaro. As part of their mission, they introduced schools and coffee-growing clinics. Thus, a Western religion was imposed on the Chagga, along with a Western medicine, Western education, and a cash crop. These developments parallel the major political reorganization effectuated by colonization and the fundamental change in the local economy. Long-distance trade became a European monopoly. Coffee growing spread rapidly over the mountain.

This general economic transformation was well under way when the colonial government passed from German hands into those of the British in 1916. Arabica coffee remains a major cash crop produced locally. Since 1961, Tanzania has been an independent nation and, among other products, relies on coffee exportation for foreign exchange.

Settlements

There are no nucleated villages on Kilimanjaro. Each household lives in the midst of its own banana-coffee garden, and the gardens, one next to another, stretch all over the mountain. The gardens are, for the most part, ringed with living fences that mark their boundaries. In the older areas of settlement, male kin tend to own and reside in contiguous homestead gardens, forming localized patrilineal clusters. Because of the enormous expansion of the population and the consequent land shortage, there are no large expanses of uncultivated or unoccupied land in the banana belt. It was otherwise in earlier times. Photographs and accounts from earlier in the twentieth century show that there were open fields between the localized clusters. Such residential arrangements were not static. A household, or several together, could break away from the localized patrilineage of which they had been members. There being no land shortage, they could, with the consent of the local chief or district head in the new location, establish themselves elsewhere and even found a new patrilineal cluster. As available land became more scarce, many households moved downmountain, and some moved up, pushing back the boundary of the forest. Thus, there are older and newer settlements on the mountain, older and newer patrilineal clusters, and substantial areas where the majority of residents are from unrelated households. Gradually, as the open land has filled up, the mobility of households has been increasingly restricted.

Economy

In the nineteenth century the Chagga were cultivators and cattle keepers. They grew many types of bananas, which were their staple food. Bananas are generally male property but are (with permission) traded by women in the markets. The Chagga also grew millet, maize, beans, finger millet (*Eleusine corocana*), cassava, sweet potatoes, yams, sugarcane, paw paws (*Carica papaya*), pumpkins, squashes, and tobacco. Many of the annual vegetable crops were grown by women and were women's property. The Chagga made (and continue to make) beer out of bananas and eleusine. In most of the populous parts of the mountain, a few stall-fed cows were kept by each household. In areas where there was more pasture, large herds of cattle were grazed. Some men owned considerable numbers of animals, but others had none. Milk was a highly valued food, as was meat. Local lineages held slaughtering feasts several times a year. There was a system of cattle lending whereby many households tended animals that were not their own. In return for caring for an animal, the borrower received the milk and the manure and, eventually, when the animal was slaughtered, was entitled to a portion of the meat. Lineage slaughtering feasts are still held today, both to coincide with major life-cycle rituals and on more ordinary occasions.

In precolonial times, in addition to production for domestic consumption, the Chagga produced food, animals, and other items for trade and tribute. Having no domestic source of iron or salt, nor an adequate supply of clay, the chiefdoms of Kilimanjaro were dependent on trade with neighboring peoples for these essential materials. They needed iron for weapons and agricultural tools, salt and clay pots for cooking. Allusion has been made to the local regional and long-distance trades in which the Chagga were actively involved in precolonial times. Warfare also played an important role in the precolonial economy. War yielded booty for the winners and often was the basis for the exaction of tribute from the losers. Moreover, the protection of traders and trade routes had military aspects.

In the colonial and postcolonial periods, the economy has changed drastically. The cropping of coffee, the advent of land shortage, the development of many small businesses, and the inflow of the wages and salaries of the many Chagga employed on and off the mountain have altered the local economic picture considerably. A subsistence dimension of the banana-vegetable-animal domestic economy persists in the household gardens, but it operates in an entirely different context from that of former times. Like banana plants, coffee bushes are male property. Access to cash is thus much more restricted for women than it is for men, even though women do more of the agricultural and domestic labor and bear the fundamental responsibility for feeding the household.

In precolonial times land was regarded as male property, inherited patrilineally by males from males or transferred inter vivos by males to males. Widows and women in other relationships to men could occupy, hold, and use land but could not obtain a transferable interest. That pattern of landholding continues, although, formally speaking, the law has changed.

Kinship

Exogamous patrilineages are the basic building blocks of the kinship system. These are sometimes called "clans" in the colonial literature. They vary in size from a few households to many dozens. Marriage is virilocal, and many lineages are localized because of the link between kinship and land tenure.

Marriage and Family

In pre-Christian days, polygynous marriage was legitimate. Over time, the churches have discouraged this practice, and monogamy (although sometimes in the form of a series of monogamous marriages) now prevails. Marriages used to be negotiated by the parents of the couple. Bride-wealth was paid and an elaborate series of ceremonies held. Some of these ceremonies persist, but indigenous cultural forms are mixed with Christian rituals. Formerly, both males and females were ritually circumcised before they were considered fit for marriage. Modified versions of these practices persist, less commonly for females than for males. Traditionally, a widow was inherited by her husband's heir. Today the husband's heir becomes the "guardian" of the widow and often takes control of whatever property rights she might have, ostensibly in her interest. Although intestate inheritance of land and most other economically significant property is from male to male, succession to such property is not just from father to son or elder to younger brother. It is complicated by the life interest of widows, by various preferred forms of primogeniture and ultimogeniture, and by the discretionary power held by the lineage over the distribution of the property of the dead.

Domestic Unit. The composition of the precolonial household changed over its life cycle and differed in polygynous households from monogamous ones. After marriage, the initial domestic unit was that of a husband, wife, and, eventually, young children. The husband later built a hut of his own, which he shared with his older sons, the wife keeping her own hut with unmarried daughters and very young sons. Households often had other single relatives (e.g., widows and widowers) attached to them. Today households are of variable composition. Many young men leave wives and children on their plots of land on Kilimanjaro while they search for salaried jobs elsewhere.

Sociopolitical Organization

Precolonial organized groups were founded on kinship, locality, age, and gender. Localized patrilineages formed the subunits within a district, and chiefdoms were composed of several districts. Chiefs were chosen within the chiefly lineage. Chiefs appointed the district heads. Lineages were led by the senior male, who was the ritual head, and also by a "spokesman," or political representative for external relations. A system of male age grades crosscuts lineages and districts. Women were also grouped in age grades. From the start of the colonial period, other organizational entities became prominent. The churches were first; later, a coffee cooperative emerged. Since independence, party (the Tanganyika African National Union, later renamed the Revolutionary party [Chama cha Mapinduzi]) and government administrative units have replaced earlier chiefs and chiefly councils. Tanzania has now introduced multiparty politics, and doubtless this will bring further changes in the future.

As coffee production gradually expanded, coffee sales became a major source of local tax revenue, enhancing local administrative resources and becoming the economic basis for secondary local institutional development. Over time, increasing numbers of Chagga received formal education. In the 1920s, with British administrative encouragement, the Chagga organized their own sales cooperative to market their coffee and regulate production. The cooperative was owned by the Chagga but managed by a European who was their employee. Despite some political ups and downs, the cooperative was, in general, very successful. An economically sophisticated and educated Chagga elite began to form. By the mid-twentieth century, political parties had taken hold that challenged local chiefs for internal political control of the mountain. The British administration periodically reorganized local administrative bodies in response to this development. In 1951, in a development that further diminished the power of the local chiefs, who by then were fairly unpopular, a paramount chief of all the Chagga was elected, backed by the Kilimanjaro Citizen's Union. The paramount, in his turn, became unpopular when he tried to make his office permanent and hereditary and sought excessive personal power. By 1961, when the British left Tanganyika (renamed Tanzania in 1964, following its union with Zanzibar), the paramount had been displaced. In any case, the new independent government abolished chieftainship; hence all the local chiefs also lost their powers. Needless to say, this move was not unwelcome in many quarters on Kilimanjaro. Local political reorganization ensued as the socialist government designed new structures. Despite considerable innovative efforts from above, however, many preexisting relationships, such as powerful kinship groupings, continued to be locally effective on Kilimanjaro.

Before 1900, conflict between chiefdoms was resolved either through chiefly diplomacy or warfare. Subsequently, colonial officials dealt with such matters administratively. Conflicts between individuals were resolved either within the lineage, between lineages, within an age grade or an irrigation consortium, or by the district heads or the chiefs. Hearings took place at every level. Fines were imposed, and persons could be expelled from whatever group was trying the case. Individuals were sometimes killed. Elements of social control were thus manifest in every group milieu. This localized control persists, with some major modifications, in the modern setting. Since the beginning of colonial times, there has been a government-designated system of officials and courts formally charged with dispute settlement and law enforcement.

Religion

In indigenous Chagga cosmology, all human activities have potential spirit-worldly significance. Thus, the seen and the unseen worlds are closely linked. Dead ancestors care how their descendants behave. Living persons are capable of invoking God or the spirits for benign or malign purposes. Incurable illness, infertility, or other misfortunes are considered likely to have been caused by human or spirit agencies. Spells, curses, amulets, and witchcraft were (and are today) commonplace, both to defend and to harm. Diviners could (and can) be consulted. Rituals mark all life-cycle events. Christian ideas and rituals are closely intertwined with indigenous conceptions and ceremonies.

Bibliography

Gutmann, Bruno (1926). *Das Recht der Dschagga.* Arbeiten zur Entwicklungspsychologie, edited by Felix Krueger, vol. 7. Munich: C. H. Beck. Translated by A. M. Nagler. New Haven: Human Relations Area Files.

Moore, Sally Falk, and Paul Puritt (1977). *The Chagga and Meru of Tanzania*. Ethnographic Survey of Africa, East Central Africa, 18. International African Institute.

Moore, Sally Falk (1986). *Social Facts and Fabrications: "Customary" Law on Kilimanjaro, 1880–1980*. Cambridge: Cambridge University Press.

SALLY FALK MOORE

Chaldeans

ETHNONYMS: none

Orientation

Today the term "Chaldean" is used to refer to a branch of the Nestorian Orthodox church that became affiliated with Rome while preserving its liturgical language and ecclesiastical customs. For example, Chaldean priests, unlike their counterparts in the Roman church, are allowed to marry. Chaldeans number at present about 200,000 Nestorian Catholics and 75,000 Jacobite Catholics, who are sometimes confused with Chaldeans. In 1646 Jacobites who were drawn to Catholicism were termed "Syrian Uniates" instead of "Chaldeans." "Uniat(e)" refers to all Eastern-rite churches that affiliated with Rome, including that of the Chaldeans. The Jacobites were part of the Chaldean church until they went their separate way.

The term "Chaldeans" was originally a designation for the inhabitants of Babylon in the first millennium B.C. First Greek and Roman writers—and, later, Alexander the Great—employed the term to refer to these people, who had invented astrology and had strongly influenced Roman writers and the leading thinkers of the East and West in postulating that astrology could ascertain the will of the gods and human destiny. The Church Fathers attacked the Chaldeans repeatedly and strongly because they believed that such theories would mitigate their own notions of how to determine the will of the one God. The earliest mention of Chaldeans occurs in the Bible, in reference to Nebuchadnezzar destroying Assyria, then conquering Syria and Palestine in 597 B.C., which events were followed by the so-called Babylonian Captivity of Hebrew notables. The latter were freed in 539 B.C. by the Persian king, Cyrus, who ended Chaldean primacy in the whole region.

The Uniates have nine Eastern patriarchs. Those of Constantinople, Alexandria, and Antioch live in Rome. In addition there are Uniate patriarchs of Jerusalem (Greek), Antioch (Syrian and Maronite), and Babylon (Chaldean). The Syrian Uniates use the liturgy of St. James, write in Karṣhūni (Arabic in Syriac script), and conduct prayers in both Syriac and Karshūni (inaudibly in Syriac). The Chaldean Uniates, on the other hand, use the liturgy of Addai and Mari, which was first adopted by the Nestorians (but in a much abridged form in its daily application, when compared to the original that is still employed by the Nestorians). Like the Maronites, they are sometimes referred to as Eastern Uniates (i.e., Eastern-rite Christians who acknowledge the primacy of the pope in Rome). The Chaldeans use one of the eighteen canonical rites that are recognized by the Holy See. They reside today in Iran, Iraq, Syria, Lebanon, and Turkey, subject to the Chaldean patriarch of Babylon. They are for the most part descended from the East Syrian or ancient Aramaean and Babylonian peoples who were Christianized when Persia ruled the East. The Persians accepted the so-called heresy of the Nestorians, and the Muslim Arabs who replaced them have allowed the Eastern Christian churches to continue to employ their rites under the protective umbrella of Islam. Each church member bears the officially recognized status of *dhimmi* (i.e., a non-Muslim permitted to retain his or her original faith).

History and Cultural Relations

Contacts with the Holy See were first initiated by the Chaldeans during the Crusades. The earliest attempt at uniting with Rome was made by Sabrisho ibn al-Masihi (1226–1257), but it was Yaballaha III (1281–1317) who first made profession of the Catholic faith in a letter addressed to Pope Benedict XI, on 18 May 1304. His avowal, however, encountered heavy resistance from Nestorian bishops, and the union with Rome was of short duration. Such a union was attempted again, by Elias, the Nestorian bishop of Cyprus. The conversion of several bishops in 1445 resulted from the union with Rome made by Timothy, also bishop of Cyprus, which union lasted only five years. A rigid policy of Latinization was applied by the doge of Venice, who succeeded the Lusignans as ruler in 1489 and who had commercial undertakings in the Mediterranean Near East.

It was following the Council of Florence that the Nestorian patriarchs developed closer ties with Rome, owing largely to increased European influence among them. Their union in the sixteenth century was a consequence of the dissatisfaction of Nestorians with having members of the same family succeed to the patriarchate, especially when incompetent members occupied the position, like Simeon V Bar Mama's 8-year-old nephew. This dissatisfaction precipitated a meeting of the bishops of Erbil, Salamas, and Azerbaijan, joined by three or four delegates from the region, in which they agreed to select another patriarch; they chose Sulāqa, an especially religious priest who had served since 1540 as the superior of the convent of Rabban-Hormizd (some 40 kilometers from Mosul, in upper Iraq).

Sulāqa came to Rome on 15 November 1552, and, on the basis of a report submitted by Cardinal Maffei, Pope Julius III promulgated a bull on 20 February 1553 proclaiming Sulāqa the patriarch of Mosul. This date became the official birthday of the Chaldean Catholic church. Sulāqa was consecrated bishop by Pope Julius III in the Basilica of Saint Peter. To help Sulāqa, the pope appointed the Dominican Ambrose Butigeg as his representative to the Chaldeans of Mosul. Sulāqa returned with Khalaf, his companion on the journey to Rome, and took up residence for his patriarchate at Amida (present-day Diyarbakır) on 12 November 1553. Seven days later, his followers recognized him as head of the Chaldean "nation." He did not survive long, however. His archenemy, the Nestorian patriarch, Simeon Denha, lured him to Amida, where the Ottoman governor of the district arranged to have him drowned in the lake, on 12 January 1555. His successor, Abdeasho IV (1555–1565), was then recognized by the pope. Another successor, Elias VIII, sent a delegation to Rome with a recommendation from the Maronite patriarch, Makhluf of Lebanon, and a profession of faith. This delegation was escorted back to Iraq from Rome by two Jesuits.

Three centuries of conflict ensued between the main church and the branches that gravitated toward Rome, during which time a number of patriarchs were unable to sign professions of the Catholic faith and receive confirmation—largely because of their early deaths—until the time of Simeon IX (d. 1600). But the mainline Nestorian church resisted strongly this schismatic tendency, and heavy pressure compelled Simeon XIII to return to the Eastern church late in the seventeenth century. Diyarbakır, a Catholic center, remained without a "Catholic" patriarch until Yūsuf (Joseph) I, archibishop of Diyarbakır, was elected patriarch in 1672. Yūsuf took the advice of the Capuchin missionaries there and withdrew from communion with Mār Ilīya (Saint Elias) in 1672. He was recognized by Pope Clement X five years later as patriarch of the Chaldean "Catholics" and was designated in 1681 by Pope Innocent XI as Mār Yūsuf, but without a see. His position was reinforced after he obtained a *firmân* (imperial order) from the Ottoman government recognizing his autonomy from the Nestorian patriarch, Elias XII Denho. He traveled to Rome to receive confirmation from Pope Innocent XI, thus formalizing the union with Rome in 1680. The title of the head of the church was henceforth to be "patriarch of Babylon," although the occupant bore the name Mār Ilīya when he was residing at Ctesiphon.

Resistance from the Nestorian church continued to be strong, and the resultant pressures obliged Mār Yūsuf to resign and return to Rome, where he died in 1707. His successor, Mār Yūsuf II (1694–1713), strengthened the ties with Rome and gained the title "patriarch of Babylon," starting a line that continued until 1828, when Yūsuf V died. When Mār Ilīya VI was accepted as Catholic and was received into union with Rome, two Uniate "Nestorian" patriarchates came into being, at some time after 1692: the Mār Shamʿun from the Sulāqa line, in Azerbaijan, and the Mār Yūsuf, in Diyarbakır.

The shift in titles and their redesignation created a great deal of confusion for scholars. The title Mār Ilīya signified descent from the old and venerated line of "Bayt al-Ab" (lit., "the House of the Father"). The title "patriarch" was hitherto accorded out of diplomacy to the Oriental Assyrians (another designation for Nestorians, because of their alleged ethnic descent from Assyrians) and in recognition of those who preceded in the Sulāqa line when they resided at Kotchannes. The title "patriarch of Babylon," moreover, was reserved for the Nestorian patriarchs of the Abūna-Basīdi family who resided at Rabban-Hormizd.

During all of these transactions and visits with Rome, the Maronites there played important roles in promoting the ties with the Holy See. Yūsuf (Joseph) al-Simʿāni (Assemani) and the Maronite patriarch served as middlemen in facilitating relationships between Rome and the breakaway Nestorians. They provided them with letters of recommendation to the Holy See and later printed their liturgical books.

Joseph III succeeded Joseph II, who had died of the plague in 1713. When Joseph III visited Mosul, he lured some three thousand Nestorians into the Catholic church, which, predictably, enraged the Nestorian patriarch. The Ottomans in the eighteenth century were under heavy pressures from the Catholic powers of Europe, who had generally surpassed them on the battlefields ever since the second siege of Vienna in 1683. The sultan's government relaxed its rules in favor of the Eastern-rite churches in Ottoman domains and made the concession to Rome of recognizing the Catholic branches at Diyarbakır and Mardin, leaving Mosul and Aleppo to the non-Uniate Nestorians.

The pressures on Joseph III caused him to journey to Rome and offer his resignation, but the pope rejected it. Meanwhile, war broke out between the Ottomans and the Persians, which kept him in Rome until 1741. He then returned to his flock and died in 1757. On 24 March 1759 the election of Joseph IV was recognized by the pope, who confirmed him as the patriarch of the United Chaldeans. He resigned in 1781 and was reinstated temporarily in 1791, then fully in 1793, as the patriarch administrator of Amid, where he died in 1796.

In 1802 the priest Augustine Hindi was named administrator of the patriarchate of Diyarbakır, and he was consecrated bishop of Mardin on 8 September 1804. He was then named apostolic delegate for the Chaldeans, a post he held for fifteen years. Rome had hoped, in denying him the patriarchate, to lure the Nestorian patriarchs of either Kotchannes or Rabban-Hormizd to create a single, united Chaldean patriarchate. Hindi did receive from Rome, however, the pallium, which carried with it the rank of archbishop. His death in 1827 ended the series of patriarchs of Diyarbakır, which had begun 147 years earlier.

John Hormizd, the last member of the Abūna family to represent the Chaldean Catholics, was appointed patriarch of Babylon in July of 1830 and so remained until his death on 16 August 1838. After once suspending him from the office, the Catholic church reversed itself and recognized Hormizd as patriarch of the Chaldeans, but only after he agreed not to admit any of his relatives to the episcopal order. In late 1844 he received an imperial firmân from the Ottoman sultan, recognizing him as patriarch of the "Chaldeans" instead of the "Nestorians," as had been previously the case. With such recognition, the Chaldean church was now firmly established as an independent entity, free of Nestorian ties. It even received recognition as a *millet* (autonomous unit), separate from the Ottomans.

The lack of success that characterized the tenure of Coadjutor Nicholas Zaya resulted in his resignation and replacement in 1847 by Yūsuf Audo, who was confirmed the following year. Audo's long pontificate yielded many converts for, as well as great dissension with Rome, a dissension that began in 1860 with the question of jurisdiction over the Malabar Christian Uniates of southwestern India. A series of less heralded patriarchs succeeded Audo, who died in 1879. The only one to achieve distinction was Yūsuf Emmanuel II Thomas, whom the Holy See named apostolic delegate for the Nestorians on 9 July 1900. Yūsuf was a popular patriarch, who served in the Iraqi senate for twenty-five years after the state's formation. His long pontificate was marked by the return to Catholicism of several Nestorian villages, two bishops, and many members of the clergy. He also witnessed the massacres of 1918, when four bishops, many priests, and up to 70,000 of the faithful are said to have perished. Joseph VII Ghanima (1948–1957) succeeded him, followed by Paul II Cheikho in 1958.

See also Jacobites; Maronites; Nestorians

Bibliography

Goormachtigh, B. M. (1897–1898). "Histoire de la mission dominicaine en Mesopotamie et en Kurdistan." In *Analecta Sacri Ordinis Fratrum Praedicatorum*. Vol. 3.

Hastings, James (n.d.). "Nestorianism." In *Encyclopedia of Religion and Ethics*. Vol. 9, 323–332. New York: Charles Scribner's Sons.

Joseph, John (1961). *The Nestorians and Their Muslim Neighbors*. Princeton, N.J.: Princeton University Press.

Louvet, Louis-Eugène (1894). *Les missions catholiques au XIXme siècle*. Lyon: Desclée de Brouwer.

The New Catholic Encyclopedia (1966). Vol. 3. New York: McGraw-Hill.

CAESAR E. FARAH

Circassians

ETHNONYM: Adyge

Orientation

Identification. The Circassians are a people indigenous to the northwestern Caucasus who are also found today as minority communities in four Middle Eastern countries: Turkey, Syria, Jordan, and Israel. They call themselves "Adyge," the term "Circassian" being the one used by outsiders ("Çerkez" in Turkish, "Sharkass" in Arabic) to refer, rather loosely, to a variety of groups from that region.

Location. The Circassians migrated into the Ottoman Empire in the late nineteenth century after the Russian takeover of their homeland. They were first settled by the Ottoman state in the Balkans but were soon displaced again as the Ottoman Empire lost control of that region. They were then settled in Anatolia and in Bilād ash-Sham (the Syrian province). The general policy of the state was to settle immigrants to act as buffers against dissident local groups and also to extend agricultural settlements and push back the "desert line"; however, specific locations were determined by local exigencies such as the availability of agricultural land. The major settlements were in the regions of the Black Sea coast, western Anatolia and Kayseri (Turkey), Aleppo (Syria), the Golan Heights (Israeli-occupied Syria), Amman (Jordan) and Tiberias (Israel). Circassians also live in the major urban centers of these areas.

Demography. The number of Circassians is difficult to determine because census data are lacking. Estimates point to about 1 million in Turkey, 60,000 in Syria, 30,000 in Jordan, and 1,500 in Israel. There are also no statistics on the rate of intermarriage with non-Circassians, which tends to vary by location, class, and urban versus rural settlement.

Linguistic Affiliation. The Circassian language, Adygebze, is one of the North-West Caucasian Group of languages and is divided into a number of different dialects. It is still spoken in all the Circassian communities, especially in the home and during community events, although the younger generation tends to feel more comfortable speaking in Arabic or Turkish, and many words have been adopted from these languages. There has been a convergence of the various dialects (notably Kabartey, Bzedugh, Shapsoug, and Abzekh) owing to intensive interaction and common residence. When Circassian is written, the adapted Cyrillic alphabet developed in the Soviet Union is used.

History and Cultural Relations

Circassian immigration into the Ottoman Empire began in 1850 and accelerated into a mass migration starting in 1864. There was an earlier Circassian presence in the Middle East, through the Mamluk "slave-dynasties" in Egypt, whose descendants, augmented by continued individual migration, came to form a Turco-Circassian elite ruling class in Egypt. This presence, although an entirely different phenomenon than the later mass migrations, points to important historical links between the Caucasus and various regional empires to which it provided slaves (both men and women) and warriors.

Circassian migration during the nineteenth century resulted from an Ottoman policy of encouraging immigration, both to overcome its shortage of manpower and to increase its Muslim population in turbulent regions. Religion was also a factor inducing the Muslim Circassians' emigration from under czarist Russian rule. In all, about 1.5 million Circassians settled in Ottoman lands. The relations that they established with their host communities were shaped by the nature of Ottoman rule and prevailing local economic conditions. The commonality of religion was an integrative force. The provincial authorities were given instructions to allocate the migrants free land and building materials and to exempt them from most forms of taxation. Soon, however, the number of immigrants overwhelmed both the facilities provided and the capacity of the provinces to absorb them. Conditions quickly deteriorated. More and more immigrants tended to drift toward the cities.

In what was to become Jordan, for example, the areas of Circassian settlement were strongholds of large nomadic and seminomadic Bedouin tribes. Conflict arose over water and pastureland. Furthermore, Circassians refused to enter into the indigenous peasant/Bedouin relationship of paying protection money. Armed clashes ensued, mostly around harvesttime, and a kind of mutual respect grew out of these clashes. Soon treaties were negotiated between various tribes and the Circassians, and some judicious marriages of Circassian women to powerful Bedouin families were arranged.

The breakup of the Soviet Union and the accessiblity of the Caucasus after 140 years now allows third- and fourth-generation Circassians to revisit their "homeland" (the republics of Adygei, Cherkessk-Karachai, and Kabardino-Balkaria, all part of the Russian Federation). An estimated two hundred families, mainly from Turkey and Syria, have migrated back, and there is intense cultural activity between various organizations in the Caucasus and ethnic associations in the Middle East, as well as families seeking long-lost kin. The new links are marked by intense nostaligia and emotion, but also by a sense of rupture caused by divergent historical experiences.

Settlements

The different settlements were formed slowly through the waves of migration and were mainly agricultural. Today some are still primarily agricultural (as in Turkey). Others have become metropolitan centers (as in Jordan), and still others are abandoned (as in Syria, where, after the Israeli occupation of the Golan Heights in 1967, the inhabitants all became refugees). Some moved to urban areas in the early days of the immigration, others came as part of a wider rural-urban migration, particularly since the 1950s.

Circassian village neighborhoods initially reflected the different dialect groups and the time of settlement. As villages grew more heterogeneous, distinct Circassian and Arab neighborhoods tended to form, although the boundaries are becoming increasingly blurred as residential and economic mobility increase. Where urban centers formed, the Circassians eventually became a numerical minority, old neighborhoods broke up, and residence became defined by class rather than ethnicity.

Economy

Subsistence and Commercial Activities. Upon settlement, the Circassians were mainly engaged in agriculture, although they gradually became drawn into the network of internal trade controlled by merchants from nearby towns and cities. In Bilād ash-Sham, although Circassians were engaged in transporting goods such as barley cultivated by Bedouins, they remained essentially suppliers of agricultural goods and did not control trade. The construction of the Hejaz railway to Mecca provided wage-labor opportunities. A few Circassians were also employed in the Ottoman administration.

The changes wrought in the geopolitics of the region in the early twentieth century, with the dismemberment of the Ottoman Empire into present-day Turkey and several mandate governments (the French in Syria and the British in Jordan and Palestine), changed the economy and nature of Circassian settlements. New opportunities, notably in the armies and bureaucracies, became available to them and their settlements become more heterogeneous. Amman, for example, became the capital of the new Jordanian state. Later, with the transformation of the peasant economy, Circassians, as others, participated in the new avenues for wage labor in industry, agro-business and so on, although the military and bureaucracy remain the main occupations for the communities in Syria and Jordan.

Industrial Arts. Circassian traditional crafts included agricultural implements, especially their distinctive two-wheeled carts, silversmithing and other metalwork, and leatherwork. Very few are still involved in crafts production today, except in the form of "folkloric" items and attempts at the revival of traditional arts.

Trade. The Circassians in the Middle East have largely not engaged in trade and attribute this to national character, saying that Circassians make good military personnel but bad traders. More likely it has to do with the nature of the opportunities that were available to them in their new environments. The Anatolian Circassians were engaged in some horse breeding and cattle trading, and some continue to work as truckers of meat and animals. Furthermore, in some places, such as Jordan, they are heavily engaged in real estate because their lands have gained in value as urban residential areas continue to expand into formerly agricultural land. The new opportunities opened up by the possibility of commercial links with the Caucasus have led some, especially in Turkey, to establish import-export companies as well as travel agencies.

Division of Labor. Previously, the division of labor reflected the nature of agriculture in the areas of settlement. Women do not seem to have worked in the fields, although they cultivated orchards and gardens and raised animals. Where herding was an important activity, women also played a role in managing herds. Young men and women had well-defined duties serving elders at formal gatherings and ceremonies. Where a more urban economy is in place, such as in Syria and Jordan, the former peasant households have been transformed; men work mostly in the military and the bureaucracy. Within the sectors made available to them by the wider economy, women have also entered the urban workforce.

Land Tenure. At the time of settlement, land was allotted to each household according to its size. In Jordan, this amount of land was 60 donums (6 hectares) for households of up to five people and 80 *donums* (8 hectares) for larger ones. Land was registered in the name of the head of the household. Later, each state undertook different types of land registration and distribution. In Jordan, land is generally privately owned, and until the 1980s, and especially in rural settlements, land was often held by the father until his death, whereupon it was divided among the children, according to Islamic inheritance rules. In those areas where land became valuable commercial property, younger family members pressured elders to divide the property among them. In a rather widespread phenomenon, many elderly women who own vast tracts of land inherited from their fathers are refusing to divide or sell them.

Kinship

Kin Groups and Descent. In the past, the basic kin units among the Circassians were the patrilineal extended family and a wider patrilineal descent group. In the Caucasus, each descent group tended to live in a separate hamlet. Emigration and settlement broke up these groups, and the new villages included many different descent groups but were often comprised of families of the same dialect group, which, in turn, represented their original region in the Caucasus. Nowadays, in places such as Jordan, descent groups are being organized in formal family associations.

Kinship Terminology. Circassian kinship terminology is extremely descriptive and distinguishes matriline from patriline for both consanguineal and affinal kin. The terms used for "father-in-law" and "mother-in-law" mean "Master" and "Lady," the same terms used to refer to members of the nobility, illustrating the strict hierarchical relations involved between in-laws. The new bride is traditionally given a new personal name upon becoming part of her husband's household and gives new names to all the members of this household, by which she henceforth calls them. Nowadays Arabic or Turkish kinship terms are increasingly replacing Circassian ones, some of them "Circassianized" through a particular pronunciation.

Marriage and Family

Marriage. Circassians are preferentially endogamous within the ethnic group but descent-group exogamous. Traditionally, marriage to kin, up to five generations bilaterally, was prohibited. This has led, in diaspora, to far-flung marriages across communities and settlements but is becoming difficult to maintain. More and more, the rule of exogamy is being ignored, although cousin marriage, which is a preferred form of marriage among Arabs, is still extremely rare among Circassians. A prevalent form of marriage is through elopement, erroneously seen as bride-capture by neighboring groups. Intermarriage with Arabs and Turks does occur, but interesting differences are found between communities. For example, in Jordan, Circassian women marry Arab men, but the reverse (Circassian men marrying Arab women) is rare, whereas in the Kayseri region of Turkey the opposite appears to hold.

Domestic Unit. The domestic unit used to be the patrilineal extended family, with each conjugal family living in a separate dwelling within a common courtyard. Circassians are largely monogamous; polygyny and divorce are rare, although remarriage after the death of a spouse is common. In general, family size—usually three to five children—is small as compared with that of the surrounding society.

Inheritance. Islamic Sharia precepts of inheritance are followed. In Syria and Jordan women inherit their share of property according to Sharia. In rural Turkey, despite the replacement of Sharia with civil codes that stipulate equal division of property among the progeny regardless of sex, it appears that women often give up this inheritance in favor of their brothers, which is common practice in the Middle East.

Socialization. Circassian families traditionally emphasize discipline and strict authoritarianism. Avoidance relationships are the rule between in-laws and between generations and different age groups. It is a source of shame for a man to be seen playing with or showing affection to his children (but not his grandchildren). Although tempered by necessities of everyday life, the same holds for relations between mothers and children. In the past, paternal uncles played an important role in instructing children in proper behavior. This behavior, both public and private, is codified in a set of rules known as Adyge-Khabze (*adyge* = mores) and is reinforced by the family as well as the kin group and the neighborhood as a whole. Nowadays ethnic associations sometimes make attempts to discuss the Adyge-Khabze with young people, and the term is almost always invoked at public gatherings. In Jordan, a Circassian school has been operating since the mid-1970s and has become an arena for socialization and reproduction of Circassian identity.

Sociopolitical Organization

Social Organization. Displacement led to the amalgamation of the different groups with one another while, at the same time, separating families and descent groups. Emigration led to the breaking up of old authority relationships and the creation of new ones. Traditionally, Circassian society was ranked into nobles, warriors, free peasants, and bondsmen—each status maintaining strict endogamy. Emigration disrupted this stratification, and land distribution tended to equalize the communities until new, class-based stratification and rural-urban differences emerged; however, the older status ranking is sometimes still a consideration in deciding on acceptable marriage partners.

Political Organization. The Circassian communities are encapsulated in different formal political systems that range from parliamentary democracies (Turkey and Israel), to one-party regimes (Syria), to constitutional monarchies (Jordan). Other than in Jordan, Circassians do not have a special quota of elected representatives in government. Informal politics of ethnicity and state policies toward minorities govern the political trends and types of participation in the communities. The ethnic associations are the primary arena for organizing the communities; elections may be hotly contested. For example, during the Abkhazian-Georgian war, aid for Abkhazia was collected by such associations. Links with the Caucasus are generally established via these associations.

Social Control. Avoidance relationships diffuse potential conflict, and control is reinforced by the strict discipline imposed through deference to the authority of elders. The latter, however, complain that the younger generation, being ignorant of customs and tradition, no longer respect them sufficiently.

Conflict. Disputes that do not involve civil law tend to be solved through negotiation and consensus by local-level leaders within the community, but intraethnic conflict sometimes involves complicated processes. In Jordan, Arab tribal law, in which not all Circassians are well versed, continues to play an important role in conflict resolution. To this end, a group of Circassian leaders in Jordan established a "Tribal Council" in 1981 to help Circassian individuals and to mediate on their behalf.

Religion and Expressive Culture

Religious Beliefs. The Circassians in the Middle East are all Muslims of the majority Sunni sect. Islam spread late into the northern Caucasus, after the sixteenth century, although a largely syncretic form of Islam, including Christian and local beliefs, continued to be practiced. Exposure to Islamic Orthodoxy occurred mostly during the immigration process, when the Ottomans sent imams to instruct the new immigrants in beliefs and practices.

Religious Practitioners. There are Circassian imams and religious specialists, but, except where there are still ethnically homogeneous villages, there are no mosques where Circassians worship separately from fellow-Muslim Arabs and Turks. Some graveyards that were established before the settlements became heterogeneous continue to be favored by Circassians for burial, even if they do not reside nearby.

Ceremonies. The main ceremonies that distinguish the Circassians from the wider society are those relating to weddings (especially when marriage is through elopement). Several days of dancing and feasting are divided into separate phases for the different age groups. Some other ceremonies (e.g., marking age grades) are now less frequently performed. Many occasions are now celebrated at ethnic organizations. In addition, the major Islamic rituals are observed.

Arts. Folk dancing figures most prominently in Circassian expressive culture, partly because of weddings and other ceremonies in which it plays a major part. Ethnic organizations have focused on folklore troupes. In some cases, notably Turkey, Circassian dances have been incorporated into the national folklore "repertoire." In other countries as well, Circassian dancing is routinely presented at national festivals and occasions.

Medicine. Besides the use of herbs and poultices, traditional Circassian medicine emphasized forbearance of pain and the value of constant entertainment in distracting the ill or wounded from dwelling on their suffering. With the encroachment of Western medicine, these practices are being abandoned. There are no specialized Circassian healers.

Death and Afterlife. Contemporary Circassian beliefs about death and the afterlife are congruent with the Islamic faith, although vestiges of distinctive beliefs in immortality are reflected in the myths of the Narts (half-divine, giant ancestors of the Circassians) and in the tales of Susoruga, who brought fire to humankind. Distinctive funeral practices are still observed, including placement of a large, open pair of scissors on the chest of the deceased and the digging of a particular type of grave.

Bibliography

Abujaber, Raouf S. (1988). *Pioneers over Jordan*. London: I. B. Tauris & Co.

Karpat, Kemal (1977). "Ottoman Immigration Policies and Settlement in Palestine." In *Settler Regimes in Africa and the Arab World: The Illusion of Endurance*, edited by Ibrahim Abu-Lughod and Baha Abu-Laban, 57–72. Illinois: Medina University Press International.

Lewis, Norman N. (1987). *Nomads and Settlers in Syria and Jordan, 1800–1980*. Cambridge: Cambridge University Press.

Shami, Seteney (1992). "19th Century Settlements in Jordan." In *Studies in the History and Archaeology of Jordan*. Vol. 4, 417–421. Amman: Department of Antiquities; Maison de l'Orient Méditerranéen.

Shami, Seteney (1995). "Disjuncture in Ethnicity: Negotiating Circassian Identity in Jordan, Turkey, and the Caucasus." *New Perspectives on Turkey* 12 (Spring): 75–95.

SETENEY SHAMI

Copts

ETHNONYM: Orthodox Coptic Christians

The Copts of Egypt are a religious minority (numbering about 6 million in Egypt) whose church they believe to have been founded by Saint Mark the Evangelist. The Coptic church is the ancient church of Egypt. Outside of Egypt, Coptic communities are found in Sudan (numbering some 100,000), the United States, Great Britain, and other European nations. The name "Copt" is derived from the Greek word "Aiguptioi" (Egyptians). The new faith engendered by Mark's teachings in the first century mingled with the beliefs of other sects, such as that of the Gnostics, and the customs and beliefs of the existing culture in Egypt in the centuries that followed. Biblical papyri and parchment codices found in Egypt provide evidence of the deep penetration of Christianity into Egypt in the early centuries after Christ's death. Constantine made Christianity the official religion of the Byzantime Empire. In A.D. 313 Alexandria, in Egypt, became the seat of Christian theological studies, and it was there that the doctrines of what was an amorphous faith were formulated into a systematic theology.

Alexandria was the place where many of the doctrines of Christianity were defined and where the distinctions between Christianity and the Coptic church originated. Constantine inaugurated an ecumenical movement intended to combat heresy with the Council of Nicaea in 325. These and subsequent councils were controlled largely by the authority of Alexandria, and, therefore, the Coptic doctrine that the father (God) and the son (Christ) are of the same essence, and that Christ's divinity and humanity are unified, was confirmed. However, at the Council of Chalcedon in 451, when Egyptian bishops were in the minority, the Coptic position was condemned. From that point on, the role of the Coptic church in the Christian world was curtailed. Two parallel lines of developement ensued: one, Melchite and Byzantine, accepted the doctrines of the Council of Chalcedon; the other, native Coptic and nationalistic, held the so-called Monophysite interpretation of the nature of Christ.

The outcome of Chalcedon was immediately felt in Egypt. The Byzantine emperors, who aimed for unity within the church, forcibly imposed that unity on the Egyptian people. Persecution of the Copts for their heresy was initiated by the political, military, and ecclesiatical leaders of Alexandria. In opposition to these Greek dictates, the Copts elected their own national patriarch, who had to move from monastery to monastery to avoid pursuing Melchite legionnaires. Excessive taxation, humiliation, and torture were inflicted on the Egyptian Copts from 451 until the Arab conquest in 641.

Muslim rule brought new problems for the Copts and created a new barrier between the Christians of the East and those of the West. Initially, the Muslim minority generally accorded the Copts a certain status as good neighbors and honest civil servants, but an uprising in 830 left Christians in a minority in Egypt for the first time since the early days of Christianity, and from the ninth century onward the Copts were persecuted by their Muslim rulers. Churches were destroyed, books were burned, and church leaders were imprisoned or put to death. By the time the British had taken Egypt in 1882, the Copts had been reduced to only about 10 percent of the total population.

Two important Coptic traditions have survived centuries of history, and exist today as salient features of Coptic culture. The first is martyrdom and the other is monasticism. The martyrs are embedded in the Coptic calendar, which is dated from A.D. 284, in commemoration of the martyrs killed for practicing their faith. In that year, the Roman emperor Diocletian began a wave of persecution that left about 144,000 Egyptian Christians dead. It lasted until 311, when his successor declared an era of toleration. Today Copts begin a new year of the martyrs each 11 September, when they remember the defiance of the early martyrs who maintained their faith in the face of death.

Saint Anthony of Egypt is credited with initiating the strongest monastic movement in religious history. Anthony, following the admonitions of Matthew, sold all of his possessions and gave his money to the poor so that he would find treasure in heaven. He fled to the solitude of the eastern desert, where he practiced a life of austerity and the mortification of the flesh. Others followed his example, and a monastic colony arose around his cave in the mountains. Somewhat later a converted Christian, Pachobius, modified monasticism by repudiating self-mortification but preserved the monastic vow of chastity, poverty, and obedience. There were numerous Pachomian monasteries, not only in Egypt but in many other places as well, and they took root in Europe by the fifth century A.D. Today the monks are the elite of the Coptic church and are symbols of sanctity as well as wielders of power.

Whereas Coptic monks are revered, Coptic clergy are not always well respected. Coptic priests perform baptisms, marriages, and burials and are given respect for those ritual acts, but the respect often ends there. Most Copts—especially educated Copts—have regarded priests as social inferiors or have been openly disdainful toward them. For the most part, priests and monks have been recruited from the lower classes. Sometimes a recurrent pattern emerges: because the clergy has little prestige, it has attracted recruits with low status, perpetuating the low status of the clergy. Those Copts with higher status tend to find positions in business and the professions.

The present population of the Copts is about 6,000,000 (Minority Rights Group 1990), but this figure may not be accurate because official census counts tend to underestimate their numbers and Coptic nationalists tend to overestimate their numbers.

Present-day Copts speak Arabic. Coptic, the liturgical language of the Coptic church, probably became extinct in the sixteenth century. Culturally, the Copts share many customs with other Egyptians and are found distributed through all layers of the social and economic fabric of Egyptian society. Although intermarriage with non-Copts is permitted, the Coptic church insists on the non-Coptic partner being rebaptized according to Coptic rites, and communion is not shared with non-Copts.

Since the early 1980s, the Copts have again suffered discrimination in Egypt: restrictions have been placed on their religious freedom, Coptic insitutions have been placed under government scrutiny, the role of Copts in the Egyptian government has been reduced, and Coptic communities have been attacked by Islamic fundamentalists. The response of the Coptic community in general has been peaceful, although a small segment seeks political autonomy and self-rule.

Bibliography

Burmester, Oswalt Hugh Ewart (1967). *The Egyptian or Coptic Church*. Publications de la Société d'Archéologie Copte. Textes et Documents. Cairo: Société d'Archéologie Copte.

Eliade, Mircea, ed. (1986). *Encyclopedia of Religion*. New York: Macmillan.

Groves, Charles P. (1964). *The Planting of Christianity in Africa*. 4 vols. London: Lutterworth Press. Originally published 1948–1958.

el-Masri, Iris Habib (1978). *The Story of the Copts*. Cairo: Middle East Council of Churches.

Meinardus, Otto F. A. (1965). *Christian Egypt: Ancient and Modern*. Cairo: Cahiers d'Histoire Égyptienne.

Minority Rights Group (1990). "Copts of Egypt." In *World Directory of Minorities*, 186–187. Chicago: St. James Press.

Wakin, Edward (1963). *A Lonely Minority: The Modern Story of Egypt's Copts*. New York: William Morrow & Co.

Dinka

ETHNONYM: Moinjaang

Orientation

Identification. "Dinka" is a term that has been used for centuries to refer to a people who speak of themselves as "Moinjaang," or "the people of the people." They live over a wide area in southern Sudan, amid the many streams and small rivers that feed into the main channel of the Nile River. The ecological year is defined by a dry season of no rain (from November to April) and the season of daily, sometimes intense rain (from May to October).

Demography. At the time of the last official census, in 1950, the Dinka were estimated to number slightly over 1 million individuals, making them the largest ethnic group in southern Sudan. Population densities vary considerably, however, in association with local ecological variation and with the seasonal movements of the Dinka with their herds of cattle.

Linguistic Affiliation. The Dinka language is most closely related to Nuer and Atuot; these languages comprise a subfamily within the larger classification of Nilotic.

History and Cultural Relations

Scholars continue to disagree about the origin of the Dinka, although there is a general consensus that they have inhabited their present country for at least 400 years, if not longer. Indeed, pictographs in temples of ancient Egypt depict cattle with striking resemblances to cattle today. Questions about the origin of the Dinka are best prefaced by questions about the origin of domesticated cattle in Africa south of the Sahara. Culturally, the Dinka are most like the neighboring Nuer and Atuot.

Settlements

Given the fact that Dinka-speaking peoples live in communities that cover considerably different ecological niches, generalizations about the "typical" Dinka settlement are difficult to make. Prior to British colonial rule, there were no "villages" per se. Instead, homesteads were clustered in nomadic territories in a pattern that allowed year-round access to drinking water and to grasslands for feeding their cattle herds. Some settlement clusters consisted of only two or three homesteads, whereas others were comprised of more than a hundred distinctive family settlements. Traditional homesteads were made of mud walls, with thatched roofs, and they lasted some twenty years. In a circular pattern around her hut, a woman cultivated her cooking gardens. Around the turn of the twentieth century, the British admiralty administration sought to cement its presence in southern Sudan by establishing a number of administrative centers. Since then, these small towns have grown considerably, establishing a mode of residence that was previously unknown to the Dinka.

Economy

The Dinka practice a mode of horticulture that complements and balances their cultural devotion to pastoralism, and it is hard to imagine a mode of livelihood that is better suited to their habitat. Millet provides the staple crop; normally there are two plantings per homestead each year. Maize, sesame, pumpkins, okra, and cassava are also cultivated. Although men engaged in the heavy work of clearing secondary forest for gardening sites, women perform the far greater part of the horticultural labor. Men in their twenties and thirties manage and tend the large herds of Dinka cattle. As the rainy season abates and the rivers and streams become more shallow, Dinka also catch many species of fish and, occasionally, hippopotamuses. Game is hunted intermittently. Few items of traditional Dinka material culture lasted longer than the people who manufactured them.

Division of Labor. The cultivation of primary food crops is largely a feminine domain, as is cooking and collecting water from bore wells or rivers. Young boys are introduced to the responsibilities of adulthood by tending small flocks of sheep and goats. Stock rearing, breeding, and tending is an adult-male responsibility. Men manufacture spears, fishing hooks, and cattle ropes from local materials, and women create cooking utensils, baskets, and sleeping mats.

Land Tenure. Access to cultivation and grazing areas is defined by membership in named patrilineal descent groups. Membership, by birth, allocates these rights to all individuals who attain adult status. Traditionally, land and cattle were owned collectively. Neither cattle nor land could be "sold" or otherwise alienated from members of patrilineal birth groups.

Kinship

Kin groups are defined in association with named, totemic descent groups and are extended bilaterally through marriage. At marriage, women leave their natal birth groups to become members of their husbands' agnatic lineages. Like those of the other Nilotic peoples of the southern Sudan and eastern Africa, Dinka relationship terminology is of the classificatory type.

Marriage and Family

Marriage. Although a small number of Dinka have "converted" to Catholicism, polygamy is the cultural ideal of Dinka men, owing primarily to economic and productive factors. Many men contract only a single marriage in their lifetime, but a significant proportion of domestic unions involve the marriage of one man to a number of women. In some chiefly families, men have anywhere from 50 to 100 wives. Due to their classification relationship terminology and also to clan exogamy, Dinka marriage customs tend to create affinal links across wide political and geographic spaces. Marriage is legally defined through the exchange of bride-wealth in the form of cattle. The ideal number of cattle with which to pay bride-wealth varies in different regions of Dinka country, but a number between thirty and forty cattle is common. In addition to the marriage of a woman to a man, the Dinka also practice some of the other forms of marriage that have been reported from other Nilotic communities, such as ghost marriage and levirate. Nearly every adult Dinka woman or man is married at least once in a lifetime.

Domestic Unit. Commensality is one of the primary bases of Dinka domesticity. Co-wives often share the responsibilities of preparing meals on a rotating basis, although a woman always sees to the needs of her own children first. Because they never learn to cook in their youth, the men are dependent upon women to prepare food for them throughout their lives. This factor of dependency is manifest in other aspects of Dinka life as well.

Socialization. A child matures in the loving and attentive company of the family's other children and step-children and a wide circle of kin. Following their initiations, young girls and boys begin to travel quite separate roads, as each interacts more intensely with members of the same sex. Boys begin to master the difficult onus of stock rearing, and girls learn the equally demanding tasks of the women's world.

Sociopolitical Organization

In all areas of Dinka settlements live *beng*, or "chiefs of the fishing spear," and trace their common agnatic heredity to the first spear master, who figures prominently in Dinka origin myths. Spear masters have a spiritual and mystical ability to provide life and assure the health of humans, plants, and animals. Traditionally, spear masters provided the sacred sanction for the regulation of political life, although the Dinka also recognized political loyalties in reference to the shared economic interests that were created through marriage. With the advent of colonial rule in the southern Sudan, British officials imposed a political order of secular chiefs that was entirely foreign to Dinka custom. The creation of a secular legal system, coupled with formal education, has all but eradicated the traditional role and status of spear masters.

Religion

Dinka religious thought posits the existence of a distant but ubiquitous divinity called Nhialac. All life emanates from and ultimately reverts to Nhialac, whereas a different stratum of spiritual agents provides the Dinka with the means of communicating with the supreme divinity. The Dinka also recognize a large number of spiritual agents that are directly susceptible to human control, through the ritual actions of diviners and healers. Traditionally, the Dinka did not imagine that another world awaited them after death, but much concern was expressed about the abilities of the "ghosts" of the recently deceased to affect the well-being of the living.

Bibliography

Deng, F. M. (1970). *The Dinka of the Sudan*. New York: Holt, Rinehart & Winston.

Deng, F. M. (1971). *Tradition and Modernization*. New Haven: Yale University Press.

Lienhardt, R. G. (1961). *Divinity and Experience: The Religion of the Dinka*. Oxford: Clarendon Press.

JOHN W. BURTON

Dogon

ETHNONYMS: Dogom, Dogono, Habbe, Hambbe, Makbe, Tombo, Tommo, Toro

Orientation

Identification. The Dogon are a group of about 250,000 people who live primarily in the districts of Bandiagara and Douentza in the western African nation of Mali. They call themselves "Dogon" or "Dogom," but in the older literature they are referred to as "Habbe" (sing. Kado), a Fulbe word meaning "stranger" or "pagan."

Location. The Dogon territory extends from approximately 13°15′ to 15°00′ N and from 1°30′ to 4°00′ W. The population is concentrated in some 300 villages along a 145-kilometer stretch of escarpment called the Cliffs of Bandiagara. Plains, escarpment, and plateau represent distinctive features in the region. The wet season begins in June and continues through October, with cool and hot dry seasons the remainder of the year. Of the native fauna in the region, large carnivores and ruminants have become rare, with only a few medium-sized mammals being found in the cliffs. Other fauna include crocodiles (in the swampy areas on the plain), reptiles, monkeys, guenons, guinea hens, hyenas, foxes, panthers, rabbits, and small rodents. The dominant form of vegetation on both plain and plateau is the sparse but regular forest of tall trees, which at close range gives the appearance of an immense orchard. Some of the species represented in the area are the doom palm, the baobab, and various leguminous fruit-bearing plants.

Demography. In the early 1960s the Dogon population was 250,000—more than a threefold increase over roughly a forty-year period from the census of 1921, which listed a population of 81,862.

Linguistic Affiliation. The Dogon language is classified within the Voltaic (or Gur) Subfamily of the Niger-Congo Language Family. Minor regional dialectal differences exist. A secret language known as *sigi so* is used by members of the men's society (*awa*) in connection with religious rites.

History and Cultural Relations

Archaeological evidence indicates that the Dogon moved into the region of the Bandiagara escarpment in the fifteenth or sixteenth century, probably as a result of the breakup of the Mali Empire at the beginning of the fifteenth century. European contact was first made in 1857. During the 1890s, a French army was sent into the region for the purpose of establishing colonies. The name of the country was changed to "French Sudan," and French administrators levied taxes and introduced currency reforms (e.g., French francs to replace the native cowrie shells). Although some Dogon accepted the new regime, many strongly opposed and resisted it for many years. Photographs of masked dancers, first taken in 1907, as well as examples of native art work, soon made their way into Europe and the United States, catching the interest and curiosity of the Western world. Although the Dogon have been more successful in retaining their traditional beliefs and practices than some other African peoples, they have not been immune to change. In 1912 a school was established for them in Sanga, followed by a Christian mission in the 1930s, and later a medical dispensary. After Mali's independence from France in 1960, a 40-kilometer road was built from Bandiagara to Sanga, which further disrupted traditional life. Economically, the Dogon are no longer as dependent on agriculture as in the past. Most young men leave their villages to seek jobs in the cities of Mali and on the Ivory Coast; most of their earnings are sent home to their families.

Settlements

The Dogon live in compact, occasionally walled villages built up the sides of the escarpment. Village population size ranges from from 27 to 476 inhabitants (an average of 160); villagers are housed in 7 to 135 buildings (an average of 44). Villages usually contain a single localized lineage whose dwellings are grouped around the "great house" (*ginna*) of the head. Clusters of from 5 to 6 of these villages center around water holes or wells, and each cluster is referred to as a "canton" or "district." Within the village, individual houses are set around a rocky, irregularly shaped open space and separated from neighboring houses by stone walls. Often the buildings are so close to one another that the floors of some houses begin where the roofs of adjacent ones end.

Economy

Subsistence and Commercial Activities. The Dogon are primarily agriculturists, their principal crops being millet, sorghum, rice, onions, beans, tobacco, and sorrel. Other crops include sesame, maize, peanuts, yams, sweet potatoes, tomatoes, peppers, okra, watermelons, papayas, some figs, gourds, and cotton. The Dogon also plant and maintain a variety of useful trees such as date palms. Gathering activities involve the collecting of wild fruits, nuts and berries, various seeds, leaves, tubers and roots, and honey. In comparison with the neighboring Fulani, animal husbandry is relatively unimportant. Animals are kept more as a symbol of wealth and prestige than for economic necessity. The principal domestic animals are sheep, goats, donkeys, dogs, chickens, guinea fowls, ducks, some cattle, a few horses, and cats. A few villages also keep bees.

Industrial Arts. Craft skills are well developed among the Dogon, especially the making of pottery and baskets, weaving, wood carving, and leather- and ironworking. Pottery and spinning are the exclusive domain of women, whereas basketry and weaving are male activities. Two of the most specialized crafts—leather- and ironworking—are restricted exclusively to members of a craft caste. The blacksmith, set apart by his caste, has no rights in the village and lives entirely on the proceeds of the sale of his goods to other villagers.

Trade. Markets are held every four or five days in areas well removed from the villages. Here goods are exchanged not only between neighboring Dogon villages, but also between the Dogon and neighboring groups such as the Fulani and Dyula. Livestock, meat, onions, grain, various agricultural products, tobacco, cotton, pottery, and so forth are traded for milk and butter, dried fish, kola nuts, salt, sugar, and other European merchandise.

Division of Labor. Work activities are clearly differentiated. Craft specialization is determined by gender and caste. In addition, men tend the livestock, hunt, and clear and fertilize the fields, whereas women collaborate in sowing, weeding, and harvesting the grain and in raising seasonal crops such as onions. Both sexes market, fish, and gather wild foods.

Land Tenure. In traditional Dogon society, land was transmitted within the family group (ginna, or lineage), and was considered inalienable property. Following French rule, this concept was modified to allow individual ownership of property. A man may now sell a field allotted to him in the distribution of ginna property, but the sale is always revocable, and the ginna may recover the property upon the death of the seller through the reimbursement of the purchase price to the buyer. Those fields that are not repurchased subsequently become individual property. Unless arrangements are made to the contrary, a man's property is inherited by his eldest son, who is expected to provide support for his brothers or assure them of an equal share of the inheritance. Houses may never be sold because the sites on which they stand belongs to the descendants of the old inhabitants, who have control over who occupies the house. Fruit trees are valued possessions, and although they may be sold, the previous owner reserves the ownership of the field in which they are planted for his own use.

Kinship

Kin Groups and Descent. The fundamental unit of Dogon social organization is the patrilineage, or ginna. Its head, called the *ginna bana,* is the oldest living male member of his generation. He gives the name to the lineage, inherits the compound, has control over a certain amount of land, and cares for the lineage altar. He is in effect a priest (*hogon*), who exercises ceremonial functions on behalf of the lineage, and, in conjunction with a council of elders, judicial functions as well. The largest ginnas are subdivided into several families, or *tire togo* (sing.). Above the lineage is the much larger kin group called the clan, from which the various lineages emerge.

Kinship Terminology. In referring to relatives, linguistic usage distinguishes between the forms of address and the specific relationship. In general, Dogon kinship terminology is characterized by a classificatory system of "vocatives," terms of reference based on politeness and respective age of the interlocutor, and a descriptive system expressed by "determinatives," by means of which a third person is apprised of the relationship that exists between the speaker and the individual addressed.

Marriage and Family

Marriage. Monogamy is the major form of marriage, although nonsororal polygyny with a limit of two wives is permitted. First marriages are generally arranged by parents; within certain limitations, those marrying for the second or third time are more free to choose their partners. Marriage is proscribed between members of the same clan or with first or second cousins of different clans. Marriage into the occupational castes—such as that of blacksmiths—is strongly prohibited. Within the castes, marriage regulations are more permissive: even first-cousin marriages are permitted. Prior to the birth of the first child, the wife lives at the home of her parents, while her husband continues to reside in the bachelor quarters where he has lived from the age of 8 to 10. Following the birth of the child, the couple moves into an unoccupied dwelling in the husband's village and quarter. Divorce is not uncommon; it occurs most often in polygynous households. When a woman leaves her husband, she takes with her only the youngest child—the remaining children stay with the husband's family.

Domestic Unit. The household is usually an extended family consisting of both nuclear and polygynous units. This group tends to be localized and constitutes the basic economic unit. The authority of the household unit is vested in the father, who controls both the economic and ceremonial functions of the family and demands unquestioning obedience from his offspring.

Inheritance. Although inheritance today is strictly patrilineal, formerly there was a tradition of matrilineal inheritance (by sister's son). A younger brother is first in line to inherit all collective property, followed by the eldest son. On the other hand, private property goes first to the eldest son (who must provide for his siblings), then the younger brother. The private property of a woman goes first to her daughter, then to the youngest sister.

Socialization. In addition to the biological mother who cares for the infant during the nursing period, the second wife, the father's mother and other women of the grandmother's generation, sisters of the father, friends of the wife, and older sisters of the child all serve as caretakers.

Sociopolitical Organization

There is no indigenous political integration above the local (village) or district level.

Social Organization. Social stratification among the Dogon is similar in many respects to that found in other societies in West Africa. One of its most distinctive features is the hierarchical series of occupational "castes" or status groups consisting of iron- and leatherworkers, *griots* (lineage genealogists), musicians, poets, and sorcerers. These caste groups live apart from the general population. Each caste is endogamous, and members do not take part in any of the common religious cults. Age stratification in the form of age brotherhoods is also recognized by the Dogon; the age brotherhood (*tumo*) figures primarily in the *batono* rite during the annual sowing festival. Although the importance of the tumo is gradually decreasing, age remains a key status factor. A men's society, frequently referred to as the "awa," or masked-dance society, is characterized by a strict code of etiquette, obligations, interdicts, and a secret language (sigi so). Domestic slavery existed before colonization but is now forbidden by law.

Political Organization. Each isolated village or district (canton) in the region has a headman or chief (hogon) who has both religious and judicial responsibilities. Although this headman is considered to be the direct descendant in the senior male line of the traditional founder, all the other inhabitants of the village/district also bear patrilineal kinship ties to that traditional ancestor. The district headman is also head of his lineage and occupies the "great house" (ginna) of that kin group. In conjunction with the council of elders, he makes decisions concerning public affairs. The hogon is assisted in office by a sacrificial totem priest (*yebene*), three bodyguards or policemen, a public crier or herald, and an ambassador who deals with other districts. Succession to office is patrilineal (by younger brother). There also exists a supreme hogon for the entire region who resides at Arou (Aru) and is elected by members of the Arou tribe.

Social Control. Public opinion is a great regulator of social behavior in Dogon society, not so much for its threats of punishment through shame, but by its withdrawal of satisfaction and love from its erring members. Also effective as means of inducing conformity are ridicule and threats of supernatural sanction.

Conflict. In the past the Dogon were considered a warlike people; they often fought with other Dogon districts as well as with their non-Dogon neighbors such as the Fulani. Each district had its own recognized war leaders. Blood alliances frequently were contracted between the Dogon and other groups such as the Bozo.

Religion and Expressive Culture

Religious Beliefs. Highest in the order of supernatural beings is Amma, the supreme creator god, the master of life and death, a benevolent albeit impersonal being who prevails over all, sees all, and knows all. He is responsible for the creation of three other subordinate beings, the worship of which is the basis of several totemic cults. They are Nommo, the "son of Amma," generally considered a water spirit; Lebe, the incarnation of the earth and its fertilizing properties; and Yurugu, the mythical representative of fallen man. The Dogon also believe in various malevolent and benevolent spirits who populate the bush, trees, and uninhabited places.

Although the Dogon recognize the creator god Amma as the Supreme Being and address prayers and sacrifices to him, the core set of beliefs and practices focuses on ancestor worship. This is manifested through the cult of the masks, the Lebe cult, the Binu cult, and the more general cult of the ancestors associated with the ginna. The spread of Islam throughout Africa has brought about some degree of change in the basic religious orientation of the Dogon. Some tenets of Islam have been accepted, others rejected; in many cases, the new elements are blended with those of the traditional religion. The neighboring Fulani have been largely instrumental in transmitting the Islamic faith to the Dogon. About 10 percent of the Dogon are Christians.

Religious Practitioners. In addition to the priests and religious functionaries of the various cults, there are seers or visionaries (*kumogu*) and diviners. Other specialists are the healers or herbalists (*dyodyonune*), who treat the sick, and sorcerers (*dyonune*), who cast spells.

Ceremonies. The principal ceremonies center around agriculture and death. The great annual Feast of Sowing (*bulu*) begins in April or May, prior to the beginning of the rainy season, in all the villages of the region. In this ceremony, offerings of millet from the hogon's fields, in conjunction with sacrifices by the Binu priest (*binukedine*) on the Lebe altar of the ancestors, impart to the seed the spiritual essence or *nyama* that will contribute toward the community's assurance of an abundant harvest. The funerary ceremonies of the Dogon consist of two parts: the initial rites, which take place immediately following death and continue for about a week, and the more elaborate *dama* rites that terminate the mourning period after an indeterminate period of time. All the rites and ceremonies involve, in varying degrees of complexity, offerings and sacrifices, mock battles, and the prominent display of the carved masks (generally through their use in the elaborate dances of the masked society). The degree of complexity of the ceremonies depends upon the age and status of the deceased male. Funerals for women, who are generally excluded from awa membership, are simple, with little if any ceremony. Once in every sixty years—roughly within a Dogon's life span—a major Sigi (Sigui) ceremony takes place. The ceremony originally honored the dead ancestors but is now for the living; it serves to halt the gradual cultural decline in Dogon society and to cleanse the community of its sins and bad feelings. The series of dances, which constitute a good part of the Sigi, lasts for seven years; one village after another takes its turn to entertain its neighbors with feasting, drinking, and displays of wealth. At this time, new masks are carved and dedicated to the ancestors.

Medicine. The Dogon attribute illness to a variety of causes, such as the weakening of the vital life force (nyama), the creation of a state of impurity in the individual through the influences of evil spirits, violation of a taboo or prohibition, and sorcery. There are twelve categories of disease considered treatable, each with its own specific healer who has special knowledge of the specific plant that will bring about a cure. Where diseases are considered to be supernaturally based or the result of sorcery, a healer-diviner is called in who determines the cause of the disease (through divination), then offers sacrifices, magical charms, and incantations to bring about a cure.

Death and Afterlife. Death is conceived as the separation from the body of the two parts that make up the personality—the nyama, or vital life force, and the *kikinu say*, or soul. Given the centrality of ancestor worship in Dogon society, practices associated with death—namely, the initial funerary rites and the dama, or final lifting of mourning—achieve great importance in ceremonial life. Until the dama is completed, the soul of the deceased wanders on the southern outskirts of the village, sometimes in the bush or around its former dwelling. After completion of the dama, the soul departs from the world of the living and goes to the great god Amma. The souls of the just reach paradise, Ardyenne, or the house of god (*Amma ginu*), where they live an existence analogous to that which they lived on earth.

Bibliography

Griaule, Marcel (1938). *Masques dogons*. Université de Paris, Travaux et Mémoires de l'Institut d'Ethnologie, 33. Paris: Institut d'Ethnologie.

Palau Marti, Montserrat (1957). *Les dogon*. Paris: Presses Universitaires de France.

Paulme, Denise (1940). *Organisation sociale des dogon (Soudan Français)*. Paris: Éditions Domat-Montchrestien, F. Loviton & Cie.

Pern, Stephen (1982). *Masked Dancers of West Africa: The Dogon*. Amsterdam: Time-Life Books B.V.

JOHN M. BEIERLE

Druze

ETHNONYMS: none

The Druze are a closed, tightly knit, Arab minority who live in southern Syria, in the mountains of central Lebanon, and in Israel, including the Golan Heights. There are also small communities in Jordan, the United States, Canada, and Latin America. In the early 1980s they numbered approximately 200,000 in Syria, 10,000 in Lebanon, 43,000 to 72,000 in Israel, and another 10,000 to 15,000 in the Golan Heights (Grimes 1988).

The Druze originated as a religious minority in the eleventh century when a small group of Muslims split off from the Shiite branch of Islam in Egypt. One of the founders, Abū ʿAlī al-Manṣūr al-Ḥākim bi-Amrih Allāh (985–1021), was accorded divine status. One of his disciples, also considered a founder of the faith, was Ḥamzah ibn ʿAlī, who established most of the doctrine that defined the new religion. Another founder, who competed with Ḥamzah for followers, was Muḥammad ibn Ismāʿīl ad-Darazī. Bloody clashes between Darazī and Ḥamzah led to Darazī's death in 1020. Al-Ḥākim and Ḥamzah died the following year, which left all three founders of the faith dead within three years of the founding of their religion.

Darazī's followers began proselytizing members of the sect in Syria. They became known as the community of Darazī, *durzi* in Arabic, and the plural form, *duruz*, took hold as their name—"Druze." After the withdrawal of Ḥamzah's successor, al-Muqtana, in 1034, Druze proselytizing ceased, and the doctrine was adopted that there could be no further admission into their ranks. The Druze then migrated northward into Lebanon, south into Galilee, and further east into Syria.

The Druze call themselves *muwaḥḥidūn*, ("declarers of oneness"), and they call their religion *dīn al-tawḥīd* (monotheism). Internally, the spiritual hierarchy of the Druze underwent a gradual change that resulted in the division of the community into two classes, the *ʿuqqāl* (knowers, sages; sing. *ʿāqil*) and *juhhāl* (the ignorant). The ʿuqqāl are those who are initiated into the doctrines of the Druze religion and who are knowledgeable about the gnostic-cosmological-moralistic writing produced by the Druze sages in the course of their history. The external signs of their status are their special garb and white turbans. The leaders of the ʿuqqāl, who are called *shuyukh* (sing. *shaykh*), are chosen from those who are considered the most learned and pious among them. Shuyukh are trained for their office at special schools. From among the shuyukh a *raʾīs* is chosen, usually a member of a leading family, as the supreme religious authority in the district.

All ʿuqqāl are expected to lead a morally impeccable life and always to behave with decorum. They must abstain from using stimulants, and from lying, stealing, and exacting revenge. They are expected to attend Friday evening services at the *majlis*, which corresponds to the Muslim mosque. They are allowed to read the Druze secret books and to know of, and participate in, the secret ritual.

The juhhāl are the uninitiated majority of the Druze community. They are held to a less strict code of behavior, and, unless they attempt to attain ʿāqil status, must remain in their "ignorant" position until death and possibly a future rebirth. The juhhāl are bound by the same laws and tenets of the religion as the ʿuqqāl.

The laws laid down by Ḥamzah in the eleventh century still apply to the Druze today. Among them are laws that establish equality between husband and wife and allow divorce only in rare circumstances, for very specific reasons. The position of women in Druze society is, therefore, on a more even level with that of men than it is in traditional Muslim societies. There is reason to believe that women, in fact, have a higher level of status than men. Almost all unmarried women work within Druze communities. When they go outside of their village, they are escorted by fathers and brothers. At work, the sexes are strictly segregated, and sometimes walls are built to keep young men and women out of each others' sight.

There are seven commandments in the Druze religion that are somewhat similar to the Five Pillars of Islam. The Druze must speak the truth among themselves (but not among outsiders); they must defend and help each other in times of crises or need (carrying arms for this purpose is sanctioned); they must renounce beliefs negating the oneness of God; they must dissociate themselves from unbelievers; they must recognize al-Ḥākim as an incarnation of God; they must be content with God's actions; and they must submit to God's will and orders.

The Druze believe that al-Ḥākim and Ḥamzah will reappear, conquer the world, and establish justice, and that the Druze living at that time will be the universal rulers. They also believe that the number of living Druze is fixed, and will always remain constant. They share with other Middle Eastern groups, such as the Baha'is, a belief in the concept of *taqiyah* (dissimulation). For the Druze, "taqiyah" means that in order for them to preserve the secrecy of their faith, they must pretend to accept the faith of the ruling majority, which for most Druze, has been Sunni Islam.

In the ten centuries following their formation as a group, the Druze have tended to settle in high mountain villages. In these protected enclaves, they have maintained their own culture, which is based primarily on their distinctive religious beliefs and perpetuated by strict endogamy. Because of their religious tenets, the Druze have insisted on self-determination and independence, and have considered all outsiders, whether Muslim or Christian, their enemies. This has resulted in numerous violent clashes with their neighbors.

The traditional culture of the Druze is threatened by the encroachment of technology and modern culture that arises from the dominant cultures within which they exist. The Druze live in uneasy compromise between their traditional values and the pressures of life in increasingly Westernized countries. Young Druze men are beginning to question the religious beliefs and practices of their elders, although there are few who have rejected the faith entirely.

If there is any large-scale rejection of the Druze religion, it will more than likely begin with the young men who have sampled the amenities of Western culture and want more from life than what can be obtained in small Druze villages. Women are not likely to lead the call for change because they seem to enjoy the protected status that they receive.

The Druze, a very old culture that began as a religious community, but have, over the centuries, become an ethnic entity. They have survived largely because of their skill at adapting to the requirements of their environment, both physical and cultural. Their traditional policy of taqiyah and accommodation to larger protective cultures has helped keep their traditions intact, but this policy may not be enough to preserve their culture in the future. If they are to maintain their identity, they must somehow accommodate the desires and demands of their more Westernized young people with the strict tenets of their distinctive religion.

Bibliography

Ben-Dor, Gabriel (1979). *The Druzes in Israel: A Political Study*. Jerusalem: Magnes Press.

Dana, Nissim (1980). *The Druse: A Religious Community in Transition*. Forest Grove, Oreg.: Turtledove Press; Jerusalem: Israel Economist.

Friendly, Alfred, and Eric Silver (1981). "Israel's Oriental Immigrants and Druzes." *Minority Rights Group Report* no. 12.

Grimes, Barbara F., ed. (1988). *Ethnologue: Languages of the World*. Dallas: Summer Institute of Linguistics.

Minority Rights Group (1994). "Druzes of Israel and the Golan Heights." In *World Directory of Minorities*, 191–192. London: Minority Rights Group.

Patai, Raphael (1986). "Druze." In *The Encyclopedia of Religion*, edited by Mircea Eliade, 503–506. New York: Macmillan.

Dyula

ETHNONYMS: Jula, Wangara

Orientation

Identification. "Dyula" is a Manding word typically referring to "traders" as a socioprofessional category, particularly to Muslim long-distance traders who speak one or another dialect of Manding. The name is used as an ethnic label by Manding-speaking minorities, particularly those living amid various Gur-speaking groups, such as the Senufo and Kulango.

Location. The Dyula are an ethnic minority in north-central and northeastern Ivory Coast, in southeastern Mali, and southwestern Burkina Faso, roughly from 8° to 12° N and from 3° to 6° W, along the southern fringes of the savanna. Nowadays many Dyula are also to be found in major towns and cities of all three countries.

Demography. The Dyula account for about 10 to 20 percent of the population of the areas they occupy. They number between 200,000 and 300,000. Since the term "dyula" is also used as a socioprofessional category, it is difficult to rely on census data for estimates, especially as many Dyula have migrated to large urban areas.

Linguistic Affiliation. The Dyula speak dialects of Manding, a northern Mande language of the Niger-Congo Family. The Dyula dialects are very closely related to certain dialects of Bamana (or Bambara) and Maninka (or Malinke), all of which are mutually comprehensible.

History and Cultural Relations

Traders from the middle Niger were drawn toward the southern reaches of the savanna and beyond toward the forest because of the presence of gold in Lobi and Akan gold fields and because of kola nuts in the forest. Particularly after the foundation of the trading town of Begho, in northwestern Ghana, around 1400, Manding-speaking traders began to settle amid various local populations, forming the southern edge of the network of a vast trading diaspora linking the West African forest and ultimately the coast with the Sahara and the Mediterranean. By the eighteenth century, there were Dyula communities along all the trade routes in the region, and these communities continued to assimilate fellow traders from elsewhere until the mid-twentieth century, by which time colonial rule had radically altered patterns of trade and migration. One of these towns, Kong, became an independent state as well as a major center of trade; it was a major power in the region, particularly during its apogee in the eighteenth century. Most Dyula communities, however, remained politically subservient to kings and chiefs of other ethnic and linguistic communities. In the last two decades of the nineteenth century, the region was torn by war: three empires—the state of Kenedugu, centered at Sikasso in Mali; the domain of Samory Toure, initially in Guinea to the west; and France—struggled for control. The great Dyula trading towns of Kong and Buna were razed by Samory, who suspected them of negotiating with the French. Following Samory's capture, France annexed the region. By and large, the Dyula submitted peacefully to the French, although, in the mid-twentieth century, many of them were active militants in the independence movement.

The Dyula recognize their cultural affinities with other Manding-speaking peoples, including the Bamana and the Maninka, and especially with trading groups such as the Maraka of the middle Niger. As an ethnic minority and part of a trading diaspora, the Dyula stress their cultural differences with their immediate neighbors—for example, the Senufo, the Kulango, or the Abron. Many Dyula are nevertheless fluent in other local languages and have usually had a vested interest in remaining on good terms with their neighbors and political overlords. Their neighbors, in turn, have relied on the Dyula as agents for buying and reselling locally produced goods and as a source for commodities produced elsewhere.

Settlements

The Dyula settled primarily, although not exclusively, along the trade routes passing through the region. The largest towns in the region—Kong (with an estimated population of 15,000 in the late nineteenth century), Buna, Bondoukou, and Bobo-Dioulasso—were major market centers inhabited mainly by Dyula. On the whole, the Dyula preferred to settle in larger villages if not towns, where there were greater commercial opportunities. Some of these communities were entirely or almost all peopled by Dyula; however, the Dyula frequently settled in multiethnic communities of various sizes, often in a spatially separate quarter. Dyula towns, villages, and quarters were in turn divided into different neighborhoods and clan wards.

Economy

Subsistence and Commercial Activities. Most Dyula were involved in trade or the production of commodities for the market on at least a part-time basis. Yams, maize, sorghum, or millet were staple crops, depending on the location, supplemented by groundnuts, tomatoes, okra, and other vegetables. Tobacco, processed as snuff, was grown as a cash crop. The Dyula were extensively involved in weaving; they enjoyed a complete monopoly over the production of cloth among the Senufo. The town of Kong, in particular, produced luxury cloths for export to other regions. The Dyula were also involved in long- and medium-distance caravan trade, as well as peddling to their neighbors imported commodities and the goods produced from them. Wealthier Dyula possessed slaves to grow their food, which afforded the traders the leisure to pursue commercial or other activities year-round. Dyula living in larger, more active commercial centers might also trade or weave all year, purchasing foodstuffs in the marketplace. Many Dyula, however, particularly those in smaller communities off major trade axes, were seasonally involved in subsistence horticulture.

Industrial Arts. The Dyula were heavily involved in the production of cloth and clothing. Spinning was a common household activity for women; in some Dyula communities, women also were involved in dyeing thread with indigo. Men wove the cloth in narrow bands, often with complex and intricate patterns, and sewed the sections into blankets or items of clothing. In the twentieth century, the Dyula were among the first in the region to purchase sewing machines. Dyula tailors are noted for their elaborate embroidery.

Trade. As specialized traders, the Dyula were involved in the buying and selling of whatever commodities were marketable. This included goods they produced themselves, principally cloth but also snuff. They were involved in the long-distance trade between the middle Niger and the forest: salt and horses were traded southward and gold and kola nuts northward, along with a variety of other commodities, including luxury cloths, shea butter, peppers, and slaves.

Division of Labor. The Dyula were part of a regional and interregional system of hereditary specialization. Broadly speaking, weaving, trade, and Islamic scholarship were the hereditary preserves of the Dyula, who were themselves divided into two hereditary categories: *tun tigi* ("warrior") and *mory* ("scholar"). These broad categories corresponded very loosely if at all with the specific occupations of individuals. Instead, specific local kin groups tended to specialize in one activity or another: a specific kind of weaving, advanced Islamic scholarship, a particular sector of trade. This system of specialization was not rigid, however, and individuals had a good deal of freedom in choosing their occupations. Weaving, warfare, and Islamic learning were specifically male activities; spinning, cooking, and child rearing specifically female. Both males and females engaged in trade. Individuals who possessed slaves assigned the relatively onerous or less remunerative tasks, but slaves did not perform any tasks that could not be or were not undertaken by free individuals.

Land Tenure. Resident members of any clan ward (*kabila*; pl. *kabilaw*) of a village had a traditional right to obtain land for cultivation. Outsiders could also obtain such rights, even permanently, by attaching themselves to a clan ward as guests (*lunanw*; sing. *lunan*). Rights over specific fields could be highly individuated, however, particularly if those fields were highly suitable for cash-crop production. Nowadays building plots in towns and, increasingly, in villages, are privately owned and registered and constitute a valuable form of landed property.

Kinship

Kin Groups and Descent. Descent groups are identified by patronyms (*dyamuw*; sing. *dyamu*), many of which are common to other Mande-speaking peoples. In any community, individuals sharing a patronym who consider themselves agnatically related together form a kabila, with a designated head, the *kabila tigi*. A large kabila is divided into segments called *so*, *lu*, or *gba*. The precise meanings attached to these latter terms vary from place to place. Many kabilaw are too small to be segmented, and a village or town can include quite a number of unrelated clan wards, some of which might bear the same patronym. Kabilaw—and even segments of them—

can be economically specialized. Internal disputes are settled by a council of the clan ward or segment as a whole.

Kinship Terminology. Kinship terminology is bifurcate merging in parents' generation, with Iroquois cousin terms in Ego's generation. Relative age is consistently stressed in Ego's and, to a lesser extent, in parents' generation.

Marriage and Family

Marriage. The most highly favored form of marriage is within the clan ward, that is, for all intents and purposes, between classificatory patrilateral parallel cousins. Marriages between relatives from different clan wards, especially matrilateral cross cousins, are also encouraged. Marriage is virilocal, except for the remarriages of older widows, who usually prefer to live with their sons. Divorce, following Islamic law, is easily obtained in principle, but couples are often pressured by their families to reconcile their differences.

Domestic Unit. The Dyula have a high incidence of polygyny. In the past, sons, even those who were married, tended to live with their father. The families of full brothers frequently remained together for some time after the father's death.

Inheritance. In principle, inheritance follows the dictates of Muslim law: all sons inherit an equal share and daughters half as much as sons. In the past, the extent to which these rules were strictly followed varied, and daughters did not necessarily receive their share. To the extent that any property was considered to be corporately rather than individually owned, it passed instead from elder to younger brother.

Socialization. In day-to-day matters, mothers and older siblings were most responsible for monitoring a child's behavior; fathers intervened more occasionally or for more serious questions. Boys from mory families were usually sent to a teacher to acquire the rudiments of Arabic literacy, if not a full-fledged religious education, whereas tun tigi boys, at adolescence, were inducted into secret *low* (initiation societies; sing. *lo*). Boys were also expected to learn specialized economic skills, such as weaving, from older kinsmen. Nowadays many children, especially in towns, attend modern schools.

Sociopolitical Organization

Social Organization. An individual's seniority is determined by generation, relative age, gender, and free or slave status. Juniors are expected to display consistent deference toward their elders, appealing to individuals even more senior or to a council of the descent group as a whole if they feel they are being unjustly treated. Rules of seniority are, in principle, applied inflexibly to designate the eldest free male of the senior generation to succeed to office within the descent group or to political office. Nevertheless, the Dyula accord considerable respect and de facto authority to any individual successful in commerce, politics, or Islamic scholarship. A distinction was drawn between slaves who were purchased (*san jon*) and slaves who were "born in the house" (*worosso*). The latter might joke obscenely at the expense of all free individuals (*horon*). Milder reciprocal-joking relationships exist between linked patronymic groups (*senanku*), between grandparents and grandchildren, between cross cousins, and between certain categories of affines (*nimogo*), specifically elder siblings' spouses and spouses' younger siblings.

Political Organization. Most Dyula communities owed political allegiance to rulers from other ethnic groups, such as the Senufo or Abron. The most notable exception was the state of Kong, where the Dyula staged a coup d'état around 1700. The Dyula who enjoyed political authority as chiefs—whether of the state of Kong, a chiefdom, or simply a village—were drawn in principle from the ranks of hereditary "warriors," called tun tigiw, or, in Kong, *sonongui*. In the late nineteenth century, many Dyula communities were annexed by the empire of Samory. Some Dyula chiefs were deposed in favor of more loyal supporters with no claims to authority. The authority of traditional chiefs was further eroded by the French and, later, by the postcolonial authorities; it is now essentially symbolic.

Social Control. The control that elders enjoyed over access to wealth and to women helped them maintain effective authority over their junior dependents. Conflicts were mediated by chiefs or adjudicated by a council of the descent group as a whole. Geographical mobility was high: malcontents could simply leave to seek their fortunes elsewhere.

Conflict. At its apogee in the eighteenth century, the state of Kong enjoyed considerable power, raiding as far as the Niger to the north and staving off the armies of Ashanti to the south. With the military decline of Kong, the Dyula there and elsewhere tended to concentrate on commercial rather than military ventures. As traders, the Dyula often had a stake in maintaining good relations with their neighbors. They were not pacifists, however; their individual or collective participation in local warfare depended on their assessment of circumstances.

Religion and Expressive Culture

Religious Beliefs. The Dyula have always been Muslim. In the past, however, the tun tigiw were not expected to conform rigorously to the same standards of Islamic practice as the mory. Instead, the tun tigiw, as members of low, participated in animal sacrifices to spirits. They might drink alcoholic beverages and observe prescribed prayer and fasting only irregularly. By about 1950, such practices were perceived as lax, as compared to other Muslim communities. The initiation societies were abolished, and a single standard of proper Muslim behavior was applied to everyone. As Muslims, the Dyula worship Allah and acknowledge the existence of angels and devils. They also acknowledge the existence of jinn, which may be Muslim or pagan and are potentially dangerous; prankish little *kongo denniw* ("bush children"); and spirits that were associated with specific initiation societies.

Religious Practitioners. Those older men learned in Arabic and Islamic theology and law were known as *karamogow* and were authorities in Islamic matters. Formerly, there also existed *lo tigiw*, elders in charge of initiation societies.

Ceremonies. Various ceremonies mark the Islamic lunar calendar year, particularly Donba, the Prophet's birthday; Tabaski, marking the season of pilgrimage and the sacrifice of Isaac; and Sunkalo, the annual fast of the month of Ramadan. Increasingly, Islamic literati decry the festivities associated with these periods, although to little avail. Weddings and funerals of important elders are also occasions for elaborate festivities.

Arts. Weaving of elaborately patterned cloths, as well as the embroidery of intricate arabesque designs on clothing, are the most highly developed Dyula art forms. The Dyula sometimes use elaborately sculpted objects—masks, loom pulleys—produced by specialists of neighboring ethnic groups.

Medicine. The Dyula resort to various herbal remedies (*fla;* lit., "leaves"), as well as to written magic formulas in Arabic. Nowadays the Dyula are quite willing to seek Western medical treatment when it is available and affordable.

Death and Afterlife. Most Dyula believe in the reality of witchcraft, of nefarious magic written in Arabic, of the deadly power of initiation-society spirits controlled by their senior members, and of dangerous local spirits, all of which may cause illness or death. These dangers are now considered remote, however, and they do not preoccupy most Dyula as they did, it would seem, in the past. As Muslims, the Dyula affirm the existence of heaven and hell in the afterlife, as a reward or punishment for behavior on earth.

Bibliography

Bernus, Edmond (1960). "Kong et sa region." *Études Éburnéennes* 8:239–324.

Launay, Robert (1982). *Traders without Trade: Responses to Change in Two Dyula Communities.* Cambridge: Cambridge University Press.

Launay, Robert (1992). *Beyond the Stream: Islam and Society in a West African Town.* Berkeley and Los Angeles: University of California Press.

Tauxier, Louis (1921). *Le noir de Bondoukou.* Paris: Leroux.

ROBERT LAUNAY

Edo

ETHNONYM: Bini

Orientation

Identification. "Edo" is the name that the people of the Benin Kingdom give to themselves, their language, and their capital city and kingdom. Renowned for their art of brass and ivory and for their complex political organization, the Edo Kingdom of Benin is one of the best known of the precolonial kingdoms on the Guinea Coast of West Africa. From at least the fifteenth century, the Benin Empire held varying degrees of authority over neighboring peoples, including the western Igbo, northeastern Yoruba, and various related Edo-speaking groups. In 1897 British-colonial forces conquered the kingdom and made it part of the Niger Protectorate. Today it is incorporated into the modern state of Nigeria.

Location. The core Edo area, about 10,400 square kilometers, is located on a rolling coastal plain crossed by rivers, in an area of tropical rain forest. About 40 percent of the region is forest reserves. Benin City, the capital, is located at 6°26′ N and 5°41′ E. The annual rainfall can be as much as 175 to 200 centimeters. The average daily temperature is about 27° C. There is seasonal variation, with a wet season from July to September and a dry one from December to February.

Demography. Accurate population figures are difficult to obtain for this area, particularly outside the capital city. In 1963 a Nigerian census indicated that Benin City had a population of 100,694. The urban population was estimated at 201,000 in 1972, and by 1976 at 314,219, indicating a growth rate of 8.5 percent for that period, on the basis of which Ikhuoria (1984, 177) estimated the city's 1980 population—of which the Edo comprised the largest number—at 425,000. Migration to Benin City continues to increase its population, which doubles in size every decade, as young people from the rural areas, as well as from different ethnic groups, come to seek employment.

Linguistic Affiliation. Edo belongs to the Edoid cluster of languages that is part of the Kwa Language Family and the Niger-Kordofanian Superfamily. Edo-speaking peoples include not only the Edo proper but also the Ishan, the Etsako, the Ivbiosakon, the Akoko Edo, the Ineme, the Urhobo, and the Isoko. Many contemporary Edo speakers speak English as well as languages of neighboring Nigerian groups.

History and Cultural Relations

The Edo have undoubtedly lived in the same area for many centuries. Connah's archaeological investigation (1975) at a site in what is today Benin City suggests that a large population with a degree of political organization may have existed as early as the end of the late eleventh century but was certainly in place by the end of the fifteenth. (Connah's radiocarbon dates from this site are 1180±100 to 1310±100). Oral traditions include references to an early dynasty of kings called *ogiso* (a term that can apply to the dynasty as a whole or to individual rulers within that dynasty), which ruled, it is suggested, until the twelfth or thirteenth century, when Oranmiyan dynasty, of Yoruba origin, took over. The fifteenth and sixteenth centuries were an age of conquest and cultural flowering. Many of the sculptures for which Benin is famous were created for the monarchs Ewuare, Ozolua, Esigie, Orhogbua, and Ehengbuda. Under the rule of these kings, the empire imposed varying degrees of domination over neighboring Yoruba-, Igbo-, and Edo-speaking populations and even extended its influence to Badagry and Ouidah (now in the Republic of Benin, which was called Dahomey until 1976). This expansion was in process when Portuguese explorers arrived in the third quarter of the fifteenth century. They were interested in spreading Christianity and developing commerce. Trade with the Netherlands, France, and England followed. Oral traditions and European records indicate that the power of the kingdom fluctuated over the centuries. A dynastic crisis in the seventeenth century led to a civil war lasting from about 1690 to 1720, which disrupted the political and economic life of the kingdom, but peace was restored by kings Akenzua I and Eresoyen in the mid-eighteenth century. Toward the end of the nineteenth century, Benin came into conflict with the British, who viewed the kingdom as an obstacle to their economic and political expansion in the area. In 1897 a British consular official insisted on visiting the city in spite of requests by the king to delay until the completion of important religious ceremonies. The consul and his party were ambushed, and most of them were killed. The British immediately assembled the "Punitive Expedition," a retaliatory force, which attacked and captured Benin City in February of 1897, setting fires throughout the urban area and taking as war booty thousands of brass and ivory sculptures. The reigning king, Ovonramwen, was sent into exile, where he died, and the Benin Kingdom was incorporated into the Southern Province of the Nigerian Protectorate. In 1914 the British amalgamated the Southern and Northern protectorates into the new country of Nigeria. In the same year, they restored the monarchy in Benin, allowing Ovonramwen's son, Eweka II, to assume the throne. They instituted a system of Native Administration (a form of indirect rule), introduced a uniform monetary system and direct taxation, established government schools, and built a communications network of roads and railways. Early in the twentieth century, the Church Missionary Society and the Society of African Missions arrived in Benin, but they had less success there than in other parts of Nigeria. Nigeria gained independence in 1960, and at that time the kingdom became part of the Western Region. Over the years, the modern political boundaries of the territory and its names have changed several times. In 1963 it was separated from the Western Region and called the Midwest Region, and then, in 1976, it was renamed Bendel State. In 1993 Bendel State was split in two, and today the Benin Kingdom is part of Edo State.

Settlements

There are several hundred villages dispersed throughout the Edo territory, varying in size from 30 inhabitants to more than 4,000. Larger villages are divided into quarters. Houses are generally constructed of mud and roofed with corrugated-iron sheets. Formerly, residences were scattered, but, with the construction of roads that started in the early part of the twentieth century, and especially with the establishment of Benin City as the state capital in 1963, villages have become increasingly aligned along the main roads. The farms are located away from the settlements.

Benin City, the capital of the traditional kingdom as well as of modern Edo State, is a large urban complex with a long history. Archaeological evidence indicates that there could have been a population concentration in that area as early as the end of the eleventh century. European visitors, beginning in the fifteenth century, found a vast palatial compound with countless courtyards, altars, halls, and passageways, all richly decorated with brass, ivory, and wooden sculpture. The king's section of the town, Ogbe—where the palace and the residences of palace chiefs, minor officials, and retainers were located—was divided by a broad street from Ore n'Okhua, where town chiefs and their retinues, minor title holders, and members of forty or fifty guilds resided, each in their own quarter. At the time of the British conquest in 1897, fires destroyed much of the traditional architecture. The city was subsequently rebuilt—to an extent along former lines. The new palace, however, is significantly smaller than the earlier one. In the area around the palace, houses are constructed of the traditional wattle and daub, but modern-style houses are favored in the other parts of the city. Migration is changing the balance between rural and urban populations. In precolonial times and through the early 1960s, most Edo lived in rural areas. Indeed, after the British conquest, Benin City suffered something of a decline. This situation changed when it became the capital of the newly created Midwest State in 1963. As a result, government establishments, urban residential areas, and commerce and industry started to develop. The military governments of 1967 to 1975 improved social services, established inter- and intracity transportation, and fostered education and health by constructing a university with a teaching hospital. The development of roads and markets throughout the region, as well as ports to the southeast of Benin City, made the capital an important node for trade. New residential and commercial areas have developed around the traditional core, some incorporating villages that used to be on the periphery of the city.

Economy

Subsistence and Commercial Activities. The basis of the economy is farming, with the main food crops being yams, cassava, plantains, and cocoyams, as well as beans, rice, okra, peppers, and gourds. Oil palms are cultivated for wine production and kola trees for nuts for hospitality rites. Farming is not an exclusively rural occupation, as many city dwellers own farms on the outskirts of the capital and commute regularly to work on them. Domestic animals include cattle, goats, sheep, dogs, and chickens. Most villages have markets, and there are also several large regional markets supplying Benin City and the other towns. In the precolonial period trade was in foodstuffs and locally manufactured products, but in the colonial period cash crops were introduced; by World War I Benin had begun to prosper from the commercial growing of timber and rubber trees. Whereas shifting cultivation used to prevail, with the introduction of cash crops it has begun to disappear in favor of crop rotation. Today all farmers grow food crops for their own consumption as well as cash crops. Rubber processing and the preparation of tropical hardwoods are major industries in the state. As Makinwa notes (1981, 31), Benin City's unique position as the state capital, coupled with the discovery of oil and a tremendous increase in its production in the late 1960s and early 1970s, drew financial resources and industries to Benin.

The urban economy is dominated by government in the formal sector and trade in the informal one. Because Benin is the capital of Edo State, the government and its agencies are the main employers for the wage-earning portion of the population. At least half of the urban work force is in clerical and, especially, sales-and-service professions. Men are typically involved in tailoring, carpentry, or electrical and mechanical repairs, and women tend to be hairdressers, dressmakers, and petty traders. Women dominate in the street and local markets in the city. Youth unemployment has become a growing problem as the influx of migrants from the villages and other parts of Nigeria steadily increases.

Industrial Arts. According to oral traditions, craft guilds have existed since the ogiso period. Members of these guilds (carpenters, carvers, brass casters, leatherworkers, blacksmiths, and weavers) live in special wards of Benin City and produce ritual, prestige, and household objects for the king and court. In the villages, there were also smiths, carvers, potters, weavers, and basket makers who created ritual paraphernalia like masks, cloth, and utensils. In the twentieth century local production of cloth, baskets, and other useful items has almost died out because of competition with European products. The changing social and economic situation has adversely affected the patronage of many of the traditional crafts, although some guild members, especially the carvers and casters, have made a successful transition to production for tourists and the Nigerian elite.

Trade. Archaeologists have uncovered evidence of long-distance trade from at least the twelfth century, but the best documentation commences with the arrival of the Portuguese in the second half of the fifteenth century and spans from that time until the present. Throughout the history of European trade, one of the sources of the king's wealth was the monopoly that he held over ivory, pepper, and certain other exports. His control extended to the markets and trade routes, which he could close whenever he wished. High-ranking chiefs of the Iwebo Palace Society administered European trade for the king, and various trading associations controlled the routes to the interior that brought products to Benin for export. These exports varied over time but also included cloth, palm oil, and slaves. In exchange, Benin imported European goods such as cloth, mirrors, coral beads, and brass and other metal objects. Since the colonial period, Benin has been tied in to the Western capitalist system.

Division of Labor. In precolonial and colonial villages, adult men tended the principal crop, yams, clearing and working the land together with male relatives, affines, or friends. Women cared for their households and grew subsidiary crops. Marketing, at least in precolonial times, was entirely in the hands of women. Within the city, the labor was divided in a similar way, that is, male guild members did the craft or ritual work, and women sold some of the products of the guild in the market. Since the colonial period, men and, to a lesser extent, women have been involved in the administrative and economic sectors of what became a regional capital.

Land Tenure. The king is considered "the owner" of all the land in the kingdom. Although this prerogative has mainly symbolic significance, the king could actually revoke rights to land in cases of insurrection or treason. Today he plays a role in the allocation of building sites in Benin City and the use of land and resources by strangers in the Edo region. The actual landholding unit is the village; its elders act as the custodians. Approval must be sought from the elders and chief for the right to use certain plots. Land is abundant, and new settlements are still being founded in the reserves of wooded land. Patterns of land use are changing, however, and, especially in the city, individual purchase is increasingly common.

Kinship

Descent is reckoned patrilineally in Edo society. Descent groups are called *egbee*, a term that refers both to the immediate lineage and to the dispersed clan of which it is part. There are about thirty-five clans, which are distinguished by exogamy, the possession of special morning salutations, and the adherence to particular avoidances of foods or activities. Unlike those of the neighboring Yoruba, Edo lineages are not landholding, nor do they have political significance, except for that of the king and a very few hereditary chieftaincy titles. The royal lineage is particularly set apart by virtue of its descent from the Yoruba culture hero Oranmiyan (called "Aranmiyan" in Edo), who founded the second Benin dynasty, which has reigned continuously since about the twelfth or thirteenth century. Kinship terminology is of the Hawaiian type.

Marriage and Family

Marriage. Polygamy is the preferred form of marriage, although in the twentieth century monogamy has come to be favored by some Christians and the educated. Marriage used to be contracted when the proposed wife was very young. There were betrothal and wedding fees. Formerly, divorce was very rare, granted only under circumstances of infectious disease or impotency, but the establishment of Native Authority courts by the British at the beginning of the twentieth century had the effect of making divorce easier to obtain. Colonialism brought Western education and Christianity, both of which are associated with a preference for monogamy. Residence is virilocal but increasingly neolocal.

Domestic Unit. The basic unit is the household, which varies in size from a single man (least common) to an extended family (most common). This family can consist of a man with his wife or wives and their children and, in some cases, married sons and their wives and children and even younger married brothers. Widowed or divorced mothers, daughters, and sisters can live there as well. If the marriage is polygamous, the wives and their children all live in separate apartments within the larger compound. Women past childbearing age often move to their own houses.

In precolonial times the family groupings in the city were much larger, since the chiefs had more wives and children and numerous slaves and servants. Thus the households of high-ranking chiefs might have included several hundred people. Today in Benin City the average size is seven to ten per household, and the number of nuclear families is increasing (Sada 1984, 119).

Inheritance. The system of primogeniture prevails among the Edo: the eldest son receives the rights to property, hereditary titles, and ritual duties. The eldest son performs the funeral ceremonies for his deceased father and inherits his father's house and lands. Although the bulk of the estate goes to the senior son, the eldest sons by the other wives of his father receive shares as well, in order of their seniority. When no sons are left, the property sometimes passes to the father's brother or sister, or sometimes to a daughter. A woman's property is inherited by her children. Royal traditions indicate that primogeniture may not always have been the rule of succession to the kingship, but it clearly has been in place since the early eighteenth century.

Socialization. In Benin the extended family is the unit of socialization within which the individual learns the necessary social and occupational skills. Babies are cared for by their mothers, grandmothers, and elder sisters. Weaning takes place when they are 2 or 3 years old, unless the mother bears another child in the meantime. Boys and girls play together until the age of 6 or 7, but then they begin to take on gender-related activities: boys accompany their fathers to the farm or, if they are artisans, to the workshop. Girls go with their mothers to the farm and learn how to sell things in the market. Formerly, the circumcision of boys and clitoridectomy of girls took place in infancy or early childhood but, in the latter case, is becoming less common. Since the early part of the twentieth century, but especially after World War II, urban crafts and small industries have adapted Western apprenticeship systems for the training of workers. Western-based education also offers avenues for the acquisition of skills. Since 1955, primary-school education in both the urban and rural areas has been free and compulsory. Secondary schools are primarily in the towns, and only the initial stages are free. Edo State has two institutions of higher education: the University of Benin, in Benin City, and Edo State University, in Ekpoma.

Sociopolitical Organization

Social Organization. The basic organizing principle within both the village and the urban ward is the division of the population into age sets. Every three years, boys who reach the age of puberty are initiated into the *iroghae* grade, whose main duties within the village include such tasks as sweeping open spaces, clearing brush, and fetching water. After the age of 25 to 30, they pass into the *ighele* grade, which executes the decisions made by the senior age set, the *edion*. The elders are exempt from physical labor and constitute the executive and judicial council of the village, led by an elected senior elder (*odionwere*).

Precolonial Benin society had a clearly demarcated class structure: a mostly urban elite, comprising the governmental, religious, and educational bureaucracies; a commoner group, consisting of lower-status urbanites, such as artisans; and the peasantry. Formerly, the king and chiefs had slaves, primarily acquired through warfare, who constituted an agricultural workforce for the elite. In contemporary society, factors such as the extent of one's Western education and the nature of one's employment—or lack thereof—play a role in determining one's position in the multidimensional system of social stratification.

Political Organization. At the summit of precolonial society was the king (*oba*), who was the focal point of all administrative, religious, commercial, and judicial concerns. He was the last resort in court matters, the recipient of taxes and tribute, the controller of trade, the theoretical owner of all the land in the kingdom, and the chief executive and legislator. As the divine king, he crystallized generalized ancestor worship in the worship of his own ancestors. It is in his office, then, that the various hierarchies met.

The members of the king's family were automatically part of the nobility. His mother was a title holder (*iyoba*) in one of the palace societies and maintained her own court near Benin City, and his younger brothers were sent to be hereditary chiefs of villages throughout the kingdom, thus constituting part of a limited, rural-based elite. Besides the king and his family, the political structure consisted of the holders of various chiefly titles, who were organized into three main orders of chiefs: the seven *uzama*, the palace chiefs, and the town chiefs. These various orders of chiefs formed the administrative bureaucracy of the kingdom, and their main concern was to augment the king's civil and ritual authority. They constituted the state council, which had an important role in creating laws, regulating festivals, raising taxes, declaring war, and conducting rituals. The king controlled the granting of most of these chiefly titles and used this power to consolidate his control over governmental processes. Once granted, a title could not be rescinded unless treason could be proven.

The kingdom was formerly divided into a number of tribute units, which corresponded to local territorial groupings. Each was controlled by a title holder in Benin City, who acted as the intermediary between the villagers and the king and whose main duty was to collect taxes and tribute in the form of money (cowries) and goods (cattle, yams, etc.). The income the king received from these sources enabled him to carry on elaborate state rituals. The king could also call on villagers to supply labor for the upkeep of the royal palace.

Kings varied over time in their ability to control the political situation. At the end of the eighteenth century, for example, senior chiefs rebelled against the king, and a long civil war ensued, which the king finally won. According to oral traditions, several obas were in fact deposed.

In contemporary Nigeria, Edo State officials consult with the Benin king and chiefs. Since 1966, the federal level of government in Nigeria has vacillated between military and civilian rule, with the exact relationship between federal and traditional authority changing under each new circumstance. In 1993 the newly established military government dissolved all existing state bodies and prohibited political activity. Supreme executive and legislative power was vested in a military-based Provisional Ruling Council and an Executive Council, both headed by the commander-in-chief, who is also the head of state. Plans for a return to civilian rule have been announced.

Social Control. The principle of the judicial system was that every head of a compound, quarter, village, or town heard cases within his jurisdiction, but serious issues—murder, treason, or succession disputes—were formerly brought before the king's council in Benin City. Trial by ordeal was used in cases of theft, perjury, and witchcraft (if the offender denied the charge). The British established a bipartite judicial system, with a supreme court administering British law and native courts for maintaining customary law. In 1947 the new Nigerian constitution established a federal system of government with a Supreme Court, a Court of Appeals, and a High Court at the federal level. Edo State, like others in the federation, has its own High Court, as well as a Customary Court of Appeal.

Conflict. In precolonial times warfare was an important component of the state polity. It apparently was the custom for kings to declare war in the third year after their succession to the throne. Ruling princes of the empire who refused to pledge their allegiance at that time were considered rebels, and war was declared against them and their towns. Economic factors were undoubtedly central to Benin's expansion: the Edo were intent on increasing their income from tribute, protecting and developing trade, and augmenting their army with captives and allies. There was a military organization involving specific chiefs who each had a core of warriors attached to his household but also recruited soldiers from their villages. For long campaigns, the soldiers built camps where they lodged and grew food for themselves.

Religion and Expressive Culture

Religious Beliefs. In the traditional Edo view, the universe is divided into two planes of existence: the visible, tangible world of everyday life (*agbon*) and the invisible spirit world (*erinmwin*) created by Osanobua and inhabited by him, other deities, ancestors, spirits, and supernatural powers. These are two parallel, coexisting realms; their boundaries, however, are not inviolable, as gods and spirits daily intervene in the lives of humans, and particularly powerful humans draw upon the forces of the spirit world to transform daily experience. The creator god, Osanobua, is rather remote; worship is more frequently directed toward the other deities, who are his children. The most important of these—according to Benin notions of seniority—is Olokun, his oldest son. Olokun, the ruler of the global waters and the provider of wealth and fertility, is the most widely venerated deity in Benin, especially among women who join local congregations to pray and sacrifice for children. Ogun, the god of iron, is the concern of all who deal with metal, including taxi drivers and mechanics. Other deities include Osun, the power inherent in leaves and herbs, the special concern of herbalists; Ogiuwu, the god of death; and Obienmwen, the goddess of safe delivery. Yoruba deities such as Eshu, the trickster; Shango, the god of thunder; and Orunmila, the deity of divination, have been incorporated into Edo religion. Congregations of worshipers and shrines dedicated to these deities are found in both the villages and the city, although Osanobua, Osun, and Ogiuwu had central shrines and chief priests in Benin City only.

An urban-rural dichotomy of religious worship was maintained through the exclusion of certain cults from the capital city. Such cults were dedicated to culture heroes—once-famous warriors, magicians, and court figures who came into conflict with the king. Fleeing from the capital, they sought refuge in their home villages and were transformed into natural phenomenona, mainly rivers. The villagers worship these culture heroes as protective deities who are concerned with fertility and health.

Aspects of the human body are endowed with spiritual power and often have shrines where they are propitiated. Important among these are the head—the locus of a person's intelligence, will, and ability to organize his life and that of his dependents—and the hand—source of the individual's ability to succeed in life in the material sense.

When the Portuguese arrived in Benin, they tried to introduce Christianity. In 1516 they built a church in the capital city and taught the king's senior son and two important chiefs how to read. Their efforts to spread the Christian faith were not successful. Missionary efforts increased substantially with colonialism, and today there are churches of every conceivable denomination in Benin City, including Hare Krishna, and some missionary outposts in villages. Church participation frequently occurs side by side with indigenous ancestral and herbal practices.

Religious Practitioners. There are two main categories of religious specialists: priest (*ohen*) and diviner/herbalist (*obo*). A priest, who can be either male or female, undergoes a long series of initiation rites before specializing in performing a wide variety of ceremonies and communicating directly, often through trance, with his or her patron deity. Such priests can be found presiding over congregations in cities and villages, as well as in the countryside. The diviner/healer, usually male, specializes in some branch of magical activity such as curing, divining, handling witches, or administering ordeals.

Ceremonies. In precolonial times there was a royal ritual cycle of ceremonies, one for each of the thirteen lunar months. Some were of a private nature, such as the sacrifices the king made to his head or his hand; others were public. Oba Eweka II curtailed many of the private ceremonies in the palace, and his son, Akenzua II, reduced and limited the public ceremonies to the Christmas vacation in order to facilitate attendance. The most important of these are Ugie Erha Oba, which honors the king's ancestors, and Igue, which strengthens his mystical powers. Domestic ceremonies mark the life cycle and the private worship of various deities and ancestors.

Arts. The Benin Kingdom is well known for its brass and ivory sculpture, which is found in museums throughout the world. These objects were produced for the king and the nobility by members of craft guilds in Benin City. Among the most famous Benin works of art are the brass (often mislabeled "bronze") commemorative heads topped by elaboratly carved ivory tusks that are placed on the royal ancestral altars and the rectangular brass plaques depicting court ceremonies and war exploits that used to decorate the pillars of the palace. In the villages, devotees of local deified culture heroes perform rituals employing a variety of different kinds of masks some of wood, others of cloth or red parrot feathers, to honor these deities and appeal for health and well-being.

Medicine. The Edo distinguish between common and serious illnesses. The former can be treated at home or by Western-trained doctors; the latter must be treated by specialists in traditional medicine, whether priests or diviner/healers. Serious illnesses (childhood convulsions, smallpox, etc.) are believed to be caused by witches or by deities angered over the violation of a taboo. Traditional medical practice centers around belief in *osun*, the power inherent in leaves and herbs that grow in the bush. Most adults have a basic knowledge of herbalism, which helps them to care for their immediate families, but there are also specialists, both priests and diviner/herbalists, who treat a variety of illnesses. Edo today distinguish between "White man's medicine," for the treatment of diseases such as measles, and "Edo medicine," which is still used for problems such as barrenness or illness created by witches.

Death and Afterlife. Death is seen by the Edo as part of a cycle in which an individual moves between the spirit world and the everyday world in a series of fourteen reincarnations. Each cycle begins with an appearance before the Creator God, at which time a person announces his or her destiny or life plan. The person's spiritual counterpart (*ehi*) is present and thereafter monitors the person's adherence to the announced plan. After death, the person and his or her ehi must give an account to the Creator God. If the account is acceptable, the person joins the ancestors in the spirit world until the time has come to be born again.

In the spirit world, the ancestors live in villages and quarters similar to those in the world of everyday life. From there, they watch over the behavior of their relations in the everyday world, punishing transgressions such as incest. Their descendants perform weekly and annual rituals to placate and implore the ancestors to bring benefits of health and fertility.

Bibliography

Ben-Amos, Paula Girshick (1980). *The Art of Benin*. London: Thames & Hudson.

Bradbury, R. E. (1957). *The Benin Kingdom and the Edo-Speaking Peoples of South-Western Nigeria*. London: International African Institute.

Bradbury, R. E. (1973). *Benin Studies*. Edited by Peter Morton-Williams. London: Oxford University Press.

Connah, Graham (1975). *The Archaeology of Benin*. Oxford: Clarendon Press.

Egharevba, Jacob U. (1968). *A Short History of Benin*. Ibadan: Ibadan University Press. Originally published in 1934.

Igbafe, P. A. (1979). *Benin under British Administration*. London: Longman.

Ikhuoria, I. A. (1984). "Rapid Urban Growth and Urban Land Use Patterns in Benin City, Nigeria." In *Case Studies in Migration and Urbanization in Nigeria*, edited by P. O. Sada and A. B. Osirike, 175–189. Benin City: University of Benin, Department of Geography and Regional Planning.

Makinwa, Paulina Kofoworola (1981). *Internal Migration and Rural Development in Nigeria: Lessons from Bendel State*. Ibadan: Heinemann Educational Books (Nigeria).

Ryder, A. F. C. (1969). *Benin and the Europeans, 1485–1897*. London: Longmans, Green & Co.

Sada, P. O. (1984). "Urban Households and Housing Conditions in Nigerian Cities with Specical Reference to Warri and Benin." In *Case Studies in Migration and Urbanization in Nigeria*, edited by P. O. Sada and A. B. Osirike, 118–131.

PAULA GIRSHICK BEN-AMOS

Ewe and Fon

ETHNONYM: Fon: Dahomeans

Orientation

Identification. "Ewe" is the umbrella name for a number of groups that speak dialects of the same language and have separate local names, such as Anlo, Abutia, Be, Kpelle, and Ho. (These are not subnations but populations of towns or small regions.) Closely related groups with slightly different mutually comprehensible languages and cultures may be grouped with Ewe, notably Adja, Oatchi, and Peda. Fon and Ewe people are often considered to belong to the same, larger grouping, although their related languages are mutually incomprehensible. All these peoples are said to have originated in the general area of Tado, a town in present-day Togo, at about the same latitude as Abomey, Benin. Mina and Guin are the descendants of Fanti and Ga people who left the Gold Coast in the seventeenth and eighteenth centuries, settling in the Aneho and Glidji areas, where they intermarried with Ewe, Oatchi, Peda, and Adja. The Guin-Mina and Ewe languages are mutually comprehensible, although there are significant structural and lexical differences.

Location. Most Ewe (including Oatchi, Peda, and Adja) live between the Volta River in Ghana and the Mono River (to the east) in Togo, from the coast (southern boundary) northward just past Ho in Ghana and Danyi on the western Togolese border, and Tado on the eastern border. Fon live primarily in Benin, from the coast to Savalou, and from the Togolese border almost to Porto-Novo in the south. Other Fon- and Ewe-related groups live in Benin. Borders between Ghana and Togo, as well as between Togo and Benin, are permeable to innumerable Ewe and Fon lineages with family on both sides of the border.

Pazzi (1976, 6) describes locations of the different groups with historical references, including the migrations out of Tado, principally to Notse, in present-day Togo, and to Allada, in present-day Benin. Ewe who left Notse spread from the lower basin of the Amugan to the valley of the Mono. Two groups left Allada: Fon occupied the plateau of Abomey and the entire plain that spreads from the Kufo and Weme rivers to the coast, and Gun settled between Lake Nokwe and the Yawa River. Adja remained in the hills surrounding Tado and in the plain between the Mono and Kufo rivers. Mina are the Fante-Ane from Elmina who founded Aneho, and Guin are the Ga immigrants from Accra who occupied the plain between Lake Gbaga and the Mono River. They encountered there the Xwla or Peda people (whom the Portuguese of the fifteenth century named "Popo"), whose language also overlaps with the Ewe language.

The coastal areas of Benin, Togo, and southeastern Ghana are flat, with numerous palm groves. Just north of the beach areas is a string of lagoons, navigable in some areas. An undulating plain lies behind the lagoons, with a soil of red laterite and sand. The southern parts of the Akwapim ridge in Ghana, about 120 kilometers from the coast, are forested and reach an elevation of about 750 meters. The dry season usually lasts from November through March, including the period of dry and dusty harmattan winds in December, which lasts longer farther north. The rainy season often peaks in April-May and September-October. Temperatures along the coast vary from the twenties to the thirties (centigrade), but may be both hotter and cooler farther inland.

Demography. According to estimates made in 1994, there are more than 1.5 million Ewe (including Adja, Mina, Oatchi, Peda, and Fon) living in Togo. Two million Fon and almost a half-million Ewe live in Benin. While the government of Ghana does not keep a census of ethnic groups (so as to reduce ethnic conflict), Ewe in Ghana are estimated at 2 million, including a certain number of Ga-Adangme who were more or less assimilated to Ewe groups linguistically and politically, although they have maintained much of their pre-Ewe culture.

Linguistic Affiliation. Pazzi's (1976) comparative dictionary of Ewe, Adja, Guin, and Fon languages demonstrates that they are very closely related, all originating centuries ago with the people of the royal city of Tado. They belong to the Kwa Language Group. Numerous dialects exist inside the family of Ewe proper, such as Anlo, Kpelle, Danyi, and Be. Adja dialects include Tado, Hweno, and Dogbo. Fon, the language of the Kingdom of Dahomey, includes the Abomey, Xweda, and Wemenu dialects as well as numerous others. Kossi (1990, 5, 6) insists that the overarching name for this extended family of languages and peoples should be Adja rather than Ewe/Fon, given their common origin in Tado, where the Adja language, mother of the other tongues, is still spoken.

History and Cultural Relations

The Adja Kingdom of Tado, in an area constantly populated since prehistory and known for metalworking and other crafts, was situated near the east bank of the Mono River, at about the same latitude as Abomey. It was probably built by immigrants from the Oyo Kingdom or from Ketu, to the east (Nigeria). Most Adja people today still live in and around Tado. Fon and Ewe peoples are the descendants of emigrants from Tado who intermarried with other groups they encountered en route to their present-day locations.

Ewe populations today are the result of various migrations moving west and toward the coast, eventually dominated by emigrants of the Adja Kingdom of Tado, who first settled in the new vassal kingdom of Notse. Early in the seventeenth century they left Notse in several groups and settled farther south and west. Their descendants eventually became the Anlo, Abutia, Be, and Kpelle, as well as the Oatchi, further south and east, in the Vogan area.

Anlo Ewe, who settled in the Volta region, in what is now the southeastern corner of the Republic of Ghana, were located in one of the strategic areas of the Atlantic slave trade. In 1683 Keta was already an important slave market. By 1727 Dutch and English slave traders were posted in Aflao, and in 1784 the Danes built a fort in Keta; Anlo territory thus became a center for the Atlantic trade. Anlo Ewe participated in the capture and sale of slaves to Europeans, and many were themselves sold into slavery and taken to the New World.

In close contact with their militarily superior and more politically centralized Asante neighbors, Anlo nevertheless were a separate polity and have maintained an Ewe identity until the present. Dominated by Akwamu during the first third of the eighteenth century, they joined with them and the army of Ouidah to war against Allada. Numerous other local wars with—and against—Akan armies involved Anlo Ewe during the seventeenth through nineteenth centuries.

Trading with Europeans was an aspect of Anlo Ewe life almost from the beginning of their settlement in the area. Bremen missionaries and other Christian emissaries set anchor in Eweland both in the Volta region and inland on the (now) Togolese side during the nineteenth century. Various Ewe populations were under close colonial supervision during the British regime on the Gold Coast and during German control of Togoland. After World War I, approximately a third of Togoland, including much of Eweland, became a part of the Gold Coast; the remainder of the country taken from the Germans became a French protectorate called Togo. Thus Eweland was split in two, and remains so today. Ewe, who were mostly "southerners," were among the first in the two countries to receive an education in British and French colonial schools.

Fon are among those who left Tado to found the Kingdom of Allada; some of them subsequently left Allada, around 1610, and migrated toward Abomey, where they succeeded in dominating the native Dahomey population some 70 years later. Fon created the royal city of Abomey (where the famous "Amazons" had their headquarters), and other Fon founded the city of Ouidah. The two cities were linked, both high places of slave commerce during the Atlantic Trade. The Brazilian Francisco de Souza, a key figure on the Slave Coast of the late eighteenth and early nineteenth centuries, established slave trading posts and built forts both in Aneho among the Mina (now in Togo) and in Ouidah among the Fon (now in Benin).

The Fon Kingdom of Dahomey, which lasted from 1625 until its defeat by the French in 1893, is legendary, thanks to numerous visitors and their accounts, from those of Bosman (seventeenth century), Norris (eighteenth century), and Burton (nineteenth century), to those of twentieth-century ethnographers, including Le Herissé (1911) and Herskovits (1938). Focal to the Atlantic trade on the Slave Coast, the kingdom was expansionist but highly centralized only in and around its main cities—Abomey, Allada, and (much later) Ouidah—high places of art, courtly ceremony, and commerce with Europeans. The kingdom was said to include a territory much larger than it could effectively control, from the Volta River in the west to Badagary in the east, and northward to the 8th parallel. Its coastline, however, extended only 16 kilometers on either side of Ouidah. Although it was thus about 39,000 square kilometers in area, the king had authority only within some 10,400 square kilometers of that territory. Numerous wars and intrigues, including captures and contests of nerves with European envoys, mark the history of the Kingdom of Dahomey. Its more cruel kings were renowned for human sacrifice (always a royal prerogative), the stunning extent of which is described in perhaps exaggerated terms by some writers (e.g., Herskovits 1938, 2:52–56).

Although many Ewe and Fon are Christian (perhaps the highest percentage among the Ghana Ewe), the majority continue to practice Vodu or Tro worship, which has remained the religion of the Adja-Tado peoples for centuries.

Settlements

Ewe and Fon live mostly in villages and towns, although there are some more isolated farming compounds. Rectangular mud brick houses and concrete brick dwellings with gabled or corrugated-iron roofs are predominant except along the ocean, where there are numerous palm-frond huts with straw- or palm-thatch gabled roofs. Small huts or buildings are often clustered in a single compound with an open court, all surrounded by a mud wall. In ocean-front fishing villages, fragile palm-frond fences give some privacy to clusters of small huts. People living in the same compound are usually members of the same patrilineage (*to-fome*), although kinship is extremely open to outside recruitment; fictive kin may even predominate in certain cases. Large villages may have central marketplaces. Today there are a number of cities and large towns in which Ewe and Fon constitute the largest portion of the population. Ewe are a majority in Tema and Aflao (Ghana) and in Lome, Kpalime, and Tsévié (Togo). Adja dominate in Tado, and Mina-Guin in the Glidji-Aneho area (Togo). Abomey, Allada, Ouidah, Grand Popo, Cotonou, and other towns in Benin are largely populated by Fon and related groups.

Economy

Subsistence and Commercial Activities. Ewe and Fon are farmers, fishermen, and market women. Nowadays they occupy all the positions and jobs to be found in government, civil service, business, and production. Staple crops are yams, maize, and manioc. (Millet was once important.) Beans, peas, peanuts, sorghum, sweet potatoes, onions, okra, peppers, gourds, papayas, bananas, plantains, mangoes, pineapples, oil palms, and some rice and cocoa are also grown. Animals raised include pigs, sheep, goats, dogs, chickens, guinea fowl, ducks, and pigeons. Fishing is of primary importance along the coast and in the Volta region. Cash crops include palm kernels, peanuts, copra, castor beans, kapok, and, by far the most important, coffee and cocoa.

Along the coast, from Accra to Porto-Novo, hundreds of thousands of Ewe and Fon women work in the ports and markets. From Lome to Cotonou, Ewe and Fon market women—both wholesalers and retailers—have a near monopoly on the internal economy. Even in small villages, many women are traders and retailers, selling anything from homemade fermented corn porridge to Coca Cola, often specializing in a single item such as fresh or home-smoked fish, imported Dutch wax cloth, fresh fruits and vegetables, or trade beads.

Industrial Arts. Ewe and Fon engage in pottery making, wood sculpting (mostly for religious use), and basketwork; in the past, every village had a blacksmith (see "Arts").

Trade. Ewe have traded with Asante and Fante, and Fon have traded with Yoruba and Hausa for as long as they have had their present identity. The slave trade and the salt trade brought other traders from the north of present Ewe and Fon regions, including as far north as Burkina Faso (formerly Upper Volta) and perhaps Mali and Niger. Portuguese traders reached the coast in the fifteenth century, even before the Ewe and Fon had migrated that far. By the seventeenth century, when the Volta region had become home to an Ewe polity and the Kingdom of Dahomey had regular relations with Ouidah, European commercial envoys were no longer a novelty on what was then called the Slave Coast. The Atlantic commerce in slaves was a significant aspect of Ewe and Fon life for two centuries.

Market activities are central in all Ewe and Fon regions. Women almost always have something to sell on market days, including foodstuffs they make themselves. They often buy their husband's or brothers' catch of fish fresh from the sea or river and take it straight to various markets. Or they smoke the fish and take them to markets farther inland. Today European, U.S., and Chinese goods are available even in small Ewe and Fon village markets more than 150 kilometers from the coast, often taken there by local women who buy the goods in coastal cities. In Togo, Ewe and Mina are said to be trading peoples willing to travel far to engage in commerce, thereby distinguishing themselves from more northern and more strictly agricultural groups who stay closer to the land.

Division of Labor. Apart from the special status of kings in the Kingdom of Dahomey and occasionally chiefs in Ewe regions, who did not perform manual labor, the main division of labor is along gender lines. Men do heavy agricultural labor such as clearing the land and staking yam vines; they fish, hunt, and build houses. Women participate in the above activities also, such as preparing the palm-frond walling or fencing necessary to hut building, taking charge of butchered animals and fish, and carrying out almost all agricultural tasks except the very heaviest. Women also carry headloads as heavy as any load men can carry. Although it is often said that only women headload, this is patently untrue. Women are in charge of most market activities, although they may hire men to help them. One of the few items usually sold by men in the market is beef, often brought by Hausa or other Muslim traders. Most other kinds of work, including cooking, may be done by women and men, and even the above-mentioned divisions of labor are not absolute. Women and children may join with men in pulling in the enormous and heavy fishing nets from the surf after a catch. Gender-specific cash savings and work collectives abound, enabling members to have their own banking as well as support in house building, clearing land, harvesting, fishing, marketing, and all other labors. Especially notable are the Fon *dokpwe,* or cooperative, and the Ewe *esodjodjo,* or *tontine* (French). Both women and men engage in child care, although women are considered to have greater responsibility in this regard. Groups of men and groups of women may take care of any and all village children in their vicinity at any given time.

Land Tenure. Anyone from a particular region can farm on land that is not occupied by anyone else. Inside a settlement, a person wishing to employ land must ask permission of the village chief or the elders of the lineage owning the land. Formerly, rights have extended only to use of land; there was no absolute right to the land itself. In the Kingdom of Dahomey, land was by definition the property of the king. In most Ewe regions, land is inherited and administrated by elders of each patriline; any lineage member may build or farm on lineage land as long as she or he respects the rights of others nearby who are already established on the land. Widows of patriline members or other persons not members of the lineage may stay on the land and farm it, but it cannot pass definitively into another lineage. Only in the last few generations has land come to be alienable from lineage tenure by being mortgaged or sold. It is possible for palm groves and other wealth on the land to be passed on matrilineally, especially in Anlo and Glidji, where Akan matrilineal practices have influenced Ewe groups. Land not already belonging to a lineage (of which there is scarcely any now) may be acquired personally through simply clearing the land, or buying it from non-Ewe or non-Fon owners; the owner may dispose of such land without consulting lineage elders. Both women and men have rights to lineage land, often now called "inheritance of land," but, in areas where land is scarce, women have difficulty claiming such rights. Where lineage land is now alienable, plot by plot (e.g., southern Togo), women may, with difficulty, have a share in the proceeds of sales.

Kinship

Kin Groups and Descent. Descent is primarily patrilineal, although among Ewe groups there are sometimes elements of double descent or of influence from Akan matriliny, such as rights of mother's brother in sister's children (including rights to pawn them). Fon have exogamous patrisibs composed of lineages, but in the Kingdom of Dahomey the royal sib had exceptional rules. Princesses married commoners and their children belonged to the royal sib, as did the offspring of royal princes. Cross-cousin marriage is preferred among most Ewe and Fon groups, particularly with mother's brother's daughter. Anlo Ewe established a clan (*hlo*) system soon after their arrival in Anlo. Long-term Anlo residents are still divided into some thirteen clans, including the Blu clan, which was specifically created for resident strangers, made "Ewe" by virtue of their clan belonging. During certain periods, there has been a preference for clan endogamy.

Kinship Terminology. Brothers, sisters, and all first cousins are referred to as *novi;* father is referred to as *to,* and mother is referred to as *no.* Classificatory mothers and fathers, siblings, and cousins are also referred to by these terms. Other terms may differ between Ewe groups and between Ewe and Fon. An Iroquois system for parents' generation is general among Ewe, except that in some regions father's brothers are *ata* rather than versions of to or *eto* (Anlo), reserved for father; and mother's sisters are *na* rather than no or *eno,* which is reserved for mother. The most significant variations are terms for father's sisters—*ete* (Anlo) or *tasi* (Guin-Mina)—and mother's brothers—*nyrui* (Anlo) or *nyine* (Guin-Mina). The Iroquois aspects are clearer in terms of address, which lump together parents, parents' same-sex siblings, and Ego's older siblings and cousins: *efo* (father or father's brothers), *fofo* or *fofovi* (younger uncle; cousin or brother older than Ego), *fogan* (older uncle or eldest brothers and cousins); *da* or *dada* (mother, mother's sisters), *davi* or *dadavi* (younger aunt, cousin or sister older than Ego), and *dagan* (older aunts and eldest cousins and sisters). Mother's brother and father's sister, however, do not have specific terms of direct address, but are addressed more formally as nyrui and ete. Fon employ descriptive terms for avuncular and nepotic kinsmen; cousin terminology is also descriptive.

Marriage and Family

Marriage. Most Ewe and Fon marriages are patrilocal, although neolocal residence has become popular in the late twentieth century. Polygyny is the rule if a man has means to marry more than one wife. It is often said that an abuse of polygyny leads wives to leave their husbands for other men, often younger and as yet unmarried, so that women also tend to have more than one husband in their lifetimes. Fon marriages are of two general types, one more prestigious than the other. Prestigious marriage includes payments by the groom to the bride's father or premarital farm labor performed by a man for his future father-in-law. Such bride-wealth or work gives a man control over his children. When this is not performed, the mother and her family have all rights over the children; thus, this sort of marriage is less desirable or prestigious for a husband. Herskovits (1938) outlines thirteen different variations of these two major marriage categories. A man must never refuse a wife offered him, and divorce may be initiated only by the wife's family. In many Ewe groups, marriage is less marked by bride-wealth or bride-service, and even if a man offers only the required drinks and cloths to his bride and her family, he may claim the children as members of his own patriline. In case of separation, a father may keep his children with him, although in many cases wives are allowed to raise the children, and rotation of children between divorced parents is perhaps as common among Ewe as it is in the United States. Among Anlo families, it is often the father's sister who arranges the marriage when a young man wishes a certain young woman to be his wife. The simple giving of gifts to the young woman and her family and the sharing of drinks and libations, often a modest affair, is, even so, a marriage ceremony and a binding ritual that links two lineages and sets in motion serious obligations. Pregnancy makes a marriage complete. In the Kingdom of Dahomey, virginity was demanded of brides in prestigious marriages. In Anlo, too, the marriage-payment might be less if the bride was found not to be a virgin; today many couples become intimate before arranging a marriage. Christian Ewe and Fon proceed according to the arrangements prescribed in their churches.

Domestic Unit. Patrilineal three- or four-generational extended family compounds, as well as agnatic extended family compounds, are common. Another model is a nuclear-family household (often with children from previous marriages) that eventually is joined by other relatives, such as the couple's younger siblings, cousins, nieces, nephews, and foster children. If the husband has not vowed monogamy, in time, other wives and their children may come to expand the compound (each wife with her own hut or little house). In many cases, other wives and their children form separate households. Adolescent boys may have collective sleeping quarters separate from their mothers and sisters.

Inheritance. Most Fon property, including land, is inherited patrilineally, although some lineage land remains. Among Ewe groups, lineage land and whatever is on it—palm groves, houses, fields, and shrines—ideally remains within the lineage, although much lineage land is being broken up and sold nowadays. Rights to lineage land are primarily patrilineal. Cloth wealth and jewelry sometimes become lineage property too, along with ancestral stools. Individual property, which may include rights to land and fields, may be inherited patrilineally or matrilineally, depending on the Ewe subgroup. (In Anlo and Glidji, for example, much private property, including oil-palm trees, is inherited matrilineally.) In some areas the eldest son inherits land rights, but livestock and other individual property go to a man's sister's son. In Lome inheritance is mixed.

Socialization. Virtually everyone, but especially older siblings, takes care of the children. Grandparents, both female and male, also spend considerable time with children. Fishermen in from the sea often sit around in groups during the afternoon, playing boardgames and watching over young children at the same time. Toddlers are passed from person to person, including adolescent boys, who appear to enjoy taking their turns. Mothers and all female relatives carry babies on their backs for much of the day; sometimes doting fathers or other male relatives also wrap babies and toddlers on their backs. Ewe adolescents experiment with sexuality early in their teen years, and nowadays pregnancy at a young age, even if the mother is unmarried, is not especially discouraged in many communities. Thus virginity is not as highly valued as it once was. Young girls help their mothers, often caring for smaller children or carrying loads to market, boys as young as 10 may go to sea with the men and go over the side of the pirogue to drive a school of fish into the nets. Inland, young boys and girls help perform agricultural tasks and care for animals. Children are present at all important social and religious events and may, at a very early age, become "spouses" of important spirits or gods, thus inheriting sizable responsibilities and the special, often prestigious, identity, that goes with them. Children as young as 10 may go into trance during Vodu (Fon and Guin-Mina) or Tro (Anlo Ewe) possession ceremonies. They also enjoy such events as recreation and take advantage of opportunities for drumming, singing, and dancing performances; teenagers and young adults may court during and after such religious rituals.

Sociopolitical Organization

Social Organization. There is virtually no formal hierarchy in many Ewe groups, except for the difference between slaves and their owners in times past. Even this crucial difference is now subject to ritual, during which some Ewe worship the spirits of their ancestors' slaves, thereby turning the tables on their past position of superiority. In Anlo there is some prestige in "royal" lineages, but there is no real class system other than that brought into existence by the capitalist economy, which now touches all Ewe and Fon to some extent, and especially those who live in towns and cities. In the Kingdom of Dahomey, the royal lineages were effectively an elite who did not labor. Both Ewe and Fon had domestic slaves, who often married nonslaves and had children with them. The children in some communities were a sort of in-between class; in other localities, they were free. In any case, after two or three generations, they were no longer tied to a slave class.

Political Organization. Although the Anlo polity was called a "state" at various periods, Green (1981, 1995) maintains it was not a true state but rather an attempt at centralization. The organizing principles were religious and clan-based rather than political or military in the strict sense. The Anlo did not have expansionist ambitions to compare with those of their Asante neighbors, who often ruled over them, or those of their Fon neighbors to the east, who maintained a royal city and a standing army. As early as the seventeenth century in the Volta region, elders were at the head of lineages, wards (lineage residential units), and villages. The *awoamefia* (political and spiritual leader, or chief priest) resided in Anloga. At the turn of the twentieth century, Ewe polities were divided into about 120 independent divisions. Each division had a number of villages, with a subchief in each one, and its own capital, with a paramount chief and military commander-inchief. Succession was patrilineal. Today political organization in villages may be quite egalitarian, although chiefs and elders (both male and female) do have more decision-making authority than younger adults. Fon villages had village autonomy before they were consolidated into a kingdom in the seventeenth century, and thus each village chief was a "king" (*toxosu*) to whom the heads of each compound answered. The Kingdom of Dahomey forced these chiefs to swear loyalty to the ruler or be sacrificed (some were sold into slavery). Sibs in Fon villages have considerable political influence, as do clans in Anlo and lineages and religious societies in other Ewe regions; the chief is hardly all-powerful.

Social Control. Although during the colonial period chiefs had considerable control (and still do as far as administrative decisions are concerned), authority is widely distributed in villages and regions. Whereas all Ewe and Fon are nominally under the jurisdiction of British- and French-inspired legal systems, the laws of the ancestors and the moral frameworks of Vodu worship tend to have just as much, if not more, authority than official law in many communities. Even in colonial and precolonial periods, the office of chief and the ranks of the elders were usually filled with men (and some women) who were linked to religious orders.

Individual behavior for many is constantly interpreted and adjusted through the lenses of Afa (or Fa) divination, which includes the "laws of destiny," or the "law-deity who brought me here" (*esesidomeda*). Thus, supernatural sanctions are more powerful than state legal systems for numerous Ewe and Fon. In the Kingdom of Dahomey, kings were tyrannical according to numerous sources; village chiefs, in keeping with earlier practices, were not. Decisions of village chiefs had to be reported to the king, however, so that final control was in his hands. The king's tribunal of chiefs was expected to judge harshly so that the king himself could demonstrate clemency by lightening the sentence. During the colonial period, there was great tension between certain Ewe Vodu orders and colonial administrators who claimed the Vodu "courts" were presuming to take the place of official courts. Numerous shrines were thus destroyed by German and British authorities. Vodu worshipers often did not consider the powers of the colonial governments to be legitimate.

Conflict. Conflict in villages is typically brought to a group of "judges," including the chief, Vodu priests, and both male and female elders. The entire village has the right to attend, and whoever wishes to speak may do so. Often divorce cases, theft, assault, and instances of injury through witchcraft do not go before official courts of law. Even cases that do go before official courts of law, including murder, may be rejudged by Vodu priests and communities because the conflict at the source of the crime is not thought to be merely personal. All conflict is a reflection of the social body in its relationship to the rest of the cosmos (see "Social Control").

Religion and Expressive Culture

Religious Beliefs. Various Vodu (Fon) and Tro (Ewe) orders are at the foundation of Fon and Ewe religion. A High God exists, according to numerous informants. Ewe may say that Mawu is the creator, similar to the Christian god, or, for some, more like the diffuse life force of the universe. For yet others, Mawu is the "mother/father" of all the Trowo (powerful spirits or deities). Among Fon, Mawu and Lisa are a couple, twins, or a female (Mawu) and male (Lisa) hermaphrodite divinity. Fon may say the world was created by Nana-Buluku, who gave birth to Mawu and Lisa. For others, Nana-Buluku, Mawu, and Lisa are all Vodus, and there is no all-powerful separate creator. Among Anlo Ewe, Nyigbla, the deity of the Sacred Forest is very important, as well as the entire pantheon of Yehve spirits, including Heviesso, god of thunder and lightning, and Avle, a goddess who sometimes impersonates men. Gu or Egu, the warrior and hunter god of iron, is central among all Ewe and Fon groups. There are a number of other Tro and Vodu orders, including Gorovodu, which is popular across Ewe and Fon populations in Ghana, Togo, and Benin. Mama Tchamba, a related order, involves the worship of the spirits of slaves from the north that Ewe once owned and married. The selfhood of each individual is involved with these major deities and spirit personalities. They are also protectors, healers, judges, and consummate performers. All Vodu and Tro orders work hand in hand with Afa (or Fa) divination, a complex interpretive framework within which each person has a life sign (*kpoli*), of which there are a total of 256. Each sign is connected to a set of plants and animals, stories and songs, dietary taboos, Vodus, and dangers and strengths, all associated with each other, as though clan-related. Events, projects, activities, and relationships also have their own Afa signs. Everything in the universe is related to Afa texts and themes, as though nature itself were divided into exogamous clans.

Many Ewe and Fon have become Christians; given their proximity to the coast, these ethnic groups were among the first to accept Christianity in the eighteenth and nineteenth centuries. Certain Christian groups originating in West Africa, such as Aladura and Celeste, have a considerable following on the coast.

Religious Practitioners. Vodu and Tro priests are usually men, but postmenopausal women may become priestesses. The great majority of spirit hosts or "wives" of the Vodus are women. Priests, priestesses, and "wives" of the Yehve deities (Sosi, Avlesi, Dasi, etc.) do not usually practice trance. Afa diviners are almost always men, although it is said that a woman can become a diviner if she wishes.

Ceremonies. Vodu and Tro ceremonies are compelling performances for both insiders and outsiders. Worshipers who begin dancing to the drum music may go into trance. Spirits who possess their "wives" may have messages for the community, may take part in judging certain cases of conflict, and may heal the sick. Above all, they are dancing gods, and there are aesthetic conventions that have long traditions. In Vodu orders where possession is not usual, ceremonies are all the more dazzling because of the perfection of their collective execution. Rows of dancers, all clothed in ceremonial attire, move across a ritual space as one person, performing specific movements. Drums always provide a sort of text or context for movement, including narrative associations and instruction. Ceremonies are events during which symbolic associations are reinforced, individual and collective identity is stated, certain aspects of identity and power are recalled and redistributed, healing and admonishment take place, and, above all, collective exhilaration, ecstasy, and awe are produced. Ceremonies are always gifts to the gods.

Afa divination involves numerous complicated rituals based on a binary system of questions and responses, and permutations of the 256 life signs associated with collections of oral texts.

Arts. Some Ewe men specialize in weaving prized *kente* cloth (similar to that of Asante), worn during all important occasions. The weaving is done on small looms that produce narrow strips of brightly colored cloth that must be sewn together to make a kente 76 to 152 centimeters wide and as long as 4.5 meters. There are numerous combinations of colors and patterns that bear great significance for the wearers. Now batik art, brought from Indonesia, is practiced in Togo and is popular among tourists. Fon artists are widely known for their appliqué hangings with legendary motifs from the Kingdom of Dahomey and Vodu culture. Elaborate engraving or carving of calabashes is another Fon art. Brass casting (using the *cire-perdue*, or lost-wax method) has been practiced by the Fon since early times. Brass workers belonged to special guilds in the Kingdom of Dahomey; they created some of the more striking objects constituting the king's wealth. Silverwork was also mastered. Both Ewe and Fon still carve wooden *bocio* figures for spiritual practices, as well as Legba statues (guardian deities) and other Vodu god-objects. Earthen Legbas are also common. Some god-objects, entirely abstract in form, are confected as a collage-sculpture, with numerous ingredients including cowry shells, goat horns, cows' tails, birds' claws, iron bells, and tree roots, all united with red clay and glazed with the blood of sacrificial animals. Drums of many different kinds are produced for specific ceremonies. Vodu costumes for spirit possession may be richly adorned with cowries sewn on in patterns. All of the objects necessary for Afa (Ewe) or Fa (Fon) divination are also created with great care and elaboration; thus they are sometimes bought by Europeans as objects of art. Stools are important to Ewe and Fon lineages. They are often carved with narrative detail so that their symbolic significance is inscribed for future generations to see.

Medicine. Today many Fon and Ewe seek medical assistance in modern clinics and hospitals and go to Western-trained doctors. They may also frequent local healers and Vodu priests who employ plants and carbonized ingredients, as well as rituals to address illness and conflicts playing themselves out in a person's body and soul. Vodu medicine is not hostile to modern biomedicine. Upon asking Afa, though divination, what to do about illness, a sufferer may be told by Afa to go to a doctor in town. Vodu medicine is particularly effective in cases of madness. Ingestion of roots and plants, as well as "speaking pain and desire" to the Vodus make it possible for the alienated to mourn losses and go on with life once again.

Death and Afterlife. Upon death, certain aspects of the person are lost forever in their individuated form, whereas other aspects, for example, the *djoto,* or reincarnation soul, will come back in the next child born to the lineage. The *luvo,* or death soul, may linger for some time after death, looking just like the person in life and frightening loved ones with demands for attention and its cravings to be still with the living. According to some informants, the person as constituted in life does not survive death, but parts of the personality may indeed continue and even join with Vodus, as part of the conglomerate energy and personality of a deity. Others say that the spirit realm mirrors human life in every aspect, so that after death individuals go on in much the same way as before. Funerals are the single most important event in a person's history, more lavish and expensive than any other celebration or feast. Groups of drummers are hired, and mourners may dance throughout the night for several nights in succession. Attending funerals and contributing to them financially and with food and drink are among the most binding obligations for lineage members, neighbors, friends, chiefs, and Vodu worshipers (above all, for those who belong to the same order as the deceased).

Bibliography

Argyle, W. J. (1966). *The Fon of Dahomey.* Oxford: Clarendon Press.

Blier, Suzanne-Preston (1995). *African Vodun: Art, Psychology, and Power.* Chicago and London: University of Chicago Press.

Green, Sandra E. (1981). "The Anlo Ewe: Their Economy, Society, and External Relations in the Eighteenth Century." Ph.D. dissertation, Northwestern University.

Green, Sandra E. (1983). "Conflict and Crisis: A Note on the Workings of the Political Economy and Ideology of the Anlo-Ewe in the Precolonial Period." *Rural Africana* 17:83–96.

Green, Sandra E. (1985). "The Past and Present of an Anlo-Ewe Oral Tradition." *History in Africa* 12:73–87.

Green, Sandra E. (1988). "Social Change in Eighteenth-Century Anlo: The Role of Technology, Markets, and Military Conflict." *Africa* 58(1): 70–86.

Green, Sandra E. (Forthcoming 1995). *Gender, Ethnicity, and Social Change on the Upper Slave Coast: A History of the Anlo-Ewe*.

Herskovits, Melville J. ([1938] 1967). *Dahomey: An Ancient West African Kingdom*. (Vols. 1, 2). Evanston, Ill.: Northwestern University Press.

Kossi, Komi E. (1990). *La structure socio-politique et son articulation avec la pensée religieuse chez les aja-tado du sud-est Togo*. Stuttgart: Franz Steiner Verlag.

Le Herissé, A. (1911). *L'ancien royaume du Dahomey*. Paris.

Manoukian, Madeline (1952). *The Ewe-Speaking People of Togoland and the Gold Coast*. London: International African Institute.

Mignot, Alain (1985). *La terre et le pouvoir chez les guin du sud-est du Togo*. Paris: Publications de la Sorbonne.

Pazzi, Roberto (1976). *L'homme evé, aja, gen, fon et son univers*. Lome: reneotyped.

Riviere, Claude (1981). *Anthropologie religieuse des evé du Togo*. Lome: Les Nouvelles Éditions Africaines.

Rosenthal, Judy (Forthcoming 1995). *Foreign Tongues and Domestic Bodies: Personhood, Possession, and the Law in Ewe Gorovodu*.

Surgy, Albert de (1988). *Le système religieux des evhe*. Paris: L'Harmattan.

Université Nationale du Bénin; Faculté des Lettres, Arts, et Sciences Humaines; Département d'Histoire et d'Archéologie (1977). *Actes du Colloque international sur les civilisations aja-ewé*. Cotonou: Université Nationale du Bénin.

Verger, Pierre (1957). *Notes sur le culte des orisa et vodun à Bahía, la baie de tous les saints, au Brésil et à l'ancienne Côte des Esclaves en Afrique*. Dakar: Mémoires de l'Institut Français d'Afrique Noire, no. 51.

JUDY ROSENTHAL

Falasha

ETHNONYMS: Beta Esráel (self-name), Esráelotch, Felasha, Kayla

Orientation

Identification. The Falasha are a northern Ethiopian highland population of Jewish belief. They are one of the dozens of small ethnic minorities in Ethiopia and have been recognized as a "nationality" in the Ethiopian constitution of 1986. More than half of this community emigrated to Israel during the late 1970s and 1980s.

Location. The traditional Falasha area lies on the central Ethiopian plateau, its elevation mostly above 2,000 meters. Roughly between 12°30′ and 14°30′ N and 37°00′ and 38°10′ E, it is located north of Gonder town, reaching up to the Tekeze River, east into western Welo (near Sequote village, and into the Shire area of Tigray Region (west of Aksum town). On the plateau, average daytime temperatures are between 16° C and 27–35° C in the dry season (from October to June, with a "small rainy season" from February to March) and slightly lower in the rainy season (May to September). Nights are cold, with temperatures around –18° C, especially in the Semyen area. Despite the "rainy season" (Keremt), rain is notoriously unreliable, and crop production is often precarious. In addition, the northern highlands have much suffered from erosion and soil deterioration. Part of the Falasha area was hard hit by the drought and famines of 1984–1985 and after.

Demography. In 1976 a voluntary-agency worker in the Falasha area conducted a census that reckoned the total number of Falasha as 28,189. This was before any emigration had taken place. The Falasha nowadays number around 30,000 to 40,000 persons, almost half of them residing in Israel. Since the start of the move to Israel, more inhabitants of the Falasha region in Ethiopia have, predictably, identified themselves as "Beta Esráel" or as being of Beta Esráel descent. They form only a tiny ethnoreligious minority within Ethiopia.

Linguistic Affiliation. The Falasha speak the Semitic languages of the majority population of their areas: Amharic and Tegreñña respectively. In the Middle Ages, and partly up to the mid-nineteenth century, they spoke Agew, a Cushitic language of the original inhabitants of the Ethiopian plateau, before the arrival of Semitic speakers of Ge'ez, Tegreñña, and Amharic, from the north. In the 1950s, owing to the emerging ties of the Falasha with Israel, some Hebrew was introduced by young teachers trained in Israel. In Israel the Falasha retain Amharic and Tegreñña among themselves, but also learn Hebrew.

History and Cultural Relations

The history and origins of the Falasha (the "Black Jews of Ethiopia") is one of the perennial subjects of scholarly and popular debate. Their Jewish beliefs (different in kind and liturgical form from "normative" Talmudic Judaism) suggest a priori an ancient link with the land of Israel and the Israelites, the popular idea being that their ancestors migrated to Ethiopia in the time of King Solomon's kingdom (e.g., as a group of highborn assistants and teachers who accompanied Menilek, who was—according to Ethiopian ecclesiastical tradition—the son of Solomon and the queen of Sheba [i.e., Ethiopia], back to Aksum from Jerusalem). The historical basis of the legend—and of various others positing an ancient link of the Falasha with the Israelites of old—is, of course, very tenuous. Indeed, recent research into the liturgical music of the Beta Esráel points to a close relationship with the Ethiopian Christian tradition, to the extent that the former has, to a significant degree, been shaped by the latter. Occasional references to "Jews" or "Israelites" in various religious and historical documents cannot be assumed to refer to the Falasha as a long-established Jewish community in Ethiopia. Deserving of more serious consideration are the accounts of medieval travelers, who mention a country where Jews lived independently in mountain fortresses, fighting with Christian emperors and defending their faith (Kaplan 1988). Even on the basis of these reports, however, one cannot conclude that the Falasha existed as a clearly identifiable Jewish population in the Ethiopian highlands, at least not before the fourteenth century. For the subsequent period, however, there are more data on groups of rebellious "Jews" (Ge'ez: Ayhud) who resisted the encroaching Christian kings trying to force them into submission and convert them to Ethiopian Orthodox Christianity. The Falasha indeed became the historic enemies (together with the Muslims) of the Ethiopian medieval emperors, certainly from the time of Ishaq (r. 1413–1438) up to that of Susneyos (r. 1607–1632). The former started a war of conquest and conversion in the area where a Judaic people or, as the Ethiopian royal chronicles often state, "former Christians, people like Jews" lived (i.e., in the area north of present-day Gonder). As a result of this war, the Beta Esráel/ Falasha lost their title to land. They became an inferior "caste," cultivating only land owned by Christians and gradually taking up crafts as additional means of livelihood. They became the blacksmiths, weavers, and potters of their area, often despised and shunned by landholding Amhara-Tigray. The corollary of this division of labor, based on conquest and religious difference, was the emergence of a "supernatural" boundary: the Falasha were often accused of possessing magical powers and the evil eye (Amharic: *buda*). In the course of the centuries, the Beta Esráel continued to fight wars to retain their independence from Ethiopian kings, who demanded political submission and tribute (Quirin 1977). Periods of relative peace (under sixteenth-century emperors Galawdewos and Fasilades) were followed by fierce battles, for example, during the reigns of kings Baede Maryam (1468–1478), Serse Dengel (1563–1597), and Susneyos. It was Susneyos who rooted out any semblance of autonomy of the Beta Esráel area and started an intensive conversion campaign. After the 1620s, the Beta Esráel became a virtually powerless minority, at the bottom end of the social hierarchy of traditional feudalist Ethiopia, and their numbers dwindled. A period of renewed interest from Western travelers and scholars was initiated by a visit of the French-Jewish Orientalist J. Halévy (1868), who prepared a report for the Jewish Alliance Israelite Universelle asking for moral, religious, and educational support for these "forgotten Jews." From that time on, albeit with ups and downs, growing Jewish interest in the Falasha and growing identification of the Beta Esráel with world Jewry and, later, the state of Israel led to a decisive rapprochement between the Beta Esráel and the Jewish people and, ultimately, to the emigration movement of recent years. The immediate causes of this movement were the sociopolitical upheaval after the Revolution of 1974 and the threats of drought and famine. The flight itself, which claimed the lives of an estimated 3,000 to 4,000 Beta Esráel, included weeks of dangerous trekking through drought- and hunger-stricken enemy territory toward refugee camps in eastern Sudan. An airlift from Sudan beginning in November 1984 and lasting until April 1985 brought many thousands to Israel, but an equal number remained in Ethiopia; thus, a truncated community continues to live in the Welo and Gonder administrative regions, in some thirty-six villages. Virtually all the Falasha in Tigray have been able to leave. Many Falasha who stayed in Ethiopia wish to go to Israel to join their relatives. Negotiations on emigration of the community were resumed after the silent rapprochement between Israel and Ethiopia in 1989 (and the restoration of various forms of assistance given by Israel to Ethiopia). In Israel, a new phase of the history of the Beta Esráel (simply identifying themselves as "Ethiopian Jews") has begun, bringing with it profound social, religious, and cultural changes challenging traditional life-styles, ideas, and norms of this once rather neglected rural Ethiopian minority (see Ashkenazi and Weingrod 1987).

Although much has been made of the Jewish belief and character of the Falasha, in a broad cultural sense (linguistically, ethnically, socially), they are primarily "Ethiopian" in character (i.e., their outlook, way of life, and economic and social organization are predominantly similar to those of the Highland Amhara-Tigray). Their Judaic tradition, however, has always stimulated a sense of separate identity, which was "reproduced" by the ethnic division of labor, supernatural beliefs, and religious differences. These elements have somewhat eroded since the Revolution because both the traditional socioeconomic stratification and superstitious beliefs were actively discouraged by the revolutionary authorities, who also denigrated traditional artisanry.

Settlements

The Falasha traditionally lived in scattered hamlets or villages in the northern Ethiopian countryside, some in all-Falasha villages, others in mixed villages, in which Amhara-Tigray Christians and (in Tigray) Muslims also lived. Although family groups (married sons of a man often chose to reside in the same village) often lived together in one area, the hamlets or villages had no clear kinship basis, the Falasha population being fairly mobile geographically. A married couple and their children inhabited the common highland *tukul* (a hut constructed of wood, straw, mud, and dried cow dung). A village had an average population of 150 to 200 persons. Before the 1960s, very few Falasha lived in towns like Gonder or Asmara (those who did, did so mainly for proximity to schools). Only in the 1960s and 1970s did some Falasha traders and laborers move to the larger villages and towns, but, especially after 1974–1975, many young men left their villages for a few years of national service in the Ethiopian army. Some became teachers, medical assistants in clinics, or clerical workers. In Israel, where Falasha, as new immigrants without resources, necessarily live in a state of dependency on government agencies, most are settled in "development towns," often in clusters of relatives and friends. Virtually none live in rural settlements. After the first years of their "absorption process," guided by state agencies, they may, if they are able to find jobs and housing, move to cities in the center of the country.

Economy

Subsistence and Commercial Activities. In Ethiopia, the Falasha were (and are) subsistence farmers and artisans (blacksmiths and potters). In the traditional prerevolutionary social order, they were tenant-peasants, eking out a living on land owned by the Amhara-Tigray; only a few Falasha families retained land rights given to their ancestors in the days of kings Fasilades and Galawdewos (sixteenth century). The main crops were the indigenous Ethiopian cereal *téff* (*Eragrostis téff*), wheat, maize, beans, and chickpeas. They also cultivated garden crops, such as spices, oilseeds, onions, and cabbage. Surpluses were marketed in the regional markets in small quantities. Livestock (cattle, sheep, goats, chickens) were raised in very small numbers. In their cultivation system (i.e., the use of ox-drawn plows and the rotation of crops), the Falasha hardly differed from the Amhara-Tigray peasants; however, their standard of living was usually lower. After the revolution of 1974, the traditional landholding system was abolished. Peasants were entitled to receive up to ten hectares for cultivation, within the framework of the new peasant associations. (All land was nationalized after the Land Proclamation Act of April 1975.) This ended the overt social inequality and exploitation of the peasants, although it did not immediately solve all problems or lead to a rise in living standards. In one village (Weleqa, near Gonder town), women earned some cash income from the sale of small black clay figures for the tourist market. This product was first introduced in the 1930s and has no traditional base whatsoever in Falasha culture. The Falasha were also well known in northwestern Ethiopia as a caste of artisans: potters and blacksmiths (and, less commonly, weavers). Because of imports of cheap iron tools and cooking utensils, however, the Falasha have been forced to subsist more and more on agriculture and some small-scale trade, which has also grown markedly. In Israel, the occupational structure of the Falasha/Ethiopian Jewish community is completely altered. Settled in urban areas, they are trained as skilled or semiskilled workers and find employment in industry, in offices, or as agricultural wage laborers. Very few have been able to set up independent private businesses. The young people, having completed high school or other training courses, quickly attain a much higher educational standard than the previous generation, improving their position in the job market.

Industrial Arts. Apart from craft work (see "Subsistence and Commercial Activities"), the Falasha had no forms of industrial art. In Israel, the women have retained and developed the production of traditional colorful basketry, although now with cotton thread instead of the tough and durable Ethiopian reeds.

Trade. In Ethiopia, the Falasha traded their surplus agricultural products at the regional open-air markets, which were held at fixed weekly intervals. There they also sold their pottery wares and iron tools. Some Falasha blacksmiths were noted for their repair work on old guns (like Männlicher, Fusil Gras, Albin, and so forth).

Division of Labor. Traditionally, the Falasha have been plow agriculturists. Men do most of the work in the fields (i.e., plowing, sowing, weeding, and harvesting—the last on a collective, mutual-help basis). Men also do the blacksmithing, weaving, and building. Women cultivate the gardens, perform the domestic tasks (preparing food, cleaning, taking care of children), draw water, and supply firewood. In addition, they produce pottery for domestic use and for sale. They also sell products in the markets. In the 1960s some Falasha men went to work as laborers in Addis Ababa and Asmara, and as sailors in Mesewa, but labor migration in general has always been insignificant. In Israel, the social structure of the Falasha community being entirely different, women are, in a way, becoming more dependent both within the household and in a wider social sense, as wage laborers competing with others in a tough job market.

Land Tenure. Before 1974, the Falasha were landless peasants paying heavy annual tributes to Amhara-Tigray landlords. Only a few Falasha had customary land-use rights. They were essentially a caste, "appended" to the Ethiopian "feudalist" system. In the Tigray region, however, many Falasha did own land. Following the introduction of wide-ranging land reform after 1975, the Falasha worked their own parcels of land within the framework of "peasant associations," which were collective communities designed to develop into full-fledged producers' cooperatives. In most of these peasant associations, Falasha lived together with the Amhara peasants on a more equal footing than they previously did, although the old fears about the Falasha possessing the evil eye are still not completely eradicated. There are also indications that religious differences and the Falasha's known desire to move to Israel continue to cause occasional friction.

Kinship, Marriage, and Family

Kinship. Although not organized in larger entities like corporative descent groups, lineages, or clans, the Falasha lived in a kinship universe where the nuclear family (*beteseb*) was the basic unit. In most respects, the Falasha resemble the Amhara-Tigray among whom they lived. Their kinship terminology is also that of the Amhara and the Tigray, an Eskimo-type bilateral terminology. As the Falasha in general did not own land, lineal-descent consciousness is less important among them than among the Amhara-Tigray, who often appealed to ambilineal descent lines to claim their rights to a particular piece of land. It is, therefore, impossible to speak of "lineages" among the Falasha, as among the Amhara. They have extensive knowledge of wider family ties—and thus of who is a Falasha/Beta Esráel. There are no fictive-kin relationships among them, although informal "adoption" is common.

Marriage. The Falasha traditionally showed group endogamy. Marrying a Christian—although not an infrequent occurrence—was actively discouraged because of traditionally strong religious boundaries in matters of food taboos, ritual purity, and so forth. The Falasha, like the Amhara, say they do not marry relatives "within the seventh degree." The marriageable age for girls ranges from 14 to 20, for boys from 18 to 28—another similarity with the Amhara-Tigray. Great value was attached to virginity: traditionally, a bride who was not a virgin on her wedding day could be returned to her parents and might be cast out from the community. Nowadays these rules have changed. Also, girls have demanded the right to choose their own partners, instead of following their parents' preference. There is also a tendency to delay the age of marriage. The rate of divorce is relatively high, and almost all adults marry more than once. (This pattern shows little change in Israel.) Settlement after marriage has been basically neolocal, depending on the preference of the male; however, most married couples remain in the village of the husband's parents for the first years after marriage.

Domestic Unit. The basic domestic unit is the nuclear family (the Falasha being monogamous)—the unit of production and consumption. Parents or married brothers and sisters may live in the same village, in separate compounds. There is mutual assistance between kin-related units, but one cannot speak of extended families in the accepted sense of the word. Widows or widowers often go to live with the eldest married son.

Inheritance. As there are few things to inherit—some cattle, utensils, tools, jewelry—there are no clearly defined rules of inheritance. If, in the "feudal" past, a family had *rist* (land-use) rights, these were transferred to the oldest son. Cash or personal belongings of the deceased would be divided among the surviving spouse and children in mutual agreement.

Socialization. In rural Ethiopian society, elder persons were respected and obeyed. Children are directed by their parents, grandparents, and village leaders. Agricultural and other skills are learned by imitation. Children, depending upon their age, are assigned specific tasks, such as herding animals, fetching wood and water, or guarding crops. Corporal punishment was an accepted means of disciplining and enforcing obedience. Primary-school education (common in most villages after the Revolution) has given the children more leverage (i.e., has led to a more "autonomous" attitude toward their seniors).

Sociopolitical Organization

The majority of Falasha belong to the peasant class (the bottom of the Ethiopian social ladder), but some are teachers, medical dressers, or government workers. In Israel, the Falasha, in accordance with their level of education and vocational training, have become part of the working class and a minority in the middle class.

Political Organization. In the Middle Ages, the Falasha were probably organized in fairly autonomous chiefdoms. In the early seventeenth century they lost all local political autonomy and became subordinate to the authority of emperor and landlords. Community affairs, disputes, and petty crime were handled by their village elders and priests. Formerly, they had local village representatives to the imperial authorities, but in the twentieth century this representation has been lost. After 1974, the Falasha were, like other rural Ethiopians, subject to—and part of—the peasant-association structures.

Social Control. In the small-scale village society of the Falasha, family honor, the normative authority of elders, and ethnoreligious-group traditions were the basis of social control. The Falasha were usually reluctant to submit cases of offense to non-Falasha courts. In postrevolutionary conditions, more appeals were made to the courts of the peasant associations and those of the *awraja* (province).

Conflict. Since the emergence of the Falasha/Beta Esráel on the historical scene in the fourteenth century, their relations with the dominant Amhara-Tigray have been tense and full of violent conflicts. Even when there were long periods of peace, cooperation, and incorporation of the Falasha into Amhara society, there remained a latent tension (religious difference, the evil-eye syndrome, social-status difference; Abbink 1987). Conflicts arising from Falasha being accused of possessing the evil eye continue to occur.

Religion and Expressive Culture

Religious Beliefs and Practices. The most remarkable aspect of Falasha culture is their peculiar form of non-Talmudic Judaism, developed in isolation from the main currents of Jewish religious thought. They believe in the God of Israel; the Old Testament commandments are their guidelines. The Falasha celebrate most festivals and fasts mentioned in the Torah, observe food taboos, and offer sacrifices, for example, on Easter (Fasika). Circumcision is carried out on the eighth day after birth, and the sabbath is closely observed. The Falasha Holy Book is the Ethiopian Bible (in Ge'ez), without the New Testament but with some Ethiopian Apocryphals. Their prayer service, prayer texts, and other religious books appear to be heavily influenced by medieval Ethiopian Christian sources. There is no clear evidence of a Hebrew tradition and of independent Jewish influence on the formation of Falasha Judaism. Some religious holidays of the Falasha are not marked by other Jews, and the Falasha traditionally did not celebrate post-Exilic festivals such as Hanukkah and Purim. Religious leadership was provided by "monks" and priests. These monks have disappeared since the late 1960s, but the priests still function as liturgical and community leaders. Since the mid-twentieth century, Falasha Judaism has been much influenced by Talmudic Judaism; religious practices not in accordance with it have, for the most part, been abandoned. In Israel, the priests are retrained as spiritual leaders. They learn rabbinical law, but few attain the status of rabbi. After arrival in Israel, Falasha immigrants are familiarized with the basics of Talmudic religious law. It is the requirement of a symbolic "conversion" that has caused the most problems in Falasha social adaptation in Israel. In addition to their Judaic belief, the Falasha traditionally shared the common Ethiopian beliefs in supernatural forces and spirits. They also consult magicians; some Falasha were themselves famous magicians, who were also revered by Christians.

Arts. Expressive arts are poorly developed among the Falasha. Except for simple decoration of pots and clothes, there are no well-developed art forms. Women used to decorate their faces and arms with tattoo patterns, like Amhara-Tigray women. There are Falasha musicians, who play the common Ethiopian instruments such as *krar, masänqo,* and *washint,* but most of their songs and dances follow the style and form of those of the Amhara-Tigray. Unique to a certain degree is their liturgical music, performed by priests during parts of the prayer service, but even this is heavily influenced by Ethiopian Christian liturgical traditions (Shelemay 1986).

Medicine. The Falasha had recourse to the spectrum of Ethiopian traditional healers, some of whom were practitoners of magic. There is also a general knowledge of the medicinal qualities of a variety of highland plants. In some villages, clinics were established, first by voluntary agencies interested in the Falasha, later by the government. Health care, is, however, far from adequate.

Death and Afterlife. The Falasha believe, in accordance with the tenets of the Bible, in life after death, and that the dead will be resurrected at the end of days. Burial takes place as soon as possible, even before all relatives may have arrived. Death is the strongest source of ritual pollution of living persons. Those having touched the corpse must remain in isolation for several days before rejoining the community. Eulogies on the deceased are given by various relatives on the day of the funeral or before. There is no particular veneration of the dead, as there is no clear idea of "lineage solidarity." Commemorative gatherings in honor of the dead person are held one week, one month, and one year after the burial.

Bibliography

Abbink, J. (1987). "A Socio-Structural Analysis of the Beta Esráel as an 'Infamous' Group in Traditional Ethiopia." *Sociologus* 37:140–154.

Abbink, J. (1990). "L'énigme de l'ethnogenèse des Beta Esráel: Une analyse anthropo-historique de leurs mytholégendes." *Cahiers d'Études Africaines* 28.

Ashkenazi, M., and A. Weingrod, eds. (1987). *Ethiopian Jews and Israel.* New Brunswick and Oxford: Transaction Books.

Kaplan, S. (1985a). "The Beta Israel (Falasha) in the Ethiopian Context." *Israel Social Science Research* 3(1–2): 9–27. Reprinted in Ashkenazi Wingrod 1987.

Kaplan, S. (1985b). "The Falasha and the Stephanite: An Episode from 'Gadla Gabra Masih'." *Bulletin of the School of Oriental and African Studies* 48:279–282.

Kaplan, S. (1988). "Some Hebrew Sources of the Beta Israel (Falasha)." In *Proceeding of the VIIIth International Conference of Ethiopian Studies, Addis Ababa, 1984,* edited by Taddesse Beyene. Vol. 1, 199–208. Addis Ababa: Institute of Ethiopian Studies; Huntingdon, U.K.: ELM Publications; Frankfurt am Main: Frobenius Institut.

Quirin, J. A. (1977). "The Beta Israel (Falasha) in Ethiopian History: Caste Formation and Culture Change, 1270–1868." Ph.D. thesis, University of Minnesota (Minneapolis). Available on Xerox University Microfilms.

Shelemay, K. Kaufman (1986). *Music, Ritual, and Falasha History.* East Lansing: Michigan State University, African Studies Center.

Shelemay, K. Kaufman (1988). "Historical Ethnomusicology: Reconstructing Falasha Liturgical History." *Ethnomusicology* 24:233–258.

J. ABBINK

Fali

ETHNONYMS: none

Orientation

Identification. The Fali belong to the vast paleonegritic group of people who are sometimes designated "Kirdi" (pagans), as opposed to the Islamized Peul or Fulbe, with whom they share the northern part of Cameroon. The name "Fali," by which they designate themselves, does not seem to be an ancient one. Indeed, it appears that, until colonialization, they were largely called by names of tribes, place-names of origin, or geographical localities. Nowadays more or less resulting from the influence of the colonial administration, they divide themselves into four large groups: the Tinguelin Fali, the Kangou Fali, the Fali of Bossoum, and those of Peské-Bori, four different appellations that correspond to as many territorial units.

Until about 1980, the Fali were easily distinguished from other peoples by their clothing. For men, that consisted of a two-piece cotton loincloth embroidered with bright colors in symbolic geometric motifs, and for women, a kind of petticoat made of bean fibers dyed black and ornamented with glass beads and cowries.

Location. Fali country stretches from 9°20′ to 10°00′ N and from 13°20′ to 13°50′ E. On the north, it is bounded by the Mandara Mountains; on the south, by the valley of the Benue; on the east, by that of the Mayo Louti; and on the west, by that of the Mayo Tiel. This is a mountainous region of about 4,000 square kilometers. The relief, not very marked but somewhat broken because of its volcanic nature, includes plateaus separated by small mountainous islands, the elevations of which vary from 600 to 1,135 meters.

The climate belongs to the tropical type in transition, with two well-marked seasons: a dry season of seven months and a rainy season lasting from July to December. Maximum temperatures on the order of 45° C are sometimes reached in the months of March and May, but they may fall to 6°C after a tornado during the rainy season.

The flora is intermediate between typical Sudanese and sub-Sahelian: a savanna with thorny shrubs. Its most northern part approaches the Chadian steppe.

The fauna was very rich until about 1970, but it has been considerably reduced by poaching and—especially—by the use of pesticides for cotton raising. The great predators—lions, panthers, cheetahs, hyenas—have today completely disappeared from the region.

Demography. In 1933 the population was estimated to be 36,000 individuals. It probably varied little until about 1960. Although their population is probably rising, the Fali in the 1990s number only about 20,000 culturally identifiable individuals.

Linguistic Affiliation. The language is classified in the Chad-Adamawa Language Group. It includes six principal dialects, two of which exist only on the Massif de Tinguelin territory nearest to the valley of the Benue and the modern city of Garoua. The Fali use Fulfuldé (the language of the Fulbe) as a vehicular language and, more rarely, they also use Hausa. In spite of their proximity to English-speaking Nigeria, the tendency among the Fali is probably toward the adoption of French.

History and Cultural Relations

Oral traditions allude to the presence of little red men, the Gwé-Gwé or Guéwé, who supposedly occupied the land before time was reckoned. This population, which has left only a mythical memory, disappeared with the arrival of the ancestors of the oldest Fali, the Ngomma. It was they who founded the modern villages of which the most ancient, now ruined,

Timpil, was the capital. Many accounts also allude to the Sao, who developed a brilliant civilization on the periphery of Lake Chad from the tenth to the sixteenth centuries and who, upon the destruction of their villages by the sovereign of Bornu, are thought to have taken refuge in the region. Their influence is proven by numerous necropolises composed of very characteristic tomb jars.

The first half of the eighteenth century (a date obtained by genealogical cross-checking) was marked by a large movement of populations, triggered by the arrival of two groups of southern origin, the Woptshi and the Tshalo. Their arrival also corresponds to a radical change in the type of burial. In the nineteenth century, following the Peul invasion, portions of neighboring ethnic groups (such as the Mundang, Njay, and Bata) attempted to incorporate themselves into the populations already in place.

In 1912 the Fali fiercely resisted the German colonizers. Under French influence (1916–1960), their territories, which were supervised but often not checked upon, consisted of independent subdivisions directly under the colonial administration (heads of subdivisions) and administered subdivisions placed more or less voluntarily under the trusteeship of Peul sultans.

Catholic and Protestant missions have had little success in making conversions. Reading and writing are taught at the village level, especially when such instruction is done as part of the Peul dependency. Primary schooling, although it scarcely touches one child out of five, is nevertheless in full swing. Some scholarships, in the form of aid to the family, permit the most gifted children access to secondary schooling, in neighboring cities. About ten brilliant successes have put Fali students into the higher-education circuit.

Settlements

The terms *hoyu* and *ara,* which designate the covered interior courtyard and the hut of each individual, respectively, also designate the house, as does the word *ba,* which applies more particularly to the group of habitations of a single lineage. The hoyu represents a family unit; it is the basis of the family. The number of persons to be lodged, rather than wealth, determines the number of huts and their importance.

A dwelling is composed of several round buildings of adobe with thatched roofs, connected to one another by a woven-straw fence. Sometimes hedges of euphorbia (*Euforbia kamerunica* and *E. hispida*) replace them or are added. Cultivated trees such as boswelia (*Boswelia dalzielli*), bougainvillea (*Bougainvillea glabra*), and flame trees (*Caesalpinea pulcherina*) provide shade and ornamentation. The buildings are placed close together, in order to leave an open area in the center. A typical dwelling unit consists of at least five parts: an entry (*atikalat*), a man's room (*ara,* the door of which faces that of the atikalat), a hut for the wife (*hoy tibuelgu*), a kitchen (*kanamju*), and an inside attic (*kulu*). Not far away, separate rooms are added for boys and girls, once they reach puberty. Young unmarried males possess a square hut, either inside the family enclosure or outside it, a few meters away. In polygamous households, each wife has a complete dwelling unit. Exterior storehouses, in which harvests (e.g., millet, peanuts) are deposited, vary in number and size, according to the ranks of the different wives to whom they belong. They vary in shape and sometimes in decoration, according to the region. They are round buildings of adobe, separated from the ground by a collections of stones. Entrance is gained from the top, by raising the movable roof.

The dwellings may also include annexes. Inside the enclosure, a storeroom-chapel shelters the "Guaw Lasindii" stones, which represent the dead of the lineage. Forges are always situated outside the smith's dwelling. They are not protected by any construction, except for a simple shelter of mats supported on stakes, while they are in use. Millet dryers, constructed in the same manner, are also placed outside. A little farther away rise the sheepfolds, which are shanties of branches where goats and sheep are penned in for the night. Shelters made of matting allow visitors and members of the household to enjoy the shade. They serve as meeting places, where people discuss or drink or where young people play music while thus preserving the intimacy of the home. Traditionally, the clay buildings were often decorated, inside and outside, with painted geometric motifs (symbolic or simply esthetic) or with imaginary scenes of a commemorative character (e.g., a hunt or a dance). Also noteworthy are the constructions that are reserved for the worship of the clan ancestors. They are enclosures covered with mats, in which two structures contain the sacred rhombs, objects of clay, and iron bracelets, as well as the clan masks.

Until 1970, the dwellings in the mountains were grouped into hamlets, according to clan or lineage. In the late twentieth century they tend more and more to include immediate family members only.

Economy

Subsistence and Commercial Activities. The Fali are farmers and hunter-gatherers. For centuries they have known how to utilize the mountains to grow the plants that constitute their basic foods—sorghum (*Andropogom shorgom*) and small millet (*Pennisetum pennicellatum*)—alternating with mixed crops such as beans (*Phaseolus sp.*), guinea sorrel (*Hibiscus sabdarifa*), sesame (*Saesamum sp.*), and peanuts (*Arachis hypogea*), to which are added numerous cucurbitaceous plants (melons, pumpkins, and so forth). When the different species of millet (*titu*) were grown primarily on a mountain slope, among piles of stones or on terraces, the other plants were cultivated around the houses.

Since they have moved into the piedmont region, however (between 1963 and 1980), the Fali, on both plain and plateau, have been able to plow land, which has made it possible for them to grow Chinese yams, taro (*Colocasia antiquorum*), sweet potatoes (*Ipomea sp.*), and even manioc (*Manihot utilissima*), although only in small quantities. Pimento (*Capsicum fastigiatum*) and okra (*Hibiscus esculentus*) stalks; some baobabs (*Adansonia digitata*), the leaves and fruits of which are edible; and papaya trees (*Carica papaya*) constitute the immediate vegetable environment of every dwelling. In addition to these types of food plants, the Fali grow others of utilitarian interest: cotton (*Gossypium sp.*); indigo (*Indigofera tinctoria*), for dyeing; euphorbias (*E. kamerunica and E. hispida*), for hunting poisons and religious medicines; cactus vine (*Vitis quadrangularis*), a sacred plant; anona (*Anona senegalensis*); and esthetic flame trees and bougainvilleas of recent introduction.

Nowadays, on the plain, the Fali are beginning to farm large areas. Use of the hoe is diminishing little by little in favor of the plow drawn by oxen. Traditional mixed crops are giving way to single-crop farming, with fallow no longer practiced for the basic food crops (millet and peanuts) or for the only income-producing crop that influences economic life, cotton. Cotton gives the Fali access to a market economy by allowing them to obtain money. Unfortunately, the clearing of land that necessitates that the farmer work farther and father away from his home has produced a seminomadism that has disrupted traditional arrangements while contributing greatly to the destruction of an already precarious ecological condition.

Hunting activities have now diminished. Antelopes, warthogs, and all large game—from panthers to servals—are still hunted with bows and arrows poisoned with *Strophantus*. Medium-size game (such as porcupines, rabbits, and wildcats) is hunted individually, with slings, sticks, or boar spears and dogs. Traditional traps—ditches, snares, and traps with radiating sharp points—as well as wolf traps of European origin are commonly used, as are locally made guns (although prohibited). The diet is also enriched with products derived from the raising of goats, sheep, and chickens, and, less commonly, with meat from a butcher shop and dried fish bought at one of the local markets. In general, the Fali are in satisfactory medical condition, with no alimentary problems.

Trade. Fali involvement in trade is extremely minor; it consists of the sale of cotton through the Sodecoton Society and millet and peanuts on the markets of villages and neighboring cities (Garoua, Gashiga, Guider, and Dembo). Necessities (fabrics, household utensils) are then purchased, as are many gadgets.

Industrial Arts. Exterior commercial exchanges rarely include goods of local manufacture. Smiths, who belong to individual clans, make weapons and tools out of used iron because ore-smelting workshops no longer exist. They make daggers, arrowheads, hoes, and scythes, mostly on a to-order basis. Smiths also repair objects of European origin, in particular bicycles and plows.

The Fali are not carvers or sculptors, except for making wooden dolls of ithyphallic aspect, which are decorated with glass beads and cowries. The gift of such a doll to a girl constitutes an engagement to be married. Another esthetic element made by the Fali is the man's loincloth, a kind of rectangular apron that extends from waist to knees, made from strips of cotton sewn together. The front part is embroidered with colored threads, which form decorative geometrical motifs that also have the value of a blazon. The posterior part, dyed with indigo, is often ornamented with glass beads and cowries. To these products can be added numerous pottery objects, often spangled with mica. The attractiveness of the body is very important to the Fali, which explains the place still occupied today by ornaments, bracelets, and necklaces, all of which are worn by men as well as by women.

Division of Labor. Sexual division of tasks is not extremely marked in agricultural labor. Perhaps this is because each woman may cultivate for her own profit a parcel of land on which she herself does all the farming work. Since the introduction of harnessed-animal labor, which is reserved for men, the woman's job has become less important. All building is done by men, except the digging of earth used as mortar; men also spin, weave, make baskets, and work on hides. To women befalls the making of all clay objects, the trimming of the stones used to crush millet and peanuts, the care and training of small children, and all household tasks. Children take care of the animals. All participate in the drudgery of carrying water and making emergency repairs to the house.

Land Tenure. The ground belongs to the Genies; humans, who came on earth afterward, are only life tenants. Nevertheless, each village possesses a certain territory in its own right, as do the clans or segments of clans that constitute its population. The lands on which the sacred enclosures of the different clans are erected can in no case be given away by others. The clan priest is their jealous guardian. Upon the death of the head of a household, his real assets (land under cultivation, planted trees) and his possessions both immovable and movable (dwellings and their contents) are transmitted from father to son by primogeniture, or from uncle to nephew; however, the wives and unmarried daughters of the dead man can continue to use them. Disputes are traditionally settled under the authority of the head of the village, who is the keeper of the law.

Kinship

The fundamental unit of social organization is the exogamous patrilineal clan, which groups together all living or dead descendants of an actual or mythical common ancestor. In actuality, however, these clans are broken up into subclans that are similar to clans, each of which has a name, a territory, a collective responsibility, a head, and its own sanctuaries and rituals. For example, a single village of five hundred inhabitants may include up to thirty clans or fragments of clans.

Kinship terminology is of the Crow-Omaha type, with clan exogamy. Only a single form of preferential marriage exists: one with a matrilateral cross cousin of the sixth degree of genealogical difference (Guilmain-Gauthier 1981). Otherwise, relationships are classificatory: within a clan, the individuals of the same generation are brothers or sisters, which does not exclude more precise appellations, such as *low mom* (brother by the same father and same mother). The terms differ according to age (*botom*): for example, *mom* (older brother), but *ka mom* (younger brother). Terms of address are often indifferent as to sex, except in certain cases: *wosom* (grandfather), *wam* (grandmother), *toy* (father), *noy* (mother), *sai* (sister), and *sata* (aunt).

Marriage and Family

Patrilocal marriage follows the rule of exogamy. Polygamy is practiced most by the noble class, and nowadays a man scarcely ever has more than four or five wives. Rather late marriage (16 years for girls and 24 for boys) takes place, in principle, after a long engagement. Despite the fact that their parents arrange the marriage, the prospective bride and groom are not obligated to acquiesce in their choice. The dowry owed to a girl's father, the payments of which can be spread over several years, is composed of services furnished (farm labor, construction), goods (animals, strips of cotton [*djolu*], clothing), and money. An average dowry corresponds approximately to 400,000 CFA francs (about U.S.$800). A married couple may divorce, under the arbitration of the head of the village. When the divorce is pronounced to be the woman's fault, the husband recovers the sum total of the dowry; in the opposite case, he loses it. In both cases, unweaned children remain with the mother; afterward they live with the father. Serious litigations that do not find satisfaction in Fali common law can be heard by the nearby Peul sultan or else in the city law court. Adultery, formerly punished by death, is today handled by fines. Corporal chastisements for the woman are also applied, with the greatest rigor, but stop short of mutilation. Child adoptions are common, both of Fali children and even of outsiders.

The domestic unit is composed of the husband, his wife or wives, their children, the paternal grandparents, and sometimes widowers or widows of the uterine line. The numerous family responsibilities that stem from this mixture of kin are generally borne well. Inheritance is governed by the rules of patrilineality.

Sociopolitical Organization

Social Organization. Fali society can be understood in concrete terms by looking at the population of a village: it is constituted of several segmented wholes that overlap or are connected, while at the same time being identified by means of predominating historical (tribes) or sociological (clans, lineages) criteria. Thus, each village can include elements of one or several tribes, essentially historical entities with a political character (Guilmain-Gauthier 1981). Each is formed by the juxtaposition—or rather the alliance—of several more or less segmented clans, which themselves break down into lineages arranged into hierarchies according to age.

Political Organization. Although the provincial administration has imposed state and national organizational structures, the Fali, like most of the ethnic groups of northern Cameroon, have kept their traditional political organization for their own internal use. Despite appearances, Fali society is quite hierarchial. It is composed of several tribes, made up of one or several noble clans (*ni haya*, "those from high up"), clans of free men and warriors (*ni fulia*, "those from down low"), and clans of slaves and foreigners (*ni palala*, "peripheral ones"). Each tribe is headed by the eldest man of the oldest lineage of one of the noble clans that are represented in the village. In spite of a flattering title, he has scarcely any authority; for alongside him there is the *wun voli* (war chief) or, more simply, *wuno* (chief), who is the true holder of power. Since he is elected from within a noble clan to which this dignity is attached, only one wuno exists per village. The supreme authority from a political point of view, he is also a religious personage, the son of ancestors who have become protectors. Because he is highly respected, he must be exemplary. He keeps no tax for himself. Formerly, if he had to decide on peace or war, he did so only with the assent of all the clan heads.

In serious conflicts that endanger a large part of the ethnic group, it used to be the case that the heads of different villages chose one of their own number to exercise a quasi-absolute power. This centralization of authority disappeared by itself when the danger was past. Nowadays the provincial administration on the district level sometimes leans on these ancient structures in order to exert its authority. It does this directly when villages have escaped from the trusteeship of the Islamized Peul (Fulbe) or indirectly by the intervention of their sultans in the opposite case. The second situation is unwillingly endured by the Fali. Their fear of seeing Islamic Peul power become preponderant led them, at the time of the last legislative elections, to vote for the RDPC, the party of President Paul Biya (a southerner and a Christian), to the detriment of the UNDP, the party of Bouba Bello (a candidate from the Islamized north).

Religion and Expressive Culture

Religious Beliefs. The Fali believe in a single god, Faw, as creator and organizer. A male being, he has willed order and harmony, and he intervenes only when they are disturbed. He is a just god, rather far away, and one whom human intelligence is incapable of depicting. Prayers are not addressed to him, but to the consecrated ancestors, who are the intercessors of men with him. Ona, the earth, is the mother goddess, around whom supernatural beings can be ranked: sacred crocodiles of heaven; guardians of light and thunder; the black snake, master of darkness; and the Genies and the bad spirits. Revealed religions have as yet had only a slight impact; there is some interest in Christian teachings, but Islam also attracts some people by appearing to be locally liberal.

Religious Practitioners. In each village there are one or several "masters of earth," a "master of rain," and a "master of hunting," as well as, in each clan, a therapist-diviner (*tondji pangu*). On the lineage level, there are also priests. The priests are more particularly responsible for domestic worship, and they should not be confused with malignant beings like sorcerers, the servants or the reincarnation of the bad dead, who are unmasked by means of ordeals. The members of a secret society—Niakt Kolshondba ("that which is not talked about now")—used to have (or may still have) the responsibility of ridding society of these injurious beings. In general, the Fali are not enclosed in the magic universe, which differentiates them considerably from members of nearby ethnic groups.

Ceremonies. All major life events are marked in a ceremonial way. Presentation to the ancestors occurs in about the sixth month of a person's life, and initiation between 12 and 17 years; in the same period and later, at about 45 years, death is endured through the ceremony of the Bashta (gift). Boys are not circumcised; girls are not excised. These characteristics again differentiate the Fali from neighboring peoples. Initiation (Tshêta Ao) consists of two parts. The first, primarily didactic and ritual, has as its setting the sacred enclosure of the clan. The second consists of a retreat in the bush of about ten days, a kind of combatant's road, which is followed in the company of an older sponsor, the *yum*. Ordeals that are extremely harsh from a physical and moral point of view introduce young people to the adult state (*tondji*). Each year, at the beginning of the dry season, the ancestors of the clan are worshiped. The ceremonies that coincide with the end of the harvest have often been confused with an agrarian religion. Ceremonies are also directed toward the Genies. Festivities of friendship, Silu Bolomji, like the preceding manifestations, call for music and dancing and are accompanied by joyful drinking of millet beer.

Arts. Sculptures are rare except for funerary representations, statuettes of baked earth, and baked zoomorphic or anthropomorphic modelings that are used as toys. Formerly, the walls of dwellings were decorated with paintings, which were mostly geometric motifs of more or less symbolic character. Sacred music, profane music, music for close by or for large spaces, vocal music (both solos and ensembles), and instrumental music are all highly developed. The principal instruments—whistles, flutes, harp-lutes, horns, drums with two laced skins—are related to paleonegritic cultures.

Medicine. The Fali make a distinction between natural illnesses (for which the physical relationships from cause to effect are known) and illnesses of supernatural origin. The former are cared for without the intervention of a specialist. The latter, which represent nearly all internal pathologies—attributed in increasing order of seriousness to ancestors, to Genies, to sorcerers, and finally to Faw—require recourse to a specialist, who is considered indispensable. He is actually the only one who can name the malady, making it possible to identify the responsible agent by divining procedures. The task thus comes back to the therapist-diviner. There is one in each clan, but his medical specialty must be practiced for the benefit of the whole village community. He recommends medications in terms of the supernatural agent that is held responsible and also of the symptoms that are observed. His services are recompensed only by modest gifts. The practice of minor surgery is fairly common. The practitioner has no other qualification than his ability.

Death and Afterlife. When death takes place, it affects only the material part of the individual. The purpose of the extremely complicated funeral rituals is to permit the soul to leave the body under conditions that are satisfactory for reaching the abode of the ancestors. The rites are also an homage to the deceased. After being washed and sometimes smeared with ocher, the corpse is placed in a sitting position with arms extended forward. It is then enveloped in strips of cotton and oxskin thongs. The hands and feet remain uncovered. While the swathing is being done in a covered enclosure, the mourners dance outside. Funeral procedures last an average of one to two days. The corpse is then lowered into a funerary well in sitting position. The festivity of the dead (Hatshu Wuta), held one month later, marks the reincarnation of the deceased as an ancestor (*manu*). Henceforth he will live out eternity under the ground, whence he will be able to come back by means of the Mask (Tiwot'u Manu). Secondary funeral procedures take place three years later for a man, four for a woman. They consist in removing the skull, which is preserved in an earthenware vessel carefully hidden in the bush. It is into the skull that thought and knowledge will be able to come back when they are entreated. These, together with vital breath, constitute the tripartite soul (*djumjum*). A period of deep mourning follows the interment until the deceased's festivity. The wife or wives, who revert to the son or brother of the deceased according to the practice of levirate, are subjected to very strict sexual prohibitions during this period of three months. These blur and disappear when the skull has been removed. Nowadays the Fali tend more and more to simplify the ritual part of the actual burial. Since 1990, some have omitted the wrapping of the corpse in strips; others have been satisfied to put the body down into a simple ditch. Three reasons can explain this abandonment of custom: the cost of the funeral procedures, the actions of Christian missionaries, and the ceaselessly growing influence of Islam.

Bibliography

Beaudelaire, H. (1946). "Eléments d'une notice sur la subdivision de Guider." *Archives de la Subdivision de Guider*. Texte dactylographié.

Bordes G., and J. G. Gauthier (1990). "Ouverture de l'économie et monétarisation des échanges chez les fali du Ngoutchoumi." *Nord Cameroun* 25:105–115.

Cardaire (Cne) (1949). "Contribution à l'étude de l'Islam noir." *Mémoire des études camerounaises*. Douala: IFAN.

Crea'ch, P. (1993). *Se nourrir au Sahel, 1937–1939: Pour mieux connaître le Tchad*. Paris: L'Harmattan.

Elridge, Mohamadou, and Modibo Bassoro (1980). *Garoua: Tradition historique d'une cité peule du Nord-Cameroun*. Bordeaux: Centre National de la Recherche Scientifique.

Essomba, J. M. (sous la direction de) (1992). *L'Archéologie au Cameroun: Actes du premier colloque international de Yaoundé (6–9 janvier 1986)*. Paris: Ed. Karthala.

Froelich, J. C. (1956). "Le commandement et l'organisation sociale chez les fali du Nord Cameroun." *Études Camerounaises* (Douala) 53–54:20–49.

Gauthier, J. G. (1963). *Une population traditionnelle du Nord Cameroun: Les fali*. Bordeaux: Institut Pédagogique.

Gauthier, J. G. (1969). *Les fali de Ngoutchoumi, montagnards du Nord Cameroun*. Oosterhout: Anthropological Publications.

Gauthier, J. G. (1989). *Les chemins du mythe: Essai sur la religion des fali du Nord Cameroun*. Bordeaux and Paris: Presses du Centre National de la Recherche Scientifique.

Guilmain-Gauthier, Ch. (1981). *Organisation et vie familiale chez les fali du Nord Cameroun*. Travaux et Documents de la RCP, 395 Centre National de la Recherche Scientifique, Laboratoire d'Anthropologie. Bordeaux.

Jansen, G., and J. G. Gauthier (1983). *Ancient Art of the Northern Cameroons: Sao and Fali*. Art ancien du Nord Cameroun: Sao et Fali. Oosterhout: Anthropological Publications.

Lebeuf, J. P. (1945). *Quand l'or était vivant*. Aventures au Tchad. Paris: J. Susse.

Lebeuf, J. P. (1961). *L'habitation des fali, montagnards du Cameroun septentrional. Technologie. Sociologie. Mythologie. Symbolisme*. Bibliothèque des Guides Bleus. Paris: Hachette.

Lebeuf, J. P., and A. Masson-Detourbet (1950). *La civilisation du Tchad*. Bibliothèque Scientifique. Paris: Payot.

Malzy, P. (1956a). Les fali du Tinguelin. *Études Camerounaises* (Douala) 54:3–37.

Malzy, P. (1956b). "Quelques villages fali du Tinguelin." *Études Camerounaises* (Douala) 51:38–41.

Meek, C. K. (1931). *Tribal Studies in Northern Nigeria*. Vols. 1, 2. London.

Passarge, S., and C. Rathjens (1920). "Eingeborenen Bevölkerung." In *Deutsches Koloniallexikon*. Berlin.

JEAN-GABRIEL GAUTHIER
(Translated by Jean H. Winchell)

Fipa

ETHNONYMS: Afipa, Wafipa

Orientation

Identification. The Fipa are a Bantu-speaking people of southwestern Tanzania in East-Central Africa. The name "Fipa" appears to have been bestowed on them by nineteenth-century traders and means "people of the escarpment." It was later adopted by German and British colonial administrators as a convenient label for this people.

Location. Ufipa (the country of the Fipa) is located between 7° and 9° S and 30°15′ and 32°15′ E. Most of the country consists of a plateau about 1,800 meters in elevation, with some adjacent territory in the Rukwa Valley to the east and along the Lake Tanganyika shore to the west. The total land area of Ufipa is about 65,000 square kilometers. The climate alternates between a six-month wet season, beginning in November, and a six-month dry season, beginning in April.

Demography. The present population of Ufipa is estimated at 200,000, with an average density of more than 8 per square kilometer. At the last tribal census, in 1967, ethnic Fipa constituted two-thirds of the then-total population of 150,000. Other numerically significant ethnic categories of the population of Ufipa are the Lungu, Nyika, Mambwe, Nyamwanga, and Wanda, all of whom are the actual or reputed descendants of Bantu immigrants.

Linguistic Affiliation. The Fipa language clearly belongs, through its grammatical structure and vocabulary, to the great family of Bantu languages whose speakers inhabit two-thirds of the African continent. Fipa is classified by linguists as belonging to a subgroup that includes Bemba, most of whose members are to be found to the south and southwest of Ufipa, in northern Zambia. Fipa itself is divided into a number of dialects, of which the most important is called Sukuuma (with no apparent connection to the people and language of a similar name in northeastern Tanzania). Most Fipa are also fluent in Swahili, the national language of Tanzania.

History and Cultural Relations

Linguistic evidence suggests that Ufipa has been largely peopled by migrants from what is now northern Zambia and southeastern Zaire. An early center of ironworking and sacral kingship appears to have been established at Milansi, a village in the middle of the Fipa plateau. A subsequent and politically dominant form of kingship gradually developed, and a centralized and hierarchic form of administration was established. It seems that early in this process the new state divided into two entities, called respectively Lyangalile and Nkansi. About 1840 the Fipa plateau was overrun by militarily superior Ngoni invaders from the south, who ruled the country until a succession dispute ended in the withdrawal of the competing factions from Ufipa. Nyamwezi traders from central Tanzania were probably in contact with Ufipa from early in the nineteenth century, and from the 1850s onward there was increasing trade between the Fipa and Zanzibari merchants from the East African coast. The missionary-explorer David Livingstone was the first European known to have visited the Fipa, in 1872. He was followed in 1880 by the Scots explorer Joseph Thomson and the German Paul Reichard. In 1890 Ufipa was incorporated into the colonial state of German East Africa; in 1919, after Germany's defeat in World War I, that state was renamed Tanganyika and administered by Britain as a mandated territory under the League of Nations. In 1961 Tanganyika, including Ufipa, became a sovereign state, and in 1963, after the union of Tanganyika and Zanzibar, the new state adopted the name of Tanzania.

Settlements

A characteristic feature of Fipa settlements is that they are strongly nucleated and widely separated from one another. Until the enforced concentration of villages that was instituted nationwide by Tanzania in 1974, the average size of Fipa settlements was about 250 inhabitants. About 700 smaller settlements, away from the major road though Ufipa, disappeared in the 1974 administrative action. In precolonial times, Fipa huts were circular, with a concentric inner corridor; today they are nearly all rectangular, although still of the same mud-and-wattle construction. Each hut is typically occupied by a nuclear family, usually with two or more children and often including one or more dependent elder kin. In 1967 the average household size was 4.9 persons.

Economy

Subsistence and Commercial Activities. Finger millet (*Eleusine corocana*) is the basic subsistence crop, supplemented by maize. The Fipa also grow lima beans, cassava, tomatoes, onions, and a wide range of green vegetables and tobacco for domestic consumption. Small livestock raised by most families include sheep, goats, poultry, and pigeons; a minority of wealthier householders raise cattle and pigs. The plateau dwellers supplement their diet with small game and with fish trapped in the numerous rivers. The Lake Tanganyika and Rukwa Valley Fipa subsist largely on fish, which they also dry and sell on the plateau. Maize and finger millet are the main cash crops of Ufipa. Before 1974, most cultivation was done with a hoe, using a form of compost mounding that is peculiar to the Fipa. With the enforced concentration of villages, however, plowing with oxen was introduced by the government and has since become the dominant means of cultivation.

Industrial Arts. Precolonial Ufipa supported flourishing ironworking and cotton-weaving industries, but these were virtually extinguished by competition from imported manufactured goods during the colonial period. Fipa women still produce pottery, woven baskets, and mats for local use.

Trade. Meat, fish, and vegetable markets are held in a few major villages. The sale of cloth, kerosene, and a variety of manufactured items is dominated by immigrant merchants, mainly East Indians, coastal Swahili, and Kikuyu from Kenya.

Division of Labor. The Fipa still generally adhere to the traditional sexual division of labor: men do the heavier work of cultivation, which today means ox plowing, and threshing, whereas women sow, weed, and winnow. Women also cook, draw water, pound and grind grain, wash clothes, and watch over children. Men build the frameworks of huts and granaries, and women plaster them. Women also brew millet beer.

Land Tenure. Before 1974, plots of land were cultivated by nuclear families and inherited by elder sons or uterine nephews upon a householder's death. With enforced villagization and the introduction of the ox-drawn plow, there has emerged a new class of rich peasants who employ wage labor.

Kinship

Kin Groups and Descent. The Fipa are grouped in cognatic kindreds, each focused on an elected leader or chairperson. These are fluid groups, whose members are drawn together by a need for mutual aid and a common interest in the accumulation and distribution of wealth.

Kinship Terminology. Although descent and inheritance are bilateral, Fipa kin terms are unilineal, distinguishing father's brother from mother's brother and father's sister from mother's sister, whereas cousin terms are of the Iroquois type.

Marriage and Family

Marriage. Nearly all Fipa marriages are monogamous; polygynous unions constitute only a small percentage. Marriage is virilocal and is usually preceded by prolonged negotiations between representatives of the kindreds of the prospective bride and groom. Bride-wealth, which traditionally consisted of iron implements, is paid today in a mixture of cattle and cash. The groom is also required to work for a season in the fields of his prospective in-laws, to prove himself able to support a wife and family. A newly married wife is not supposed to speak to her parents-in-law until she has borne a child. Divorce is comparatively rare.

Domestic Unit. The nuclear family of husband, wife (occasionally wives), and children is the basic unit of social organization. All members of the family work together on a common plot and eat together.

Inheritance. Upon the death of an adult, his or her property is assigned to one or more kin at a general meeting of householders belonging to the kindred. In the case of a man, the meeting can also assign his widow to a suitable heir, usually a brother of the deceased; however, the widow has the right to refuse to be inherited and to become an independent householder in her own right instead.

Socialization. Children are raised and instructed in social norms by their parents, elder siblings, and paternal and maternal uncles and aunts. There is an egalitarian, joking relationship between grandparents and grandchildren, as there is between cross cousins. The main emphasis in child socialization is on sharing and nonviolence. Children are rarely beaten.

Sociopolitical Organization

Social Organization. In precolonial times, Ufipa was divided between two indigenous states, Nkansi and Lyangalile, ruled by related dynasties, who called themselves the *aTwa* (sing. *unnTwa* or *mTwa*), not to be confused with the similarly named Pygmy or Pygmoid peoples of Central and East Africa. These states appear to have been, to a large extent, meritocracies, in that apart from the office of the monarch and a few other and largely symbolic titles, any political office was open to able and ambitious commoners. Contemporary documents and oral traditions portray a mobile, commercially oriented, prosperous, and peaceful precolonial society. These are still basic characteristics of Fipa society today. Above the level of the domestic unit, the village remains the fundamental unit of society, pervaded by an ethos of communal solidarity and equality, notwithstanding considerable differences between householders in terms of wealth and status in the larger social world. Within the village, relative age remains the major determinant of a person's status.

Political Organization. In the precolonial order, which continued under the British system of "indirect rule" and throughout the early years of independence, each village was governed by an elected head chosen from among the constituent householders. Since 1974, this office has been succeeded by that of the local chairperson of the Tanzanian governing party, the Chama cha Mapinduzi (CCM), or Revolutionary party. The long era of one-party rule in Tanzania seems set to end with the holding of multiparty elections in October 1995. The remaining political and judicial powers of the indigenous Fipa royals were abolished at the time of Tanganyika's independence in 1961 and were assigned to centrally appointed commissioners.

Social Control. The basic source of social control in Ufipa remains the pervasive ethos that powerfully inhibits most Fipa from resorting to physical violence in interpersonal relations. Any such behavior is condemned as "subhuman" and can result in the social ostracism of the offender.

Conflict. Although armed conflict appears to have been endemic early in Fipa precolonial history, by the mid-nineteenth century the people were famous in the region for their pacific nature, and this characteristic is still apparent.

Religion and Expressive Culture

Religious Beliefs. The traditional religion of the Fipa was based on a network of territorial spirit shrines, administered by hereditary priests. These spirits were associated with prominent natural features such as hills, lakes, or large trees, and were commonly incarnated in pythons.

Today about 70 percent of Fipa are nominally Christian—most of these being Catholic—and 5 percent are Muslims. Worship of the traditional divinities has almost entirely lapsed. The most commonly invoked supernatural beings are ancestral spirits—who are intrinsically benign but may inflict sickness on erring descendants—and the intrinsically malign spirits of deceased sorcerers, creditors, suicides, and women who have died in labor.

Religious Practitioners. There are among the Fipa numerous indigenous experts in magico-medicine. Their craft centers on divining the occult causes of their clients' afflictions and dispensing treatment. These practitioners are also consulted by people who wish to obtain some benefit, such as wealth, employment, or a love partner.

Ceremonies. There was formerly an annual New Year ceremony at the beginning of the rainy season in early November, but this is no longer observed. The major ceremonial occasions observed by the Fipa today are the life-cycle rituals of birth, marriage, and death.

Arts. The Fipa have produced little or no sculptural art. Artisans formerly made a range of musical instruments, including flutes, lyres, and drums. Oral art—especially storytelling and the exposition of proverbial lore—is the major form still practiced.

Medicine. Sickness and death are attributed to sorcery or to the action of spirit agencies. Resort to the skills of indigenous practitioners is the main defense against these dangers.

Death and Afterlife. After death, a person's spirit is supposed to reside in an underworld and may decide to reincarnate in the same family after a lapse of two or more generations. After the identity of a reincarnating spirit has been established by divination, the newborn is given the name of his or her putative ancestor.

Bibliography

Lechaptois, A. (1913). *Aux rives du Tanganika*. Algiers: Maison Carrée.

Robert, J. M. (1949). *Croyances et coutumes magico-religieuses des Wafipa païëns*. Tabora: Tanganyika Mission Press.

Willis, R. G. (1966). *The Fipa and Related Peoples of Southwest Tanzania and Northeast Zambia*. London: International African Institute.

Willis, R. G. (1978). *There Was a Certain Man: Spoken Art of the Fipa*. Oxford: Clarendon Press.

Willis, R. G. (1981). *A State in the Making: Myth, History, and Social Transformation in Precolonial Ufipa*. Bloomington: Indiana University Press.

ROY G. WILLIS

Fulani

ETHNONYMS: Bororo'en, Fellaata, Fellah, Filani, Fula, Fulata, Fulbe, Hilani, Peul, Toroobe

Orientation

Identification. "Fulbe" is the preferred self-name of the group the Hausa term the "Fulani" or "Hilani." In French countries, they tend to be termed "Peul" or "Fulata." Because of their spread over a wide area and their assumption of cultural traits from surrounding groups, there is great confusion regarding the nature of Fulani ethnicity. This confusion is reflected in the confounding and conflating of names for particular segments or local groups of Fulbe, such as Toroobe and Bororo'en, with the entire ethnic group.

Location. The Fulani live in an area that stretches from Ouadaï, a city east of Lake Chad, to Senegal's Atlantic shore. There are groups of Fulani as far east as the border of Ethiopia.

Demography. Estimates of the number of Fulani vary. A major problem in reckoning the population is that Fulani are found in twenty nations in a wide swath of Africa—from Mauritania and Senegal to Sudan, Ethiopia, and Kenya. Only Liberia may not have any Fulani settlements. It seems reasonable to accept an estimate of 7 to 8 million nomadic Fulani and 16 million settled Fulani.

Linguistic Affiliation. The language is variously known as "Fulfulde," "Pulaar," "Fula," or "Peul," among other names. It belongs to the West African Subfamily of the Niger-Congo Group, along with Wolof, Serer, and Temne. There are many variations and dialects of Fulfulde. The influence of surrounding peoples is clearly seen in its local variations. Fulfulde is generally written in Roman script, although in the past it was written in Arabic.

History and Cultural Relations

A search for the origin of the Fulani is not only futile, it betrays a position toward ethnic identity that strikes many anthropologists as profoundly wrong. Ethnic groups are political-action groups that exist, among other reasons, to attain benefits for their members. Therefore, by definition, their social organization, as well as cultural content, will change over time. Moreover, ethnic groups, such as the Fulani, are always coming into—and going out of—existence.

Rather than searching for the legendary eastern origin of the Fulani, a more productive approach might be to focus on the meaning of Fulani identity within concrete historical situations and analyze the factors that shaped Fulani ethnicity and the manner in which people used it to attain particular goals.

People whom historians identify as Fulani entered present-day Senegal from the north and east. It is certain that they were a mixture of peoples from northern and sub-Saharan Africa. These pastoral peoples tended to move in an eastern direction and spread over much of West Africa after the tenth century.

Their adoption of Islam increased the Fulanis' feeling of cultural and religious superiority to surrounding peoples, and that adoption became a major ethnic boundary marker. The Toroobe, a branch of the Fulani, settled in towns and mixed with the ethnic groups there. They quickly became noted as outstanding Islamic clerics, joining the highest ranks of the exponents of Islam, along with Berbers and Arabs. The Town Fulani (Fulbe Sirre) never lost touch with their Cattle Fulani relatives, however, often investing in large herds themselves. Cattle remain a significant symbolic repository of Fulani values.

The Fulani movement in West Africa tended to follow a set pattern. Their first movement into an area tended to be peaceful. Local officials gave them land grants. Their dairy products, including fertilizer, were highly prized. The number of converts to Islam increased over time. With that increase, Fulani resentment at being ruled by pagans, or imperfect Muslims, increased.

That resentment was fueled by the larger migration that occurred during the seventeenth century, in which the Fulani migrants were predominantly Muslim. These groups were not so easily integrated into society as earlier immigrants had been. By the beginning of the eighteenth century, revolts had broken out against local rulers. Although these revolts began as holy wars (jihads), after their success they followed the basic principle of Fulani ethnic dominance.

The situation in Nigeria was somewhat different from that elsewhere in West Africa in that the Fulani entered an area more settled and developed than that in other West

African areas. At the time of their arrival, in the early fifteenth century, many Fulani settled as clerics in Hausa city-states such as Kano, Katsina, and Zaria. Others settled among the local peoples during the sixteenth and seventeenth centuries. By the seventeenth century, the Hausa states had begun to gain their independence from various foreign rulers, with Gobir becoming the predominant Hausa state.

The urban culture of the Hausa was attractive to many Fulani. These Town or Settled Fulani became clerics, teachers, settlers, and judges—and in many other ways filled elite positions within the Hausa states. Soon they adopted the Hausa language, many forgetting their own Fulfulde language. Although Hausa customs exerted an influence on the Town Fulani, they did not lose touch with the Cattle or Bush Fulani.

These ties proved useful when their strict adherence to Islamic learning and practice led them to join the jihads raging across West Africa. They tied their grievances to those of their pastoral relatives. The Cattle Fulani resented what they considered to be an unfair cattle tax, one levied by imperfect Muslims. Under the leadership of the outstanding Fulani Islamic cleric, Shehu Usman dan Fodio, the Fulani launched a jihad in 1804. By 1810, almost all the Hausa states had been defeated.

Although many Hausa—such as Yakubu in Bauchi—joined dan Fodio after victory was achieved, the Fulani in Hausaland turned their religious conquest into an ethnic triumph. Those in Adamawa, for instance, were inspired by dan Fodio's example to revolt against the kingdom of Mandara. The leader was Modibo Adamu, after whom the area is now named. His capital is the city of Yola. After their victories, the Fulani generally eased their Hausa collaborators from positions of power and forged alliances with fellow Fulani.

Settlements

For the fully nomadic Fulani, the practice of transhumance, the seasonal movement in search of water, strongly influences settlement patterns. The basic settlement, consisting of a man and his dependents, is called a *wuru*. It is social but ephemeral, given that many such settlements have no women and serve simply as shelters for the nomads who tend the herds.

There are, in fact, a number of settlement patterns among Fulani. In the late twentieth century there has been an increasing trend toward livestock production and sedentary settlement, but Fulani settlement types still range from traditional nomadism to variations on sedentarism. As the modern nation-state restricts the range of nomadism, the Fulani have adapted ever increasingly complex ways to move herds among their related families: the families may reside in stable communities, but the herds move according to the availability of water. Over the last few centuries, the majority of Fulani have become sedentary.

Those Fulani who remain nomadic or seminomadic have two major types of settlements: dry-season and wet-season camps. The dry season lasts from about November to March, the wet season from about March to the end of October. Households are patrilocal and range in size from one nuclear family to more than one hundred people. The administrative structure, however, crosscuts patrilinies and is territorial. Families tend to remain in wet-season camp while sending younger males—or, increasingly, hiring non-Fulani herders—to accompany the cattle to dry-season camps.

Town Fulani live in much the same manner as the urban people among whom they live, maintaining their Fulani identity because of the prestige and other advantages to which it entitles its members. In towns, Fulani pursue the various occupations available to them: ruler, adviser to the ruler, religious specialist, landlord, business, trade, and so forth.

Economy

Subsistence and Commercial Activities. The Fulani form the largest pastoral nomadic group in the world. The Bororo'en are noted for the size of their cattle herds. In addition to fully nomadic groups, however, there are also semisedentary Fulani—Fulbe Laddi—who also farm, although they argue that they do so out of necessity, not choice. A small group, the Fulbe Mbalu or Sheep Fulani, rely on sheep for their livelihood.

The Toroobe are outstanding clerics in the Sunni branch of Islam. They have generally intermarried with Hausa and no longer speak Fulfulde. They are found practicing other urban trades: teaching, serving in government positions, engaging in legal activities, renting property, financing trade, and so forth.

Many of the other Town Fulani were actually slaves of the Fulani who now identify with the group because of their high prestige. These urban dwellers engage in all the trades one finds in Hausa towns from crafts to long-range trade throughout Africa and the world.

Industrial Arts. The Fulani are not particularly noted for industrial arts, except for those associated with cattle. They do engage in leatherworking and some craft production. Many of their former slaves who have assumed Fulani ethnicity follow the basic crafts of other West Africans: silver- and goldsmithing, ironworking, basket making, and similar crafts.

Trade. The Fulani are engaged in long-distance trade, generally involving cattle, with their Hausa colleagues. Often the Hausa are also butchers who control West African cattle markets by controlling access to Fulani cattle.

Division of Labor. Herding cattle is a male activity. Tending and milking cattle, however, are women's work. Women may also sell dairy products; their graceful movement with containers of milk or cheese is a common sight in West African towns. Adolescent males traditionally have been in charge of moving the herds, whereas their elders deal with the political decisions and negotiate with sedentary people for the safe movement of the herds through farmlands.

Land Tenure. Land is held by—and inherited through—the patrilineage. As the Fulani have become increasingly sedentary—generally as a result of the pressure of the modern nation state and its centralized control—rights in land have become increasingly important.

Kinship

Kin Groups and Descent. The Fulani are patrilineal and patrilocal. Kinship and seniority are vital to their way of life. The basic elements of kinship are sex, age, and generation. Full siblings tend to unite against half-siblings, although half-siblings with the same mother do share a special bond.

The Fulani have a principle of generational seniority that is embodied in the general organization of lineages. There are four general lineages, all traced to descent from a common ancestor and his sons; however, everyday groups cut across these *yettore* lines. Such groups developed to meet historical needs.

Over time, patrilineages—much shallower than the four general lineages—emerged. These patrilineages, in turn, are intersected by territorial groups under men called "guides."

Patrilineages are named and consist of three ascending generations. They are coresidential, and members cooperate in pastoral pursuits. The patrilineage controls marriage and is endogamous. A clan is a cluster of lineages, and the clan members generally share a wet-season camp.

Kinship Terminology. There is a good deal of ambiguity in the Fulani use of kinship terms. Thus, any of these terms can be used to refer to a specific person or a range of people. Part of this ambiguity results from the Fulani preference for close marriage so that any person might, in fact, be addressed or referred to by any of several terms.

Goggo is used for father's sister or paternal aunt. *Bappanngo* is father's brother, whereas *kaawu* refers to mother's brother; *dendiraado* designates a cross cousin, and *sakike* is a sibling. *Baaba* is father, and *yaaye* is mother; *biddo* or *bu* is a child. These terms are often combined, however. Thus, *sakiraabe* refers to both siblings and cousins of all sexes. A true sibling if elder is termed *mawniyo;* if younger, *minyiyo*. *Maama* refers both to grandparents, of either sex, and their *sakiraabe* and their grandchildren. When it is necessary to distinguish male from female, a term may be added: *biddi* for male, and *dibbo* for female.

Marriage and Family

Marriage. Ideally, the Fulani do not practice birth control because the perfect or model Fulani marriage will produce many children. Toward that goal, the Fulani marry young. No special value is placed on virginity, and women are not shy about boasting about their various experiences. In fact, the Fulani expect young women to bring sexual experience to marriage. There are even special dances in which women select mates, with the proviso that the mate selected not be her fiancé or a particular category of relative—one to whom she could be affianced, for example.

At the same time, a woman is expected to display appropriate modesty whenever the subject of marriage arises, for marriage confers on her a special status. There has been some confusion regarding what constitutes the marriage ceremony among the Fulani. Because neither bride nor groom may be present at the ceremony, owing to shame-avoidance taboos, the significance of the cattle ceremony (*koowgal*) has often been overlooked. In that ceremony, the bride's father transfers one of his herd to the groom, legalizing the marriage. There may also follow a more typical Islamic ceremony, termed *kabbal*. Again, neither bride nor groom may actually be present at the ceremony.

An important public acknowledgment of the marriage is the movement of the bride to her husband's village, termed *bangal*. The women of that village come to greet her, and the welcome is a rite of passage for the bride. The bride's status increases with each child she has, especially with the birth of males.

The Fulani prefer endogamy. Their first choice of a marriage partner is a patrilateral parallel cousin. If that is not possible, their other choices are for the partners to share a great-grandfather, a great-great grandfather, or a patrilateral cross cousin.

Domestic Unit. A man is allowed four wives. Each wife brings cattle with her to the marriage. It is a major obligation for a woman to milk the cattle and prepare the dairy products. A woman receives respect from her sons and daughters-in-law.

Inheritance. Lineage members inherit cattle and widows. Among Town Fulani, inheritance generally follows Islamic prescriptions, with the exception that generally women do not contest their inheritance with their full brothers.

Socialization. At 2 years of age, children are weaned. A child's father remains distant throughout its life. Women provide for children's needs. Thus, a mother and her daughters tend to the needs of her sons. A young girl first plays at carrying dolls on her back and then moves on to carrying her baby brother.

Among the Pastoral Fulani, baby girls are given amulets for fertility and boys for virility. Mothers take care to preserve and shape their children's conformity to the Fulani ideal notions of beauty. Mothers attempt to lengthen their children's noses by pressing them between their fingers, stretching, and squeezing hard. They also attempt to shape their children's heads into the ideal round shape.

Acquiring a culture is perceived as acquiring something that is found. The Fulani term is *tawaangal*. There is a sense that no one invented nor can change these traditions, for they define what it is to be Fulani.

Young children are treated with great gentleness and are rarely disciplined. Adults seek to avoid giving them any emotional shocks. Most training is given by a child's mother and the other women of the compound. They are believed to be more capable of patience and reciprocity. Young girls are initiated into their adult work through games. The young girl carries her doll. At 2 or 3 years old her ears are pierced, six holes in her right ear and six in her left. Almost as soon as she can walk well, she is placed into the middle of a circle of dancing women who begin to teach her to dance and praise her efforts lavishly.

Indeed, the transition to adulthood proceeds in smooth steps. At about 5 years of age, girls are taught the rules of the moral code *-mbo*. There are to be no sexual relations of any kind with brothers. A woman may not look at her fiancé in the face. She must demonstrate respect for elders and must never mention her future parents-in-law. Women have two essential roles in Fulani society, that of sister and daughter. Either at her naming ceremony or just before she leaves her father's home for her husband's, a woman's father presents her with a heifer. There is shame for a man on entering his daughter's home; however, the strong affection he demonstrates for his grandchildren is meant to show his affection for his daughter as well.

Young boys play at taking care of the cattle and performing men's work. Mothers come to rely more on sons than on daughters because daughters will leave the compound upon marriage.

Sociopolitical Organization

Social Organization. The Fulani are many different people. Among those who term themselves "Fulani" are former slaves and members of castes or guilds, such as blacksmiths or bards. It is important to note that the Fulani hold that belonging to society itself is dependent on the will of the individual.

Political Organization. Fulani tend to be the ruling caste among Islamic communities in the northern areas of West Africa. They control the various northern emirates in what was Northern Nigeria, for example. They also play a major role in the modern governments of many West African states.

Among the Cattle Fulani, a leader (ardo) of a territorial group has a major role. Patrilineages play an important part in regulating day-to-day matters and in controlling cattle. They also govern marriages and widow inheritance.

Conflict. Kinship and regional groups regulate conflict within and between groups. The Fulani often come into conflict with settled populations among which they pass. Alliances with Town Fulani help resolve a number of disputes between Fulani and their neighbors. The Fulani are quick to resort to combat in the defense of their interest but also have a reputation for waiting for the opportune moment to seek revenge if the situation demands patience.

Religion and Expressive Culture

Religious Beliefs. Over 90 percent of the Town Fulani are Muslims. It is, in fact, rather difficult to discover any Fulani—Town or Cattle—who admits to not being Muslim, no matter how lax his or her practice may be. The Fulani share many beliefs with other West African Muslims. They use Islam both as a means to distinguish themselves from others, through the reputation of Fulani clerics, and as a link to members of other African groups.

At the same time, there is belief in the steady-state nature of culture that preceded Islam. Culture is seen to be unchanging and constant from generation to generation. The only improvement a Cattle Fulani sees possible is to have more children than his or her parents. Otherwise, the appropriate thing to do is to live according to the code of the ancestors.

That code stresses the symbolic importance of cattle in defining Fulani ethnicity. There is also a requirement to respect one's seniors and to love one's mother. The ethos of the Fulani is best summed up in the concept of *palaaku*. It portrays the ideal Fulani as one who has stoic sobriety, reserve, and strong emotional ties to cattle. At the same time, the model Fulani is gentle in demeanor. His carriage conveys a proud reserve, almost a disdain toward non-Fulani. It is said that no one knows what a Fulani is thinking. The true Fulani is physically as well as psychologically distant from other people, especially non-Fulani. Moreover, he is enjoined from displays of strong emotions. His demeanor is taciturn, loathing the boisterousness of others. Wealth is not to be vulgarly displayed but carefully and quietly tended.

The Fulani have a number of taboos. They may not pronounce the name of a spouse, a first son, a first daughter, a father or mother, or a parent-in-law or the names of the parents of any beautiful girl or young woman. In addition to observing the usual Islamic dietary laws, they may not eat goat meat, lest they become lepers.

Religious Practitioners. As Muslims, the Fulani share with other Muslims reliance on traditional Islamic religious practitioners and are themselves prominent members of the Islamic clerical class. In common with other West Africans, however, Fulani will frequent local religious practitioners who have established reputations for their curative powers and supernatural abilities.

Ceremonies. Various life-cycle events—naming, acceptance of young girls into the group, marriage, first child, and so on—are marked by ceremonies. The Shar'o ceremony demonstrates to the community that a young man has come of age. In it, adolescent friends take turns beating each other across the chest with their walking sticks. No sign of pain or discomfort can be shown. Although adolescents have died in this ceremony, young men are eager to participate and display their scars with pride throughout their lives.

Arts. The Fulani are noted for their oral literature, which celebrates the concept of palaaku and serves to define Fulani identity. Fulani oral literature has been influenced both by surrounding peoples and by Islam. The major categories of Fulani literature are poetry, history, story, legend, proverb, magic formula, and riddle. Many of these genres are sung, either by amateurs or by professionals.

Medicine. The Fulani participate in a number of medical systems. One is an Islamic system, basically derived from the Arabs and through them from Greco-Roman sources. They share many traditions with the groups among whom they live. Since the onset of British colonization—around the turn of the twentieth century—they have been exposed to Western medical practices. In common with other West Africans, they have incorporated elements from these various systems in a rather syncretistic and pragmatic fashion.

Death and Afterlife. If one lives up to the palaaku code and obeys Allah's laws, there will be rewards in the afterlife. The Fulani, in common with other Muslims, believe in an afterlife of material rewards for the followers of Allah.

Bibliography

Azarya, Victor (1978). *Aristocrats Facing Change*. Chicago: University of Chicago Press.

Ba, Amadou Hampata (1990). "Out of the Land of Shadows." *UNESCO Courier*, May, 22–25.

Dupire, Marguerite (1973). "Women in a Pastoral Society." In *Peoples and Cultures of Africa*, edited by Elliott P. Skinner, 297–303. Garden City, N.Y.: Doubleday.

Eguchi, Paul K. (1993). "'Fulbe-ness' in Fulbe Oral Literature of Cameroon." In *Unity and Diversity of a People: The Search for Fulbe Identity*, edited by Paul K. Eguchi and Victor Azarya, 181–200. Senri Ethnological Studies, no. 35. Osaka: National Museum of Ethnology.

Eguchi, Paul K., and Victor Azarya, eds. (1993). *Unity and Diversity of a People: The Search for Fulbe Identity*. Senri Ethnological Studies, no. 35. Osaka: National Museum of Ethnology.

Frantz, Charles (1981). "Settlement and Migration among Pastoral Fulbe in Nigeria and Cameroun." In *Contemporary Nomadic and Pastoral Peoples*, edited by Philip Carl Salzman, 57–94. Studies in Third World Society, Publication no. 17. Williamsburg, Va.: College of William and Mary, Department of Anthropology.

Hopen, C. Edward (1984). "Fulani." In *Muslim Peoples: A World Ethnographic Survey*. 2nd ed., rev. and expanded, edited by Richard V. Weekes, 257–261. Westport, Conn.: Greenwood Press.

Riesman, Paul (1977). *Freedom in Fulani Social Life: An Introspective Ethnography*. Translated by Martha Fuller. Chicago: University of Chicago Press.

Salamone, Frank A. (1985). "Colonialism and the Emergence of Fulani Ethnicity." *Journal of Asian and African Studies* 20: 170–201.

Schultz, Emily A. (1981). *Image and Reality in African Interethnic Relations: The Fulbe and Their Neighbors*. Studies in Third World Society, Publication no. 11. Williamsburg, Va.: College of William and Mary, Department of Anthropology.

Stenning, Derrick J. (1959). *Savannah Nomads: A Study of the Wodaabe Pastoral Fulani of Western Bornu Province, Northern Region, Nigeria*. London: International African Institute; Oxford University Press.

Wilson, Wendy (1990). "Women Pastoralists and Project Participation." *Sage* 7:18–23.

Wilson-Haffenden, James Rhodes (1967). *The Red Men of Nigeria: An Account of a Lengthy Residence among the Fulani or "Red Man," and other Pagan Tribes of Central Nigeria*. London: Cass.

Wyatt-Brown, Bertram (1988). "The Mask of Obedience: Male Slave Psychology in the Old South." *American Historical Review* 93:1228–1252.

FRANK A. SALAMONE

Ganda

ETHNONYMS: Buganda, Luganda

The Ganda are a group of people who live in the province of Buganda in Uganda. The Ganda refer to themselves as "Baganda" (sing. Muganda), and they refer to their language as "Luganda." Luganda is a Bantu language. Linguistically, Luganda can be placed within the Interlacustrine Group of the Northern Zone of Bantu languages or within the Central Branch of the Niger-Congo Language Family.

Buganda is one of four provinces within the country of Uganda. It is located on the northern and western shores of Lake Victoria, from 2° N to 1° S. It stretches for about 320 kilometers along the shore and extends inland about 130 kilometers. The land area of Buganda is about 45,000 square kilometers, and the elevation averages about 1,200 meters above sea level. The Ganda occupy the northwestern shore of Lake Victoria, a region characterized by flat-topped hills separated from each other by swampland.

Although the number of Africans living in Buganda, according to the 1950 census, was 1,834,128, only 1,006,101 of these people were ethnically Ganda. The overall density was 42 persons per square kilometer. At about the time of European contact (c. 1862), there were 3,000,000 Ganda. Civil wars, famine, and disease had reduced their number to about 2,000,000 by 1911. In 1986 their population was estimated at 2,352,000 (Grimes 1988).

Along with Bunyoro, Toro, Ankole, and Kiziba, Buganda is one of the Lacustrian kingdoms. The Ganda are people of mixed origins, whose ancestors migrated to their present location over the past 600 years. Historically, they were known as a warlike people who conquered many of their neighbors. At the time of White contact, the Ganda kingdom was at the height of its power.

The first contact with Westerners occurred in 1862, and missionaries arrived in Buganda soon thereafter. In the Buganda Agreement of 1900, Buganda was designated a province of Uganda. In 1962 the status of Uganda changed from that of a British protectorate to an independent nation and a member of the Commonwealth of Nations. In the Uganda Agreement, the position of the king (*kabaka*) was confirmed, and the native system of administration was preserved. The central government of Buganda Province consists of the kabaka, three ministers, and a legislative assembly (*lukiiko*). For administrative purposes, the province is divided into counties, subcounties, and parishes.

The Ganda are primarily an agricultural society; their staple crops are bananas and yams. Cotton was introduced as a market crop early in the twentieth century. In addition, sweet potatoes, taro, manioc, maize, millet, peanuts, beans, squashes, gourds, sesame, tomatoes, and sugarcane are grown. Ownership of cattle is a sign of wealth, and goats, chickens, and a few sheep are also kept. The banana has been of great importance in Ganda life. Typically, each household had a banana grove, which supplied the major food needs of the family. A grove could produce for as long as seventy years and required only a little weeding and mulching, work that was commonly done by women. According to the Ganda, one woman working in a banana grove provided food for ten men. Because of the banana, the Ganda have not needed to follow a pattern of shifting agriculture, and the land has been able to support a fairly dense population.

Traditionally, villages consisted of a number of households, each one surrounded by its banana gardens, spread out over the top of a hill. Villages were made up of between 60 and 100 adult males, together with their families, in a hierarchical system. All land was considered to be owned by the kabaka, who appointed local chiefs to administer specific territories. The chiefs, in turn, had subchiefs under them. At the bottom of this hierarchy was the village headman.

Land was controlled by patrilineal clans, each of which was protected by a major and a minor totem. Clan estates were administered by the heads of the clans, who were confirmed by the kabaka. Tribute—in the form of goods and services—flowed from the clans, to the chiefs, to the kabaka. For the kabaka, clan affiliation was different. There was a royal family, rather than a royal clan, and the children of the kabaka were affiliated with their mothers' clans. The succession to the kingship was in the male line: sons, grandsons, and brothers were eligible to inherit the title. In addition to his role as monarch, the kabaka was the head of all the clans in the kingdom. Through this latter role, the position of the king was reinforced, insofar as he was directly related to every family in the kingdom. Because of the kabaka's dual function, the Ganda consider it inconceivable for their society to exist without a king. Nevertheless, the chieftainship has declined in importance, and villages have become more dispersed and now lack the central focus of a chief's house. The residents of a village no longer get together except for marriage feasts and funerals.

The traditional religion of the Ganda was based on beliefs in the spirits of the dead. Prophets and mediums were able to consult with these spirits, which had influence over the affairs of the living. Although all of the Ganda are now considered to be Christian or Muslim (a small minority), vestiges of the traditional religion can still be observed. For example, sorcery, traditional medicine, spirit possession, and ancestor worship are some of the elements of the traditional religion that are sometimes practiced today.

Bibliography

Apte, David E. (1967). *The Political Kingdom of Uganda: A Study in Bureaucratic Nationalism*. 2d ed. Princeton, N.J.: Princeton University Press.

Fallers, Margaret Chave (1960). *The Eastern Lacustrine Bantu (Ganda and Soga)*. London: International African Institute.

Grimes, Barbara F. (1988). *Ethnologue: Languages of the World*. Dallas: Summer Institute of Linguistics.

Mair, Lucy Philip (1934). *An African People in the Twentieth Century*. London: G. Routledge & Sons.

Mair, Lucy Philip (1940). *Native Marriage in Buganda*. London: Oxford University Press for the International Institute of African Languages and Cultures.

Ray, Benjamin C. (1991). *Myth, Ritual, and Kingship in Buganda*. New York: Oxford University Press.

Richards, Audrey Isabel (1960). "The Ganda." In *East African Chiefs: A Study of Political Development in Some Uganda and Tanganyika Tribes*, edited by Audrey I. Richards, 41–77. London: Faber & Faber for the East African Institute of Social Research.

Richards, Audrey Isabel (1966). *The Changing Structure of a Ganda Village: Kisozi 1892–1952*. Nairobi: East African Publishing House.

Richards, Audrey Isabel, ed. (1954). *Economic Development and Tribal Change: A Study of Immigrant Labour in Buganda*. Cambridge: W. Heffer and Sons for the East African Institute of Social Research.

Roscoe, John (1911). *The Baganda: An Account of Their Native Customs and Beliefs*. London: Macmillan.

Southwold, Margin (1965). "The Ganda of Uganda." In *Peoples of Africa*, edited by James L. Gibbs, Jr., 81–118. New York: Holt, Rinehart & Winston.

Ghorbat

ETHNONYMS: Ghurbat, Gurbet, Qorbat

Orientation

Identification. The term "Ghorbat" is applied to several non-food-producing, itinerant populations of fairly low status throughout the Middle East and even beyond, in parts of formerly Soviet Central Asia and the Balkans. These peripatetic populations have usually been dubbed "Gypsies." In prerevolutionary Afghanistan (i.e., prior to 1978) "Ghorbat" was the self-applied ethnonym of a predominantly itinerant and endogamous community of artisans and petty traders; nongroup members were, however, often unaware of this ethnonym and classified this population as "Jat" or, in Pashto-speaking areas of the country, as "Jaṭ." In the late nineteenth and early twentieth centuries, in the border areas between Afghanistan and Pakistan, all those who were neither Pashtun, nor Baluch were contemptuously termed "Jaṭ" by members of these two communities. Even in the 1970s in Afghanistan, "Jat" and "Jaṭ" were pejorative terms and subsumed six distinct endogamous, itinerant communities, whose members offered goods and services for sale; the Ghorbat were one such community. The etymology of the term "Ghorbat" is uncertain, but it could derive from the Arabic/Persian words for "stranger," "exile," "the west," or even "poverty."

Location. In the 1970s the Ghorbat lived scattered throughout the major part of Afghanistan; 51 percent of the families were entirely nomadic, and 32 percent were entirely sedentary; 17 percent were partly sedentary—in the summer months, while the men migrated, women and children stayed home. For migration, pack animals had been very largely replaced by state bus transport. The migration pattern of the itinerant Ghorbat was seasonal: in winter, movement was from colder to warmer regions; it followed the agricultural cycles—in particular, the wheat-harvesting cycles of various regions. After the harvest of wheat, millet, and rice, the sieves manufactured by the Ghorbat were required by farming households. Following the harvests, marriages and other life-cycle festivities were performed in rural areas, which increased the demand for cloth, tambourines, and other products sold by the Ghorbat. In former times, before the Afghan government prohibited it, the Ghorbat also practiced bloodletting in autumn; they still offered traditional cures for petty ailments, especially those commonly contracted in winter. There was a shortage of ready cash in the Afghan countryside, and, after the harvests, villagers were in an easier position to pay the Ghorbat for their goods and services with agricultural produce. Some of these products, such as wheat, rice, and raisins, were partly consumed by the Ghorbat over the rest of the year; the excess, as well as products that they could not process themselves—such as cotton—or products that could not be conserved for long—such as cherries—were resold at a profit in urban centers. In the 1980s the location of the Ghorbat within Afghanistan was not known, but some families were reported to have been seen in Pakistan.

Demography. In 1976–1977 the Ghorbat community in Afghanistan consisted of roughly a thousand nuclear families, of which some six hundred were nomadic or seminomadic; average family size was 5.0 individuals. They thus formed the largest nonpastoral, itinerant community in the country.

Linguistic Affiliation. All Ghorbat spoke Qazulagi (also called Ghorbati), their mother tongue, in addition to the two most commonly spoken languages of Afghanistan—local variants of Persian—and sometimes Pashto. Qazulagi shares its basic structure with Persian; its vocabulary and syntax also contain numerous elements of rural Persian as spoken in various parts of Afghanistan. The vocabulary also includes a large number of Persian words incomprehensible to the normal Afghan, owing to a manipulation of phonemes, as well as words of Indic, Arabic, and Turkish origin. Some 60 percent of the vocabulary is of an as yet unknown origin. About one-third of it also has also been recorded by various scholars among other peripatetic communities elsewhere in the Middle East and in Soviet Central Asia.

History

Ghorbat history is based entirely on oral traditions. These stories invariably point to an Iranian origin, and, like the folk histories of many other peoples of the region, that of the Ghorbat posits a link with Sāssānian epic heroes and royalty. The ancestors of the Ghorbat are said to have been gold- and silversmiths who, for political and religious reasons, fled eastward into Afghanistan at a mythical point in time located simultaneously in the Sāssānian era and at the time of the prophet Mohammed. In the 1970s they were Afghan citizens, held identity cards, and were conscripted.

Settlements

The Ghorbat had two basic types of settlements—camps and houses. Nearly half of the itinerant families spent five to seven months in houses and the rest of the year in tents; fewer than 10 percent lived in camps throughout the year. Ghorbat tents were formerly stitched by the women; since the 1960s, however, they have been bought at intervals of three to four years and were, in principle, indistinguishable from the white canvas cloth tents used by other peripatetics, as well as by migrant labor in Afghanistan. Each tent was occupied by a nuclear family and surrounded by a low mud-and-stone wall, which helped keep out rain. Although a camp could include up to twenty-six tents, the commonest were those with two tents; whatever their number, the tents were positioned in such a manner as to leave some space free for communal use in the middle of the site. In all circumstances, the back flap of each tent was visible from at least one other tent. This was a security measure—household goods and equipment were stored in the back quarter of tents. Depending on the size and the duration of the camp, up to seven temporary structures could be constructed by the Ghorbat on their campsites. These were for common use and included a garbage pit, a place for prayer, and sometimes an oven for baking bread. Camping regions did not vary over the years, but precise camping sites depended in rural areas on the availability of fallow fields, as well as on the requirements of a family's eventual pack animals. In the vicinity of towns, government wastelands were used as campsites, but after 1975 camping in these areas was prohibited, and it was increasingly difficult to find suitable sites. Houses inhabited by the Ghorbat usually belonged to a group member. These houses were situated in specific areas of some of the larger towns, and always several families lived in two or more contiguous houses. Architecturally, these houses were not substantially different from neighboring ones occupied by non-Ghorbat.

Economy

Subsistence and Commercial Activities. The itinerant Ghorbat manufactured mainly sieves and tambourines but also bird cages and some traditional cosmetics; the peddling of these products in addition to cloth, haberdashery, trinkets, and certain services ensured their subsistence. Four major types of sieves (with eleven subcategories) and three sizes of tambourines (of three different qualities each) were made. Rattle-drums were also made. The sieves were for agricultural and household use and consisted of a circular frame of willow wood over which thongs of sheep- or goatskin were interwoven; the tambourines were also made of willow and sheep or goat hide. In addition, the Ghorbat often also stretched the skins over clay arm-drums made by potters. The bird cages were made of cedar and either split bamboo or long olive twigs. The entire manufacturing process was manual. Increasingly, industrially manufactured imported sieves tended to reduce the demand in urban kitchens for the traditional flour sieve made by the Ghorbat. In the early 1970s a few young men abandoned these traditional occupations and took low-wage labor, opened small shops, or sold their services as carpenters or other sedentary artisans. An entire section of the long sedentarized Ghorbat of Kabul city worked as animal traders and cobblers and did various other jobs. No Ghorbat owned agricultural land, and the only domestic animals were a few dogs, hens, and, decreasingly, donkeys as pack animals.

Division of Labor. Ghorbat men were in charge of manufacturing sieves, tambourines, and cages. Women were traditionally responsible for peddling these and other goods and services (including, at times, matchmaking and moneylending) from door to door; they sometimes lent a hand in making tambourines too. Women and men shared a large number of household chores.

Kinship

Kin Groups and Descent. The Ghorbat were divided into three major lineages, which were further divided into a total of eighteen patrilineal descent groups. Following the principle of segmentary systems, each of these descent groups was further divided on an average every second generation.

Marriage and Family

Marriage. Ghorbat lineages are, on the whole, endogamous. In keeping with the general Middle Eastern pattern, patrilateral parallel-cousin marriages as well as exchange marriages between sibling pairs were preferred, but in reality such unions constituted only about 17 percent and 18 percent respectively of all marriages. In such marriages, bride-price was lower than usual. In accordance with Islam, marriage was considered a contract, and divorce and widow remarriage were permitted, although not frequent. Cases of polygyny were extremely rare. The vast majority of marriages were arranged by the parents, and the residence pattern was virilocal.

Domestic Unit. The nuclear family was the minimal unit of production and consumption. It usually consisted of a married couple with their two unmarried children.

Inheritance. The Ghorbat followed fairly strictly the Islamic laws of inheritance prevalent in Afghanistan regarding the disposal of almost all of a man's personal possessions (clothes, tools, cash, etc.); a woman's jewelry was distributed equally among all her living children. The tent of a Ghorbat was inherited by his child/ren living in it at the time of his death; his widow had the right, if she wished, to continue to live in it—she would then have to be cared for by the inheritor(s). The same applied, in principle, to a house and its parts. The clientele a woman peddlar had built up over the years, and which was the major source of subsistence for her family, was "inherited" equally by all her daughters.

Socialization. Infants and children were raised by both parents (although more by the mother), siblings, and other members of the camp and/or extended family. Among the nomadizing families, physical punishment was never used in child rearing.

Sociopolitical Organization

The Ghorbat community was, in principle, egalitarian, although, in exceptional situations, hierarchical feelings could develop between lineages, and even within lineages between descent groups. There was no superordinate political structure and no permanent or hereditary positions of leadership or decision-making power at any level; the only few commonly recognized offices of authority were temporary and specifically goal oriented.

Social Control and Conflict. Social control was maintained by a value system that placed a premium on compromising, and thus minimizing conflict. Institutions of mutual financial and social help gave additional support to this system. Given the marginal socioeconomic position of the community as a whole, the Ghorbat were also obliged to avoid conflicts with the greater society; this was achieved largely by acquiring locally influential rural and urban clients, who, on occasion, interceded on their behalf and helped in other ways. The go-betweens in such situations of potential conflict with outsiders were usually Ghorbat women.

Religion and Expressive Culture

The Ghorbat were Shia Muslims, except for those in Kandahār, in the south, and some in Mazār-i-Sharīf, in the north, who were Sunni. Apart from Islamic ceremonies, and festivals, they also celebrated Nawroz, which was commonly marked in Afghanistan as New Year's Day (21 March).

Arts. Tattooing was fairly common. The Ghorbat painted their tambourines with various, predominantly floral, motifs and then sometimes decorated them with little jangles or bells.

Death and Afterlife. Beliefs and practices did not diverge basically from general Islamic patterns in the area.

Bibliography

Olesen, Asta (1977). *Fra Kaste til Pjalteproletariat? Etnisk erhvervsspecialisering i Østafghanistan, belyst ved udviklingen i kornrenseres, sigtemageres og småhandelsfloks vilkår.* Århus: Århus University.

Rao, Aparna (1982). *Les Ġorbat d'Afghanistan: Aspects économiques d'un groupe itinérant "Jat."* Paris: Eds. ADPF/Institut Français d'Iranologie de Téhéran.

Rao, Aparna (1986). "Roles, Status, and Niches: A Comparison of Peripatetic and Pastoral Women in Afghanistan." *Nomadic Peoples* 21–22:153–177.

Rao, Aparna, and Michael J. Casimir (1988). "How Non-Food-Producing Nomads Obtain their Food: Peripatetic Strategies in Afghanistan." In *Coping with Uncertainty in Food Supply*, edited by Igor De Garine and G. A. Harrison. Oxford: Clarendon Press.

APARNA RAO

Gusii

ETHNONYMS: Abagusii, Kisii, Kossowa, Wakisii

Orientation

Identification. "Gusii" or "Abagusii" is the people's name for themselves. A Gusii individual is an "Omogusii." "Kisii" is the Swahili name that the British colonial administration used, and it is still the common name used by other inhabitants of Kenya. The Gusii are divided into seven clan clusters: Kitutu (Getutu), North Mugirango, South Mugirango, Majoge, Wanjare (Nchari), Bassi, and Nyaribari.

Location. Gusiiland is located in western Kenya, 50 kilometers east of Lake Victoria. Since precolonial times, abundant rainfall and very fertile soils have made Gusiiland one of the most productive agricultural areas in Kenya. The proportion of cultivable land ranges between 70 and 80 percent. The region is demarcated by the coordinates 0°30′ and 1°00′ S and 34°30′ and 35°00′ E. In 1989 Kisii District was divided in two; one segment retained the old name, and the other was called Nyamira. The Gusii are still the sole ethnic group inhabiting these districts. The area is a rolling hilly landscape on a deeply dissected peneplain at elevations of 1,190 meters in the far northwestern corner of the territory and up to 2,130 meters in the central highlands. The mean maximum temperatures range from 28.4° C at the lowest elevations to 22.8° C at the highest. The mean minimum temperatures are 16.4° C and 9.8° C, respectively. Rain falls throughout the year; the annual average is between 150 and 200 centimeters. There are two peak seasons of rainfall: the major rainy season (March to May) and the minor rainy season (September to November). In the nineteenth century much of present-day Gusiiland was covered by moist montane forest. Today all forest has been cleared; scant indigenous vegetation remains, and no large mammals are found.

Demography. In 1989 the number of Gusii was 1.3 million, and population densities ranged from 200 to over 600 persons per square kilometer. This population, increasing by 3 to 4 percent per year, is among those exhibiting the most rapid growth in the world. The average woman bears close to nine children. Infant mortality is low by sub-Saharan African standards about 80 per 1,000 live births.

Linguistic Affiliation. Ekegusii is a Lacustrine Bantu language.

History and Cultural Relations

At the end of the 1700s, Bantu-speaking populations were dispersed in small pockets at the northern, southern, and eastern margins of the Kisii highlands and in the Lake Victoria Basin. Around 1800, the highlands above 1,515 meters were probably uninhabited from the northern part of the Manga escarpment southward to the Kuja River. At that time, the lowland savanna was being settled by large numbers of agropastoralist peoples ancestral to the present-day Luo and Kipsigis, dislodging the smaller Bantu groups from their territories on the savanna. The Gusii settled in the Kisii highlands, whereas other culturally and linguistically related groups remained along the Lake Victoria Basin or settled in the lower savanna region at the Kenya-Tanzania border (as did the Kuria, for example). The establishment of the British colonial administration in 1907 was initially met by armed resistance, but it ceased after World War I. Unlike other highland peoples in Kenya, the Gusii were not subjected to land alienation. The seven subdivisions of Gusiiland were converted into administrative units under government-appointed chiefs. The first missions were established by the Catholics in 1911 and the Seventh Day Adventists in 1913. Mission activity was initially not very successful; several stations were looted. Since Kenyan independence in 1963, schools have been built throughout the area; roads have been improved, and electricity, piped water, and telephones have been extended into many areas. By the 1970s, a shortage of land had begun to make farming unprofitable, and the education of children for off-farm employment became more important.

Settlements

Before the colonial period, the extended polygynous family was spatially divided into two components: the homestead (*omochie*), where the married men and women and their unmarried daughters and uncircumcised sons lived, and the cattle camps (*ebisarate*), located in the grazing areas, where most of the cattle were protected by resident male warriors. The British abolished the cattle camps in 1913. In the late nineteenth century most Gusii were settled in dispersed farmsteads, although the North Mugirango built fortified villages for protection against Kipsigis raids. A homestead consisted of the wives' houses. The compound had several elevated granaries for finger millet. The traditional Gusii house (*enyomba*) was a round, windowless structure with a framework of thin branches, walls of dried mull, and a conical, thatched roof. Today the Gusii continue to live in dispersed homesteads sited in the middle of the farm holdings. Modern houses are rectangular, with thatched or corrugated-iron roofs, and cooking has been moved from the house to a separate kitchen structure.

Economy

Subsistence and Commercial Activities. The precolonial staple crop was finger millet, which was grown together with sorghum, beans, and sweet potatoes. Cultivated-plant food was complemented by meat and milk from livestock and by wild vegetables. At the end of the nineteenth century, the cultivation period was two years, with a fallow of three to six years. By the 1920s, maize had overtaken finger millet as both a staple-food crop and a cash crop. Other important contemporary crops include cassava, pigeon peas, green grams, onions, bananas, potatoes, and tomatoes. Coffee was already being grown on a limited basis in the 1930s, and, by the 1950s, Gusiiland had become established as a producer of coffee and tea. Iron hoes and ox-drawn plows are still used in cultivation. Livestock were formerly more numerous, but farmers still raise cattle (both of local zebu and of European stock), goats, sheep, and chickens. The high population density has forced the Gusii to utilize every available space for agriculture, and most families today are unable to produce enough food for their subsistence needs. In addition to farming, many Gusii engage in employment or business, either locally or in the large urban centers.

Industrial Arts. In precolonial Gusiiland, iron tools, weapons, decorations, wooden implements, small baskets for porridge, and poisons were all produced locally. Pottery making was limited; most pottery and basketry was obtained through trade with Luoland. The most notable—in terms of technical complexity and product value—of the Gusii industries were the smelting of locally obtained ore and the manufacture of iron implements. Blacksmiths did not form a special caste, as is often the case in African societies. Smithing was a remunerative industry, reserved for men, and blacksmiths became wealthy and influential.

Trade. Precolonial Gusii exchange took place within the homesteads. Tools, weapons, crafts, livestock, and agricultural products were exchanged, and goats and cows were often used as the media of exchange. During the nineteenth century, regular barter between the Luo and the Gusii, conducted by women, took place at periodic border markets. In addition, there was a regular and voluminous trade of Gusii grain for Luo livestock that took place at Gusii farms. Luo traders still arrive in Gusiiland on donkeys loaded with salt and pots. The network of markets, shops, and cash-crop purchasing centers that connects Gusiiland with the rest of Kenya has continued to grow. In 1985 the major urban center was Kisii Town, which features numerous marketing facilities, shops, and wholesalers.

Division of Labor. In the late nineteenth century women were primarily responsible for food cultivation and processing, cooking, brewing, fetching water and fuel, and cleaning house, whereas men were concerned with waging war, building houses and fences, clearing new fields, and herding. Although women performed most of the cultivation, men participated to a much higher degree than is the case today. Herding was undertaken by boys and young unmarried men in the cattle villages; initiated unmarried daughters assisted in cultivation. Since the early colonial period, the division of labor has gradually changed, to the disadvantage of women: men have withdrawn from cultivation, but women are obliged to perform most of the same tasks that they undertook during the precolonial era, in addition to cultivating the men's cash crops.

Land Tenure. Until the 1940s, land was held corporately by lineages and clans. Grazing was communal, and arable land was divided into plots with strict use rights that pertained to each household of the polygynous family. Local populations also included families belonging to other clans—"dwellers" (*abamenyi*), who had limited tenure. Land was not inherited or alienated through transactions. Today all land is registered in individual men's names, but the land market is still limited, and sales are uncommon. Through inheritance, men have ultimate rights to the management and use of land. Women still have no birthright to their parents' land. The vast majority of women can obtain access to land only through marriage; however, a few employed women are able to buy land in other districts. Since the initial registration, land has not been surveyed, and much of it is still registered in the name of a dead father or grandfather. A man usually transfers land to his wife and sons when the eldest son marries. Ideally, land is divided equally between wives, under the supervision of and witnessed by local male elders. After division, the husband often retains a small plot (*emonga*) for personal use.

Kinship

Kin Groups and Descent. During the precolonial period, the exogamous, patrilineal clan (*eamaate*) was the largest cooperative unit. Clans were part of clan clusters, which had birds or animals as totems but lacked any common organization. At the lineage (*riiga*) level, patrilineal descent and marriage defined commonly recognized access to land and provided the rationale for corporate action. During the colonial period, indigenous political and social organization became conceptualized as a segmentary lineage system in which units from the clan cluster, clans, and clan segments became defined according to a genealogical grid with an eponymous ancestor at the top.

Kinship Terminology. Gusii kinship terminology is classificatory, merging lineals with collaterals. Specific lineal terms are used to denote the immediate family: *tata* (own father), *baba* (own mother), *momura one* (own son), and *mosubati ominto* (young woman of our house). All other women and men of Ego's generation, however, including "real" brothers, are called *mamura ominto*. In the mother's family, the reciprocal term *mame* is applied to mother's brothers, their wives, and to sister's children. In any clan in which Ego has kinship connections, individuals of Ego's parents' generation are called *tatamoke* (small father) or *makomoke* (small mother). All members of the descending generation are *omwana one* (my child), those of the grandchildren's generation are *omochokoro*, and those of the grandparents' generation are *sokoro* (grandfather) and *magokoro* (grandmother). Gusii terminology also distinguishes links that have been established by a transfer of marriage cattle.

Marriage and Family

Marriage. Marriage can be established only through the payment of bride-wealth, in the form of livestock and money, by the husband to the wife's family. This act establishes a socially sanctioned marriage, through which a woman and a man become socially defined mothers and fathers. Residence is at the husband's home. Divorce was and still is rare; it entails the return of the bride-wealth. At the death of a husband, the widow chooses a leviratic husband among the deceased's brothers. Until the 1960s, everyone got married as soon as possible after puberty; by the end of the 1960s, elopements had started to increase in number because of a decline in the demand for wives. The period between the inception of a cohabiting union and the payment of bride-wealth has become progressively more and more extended. In 1985 at least 75 percent of all new unions between women and men were established without the payment of bride-wealth. Without this payment, the union is without social and legal sanction; consequently, there now exists a socially and economically marginalized stratum of single mothers who have no access to land. A related development has been the decline in the value of bride-wealth payments for peasant women, from about thirteen adult zebu cows in the first half of the 1950s to about three by 1985. Employed women—such as nurses and lawyers—fetch higher bride-wealth payments, around the value of fifteen to forty-five zebu cows (although their bride-wealth is frequently paid in cash and European cows).

Domestic Unit. Traditional Gusii households are based on nuclear or polygynous families. Each wife maintains her own household, and, in polygynous families, there is little cooperation between co-wives. With the decline in polygyny, a domestic unit typically has come to consist of a wife, a husband, and their unmarried children. It may also include the husband's mother and, for shorter periods, younger siblings of the wife. Until the birth of the first or second child, a wife and her mother-in-law may cook together and cooperate in farming. Married sons and their wives and children usually maintain their own households and resources.

Inheritance. According to customary law, which is still the effective rule for the majority, only men can inherit. Sons inherit only the cattle, land, and other assets that belong to their own house (enyomba). All the resources that are owned by the father, such as personal cattle or business establishments, should be divided equally between houses, irrespective of the number of sons in each. Although national law recognizes the equal inheritance rights of daughters, customary law has seldom been challenged (see "Land Tenure").

Socialization. Mothers have the ultimate responsibility for the care and socialization of their children, but they delegate a great deal of caretaking and training to other children in the homestead. Mothers seldom show physical or verbal affection for children, and fathers take very little part in child rearing. Gusii infants are raised to understand how to behave according to the codes of shame and respect that apply to their relationships to persons in adjacent generations. The grandparents play a supportive role and are supposed to inform grandchildren about proper behavior and sexual matters.

Children cease sleeping in their mother's house when they are still very young. After the age of 8, boys gradually start to sleep in a special house for unmarried sons. After initiation, at the age of 10 or 11, a son cannot sleep in his mother's house at all. At the age of 6, a girl starts to sleep either in the house of one of her mother's co-wives or that of her grandmother. Initiated girls must sleep in the house of a postmenopausal woman, usually the paternal grandmother.

Sociopolitical Organization

Social Organization. Except as a unit of exogamy, the clan today seldom appears as a social group for coordinated action. In elections to parliament, county councils, and cooperative boards, clans provide voting blocks for their own candidates. The lineage is also losing its importance as a field for social action. Regular social and economic interaction is limited to the sibling group. Socioeconomic stratification is rapidly emerging, but there is no formal hierarchy. There is a marked trend toward intermarriage between persons of similar economic and social status.

Political Organization. Precolonial political power and authority were vested in local male elders' councils and in the big-men who dominated their neighborhoods. In the absence of crosscutting forms of social organization, political life was factionalized into descent-based groups of varying ramifications. Only the Kitutu clan cluster developed a rudimentary political office of chief, *omogambi* (lit., "giver of verdicts"). Women were alienated, and geographically separated, from their natal clans and were thus in a position of little influence and power during the first years of marriage; however, older women, who had gained power by dint of the number of their sons and daughters-in-law, were often in charge of negotiations between fighting parties. Men continue to dominate political life, and leadership is nowadays based on elected office in local government bodies and in administration as chiefs and assistant chiefs.

Social Control. During the precolonial period, disputes over cattle and land, crimes, and other misdeeds were handled by local male elders' councils and by big-men. Today local disputes are handled by a meeting of local male elders and the assistant chief (*baraza*). Crimes and disputes can also be taken to the court system.

Conflict. During the nineteenth century, interclan relationships were often hostile and resulted in raids for cattle and pastureland. Gusii relationships with neighboring groups varied over time but were generally peaceful and cooperative with the Luo groups and perpetually hostile with the Kipsigis. After 1918, the British administration suppressed armed conflicts in the area. There was, however, a resurgence of armed conflict, over land, between the Gusii and the Maasai during the 1960s.

Religion and Expressive Culture

Religious Beliefs. Before the advent of Christianity in the region, the Gusii believed in the existence of one God, who was the originator of the world but did not directly interfere in human affairs. It was the concept of an ancestor cult that, together with their ideas about witchcraft, sorcery, and impersonal forces, provided a complex of beliefs in suprahuman agencies. The ancestor spirits (*ebirecha*) existed both as a collective and as individual ancestors and ancestresses of the living members of a lineage. They were not propitiated until there was tangible evidence of their displeasure, such as disease or death of people and livestock or the destruction of crops. Most Gusii today claim to be adherents of some Christian church. There are four major denominations in Gusiiland: the Catholic, Seventh Day Adventist, Swedish Lutheran, and Pentecostal Assemblies of God. Active Seventh Day Adventists are oriented toward European family ideals, and they practice a form of Protestant ethic. Although the churches are very active, certain aspects of non-Christian beliefs still permeate the lives of most Gusii. Afflicted by misfortune, many Gusii visit a diviner (*omorgori;* pl. *abaragori*), who may point to displeased spirits of the dead and prescribe sacrifice to placate them.

Religious Practitioners. Abaragori, who are usually women, determine the cause of various misfortunes. Diverse healers also exist, such as the *abanyamoriogi* (herbalists), who use various mixtures of plants for medicines. *Ababari* (indigenous surgeons), set fractures and treat backaches and headaches through trephination. *Abanyamosira* (professional sorcerers) are normally hired to protect against witchcraft and to retaliate against witches. An *omoriori* (witch smeller) ferrets out witchcraft articles (e.g., hair or feces of the victim, dead birds, bones of exhumed corpses) that may be buried in a house. A witch (*omorogi*) can be a man or a woman but is usually the latter. Witches are believed to operate in groups; they dig up recently buried corpses in order to use the body parts as magical paraphernalia and to eat the inner organs. Witches usually kill their victims through the use of poisons, parts of corpses, and people's exuviae. Witchcraft among the Gusii is believed to be an acquired art that is handed down from parent to child.

Ceremonies. The most elaborate and socially important ceremonies are associated with initiation and marriage. Initiation involves clitoridectomy for girls and circumcision for boys. The ceremony prepares the children as social beings who know rules of shame (*chinsoni*) and respect (*ogosika*). The girls are initiated at the age of 7 or 8 and the boys a few years later. Initiations are gender segregated, and the operations are performed by female and male specialists. Afterward there is a period of seclusion for both genders. The traditional wedding is no longer performed. It was an extremely elaborate ritual that lasted several days. The rituals emphasized the incorporation of the bride into the groom's lineage and the primacy of male fertility. Among wealthier people, it has been replaced by a wedding in church or before an administrative official.

Arts. The Gusii soapstone carvings have received international distribution and fame. The stone is mined and carved in Tabaka, South Mugirango, where several families specialize in this art. The craft is bringing in a sizable income to the area through the tourist trade.

Medicine. Kisii Town has a government hospital and several private clinics, as well as private practitioners. There are also a number of clinics and health-care stations throughout Gusiiland. (For traditional medicine and health care, see "Religious Practitioners.")

Death and Afterlife. Funerals take place at the deceased's homestead; a large gathering is a sign of prestige. Women are buried beyond the yard, on the left side of the house, whereas men are buried beyond the cattle pen, on the right side of the house. Christian elements, such as catechism, reading out loud from the Bible, and singing hymns, are combined with the traditional practices of wailing, head shaving, and animal sacrifices to the dead. The preferred person to dig the grave is the deceased's son's son. Before burial, the corpse is dissected in order to ascertain whether death was caused by witchcraft. After burial, the widow/widower is in a liminal state and cannot move far from the homestead until after a period of a few weeks to two months, when ritual activities, including a sacrifice, are performed. One basic theme of the funeral is the fear of the dead person's spirit. The deceased, enraged at having died, may blame the survivors and must therefore be placated with sacrifices.

Bibliography

Hakansson, N. Thomas (1988). *Bridewealth, Women, and Land: Social Change among the Gusii of Kenya*. Uppsala Studies in Cultural Anthropology, no. 9. Stockholm: Almkvist & Wiksell International.

Hakansson, N. Thomas (1994a). "Detachable Women: Gender and Kinship in Process of Socioeconomic Change among the Gusii of Kenya." *American Ethnologist* 21:516–538.

Hakansson, N. Thomas (1994b). "Grain, Cattle, and Power: The Social Processes of Intensive Cultivation and Exchange in Precolonial Western Kenya." *Journal of Anthropological Research* 50:249–276.

Hakansson, N. Thomas, and Robert A. LeVine (1995). "Contradiction and Change: Gender and Divergent Life-Course Strategies among the Gusii." In *African Families and the Crisis of Social Change*, edited by Thomas Weisner, Candice Bradley, and Philip Kilbride. New York: Greenwood Press. In press.

LeVine, Robert A. (1959). "Gusii Sex Offenses: A Study in Social Control." *American Anthropologist* 61:965–990.

LeVine, Robert A. (1982). "Gusii Funerals: Meanings of Life and Death in an African Community." *Ethos* 10:26–65.

LeVine, Robert A., and Barbara B. LeVine (1966). *Nyansongo: A Gusii Community in Kenya*. Six Cultures Series, vol. 2. New York: John Wiley & Sons.

LeVine, Robert A., Sarah LeVine, P. Herbert Leiberman, T. Betty Brazelton, Suzanne Dixon, Amy Richman, and Constance H. Keefer (1994). *Child Care and Culture: Lessons from Africa*. Cambridge: Cambridge University Press.

LeVine, Sarah (1979). *Mothers and Wives: Gusii Women of East Africa*. Chicago: University of Chicago Press.

LeVine, Sarah, and Robert A. LeVine (forthcoming). *Stability and Stress: The Psychosocial History of an African Community*.

Mayer, Philip (1949). *The Lineage Principle in Gusii Society*. International African Institute Memorandum no. 24. London: Oxford University Press.

Mayer, Philip (1950). *Gusii Bridewealth Law and Custom*. The Rhodes-Livingstone Papers, no. 18. London: Oxford University Press.

N. THOMAS HAKANSSON

Hausa

ETHNONYMS: Afnu (the Kanuri term) or Afunu; Arna or Azna, Bunjawa, Maguzawa (non-Muslims); Aussa, Haoussa, al Hausin

Orientation

Identification. The Hausa constitute the largest ethnic group in West Africa. The term "Hausa" actually refers to the language and, by extension, to its native speakers, of whom there are about 25 million.

Location. The Hausa are scattered across the savanna of northern Nigeria, the adjacent area of Niger, and, as a result of extensive migration, in enclaves in various African cities as far south as the Atlantic coast. The focal homeland covers an area about 640 kilometers wide, from Lake Chad to the east to the Niger River in the west. It extends from 11° to 14° N and from about 2° to 14° E. The annual rainfall ranges from about 50 centimeters in the north to 100 centimeters in the south.

Demography. There are approximately 22.5 million Hausa in West Africa. According to the last census, carried out in 1963, 80 percent of the Hausa are rural, 20 percent urban. Even with the tremendous urbanization of the 1970s and 1980s, economic problems have led to return migrations to the countryside. Thus, the 80:20 ratio may still stand. Among the Hausa, there is high infant mortality. If a child survives his or her first two years, he or she will probably live to age 50. Risk decreases until one reaches middle age, but many Hausa survive into their 70s and 80s.

Linguistic Affiliation. A Chadic language, Hausa is related to Arabic, Hebrew, Berber, and other Afroasiatic Family members. Proper tone and stress are imperative. Hausa, which was originally written in Arabic script, has a centuries-old literary tradition, but it is also the language of trade and, next to Swahili, is the most widely spoken African language.

History and Cultural Relations

Hausa history is one of immigration and conquest. The Hausa nation has evolved from the incorporation over hundreds of years of many different peoples who joined the original stock. They are united by a common language and adherence to a common religion, Islam. According to tradition, the Hausa people derive from the Hausa *bakwai*, the "true" seven states, of which Daura (named after its female founder) is considered the most senior. In the myth of origin, Bayajidda, the son of the king of Baghdad, arrived in Daura via Bornu. He killed the snake that occupied the well, impeding the townspeople's access to the water. As a reward, Bayajidda married the queen. Their son Bawo was the progenitor of six sons, thereby founding six states—Daura, Katsina, Zazzau (Zaria), Gobir, Kano, and Rano. Bayajidda's son by his first wife, Magira (a Kanuri woman), founded Biram, the seventh state.

In fact, it is not known when the movement of peoples actually occurred; neither has the migrants' place of origin been pinpointed. The seven Habe kingdoms were formed by a coalescence of strangers with local folk. The emergence of states in Hausaland was apparently associated with the establishment of capital cities as centers of power. They were different from earlier settlements in that they were cosmopolitan, fortified, and each the seat of a king who was recognized as the superior power throughout the surrounding area.

Before 1804, Habe kings ruled over Hausaland; following 1804, the Fulani took over, and by mid-century the Hausa were stratified into three tiers: the hereditary ruling Fulani, the appointive ruling class dominated by Fulani, and the Habe commoners.

Hausa relations with others are considerable, because of their extensive involvement with trade and Islam. There is considerable exchange with the Kanuri to the east, the nomadic Tuareg, and southern Nigerians (Igbo, Yoruba); in their diaspora settlements, other ethnic groups that share their cultural orientation, such as the Wangara, the Zabarama, the Adar, the Nupe, are often lumped together with them as "Hausa."

Settlements

The Hausa classify their settlements as cities, towns, or hamlets. The cities have wards for foreigners, including Tuareg, Arabs, Nupe, Kanuri, and others. The capital cities are walled, and residents live in walled compounds with interior courtyards. Those of the well-to-do are whitewashed and decorated with plaster arabesques. The women's quarters are separate. Urban compounds may house sixty to a hundred persons. Although the Hausa accord urban living the most prestige, they are primarily rural. Each village contains a capital, as well as several hamlets; the capital is divided into wards, housing families of the same occupational group. Traditional village compounds are walled or fenced; materials range from baked clay to mud or cornstalks. Compounds characteristically contain an entrance hut, an open shared cooking and work area, a hut for the compound head, and separate huts for each of his wives. Newer housing is rectangular and concrete. The number of people living in a rural compound ranges from one to thirty, the average being ten.

Economy

Subsistence and Commercial Activities. Agriculture is the main economic activity. Grain is the staple diet, including Guinea corn, millet, maize, and rice. The Hausa also grow and eat root crops and a variety of vegetables. Cotton and peanuts are processed and used locally, but part of the harvest is exported. The Hausa practice intercropping and double-cropping; their main implement is the hoe. The Cattle Fulani provide the Hausa with meat, yogurt, and butter.

Most men also practice a second occupation; ascriptive and ranked, these include aristocratic officeholder, scholar, Islamic cleric (imam), artisan, trader, musician, and butcher. As good Muslims, the urban women are in seclusion (rural women much less so), and therefore dependent upon their husbands for their maintenance; they are economically active from behind the compound walls, however, primarily in order to finance their daughters' dowries. Their work, which includes sewing and selling prepared food and jewelry, is an offshoot of their domestic persona.

Industrial Arts. There are full-time specialists only where there is an assured market for craft products. Men's crafts include tanning, leatherworking, saddling, weaving, dying, woodworking, and smithing. Iron has been mined, smelted, and worked as far back as there are Hausa traditions. Blacksmiths have a guildlike organization, and many are hereditary.

Trade. Trade is complicated and varied. Some traders deal in a particular market, as distinguished from those who trade in many markets over a long distance. This dual trade strategy, augmented by the contributions of the Cattle Fulani, enabled the Hausa to meet all of their requirements, even during the nineteenth century. The markets are traditional to Hausa society and carry social as well as economic significance; male friends and relatives meet there, and well-dressed marriageable young women pass through, to see and be seen. The Hausa differentiate rural from urban settlements in terms of the size and frequency of the markets.

There is also customary exchange that takes place outside of the market. Gift exchanges are practiced at life-cycle celebrations such as childbirth, naming, marriage, and death; other exchanges are framed by religion (alms, tithes, fixed festivals) and politics (expressing relations of patronage/clientage).

Division of Labor. Hausa society traditionally observes several divisions of labor: in public administration, it is primarily men who may be appointed, although some women hold appointed positions in the palace. Class determines what sort of work one might do, and gender determines work roles. When women engage in income-producing activities, they may keep what they earn. Because of purdah, many women who trade are dependent upon children to act as their runners.

Land Tenure. The rural householder farms with his sons' help; from the old farm, he allocates to them small plots, which he enlarges as they mature. New family fields are cleared from the bush.

Kinship

Kin Groups and Descent. Although the domestic group is based on agnatic ties, and even as Hausa society is patriarchal, descent is basically bilateral; only the political aristocracy and urban intelligentsia observe strict patrilineality, everyone else practicing bilaterality.

Kinship Terminology. Hausa kinship terminology cannot be classified according to standard anthropological categories because of the number of alternative usages. For example, a man's siblings and his parallel or cross cousins are called *'yanuwa* (children of my mother); cross cousins, however, are also referred to and addressed as *abokan wasa* (joking relations), and special terms distinguishing elder and younger brother and sister may also be applied to both parallel and cross cousins.

Marriage and Family

Marriage. Adult Hausa society is essentially totally married. Ideal marriage is virilocal/patrilocal, and it is polygynous: a man is allowed up to four wives at a time. The term in Hausa for co-wife is *kishiya,* from the word for "jealousy," often but not always descriptive of co-wife relations. Once men begin to marry, they are rarely single despite divorce because most are polygynous; nearly 50 percent of the women are divorced at some point, but there is such pressure to be married and have children that they tend not to stay unmarried long. Important social distinctions identify women in terms of their marital status. By custom, girls marry at the age of 12 to 14. There is some disagreement in the literature regarding the respectful nature of singlehood. Divorce is a regular occurrence, not surprisingly, given the brittle and formal relationship between spouses. Both men and women have a right to divorce, but for men it is easier. After divorce, most weaned children are claimed by their father.

Marriage is marked by bride-price, given by the groom's family to the bride, and a dowry for the bride provided by her family. Marriage is classified according to the degree of wife seclusion and according to whether it is a kin or nonkin union. Bilateral cross-cousin marriage is preferred.

Domestic Unit. The ideal household is the agnatically based *gandu* (family farm), formed by a man with his sons and their wives and children. After the senior male's death, the brothers may stay on together for a time. More frequently, each brother's household becomes a separate economic unit.

Inheritance. Consistent with Islamic practice, a woman can own and inherit in her own right, but her inheritance rights are subordinate to those of men. All of the wives married to a man at the time of his death are entitled, together with their children, to share one-quarter of his total estate if there are no agnatic descendants, or one-eighth of his estate if there are agnatic descendants. Women own property such as houses and land together with consanguines, even after marriage, and they inherit only half as much as their brothers.

Succession to leadership of the agnatic group and leadership of the compound is collateral. Farmland is inherited in the male line, the gandu being collectively owned by brothers.

Socialization. Women observe a postpartum taboo on sexual intercourse for a year and a half to two years, during which time the child is breast-fed. Toddlers are weaned onto soft foods and then to the standard diet. An older sister carries the infant on her back when the mother is busy, which extends into a special attachment between an adult man and his elder sister.

From infancy, boys and girls are treated differently. Boys are preferred; as they age, they learn that they are superior to girls and consequently to distance themselves from them and identify with things masculine. It is imperative for boys to separate from their mothers. Girls are trained to self-identify in terms of their sex role: domestic (female) skills are taught to young women as they mature. They are admonished to be submissive and subordinate to males. As children, boys and girls are rigidly sex-stereotyped into appropriate behavior.

Sociopolitical Organization

Social Organization. One of the most salient principles in Hausa society is the segregation of adults according to gender. Throughout Hausaland, seclusion of married women is normative, and the extradomestic impact of sexual segregation and stratification is that women are legal, political, and religious minors and the economic wards of men. Although women are central to kinship matters, they are excluded from extradomestic discussion and decision making. Both within the household and in the public domain, patriarchal authority is dominant and reinforced by spatial separation of the sexes.

The senior wife of the compound head, the *mai gida,* is the *uwar gida.* She may settle minor disputes among residents and give advice and aid to the younger women. Domestic authority rests with the male head of compound/household.

From childhood, males and females develop bond friendships with members of the same sex, a practice continued into adulthood and marked by reciprocal exchanges. Given their seclusion, women tend to formalize their bond ties more than men do. Formal relationships that emphasize differences in status (patron/client) are also established by women, as they are by men.

Political Organization. Organizational structure is hierarchic; the centralized kingdoms, known as emirates, are the primary groupings; districts are secondary and village areas tertiary.

The institutions of kinship, clientship, and office (and, in the past, slavery) in the emirates, have provided the fundamentals of Hausa government from the sixteenth century until the middle part of the twentieth century. Rank regulates relations between commoners and rulers.

"Traditional and modern government proceeds through a system of titled offices . . . , each of which is in theory a unique indissoluble legal corporation having definite rights, powers and duties, special relations to the throne and to certain other offices, special lands, farms, compounds, horses, praise songs, clients, and, formerly, slaves" (Smith 1965, 132). In most states, major offices are traditionally distributed among descent groups, so that rank and lineage intertwine. The traditional offices differed in rewards, power, and function, and were territorially based with attendant obligations and duties. Within communities, the various occupational groups distribute titles, which duplicate the ranks of the central political system.

Clientship links men of unequal status, position, and wealth. It is a relationship of mutual benefit, whereby the client gains advice in his affairs at the minimum and protection, food, and shelter at the maximum. The patron can call upon the client to serve as his retainer.

In applying his notion of government to Kano, the Fulani religious and political leader Usman dan Fodio, when he launched his successful jihad against the king of Gobir in

1804, he followed the basic premise of a theocracy within a legalistic framework; government, and its chief agent, the emir, were perceived as an instrument of Allah.

Social Control. Legal affairs fall under the jurisdiction of the emir, and he is guided by Islamic law. The Quran, the word of Allah, and its *hadith,* the traditions of the Prophet Mohammed, along with the dictates of secular reasoning provide answers to legal questions. The Sharia, the canon law of Islam, is fundamentally a code of obligations, a guide to ethics. Sanctions of shame and ostracism compel conformity to Hausa and Islamic custom.

Conflict. When disputes arise, the Hausa may opt to go to court, submit to mediation, or leave it to Allah. The basic process involves deference to mediation by elders.

Religion and Expressive Culture

Religious Beliefs. About 90 percent of the Hausa are Muslims. "The traditional Hausa way of life and Islamic social values have been intermixed for such a long time that many of the basic tenets of Hausa society are Islamic" (Adamu 1978, 9). Islam has been carried throughout West Africa by Hausa traders.

Adherents are expected to observe the five pillars of Islam—profession of the faith, five daily prayers, alms giving, fasting at Ramadan, and at least one pilgrimage to Mecca (the hajj). Within Hausa society, there are sects (brotherhoods) of adherents; of these, the Tijaniya, Qadriya, and Ahmadiyya have been important. Wife seclusion is basic to the Hausa version of Islam, although it is believed that the institution is more a sign of status than of religious piety.

Even among some Muslims, as among the Maguzawa pagans, spirit cults persist. One, the Bori, has more female than male adepts; cultists are believed to be possessed by particular spirits within the Bori pantheon.

Religious Practitioners. Although such personnel as imams and teachers (*mallamai;* sing. *mallam*) have no churchly functions or spiritual authority, they do tend to assume or accept some measure of spiritual authority in certain contexts.

Ceremonies. Men are enjoined to attend Friday prayers at the mosque. Men and women celebrate the three main annual festivals of Ramadan, Id il Fitr, and Sallah. Life-cycle events—birth, puberty, marriage, death—are also marked.

Arts. The arts are limited to those forms allowed by Islam; the Hausa use Islamic design in their architecture, pottery, cloth, leather, and weaving. Music is an integral part of Hausa life and can be classified in terms of function and audience: for royalty, for dancing pleasure, and for professional guilds. Each category has its own instruments, which include drums as well as string and wind instruments. Poetry exists in an oral tradition, as practiced by the praise singers and the oral historians, and also in the written tradition of the learned.

Medicine. There is a tricultural system that consists of strong traditional roots set in the framework of a predominantly Islamic mode, now augmented by Western medicine. The Bori spirit-possession cult is relied upon for various kinds of curing, and this involves diagnosing the particular spirit giving the sick person trouble.

Death and Afterlife. Burial is in the Islamic manner. Upon death, the individual passes on into the realm of heaven (paradise) or hell, consistent with Islamic teaching.

Bibliography

Adamu, Mahdi (1978). *The Hausa Factor in West African History*. London: Oxford University Press.

Coles, Catherine, and Beverly Mack, eds. (1991). *Women in Twentieth Century Hausa Society*. Madison: University of Wisconsin Press.

Hill, Polly (1972). *Rural Hausa: A Village and a Setting*. Cambridge: Cambridge University Press.

Paden, John (1974). *Religion and Political Culture in Kano*. Berkeley and Los Angeles: University of California Press.

Smith, Mary F. (1981). *Baba of Karo*. New Haven: Yale University Press. Originally published in 1954.

Smith, M. G. (1965). "The Hausa of Northern Nigeria." In *Peoples of Africa*, edited by James L. Gibbs, Jr., 119–155. New York: Holt, Rinehart & Winston.

DEBORAH PELLOW

Hazara

ETHNONYMNS: Hazaragi, Hezareh, Hezare'i

Most Hazara live in central Afghanistan in an area known as the Hazarajat. Others live in areas north of the Hindu Kush. The Hazarajat and other Hazara territories are mountainous. The climate is severe in winter, with heavy snowfall; summers are mild but short, particularly at higher elevations. The Hazarajat, considering its harsh terrain, is densely populated.

The Hazara are roughly estimated to number between 1 and 1.5 million in Afghanistan and between 17,000 and 70,000 in Pakistan, but some estimates suggest a total of 6 million Hazara. Other ethnic minorities are sometimes considered to be Hazara or Hazara-related. The Taimani, who live at the eastern and western edges of the Hazarajat, are related to the Hazara, but the Taimani on the western edge are associated with the Aimaq. The Tatars, sometimes known as Tajiks, were once called Hazara Tatars and are considered physically and culturally similar to the Hazaras. The Moghols (Mongols) of Ghor, although probably related, are considered ethnically distinct from the Hazara.

Hazara are thought to have several affinities with the Mongols, including physical appearance, language, and kinship system. Although the Hazara lack the characteristic epicanthic eyefolds, many believe they are clearly Mongoloid. Hazaragi, the traditional language of the Hazara, is an Indo-Iranian language with many Mongol loanwords. Hazaragi is spoken in the home and, in the more isolated areas, it is also the language spoken in public affairs. Another indication of Mongol influence is the Hazara designation of older and younger siblings by different terms.

The term *hazara* is a Mongol-Persian blend. It means "thousand" in Farsi, and is believed to be the Persian equivalent of the Mongol word for thousand, *minggan*. The Mongols called a fighting unit by this term because the unit consisted of a kinship group that provided a thousand horsemen. Therefore, the word actually means "tribe." After the Hindu Kush Mongols acquired Farsi, the Farsi equivalent replaced the Mongol word. By the fifteenth century, "hazara" meant "mountain tribe," and, later, it came to refer to the group now known as "Hazara."

The Hazara were traditionally nomads who subsisted by herding sheep and goats; they also raised horses for fighting feuds. Mixed grain farming is now their primary subsistence activity. Most of the farming takes place on the alluvial floors of the valleys, but the higher ground is also used in various ways. Irrigation is used wherever possible. Small numbers of sheep and goats are herded in the valleys in winter, in the mountains in summer. Major crops include wheat and barley; fava beans are planted in rotation whenever necessary. Milk products are the main source of protein. Wool is a source of fiber, and Hazara women make woolen rugs of the Gilam type.

Hazara kinship is organized in lineages; descent is traced through the male line. The males in a specific area consider themselves descendants of a common ancestor. Although memory of tribal lineages traditionally extended back seven or eight generations, people probably remember no more than half that number today. Leading men within a village resolve any social conflicts by consensus.

The Hazara prefer to marry first cousins on their father's side, as is the Muslim practice, and there are many intravillage marriages. Hazara seldom marry outsiders, and, when they do, it is usually women who are given to men of other groups. The children of such unions are not usually considered Hazara.

Tribal authority was formerly vested in mirs or khanates, but, after the Hazara-Afghan war of 1891, Hazara power was weakened. There are two kinds of political leaders today, the *khanawada*, or khan, and the *araab* or *malek*. The khanawada's influence is based on personal wealth, kinship, and social alliances. The araab is an appointed representative. Holders of these positions are generally relatives and allies.

The sayyid, an Islamic authority, is also an influential person among the Shia Hazara. Sayyids claim descent from the Prophet Mohammed and are highly venerated by the Hazara. A group of sayyids live among the Hazara, and, because they take wives from the Hazara, they now resemble the Hazara in culture and appearance. These authorities use their sacred status to serve the religious needs of the people, and they are part of a large informal network that has been mobilized to exert influence on public affairs.

The Hazara are one of Afghanistan's most impoverished ethnic groups and one of the most resistant to central-government control. Although there have been few studies in recent years, it is believed that the Hazara have been virtually free of government control since the Soviet invasion of Afghanistan in 1979 and the civil unrest following the end of Soviet occupation.

Bibliography

Aslanov, M. G., et al. (1969). "Ethnography of Afghanistan." In *Afghanistan: Some New Approaches*, edited by G. Grassmuck, L. W. Ademec, and F. H. Irwin. Ann Arbor: University of Michigan Press.

Bacon, Elizabeth E. (1951). "An Inquiry into the History of the Hazara Mongols of Afghanistan." *Southwestern Journal of Anthropology* 7:230–247.

Canfield, Robert L. (1975). "Suffering as a Religious Imperative in Afghanistan." In *Psychological Anthropology*, edited by Thomas Williams. The Hague: Mouton.

Canfield, Robert L. (1984). "Hazaras." In *Muslim Peoples: A World Ethnographic Survey*, edited by Richard V. Weekes, 327–332. Westport, Conn.: Greenwood Press.

Davydov, A. D. (1965). "Rural Community of the Hazaras of Central Afghanistan." *Central Asian Review* 14(1): 32–44.

Dupree, Louis. (1979). "Further Notes on Taqiyya: Afghanistan." *Journal of American Oriental Society* 99(4): 680–682.

Ferdinand, Klaus (1965). "Ethnographical Notes on Chahar Aimak, Hazara, and Moghol." *Acta Orientalia* 28(3–4): 175–204.

Grimes, Barbara F. (1988). *Ethnologue*. Dallas: Summer Institute of Linguistics.

Kakar, M. Hasan (1973). *Pacification of the Hazaras of Afghanistan*. New York: Afghanistan Council of the Asia Society.

Herero

ETHNONYMS: Dama, Damara

Orientation

Identification and Location. In Otjiherero, the Herero language, "Ovaherero" means the "Herero people," and "Omuherero" refers to a single Herero person. The Herero are a Bantu group living today in Namibia (formerly South-West Africa) and in the Republic of Botswana (formerly Bechuanaland) in southern Africa. Those in Botswana are located in and around the Kalahari Desert and are descended from a group of Herero who escaped from South-West Africa after an unsuccessful war against German colonialists in 1904. The majority of Herero, numbering over 30,000, remained behind, were incarcerated, and were subjected to forced cultural assimilation. This description treats the Herero in general before the 1904 war, together with the Herero of Botswana after that time, as an ethnographic unit. The Herero of Namibia, who have been dominated by and incorporated into a European-based tradition, are not discussed here.

Demography. The government of the Republic of Botswana discourages "tribalism" and does not identify the "ethnicity" of its citizens, rendering an accurate count of the Herero impossible. Modern estimates range between 7,000 and 8,000 persons, the greatest percentage of whom live in western Botswana on the northern fringe of the Kalahari, in Ghansi District and in Ngamiland District. Makakun, the first Herero settlement in Botswana after the flight from Namibia and still the largest Herero area, is located west of Lake Ngami, in Ngamiland.

Linguistic Affiliation. The Herero speak a form of southwestern Bantu that is shared most closely by two other major groups, the Ovambo (or Ambo) and the Ovimbandu (or Umbandu), both of which are found in Angola, north of Namibia. The Herero Branch of southwestern Bantu consists of four major groups of speakers: the Mbanderu, the Himba, the Tjimba, and the Herero proper.

History and Cultural Relations

The Herero are thought to have migrated westward from the lacustrine area of eastern and central Africa and then southward, entering the Kaokoveld, in what is now northern Namibia, around 1550. After some years in the Kaokoveld, they began a gradual push south, spreading as far as present-day Windhoek by about 1750. In their diffusion throughout Namibia, Herero came into conflict with other native occupants of the territory, most notably the Hottentots. Beginning about 1825, a state of war existed off and on between the Herero and the Hottentots; by 1870 the Herero had established their supremacy, and a relative peace prevailed in Namibia during the next decade, followed by war again in 1880. In 1884, when the land became a German territory known as South-West Africa, the Germans used these intertribal conflicts to help establish their authority. They sided with the Herero, providing them arms and advice, while planning to use them to subjugate the Hottentots and other local groups, and then to disarm the Herero. In return for German help, some Herero leaders ceded the mineral rights in their pastureland. Simultaneously, European farmers and traders were moving into South-West Africa in increasing numbers and settling the land, thus restricting Herero access to water and pasturage for their herds. By the 1890s, when the Hottentots had by and large been subjugated and the Germans had adequately established themselves in the territory, they turned their efforts more directly to domination of the Herero. During the next several years, the Herero were gradually deprived of their livelihood and their nomadic freedom, prompting the Herero uprising in January 1904. At the battle of Waterberg in August, the Herero were decisively defeated. About 2,000, in a number of small groups, escaped eastward across the Kalahari into what was then the British protectorate of Bechuanaland, arriving with few or no cattle. In a strange land and without an economic base, Herero went to work for the Tswana, the numerically dominant tribal group in the country. Because the territory was a British protectorate (1885–1966) under "indirect rule," the incoming Herero applied to the local hereditary Tswana chief for permission to settle, and it was in the chief's jurisdiction that they resided. Herero entered the employ of Tswana (who, although horticulturists, kept some cattle), selling their labor and expertise as herders. In return, they received milk, crops, and an occasional calf. From the milk they made butter, which they sold back to Tswana. Herero ate sparingly, selling the extra food. With the proceeds, they bought additional cattle or acquired the stud services of bulls from Tswana herds—and undoubtedly they stole an animal here and there. The result of these activities was that in the 1930s, after about a generation in Botswana, Herero had amassed herds of sufficient size to assert economic independence from their former Tswana employers and reestablish pastoralism as their way of life. Today, despite their small population, the Herero are economically successful, and their contribution to Botswana's beef industry is indispensable to the national economy. Their transition from traditional pastoral nomads, with what has been called in East Africa the "cattle complex," to participants in a European-influenced economy, in which cattle are primarily market commodities, has produced profound changes in Herero society.

Settlements

Although nomadic in precontact times, the Herero today are sedentary, and their primary residential unit is the "homestead" (*onganda;* pl. *ozonganda*), consisting of a number of sun-hardened clay huts (*ozondjuo;* sing. *ondjuo*) arranged formerly in a closed circle but nowadays in a line or an arc. At the center of the traditional onganda were animal corrals, constructed of thornbushes. Just to the east of the cattle corrals was the "sacred hearth" (*okuruo*), consisting of an upturned bush and a small fire that burned continually in honor of the ancestors. To the east of the okuruo was the hut of the "great wife" of the homestead head, the senior male, who was referred to as *omuini,* or "owner" of the homestead. A series of huts extended in northwesterly and southwesterly arcs from the senior wife's hut to form a circle around the corrals; all huts opened to face the corrals. The entire homestead was surrounded by dead thornbush branches as protection from raiders and predators. This circular pattern also emphasized the cultural focus of Herero society. Cattle were considered sacred gifts from the ancestors, and all ritual activities were conducted at the okuruo, which symbolized the coherence of Herero society and the direct connection with the Herero then had with their forebears. Today, however, cattle are considered secular commodities to be sold at market for profit, belief in the ancestors no longer plays a large role in Herero life, traditional rituals have given way to secular ceremonies, and, consequently, the "sacred hearth" has disappeared. Huts are no longer arranged in any special pattern, although their openings still face the corrals, given that cattle remain the bedrock of Herero economy. The Herero also maintain cattle posts, extensions of the permanent homesteads, to help distribute cattle over wide areas and thus exploit large tracts of pasturage in an arid habitat.

Economy

Subsistence and Commercial Activities. Cattle herding remains the primary subsistence activity, but Herero are also engaged, in decreasing order of importance, in trading, hunting, and cultivation. Cattle management may be characterized as laissez-faire. Except for the rainy season (October or November through early or mid-April), adult cattle are not penned up at night. They graze freely on their own, returning every three or four days to a well near the homestead for water. When grass becomes too thin in a given area, a herdsman leads the animals to another unoccupied area. During the rainy season, however, the herd must be watched more closely. In the dry season the herd tends to stay together because good pasturage occurs in relatively isolated and well-delineated areas, but during the rainy season more good grass is found over a wider area, and individual animals may wander and become separated from the herd. With few naturally occurring watering spots in the Kalahari, the Herero must dig wells. One well provides drinking water for the people of a single homestead; another, larger well provides water for the animals that are kept by a cluster of three to five homesteads, located within several kilometers of each other. Horses and donkeys are watered with the cattle, but sheep and goats usually do not approach the well until after most of the larger animals have left. Tubs of water are also filled each day by women and children and are kept at the homestead for the animals that remain there. The Herero keep dogs, for hunting, and chickens, whose eggs are eaten (as are the chickens themselves when they die, although they are not killed for consumption). Cattle, goats, and sheep are also eaten, as is some wild game, whereas horses, donkeys, and dogs are not. Although of minor importance to the Herero economy and diet, hunting is considered an exciting and psychologically satisfying pursuit by these formerly nomadic warriors and raiders. Winter (May to August) is the most active hunting season; the weather is cooler, and meat can be kept longer without spoiling. In addition to meat for consumption, the Herero hunt to acquire commodities (meat, hides, horns) to barter for such staples as sugar, tea, salt, and tobacco. The Herero engage in this activity only if early rains indicate a lengthy wet season. On average, only one homestead in a cluster has a field. Both horticulture and agriculture are practiced; planting is in November and December and harvesting in April. Crops, chief among which is maize, are grown mainly for consumption by the cultivators themselves, but any surplus is sold or traded to neighbors.

Industrial Arts. Nowadays the Herero manufacture little, either for their own use or for sale or trade, except for an occasional three-legged, triangular chair, for which they were once well known.

Trade. Trade has always been an important element in the Herero economy. Before the arrival of Europeans, the Herero traded animal products with other groups, such as the Ovambo and Bergdama, for axes, iron for weapons and ornaments, and salt. With Europeans, the Herero traded sheep, oxen, butter (which the Herero did not consume, but used as a cosmetic and sunscreen), pelts, and ivory in return for barrels, wagons, metal implements, rifles, salt, and whiskey. Today the Herero are thoroughly dependent on markets. They travel to towns to sell their cattle and the products derived from both domestic and wild animals, and they frequent general stores to purchase such items as canned food and fresh produce, tobacco, clothes and material for clothes, furniture, tools, gasoline, paraffin, soap, matches, and machine parts for well pumps. Some Herero even own motor vehicles, and nearly every homestead has at least one portable radio. Gone are the leather aprons and white-plumed headdresses of former times. Men wear contemporary Western clothes, and women make their own brightly colored versions of the high-necked, long-sleeved, long-hemmed "Mother Hubbards" that were worn by the wives of colonial missionaries. Weekly visits by a goods-laden truck from a general store provide occasions for the residents of an area, both Herero and non-Herero, to gather, gossip, haggle, and flirt.

Division of Labor. Herding remains today primarily a male activity, the only cattle-related female chore being the daily milking. Women and children see to the daily watering of sheep and goats at the homestead, and women are responsible for domestic activities, care of young children, and tending and harvesting the small fields of crops when these are present. Men conduct trading activities regarding cattle and the products of the hunt, but women do most of the bartering of other goods. Cooperative activities that involve large numbers of people (such as watering herds, care of livestock wells, and hunting) are undertaken by the men of a homestead cluster and other neighbors. Formerly, according to the Herero, large-order cooperation occurred only between agnatic (patrilineal) relatives; thus, they say, kin tended to live near each other to facilitate joint activity. Nowadays those who live near each other, regardless of their relationships or the absence thereof, are those who cooperate. Research conducted during the 1970s indicated that, contrary to Herero claims, this may have largely been the case even in the past (Vivelo 1977).

Land Tenure. In precontact times, the land upon which Herero cattle grazed at any given time was Herero land. After the arrival of Europeans in South-West Africa, Herero access to open territory became increasingly restricted as the settlers staked out exclusive claims to the land. By the time of the 1904 war, the Herero were confined by the growing European population to the areas around a few permanent or semipermanent waterholes. Today all land is owned by the state but is leased to local residents, through the offices of district land boards, for ninety-nine-year terms. Inheritance of rights in land is determined by civil law, according to which the land passes from elder to younger brother or from father to son.

Kinship

The Herero practice double descent; that is, descent is reckoned both patrilineally and matrilineally. Every Herero is linked to a series of male ancestors through his or her father and to a series of females through his or her mother. Herero descent-ordered units consist of *otuzo* (sing. *oruzo*), or patrisibs, and *omaanda* (sing. *eanda*), or matrisibs, which are internally differentiated into patrilineages and matrilineages, respectively. (Patrisibs are classified into six phratries, and matrisibs into two.) In Otjiherero, the term for patrilineage and homestead is the same (onganda), as is the term for matrilineage and hut or household (ondjuo), which reinforces the view that Herero kin relations are connected to, and possibly derived from, coresidence.

Kinship Terminology. Herero kinship terminology is of the Iroquois, or bifurcate-merging, type.

Marriage and Family

Marriage. Today ethnic endogamy is giving way to intertribal marriage, and children of such unions suffer no social stigma. A Herero man may also keep concubines, women to whom he is not formally married, who live either in his homestead or in their natal homesteads. The children of such a union belong to the man's patrisib if he pays child-wealth to the mother's father, or to the mother's patrisib if he does not. Wives live in their husbands' homesteads, and a married couple usually lives in the man's father's homestead, although sometimes poor matrilineal relatives may also be found in a homestead. Because formal marriages are not validated by civil ceremony as opposed to tribal ritual, divorce is similarly conferred by the Botswana courts and is not difficult to obtain.

Domestic Unit. The primary domestic unit is the individual household within a homestead, in which a woman and her children reside. In a monogamous marriage, the husband lives in the same house; in a polygynous union, the man has no house of his own, but rotates among those of his wives.

Inheritance. In former times, when "sacred" cattle were distinguished from "secular" cattle, the former were inherited patrilineally, first from elder brother to younger and then from father to son, and the latter were inherited matrilineally from mother's brother to sister's son. Today, under the influence of Botswana's legal system, inheritance of all property is largely from parent to child.

Socialization. Care of children is chiefly a female responsibility. Girls remain with their mothers, often looking after younger siblings, until they are married and move away. Boys assist with chores around the homestead under the direction of any resident adult, but most of their day is spent in leisurely play. Girls are considered marriageable at about age 16, and premarital sex is permitted among young people of marriageable age. Most Herero children acquire only enough formal schooling to learn basic reading and writing.

Sociopolitical Organization

Previously, leadership among the Herero depended on a combination of descent, wealth in cattle, success in warfare, and personality characteristics, and it carried little real authority. In precontact times, Herero society consisted of autonomous herding units, each headed by an elder male, or omuini, each ranging over large tracts of land in search of pasturage and water. At the end of their migratory period, these units set up homesteads around major water sources, and although they still practiced nomadism, their movement tended to be more regular and less far-ranging. They gathered in neighborhoods or clusters of homesteads around a dependable water supply and formed alliances for military and economic purposes. In each cluster, an *omuhona,* or headman, emerged, one of the homestead heads who had distinguished himself as a military leader and who was respected for his fairness and good judgment. An omuhona's authority was limited, however; he led only because others saw an advantage in following him. When the Herero settled in the new land, they lived under the political jurisdiction of Tswana chiefs. As they grew in number and economic independence to be recognized as a separate group, with their own settlements, local Herero headmen were designated by the Tswana chiefs. Nowadays headmen are appointed by the Botswana state administration, and they function as the lowest-level bureaucratic authority, serving as spokespersons for the state, rather than for indigenous leaders and constituents. They handle local disputes of a relatively trivial nature; more serious conflicts and social control in general are the purview of the police and district commissioners.

Religion and Expressive Culture

Religious Beliefs. Traditionally, all important social occasions and all stages in the Herero life cycle were validated by religious ceremonies that invoked the ancestors. Because cattle were a gift from the ancestors and were kept in their honor, all important rituals involved the use, often the sacrifice, of animals. Today the connection with the ancestors has been broken. The most valued legacy of the ancestors has, in the Herero view, been profaned. Cattle are no longer treated as sacred commodities, but as secular property. When cattle were the exclusive property of a group of people with common descent (i.e., persons who shared the same ancestors), their sacred nature was preserved. Now that cattle are sold to nonrelatives, the ancestors' gift has been rejected, which means that the ancestors and the way of life they bequeathed to their descendants have also been rejected. Decreased reference to the ancestors has led to the disappearance of religious ritual. Without ritual, the place where ritual was conducted (the okuruo) became superfluous. Today Herero society may be justifiably characterized as secular. Although some Herero are nominally Christian, most disavow any religious belief.

Ceremonies. The only ceremonies in which Herero engage today are what they call "celebrations." On the occasion of a girl's coming-of-age or a marriage or some other notable happening, and sometimes for no reason at all, Herero will summon their neighbors (including non-Herero), kill a goat, cook the meat, and sit around the fire drinking store-bought beer, eating, and singing songs (some secular, some derived from Christian hymns). Men, women, and children will eat, sing, and chatter long into the night.

Arts. The Herero practice no arts other than occasionally to adorn the exteriors of their huts with individualistic designs (handprints, geometric patterns).

Medicine. The Herero no longer practice any native medicine; they rely on the services of Western physicians and nurses.

Death and Afterlife. The Herero bury their dead, as they always have always done, but today the funeral rites are simple and secular, and interment is in government-approved cemeteries. The Herero believe that a soul survives the body and upon death goes to a place in the sky, but they profess to know nothing about this place or what happens there, and they say that they are content to wait and find out when they die, rather than to speculate.

Bibliography

Gibson, Gordon D. (1952). "The Social Organization of the Southwestern Bantu." Ph.D. dissertation, University of Chicago.

Gibson, Gordon D. (1956). "Double Descent and Its Correlates among the Herero of Ngamiland." *American Anthropologist* 58:109–139.

Gibson, Gordon D. (1959). "Herero Marriage." *The Rhodes-Livingstone Journal* 24:1–37.

Vivelo, Frank Robert (1977). *The Herero of Western Botswana: Aspects of Change in a Group of Bantu-Speaking Cattle Herders*. American Ethnological Society Monograph 61. St. Paul, Minn.: West Publishing Co.

FRANK ROBERT VIVELO

Ibibio

ETHNONYMS: none

Orientation

Identification. The name "Ibibio" identifies the largest subdivision of people living in southeastern Nigeria, in Akwa Ibom State, and it is generally accepted and used for both ethnic and linguistic descriptions. Like their Igbo neighbors, the Ibibio people originally shared no common term that identified them as a whole. The name "Agbisherea" was first used by European explorers in the nineteenth century to describe Ibibio inhabitants, but apparently died out soon after. Some Igbo-speaking people refer to their Ibibio-speaking neighbors as "Mong"; others call them "Kwa."

Location. The Ibibio are located to the south and southeast of the Igbo, in southeastern Nigeria. This includes the former Calabar Province (the Itu Mbuzo subgroup is in the Bende Division), Owerri Province, and certain villages of the Obong. The Eastern Ibibio, or Ika, have attached their village groups to the Ndokki Igbo of Owerri.

Demography. The Ibibio numbered over two million in the 1963 census and fell into the following six major divisions: Riverain (Efik), Northern (Enyong), Southern, (Eket), Delta (Andoni-Ibeno), Western (Anang), and Eastern (Ibibio proper). These main groups are further divided into groups that are identifiable by geographical location. The Efik reside mostly in the Calabar Province, and are divided into Enyong (Aro), Calabar, Itu, and Eket groups. The Riverain area also includes the Cameroons, inhabited by the Kumba and Victoria groups. The Eyong are divided into the Enyong (Aro) and Ikot Ekpene of Calabar Province and the Bende division of Owerri Province. The Eket division resides in Calabar Province. The Adoni-Ibeno are divided into the Eket and Opopo of Calabar Province. The Anang are divided into the Abak and Ikot Ekpene of Calabar Province, and the Aba of Owerri Province. The Ibibio proper are divided into the Uyo, Itu, Eket, Ikot Ekpene, Enyong (Aro), Abak, Opopo, and Calabar groupings. They also make up the Aba division of Owerri Province.

Linguistic Affiliation. The Ibibio speak dialects of Efik-Ibibio, a language of the Kwa Branch of the Niger-Congo Family. Being the best-known dialect, Efik has been established as the literary language, and is understood by most educated Ibibio. Because of its remarkable assimilative power, Efik spread throughout the Cross River area and even into the Cameroons.

The most basic difference among the many dialects of Ibibio is in the vocabulary. To a lesser extent, the sound system, tone, and grammar can be distinguished. Comparative studies have shown considerable similarity between the Efik and the Ibibio proper, Oron, Eket, Anang, and Ibeno dialects.

History and Cultural Relations

Historical records indicate no traditional migratory pattern among the Ibibio proper and the Anang; they appear to be longtime occupants of their present habitat. All of the other Ibibio-speaking groups were derived from the Ibibio proper. Direct references to the Ibibio are found in early historical records. This is presumably because of their activity in the slave trade. Their history is associated with the Calabar and Efik of the lower Cross River area. (The name "Efik" refers not to the Ibibio subdivision, but to the indigenous groups among whom the Efik Ibibio settled.)

The first Christian mission was erected in Calabar circa 1846. During the latter half of the nineteenth century, numerous military expeditions were undertaken to bring the Ibibio under British rule. As a direct result of the conquest, military posts were set up in 1903 in Ikot Epene, Itu, and Uyo.

Economy

Subsistence and Commercial Activities. Like their Igbo neighbors, the Ibibio are primarily rain-forest cultivators of yams, taro, and cassava. They engage in subsistence agriculture. Other food crops include plantains, chilies, maize, beans, and pumpkins. Most of Ibibio wealth comes from the export of palm-oil products, distributive trading among themselves, and town wage labor.

Industrial Arts. The Ibibio, especially the Anang, are well known for their skill in wood carving and are considered masters of an adroit professional technique. Weaving is generally done by youths of both sexes, whereas women are responsible for mat making.

Trade. The Efik engage in trading fish and palm oil in considerable amounts.

Division of Labor. As with the Igbo, yams are traditionally considered to be the chief crop of men, and cocoyams the chief crop of women. Men do most of the clearing, planting, and harvesting of the yams. Women weed, plant, and tend other crops. They also collect the harvested yams into baskets and carry them to the market.

In collecting the produce from palm trees, men generally do the climbing, and the women collect and carry the fruit to the market. The extracting and processing of palm oil is usually done by women, who retain the palm kernels. Also, raffia palms may be tended by men, but are usually owned by women, and are used to make wine, mats, and poles.

Land Tenure. With a strong emphasis on the patrilineage, the male members form the dominant nucleus of the hamlet and have collective rights to its land. The lineage head allocates the land for farming among its members on a yearly basis (see also "Social Control").

Kinship

Kin Groups and Descent. Although not as extensively studied, the Ibibio appear to have shared the same settlement patterns and territorial organization as their Igbo neighbors. Ibibio villages generally consisted of compounds of rectangular constructions, each with several rooms, arranged around a courtyard or common meeting place. Their villages usually held about five hundred people, and were divided into physically distinct hamlets that contained separate patrilineages. The hamlets were part of a larger settlement, which was represented by a secular leader who was generally the senior male member of the group. In patrilineal descent groups, the men traced their descent to a single male ancestor. Women continued to claim the support of their own lineage head after they were married.

Kinship Terminology. The *ete otun*, or secular leader, is distinguished from the *ete ekpuk*, the ritual leader. The ete otun may not rightfully act without the latter's consent.

Marriage and Family

Marriage. Betrothal before the age of 14 was common. Marriage payments were made to the prospective bride's parents. The marriage payment was shared among the bride's kin, with the father keeping the largest share. The marriage payment traditionally had to be completed before the marriage could be consummated; it was supplemented by services rendered by the husband to the bride's father.

Domestic Unit. Men and women had separate houses grouped in compounds usually composed of the houses of a single household (i.e., a man, his wives, and other dependent relatives). Several of these made up a family (*nnung*), whereas many such families made up a compound (*ekpuk*).

Inheritance. As with the Igbo, personal property is inherited by the deceased father's eldest son.

Socialization. Ibibio men and women are formally grouped into age sets, the status of which increases with seniority. They are informally established for youths around the age of 10, and are formally recognized when its members are about 12 years of age. Members of the young sets are given instruction in morality and native laws. To this end, age sets function as self-disciplinary institutions and guardians of public morality.

Sociopolitical Organization

Social Organization. Restricted title associations are important marks of prestige among the Ibibio. The principal women's society is the Ebre society. The principal men's society is the Ekpo society.

Political Organization. The lineage head (ete ekpuk) and the town head (*obon ison*) are traditionally regarded as the main sources of justice for their respective groups, but the *ade facto* (council of elders) also meets for judicial purposes in the village court.

Social Control. As among the Igbo, cooperation and social control outside the family is most effectively achieved within the patrilineal and exogamous lineage. The ete ekpuk maintains moral authority and ritual obligations over a wide field, as he is the guardian of the ancestral shrines. In theory, he maintains the right to assign farming plots on lineage land, although in practice these duties are usually carried out by the ete otun (see also "Socialization").

Religion and Expressive Culture

Religious Beliefs. Although religious rituals concern several deities and spirits of ancestors, it has been argued that, like the Igbo, the Ibibio believe in a Supreme Being, Abassi, who is the sky god. Abassi is generally regarded as the creator of human beings. As in Igbo religious culture, there is no specific cult or priesthood established for this supreme deity. An Ibibio myth attributes the distancing from the earth of the abode of this sky god to the pounding of an old woman's pestle.

Death and Afterlife. Worship of the ancestors is a very important part of Ibibio religious culture. Sacrifices are often made at the ancestral shrine, which is kept at the house of the eldest member of the lineage group. Disgruntled ancestors may wander among the living, causing harm until the ceremony of Obio Ekpo ("world of the dead") is performed so that the spirit can enter the world of the dead. The Ibibio have a concept of good (*eti*) and evil/bad (*idiok*). A person has two souls, the immortal soul (*ukpong*) and the animal-linked soul (*ukpong ikot*), which can live in lions, leopards, bush pigs, antelopes, and pythons. The latter also dies at death, whereas the former is reincarnated or becomes a malevolent ghost troubling the living.

Bibliography

Forde, D., and G. I. Jones (1962). *The Ibo and Ibibio-Speaking Peoples of South-Eastern Nigeria: Ethnographic Survey of Africa.* London: Stone & Cox.

Horton, R. (1976). "Stateless Societies in the History of West Africa." In *History of West Africa,* edited by J. F. Ade Ajayi and Michael Crowder. Vol. 1, 72–113. London: Longman.

Offiong, D. A. (1991). *Witchcraft, Sorcery, Magic, and Social Order among the Ibibio of Nigeria*. Enugu: Fourth Dimension.

IFI AMADIUME

Igbo

ETHNONYMS: Ala Igbo, Ani Igbo, Ibo, Ndi Igbo

Orientation

Identification. Igbo is the language spoken in Ala Igbo or Ani Igbo (Igboland) by the people who are collectively referred to as "Ndi Igbo"; their community is known as "Olu no Igbo" ("those in the lowlands and uplands"). Before European colonialism, the Igbo-speaking peoples, who shared similarities in culture, lived in localized communities and were not unified under a single cultural identity or political framework, although unifying processes were present via expansion, ritual subordination, intermarriage, trade, cultural exchange, migration, war, and conquest. Villages and village groups were generally identified by distinct names of their ancestral founders or by specific names such as Umuleri, Nri, Ogidi, Nnobi, Orlu, Ngwa, Ezza, and Ohaffia.

There are several theories concerning the etymology of the word "Igbo" (wrongly spelled "Ibo" by British colonialists). Eighteenth-century texts had the word as "Heebo" or "Eboe," which was thought to be a corruption of "Hebrew." "Igbo" is commonly presumed to mean "the people." The root *-bo* is judged to be of Sudanic origin; some scholars think that the word is derived from the verb *gboo* and therefore has connotations of "to protect," "to shelter," or "to prevent"—hence the notion of a protected people or a community of peace. According to other theorists, it may also be traced to the Igala, among whom *onigbo* is the word for "slave," *oni* meaning "people."

Igbo-speaking peoples can be divided into five geographically based subcultures: northern Igbo, southern Igbo, western Igbo, eastern Igbo, and northeastern Igbo. Each of these five can be further divided into subgroups based on specific locations and names. The northern or Onitsha Igbo are divided into the Nri-Awka of Onitsha and Awka; the Enugu of Nsukka, Udi, Awgu, and Okigwe; and those of the Onitsha town. The southern or Owerri Igbo are divided into the Isu-Ama of Okigwe, Orlu, and Owerri; the Oratta-Ikwerri of Owerri and Ahoada; the Ohuhu-Ngwa of Aba and Bende; and the Isu-Item of Bende and Okigwe. The western Igbo (Ndi Anioma, as they like to call themselves) are divided into the northern Ika of Ogwashi Uku and Agbor; the southern Ika or Kwale of Kwale; and the Riverrain of Ogwashi Uku, Onitsha, Owerri, and Ahoada. The eastern or Cross River Igbo are divided into the Ada (or Edda) of Afikpo, the Abam-Ohaffia of Bende and Okigwe, and the Aro of Aro. The northeastern Igbo include the Ogu Uku of Abakaliki and Afikpo.

Location. Today Igbo-speaking individuals live all over Nigeria and in diverse countries of the world. As a people, however, the Igbo are located on both sides of the River Niger and occupy most of southeastern Nigeria. The area, measuring over 41,000 square kilometers, includes the old provinces of Onitsha, Owerri, East Rivers, Southeast Benin, West Ogoja, and Northeast Warri. In contemporary Nigerian history, the Igbo have claimed all these areas as the protectorate of the "Niger Districts." Thus began the process of wider unification and incorporation into wider political and administrative units. Presently, they constitute the entire Enugu State, Anambra State, Abia State, Imo State, and the Ahoada area of Rivers State; Igbo-speaking people west of the Niger are inhabitants of the Asaba, Ika, and Agbo areas of Delta State.

Demography. In 1963 the Igbo numbered about 8.5 million and by 1993 had grown to more than 15 million (some even claim 30 million, although there has been no widely accepted census since 1963). They have one of the highest population densities in West Africa, ranging from 120 to more than 400 persons per square kilometer. Igbo subcultures are distributed in six ecological zones: the northern Igbo in the Scarplands, the northeastern Igbo in the Lower Niger, the eastern Igbo in the Midwest Lowlands, the western Igbo in the Niger Delta, the southeastern Igbo in the Palm Belt, and the southern Igbo in the Cross River Basin.

Linguistic Affiliation. Igbo is classified in the Kwa Subgroup of the Niger-Congo Language Family, which is spoken in West Africa. It is thought that between five and six thousand years ago, Igbo began to diverge from its linguistic related neighbors such as the Igala, Idoma, Edo, and Yoruba languages. There are many dialects, two of which have been widely recognized and are used in standard texts: Owerri Igbo and Onitsha Igbo. Of the two, Owerri Igbo appears to be the more extensively spoken.

History and Cultural Relations

Contemporary views in Igbo scholarship dismiss completely earlier claims of Jewish or Egyptian origin—that is, "the Hamitic hypothesis"—as "the oriental mirage." Instead, there are two current opinions as a result of evidence derived from several sources that take into account oral history, archaeology, linguistics, and art history. One suggests the Awka-Orlu uplands as the center of Igbo origin, from which dispersal took place. The second and more recent opinion suggests the region of the Niger-Benue confluence as the area of descent some five thousand years ago, and the plateau region, that is, the Nsukka-Okigwe Cuesta, as the area of Igbo settlement. This first area of settlement would include Nsukka-Okigwe and Awka-Orlu uplands. The southern Igbo would constitute areas of later southward migration.

Until about 1500, major economic, social, and political transformations led to continuous outward migrations from overpopulated and less fertile Igbo core areas to more fertile lands, particularly east of the lower Niger River. The Igbo had cultural relations with their various neighbors, the Igala, Ijaw (Ijo), Urhobo, Edo, and Yoruba. From 1434 to 1807, the Niger coast was a contact point between European and African traders. This was also the period of trade in slaves; this activity resulted in the development of many centralized states owing to greater economic accumulation and the development of more destructive weapons of war. The Portuguese came to Nigerian coastal towns between the fifteenth and sixteenth centuries; they were the first Europeans to make contact with the Igbo. The Dutch followed in the seventeenth century, and the British came in the eighteenth century. In the late nineteenth century, mission Christianity and colonialist interest worked together for the colonization of Igboland. The Church Missionary Society and the Catholic Mission opened their missions in Onitsha in 1857 and 1885, respectively.

Economy

Subsistence and Commercial Activities. Subsistence farming characterizes agriculture among traditional Igbo people. The chief agricultural products include yams, cassava, and taro. Other important subsidiary crops include cocoyams, plantains, maize, melons, okra, pumpkins, peppers, gourds, and beans. Palm products are the main cash crops. The principal exports include palm oil and, to a lesser extent, palm kernels. Trading, local crafts, and wage labor are also important in the Igbo economy. High literacy rates among the Igbo have helped them obtain jobs as civil servants and business entrepreneurs since Nigeria gained independence in 1960.

Industrial Arts. The Igbo blacksmiths of Awka are renowned for their ironsmithing. Men's wood carving and women's pottery and patterned woven cloth are of very high quality, and Igbo carpenters can be found all over Nigeria. The stylized character of Igbo masks consists of figures with beak noses, slit eyes, and thin lips.

Trade. The Ikwo and Ezza in the Abakaliki Division of Ogoja produce a substantial surplus of yams for trade. Women dominate rural retail-market trade. Trading is a major social and economic function of women in traditional Igbo society. Women engage in all sorts of economic activities to make money to purchase the essentials they need. They make mats and pottery and weave cloth. Women do most of the petty trade, which is very active. The manufacture and trade of pottery are almost exclusively the domain of women. Igbo also process palm oil and palm kernels, which they market with the surplus crops from their farm stock, and generally monopolize the sale of cooked foods. They mine and sell salt.

Division of Labor. There is a sexual division of labor in the traditional setting. Men are mainly responsible for yam cultivation, and women for other crops. Usually, the men clear and prepare the land, plant their own yams, cut stakes and train the yam vines, build the yam barns, and tie the harvest. The women plant their own varieties of yam and "women's crops," which include cassava, cocoyams, pumpkins, and peppers. They also weed and harvest the yams from the farm. With regard to palm products, the men usually cut the palm fruit and tap and then sell the palm wine. They also sell palm oil, which the women prepare. In general, women reserve and sell the kernels.

Land Tenure. Most farmland is controlled by kinship groups. The groups cooperatively cultivate farmland and make subsequent allocations according to seniority. To this end, rights over the use of land for food cultivation or for building a house depend primarily on agnatic descent, and secondarily on local residence. It is Igbo custom that a wife must be allocated a piece of land to cultivate for feeding her household.

Kinship

Kin Groups and Descent. Igbo society places strong emphasis on lineage kinship systems, particularly the patrilineage, although some Igbo groups, such as the Ohaffia, have a matrilineal descent system, whereas groups like the Afipko Igbo have a double descent system. In all the Igbo groups, one's mother's people remain important throughout one's life.

Kinship Terminology. The *umunna,* children of one father or a localized patrilineage, is made up of specific compound families, which consist of even more basic matricentric household units of each mother and siblings. The umunna is made up of both male and female cognates of an Igbo man's father's lineage. All blood-related kinship groups are bound in the morality or ethics of *umunne,* the ritualized spirit of a common mother. *Ndi-Umune,* or *ikwunne,* is the term used to describe the mother's agnates.

Marriage and Family

Marriage. Marriage is not a matter for the man and woman alone; it concerns the close kin of both. Marriage arrangements are negotiated between the families of the prospective bride and groom. With regard to the paternity of the wife's children, they belong to the lineage of the husband. When a woman has children out of wedlock, however, they belong to her natal lineage, and not to that of the children's father. Igbo have also institutionalized marriage options permitting "female husbands" in woman-to-woman marriages, in special circumstances. Some daughters with a male status (i.e., "male daughters") do not even have to marry to procreate.

Although females are brought up looking forward to this dual role, it would be misleading to think that the major roles of women in Igbo society are as wife and mother, since Igbo women are prominent in public life as an organized force in both economics and politics. A significant part of a young girl's or a young man's childhood training is geared toward their future roles in the family and as useful and responsible citizens. Women are fully involved in matchmaking and usually participate directly or indirectly in the actual negotiations of marital arrangements for their sons or their daughters, in cooperation with the male members of the families concerned. Women have powerful and active behind-the-scene roles in seeking out the girls they would like their sons to marry. The approval of the mother is vital because the young bride is generally expected to live with her mother-in-law and to serve her for the first few months of marriage, until the new couple can set up an independent household and farmland.

Domestic Unit. Most Igbo lived in villages made up of dispersed compounds. A compound was typically a cluster of huts belonging to individual household units. The typical Igbo village consisted of loose clusters of homesteads scattered along cleared paths that radiated from a central meeting place. The village meeting place usually contained the shrines or temples and groves of the local earth goddess and also served as the market. Large communities often had two such units. Most local communities contained anywhere between 40 and 8,000 residents. Homesteads were generally comprised of the houses of a man, his wives, his children, and sometimes his patrilineal cousins. They were often surrounded by mud walls and were nearly always separated from neighboring homesteads by undergrowth or women's gardens. Northern Igbo women normally decorated the mud walls of their houses with artwork. In the south, houses were made of mud on a stick framework; usually either circular or rectangular, the houses were thatched with either palm leaves or grass and were floored with beaten mud. Co-wives had their own rooms, kitchens, and storerooms. Young children and daughters usually stayed with their mothers, whereas the males lived in separate houses. Population pressure and European architecture has forced significant changes in these old settlement ideals, introducing (cement) brick houses lacking aesthetic appeal.

Inheritance. The bulk of inheritance allotments are granted to the eldest son, who, at the time of the inheritance, becomes responsible for the welfare of his younger siblings. If the eldest son is a minor at the time of his father's death, a paternal uncle will take charge of the property and provide for the deceased brother's family. There is also marriage by inheritance, or levirate—a widow may become the wife of her brother-in-law. In some localities, widows may become the wives of the deceased father's sons by another wife.

Sociopolitical Organization

Social Organization. Traditional Igbo social life is based on membership in kinship groups and parallel but complementary dual-sex associations, which are of great importance to the integration of society. The associations take several forms, including age grades, men's societies, women's societies, and prestige-title societies such as the Nze or Ozo for men and the Omu, Ekwe, or Lolo for women. The interlocking nature of these groups prevents the concentration of authority in any one association. Age sets are informally established during childhood. Respect and recognition among the Igbo are accorded not only on the basis of age, but also through the acquisition of traditional titles. In Igbo society, an individual may progress through at least five levels of titles. One could liken the acquisition of titles to the acquisition of academic degrees. Titles are expensive to obtain, and each additional title costs more than the preceding one; they are, therefore, considered a sure means to upward mobility.

Political Organization. The basic political unit among the Igbo is the village. Two types of political systems have been distinguished among the Igbo on both sides of the Niger River: the democratic village republic type, found among the Igbo living to the east of the Niger River, and the constitutional monarchy type, found among Igbo in Delta State and the riverine towns of Onitsha and Ossomali. Most of the villages or towns that have the latter type of political system have two ruling monarchs—one female and one male. The *obi* (male monarch) is theoretically the father of the whole community, and the *omu* (female monarch) is theoretically the mother of the whole community; the duties of the latter, however, center mainly around the female side of the community.

Women engage in village politics (i.e., manage their affairs, separately from the men). They do this by establishing their own political organizations, which come under an overall village or town Women's Council under the leadership of seasoned matriarchs. It was this organizational system that enabled Igbo women and Ibibio women to wage an anticolonial struggle against the British in 1929 known as the Women's War (Ogu Umunwayi).

Both types of political systems are characterized by the smallness in size of the political units, the wide dispersal of political authority between the sexes, kinship groups, lineages, age sets, title societies, diviners, and other professional groups. Colonialism has had a detrimental effect on the social, political, and economic status of traditional Igbo women, resulting in a gradual loss of autonomy and power.

Religion and Expressive Culture

Religious Beliefs. Although many Igbo people are now Christians, traditional Igbo religious practices still abound. The traditional Igbo religion includes an uncontested general reverence for Ala or Ana, the earth goddess, and beliefs and rituals related to numerous other male and female deities, spirits, and ancestors, who protect their living descendants. Revelation of the will of certain deities is sought through oracles and divination. The claim that the Igbo acknowledge a creator God or Supreme Being, Chukwu or Chineka, is, however, contested. Some see it as historical within the context of centralized political formations, borrowings from Islam and Christianity, and the invention of sky (Igwe) gods. The primordial earth goddess and other deified spirits have shrines and temples of worship and affect the living in very real and direct ways, but there are none dedicated to Chukwu. Ala encapsulates both politics and religion in Igbo society by fusing together space, custom, and ethics (*omenala*); some refer to Ala as the constitutional deity of the Igbo.

The Igbo concept of personhood and the dialectic between individual choice/freedom and destiny or fate is embodied in the notion of *chi*, variously interpreted as spirit double, guardian angel, personal deity, personality soul, or divine nature. Igbo have varied accounts of myths of origin because there are many gods and goddesses. According to one Igbo worldview, Chukwu created the visible universe, *uwa*. The universe is divided into two levels: the natural level, uwa, or human world, and the spiritual level of spirits, which include Anyanwu, the sun; Igwe, the sky; Andala (or Ana), the earth; women's water spirits/goddesses, and forest spirits. Through taboos, the Igbo forge a mediatory category of relations with nature and certain animals such as pythons, crocodiles, tigers, tortoises, and fish.

Religious Practitioners. There are two different kinds of priests: the hereditary lineage priests and priests who are chosen by particular deities for their service. Diviners and priests—those empowered with *ofo*, the symbol of authority, truth, and justice—interpret the wishes of the spirits, who bless and favor devotees as well as punish social offenders and those who unwittingly infringe their privileges, and placate the spirits with ceremonial sacrifices.

Death and Afterlife. The living, the dead, and the unborn form part of a continuum. Enshrined ancestors are those who lived their lives well and died in a socially acceptable manner (i.e., were given the proper burial rites). These ancestors live in one of the worlds of the dead that mirrors the world of the living. The living pay tribute to their ancestors by honoring them through sacrifices.

Bibliography

Achebe, Chinua (1958). *Things Fall Apart*. London: Heinemann.

Afigbo, A. E. (1971). *The Warrant Chiefs: Indirect Rule in Southern Nigeria, 1891–1928*. New York: Humanities Press.

Afigbo, A. E. (1981). *Ropes of Sand: Studies in Igbo History and Culture*. Ibadan and Oxford: Ibadan University Press and Oxford University Press.

Amadiume, Ifi (1987a). *Afrikan Matriarchal Foundations: The Igbo Case*. London: Karnak House.

Amadiume, Ifi (1987b). *Male Daughters, Female Husbands: Gender and Sex in an African Society*. London: Zed Books.

Anyanwu, U. D. and J. C. U. Aguwa, eds. (1993). *The Igbo and The Tradition of Politics*. Enugu: Fourth Dimension.

Arinze, F. A. (1970). *Sacrifice in Ibo Religion*. Ibadan: Ibadan University Press.

Basden, G. T. (1966). *Niger Ibos*. London: Frank Cass.

Cole, Herbert (1982). *Mbari: Art and Life among the Owerri Igbo*. Bloomington: Indiana University Press.

Cole, Herbert, and Chike Aniakor (1984). *Igbo Arts: Community and Cosmos*. Los Angeles: University of California, Museum of Cultural History.

Forde, D., and G. I. Jones (1962). *The Ibo and Ibibio-Speaking Peoples of South-Eastern Nigeria: Ethnographic Survey of Africa*. London: Stone & Cox.

Green, M. M. (1947). *Ibo Village Affairs*. New York: Praeger.

Henderson, Richard N. (1972). *The King in Every Man*. New Haven: Yale University Press.

Hodder, B. W. (1969). *Markets in West Africa: Studies of Markets and Trade among the Yoruba and Ibo*. Ibadan: Ibadan University Press.

Horton, R. (1976). "Stateless Societies in the History of West Africa." In *History of West Africa*, edited by J. F. Ade Ajayi and Michael Crowder. Vol. 1, 72–113. London: Longman.

Isichei, Elizabeth (1976). *A History of the Igbo People*. New York: St. Martin's Press.

Isichei, Elizabeth (1978). *Igbo Worlds: An Anthology of Oral Histories and Historical Descriptions*. Philadelphia: Institute for the Study of Human Issues.

Leith-Ross, Sylvia (1939). *African Women: A Study of the Ibo of Nigeria*. London: Faber & Faber.

Metuh, E. I. (1981). *God and Man in African Religion: A Case Study of the Igbo of Nigeria*. London: Chapman.

Nsugbe, Philip (1974). *Ohaffia, A Matrilineal Ibo People*. Oxford: Clarendon Press.

Nzimiro, Ikenna (1972). *Studies in Ibo Political Systems*. Berkeley and Los Angeles: University of California Press.

Ohadike, D. C. (1994). *Anioma*. Athens: Ohio University Press.

Onwuejeogwu, M. A. (1981). *An Igbo Civilization: Nri Kingdom & Hegemony*. London: Ethiope Publishing.

Uchendu, V. C. (1965). *The Igbo of Southeast Nigeria*. New York: Holt, Rinehart & Winston.

IFI AMADIUME

Iraqw

ETHNONYMS: Mbulu, Wambulu

Orientation

Identification. The Iraqw are an agrico-pastoral people who live in north-central Tanzania. No comprehensive ethnography has been written to date about them, although various aspects of their culture have been studied by anthropologists.

Location. The Iraqw inhabit the Mbulu and Hanang districts of the Arusha region in northern Tanzania. Their population is concentrated primarily in Mbulu district on the Mbulu Plateau between Lakes Manyara and Eyasi. The topography of this area varies from the mountainous homeland of Iraqwa Da'aw (2,000 meters) to the lower-lying savanna (1,000 meters). The average annual rainfall in areas of higher elevation is 60 to 90 centimeters, but in the lower elevations of the southwestern part of region the range is from 30 to 60 centimeters. The rainy season begins in November and continues through to April. The dry season is from May to the beginning of November. Temperatures average 18° C.

Demography. In the 1967 population census of Tanzania, the Iraqw numbered 198,560, making them the sixteenth-largest ethnic group in a country of more than 120 groups. The Iraqw are the largest population group in the Arusha region, and, with a population expanding by 3.5 percent each year, they have one of the highest birthrates in Tanzania. It is estimated that in 1990 the population totaled around 350,000 people. Within Mbulu District, highest population densities are found in the Endagikot, Daudi and Karatu divisions.

Linguistic Affiliation. There is debate about the linguistic classification of the Iraqw. Some experts have designated their language as "Southern Cushitic." Whiteley (1958), however, has disputed this classification, finding no connection with the Cushitic languages of Ethiopia. He claims that certain features of the language are comparable to those of Hamitic and Semitic languages.

History and Cultural Relations

It is not known when or how the Iraqw came to settle in Mbulu District; however, they refer to the mountainous region of Iraqwa Da'aw in Kainam Ward as their "homeland." Until the late 1890s, the population was concentrated in this area to avoid conflict with the hostile neighboring communities of Maasai and Barabaig. During both the German and British colonial periods, as a rinderpest epidemic and colonial pacification weakened the Maasai and Barabaig, the Iraqw were able to migrate both north and south out of their homeland.

With the expansion of their territory, the Iraqw have come to interact and coexist with the Datoga, the Barabaig, the Gorowa, the Mbugwe, the Alawa, and the Burungi. In the southern part of Mbulu District, the Iraqw employ Nyaturu from Singida District as seasonal laborers.

Settlements

Before independence, Iraqw villages varied greatly in size, ranging from 40 to 400 inhabitants. Since 1974, the Iraqw have been moved into eighty-six villages in Mbulu District. In the northern part of the district, the villages have an average population of 2,500 people in 400 households. In the southernmost part of Mbulu, the villages average 1,500 people in some 225 households. The household typically consists of a man, his wife, and their children. It is the primary economic unit: each has its own agricultural plots and livestock. Every village is named and has a definite boundary. Houses within the village are dispersed.

House types vary by geographical conditions within Mbulu District. There are three basic types of houses. The subterranean house, which is dug into the side of a slope and has an earthen roof, was thought to be built as a defense against raids by the Maasai. Another type, which is most common in Mbulu District, is the round, grass-thatched and mud-plastered house. These houses have a small entryway and, usually, no windows. Most houses face west. Inside, the house is divided into rooms and there is a sleeping platform covering part of the main living space. Immediately inside the entryway is a room where the livestock are brought for the night. Outside the entrance is a courtyard of packed earth. A Swahili-style dwelling has appeared in Mbulu, and it is being encouraged by the Tanzanian government. Square or rectangular, its peaked ridge roof is of thatch or sheet metal, and it has several windows.

Economy

Subsistence and Commercial Activities. Maize is the staple crop of the Iraqw; it is supplemented with beans, sorghum, and millet (the latter two are used primarily for brewing beer). Other food crops are pumpkins, sweet potatoes, European potatoes, onions, and various legumes. Households generally have about 1.2 hectares of land. In areas of high rainfall, such as in the wards of Kainam, Murray, and Karatu in central and northern Mbulu, households can obtain a harvest twice a year. The Iraqw intercrop maize and beans, and maize and sorghum, and sow pumpkins, sweet potatoes, and gourds between the rows of each crop. Millet is usually planted in separate areas. Cash crops include wheat, maize, beans, onions, garlic, European potatoes, and pyrethrum. Typically, an Iraqw household keeps several cows, a few sheep and goats, and chickens. Pigs are often raised for sale, and donkeys are kept for transportation.

Grazing land is divided into private and public pastures. Private pastures are limited to land around the homestead, but the public grazing land of the village can be at some distance from the homesteads. Cattle are a symbol of a family's wealth and are one of the principal investments of the household. As it is difficult for one family to keep a large number of cattle, a system of lending has developed that both reduces the risk of spread of disease and establishes a patron-client relationship with those who have fewer cattle. In exchange for taking care of another's cattle, a family has the right to the milk of the cows and to some of the newborn calves. Livestock are also sold in the market.

Industrial Arts. Blacksmiths and potters were the only full-time specialists in precolonial Iraqw society. Smithing, which is practiced by very few Iraqw, is a male profession. Pottery making is the domain of women. Unglazed earthen pots are fashioned in various shapes and sizes without the use of a wheel. Women also make reed mats, which are sold in the towns. Various articles such as beer filters, furniture, hatchets and hoes, leather goods, and musical instruments are also made by the Iraqw.

Trade. Cattle markets are an important locus of economic activity in Mbulu District. Many Iraqw earn the greater part of their income from these markets. In addition to livestock, the Iraqw sell agricultural products, both at local markets and to Asian merchants.

Division of Labor. Gender and age are the bases for the Iraqw division of labor. On the Iraqw homestead, women sow the fields and harvest the crops, although men may assist if there is a shortage of labor. Hoeing, weeding, and threshing of sorghum and wheat are men's tasks. Young girls are responsible for taking the livestock out of the house in the morning, collecting the night's manure, and spreading it in the sun to dry. Children and married women take care of the calves and the wounded cattle, goats, and sheep; the young, unmarried men are responsible for herding. Women cook, keep house, and care for the children. They collect firewood, draw water, milk the cows, and plaster the house walls. Possessions and space within the house are strictly divided by gender. Men own—and are the only ones allowed to touch—spears, bows, arrows, and shields. Only women may touch the cooking pots, the hearth, and the stone mills. In addition, there is one room inside the house that men are forbidden to enter. Elder men are the principal actors in the political and social spheres. Although the majority of religious specialists are men, women do serve as diviners and rainmakers. The roles of county leader and elder are accorded only to men.

Land Tenure. Cropland and small grazing plots are held by individual heads of families. Villages and sometimes larger political units have control over more extensive areas of communal grazing land. Individuals maintain their rights to land by keeping it under cultivation. If a family migrates to another area, the head of the household may transfer his rights to his land on a permanent or temporary basis, or he may lend land. Transference of rights requires a public agreement before the elders, but lending is carried out informally. If a man returns to his land, the other occupants must leave. The first man to move to new, unoccupied territory is responsible for allocation of land to all incoming settlers. He is not considered the owner of the new territory but, rather, its overseer and protector. After all the land is distributed, the original pioneer no longer has any control over it.

Kinship

Kin Groups and Descent. The Iraqw are divided into more than 200 patrilineal clans, each named after the original founder. These clans are not localized but are spread out all over the territory, as a result of the Iraqw pattern of residence. Except for establishing rules for exogamous marriage, the clan lacks a prominent role in Iraqw daily life. The most important kinship unit within Iraqw society is the household. Communities are formed on the basis of shared space rather than shared kinship.

Marriage and Family

Marriage. Polygyny is accepted, but very few men have more than one wife in Iraqw society. Generally, marriages are arranged by fathers rather than the couple themselves. The wedding involves a huge feast at which the bridegroom's family gives the bride a cow, a goat, a sheep, and a bottle of honey as bride-price to the bride's father. Bride-price is only returned to the groom if there is a divorce. Residence after marriage is neolocal. The Iraqw also practice levirate; children born to a woman after her husband's death are considered to belong to the deceased man. Ghost marriage, whereby women are married to the name of a deceased man and any children she has belong to that name, is also practiced.

Domestic Unit. The domestic household is the primary economic unit. Each household has its own fields and livestock. If a man has more than one wife, separate houses may be built for each.

Inheritance. The Iraqw do not follow strict rules of inheritance. In theory, the wife inherits all of the property of her husband and passes it on to her sons. In general, the youngest son inherits the farmland and most of the property; however, this transfer of the rights to land to a son must be approved by the village elders (Thornton 1980).

Socialization. Circumcision is a large, collective ritual performed on children ranging from 3 to 10 years old. Beer is brewed for the occasion, and gifts are presented to the initiates from relatives and friends. After boys are circumcised, they become official members of a youth group (*masomba*) and are expected to take on greater responsibilities with regard to work and social obligations. A male will remain in the group until he is around 40, when he is considered an elder, or *barise*. Until the 1930s, when the rites were abolished by the colonially appointed chief, girls were circumcised in the *marmo* ritual. More elaborate than male circumcision, this rite involved ritual seclusion for the girls, during which they were instructed in sexual lore and their duties as a wife. Following seclusion, they were circumcised and then permitted to marry.

Sociopolitical Organization

Social Organization. Although the Iraqw recognize kinship units, the most important social and political groups are based on age and gender and local spatial relations. The young men of the masomba must participate in cultivation, house building, cattle raising, and protection of their livestock and comrades from attack. They also organize dances. Membership in this group is based on age and on locality. Usually a masomba consists of twenty or so young men from neighboring houses. The elders are in charge of the organization of ritual, the settling of disputes, the establishment of local boundaries, and convening meetings to discuss the community's welfare.

Political Organization. In precolonial Iraqw society there was no formal structure of authority. Villages consisting of neighborhood groups are the minimum local social and political unit. Neighbors assist each other in farm work and in mutual defense and assistance. Villages put on harvest rites and hold beer parties and festivals and feasts for the ancestors. Above the level of the village, is the county or section (*aya* in Iraqw). Within the county, elders from all the villages hold regular meetings to settle disputes and to organize the rituals that maintain the well-being of the county. At the head of the council of elders for a particular county is an elder known as the *kahamusmo*. He is responsible for calling meetings, supervising rituals, and for allocation of new land to incoming settlers. Upon his death, this position passes to the man whom the kahamusmo designated as his successor. Often this will be his eldest son.

Social Control. The principal means of social control is public opinion. An individual who does something wrong is openly criticized by neighbors and relatives. Where more definite action is called for, elders will prohibit people from speaking to wrongdoers and, in extreme cases, may banish them from the community. Banishment is communicated by the elders' act of placing a thorn branch across the doorway of the offender during the night. Failure to leave after this warning may result in the person's house being burned to the ground.

Conflict. The Iraqw are a peaceful people who have, for the most part, avoided conflict. They have not engaged in cattle raids on their neighbors. Internal fighting was rare, but when bloodshed did occur, the patrilineal relatives of the guilty party had to pay "blood-wealth" to the family of the victim.

Religion and Expressive Culture

Religious Beliefs. Christianity and, to a much lesser extent, Islam have gained wide acceptance in Iraqw society; however, many of the precolonial beliefs are still maintained. Lo'a, a female deity, is associated with the sky, the sun, and the rain. *Netlangw*, or earth spirits, live in stream beds and springs. Lo'a and the netlangw are considered to be in opposition. Lo'a is more remote than the earth spirits, but sacrifices are made to her for prevention of disease and for gratitude for the harvest. Both Lo'a and the netlangw are addressed in prayers.

Ancestors can influence the living and are thought to appear in the form of a hyena. Although there is no ancestor cult, sacrifices to the ancestors are made when it is feared that they are angry. Ancestors only cause trouble to their immediate relatives. Witchcraft is not a prominent feature of the Iraqw religion, but Iraqw do believe that certain people are capable of performing witchcraft and bringing misfortune to others through the manipulation of animals.

Religious Practitioners. The principal religious specialist in Iraqw society is the diviner or rainmaker (*qwaslare*). These experts, who can be men or women, are responsible for deciding what rituals must be carried out for the benefit of both individuals and for the county. The knowledge of divination is usually transmitted along kinship lines. Diviners do not request payment, but people give them presents or assist them in cultivation in return for their efforts. Individuals who can divine for the county as a whole are thought to come only from the Manda clan.

Ceremonies. Sacrifices are made to Lo'a, the netlangw, and to the ancestors. In addition, the Iraqw hold a countrywide, boundary-defining ritual to purify the land. Harvest rites are also held in gratitude to Lo'a.

Arts. Iraqw women make many different types of pottery and weave mats from reeds. Musical instruments are also made.

Death and Afterlife. At death, people become ancestors and go to live in an underworld that is nearly identical to the world of the living.

Bibliography

Fukui, Katsuyoshi (1969). "The Subsistence Economy of the Agrico-Pastoral Iraqw." *Kyoto University African Studies* 4:41–76.

Raikes, Philip (1975). "Wheat Production and the Development of Capitalism in North Iraqw." In *Rural Cooperation in Tanzania*, edited by Lionel Cliffe, et al. Dar es Salaam: Tanzania Publishing House.

Thornton, Robert J. (1980). *Space, Time, and Culture among the Iraqw of Tanzania*. New York: Academic Press.

Wada, Shohei (1969a). "Local Group of the Iraqw—Their Structure and Functions." *Kyoto University African Studies* 3:109–131.

Wada, Shohei (1969b). "Territorial Expansion of the Iraqw—Land Tenure and Locality Group." *Kyoto University African Studies* 4:115–132.

Whiteley, W. H. (1958). *A Short Description of Item Categories in Iraqw*. London: School of Oriental and African Studies.

Winter, Edward (1966). "Territorial Groupings and Religion among the Iraqw." In *Anthropological Approaches to the Study of Religion*, edited by M. Banton. London: Tavistock.

Winter, Edward (1968). "Some Aspects of Political Organization and Land Tenure among the Iraqw." *Kyoto University African Studies* 2:1–29.

Yoneyama, T. (1969). "The Life and Society of the Iraqw." *Kyoto University African Studies* 4:77–113.

Yoneyama, T. (1970). "Some Basic Notions among the Iraqw of Northern Tanzania." *Kyoto University African Studies* 5:81–100.

KATHERINE A. SNYDER

Iteso

ETHNONYMS: Bamia, Itesyo, Omia, Wamia

Orientation

Identification. The Iteso comprise the second-largest ethnic group in Uganda and a significant portion of the non-Bantu-speaking minority in Kenya's Western Province. The Iteso of Uganda have not been well described, but significant studies exist of the political and economic dimensions of colonial rule in their territory. For the Iteso of Kenya, there are substantial studies of social organization, social change, and ritual processes. The Iteso have an undeserved reputation in Kenya for cultural conservatism, whereas in Uganda they have been described as being among the most economically adaptable of people. In common with many of the peoples of the Kenya-Uganda border region, they have a history of extensive multiethnic contact and have come to share many customs with neighboring peoples, although not at the expense of their identity or cultural distinctiveness.

Location. In Uganda the great majority of Iteso occupy Soroti District and some of the adjacent areas in the northeastern part of the country. Farther east and south, they constitute about half of the population of Bukedi District. These Iteso are separated from their more northern Ugandan colleagues by Bantu-speaking peoples, notably the Gisu, Banyole, and Bagwere. They are not separated spatially from the Kenyan Iteso of Busia District in Western Province, with whom they share a common border. The Iteso of Soroti District, Uganda, are called the Northern Iteso in the ethnographic literature; the Iteso of Bukedi District, Uganda, and Busia District, Kenya, are called the Southern Iteso. The Southern Iteso occupy the foothills of Mount Elgon and the surrounding savanna. The Northern Iteso environment varies from low and wet near the shores of Lake Kyoga and its neighboring swamps to high and arid in the north. In both areas, annual rainfall is separated into two wet seasons—the "short" and "long" rains. It varies considerably from year to year and locality to locality, averaging 150 centimeters a year in Kenya. The Iteso have always moved their households in response to changes in economy, politics, and climate. After the 1950s, land scarcity and colonial (later state) control prevented the Iteso from adapting their economy to the environment.

Demography. The latest reliable census for Uganda (1969) lists 600,000 Iteso living in Soroti District and 65,000 living in Bukedi. Approximately 150,000 Iteso resided in Kenya in 1979. Population densities range from about 32 per square kilometer in the more arid portions of northern Uganda to over 500 in the densely populated areas of Kenya. In Kenya, where the population has increased dramatically in the late twentieth century, the majority of Iteso are now under 15 years of age. Life expectancy has also increased, but recent figures are not available. Until the 1960s, half of all children died before reaching adulthood.

Linguistic Affiliation. The Iteso speak an Eastern Nilotic language. The Eastern Nilotic Branch of Nilotic is divided into the Teso-speaking and Maa-speaking (Maasai) branches. The Teso Branch is further divided into speakers of Ateso (the language of the Iteso) and those of the Karamojong cluster, including the Turkana, Ikaramojong, Jie, and Dodoth in Kenya and Uganda.

History and Cultural Relations

Iteso traditions relate that they originated somewhere in what is now Sudan and moved south over a period of centuries. It is not possible to calculate the time of this movement. A body of Iteso is said to have separated from the Karamojong and moved further south. This may have been a very early separation because the clan names and ritual customs associated with the second of two distinctive groups of Karamojong and Jie people are not found among the Iteso. Unlike the other Teso-speaking ethnic groups, the Iteso have never been transhumant or nomadic; agriculture has played as significant a role in their social, economic, and expressive lives as cattle have among the other groups.

Iteso clan names reveal a history of long-standing ethnic interactions. Names of Bantu and Northern Nilotic origin are found among them. The Iteso were probably well established in their northern Uganda heartland by the mid-eighteenth century, when they began to move farther south. The history of the Iteso and neighboring peoples has not been extensively documented. Traditions recorded among the JoPadhola indicate there were two waves of Iteso migration. The first was family based and peaceful. It was followed by a more extensive and aggressive migration that left the Iteso in control of a large swath of territory that by 1850 extended as far as the western highlands of Kenya. European travelers record extensive fear of Iteso warriors; nonetheless, the Iteso soon suffered reverses that caused them to draw back to their current territory in Kenya. Since then, the Northern and Southern Iteso territories have been separated. Relations with other societies throughout the precolonial period were alternately peaceful and acrimonious. As a result of spatial intermixture and intermarriage, Iteso elements and customs can be found among neighboring peoples and vice versa. Intermarriage has always been extensive. It is likely that ethnic identity hardened during the colonial period, as it has since, when resources such as land were newly defined as belonging to "tribes."

The Iteso in Kenya and Uganda were conquered by African colonial agents of the British and indirectly ruled through them. Western Kenya was transferred from Uganda to Kenya in 1902. As a result, the economic and political histories of the Northern Iteso and the part of the Southern Iteso living in Kenya have taken vastly different courses. At independence, the Ugandan Iteso were far more wealthy than their Kenyan counterparts. This difference resulted from the status of Uganda as a protectorate reserved for "African development" and Western Kenya's status as a labor reserve for the European-owned farms in the "White Highlands." As a minority people in Kenya, the Iteso are not well known and have been viewed with some suspicion by surrounding peoples. On the other hand, the Kenyan Iteso have not suffered from the political destabilization in Uganda since 1970. Events in the colonial period and since have elaborated cultural differences among the Iteso that were regional in origin. The language of the Northern Iteso, for example, was extensively influenced by the Baganda people, who ruled the Iteso on behalf of the British colonial regime, whereas that of the Southern Iteso is in some ways closer to Turkana. As a result of living among Bantu- and Nilotic-speaking peoples, the Southern Iteso have probably been subject to a greater variety of cultural influences. The economic infrastructure is far more developed in Kenya than in Uganda, and cash income is also higher, reversing a pattern found in the 1960s. The Kenyan Iteso undertook considerable labor migration: most men between the ages of 60 and 80 have worked outside their home territory; many served in places such as Burma during World War II. In the early 1980s government-sponsored cooperatives that ran cotton ginneries in western Kenya failed to pay for cotton delivered by the Iteso and others. Consequently, they began experimenting with new cash crops, such as tobacco, grown with the aid of loans from large agricultural companies. In the early 1990s there was a partial revival of cotton growing, and the ginneries have been resuscitated.

Settlements

The culture and social organization of the Northern Iteso has been sparsely studied. The material that follows refers primarily to the Southern Iteso. Settlements are dispersed: each household is usually situated at the edge of its own land but is frequently adjacent to other households. In the immediate precolonial period, Iteso households were combined into larger settlements centered around an important person called the *lok'auriaart,* "man of the cattle-resting place." For a considerable period of time after the establishment of colonial rule, these important men dominated decisions to settle, but households were increasingly dispersed. The primary organization in terms of which households currently cooperate and interact is the *adukete,* "those who have built together." This is a loosely defined territorial unit whose members do not always agree about its membership, not unlike an urban neighborhood. It is a network rather than a corporate group. Members of the adukete feel an obligation to help one another and settle disputes among themselves. Because people no longer move their households at will, there is a greater tendency for members of the same lineage to live near one another in settlements.

Economy

Subsistence and Commercial Activities. Eleusine (finger millet) and sorghum are major food crops. In the 1920s colonial officials introduced cassava as a supplement to these staples and as a famine-relief food. Cassava, which the Iteso cook with finger millet and sorghum, is planted in fields that would otherwise be fallow. Women grow vegetables in gardens next to their sleeping houses and gather various wild foods, especially mushrooms and flying ants, a delicacy. Men herd cattle, and the grazing of animals was regarded as a commonly held right until the late 1960s and early 1970s; there have been conflicts over the right to graze since then, and some people have fenced their fields. The primary cash crop was cotton, which was grown by men and women in separate plots (and for individual income) during the short rains. As a result, the labor demands for cash crops did not conflict with demands for subsistence farming. Many households have teams of oxen and plows; others trade their labor for the use of a richer household's teams. Newly introduced cash crops such as maize and tobacco are grown during the long rains and have caused considerable concern about how people will manage the conflicting demands of cash and subsistence farming. The primary commercial activities are trading in cattle, owning small shops, and (in Kenya) employment in such public-sector jobs as local administration and schoolteaching.

Industrial Arts. The primary occupations are carpentry, tailoring, butchery, and various indigenous skills, such as making the boards used for *elee*, a game of calculation played with seeds, which is the Iteso national pastime. Few of these are full time occupations. In some areas there are women potters, but blacksmithing is unknown. The Iteso of Kenya traded with the Samia people for their iron goods in the precolonial period.

Trade. There were a few markets at independence; some have grown much larger with the addition of government facilities such as schools and dispensaries. Market and cattle-trading days rotate among different major markets. These have also become centers for an extensive trade in dried fish and goods such as used clothing imported from the United States. Gas-operated grinding mills are now frequently found at market centers. Women pay for the grinding of foodstuffs through the sale of beer they have brewed and small amounts of grain and vegetables.

Division of Labor. The division of labor among the Iteso is characterized by the radical separation of the sexes in subsistence and ritual activities. Men are responsible for building houses and clearing land. Both men and women plant, weed, and harvest, but women are solely responsible for processing food crops, including threshing, grinding, and cooking. Although public rituals have largely disappeared among the Iteso, domestic and life-cycle rituals are regularly performed by women. Ritual is defined as part of their work—protecting the lives and health of the children of their households. Within neighborhoods, households regularly cooperate in tasks such as harvesting cotton; in this way, individual harvests are quickly garnered, and labor is fluidly distributed in a period of peak demand. The social mechanism underlying this cooperation is the beer party, which is also a context for cooperation between husbands and wives. People who do not work cooperatively and attend beer parties are judged to be *epog* ("proud" and thoughtless of other people's needs)—a very serious insult to the Iteso.

Land Tenure. Land was freely available during the precolonial period. Only improvements—for example, trees planted on the land—were owned. Today such trees are a source of considerable conflict because people own trees on land belonging to someone else. Land was first sold in the mid-1950s, but registration did not begin until the early 1970s. Land was never held by corporate groups such as lineages, and thus the transition to individual landholdings was accompanied by less conflict than elsewhere in Kenya. Important men anticipated the impending land scarcity and moved their former clients to large, newly claimed land parcels. For the first time, some Iteso in Kenya are unable to grow enough food to feed themselves. They have to work at very low rates for wealthier, usually salaried, people.

Kinship

Kin Groups and Descent. The Iteso are a patrilineal people with three levels of patrilineal descent, each defined by the activities associated with it. The nominal clans are nonexogamous name-bearing units associated with Iteso historical narratives and ideas about the inheritance of character. Nominal clans are divided into clans, within which marriage is forbidden. These exogamous clans are further divided into lineages, with genealogies three to five generations deep, whose primary duty is to supply support and attendance on ritual occasions such as funeral rites. The more closely related descent groups are bound by ties of sentiment but also divided by intrahousehold conflicts over property, which have emerged in the late twentieth century. Descent groups are not property-holding units but do figure significantly in Iteso definitions of their social universe.

Kinship Terminology. The Iteso use Hawaiian cousin terminology with bifurcate terms for the first ascending generation and descending generation from Ego.

Marriage and Family

Marriage. Marriages are defined from two points of view: they are alliances between spouses but also between two exogamous clans. The first alliance is evident in the practical arrangements of setting up a household, and the second is expressed in ritual and healing practices. More than one-third of all men and a majority of all women are married polygynously. Although the number of men with four or more wives has decreased since the precolonial and early colonial period, it is possible that the total number of people married polygynously is increasing in the rural areas, as in many other Kenyan societies. The amount of bride-wealth has remained the since the mid-twentieth century, but the time taken to hand over the ten to fifteen head of cattle has changed, from almost immediately after the birth of the first child to an extensive period of more than twenty years. Postmarital residence tends to be virilocal for women and neopatrilocal for men, who soon move into a new home on family land. Divorce is rare; even marriages said to end in divorce are often reconciled when the estranged wife returns after an extended period of time. Bride-wealth helps constrain the incidence of divorce because a man who receives cattle through his sister's marriage would have to return the bride-wealth (on which his own marriage depends) if her divorce were finalized. The result is a series of disrupted marital exchanges.

Domestic Unit. Domestic groups are established among the Iteso when a man marries a woman for the first time. Shortly thereafter they set up a spatially independent household, but under normal conditions, the husband's mother supervises her daughter-in-law. Most Iteso men strive for more than one wife; polygynous unions are frequent, but in the late twentieth century they have been opposed by women. Households are composed of separate "houses" composed of mothers and their children. Cattle from bride-wealth are supposed to belong to this "house." Relations between full siblings are the most solidary in Iteso society. Children leave their natal household at marriage, and women most often go to live with their youngest son when he has married, effectively separating husband and wife at the end of their married life. As a result, Iteso households are complex but not generationally extended. Scarcity of land may change this pattern in areas where population is especially dense.

Inheritance. Men leave three kinds of property: land, cattle, and personal property such as shops and cash. Sons assume the right to family land when they marry; when an elder dies, any remaining land is divided among his unmarried sons. Cattle are inherited by the sons of each mother. Men may control the cattle that come into "houses" through their daughters' marriages, but at death only the full brothers of the married daughter have inheritance rights to these cattle and to cattle assigned to their mother from their father's residual herd. Male children without the cattle they must have before they can marry may be given excess cattle belonging to another "house." Other property is divided equally among all the sons. Women do not inherit male property, only female personal property such as clothing and household effects.

Socialization. Socialization is not elaborately ritualized among the Iteso. Weaning occurs at about 1 to 2 years of age. Children are indulgently treated until they go to school or begin to take up work tasks. Marriage is the most abrupt transition for women; it is somewhat traumatic—especially if it is with a much older man. Men's status transitions are easier because they do not move far away from their natal households. Attending boarding school, which is common in Kenya for the children who manage to get to a secondary school, may likewise be a traumatic experience. The primary context for local cultural learning was the grandmother's hut, where many children used to spend considerable time learning folklore and customs, enjoying storytelling and the expressive arts. The expansion of schooling has severely attenuated this significant setting for socialization. As a result, many young people currently grow up with very limited knowledge of their culture. Formal schooling will probably bring about extensive changes in the body of Iteso knowledge.

Sociopolitical Organization

Social and Political Organization. The Iteso live in territorial units of increasing scale: the household; the neighborhood; government-defined units (the headman's area and the sublocation); the location (headed by a government-appointed chief); and the division, which also tends to correspond to the constituency for the Iteso member of parliament. In addition, the Iteso of Kenya recognize three dialect groups, which have had different external cultural influences.

The precolonial Iteso were organized into territorial units called *itemwan* ("fireplaces"—called "sections" in the anthropological literature; sing. *item*), which were the largest-scale political units and were organized for defense and political expansion. An itemwan may have been led by a successful war leader. The age system appears to have been extremely different from one part of the Iteso territory to another. One constant element was the rituals associated with retirement from the status of elder. After performing them, retired men could no longer marry and were believed to have privileged access to the divinity.

Women's forms of social organization include special, ritually defined friendships, labor cooperatives, groups formed to heal illness caused by spirit possession, and, since the mid-1980s, church groups.

Social Control. The feud functioned as a significant mechanism for social control among the Iteso during the precolonial period. All members of a lineage were held responsible for the actions of their fellow lineage members. Witches and deviants, such as persons who committed incest, were either expelled or punished. Since the advent of colonial rule, neighborhood disputes have been adjudicated by a council of male elders and the headman. Disputes that cannot be settled at this level can be taken to the chief's meeting or to the district court. Values associated with ideals of male and female achievement, particularly those connected with childbearing, are very significant for the Iteso. Even the words for "adult male" and "husband" and "adult female" and "wife" are the same. All adult Iteso strive to become successful parents, and their sense of efficacy is tied to their reproductive status. Women are closely supervised from marriage through the end of their fertile period. One of the consequences of joining a cult of spirit possession is to provide contexts in which male supervision of female activities is not appropriate.

Conflict. The Iteso are a very egalitarian people and have a quite justified reputation for independent action. They tend to settle conflicts before they reach the formal legal system. There are a number of sources of conflict. The first is interethnic: the Iteso still see themselves as disputing with their traditional enemies. Territorial disputes occur pertaining to the number of seats the Iteso should have in parliament and to the boundaries of the location in which they live. During the 1970s, when land was first registered, land disputes were a major source of conflict—especially between sets of half-siblings or the descendants of in-laws who had chosen to live together. Disputes between neighbors (over cattle grazing) and between husbands and wives (over the allocation of labor) are now frequent. These are the product of land scarcity and changing patterns of cash cropping, which now conflict with the labor demands of subsistence.

Religion and Expressive Culture

Religious Beliefs. The Iteso believe in a divinity with different aspects, variously called *akuj*, "high," or *edeke*, "illness." Other entities in their pantheon included the Ajokin, little spirits of the bush, who invited people who met them to feast, providing they kept the invitation a secret. Under missionary influence, the Ajokin have come to be identified with the devil. Ipara, spirits of the dead, figure prominently in their lives, but there are no special shrines for propitiation. The Ipara are selfish and do not enforce good behavior so much as demand propitiation. When they possess people, the Ipara bring with them exotic spirits from other cultures who harm or make ill the people possessed. Catholic missionaries have had considerable influence among the Iteso, and almost all of them had been baptized by 1990. Women are especially involved in the church. The African priests at the missions have successfully advocated the organization of local cooperative groups called "Christian communities."

Religious Practitioners. Most Iteso religious practices are either associated with transitions in the life cycle or are ways of managing misfortune and illness. Women are the primary religious practitioners. The performance of domestic rituals is defined as part of their "work." In addition to domestic ritual, women predominate in cults of spirit possession. Men serve as diviners and healers, and some specialize in "blocking" the effects of the spirits of the dead. In the precolonial period, men who had been retired through the age system acted as intermediaries between the divinity and the people.

Ceremonies. Domestic ceremonies take place in the household and include naming rituals, the complex rites associated with marriage and birth, and rituals held to heal ill children. Mortuary rituals also take place within the household and involve a series of ceremonies that invoke the entire complex of social relations of the dead person. The rituals of the age system took place outside the home in the "bush" and were organized in terms of the symbolic attributes of various animals. Domestic rituals and healing rituals such as those associated with spirit possession draw on much the same symbolic repertoire, a good deal of which involves the ritual dramatization of female agricultural and child-rearing tasks.

Arts. The plastic arts include pottery making by women and musical-instrument making by men, some house decoration, and, traditionally, cicatrization for women. These are all purely aesthetic and have no religious significance. The verbal arts—which include a cycle of trickster tales, proverbs, female storytelling, and male rhetoric—are far more developed.

Medicine. Iteso medical practices are derived from multiple sources and include a range of Western medicines purchased at stores or obtained at government clinics; locally known herbal cures; and resort to religious practitioners, such as curers of illnesses caused by spirits of the dead.

Death and Afterlife. At death, the body is separated from its *eparait* (spirit), which goes to live in the bush. The spirit ideally moves deeper and deeper into the bush, but in practice many spirits return to bother the living. Spirits of the dead are greedy: they require offerings of food and drink. As a result of mission influence, spirits of the dead have come to be associated by some Iteso with the Ajokin, little creatures of the bush, and both of these have come to be associated with the devil. The skeletons of dead people are exhumed after a number of years so rituals can be performed to "cool" them and make them more kindly disposed to the living. Older Iteso are very concerned that their children will bury them in coffins and prevent this practice, thus suffocating the dead in the earth. Funeral rituals are a major focus of Iteso ritual life, and many Iteso point out that they are a primary reason for having children: "Without children, who will sacrifice at the head of your grave?"

Bibliography

Gulliver, Phillip H., and Pamela Gulliver (1953). *The Central Nilo-Hamites*. London: International African Institute.

Karp, Ivan (1978). *Fields of Change among the Iteso of Kenya*. London: Routledge & Kegan Paul.

Karp, Ivan (1987). "Beer Drinking and Social Experience in an African Society." In *Explorations in African Systems of Thought*. 2nd ed., edited by Ivan Karp and Charles S. Bird, 83–119. Washington, D.C.: Smithsonian Institution Press.

Karp, Ivan (1988). "Laughter at Marriage; Subversion in Performance." *Journal of the Folklore Institute* 25(1–2): 35–52.

Karp, Ivan (1989). "Power and Capacity in Rituals of Possession." In *Creativity of Power*, edited by W. Arens and Ivan Karp, 91–109. Washington, D.C.: Smithsonian Institution Press.

Vincent, Joan (1982). *Teso in Transformation*. Berkeley and Los Angeles: University of California Press.

IVAN KARP

Jacobites

ETHNONYMS: none

Orientation

The Jacobites, today numbering some half a million, adhere to a branch of Christianity that is most commonly known as the Jacobite church. They are to be found mostly in northern Iraq and southeastern Turkey. Following the Mongol invasions in 1258, some emigrated to northern Mount Lebanon, where they settled among the Maronites, their spiritual cousins. There are settlements in northern Syria—around Homs (Emessa) and Hama and also in Damascus—organized into some six parishes and subscribing to the Catholic branch. Those around Aleppo date from after World War I. Jacobites in Syria numbered some 100,000 in the mid-1970s, with about a quarter of them being Catholic.

History and Cultural Relations

The Jacobites have been referred to historically as members of the "West Christian Church," also of the "Syrian Orthodox Church of Antioch and all the East." Jacobite missionary activity, dating back to the earliest centuries of Christianity, led to the establishment of a branch in the Malabar region of southwestern India. The apostle Saint Thomas is credited with laying the foundation for the Malabar church.

The Jacobites came into being under this name as a consequence of the intense Christological controversies that took place during the fourth and fifth centuries, when the Arian heresy—which stressed that only the Father was the true God, the Son being subordinate—prevailed (not to be overturned until the Second Ecumenical Council at Constantinople in 381). Grounded as they were in the Aramaic culture and history of the Syro-Iraqi region, it was inevitable that they would be drawn away from the Greco-Roman church, which eventually triumphed as the official religion of the empire.

The Jacobites were one of the Eastern churches that espoused Monophysitism, a by-product of the Council of Chalcedon of 451, which was declared heretical when Emperor Justin I caused fifty bishops who espoused Monophysitism to be excommunicated at the Synod of Constantinople, in 518. Monophysites henceforth were to be suppressed at the highest level of the state church. Reprieve was gained under the Empress Theodora, who urged a policy of reconciliation on her husband, Emperor Justinian, and who was therefore hailed as a champion of Monophysitism. This policy changed quickly under Justin II, however.

The Monophysites of Syria came to be known as Jacobites, probably named after Jacob Baradai, a monk who lived in a monastery near Edessa (present-day Urfa). He journeyed to Constantinople in 540 to plead the cause of Monophysitism. Imprisoned for fifteen years with other bishops who shared his convictions, he was subsequently consecrated bishop of his sect and sent to Syria to organize it. He later consecrated Servius, who was to succeed Severus as patriarch of Antioch in 512. Some say he ordained two patriarchs, eighty-nine bishops, and countless members of the clergy. He is often called "Bishop of Edessa," but, as attested by the chronicler Gregory Bar Hebraeus, he had no fixed see. According to another tradition, the name derived from Jacob, the biblical patriarch. One Jacobite deacon alleged that his people were descendants of Jewish converts to Christianity, and still another source claims that the name came from Saint James, brother of Jesus and first bishop of Jerusalem. Regardless of the name's origin, before long the Arab tribes in the region that had been Christianized came under the leadership of this church, including the two dominant ones—the Taghlib in lower Iraq and the Banu Ghassān in lower Syria. They anchored the see of their faith at Antioch and, like the Syrian Orthodox and Byzantine-rite patriarchates, refused to surrender to the dictates of Constantinople.

Antioch had been the preeminent seat of early Christianity (it was the place where Christians first declared themselves), and it remained so until the Council of Chalcedon in 451, which sought to diminish its centrality by elevating the bishopric of Jerusalem to a patriarchate. The Jacobites were driven from Antioch after the death of Severus in 538. The term "Jacobite" was not even their own choice, but was given to them by their Greek Orthodox rivals. They readily accepted it, however.

The Jacobites' conflict with the Greeks, as with the other Eastern Christians who were opposed to them, was both theological and national, or ethnic: it was a contest between Syriac thought and Hellenistic culture. Moreover, the Christianity of Antioch was greatly influenced by the Jewish faith, as preached and practiced by Jesus, his disciples, and followers. The schism of Chalcedon stimulated the rise of Syriac as a religious and ecclesiastical language, whereas the Orthodox Antiochans pursued a Greek liturgy. The Greek version of Christianity persisted under the Byzantine Empire and even after the Ottomans had conquered their capital in 1453. The Jacobite version, on the other hand, was most powerful during the time when the Muslim Umayyad Empire thrived in Syria (661–750). The Jacobites and the Nestorians were favored by the Muslims over those who owed allegiance to Constantinople.

In Syria proper, there was an ongoing contention between Jacobite and Orthodox Christians that lasted over a hundred years after the Council of Chalcedon. The patriarchs of Antioch were sometimes Orthodox and sometimes Monophysite. Most famous of the latter was Severus, who controlled the city itself from 513 to 518. He was an author who wrote in Greek, a great admirer and quoter of Ignatius's *Epistles*, and a leader of the Monophysite party until his death, following which there was to evolve a double patriarchate: one at Antioch for the Jacobites, and the other for the Syrian Greek Orthodox.

The final breach between Monophysitism and Orthodoxy took place during the reign of Justinian's successor, Justin II, who, according to a contemporary account of John of Ephesus, persecuted the Monophysites. John hailed from Amida (present-day Diyarbakır) and served as bishop during the sixth century. He wrote in Syriac, thus earning the distinction of being the first Syriac historian. Even when driven from Antioch, Jacobite patriarchs continued to style themselves "of Antioch," although they now resided elsewhere, in Malatya, Diyarbakır, and, since the twelfth century, at the monastery of Zaʿfarān (Saffron) near Mardin.

Jacobites were intellectually active and demonstrated their historically close affinity with Hellenistic culture. The principal writer of the period was James (Jacob) of Edessa (d. 708), a poet, commentator, and letter writer, as well as a voluminous translator of Greek works into Syriac. Most eminent among all Jacobite writings in the medieval era is the *Chronicle* of Gregory Bar Hebraeus (d. 1286), a brilliant scholar of Jewish parentage who served as metropolitan of Mosul after holding other sees. A lesser-known writer was Dionysius Bār-Ṣalība, metropolitan of Amida, a theologian and commentator of the eleventh century. Jacobite writers gained prominence under the Muslims in science, medicine, and literature, to whose Islamic civilization they contributed in no small measure.

The Crusades and the reliance of the Crusaders in Edessa, Antioch, and Jerusalem on native Christian sects—no matter how "heretical"—served in the long run to damage the Jacobites' native-church status with the Muslims. Unlike the Armenians and Maronites, however, the Jacobites did not strike up military alliances with the Crusaders, nor did they fight in their ranks, which enabled them to escape significant Muslim vengeance under the Mamluks. A temporary reprieve from persecution came with the Mongols, who conquered Baghdad in 1258 and ended the ʿAbbāsid caliphate, because of the strong influence of Nestorian Christianity among them.

Following the defeat of the Mongols, native Christian churches were once again chastised by the Mamluk sultans, who issued Jacobite patriarchs strict orders not to have any traffic with foreign Christian leaders. Jacobite communities sustained the greatest damage of all when Timur Lang (Tamerlane) conquered the area in the late fourteenth century and caused the death of the majority of Jacobites in the region of Ṭūr ʿAbdīn; they were reduced to the status of a minority sect in the region between Mardin and Mosul, where they once were a majority.

Henceforth Jacobites were to be concentrated east of Aleppo and west and north of Mosul, with Ṭūr ʿAbdīn becoming their strongest center. From northern Mesopotamia, they spread into Iran, where Nestorianism was flourishing. Carmelite missionaries discovered Jacobite communities in Shīrāz and Eşfahān in the seventeenth century and quickly turned them (some six hundred households) into Catholics. Aleppo (ancient Beroea) had had a Jacobite archbishop since 543, and, after the Arab conquest, Maronite and Melchite Christians also anchored bishoprics in the city, which had become an important center of anti-Chalcedonian Christians. As the city developed into one of the richest trading centers of the Ottoman Empire, attracting a large foreign commercial presence, the Catholic missions that had been established there succeeded in turning the anti-Chalcedonian Christians into followers of Rome. These Uniates, as they were then called, were to be known after the eighteenth century as "Syrian Catholics," to distinguish them from their brethren, who were now termed "Syrian Orthodox" (not to be confused with the Byzantine-rite Orthodox).

Jacobites spoke a vernacular Syriac in the early centuries; following the Arab conquests, they switched to Arabic and took Arabo-Islamic names. Indeed, they had adopted the language even before its alphabet. During the late nineteenth and early twentieth centuries, Jacobites formed important elements in cities like Mosul, Mardin, Urfa, Diyarbakır, Aleppo, and Baghdad. Interfaith relations were cordial and respectful, because the Jacobites were loyal to local administrations. One Episcopal missionary, Horatio Southgate, claimed that Muslims frequented Jacobite churches and even shared in revering their "holy men" and saints, most probably because of the Christian ancestry of those who had converted to Islam. Mardin served at this time as the center of the sect.

Administratively, the Jacobites were subject to their own clergy in civil as well as in spiritual matters, a system that derived from the *millet* (autonomous unit) structure that they had enjoyed under the Ottomans. Their link with the Sublime Porte (the Ottoman sultan's ministerial government) came via the Armenian patriarchate, and it was not until 1882 that they achieved a separate millet status, thanks largely to pressures from Great Britain. Theologically, they shared more with Coptic Monophysites than with Armenian Monophysites.

Oswald Hutton Parry, a Western observer, has described firsthand (Parry 1895) the organizational hierarchy of the Jacobite church, which was based in the nineteenth century in Mosul (or Mār Mattai), with bishops at Jerusalem, Damascus, Homs (Emessa), Edessa (Urfa), Amida (Diyarbakır), and Ṭūr ʿAbdīn (Jabal Ṭūr). The bishop of Mār Mattai had no independent see, and his entourage in 1887 consisted of only one monk in residence.

According to Parry, the patriarch was elected by the people, and the election was confirmed by the bishops who resided near Mardin. It was not uncommon for the *maphrian* to be promoted to the position of patriarch. The patriarch consecrated the bishops, who had to be either monks or widowed priests. Those chosen from the rank of monks were called *matrān;* those chosen from widowed priests were known as *asgaf:* they held a slightly lower rank than matrān and did not qualify for the patriarchate or maphrianate. Patriarchs and bishops were legally permitted to serve as judges for their own people in cases governed by personal law (i.e., marriages and divorces). Bishops had to be at least 35 years old to be ordained; deacons could be 20 or younger if they were able to read the Psalms in Syriac. Parish priests were elected by the parish councils. Deacons engaged in secular work during the week.

Jacobite monasteries were widespread; each came under the jurisdiction of the diocesan bishop unless it contained the tomb of a patriarch or archbishop, in which case it came under the governance of the patriarch. Monks were often laymen.

The Jacobites share the Syriac liturgy—with some variations—with Maronites, Uniate Syrians, and Malabar Jacobites. Leavened bread is used in the Mass, and the leaven is handed down from generation to generation. The Eucharist is reserved for the sick, but only for communion on the same day. Upon baptism, a child is blessed with *myron* (from Greek: lit., "sweet oil"; consecrated only by the patriarch and other primates of the church) immersed in water thrice, annointed all over the body with oil, clothed, and confirmed. Confession is mandatory before communion on Maundy Thursday, Christmas, and Pentecost. Lent and Advent are observed as strict fasts; other such fasts include the Apostles' Fast, Pentecost, Mary's Fast (1–15 August), and those held on Wednesdays and Fridays during each week of the year (from sunset to sunset).

Today Jacobites still inhabit an area encompassing northern Iraq and Harput and Diyarbakır in Turkey. They number over two hundred thousand in Turkey, with almost an equal number in Iraq and Syria. There are sizable numbers around Mosul and Damascus, with the largest groupings in Jabal Ṭūr, north of the Mardin-Jazīra-Nusaybin line. They have important businesses (largely jewelry) and churches in İstanbul. Syriac is spoken vernacularly in southeastern Turkey, where Jacobites are heavily concentrated, and where some of the oldest and best-known churches are located.

The Uniate branch of the Jacobite church resulted from the work of Jesuits when they first came to Mesopotamia, in 1540. After the Union of Florence in 1439, many Jacobite clerical leaders became affiliated with Rome through their patriarchs. The split that took place between Mardin and Ṭūr ʿAbdīn at the beginning of the seventeenth century contributed to the move. Mardin, with its important cultural center at Zaʿfarān, drew Diyarbakır and Aleppo into its orbit. The permanent split began with the visit of André Akhijian, a young Jacobite monk from Mardin, to Rome in 1642. He was consecrated bishop in 1656 at the special request of the French consul, Victor Piquet, and succeeded Patriarch Sham un in Aleppo in 1659. A patriarchate in that city dates to 1646.

Maronites of Lebanon were instrumental in the creation of the Catholic patriarchate among the Jacobites, as they had been in creating one among the Nestorians, but this action intensified the opposition of their Orthodox brethren, and, between 1702 and 1755, the Jacobites were forced to endure many hardships, in spite of the support of the Maronite patriarch and his bishops. Often they could not elect their own patriarch, obliging Rome to appoint a vicar for them, which in turn obligated him to reside in Shabbaniya, in Lebanon, in order to enjoy the protection of the Maronites, who built a home there for him.

It was not until the election of Michael Jarwah as patriarch in 1738 that the Catholic branch took hold. Jarwah had endured much suffering and exile, ending up as a refugee at Saint Anthony's Maronite monastery in Bayt Shabāb (Lebanon). He was given a school in Sharfa by the Maronite patriarch, Estepahn al-Duwayhi, and, through a generous endowment of the Maronite Khāzin feudal family, he was able to establish his patriarchal see as the most important Syrian Catholic center in the East.

In 1831 Armenian Catholics were represented by a patriarch who was not affiliated with the Latin church. The Sublime Porte recognized this patriarchate as being independent of Rome, thus establishing the precedent for other independent Catholic communities to break away from the jurisdiction of their patriarch. "Latinization," a controversial issue, was resisted by most native Catholics. The Sacra Congregatione della Propaganda Fide of Rome, in a decree dated 20 November 1838, permitted the sultan's Catholics to choose one of the rites for themselves and barred them access to the Latin rite, in order to satisfy their resentful bishops. The door was thus opened to all Ottoman subjects who had embraced Catholicism to receive legal status of their own. So the "Jacobite" Catholics were formally recognized as a separate and distinct community when Peter Jarwah was granted civil as well as spiritual jurisdiction over his flock in 1843.

Atrocities in their Anatolian habitat and the promise of economic opportunities drew a larger number of Jacobites to Lebanon after 1890. They settled in key cities like Beirut, Zahlé, and Tripoli, as well as in the Bekáa Valley. After World War I, the Syrian Catholic patriarch established his residence in Beirut, his predecessor having left Mardin under pressure from the Orthodox Jacobites. One of them, Jibrāʾīl Tabbūni, was made a cardinal of the Roman Catholic church in 1929.

Horatio Southgate was sent to the region by the Board of the Episcopal church in 1835 with the view of founding a mission to the Jacobites; a one-man mission was established in 1839, with residence at Mardin. The Episcopal missionary worked his way into the grace of the patriarch by alleging that there were no theological differences between Jacobites and Episcopalians. His purpose, as he declared it, was to rescue the Jacobites from absorption by the Roman church.

In consequence of the increased Protestant missionary activities among the Jacobites and other native Christian churches in the East, coupled with the intense pressures upon the Ottoman government by European Protestant powers, first Grand Vizier Reşid Paşa, in November 1847, and then, in November of 1850, Sultan Abdülmecid himself, issued charters declaring Ottoman subjects espousing Protestantism to be a separate community, entitled to the same rights accorded other non-Muslim subjects of the sultan.

Bibliography

Assemani, Joseph Simon (1730). *De Syris Monophysitis Dissertatio. Bibliotheca Orientalis*. Vol. 2. Rome.

Brightman, F. E. (1847). *Liturgiarum Orientalium Collectio*. 2 vols. Frankfurt am Main and London.

Denzinger, H. (1863–1864). *Ritus Orientalium*. 2 vols. Würzburg.

Joseph, John (1983). *Muslim-Christian Relations and Inter-Christian Rivalries in the Middle East: The Case of the Jacobites in an Age of Transition*. Albany: State University of New York Press.

Parry, Oswald Hutton (1895). *Six Months in a Syrian Monastery*. London.

Renaudot, Eusebe (1847). *Liturgiarum Orientalium Collectio*. 2 vols. Frankfurt am Main and London.

CAESAR E. FARAH

Jews, Arabic-Speaking

ETHNONYMS: Names among Jewish groups of the Fertile Crescent are based on locale. Examples are Halabiye (Aleppians) and Shawam (Damascenes). Among Arabic speakers, Arabic-speaking Jews are referred to as "Yahud awlad al-ʿarab" (lit., "Jews who are children of the Arabs," or Arabophone Jews).

Orientation

Identification. From the beginnings of the Diaspora until 1948, there were substantial Jewish communities throughout southwestern Asia. The Jewish communities in Arabic-speaking areas of Iraq, Syria, Lebanon, and Egypt, as well as those in southeastern Anatolia, were predominantly Arabic speaking, as were some Jews in pre-1948 Palestine. No single name encompasses these communities. They are ritually Sephardic. Jews in most locales have Arabic speakers of other religions as coresidents. In southeastern and south-central Anatolia, coresidents include Turks and Kurds. Formerly, there were also considerable numbers of Armenian Christians in Anatolia and Aleppo. The Jewish communities are discontinuously distributed.

Location. Arabic-speaking Jews lived in villages, towns, and cities in an area extending from Baghdad (33°20′ N, 44°30′ E) to Cairo (30°01′ N, 31°14′ E) in the west and south, and as far as Diyarbakır (37°55′ N, 40°18′ E) in the north.

Demography. Figures for the premigration period are in dispute, but the early twentieth century was marked by lowering infant-mortality rates, and also by emigration and high death rates in the period from 1910 to 1920, owing to war, famine, and influenza. The Ottoman census in 1893 can serve as a baseline, although it may be an underestimate. Females sometimes were not counted, and the considerable number of minority members carrying foreign passports were not included with local Jews or Christians. For the Arab provinces (excluding Egypt), there were 32,867 Jews out of a total population of 1,965,085. Estimates of the numbers of Jews in Iraq, Egypt, and Syria-Lebanon total 180,000 in 1917, 261,000 in 1947, and 5,700 in 1972 (5,000 of whom were in Syria and Lebanon). After the almost total emigration from Lebanon, this population is lower today. Figures for the earlier period include the Jews of Iraqi Kurdistan and the Ashknenazic Jews in Egypt but exclude the Jews in Palestine/Israel.

Linguistic Affiliation. The traditional domestic language was Eastern Arabic. The dialects that were spoken by Jews in Syria and Egypt were urban dialects of those areas, whereas an Iraqi urban dialect was spoken in Baghdad and by eastern Anatolian Jews. The dialects spoken by the Jews were also based on Hebrew as a source of vocabulary. Because of immigration, large numbers of Jews in Egypt and Palestine were non-Arabic speakers. After 1920, Hebrew became the language of Palestinian Jewry.

History and Cultural Relations

The Fertile Crescent is the region where Judaism originated. With the beginnings of the Diaspora in the sixth century B.C., and, certainly by the second century B.C., there were Jewish populations throughout the region, especially in Babylonia (now southern Iraq). From the beginning to the present, Jews have lived side by side with peoples of other religions.

From the sixth century B.C. until well after the Arab conquest in the seventh century of the Christian Era, Aramaic was the primary language of Jews in the Fertile Crescent, whereas Egyptian Jewry was Greek speaking. Although there were some Jews living in cities, most Jews in this period were rural cultivators. By the ninth century, Jews were increasingly becoming urbanites, specializing in crafts and trade. There were, at that time, some speakers of Arabic.

Jews, like their coresidents, flourished during the Umayyad and ʿAbbāsid periods, but the Fertile Crescent in general went into a decline with the breakup of the ʿAbbāsid and Fāṭimid monarchies in the eleventh century and suffered from internal disorder and invasions by the Turks, the Crusaders, and the Mongols. During the late fifteenth and the sixteenth centuries, communities of Jews in Egypt, Palestine, and Syria were augmented by the settlement of Jews from Spain and Sicily. These newer immigrants helped to give the Jewish communities importance in trade relations with Europe.

In the nineteenth century the European Industrial Revolution caused Middle Easterners to import more and more products from Europe. Many artisans were forced out of business as local merchants imported increasing quantities of foreign goods, beginning with textiles. A substantial number of non-Arabic-speaking Jews emigrated to Egypt and Palestine during the nineteenth century. There were many emigrants from the Jewish communities of the Fertile Crescent. Many Baghdadi Jews moved to India and the Far East. Both Aleppo and Baghdadi Jews established trading firms for goods exported from Manchester, England. During the late nineteenth and early twentieth centuries, Cairo, Alexandria, and Beirut flourished as new trading centers and were the targets of many ambitious Jews from elsewhere. Other Jews from the Fertile Crescent found homes in Palestine/Israel, and from 1900 on, many Syrian Jews emigrated to the Americas.

After World War II, the conflict between Zionism and Arab nationalism came to a head. By 1950, the majority of Jews from Syria and Iraq had emigrated to Israel and elsewhere. After the 1956 Suez War, Egypt was largely emptied of its Jewish population. Lebanon received several thousand Jewish immigrants during the 1950s, but most left during the Lebanese Civil War, which began in 1975. Several thousand

Jews remain, mainly in Syria, as a result of government policies that prohibit Jewish emigration.

The Arabic-speaking Jews of the Fertile Crescent were an integral part of the Jewish Diaspora. The Jewish communities there were hosts to traveling Jewish merchants and to pilgrims to and emissaries from the Holy Land. Hebrew books, many of which were printed in Europe, circulated throughout these countries. In their vernacular culture, the Jews of the Fertile Crescent had ties with their Gentile neighbors and shared many patterns of behavior with them. In modern times, European culture, especially that of France, was transmitted to the Jews in this part of the world.

Settlements

Throughout their history, the vast majority of Jews have lived in large cities and market towns. They lived in neighborhoods that were largely Jewish, but in most cities they had neighbors who adhered to other religions. Preference was given to living in courtyards with coreligionists, but non-Jews might live on the same street.

Economy

By the nineteenth century, most Jews, even those who lived in rural areas, were working as artisans and traders, although some village Jews may still have been full-time cultivators. Many Jews were itinerant peddlers and artisans who traveled from the cities to rural areas.

Trade. In urban areas, the locale of trade was primarily the market area, in which different crafts and specialities had their own streets and alleys. Foreign goods were generally given to peddlers and retailers on consignment by large wholesalers. In rural areas, Jewish peddlers would sell to Gentile cultivators on credit and receive payment either in kind or in cash at harvesttime.

Division of Labor. Almost all extradomestic tasks, including the marketing of goods, were done by men, at least in middle-income families. Poor women did work for wages, particularly by sewing and performing domestic labor. The Jewish women who worked as dancers in Damascus were drawn from the poorer classes. Some female teachers from Europe and Palestine taught in the more "modern" schools. In Egypt, with its large cosmopolitan population, some women were included in the professions.

Kinship

Kin Groups and Descent. Some patrilineages have permanent family names that indicate ramification. For instance, one family of Kohanim (families descended from the Aaronide priests) is called "Dwek HaKohen." One branch of the Dwek may be the Dwek Halusis, while another may be the Dwek Kassab. These are not corporate groups, however, with fixed membership and estates.

Kinship Terminology. Like other speakers of Arabic, these Jews use the bifurcate-collateral system of differentiating siblings of the father from siblings of the mother and the Sudanese terminology of designating the father's brother's son as *ibn ʿamm*, the father's brother's daughter as *bint ʿamm*, the mother's brother's son as *ibn khal*, the father's sister's daughter as *bint ʿammti*, the mother's sister's son as *ibn khalti*, and so on.

Marriage and Family

Marriage. According to Jewish law, uncles may marry nieces, but aunts may not marry nephews. Marriage with all four first-cousin-types is permitted. Polygyny is also permitted, although restricted by clauses in the marriage contract. Polygyny has traditionally been infrequent, however. Levirate marriage with the widow of a childless brother could occur. Divorce was permitted, but unlike a Muslim, a Jewish man could remarry his former wife only if she had not married another man before such remarriage.

Domestic Unit. Most households were composed of either nuclear families or small extended families. Wealthy households also included servants.

Inheritance. Inheritance in Jewish law favors the males. Traditionally, sons and their descendants inherited from the father; daughters only inherited when there were no sons or male heirs to the sons. A husband might inherit from his wife, but she could not inherit his estate. The marriage contract was intended to ensure her subsistence. If a man had no children, his brothers inherited his estate. The firstborn son received a double portion. Some families did have special rights to particular positions in the Jewish communities and to quasi-official posts. For a long time, a family claiming descent from King David supplied the exilarchs (*resh galutha*) who were the recognized heads of the Jewish community under the Sāssānians and under the Umayyad and ʿAbbāsid caliphs. Members of the Ha-Dayyan family in Aleppo, which claims descent from the exilarchs, are still alive. They supplied leaders to the Mustarib segment of Aleppine Jewry until World War I. The Laniado family has long been the leading rabbinic family among Sephardic Jews of Aleppo. For many generations, the family of Moses Maimonides led the Jews of Egypt. Some Jewish families inherited preferences for such positions as the customs collector and the *sarraflik* (the governor's financier).

Socialization. Emphasis has generally been placed on respect for elders, traditional religion, and conformity to social rules. Sons kissed their fathers on the hand on ritual occasions. Corporal punishment, including bastinado (*falaqa*) was used in schools. Fathers might also bring adolescent sons to their schoolteachers to discipline them. Boys were sent to schools to learn Hebrew, the Pentateuch, and prayers, usually by rote. Larger communities, such as Aleppo and Baghdad, had advanced rabbinic schools (*midrashim*), where Talmud was taught. Girls were generally trained at home by their mothers and were subject to the discipline of both their parents and their older siblings. Beginning with the nineteenth century, there were Western-style schools for boys and girls, run either by Christian missions or by the Alliance Israelite Universelle.

Sociopolitical Organization

The Fertile Crescent was part of the Ottoman Empire from 1517 to 1917, when the various Arab provinces of the empire were divided between the British and the French. Under all of these regimes, the Jews were recognized as a religious grouping and were generally granted the right to deal with matters of personal status and other matters through their own officials. Until the post–World War II period, separate rabbinic courts adjudicated such matters, but such courts have since been abolished in some countries of the area.

Under the Ottomans, a hierarchy stretched from the sultan, through governors, down to the village or neighborhood headmen. Jews and members of other "protected" minorities (especially Christians) were obliged to follow Ottoman law and to maintain low profiles. They also had to pay special taxes. They could not build conspicuous houses of worship, and they had to show deference to Muslims. In return, the minority communities were granted considerable autonomy. In areas pertaining to their internal affairs, they were under the authority of their religious leaders.

From 1839 on, the Ottoman government maintained a hierarchy of "chief rabbis" comparable to Christian bishops. The term for chief rabbi was *hakham bashi*. Although the chief rabbi was nominated by the notables of the local community, his appointment had to be confirmed by the governor and the central government. This system remained in place under the successor states. Until World War I, the hakham bashi represented the Jews on municipal councils. Each neighborhood had a headman (*mukhtar*). In mixed neighborhoods and villages, there might be a headman to represent each major religious group.

Social Control. Within the Jewish communities, the rabbis have exercised a high degree of control, including the use of excommunication (ostracism) and the application of corporal punishment to enforce their decisions. In families, senior males exercised authority over women and children.

Conflict. Within the Jewish community, one line of conflict was between veteran residents and newcomers, as between the "Arabized" Mustaribim and the immigrants from Spain and Sicily in the sixteenth century or, in recent times, between Jewish Ottoman subjects and the Jews who held foreign passports. At times, there also were quarrels between powerful wealthy individuals and the rabbinic authorities.

The nature of the relations between Jews and their Gentile neighbors has varied. In the nineteenth century Jews generally had better relations with the Muslim majority than with Christians, who were directly in competition with Jews for similar quasi-governmental niches. Right after World War I, there was considerable friction in Aleppo between Jews and newly arrived Armenian refugees from Anatolia. Since the 1930s, Jewish relations with Muslims have been embittered by the Arab-Israeli conflict.

Religion and Expressive Culture

Religious Beliefs and Practices. Rabbinic Judaism is the religion of the people being considered here. In Egypt, there are still small numbers of non-Talmudic Qaraites Talmud, and several hundred Samaritans persist in Nablus. Members of both groups can also be found in Israel today.

Judaism is a monotheistic religion, but traditionally it has recognized angels and saintly individuals as having extraordinary influence with God. Rabbis may be asked to write talismans against the evil eye and other ills.

Like orthopraxic rabbinic Jews elsewhere, Arabic-speaking Jews observe the Sabbath from sundown to sundown by abstaining from what is defined as "work" in the Talmud. This abstention includes the preparation of special Sabbath dishes, which can be kept warm overnight in an oven called a *hamin*.

Religious Specialists. Rabbis, generally called *hakhamin*, are trained in Jewish law. Some are also mystics initiated in the cabala. There is no clear distinction between the legally learned and the mystical-magical religious leaders.

Ceremonies. The yearly cycle of festivals and fasts follows the Jewish calendar, beginning with Rosh Hashanah and ending with the penitential prayers that lead to the New Year. Similarly, Jews follow a life cycle of rites of passage, from prenatal rituals and infant-male circumcision to burial and mourning.

Arts. As artisans and as consumers, Jews have generally utilized decoration in clothing and homes resembling that of their neighbors. Through sumptuary codes, the Muslim states have at times imposed particular forms of clothing on Jews. Some varieties of goods were made locally by Jewish artisans, whereas other varieties were made by coresidents of other religions.

In song, the Jews of Aleppo and Damascus combined Hebrew poetry with Arabic and Turkish melodic modes. Such songs would be sung at the synagogue and also on ceremonial occasions. These songs are generally called *pizmonim* (Hebrew: poems). Some are sung before dawn on the Sabbaths between Sukkoth and Passover as petitionary prayers (Hebrew: *baqashot*).

Medicine. Although Western medicine has been used in the twentieth century, it has been supplemented by traditional cures, including talismans prepared by rabbis, visits to shrines, bleeding by leeches, and the like.

Death and Afterlife. Traditional beliefs assumed bodily resurrection of the dead at the End of Days, reward and punishment, and the possibility of reincarnation. The dead were buried within twenty-four hours after death, if possible, in Jewish cemeteries.

Bibliography

Ben-Jacob, Abraham (1965). *A History of the Jews in Iraq: From the End of the Gaonic Period (1038* C.E.*) to the Present Time* (in Hebrew). Jerusalem: Ben Zvi Institute.

Cohen, Hayyim J. (1973). *The Jews of the Middle East, 1960–1972*. Jerusalem: Keter Publishing Co.

Goitein, Shlomo D. (1969–1989). *A Mediterranean Society*. Berkeley and Los Angeles: University of California Press.

Shamir, Shlomo, ed. (1987). *The Jews of Egypt: A Mediterranean Society in Modern Times*. Boulder, Colo.: Westview Press.

Zenner, Walter P. (1982). "Jews in Late Ottoman Syria." *In Jewish Societies in the Middle East*, edited by Shlomo Deshen and Walter P. Zenner, 155–210. Lanham, Md.: University Press of America.

WALTER P. ZENNER

Jews of Algeria

ETHNONYMS: Maghrebi Jews (Arabic *maghreb:* west), North African Jews, Pieds-Noirs, Sephardic Jews, Sfardim

Orientation

Identification. The Jews of Algeria are a very diverse cultural group, owing in part to Algeria's turbulent history. They have experienced the several cultures and languages under diverse rulers, beginning with the autochthonous Berbers, and followed by the Romans, the Byzantines, the Arabs, the Turks, and, finally, the French and the Europeans. Today they constitute the most Westernized Jewish community originating from North Africa and are established mostly in France. Small groups have also immigrated to Israel and to North and South America.

Location. The Jews of Algeria have long lived in the central part of North Africa, between Morocco on Algeria's western border and Tunisia on its east. The largest Jewish communities in Algeria were established in the major cities of the Mediterranean coast (Oran, Algiers, Bejaïa, Annaba, Mostaganem), as well as in cities of the hinterland like Tlemcen and Constantine. There were also Jews in the remote southern fringes of the Sahara, in Biskra, Bou-Saada, Djelfa, and in the Mzab, in Ghardaïa. Less than one hundred Jews are left in Algeria today, after their emigration en masse in the early 1960s. Most live in Algiers and in Oran.

History and Cultural Relations

The presence of Jews in Algeria spans from the pre-Roman period to the early 1960s, when Algeria became independent. Before the Roman Empire took over these remote coasts of northern Africa, descendants of Jews who had fled Palestine after the destruction of the first and second temples of Jerusalem had settled among the Berber tribes of central Maghreb, some of whom had converted to Judaism over several centuries. Jews spoke the Berber language, especially in the eastern part of Algeria, in Kabyle lands, and even prayed in Berber, as evidenced in certain Berber versions of liturgical documents such as the *Passover Haggadah*. During the Arab conquest of Africa in the seventh century, Berbers and Jews fought together against the invaders, an episode recounted at length by the Muslim medieval historian Ibn-Khaldun. According to this author, a Jewish Berber "queen," named Kahina ("the Priestess"), at the end of the seventh century led the autochthonous armies that fiercely resisted the Arabization of the Maghreb. Most Berbers were converted to Islam a few decades later, and the Jews of Algeria started their cultural and linguistic assimilation into the Arab world. They rapidly began developing familiarity with Arabic literature, grammar, and science; in some areas, Jewish communities spoke Judeo-Arabic as their daily language. Despite this deep penetration of the Arabic culture into Jewish habits, the Jews of Algeria remained committed to their religious tradition, and some of their rabbis became widely noted for their Talmudic commentaries and the contacts they had with Palestinian and Babylonian sages. In eastern Algeria, the Karaite dogma (a Jewish sect recognizing only the Bible as their religious canon) had also developed, and had prospered until the early twentieth century. The other major breakthrough in Algerian Jewish history occurred after 1391 when refugees fleeing Catholic Spain arrived en masse into the North African haven. They brought their theological knowledge, their sages, and a more Europeanized Jewish tradition. They were rapidly integrated into the local Jewish leadership. Finally, more European Jews immigrated to Algeria in the seventeenth and eighteenth centuries, coming from Italy. The languages spoken by the Jews in Algeria at that time were—and still are—Berber, Arabic, Spanish (or Ladino, a Judeo-Spanish language), Italian, and Hebrew. Most of these communities were subject to the status of *dhimmi* imposed by the Turks in the sixteenth century on all non-Muslim groups living under Muslim rule. As for the Jews, this status included such restrictions as residential segregation, compulsory clothing stigmas, and posture prohibitions: Jews could not mount horses, carry arms, or be in a posture physically superior to Muslims. The colonization of Algeria by the French, which began in 1830, put an end to this position of inferiority. When, in 1870, Jews were given French citizenship, they began their progressive integration into French language, culture, and social values, principally by their entry into the French school system. This process was completed when most Algerian Jews, not finding their place in the newly independent Algerian nation, left for France, beginning in 1961. A small number among them went to Israel, and to North and South America. Around 150,000 Algerian Jews arrived in France in the early 1960s. This wave of immigration brought significant changes to the French Jewish community.

Settlements

The emigrants to France following Algerian independence settled in large numbers in Paris and its suburbs, in the major cities of the Mediterranean coast, and in such cities as Bordeaux, Toulouse, and Lyon. Those who came from the Mzab chose the Alsatian city of Strasbourg, which had a strong Jewish community.

Economy

Until World War II, Algerian Jews lingered on the lowest layers of the social and economic ladder. Typical Jewish occupations were artisan, jeweler or cobbler, petty merchant, and unskilled worker. Since their integration into the French education system, Algerian Jews began to move upward and to enter new occupations such as public service; some worked in the French postal system, others in the national police. The luckiest among them, children of wealthy traders who were sent to France to study in its universities, began to enter the legal and medical professions. Others enjoyed careers as teachers. The most significant change in the economic position of Algerian Jews after World War II was generated by the entrance of women into the secular education system and into the labor market. Traditionally, women had worked at home, as seamstresses, but in the postwar period nursing and clerical and administrative work became available. By the time of the large emigration to France, in the early 1960s, Algerian Jews had penetrated most sectors of the labor market—except the army and agriculture, where Jewish presence was insignificant. As native French speakers, Jews readily assimilated into the French economic and social system. Algerian Jews are now found in high positions in the French government (in some ministries, in the President's cabinet) and are quite visible also among the academic elite.

Kinship, Marriage, and Family

Kinship. The traditional kinship system and family organization among Algerian Jews was based on a strong patrilineal and patriarchal pattern. The father headed the family even after the marriage of his children, especially when he had sons. On the surface, wives appeared to be totally subjugated by their husbands, but in reality they had much authority over domestic affairs and the education of children. Professional training was acquired within the family, and occupations were transmitted from father to son—to the eldest son in particular. Fathers encouraged their sons to live in the paternal home after they married. In many small towns, some households consisted of an extended family including the nuclear group of parents and their children, a married son, his spouse, and their children. These patterns changed significantly with the progressive Westernization of the Jews and their integration into the French education system. Emancipation began for women as they received secular education, leading to economic independence. Extended family households shattered as they faced economic difficulties. Fathers slowly lost their authority over the households, and the rule of patrilocal residence began to erode. These developments were particularly marked in large urban communities, among wealthy families who had adopted the French way of life, and after World War II, when Jewish women had almost totally acquired their emancipation and when Jews began to move up the socioeconomic ladder.

Marriage. The traditional marriage system, which existed until about the 1960s, was characterized by the dowry and a strong endogamic rule. These two principles underwent major changes with the Westernization of Algerian Jews and their socioeconomic advancement. As endogamy was not only ethnico-religious but also socioeconomic, wealthy Jews married into wealthy families, and matrimonial selection among the poor was confined to the lowest social categories. In the working-class milieu, the dowry was not required when families had no means to provide it or when parents were eager to expedite their children's marriage, under fear of intermarriage. Also, because potential brides were being educated and entering the labor market, dowries proved to be unnecessary. Similar to other emancipated minorities, Algerian Jewish women, once integrated into French society, tended to postpone marriage until after education and embarking on an occupation. The demographic result of the social emancipation of Algerian Jews was thus a significant decline in fertility rates; another was the increasing rate of intermarriage with Christians (but intermarriage with Muslims remained rare among Algerian Jews).

Religion and Expressive Culture

Yet another result of the emancipation and Westernization of Algerian Jews can be found in religious practices. When families Frenchified their way of life, they tended to relinquish religious observance. The observance of Sabbath prescriptions and dietary laws were the first to be affected by this process. Some nonkosher food items are now tolerated in the daily diet, although they will never be included in a festive meal such as the Sabbath dinner or other ritual-table reunions. Although religious practice has decreased since the mid-twentieth century, some major rituals—such as Yom Kippur—and the great festivals of the Hebrew New Year, the Passover seder, and most rituals of the life cycle continue to be observed. These rituals have resisted the erosion of secularization because they have always required well-attended family reunions. The family is what perpetuates major rituals, and it is strengthened through the celebration of these convivial kin gatherings. One of the most dramatic of family ritual reunions is the wedding celebration. The Middle Eastern characteristic still alive in the celebration is the ceremony of the Henna, named for the vegetal substance that is spread on the hands of the spouses and of their single siblings. The Henna is celebrated a few days before the religious ceremony in the synagogue, which is structured according to the canonic rule of Hebrew law. By contrast, the Henna is not a religious ritual. It is a traditional and popular celebration that includes a banquet of traditional North African delicacies, Middle Eastern folk music, and the exchange of gifts and jewelry between the bride and the groom.

Bibliography

Bahloul, Joëlle (1983). *Le culte de la table dressée: Rites et traditions de la table juive algérienne*. Paris: A. M. Métailié.

Friedman, Elizabeth (1988). *Colonialism and After: An Algerian Jewish Community*. South Hadley, Mass.: Bergin & Garvey.

Hirschberg, H. Z. (1974–1981). *A History of the Jews in North Africa*. 2 vols. Leiden: E. J. Brill.

JOËLLE BAHLOUL

Jews of Iran

ETHNONYM: Yahundai

Orientation

Identification. Until mass emigration began in 1948, Jews constituted one of the largest and longest-settled non-Muslim populations in Iran. Dispersed in every city and town in the country, Iranian Jews were almost always a minority except in a few rural settlements, where they occasionally constituted a majority. Jewish communities of Afghanistan, Daghestan, and Central Asia were culturally and linguistically very closely related to those of Iran.

Location. Iran is bounded on the north by Azerbaijan, the Caspian Sea, and Turkmenistan; on the east by Afghanistan and Pakistan; on the south by the Persian Gulf; and on the west by Iraq and Turkey. Much of Iran consists of mountains and high plateaus, and lacks navigable rivers. The climate ranges from semitropical along the Caspian to true desert in the east. Precipitation varies greatly but is limited to the cold season, (i.e., from October to March).

Linguistic Affiliation. All Iranian Jews speak Farsi, an Indo-European language. Each community also has its individual Jewish dialect, often mutually unintelligible to Jews from other regions. These dialects are grammatically and phonetically distinctive from standard Farsi and utilize Hebrew loanwords and metastasis. A mutually intelligible trade jargon, *letra'i*, consisting of mostly Hebrew vocabulary embedded in Persian grammar, was regularly spoken by Jewish merchants engaged in both local and intercity commerce. Jewish goldsmiths had their own jargon, *zargari*, which interpolated nonsense syllables into the flow of speech. A liturgical formalized version of Judeo-Persian is used in synagogue worship, and literature is written in Hebrew characters.

Demography. Until 1979, the Jewish population of Iran was usually estimated at 80,000 to 100,000. Prior to the establishment of Israel in 1948, substantial numbers of Jews were to be found in nearly every city. Rural Jews were found in Fārs Province and Kurdistan. Eşfahān and Shīrāz were traditionally the two largest settlements. In the late nineteenth and early twentieth centuries, Tehran's growth attracted large numbers of provincial Jews. From the 1950s to the 1970s, Tehran had over 50,000 Jews, Shīrāz about 8,000, and Eşfahān 3,000. During that period, increasing fertility and lower mortality were offset by emigration. The Iranian Revolution caused large numbers of Jews to emigrate; estimates of the remaining population are approximately 30,000: 8,000 in Shīrāz, 20,000 or more in Tehran, and less than 2,000 scattered among the other cities and towns. Important communities of Iranian Jews are also to be found in Los Angeles and New York, and large numbers are settled all over Israel. The total number of Iranian Jews may be in excess of 300,000.

History and Cultural Relations

Jews probably first came to Persia (ancient Iran) during the eighth century B.C.E., as a result of Assyria's conquest of Israel. Various traditions ascribe Jewish settlement of Eşfahān to Nebuchadrezzar, king of Babylon, after his conquest of Judah in 586 B.C.E. The biblical books of Daniel and Esther allude to large and sometimes influential Jewish communities in Achaemenian Persia. Under the Sāssānians (226–646 C.E.), Iranian Jews were ruled by a Jewish royal figure, the exilarch, living in Babylonia. Eşfahān was ostensibly a center for Talmudic study. Jews clashed with Zoroastrians over a number of ritual practices in the late fifth century. Mounting suppression of Jewish ritual practices finally culminated in anti-Jewish riots and expulsion of Jews from Eşfahān. After the Arab conquest in 642, Iranian Jews fared rather well. Jewish travelers of the ninth to eleventh centuries described large tracts of Jewish-controlled territory in the Zagros Mountains and refer to Jewish tribal entities engaged in pastoralism. Arab historians of the period refer to the area as "Yahudiya" (lit., "Jew land"). Jews helped found the city of Shīrāz in the eighth century. Iranian Jews were instrumental in international commerce and set up widespread credit networks. A series of messianic movements occurred in the north of Iran and were forcibly suppressed. Jews fared well under the Mongols and were influential in government in the thirteenth and fourteenth centuries. It was during this period that there was a flowering of Judeo-Persian religious literature. In 1502, under the Safavids, Shia Islam became the state religion. Jews were more formally treated as dhimmi, a "protected" minority. They were numerous regulations imposed upon Jews, including special dress, colored markers, and restrictions on touching food. In the seventeenth century large numbers of Jews were forcibly converted to Islam, first under Shāh Abbas I and later under Shāh Abbas II. Subsequently they were allowed to return to Judaism, but many did not. During the eighteenth and nineteenth centuries, conditions for Iranian Jews changed with the rulers. Under the Afghans (1736–1747) and Zands (1750–1794), conditions were good, whereas under the Qajars (1796–1925), Jews often suffered extensive abuse and discrimination. In the late nineteenth century European Jews intervened in Iran and sought to protect indigenous Jews from violence. Alliance Française Universelle established schools in the larger Jewish communities and sponsored European-type education for Jewish children. Anti-Jewish pogroms in Fārs Province prior to World War I marked an attempt by local politicians to use indigenous Jewish ties with Europe in an effort to influence European governments. Under the Pahlavis (1925–1978), most discriminatory legislation against Jews was lifted, and Jews were free to participate in almost every aspect of commerce and government. From 1948 to 1978, there were waves of Jewish emigration from Iran to Israel. The last large-scale emigration began in the autumn of 1978 and lasted through the spring of 1979, when large numbers fleeing the Revolution and the Islamic regime established after the demise of the Pahlavis fled to Israel, Europe, and the United States. Under the Islamic government, a number of important Jewish leaders were executed, Jews were harassed, and Jewish schools were forced to integrate Muslim students, teachers, and curricula into their programs. Foreign Jewish-aid organizations were forced out, and some discriminatory restrictions were imposed on Jews. Small-scale Jewish emigration continues, but the remaining community seems to have established a viable socioeconomic niche, and blatant hostility seems to have subsided.

Jews have long been treated as dhimmi; however, this status of "protected minority" has been precarious ever since Imami Shiism became the state religion nearly 500 years ago. In fact, Jews are considered *nagas* ("polluting") in Shiite terms, and, from time to time, various forms of discriminatory legislation have been adopted. Direct physical contact between Jews and Muslims was traditionally forbidden, and indirect contact such as food handling or sitting on the same carpet was prohibited by strict Muslims. Jews had to wear identifying dress. They were unable to engage in certain occupations, such as agriculture, and tended to enter service or middleman occupations and certain crafts such as goldsmithing. Under the Pahlavis, most of these discriminatory practices were officially eliminated, although the behavior was not totally extinguished. It is not clear whether restrictions were reimposed under the Islamic Republic. Until the late twentieth century, Jews competed economically against other minorities, especially Armenians, and did not generally enjoy good relations with them. They interacted far better with Bahais, some of whom had converted from Judaism.

Settlements

Ninth-century travelers reported large numbers of rural Jews, many of whom were pastoralists. Since the eighteenth century, at least 80 percent of Iranian Jews have been urban. Their quarter, the *mahalleh*, was largely homogeneous and usually close to the seat of political power. Housing was traditionally mud-brick with flat roof (except for Kermān, where dome construction was more common). Entrances were low as a defense against forced entry. Alley-neighborhoods were common and kin often lived nearby. The Jewish quarter tended to be self-reliant, distributing foods raised outside and supplying most communal services needed: education, meat slaughtering, ritual bath, synagogue, and so forth. In the late Pahlavi period, most urban Jews lived in newer areas of the cities, recreating some of the institutions left behind in the mahalleh.

Economy

Subsistence and Commercial Activities. Subsistence was provided by manual labor and middleman occupations. Diet was heavily dependent on rice, bread, and vegetables. Dairy products processed by local Jews, as well as meat, chicken, and beef ritually slaughtered and distributed by Jewish butchers, were part of the diet. Meat was consumed at least twice a week. The diet began shifting in the late 1960s as processed foods such as pasta, vegetable oil and fat, soft drinks, candy, and ice cream became more available. Among the Western-educated, European, American, and Israeli cuisine became more common. The basic diet, however, remained unchanged.

Lacking banks, fearing robbery, and having been precluded from investing in land, most Jews traditionally disposed of spare cash through moneylending. Many served the community as butchers, ritual slaughterers, and other religious functionaries. Others worked as metalsmiths, masons, drapers, musicians, druggists, doctors, and liquor and carpet merchants. In more recent times, with the breadth of economic opportunity broadly expanded, many more Jewish professionals and entrepreneurs have emerged. Teaching and civil service have provided new opportunities. Others have become automobile dealers and international shippers. Many of the poorest Jews have emigrated; the prerevolutionary community was, for the most part, economically comfortable.

Industrial Arts. The traditional cottage industries of Iranian Jews included warp winding and the manufacture of wine and liquor, jewelry, musical instruments, ritual artifacts, and mosaics. More recently, coppersmithing, "antiques," and tourist items for foreign Jews were also made by Jewish artisans.

Trade. Although a few rural Jews traditionally engaged in farming, most were peddlers. Urban Jews, too, were usually middlemen, plying their merchandise in nearby villages and among distant pastoralists or visiting the homes of perspective buyers within the city. Most have shops along the main streets or booths in the bazaar. Some sell from pushcarts. In Pahlavi times, large Western-style automobile showrooms, stores, and movie theaters were owned by Jews.

Division of Labor. In the past, Jewish women's occupations were limited to peddling, spinning cotton, midwifery, healing, and sewing. Since the early 1960s, many women have obtained high school and college educations and entered nursing, laboratory technology, teaching, librarianship, and business.

Land Tenure. Iranian Jews were generally not permitted to own land until 1925. Since then, Jews have invested heavily in urban property and rural agricultural holdings. Most own their own homes outright or lease by "key" money.

Kinship, Marriage, and Family

Kinship. Among contemporary Iranian Jews, the nuclear family is basic, but the *khanevadeh* (patrilateral extended family), which generally consists of three generations, is the most important unit of family obligation. When the khanevadeh is a residence unit (as it commonly was in the past), extended corporate responsibility is usual. In recent times, more of the responsibilities have been assumed by the *famil* (bilateral kindred). The famil is loosely defined but usually includes consanguines who are removed from Ego and affines by no more than four degrees. Kindred responsibilities are most associated with life-cycle events, but business associates and mates are often preferentially selected from this group. Descent is agnatic, and lack of sons is deemed calamitous, but lineage links are rarely traceable for more than three or four generations.

Kinship Terminology. Kinship terminology is bifurcate collateral; cousin terminology is of the Sudanese type. Fictive terminology is frequently adopted for enhancing business relationships.

Marriage. Marriages were traditionally arranged while the bride was prepubescent. The age difference between husband and wife was frequently ten years or more. Spouses were often close kin; unions between first cousins and between uncles and nieces were especially preferred. Postmarital residence was exclusively patrilocal. In the 1960s brides were usually in their late teens, often high-school graduates, and the age difference between spouses was somewhat reduced. Dowry remains the norm, and with large numbers of young males emigrating from Iran, dowries are said to have reached monumental proportions. Patrilocality is still fairly common, at least for the first year or until a child is born. Divorce is uncommon among Iranian Jews.

Domestic Unit. The khanevadeh was formerly the most prevalent type of domestic unit, but, since the 1960s, households have tended to be nuclear, and family size has been greatly reduced. Traditional households of as many as twenty-five to thirty individuals often included several nuclear or extended families, sometimes unrelated (sometimes not even all Jewish) but often sharing domestic responsibilities. Among emigrants to the United States, extended-family households have sometimes served as a temporary buffer to confronting the economic and socially assimilatory pressures of American life.

Inheritance. Patrilineal inheritance is the rule; all sons inherit equal shares. Daughters receive dowries in lieu of inheritance; they only inherit if there are no sons. A "law of apostasy" used to give the entire estate to any son who converted to Islam, but that law was effectively revoked under the Pahlavis.

Socialization. Sons are favored by parents, but mothers like having daughters to assume domestic responsibility. Corporal punishment is rare and almost never across gender lines. Both parents are much respected, but affection for the mother, as well as her demands on her children, are exceptionally strong. Sons' educations is a father's responsibility; daughters are still primarily a mother's concern. Sibling responsibility remains very powerful, especially across gender lines; brothers can veto their sisters' marriages and resort to corporal punishment of unmarried siblings. On the other hand, sibling mutual responsibility transcends marriage, and ties often remain close and affectionate.

Sociopolitical Organization

Iran has long had authoritarian government. Under the Pahlavis and thereafter, Jews were permitted to elect a parliamentary representative, but they have had very little direct national or local political influence.

Social Organization. Jewish communities are not really stratified, but there is a hierarchically structured ranking system. From the 1950s to the 1970s, the economic structure of the community shifted from a few rich and more poor to a larger proportion of wealthy and "middle class." Social mobility within the community is easy, and ranking is constantly fluctuating.

Political Organization. Traditionally, a dual organization was common in larger urban communities: a publicly visible council of community notables with responsibility to the authorities, and a "council of the pious" composed of community religious figures and ritual functionaries. The latter was frequently more important in community matters. Under the Pahlavis, each community elected an *anjoman* (council), which gradually assumed full political responsibility for the community, both internally and externally. The anjoman often preferred to defer action, whenever possible; its activities usually had little impact on most people. Group decisions are arrived at by consensus.

Social Control. *Ta'arof,* formal Iranian manners, based on honor exchange and mutual "offering" was traditionally a most important mechanism for regulating interpersonal relations; public opinion always influences behavior. Mediation is the most common means of settling disputes. Recourse to a Jewish court is a last resort. Use of state courts for resolution of intracommunal matters is considered reprehensible.

Conflict. Because Jews have rarely been treated equitably under the law, external conflict has never been handled well. Where possible, Jews maintain low visibility and rarely resort to violence, no matter the provocation.

Religion and Expressive Culture

Religious Beliefs and Practices. Iranian Jews follow the *mizrahi*, or oriental tradition of Jewish observance. Sephardic influence has affected the ritual tradition over the past 200 years, but practices remain locally and regionally distinctive from the Great Tradition. Judaism is very important for most Iranian Jews, although piety and observance varies inversely with assimilation. The *knisa*, "synagogue," is not only the most important community religious institution, but remains its primary social institution even in the current Iranian Jewish diaspora. Many men attend synagogue daily, and almost all do so on the Sabbath—Friday night to Saturday night. Holyday attendance is likewise high. Women participate less regularly. Rosh Hashanah and Yom Kippur are the most important holy days and are occasion for *ziyarat* ("pilgrimage") to the shrine of Serah bat Asher in the village of Lenjan, near Eşfahān. The other holy days are more specifically family- and home-oriented. Each community has numerous ritual functionaries, but few of them, aside from religious teachers, earn their primary income from this service. Observance of the *kashrut*, the dietary laws, and separation of spouses during and after menses, are the norm.

Arts. Jews have long been among the leading musical performers, dancers, and instrument makers. There are specialized ritual-art forms for local use and the tourist trade.

Medicine. Jews have been fortune-tellers, herbalists, bonemenders, midwives, and doctors. Some continue these traditional practices. Since the 1960s, many have become Western-trained doctors, dentists, nurses, and medical technicians.

Death and Afterlife. Death is an expected conclusion of life and an occasion for family solidarity. Burial takes place within twenty-four hours of death, and formalized wailing by females is ceremonially appropriate. Customary Jewish mourning rituals continue for a full year. Prayers are recited weekly on the day of the parent's death, special study occurs in the house of the deceased every Sabbath, and *yeshuva* ("sitting") is held, with study, prayer, and feasting in the house of the deceased on new moons and certain holy days. Death is thought to revisit susceptible households, so amulets are used to keep it away. Belief in spirits is common and similar to that among non-Jewish Iranians.

Bibliography

Loeb, Laurence (1977). *Outcaste: Jewish Life in Southern Iran*. New York, London, and Paris: Gordon & Breach.

Pliskin, Karen (1987). *Silent Boundaries: Cultural Constraints on Sickness and Diagnosis of Iranians in Israel*. New Haven: Yale University Press.

LAURENCE I. LOEB

Jews of Israel

ETHNONYMS: Yahudim (pl.), Yisraelim (pl.)

Orientation

Identification. The state of Israel came into formal existence on 14 May 1948. The United States recognized the new state on the same day, and the Soviet Union followed on 18 May. On 15 May 1948 the new state was invaded by the armies of Egypt, Iraq, Jordan, Syria, and Lebanon, along with smaller numbers of troops from other Arab countries. Hostilities continued until January 1949, when a cease-fire was negotiated. The boundaries determined by the cease-fire defined the state of Israel until the 1967 War (the "Six Day War"), when additional territories (East Jerusalem, the West Bank, the Golan Heights, and the Gaza Strip) came under Israeli control. On 11 May 1949 Israel was admitted to the United Nations as a member state.

Location. Israel is located in southwestern Asia, at the eastern end of the Mediterranean Sea, at approximate latitude 31°30′ N and longitude 35°00′ E. It is bounded on the north by Lebanon, on the northeast by Syria, on the east and southeast by Jordan (the Dead Sea and the Gulf of ʿAqaba), on the southwest by Egypt (the Sinai Peninsula), and on the west by the Mediterranean Sea. Pre-1967 Israel had an area of approximately 20,700 square kilometers (about the size of the state of New Jersey). The territories captured after the 1967 War total about 7,500 square kilometers, including East Jerusalem which, along with the Golan Heights, Israel has formally annexed. Geographically, Israel is divided into four regions: the coastal plain, the central highlands, the Jordan Rift Valley, and the Negev Desert. The highest point in Israel is at Mount Meron (1,208 meters), in the Galilee (the central highlands) near the city of Safad. The lowest point is at the Dead Sea (in the Jordan Rift Valley) which, at 399 meters below sea level, is the lowest point in the world. Israel, located between a subtropical arid zone to its south and a subtropical wet zone to its north, has a Mediterranean climate with short, cool, and rainy winters and long, hot, and dry summers. About 70 percent of the rainfall occurs between November and March, but it is unevenly distributed, diminishing sharply to the south. During January and February, precipitation may take the form of snow at the higher elevations (including Jerusalem). About a third of the country (areas receiving more than 30 centimeters of rainfall a year—the coastal plain, the Jezreel Valley, and the Galilee) is cultivable.

Demography. At the end of 1987, the total population of Israel was 4,389,600, of whom 82 percent (3,601,200) were Jews. (About 27 percent of the world's Jewish population lives in Israel.) The Jewish population in the late 1980s grew at the rate of about 1.4 percent (compared to about 3 percent for the non-Jewish population). With a median age of about 27.6 (1986), the Jewish population is relatively young, but not so compared to Muslims (whose median age in the same year was 16.8). The Jewish population is skewed in age toward the very young and the very old; a relatively small percentage is in the 35–50 age group. This skewing is because of the effects of large-scale immigration in forming the Jewish population of Israel. Between 1948 and 1960, immigration accounted for almost 70 percent of the annual average population-growth rate. Many of these immigrants were older, and those who were younger were often single people who deferred marriage and child rearing until after their settlement.

Linguistic Affiliation. Hebrew is the major official language of Israel and the predominant language of Israel's Jews. Arabic is spoken by Israel's Arab minority, most of whom are bilingual in Hebrew as well. Arabic is also an official language and may be used in courts and the parliament (Knesset). The successful revival of Hebrew as a modern, spoken, and "living" language, a major thrust of the Zionist cultural program, was one of its major accomplishments. Nevertheless, because so many in the population are immigrants, many other languages are spoken by Jews, especially older people or recent immigrants. These include Arabic (or dialects of Judeo-Arabic), Yiddish, Ladino, Persian, English, Russian, French, Spanish, and other European, African (e.g., Amharic) and Asian (e.g., Malayalam, of Cochin, India) languages.

History and Cultural Relations

The connection of the Jewish people to the land called "Palestine" by the Romans is one of the oldest religio-political claims in the world. Jews (and many Christians as well) will point to God's promise to Abraham in Genesis 15:17 and Deuteronomy 1:7 and 11:24 as proof of the sacred "birthright" of Jews to what they call the Land of Israel (Eretz Yisrael). Jewish presence in Palestine has been constant (if very small in number), even after the final Roman suppression of the Jewish revolt in 135 C.E. Throughout premodern times, pious Jews lived in Palestine, concentrated in the four "holy cities" of Jerusalem, Hebron, Safad, and Tiberias. They were supported by funds, called *halukkah,* collected by special emissaries sent from Palestine to Jewish diaspora communities.

The history of modern Israel, however, begins in the nineteenth century with the articulation in Europe of a program for Jewish national and cultural revival, called Zionism ("Zion" being one of the biblical names for Jerusalem). Zionism was a reaction to virulent and increasingly violent European anti-Semitism (which culminated in the terrible Holocaust of 1933–1945), but it was also a response to the nationalist movements of other, especially eastern and southern, European peoples throughout the nineteenth century. Zionism stressed the physical relocation of Jews to Palestine (in Hebrew, Aliya), and in 1882 the first wave of these "modern" immigrants—politically and ideologically, rather than religiously, motivated—arrived. This first wave effectively doubled the Jewish population of Palestine (from about 24,000 in 1881). Immigration continued to come in waves, mostly from eastern and central Europe, until the eve of World War II. Immigration was greatly curtailed by the war and, later, by restrictive British policies (Palestine had been a British Mandate since 1919), which sought to assuage Arab fears, which were based on the fact that, by early 1948, the Jews had succeeded in establishing a society in Palestine (called the Yishuv) that was in many ways autonomous and independent of both Arab society and British colonial constraints and that had many of the institutions of a state already in place. On the day Israel declared its independence, there were about 650,000 Jews in the country. Virtually the first act of the new government was to open its borders to unrestricted Jewish immigration. There was a massive influx between 1948 and 1960 from Middle Eastern and North African countries—almost the entire Jewish populations of Yemen, Aden, Libya, and Iraq, and large numbers from Egypt, Syria, Morocco, and Tunisia. Today these so-called "Oriental" (Afro-Asian) Jews and their children constitute the majority of the Jewish Israeli population, outnumbering Jews of European and North American origin. Nevertheless, it was not until 1975 that native-born Jewish Israelis (called "sabras") outnumbered immigrants of any kind.

Settlements

The Jewish population of Israel is overwhelmingly urban (about 90 percent), concentrated along the Mediterranean coast and in the three major cities—Tel Aviv, Jerusalem, and Haifa. About twenty-seven smaller cities called "development towns" were planned by the government, starting in the mid-1950s, as ways to settle large numbers of Oriental Jews, promote light industry, and disperse the population from the coastal strip. Today these areas, among the poorest Jewish areas in Israel, are sites of ethnic unrest. Of the small proportion of Jews who reside in rural areas, the majority live in collective (kibbutz) and cooperative (moshav) communities. The kibbutz, especially, is known worldwide as a distinctive Israeli institution whose members (*kibbutznikim*) historically have played a significant role in Israeli society. Nevertheless, today only about 3.5 percent of Israeli Jews live on the kibbutzim and 4.5 percent on the moshavim.

Economy

Subsistence and Commercial Activities. Israel's economy in the past was influenced heavily by the centralized and socialist tendencies of the Labor governments that ruled the country between 1948 and 1977. Between 1977 and 1992, Likud-led governments favored privatization of enterprises and limitations on the large public sector. Labor was returned to power in 1992.

Industrial Arts. The importance of Israel's industrial sector has continued to grow (proportional to agricultural production), and by the early 1980s industrial exports accounted for close to two-thirds of total exports. Tourism remains a major source of employment and foreign exchange.

Trade. Israel's merchant marine (numbering about 100 ships) is vital both to its economy and, given hostile relations with surrounding Arab countries, its sense of security. Israel's small size, lack of natural resources (particularly petroleum and water), and heavy commitments to defense expenditures have constituted obstacles to sustaining economic growth, and the country has become increasingly dependent on foreign inflows of capital, especially foreign aid from the United States.

Division of Labor. About 40 percent of the Jewish civilian labor force is female. The other great division of labor is between Jews and Arabs, with the latter concentrated in construction and agriculture. Occupational differences are also evident between Jews of Afro-Asian origins ("Orientals") and those of Euro-American descent (called "Ashkenazim"): about 65 percent of all Ashkenazim are concentrated in white-collar professions, whereas about 55 percent of Oriental Jews are concentrated in blue-collar occupations.

Land Tenure. Most of the land in Israel is owned by the state or state-sponsored institutions and is conceived as held "in trust" on behalf of the entire Jewish people.

Kinship

Kin Groups and Descent. Extended kin groups based on descent are not important among Jewish Israelis. Kinship is bilateral, and the nuclear family is its most important unit. Remnants of other patterns—for example, patronymic kin groups (*hamula*, pl. *hamulot*)—can be found in some moshav communities settled by North African Jews.

Kinship Terminology. Kin terms conform to Western (cognatic) systems, translated appropriately into Hebrew.

Marriage and Family

Marriage. The median age of marriage in 1986 for Jewish men was 26.4, for women 23.1. (Many men defer marriage until after their mandatory service in the Israel Defense Forces.) The age is considerably younger among ultra-Orthodox Jews, who are effectively exempted from army service, and for whom the biblical injunction to "be fruitful and multiply" is very important.

Domestic Unit. The nuclear family is the main domestic unit. The average family size is 4.7 among Jews of Oriental origin, versus 2.8 for Ashkenazim.

Inheritance. Inheritance, like all matters of personal-status law in Israel, falls for Jews under the jurisdiction of rabbinical courts that apply (sometimes controversially) rabbinic law (*halakha*).

Socialization. Education in Israel is free and compulsory through tenth grade, tuition in high school (since reforms in 1984) has been set at about U.S.$10 monthly. Preschool is available to children between ages 3 and 6 and (given the high percentage of working women) is widely used. Education is sharply divided into three separate tracts: state-supported secular schools (about 72 percent of primary-school students), state-supported religious systems (about 22 percent), and a number of traditional, private religious schools (the yeshivas, or Talmudic academies) that cater to the ultra-Orthodox. These enroll about 6 percent of primary-school students. For the vast majority of Israel's Jews, service in the Israeli army is a crucial part of their transition to adulthood.

Sociopolitical Organization

Social Organization. The key to Israeli Jewish social organization is the fact that Israel is overwhelmingly a nation of immigrants, who, despite their common identity as Jews, come from very diverse social and cultural backgrounds. The goals of Zionism included the "fusion of the Exiles" (as Diaspora Jews were called), and although great strides toward this fusion have occurred—the revival of Hebrew has been mentioned—it has not, on the whole, been achieved. The immigrant groups of the 1950s and 1960s are the ethnic groups of today. The most important ethnic division is that between Jews of European and North American background, called "Ashkenazim" (after the old Hebrew name for Germany) and those of African and Asian origins, called "Sephardim" (after the old Hebrew name for Spain, and referring technically to Jews of the Mediterranean and Aegean) or "Orientals" (in modern Hebrew *edot hamizrach;* lit., "communities of the East"). The problem, as most Israelis see it, is not the existence of Jewish ethnic divisions per se, but the fact that they have become linked over the years to differences in class, occupation, and standard of living, with Oriental Jews concentrated in the lower strata of society.

Political Organization. Israeli is a parliamentary democracy. The whole nation acts as a single constituency to elect a 120-member parliament (the Knesset). Political parties put forth lists of candidates, and Israelis vote for the list, rather than individual candidates on it. A party's representation in the Knesset is based on the proportion of the vote it receives. Any party receiving at least 1 percent of the national vote is entitled to a seat in the Knesset. The majority party is asked by the president (the nominal head of state, chosen by the Knesset to serve a five-year term) to name a prime minister and form a government. This system entails coalition formation, and means there are many small political parties, representing all shades of political and ideological opinion, that play a disproportionate role in any government.

Social Control. There is a single national police force and an independent, paramilitary, border police. National security is considered a top priority in Israel and, within the country, is the responsibility of an organization called the Shin Bet. The Israeli army has enforced social control in the Territories, particularly after the Palestinian uprising (*intifada*) of December 1987. This new role for the army has been very controversial within Israel.

Conflict. Israeli society is characterized by three deep cleavages, all of which have entailed conflict. In addition to the cleavage between Ashkenazim and Oriental Jews, and the deeper one between Jews and Arabs, there is a division in the society between secular Jews, the Orthodox, and the ultra-Orthodox. This last division cuts across Jewish ethnic lines.

Religion and Expressive Culture

Religious Beliefs. Judaism is the dominant religion, although the majority (about two-thirds to three-fourths) of Israeli Jews are nonobservant. There are ritual and liturgical (and, some claim, stylistic and emotional) differences between Ashkenazi and Sephardi traditions.

Religious Practitioners. Rabbis are the predominant Jewish religious practitioners. Religious-court judges serve as state civil servants. There is a Ministry for Religious Affairs and a Chief Rabbinate, the latter divided into Ashkenazi and Sephardi offices.

Ceremonies. All of the holidays of the Jewish religious calendar are celebrated in Israel. Some ethnic festivals (e.g., the North African Mimouna) are also celebrated, and some national holidays—for example, Israeli Independence Day (Yom Haatzma'ut) and Remembrance Day—are given a semisacred status.

Arts. Both the "high arts" (classical music, dance, theater, and literature) and folk arts (dance, especially) are highly extolled.

Medicine. Good medical care is widely available, and medical insurance (*kupat holim*) covers virtually all Israelis.

Death and Afterlife. Traditional Jewish death rites are simple. At the grave site, a kaddish is said; on various occasions from then on it will be repeated by close relatives to memorialize the deceased. A seven-day full mourning period (*shivah*) follows. (Lesser mourning lasts thirty days, a full year for one's parents.) The anniversary of the death (*yahrzeit*) is celebrated by close relatives. The soul (*nefesh*) of the deceased is thought to return to God.

Bibliography

Avruch, Kevin (1981). *American Immigrants in Israel: Social Identities and Change*. Chicago: University of Chicago Press.

Deshen, Shlomo, and Moshe Shokeid (1974). *The Predicament of Homecoming: Cultural and Social Life of North African Immigrants in Israel*. Ithaca, N.Y.: Cornell University Press.

Elazar, Daniel (1986). *Israel: Building a New Society*. Bloomington: Indiana University Press.

Spiro, Milford E. (1970). *Kibbutz: Venture in Utopia*. Cambridge: Harvard University Press.

Weingrod, Alex, ed. (1985). *Studies in Israeli Ethnicity*. New York: Gordon & Breach.

KEVIN AVRUCH

Jews of Kurdistan

ETHNONYMS: In Kurdistan: Hōzāyē (by the Jews themselves), Hūdāyē (by the Christians), Juhū (by the Kurds); in Israel: Kurdim.

Orientation

Identification. Kurdish Jews, a largely rural people, have lived in the mountains and plains of Kurdistan since time immemorial. They have been geographically isolated throughout much of their history and are thought to have retained some old Jewish traditions. Their Neo-Aramaic language is a survival of old Aramaic, which was the dominant language in the Middle East before being gradually superseded by Arabic after the Islamic conquest of the area during the seventh century A.D. Most of the Kurdish Jews emigrated to Israel during 1950–1951.

Location. Kurdistan is a geographic-ethnic term referring to a large territory (about 960 kilometers long and 190 to 240 kilometers wide) in central Southwest Asia, divided at present among Iraq, Turkey, and Iran. The Kurds are a nation without a politically recognized homeland (in spite of their continuous struggle for centuries to have one). Kurdistan consists mostly of a rugged chain of mountains, with the exception of some lowland areas on the fringes. The climate is characterized by heavy snows during the winter, followed by spring rains and heavy runoff down the slopes, creating rapid torrents and swollen rivers. This combination of rugged terrain and harsh weather makes the region an inaccessible and almost impregnable fortress. Hence, day-to-day control by remote governments has always been tenuous at best. Kurdistan has consequently served as a refuge for various religiously and politically dissident groups throughout the ages.

Demography. At present there are about 2,400,000 Kurds in Turkey, 2,200,000 in Iraq, 2,000,000 in Iran, and smaller numbers in Syria and Russia. The total number of Jews in Kurdistan, before the mass emigration to Israel, was about 25,000, sparsely scattered in about 200 villages and little towns. Their number in Israel (including those born there) today is estimated at 100,000. Because of their strong sentiment for Jerusalem, many live there or in the nearby villages. Others have settled in rural areas near Haifa, the Jordan Valley, and the Lakhish region.

Linguistic Affiliation. The Muslim Kurds speak Kurdish, an Indo-Iranian language that has several regional dialects. Most Christians and Jews speak various Aramaic dialects containing many Kurdish, Persian, Turkish, and Arabic loanwords. The Jewish dialects also include many Hebrew loanwords. Because the topography and climate make travel and communication very difficult, almost every village and town had its own dialect. Wherever there was a Jewish community, there was usually a distinctive Jewish dialect, as well as a Christian one, which were, however, mutually intelligible. The farther two places were from each other, the less mutually intelligible their dialects would be. Practically all the Jewish men and many women also spoke Kurdish, which they used when talking with Kurds at the marketplace and during other social and commercial encounters. Kurdish was also the language of folk songs and other types of folklore traditions.

Hebrew was the language of recitation for religious rituals, blessings, and prayers. The learned men also used Hebrew for their traditional forms of writing, including personal correspondence. Hebrew expressions were used by Jews engaged in commerce as a secret in-group language when they did not want the Gentiles to understand. Arabic was used only for official purposes or when talking with nomadic Arabs. Many Jews in the larger towns, however, have shifted from Aramaic to Arabic (in Iraq), Persian (in Iran), and Turkish (in Turkey).

History and Cultural Relations

According to their oral tradition, Kurdish Jews are the descendants of the Jews exiled from Israel and Judea by the Assyrian kings (2 Kings 17:6). Several scholars who have studied the Jews of Kurdistan tend to consider this tradition at least partly valid, and one may safely assume that the Kurdish Jews include, among others, some descendants of the ancient Jewish exiles, the so-called Lost Ten Tribes. Christianity was successful in this area, partly because it was inhabited by Jews. Christianity, which usually spread in existing Jewish communities, was accepted in this region without difficulty. The first substantial evidence of Jewish settlements in Kurdistan is found in the reports of two Jewish travelers to Kurdistan in the twelfth century. Their accounts indicate the existence of a large, well-established, and prosperous Jewish community in the area. It seems that, as a result of persecutions and the fear of approaching Crusaders, many Jews from Syria-Palestine had fled to Babylonia and Kurdistan. The Jews of Mosul, the largest town, with a Jewish population of about 7,000, enjoyed some degree of autonomy, and the local exilarch (community leader) had his own jail. Of the taxes paid by the Jews, half were given to him and half to the (non-Jewish) governor. One account concerns David Alroy, the messianic leader from Kurdistan who rebelled, albeit unsuccessfully, against the king of Persia and planned to redeem the Jews from exile and lead them to Jerusalem.

Stability and prosperity, however, did not last long. The reports of later travelers, as well as local documents and manuscripts, indicate that Kurdistan, except for some short periods, suffered grievously from armed conflicts between the central government in Turkey and the local tribal chieftains. As a result, the Muslim, as well as Jewish and Christian populations declined. Many localities that had earlier been reported to have large Jewish populations were reduced to a few families, or none at all. The U.S. missionary Asahel Grant visited the once important town of Amadiya in 1839. He found hardly any inhabitants: only 250 of 1,000 houses were occupied; the rest were demolished or uninhabitable. In more recent times, Amadiya has had only about 400 Jews. Nerwa, once an important Jewish center, was set on fire by an irate chieftain just before the outbreak of World War I, destroying, among other things, the synagogues and all the Torah scrolls therein. As a result, with the exception of three families, all the Jews fled the town and wandered off to other places, such as Mosul and Zakho. In modern times, the latter has been one of the few places in Kurdistan proper with a substantial Jewish population (about 5,000 in 1945).

Kurdistan is a unique synthesis of several cultures and ethnic groups. In the past, it bordered the great Assyrian-Babylonian and Hittite empires; later it adjoined Persian, Arabic, and Turkish civilizations. Kurdistan embraces a great variety of sects, ethnic groups, and nationalities. Apart from the Kurdish tribes (mostly Sunni Muslims, and the rest Shiites) that form most of the population, there are various Muslim Arab and Turkish tribes, Christians of various denominations (Assyrians, Armenians, Nestorians, Jacobites), as well as Yazidis (followers of an ancient Kurdistani religion), Mandeans (a Gnostic sect), and Jews. The Jews had—albeit at times quite limited—cultural ties with the Jews of the larger urban centers of Iraq (Mosul, Baghdad), Iran, and Turkey, and especially with the Land of Israel (Palestine). Many Kurdish Jews had relatives who sought employment in the larger urban centers. Individuals, families, and sometimes all the residents of a village had been emigrating to the Land of Israel since the beginning of the twentieth century. These trickles culminated in the mass emigration of the entire Jewish community of Iraqi Kurdistan to Israel during 1950—1951.

Economy

In general, living conditions were quite meager and unstable. Many of the Kurdish Jews were farmers, shepherds, rafters, and loggers—occupations almost unknown in other Jewish communities in the East or West. In past centuries, there were more villages populated entirely by Jews than there were later; some villages remained entirely Jewish until the mass emigration to Israel. In larger centers, Jews traded in grain, cotton, wool, furs, cattle, gum, gullnuts (from which ink was made), sesame, dried fruits, and tobacco. Many had vineyards and orchards. Jewish artisans included weavers, dyers, shoemakers, tailors, and a few silversmiths and goldsmiths. In the twentieth century, for security reasons and owing to improvements of transportation (e.g., the use of motorized vehicles), many Jews (as well as others) gradually left the villages and the hardships of farming. Moving to urban centers, they looked for an easier life as shopkeepers, merchants, and butchers. The towns, with their large synagogues and numerous religious functionaries, were more suited to Jewish life and provided greater security against attacks by nomadic tribes and brigands, as well as relief from the natural calamities of the rugged areas. A common sight in the larger towns, such as Zakho, were poor peddlers traveling in companies of two or more, riding donkeys and mules and selling certain groceries (e.g., tea and sugar) and notions (e.g., needles, buttons, and thread). This occupation was extremely dangerous because their routes were often infested with robbers; many lives were lost at the hands of Kurdish brigands. Another dangerous occupation among the poor was rafting and logging. About seventy families in Zakho made a meager living from transporting logs, used for construction and carpentry, on the torrential rivers. Other common skills were spinning (done mostly by women), weaving of light rugs and clothing, and dyeing of woolens. Weaving was common in the urban centers as well as the rural areas. In general, the occupations of the Kurdish Jews were typical of a rural or small-town society, and, therefore, few wealthy merchants were found among them. Money in general was scarce in Kurdistan, and so were items of luxury. Much of the trading was by way of barter—for example, shoes could be exchanged for chickens, notions for farm produce. Some Kurdish Jews, after their emigration to Israel, continued to work as farmers in rural areas around Jerusalem and the Jordan Valley. Of those who settled in the cities, principally Jerusalem, many women worked as maids, and most men worked first at hard manual labor, as porters, masons, and stonecutters. A few who started as common laborers in the building trade are now among the wealthiest people in Israel; they own luxurious hotels, restaurants, and supermarkets. Much of the construction business in Jerusalem was—and still is—dominated by Kurdish Jews. Some have become prominent in the Israeli army or have become high government officials or members of city councils.

Kinship, Marriage, and Family

The Kurds are a distinct, non-Arab ethnic group, mostly Sunni Muslims, with their own language, customs, dress, and ways of life. Originally the Kurds formed a mostly rural society. Traditional tribal villages included nomadic or seminomadic groups, but an increasing number of Kurds now live also in towns and work at various urban trades. Yet most Kurds, urban and rural alike, still associate themselves with specific tribal groupings. Throughout Kurdistan, marriage between cousins, or at least within the tribal clan, is preferred, and marriage with the father's brother's daughter is regarded as ideal. Such marriages are, nevertheless, accompanied by the payment of a bride-price (a substantial sum of money) to the father of the bride. These customs were prevalent among the Kurdish Jews as well. Such marriages assured the strengthening of kinship ties and the obedience of the bride to her husband and her mother-in-law, who was the "boss" in the extended family, in which all lived under the same roof. In the case of rich families, it kept the family's wealth within the family. It was usually beneficial for the bride as well: she did not have to wander to another tribe or village, and, as a relative, she was treated kindly and favorably. She stayed close to her parents and her previous home, which was an important moral support for young brides, who were often married at the age of 15 to 16, sometimes to much older husbands. Monogamy was the common norm, although some practiced polygamy. Soon after the wedding, the new bride had to be quickly "incorporated" into a very busy joint-family household, succumbing to endless chores and hard work. She was expected to bear a child, preferably a son, during each of her fertile years. There was a high rate of child mortality, however, and the chances of survival for the newborn were about fifty-fifty. Even though Kurdish society is patriarchal and patrilineal ties are very important, Kurdish women enjoy more freedom and a wider participation in public life than do rural Arab, Persian, and Turkish women. Kurdish women are also freer in their behavior toward males and rarely wear the veil, which is commonly worn by women in the Muslim world.

Religion and Expressive Culture

Religious Beliefs and Practices. The level of spiritual life in any society depends largely upon its physical security, economic conditions, population size, and communication, as well as contact with other societies. In the case of the Jews of Kurdistan, all these factors are mostly negative. Life in the area was often precarious. It was common for population remnants to migrate from place to place because of natural disasters (floods, plagues) and destruction or devastation by tribal chieftains. The Jewish population in any one locality would often dwindle from several hundred or several thousand to a few families. Yet, during some short, less troubled periods of relative security, a few centers of learning did flourish. The Kurdish Jews, as in any traditional rural society, were deeply religious, observing what they knew of Jewish law quite strictly. Although many could not read Hebrew prayers, almost everyone attended services in the synagogue, not only on the Sabbath and Jewish holidays, but also on weekdays. All Jewish holidays were observed and celebrated with great joy. In spite of the general preoccupation with daily routine practices, the moral principles and customs of Judaism were learned as well, being transmitted orally from generation to generation, often through the sermons in the synagogue. The sermon played a most important role in the religious and national edification of isolated communities such as Kurdistan, where books were rare and the rate of illiteracy was high. The sermon included tales and legends of the life and deeds of the patriarchs, ancient kings and heroes, prophets and rabbis, mystics, and ordinary pious men and women, all carefully selected to fit the particular audience. The legends were not only fascinating in themselves but also taught ethical principles, repentance for misconduct, and steadfast devotion to the faith of the fathers. The miracles and salvations so often mentioned in these sermons gave the Jewish community much comfort, as well as strength to endure the hardships of daily life in exile and to maintain hope of redemption and the coming of the Messiah. The ties to the Land of Israel, the land of their roots, were indicated in religious literature and in various customs, for example, the attributing of biblical names to localities in Kurdistan (e.g., Ekron, for the local town of Aqra and calling Zakho "the Jerusalem of Kurdistan"). All Jewish dead were placed in their graves with their feet facing in the direction of Jerusalem, probably to hasten their arrival there on the Day of Resurrection. The religious practices of the Kurdish Jews included, in common with other Middle Eastern and North African Jewish and non-Jewish communities, the visitation and veneration of local shrines or tombs assumed to be the burial grounds of holy persons.

Medicine. The shrines were visited in groups or by individuals, such as barren women or parents of paralyzed children, who beseeched the holy men to intercede on their behalf and cure their illnesses. A variety of amulets prepared by living mystics were used for healing all sorts of psychological-physical aliments or for restoring love relations, such as in the case of a wife who was no longer loved by her husband. Popular folk medicine included bloodletting by razor cuts on the back, the application of leeches, and the preparation of herbal drinks and homemade creams.

Handicrafts and Oral Arts. Like those of other rural societies, the arts of the Kurdish Jews were mostly practical crafts: weaving various types of carpets, producing woolen textiles, and knitting items such as socks, gloves and hats, silk-embroidered scarfs, and handkerchiefs. People who could not afford to buy new clothes would simply dye the old ones in strong, bright colors such as indigo and crimson, to give them a new look. A few people were gold- and silversmiths. During weddings and others festivities, women wore gold or silver jewelry, such as nose- and earrings, necklaces, and hand and foot bracelets with little bells. Small children wore various types of silver pendants, some with Hebrew inscriptions, as well as little gold and silver bells, to protect them from the evil eye and evil spirits. At celebration times, men would wear fine woolen baggy suits, a very elaborate headdress, and belts with daggers in silver-decorated sheaths. Some old men had very fancy smoking pipe with long tubes.

A few men and women excelled in the oral arts of storytelling and singing. The rich oral folk literature provided the most popular pastime for Kurdish Jews. Some of the best narrators of these Kurdish tales were Jewish, and they were sought after by Jews and Muslims alike. The general content of the stories was often well known to the audience, but an artistic narrator could captivate his listeners again and again. The storyteller made the story come to life by gesticulating and making facial expressions, by changing voices, and by producing sound effects, such as the fast running of a gazelle or the galloping of a horse. The stories varied in length and in subject matter—from serious heroic adventures or misfortunes, tragic love stories, and imaginative moralistic tales to humorous, erotic, supernatural, and entertaining anecdotes. Sometimes the narration would extend over several long winter nights—the narrator always stopping at a critical point to leave the audience in suspense until the next evening. Singing was common during work (especially during group work such as wheat grinding), at celebrations, and during mourning periods. Women excelled as chanters at funerals, moving mourners to loud weeping. Those with pleasant "professional" voices sang for an audience, but almost everyone sang anywhere—walking down a street or when alone in the countryside. Singing was usually unaccompanied by musical instruments, except during wedding celebrations and other occasions for dancing, in which cases a wooden flute and a large kettle drum were played.

Bibliography

Ben-Jacob, Abraham (1972). "Kurdistan." In *Encyclopaedia Judaica*. Vol. 10, 1295–1301. Jerusalem: Keter.

Bois, Th. (1981). "Kurds, Kurdistan." In *Encyclopedia of Islam*. New ed. Vol. 5, 438–486.

Sabar, Yona (1982). *The Folk Literature of the Kurdistani Jews: An Anthology*. New Haven: Yale University Press.

YONA SABAR

Jews of the Middle East

ETHNONYMS: Jews of Islam, Oriental Jews

Orientation

Prior to 1948, Jewish communties were found discontinuously in an area stretching from southwest Asia across North Africa, from Tajikistan and Uzbekistan in the north to Yemen in the south, and from Afghanistan in the east to Morocco in the west. The label "Oriental Jews" is sometimes applied to Jews in this region, although it also includes Jews of India. The label "Jews of Islam" is also used, but some communities exist in regions where Christianity is the dominant religion, such as in Soviet Georgia. Obviously, when applied to Jewish communities, the term "Middle East" applies to lands not generally thought of as Middle Eastern, such as Uzbekistan. In general, in the Middle East and elsewhere, Jewish cultures can be viewed as both subcultures within a larger "Jewish civilization" and as minority groups in the society where they live.

Of the various criteria used by anthropologists to delineate culture-bearing units, four apply to the Jews of the Middle East: religion, region, language, and economic-ecological position.

Religion

Traditionally, people identified as Jews were those who adhered to the laws of the Pentateuch, as revealed by Moses, and who retained and read the Scriptures in Hebrew. They saw themselves as the descendants of the Hebrew patriarchs; even those who converted to Judaism were symbolically inducted into the family of Abraham, Isaac, and Jacob. In the twentieth century there are several groups who still define themselves in this way. One of these is the Samaritans, few in number (152 in 1901; 430 in 1970) who live in Nablus on the West Bank of the Jordan River and in Holon, Israel. Technically, they are not Jews, albeit Israelites, as the Samaritan Canon of Scriptures accepts only the Pentateuch and the Books of Joshua and Judges as divinely revealed, and they continue to practice animal sacrifice at Passover.

The Jews, in the sense of those who accept the full Hebrew Scriptures or Old Testament, include the Beta Israel of Ethiopia, who may have become isolated before the full crystallization of postbiblical Judaism, the Rabbinites, and the Karaites (Qaraites). These latter two groups can be understood only in relation to one another. The Rabbinites, who include the overwhelming majority of Jews in the world today, trace themselves back to the Pharisees of Judea, during the Maccabeean and Roman periods. The Pharisees and their successors developed a tradition of the interpretation of the laws of Moses, which became codified in the Talmudic literature. Many features of contemporary Judaism stem from this branch of Judaism including, among others, the substitution of fines and payment of compensation for body mutilation to enforce the *lex talionis*, lighting of candles to begin the Sabbath and holidays, the Seder ceremony to mark Passover, keeping Sabbath dishes warm, the Hebrew prayer book, and Talmudic study and argumentation.

During the seventh and eight centuries A.D., those who argued that the Pharisaic-Rabbinic interpretation constituted a deviation from revealed Scripture formed a sect called the "Karaites" ("Scriptualists"). In the twentieth century Karaites lived in Lithuania, Crimea, and Egypt, although most of those in Egypt have emigrated to Israel or North America. In Egypt in particular, there was much contact between the Karaite and Rabbinite Jews, whereas relations between the two groups in czarist Russia were marked by tension, hostility, and social distance. Unless otherwise noted, the remainder of this article pertains only to Rabbinite Jews.

During the twentieth century, Rabbinite Jews have been divided into two groups: those who attempt to adhere to traditional beliefs and practices (traditionalists, Orthodox, orthopraxic) and those who, as "moderns," no longer accept the Torah (the laws of Moses) as divinely revealed. In both Israel and North America, the latter are the majority, either alone or when counted in combination with individuals who do not observe the tradition strictly, regardless of their beliefs.

Region

Cultural differences between rural and urban, coastal and oasis communities (as well as along other parameters) differentiate Jewish groups from one another. Jews living in rural areas share many characteristics with Jews from other rural areas, as do Jews from different cities or those who reside along different trade routes.

Certain ritual differences can be understood in terms of regional differences. The differences between the "native" residents of a particular city and new immigrants are sometimes marked by the continued use of certain rituals by one group or the other. For example, during the Middle Ages the Rabbinites in Cairo were divided by use of either an Iraqi synagogue, later frequented by Jews from Spain, or use of the Palestinian synagogue, which was also used by North African sojourners and immigrants. Similarily, Jewish families in Aleppo, Syria, know if they are of Sephardic origin or of Mustarib origin.

The distinction between Sephardim and Ashkenazim is similar. The groups each recognize the other as legitimately Jewish, while noting cultural differences resulting from the disparate locations of the original groups. The Sephardim had lived on the Iberian Peninsula, which medieval Jews called "Sephard," whereas Ashkenazim had lived in Germany, called "Ashkenaz" in medieval times. The differences between the two groups came to involve liturgical matters, language (both the domestic language and the pronunciation of Hebrew), and the interpretation of laws. For example, the order of prayers in the prayerbooks varied slightly; Ashkenazim, but not Sepahardim, generally prohibited polygynous marriage and the levirate; and the Passover diet was more restricted for the Ashkenazim than for most Sephardim.

Because of the dissemination of Sephardic publications, most Jews in the Middle East came to use the Sephardic prayer book and to follow the Sephardic interpretation of the laws, contained in Joseph Karo's *Shulhan Arukh*. Thus, these Jews have often been classified as Sephardim, whether or not their ancestors actually lived in Spain.

Language

Jewish groups can be differentiated from each other and from non-Jewish groups by linguistic criteria. In some places, Jews spoke a domestic language different from that of their neighbors. Everywhere in the Middle East and Europe, Hebrew was used by Jews in prayer and for internal legal matters and sometimes for literature, usually religious, but sometimes secular as well. Aramaic, the language of the Talmud, was used for sacred purposes. Hebrew was an important source of words for jargons and argots, even among the uneducated. Until modern times, Jews wrote using Hebrew characters, whether they were writing in Yiddish, Judeo-Spanish, Arabic, Aramaic, or Persian.

In Arab and Persian lands (including parts of Afghanistan and Central Asia), Jews generally spoke dialects intelligible to the coresident populations, but in the Balkans and Anatolia, as well as in Kurdistan and Azerbaijan, Jews spoke a distinct domestic language.

Classification of Jewish populations by domestic language (the language used for day-to-day affairs) provides a convenient taxonomy of groups.

Yiddish, the Germanic language used by East European Jews, was spoken by Eastern European Jews in Palestine. Although now replaced largely by Hebrew, some ultraconsevative Jews in Israel continue to use it.

Ladino (also called "Judezmo" and "Hakatia") is the Judeo-Spanish language spoken by Jews in the Balkans, Anatolia, and northern Morocco and by their descendants in Palestine/Israel and Egypt. In the Balkans, there are also communities of Romaniot Jews who still use a Jewish dialect of Greek.

In North Africa, the countries of the Fertile Crescent, and Yemen, Jews spoke various dialects of Arabic. The extent to which these dialects should be classified as Judeo-Arabic varies from place to place.

Aramaic (also called "Syriac") was the dominant language in the Fertile Crescent (except for Egypt) from the sixth century B.C. until the seventh to eight centuries A.D., when it was superseded by Arabic. Forms of Aramaic are still used in a few small Christian groups such as the Nestorians and Jacobites, as well as by their Jewish neighbors in Kurdistan and Azerbaijan. Jews call this language either Targum or Jebali. Muslims in these areas speak either Turkic or Indo-European languages.

Persian (variously called "Farsi," "Dadi," "Tat," or "Tajik") is spoken by the Jews of Iran, Afghanistan, Tajikistan, Uzbekistan, and Daghestan. In Soviet Central Asia, Jews tended to adopt the Russian culture earlier than their Muslim neighbors.

Georgian (Gruzini), the language of Soviet Georgia, is spoken by Jews in and from that region.

Finally, it is likely that some small Jewish communities adopted languages other than these from their neighbors.

Economic-Ecological Position

In the Middle East, Jews were generally differentiated from their neighbors by partial or full occupational specialization. Some rural Jews were cultivators, but many Jews—even in rural areas—were engaged in other occupations, although other groups might also be involved in this same work. For example, in the Middle Ages, Jews as well as other peoples were traders and artisans, and, in modern times, both Jews and Armenians have specialized in the working of precious metals. Thus, whereas Jewish communities might be associated with a particular occupation or trade, it does not mean that they alone engaged in that activitity. Still, some Jewish communities were marked by a trend toward occupational uniformity, exhibited by the silversmiths of Habban in South Yemen or the residents in a weaver's village near the northern Yemeni coast. These occupational roles had important implications for community life. For example, in communities where Jewish men specialized in itinerant occupations—such as peddling or rural artisanry—the men often had to spend much time apart from their wives and families.

Bibliography

Cohen, Hayyim J. (1973). *The Jews of the Middle East, 1960–1972*. Jerusalem: Keter.

Deshen, Shlomo, and Walter P. Zenner, eds. (1982). *Jewish Societies in the Middle East*. Lanham, Md.: University Press of America.

Encyclopaedia Judaica (1972). Jerusalem: Keter.

Zenner, Walter P. (1978). "Jewish Communities as Cultural Units." In *Community, Self, and Identity*, edited by B. Misra and J. Preston, 161–172. The Hague: Mouton.

Zenner, Walter P. (1982). "The Jewish Diaspora and the Middleman Adaptation." In *Diaspora: Exile and the Jewish Condition*, edited by E. Levine, 141–156. New York: Jason Aronson.

WALTER P. ZENNER

Jews of Yemen

ETHNONYMS: Teymanim, Yehudei Teyman

Orientation

Identification and Location. Jews have lived in Yemen, a large and rugged country in the southwest part of the Arabian Peninsula, for at least 1,500 years. They identify themselves and are identified by others, as part of the widespread Jewish people. They maintained their specifically Jewish culture, based on the books, practices, beliefs, worship, and lore of Judaism. This is what distinguished them as a separate people from their Muslim Arab neighbors for so many centuries.

Demography. At the end of the nineteenth century, there may have been 60,000 Jews living in Yemen, but as of 1881 a movement began among them to emigrate to Palestine (which they called the "Holy Land" and the "Land of Israel" or the "Land of Zion"). In 1949–1950 almost all the remaining Jews of Yemen, about 49,000, left Yemen for Israel, leaving only a few hundred. Today there may be more than 2,000 Jews in Yemen, but over 165,000 in Israel trace their roots to Yemen.

Linguistic Affiliation. In Yemen, Jews spoke Arabic, but Jewish men knew how to read and write Hebrew and used it primarily as a language for religious worship and study. Today, in Israel, they speak only Hebrew. (Both Arabic and Hebrew belong to the Semitic Group of languages, of the larger Afro-Asian Language Family.)

History and Cultural Relations

It is not clear when the Jews first settled in southwestern Arabia, but they were certainly there by the sixth century of the Christian era. They comprise part of the Jewish dispersion (diaspora) from ancient Palestine (the Land of Israel) after the Roman conquest and may have been settlers derived directly from there or more indirectly from Babylonia (Iraq) and Egypt. Local converts may have augmented their numbers. Although geographically and socially remote from most of the rest of the Jewish world, they managed to maintain some links, through letters and occasional travelers, with other Jewish communities, especially those of North Africa and the Middle East. Their religious life remained virtually identical, in its major elements, to that of Jews in the rest of the world. On the other hand, although they lived in close proximity to their Muslim Arab neighbors and shared many aspects of daily life, economy, and material culture with them, they remained quite distinct from them. This was particularly the case with their religious beliefs, practices, and organization, as well as their arts and expressive culture. The Jews were categorized under Muslim law as *dhimmi*, a group tolerated and permitted to practice its own religion, but liable to special taxes, without political or legal rights, under the control of Muslim "patrons," and subject to special laws keeping them in a clearly inferior position to Muslims. Their history within Yemen is largely the story of better or worse times, depending upon their treatment by various indigenous Shiite Muslim rulers or the Ottoman Turkish powers that fought with the former for control. In their great exodus of 1949–1950, Jews virtually disappeared from Yemen.

Settlements and Economy

The Jews of Yemen are said to have lived in about a thousand different localities, some in cities such as Sanʿa (the capital), Dhamar, and Amran, but mostly in small villages throughout the land. Whether in small rural settlements or the cities, most Yemenite Jews were artisans, producing the goods needed by the Arab farmers and nobles. They engaged in a wide range of manual trades, including blacksmithing, silversmithing, tailoring, pottery, charcoal making, soap making, masonry, stonecutting, carpentry, building, milling, baking, and candy making. Certain skilled men acted as scribes, producing the scrolls containing the Five Books of Moses (Torah), as well as other religious works and amulets. Some Jews worked as porters, donkey drivers, peddlers, shopkeepers, and traders. Although Yemen was an agrarian society, few Jews actually farmed. Some did own land, which they leased to Arab farmers, and some owned livestock in partnership with their Muslim neighbors. The Jews might be treated as a pariah group and were sometimes forced to do work considered degrading to Muslims, such as cleaning latrines and sewers, removing carrion and manure from the streets, or burying non-Muslim travelers who died in Yemen.

Community Organization and Religious Life

Although the Jews had no political or legal rights and were under the protection and control of local notables as well as the ruling imam, they had a degree of autonomy in their own community. Aside from local "headmen," who represented their communities before the authorities, most leadership came from religious leaders. In Sanʿa, the largest population and political center, there were some learned rabbis and wealthy men with political influence, but everywhere there were men with Jewish learning and the ability to teach, organize Jewish community life, build synagogues, and lead congregations. Above all, the life of the Jews centered around their religiously mandated practices (*mitsvot*, in Hebrew), which included religious instruction for boys; public worship daily, on the Sabbath, and on holy days; the maintenance of a ritual bath; provision of properly slaughtered and butchered kosher meat; and arrangements for properly administered life-cycle rites (ritual circumcision, marriage, funerals, and mourning). Most leaders and teachers were volunteers, devoting their time, learning, and expertise to these purposes—usually without pay—as their religious duty, and for the esteem and honor that fulfilling these needs brought. Conflicts within the Jewish community usually arose from disagreement about practices or from rivalry among aspiring leaders.

Women

Whereas men were expected to read and write Hebrew, participate in public worship, and be very knowledgeable about the Torah, women were not. According to Jewish law, they could not participate in synagogues; therefore most were not taught. They were, however, expected to know Jewish law relating to what was considered their own realm: personal purity, the dietary laws, and maintaining the proper conditions for celebrating the Sabbath and festivals at home. From all accounts, the women were fully supportive of these arrangements and of their own role in the Jewish community.

Exodus and Emigration to Israel

The Jews of Yemen always maintained the idea that they were living in exile (*galut*) from their true home, the Land of Israel (or Zion). When the new Jewish state of Israel was established in 1948, it became possible for them to put their ideology into practice. Almost all the Jews of southern Arabia left for Israel, walking or riding to a point near Aden, where they met Israelis who arranged to transport them to the Holy Land in airplanes. (The airlift was called "On Wings of Eagles," after prophecies in the Bible.)

The Yemenite Jews in Israel

Identification. Today the Yemenite Jews in Israel have three basic identities: as Jews, as Israelis, and as Jews from Yemen. Any one of the three may take precedence in a given situation, but all are important to them.

Settlements and Economy. The Yemenite Jews arrived in Israel with little preparation for life in an industrial state. None had a modern education or technical training. They had a very strong work ethic, however, and willingness to take on jobs others might consider demeaning. About 28 percent went to settle in more than fifty newly created cooperative villages (*moshavim*) and learned to become farmers. (Most of these families still have homes and farms in the villages, although many of their children have been well educated and have moved to urban occupations.) The other immigrants went to live in towns and cities. Many men went to work in the building trades or in industry, often learning skilled trades within a few years. Some worked in sanitation. Women, who had not usually worked outside of their homes in Yemen, were often employed as housekeepers in private homes, offices, and institutions. The younger the immigrants were when they arrived, the more likely they were to get some schooling, perhaps enough to become teachers or clerks. Today Yemenite Jews in Israel can be found in many occupations, especially as teachers, bureaucrats and organizers, skilled workers in industry, engineers and technologists, artists and musicians, and members of the military forces. There are growing numbers of professionals among them.

Sociopolitical Life. Yemenite Jews are integrated into Israeli society and participate in all the institutions of the state. Although there have been Yemenite political parties contesting national elections, these have usually not fared very well. Nevertheless, Yemenites are increasingly gaining political office, especially on municipal and regional councils and workers' councils, not on the basis of ethnic appeals but as members of the established parties. They tend to split their loyalties between the Labor party, the Likud, and the National Religious party.

Community Life. An outstanding aspect of Yemenite life in Israel is their tendency to form their own neighborhoods. This is particularly important because they generally remain devoted to the practice of the Jewish religion, in the form that they knew it in Yemen. They maintain their own synagogues, employing their distinctive melodies and pronunciation of liturgical Hebrew, which they prize. Because an observant Jew is strictly forbidden to ride on the Sabbath and most holy days, a religious Yemenite family must be within walking distance of a Yemenite synagogue. Because there must be a congregation to support such a synagogue, there must be a sufficiently large population in the area. The Sabbath and other holy days are spent visiting family and friends, often participating in distinctive Yemenite social and ritual gatherings to eat and drink. They continue to celebrate the life-cycle rituals very much as they did in Yemen, and this, too, requires a group of like-minded neighbors. In Israel as in Yemen, community life centers on the family, the synagogue, and the observance of the cycles of religiously mandated activities.

Religion and Expressive Culture. The importance of Judaism for most Yemenites can not be overstressed. Their distinctive expressive culture is based largely on their Judaism. Yemenite men tend to be extremely knowledgeable about religious practice, and most can direct synagogue services themselves. Their synagogues do not depend on the services of rabbis; members of the congregation take turns leading public worship. As in Yemen, this often results in rivalries and conflict. Yemenite communities usually contain a number of small synagogues competing for worshipers and honors. Religion is taken very seriously, the synagogue being the locus of much of the social life of the men. In addition to weekly and annual occasions for worship and celebration, men and women are frequently called upon to participate in birth, marriage, and death rituals. These are celebrated with the participation of kin, friends, neighbors, and more distant fellow Yemenites. Food, ritual, poetry, music, and sometimes dance and costuming, may be accompaniments to these rituals. They pride themselves upon their abilities and their loyalty to these traditions. Marriages, in particular, are celebrated with a number of events, often lasting over several weeks. The *h'inna* celebration preceding marriage is basically a women's party, during which the bride-to-be is dressed in extraordinary costumes and jewelry, and women drum and sing special songs and dance. (These days men usually join in as well.) From Yemen they brought a corpus of poetry (based on religious themes), musical style and melodies, and distinctive dance traditions and costumes. All of these are maintained in Israel today. While almost anyone may dance or sing, there are organized amateur dance groups and many professional performers and composers. New works are always being created on the base of the old forms. Professional musicians often achieve considerable prominence for their Yemenite works, as well as for their performance of other genres. Even before Israel became a state, in the 1920s and 1930s, Yemenite traditions and performers contributed much to the development of Jewish music, dance, and decorative arts.

Bibliography

Ahroni, Reuben (1986). *Yemenite Jewry: Origins, Culture, and Literature*. Bloomington: Indiana University Press.

Lewis, Herbert S. (1989). *After the Eagles Landed: The Yemenites of Israel*. Boulder, Colo.: Westview Press.

"Yemen." (1972). In *Encyclopaedia Judaica*. Jerusalem: Keter.

HERBERT S. LEWIS

Kanuri

ETHNONYMS: Beri-beri, Bornu, Yerwa

Orientation

The Kanuri are the dominant ethnic group of Borno Province in northeastern Nigeria. They number over 3 million in Nigeria, about 500,000 in Niger, 100,000 in Chad, and 60,000 in Cameroon. They are called "Beri-beri" by the Hausa, but they seldom use the term themselves. Bornu Emirate, the major division of the province and the Kanuri homeland, has a history as a political entity that stretches back at least 1,100 years. It has been a Muslim emirate since the eleventh century. Bornu Emirate is located between 11°00′ and 13°00′ N and 11°00′ and 13°30′ E. It is bordered on the north by the Republic of Niger, on the northeast by Chad, and on the east by Cameroon. Kanuri may be found in all of the major cities of northern Nigeria and in the neighboring sections of Chad and Niger. The southwestern section of the Republic of Niger is predominantly Kanuri.

The Kanuri language has the largest number of speakers of the Central Saharan Language Family, which has speakers from northern Nigeria to the Central Sudan. Kanuri is unrelated to Hausa, which is the most commonly spoken language in northern Nigeria. Most Kanuri can speak some Hausa.

The climate of the Kanuri region is typical sub-Saharan savanna. Rainfall averages 56 to 69 centimeters per year, nearly all of it falling from June to September. The harmattan, the wind off of the Sahara, blows cool from mid-December to mid-March, and then may heat up to 38° C. The temperature may remain that high for weeks at a time, until the rains start in June. Most of Borno is flat, except for the southwest, where the rugged Bauchi plateau rises steeply. The eastern part, on the shores of Lake Chad, is marshy. Because of the flatness of the terrain, the summer rains create swamps, and travel becomes impossible. The soil is sandy and is covered with scrub brush, scattered thorny trees, and occasional baobabs. There are also large flat surfaces of hard green clay at the bottoms of ridges, which provide material for buildings and pottery.

History and Cultural Relations

Although there are semilegendary views about early Kanuri roots in Yemen, little is known of the earliest phases of Kanuri culture. Contemporary Kanuri are the descendants of the ruling Saifawa family of the Kanem Empire. As a result of civil war, this family left Kanem in the fourteenth century and, after nearly a century of internal strife, established a new empire southwest of Lake Chad. This empire was and is known as Bornu, although Borno is now its official name. The area to which the Saifawa moved was inhabited by various peoples about whom little is known. Now they are known collectively as the Sau—reputedly a race of giants. For a period of several centuries, the efforts of the Saifawa to consolidate their power and expand their kingdom's boundaries led to the incorporation of many distinctive groups within Kanuri society. This process has not ended. Intermarriage, commerce, politics, and other factors have combined to produce a people who are culturally heterogeneous.

The Kanuri have had a strong influence on surrounding peoples, which include the Budum of Lake Chad, the Mandara and Kotoko (or Mogori) who live southeast of the Kanuri, the Marghi of the Damboa district, the Babur in the hills south of the Kanuri, the Bolewa located southwest of the Kanuri, and the Bede of Gashua, within the Kanuri territory. All of these groups have acquired various aspects of Kanuri culture, mainly the Kanuri language and Islam. Many, including the Hausa, were at one time subjects of the Kanuri Empire.

Economy

The Kanuri are sedentary hoe agriculturists, although almost all of the men practice some other occupation as well. The economy is complex, with commerce, transportation, and construction constituting the other main elements of the private business sector. Government and public-service jobs provide another major source of employment today; manufacturing and industry are still relatively unimportant.

Millet is the staple food crop, supplemented by guinea corn (sorghum). Groundnuts (peanuts) are grown for sale. Hunting is of minor significance, but fish are an important resource to villages along the shores of Lake Chad and the Yobe River. Horses are symbols of prestige. Most households use donkeys as draft animals. Sheep and goats are commonly kept. For beef, most Kanuri rely on the pastoral Shuwa and Fulbe (Fulani, Peul) cattle herders, with whom they exchange grain and craft work for the beef they need. In a few areas, the Kanuri keep large herds of cattle.

The Kanuri diet consists of large quantities of millet, served either as porridge or as dumplings. A vegetable soup, also containing meat, groundnut oil, salt, and other condiments—especially red peppers—is poured over the millet. The diet is universal, but the soup contents vary according to socioeconomic class. Cooked foods are sold in the markets, and a wide range of canned foods are available to city dwellers. Goats and sheep are slaughtered for religious ceremonies. Islamic food taboos are observed.

Kinship, Marriage, and Family

The basic socioeconomic unit is the virilocal extended family, each of which occupies a single walled compound. Although this type of unit is the ideal, neolocality is actually more common. In the case of traditional aristocracy and royalty, the households included slaves, concubines, and numerous retainers and adopted children in addition to the nuclear family. At this social level, the household is not strictly a kin group, although the relations are patterned on kin relations, and kin terms are used.

Social relations in Kanuri society are generally patterned upon those of the idealized family, the most common being the father-son/superior-subordinate relation. A man's prestige is based on the size of his household and the number of his patron-client relationships. His followers provide farm and household labor, support, and defense; in return, he provides food, clothing, bride-price, and possibly a bride, to each of them. Given that a man's status increases or diminishes with that of his household, regardless of his position within it, there is a premium on loyalty to the master.

For men, marriage usually occurs first at about age 20, and for women, at about age 14. The preferred marriage for a man is to a young virgin, 10 to 14 years of age. But this is a very expensive form of marriage, and most men cannot afford it as a first marriage, when they are themselves usually in their late teens to mid-twenties. The more common first marriage is to a divorcée, for whom the bride-wealth payments are much lower. The rate of divorce is extremely high, approaching 80 percent of all marriages. In case of divorce, children stay with the father. Marriage between cousins sometimes occurs, a form that also results in a reduced bride-price.

In accordance with Islamic law, polygyny is permitted. Concubinage is also practiced, although far less commonly than polygyny. Ideally, married Kanuri women are secluded. This practice is rare in rural areas, where the economic role of women is vital, but it is rather common in large cities, such as Maiduguri.

Although agnatic relations take precedence for legal matters and inheritance, kin relations are recognized through both lines. Kin terms make no distinctions for agnates above the parental generation or for cousins, who are all classed as brothers and sisters. Agnates generally live together in their own wards within a city, town, or village. Although there are no corporate lineages as such, in the eyes of the law these groups of neighboring agnates are treated as corporate units, in the sense that they are responsible for the actions of their members. People without agnates upon whom they can depend are social outcasts.

Sociopolitical Organization

The Kanuri live in settlements ranging in size from the large city of Maiduguri—which is the capital of Borno and has a population of 80,000—to tiny hamlets of three or four households. About two-thirds of the population live in villages of from 1,000 to 5,000 people. About one-quarter live in cities of more than 10,000. Hamlets are found about every 1.5 to 3 kilometers, and larger villages every 8 or 10 kilometers. Settlements are composed of walled compounds, made up of mud- or grass-mat-walled houses, with thatched conical roofs. Farms extend in a circle from the settlement, with scattered farms, pastures, and free land beyond.

Before European contact, Bornu was a feudal state, with royal lineages, a landholding aristocracy, peasants, and slaves. Today, in almost all cases, important political leaders are descendants of the aristocratic lineages, but popular elections have added commoners to their ranks. When the British took control at the beginning of the twentieth century, they abolished slavery and took over the top decision-making positions, but they left most of the social system intact. In small villages, there is little or no labor specialization, and differences in wealth are slight. In towns and cities, however, social stratification is pronounced, and differences in wealth may be great. New trading opportunities, Western education, and political power through election and financial support of others have all served to create a situation in which there are many commoners who have become as wealthy as the aristocrats.

Relationships between social unequals, in which each person has diffuse obligations to and expectations of the other, is still an integral part of Kanuri culture today. In the past, the principal contrast was between the nobility and royalty, on the one hand, and commoners, on the other. Today this contrast is being transformed to one between the modern, educated, bureaucratic elite and the traditional, illiterate peasantry. Occupations that are related to politics and religion have high status, whereas those that are associated with things thought to be dirty have low status. Quranic scholars and individuals with political positions have high status, but barbers, blacksmiths, well diggers, tanners, and butchers have very low status. In between are the great bulk of commoners who are farmers, artisans, and traders. Musicians (classed as beggars) and moneylenders (who, because they charge interest, are viewed as violators of Islamic law) hold the lowest status of all.

Another major dimension of social inequality in Borno is between men and women. In a pattern that reflects Islamic law as it is interpreted locally, women are legally and socially inferior to men, and they are considered a major source of instability. Accordingly, various civil and social rights are denied to women.

The Bornu Emirate is a political entity and is viewed as such by its inhabitants. Its present political structure is a result of the colonial era, but is still largely based on precolonial values, traditions, and ideology. The *shehu,* or king, is both the political and the religious leader of the emirate. There are twenty-one districts, each with a district head—usually a member of the aristocracy—and a district capital. The districts are composed of villages, each with its own headman (*lawan*), and of towns and cities, each of which may have more than one headman. Villages, towns, and cities are composed of wards and surrounding hamlets. Wards and hamlets are each run by a *bullama,* usually the founder or senior male.

Religion

The Kanuri have been Muslims since the eleventh century. Law, education, and social organization are the parts of their culture that have been most affected by Islam. The Malakite version of Islamic law is administered by an *alkali* (judge) who has been trained at the Kano Law School. Traditional education is in the Quran. Social organization emphasizes the importance of the nuclear family and the supreme authority of the father.

Today Islam is the central ideological force in the daily lives of the Kanuri, affecting the thinking and behavior of the people in every way. The full ritual calendar of the Muslim year is followed, the fast is faithfully kept by all who are required to do so by traditional laws, and the other pillars of Islam are religiously followed by the great majority. Despite the strength of this orthodoxy, a few superimposed superstitious practices, such as the wearing of charms and amulets, are considered by most of the populace as acceptably Islamic. Of the various Sufi brotherhoods in Nigeria, the dominant one in Borno appears to be that of the Tijaniya.

Bibliography

Botting, Douglas (1961). *The Knights of Bornu*. London: Hodder & Stoughton.

Cohen, Ronald (1960). *The Structure of Kanuri Society*. Ann Arbor: University Microfilms.

Cohen, Ronald (1961). "The Success that Failed: An Experiment in Culture Change in Africa." *Anthropologica*, n.s. 3:21–36.

Cohen, Ronald (1967). *The Kanuri of Bornu*. New York: Holt, Rinehart & Winston.

Low, Victor N. (1972). *Three Nigerian Emirates: A Study in Oral History*. Evanston, Ill.: Northwestern University Press.

Murdock, George P. (1959). *Africa: Its People and Their Culture History*. New York: McGraw-Hill.

Peshkin, Alan (1970). "Education and Modernism in Bornu." *Comparative Education Review* 14:283–300.

Peshkin, Alan (1972). *Kanuri Schoolchildren: Education and Social Mobilization in Nigeria*. New York: Holt, Rinehart & Winston.

Rosman, Abraham (1966). *Social Structure and Acculturation among the Kanuri of Northern Nigeria*. Ann Arbor: University Microfilms.

Tessler, Mark A., William M. O'Barr, and David H. Spain (1973). *Tradition and Identity in Changing Africa*. New York: Harper & Row.

Karaites

ETHNONYMS: Ba'ale Mikra, Binei Mikra, Israelite Karaites, Karaim, Karaite Jews, Qaraites

Orientation

Identification. The name "Karaite" is derived from the Hebrew word, *kara*, "to read," emphasizing the adherence of the group to the Pentateuch, Prophets, and Writings to the exclusion of the Talmud, or postbiblical rabbinic commentary, which the Karaites reject as a source of divine law. An alternative meaning of "kara" is "to call, to invite," which signifies the missionary efforts in which Karaites once engaged to draw people to their faith. The origins of Karaism are disputed. Some trace the roots of Karaism to one of the non-Pharisaic groups in the Second Temple period such as the Sadduccees, Essenes, or Dead Sea Scroll Covenanters. Others attribute the "founding" of Karaism to Anan ben David, a candidate for the exilarchate, the position of chief representative of Jewry, in Baghdad during the eighth century. In any case, questions of sources, authority, and interpretation of the Law are one of the few issues that have given rise to separate movements within Judaism, and such is the basis of the dispute between Karaites and Rabbinites, or Talmudic Jews. The Karaites are the oldest surviving Jewish group that opposes rabbinic Judaism.

Location. The majority of Karaites are found in Israel. Israeli Karaites are mostly of Egyptian origin, although a very small group of them immigrated from Hitt, Iraq.

Demography. It is difficult to ascertain the numbers of Karaites who resided in Egypt in the twentieth century because population statistics vary. The Egyptian census recorded 4,507 Karaites in 1927; 3,260 in 1937; and 3,486 in 1947. A Karaite source estimates that there were 4,000 to 5,000 Karaites living in Cairo in 1952. The same source indicates that between 1948 and 1956 fewer than 100 Karaites left Egypt, despite a bomb that exploded in the Karaite quarter of Cairo in 1948, killing 17 Karaites. In 1956, however, after Abdul Nasser expelled foreign nationals from Egypt in retaliation for the invasion of his country by France, Britain, and Israel during the Sinai Campaign, many Karaites who were not forcibly deported nevertheless chose to leave. By 1959, less than 2,000 Karaites remained. The second major exodus of Karaites followed the Six Day War (5–10 June 1967). As a result of that conflict, young Karaites and Rabbinites were imprisoned in Egypt for two years. By 1970, no more than 300 Karaites remained. In the late twentieth century only a handful of Karaites, all elderly, are to be found in Cairo.

The population figures on Karaites in Israel are not exact because, for both political and religious reasons, the Karaites do not allow themselves to be counted. Population estimates range from 8,000 to 25,000. Approximately 1,000 Karaites of Egyptian origin live in the United States. Significantly smaller numbers are scattered in other countries, including Canada, France, Switzerland, England, Brazil, and Australia. Karaite communities once established in Eastern Europe have largely disappeared, although 100 families still remain in İstanbul.

Linguistic Affiliation. Karaites in Israel speak Hebrew and Arabic. Karaites who came from Poland, Lithuania, and the

Crimea spoke their own Turkic language, Karaimic or Karay, which contained some Hebrew words and was written in Hebrew script.

History and Cultural Relations

Several major factors contributed to the crystallization of Karaism as a distinct branch of Judaism, beginning in the eighth century. The spread of Islam and the messianic atmosphere that it created influenced the spirit of the Jews in newly Islamicized countries. The conformity to the Babylonian Talmud enforced on Jews living on the peripheries of the Diaspora opened up the possibility of questioning the right of one Jewish administration to have authoritative control over the entire domain of Jewish Law. Finally, the tolerance of Muslim rulers to religious diversity made it feasible for religious dissenters to declare their independence from the dominant group; however, whereas the Karaites expressed their opposition to rabbinic authority in the form of messianic asceticism, the content of their beliefs and practices had its foundation in pre-Islamic Judaism.

Karaism eventually spread east to Persia and west to Palestine, Egypt, and Spain. Palestine, in particular, became an important center for Karaites in the tenth century, owing to an emphasis on Avelei Zion (mourners of Zion), who called for a return to Jerusalem. Karaites also settled in Turkey; in the twelfth century Karaites began to move into the Crimea and, later, into Lithuania and Poland.

Karaite settlement in Egypt can be traced back to around the ninth century. Karaites were relatively affluent and influential members of the Jewish community during the first several hundred years of their movement's formal existence. *Ketubot* (marriage contracts) stipulating the rights of Karaite and Rabbinite partners were found in the Cairo Geniza and provided evidence for the occurrence of "mixed" marriages. During this period, the Rabbinites also adopted certain Karaite practices such as purifying themselves with running water rather than immersion in the *mikva*, or ritual bath. When Maimonides, a highly regarded Rabbinite religious scholar, came to Cairo in the late twelfth century, he severely admonished the Rabbinites for imitating Karaite customs, and his anti-Karaite polemics prevailed. For the most part, social distance between the two communities continued into the twentieth century, in spite of the fact that Karaites and Rabbinites lived in adjacent quarters in Cairo—Harat al-Yahud and Harat al-Yahud al-Qarain.

The economic position of the Karaites fluctuated with the times, but their political security remained relatively constant until 1956. For example, during Mamluk rule in Egypt (1260–1517), the Karaites were recognized as a distinct group within the Jewish community and fell under the protection of the *dhimma*, or "People of the Book," as did the Rabbinite Jews. They continued to be granted autonomous status as a religious group under the *millet* system of the Ottomans and to function, more or less, as an independent religious community until their immigration to Israel in the 1950s. Despite their separate status, however, Egyptian Karaites always regarded themselves and were regarded as Jews by both Rabbinite and Muslim Egyptians.

The majority of the world's Karaites now live in Israel. They came to Israel under the Law of Return (a law that grants automatic citizenship to Jews); they participate in the military and are enrolled in the same educational institutions as Rabbinites. Nevertheless, the Karaites have faced many obstacles to maintaining a distinct identity within Israeli society. These obstacles include discrimination they have encountered as Middle Eastern Jews, the unwillingness of the Chief Rabbinate to recognize or support trends within Judaism that deviate from Orthodoxy, and the influence of secularism. Karaite leaders have taken measures to counter these forces by organizing summer camps, after-school religious instruction, parties for youth, and international conferences to renew and strengthen ties with other Karaite communities, and by publishing a bimonthly bulletin.

Settlements

In Israel, Ramla is the administrative and spiritual center of the Karaite community and houses the office of the Karaite chief rabbi. A community can also be found in Jerusalem, where a Karaite synagogue, allegedly dating to the time of Anan ben David, is located in the Jewish Quarter of the Old City. This synagogue is a subterranean structure. The reasons for the underground site cannot be substantiated, but several interpretations are available. A political reason given is that Islamic authorities made it illegal for Jews to erect synagogues at the time of construction; others suggest that the underground site is a metaphorical application of a biblical passage, "From the depths, hear us, oh Lord." In addition to Ramla and Jerusalem, Karaites are concentrated in Ashdod, Bat-Yam, Beersheva, Kiryat Gat, Ofakim, and the agricultural settlements of Moshav Masliach and Moshav Renan.

Economy

The majority of Karaites in Cairo worked as artisans—primarily as gold- and silversmiths—or engaged in trade or peddling. Some attained positions as doctors and lawyers or entered the commercial middle class. In Israel, most Karaites hold working-class occupations such as construction or factory work or middle-class occupations such as teaching or permanent military personnel.

Kinship, Marriage, and Family

Kin Groups and Descent. The Karaites trace descent patrilineally: a child must have a Karaite father to be considered a Karaite. Karaites base this practice on the fact that, in the Bible, tribes are given male names and that biblical characters are always referenced by their fathers' names. Because the Karaites do not presently allow converts, membership in the group is determined by birth only.

Marriage. Historically, Karaite-Rabbinite marriages occurred, but the Karaites are currently an endogamous group, at least ideologically. Karaites have a category of forbidden marriages called *gilui ariyot* (incest) that differs from that of the Rabbinites and is cited as a central obstacle to intermarriage. In this category, men are prohibited from marrying their father's sisters or mother's sisters, and women are prohibited from marrying their father's brothers or their mother's brothers. The offspring of such unions would be considered *mamzerim* (bastards) and would be forever forbidden from taking a marriage partner. Among the Rabbinites, the prohibition applies exclusively to men. Moreover, unlike Rabbinites, Karaites do not require levirate marriage.

For a marriage to take place, three conditions must be met. These include a written contract, *mhar* (bride-price), and sexual consummation. In Egypt, the Karaite community permitted its members to practice polygyny, although actual occurrences were relatively rare. In Israel, polygyny is illegal. If a marriage is unsuccessful, Karaite law grants women the same rights to divorce as men. In the event that a husband refuses to deliver a *get* (bill of divorcement) to his wife, and the Karaite *beit-din* (religious court) agrees that a divorce is justified, then it will grant the couple a divorce by judicial decree. In Israel, because the Orthodox Chief Rabbinate has exclusive legal authority in matters of personal status concerning Jews, the Karaite beit-din is currently operating in a de facto rather than a de jure manner.

Domestic Unit. The Karaite family is basically patriarchal. Among the very religious, menstruating women must sleep and sit in separate spaces from men and are prohibited from entering the kitchen and engaging in food preparation for a seven-day period. These practices highlight the centrality of men in ritual roles because the practices are intended to help guard men from impurity so that they may participate in synagogue services. In Egypt, where Karaites often lived in extended families, postmenopausal women would commonly assume all household chores while younger women were menstruating; in Israel, where the nuclear family is more the norm, men and boys sometimes assume these domestic duties.

Despite the fact that the women's movements are restricted in certain areas, unlike the Rabbinites, Karaite men do not recite prayers thanking God that they were not born women. Karaite women are also allowed relative freedom of dress and may dispose of property without their husbands' permission.

Religion and Expressive Culture

Religious Beliefs. The main principle underlying Karaite Judaism can be summed up by a statement attributed to Anan ben David: "Don't rely upon me, but study diligently the Holy Scripture." Hence, according to Karaite belief, every person has the ability to comprehend the word of the Torah, and intermediaries are not required to mediate between humans and God. As a result, rabbis are never elevated to saintly status as they are in some Ashkenazi and Sephardi Jewish traditions. Additionally, although Karaites do have books of commentary, they are not regarded as binding documents that dictate human action.

The Karaite religion has three basic components. The first is the written text of the Bible. The Torah is regarded as perfect and complete on the basis of the following passage: "Ye shall not add unto the word which I command you, neither shall ye diminish from it, that ye may keep the commandments of Jehovah, your God, which I command you" (Deuteronomy 4:2). The second is *hekesh*, or analogy. For example, the Bible forbids marriages between a man and his mother's or father's sister, so by analogy, a woman is forbidden to marry her father's brother or mother's brother. The third is *sevel hayerusha* (lit., "burden of inheritance"). These are customs that have been transmitted from one generation to another that are viewed as not contradicting or concealing the intent of the biblical text. For example, when a boy is circumcised on the eighth day as commanded by the Torah, the baby is placed on a velvet pillow and introduced to the mother several times by another relative prior to the actual procedure. In Egypt bar mitzvahs were not held for boys coming of age, but in Israel Karaites frequently hold bar mitzvahs, because of pressures to conform, and the practice may become integrated into their sevel hayerusha.

Karaite interpretations of biblical commandments sometimes vary from those of Rabbinite Jews. For example, the passages from Deuteronomy (6:8–9 and 11:18–20), "And thou shall bind them for a sign upon thine hand, and they shall be as frontlets between thine eyes" and "And thou shall write them upon the posts of thy house and on thy gates," are taken allegorically to mean that one must always keep God's commandments in mind. Thus, it was not Karaite custom to use *tefellin* (phylacteries) or *mezuzot* (doorpost scrolls; sing. *mezuzah*). In Israel, however, Karaites have developed a modified form of mezuzah in the shape of the Ten Commandments.

Karaite interpretations of the Bible may also be more literal than those of Rabbinite Jews. For example, the passage from Exodus that prohibits the seething of a kid in its mother's milk is taken at its word and does not require the separation of all meat and all milk.

The Karaites formally oppose any practices related to astrology, divination, luck, or fate. Nevertheless, some Karaites adopted folk beliefs and practices from their Egyptian surroundings, such as the use of amulets to ward off the evil eye or determining one's future through the reading of coffee grinds.

Religious Practitioners. In Egypt, Karaite religious practitioners were called *hakhamim* (sages or wise ones). The leader of the community was addressed as *hakham akbar* and oversaw the activities of the religious court and the religious council. These leaders were not always of Egyptian origin and sometimes came from as far away as Crimea or Turkey.

In Israel, hakhamim are also referred to as rabbis. A chief rabbi is elected by a Karaite religious council comprised of *shohetim* (ritual slaughterers), *mohelim* (circumcisers), and rabbis. In 1991 Karaites opened a *beit midrash* (house of study) in Jerusalem to train future rabbis. Prior to that, Karaite rabbis were trained through apprenticeship to other rabbis.

Ceremonies. The Karaite synagogue is treated, as much as possible, as a microcosm of the Temple on the basis of a passage from Ezekiel (11:16), "Although I have removed them far away among the nations, and although I have scattered them among the countries, yet will I be to them a minor sanctuary in the countries whither they are come." The Karaites make every effort to maintain their synagogue in a state of purity for worshipers at the time of daily prayers, Shabbat (Sabbath), and holidays. Menstruating women and women who have just given birth are not allowed to enter the synagogue. Likewise, people who have recently engaged in sexual relations or come in contact with the dead are forbidden entry to this holy site. Those who do enter, males and females alike, must cover their heads and remove their shoes because it is written, "put off thy shoes from off thy feet; for the place whereon thou standest is holy ground" (Exodus 3:5). The synagogue floor is covered with rugs and the worshipers pray facing Jerusalem and prostrate themselves facing the Ark as the priests prostrated themselves toward the Temple altar.

The Karaites attempt to structure their prayer services after Temple activities. Two services are held every day, one at sunrise and one at sunset, to correspond with the times that sacrifices were performed at the Temple. On Shabbat and holidays, additional prayers are recited to replace the extra sacrifice that would have been offered. On these days a Torah scroll referred to as the "Sefer Kourban" (Sacrifice Book) is also removed from a glass case and opened in lieu of the Temple sacrifice.

Shabbat is viewed as a time for spiritual pleasures rather than worldly pleasures. Unlike the Rabbinites, the Karaites strictly forbid sexual intercourse on Shabbat because it generates impurity and is considered a form of labor. Shabbat candles are not lit, and any use of fire is prohibited. Food is eaten cold.

The Karaite calendar is based on the actual observance of the new moon or the possibility of the observance of the new moon based on available scientific data. Holidays can fall on any day of the week, with the exception of Shuvuot (Feast of Weeks) because it is stated in Leviticus that the Omer should be counted from "the morrow of the Sabbath" (23:15). Passover and Sukkot (Feast of Tabernacles) are observed for seven days rather than eight.

Therefore, the dates of holidays do not necessarily coincide with those of the Rabbinites. The *shofar* (ram's horn) is not blown on Yom HaTeruah (Day of Shouting or Cheer, known to Rabbinites as "Rosh Hashannah") because neither the Temple nor the Temple altar are still standing. Hanukkah is not celebrated because it is a holiday of postbiblical origin.

Passover is a very central holiday for Egyptian Karaites because it serves as an allegory for their own historical exodus from Egypt. During the Passover seder, or meal, which is only held one night, the Karaites read from their own Haggadah that retells the story of the hasty departure of the Jews from Egypt in biblical times. Instead of wine, they drink a homemade grape juice from red, seedless raisins because they say that the juice would not have had an opportunity to ferment, and they eat bitter herbs and lamb. During Passover week, Karaites refrain from eating leavened bread, anything derived from soaked grains, or food prepared outside of the home.

Arts. The Karaites have a body of literature that addressed issues of Karaite law (*halakhah*). Two of the authors that continue to be studied and cited frequently by contemporary Karaite scholars are Aaron ben Elijah, known as the "latter," who wrote *Gan Eden* and *Keter Torah* and lived in the fourteenth century in Nicomedia and Constantinople, and Elijah ben Moses Basyatchi who wrote *Aderet Eliahu* and lived in the fifteenth century in Constantinople.

Another aspect of the arts that plays a central role in Karaite life is traditional Karaite music. Music is an integral part of Karaite services and life-cycle ceremonies and consists of two broad categories. The first is that of synagogue liturgy and is derived primarily from the Psalms; the second is a body of poetic texts sung after services or for occasions such as weddings or circumcisions. The musical style creates an atmosphere of community and cohesion, but the unique contributions of talented participants are also highlighted, and women as well as men are allowed to display their knowledge and skills.

Bibliography

Colligan, Sumi (1980). "Religion, Nationalism, and Ethnicity in Israel: The Case of the Karaite Jews." Ph.D. dissertation, Princeton University.

El-Kodsi, Mourad (1987). *The Karaite Jews of Egypt from 1882–1985*. Lyons, N.Y.: Wilprint Press.

Hirshberg, Jehoash (1989). "The Role of Music in the Renewed Self-Identity of Karaite Jewish Refugee Communities from Cairo." *Yearbook for Traditional Music* 21:36–56.

Kramer, Gudrun (1989). *The Jews in Modern Egypt, 1914–1952*. Seattle: University of Washington Press.

Mann, Jacob (1935). *Texts and Studies in Jewish History and Literature*. Vol. 2. Philadelphia: Jewish Publication Society.

Nemoy, Leon (1952). *Karaite Anthology: Excerpts from the Early Literature*. New Haven: Yale University Press.

SUMI COLLIGAN

Karamojong

ETHNONYMS: Karimojong, Ngakarimonjong

The Karamojong are a pastoral group who inhabit the plateau region of Uganda. Linguistically, the Karamojong belong to the Central Group of the Nilote Language Family, which also includes several neighboring groups that speak a mutually intelligible dialect. The related groups include the Teso, Iteso, Jie, Dodoz, Topoza, Jiye, Nyangatom, and Turkana. In 1986 the Karamojong numbered about 300,000, which included 50,000 Jie.

The habitat of the Karamojong is a plateau 1,120 to 1,360 meters high; there are steep hills throughout, and higher mountains border the plateau. It is a region characterized by thorny plants and grasses. The savanna becomes green with the first rainfall, in April, but dries up again in November, when the rain stops. The dry season is very windy, and there is no surface water, except for puddles left over from the rainy season, which quickly dry up. River beds fill up in a few hours during storms, and dry up again after the storms pass.

The Karamojong pattern of land use is closely related to their habitat. There are two primary patterns of land use, which are reflected in two distinct types of settlement. Permanent settlements have internal compounds, sleeping houses, and granaries with large storehouses. Temporary camps are primarily a complex of corrals to contain cattle, sheep, and goats, and they usually have only temporary shelters for humans.

The permanent settlements are in the central part of Karamojong territory and are the locii of cultivation and continuous habitation. Their position is fixed by the availability of reliable permanent water, and their mobility is limited by the need to store gardening implements and grain. Women carry out most of the activities related to these permanent settlements. With the exception of some milk products, the only food consumed in the permanent settlements is generally the product of women's agricultural efforts. The camps are in the eastern and western portions of Karamojong territory. They are very mobile because of the need to respond to changes in grazing conditions and the availability of water. Men carry out most of the activities of the camp, which are primarily pastoral, and the food consumed—primarily milk and blood—is almost exclusively produced from the herd.

The staple crop is sorghum, which is planted with cucumbers and marrows. Beans and gourds, and sometimes maize and millet, are also grown. Because of their environment, the Karamojong cannot subsist by cultivation alone; they therefore attach greater economic importance to raising livestock. Their form of pastoralism is to exploit the products of the stock rather than slaughter the stock. They consume milk, milk products, and blood rather than meat, which is eaten only at public ceremonies or when an animal dies.

Cattle are a key element of Karamojong culture. They are highly valued both in economic and social terms. Milk, blood, and meat provide sustenance; fat is both a food and a cosmetic; urine is used as a cleanser; hides make sleeping skins, shoulder capes, skirts, bell collars, sandals, armlets, and anklets; horns and hooves provide snuff holders, feather boxes, and food containers; bags are made from scrota; intestines are used for prophecy; chyme has a ceremonial function (anointing); and droppings are used for fertilizer.

Cattle are literally wealth; they are used to establish families, acquire political supporters, achieve status, and influence public affairs. The payment of cattle, as bride-wealth, to a girl's kin is an essential step in arranging a marriage. A man is only the genitor, not the father, of children he engenders, unless he transfers cattle in a bride-wealth for their mother. Furthermore, the acquisition of an extended range of kinsmen through affinity is almost as significant as the acquisition of a bride and, potentially, a family. In other words, the more cattle a man provides in bride-wealth the more kinsmen he creates who receive a share of cattle, and the larger his range of affinal ties—a very important social asset.

Although the family and the clan, which usually extends only three generations, are the primary social units, two other units are of central importance in Karamojong society, and provide the basis for political action. Territoral groups create units of common interest, allegiance, and action. Age groups, by allocating authority, determine the roles of individual members of territorial groups in any corporate action.

Territorial groups range in size from small settlements and neighborhoods, to larger localities (consisting of several neighborhoods), to subsections, and finally to sections or tribal groups. The Karamojong neighborhood is made up of a small number of settlements, the members of which recognize social ties with each other, offer mutual hospitality, utilize common natural resources, take common ritual action, and meet together frequently for social interaction. This is the setting where most face-to-face encounters take place. Subsections are enduring social groups; their continuity derives from coresidence, corporate activity, and the establishment of a distinctive name that ties each to some natural object. Subsections are also religious congregations, each with its own ritual specialist and ceremonial grounds.

Karamojong adult males are organized into a series of groups based on varying degrees of common age. These age sets are an integral part of Karamojong social organization and provide the basis for political authority. The highest sources of authority are the elders of a community. The channels of authority are provided by the relationships that are created by the organization of people into age categories. The use of authority is occasioned by public ritual gatherings, council meetings, and public disputes. Decisions and sanctions of the elders are carried out because subsenior age sets adhere to the norms of obedience established with age rankings. The elders are also considered to have divine authority—or at least to be closely linked to divine authority. The consequence of violating the elders' authority is punishment inflicted by younger obedient men, or by deity, leading to the misfortune or death of the disobedient and their dependents.

Bibliography

Dyson-Hudson, Neville (1966). *Karimojong Politics*. Oxford: Clarendon Press.

Gourlay, K. A. (1966). *The Making of Karimojong' Cattle Songs*. Nairobi: University of Nairobi, Institute of African Studies.

Grimes, Barbara F., ed. (1988). *Ethnologue: Languages of the World*. Dallas: Summer Institute of Linguistics.

Novelli, Bruno (1989). *Aspects of Karimojong Ethnosociology*. Museum Combonianum no. 44.

RONALD JOHNSON

Khoi

ETHNONYMS: Herders of southern Africa, Khoikhoi (Khoekhoe) Hottentots, Khoisan

Orientation

Identification. "Hottentot" was the collective name given to indigenous herders of southern Africa by early travelers from Europe. As herders, they were distinguishable from both the hunter-gatherer "Bushmen" (or San) and from crop farmers (Bantu-speaking people). They had no collective name for themselves, but they identified strongly with various clan names, such as "Chochoqua," "Goringhaiqua," or "Gorachoqua." Twentieth-century scholars have tended to identify a number of ethnic divisions within the Khoi that are associated with geographically and socially distinct regions: "Cape Hottentots," "Eastern Cape Hottentots" (sometimes classified together as "Cape Khoikhoi"), "Korana" (!Kora), and "Naman" (Nama).

The term "Hottentot"—and especially its abbreviated version, "Hotnot"—have acquired derogatory connotations, and the preferred terms "Khoi" or "Khoikhoi" (meaning "the real people") are most commonly used in the literature today.

Location. At the time that the first European settlers arrived in southern Africa (mid-seventeenth century), Khoi populations were located around the Cape of Good Hope and along and inland from the southwestern and western coasts—roughly south from 22° N and west from 25° E. This whole area is a winter-rainfall region, but, whereas the southwestern parts have an annual rainfall of up to 76 centimeters per year, much of the northern and inland areas are semidesert with sparse and irregular rainfall (less than 13 centimeters per year). Archaeological evidence suggests that the Khoi had previously been more widely distributed (especially to the east), but had been displaced by the arrival of crop farmers (Bantu-speaking people) whose southward migration eventually ended around A.D. 500 on the boundary between the summer and winter rainfall regions (near present-day Port Elizabeth). European settlement at the Cape similarly resulted in the rapid displacement of Khoi populations, who were eventually forced into the most arid and remote areas. Today Khoi herders are found only in isolated reserve areas in South Africa and Namibia.

Demography. Although some historians (e.g., Stow) have estimated the total Khoi population in the mid-seventeenth century at less than 50,000, it is unlikely that their number was less than 200,000. The main reason for this lack of agreement seems to be the different definitions of the population in question. For example, some estimates excluded population north of the Orange River, while others included the Einiqua (about whom very little is known). There is widespread agreement, however, that this population was decimated during the eighteenth century—by the smallpox epidemics, through intermarriage with other populations, and through incorporation into settler society. The 1805 Cape census recorded only 20,000 "Hottentots," but this figure included people of mixed descent and excluded significant populations that were not yet part of Cape Colony. Present population estimates are similarly hampered by the problem of definition: most descendants of the Khoi are wage laborers who have been incorporated into the broader category of "Coloured" and do not identify themselves as either "Khoi" or "Hottentot." If the term "Khoi" is used in the narrower sense, however, to refer only to those descendants of the indigenous herders who continue to practice a herding life-style on communal lands, the current population (in South Africa and Namibia) is well below 20,000.

Linguistic Affiliation. The languages spoken by the Khoi and the San (Bushmen) were part of a broad family of Khoisan languages (clearly distinguishable from the Bantu languages spoken by the neighboring agricultural Nguni and Sotho). The Khoisan languages, well-known for the prevalence of a range of different clicks, can be subdivided into Khoikhoi (Hottentot) and San (Bushmen) languages. Whereas all Khoi herders spoke one of a number of mutually understandable Khoikhoi languages, some groups of San hunters also spoke Khoikhoi languages. Khoikhoi languages have largely been replaced by Afrikaans and are rapidly disappearing in South Africa today—very few young people, even in the reserve areas, retain more than a smattering of their traditional language. In Namibia, it is still the mother tongue of most of the few thousand remaining Khoi herders.

History and Cultural Relations

Khoi herders have lived in southwestern Africa for at least 2,000 years. Until recently, it was generally accepted that a distinct group of herder Khoi, originating in Central Africa, had migrated south with their herds of fat-tailed sheep, eventually displacing hunting populations in those areas where they chose to settle. Contemporary theories acknowledge that, given the close linguistic, cultural, and racial links between the Khoi and the San, the emergence of a herding life-style was more complex than this simple model would suggest.

Some San hunters were incorporated into Khoi populations, and some Khoi herders lost their stock and became hunters. It is also possible that some San populations acquired stock and thus adopted a herder life-style. Notwithstanding such fluidity, there is much evidence that Khoi and San saw themselves as being different. In particular, the Khoi viewed people without stock as inferior and despised those hunters who stole their stock. A system of clientship developed whereby individual San (commonly referred to as "Sonqua") were adopted as servants by the pastoralists.

European settlers were initially interested in the Khoi as trading partners. To provide fresh supplies to ships rounding the Cape, Europeans obtained stock through barter. Khoi were very careful of their breeding stock and did not ordinarily kill cattle for food; tensions arose as they became increasingly reluctant to part with their animals. When settlers themselves began to farm, the resultant struggle over land increased tensions and led to open conflict. Gradually, the Khoi herders were displaced from the area around the Cape and forced to retreat to more remote and arid regions. While it is true that their numbers were decimated by smallpox epidemics, many were also incorporated into settler society as domestic and farm workers. At the same time, some settlers moved away from the Cape, intermarried with Khoi women, and adopted a life close to that of the Khoi pastoralists. Their descendants became known as "Basters" (bastards)—people of mixed descent—who learned to speak Dutch (later Afrikaans) and were educated in Christianity.

There was significant interaction between the remaining "pure" Khoi and the Dutch-speaking Basters; gradually, therefore, no clear division could be drawn between the two. In some instances, Khoi and Basters combined into single sociopolitical groupings.

By the turn of the twentieth century, little remained of the traditional pastoral life-style of the Khoi. In many areas, however, descendants of the Khoi had managed to retain rights to land by recognizing that missionaries could offer some protection from encroaching Dutch farmers. By 1900, numerous mission stations had been established, and these areas eventually became the reserves where seminomadic pastoralism is still practiced today.

Settlements

Unlike the San, who lived in very flexible and mobile bands generally numbering fewer than 50 persons, the basic village encampment (or *kraal*) of the precolonial Khoi was significantly larger, incorporating well over 100 persons (some villages included several hundred). The basic housing structure was a round hut (*matjieshuis*) made of a frame of saplings that was covered with reed mats. Each village encampment consisted primarily of members of the same patrilineal clan.

Economy

Subsistence and Commercial Activities. Although subsistence activity was centered on the care of herds of sheep and cattle, hunting and the collection of wildplant foods were also important. In general, cattle were only slaughtered for ritual purposes, but their milk was an essential part of the diet. The Khoi used oxen to carry loads and to ride on. Fat-tailed sheep were slaughtered more regularly (their fat was highly prized), and their skins were used for clothing. Ewes were also milked.

A majority of the contemporary population in the reserves is still involved with herding (primarily of sheep and goats) on communal land. Today most of the produce is sold outside the reserves. Notwithstanding the significance of herding, wage labor outside the reserves is the major source of income.

Industrial Arts and Trade. The Khoi manufactured skins into clothing, bags, and blankets, and threaded reeds together to make sleeping mats and mats to cover their round houses. Mat houses provided very practical accommodation, especially in warmer climates. During warm days they offered a cool, relatively bright shelter, with the crevices between the reeds allowing air to circulate. During the rains, the reeds would swell as they absorbed water and therefore offer good protection against leaks. During the cold months, the inside of the house could be lined with skins to offer extra insulation against the elements. This structure also had the advantage that it could be dismantled and reerected every few months in response to the changing seasons or when grazing in the surrounding area became depleted.

The Khoi made pottery, some of which had distinctive pointed bases and handles, which could be tied to their oxen when moving, or to hut poles. They made spears with fire-hardened tips, but generally used iron tips, which they obtained from neighboring Bantu-speaking peoples or, more recently, from European ships and settlers.

Division of Labor. Women milked the cows and ewes and collected plant foods; herding and hunting activities were the preserve of men. The construction of mat houses was a task shared by men and women: men cut and planted the saplings and tied them together with leather thongs to form a frame, and women collected the reeds and manufactured the mats. With the introduction of modern dwelling structures, women have largely taken over the entire task of constructing traditional homes, and men have become responsible for the erection of modern (primarily corrugated-iron or brick) housing. Many contemporary households in the reserves have both modern and traditional structures—the latter being reserved for cooking activities (the domain of women).

Land Tenure. In precolonial times, several clan-based villages were united into much larger units called tribes or hordes, which ranged in size from a few hundred to several thousand individuals. The most significant aspect of tribal integrity related to the various clans' unrestricted access to communal tribal land. Local clans could move around and utilize pasture, water resources, game, and wild fruit and vegetables within the tribal area (although individual clans tended to move in a regular pattern in a specific tract of tribal land). The relatively low population density prior to the arrival of Europeans meant that there was limited competition for any given piece of land, and the extent of tribal land was thus defined not so much in terms of exact boundaries as with reference to land around key water holes as well as areas with better pasture.

The communal character of land tenure has been retained in most of the contemporary reserves, and local populations have resisted government's attempts to create individual farms. Although specific plots of land are allocated to individual farmers in some of the reserves (where crop cultivation is possible), such plots are not privately owned and remain under the control of the local communities.

Kinship

Kin Groups and Descent. The exogamous patrilineal clan was the basic unit of social organization. Although tribal groupings were unstable and mobile, and were not composed exclusively of clan members, the Khoi kept detailed oral genealogies of the origins of various clans and of the relationship between them. This knowledge was very important, since precedence within tribes and clans was by primogeniture.

During most of the twentieth century, descent has been used as an important indication of status—higher status being associated with "White" blood. More recently, the opposite trend has been emerging: people are keen to emphasize their Khoi history.

Kinship Terminology. Individuals were given both patrilineal clan names and "great names"—names inherited by a group of brothers from their mother, or of sisters from their father. In this way, men shared their name with their maternal grandfather, and women with their maternal grandmother. These names were closely associated with the pattern of institutionalized joking and avoidance relationships between kin.

Marriage and Family

Marriage. Clans were exogamous, and men from one clan thus had to seek wives in another. Given the geographical proximity of related clans, it was possible for many men to find wives within the tribe; however, marriage between members of different tribes was also common. Marriage served as a powerful social mechanism to unite members of the tribe or to link different tribes together. This bond was reinforced by the custom that the bridegroom had to spend the first few months of marriage (often until the birth of the couple's first child) living at the village of his parents-in-law. (This practice has sometimes been referred to as bride-service). Thereafter, residence was patrilocal. Marriage usually involved the transfer of cattle from the groom's family to the bride's parents. Polygyny was permitted but not very common.

Inheritance. Individual clans or tribes controlled access to land and the resources on it, but there was a clear understanding that land could not become the property of individuals. By contrast, all stock were individually owned, and a wealthy stock owner was accorded high status. Wealthier stock owners almost invariably acquired their stock through inheritance. Customary inheritance patterns varied: in some tribes, the inheritance was shared among all the children; in others, only sons inherited; in yet others, the eldest son was the only heir.

Socialization. Parents were responsible for training their children in the basic subsistence skills, following the basic sexual division of labor. Very close relationships existed between grandparents and their daughters' children, and between children and their mother's brothers. Relationships between brothers and sisters and between a father's sister and her brother's children were respectful and formal.

Sociopolitical Organization

Social Organization. Although precolonial village encampments generally included some members of other clans, as well as some dependents or servants (San or impoverished Khoi from other clans), patrilineal descent formed the basis of social organization.

Political Organization. Each village recognized the authority of a headman, a hereditary position passed on to the eldest son of the founding ancestor and so forth for every generation. Headmen provided leadership regarding decision making within the village (e.g., determining when and where to move), as well as acting as mediator or judge in criminal or civil disputes. Although villages enjoyed a fair degree of autonomy, several villages were united to form a horde or tribe. As with clan-based villages, tribes had a kinship base. They were composed of a number of linked clans, with the seniority of one of the clans being recognized. (In one example, five of seven clans were descended from one of five brothers, with the remaining two being offshoots of these. The clan descended from the eldest brother was the senior clan.) The head of the senior clan was acknowledged as the chief of the tribe. The tribal chief controlled access to the tribal resources, but there was a clear recognition that neither the land, nor the resources left on it, could become the property of individuals (and this included the chief). Chiefs commanded a great deal of respect through their individual ability and effort (often accumulating very large herds), but they still remained dependent on the wishes of the tribal council, a group consisting of the headmen of all the other clans. Colonial governments succeeded in coopting many leaders (chiefs or headmen) by formally recognizing their position as "captains."

Social Control. Criminal and civil disputes were handled by the chief and his council (or, in some cases, by the village headmen). More recently, however, such cases have been handled by the captain (i.e., a government appointee), by management boards in the various reserves, or by state courts.

Conflict. During precolonial times, relations between Khoi and San groups were often strained. Khoi accusations that San had stolen their livestock sometimes resulted in open warfare. The pressure on land associated with European settlement gave rise to warfare not only between Khoi and the Dutch farmers, but also between different Khoi tribes. It is generally assumed that Khoi political groupings were too small and weak to offer much resistance to the settlers (who had access to firearms and horses). The Khoi did offer significant resistance, however. Various tribes could and did unite against the common enemy, the most notable episode being the Khoikhoi War of Independence (1799–1803). Although ultimately unsuccessful, it showed that the Khoi were capable of mobilizing the support of many different tribal groupings (in this particular case, they also joined forces with Bantu-speaking Xhosa) and of presenting a united force.

Religion and Expressive Culture

Religious Beliefs. Khoi have been under missionary influence for a considerable length of time, and relatively little information regarding religious beliefs is available. A range of myths that have been recorded shed some light on pre-Christian beliefs. Special significance was attached to the moon (it has been claimed that the Khoi "worshiped" the moon) and to two central good beings, Tsûi-//goab (the deity) and Haiseb or Heitsi-eibib (the folk hero). The Khoi also believed in ghosts and witches, but not in the power of ancestors; however, there is some evidence that the spirits of the dead were involved in curing rituals.

Religious Practitioners. Some individuals played a dominant role in healing or rainmaking rituals, but it would be incorrect to view them as specialist religious practitioners. There is some mention of magicians, but very little is known of the methods they employed.

Ceremonies. The central theme of virtually all Khoi ritual was the idea of transformation or transition from one status to another. Most rituals marked the critical periods of change in a person's life—birth, puberty, adulthood, marriage, and death. In all of these rituals, the concept of *!nau* was central. !Nau was seen as a state of particular vulnerability and danger. The ceremonies all involved a period of seclusion associated with increased !nau. During these periods of social withdrawal, certain substances (notably water) were avoided, whereas others (such as fire or the *buchu* plant) were associated with protection. Of particular interest is the part played by livestock—not only in feasting associated with the rituals, but in the rituals themselves. In contrast with water, domestic stock seemed always to be associated with protection (e.g., feeding babies with the milk of cows or ewes, or the wearing of parts of a slaughtered animal, as in the case of female puberty rituals).

Medicine. Besides the healing rituals (often taking the form of trance-dancing), much use was made of the medicinal properties of various plants. All adult Khoi possessed a basic knowledge of plant usage, but certain individuals were seen to have developed higher levels of expertise. Some of this knowledge remains important today.

Death and Afterlife. Besides natural causation, death under exceptional circumstances was often attributed to the evil being //Gâuab, to ghosts, or to the violation of certain ritual avoidances. Burials took place as soon as possible after death. The Khoi did not have a well-developed conception of an afterlife, and funeral ceremonies were appropriately unelaborated.

See also San-speaking Peoples

Bibliography

Barnard, Allan (1992). *Hunters and Herders of Southern Africa: a Comparative Ethnography of the Khoisan Peoples*. Cambridge: Cambridge University Press.

Carstens, W. Peter (1966). *The Social Structure of a Cape Coloured Reserve*. Cape Town: Oxford University Press.

Elphick, Richard (1977). *Kraal and Castle: Khoikhoi and the Founding of White South Africa*. Johannesburg: Ravan Press.

Engelbrecht, J. A. (1936). *The Korana: An Account of Their Customs and Their History, with Texts*. Cape Town: Maskew Miller.

Hoernlé, A. Winifred (1913). *Richtersveld: The Land and its People*. Johannesburg: Council of Education, Witwatersrand.

Marais, J. S. (1968). *The Cape Coloured People: 1652–1937*. Johannesburg: Witwatersrand University Press.

Schapera, I. (1930). *The Khoisan Peoples of South Africa: Bushmen and Hottentots*. London: George Routledge & Sons.

Smith, Andrew B., ed. (1995). *Einigualand: Studies of the Orange River Frontier*. Cape Town: University of Cape Town Press.

Stow, George W. (1905). *The Native Races of South Africa: A History of the Intrusion of the Hottentots and Bantu into the Hunting Grounds of the Bushmen, the Aborigines of the Country*. London: Swan Sonnenschein.

Wilson, Monica, and Leonard Thompson, eds. (1969). *The Oxford History of South Africa*. Oxford: Clarendon Press.

EMILE BOONZAIER

Kikuyu

ETHNONYMS: Gekoyo, Gigikuyu, Gikiyu

Orientation

The Kikuyu, a major ethnic group of Kenya, numbered about 4.4 million in 1987, accounting for about 20 percent of Kenya's population of 25 million. The Kikuyu refer to themselves as "Mugikuyu" (sing.) or "Agikuyu" (pl.). The Kikuyu language, which has three predominant dialects, is linguistically related to other Bantu-speaking groups in central Kenya, including the Kamba, Embu, Mbere, Tharaka, and Meru.

History and Cultural Relations

The Kikuyu share common historical roots with the Kamba, Embu, Mbere, Tharaka, and Meru. All of these groups date back to a prototype population known as the Thagicu. Migrating from the north, the Thagicu settled in the Mount Kenya region sometime between the twelfth and fourteenth centuries. As splinter groups formed, one of the groups migrated south and settled on the southwestern slopes of Kirinyaga (Mount Kenya). Archaeological evidence suggests that the people who settled there hunted game, herded sheep and goats, and worked with iron to make simple tools and weapons.

There were additional Bantu migrations from the northeast, followed by periods of settlement, intermarriage, and further splintering of the Thagicu in the fifteenth and sixteenth centuries. The Kikuyu trace their descent from one of the splinter groups that settled at the convergence of the Tana (Thagana) and Thika rivers. From the settlement at Ithanga, subgroups migrated in several directions, some north to Nyeri, others northeast to Kirinyaga, and some south to Murang'a over the next two centuries. Some migrated further south than Murang'a, toward Kiambu, in the eighteenth century, and came into contact with a hunting people they called the Aathi. They intermarried with the Aathi and acquired land from them in exchange for goats.

As different Kikuyu settled in different areas, a clan structure emerged. Each clan traced its descent back to a specific female ancestor. According to Kikuyu mythology, there were nine (or nine plus one) original clans. Two clans, the Acera and Agaciku, are thought to have formed through contact with neighboring Kamba. The largest clan is the Anjiru; its members were formerly renowned as great warriors and medicine men. The Aithaga clan was known for its ironworks, and its members were also thought to have the power to control rain. Other clans include the Ambui, Angari, Aithiegeni, Aithirandu, and Aithanga. According to Kikuyu myths, Kikuyu and Mumbi were the male and female progenitors of the nine clan ancestors.

Economy

The Kikuyu were originally hunter-gatherers, but they gradually adopted horticultural practices. The first crops grown by the Kikuyu were cocoyams, sweet potatoes, bananas, and millet. The cultivation of crops was traditionally segregated by gender. Men cultivated yams and bananas, whereas women grew sweet potatoes and millet. Women also gathered a variety of wild spinachlike greens, tubers, such as arrowroot (taro), and berries. Sugarcane was grown and honey collected from hives in the forest for the production of beer. Maize was introduced early in the nineteenth century and has become a major staple crop. When it is used for domestic consumption, it is usually grown by women, but when it is sold as a commodity, it is more often grown by men.

Many foods have been added to the traditional crops of the Kikuyu. European potatoes, cassava, and rice have been added to the cultivated crops, as well as legumes, which include dwarf beans, cowpeas, pigeon peas, kidney beans, lentils, and garden peas. Today Kikuyu also grow cabbage, tomatoes, onions, carrots, kale, and swiss chard. They season their foods with salt, chili peppers, or curry. A great variety of fruits is grown in the area. In addition to bananas, these include passion fruits, mangoes, papayas, loquats, plums, pineapples, oranges, and avocado pears. Women and children especially enjoy fruits, which they sell in local markets.

Although Kikuyu were formerly hunters, Kenyan game laws prohibit them from hunting today. Meat of wild game (antelope, impalas, bushbucks) and from herd animals (goats, sheep, and African cattle) was the prerogative of men. Pork and fish were prohibited, and game birds and other fowl were eaten only occasionally; eggs were not a part of the diet. Women rarely ate meat and then only when it was handed to them by their husbands. Today meat is served only on special occasions—to celebrate a ceremony, such as Irua (circumcision), or to welcome an important visitor. Cash crops, such as tea, coffee, and rice, were not grown until the 1940s, and, in some areas of Kenya, much later, but they have become an important part of the economy.

Kinship, Marriage, and Family

The nuclear family, which consists of a husband and wife, or wives, and children, is the basic social unit of Kikuyu society. As children grow up and form their own families, a subclan (*mbari*) is formed. Each mbari contains a hundred to a thousand families, and each member of an mbari knows from which ancestor, or which daughter of Kikuyu and Mumbi, they originate. The Kikuyu family is considered to be circular, rather than linear as in Western cultures. Each new generation replaces their grandparents, who are then free to become ancestors. The need to replace four grandparents is an important reason for having a minimum of four children, and more children gives honor to the parents' siblings.

Extended families living together form a homestead (*mucii;* pl. *micii*), and several micii together form into larger units, roughly equivalent to villages or hamlets.

Ideally, the mucii includes the paternal head of the family, his wives or wife, their unmarried children, often his married sons, and sometimes single male or female relatives. The Kikuyu are traditionally polygynous, but with the influence of Christianity and Western education, the trend has been toward monogamy. If a man chooses to marry more than one wife, theoretically he must provide *ruracio* (bride-wealth) and a separate house for each within the homestead.

Sociopolitical Organization

The concept of *mariika* (age sets; sing. *riika*) is of central importance within Kikuyu society. Mariika provide a way of keeping track of groups of people (both male and female) who were circumcised in different years. The circumcision group (generation) is given a name that identifies it with a particular event or characteristic of the group. Members of a particular riika, circumcised at the same time, were given a rank in the age groupings. The rank defined the behavior of individual members within a riika and their behavior toward members of other age groups, both younger and older. The older a riika became, the more respect it was given. Mariika function as agents of gender-segregated social control.

A strong bond of friendship forms between members of the same riika during Irua (circumcision ceremonies) and continues as a form of mutual social aid throughout their lives. Younger Kikuyu, however, are usually circumcised in hospitals today, and have a much weaker concept of mariika than earlier generations. In place of Irua, modern young Kikuyu find peer bonds in the school setting. Furthermore, the strict social segregation between the sexes seems to be breaking down as young people of both sexes come into contact with one another in primary classrooms, on the playground, and through church activities.

In the past, the transition from one life stage to another in Kikuyu society was marked by rites of passage. Each stage was given a special name for both males and females. Stages of life for the Kikuyu included newborn, infant, uncircumcised boy or girl, circumcised boy or girl, married, married with children, and old age.

Political authority in precolonial Kenya was decentralized. No kings, chiefs, or bureaucratic institutions existed. For the most part, political authority was collective at every level, and decisions were generally reached by the oldest males of kin groups or political units in council. Although the councils made some important decisions for the group as a whole, their primary role was judicial—the settlement of disputes between kin groups. The collective prestige of the elders in council, as the representatives of tradition and the ancestors, gave their words weight and their decisions authority. Women also had a council, the function of which was to deal with domestic concerns, matters of the farms, and the discipline of female social and ritual life. Women were excluded from politics and were usually prevented from holding rights in land.

The imposition of foreign rule on the Kikuyu drastically altered their social and political structures and disrupted their traditional ways of life. European settlement policies had an even more drastic effect on the Kikuyu as land was virtually taken away from thousands of resident Kikuyu without adequate compensation.

Religion and Expressive Culture

In the traditional religion of the Kikuyu, the elders, or the older people within a clan, were considered to be the authority of God (Ngai). They used to offer to Ngai propitiatory sacrifices of animals, in chosen places that were considered sacred, usually near a fig tree or on the top of a hill or mountain. Even today there are large sacred trees where people sometimes gather for religious or political meetings or particular feasts. Mount Kenya, especially for the clans who live on its slopes, is considered the home of God.

The medicine man was a powerful person in traditional Kikuyu society. People would come to him to learn the future, to be healed, or to be freed from ill omens. The primary apparatus of the medicine man consisted of a series of gourds, the most important of which was the *mwano,* or divination gourd. It contained pebbles picked up from the river during his initiation, as well as small bones, marbles, small sticks, old coins, pieces of glass and any other object that might instill wonder in the eyes of his patients.

With European contact and the arrival of missionaries at the end of the nineteenth century, conversion of the Kikuyu to Christianity began with the establishment of missions throughout Kenya. Conversion was slow for the first thirty or forty years because of the missions' insistence that the Kikuyu give up a large part of their own cultures to become Christians. Although many Kikuyu became Christians, resistance to changing their customs and traditions to satisfy Western religious standards was very strong. Many Kikuyu took a stand over the issue of female circumcision. Missionaries insisted that the practice be stopped, and the Kikuyu were just as adamant that it was an integral part of their lives and culture. The issue eventually became tied to the fight for political independence and the establishment of Kikuyu independent schools.

The Kikuyu have no unique written language; therefore, much of the information on their traditional culture has been gleaned from their rich oral traditions. The oral literature of the Kikuyu consists, in part, of original poems, stories, fables, myths, riddles, and proverbs containing the principles of their philosophy, system of justice, and moral code. An example of Kikuyu music is the *Gicandi,* which is a very old poem of enigmas sung by pairs of minstrels in public markets, with the accompaniment of musical instruments made from gourds.

Bibliography

Clough, Marshall (1990). *Fighting Two Sides: Kenyan Chiefs and Politicians*. Niwot, Colo.: University Press of Colorado.

Davison, Jean (1989). *Voices From Mutira: Lives of Rural Gikuyu Women*. Boulder, Colo.: Lynne Rienner Publishers.

Hedlund, Hans G. B. (1992). *Coffee, Co-operatives and Culture: An Anthropological Study of a Coffee Co-operative in Kenya*. Nairobi: Oxford University Press.

Kenyatta, Jomo (1979). *Facing Mount Kenya: The Traditional Life of the Gikuyu*. London: Heinemann.

Muriuki, Godfrey (1985). *People Round Mount Kenya; Kikuyu*. 2nd ed. London: Evans Bros.

Presley, Cora Ann (1992). *Kikuyu Women, the Mau Mau Rebellion, and Social Change in Kenya*. Boulder, Colo.: Westview Press.

Prins, Adriaan Hendrik Johan (1970). *East African Age-Class Systems: An Inquiry into the Social Order of Galla, Kipsigis, and Kikuyu*. Westport, Conn.: Negro Universities Press.

Kipsigis

ETHNONYM: Lumbwa (an opprobrious name given to the Kipsigis by the Maasai that appears in many early texts)

Orientation

Identification. Kipsigis are the southernmost and most populous of the Kalenjin peoples of Kenya. The term "Kalenjin" (lit. "I say to you") was coined in radio broadcasts and at political rallies during the late colonial period, at a time when political events spurred a growing awareness of the close cultural, historical, and linguistic ties between Kipsigis and neighboring peoples to the north. Within the broader political and cultural context of present-day Kenya, the Kalenjin are recognized as a distinct population that shares a common cultural heritage and common political interests.

Location. The Kipsigis occupy a portion of the highlands in southwestern Kenya that is roughly contiguous with the present boundaries of Kericho District. The terrain is composed of steep ridges, interspersed with numerous rivers and streams, which gradually give way to gently rolling hills and grasslands. Elevations reach nearly 2,100 meters along the eastern extent of Kipsigis country and about 1,450 meters elsewhere. Rain falls most abundantly during two rainy seasons, ranging from 180 to 190 centimeters a year in the high country to 100 centimeters a year in the grasslands. Temperature does not vary markedly by season, but it does fluctuate between daytime highs averaging about 30° C and nighttime lows of about 9° C.

Demography. A precise population figure for the Kipsigis is unavailable because the most recent Kenyan census data do not distinguish the Kipsigis as a separate population group. Informed sources estimate a population of no less than 600,000, which is at least a threefold increase since 1962. The vast majority of this population lives within Kericho District, an area of 4,909 square kilometers. Few Kipsigis elect to live in the market towns and administrative centers throughout the district, although it is not uncommon for young men and, with increasing frequency, young women, to leave the district to take advantage of educational and employment opportunities in other parts of Kenya. Population density within the countryside falls in the range of 80 to 150 per square kilometer.

Linguistic Affiliation. Kipsigis is a tonal language. Classified as Nilotic, it is grouped within the Eastern Sudanic Branch of the Nilo-Saharan Language Family.

History and Cultural Relations

Kipsigis say that both they and the Nandi come from a place called "To," which some of them locate in the vicinity of Lake Baringo. In the course of their southward migration, sometime between the seventeenth and early nineteenth centuries, the Kipsigis and the Nandi separated. Today the Nandi are their immediate neighbors to the north. Pushing farther south, Kipsigis displaced the Luo, Kissi, and Maasai, the descendants of whom are currently their neighbors to the west and south. The Kipsigis once called these people *puniik*, meaning "enemies" or "strangers," although relations with these populations were never completely hostile. Relations with the Maasai were often characterized by fierce competition for grazing land. Despite reciprocal cattle raids, Kipsigis and Maasai intermarried and occasionally adopted one another's children. Exchange with the Kissi seems to have been more frequent, particularly in times of famine, when Kipsigis would exchange cattle for Kissi grain. There are a number of Kipsigis clans of Kissi origin. Okiek hunters occupy the forest to the west. Like the Nandi, the Okiek are Kalenjin speakers. Both groups have maintained intimate cultural and political relations with Kipsigis—they intermarry, share clan affiliations, participate in joint initiation ceremonies, and, in the case of the Okiek, they previously exchanged forest products for Kipsigis grain. Indeed, before the imposition of colonial administration, ethnic boundaries between the Kipsigis and their neighbors seem to have been quite fluid and permeable. The arrival of the British (around the beginning of the twentieth century) radically transformed Kipsigis society. White settlers alienated nearly half of Kipsigis land. Through a series of pressures and inducements, the Kipsigis were gradually drawn within the orbit of the colonial market economy. In the late twentieth century structural changes in the regional economy forced thousands of western Kenyans, mostly Luo people, to come to Kericho in search of employment. Many find work on Kipsigis farms, and they may spend years working for the same family.

Settlements

Kipsigis country is a patchwork of contiguous small farms, ranging from less than 1 to more than 12 hectares. Most families live on farms of between 3 and 6 hectares. These farms are grouped into communities called *kokwotinwek* (sing. *kokwet*). These are not nucleated villages; in fact, one who is unfamiliar with a particular kokwet cannot easily discern its boundaries, although certain physical features—such as roads, streams, or marshes—often separate one kokwet from the next. The kokwet provides a pool of neighbors with whom one is expected to cooperate in certain kinds of farm work and to rally behind in times of sickness or need. In the past, kokwet membership was largely elective, at least for married men, given that residence was ideally neolocal. Today land scarcity prohibits such mobility. It is unlikely that a young man can find, let alone afford, a piece of land away from his father's farm, and therefore the kokwet is becoming a less fluid social unit. A mature Kipsigis homestead generally has three house types: a father's house, rectangular in design, often covered by a corrugated tin roof; a kitchen building, which is round, with a thatched roof, where children and unmarried daughters sleep; and a bachelors' house, where initiated young men sleep. Most Kipsigis houses are of mud-and-wattle construction; however, some prosperous farmers are now building stone houses that incorporate various features of European design.

Economy

Subsistence and Commercial Activities. Although the Kipsigis have always cultivated a range of food crops, they are generally—but perhaps anachronistically—identified as "cattle-raising people." Nearly every adult male owns at least one cow. Milk is a favored food and is considered crucial for the welfare of young children. Livestock, which include goats and sheep, are a unique form of value, insofar as they remain an important part of bride-wealth payments. Nevertheless, livestock are but one component of a mixed farming regime. Like other farming activities, herd-management decisions are heavily influenced by market factors and cash requirements. There is a growing market for milk, which is sold through cooperatives to the government creamery, and a brisk trade in livestock at weekly cattle markets. Maize has largely replaced finger millet and sorghum as the staple food, although the latter are often grown on small plots for home consumption. Maize is also an important cash crop. Given an average harvest, nearly every farmer has some surplus to sell to the state-run cereal board. Some farmers grow maize on a commercial scale. A variety of vegetables is grown in kitchen gardens. At higher elevations, where soil conditions and rainfall are favorable, most farmers grow tea on plots that generally range between 0.2 and 2.4 hectares. Green leaf is plucked throughout the year and sold to state-run factories, where it is processed. The Kipsigis themselves buy their tea at local stores. Served with milk and copious amounts of sugar, tea has become a mainstay of their diet.

Industrial Arts. The Kipsigis are renowned for building handsome and durable houses. Many are competent tanners and leatherworkers. Some women still construct delicately woven food baskets and decorate gourds, which serve as milk containers.

Trade. Small stores, rarely more than 1.5 kilometers or so apart, sell the basic items—cooking oil, salt, sugar, tea, kerosene—that are consumed in nearly every household. Often the proprietors also run a diesel-powered mill that neighborhood women use to grind their maize. Market towns, which are usually within walking distance of many kokwotinwek, offer a wide range of consumer products and services that are provided by commercial artisans. There is a growing cadre of Kipsigis entrepreneurs who run all sorts of businesses; the transport business is the most popular. Weekly cattle markets are lively events: women come to buy and sell fruits and vegetables, itinerant traders buy livestock from farmers and bring them to market, and other farm products are sold directly to government marketing boards.

Division of Labor. Women do all the cooking, which includes the ancillary tasks of collecting water and firewood. They tend the kitchen gardens and often grow small plots of finger millet and sorghum. Women are also the caretakers of children. Men build houses, repair fences, and clear rough land. They provide veterinary care for livestock and, when the situation demands, perform autopsies. Major agricultural tasks involve the entire family and, frequently, cooperative work groups composed of kokwet members. Plowing with oxen is men's work. Planting maize is done by all available family members. Weeding is generally done by women. Maize is harvested by work groups composed of both men and women, who move in a round from one farm to the next. Plucking tea, which is a daily chore on plots of more than 0.4 hectares, is shared by all available hands. Many farmers also engage migrant workers to pluck their tea.

Land Tenure. By the 1950s, virtually all agricultural land was claimed as private property. Land is owned almost exclusively by men, but it is difficult for a man to sell his land if his wife or elder sons object. Title deeds devolve to a man's sons. The rights of unmarried daughters and their children to stay on the farm are recognized; however, there is as yet no consensus regarding what portion of the farm, if any, such women or their children can claim.

Kinship

Kin Groups and Descent. The Kipsigis have more than 200 exogamous patrilineal clans, which serve as descent groups. Clans are not localized and have a rather diffuse corporate character. Clansmen are expected to make homicide payments when one of their own is held responsible for a death. Close clansmen often take a keen interest in one another's careers and home affairs and may be called on when disputes develop within the family concerning inheritance of land or livestock, but clan identity as such has little influence in day-to-day affairs.

Kinship Terminology. The Kipsigis employ a modified Omaha kinship terminology.

Marriage and Family

Marriage. The Kipsigis are polygamous. Rates of polygamy may be declining, however, as people continue to adjust to structural changes within the local economy. Christian strictures against polygamy also influence marriage patterns for many Kipsigis. Bride-wealth payments include livestock and cash. Kipsigis say it is best if co-wives live far apart, but the increasing cost and scarcity of land make such arrangements impracticable for most. Men are expected to supply stock to each house, so that each wife will have cows to feed her children. Over the years, women develop a proprietary interest in these herds, which come to include bride-wealth cattle from their daughters' marriages. If a woman has no sons, she may use some of these cattle to "marry" another woman. According to convention, she will choose her "wife's" principal lover, whose status is acknowledged with the payment of one cow. Children born from such marriages take the clan identity of the cow giver's husband. Divorce is exceptionally rare, even in cases where husband and wife have been separated for many years.

Domestic Unit. Every married woman keeps her own house, in which the cooking is done and the young children sleep. As a man's family matures, certainly before his daughters reach puberty, he will build his own house nearby. Once initiated, young men move to separate sleeping quarters some distance from the main family compound. Older brothers who have married before a farm is subdivided build separate compounds for their families. Each household operates as a relatively autonomous family unit.

Inheritance. When a man is close to death, custom dictates that he call his sons together and instruct them about the disposition of his property, which, these days, may include certain off-farm assets. The livestock that a man has acquired by his own efforts—by purchase or by patient husbandry—are divided equally among all his sons. Bride-wealth cattle, however, are attached to the households from which his married daughters have departed, so that brothers from different houses may be more or less fortunate in the number of cattle they inherit. In cases where extended families occupy one farm, each household ideally receives an equal share of the land, which, over time, will be divided evenly between the sons of each house. If a man has more than one farm, each will be regarded as a separate estate to be shared exclusively by the members of the household who live on that farm.

Socialization. Young children are nursed, fed, dressed, bathed, and watched over by women. Fathers take a keen interest in their children, but physical contact and displays of affection are generally restrained. As a rule, young girls are given household chores at an earlier age than their brothers. Shortly after puberty, boys and girls undergo separate initiations, which coincide with a one-month break in the school calendar. Boys are circumcised, and girls have parts of the clitoris and labia removed. Boys return from initiation with an ascetic bearing that signifies their ascent from childish things and childish behavior. They are expected to remain aloof from their mothers and sisters, who in turn treat them with respect. Girls return from initiation with the expectation they will soon be married, a situation that is often forestalled these days by their continued education. Kipsigis who belong to certain Protestant sects do not send their daughters for initiation; some are developing a "Christian" version of initiation for their sons.

Sociopolitical Organization

Social Organization. There are seven sequentially recurring age sets, called *ipinda*. One is free to dance, drink, and carry on with age mates but ought to be more circumspect in the company of seniors. Men should not marry the daughters of their age mates. Women are also initiated into age sets, but they take the age-set status of their husbands when they marry. Kipsigis men also belong to patrilineal associations called *boriet*, which, in the past, served as regiments in times of war. The kokwet is the hub of community life. People call on their fellow kokwet members for mutual aid. Members of the kokwet or of neighboring kokwotinwek also cooperate in public projects such as building schools. Church groups, particularly those formed by Protestant sects, are becoming important forms of association. Church women have organized cooperative groups that crosscut kokwet ties. The social and economic distance between prosperous farmers and those who are less fortunate is growing. The social implications of such differentiation are as yet unclear, but the emergence of a landless or land-poor rural proletariat seems a likely prospect.

Political Organization. Kipsigis place great value on personal autonomy and are reticent to interfere in one another's affairs. Men may be respected for their achievements and admired for their persuasive oratory, but they do not receive consistent support for their positions at public gatherings. Cliques and political factions are ad hoc and unstable. The basic forum of political participation is the kokwet council, which is composed of all adult men within the kokwet. These men appoint a "village elder," who serves as a liaison to the local subchief appointed by the Kenyan government. The subchief or the local chief may call a kokwet meeting to communicate government policy.

Social Control. Kipsigis place great stock in their notion of respect. A sister respects her brother by dropping her playful attitude toward him once he is initiated. A man respects his mother-in-law by keeping his distance from her. Elders always command respect. Losing one's temper is considered an unfortunate and embarrassing lapse. Angry words are rarely spoken; they may cause physical harm. Serious arguments are mended by a formal apology. The ultimate sanction of serious misconduct is a father's or elder's curse. It is believed that some elders have the power to curse even unknown culprits to death. Criminal conduct is defined by the Kenyan government, and local administration police handle it.

Conflict. In cases of chronic marital discord, a man may send his wife back to her natal home, or she may elect to go herself. Disputes between neighbors involving boundaries, property damage, and the like are heard by the kokwet council. Jealousy or hidden enmity may provoke witchcraft, which can be directed at people or cattle, but witchcraft accusations are rare. Sanctions include shunning or, in extreme cases, banishment. Cattle raiding, a once-popular pursuit of Kipsigis warriors, is no longer tolerated.

Religion and Expressive Culture

Religious Beliefs. Many Kipsigis are Christians; they hold their faith with varying degrees of orthodoxy. Non-Christians believe in a watchful but distant god, whose main manifestation is the sun. Kipsigis are likely to trace personal misfortune to transgressions committed by themselves or by one of their close kin, particularly a parent.

Ceremonies. Kipsigis have ceremonies to "greet" a mother and her newborn child and also to celebrate the completion of a new house. Marriage ceremonies have become elaborate affairs, particularly in Christian families. There are joyful and sometimes raucous public ceremonies held during the first and final states of initiation.

Arts. The Kipsigis are great singers. Choral groups often compose original songs, which are performed at ceremonies and various public events. There is a small but well-established Kalenjin music industry. Popular singers combine upbeat Western and indigenous musical styles.

Death and Afterlife. The Kipsigis bury their dead quickly. The eldest son will bury his father, and the youngest son will bury his mother. After a death, the immediate family will retreat from public life to mourn. The spirit of a recently deceased patrilineal relative is believed to be reincarnated in a newborn child.

Bibliography

Komma, Toru (1984). *The Women's Self-Help Association Movement among the Kipsigis of Kenya*. Senri Ethnological Studies, no. 15. Osaka: Nation Museum of Ethnology.

Manners, Robert A. (1967). "The Kipsigis of Kenya: Culture Change in a 'Model' East African Tribe." *In Contemporary Change in Traditional Societies*. Vol. 1, *Introduction and African Tribes*, edited by Julian H. Steward. Urbana: University of Illinois Press.

Orchardson, Ian Q. (1961). *The Kipsigis*. Abridged from the original manuscript by A. T. Matson. Nairobi: East African Publishing House.

Peristiany, John G. (1930). *The Social Institutions of the Kipsigis*. New York: Humanities Press.

MICHAEL M. DONOVAN

Kongo

ETHNONYMS: Bembe, Kongo, Kunyi, Manianga, Mboma, Mpangu, Ndibu, Ntandu, (N)Sandi, Solongo, Vili, Yombe, all with or without the plural prefix "Ba." "MuKongo" or "Mwisi Kongo" refers to an individual. The people call their homeland "Kongo." The language is KiKongo (KiBembe, etc.)

Orientation

Identification. The BaKongo, numbering three to four million, live in west-central Africa, in a roughly triangular area extending from Pointe-Noire, Congo, in the north, to Luanda, Angola, in the south, and inland to Kinshasa, Zaire. The unitary character of the Kongo group and the identity of the various subgroups are artifacts of colonial rule and ethnography.

Location. Neither the internal nor the external boundaries of the Kongo group can be defined with any precision. The northern part of the Kongo territory is forested, whereas the southern is mainly savanna grasslands with forest galleries. The Zaire (Congo) River fights its way to the sea by a series of cataracts from Malebo Pool, between Kinshasa and Brazzaville, through the rugged Crystal Mountains, whose elevations range from 200 to 400 meters. The vegetation does not differ from that of other parts of tropical Africa; the soil is predominantly lateritic, varying in fertility from the forested bottomlands to the coarse grass and sparse orchard-bush of nearly barren hills. The long dry season lasts from mid-May to September, the short rainy season from October to mid-December, the short dry season from mid-December to February, and the long rainy season from February to mid-May. The average temperature in Brazzaville is 25° C. Because the upper waters of the Zaire extend north of the equator, the flow of the river is fairly constant; high water levels occur in mid-December, low water levels between 15 July and 15 August. Until about 1900, the fauna included lions, hippopotamuses, leopards, elephants, several species of antelope, chimpanzees, giant otters, buffalo, gorillas, and snakes of many kinds, poisonous and nonpoisonous. Animals frequently hunted included wild pigs, cane-cutter rodents, civet cats, bats, and field rats. Fish abound in the rivers. Virtually all large animals except crocodiles have now been killed off by hunters and, since 1970, as a consequence of increasingly rapid destruction of forest habitats. Natural resources include petroleum (in the Cabinda enclave, on the coast) and noncommercial amounts of gold, bauxite, and copper.

Demography. In 1960 the Kongo population in Zaire (Belgian Congo) was approximately 951,000, not including the city of Kinshasa, whose population of 70,000 was about half Kongo. A similar number of BaKongo were located in Congo (formerly the French colony of Moyen Congo), with a corresponding concentration in Brazzaville. By 1970, the population of the major urban areas had tripled; it continued to grow thereafter, although, since 1990, there has been some return to rural areas, for economic and political reasons. Demographic information pertaining to the BaKongo of Angola is lacking; northern Angola was embroiled in civil war during most of the thirty years after 1960, when thousands of Kongo refugees moved temporarily to Zaire. In general, the BaKongo of Zaire are much better documented than those of either Angola or Congo.

Linguistic Affiliation. KiKongo is a Western Bantu language whose several dialects constitute Group H of M. Guthrie's classification. A form of KiKingo, called KiLeta, functions as a lingua franca for many Kongo-related peoples further east. The younger generation of BaKongo in Congo and Zaire, especially in the cities, speak only Lingala, which is increasingly becoming the national language of Zaire.

History and Cultural Relations

The legendary origin of most of the Kongo peoples is Mbanza Kongo, the capital of the Kongo Kingdom, founded perhaps in the thirteenth century but long since reduced to a village—São Salvador—in northern Angola. In 1485 the Portuguese sailor Diego Cão brought the first Europeans to Kongo. Shortly afterward, most of the nobility converted to Christianity. During the sixteenth century, Kongo maintained diplomatic relations with Portugal and the Vatican.

The growth of the Atlantic slave trade in the seventeenth century favored the development of petty states on the coast, notably the kingdom of Loango in modern Cabinda. Increasing Portuguese intervention in Kongo politics, culminating in the defeat of the Kongo king in 1665, brought to an end the relatively centralized period of Kongo government, despite an effort in 1704, led by the prophet Beatrice Kimpa Vita, to revive the kingdom. By the eighteenth century, the typical Kongo settlement was a village of from 200 to 500 inhabitants. The BaKongo were thereafter increasingly integrated into the Atlantic commerce. Their main function was to act as porters and middlemen between the European stations on the coast and the Tio and BoBangi traders at Malebo Pool, where navigation downstream on the Zaire ceased to be possible. The population was stratified into free and slave. From the effective end of the slave trade in 1863 until the creation of the Free State in 1885, slaves were used mostly for agricultural production intended for the European settlements on the coast.

When the European powers divided Africa among themselves in 1885, the Zaire Basin, named the "Congo Free State," was allotted to Leopold II, king of the Belgians. His agents, led by Henry Morton Stanley, took over the interior, including the territory of the BaKongo, where they set up police posts, established trade routes of their own, and more or less forcibly recruited much of the male population as porters and laborers. Similarly violent processes of occupation in the neighboring French and Portuguese colonies, with associated epidemics of sleeping sickness, killed off as much as three-quarters of the population.

In 1908 international protest and fiscal mismanagement forced Leopold to hand over his colony to Belgium, as the Belgian Congo. Effective administration of all three colonial territories was in place by about 1920. Thereafter, the combined effect of state and, more especially, Catholic- and Protestant-mission education, helped to make the BaKongo one of the most Westernized and most influential groups in French Congo, Belgian Congo, and Angola, although they never formed a coherent international bloc. In 1960 Kongo politicians emerged as heads of newly independent states in both Kinshasa and Brazzaville, only to be replaced during subsequent civil strife.

Settlements

Besides the capital cities of Brazzaville (Congo) and Kinshasa (Zaire), the principal urban centers are the ports of Pointe-Noire, Matadi, and Boma. BaKongo predominate in the many towns of their home region but are also found in towns and cities throughout their respective countries. In their own rural areas, BaKongo live in scattered villages varying in population from a few dozen to a few hundred persons. Constructed of adobe, burned brick, or wattle and daub, with roofs of thatch or corrugated iron, the houses shelter single individuals or married couples. Usually, there are two rooms, the inner one reserved for sleeping and storage. A separate kitchen at the back of the house is the center of the female domain.

Economy

Subsistence and Commercial Activities. Most men and many women work, or seek work, in urban areas for most of their working lives. The rural population consists disproportionately of children and elderly people. In urban areas, wages are rarely sufficient to support even a single individual; therefore, people depend on innumerable petty occupations, legal and illegal, to make ends meet. In rural areas, families export as much food to town as they can, earning cash with which to pay taxes and school fees and to buy hardware, clothes, and small luxuries. Domestic animals include goats, sheep, pigs, and poultry; commercial cattle ranches supply meat to the towns. The BaKongo grow manioc, several kinds of yam, maize, peanuts, and various pulses, as well as bananas, avocados, citrus fruits, and palm nuts. A major handicap to the rural economy is the expense and unreliability of transportation. After 1985, the national economy virtually disintegrated, leaving most BaKongo, urban and rural, in dire straits.

Industrial Arts. In rural areas, some men weave baskets and mats, and a few continue the traditional techniques of ironworking; a few women make pots.

Trade. Villages within reach of a truck route may hold a market on Saturdays. Unlicensed traders bring manufactured goods from town for sale or barter, and may make cash advances to rural producers. In town, most women supplement their incomes by buying goods in small quantities and selling still smaller amounts, but a certain number have become successful wholesalers and importers.

Division of Labor. Although both women and men work for wages when they can, men predominate in the better-paying and more prestigious occupations. In rural areas, men cultivate forest crops, including fruit trees, whereas savanna crops are appropriate to women. Men hunt; women fish and catch small rodents.

Land Tenure. In principle, in Zaire all land belongs to the state, from which commercial developers may obtain use rights. In practice, in rural areas unattractive to capitalists, traditional rules of land tenure prevail. Land is owned by matrilineal descent groups called "houses" and is available for use to the members of the house, to in-marrying women, and to the children and grandchildren of male members. Fruit trees, also inherited matrilineally, are owned separately from the land on which they stand.

Kinship

Kin Groups and Descent. In Zairean law, all traditional kinship groupings have been abolished and replaced by a modified type of European family. In practice, every MuKongo identifies himself by reference to his mother's clan and the village in which it is domiciled. Exogamous local sections of each matrilineal clan are divided into landowning houses, and these, in turn, into lineages functioning as inheritance groups.

Kinship Terminology. BaKongo can trace their relationship to others through only one of several routes, depending on the situation. Two persons occupying the same status with respect to any third party are said to be "siblings," *mpangi*. When reckoning is by clans, this principle generates a terminological pattern of the Crow type, in which mother's brother's daughter is equated with "child," *mwana*, and father's sister's daughter with "father," *se*. When reckoning is traced from individual to individual, the pattern becomes Hawaiian, meaning that all cousins are called "sibling." Most kinship terms apply to relatives of either sex.

Marriage and Family

Marriage. Monogamy is required by law, but many men have long-standing, quasi-domestic relationships with more than one woman. Traditionally, marriage with a classificatory patrilateral cross cousin was preferred, but no one may marry into a closely related lineage. Couples are expected to go through traditional wedding formalities, but official recognition is extended only to legally registered marriages. A man is obliged to support his children, whether he married their mother or not, and there is no status of illegitimacy.

Domestic Unit. By tradition, a married woman and man have separate budgets, the wife being responsible for the provision of food (except meat) and the husband for clothes and other bought goods. Each disposes independently of any surplus, but in Zaire the government favors making women dependent on their husbands. Children are raised cooperatively by neighboring and related women.

Inheritance. Increasingly, especially in urban areas, children inherit from their fathers.

Sociopolitical Organization

Social Organization. Matrilineal descent groups of every level are led by a headman (*nkazi*) with at least nominal authority. Civil affairs, subject to traditional or "customary" regulation (*fu kia nsi*), are managed by committees consisting, as appropriate, of representatives of an individual's father's and mother's clans, along with patrifilial children and grandchildren. Such bilateral committees also represent the individual or his lineage at weddings, funerals, and lawsuits. In the conduct of such affairs, the skill of the orator (*nzonzi*), that is, the ability to influence the gathering by authoritative references to tradition and apt proverbs, is greatly esteemed. Official communications and conclusions are registered by exchanging symbolic gifts of food and money.

Political Organization. Indigenous chieftainship no longer has any effective existence, although, in Zaire, the government, for its own purposes, occasionally convenes people it regards as "customary chiefs." Local politics focuses on rights to land—that is, the rights of the "first occupant." Others who wish to use the land, acknowledging the primacy of the owning house, are supposed to be the descendants of slaves or refugees. Arguments about who is a slave and who is not depend on the recitation of tradition and pedigree, supported by the testimony of neighboring descent groups, and may drag on for generations. The basic unit of rural government in Zaire, roughly corresponding to a U.S. county, is the "collectivity," known in colonial times as the "sector" and, later, as the "commune." Its officers, elected or appointed as the policy of the day may decree, form the lowest rank of the national territorial bureaucracy, which is responsible for local taxation, road maintenance, and public order. The Kongo area in northern Angola has been ravaged by civil war for decades.

Social Control. Elders are believed to exercise a kind of witchcraft on behalf of their dependents, but also to use it against them should they feel that their wishes have been ignored. They may also be accused of misusing this power. Witchcraft capacity (*kundu*) is said to be acquired from other witches for a fee, ultimately requiring the sacrifice of a relative to be "eaten" by the witch coven.

Conflict. The BaKongo have a reputation as a nonviolent people. Physical violence is, in fact, rare among them, although they think of themselves as under constant attack by hostile relatives and neighbors, "witches" exercising occult powers. Appropriate committees of elders mediate disputes, and diviners may be consulted in serious cases; often the diviner is a "prophet" (*ngunza*) of a Christian denomination.

Religion and Expressive Culture

The BaKongo are Christians, mostly Catholic, but with a strong Protestant minority in all three countries, affiliated with British, U.S., and Swedish evangelical missions. Church-related schools and hospitals provide the best available education and medical care. Between 10 and 15 percent of the population belong to local Pentecostal churches, most of which trace their origin to the celebrated Kongo prophet Simon Kimbangu, who preached and healed the sick for a few months in 1921 before being imprisoned for life by the Belgian authorities. His son Joseph Diangienda (deceased) founded and led the now international Church of Jesus Christ on the Earth by the Prophet Simon Kimbangu. Kimbanguist-related movements have included Khakism in Congo in the 1930s and Tokoism in Angola in the 1950s.

Arts. Indigenous arts, including sculpture and music, have been almost entirely suppressed by European influence. The traditional pentatonic scale can still be heard in the songs of women, especially as sung at funerals and in connection with the cult of twins. A variety of percussion instruments and idiophones (drums, silt gongs, clapperless bells, rattles) are employed at parties and religious services. In Kinshasa, the BaKongo contribute substantially to Zaire's internationally famous popular dance music.

Medicine. BaKongo of all walks of life commonly consult healers and magical experts (*nganga*) to deal with not only illnesses but also afflictions such as marital disputes, unemployment, traffic accidents, and theft. Such experts, concentrated in the towns, include non-BaKongo. A distinction is made between afflictions sent by God, which are "natural," and those in which an element of witchcraft is involved. Sufferers and their families commonly essay a series of treatments for the same problem, visiting both the diviner and the hospital.

Death and Afterlife. Funerals are important occasions of social gathering and family expenditure. Ideally, the bodies of the dead should be taken back to their natal villages if death occurs in town. Cemeteries are considered to be dangerous places, not to be visited casually. The land of the dead is thought of as situated on the other side of a body of water, sometimes identified with the Atlantic. The life of the dead continues that of the living in another place but inverts it, in such a way that to the dead, who become white, nighttime is daylight. All exceptional powers among the living are thought to be obtained from the dead, either legitimately, as in the case of chiefs and elders, or illegitimately, in the case of witches. In modern belief, benevolent powers from the land of the dead tend to be consolidated under the name "Holy Spirit," and evil powers as "Satan."

Bibliography

Bockie, Simon (1993). *Death and the Invisible Powers: The World of Kongo Belief*. Bloomington: Indiana University Press.

Dupré, Georges (1985). *Naissances d'une société: Historique et histoire chez les Beeme du Congo*. Paris: OSTROM.

Janzen, John M. (1978). *The Quest for Therapy in Lower Zaire*. Berkeley and Los Angeles: University of California Press.

MacGaffey, Wyatt (1970). *Custom and Government in the Lower Congo*. Berkeley and Los Angeles: University of California Press.

MacGaffey, Wyatt (1986). *Religion and Society in Central Africa*. Chicago: University of Chicago Press.

Thornton, John K. (1983). *The Kingdom of Kongo*. Madison: University of Wisconsin Press.

WYATT MACGAFFEY

Konso

ETHNONYMS: none

Orientation

Identification. The Konso are comprised of three groups living in southern Ethiopia—the Garati, the Takadi, and the Turo—that speak three very similar dialects. The name "Konso" may have been given to them by outsiders, such as the Borana Galla: it resembles the name of a very prominent hill overlooking two of the most important markets, which have a long history of trade with the Borana and the Arussi.

Location. The Konso territory is a range of mountains about 50 kilometers south of Lake Shamo, in a bend of the Sagan River in the Rift Valley of southern Ethiopia, 5°30′ N, 37°30′ E. The area of cultivation is approximately 650 square kilometers, and the elevation ranges from about 410 to 545 meters. Annual rainfall is about 66 centimeters, and there are two rainy seasons, one from February to May, and the other from October to December. The climate is dry montane, and temperatures vary from below 16° C at night in the higher regions during the rainy seasons to over 32° C in the lower regions during the dry seasons. Until the arrival of firearms, elephants and rhinoceroses were common in the lowlands; they have long since disappeared, but lions and leopards, crocodiles, pythons, ostriches, zebra, hyenas, and monkeys still exist there, as well as a variety of other animals, such as wild pigs and several species of the deer family. Bird life occurs in numerous forms, including guinea fowl and francolins.

Demography. In 1967 the population was between 55,000 and 60,000, and this estimate is not likely to have changed significantly in the last hundred years. Population density is therefore about 77 to 96 per square kilometer.

Linguistic Affiliation. The Konso language is a member of the East Cushitic Family, Lowland Group.

History and Cultural Relations

Konso traditions suggest a complex pattern of migration into their present territory over the last thousand years, but the predominant cultural influence has been that of the Borana. Close similarities also exist with the neighboring Gauwada, Gidole, and Burji. The Konso were conquered by the army of Emperor Menelik II in 1897, and since that time have been subject to the Ethiopian state. No attempt was made to convert them to Coptic Christianity, however, and government authority has been limited to collecting taxes, preventing warfare, and the introduction of Ethiopian courts of law and police. The inclusion of the Konso within the Ethiopian state encouraged the growth of trade and the use of money, but markets are an ancient feature of Konso society, and they have long been familiar with salt-bar currency and the Maria Theresa dollar. Salt was the most significant import in precolonial times; it was exchanged for coffee and craft products. The Norwegian Lutheran Mission arrived in 1954 and established a school and clinic; a government school was also established a few years later. Until about the mid-1960s, road communications were poor, and the Konso were consequently isolated from social developments in other parts of Ethiopia. Major roadworks were undertaken in the mid-1980s.

Settlements

The Konso live in about thirty-five walled towns, with average populations of 1,500 and a maximum of about 3,000, covering from 6 to 14 hectares, often on the summits of hills or at other easily defensible sites. The walls are without mortar, 3.0 to 4.5 meters high; they are intended only to deter a surprise attack, not to resist a siege. They are usually surrounded by a dense belt of vegetation as a further deterrent to attack. Each town is separated into two divisions, and a man who is born in one is forbidden to live in the other. The divisions have no other social function, however. They are divided into wards, which may contain twenty to eighty homesteads. The average population of a homestead is five, comprising a married man, his wife, and their children. Homesteads are always on two levels; ideally, the upper level is for humans and the lower level for animals. Each homestead contains sleeping huts, kitchen, granaries, and animal stalls and is surrounded by a wooden fence. These fences form continuous walls along the paths within the towns. There are also numerous public meeting places (at least one for each ward), where men sit during the day and where ceremonies take place. Each public place has a men's house, where the married men usually sleep at night, together with the bachelors, but these houses are unoccupied during the day.

Economy

Subsistence and Commercial Activities. The Konso are intensive agriculturists, using animal and human manure and terracing to preserve the soil. Two-pronged hoes and digging sticks are the main agricultural implements. The principal crops on the lower slopes are sorghum, of which at least twenty-four varieties are grown, and maize; on higher ground, the staple crops are wheat and barley. The Konso also grow peas, chick-peas, beans, finger millet, yams, taro, Indian turnips (*Araceae arisaema*), and another tuber, Taccaceae (*Tacca involucrata*). Tree foliage is an extremely important source of food and the Moringaceae (*Moringa stenopetala*) is cultivated for this purpose at each homestead. Ensete (*Ensete edulis*, or "false banana") is grown, but is of little importance. Honey is collected from hives that the Konso place in trees. Cotton is of great economic importance, tobacco is popular, and coffee is also grown. Cattle, sheep, and goats are raised, but the little milk that is produced is made into butter or given to the children. Chickens have always been kept, but only for their feathers. All birds and eggs are forbidden foods, as are most wild animals and fish. Hunting for food and collecting are of little or no significance.

Industrial Arts. The basic crafts are ironworking, weaving, pottery making, and tanning, and their practitioners form a despised hereditary caste. Men work as smiths and weavers, their wives as potters and tanners. There is no restriction on smiths becoming weavers or vice versa, and the same is true of potters and tanners. The spinning of cotton is practiced freely by all men who choose to do so, and some farmers have taken up weaving, to general disapproval. The artisans have never owned land, and intermarriage with farmers is forbidden them. There is no residential segregation of artisans, however, and in dress and appearance they resemble the farmers.

Woodworking, including the making of bowls, troughs, and beehives and the carving of memorial statues, is practiced by farmers. Baskets are also made, and gourds are widely used as containers.

Trade. A traditional market is held every day at a different location, outside one of the towns. Here the artisans sell their wares, and farmers also sell grain, tree foliage, honey, butter, and other agricultural produce. Animals are slaughtered for meat at these markets; in the past, only artisans were butchers, as the slaughter of animals for sale rather than ceremonial use was deprecated. The Borana and Arussi Galla often attend these markets, to which they traditionally brought salt in exchange for coffee and craft products.

Division of Labor. Ironworking, weaving, building houses, collecting honey, repairing terraces, tending livestock, felling trees, and all other heavy or dangerous outdoor work are male activities. Pottery, tanning, fetching water, preparing food (especially beer), and child rearing are female activities. Men and women both work in the fields, but threshing wheat and barley and bird scaring in the harvest season are male activities. Men and women both attend markets as vendors and purchasers.

Land Tenure. Land may be owned and inherited only by men, although women may rent it if they are widowed. Plots of land are owned individually and may be bought and sold.

Kinship

Kin Groups and Descent. The Konso are divided into nine dispersed patrilineal exogamous clans, which form three groups associated with God, the Earth, and the Wild. It is likely that in the past they were of segmentary organization, as is the case with other East Cushitic peoples, but nowadays there are no remembered genealogical links between the clan and the component lineages. The head of each lineage is the *pogalla* (pl. *pogallada*), who is descended by primogeniture from a known founder. The pogalla is responsible for blessing the lineage, for settling disputes between its members, and for representing them in disputes with members of other lineages. He is usually wealthier than most of its other members, because eldest sons inherit twice the share of their brothers. Both the pogalla and other wealthy members of the lineage may be called upon to assist poorer members, and the lineage will help to pay any fines imposed on members by the town. The Konso say that lineage members do not like to live close together, and there is a clear tendency for them to live some distance apart, often in different wards. Many accusations of witchcraft are made between members of the same lineage.

Kinship Terminology. Kinship terminology is of the Omaha type.

Marriage and Family

Marriage. Polygyny is permitted, but only about 10 percent of Konso men have sufficient wealth to support more than one wife. There is also considerable jealousy between co-wives, who have separate establishments. Marriages are arranged by parents but, usually, only at the request of the young man and with the consent of the girl. Bride-wealth is not an important aspect of marriage and is not thought of as a compensation for rights over the bride or her children transferred in marriage, but only as establishing friendship between the groom and his father-in-law. Divorce is easy in theory, but in practice it seems to be rare. For the Konso who live in Garati, all parallel-cousin marriage is prohibited, but marriage is allowed with cross cousins as long as they are not eldest daughters, whereas in Takadi and Turo, all cross-cousin marriage is forbidden, as well as all parallel-cousin marriage. A man may marry his deceased wife's sister, and a woman whose husband dies may marry his brother, but if the husband was an eldest son who died without an heir, his wife is expected to bear a son in his name by one of his brothers. The wife of a pogalla is not supposed to marry again. More than 50 percent of marriages take place within the town, and those outside the town are with members of friendly towns near at hand. Residence is patrilocal.

Domestic Unit. The domestic group of husband, wife, and children is the basic unit of production. The eldest son lives in his father's homestead after marriage, but younger sons are expected to set up new homes after they marry. In polygynous marriages, the senior wife lives in her husband's homestead, but junior wives have separate establishments, where they live with their children and are visited periodically by their husband. The family is under the authority of the husband.

Inheritance. Property is inheritable only within the lineage. The eldest son inherits his father's homestead and twice the share of land that is inherited by each of his younger brothers. If a man dies without heirs, the nearest male relative within the lineage will inherit. Women cannot inherit any form of property, nor can they transmit property rights.

Socialization. The mother is primarily responsible for disciplining the children, and her brothers may also punish them. The relationship between grandparents and grandchildren is more relaxed than that between parents and children, yet great respect is given to the grandfather in particular. Older siblings, usually sisters, are delegated to look after small children, and, given the crowded and populous nature of Konso towns, it is easy for children to play together in groups. Adolescent boys sleep in the men's houses with the older married men, where they become acquainted with Konso traditions.

Sociopolitical Organization

Social Organization. Although wealth is admired, Konso society is basically egalitarian, and the only major difference of status is that between farmers and artisans. Generational seniority, rather than inherited status or kinship, is the most important principle of Konso social organization, although the pogalla is greatly respected. Each region has its own system of age grouping, according to which a man enters the system a fixed number of grades behind that of his father, rather than being automatically initiated into the most junior grade. After a fixed period of years, everyone is promoted simultaneously into the next grade. In Garati, this interval is eighteen years, in Takadi nine, and in Turo five. This type of age-grouping system is known as *gada* and is distinctive of peoples speaking East Cushitic languages. The systems stratify society into three categories: boys, not allowed to marry or to take part in councils; warriors, who may marry and take a junior part in councils; and elders, whose functions are judicial and religious. The systems are primarily concerned with men rather than women; women are excluded from the Takadi and Turo systems once they have reached the grade in which marriage is allowed, and although in Garati they retain the same grades as men, this is only in relation to their maternal role. The members of each grade are grouped into age sets, but every town has its own sets, and the grades are not corporate groups.

Political Organization. Each region has a priest, who lives in isolation, and whose function it is to bless the towns of his region and to perform the ceremonies that are associated with the gada system. In the past, when warfare broke out between towns, he would send his deputies, drawn from the most important lineage heads of the region, to run between the opposing warriors and cast down their staves, and, ideally, this was supposed to prevent further fighting. The regional priests lacked political authority, however, and the towns were autonomous units in this respect. Each town has a council of elders, drawn from the ward councils. Councilors are elected informally on the basis of their personal qualities, and traditionally they acted as a court to hear civil and criminal cases.

Social Control. Formerly, thieves could be punished by whipping or, in extreme cases, by execution, administered by the warriors. Today, however, the Ethiopian courts have taken over much of the administration of justice, but towns still fine those who disturb the peace by quarreling or by other antisocial behavior. Expulsion from the town is another sanction that was traditionally employed. Those who are quarrelsome or uncooperative, especially to fellow ward members, may be ostracized and denied help—for example, in the form of fetching water in time of sickness or burying their dead—by the ward. Civil claims for compensation are also the responsibility of the councils. In some towns there is an annual ceremony at which leaders from both elders' and warriors' grades exhort their fellow townsmen to behave responsibly and to respect traditional values. These values emphasize peace and truth above all else, and public opinion is an extremely powerful force in maintaining them. The Ethiopian government has authorized a headman (*balabbat*) in each town, who is always an important lineage head. He has no real authority, but the Konso consider him their chosen representative in dealings with the government.

Conflict. The Konso admire bravery, and in the public places there are many "stones of manhood" commemorating victories over other towns. They believe that conflict displeases Waga, the Sky God, however, and that blood defiles the earth; therefore warfare and violence should be resolved by ceremonial reconciliation. Barbed spears are forbidden, and although the Konso are familiar with bows and arrows, these have never been made. Only in rare instances were towns burned during warfare, which was conducted with spears and stones in the open fields. Towns formed stable alliances for military purposes. Homicide was the only crime that could not be punished or expiated by compensation. The victim's closest agnates had the duty of killing the murderer, and this act of vengeance was supposed to settle the matter and not produce a feud.

Religion and Expressive Culture

Religious Beliefs. Waga, the Sky God, is believed by many to have created humans in the beginning, and each person at conception. He once lived on earth among the Konso, but he was offended by a woman and so went to live far away. He is still concerned with human affairs, however, and he punishes sinners with sickness, sterility, and death and may even withhold rain from towns in which there is too much quarreling. The elders are God's deputies on earth. There is no idea of private prayer to God; his benefits are requested by the performance of ritual. Opposed to God are many evil spirits, who live in the lowlands and under certain trees and also in the vicinity of the towns, where they are especially active at night. They can cause insanity and sickness, and some people are said to be possessed by them, and, in consequence, they, too, are feared. Another kind of spirit, not considered evil but potentially dangerous if annoyed, lives in wells. The Konso also believe that the soul survives death as a ghost and retains some contact with the living, mainly through the dreams of the lineage head. Ghosts may be heard talking or flapping about at night, and in a few cases they may cause sickness, but there is no cult of the ancestors. To dream of the dead is dangerous for ordinary people and may be an omen of their own death. Beliefs about the evil eye are very important: someone with the evil eye can cause food to stick in the throat, beer to spoil, crops to dry up, and children and calves to refuse to suckle. The motive for use of the evil eye is said to be spite and envy, which can be detected by a habit of praising the fields, stock, or children of others. Many magical substances are used both for hostile and protective purposes. Women are closely associated with the earth, which is a cosmological element, distinct from but complementary to God, who is associated with men. God is not regarded as the creator of the earth, but he nourishes it with rain. Earth is the source of food, whose preparation is exclusively reserved for women, whose symbol on graves and elsewhere is a clay pot. It will be recalled that nine clans are divided into three groups, associated with God, the Earth, and the Wild. God is the source of the social and moral order, whereas the Earth and women supply the physical necessities of life. The Wild is associated with the dangerous forces of spirituality, not only with those of a hostile nature—such as evil spirits and madmen—but also with priests. It is considered dangerous for priests to live in the towns, although most of them now do so, and the most sacred places are always outside the towns and overgrown with wild vegetation that must not be cut.

Religious Practitioners. The main division of Konso religious practitioners is between priests and diviners. The function of priests, always men, is to bless their lineage, ward, town, or region, and this function is performed in public rituals by holders of inherited office. On the other hand, the diviner, who may be female or male, is a private consultant who has acquired occult powers, and his or her advice is sought in secret, not only to discover the mystical source of illness or other misfortunes but also to cast spells on one's enemies. Dream diviners may be priests, but most diviners are feared because it is believed that they are possessed by evil spirits.

Ceremonies. Symbolism and ritual are more important than myths as expressions of the Konso worldview. Almost all rituals involve sacrifice and blessing; they are conducted in sacred places from which women and children are excluded, although they may be spectators. The most elaborate ceremonies occur in the gada system of each region, at the time when everyone is promoted to the next grade. In Takadi, the land is ritually purified of sin in the year after this ceremony. The warrior grade is represented by a dead juniper tree, placed in one or more sacred places in a town, and the erection of these trees is accompanied by a complex ritual. Each year, the pogalla blesses his lineage, their crops, and livestock, and, in Garati, the mothers of those in the warrior grade perform a ceremony to bless their sons, the only occasion on which women assume such a role. In some towns, the men leave the town each year, to hear speeches on good conduct, and then return through a ceremonial gate formed by the most important pogallada holding their staves over the path. This ceremony is regarded as a ritual purification. When a child is born, it is secluded with the mother for three months and then, in a complex ritual, named. Death involves mourning at the house of the family and the digging of the grave by men of the ward; after a few months, a bullock should be sacrificed. Marriage involves very little ceremony.

Arts. Apart from the carving of wooden statues to honor successful men, the Konso have little in the way of art.

Medicine. The Konso have made scant use of plants for medicinal purposes, but they are aware of the technique of variolation as a primitive form of vaccination to prevent smallpox.

Death and Afterlife. The person is comprised of flesh, "vitality" (seen as the pulse), which disappears, and of the soul, which becomes a ghost. There are no rewards or punishments in the afterlife.

Bibliography

Hallpike, C. R. (1968). "The Status of Craftsmen among the Konso of Southwest Ethiopia." *Africa* 38:258–269.

Hallpike, C. R. (1970a). "Konso Agriculture." *Journal of Ethiopian Studies* 8:31–43.

Hallpike, C. R. (1970b). "The Principles of Alliance Formation between Konso Towns." *Man*, n.s. 5:258–280.

Hallpike, C. R. (1972). *The Konso of Ethiopia: A Study of the Values of a Cushitic People*. Oxford: Clarendon Press.

C. R. HALLPIKE

Kpelle

ETHNONYMS: Gerse, Guerze, Kpese, Pessy

Orientation

Identification. The Kpelle are the largest ethnic group in the West African nation of Liberia and a significant group in neighboring Guinea. Whereas the Kpelle of Guinea (called "French Kpelle" by Liberians) are poorly described, the Liberian Kpelle have been more thoroughly studied. They are arguably the most rural and conservative of the major Liberian peoples.

Location. Most Kpelle inhabit Bong County and adjacent areas in central Liberia. The terrain is primarily rain forest crisscrossed by hills, with swamps and rivers in lowland areas. Annual rainfall varies from 180 to 300 centimeters, the bulk falling from May through October, the Kpelle rainy season. There is often a brief period of diminished rainfall, however, usually in July, called in Liberia the "mid-dries." The average low temperature in a typical year in the Kpelle area is 19° C, the average high 36° C.

Demography. There are over 300,000 Kpelle in Liberia and approximately 100,000 in Guinea. In Liberia they constitute about 20 percent of the total population; about 15 percent of Liberian Kpelle can be classified as urban dwellers, whereas the rest are rural. Population density ranges from 10 to 40 per square kilometer in Kpelleland, with greatest concentrations along the main roads; average density is 14 per square kilometer. Life expectancy at birth is under 40 years; between 16 percent and 55 percent of all children born do not reach adulthood.

Linguistic Affiliation. The language, also called Kpelle, is monosyllabic and tonal; it is classified in the Mande Family of the Niger-Congo Stock.

History and Cultural Relations

The Kpelle migrated from the savanna area of the western Sudan to what is now Liberia shortly before the end of the sixteenth century, perhaps fleeing conflicts among the Sudanic states. Having mastered slash-and-burn agricultural techniques and acquiring new forest crops, they easily overrode the foraging Kwa-speaking peoples already there and quickly expanded into much of their present territory. In 1820 the first Afro-American settlers arrived in Liberia as the Kpelle were expanding south and west. In the 1920s Firestone leased land at Harbel and planted the first rubber trees there. The demand for tappers prompted the first Kpelle labor migrations. A second wave of labor migrations, in the 1960s, coincided with the opening of large iron mines in the western parts of the republic. Urban migration has accelerated since the 1970s; there are now distinct Kpelle communities in Monrovia.

The Kpelle interact most frequently with the neighboring Mende, Loma, Mano, and Bassa. They share the Poro complex of secret ritual societies with all of these peoples except the Bassa; initiates may even attend certain secret rituals in these other ethnic areas. The Kpelle also trade with the Muslim Vai and Mandingo, who frequently live among them in small numbers, as do some Lebanese merchants and U.S. missionaries and Peace Corps volunteers. An Episcopal-controlled four-year college is located in the middle of Kpelleland. The huge Firestone rubber plantation has been evacuated and left untended owing to the Liberian civil conflict that began in December 1989.

Settlements

The traditional Kpelle house is a round one-room, wattle-and-daub hut with a conical thatched roof; however, this type, although found everywhere, nowadays predominates only in relatively remote, unacculturated villages. More common is the square house with three rooms and an open porch, or a rectangular house with two rooms and a very wide open porch. Zinc roofs are gradually replacing thatch, especially where cash employment is common.

Kpelle villages generally accommodate between 50 and 600 persons living in 10 to 150 huts; these numbers may be considerably higher if the village is an important one or is located on a motor road. Villages are often surrounded by considerably smaller farm hamlets; in addition, some families or even individuals live alone, away from a village or hamlet. Larger villages, called "towns" by the Kpelle, are divided into "quarters," named subunits with their own quarter-chiefs. Farms are located away from villages, sometimes at a considerable distance. Villages are generally several kilometers apart, with farm hamlets, if any, dispersed around each village and uninhabited bush between each village-hamlet cluster. Many Kpelle today live as refugees in Guinea and Monrovia because of the civil war.

Economy

Subsistence and Commercial Activities. Dry swidden rice is the Kpelle staple and the focus of Kpelle life. The Kpelle conceptualize the word "work" to mean "rice cultivation." One crop a year is harvested in an annual slash-and-burn cycle; land is generally used once and then left fallow for at least seven years. Cassava (manioc) is the second-most important staple crop. The Kpelle also grow a variety of other foodstuffs, including yams, potatoes, plantains, greens, peanuts, eggplants, okra, tomatoes, sesame seeds, peppers, onions, oranges, grapefruits, mangoes, bananas, pineapples, and papayas. Hunting and trapping contribute occasional meat to the diet, although fishing contributes a larger proportion of protein sources. Gathering is far more important, providing palm wine, palm nuts (for palm oil), kola nuts, and many wild fruits, fungi, vegetables, herbs, roots, and greens. Cash cropping of sugarcane, rubber, cacao, and coffee did not begin until the 1960s. A decreasing few Kpelle spin and weave native cotton into homespun cloth, and a few fairly affluent men distill sugarcane juice into rum, but most Kpelle acquire cash through wage labor on rubber farms and in iron mines. Most Kpelle have no domestic animals; those who do keep goats, sheep, and chickens slaughter them only for religious sacrifice or to honor a high-status visitor. A few wealthy families have some cattle or a few pigs.

Industrial Arts. Although there are no full-time specialists, most villages have weavers, tailors, furniture makers, mask and fetish sculptors, and a blacksmith. The art of smelting iron from ore is now virtually forgotten but was once a highly valued skill.

Trade. Markets were introduced by the Americo-Liberians and are still not found in remote roadless parts of Kpelleland, but, in less remote areas, lively weekly markets are an important event. In large commercial towns lining the major arteries, one may find market produce nearly every day, in addition to many Lebanese- and Syrian-run shops.

Division of Labor. The Kpelle division of labor is determined primarily by gender. Men clear the bush, and women plant. Men hunt and occasionally fish and gather palm wine, palm nuts, and kola nuts. Women do most of the fishing and gathering. Women weave nets and most baskets, whereas men plait mats, make furniture, weave some types of mat, and, where it is still practiced, weave homespun cloth. Although all Kpelle are farmers, some further division results from knowledge of politics and "medicine" (or "magic"). A chief, for example, may be somewhat better off than others. Medicine men, medicine women, and shamans of various types also often enjoy considerable prestige and influence, particularly within the framework of the numerous secret (or sacred) societies. The blacksmith, for example, is always a powerful medicine man who is believed by many to be an important ritual leader within the Poro society for men. Wealthy, influential men are called "outstanding men" or "big shots" and are very much admired and often envied.

Land Tenure. Because population density is low, there is little land pressure in most of Kpelleland. The first man to settle in a previously uninhabited area is called the "owner of the land," a title with ritual as well as secular significance. He, or if deceased, his descendant, allots land to those who ask, and permission is rarely refused.

Kinship

The only significant kin group is the patrilineage, which is weak in function and shallow in depth, extending only three or four generations. Iroquois cousin terminology with bifurcate-merging avuncular terms is used.

Marriage and Family

Marriage. Although monogamy has become more common in the late twentieth century, polygyny remains the preferred marital type. Anthropologist James Gibbs (1965) describes six types of union recognized by the Kpelle, ranging from the most prestigious (full bride-price paid outright with patrilocal residence) to casual liaisons. The Kpelle prefer marriage with bride-price, although bride-service is acceptable as well. Patrilocal postmarital residence is preferred, but neolocality associated with bride-service is quite common for very young couples. At least 20 percent of Kpelle marriages end in divorce, which can be quite complex and protracted. Grounds include infertility and adultery for husbands, and physical abuse and nonsupport for wives. Divorce negotiations involve property, especially when substantial bride-price is involved.

Domestic Unit. The polygynous family, with each wife and her children having their own hut, is the ideal form, but it is quite rare. It is more likely that all members of a polygynous family live in the same house, with each wife having her own room. Often one wife will live elsewhere, even several kilometers away. Monogamous nuclear and extended families are on the increase.

Inheritance. A man's authority, property, and younger wives are inherited either by his oldest surviving brother or his oldest son. Obligations, debts, personality, and food taboos, among other things, are inherited patrilineally.

Socialization. Until age 2, children are very much indulged; from age 2 to 6, they are trained through threats and ridicule; after age 6, corporal punishment is frequently used. At all ages, curiosity is stifled and innovation actively discouraged. Boys are circumcised when they are young. At some point between the ages of 7 and 20, boys are initiated in seclusion and en masse into the secret men's society called Poro. While Poro school used to last up to four years, nowadays it is generally much shorter. Physical initiation features scarification on the back and often on the chest and stomach as well. Also between the ages of 7 and 20, girls are initiated into the women's Sande society, a process that traditionally lasted up to three years. Clitoridectomy and labiadectomy are central features of female initiation. For both sexes, initiation is carried out by masked figures.

Sociopolitical Organization

Social Organization. Although residence and many activities tend to be built on the patrilineages, associations are more important in Kpelle social organization. The first is the *kuu,* which is an ad hoc cooperative work group of kin, friends, and neighbors. The two primary kuu types are those that are formed to clear the forest for a rice farm and those that are called together to build a house, but work groups are also created for other purposes. Even more significant are the many secret societies, especially the Poro (for men) and Sande (for women), which pervade many aspects of life. They function as religious, social, political, legal, and educational institutions. In addition, there are numerous exclusive specialized societies devoted to various forms of magic ("medicine")—for example, controlling snakes, lightning, or witches.

Political Organization. The Kpelle are organized into several petty chiefdoms without any overarching political structure above the local chiefdom. Since the pacification of the interior by the Americo-Liberian government's Frontier Force, these chiefdoms' heads have been called paramount chiefs. Under each are several clan chiefs—but "clan" in this context simply refers to a district and has nothing whatsoever to do with kinship. Under each clan chief are the various town chiefs, and under them, quarter chiefs, if any. The Poro Society acts as a sort of shadow government; chiefs at any level can accomplish little without Poro backing.

Social Control. Beyond enculturation, conformity is achieved largely through social pressure, especially the fear of being accused of witchcraft. The Poro and Sande also keep their members in line, even trying and torturing individuals for serious violations of norms. In secular matters, most cases are adjudicated in informal hearings, often convened by the village chief. Nowadays more serious cases go through the Liberian courts, although traditional ordeals are often employed.

Conflict. The Kpelle engaged in sporadic warfare until the late 1930s. "War chief" was a traditionally recognized and prestigious office; it is now defunct, although it may still have ritual significance within the Poro.

Religion and Expressive Culture

Religious Beliefs. Whereas some 10 to 25 percent of the Kpelle are nominal Christians (usually Lutheran) in those areas where missionaries are very active, and whereas a handful embrace Islam, the vast majority hold traditional animistic beliefs. Kpelle religion is rather inchoate, focused vaguely on God, the ancestors, and forest spirits and more sharply on the secret medicine societies and the masked spirits who operate within those societies. The Kpelle recognize a High God who created the world and then retired. They believe in a variety of lesser spirits or genii, including ancestors, personal totems, water spirits, and spirits in magically powerful masks. Witchcraft and sorcery figure prominently in the belief system.

Religious Practitioners. The Kpelle recognize three principal types of shaman (medicine person of either sex): those associated with the Poro and Sande societies, those associated with other specific medicine societies, and those who are independent. The first two types mainly conduct rituals; the third type, and occasionally the second, primarily heal. The Kpelle also utilize diviners who analyze problems for a fee.

Ceremonies. Sacrifices are made to ancestors and other spirits, often at crossroads. Rituals and ritual knowledge are secret and, in general, associated with the secret medicine societies. Accordingly, most important Kpelle rituals are not accessible to observers. One exception is the coming-out ceremonies following initiatory seclusion.

Arts. The Kpelle design various musical instruments, weave homespun cloth and several types of mat, and carve crude sculptures. Their most beautiful and refined artistic creations are the elegant and awesome spirit masks associated with the secret societies.

Medicine. The Kpelle deal with disease and with spirits through magic and medicine, both of which are implied by the word *sale.* Depending on whether a malady is determined to be caused by spiritual (e.g., witchcraft) or other agency, the appropriate type of specialist is consulted for treatment.

Death and Afterlife. Death is a passing into a spiritual realm that coexists with the material realm. The deceased become ancestors, who seem to become increasingly vague and to move further away from villages and into the bush as their memory becomes less distinct in the minds of their living relatives.

Bibliography

Bellman, Beryl (1975). *Village of Curers and Assassins.* The Hague: Mouton.

Bledsoe, Caroline H. (1980). *Women and Marriage in Kpelle Society.* Stanford, Calif.: Stanford University Press.

Erchak, Gerald M. (1977). *Full Respect: Kpelle Children in Adaptation.* New Haven: HRAF Publications.

Gibbs, James L., Jr. (1965). "The Kpelle of Liberia." In *Peoples of Africa,* edited by James L. Gibbs, Jr., 197–240. New York: Holt, Rinehart & Winston.

GERALD M. ERCHAK

Kurds

ETHNONYMS: none

Orientation

The Kurds have inhabited an area of rugged mountains and high plains at the headwaters of the Tigris and Euphrates rivers for over two thousand years. They are believed to be descended from the Medes who overthrew Nineveh in 612 B.C. Their traditional mode of subsistence is pastoralism and agriculture.

The territory Kurds conceive of as Kurdistan ("the land of the Kurds") is distributed across the present borders of Turkey, Iraq, Iran, and Syria. There are other pockets of Kurds living in these countries, but outside of Kurdistan. A large group of Kurds can also be found in contiguous parts of the former Soviet Union. The terrain of Kurdistan is formed by the Eastern Taurus and the Zagros mountains and includes the steppelike plateaus to the north and the foothills of the Mesopotamian plains to the southwest. The climate is prone to extreme temperature fluctuations, from −30° C in the winter, to 45° C during the summer. Some mountain villages are completely isolated by heavy snows for up to six months of the year.

Kurdish, an Indo-European language, is most closely related to Persian. It consists of four main dialects (northern, middle, and southern Kurmanji, and Gorani), which in turn include several local dialects.

Estimates of the number of Kurds living in Turkey, Iran, Iraq, Syria and the former USSR are unreliable owing to the census policies of the various countries. Estimates of the Kurdish population in the mid-1970s for all these countries combined ranged from 13.5 to 21 million.

History and Cultural Relations

The Kurds have a long and eventful history. The Greek historian Xenophon recounted his encounters with the "Karduchi" as early as 375 B.C. The Arabs who brought Islam to the area in the seventh century A.D. were the first to refer to "Kurds." Many important figures in the history of the Ottoman and Persian empires were Kurds, and the remote area inhabited by Kurds served as a buffer between empires. The Kurds have long fought for autonomy, either as self-governing provinces or as an independent nation-state.

This history has profoundly affected almost every aspect of Kurdish life and culture. Rapid social change has been occurring in the countries that divide Kurdistan, which affects the Kurds as well. The policies of the various governments have also had quite different kinds of impact on the Kurds. Whereas the Turkish government outlaws the use of the Kurdish language in public and the publication or possession of Kurdish writings or audio recordings, the Iraqi government allowed the use of Kurdish as the language of instruction for Kurdish schoolchildren during the 1970s and 1980s. Thus, the development of Kurdish literature prospered in Iraq but was severely hampered in Turkey. In addition to dialectal differences, written communication is further complicated by the use of the Latin, Arabic, and Cyrillic alphabets in the different countries. These examples illustrate the complexity of the situation and serve as a caution against overgeneralization.

Settlements

Traditionally, Kurds were either nomads who lived in tent camps and moved their herds between summer and winter pasturage, or settled agriculturists who lived in villages on the plains or in mountain valleys. Today most Kurds have settled. Those who have not live in heavy, black woolen tents, which remain standing at the winter pasturage, and use lighter tents when traveling to and from summer pastures higher in the mountains. Camps may consist of an entire clan or of a group of families who join to herd their flocks together.

Kurdish villages consist of low clay or stone houses with flat roofs. They are often built up the sides of a slope such that the roof of one house serves as a terrace for the house above it. Some villages correspond to lineages, others contain members of several lineages or of both tribal and nontribal groups; many are not organized along any kind of kinship tie. Villages often own communal pasture land, and, in some villages, private property may be sold only to fellow villagers. Kurdistan also contains several urban centers where large landowners, professionals, government workers, and laborers reside.

Economy

The nomadic pastoralists raise sheep and goats and trade wool, meat, and dairy products for grain, tea, sugar, and other consumer products available through the local markets. Other domesticated animals include cattle, donkeys, mules, and horses.

In the agricultural villages, wheat, barley, and lentils are the staple crops. Tobacco is raised as a cash crop, and walnuts, fruits, and vegetables are cultivated according to local conditions. Most agriculturists also have livestock.

Domestic industry consists of spinning, weaving, plaiting ropes, and the production of unglazed clay storage vessels.

The distribution of labor is based on the distinction between male and female tasks and that between peasants and aristocratic landowners. Women are responsible for milking and the processing of butter and cultured milk. In addition to preparing food, housekeeping, and child care, they collect firewood and manure for use as fuel, fetch water, clean grain, spin, weave, make cigarettes, harvest tobacco, carry the harvest to the threshing floor, and may help with plowing. Aristocratic women perform tasks within the home but have servants to do the work away from home, such as milking and fetching fuel.

Men plow, sow, and harvest, transport surplus grain to the town market, and make whatever purchases are needed at the market. Usually one shepard is employed to herd the flocks for the entire village. Traditionally, the *agha* (lineage, clan, or village leader), was responsible for the upkeep of a guest house in which visitors to the village were lodged and entertained and where village men met to discuss recent events. In return for this service, the agha was paid a tribute of approximately 10 percent of the villagers' harvest. Village guest houses are no longer as important as they once were. As the village leaders have moved away to the larger towns, the village guest houses have begun to disappear, and the men socialize instead at local tea houses.

Kinship

Kurdish kin groups are based on patrilineal descent. Several generations of one man's descendants through the male line constitute a lineage. Several such lineages compose a clan. It is assumed that all members of a clan are related through a common male ancestor, but outside groups may attach themselves to a powerful tribe and, after several generations, be incorporated as full members into a clan and tribe. A tribe consists of several clans.

Kurdish kinship terminology does not distinguish between maternal and paternal grandparents. It does distinguish between father's and mother's brothers, and between their children. Father's sisters and mother's sisters, however, are categorized together, as are their children.

Marriage and Family

Kurdish marriages are arranged between the families of the bride and groom. Ideally, a man will marry his father's brother's daughter, to whom he has "first rights." The majority of Kurdish marriages in the 1960s were reported to be between the children of two brothers. This lineage endogamy "keeps the family together" but also weakens the ties between lineages, thus increasing the likelihood of conflict. If marriage to father's brother's child is not possible, the next best choice is one of the other cousins.

Marriage negotiations are first carried out between the women of the two families, and then finalized by the men when a marriage settlement is drawn up. It states the size of the bride-wealth and how it will be used. If the groom does not pay the agreed-upon bride-wealth or does not support and clothe her according to the standards of her own family, the bride has grounds for divorce. The only other way she may obtain divorce is by repayment in full of the bride-wealth, unless otherwise stipulated in the marriage settlement. The man may divorce his wife merely by renouncing her three times.

According to the Quran, a man may have up to four wives provided he can support them all and spends equal time with each; however, few men can afford even two wives. A childless marriage is the most common grounds for divorce or the taking of a second wife.

The wedding entails the fetching of the bride to the groom's home, where the new couple will live until they establish their own home. A Kurdish household thus consists of a man, his wife (or wives), children, and eventually daughters-in-law and grandchildren. In the case of polygyny, each wife may have her own section of the house, which she runs independently.

Inheritance from the father is divided equally between the sons. Daughters do not inherit.

Sociopolitical Organization

Tribal organization based on patrilineal descent is typical of Kurdish nomadic pastoralists. Pasturage is collectively held by the clan within the tribe's territory, and migrations are coordinated at the tribal level. Among the seminomads and in the sedentary villages, clans and lineages come into play only in response to conflict, often in the form of blood feuds; however, not all sedentary agriculturists are organized along kinship lines. A traditional distinction was made between tribal agriculturists, who owned the land they worked, and nontribal peasants, who were subservient to the landowning tribals. These peasants did not own the land—they were bound to it and "belonged" to the tribal leader who controlled it. They owed him their labor and/or a percentage of their crops. Thus, Kurdish society includes both tribal and feudal systems, with clan, lineage, or village leaders serving as feudal lords.

As most Kurds have settled and become agriculturists, and because of the impact of government policies such as land reforms, changes have occured in Kurdish social organization. Through his contacts with government authorities, the agha was able to register communal lands in his own name. Thus, whereas in some areas village membership includes the right to a plot of land, in others entire villages are owned by a single absentee landlord, for whom the villagers work as sharecroppers or wage laborers. The mechanization of agriculture has reduced the need for village labor, and villagers have sought wage employment in urban centers both within and outside Kurdistan. The following recent events have clearly also had a major impact on Kurdish social organization: the Iran-Iraq War, the forced resettlement of tens of thousands of Iraqi Kurds, Iraq's gas-bombing of Kurdish towns and villages, the Gulf War and the resultant flight of Kurds to Iran and Turkey, and the establishement of a U.N.-enforced safe haven; however, the long-term consequences of these events remain to be determined.

Because of its rugged terrain, Kurdistan acted as a buffer area between a series of competing empires. Kurdish political organization is therefore best understood as a response to the state. Kurdish tribal leaders were able to increase their power vis-à-vis one another by leading warriors in the service of the various empires. Their loyalty to the state was rewarded with titles and the backing of the central government in local disputes. Other tribal chiefs could submit to this paramount chieftain or establish relations with the competing states. Eventually, confederations of tribes arose that were ruled by a single *mir*. These emirates encompassed large territories and were granted considerable autonomy. In the 1500s many of the Kurdish emirates were incorporated into the Ottoman Empire. The mirs maintained local autonomy but were under the administration of regional governors who reported directly to the sultan. The emirates were abolished in the 1800s, and local rule reverted to several paramount chieftains.

In the 1900s government control penetrated further into the local level, and administrators dealt directly with the leaders of individual tribes and villages. Thus, Kurdish leaders are now found at the local level, and their influence is derived from personal attributes such as generosity, honor, and the ability to persuade and to deal with government officials. Tribal and lineage leadership is inherited, although there may be several contenders within the family, and other families may challenge and take over the position. Larger tribes generally choose their leader from a royal lineage, but different branches of the lineage may compete for the title. The *shaykh* (pl. *shuyukh*) also plays an important role (see "Religion and Expressive Culture").

The Kurds have been much affected by the different national policies and are now engaged in a long-term effort to gain some form of self-rule. Demands range from local autonomy to the formation of a Kurdish nation-state. Political parties and demands, guerrilla forces, and support from foreign governments are all part of modern Kurdish politics.

Religion and Expressive Culture

The Kurds converted to Islam in the seventh century A.D. Most Kurds are orthodox Sunni Muslims of the Shafi school; however, in southeastern and southern Kurdistan, some tribes are Shiite. Also found in southeastern Kurdistan is the Ahl-e Haqq sect, which, although based on Ismaili Shiism, is considered heretical by other Muslims. The Alawites (Alevis) of northwestern Kurdistan also practice an unorthodox form of Shiism. The majority of Alawites are Turks, but many are Kurds, some of whom speak the Zaza dialect. A syncretistic form of religion found only among the Kurds is the Yezidi sect. It is believed to be derived from Zorastrianism but influenced by Ismaili Shiism. Its practitioners have been referred to as devil worshipers and are subject to severe persecution. In addition to Muslims, groups of Jews and Christians (Armenians, Assyrians, and Syriacs) have lived among the Kurds.

Sharia (Islamic law) was enforced in religious courts throughout the Ottoman Empire. With its fall and the secularization of the Turkish state, the only clerics left are the mullahs. They continue to provide religious instruction and lead religious ceremonies at the village level. Their prestige and influence are no longer guaranteed, however, but is based upon their personal integrity and wisdom.

In addition to the clerics and the shuyukh, there are those who maintain that they are descendants of the Prophet Mohammed. Many of them are poor, living on a claim to financial support on the basis of their descent; some serve as itinerate peddlers of religious amulets and as soothsayers. They are accorded little respect unless they are also wealthy or powerful; in this case, their descent increases the prestige they have obtained through other channels.

The shuyukh obtain prestige and power as holy men and leaders of religious brotherhoods (Sufi or Dervish orders). After receiving instruction in the religious order, a man may be declared a shaykh by an already established shaykh. A shaykh's ability to perform miracles serves as proof that he is indeed a "favorite of God." This ability is believed to continue after death, giving rise to pilgrimages to the tombs of powerful shuyukh. Before the emergence of modern political parties, Dervish orders in Kurdistan—the Qadiri and the Nagshibandi brotherhoods—provided a basis for a level of organization wider than the tribe but independent of the state (van Bruinessen 1992, 210). For this reason, shuyukh performed an important function as mediators after the destruction of the emirates. They have thus been able to gain substantial power as leaders, especially in areas where tribal organization dominated and blood feuds prevailed.

In addition to the observances of the Islamic calendar, Kurds celebrate events of the pastoral seasons, which provide occasions for the strengthening of social bonds and negotiation of marriages. The Kurdish new-year celebration, Newroz, takes place on 21 March and commemorates the people's rebellion against a cruel and unjust king, and the return of light. Fires are lit on mountaintops and in villages, and a feast is held, followed by a ceremony mourning the dead. The Kurds consider Newroz their "national holiday," which they claim to have celebrated for over 2,500 years.

The Kurds are renowned for the rich colors and intricate designs of their wool rugs. These continue to fetch high prices on the international market but are sold by traders in urban centers far from Kurdistan.

The Kurds also have a rich oral tradition. Professional troubadours traveled from place to place recounting legends and singing ballads and epic tales. The art of storytelling was much appreciated until the radio and increased literacy began to compete. Kurds have therefore begun to write down their oral legends and songs in an effort to preserve them. Kurdish written literature consists predominately of classical poetry dating from as far back as A.D. 1200. After the division of the Ottoman Empire, the new nation-states restricted or forbade the publication of Kurdish literature. Only in Iraq could it continue to develop freely. Kurdish exiles in Europe are now attempting to further the analysis and development of their literature.

The Kurds maintain that to be a Kurd is "to look Death in the eye" because expressing and passing on their culture has often entailed breaking laws and engaging in armed resistance. As agonizing as was the plight of Iraqi Kurds in the aftermath of the Gulf War, it was merely another chapter in the ongoing Kurdish struggle for self-rule in the face of the repression and violence employed by the various national governments to assimilate and/or control them. Men speak of having many children to ensure that some Kurds survive the violence to carry on the culture.

Kurdish funerals occur immediately after death. The corpse is washed by a member of the same sex, wrapped in white cotton, and covered with a prayer rug. It is carried to the mosque, where a blessing is given, according to the Shafi rite. It is then buried, facing Mecca, stones marking the head and feet. Following a death, friends and relatives visit the family of the deceased, to pay their respects. While in mourning, a person will not make visits outside the home unless there is a death in the family.

Bibliography

Barth, Fredrik (1953). *Principles of Social Organization in Southern Kurdistan*. Oslo: Universitetsforlaget.

Busby, Annette (1994). "Kurds: A Culture Straddling International Borders." In *Portraits of Culture: Ethnographic Originals*, edited by Melvin Ember, Carol Ember, and David Levinson. The Source One Custom Publishing Program. Englewood Cliffs, N.J.: Prentice-Hall.

Chaliand, Gerard (1980). *People Without a Country: The Kurds and Kurdistan*. London: Zed Press.

Entessar, Nader (1992). *Kurdish Ethnonationalism*. Boulder, Colo., and London: Lynne Rienner Publishers.

Hansen, Henny Harald (1961). *The Kurdish Woman's Life*. Copenhagen: Nationalmuseets Skrifter.

Leach, Edmund R. (1940). *Social and Economic Organization of the Rowanduz Kurds*. Monographs in Social Anthropology, no. 3. London: School of Economics and Political Science.

McDowall, David (1992). *The Kurds: A Nation Denied*. London: Minority Rights Publications.

Olson, Robert (1989). *The Emergence of Kurdish Nationalism, 1880–1925*. Austin: University of Texas Press.

van Bruinessen, Martin M. (1992). *Agha, Shaikh, and State: The Political Structures of Kurdistan*. London and Atlantic Heights, N.J.: Zed Press.

ANNETTE BUSBY

Lango

ETHNONYMS: Jo Lango, Langi

Orientation

Identification. The Lango are one of the largest of the non-Bantu ethnic groups in Uganda. They are often classified together with their western neighbors, the Acholi, although they have long regarded themselves as being distinct from them. In the past, the Lango were generally regarded as the residents of a rural hinterland and as people whose activities had little effect on the nation as a whole, but, since Uganda's independence, the Lango have become integrated into national political life.

Location. The Lango live between 1°30′ N and 2°44′ N and between 32°15′ E and 33°15′ E. Their territory covers 14,820 square kilometers, including 1,300 square kilometers of open water and swamp. The gently rolling savanna of Lango territory lies at an elevation of 900 to 1,200 meters. Neighboring ethnic groups are the Acholi to the west, the Iteso to the east, and the Karamojong to the north.

Demography. There are about 410,000 Lango in Uganda. The population is most dense in the southern part of Lango territory, in the area between Lira and Lake Kyoga, where it reaches about 48 per square kilometer. In the northern and western portions of the Lango District, the population density is about 16 per square kilometer.

Linguistic Affiliation. Lango is a Nilotic language that is mutually intelligible with Acholi. Lango, Acholi, Luo, and Alure are usually classified together as the Southern Luo languages, which means that the Lango are linguistically related to the Luo of Kenya.

History and Cultural Relations

The Lango settled into their present location after first moving southward as part of the southerly migration of Luo-speaking Nilotic people, which probably took place in the fifteenth century. There is evidence that cultural distinctions between the Lango and the Acholi were well established by the early nineteenth century. The relationship between the Lango and their Paranilote-speaking neighbors to the northeast, the Karamojong, is unclear. Many Lango clan names resemble Karamojong clan names, and Lango cultural practices such as totemic observances and age grades, are similar to Karamojong practices and may have been borrowed from them.

The two most salient features of the history of the Lango within the nation of Uganda are that they are not Bantu and that they have had a stateless society. When the British came to Uganda in the mid-nineteenth century, the center of colonial power was established on the shores of Lake Victoria in the kingdom of Buganda, 320 kilometers south of Lango territory. The Ganda and the other Bantu kingdoms in the southern part of Uganda gained the respect of the British in large measure because of their well-organized states. The non-Bantu societies to the north of the "Bantu line" were stateless, and, for most of the colonial period, they were regarded as the poorest, the least tractable, and the most warlike societies of Uganda. By creating most of its important institutions in the south of the country, the colonial administration heightened the differences between the north and the south, and the Lango were effectively left out of colonial development.

Contact between Lango and Ganda during the colonial period was characterized by bitterness and a lack of understanding that persist even now. Antagonism between these two societies was particularly strong during the mid-1960s, the years immediately following Uganda's independence. A Lango, Milton Obote, led the Uganda People's Congress and became prime minister; he found himself opposed to the political power of the Ganda Kingdom, the people of which had organized themselves into a political party, the Kabaka Yekka. Ensuing political events—the overthrow of Obote, the divisive reign of Idi Amin during the 1970s, and the long years of civil war—involved the Lango people in a series of opposition movements and guerrilla skirmishes. They have undergone considerable economic hardship and have all but lost any effective political voice in the national government.

Settlements

In precolonial times, the Lango lived in villages of about a hundred people. These were abandoned in the twentieth century, and households came to be widely dispersed. This shift in residence patterns may have been stimulated by the cessation of intervillage warfare. The standard pattern now is for a household to be built in a small clearing and to be surrounded by fields and grasslands. As sons marry, they may build households nearby in separate clearings, far enough from other households so as to be barely visible. The clearing might be more than 20 meters in diameter; its principal building is the sleeping house, which is likely to be about 6 meters by 6 meters. Roofs are almost always thatched, but houses of wage earners often have corrugated metal roofs.

An area of about 2.6 square kilometers, which might include twenty households, is loosely organized as a neighborhood, or *wang tic*. Three or four men representing the most prominent clans in the neighborhood serve as an informal neighborhood council, but the wang tic is not an officially recognized entity. The local administrative official, the *jon jago,* administers an area of about 80 square kilometers. Schools, courts, police, and medical services are often located at the headquarters of the jon jago. The next level of government is that of the county, and there are seven counties in Lango District, which has its headquarters in Lira, in the approximate center of the district.

As the colonial administration established itself, and as commerce and transport became important, there arose a number of trading and administrative centers that have become important foci of activity for the Lango. The most important of these is Lira, which is the site of a large hospital, numerous secondary schools, an airport, a prison, cotton ginneries, banks, churches, and retail shops.

Economy

Subsistence and Commercial Activities. The Lango subsistence system is classified as a "mixed" system (i.e., a combination of pastoralism and agriculture). Millet and sorghum are the two principal food crops, and, because they are the crops that the Lango have grown for the longest period of time, these foods are integrated into religious and symbolic conceptions more than other food crops are. Other important crops are maize, groundnuts (peanuts), potatoes, and cassava. Lesser crops are bananas, tomatoes, sesame (*simsim*), cowpeas, and various leafy greens. Most Lango labor goes into agricultural activities, but only half of the labor goes into the production of food; the other half of the agricultural labor goes into the production of cotton, which is the principal source of income for Lango peasants. After the introduction of cotton in 1912, the Lango people became integrated into the world industrial economy for the first time. The cotton was shipped to British textile mills, and the Lango were able to use cash from its sale to pay taxes and the school fees of their children.

Pastoralism requires much less labor than agriculture, but it figures very prominently in Lango cultural life. The Lango exemplify the East African cultural traits that Melville J. Herskovits long ago dubbed "the cattle complex." Social status is marked by the number of cows a man has; cattle are used to pay bride-wealth, and they are prized for various attributes, such as loyalty or bravery, which are sometimes imputed to particular animals. As a source of food, Lango cattle are of limited value. They provide very little milk, but surplus cattle are slaughtered for feasts, and some are sold to traders who ship them to southern Uganda. Since about 1950, there has been a shift in attitudes: cattle are no longer regarded as a commodity that should be kept for the conspicuous display of prestige or for social exchange but as a commodity that can be sold for profit. During the civil wars of the 1970s and 1980s, however, most cattle were slaughtered, and at present the Lango have very few cattle and are thus unable to use them for ritual purposes and exchange, as they had in the past.

In the southern part of Lango territory, near Lake Kyoga, there is a lacustrine adaptation that is centered upon fishing. The lake is an abundant source of Nile perch and other fish, and these can be caught with traps, lines, and spears.

Industrial Arts. There are no Lango artifacts that are made by full-time specialists. In the past, blacksmiths and iron smelters were specialists, but their techniques have long been forgotten. Coiled pottery is made by women who happen to reside near suitable deposits of clay. Some people are known to be especially good at fashioning drinking straws out of reeds, or thatching roofs, or carving wood, or weaving grass mats, but they are not full-time specialists, and in fact many adults can perform these tasks to some degree. The introduction of trade goods and new forms of technology has led to a number of new crafts. In the trading centers, one finds tailors, bicycle repairers, furniture makers, motor mechanics, and carpenters.

Trade. A well-established long-distance trade network existed in precolonial times, involving sesame, which was traded northward into Sudan, much of it ending up in Egypt. The sesame trade dwindled in the twentieth century, but a new and much more complex form of trade was introduced during the colonial period. East Indian traders controlled this trade at both the wholesale and retail level. They operated numerous small shops throughout Lango District and sold such necessities as clothing, matches, kerosene, metal sheeting, bicycles, and pots and pans. The expulsion of East Indians from Uganda by Idi Amin has greatly disrupted this trade network. Supplies are now irregular, stocks are low, and money is scarce. There is also a system of local markets, which are held throughout Lango territory. These markets allow people to dispose of surplus crops or cattle, and they work well in distributing foodstuffs and permitting Lango people, particularly women, to earn small amounts of cash.

Division of Labor. The division of labor in Lango is based mainly on age and sex. As soon as they are 6 or 7 years old, girls assist in household tasks and in caring for younger siblings. Young boys look after cattle, and, by the time they are 10, they may be put in charge of a small herd. Girls often marry when they are 15, and they then take on the responsibilities of growing and preparing food for their households. Adolescent boys are allotted their own fields, so that they can begin their lives as active cultivators. As adults weaken because of age, their productive capacities diminish, and old people find themselves dependent on others for food, with the result that they are often malnourished and embittered.

The sexual division of labor involves men doing the heavy agricultural labor and women doing much of the rest. Men cut trees and brush to clear the fields and hoe the soil at the beginning of the rainy season. They also sow the crops and plant the potatoes and cassava, but after the food crops have been planted, the responsibility of weeding and harvesting falls mostly to women. The crops are said to belong to the women, who must dry them, store them, prepare them for consumption, and sell any surplus. Although women have considerable control over the food crops, men control the cotton. They weed, spray, and harvest the cotton crop, and they control the cash derived from its sale.

Land Tenure. There is some variation in the forms of land tenure in different parts of Lango territory, depending mostly on population pressure. In the southern region, where land is scarce, there has been a tendency for fields to be small. In the northern part of Lango District, land is more available, and, until the 1970s, men had little trouble finding land to cultivate. Throughout the territory as a whole, there is no fixed ownership of land. People have usufruct rights to a parcel of land, but they do not actually own it. Attempts by the government to survey the land and establish a system of landownership have been steadfastly resisted by the Lango, who see landownership as the end of communalism and who fear that acquisitive individuals will take over large tracts of land. The Lango usufruct system, which worked well in the past, merely entails a young man asking the other men in his neighborhood if he may use a piece of land. As his household expands, and as he intensifies production, he may add additional fields, but his acquisitions are always limited by his ability to work the land. Neighborhood elders sometimes fail to give permission, and, occasionally, a man who causes trouble in the community is stripped of his land and must leave to take up residence in another neighborhood. Population pressure and soil erosion have made this system of usufruct less practicable than it was in the past, and conflicts over land are becoming more numerous.

Kinship

Kin Groups and Descent. Descent is patrilineal, and localized descent groups of four generations play an important role in neighborhood affairs. A patrilineage called the *jo doggola* ("people of the doorway") is made up of about six generations and is the largest corporate descent group. Its members may be dispersed over an area of 50 square kilometers, but they participate jointly in a number of activities. There may be eighty adult male members of this lineage who can be called upon to pay blood money in the event that one of its members is deemed responsible for the death of a nonmember. Members of the jo doggola also attend important rituals, such as funerals and marriages, and the failure of one section of the lineage to attend such a ritual is often an indication of impending fission within the lineage. Lineage fission is brought on in several ways: the lineage can grow so large that members cannot keep track of one another, the membership can become too widely dispersed, or conflicts can take place. Typically, these conflicts occur between two senior brothers quarreling over cattle or over the rights to use certain fields. Within the jo doggola, people have a clear sense of genealogical relationships, but beyond six or seven generations genealogical knowledge becomes unclear. Nevertheless, a vague sense of kinship does persist among people who are patrilineally related, however distant the relationship may be. Each person sees himself or herself as belonging to a named patrilineal group that includes a large number of people and is made up of many different jo doggola. These clans, or sibs, are typically found throughout Lango territory, although they are unevenly represented in different locales. The members of a particular sib often claim a totemic relationship with a particular species and follow a number of ritual avoidances. At present, the only real importance attached to sib membership is in connection with marriage, in that a man and a woman of the same sib are believed to be patrilineally related to one another and therefore cannot marry.

Kinship Terminology. Kinship terminology is of the Omaha type.

Marriage and Family

Marriage. The Lango practice polygyny and attach considerable importance to bride-wealth. Men commonly extol polygyny as an ideal, but in the 1960s only about 20 percent of the men who were married at any given time were married polygynously. Men commonly find it difficult to arrange for the bride-price for a second wife, and many women do not want to be married as a second or subsequent wife; hence, polygynous marriages are not always possible. Another important factor is population pressure. In some locales, there is not enough land available for men to have more than one wife, given the fact that men are expected to provide all of their wives with fields of approximately equal size for cultivation.

One of the difficulties in polygynous marriages is the relationship between co-wives. A woman who allows her husband to marry a second wife often does so with the expectation that she will have some authority over the junior wife; thus the junior wife enters the marriage in a weak position. A woman who has failed to bear children in a previous marriage or who has the reputation of being troublesome or lazy is more willing to be married polygynously. Such a woman also commands a relatively lower bride-price.

The bride-price in Lango is about fourteen head of cattle and a significant amount of other goods such as goats, cloth, cooking pots, and hoes, which are paid to the family of the bride. The problem of accumulating the bride-price can be very complicated, and boys must start planning how to solve it during their adolescence. A boy may obtain the support of his mother, who will attempt to get some of the cattle from her husband's herd for the boy's bride-price. Boys also are linked to their sisters; they must wait until their sisters are married so that they can obtain part of their bride-prices to pay for their own marriages. One other possibility is for boys to solicit cattle from members of their lineage or from their mothers' brothers. A kinsman who sponsors a marriage may expect the young man to reside near him after marriage and to serve as his dependent. Thus, men who have no sons sometimes acquire the loyalty of young members of their own lineage by sponsoring their marriages. If a man sponsors the marriage of his sister's son, the children born to the marriage will belong to the lineage of the sponsor (i.e., they will belong to the descent group of their father's mother's brother). This, of course, is a deviation from the normally strict rule of patrilineal descent, but the Lango see this arrangement as entirely consistent. They say that a child belongs to the descent group of the person who paid the bride-wealth of its mother. Normally, a woman's husband receives the bride-price from his own descent group, and a boy is discouraged from asking his mother's brother for bride-wealth. Children born to a woman for whom no bride-wealth has been paid belong to their mother's descent group (i.e., the descent group of her father). If a man subsequently marries the woman by paying bride-wealth, he may pay an additional amount to her father and procure her children for his own descent group. Because of the difficulty that is encountered in paying bride-wealth, a young man cannot reasonably expect to be married before he is 21, whereas girls commonly marry at about age 16.

Domestic Unit. The domestic unit consists of a woman and her husband, together with her unmarried children and, possibly, a young married son and his wife who live in a small, temporary house near the young man's mother's house. If a man is married polygynously, each wife has her own house and resides in a separate clearing. This means that a man must clear land and build a house for each woman he marries. The households of co-wives are usually within 50 meters of one another, but each household functions independently. A man alternates between the households of each wife, sleeping for three nights with one before moving to the next for three nights. The domestic cycle begins when the man takes a wife and establishes a new household with her.

Inheritance. There are few formal rules of inheritance among the Lango, although there are certain principles in operation. Old men are usually dependent on their offspring, and, by the time they die, they no longer have significant possessions. Cattle are the only significant wealth that figures in inheritance, and when a man who owns cattle dies, it is expected that his cattle will be divided among his sons in such a way that the oldest son receives somewhat more than all the others. In practice, this principle can lead to great problems. If a man has more than one wife, the sons of the senior wife are likely to claim a larger share, and a conflict may ensue between the two wives and among their offspring.

Socialization. There is a postpartum sex taboo of one year; hence, children tend to be spaced about two years apart, although this pattern is affected by a high infant-mortality rate. Children are not weaned until the mother becomes pregnant again, or until the mother decides that nursing is no longer practical. Boys are treated more leniently than girls and are given fewer responsibilities in childhood. Tension is likely to develop between boys and their fathers as boys reach adolescence and begin to press claims for their fathers' cattle so as to accumulate the necessary cows for bride-wealth. Mothers commonly side with their sons in these disputes, and as sons draw away from their fathers, they draw closer to their mothers, who see sons as a source of support in their own struggles with their husbands over money and other resources.

Sociopolitical Organization

Social Organization. The key to understanding Lango social organization is to recognize that it is both patrilineal and patrilocal (see "Kin Groups and Descent"). Men tend to reside near their fathers; hence, there are clusters of patrilineally related kinsmen in each neighborhood. Men often marry women who live 8 to 24 kilometers away from their own neighborhoods, and, consequently, women are introduced to their husbands' neighborhoods at marriage. Lango ideology is also "patricentric," in that people see a strong relationship between patrilineages and particular locales, and they regard males as being fixed in particular locales, in contrast to women, who change residences at marriage. Women often describe themselves as "strangers" in their husbands' neighborhoods. The Lango exemplify the classical problem that has been examined by anthropologists: that of the incorporation of women into the residential and kin groups of their husbands.

In addition to lineages, social organization in the neighborhood involves a corporative work group that cuts across kinship ties. All the members of a neighborhood are expected to assist one another in cultivating and harvesting, and a person who works alone jeopardizes his rights to land within the neighborhood. This neighborhood work group often meets informally for work followed by beer drinking, and it is probably the most important group to which a man belongs. In the past, there were age grades in Lango, but this seems to have died out sometime in the middle of the twentieth century. Another entity that is fast fading away is the traditional group comprised of the elders of five or six different patriclans that were linked together for certain ritual purposes. In the past, these ritual linkages were also associated with military alliances, but the necessity for such alliances died out shortly after the imposition of colonial rule.

Political Organization. Traditionally, a local-level leader was called a jon jago, and a higher-level leader was called a *rwot,* but they were really ad hoc war leaders rather than chiefs. These leaders were important primarily during times of conflict, when they could organize armed groups, sometimes raiding rival groups to acquire cattle, territory, or wives. The jon jago served as a client to a rwot, who might exert influence over an area of 260 square kilometers. These leaders did not preside not over a state organization; Lango was a stateless society, and the relations between individuals and groups were largely determined by kinship groups. The imposition of colonial rule after 1910 led to the creation of a formal governmental apparatus in which local chiefs served under county chiefs, who in turn served under a district commissioner.

Social Control. Traditionally, social control was effected by kin groups as well as by local councils of elders from several different kin groups. Men could be banished from a community and stripped of their rights to use land. Accusations of sorcery were sometimes used against people, and various forms of physical punishment were imposed upon people who committed offenses; for example, a woman who committed adultery might have her nose cut off by her husband's kinsmen. Since the imposition of colonial rule, social control has mostly been relegated to the formal legal system. People regularly take one another to court for a wide range of offenses.

Conflict. The two principal sources of conflict are marriage and cattle, and the two come together in questions of bride-wealth. There is often a permanent state of conflict between affines over claims that the bride-wealth payment was insufficient. Death is another serious source of conflict, because the Lango believe that a death is always caused by someone. Disputes between lineages are no longer as serious as they were in the past, when long-lasting feuds were common and sometimes led to hostilities.

Religion and Expressive Culture

Religious Beliefs. Lango religious beliefs are very diffuse and have been affected by the introduction of Christianity as well as by contact with neighboring societies. The Lango believe in a creator spirit called Jok, who is regarded as an all-powerful deity, and who is often equated with the Judeo-Christian God of the missionaries. There are also lesser deities—the spirits who bring sickness and cause trouble; the term for these deities is also "jok." These spirits are of two sorts. The first, associated with the wind, are seen as free-floating spirits who dwell in out-of-the-way places and attack people, often for no good reason. They are harmful and capricious, and people believe that it is important to take precautions against them. The other sort of jok is the shadow, or soul, of a deceased person.

Ceremonies. Most Lango ceremonies are either rites of passage or rituals associated with problems of spirit possession and fertility. Beginning around 1920, rituals that centered on spirit possession spread from the neighboring Bunyoro people into the western part of Lango District. The spirit-possession rituals had great appeal to women, and women were predominant in many of the possession activities, both as patients and as the principal performers. As possession rituals became more popular in the 1940s and the 1950s, the traditional rituals, which had mostly been performed by men, began to decline. Younger men lost interest in the traditional rituals, which came to be held less often. Since the 1960s, women have been more active than men in performing rituals, most of which involve an attempt to cure someone—typically, a woman—who is believed to have been possessed by a spirit.

Arts. Plastic arts are nearly nonexistent; for example, there is no tradition of wood carving except for the occasional carving of some useful object, like a stool.

Music and dance are important aspects of Lango life; the finger piano, drum, and flute are the principal instruments. Singing is done mostly by women, some of whom are recognized as virtuoso solo singers, but groups of people also enjoy singing in unison. Groups of young people compete with one another in public dance contests.

Medicine. Many plants are believed to have medicinal properties, and certain individuals have a knowledge of these plants. With the increasing popularity of spirit-possession rituals, however, curers have made less use of plants and have come to rely more heavily on the belief that illness is caused by spirit possession. The decline in the use of medicinal plants is also related to the declining popularity of the traditional rituals performed by men. The men who performed these rituals were also experts in the use of medicinal plants, and, as interest in the rituals waned, fewer men acquired expertise in the use of medicinal plants. Many traditional medicines have also been replaced by Western medicines, which were widely available to the Lango from the 1940s until the early 1970s. Since the 1970s, Uganda's political unrest has led to a deterioration of the government medical system, and there some indication that the use of traditional medicines is being revived. There is particular concern over the AIDS epidemic in Uganda, and there has been a renewed use of magical cures and folk medicines throughout Lango territory.

Death and Afterlife. The Lango believe that the soul, or shadow, departs from the body as it is being placed in the grave and takes up residence in the bush, near the living kin of the deceased. These shades often dwell in caves, in rocky outcroppings, or near sources of water, and they continue to maintain an active interest in the affairs of their living kin. There is no notion of the afterlife as a reward for a virtuous life or as a punishment for evildoers. Instead, the afterlife represents another stage in social life, because death merely transforms a person into an ancestor spirit, which then plays a role in the ritual life of the community. In general, the importance of an ancestor spirit is a reflection of the importance of that person during life; thus, children and women are not as likely to be regarded as prominent ancestors.

Bibliography

Curley, Richard T. (1973). *Elders, Shades, and Women: Ceremonial Change in Lango, Uganda.* Berkeley and Los Angeles: University of California Press.

Driberg, Jack H. (1923). *The Lango: A Nilotic Tribe of Uganda.* London: T. Fisher Unwin.

Haley, T. T. S. (1947). *The Anatomy of Lango Religion and Groups.* Cambridge: Cambridge University Press.

Herskovits, Melville J. (1926). "The Cattle Complex in East Africa." *American Anthropologist* 28:230–272, 361–380, 494–528, 633–664.

Tosh, John (1978). *Clan Leaders and Colonial Chiefs in Lango, c. 1800–1939.* Oxford: Clarendon Press.

RICHARD T. CURLEY

Lobi-Dagarti Peoples

Orientation and Ethnonyms

The group known to French writers, following the usage of Labouret (1931) and Père (1988), as the "Lobi" are found distributed between 9°00′ and 11°00′ N and 2°30′ and 4°00′ W. They are divided among three contemporary nations: Burkina Faso (formerly Upper Volta), in South-West Department; Ghana (formerly Gold Coast), in the districts of Lawra, Wa, and Bole; and Ivory Coast, in the districts of Bonduku and Buna.

The terms "LoDagaa" and "Lobi-Dagarti" (or Dagara) are used for a cluster of peoples situated across the frontier of Burkina Faso and Ghana, originally grouped together by Labouret, following the usage of Delafosse and other francophones. In this cluster, Labouret included the "true Lobi" (or those the Birifor call the "LoWilisi") around Gaoua, who (according to Westermann and Bryan 1952) speak a Dogon-type language (the inclusion of Dogon is disputed); the Birifor (or LoBirifor) to their east, who speak Dagara, a Mole-Dagbane language; and four smaller groups: the Teguessié, the Dorossié, the Dian, and the Gan. The Teguessié (or Tégué) speak a language of the Kulango Group and are sometimes thought of as the autochthons; they were Masters of the Earth in much of the area. The other small groups speak languages related to Lobiri, as do the Padoro and possibly the Komono; Dian and Lobiri (in the east) are more closely related, as is the western group.

Subsequently, Père (1988) adopted the francophone use of Lobi ("la région Lobi") to cover the peoples of the Gaoua District of Burkina Faso, including not only the Jãa (Dian); the Gaàn (Gan); the Teésé (Teguessié); the Dɔ̀csè (or Dorossié, but also the Kùlãgo [Kulango]); the Dagara (divided into Dagara Lobr and Dagara Wiili [Oulé]); and the Pwa (formerly known as the Pugula or Pougouli), who speak a Grusi language. Indeed, because she is dealing with the region, she also includes the Wala and the Dagara-Jula in her account.

The problems of ethnic classification in this area are several. In the first place, names differ, depending on whether they are used by francophones or by anglophones. The Lobi described by Rattray (1932) include the Birifor as well as the Dagara of Labouret. Second, the names have changed over time. People who were known as "Lobi" in the Lawra District of Ghana at the beginning of the nineteenth century are now "Dagara." Third, the names themselves often do not describe distinct ethnic groups. There are many differences in custom and organization between neighboring settlements, and these settlements may be referred to by the two quasi-directional terms, "Lo" (Lobi, west) and "Dagaa" (east), to distinguish different practices (for example, the use of xylophones). A settlement may identify with its eastern neighbors on one occasion (as Dagaa) and with its western ones (as Lo) on another. This actor usage has led Goody to identify a spectrum of peoples, the LoDagaa, who use these names for reference to themselves and others. They are, from west to east, the true Lobi, the Birifor or LoBirifor, the LoPiel (around Nandom) and the LoSaala (around Lawra), the Dagara (around Dano), the LoWiili (around Birifu), both DagaaWiili (around Tugu), and the Dagaba or Dagarti. The Wala speak the Dagaba language and constitute a small state that has its origins eastward in Dagomba. That state established itself as ruler over the southern Dagaba and some Grusi-speaking peoples. In the west, a branch of the ruling dynasty extended across the Black Volta to Buna, where they adapted the local Kulango language. The LoPiel and the LoSaala are known to francophones as "Dagara" (or Dagara-Lobr), and they now generally use this term rather than "Lobi" for self-reference because they have been forced to classify themselves unambiguously for administrative purposes. That change is widespread because "Dagara" is often a more prestigious term than "Lobi." The latter is associated in many people's minds with the large lip plugs of gourd or metal that are worn in the west (the easterners wear thin metal plugs) and with the stress that the westerners place on matrilineal inheritance, about which modernizers (church, schools, law, some administrators) generally feel hostile and ambivalent.

Given these contextual, overlapping, and changing usages by the peoples themselves, actor names are rarely satisfactory to indicate "tribal" groups, by which we refer to larger groupings of settlements with relatively homogeneous practices. These groups can be distinguished, roughly from east to west, as the Dagaba or Dagarti (around Jirapa); the LoPiel (around Nandom) and the LoSaala (around Lawra), both "Dagara Lobr" in French; the DagaaWiili (around Legmoin and Tugu) and the LoWiili (around Birifu), both "Dagara Wiilé" in French; the Birifor or LoBirifor (around Batié and in western Gonja); and the Lobi or LoWiilisi (around Gaoua). There are, in addition, the smaller populations of Gan, Dorossié, and Gian, who speak Lobi languages, and Teguessié, and who speak Kulango. These groups can be collectively designated as the LoDagaa or Lobi-Dagarti cluster, there being no reason to exclude the other Dagara-speaking peoples once the Birifor have been included among the Lobi.

Demography. Exact population figures are not readily available because these peoples are divided among three nation-states. Westermann and Bryan (1952) derived the following data from Labouret, Rattray, and early censuses: Lobi, 211,000; LoBirifor, 48,696 plus 40,520 in Ghana; Dagari/Dagarti/Wiili, 75,000 in Burkina Faso, 119,216 in Ghana; Wala, 25,923; Teguessié, 2,000; Dorossié, 7,500; Dian, 8,380, and Gan, 5,350. These figures should probably be doubled.

It is difficult to reconcile these numbers with the ones Père gives for the population of the Gaoua "circle" in 1975, namely, 180,288, of whom approximately 90,000 were "true Lobi" (with about another 75,000 in Ivory Coast, according to de Rouville); 60,000 were Birifor and 18,000 Dagara (Wiili).

History and Cultural Relations

The Lobi-Dagarti peoples are without any overarching tribal organization or, strictly speaking, any territory. They move not as large units, but as family groups, sometimes into other ethnic areas, where they may be absorbed into the local population. Most of the groups to the west of the Black Volta claim to have been formerly settled to the east of the river, in what is now Ghana. From the eighteenth century on, they have moved across the river. There appear to have been Lobi as well as Dagaba in the Wa area when the ruling dynasty arrived; the Jãa were certainly settled in the Lawra area until, attracted by a sparsely populated region with plenty of farmland and forest produce and under pressure from other LoDagaa, mainly from the south and southwest (but even from west of the river), they crossed the Black Volta. A minority of clans trace their origins from other regions.

One of the factors leading to the movement has been the search for more and better land, following earlier hunting expeditions. Another factor has been the raids mounted by the states of the region (as well as by the occasional freebooters and adventurers) in their search for slaves, partly for their own use but mainly to supply the Asante and, through them, the Europeans in the south. The invaders on horseback terrified the inhabitants, who sometimes retaliated with poisoned arrows. Mainly, however, they fled, using the larger rivers. A number of characteristics—their dispersed settlements of fortress-type houses, the women's lip plugs, their rejection of cloth, and their general aggressiveness—have been attributed to the effects of such raids. In the late twentieth century houses are smaller, the manner of dress is more "European," and less hostility is displayed.

The establishment of the international boundary has brought about a decline in east-west migration. The main movement of the Lobi in the late twentieth century has been of two kinds. The first has been from the Lawra District to the vacant lands southward on the road to Kumasi, which many men have traveled in the dry season as migrant laborers. Settlements that produce food for sale in the markets have grown up from Wa south to the northwest of Asante. The second movement, beginning in 1917, has been eastward across the Black Volta from the francophone territories to Ghana, where there were fewer calls by the government on labor services. Many Birifor moved into the sparsely populated lands of western Gonja, which had been decimated as a result of Samori's wars at the end of the nineteenth century. These migrants have proved to be much more aggressive, market-oriented farmers than their hosts, with whom there has been some conflict over taxes and representation.

Settlements

Settlements in the area consist of named units that are usually centered on a specific parish or ritual area of an Earth shrine. These settlements are inhabited by members of several exogamous lineages housed in fortress-type compounds with 2.5-meter-high walls, a flat roofs, and entrances reached (at least formerly) by wooden ladders to the roofs. These houses are some 100 meters apart and contain an average of 15 persons, but they vary in size, depending on the state of the developmental cycle of the domestic group. Around the walls lies the compound farm, which is fertilized by human detritus and is used by the women to plant their soup vegetables. It is adjoined by home farms; bush farms lie much farther away. The settlements consist of some 250 to 750 inhabitants.

Economy

Subsistence and Commercial Activities. The economy is essentially one of the hoe farming of cereals (sorghum, pennisetum [pearl millet], maize), together with some yams, especially in the southern areas that are occupied by migrants. In addition, people grow squashes, peppers, beans (including Bambara beans), groundnuts, and a little rice. Some of this produce is sold in the local markets, especially sorghum in the form of beer. Most compounds also possess a herd of cows, and some sheep, goats, guinea fowl, and chickens, which are mainly killed as sacrifices to be distributed.

Industrial Arts and Trade. Lobi women produce a certain amount of gold, which finds its way into the hands of Dyula traders. Associated with earlier gold workings, it has been suggested, are the ruins of stone houses. Since the advent of colonial rule, the relative peace that it brought about and the cheaper iron tools that it provided have led to increased production, evidence of which can be seen in the markets. That increase is also true for livestock. Along with wage labor (performed either locally or as migrants), these developments have increased purchasing power. Whereas little was imported earlier except salt, now large amounts of cloth are brought in, and other manufactured objects, such as matches, bicycles, transistor radios, and household utensils, are used in considerable quantities. Local craft production consists of iron implements, brass bangles and other ornaments, musical instruments, some wood carvings, and woven mats.

Today migration—both of the uneducated, seeking work as laborers, and of the educated, who generally work in the towns—is frequent. The age of migrants is now much lower than formerly, and the duration of their absences is much greater. The result is that larger numbers of houses are inhabited by old men, women, and children who have to carry out the agricultural work without the help they would have received from the migrants. Thus, the sexual division of labor has been altered. The south, however, is beginning to lose some of its attraction as the international economy affects the recruitment of labor, potential recruits are frightened by tales of AIDS.

The LoDagaa (including the Lobi) were not themselves traders (except in the state of Wa), but major north-south trade routes of Dyula and Hausa merchants ran through the area from the forest to the Sahel.

Division of Labor. Farming was mostly done by men, but women helped with the planting and the harvesting. In some places, women would organize men to farm for a friend by brewing plenty of beer. Women cultivated soup vegetables, collected forest produce, carried loads, gathered firewood, fetched water, extracted oil, and prepared food and beer. Grinding grain, in particular, was a lengthy process. Their workload is now changing as a consequence of the introduction of wells and mills. Men carried out the heavy agricultural work, looked after livestock, and hunted. Both sexes took part in house building during the dry season.

Land Tenure. Land tenure took the form of a hierarchy of rights distributed within the lineage. At one level, land was "owned" by the wider patrilineage, and if any land was not being farmed, other members had a claim to use it. Use rights were exclusive and more important where land was scarce or especially valuable (because of water). Where population density was low, it sufficed to approach the local Master of the Earth, who would perform a simple sacrifice.

Kinship

Kin Groups and Descent. Across the LoDagaa cluster, roughly from east to west, there is an increasing emphasis on the role of matrilineal descent groups. In the east, the Dagaba are organized on the basis of patrilineal descent groups alone. Several of these exogamous units exist in each parish. These lineages, which trace patrilineal relationships between their members, belong to wider named clans, segments of which are found in widely dispersed settlements, even those of different "ethnic" groups, roughly tracing out lines of migration. Groups to the west also have matrilineal clans, and all except the Wiili (and formerly even some of the LoWiili) inherit land and immovables agnatically and inherit movables (wealth, cattle) through the uterine line. Hence, the patriclans are locally based, but the matriclans are dispersed. These groups are therefore variants of classic double-descent systems.

Patrilineal clans are numerous, each with its own prohibitions, often against the killing of a totemic animal or the eating of foods in a particular way. The clans are paired in joking relationships, and their ritual foci are lineage shrines. Among the Lobi and, to some extent, the Birifor, although patrilineal clanship is concealed, it is significant in landownership and in some ritual affairs, especially in the Dyoro initiations. The matriclans, right across the cluster, are basically four in number—Some, Da, Hienbe, and Kambire. The first two and the last two are paired in joking relationships, which are particularly important at funerals. These dispersed matriclans have particular loci where sacrifices are occasionally performed.

Kinship Terminology. In a double-descent system, one can refer to any kin either in the patrilineal or in the matrilineal mode. The patrilineal mode is Omaha, whereas the matrilineal one is Crow. The dominance of these different modes depends upon the strength of the relevant groups.

Marriage and Family

Marriage. In the eastern groups, marriage is strictly virilocal and is effected by the transfer of bride-wealth in cowries and subsequently in cattle. The transfers take place over time, as the marriage is consolidated with the birth of children. Traditionally, the groom also had to bring parties to farm for his in-laws from time to time, although among the educated this practice tends to get commuted into a monetary payment. Each marriage invokes the construction of a new sleeping room and cooking hearth. Among the Birifor and the Lobi, when a fiancé comes to farm, he may eventually be allowed to spend the night with his future wife and, later, to have her visit his own house in return for further work. She did not usually reside permanently in her husband's house until after the birth of their first child. Initial bride-removal without bride-service, as in some cross-"ethnic" marriages, entailed a very heavy payment of five cattle, a form of marriage that is becoming more common. The children are members of both their patrilineal and their matrilineal clans. Nowadays marriage by elopement is more common, with the wife joining her husband straightaway and the bride-wealth being eventually paid.

Domestic Unit. The domestic unit is generally built on agnatic ties, given that wives join their husbands at marriage, but among the Lobi and Birifor, men do extensive bride-service, and some young children may grow up with their mother's brothers before their mother leaves for her husband's house. In most cases, the farming group is small. A man and his sons may farm together for a longer period among the groups in which patriclans dominate. The dwelling group that occupies a compound may consist of several farming groups, and each farming group may be divided into smaller eating groups.

Inheritance. Among the Dagaba and the Wiili, a man's property passes first to his full brothers, if they are farming together, and then to his sons. Among the LoPiel, the LoSaala, the Birifor, and the Lobi, land passes in the paternal line, whereas movable property is transmitted first to uterine siblings and then to sisters' sons, leading to earlier splits in the domestic groups and to tensions between a man and his mother's brothers. A woman's property generally goes to her daughters if it is sex-linked, but livestock may go to her sons.

Socialization. Young children are looked after by their mothers and are breast-fed until they can walk and talk, when they "become humans" and are thus entitled to a proper burial (see "Death and Afterlife"). Later on, they are cared for by elder sisters or relatives, who involve them in their play. Boys go off in groups to herd cattle, whereas girls play more domestic games around the compound, helping their mothers from time to time by fetching water or grinding and pounding cereals. Among the Lobi, girls also look after cattle, although boys and girls pass this responsibility to their juniors when they are initiated into the Dyoro society.

Sociopolitical Organization

Political Organization. Except for the Wala and the Gan, the peoples of this group lacked chieftainship and central political organization until the coming of colonial rule. Before that, settlements were basically parishes, ritual areas under the supervision of a Master of the Earth, who conducted expiatory and other sacrifices in a sacred grove on behalf of the community. Particularly severely reproved was the shedding of the blood of any member of the community. In addition to the Master of the Earth, there was a leader in armed conflict (and the hunt), the Master of the Bow. The Earth priest was always advised by the heads of the constituent lineages of the settlement, who made up an informal moot and entered into complex patterns of reciprocal action in funerals and on other ritual occasions. A powerful man in the settlement might, on occasion, build up both riches and a following, and thereby temporarily gain influence over community affairs. On some of the trade routes running north and south, Muslim merchants established settlements and engaged in local as well as long-distance trade. Today all areas have had chiefs imposed upon them by the government authorities.

Social Control and Conflict. In earlier times, the absence of central authority meant that the feud played an important part in the settlement of disputes. Men always traveled equipped with bows and poisoned arrows, a practice that early colonial administrators tried to modify with varying success, especially in Lobi country. The main causes of conflict were rights to women and access to forest products. Within the parish, conflicts of this kind were rare because of kin ties and respect for the Earth shrine. Strong sanctions existed against adultery, theft, and other delicts, which were settled within and between local lineages. More recently, local chiefs and headmen have exercised supervision on behalf of the government, and local courts of law have been established.

Religion and Expressive Culture

Religious Beliefs. The religion of the LoDagaa cluster centers on the Earth and the ancestors. The worship of the Earth (which is conducted by the Master of the Earth on behalf of the parish) relates to the fertility of the soil and, indeed, to all of its uses; it would be offended by having anyone who suffered a bad death interred within it or by having the blood of any member of its congregation shed upon it. The Earth looks after the community, but the ancestors supervise the lineage and are concerned with matters relating to the household and kin, that is to say, with a very wide range of human activity. Whereas the Earth is propitiated at a stone in a sacred grove, the ancestors are worshiped at anthropomorphically carved wooden shrines—one for each male who leaves behind sons; these are kept in a corner of the byre where the cattle are stalled.

There are a multitude of other supernatural agencies, the most important of which is the rain shrine, which draws its strength from the power of thunder and lightning. Most of the "medicine shrines" circulate throughout the region, and a selection will have been acquired by any of the more established houses—and even by distant clients. In the long run, their popularity waxes and wanes.

As intermediaries between humans and these deities, there is a body of beings of the wild—hill and water spirits—whose home is the bush (as that of humans is the cultivated lands) and whose flocks are the wild animals. In their rooms, most senior men and women have shrines to these spirits, by whom they have been "caught." They are associated with divination because they can reveal the truth through dreams and in other ways. They are also the ones who have, with the blessing of the High God, introduced humans to the main aspects of culture: the growth of crops, the making of food, the smelting of iron, hunting, and so forth.

The High God is characteristically "otiose" and has no altar, no means of communication. Muslims and Christians in the area are characterized as "praying to God"; for others, such a God is too far removed from human ways. Nevertheless, the myth of the Bagre society emphasizes the High God's role as Creator, and members of various syncretic cults, together with those who were converted en masse to Christianity, emphasize that potentially this God could play a greater part than was traditionally assumed.

Since the 1930s, mass conversions to Catholicism have taken place, beginning among the LoPiel population around Dissin. Since then, the religion has spread widely; churches and hospitals have been constructed and priests trained. Until the late twentieth century, Protestant sects had made little headway in the area, but conversions have recently been made among the Lobi. Islam was formerly confined to small trading settlements and to the major towns, such as Wa and Buna; it has made a few converts in the villages but remains largely identified with the states of the region.

Religious Practitioners. Practically every adult is an officiant at some shrine or another, but the main figure is the Master of the Earth. Some individuals develop special reputations as diviners. All are involved in sacrifices to the ancestors, to the beings of the wild, and to medicine shrines.

Ceremonies. Annual ceremonies are performed at household shrines, especially at the end of the farming season. It is toward this time that, among the central groups, neighbors dance in the marketplace to celebrate the flowering of the guinea corn. Not long afterward, lineages perform special sacrifices to clan deities, a time when they also poison their arrows. Traditionally, success in the hunt also elicited special ritual performances, as did killing someone in war, whether friend or enemy.

Birth and marriage were accompanied by little ceremonial. Death and burial, on the other hand, were occasions; the funeral ceremonies, which resulted in redistribution of the property of the dead (including sexual rights) and the creation of an ancestor shrine (if there were offspring), lasted for many months and brought mourners from far and wide.

The major ceremonial sequences, however, were those associated with secret societies: the Bagre in the east and the Dyoro in the west. The Bagre is performed by lineages when they have sufficient neophytes (and enough grain) to carry out a performance, with the participation of their neighbors as officiants. During the course of the long sequence of rites, the neophytes are placed under a series of taboos, from which they are gradually released. The rites are accompanied by an extensive recitation concerning the creation of culture. The Dyoro ceremony involves a visit by patrilineages to special centers, where the ancestors lived before reaching the banks of the Black Volta and where the principal rites of initiation take place. Indeed, the ritual reenacts the long-ago migration of the patriclan and so preserves a little of its history. In the ceremony, which takes place every seven years, the initiates are killed off and revived.

Arts. Labouret noted the general features of the culture of this area (except for that of the Muslims). Clothing was absent except for the penis sheath for men and leaves for women (although this has largely changed). Women wore lip plugs and practiced excision, but there was no male circumcision. Separate flat-roofed compounds were constructed of clay and served as small fortresses. The spectrum of peoples in the area have similar techniques of metalworking and pottery making (including the lost-wax process); use bows, quivers, and arrows poisoned with *Strophantus hispida;* make three-footed stools, sometimes carved; and maintain secret societies and the use of the bullroarer.

Different types of xylophone serve as ethnic identifiers, but the social systems have many common elements. Most significant are the similarities and variants in social organization, in political systems, in religion, and in kinship.

The LoDagaa have expert xylophone players who perform at funerals, at the Bagre, and for dances of various kinds. They produce some carving: ancestor shrines, beings of the wild, deities, stools, and walking sticks. The Lobi formerly made masks based on Baule designs, at the instigation of Commandant Labouret. The LoDagga make many large clay sculptures of beings of the wild and of minor deities. There is virtually no painting, except for the application of white clay on the human body during funeral and Bagre ceremonies. Some practitioners carve figurative and decorative patterns on gourds.

Medicine. There are no specialist herbalists among the LoDagaa, although some men and women are recognized as knowing more than others. Some curative medicines ("medicines" are used for different purposes) are associated with shrines, others are "invented" by individuals going to the woods, and still others have been of long-standing use and are known to most households. Women's knowledge centers mainly around medicines relating to childbirth and female complaints.

The medical system is open-ended, and there has been no problem in assimilating European cures, especially pills and injections. Today there is a wide network of government and missionary hospitals and clinics. Many tropical diseases have been more or less brought under control (for example, cerebrospinal meningitis, leprosy, and sleeping sickness), but malaria has made an unwelcome comeback.

Death and Afterlife. Death, particularly of infants, was frequent. Those who have not yet been weaned are not mourned in the usual way, except by their mothers, because they are deemed to be wandering spirits, rather than humans. Precautions are taken against their return to this earth. For all others, however, the funeral rites are long and complex, and they involve the participation of many people. The burial performance takes three or four days, depending on whether the deceased is a male or a female, and that performance is followed over the next year by a series of rites that gradually release the widow (or widower) and the property and personality of the deceased and dismiss the soul to "God's country." The dead travel across the river of death with the aid of a ferryman; during the trip, those who have led evil lives may be punished for their misdeeds. In the course of the series of funeral ceremonies, a dead man also becomes an ancestor, with a shrine that will thereafter receive regular offerings of food and drink from his descendants, especially from those who have inherited from him.

Bibliography

Evans, P. A. (1983). "The LoBirifor/Gonja Dispute in Northern Ghana: A Study of Interethnic Political Conflict in a Post-Colonial State." Ph.D. dissertation, University of Cambridge.

Fiéloux, M. (1980). *Les sentiers de la nuit: Les migrations rurales des groupements lobi de la Haute Volta vers la Côte d'Ivoire.* Travaux et Documents, no. 110. Paris: Office de la Recherche Scientifique et Technique Outre Mer (ORSTOM).

Goody, Jack (1954). "The Ethnology of the Northern Territories of the Gold Coast West of the White Volta." London: Colonial Office. Mimeographed.

Goody, Jack (1956). *The Social Organization of the LoWiili.* London: HMSO.

Goody, Jack (1962). *Death, Property, and the Ancestors.* Stanford, Calif.: Stanford University Press.

Goody, Jack (1972). *The Myth of the Bagre.* Oxford: Clarendon.

Hagaman, B. L. (1977). "Beer and Matrilyny: The Power of Women in a West African Society." Ph.D. dissertation, Northeastern University.

Kambou, J.-M. (1971). "La pénétration française en pays lobi, 1897–1920." Mémoire de maîtrise, Université de Paris I.

Labouret, H. (1931). *Les tribus du rameau lobi.* Paris: Institut d'Ethnologie.

Labouret, H. (1958). *Nouvelles notes sur les tribus du rameau lobi: Leurs migrations, leurs parler et ceux de leurs voisins.* Mémoires de l'IFAN, 54. Dakar.

Meyer, P. (1981). *Kunst und Religion der Lobi.* Zurich: Museum Reitburg.

Père, M. (1988). *Les lobi: Tradition et changement (Burkina Faso).* 2 vols. Laval: Siloë.

Rattray, R. S. (1932). *The Tribes of the Ashanti Hinterland.* Oxford: Oxford University Press.

Rouville, C. de (1987). *Organisation sociale des lobi: Une société bilinéaire de Haute-Volta, Côte d'Ivoire.* Paris: L'Harmattan.

Savonnet, G. (1976). *Les birifor de Diépla et sa région, insulaires du rameau lobi (Haute Volta).* Atlas des Structures Agraires au Sud du Sahara, no 12. Paris: Office de la Recherche Scientifique et Technique Outre Mer (ORSTOM).

Spini, T., and G. Antongini (1981). *Il cammino degli antennati: I lobi dell' Alto Volta*. Bari: Laterza.

Westermann, D., and M. A. Bryan (1952). *The Languages of West Africa*. London: International African Institute.

JACK GOODY

Lozi

ETHNONYMS: Barotse, Barozi, Barutse, Kololo, Marotse, Marutse, Rotse, Rozi, Rutse, Silozi, Tozui

Orientation

Identification. Concentrated around the Zambezi River plain lying at 14°30′ to 16°00′ S by 23°00′ E, the Lozi consist of a number of interrelated ethnic groups located along the Zambezi River in Barotse Province of western Zambia. As used here, the term "Lozi" refers both to the Lozi proper and to those groups that have become subject to and assimilated into the Lozi proper. These groups include the Kwanda, Makoma (Bamakoma), Mbowe (Mamboe), Mishulundu, Muenyi (Mwenyi), Mwanga, Ndundulu, Nygengo, Shanjo, and Simaa. In addition to being members of the Lozi-dominated Barotse Kingdom, these peoples share similar customs, speak the Lozi language (Kololo), and intermarry. The Barotse Kingdom incorporated a number of other ethnic groups, such as the Tonga, Lukolwe, and Subia, but these groups have remained somewhat distinct in language and customs.

Demography. Population data for the Lozi are poor, based mainly on estimates, and do not lend themselves to an assessment of demographic trends. Figures for the whole of Barotse Province (including non-Lozi) place the population at 295,741 in 1938 and 361,905 in 1963. The 1938 estimates suggest figures of about 67,000 for the Lozi ethnic group itself and 105,000 for the Luyana group (the Lozi and related groups that consider themselves to have common origins). If assimilated peoples are included, the Lozi population in 1938 reached over 160,000. More recent estimates place the Lozi at 380,800 in Zambia (1986); 8,070 in Zimbabwe (1969), and 50,000 in Mozambique (1988).

Linguistic Affiliation. Lozi (Kololo) is the common language of Barotse Province, although many inhabitants speak other Bantu languages as well. Lozi has been classified as a Bantu language of the Benue-Congo Family, within the larger Niger-Congo Group. The Lozi language derives largely from the Sotho dialect spoken by the Kololo, who conquered the Lozi, but it exhibits some modifications, especially in phonetics and vocabulary.

History and Cultural Relations

The history of the Barotse Kingdom begins with the southward movement of the Luyi people sometime around 1600. Luyi history is characterized by a series of expansionary conquests and the absorption of numerous other peoples under their rule. Luyi domination was temporarily interrupted when they were conquered by the Kololo, a group of invaders from the south, who ruled the kingdom from 1838 to 1864. In 1864 one of the Luyi (now known as Lozi) princes reestablished his group's dominance by conquering the Kololo. By then, however, British and Portuguese interests had begun to penetrate the area. The first treaties between the British and the Lozi, signed in 1890 and 1900, placed the Lozi under the authority of the British South Africa Company, but allowed them considerable autonomy in self-government. During the twentieth century, there were a series of changes in the larger political institutions to which the Lozi were subordinate. From 1924 to the 1950s, they were a part of Northern Rhodesia, under the rule of the British Colonial Office. Subsequently, they were incorporated into the Federation of Rhodesia and Nyasaland, and in 1964 Barotse Province became part of the newly proclaimed Republic of Zambia. Each of these political developments brought changes to the sociopolitical organization of the Lozi; the indigenous political organization increasingly lost power and functions, and the territorial extent of Lozi domination was constricted.

Settlements

The Lozi occupy small, compact villages, often surrounded by a fence or palisade and usually arranged with a cattle corral or open plaza in the center. Although village sites persist over time, there is a great deal of flux in village population. Flooding of the Zambezi River necessitates abandonment of villages in the flood plains during part of the year. In some cases, all or most of a village's population will move together to their lands on higher sites. Sometimes, however, the entire village will disperse, with its members joining kin from other villages. Besides this annual flux, there is a continual flow of people from one village to another for various reasons. The prevailing house type is that of a round hut with a low cylindrical wall of rush mats or of wattle and daub and a conical thatched roof.

Economy

Subsistence and Commercial Activities. In a habitat characterized by great seasonal and ecological variation, it is not surprising that the Lozi subsistence economy is both mixed and complex. Lozi agriculture produces such staples as bulrush millet, cassava, sorghum, and maize, plus a number of lesser crops, including groundnuts, sweet potatoes, beans, and melons. Agricultural crops, methods, and intensity vary with the location of the plot, the type of soil, the amount of moisture, and the population's needs. Most cultivation is done with hoes, the plow being a relatively recent, and not always practical, introduction. Fallowing, manuring, crop rotation, and construction of drainage ditches are known to the Lozi and applied where deemed necessary. Most Lozi also keep domestic animals—cattle in particular, but also poultry, goats, and sheep. Hunting, collecting, and fishing are all important adjuncts to the subsistence economy, and the Lozi use a variety of technical equipment in these activities.

Industrial Arts. The Lozi are skilled ironworkers. Blacksmiths smelt the iron ore obtained from stream and river beds and from swamp soils to produce axe, hoe, and mattock heads, snuff spoons, crocodile hooks, knife blades, dagger blades, iron ankle-rings, hammers, and other items. A skilled and experienced blacksmith will often embellish his work with punched ornamentations or bosses. Many utilitarian pots are vase shaped and without handles; some of these are decorated around the neck with patterns of a lighter or darker color, others are highly polished to give the appearance of glaze. Large urn-shaped maize bins are made of unbaked clay and also have clay lids. On the front of these vessels, close to the bottom, is a semicircular opening protected by an interior slide, which may be lowered or raised by horizontal handles.

The average Lozi can carve a knobkerrie or a handle for an axe or a hoe; the Lozi also produce excellent dugout canoes. Many of the wooden artifacts used by the Lozi, such as stools, bowls, and dishes, are probably obtained in trade from neighboring tribes.

Trade. Traditionally, economic exchange was carried on through barter and redistribution by the king, and trade between the Lozi and surrounding bush tribes formed a very important part of the economy. Fish and cattle, held in abundance by the Lozi, were bartered for bulrush millet; cassava meal; iron; many types of woods, bark, and grasses; and various tribal specialties of the bush people. Trade between the Lozi and the outside world began to develop in the nineteenth century, particularly with Arab and European traders. Although Loziland had few profitable exports, owing to its remoteness from the outside world, the Lozi did have ivory, beeswax, and slaves, which were exchanged for luxury items of the industrialized world. As the economic balance changed during World War II, cattle and dried fish began to be exported to centers of industry in the Rhodesias (now Zambia and Zimbabwe). Today the Lozi are part of a full-fledged cash economy with market mechanisms.

Division of Labor. The division of labor in subsistence pursuits largely follows sex lines. Men are responsible for livestock, hunting, most of the fishing, and the more arduous agricultural tasks; women do most of the work in agriculture and collecting, a little fishing, and most of the routine domestic chores. Occupational specialization was limited in the past, but has become increasingly important. Migration for wage labor opportunities has become a major means of support for the Lozi.

Land Tenure. In traditional Lozi society, all land and its products belonged to the king, and the king was obligated to provide his subjects with land and protection. In addition, every subject had the right to fish in public waters, hunt on public lands, and to use the natural raw materials of the land (e.g., clay, iron ore, grasses, reeds, trees). In return for the use of the land and its products, the king had the right to claim the allegiance of everyone living on his land, to demand tribute from their produce, to control the building of villages, and to pass laws affecting land tenure and use. In addition, the king retained direct control over unallocated land, had residuary rights to land for which an heir could not be found, and potentially had the right to give unused land to landless people or to use it for his own purposes or for public works. Land allotted by the king to villages was held in the name of the village headman, who, in turn, distributed parcels of land to his fellow villagers.

When an individual is given land from the king, he doesn't really own it. He has ownership of, or access to, that land only as long as he occupies his position within the village. Valued property, such as garden plots and fishing sites, were attached to particular villages and, specifically, to certain individuals or families within those villages. If a man leaves a village, he loses his rights to all land within that village. Once land has been acquired by right of blood or adoption, a family member (male) has the right to use it and to transmit it to his own heirs, and this right is protected by the courts, even against the wishes of the headman.

Kinship, Marriage, and Family

Kinship. The Lozi possess no unilinear kin groups. Despite a slight patrilineal bias, kinship is reckoned bilaterally, with relations traced as widely as possible through both consanguineal and affinal ties. They have eight noncorporate name groups called *mishiku* (sing. *mushiku*), and a man can claim membership in any or all of them, provided that he is a direct descendant in any line of a person who was a member.

Marriage. Marriages are legitimated by the payment of a small bride-price. The practice of bride-service has fallen out of use, and postmarital residence is usually in the community of the groom. Polygyny is common, but the Lozi do not practice polyandry. Co-wives are accorded relatively equal status, although they are ranked according to order of marriage. The senior wife has a few privileges, such as first consideration in the distribution of food produced by the husband, but she has no authority over her co-wives. Neither levirate nor sororate are practiced. Divorce rates are high, and an individual Lozi may have had several partners during his or her lifetime. Marriages between close relatives, extending to third cousins, are prohibited; some cousin marriages occur despite this prohibition, but with the proviso that they may not be dissolved by divorce.

Domestic Unit. Residence patterns in marriage are loosely structured. Formerly, initial residence was matrilocal, whereas permanent residence later on was usually patrilocal. However, a man could take up residence in the village of any grandparent, and possibly even in the wife's father's village, if there were no available locations in his father's village. Incidences of avunculocal residence have also been reported for the Lozi.

The nuclear family constitutes the basic economic unit of Lozi society. In polygynous marriages, each wife has a separate dwelling and her own gardens and animals to tend. She has the rights of disposition of her own produce and receives a share of the husband's produce. Cooperation in production and consumption between co-wives is highly variable. The traditional ideal is that each wife produces only for her husband and her own children, but it appears that there has been an increased tendency away from this ideal of separateness. In the past it was common for one wife to prepare food for the whole polygynous unit.

Sociopolitical Organization

During the days of the Lozi Kingdom, there was no higher territorially based organization than the village, except for the kingdom as a whole. Beginning with British rule, however, territorial organization was introduced, with villages organized into districts, districts organized into Barotse Province, and the province, in turn, forming a part of a larger political unit or state. In contrast, the Lozi Kingdom was hierarchically organized into a system of nonterritorial political sectors. Members of a sector owed allegiance to the sector head, a man who held a senior title in the Lozi court. These sectors were dispersed throughout the kingdom and served as judicial, military, and administrative units.

The Lozi Kingdom was highly stratified socially. At the top was the royalty (*linabi* and *bana bamulena*), composed of all those who could trace their descent from a king bilaterally within four to five generations. Husbands of princesses and commoners related to royalty were also of high status. Below them were the ordinary commoners. Slaves and serfs formed the lowest strata. (The institutions of serfdom and slavery were abolished in 1906.) The king was the ultimate authority. In earlier times, a chief princess held almost equivalent power over the southern portion of the kingdom, but British rule eroded her powers. In addition, the Lozi courts had a number of stewards, councilors, and members of royalty, all of whom participated in decision making. The most important office next to that of the king was that of *ngambela*, chief councilor, sometimes referred to as the "imperial chancellor," a commoner who represented the commoners' interests in the court. Allocation of power within the Lozi power structure was highly complex and dichotomized. Commoner interests were balanced against royal interests from the top down.

The prerogatives and functions of the king and his courts have undergone steady erosion since the beginning of British colonial rule. As part of a larger political unit, the king was no longer the ultimate power. Power in judicial matters was first limited to minor legal cases and later placed completely within the Zambian judicial system. Similarly, the right to collect tribute was taken from the king. By 1965, most of the governance of the Lozi was through Zambian national agencies, and the right to distribute land rights was virtually the only power that the king could still exercise.

Sanctions maintaining relationships among the Lozi are general and diffuse; breaches of their rules lead to far more serious consequences than a lawsuit in court. Penalties applied to an erring kinsman may range not only from loss of rights to cattle and land, but also the loss of support from fellow kinsmen in various economic endeavors. Conscience and sentiments are major factors in inducing conformity and in making redress for wrongs. Generally, the settlement of everyday problems and the administration of justice is handled at the village level. Should the verdict not satisfy the parties involved, the case is passed along to the next level in a hierarchial court system, until satisfaction is obtained.

Historically, warfare was very common among the Lozi. Lozi kings fought not so much to enrich themselves, although they obviously increased their power and prestige through successful military operations, but to obtain land and cattle, to add to their subject population, and to extend the area of tribute-exchange in which the conquered shared. At the height of their power, the Lozi ruled over some twenty-five tribes of from 300,000 to 400,000 people spread over an area of some 200,000 square kilometers. After British rule was established in 1890, the Lozi domain was restricted to Barotse Province of Rhodesia (later, Zambia). In traditional society, rebellion against the authority of the king was common. Often contenders for power were the king's councilor or groups of councilors, who had enlisted a prince of the royal family on their behalf. When a group of councilors mutinied against a king, because of the king's policies or because he favored another group of councilors, they attacked neither the kingship itself nor the rights of the royal family to it. Each party put forward its royal candidate for the throne and fought in his name. Clearly, commoners could only seek power by serving their own royal candidate for the kingship.

Religion and Expressive Culture

Religious Beliefs. The Lozi are primarily monotheistic, but they retain a number of beliefs about spirits and other supernatural beings. Elaborate rituals and offerings are focused on the burial sites of former kings and chief princesses. Priests mediate between the Lozi and the spirits of their former rulers. There is a different set of beliefs and practices concerning commoner ancestors, and rituals concerning these spirits takes place on an individual level. Sorcery, divination, exorcism, and the use of amulets are all elements in the Lozi religious system.

Ceremonies. The Lozi ceremonial calendar is largely defined by the state of the flood. The two great national events of the year are the moves of the king between his home on the plain at the time of rising flood, and his eventual return after the flood waters fall. The initial move is made following the appearance of the new moon and after sacrifices are made at all the royal graves. Amid the booming of the royal drums, the king, traveling on the royal barge and accompanied by the princes and councilors of his court, proceeds to one of his capitals located on high land above the floodplain. This procession is followed by the migration of the commoners in their dugout canoes. As the flood recedes, the king is enjoined by the royal drummers to move back to the plain so that the people can return to their normal economic pursuits. At this time, the king makes his return journey along a canal dug by one of his predecessors. This trip is accompanied with far less ceremony than the original voyage entailed. Upon the return of the king to his capital, much dancing, especially of the *ngomalume* (royal dance) variety, takes place.

Arts. Lozi artistic expression includes ironic folktales, maxims, and songs about people, objects, and places, all of which are rich in historical allusion and proverbial wisdom. There is a band of musicians within the king's court; they sing as well as play musical instruments. These musicians perform on state occasions, or otherwise at the king's command. The instruments used by this band include a wide variety of drums (kettle, friction, small tube-shaped drums, and war drums), marimbas, the *kangomhbro* or *zanza* (ten pieces of metal fixed around a plate of hardwood on an empty calabash), various stringed instruments made of the ribs of fan palms, iron bells, rattles, and pipes of ivory, wood, or reeds.

Medicine. Diviners usually dance to work themselves into a frenzy and into a state of spirit possession to cure their patients. According to the Lozi, almost all disease is caused by sorcery. To combat these diseases, a witch doctor (*naka*) is called in to perform rites of exorcism over the patient. The naka, who possesses real if limited medical knowledge, may be a member of the local community or may be invited from a neighboring village or from an outside tribe. The diseases treated by exorcism are psychic disorders that are usually attributed to possession by a malevolent spirit. These disorders are called *maimbwe*, *liyala*, *macoba*, and *kayongo*. The method of curing involves exorcistic dancing combined with the inhalation of the vapor from boiling concoctions of bark, roots, and leaves. There are also a number of less common curing ceremonies, such as the one performed when a child becomes possessed by a hunter ancestor.

Death and Afterlife. At the point of death, the individual's eyes and mouth are kept open. When death occurs, the body is flexed so that the knees come up under the chin. The body is then removed from the hut through a special opening cut in the side of the dwelling for this purpose. As the body is taken to the cemetery for burial, spells are scattered on the road to prevent the return of the ghost to haunt the village. Men dig the grave while women stand around the grave site and check to see if the grave is deep enough. Men are buried facing east, whereas women face the west. When the grave is ready, two relatives of the deceased climb into the grave to receive the body. The personal possessions of the deceased are then placed around the corpse. Relatives kneeling around the open grave then gently push dirt into the hole, while those within place dirt around the body. The grave is then completely filled. On top of the grave are placed a broken anthill and a wooden plate or some other object that has been broken with an axe stroke (dead like its owner), in the belief that they will accompany the individual to the other world. The grave of a person of status, which is situated to the side of the commoner's cemetery, is surrounded by a circular barrier of grass and branches. After returning to the village the people mourn for several days. As a sign of grief, the kin of the deceased wear their skin cloaks inside out. The hut of the deceased is pulled down, the roof being placed near the grave, while the remaining possessions of the dead person are burned so that nothing will attract the ghost back to the village. Sons and brothers of the deceased build miniature shelters in their courtyards, bearing the name of the dead, in which the spirit may come and find protection. At times of sickness or disaster, the kin of the deceased go to these shelters to worship and seek the spirit's aid.

The funeral rites for a king are far more elaborate. Before his death, each king selects or builds a village in which he will be buried, peopling it with councilors, priests, and other personnel. At his death, the king is buried in a huge grave at this site. This is then surrounded by a fence of pointed stakes and the markings of royalty erected around the location. Trees, obtained from the bush, are planted at the royal grave so that from a distance the site stands out distinctly on the flat plain. The Lozi believe that these royal graves are infused with great supernatural power, affecting the lives not only of the royal heirs but of all the inhabitants of Loziland. Each grave has its resident priest, who makes offerings at the site. The royal ancestors are believed to act as intermediaries between Nyambe (the supreme god) and man.

At death, the spirit of the deceased goes to a "halfway house" on the way to the spirit world. Here the deceased, if a man who has the appropriate tribal marks (*matumbekela*) on his arms and holes in his ears, is received by Nyambe, or if a woman, by Nasilele (Nyambe's wife), and then placed on the road to the spirit world proper. If matumbekela and holes through the ears were lacking, the man was given flies for food and not welcomed; he was put on a road that meandered and became narrower and narrower until it ended in a desert where the man would die of hunger and thirst.

Bibliography

Gluckman, Max (1965). *The Ideas in Barotse Jurisprudence*. New Haven: Yale University Press.

Kalaluka, Likando (1979). *Kuomboka: A Living Traditional Culture among the Malozi People of Zambia*. Lusaka: Neczam.

Murdock, George Peter (1959). *Africa: Its Peoples and Their Culture History*. New York, Toronto, and London: McGraw-Hill.

Murray, Lynn Loreen (1972). *The Origins of North-Western Rhodesia*. Kingston, Ont.

RONALD JOHNSON

Luba of Shaba

ETHNONYMS: Baluba, Central Luba, Luba Katanga, Luba Lomami, Luba Samba, Luba Shankadi

Orientation

Identification. The patrilineal Luba of Shaba differ in their descent system from the Eastern Luba (the matrilineal Luba-Hemba, living east of the River Zaire); by their culture and language, they are distinct from the Western Luba (Luba of Kasai).

Location. Luba country stretches from the River Lwembe to about 50 kilometers east of the Zaire River, between 6°30′and 10°00′ S in north-central Shaba, in southern Zaire. Except for the Upemba Depression, where the Zaïre River flows through a system of marshes and lakes, the area is a wooded savanna. Annual rainfall exceeds one meter; the rainy season begins in October and ends in May, with a short break in January. The temperature keeps close to its annual average of 24°C.

Demography. The Luba form the largest ethnic group of Shaba. Their population is estimated at 1,100,000, which would represent an average density of 12 people per square kilometer. Outside urban centers, high densities are found in the northern end of the Upemba Depression.

Linguistic Affiliation. Kiluba is a tonal language. It is classified in the Western Bantu Language Group.

History and Cultural Relations

Excavations of graves in the Upemba Depression show that as early as the eighth century A.D., a social stratification had developed in the region: some of the tombs show more wealth than others and contain artifacts that are nowadays connected with power (ceremonial axes, hammers/anvils). Power was probably transmitted hereditarily, as some children were buried with a great number of valuable objects. Archaeological research has revealed an outstanding cultural continuity from that era until now.

According to the genesis tradition of the kingdom, an aristocratic hunter hero coming from the East (Mbidi Kiluwe) met an aboriginal ruler (Nkongolo); unaware of the demanding customs of sacred kingship, notably of the meal rituals, he married the two sisters of this ruler and went back alone to his country. One of the sisters gave birth to a son (Kalala Ilunga) who eventually became a mighty warrior whom the ruler planned to kill. The young man had to flee to his father's country. Later, he came back, beheaded his maternal uncle, and became the first king of the Luba. These traditions gave rise to a controversy between, on the one hand, structuralists, who argue that the epic is representative of mythic ground shared by many Bantu-speaking peoples, and on the other hand, Africanist historians, who consider either that the epic contains traces of ancient historical facts or that it is a political charter legitimizing the prerogatives of the dynasty. However that may be, the Luba Kingdom was founded in the eighteenth century or before, in the vicinity of the present town of Kabongo. It exerted a strong political influence on its neighbors and was the main reference point for many rulers' genealogies and many religious institutions of the Eastern Savanna peoples. Until 1870, the Luba king—the *mulopwe* (pl. *balopwe*)—had at his disposal a powerful army able to wage war hundreds of kilometers from the capital. But the kingdom did not rest on a firm centralized administrative apparatus: royal authority was mostly effective in the capital's region; beyond that center lay "chiefdoms," which had more autonomy the farther they were from the capital. Each was governed by a local rulers—also called a mulopwe—whose ritual life was similar to the king's. These chiefs had to bring tribute to the king as acknowledgment of his hierarchical seniority. The kingdom began to collapse by 1870 on account of an unending succession struggle and of repeated attacks by Angolan slave traders and Tanzanian conquerors who took advantage of their firearms. Belgian colonizers settled around 1900 and hastened the fall of the kingdom by dividing its center into two large territories, the government of which was assigned to two rival heirs from the ancient dynasty: Kabongo and Kasongo Nyembo. Moreover, about twenty Luba chiefdoms were acknowledged as fully independent from those two rulers.

After the independance of the Congo, the Luba led a harsh war against their southern neighbors who supported the Katanga secession (1960–1963).

The expansion of the kingdom (up to an area of about 200,000 square kilometers) and of long-distance trade stimulated contacts between the Luba and their neighbors. Nowadays political ties have come to an end, but Luba influence is still noticeable, notably in the regalia and religious practices.

Settlements

An adobe building with a metal roof and a few partition walls more and more often takes the place of the ancient four-cornered house with a thatched roof and walls of branches plastered with clay. Small villages are sometimes exclusively inhabited by members of the same lineage, but the larger ones are divided into lineage quarters. The total population of a village varies considerably: a few thousands along the main streams, as a result of conurbation processes, sometimes well under a hundred in the countryside. Formerly, the capital used to be densely populated. The layout of the houses of the chief, his wives, and his dignitaries followed a definite checkered plan.

Economy

Subsistence and Commercial Activities. The Luba practice slash-and-burn agriculture; fields are abandoned after a few seasons. The most cultivated plants are cassava and maize; to a lesser extent, one also finds sweet potatoes, peanuts, tomatoes, onions, beans, cucumbers, tobacco, and sesame. Millet and sorghum are now mainly used for brewing beer. Two species are often cultivated on the same field. The main crops are produced by June. One can find banana, mango and *Elaeis*-palm plantations, as well as wild olive trees surrounding some villages. (Oil is derived from the fruits of the latter two.) Cotton cultivation has vanished since independance. In the Upemba Depression and, to a lesser extent, along the Zaire River, fishing is the principal economic activity. Everywhere hunting is a secondary activity. Great collective hunts take place when the savanna is set on fire, at the end of the dry season. The Luba breed sheep, goats, pigs, and some poultry, all of which are eaten on special occasions; they also breed dogs for hunting.

Industrial Arts. Among the Luba of Shaba there are blacksmiths, potters, woodworkers, sculptors, and weavers of mats, baskets, and nets. Salt making is still a viable activity in the marshes south of Kabongo. Once flourishing, the industries of iron smelting and of raffia-fiber cloth weaving have now disappeared.

Trade. The discovery of copper crosses in eleventh-century graves proves that as early as this era, a long-distance trade connected the Upemba Depression with the Copperbelt. This trade intensified from that time onward, and it is also via the Copperbelt that the Luba acquired the glass beads and shells that were to become the means of exchange during the eighteenth and nineteenth centuries. The currencies used for commercial and ritual purposes, although distinct, could be exchanged for each other. The Luba also traded with populations to the north and to the east: the Songye of Kasai bartered raffia cloths and other finished products for iron, copper, salt, and fish from the Luba. Commercial trips were undertaken by groups of usually less than twenty people. In the past, there were no marketplaces, as there are nowadays in the centers.

Division of Labor. Men deal with political affairs, hunt, fish, fight, clear the bush, rear animals, make nets and fashion wooden tools, and build the framework of the house. Women do the rest of the agricultural work, brew beer, make pottery, deal with the children and the home, and tend the poultry. Children and adolescents are compelled to perform few tasks, although girls soon help their mothers at home. Political leaders, religious specialists, and specialized workers are the only people not to follow the common pattern of labor.

Land Tenure. The first man to settle on a land is its "owner," and this title is transmitted to his successor. This dignitary has a right to a share of all that is taken from his land, whatever it may be: game, gathered or cultivated plants, salt, or iron ore. This right applies also to the lakes. As land suitable for cultivation is not scarce, its use is not the privilege of the lineage to which the landowner belongs.

Kinship

Kin Groups and Descent. The patrilineages (*bisaka;* sing. *kisaka*) may have alimentary taboos and may "own" some land or lakes. The patrilineal ideology is not very developed: for example, a person's protective spirit, after which that person is named at birth, may come from either his paternal or his maternal family.

Kinship Terminology. The Luba of Shaba use Hawaiian cousin terminology and bifurcate-merging avuncular terms. Joking relationships are maintained with maternal uncles and with all grandparents.

Marriage and Family

Marriage. Large-scale polygyny was the appanage of the ancient sacred chiefs, small-scale polygyny is the ideal of every man; monogamy is the norm and is gaining ground with Christianization. The matrimonial alliance follows a semicomplex pattern: the prospective wife may not come from any of Ego's grandparents' lineages, nor have a common great-grandparent with him, nor be a close relative by marriage (wife's sister, sister's husband's sister, brother's wife's sister, and so forth). After having paid most of the bride-wealth (a gun; formerly, precious beads), the husband brings his bride to live near his parents. Divorce calls for the repayment of all or part of the bride-wealth. The responsibility for the death of a wife is ascribed to her husband, who has to pay heavy death-dues to his in-laws.

Domestic Unit. The household includes a dwelling for the husband and one for each of his wives. Young children live at their mother's house. If the owner is an important man, these houses are surrounded by an enclosure, and there is a special kitchen for his meals; among the most traditional people, next to the kitchen there are little huts for the ancestors' worship.

Inheritance. The possessions of a man are inherited by his brothers and his sons, the eldest taking precedence over the youngest. Levirate is frequent, and a sister's son may sometimes inherit one of his uncle's widows.

Socialization. Children stand close by their mother and are very protected until the age of weaning, at around 2 years old. Then, until the age of 7 or 8, they play with other youngsters, near their mothers. Girls begin to learn to do housework. By the age of 8 or 10, punishments are harsher; sexual dichotomy increases, especially in the games. Formerly, during the dry season, children built mock villages where they would imitate the adults' lives. Education tends to minimize the competitive spirit, for which there is no place in the games, and to emphasize conformity. Until the 1950s, children had to undergo a complex ritual initiation of several months, which was not the occasion for any utilitarian teaching. Circumcision (*mukanda* in the west, *disao* in the east) was collective and followed by a long seclusion in a camp out of the village; nowadays the operation is carried out individually and casually on youngsters. The girls' initiation (*butanda*) was individual and took place long before puberty in the village; in the next years, the girl was tattooed and underwent manipulations aimed at developing her sexual organs. These manipulations are still usual practice.

Sociopolitical Organization

Social Organization. The main cooperative work group is that of brothers, in particular for the building of a house. There is not much cooperation in the agricultural work. The secret societies are less powerful than in the past: the most important of them is the Mbudye society, which formerly was closely associated with political power. Synchretic churches have multiplied; among them, the Jamaa is a Catholic movement inspired by Father Tempel's famous book, *Bantu Philosophy;* it is focused on the union of the community and of the married couple.

Political Organization. Before taking up his function, a potential chief (mulopwe) undergoes a test to show that the tutelar spirits of the chiefdom accept him. The critical point of the enthronment process is a four-day seclusion, during which the recipient has incestuous intercourse with a female relative and gains a new spiritual identity through close contact with some relics of his predecessors. He formerly had to be smeared with human blood to gain his full status. A chief has to submit to many prohibitions: he may not touch a lake, nor see a corpse, nor share his meal with anyone. In a mystical way, he is responsible for the well-being of his subjects, who are his "children"; in the past, he was killed as soon as he became mutilated or in poor health. Chiefs are surrounded by a court of dignitaries, whose functions are more or less specialized. The subdivisions of the chiefdom are controlled by local lineage headmen or secondary chiefs appointed by the court; they are responsible for the sending of tribute, the composition of which depends on the region's specialities. This tribute is the main sign of one's submission to the chief.

Social Control. Having created life, the parents have a right to be respected: children who fail to perform their duties to their fathers may be struck by illness or great misfortunes, sent by their ancestors. Outside of this domestic setting, minor offenders are tried by judges from the village or by lineage elders; the more important cases are settled by the sacred chief, helped by his counselors. In the past, ordeals (by poison, etc.) were often imposed by ritual specialists on offenders.

Conflict. The expansion of the kingdom was the result of a warlike and matrimonial policy. In the past, after the death of a king, his potential heirs had to fight. The war dignitaries, once numerous, have become scarce since the pacification.

Religion and Expressive Culture

Religious Beliefs. Three categories of spirits are at the heart of the Luba religious system. The first are the ancestors; they are most commonly encountered in a relative's dream, coming as a favor to announce to a man or his wife that the wife is pregnant. The ancestor is then expected to protect the fetus, being "godfather" to the unborn. Territorial spirits (often called *mikishi* [sing. *mukishi*]) are responsible for the plentifulness of game and fish. The third type (*bavidye;* sing. *vidye*) are mighty spirits able to possess human beings. Some traditions include a "great vidye," the creator of everything, although he does not receive any worship. Sorcery is particularly feared and harshly condemned.

Catholic and Protestant missions have settled in many regions of Lubaland; their influence is felt everywhere, but it has not put an end to the belief in the power of the spirits and of the sorcerers.

Religious Practitioners. Many specialists communicate with the spirits. The head of the household leads the familial ancestors' cult; he prays to them in front of their little huts in his courtyard when there is a problem or at the new moon, which is the day of the spirits. Among the lineages possessing some lake or some land, a *kitobo* priest is in charge of offering beer to the territorial spirits when the game or fish disappear. Professional mediums (male and female) are possessed by the mighty spirits. When they go into trance, the spirits speak through their mouth; they carry out divination and are in charge of locating sorcerers and their charms.

Ceremonies. The enthronement and the funeral of the mulopwe, of his dignitaries, and of the kilumbu are occasions for great ceremonies. The public announcement of a woman's first pregnancy, birth, marriage, funeral, and the end of mourning are regarded as being important steps in one's ritual life cycle. In the past, the coming of the first teeth, the boys' circumcision, the girls' initiation, the harvest of the first crops, and the great hunts at the end of the dry season were occasions for collective rites.

Arts. Luba wood sculptures (caryatid stools, bowl bearers, bowstands, cups, staffs, spears, paddles, axes, etc.) have earned their excellent reputation, but they are mostly ancient works. They are intended for the mulopwe, his court, and the ritual specialists. To gain any efficaciousness, a statue has to be activated by a ritual specialist, who introduces some charms into it so that it can serve as a receptacle for spirits. The Mbudye society uses a wood board ornamented with patterns of beads or other elements as a mnemonic device to relate the kingdom's history. The exact use of the numerous masks has not been cleared up; they seem to be connected with secret societies and with the circumcision ceremonies. Chiefs had their musicians.

Medicine. Every sickness is supposed to have originated from a spiritual cause, and a divination process is employed to discover it. The sick person either has to apply to the spirits responsible for his misfortune and to submit to some ritual obligations in connection with them, or must have a charm made up to protect him from the harm of the sorcerers.

Death and Afterlife. Some people, even if sociable during their lifetime, become malevolent after their death. Expulsion rites are then required. In the past, the Tusanji secret society was responsible for neutralizing malignant spirits, by unearthing their corpses and ritually eating them. Usually, however, the spirits of the dead are benevolent and protect the members of their family who are still alive. Dead people who have no link with the living and who do not give their names to newborns sink into a deeper afterworld, more gloomy than the first (which is described as a continuation of earthly life).

Bibliography

Burton, William F. P. (1961). *Luba Religion and Magic in Custom and Belief*. Tervueren: Musée Royal de l'Afrique Centrale (MRAC).

Nooter, Mary (1991). "Luba Art and Polity: Creating Power in a Central African Kingdom." Doctoral thesis, Columbia University.

Petit, Pierre (1993). "Rites familiaux, rites royaux: Étude du système cérémoniel des Luba du Shaba (Zaïre)." Doctoral thesis, Université Libre de Bruxelles.

Petit, Pierre (1995). "The Sacred Kaolin and the Bowl-Bearers (Luba of Shaba)." In *Objects-Signs of Africa,* edited by Lucde Heusch, 111–131. Tervueren: Musée Royal de l'Afrique Centrale (MRAC).

Reefe, Thomas Q. (1981). *The Rainbow and the Kings: A History of the Luba Empire to 1891*. Berkeley and Los Angeles: University of California Press.

Theuws, Jacques A. (Th.) (1962). *De Luba-Mens*. Tervueren: Musée Royal de l'Afrique Centrale (MRAC).

PIERRE PETIT

Lugbara

ETHNONYM: Logwari

Orientation

The Lugbara people live on the plateau of the Nile-Zaire watershed in northwestern Uganda and northeastern Zaire. In the 1950s they numbered 244,000, of whom 183,000 lived in Uganda. They speak a cluster of dialects of the Eastern Sudanic Language Group, closely related to Madi, Logo, `Bale (Lendu), and Keliko and distantly related to Azande and Mangbetu. They and the Madi, to their east, are the only representatives of this language group in eastern Africa. They refer to themselves today as "Lugbara" but also as "Urule'ba" ("High people") and "Andrale'ba" ("Low people"), others of the former being the Keliko and Logo to their west and others of the latter being the Madi to their east. Their plateau is very distinct from the landscapes of most of their neighbors, and they are conscious of their singular identity geographically, linguistically, and culturally.

History and Cultural Relations

The Lugbara came under colonial rule in 1900, as part of the Congo Free State. Arab slavers were active to the north and west during the nineteenth century, but the Lugbara escaped actual slave raiding because of their terrain and their military fierceness. Belgian administration was slight—and ceased upon the death of King Leopold II. The Lugabara were then handed over to Anglo-Egyptian Sudan, after which Lugbara country was harassed by European elephant hunters until it was transferred to the British administration of Uganda in 1914, as part of the new West Nile District. After the independence of Uganda in 1962, the Lugbara were largely ignored during the first regime of Milton Obote, offered many favors by Idi Dada Amin (who came from West Nile District), and subjected to brutal near-genocide under the second Obote regime. Today the Lugbara population is certainly far less than in the early 1950s, and their social economy and organization have altered markedly from their preindependence form.

Economy

The Lugbara plateau is extremely fertile, supporting, in its center, a population density of more than 80 to the square kilometer during the 1950s. The Lugbara are highly efficient peasant farmers, their staples being grains (traditionally millets and sorghums, now with some maize), root crops (traditionally sweet potatoes, now also cassava), and legumes of many kinds. With increasing dependence on cassava, the formerly highly nutritious diet of the Lugbara has been drastically worsened. Cash crops were encouraged during the colonial period, but, owing to edaphic and climatic factors and the long distance to the nearest markets for cash crops (some 800 kilometers to the south), few have been profitable. Groundnuts, sunflower, cotton, and tobacco have all been tried, only the latter two with success. The main export has been that of male labor to the Indian-owned sugar plantations and the African-owned farms of southern Uganda; about one-quarter of the men are absent at any one time. Until the Obote atrocities of the 1970s, the Lugbara peasant society could maintain its members on a level of nutrition and health that was at least equal to those of most Third World societies.

The Lugbara keep some livestock: cattle, goats, sheep, fowl, dogs, and cats; before the cattle epidemics of the 1980s, they had far greater herds. Cattle, goats, and sheep are not killed for consumption, but rather for ancestral sacrifices (although the meat is actually consumed by those attending); the sale of hides and skins earns valuable income.

Traditionally, local exchange of surplus foodstuffs was in the form of gifts between kin and barter with others. Small local weekly markets came into being during the 1920s, with the introduction of cash, maize (used for beer brewing), and consumer goods such as kerosene, cigarettes, and cloth. (As late as the 1950s, women wore only pubic leaves and beads, and elder men, animal skins.)

The division of labor is sharply defined. Men and women share agricultural tasks, the men opening the fields and the women doing most of the remaining work. Men hunt and herd cattle; women do the arduous and the time-consuming everyday domestic tasks. Formerly, men were responsible for the physical protection of their families and for waging feuds and war. Men hold formal authority over their kin, but older women informally exercise considerable domestic and lineage authority. Land is held by lineages, as land is traditionally not sold or rented. Women are allocated rights of use by their husbands' lineage elders.

The country is open, composed of countless small ridges with streams between them; the compounds and fields are set on the ridges. Houses, round and made of mud and wattle and thatch, are dispersed throughout the almost continuous fields. Few settlements today have more than three or four houses. A century ago compounds were large for defense, but colonial administration removed the threat of war and feud. A house is the dwelling place of one wife and her children. If she is the only wife, her husband also sleeps there. If a man has more than one wife, he moves from one house to another in turn. The house, and especially its hearth, is very much a female domain. A compound, of one or more women's houses, is typically surrounded by a euphorbia fence, often with a nearby cattle kraal; beyond lie fields. The fields vary in type: small gardens typically on the sites of earlier houses, home fields under permanent cultivation and often irrigated, and farther fields under shifting cultivation, the fallow used for grazing. Stretching out beyond the fields is untilled grazing land, and near the edges of the country are wide extents of bush and forest, used for hunting.

Kinship and Marriage

The Lugbara recognized patrilineal descent, claiming a single origin from two brothers—Heroes—who entered the country from the north, found and cured many leper women, and then married them, their sons becoming the founders of some sixty clans. Genealogies from the founders to the present are usually between nine and twelve generations in depth.

The Lugbara have never formed a single polity and have lacked kings or traditional chiefs. The largest indigenous autonomous group is known as *suru* ("group" or "category"); it has an average population of some 4,000 people. The suru is formed of the members of a single clan, with many categories of attached groups; not all the members of a given clan will live in the same clan territory, which is given the clan name. The core members of this territory, a single jural community, may be referred to as a subclan. A clan is ideally exogamous; internal disputes should be settled by ritual or feud, in which women and children are not harmed, rather than by warfare, as between neighboring jural communities, in which women and children might be captured. The subclan territory is divided into smaller territorial units, there usually being three or even four levels; the smallest is the household occupying a single compound. These units are likewise each formed around a patrilineal lineage, a segment of the subclan; those who form the core of the household are a minimal lineage. The whole forms a segmentary lineage system. The lineage comprises kin who can trace their exact relationships, whereas those beyond it cannot do so. Lugbara recognize this distinction by referring to a lineage as *ori'ba* ("ghost people"), who together sacrifice to a single ancestor. Today this traditional pattern has become largely weakened and even destroyed by overcrowding, the events of Obote's genocide and later famines, and the consequent movements of populations.

Marriage is forbidden between members of the same clan or with a man's or woman's mother's close kin. It is effected by the transfer of cattle bride-wealth from the groom's to the bride's close patrilineal kin. Polygyny is a male ideal, about a third of the men having more than one wife; most secondary wives, however, are those inherited from their brothers or fathers' brothers. Divorce, which is relatively unusual, may traditionally be made only by the husband, the cattle being returned except for one beast for each child born; the most common grounds are adultery and the wife's barrenness.

The household is a close-knit and mutually dependent unit. The socialization of children is traditionally by parents and older siblings. There are no forms of initiation at puberty, but children of about 6 undergo forehead cicatrization and excision of the lower four incisors.

Political Organization

The segmentary lineage system was traditionally self-controlling. The rainmaker ("chief of rain," the genealogically senior man of each subclan) was the only holder of political authority until colonial administration and is still today the only one whose authority is freely accepted. Otherwise, only the heads of minimal lineages—"big-men"—held local authority. Disputes between households and small groups were settled by feud, which was fought subject to strict rules of conduct; feuds were brought to a close by the subclan rainmaker's threatening a curse upon the participants unless they settled their dispute. Between jural communities, disputes were settled by war, which ended through the joint action of the two rainmakers involved. Disputes were almost always over repaying bride-wealth, trespassing, or stealing livestock.

The Belgian administration appointed locally influential men as chiefs, making them responsibile for controlling feuding and warfare to the best of their abilities. The British, who marked boundaries between clusters of jural communities and divided the country into chiefdoms and subchiefdoms, continued the system of appointing influential local leaders. Over time, many units were amalgamated, and, by the 1950s, there were five Lugbara chiefdoms in Uganda and the same number in the Belgian Congo, each chiefdom comprising some five or six subchiefdoms, all under appointed chiefs; below the chiefs were headmen. During the 1950s, the British administration introduced elections for these offices, with some success; in general, however, those elected were looked upon as "Europeans" and often as exploiters who worked under the supervision of European district officials. The European officials numbered one district commissioner and two assistants for the district, of which the Lugbara comprised something over half the population.

Religion and Expressive Culture

The Lugbara recognize a single deity, Adroa (also known as Adro), who created the world and its inhabitants. Two Heroes then formed Lugbara society itself. Beneath Adroa are two categories of spiritual beings: the spirits and the ancestors. Spirits are known as *adro*, a word of complex meaning that essentially refers to a source of power. The spirits are of many kinds and have different degrees of power over human beings. First are the numberless spirits of sickness and disaster, their motives unknowable to the living (although female diviners are thought able to make some contact with them). Second are the spirits that inhabit the bodies of the living, together with the soul. The spirit in the body leaves at death, dwelling in the forests with an immanent aspect of the Adroa. These spirits take the form of small human beings, and both they and Adroa kill on sight.

Ancestors who left male children are "ghosts"; they send sickness to their descendants as response to disobedience. Sacrifices of meat, blood, and beer are offered to the ghosts individually, by elders. The ancestors without male children form a collectivity to which grains and milk are offered, as do the spirits.

Living elders act as priests for their lineages and also as oracles who discover the identity of the ghosts sending sickness. Today many people attend government and mission clinics to ensure physical healing, but the clinics cannot discover the underlying mystical causes of sickness. Diviners, mainly women, are possessed by—and can contact—spirits in order to ascertain the causes and suggest means of removing them. Prophets have appeared at moments of crisis; they bring with them extremely powerful spirits who give divine messages regarding the reorganization of traditional systems of authority. The most famous was the prophet Rembe, who led an anti-European healing cult in 1916. Lugbara also believe in specters of the recently dead.

The most important rites of sacrifice are those to the dead, especially senior men and women; rites of birth and marriage are little elaborated. Sacrificial rites are a central aspect of the authority of the elders, who control them and so gain sanction for the authority given them by their dead forebears. Death rites, mainly in the form of death dances, are highly elaborate; they reestablish the disturbed distribution of lineage authority. There is only a vaguest belief in a land of the dead, but none in a journey to it after death.

Lugbara beliefs in witches and sorcerers, which are clearly distinguished, are strong. Witches are men, especially elders, who pervert their legitimate lineage authority for their own selfish ends. Sorcerers—women and young men—lack legitimate authority and are thus thought to use "medicines" and poisons. Both witches and sorcerers are feared but can be dealt with by diviners, who can identify them. Witchcraft is linked to the lineage system; as that system has weakened in the late twentieth century, beliefs in sorcery have been strengthened.

Christian missions (Italian Verona Mission and the Africa Inland Mission) entered the area soon after 1914 but made few converts until the latter half of the century; today most Lugbara are Catholics. There is little adherence to Islam except for the "Nubi" in the few small townships.

The Lugbara do not practice painting or elaborate carving in wood or metal, their main aesthetic products being fine basketry and pottery. Ironworking for tools and weapons is by a specialists' ethnic group (Ndu) regarded with awe and some fear, who live dispersed among the Lugbara settlements.

Bibliography

Middleton, John (1970). *The Study of the Lugbara*. New York: Holt, Rinehart & Winston.

Middleton, John (1987). *Lugbara Religion*. Rev. ed. London: Oxford University Press for International African Institute.

Middleton, John (1992). *The Lugbara of Uganda*. Rev. ed. New York: Holt, Rinehart & Winston.

JOHN MIDDLETON

Lunda

ETHNONYMS: Akosa, Aluunda, Aruund, Eastern Lunda, Imbangala, Ishindi Lunda, Kanongesha Lunda, Kazembe Mutanda Lunda, Luapula Lunda, Lunda-Kazembe (Cazembe), Lunda-Ndembu, Luunda, Musokantanda Lunda, Ndembu, Northern Lunda, Ruund, Southern Lunda, Western Lunda

Orientation

Identification. "Lunda" is the most widely used English term to refer to literally hundreds of social groups whose oral histories link them in varying ways to a far-flung empire that controlled trade and tribute in much of Central Africa from the sixteenth through the nineteenth centuries. Local names for groups tend to reflect either geographical position, topographical features, or names of founding lineages of local ruling dynasties.

Location. The Lunda are broadly distributed in eastern Angola, southern Zaire, and northern and western Zambia. Most of this territory is characterized by high plateau ranging between 1,200 and 1,500 meters above sea level. The vegetation-soil types are generally described as Northern Brachystegia woodlands on clayey plateau soils in the extreme north, Northern Brachystegia woodlands on Kalahari Contact soils in the central region, and Cryptosepalum forest and Cryptosepalum-Brachystegia woodland on upland and central sands in the south. The landscape, however, is broken up into myriad micro-ecological niches, corresponding to bands of changing soil type and variations in elevation. The most common are thick forest, forest of low stunted trees, gallery forest along rivers, grassy plains, and sparse shrub land at the edge of plains. There are three rather distinct seasons. There is a rainy season that runs from roughly September to April, during which time 15 to 28 centimeters of rain may fall. May to July is the cold, dry season, during which time the temperature regularly drops down to around 4° C, and night frost sometimes occurs in low-lying valleys. August to September is the hot dry season, with temperatures regularly soaring into the 30s (C).

Demography. No reliable census figures exist for the number of individuals who consider themselves Lunda. A rough estimate is 500,000 in Angola, 750,000 in Zaire, and 200,000 in Zambia. Population densities range as low as 0.8 persons per square kilometer in some rural areas, but reach extremely high ratios in urban areas of all three countries.

Linguistic Affiliation. The Lunda language is Western Bantu at its root, with some overlay of Eastern Bantu and with local influences from the languages of people who existed in Central Africa before the Bantu expansion. A core vocabulary is mutually intelligible over vast areas, but understanding decreases as one moves away from the central point. Some groups, such as the Luapula Lunda, have almost completely adopted the language of the people among whom they settled.

History and Cultural Relations

Before the sixteenth century, the basic institution of the Lunda was believed to have been the segmentary matrilineage. Each lineage segment occupied its own small territory (*mpat*), mostly along the Kalanyi River in present-day Zaire. They raised millet and sorghum as well as other crops, but fishing was the activity for which they were most noted. Each mpat was probably centered on an ideal location for fishing, with crops being planted in the fertile alluvial soils along the riverbank. By all indications, this system was extremely productive; Lunda territory was dotted with a rapidly expanding number of independent domains, each with its own headman.

Shortly after 1600, a centralized polity emerged that attracted traders from both the Atlantic and Indian Ocean coasts of Africa. The Lunda capital was located at Musumba, in present-day Zaire, but several major Lunda clusters existed with populations exceeding 10,000 people each. With four large standing armies, an array of titled court figures and a large complex bureaucracy, the Lunda became an empire capable of controlling the terms of trade and exacting tribute over a wide area.

The Lunda have a long history of spawning émigrés who, through political manipulation or outright conquest, have reformulated the social and economic landscape of Central Africa. During the 1600s, one set of émigrés left the Lunda center, traveled west, and played a seminal role in the formation of the Kasanje Kingdom in Angola. Another set of émigrés traveled south to form the Luvale ruling dynasty. During the mid-1700s, royal lineages from the Lunda center traveled south to form the polities of Kanongesha, Ishindi, Musokantanda, and Kazembe Mutanda. A fifth group traveled east and established a polity along the Luapula River in Zambia. The impetus for most of this movement was the attempt to control strategic positions in the rapidly expanding long-distance trade network. Caravans from both coasts, with up to a thousand merchants and carriers, were crisscrossing Central Africa on a regular basis in search of marketable commodities, and in need of vast quantities of food. Some Lunda groups specialized in providing ivory, slaves, copper, wild rubber, and other goods that fueled the trade. Other groups ventured into the commercial production of food. Still others grew wealthy by levying taxes on the movement of men and materials through their territory, particularly at strategic river crossings. Most of these polities remain in direct tributary relations with the Lunda center at Musumba.

With the formal establishment of colonialism in the late 1800s, the Lunda were subjected to a tripartite division among the European powers of England, Portugal, and Belgium (later France). The long-distance caravan system was curtailed. The Lunda in each of the three colonial territories were relegated to the margins of newly emerging centers of economic activity. Little has changed in the era of independence.

Settlements

The traditional village was a collection of small circular clay houses with straw-thatched roofs, arranged in a circle around a central meeting house. Members of alternate generations would build on opposing hemispheres of the circle. Banana, tobacco, and a few specialty crops would be planted around the periphery, with the main food gardens fanning out some distance from the village. Hectares of forest would separate individual villages. Villages would range in size from less than a dozen individuals to several hundred people in the villages of chiefs or senior headmen. More than 10,000 people were known to have occupied the court of the paramount chief at Musumba.

Today villages of square or rectangular houses tend to form straight lines along roadways and major paths, clustering at crossroads. Small towns, where life takes a more urban tempo, dot Lunda territory.

Economy

Subsistence and Commercial Activities. Subsistence production consists mainly of cassava—the basic staple—supplemented by maize, bananas, pumpkins, pineapples, sweet potatoes, yams, beans, groundnuts, tomatoes, cabbages, and a wide variety of other vegetable crops. Millet and sorghum, once the major food crops, are today grown primarily by women, for the production of alcoholic beverages. Goats, sheep, pigs, chickens, and a few cattle are present in most areas. Game is fairly abundant and is secured either through hunting or trapping. Honey, mushrooms, fruits, berries, and other wild foods are regularly gathered in the forest. Fishing with hook and line, nets, and traps is a popular activity.

Cassava, maize, pineapples, and sunflowers are the major

commercial crops. Since the mid-1980s, fish farming has become an increasingly widespread activity.

Industrial Arts. Traditionally, the Lunda were well known for copper- and ironsmithing, pottery, basket making, mat weaving, and woodworking. Local craft production, however, declined precipitously under colonial rule and persists today at a very low level.

Trade. Precolonial trade was characterized by a vast array of goods from both Europe and the Indian Ocean nations flowing into the Lunda region in exchange for copper, iron, ivory, skins, slaves, honey and wax, rubber, and food. During the colonial era, 1884–1964, external trade was forcefully curtailed. Today there is extensive interregional trade between Lunda in Angola, Zaire, and Zambia, exploiting the differing price structures of each country. The trade consists mainly of foodstuffs, particularly dried fish and game meat, in exchange for manufactured commodities such as sugar, salt, cooking oil, clothing, and household utensils.

Division of Labor. Males, females and children all plant cassava extensively. Men are responsible for cutting trees and clearing the fields. Women do all the processing and cooking. Men are responsible for providing the household with protein foods, either by hunting, trapping, fishing, raising domestic stock, or through cash purchases. Men are also responsible for all village construction and for providing tools, as well as some clothing, for wives and children. Women provide most of the child care, with some assistance from husbands and older children. Women also secure and maintain the cooking and other household utensils.

Land Tenure. Land is rather abundant throughout most of the Lunda territory and is, therefore, rarely a subject of dispute. Traditional use rights are established by requests made to local chiefs and senior headmen. Requests for land are generally denied only if a prior claim exists. Owing to the practice of shifting cultivation, fields as well as entire villages move frequently, and land is not generally considered an inheritable commodity. Access to land in or near towns is granted through local government councils, often on a ninety-nine-year lease basis. The civil war in Angola has, since 1975, made all land tenure uncertain in that country. Zambia has held national discussions on the future of land tenure in rural areas.

Kinship

Kin Groups and Descent. Most Lunda are matrilineal, but only the lineages of chiefs or certain headmen are remembered with great genealogical depth. Most matrilineages, however, are quite extensive geographically. Attendance at weddings, funerals, and initiation ceremonies serves to keep individuals in touch with matrikin over vast areas of Angola, Zaire, and Zambia. The matrilineage rarely acts as a corporate group, but it does provide a potential network for support and hospitality should the need arise. Personal relations cultivated over time, rather than cultural prescriptions, determine the degree of closeness and frequency of social interaction.

Kinship Terminology. The Lunda use an Iroquois kinship terminology system. The major features include a merging of same-sex siblings by the descending generation. Both mother and mother's sister are called by the same term, *mama*. Both father and father's brother are called *tata*. Distinctions are made for the father's sister (*tatankaji*) and mother's brother (*mandumi*). Likewise, cross cousins (children of mother's brother or father's sister) are distinguished from parallel cousins (children of mother's sister or father's brother). The latter are addressed using sibling terms. Hierarchy based on age defines relationships among the Lunda. Most kin terms reflect, or are appended by terms that reflect birth order or relative age—for example, *yaya* (older brother or sister), *mwanyika* (younger brother or sister), *-mukulumpi* (-the elder), *-kansi* (-the younger).

Marriage and Family

Marriage. Traditionally among the Lunda there has been a slight preference for cross-cousin marriages. Little pressure is exerted, however, and individuals generally enjoy a great deal of latitude in the choice of marriage partners. Many marriages take place across ethnic boundaries. In the past, couples would live uxorilocally for the first few years of marriage, with the husband performing bride-service for his in-laws by assisting with agricultural tasks and village construction. Later the couple would reside patrilocally. Today a wife generally moves to her husband's village immediately upon the completion of an exchange of bride-wealth and the performance of a simple ceremony. Bride-wealth may consist of agricultural commodities, tools, household utensils, clothing, and a small amount of cash. Couples today may also choose to marry in civil ceremonies in town, or in Christian ceremonies in any of the numerous churches in Lunda territory, with or without bride-wealth. The Lunda possess one of the highest rates of divorce noted in the anthropological literature. In the 1950s it was recorded that nearly 66 percent of all marriages ended in divorce. By the 1980s, the divorce rate had dropped to around 33 percent. Polygyny is permitted, but probably less than 1 in 50 men actually has more than one wife at a time.

Domestic Unit. Ideally, each mature adult has his or her own house. Children tend to sleep with their mother when they are very young, with a grandparent in their preteen years, and in single-sex "dormitories" as young adults. Houses are grouped together into distinct villages, the core of which is usually a set of matrilineally related males, ideally uterine brothers and their wives and children. Extended and classificatory kin, as well as friends and visitors, are also present in most villages. In some respects the matricentric bond can be viewed as the basic unit of society. Because divorce and remarriage are frequent, women with their children oscillate between the villages of their matrilineal kin and those of their successive husbands. There is strict division of labor by gender; the labor of children is under the control of the mother. Productive individualism is the norm, but consumption tends to be communal. Households could be defined as those who habitually dine from the same pot.

Inheritance. Titles, positions of leadership, cash, and other precious articles are inherited matrilineally. Individuals are traditionally buried with their few utilitarian personal possessions, such as tools, clothing, and household utensils. Standing crops and domestic stock are consumed by the funeral party.

Socialization. Boys remain under the authority and guidance of their mothers until they have undergone the circumcision rite. Girls remain with their mothers until they marry. Older siblings play an active role in supervising and educating younger siblings. The grandparent-grandchild relationship is extremely close. They are permitted a degree of informality and intimacy denied in other relationships. In theory, at least, a grandparent cannot deny any request made by a grandchild. Traditionally, every adult in a village was said to be responsible for educating and socializing every child in the village. Today, however, public schools and churches play an increasingly important role in shaping the ideas and ideals of the youth.

Sociopolitical Organization

Social Organization. Lunda individuals tend to be embedded in social networks made up of numerous distinct, yet often overlapping, social units. These include the household, the village, the matrilineage, local cohorts, ritual cults, religious communities, occupational associations, civic clubs, and perhaps political parties. These social units vary in their methods of recruitment, the claims they make on the individual, and the benefits they offer in return. Individual commitment to particular social units varies over the course of a lifetime as people's ambitions, capacities, and strategies change. Lunda enjoy a great deal of flexibility in residential affiliation and choice of personal association. The social landscape is fluid and ever-changing.

Hierarchy, expressed in an idiom of age, is the dominant feature of traditional social organization. Notions of hierarchy are embedded in the language; they are expressed in routine greetings, and they set the norms of daily social interaction. The hierarchy extends from the most recently born up to the paramount chief. It cuts across lineages, villages, and national boundaries.

Political Organization. Historically, the Lunda are remarkable for their drive to maintain local autonomy while simultaneously building up wide-ranging social, economic, and political networks. During the sixteenth through nineteenth centuries, the Lunda king at Musumba (Mwantiyanvwa) was able to exact tribute from wide areas of Central Africa. Otherwise, he made few demands and exerted little influence on daily village life. Headmen oversee the affairs of each village. The longest-standing headman in a particular area is generally recognized as the senior headman. Subchiefs preside over clearly defined territories. The power of headmen, senior headmen, and chiefs resides in their ability to mobilize a consensus on local issues. They possess little coercive force and cannot dictate the course of events. Shifting agriculture and residential mobility enable individuals to simply leave the territory of an unpopular leader.

Today the central governments of Zaire and Zambia continue to recognize traditional leaders as the custodians of rural lands. There are, however, national structures (i.e., executive, legislative, and judicial bureaucracies of government) superimposed on the traditional framework, as well as representatives of the ruling political party. In reality, the relationship between government bureaucrats, party functionaries, and traditional leaders is fluid, highly variable, and often quite volatile. Functional power tends to gravitate toward the most powerful local personality rather than toward particular positions.

Conditions brought about by the civil war in Angola have not been conducive to the formation of any stable political organization among the Lunda of that country.

Social Control. Most petty crimes and misdeeds are handled by informal local gatherings presided over by headmen, senior headmen, and chiefs. The focus is primarily on restitution, through the imposition of fines paid to the aggrieved party. Individuals dissatisfied with the outcome of local negotiations may carry the case first to local constitutional courts, and then to higher courts of appeal. There is a clear preference, however, for dealing with these problems locally, as constitutional courts tend to punish offenders by imposing fines paid to the court or by incarcerating the offender, rather than requiring restitution to the aggrieved party. Serious crimes, as well as those committed in urban areas, are mandated directly to constitutional courts.

Conflict. Most of Lunda territory is lightly policed, and serious conflicts are rare. The local docket is dominated by cases of untethered domestic animals straying into neighbors' gardens, accusations of adultery, and the occasional drunken brawl, most of which are swiftly resolved. In Angola, however, conflict of a military nature was a constant concern during the civil war.

Religion and Expressive Culture

Religious Beliefs. Traditionally, it was believed that Nzambi, the supreme deity, created the universe and all its inhabitants. He endowed each type of living entity with a unique set of capacities that alone determine its fortune. Humans were uniquely blessed with the gift of intellect. Nzambi plays no role in the day-to-day interaction of his creation, nor does he favor any one of his creatures over the others. He requires no formal worship. Human appeals for supernatural intervention are directed mostly toward the ancestors. The spirits of the dead tend to remain in the area where they resided during life, and they continue to be concerned with the welfare of their living kin. Ancestral spirits particularly wish to be remembered for their contributions to the world of the living. Remembrance takes three forms: mentioning an ancestor's name in daily conversation, propitiating an ancestor during communal meals, and naming a newborn after a favored ancestor. Neglected ancestors are said to afflict their living kin with a range of diseases, primarily infertility for women and lack of hunting success for men. Ancestors may also afflict kin who are not living properly (e.g., quarreling and not sharing).

The Lunda metaphysical world is also inhabited by a variety of invisible beings with sinister intent toward humans. These beings, under the nominal control of human witches, can likewise cause debilitating illness and even death if not discovered and neutralized.

The twentieth-century influx of U.S. and European missionaries into Lunda territory has led to a proliferation of religious beliefs. Evangelical Protestant, Catholic, and independent churches now dot the landscape. The earliest missionaries adopted the local term, Nzambi, to refer to the High God, implying in some respects that they were not attempting to introduce a new God but were simply bringing new information about the old Lunda High God. All local religions thus proclaim Nzambi as the supreme deity. They differ, however, in their beliefs about Nzambi's secular and spiritual requirements, preferred forms of worship, areas of intervention, and the benefits offered.

Religious Practitioners. Traditionally, it was the task of diviners to ascertain whether it was an ancestor or an invisible being who was responsible for a particular human affliction. A *chimbuki* (medicine man) would then be responsible for performing an elaborate ritual that would appease and neutralize the afflicting entity. The chimbuki would be assisted in the ritual by a coterie of individuals who have themselves been afflicted, yet survived the same sort of metaphysically induced illness being experienced by the patient. Herbal medicines (both ingested and applied to the patient's body), the manipulation of symbolic objects, and the adherence to strict taboos on foods and personal behavior are the dominant features of such rituals.

Today priest, pastors, deacons, and spiritual counselors of various sorts compete for prominence with traditional healers. The majority of Lunda regularly attend one of the Christian churches in their area, yet most still rely on herbal medicines and participate in traditional healing rituals.

Ceremonies. In addition to the vast repertoire of curing rituals, the Lunda perform ceremonies to mark most important transitions in life (i.e., birth, marriage, coming of age, and death). The boys' initiation rite (*mukanda*) and the girls' initiation rite (*nkanga*) are the most elaborate. Mukanda today is a month-long ritual during which time groups of boys, mostly between the ages of 10 and 15, are isolated in forest camps where they are first circumcised, then instructed and tested in productive skills, cultural history, and social etiquette. They are also subjected to hard labor and harsh discipline. Mukanda begins and ends with a public ceremony that entails round-the-clock singing, dancing, feasting, storytelling, and perhaps the appearance of masked figures believed to be the embodiment of nature spirits. Mukanda is heavily laden with symbolism meant to signify the cultural unity of all Lunda men, at one level, and the interrelatedness of all Lunda, male and female, at another. Upon completion of mukanda, a boy received the full complement of rights and duties bestowed on all adult Lunda males.

Nkanga differs markedly from mukanda. Girls are initiated individually in the village, rather than in groups in the forest. They are relieved of all physical labor, pampered, groomed, and sung to, for up to three months. They are not subjected to any physical operation. Like the boys, however, they are instructed in productive skills, cultural history, and social etiquette. Much of the instructional focus and symbolic expression is on augmenting reproductive capacity and on child-rearing competency. For most of nkanga, a girl remains isolated from males in a small seclusion hut, where she is regularly visited by elder women from the surrounding area. A young attendant is assigned to each girl, to be her constant companion and to attend to her every need. A girl is to remain silent throughout nkanga, speaking only in whispers to her attendant should the need arise. Nkanga, likewise, begins and ends with a well-attended public ceremony characterized by great revelry, most notably the singing of ribald songs extolling female virtues while denigrating male vices. Symbolically, nkanga possesses many levels of meaning. It expresses the unity of females in opposition to males, while simultaneously asserting the unity of all Lunda under matrilineal principles of social organization. Like mukanda, nkanga also symbolizes the death of one's former self, and rebirth as a new social persona. Gifts, primarily clothing and cash, are heaped on the new adult member of society.

Arts. A few professional wood-carvers and basket makers continue to produce locally. Most decorative objects, music, and performances, however, are produced by dedicated amateurs, solely for local enjoyment.

Medicine. The Lunda can be described as botanists par excellence. Nearly a hundred different medicinal plants have been recorded as being in use, from which herbal specialists can concoct a vast array of composite remedies. Even very young children tend to be competent in the preparation of herbal remedies for such simple ailments as headaches, stomach aches, colds, influenza, and muscle aches and pains. The local population also accepts and seeks out Western pharmaceutical drugs, viewing them as being akin to traditional herbal preparations, albeit more powerful because they are believed to be more concentrated, especially injections. Nevertheless, most individuals in rural areas still try one or more herbal preparations before resolving to visit a clinic. This is so in part because most traditional medicines can be gathered in the course of daily activities such as going to the fields and gardens, drawing water from the river, trekking to distant pastures to round up the goats and sheep, or going to the bush to hunt, trap, or fish. A visit to one of the few clinics in the area, however, tends to break up the daily routine, often forcing people to walk great distances, to wait in long lines, perhaps only to receive pills instead of the much more highly desired injections. Elaborate curing rituals are the prescribed medicine for spirit-induced ailments.

Death and Afterlife. Death may be attributed to either natural or supernatural causes. It is invariably accompanied by accusations of witchcraft, threats of retaliation, the questioning of long-standing relationships, and, occasionally, divination to ascertain the true cause of death. In the case of married individuals, the surviving spouse is generally required to pay a substantial sum (*mpepi*) to the lineage of the deceased, regardless of culpability. Individuals are buried in cemeteries shared by clusters of villages. A complex cleansing ritual is performed to remove the aura of death from the village and to appease the recently departed and ease his or her passage into the afterlife. Traditionally, it was believed that the spirit of a deceased individual remained in the area he or she inhabited during life, watching over living kin and reestablishing contacts with friends and relatives who had died earlier. Today the multiplicity of ideas about the afterlife spawned by various Christian denominations competes for prominence with traditional notions.

Bibliography

Bustin, Edouard (1975). *Lunda under Belgian rule: The Politics of Ethnicity*. Cambridge: Harvard University Press.

Chinyanta, Munona (1989). *Mutomboko Ceremony and the Lunda-Kazembe Dynasty*. Lusaka: Kenneth Kaunda Foundation.

Cunnison, Ian G. (1959). *The Auapula Peoples of Northern Rhodesia: Custom and History in Tribal Politics*. Manchester: Manchester University Press.

Dias de Carvalho, Henrique A. (1890). *Ethnographia e historia tradicional dos povos da Lunda*. Lisbon: Imprensa Nacional.

Hoover, J. Jeffrey (1978). "The Seduction of Ruwej: Reconstructing Ruund History (the Nuclear Lunda: Zaire, Angola, Zambia)." Ph.D. dissertation, Yale University.

McCulloch, Merran (1951). *The Southern Lunda and Related Peoples (Northern Rhodesia, Belgian Congo, Angola)*. London: International African Institute.

Poewe, Karla, O. (1981). *Matrilineal Ideology: Male-Female Dynamics in Luapula, Zambia*. New York: Academic Press.

Pritchett, James A. (1989). "Continuity and Change in an African Society: The Kanongesha Lunda of Mwinilunga Zambia." Ph.D. dissertation, Harvard University.

Schecter, Robert E. (1976). "History and Historiography on a Frontier of Lunda Expansion: The Origins and Early Development of the Kanongesha." Ph.D. dissertation, University of Wisconsin.

Turner, Victor W. (1957). *Schism and Continuity in an African Society: A Study of Ndembu Village Life*. Manchester: Manchester University Press.

Turner, Victor W. (1967). *The Forest of Symbols: Aspects of Ndembu Ritual*. Ithaca, N.Y.: Cornell University Press.

Turner, Victor W. (1968). *The Drums of Affliction: A Study of Religious Processes among the Ndembu of Zambia*. Oxford: Clarendon Press.

JAMES ANTHONY PRITCHETT

Luo

ETHNONYMS: Dholuo, Nilotic Kavirondo

The Luo live primarily within the Kenyan province of Nyanza. In 1987 they numbered about 3.2 million, of whom about 200,000 lived in Tanzania and another 200,000 in other countries, outside Kenya. They belong to a larger grouping of Nilotic peoples of East and Central Africa. The Luo have migrated from the Bahr al-Ghazal region of Sudan over the past 500 years. Throughout the mid- and late twentieth century, they have lived in densely settled land of separated farmsteads, in three districts around Lake Victoria. The landscape varies from flat and dry by the lake to green and hilly in the eastern uplands. The Luo are homogeneous in language, and Luo communities are linked by marriage and other kin ties. Their neighbors include the Nandi, Gusii, Maasai, and Kuria, and they also have dealings with migrant Indian, Middle Eastern, and Somali traders in the towns.

Although the Luo farm the land in order to produce an adequate food supply, they are first and foremost cattle herders. Their love of herds is a fundamental social reality, and cattle herding is therefore a fundamental aspect of their social structure. In the latter half of the twentieth century, about a third of the middle-aged men have lived outside the Luo homeland while seeking wage labor in Kenya's plantations, towns, and cities. Within Nyanza Province, several large sugar plantations provide some manual jobs.

The Luo provide a classic example of a segmentary lineage society with kin-group formation based on patrilineal descent. Patriliny, bride-wealth, and polygyny all reinforce each other. The Luo are patronymic in naming and virilocal in postmarital residence; one-third of Luo families are polygynous.

Reproduction is a key underlying concern. It is a basis of the value system by which men judged exchanges in the past. Products of exchange progressed from cultivation to chickens, chickens to goats, goats to cows, and finally, cows to women. Fertility is at least as much a woman's concern as it is a man's. The success of marriages and the wives' social status both depend on their producing children.

Wives keep separate houses within the circular homesteads of the larger polygynous families; they farm separate fields and maintain separate granaries, but their husbands are normally considered the heads of the homesteads. Farmwork is assigned according to gender: women shoulder the time-consuming task of caring for the basic staple crops, whereas men are responsible for the cash crops—and generally do less of the farmwork.

Age is deeply respected in Luo culture. Elder men control the allocation of bride-wealth cattle, land, and, to some extent, labor and cash. According to Luo ideology, age, wealth, and respect come together, and it is considered natural that elders control family resources. Elder men are also the representatives of their families to the outside world.

Ancestor worship played a predominant role in the traditional religion of the Luo. Ancestral and other spirits were active forces in their world, and they are still evident within the belief system of many Luo. Since well before the twentieth century, however, British, American, and other Catholic and Protestant missions, as well as many independent African Christian churches, have all competed for converts in Luo territory. The organization of local independent churches reflects the segmentary lineage system that is so important in Luo life. Although the Luo are predominantly Christian, their religious beliefs and practices are a mixture of traditional indigenous elements and newer, exogenous elements.

Bibliography

Ocholla-Ayayo, A. B. C. (1980). *The Luo Culture: A Reconstruction of a Traditional African Society*. Wiesbaden: Steiner.

Shipton, Parker (1989). *Bitter Money: Cultural Economy and Some African Meanings of Forbidden Commodities*. American Ethnological Society Monograph Series, no. 1. Washington, D.C.

Lur

ETHNONYMS: Lor, Lori

Orientation

The Lur are found mainly in three regions of Iran—Lorestān, Bakhtīarī, and Kohkīlūyeh, all of which are located along a northwest-southeast axis of the Zagros mountain range and its southern foothills. These mountains are 160 to 320 kilometers wide, and extend southeastward from Lake Van in Turkey to near Bandar ʿAbbās in southern Iran, a distance of about 1,600 kilometers. The valleys within this mountain range have rich pastures that have been used by several nomadic pastoral societies, including the Lur.

Generally speaking, the Lur speak Luri, an Indo-Iranian dialect closely related to modern Persian (Farsi). Modern Luri is viewed as the continuation of an old dialect closely related to old Persian, or as a derivation from the Middle Persian that developed in pre-Islamic times. An alternative theory suggests that modern Luri developed from New Persian during the tenth century A.D.

There are three primary languages spoken by Lur today. Luri, a dialect of Farsi, is spoken by almost 90 percent of the inhabitants of Kohkīlūyeh. A Turkic language (which seems intrusive to the region) is spoken by the Qashqa'i pastoral nomads, who migrate annually into the area with their flocks of sheep. Farsi, the official language of government bureaucracies and non-Lur civil servants, is gaining in importance and popularity owing to compulsory education and government programs. Men, who, unlike women, have extensive contacts outside their communities, are often bilingual in Luri-Farsi and Turkic-Farsi.

History and Cultural Relations

The Lur may have migrated from Syria into the western Zagros Mountains some time after the Arab invasion of Iran in the seventh century A.D. Another theory suggests that the Lur were indigenous nomadic herders who inhabited the area since early times and spoke an Indo-Iranian language. Adherents of the latter theory believe that the Lur were the descendants of the Parsua, who inhabited what is now Lorestān and Bakhtīarī in 800 B.C. The Parsua established the Persian Empire (550–330 B.C.) and are thus considered among the indigenous Persians.

The traditional homeland of the Lur is the Zagros Mountains, but there are Lur communities scattered in many parts of Iran. The Lur are believed to constitute about half of the population of Īlām and the entire population of Lorestān, Bakhtīarī, Kohkīlūyeh, and Boyer Ahmadī. In addition, they occupy almost one half of Khūzestān, one third of Hamadān and Bushehr, and a significant portion of Fārs. There are also Lur communities elsewhere in Iran, and a significant population living in Iraq.

The traditional territory of the Lur was divided in the tenth century into what has become known as the Lorestān-e-Bozorg (the large Lorestān), which is now the Bakhtiari territory, and the Lorestān-e-Kuchak (the small Lorestān), which is now the governorship of Lorestān. Probably because of conflict between different tribes within the areas, each of the two Lorestāns was further subdivided into smaller political units. The Lorestān-e-Kuchak consists of two ecological and cultural zones: Pusht Kuh ("behind the mountain") and Peesh Kuh ("in front of the mountain"). Pusht Kuh is actually a transitional zone between Lorestān proper and central Kurdistan. The Bakhtiari of Lorestān-e-Bozorg were also split into two tribal blocs, Haft Lang and Char Lang. Kohkīlūyeh is an administrative district in southwest Iran covering an area of about 15,000 square kilometers. This region lies within the southwestern segments of the Zagros arc.

The inhabitants of Pusht Kuh include Kurds, Lur, and Arabs, who have strong cultural and linguistic affinities with the more dominant Kurdish populations to the north. This segment of the population numbers about 120,000 (Fazel 1984) and has a greater degree of religious diversity than the other Lur populations. The major religious groups here include the Shia Ithna Ashari (to which most Lur belong), Ali Allahi, the Sunnis, and Christian Assyrians. The population of the Lur of Peesh Kuh, or Lorestān proper, is estimated at 230,000 (Fazel 1984). The Peesh Kuh Lur are much more homogeneous than the Pusht Kuh Lur, and are very similar to the Bakhtiari, especially the Chahar Lang Bakhtiari. The Haft Lang Bakhtiari have more in common with Kohkīlūyeh Lur. The Lur of Bakhtīarī numbered approximately 680,000 in 1982 (Grimes 1988) and those of Kohkīlūyeh approximately 270,000 (Fazel 1984). The total population of Lur in Iran was estimated at about 3,000,000 in 1982 (Grimes 1988).

The reigns of Reza Shah (1925–1942) and Moḥammad Reza Shah (1942–1979) brought drastic changes to the lives of the Lur and the other tribal groups in Iran. For the most part, the policies of both leaders included the elimination, pacification, or settlement of the tribes. During Reza Shah's reign, tribal leaders were executed, and migrations between summer and winter camps were banned. The resulting loss of 90 percent of the livestock inflicted extreme hardship on the tribes. The land reforms of the Pahlavi regime, intended in part to settle the tribes, created ecological disasters as impoverished nomads began a frantic conversion of steep mountain pastures into farmlands in order to qualify for individualized ownership of land. Similarly, the introduction of a national system of education undermined the normative foundation of the traditional socioeconomic systems; thus, literacy also brought alienation from the only life-style that was available.

The Revolution of 1978–1979 ended the Pahlavi regime and some of the problems it had created for the tribes. Postrevolutionary changes are proceeding in the context of the Islamization of society, enforced by strict guidelines from the central government. As a result, tribal religious leaders have been given a critical role in supervising and implementing Islamic guidelines in education, commerce, and aspects of social behavior. Lack of reliable information from Iran prevents an assessment of what effect these changes are having on the Lur and the other tribes of Iran.

Economy

The traditional subsistence activity of the Lur is pastoralism. As much as half of the Lur population may be engaged in nomadic herding of sheep and goats, although some experts believe the proportion of pastoralists is now much smaller. Like most nomads of the Zagros, Lur herders spend six to eight months with their flocks in the low-lying pasture lands, usually from October to April. In the dry season (May to September), the herders move to high mountain pastures. The longest migration takes about 25 days and covers a distance of about 240 kilometers. The more settled Lur emphasize agriculture over herding; wheat and barley are the major crops. They tend to live in permanent villages year-round, whereas the nomadic groups live in permanent buildings only in the winter. For the other eight months of the year, the nomads live in black goat-hair tents, which are made by women.

The Lur take their agricultural and pastoral products to markets, where they purchase goods manufactured elsewhere in the country. Itinerant traders and merchants have established long-standing commercial relations with the Lur, especially with the pastoralists. They extend credit to their trading partners during the fall and winter season and collect the debts in summer, when the surplus dairy products and animals born in the previous winter become available for the market. High interest rates, however, sometimes 100 percent semiannually, have greatly undermined the economic base of the nomadic household. Nearly 30 percent of the region's herds of sheep and goats are owned by urban-based merchants. Most households are burdened with perpetual indebtedness. Despite this systematic exploitation, the Lur nomads, along with other pastoral groups, continue to provide meat, dairy products, wool, and hides for the rest of the nation.

The Lur believe that their success as herders is determined by personal qualities and luck. It is only the wealthiest portion of the population, however, that is usually able to maintain or increase its wealth. The majority of the population requires economic support from the upper strata of society, which control larger herds, require labor for their herds, and can provide work and salaries for those of the lower strata. Lower-strata members have fewer animals, must work for others to make up for their lack of sufficient capital in animals, and are usually obliged to offer the labor of their sons to larger herd owners, so that control over their sons is also weakened. Lur claim that as equals they are free to opt out of dependent contractual relationships, but doing so means that they must find support from another source, which is usually not easy to do.

Sociopolitical Organization

The most inclusive political unit of the Lur is the tribe, or *il*, which is composed of several genealogically distinct subtribes, each a federation of localized kinship groupings called an *oulad*. Oulad members trace descent through the male line, to an ancestor whose name has become the referent or label for the whole group. An oulad, in turn, is an aggregate of several migratory camp units or settled hamlets, the size of which varies from three to eight tent households. The tent household, composed of a husband and wife and their children, with a flock of sheep or goats, is the basic social and economic unit of the Lur.

Traditionally, each tribe is headed by a hereditary chief, or khan, who is recruited by a special oulad. Aided by an army of retainers, the khan ensures peace and security within his jurisdiction by maintaining a balance of power among the component subtribes, arbitrating potentially disruptive disputes that cannot be resolved at the local level, and representing the tribe in matters involving the state or the neighboring sedentary communities. The financial support of the khan's administrative apparatus is provided by an annual tax on grain and animals.

Religion

The religion of the Lur is based almost exclusively on the beliefs of the Shia sect of Islam. They have a very pragmatic belief system, with simple religious observances as compared to the highly esoteric Islam of the urban centers. Most religious practitioners are *sadaat* (sing., *sayyid*), who claim descent from the prophet Mohammed. Few sadaat are literate, and those who are rarely achieve high status within their community.

Shrines dedicated to holy men who were founders of various sadaat descent groups are scattered throughout the region. Because the shrines are believed to have curative powers, many people with physical and psychological ailments visit them seeking cures. Legal disputants also sometimes use the shrines to solemnize their testimonies.

The Lur system of values is based on the Islamic faith, but Lur values are also revealed by a rich body of folklore that glorifies the history of each group and describes the adventures of culture heroes. Personality characteristics that are considered important in these stories include honor, loyalty, generosity, and, most important, bravery in battle.

Bibliography

Amanolahi, Sekandar (1988). *Tribes of Iran*. Vol. 1, *The Tribes of Luristan, Bakhtiari, Kuh Gilu, and Mamasani*. New Haven: Human Relations Area Files.

Barth, Fredrik (1960). "Nomadism in the Mountain and Plateau Areas of South West Asia." In *Problems of the Arid Zone*, 341–355. Proceedings of the Paris Symposium on the Problems of the Arid Zone (1960). Paris: UNESCO.

Eickelman, Dale F. (1989). *The Middle East: An Anthropological Approach*. 2nd ed. Englewood Cliffs, N.J.: Prentice-Hall.

Fazel, G. Reza (1984). "Lur." In *Muslim Peoples: A World Ethnographic Survey*, edited by Richard V. Weekes, 446–451. Westport, Conn.: Greenwood Press.

Fazel, G. Reza (1985). "Lurs of Iran." *Cultural Survival Quarterly* 9(1): 65–69.

Grimes, Barbara F. (1988). *Ethnologue: Languages of the World*. Dallas: Summer Institute of Linguistics.

RONALD JOHNSON

Luyia

ETHNONYMS: Abaluhya, Abaluyia, Baluyia, Bantu Kavirondo, Luhya

Orientation

Identification. "Abaluyia" is the preferred name for the people once called the "Bantu Kavirondo" because of their proximity to Lake Victoria's Kavirondo Gulf. "Abaluyia"

refers to the nation, tribe, or ethnic group, "Omuluyia" to an individual, and "Luluyia" to the language they speak. There are seventeen Luluyia-speaking subnations in Western and Nyanza provinces of Kenya: Bakhayo (Abakhayo), Bukusu (Babukusu, Kitosh [derogatory], Vugusu), Banyala (Abanyala), Basonga (Abasonga), Banyore (Abanyore), Batsotso (Abatsotso), Idakho (Abetakho, Babetakho), Isukha (Abesukha, Babesukha), Kabras (Abakabras), Kisa (Abakisa, Bakisa), Logoli (Avalogoli, Maragoli), Marachi (Abamarachi, Bamaraki, Marach), Marama (Abamarama, Bamarama), Samia (Abasamia, Basamia), Tachoni (Abatachoni, Kitosh), Tiriki (Batiriki), and Wanga (Abawanga, Bawanga). Some Luluyia speakers are found in eastern Uganda: the Gisu (Abagisu, Bagisu, Bamasaba, Masaba), Gwe (Abagwe), Nyole (Abanyole, Abanyuli), and Samia. The ethnic label "Abaluyia" is Kenyan, however, and is not used by Ugandan Luluyia speakers. The label has been associated with this part of Kenya since the 1930s, and elders from the region accepted the designation during the 1960s.

Location. The Abaluyia region, which includes eastern Uganda, extends roughly from the equator to 1°10′ N and from 34°00′ to 35°15′ E. It is bounded on the south by Nyanza Province and Lake Victoria (elevation 1,127 meters), on the north by Mount Elgon (elevation 4,296 meters), and on the east by the Rift Valley. The majority of the Abaluyia live in Western Province, Kenya, which consists of four districts: Bungoma, Busia, Kakamega, and Vihiga. Most of the region (90 percent) is highly suited for agriculture, but there are interspersed rocky and sandy areas. Temperatures range from about 32° C in the south to 5–10° C near Mount Elgon. There are two rainy seasons, the long rains from March to June or July and the short rains from August to October. Rainfall ranges from 76 centimeters per year in the southernmost region to 155 centimeters per year around the area of the Kakamega Forest—a 315-square-kilometer, isolated primeval rain forest teeming with many unique plant, primate, bird, and insect species. Large carnivores (e.g., leopards), large mammals (e.g., elephants), and ruminants (e.g., gazelles) were once common throughout western Kenya, but they have been gone since at least the 1950s or 1960s. Although eucalyptuses and euphorbias are common, deforestation of the entire region, including the Kakamega Forest, poses a serious threat.

Demography. Wagner (1949) estimated that there were less than 350,000 Abaluyia in 1937. The Abaluyia, with a total population of 3.5 million, are now the second-largest ethnic group in Kenya. There are at least 1.5 million Luluyia speakers in Uganda, but—unlike the Kenyan Abaluyia—they do not consider themselves a single ethnic group. Population densities range from more than 2,000 persons per square kilometer in the south (Vihiga District) to less than 200 persons per square kilometer near Mount Elgon. Although there is now some evidence of fertility decline, total fertility rates, until the late 1980s, exceeded nine and ten births per woman of childbearing age.

Linguistic Affiliation. Luluyia is a Western Bantu language. The Abaluyia subnations speak mutually understandable dialects, but subnations that border each other are more likely to understand one another's dialect. Some of the dialects (Lubukusu, Kisamia) are tonal. Many contemporary Luluyia speakers also know English, Kiswahili, Dholuo, and/or Luganda.

History and Cultural Relations

Luluyia-speaking groups have occupied the same East African region for up to 500 years; they displaced long-established foraging and herding peoples. The Abaluyia subnations, most of which probably originated from central Africa, were originally clans with diverse historical origins that grew large and then split into subclans. The eighteenth and nineteenth centuries were characterized by widespread warfare between Abaluyia subnations and neighboring ethnic groups, especially the Buganda, Luo, Nandi, Maasai, and Iteso. The Bagisu, Bakhayo, Bukusu, Banyala, Batsotso, Kabras, Nyole, Marachi, Marama, Samia, and Tachoni constructed fortressed settlements during this period. These were walled with thorns and surrounded by moats.

During the colonial period (1895–1963), the British, whose goal was to pacify the area and facilitate the completion of the Uganda Railway, made several unsuccessful attempts to unite politically the Luluyia-speaking subnations. In 1895 the Bukusu waged an unsuccessful war of resistance, the Chetambe War, against the British. The first train reached Kisumu in 1901. The Abaluyia region was split in two in 1902, when the British established the current boundary between Kenya and Uganda. As a result, the subnations in Kenya and Uganda have different colonial histories and different political economies. In 1909, in a futile attempt to unite the subnations, the British anointed Nobongo Mumia of the Wanga "kingdom" the "supreme" chief. The Abaluyia, however, never had a single paramount chief prior to British colonial rule. The Ugandan Nyole were dominated by the Baganda; various clan leaders in Kenya aligned themselves with or resisted the British. The Kenyan Abaluyia did not develop a unified ethnic identity until the 1930s, and the Ugandan Luluyia speakers have never had a single ethnic identity.

The Friends African Mission, the Mill Hill Mission, the Church of God, and the Church Missionary Society (Anglican) were all established in the region between 1902 and 1906; mission schools were established shortly thereafter. A brief gold rush (1929–1931) was followed by land confiscation and alienation. Today nearly all Abaluyia are Christians, although some Abaluyia—especially around Mumias town—practice Islam. Universal primary education has been achieved in much of western Kenya.

Settlements

Precolonial Abaluyia villages were loosely organized around single localized lineages (*enyumba;* pl. *tsinyumba*). Abaluyia homesteads consisted of circular compounds surrounded by euphorbias, thorns, or clay walls. Structures within the compounds followed a prescribed layout, although there were variations. Houses were circular with thatched roofs. The first wife's house was directly opposite the gate, with the houses of junior wives organized to the left and right, according to seniority. The married sons' houses were near the gate and were arranged according to birth order. Because unmarried children who had reached puberty were not permitted to sleep under the same roof as their parents, unmarried sons slept in special houses called *chisimba* (sing. *esimba*). Girls, and sometimes younger boys, slept with classificatory grandmothers in girls' houses (*ekogono* or *eshibinze*). The compound usually had one or more elevated granaries, and animals were often kept in separate structures. Nowadays settlements are organized more like neighborhoods. Mud houses are usually square and often roofed with iron sheets. Modern block houses with tile roofs line the major roads. Compounds are often crowded and may be laid out less formally. They are surrounded by euphorbias, shrubs, rows of trees, or fences. In some places, girls' houses no longer exist: girls sleep in their mothers' kitchens, but older boys continue to sleep in separate dwellings. Granaries are still common in the Bukusu area but are rare in Maragoli and Banyore.

Economy

Subsistence and Commercial Activities. The Abaluyia are now primarily farmers who keep cattle, but in precolonial times men hunted, and animal husbandry was even more important. The Banyala and the Samia were known for their expertise in fishing, and quail and insects were eaten throughout the region. Finger millet, sorghum, sesame, pumpkins, sweet potatoes, yams, beans, and bananas were the most important crops in precolonial times. Nowadays the main crop is maize intercropped with beans; millet and sorghum are less common. In addition to the traditional crops, other important contemporary crops include green beans, red beans, bananas, groundnuts (peanuts), *sukuma wiki* (kale), cabbages, potatoes, and cassava. The major cash crops are tea, coffee, sugarcane, cotton, and sunflower seeds. Farms are tilled entirely with iron hoes in the hillier, more densely populated areas, whereas hoes are commonly used with ox-drawn plows and tractors in the northern and western regions. Cattle (zebu, mixed, and grade), goats, sheep, chickens, ducks, and turkeys are common.

Industrial Arts. Formerly, the important crafts were blacksmithing, pottery, basketry, woodworking (particularly, the manufacture of drums), and weaving. Blacksmithing had been passed down patrilineally in some clans. The Samia (especially the Abang'aale clan) were particularly well known for blacksmithing and mining of iron ore. Manufacture of pottery was more often a woman's than a man's task—although Bukusu women of childbearing age could not quarry clay. Pots, which were usually traded and owned by women, were considered utilitarian. There was not much specialization in the manufacture of everyday wood tools (e.g., hoe handles), but specialists still make drums, lyres, stools, and wood carvings.

Trade. The subnations of the Abaluyia traded among one another during the precolonial era. Iron hoes, spear points, and ivory, for example, could be traded for grains or animals. Precolonial trade covered a distance of no more than 72 kilometers, but there were three precolonial markets where Luo, Nandi, and Abaluyia came together to trade baskets, wooden tools, quail, and various foodstuffs for cattle, fish, tobacco, and so forth. During the colonial era, various weekly regional and local market centers developed, where local and European goods could be bought or bartered. Wagner counted sixty-four recognized markets in 1937. By 1990, in addition to dozens of rural, market, and local trading centers, there were at least ten urban centers in Western Province, Kenya, where one could buy everything from Diet Coke to Michael Jackson tapes.

Division of Labor. In precolonial times, hunting and warfare were important men's work. Horticulture was mainly women's work. Men cleared fields, but women usually prepared soil, planted, weeded, and harvested. Only men planted trees, although women cared for them. Large animals were the domain of men and unmarried boys. Traditionally, the men milked the cattle in most of the subnations, but nowadays women often do it. Women owned and cared for poultry. Both women and men were involved in marketing: the women sold pots, products grown in kitchen gardens, dried fish, fruits, and grains bought from farmers in other regions. Only men took animals to market. House building has many stages, each with a division of labor; however, women generally repaired walls and floors, whereas men prepared thatching materials. Children contributed to subsistence: girls mainly in the home and fields, boys mainly with the herds. Boys and girls helped out with other tasks, such as tending younger children, gathering wood, and fetching water. Girls helped their mothers in selling. Nowadays men's and women's roles are more varied. Although the sexual division of labor at home has not changed much, both men and women have a broader range of occupational opportunities. Schoolteacher, agricultural-extension worker, and sugar-factory worker are common occupations of rural Abaluyia. The sexual division of labor in agriculture has changed somewhat as agriculture has intensified. Modern Abaluyia children usually attend school and are less available to perform chores.

Land Tenure. Traditionally, land was inherited patrilineally. Among the Kenyan Abaluyia, families owned land, and this land was referred to as the *omulimi gwa guga* (lands of the grandfather). A man apportioned his land to sons as they married but could not alienate the omulimi gwa guga. Women had use rights on their husbands' farms but could not inherit land. Mothers could, however, hold land in trust for sons. When his mother died, the last-born son would inherit the land she farmed. Communal lands, such as surplus lands or those used for grazing, were under the control of the clan and administered by the *luguru* (headman). Women are permitted to inherit land in contemporary Kenya but more often acquire land by purchasing it themselves. Communal grazing lands are now rare because of population pressure. Most land is registered, and buying and selling of land are individual affairs. Land disputes are handled in courts or in sublocation meetings convened by assistant chiefs.

Kinship

Kin Groups and Descent. The exogamous patrilineal clan (*oluyia*) is the fundamental unit of Abaluyia social organization. Clans may also have several exogamous subclans. There were at least 750 Abaluyia clans by the mid-twentieth century. Each clan has an animal, plant, or bird totem, as well as an ancestor for whom the clan is usually named.

Kinship Terminology. The Abaluyia use an Iroquoian system that incorporates classificatory kinship terminology. Grandparents and grandchildren are called by the same kin terms—*guga* for grandfathers, grandsons, and great-grandsons, *guku* for grandmothers, granddaughters, and great-granddaughters. Distinctions are made for the father's sister (*senje*) and mother's brother (*khotsa*), but clan relatives of the same generation (e.g., women and female in-laws) are called by the same term (in this case, *mama*). Cousins are addressed by sibling terms, but, in some places, cross cousins are distinguished in reference.

Marriage and Family

Marriage. Traditional Abaluyia marriage is patrilocal. Polygyny rates vary among the subnations, and bride-wealth, consisting of animals and money, is usually exchanged. Many types of exchange occurred during the marriage process, and male elders conducted the negotiations. Wives were chosen for their good character and the ability to work hard. Men were also chosen for these qualities, as well as soberness and ability to pay bride-wealth. After marriage, co-wives usually had separate dwellings but would often cook together. New wives were not permitted to cook in their own houses until their own cooking stones were set up in a brief ceremony. This was often after the birth of one or several children. Childlessness was usually blamed on the woman. In some subnations, a woman whose husband died lived in a state of ritual impurity until she was inherited by the dead husband's brother. Divorce may or may not have involved return of bride-wealth cattle. In the case of divorce or serious witchcraft accusations, the woman could return to her natal home without her children, who remained with their fathers.

Abaluyia women in contemporary Kenya choose among a variety of marriage options, including the traditional bride-wealth system, Christian marriage with or without bride-wealth, elopement, and single parenthood. Women with more education may command a higher bride-wealth. Bride-wealth in Bungoma remains stable, but in Maragoli and some other regions, bride-wealth may be declining or disappearing.

Domestic Unit. A married man heads one or more households. A typical household consists of a husband, a wife, and their children. Other family members may join these households, including the wife's sisters, the husband's other children, and foster children. Since mature relatives of adjacent generations do not sleep in the same house, grandmothers and older children often occupy adjacent houses; however, all usually eat from the same pot. These rules have not changed much, although many rural households are now headed by women because of long-term male wage-labor migration.

Inheritance. Land is inherited patrilineally (see "Land Tenure").

Socialization. Abaluyia communities are characterized by a high degree of sibling involvement in caretaking, under the general supervision of the mothers and grandmothers in the homestead. Although mothers play a primary role in child rearing, small children and infants may be left with older siblings while their mothers do other work. Although fathers play a minimal role, they are often the ones who take children for medical care. Grandparents and grandchildren have close relationships. Until the mid- to late twentieth century, girls learned about marriage and sexuality from their grandmothers. In the Abaluyia subnations that circumcise, boys are admonished by male elders and taught to endure the pain of circumcision without flinching, a sign that they have the strength of character to endure other hardships they may face. Contemporary Abaluyia grandparents play an even greater role in child rearing because they are thrust more and more into foster-parent roles.

Sociopolitical Organization

Social Organization. Although some clans were known for particular roles and strengths during the eighteenth through early-twentieth centuries, leadership has come from a variety of clans and subnations over the years. The range of social stratification among the Abaluyia extends from the landless to poor, middle-level, and rich farmers, depending upon such factors as the size of the plot owned and the number of animals kept. There is a developing class system but no formal hierarchy.

Political Organization. Prior to the colonial period, the highest level of political integration was the clan, and the clan headman was the most powerful figure. In some of the subnations, patron-client relationships developed between powerful clan heads and landless men who would serve as warriors. These big-men later gained power through alliances with the British, but there were no precolonial chiefs among the Abaluyia. Nevertheless, some clans and individuals were viewed as having particularly good leadership abilities. In Kenya, the traditional headman system changed in 1926 with the institution of *milango* headmen (usually, they were also luguru headmen), then the *ulogongo* system in the 1950s. Currently, villages are headed by luguru, sublocations are headed by government-hired and -paid assistant chiefs, and a paid chief leads at the location level.

Social Control. Crimes, misdeeds, land disputes, and the like were originally handled by the clan. Nowadays, in Kenya, these matters proceed initially to the headmen and assistant chiefs, who deal with local disputes at a monthly *baraza* (community meeting). Unresolved cases may be taken up by the location chief, district officer, or district commissioner; final recourse may be sought in the Kenyan court system.

Conflict. During the eighteenth and nineteenth centuries, Abaluyia subnations and clans often raided and warred against each other and against their non-Abaluyia neighbors (see "History and Cultural Relations"). This warfare accelerated toward the end of the nineteenth century with the arrival of the British and the introduction of firearms. Pax Britannica was achieved in 1906, but feuds and rivalries continued within clans and subclans even into the postcolonial era. The Marachi and Wanga eventually formed military alliances with the British, but others, such as the Bukusu, waged wars of resistance. Conflicts are now rare, although political events in Kenya in the 1990s have resulted in some interethnic fighting at the margins of the Abaluyia region.

Religion and Expressive Culture

Religious Beliefs. There is a sharp distinction between precolonial religious beliefs and contemporary ones. Prior to missionization, the Abaluyia believed in a High God, Were, as well as in the concept of ancestral spirits. Some said that Were lived on Mount Elgon. Ancestral spirits had power in everyday life and could cause illness and death. After 1902, the first U.S. Quaker missionaries arrived in Kaimosi and began to convert the Tiriki and Maragoli with varying success (see "History and Cultural Relations"). Other missions followed, and the schooling and wage-labor opportunities available to the converted were very attractive to the ambitious. By the 1930s, at least six Christian missions were in place in western Kenya, boasting 50,000 converts. Nowadays, worshipers of ancestral spirits are rare; nearly everyone is a Christian, Muslim, or self-described "backslider." It is important to note, however, that missionary teachings have not abolished certain traditional practices; for example, beliefs in ancestral powers are still widespread.

Religious Practitioners. Traditional practitioners included garden magicians and rain magicians. Witchcraft, sorcery, and traditional healing continue to play a role in Abaluyia communities. Both men and women can be healers or practice witchcraft. A common witchcraft accusation is that a person is a night runner—that is, he or she keeps a leopard in the house and runs naked at night rattling neighbors' doors and windows. Untimely deaths may be blamed on witchcraft and sorcery. Beliefs in poisoning or nonspecific causation of death, illness, or misfortune by witchcraft or sorcery are common. Traditional healers undergo a kind of ritual healing themselves and are indoctrinated by other healers. Healers may also have expertise with herbal medicines.

Ceremonies. Transitions from one life stage to the next are the most celebrated events. The important transitions for women are coming of age, marriage, and giving birth, whereas initiation is the most important event for men. In some subnations (Batsotso, Banyore, Kisa, Marama, and Wanga), six lower teeth were extracted in childhood; others extracted only one (Idakho, Isukha) or two (Bukusu). The extraction of teeth varied widely and was probably borrowed from neighboring ethnic groups. Men and women were often scarified at marriage, but now only the very old have any scarification. Male circumcision is important in the Bukusu, Banyore, Batsotso, Banyala of Kakamega District, Idakho, Isukha, Kabras, Kisa, Logoli, Marama, Tachoni, Tiriki, and Wanga subnations. The Gisu also circumcise. Some subnations neighboring the Luo do not circumcise, including the Bakhayo, Basonga, Gwe, Marachi, Samia and some Banyole. Circumcision ceremonies vary between subnations, although the stages usually consist of a period of preparation, the circumcision day, and a subsequent period of seclusion. The Bukusu and Tachoni have cyclical age-set systems with names that repeat about every one hundred years. Bukusu and Tachoni circumcise every two years. Some Abaluyia subnations are similar to the Logoli, who circumcise once every ten years and whose circumcision groups are named after a current event. Traditionally, boys were usually circumcised between ages 12 and 18 but could be circumcised earlier or later. A requirement of a traditional circumcision is demonstration of bravery. Even a flinch or change of expression can result in lifelong shame and disgrace. Nowadays circumcisions are done at younger ages, and boys may be circumcised in hospitals. Female circumcision was once practiced only by the Tachoni and the Bukusu, who probably adopted it from their Kalenjin neighbors.

Arts. There are few specialized arts in the Abaluyia region. Houses are sometimes painted on the outside, especially during the Christmas season.

Medicine. Contemporary Abaluyia seek medical assistance in a variety of settings, including hospitals and clinics, and from both community health workers and traditional healers (see "Religious Practitioners").

Death and Afterlife. Death may be attributed to both natural and supernatural causes. The deceased are usually buried on their own compounds. Abaluyia funerals typically involve a period of wailing immediately after the death, a time when the body of the deceased can be viewed, and the funeral itself. During the period after the funeral, animals are slaughtered, widows' roles are considered, and some family members shave their heads. In some Abaluyia subnations, the announcement of the death of an important man or woman may have been accompanied by a cattle drive. Funeral celebrations can involve great expense and last for several days and nights, often accompanied by dancing and drums. Widows are ritually unclean for a period after the death of their spouses and are subject to a number of prohibitions. Traditionally, the widow sometimes wore her dead husband's clothes until she was inherited by his brother. Musambwa were believed to have an active role in the world of the living, and, in former times, people would call upon them to change their fortunes. Illness and death were attributed to angry musambwa.

Bibliography

Bradley, Candice (1993). *Bibliography of Western Province, Kenya.* African Studies, University of Wisconsin.

de Wolf, Jan Jacob (1983). "Circumcision and Initiation in Western Kenya and Eastern Uganda: Historical Reconstructions and Ethnographic Evidence." *Anthropos* 78:369–410.

Makila, F. E. (1978). *An Outline History of the Babukusu of Western Kenya.* Nairobi: Kenya Literature Bureau.

Munroe, Robert L., and Ruth H. Munroe (1989). *Logoli Time Allocation.* Cross-Cultural Studies in Time Allocation, vol. 5. New Haven: HRAF.

Osogo, John (1965). *Life in Kenya in the Olden Days: The Baluyia.* Nairobi: Oxford University Press.

Sangree, Walter H. (1965). "The Bantu Tiriki of Western Kenya." In *Peoples of Africa,* edited by J. Gibbs. New York: Holt, Rinehart & Winston.

Ssennyonga, Joseph (1978). "Population Growth and Cultural Inventory: The Maragoli Case." Doctoral thesis, University of Sussex.

Wagner, Gunter (1949–1956). *The Bantu of Western Kenya.* 2 vols. London: Oxford University Press.

Wandibba, Simiyu (1985). *History and Culture in Western Kenya: The People of Bungoma District Through Time.* Nairobi: Gideon S. Were Press.

Weisner, Thomas S. (1979). "Urban-Rural Differences in Sociable and Disruptive Behavior of Kenya Children." *Ethnology* 18:153–172.

Were, Gideon S. (1967). *A History of the Abaluyia of Western Kenya c. 1500–1930.* Nairobi: East African Publishing House.

Whyte, Michael A., and Susan Reynolds Whyte (1984–1985). "Peasants and Workers: The Legacy of Partition among the Luyia-speaking Nyole and Marachi." *Journal of the Historical Society of Nigeria* 12:139–158.

CANDICE BRADLEY

Maasai

ETHNONYMS: Ilmaasai, Masai (also Maa, which refers to all those peoples who speak the Maasai language)

Orientation

Identification. The Maasai comprise a federation of tribal sections whose economy is based on nomadic pastoralism. Most prominent among them are the Purko and Kisonko, and also among the core groups are the Damat, Kaputiei, Keekonyukie, Loita, Koitokitok, Loodokilani, Matapato, Salei, and Serenket. More peripheral, and with different clans but sharing the Maasai age system, are the Dalalekutuk, Laitayok, Moitanik, Siria, and Uasinkishu, and also the agricultural Arusha. More peripheral still, with their own independent age systems, are the Parakuyu, Samburu, and Tiamus. Because each tribal section is effectively autonomous, both economically and socially, there is a considerable diversity in custom between sections.

Location. The designated Maasai region covers some 100,000 square kilometers, divided between southern Kenya, where most of the Maasai live, and northern Tanzania, where the land is more arid and the population sparse. The principal rains come in the spring. The dry season typically covers the six summer months, extending occasionally to periods of eighteen months or more when the rains fail in some part of the region.

Demography. There are rather more than one-quarter of a million Maasai, with a broad balance between the sexes. A high rate of polygyny is achieved by delaying the age of marriage of young men as compared with that of girls. During their extended period of bachelorhood, youths are still regarded as warriors (*moran*).

Linguistic Affiliation. Maa (Maasai) is classed as a Paranilotic language.

History and Cultural Relations

According to oral traditions, the Maasai migrated from the north to their present area, probably before A.D. 1800, and adopted a boy they found there, who became the ancestor of the Loonkidongi dynasty of prophets. From this time on, and under the patronage of successive prophets, these oral traditions relate to the military dominance of the Maasai over their neighbors, who emulated Maasai warrior practices. This military emphasis led in the earlier period to internecine competition between the Maasai and the more peripheral Maa peoples, and then, following a disastrous cattle epidemic and famine in the 1880s, to civil war among the Maasai proper, who were seeking to recover their fortunes at each other's expense.

The civil wars were ended by colonial intervention in the areas, which were split between British and German rule—now Kenya and Tanzania, respectively. The two halves have developed separately since then, while retaining close cultural links as "one people." In Kenya, it was largely Maasai land that was alienated for European colonization through two controversial treaties. These treaties confined the Maasai to their present reserve, where they have remained largely isolated from change, even since independence in 1963. A volume on the (Kisonko) Maasai written by a German military administrator, M. Merker (1904), provides the most lucid account of the Maasai of early colonial Tanzania. Since then, the demise of the system of warrior villages in Tanzania suggests greater administrative interference into their internal affairs than was the case in Kenya. More recently, the Maasai as a nomadic people have proved an intractable problem for the Tanzanian government's policy of accommodating dispersed populations in settled villages during the 1970s ("villagization").

Settlements

The significant residential groupings are the locality, the village, and the polygynous homestead, or joint family. The locality typically corresponds to a natural water-catchment area, within which interaction is most frequent and elders meet to discuss the issues that affect the community at large and the villages within it. Villages are dispersed throughout the locality, but have little social identity of their own. They are built primarily as a protection against the dangers of the bush at night. During the day, the cattle go out to graze, and social life extends to the wider neighborhood and locality. The significant unit within the village is the cluster of huts and stock corrals that comprise the joint-family homestead, of which there are typically four or five within each village. It is the joint family that has the greatest continuity, and the family head has almost total autonomy in handling its internal affairs. Such families may migrate to another locality at any time, leaving their huts and village space to be occupied by any newcomers to the village. Huts and villages tend to be more substantial and permanent in the less nomadic, upland areas.

Contrasting with the elders' villages, both ideologically and in size, are the warrior villages (*manyat*), which are built to protect the area from marauders. Typically, there are three or four warrior villages in any tribal section, and the warriors who are associated with them claim considerable autonomy from the elders and adopt a contrasting life-style that emphasizes their dependence on one another and their lack of domesticity.

Economy

Subsistence and Commercial Activities. The life-style of the Maasai is oriented toward their herds of cattle, although sheep and goats play an important part in their diet, especially during the dry season, when milk is scarce. The need to graze stock necessitates dispersal over the widest area that is consistent with the availability of grazing and access to water, especially in the dry season. Traditionally, in the most severe famines, Maasai could merge temporarily with neighboring Dorobo hunters and gatherers. During the twentieth century, as the area that is suitable for hunting has contracted and as opportunities for employment have opened up, many of those whom circumstances have squeezed out of the Maasai pastoral economy have drifted toward the fringes of urban society, seeking employment—notably as security guards.

Industrial Arts. Blacksmiths, especially in the past, produced spears and ornaments. Associated with the dirt of their craft, they were despised and not allowed to intermarry with Maasai, who were not involved with blacksmithing.

Trade. Traditionally, sheep and goats were traded with neighboring peoples for vegetable produce. Although the opportunity to migrate for wage labor had been available earlier, it was not until the 1960s that Maasai, who traditionally sold their stock only from absolute necessity, entered the monetary economy; they remain essentially self-sufficient.

Division of Labor. Boys herd the stock, assisted by older males and girls as the need arises, and under the overall supervision of the family head. At night, responsibility for the herds passes to the women. Women also look after their dependent children, maintain the domestic supply of firewood and water, and milk the cattle. Warriors are expected to defend the herds.

Land Tenure. Each tribal section claims sole grazing rights in its own territory, and individual elders may develop and claim wells for watering stock. In times of need, however, it is a major premise that Maasai land and water belong ultimately to all Maasai and that no one should be denied access, even across the boundaries between tribal sections. This principle conflicts with two economic trends that began in the 1960s and have been steadily gaining force, which entail a shift toward local ownership of land: the encroachment of agriculture and the government's attempts to confine Maasai to group ranches. Neither of these developments is consistent with the erratic nature of droughts.

Kinship

Kin Groups and Descent. The Maasai are a patrilineal people, with shallow dispersed lineages that extend for only one or two generations beyond the oldest living elders. These lineages are identified with the membership of a clan. Today the bonds and restrictions of clanship are weak, and clan membership tends to acquire significance only by default, as, for example, when the members of a migrant family find themselves isolated from close friends or kin.

Kinship Terminology. Although kinship terminology is broadly of the Omaha type, there is a general preference to address others by the use of teknonyms or, among close kin and affines, to establish gift terms that emphasize mutual respect.

Marriage and Family

Marriage. Marriages are arranged by the elders, without consulting the bride or her mother. Polygyny is an ideal that is achieved by most older men. As a result of their being younger than men at the time of marriage, most women become widows, and it is understood that they should not remarry.

Domestic Unit. The father is the key figure in the patriarchal family, and, theoretically, his control is absolute—subject only to interference by close senior elders in situations of crisis. Traditionally, as long as the father was alive, no son had final control over his cattle nor over his choice in marriage; this is still the norm in pastoral areas, away from the townships. In practice, as they age, older men rely on their sons to take over the management of the family, and it is the subservience of women that is the most permanent feature of the Maasai family. After her husband's death, even a forceful widow is subordinate to her sons in the management of her herd, and she finds herself wholly unprotected if she has no sons.

Inheritance. At marriage, a bride is allocated a herd of cattle, from which all her sons will build up herds of their own, overseen by their father, who also makes gifts of cattle to his sons over the course of his life. When the parents die, the oldest son inherits the residue of his father's herd, and the youngest inherits the residue of his mother's allocated cattle. Daughters inherit nothing at all.

Socialization. The warrior village plays a key role in the socialization of men. Boys are taken away by their older warrior brothers as herders and are taught to respond to the discipline of the warrior village. Then, in due course, as warriors within their own village, they are expected to develop an unquestioning acceptance of the authority of their peers to emerge to elderhood with a strong sense of loyalty to this peer group.

A girl's childhood is dominated by a strict avoidance, even a fear, of her father and other elders. Her marriage prospects and her family's reputation hinge on her ability to develop an acute sense of respect. She is socialized to accept her subservience to her future husband—himself an elder—and to the elders at large.

Sociopolitical Organization

Social Organization. The most distinctive feature of Maasai society is the age system, which stratifies adult males into age sets, spaced apart by about fifteen years. Each age set is further divided into two successive subsets, the "right-hand," followed by the "left-hand." Of primary importance in the community is the subset of warriors who have been most recently initiated. In their physical prime, they form their warrior villages during this period, until the next subset captures the limelight. It is the establishment of such successive arrays of warrior villages, every seven years or so, that symbolizes the autonomy of the warrior ideal and the temporary independence of each warrior from his father. This independence extends to those mothers of moran who are "seconded" to the warrior villages of their sons.

Each warrior village is a cultural ideal that proclaims the close fraternity among all warriors. They disown any individual claims to property and are obliged to share their time, their food, and even the girls who are their mistresses. The restrictions on their diet and behavior keep them in each other's company, reinforcing their dependence on their peers.

The warrior villages of one subset are abandoned before the initiation of the next subset of warriors, and retirement to elderhood entails a dispersal into smaller and often more remote villages, in order to exploit fully the available grazing lands and water for livestock. As elders, the mens' prime concern is to establish their families and herds. The transition to elderhood thus entails a transformation from a young man who had been heavily dependent on his peers to a self-reliant and self-interested veteran. The independence of each stock owner within the elder's village is popularly seen as the converse of the close dependency that was nurtured within the warrior village, just as the image of the patriarch is the converse of the popular image of the selfless warrior.

Political Organization. Authority within the age system resides in the linkage of alternating age sets (A-B-C-D-E-F . . .), whereby elders of age set A bring a new age set, C, to life in a ceremony that includes the kindling of a fire: they then become the "firestick patrons" of the members of age set C and are responsible for promoting them as warriors in stages toward elderhood. Similarly, C will eventually be patrons to age set E, creating a linkage of age sets, A-C-E- . . ., which is separate from a parallel firestick linkage among age sets B-D-F. . . . This dual system of accountability entails an ambivalent combination of rivalry between adjacent age sets (especially in the south) and of hostility between young and old (especially in the north).

Social Control. Social control among the Maasai rests ultimately on the general belief in the power of elders to bless and to curse, which is linked to their moral superiority in all spheres. The power of firestick patrons over warriors, of fathers over their children, and of all senior kin resides in their power to curse.

Conflict. Conflict among the Maasai focuses primarily on various aspects of warriorhood. The warriors are seen as the defenders of Maasai herds even today, although cattle raiding occurs only on a minor scale as compared with what went on in the past. More pressing are the problems that are internal to the Maasai, those of accommodating the warriors. On the one hand, there is a strained relationship between warriors and elders over stock theft and adultery by the warriors, both of which stem from their prolonged bachelorhood and from the food shortages they often endure, in contrast to the lives led by the wealthy and polygynous elders. On the other hand, there is the rivalry that exists between successive subsets of warriors. The privileges that are claimed by each subset of warriors in their prime are denied their successors until these novices are capable of assuming them in a display of force. This rivalry can lead to fierce infighting. The succession of age sets and subsets is far from smooth, therefore, and the warrior ideal continues to dominate, even after almost a century of peace.

Religion and Expressive Culture

Religious Beliefs. The Maasai believe in an omnipresent God (Nkai), but they have no means of knowing their God's form or intentions. Inasmuch as God has human attributes, they might be described as those of extreme age. Respect for the knowledge of the oldest living men and for their ritual power to bless and to curse is magnified in the profound respect for their all-powerful and all-knowing God.

Pronounced beliefs in sorcery are also evident, particularly at times of misfortune and at major sacrifices. The characteristics of the supposed sorcerers may be viewed as a grotesque caricature of the competitive instincts that are popularly attributed to individual elders, emphasizing their greed and envy of the good fortune of others.

Religious Practitioners. The widespread concern with sorcery is associated with the Loonkidongi dynasty of prophets. Each tribal section has its own prophet, who is seen as helping its members to cope with the endemic sorcery, by providing them with protective medicines and advice for their ceremonies. The prophet is regarded with awe as a type of all-seeing godfather, but his power to curb sorcery is also thought to derive from his knowledge of sorcery as a Loonkidongi, and popular attitudes toward other members of this dynasty are highly ambivalent. The Loonkidongi tend to live in small colonies on the borders between Maasai tribal sections, where they are suspected of providing a breeding ground for discontent, practicing sorcery among themselves, and even secretly selling evil charms to would-be Maasai sorcerers.

Ceremonies. The promotion of warriors to elderhood entails a series of extended ceremonies. The first of two high points of this process is the *eunoto* ceremony, when warriors are "raised" to senior-warrior status. For this occasion, they come from their separate villages and form a single village. They are led by a ritual leader (*olotuno*), who is sometimes thought to shoulder the misfortunes of his peers and is therefore destined to an early death or an impoverished life. Shortly after the eunoto, the warriors abandon their warrior village and return with their mothers to their fathers' villages. The second high point of their career as an age set is the *olghesher* ceremony, which finally unites the "right-hand" and "left-hand" subsets, promoting them jointly to senior elderhood. They are now endowed with the power to bless and to curse and to become firestick patrons of the next new age set.

Their age-set rituals also serve to unite the Maasai federation as a people. The Keekonyukie section in the north and the Kisonko section in the south each have a central role in unifying the Maasai through synchronizing their shared age system. At the inception of each age set, all Maasai are oriented toward the north, waiting for the ritual cue from the Keekonyukie, when boys from the northern tribal sections compete to seize an ox's horn. Only after this ritual has occurred can the new age set be inaugurated in other tribal sections. About twenty-five years later, it is the Kisonko who must first perform olghesher, finally promoting the whole age set and giving it a name that is adopted by all Maasai. Meanwhile, other tribal sections must wait in turn for this lead before they too can follow suit. These two ritual cues, alternating between north and south and between firestick linkages in a fifteen-year cycle, provide a common orientation in space and in time for the Maasai, punctuating their life courses as individuals and reiterating the unity of all Maasai.

Women's ceremonies invariably stem from a widespread concern for their fertility, and, at such times, their dancing is a central feature. These dances sometimes amount to a display of anger and even violence against the elders, and they provide an arena within which women's subservience is temporarily reversed. Even elders share in the belief that these dances will restore fertility and bring the community back to harmony.

Arts. Visual arts among the Maasai focus predominantly on body decoration and on the beaded ornaments that are displayed by warriors and complemented by the beaded ornaments of girls and young women—notably in the trousseau of a bride. These decorations are prominently displayed in their dances, which are themselves a popular art form, frequently with a competitive idiom. Elders do not perform in display dances, but their oratory has many parallels with dance, with gestures used to delineate the space around them and to structure their rhetoric, holding the attention of the audience with a display of the panache that they learned as warriors in their youthful dancing.

Medicine. In addition to the prophets, lesser members of the Loonkidongi dynasty serve as diviners who claim the power to diagnose illnesses and the causes of misfortune and to prescribe a range of herbal medicines and ritual cures. Their secrets are carefully withheld from other Maasai and are linked to a range of "poisons" that are associated with their powers of sorcery, if they are provoked.

Death and Afterlife. There are no elaborate mortuary practices among the Maasai and no beliefs in afterlife. For a parent, however, there is a sense akin to immortality in leaving behind a family whose very existence stems from a life that has been dedicated to care and attention. To leave no successors is to face oblivion in the fullest sense, and it may be taken as a sign of having been cursed.

Bibliography

Gulliver, P. H. (1962). *Social Control in an African Society: A Study of the Arusha, Agricultural Maasai of Northern Tanganyika.* London: Routledge & Kegan Paul.

Merker, M. (1904). *Die Maasai.* Berlin: Dietrich Reimer.

Spencer, Paul (1976). "Opposing Streams and the Gerontocratic Ladder: Two Models of Age Organization in East Africa." *Man* 11:153–175.

Spencer, Paul (1988). *The Maasai of Matapato: A Study of Rituals of Rebellion.* Manchester: Manchester University Press.

PAUL SPENCER

Mamprusi

ETHNONYM: Dagbamba

Orientation

Identification. The people now known as the "Mamprusi" occupy the East and West Mamprusi districts of northern Ghana. Their name is linked to "Mamprugu," the name of the kingdom with which they are associated. Until recently, "Mamprusi" was a term mainly used by outsiders. They called themselves "Dagbamba," a term also used by their southern neighbors, known in English as "Dagomba." Mamprusi called these people "Yooba" (people of the forest) or "Weiya," in reference to the marshy areas also occupied by these neighbors. Similarly, their northern neighbors, the Mossi, were named for the grassy bush (*moo*) that characterizes the ecological zone to the north. Mamprusi usage of the term "Dagbamba" as an autonym, combined with their reference to their neighbors in terms of a characteristic habitat, reflects their view of themselves as inhabiting a central and civilized place in the universe of peripheral peoples. Since their southern neighbors have appropriated the name "Dagbamba" and its English equivalent "Dagomba," the former Dagbamba have become Mamprusi.

Location. The East and West Mamprusi districts (formerly the South Mamprusi District) extend west some 320 kilometers from the international border dividing Ghana and Togo. Some 80 kilometers separate the Nasia River, in the south, from the White Volta River, which marks the northern boundary of this area. In the northeast of the region, the Gambaga escarpment rises 450 meters above sea level at the southward bend of the White Volta River, and continues eastward into Togo. It is likely that in the precolonial period, the Mamprusi zone of influence followed this escarpment.

The region falls within the climatic zone of the Guinea Savanna. The rainy season falls between April and September, and there are no second rains. January and February are characterized by a harmattan season, during which a cold, dry wind sweeps through the country. South of the Gambaga scarp, wooded slopes contract with the arid land and lathyritic soils, lying immediately to the north, or the deforested continuation of the scarp to the northwest. In the south, southeast, and western margins of the districts, land is periodically flooded by tributaries of the Nasia, Oti, and Volta rivers. In the 1960s the Mamprusi districts marked the northern margin of the yam-growing region of Ghana. Deforestation, periodic drought, and increased population pressure have caused some damage to the environment since then, and yams are now said to be much more difficult to grow. Land-fallowing periods are generally shorter than they were in the 1960s, and there is less uncultivated land.

Linguistic Affiliation. Mampruli is one of a number of Mole Dagbani languages spoken in Ghana, Burkina Faso, and Togo. Many languages of this group are spoken by contiguous populations; neighboring peoples are likely to speak mutually intelligible variants of a common tongue. Given frequent intermarriage of Mamprusi with their non-Mamprusi neighbors, many Mamprusi speak several Mole-Dagbani languages. Those who have traveled south, in Ghana, often speak Twi. Many traders speak Hausa, and all schoolchildren learn some English. Familiarity with French is increasing. Muslims are learning to speak as well as to read Arabic.

Demography and Settlement Patterns. In 1960 the population of the Mamprusi districts was roughly 104,436 in an area of 7,790 square kilometers. Population increase has raised the density from 14 persons per square kilometer in the 1960s to over 20 in the 1980s. In the 1960s most Mamprusi lived in settlements of 500 persons or fewer, but, by the 1990s, several large villages with populations of more than 10,000 had emerged. The relative proportion of different ethnic groups in the population has remained roughly constant, with the exception of an influx of Yoruba and Mossi peoples, who were expelled from Ghana in 1973. The Mamprusi, although still less than a majority of the population, continue to constitute the largest single ethnic group. Mamprusi settlements, in contrast with those of neighboring peoples, are nucleated rather than dispersed; often they are clustered near a chief's compound. Larger settlements are divided into sections (*foanna;* sing. *foango*). In the neighborhood of Nalerigu, the present capital of the Mamprusi ex-kingdom, there are the remains of an ancient wall that appears to have partially surrounded the king's village, leaving it open to the north and northeast, where the land rises rapidly, but protecting the lower-lying parts of the village. The wall enclosed streams and farmland as well as a residential area.

History and Cultural Relations

The Mamprusi kingdom is one of several related states founded in the distant past by descendants of Na Gbewa, who, legend has it, entered the area from the northeast in flight from a pursuing army. Mamprusi legend identifies this time as just shortly after the beginning of the world and identifies the people who gave the Na Gbewa refuge as the original inhabitants of the region. Historians suggest that a founder of Mamprusi kingship may have arrived in the area in the fourteenth century, at a time that would coincide with the collapse of Fulani emirates in what is now northern Nigeria and the dispersal of princes and their followers from that region. Mamprusi traditions are vague as to the birthplace of Na Gbewa but emphatic about the location of his burial site at Pusiga, northeast of the present capital. This is said to be where Na Gbewa first stopped and founded the original capital. When he was very old, the succession was contested and his favorite son slain by a rival prince. On hearing the news of his son's death, Na Gbewa disappeared—he was swallowed into the earth at the site of his palace, a place in the bush where sacrifices are still made to his spirit. In the course of the conflict that followed his death, his kingdom was divided; elder and younger brothers became kings of the Mamprusi and Dagomba peoples, respectively. Mossi kings are descendants of a latter Mamprusi king's daughter who eloped from her father's village at a time when the capital had been moved from Pusiga to Gambaga.

The configuration of relationships among Mamprusi, Dagomba, and Mossi kingdoms that arises from this history is expressed in the Mamprusi view of Dagomba kings as their junior brothers and Mossi kings as grandsons of their own king. This amounts to an assertion of Mamprusi seniority. In the past, this presumed seniority was translated into particular forms of conventional behavior held to be appropriate among kin when Mossi, Dagomba, and Mamprusi met one another, particularly in market situations but also in political/ritual contexts.

East and West Mamprusi districts extend over five territorial segments, or provinces, of the former kingdom. Each of these, like the kingdoms founded by different descendants of Na Gbewa, is regarded as the inherited domain of a distinct patriline founded by the son of a Mamprusi king. (It should be emphasized that the notion of domain does not, in this context, imply exclusive rights to use or dispose of land, but rather political authority with respect to the population.) The central area includes the king's village at Nalerigu and other settlements where members of the kings patrilineage hold chiefly office. To the west, from north to south, are the provinces of Kpasinkpe, Wungu, and Janga. To the east, the province of Yunyo separates Nalerigu from the Togo border. The paramount chief of each of these provinces is political head of a corresponding patrilineage, which provides royal chiefs in that province. The Mamprusi king's title, *nayiiri*, (*na* = "king" or "chief"; *yiiri* = "house") is unique, and, unlike that of the provincial paramounts or those of the Mossi and Dagomba kings, it is not linked to the name of any particular territory. It implies his position at the very center of the polity, where he is the source of *naam*, the mystical aspect of chiefly power.

The precolonial history of the Mamprusi is as yet known only through the occasional written records made from legend. At the turn of the twentieth century, the Mossi, Dagomba, and Mamprusi kingdoms were invaded by British-, French-, and German-led troops. A first treaty with the Mamprusi king was made by George Ekom Fergusen—and contested by the French. Later, British troops led by a certain Capt. Stewart settled in Gambaga (1897–1902), where he negotiated with French officers in the Mossi kingdom of Tengkudugu to the northeast and with Germon officers to the east, across what is now the Togo border. A final settlement in Vienna in 1902 established the present boundaries between Togo and Ghana in the east, and between Ghana and Burkina Faso in the north.

Economy

Subsistence and Commercial Activities. Agriculture and animal husbandry provide subsistence for most of the population. Sheep, goats, pigeons, fowl, and guinea foul are kept by most households, and wealthier families have cattle. Chiefs may have horses for ceremonial use, but horses and donkeys (formerly important beasts for transport) are bred farther north, in Mossi territory. Increased population density has led to greater pressure on land. Grazing land, formerly used by transhumant Fulani herders, is now scarce. Fallowing periods are shorter, and, in some areas, drought has led to the destruction of ground cover. Traditionally, millet, guinea corn, and sorghum were the major cereal crops, but maize is now increasingly cultivated despite widespread recognition that it is of less nutritive value than traditional crops that require longer growing seasons. Rice, which has a long history of cultivation as a minor crop, has been introduced in new varieties as a cash crop.

Division of Labor. Mamprusi used to claim that their women did not farm, by which they meant that their wives did not hoe, as do women of neighboring peoples, but helped in the sowing and harvesting of crops; however, famine conditions during the early 1980s resulted in the use of all available labor in agriculture. Men and women now both participate in all phases of the farming cycle other than firing the bush and clearing land for cultivation, which is the work of men. Dawadawa pods and shea nuts, collected by women, are still an important source of food, and their elaborate processing is a task for women. Building houses is men's work. Women finish the floors and walls. Baskets, pots, and locally woven cloth are made by neighboring peoples, and certain foodstuffs (e.g., smoked fish) are also bought from neighbors rather than produced by Mamprusi. Literate adults who have been through the Ghanaian school system are employed by local government offices or work for foreign missionaries and nongovernmental organizations. Local salaries are usually insufficient, however, and farming is a necessary adjunct to most other occupations.

Trade. Women are expected to trade as an extension of their domestic duties. Traditionally, they received cereal from their husbands to make the staple porridge but were expected to collect or trade for ingredients to make soup to accompany the porridge. Shea butter and dawadawa flour, firewood, and millet beer were prepared by women, both for domestic use and trade. Some women are engaged in large-scale trade of grain and yams, cooked food, beets, kola nuts, smoked fish, and imported manufactured goods. Mamprusi men may engage in trade as a full-time alternative to agriculture. Specialists trade in salt, kola, cattle, yams, and, now, manufactured goods. Although women own livestock, they never buy live animals themselves; even hens and guinea fowl are bought and sold by men. Local markets are held either on every third or every sixth day, and specialist traders follow particular sets of markets, which constitute local market cycles. Major market towns have a permanent market site, daily markets, a few small stores, and beer bars. Smaller villages have only periodic markets.

Land Tenure. Traditionally, Mamprusi have regarded land as belonging to the ancestors and to future generations; hence, the sale of land is considered an offense against the ancestors. In urban areas, houses are sold, but this is considered sale of the construction alone. Use rights to cultivate land belong to the person who has cleared it. Usufructuary claims to land may be inherited within a family, but unused land reverts to the community, to be allocated by village chiefs and elders. Until the late twentieth century, there had been relatively little pressure on land, and the only major conflicts over land use occurred between neighboring village communities. Formerly, these conflicts might be resolved by the movement of farmers to unused land and the relocation of village communities. This has become more difficult with increased population density and capital investment in unmovable village infrastructure (e.g., school, clinic, government office, market, church/mosque, water pipes).

Kinship

Kin Groups and Descent. The calculation of patrilineal descent is significant at both the domestic and political levels. The royal patriclan descended from the first king, Na Gbewa, is constituted at present by the five patrilineages that articulate the territorial framework of Mamprusi political organization (see "History and Cultural Relations"). Each royal lineage provides a chief for the capital village in its respective province; the centrally localized lineage provides the king. Chiefs of the capital villages in each province are selected and installed by the king and his court, but they, with their courts, in turn select and install village chiefs within their provinces. Although each lineage is localized in a corresponding province, its constituent segments are dispersed throughout the many small settlements of that territory. Villages may contain a variety of commoner kin groups and one or more segments of a royal lineage, or they may be made up of a single extended kin group consisting solely of either royals or commoners.

The patrilineages that form the royal clan are subdivided into "gates" (*zanoaya;* sing. *zanoari*); many commoner lineages are similarly organized. A gate consists of agnates who trace connection through three generations of deceased patrikin. Within a gate, office is inherited, and gate numbers cooperate in the performance of funerals. Members of the same gate sacrifice together to their common ancestors. The distinction between royals (*nabiisi*) and commoners (*tarima*) depends on patrilineal filiation, and Mamprusi claim that all patrilineal descendants of kings, however distantly related, are royal. Large numbers of commoner gates probably have royal origins. Although it is said that royals should not intermarry, neither at clan nor at lineage levels are Mamprusi royals an exogamous group. The exogamous unit is the gate. Beyond this range of patrikin, marriages occur, although one or both partners may relinquish royal status in establishing the union. Where intermarriage occurs between members of different royal lineages or different gates of a single lineage, one segment will be regarded as royal, while the other will be classified as commoner. If royal descent is not reaffirmed by tenure of royal office, royal status is eventually lost. Thus, the commoner population consists of descendants of royals who have lost claim to royal office as well as immigrants from a variety of different ethnic groups, most notably Tampollensi, Tchokossi, Kantonshi, and other neighboring peoples. Some commoners claim autochthonous origins. Commoners hold office as elders in the chiefly courts and may also hold chiefly office, although their chiefships, unlike those of royals, are not ranked; they are regarded as nonresident elders of a royal chief's court.

Kinship Terminology. The Mamprusi classificatory terminology distinguishes three generations, and great-grandparent/great-grandchild relationships can be described. In Ego's generation, men distinguish senior brother (*bere*) from junior brother, who is classed together with sisters as junior sibling (*tizoa'*). Female (*tizo-pwa'a*) and male (*tizo-doo*) junior siblings can be identified. Women class their senior sisters and brothers together (bere) and their junior brothers and sisters together (tizoa'). In the first ascending generation, Ego categorizes siblings of the same sex as a parent, depending on their age relative to the parent. The categories senior father (*bakpema*) and junior father (*bapura*), or senior mother (*makpema*) and junior mother (*mapura*) include all persons for whom Ego's parents use sibling terms. Special terms distinguish a mother's brother (*nyahaba*) and a sister's child (*nyahanga*). A father's sister (*piriba*) refers to her brother's child as child (*bia*). Ego refers to his own children and to those of persons he calls by a sibling term, as child (bia); male child (*bi-dibiga*) and female child (*bipunga*) may be distinguished. The child of any person called child will be called grandchild (*ya'anga*), for which the reciprocal is female grandparent (*yapwa'a*) or male grandparent (*yadoo*). The term for grandparent (*yaaba*) is also used for ancestor. Affines distinguished in Ego's generation include husband (*sira*), wife (pwa'a), sister's husband (*datyia;* pl. *datyisi*), and brother's wife (*pwaatia;* pl. *pwaatyisi*). A woman calls her husband's brother "husband" (sira) but usually specifies his relative age with respect to her husband (*sira-kpema* = senior husband; *sira-pira* = junior husband). A man calls his brother's wife, wife (pwa'a). All the above terms are used both in address and reference and replace personal names in most contexts.

Marriage and Family

Marriage. In theory Mamprusi royals must marry commoners. In effect, they seek to spread their matrimonial alliances as widely as possible. Among royals and commoners members of the same gate are forbidden to marry, and marriage to patrikin with whom precise genealogical connection can be traced is frowned upon. Matrilateral cross-cousin marriage—that is, marriage to a cross cousin who is not the child of a parent's own sibling—is regarded as a good marriage, particularly by Mamprusi Muslims. Men aspire to polygynous marriages. Chiefs and important commoners have many wives. Mamprusi frown upon sororal polygyny, saying that marriage with two women from the same house leads to quarrels among the wives and difficulties in management for the household head. Marriage is established by gifts of kola. Two prestations of kola are sent by the head of the husband's gate to the head of the wife's gate. Both are sent via the chief or chiefs of the villages in which the partners reside. The first, message kola, establishes that the woman has spent the night with her future husband. If this kola is accepted, the pardon kola follows. The marriage kola is distributed to members of the woman's gate, and a portion of both prestations is taken by the chief or chiefs and distributed to elders. Chiefs thus involved will subsequently mediate in disputes arising within or from the marriage. The exchange makes children legitimate members of the father's gate. A son-in-law acquires important ongoing responsibilities with regard to his wife's kin. He must attend the funeral of senior members of her gate and give her grain, a sheep, and cash to contribute. He must raise a group of dancers and gun bearers to celebrate the deceased. A husband's failure to provide the requisite funeral contribution is grounds for divorce. When, as frequently happens, Mamprusi men marry women of neighboring ethnic groups, they follow the woman's group's customs for establishing the marriage.

A determined woman can now leave a marriage she dislikes. This is said to be the result of modern government intervention, but it seems likely that even formerly, it was not impossible for a woman to leave one husband for another. It is more difficult however, for her to return to her kin. Men also cannot easily dismiss a wife of long standing. Although marriage is unstable in the first years, it becomes more stable after the birth of children. After a husband's death, his widow may choose to marry one of his brothers, but cannot be forced to do so against her will. Young widows may return home and accept gifts from suitors, which they will use to trade. They are then supposed to choose a husband and return the gifts to the rejected suitors. An elderly widow is household head if she has a married son with whom she lives in her deceased husband's house. A widow without sons will reluctantly return to her own kin.

Domestic Unit. The core of the household is the patrilineal family. Royal households normally include a polygynous household head, perhaps with his younger married sons and unrelated dependents. Commoner households more often include older married brothers with children, and often three generations of agnates reside together. Older men are often polygynous; important chiefs and wealthy commoners have many more than the maximum of four wives permitted Muslims. Marriage is invariably patri-virilocal. A woman retains membership in her natal lineage. Although she normally will be buried in her husband's house, a final funeral is performed for her in her natal home.

Although women observe an etiquette of respect when dealing directly with their husbands, and the male household head is treated with deference by resident family members, women control the domestic domain. Significantly, a male household head is said to be subordinate to his father's sister if such a relative is in residence. The internal hierarchy of the household is based on the ranking of women in polygynous marriages. A senior wife has authority over junior wives, and their children sleep in her room. She supervises their collective performance of the major domestic tasks and may also organize trading enterprises. Mothers-in-law have authority over their husband's wives.

Sociopolitical Organization

The king (nayiiri) sits with his court in his palace (*nayiini*) at the village of Nalerigu, roughly in the territorial center of the former kingdom. Although aspects of the kingship are replicated in the paramount chiefship of each province, only the king's palace contains the regalia used to install the king and to invest the heads of the other royal provinces. Each king is regarded as embodying all preceding kings, and his court is, directly or indirectly, the source of kingship/chiefship (naam) throughout the kingdom. It is the most elaborate and largest court containing offices represented in smaller numbers in all other royal courts. Of these, the Master of Horses (*wudaana*) and the Master of Spears (*kpanaraana*) are most common. Courts also include gun bearers, drummers, and local earth-priests, as well as Muslims. Also numbered among the king's elders are all the household heads of a settlement, special drummers and officeholders responsible for his clothing and regalia, successors to the titles of former executioners, and eunuchs.

Courts allocate land and deal with disputes arising from land claims and litigation arising from marriage, as well as other domestic and civil disputes. Most disputes are dealt with first in a chief's court rather than in government courts. Chiefly courts deal with funerals and succession to office, organize annual calendrical celebrations, perform sacrifices on behalf of the community to earth and ancestor divinities, and mediate between the local communities and national government. Special commoner-chiefs deal with witchcraft accusations and have custody of convicted witches.

Commoner elders in the king's court play a crucial role in the selection of each new king and are involved in the selection and installation of royal chiefs. Succession to royal office is competitive; numerous candidates present themselves, and, through gifts and persuasion, attempt to influence the court in their favor. Office should circulate through the various gates of a royal lineage, and a son should not succeed his father in office. The participation of commoners—as king/chief makers and as followers of rival princes in competitions for royal office—balances the hegemony of royals and acts as a check on the abuse of power by one segment of the royal lineages. All offices are held for life; therefore much of the court endures beyond the reign of a particular king or chief.

Since 1957, numerous local institutions have been set up in the Mamprusi districts by the Ghanaian government to extend the processes of technological and social transformation begun during the colonial period. Police and army units represent the central government, as do schools and local government offices. Roads, a postal system, telephone communication, and bus transport connect the Mamprusi districts with the rest of the world. Increased trade with southern Ghana has resulted in the expansion of markets and increased distribution for commodities made elsewhere.

The north of Ghana has been the scene of numerous small-scale conflicts since the late 1960s, most of which have not involved Mamprusi. One of the longest-standing conflicts involves people resident immediately to the north who claim Mamprui identity and are descended from royal Mamprusi who emigrated to that area prior to the British conquest. They speak Hausa or Kusal rather than Mampruli, and, although they consider themselves Mamprusi, they should be considered separately from the ethnic group residing in the Mamprusi districts.

Religion

Kingship. Mamprusi kingship is both a religious and a political institution. The king and royal ancestors are held responsible for the fertility of land and people. Respect for a village chief is a manifestation both of political allegiance and reverence for the kingship. The king embodies the royal ancestors and owns all the land and everything on it; royal chiefs replicate his powers on a more limited scale. The living king and royal chiefs delegate responsibility to members of other king groups, which have other divinities, and those, too, are regarded as having a part to play in providing for the general welfare.

Commoner Divinities. The ancestors of commoners are called upon to support the polity during certain annual ceremonies and in other circumstances that affect the polity. During natural disasters such as drought or political trauma such as the interregnum and—particularly important—at the installation of a new king, commoner-elders request support from their ancestors for the wider community. After his installation, the king should provide animals for sacrifice by commoners at earth-shrines and elsewhere. At the village level, local commoner priests ritually ratify a chief's investiture, which is performed by a royal court, and sacrifice at local shrines on his behalf.

Islam. The historical connections between the Mamprusi and Islam are unclear. In major market towns and the capital village, a few Muslim families are clearly distinguished from other Mamprusi. Muslim men marry non-Muslim women, and their wives tend to adopt Islam. They trace their origins to royals who did not achieve office or to immigrant traders. The oldest Muslim community is located in Gambaga, a major market in the precolonial period. Muslims there provided services for the caravan trade and were, until the late twentieth century, dyers. The king's *liman* resides in Gambaga. Liman Baba, who acted as a go-between for Na Barga, the reigning king when the British arrived, is also mentioned in reports from Kumasi. He clearly was an important and literate figure of the period. At present, Muslims participate at court and in domestic rituals performed at death and naming. It is traditionally forbidden for the king to be a Muslim, but, during the late twentieth century, kings have been converted to Islam. Since the 1960s, evangelical Muslims have been active and the number of mosques and the diversity of Muslim communities has increased in the Mamprusi area.

Christianity. The first Christian mission in the Mamprusi region was probably the Assemblies of God, established around 1925. After independence, the Baptist Mission Hospital was built in Nalerigu, the king's village, with funds from the United States; since then, both British and U.S.-based missions have established themselves. Ghanaian churches have also founded congregations.

Bibliography

Allan, W. (1965). *The African Husbandman*. New York: Barnes & Noble. Rev. ed. 1967.

Arana, E., and M. Swadesh (1967). *Diccionario analítico del mampruli*. Mexico City: Museo de las Culturas.

Drucker-Brown, S. (1975). *Ritual Aspects of Mamprusi Kingship*. African Social Research Document 8. Cambridge: African Studies Center.

Drucker-Brown, S. (1982). "Joking at Death: The Mamprusi Grandparent-Grandchild Joking Relationship. *Man*, n.s. 16:714–728.

Drucker-Brown, S. (1984). "Calendar and Ritual among the Mamprusi." *Systèmes de pensée en Afrique Noire*. Vol. 8. Paris: Centre National de la Recherche Scientifique (CNRS).

Drucker-Brown, S. (1986). "The History of Magazi Akushi and the Mamprusi Muslims of Gambaga." *Cambridge Anthropology* 11:78–83.

Drucker-Brown, S. (1989). "Mamprusi Installation Ritual and Centralization: A Convection Model. *Man*, n.s. 24:185–201.

Drucker-Brown, S. (1992). "Horse, Dog, and Donkey: The Making of a Mamprusi King." *Man*, n.s. 27:71–90.

Drucker-Brown, S. (1993). "Mamprusi Witchcraft, Subversion, and Gender Relations." *Africa* 6:531–550.

Drucker-Brown, S. (1994). "The Divorce of Zanjiili's Daughter." *Droit et Culture* (Paris) 27.

Drucker-Brown, S. (1995). "The Court and the Kola Nut: Wooing and Witnessing in Northern Ghana." *Journal of the Royal Anthropological Institute* 1(1): 129–144.

Drucker-Brown, S. (Forthcoming 1995). "Communal Warfare in Northern Ghana: Unaccepted War." In *Warfare: A Cruel Necessity?*, edited by R. Hinde and H. Watson, chap. 2.

Fage, J. S. (1964). "Reflections on the Early History of the Mossi-Dagomba Group of States." In *The Historian in Tropical Africa*, edited by J. Vansina, R. Mauny, and L. V. Thomas. London: Oxford University Press for International African Institute.

Naden, T. [n.d.]. *Kinship Terminologies in Northern Ghana*. Legon, Ghana: Ghana Institute of Linguistics.

SUSAN DRUCKER-BROWN

Mandaeans

ETHNONYMS: none

The Mandaeans are a group of people defined primarily by their religious affiliation, which differs from that of their mainly Muslim neighbors in Iran and Iraq. Mandaean religion is related to the gnosticism of the third and fourth centuries, and it has affinities with both Judaism and Christianity. Based on evidence from Mandaean language and literature, it is thought that they migrated from the Jordan Valley eastward to Haran in the first century. From Haran, which is on the border between present-day Turkey and Syria, they moved on to southern Babylonia, where they have remained. Today they live along the rivers and waterways of southern Iraq and Khūzestān, Iran. The Mandaean language is related to Aramaic and contains West Syrian linguistic elements, which supports the belief that they migrated from west to east.

With the Islamic conquest in the seventh century, Muslim leaders declared that all religious groups must have a holy book and a prophet if they were to avoid being forcibly converted to Islam. The Mandaeans, then, proclaimed *Ginza* to be their holy scripture and John the Baptist to be their prophet. *Ginza* is a collection of mythological, revelatory, and hymnic writing divided into *Right Ginza* (material world) and *Left Ginza* (afterworld). The *Right Ginza* contains prose primarily concerned with the world of humans, and the *Left Ginza* contains verse primarily concerned with the fate of souls.

Ginza and other Mandaean holy books reflect the dualism that is inherent in all Mandaean beliefs and traditions. At least one of the major texts of Manichaeism, which is based on dualism, can be traced to a Mandaean original dated at about 250 A.D. In Mandaean dualism, diametrically opposed entities clash with each other—but are also intertwined and, to some extent, recognize the others' claims. Good and evil, light and darkness, soul and matter struggle with each other for control of the world. Mandaean mythology includes a preexisting lightworld (heaven), creation of the earth and humans, and the soul's journey back to the lightworld.

Mandaean rituals are also based on dualistic principles and center around the practice of baptism. Repeated baptisms take place on Sundays and specific festival days. There are two minor rites of ablution performed by individuals (not priests) and more important baptisms performed by a priest. Lay members get baptized as often as they want to, and baptisms are required at specific occasions, such as marriage, after childbirth (for a woman), and immediately before death (as close as can be predicted). Water acts to clean away sins and impurities; it also represents the lightworld as reflected in the earthly world. Because the baptismal river water symbolizes the lightworld, baptism becomes a kind of ascension preparing the individual for ascension at life's end. A more complicated, lengthy, and secret ritual is performed for the dead by priests.

The Mandaeans have never aspired to secular power or political expansion. As a non-Muslim minority within an Islamic society, the Mandaeans have not flourished, but they have generally been allowed to live in peace. An outbreak of cholera eliminated the priestly class in the 1830s, but they were replaced with new priests from the laity. With the rise of secularism, some scholars thought that they might be on the brink of extinction, but, with a renewed interest in traditional cultural and religious values and practices among this endogamous group, a Mandaean revival seems to be occurring.

Bibliography

Drower, Ethel S. (1937). *The Mandaeans of Iraq and Iran: Their Cults, Customs, Magic, Legends, and Folklore*. Oxford: Clarendon Press. Reprint. 1962. Leiden: E. J. Brill.

Eliade, Mircea, ed. (1986). *The Encyclopedia of Religion*. New York: Macmillan.

Grimes, Barbara F., ed. (1988). *Ethnologue: Languages of the World*. Dallas: Summer Institute of Linguistics.

Macuch, Rudolf (1965). *Handbook of Classical and Modern Mandaic*. Berlin: de Gruyter.

Mande

ETHNONYMS: Manding, Mandingue

"Mande" is a term that has been used to identify the culture that embraces the western third of Africa's great northern savanna and coastal forests. In a narrow sense, "Mande" identifies a geographic homeland, with boundaries that vary according to regional beliefs and politics. This homeland is centered along the common border between Mali and Guinea. From this core area, the Mali Empire coalesced and spread eastward into Burkina Faso; westward into Guinea and Senegal, Gambia, and Guinea Bissau; and southward into Sierra Leone, Liberia, Ivory Coast, and Ghana. The Mali Empire was the source of the Mande diaspora; therefore, in a broad sense, "Mande" refers to the areas of these countries that are occupied by Mande language speakers.

The Mande are comprised of a number of different ethnic groups including—but not limited to—the Bamana (or Bambara), Maninka (or Malinke), and Dyula, who constitute the linguistic and cultural nucleus; the Somono, Bozo, and Wasuluka, who are close to the nucleus; the Kagoro, Khasonke, Mandinko, Marka, and Soninke, who are savanna groups; and the Kuranko, Kono, Vai, Susu, and Yalunka, who are forest groups. The largest group, numbering more than 1.6 million, is that of the Bamana. Some of the smaller groups, such as the Bozo and the Yalunka, have fewer than 50,000 members each.

There is tremendous regional variation among the Mande, both in dialect and in culture. There are many different dialects of Mande, and some, such as Maninka and Mandinko, are mutually unintelligible. Some aspects of culture, such as the practice of Islam, also vary greatly from area to area and even from community to community.

All Mande are primarily agriculturists, and most are full-time subsistence farmers. Many towns are surrounded by women's garden plots and by much larger family fields. Rice is an important staple crop. During planting and harvesting, much time is spent in the fields. During other seasons, there is time for other activities, and some farmers have part-time businesses to supplement their harvests.

All of the Mande groups have similar social systems. Until the advent of colonialism in the nineteenth century, the Mande were divided into three main groups: farmers and nobles, specialized professionals, and slaves. This social structure probably developed with the founding of the Mali Empire in the thirteenth century. The ways in which membership in and interaction among these groups were defined varied between ethnic groups and changed rapidly over time. After the turn of the twentieth century, European colonialists drastically changed the social structure of the Mande by outlawing slavery; however, the position of slave still persists within a castelike system in Mande society.

The Mande are a patrilineal group, with the oldest male acting as lineage head. A minor lineage is often defined territorially as the houses of a man and his immediate family. A major lineage includes the houses of genealogical brothers and their families. A hamlet is the next larger unit, containing the houses of men of the same clan name. The men of a hamlet attend ritual meetings together and are arranged roughly according to seniority based on age. The hamlet also defines an exogamous group, wherein the men of one hamlet give their daughters in marriage to the men of other hamlets.

Heavy farmwork is done by men; women have both farm and domestic duties. Women perform much of the time-consuming work, such as cooking, cleaning, and child rearing. Whereas men usually occupy the village-based leaderhip positions, such as headman and imam, or religious leader, the women of a village often have their own organization, with a leader who corresponds to the male religious leader. This "circumcision queen," as she is sometimes known, is responsible for the girls' circumcision ceremonies and is acknowledged as an expert on health, medicine, and the raising of children.

Bibliography

McNaughton, Patrick R. (1988). *The Mande Blacksmiths: Knowledge, Power, and Art in West Africa*. Bloomington: Indiana University Press.

Schaffer, Matt (1980). *Mandinko: The Ethnography of a West African Holy Land*. New York: Holt, Rinehart & Winston.

Mangbetu

ETHNONYMS: Amangbetu, Kingbetu, Mambetto, Mangbettu, Nemangbetu

Orientation

The Mangbetu live in the northeastern corner of Zaire. They are distinctive in that they are the founders of one of the few centralized political systems in Central Africa. The territory that was eventually ruled by Mangbetu stretched about 300 kilometers east from the Uele River Basin and about 150 kilometers north from the Nepoko River. The number of people under Mangbetu control has been estimated at between 80,000 and 150,000. A 1959 census reported about 150,000 people in Mangbetu territories, and a 1985 count lists 650,000 Mangbetu speakers in Zaire.

The land occupied by the Mangbetu is a transitional zone in which environmental conditions vary considerably from north to south. Within 200 kilometers north to south, rainfall patterns range from almost no dry season to a dry season of three to four months; vegetation ranges from tropical forests, to forest-savanna mixture, to gallery forests, to wooded savanna. In this ecological zone, there is a variety of wild plant and animal life that exceeds that of the more uniform forest in the south or the savanna in the north. The Mangbetu, for example, traditionally hunted both the okapis of the forest and the zebras of the savanna.

A large range of domesticated plants can be found in the region as well. The long annual rainy season provides plenty of moisture for crops. In the dry season, there is ample time to cut down, dry, and burn trees for gardening. Numerous forests provide land for shifting agriculture. Regularly planted crops include grains (e.g., sesame, millet, maize), African and Asian yams, oil palms, sweet manioc, and the Mangbetu staples—sweet potatoes and plantain bananas.

The favorable environment of the forest-savanna ecosystem has been attractive to a large variety of human groups. Immigrants from east and west tended to remain in this abundantly rich area rather than to move on. Immigrants from the north were drawn to the area by its resources and were blocked from moving farther south by the forest barrier. The resulting clashes and intermarriages have contributed to the region's ethnic and cultural variety. There are at least fifteen dialects belonging to three different language families, which, in turn, are parts of two major linguistic groupings (Keim 1979). The Mangbetu, along with five other groups, speak the Kere language (more often known as "Mangbetu"). Kere is classified as being in the Central Sudanic Language Family, which is part of a larger grouping of Chari-Nile languages.

History and Cultural Relations

At the beginning of the nineteenth century, the Mangbetu were only one of many small groups of people that were settling on the northern edge of the Zaire rain forest. At that time, the Mangbetu leader, Nabiembali, gathered a following of warriors and moved north across the upper Bomokandi River to subdue groups of Mangbele and Mabisanga. Not long afterward, he continued Mangbetu expansion by conquering other peoples in the area, among them groups of Madi, Bangba, Mayogo, Mayvu, Makango, and Barambo. The major significance of Nabiembali's conquests was that he incorporated non-Kere-speaking peoples into his kingdom. His conquests represented the first time that power had been wielded on a territorial basis.

The Mangbetu are basically patrilineal. At the same time, the maternal uncles of a man are very important. It was formerly a common practice for a strong nephew to be accepted as a ruler over his maternal kin. The nephew's son then became heir to his father's power. Tied in with these practices was the tradition of giving women to unrelated groups or exchanging women with them. This practice was accepted throughout the region as a form of peacemaking or alliance, but Nabiembali—and the Mangbetu who followed him—turned the custom into an institution of control over the many ethnic groups that were represented among their subjects. One of the primary advantages of this practice was that it could give a weak clan a strong leader, through the clan's maternal ties; however, Nabiembali used the practice in reverse. He developed a strategy of marrying many wives, not only to increase productivity, display his wealth, and have many sons, but also to legitimize his conquests and extend his control. His policy worked to the extent that some of his sons were accepted as rulers among their mothers' peoples. However, because his sons sought to extend their own power and the influence of their maternal clans (over which they ruled), and because they challenged the authority of their father, both centralized power and the extent of Mangbetu rule were eventually weakened.

The justification of Mangbetu leadership was related to two concepts, *nataate* and *nakira*. "Nataate," loosely translated, refers to one's capacity to do, or one's social skills. "Nakira" refers to one's intelligence or one's technical and mental skills. Nataate is the dynamic power that exists within a person and makes him respected by others. Nakira is the ability one has in almost any endeavor, but particularly in dancing, singing, and public speaking. The Mangbetu criterion for succession was a combination of hereditary links and ability. Superior nataate and nakira were considered seriously in the choice of a successor to the ruler; therefore, an incompetent firstborn son might be rejected in favor of a more competent younger brother. In practice, many succession problems resulted from this imprecise formula for the transfer of power.

The Mangbetu achieved a very high level of technological and material development, as indicated by early reports from European explorers. For example, Georg Schweinfurth, the first European to reach the area, visited Mbunza, the Mangbetu ruler, in 1870, and described thousands of subjects at Mbunza's court as well as hundreds of nobles and courtiers. Within the capital, there were many large buildings; smaller huts filled with animal skins, feathered hats, and necklaces; and an armory of iron spears, piles of knives, and hundreds of polished copper lances. Mbunza's household included musicians, eunuchs, jesters, ballad singers, dancers, and bodyguards. Surrounding the capital were large, cultivated fields and orchards of oil palms and other trees (Schweinfurth 1874).

Much of the Mangbetu material culture was probably borrowed from conquered peoples, but the Mangbetu encouraged the development of all the arts of the peoples under their control. Examples of their crafts include intricately forged chains and knives with carved ivory handles; geometric decoration of bodies, pots, mats, and houses; a distinctive coiffure that emphasized their artifically elongated heads; carefully carved stools, dishes, gongs, trumpets, and canoes; and finely formed human heads made out of clay and wood.

Religion

The religion of the Mangbetu is reflected in their material culture. The material wealth of "great rulers" included many items that were reserved for their exclusive use and that symbolized their links with divine authority. For example, the skin, tails, teeth, and claws of leopards were sacred and were reserved for the use of the king alone; the *nekire* (whistle) and *bangbwa* (war drum) were used exclusively by the king to protect his people or goods or to bring good luck. The king was also believed to have the ability to control rain, which he used not to help with the crops but to permit outdoor gatherings and to serve as a weapon in war.

In the nineteenth century another supernatural force entered into Mangbetu society, possibly in the context of a secret society that was focused on Mangbetu opposition to colonialism, but perhaps even earlier, in the 1850s. In the beginning, this force, called *nebeli,* seems to have been a potion that could attract animals to traps and subdue feared animals. Later, it was used to defeat enemies. Eventually, its use was incorporated into the rituals of a secret society, also known as nebeli, the purpose of which was to protect the larger community and its culture. Most Mangbetu leaders of the twentieth century were nebeli members, and most used the society to strengthen their rule over their subjects.

Belgian colonialism, beginning early in the twentieth century, drasticallly changed Mangbetu society. Generally speaking, there was acceptance of Belgian rule without full Mangbetu cooperation or participation in the Belgian administrative system. The Mangbetu and their subjects accepted Christianity very slowly and sent few of their children to European schools. Mangbetu production of cash crops was lower and more painfully extracted than elsewhere in the Belgian colony. When towns grew up around administrative and commercial centers, the Mangbetu participated in relatively small numbers. By contrast, other groups, especially the Budu, became clerks, servants, drivers, laborers, vendors, and students.

A prevailing explanation for Budu successes (and Mangbetu failures) is that the Budu were under attack from the Mangbetu at the time of colonial contact, and so conformed to European wishes in order to save themselves. Conversely, the Mangbetu, who were proud conquerors, withdrew in defiance and preferred to reminisce about past glories and plot a return to power. It is clear that Mangbetu prestige suffered with their loss of slaves, the end of raiding, the disgrace of being conquered, and other such humiliations, but colonial policies also kept the Mangbetu from developing more successfully. By prohibiting the entrepreneurial activity of lineages, by reducing the prestige of the Mangbetu court, by regulating succession, and by reinforcing the power of the "great rulers" to keep subjects in line, the colonizers effectively suppressed Mangbetu culture.

Bibliography

Anstey, Roger (1962). *Britain and the Congo in the Nineteenth Century*. London: Oxford University Press.

Denis, Paul (1961). *Histoire des mangbetu et des matshaga jusqu'à l'arivée des belges*. Archives d'ethnographie, no. 2. Tervueren: Musée Royal de l'Afrique Centrale.

Keim, Curtis A. (1979). *Precolonial Mangbetu Rule: Political and Economic Factors in Nineteenth-Century Mangbetu History (Northeast Zaire)*. Ann Arbor, Mich.: University Microfilms International.

Kottack, Conrad (1972). "Ecological Variables in the Origin and Evolution of African States: The Buganda Example." *Comparative Studies in Society and History* 14:351–380.

Miracle, Marvin (1967). *Agriculture in the Congo Basin: Tradition and Change in African Rural Economies*. Madison: University of Wisconsin Press.

Murdock, George P. (1959). *Africa: Its Peoples and Their Culture History*. New York: McGraw Hill.

Richards, Audrey I. (1960). *East African Chiefs*. New York: Praeger.

Schweinfurth, Georg (1874). *In the Heart of Africa: Three Years' Travels and Adventures in the Unexplored Regions of Central Africa from 1868–1871*. Translated by Ellen E. Frewer. 2 vols. New York: Harper & Bros.

Sundstrom, Lars (1974). *The Exchange Economy of Pre-Colonial Tropical Africa*. New York: St. Martin's Press.

RONALD JOHNSON

Maronites

ETHNONYMS: none

Orientation

The Maronites are an ancient East Christian sect that derives its name from John Maron, a learned monk who was named patriarch of Antioch, around the turn of the eighth century. Some Maronite authors claim, however, that the name derives from Maron, or Maro of Cyrrhus, a monk who was born near Apamea on the River Orontes, in northern Syria (and who died there, at some time before 423). He was a renowned ascetic who prayed on a mountaintop. Endowed with extraordinary spiritual powers, he attracted many disciples. These authors claim that he was a friend of Saint John Chrysostom, father of the liturgy that is still used in both the Greek and the Roman churches, and an upholder of orthodoxy when Monothelitism (the view that Christ had but one will) was the issue of debate. His followers built a monastery next to his tomb, and it became the nucleus of the Maronite church, which gained lasting approval from Pope Benedict XIV in 1753. Indeed, the Maronite church was the first Syrian church to join Rome, and thus it became the first Uniate of the East.

Maronites today number about 1,300,000. Half a million of them reside in Lebanon, which has served as their national home ever since they left northern Syria. Other centers of residence include Syria, Palestine, Cyprus, Egypt, and the Americas, where some 200,000 constitute the core of the early emigrants from the Syro-Lebanese region, who left when it was still under Ottoman rule. They have established official bishoprics in Aleppo, Tripoli, Jubayl (ancient Byblos) and Botra, Baʿalbek (ancient Heliopolis), Damascus, Beirut, Tyre, Sidon, Cyprus, and also in North America, where they have independent churches in the principal cities of the continent.

History and Cultural Relations

The earliest information that is available on the Maronite sect was recorded by Theodoret, bishop of Cyrrhus (d. 458). Early in the sixth century, Maronite monks were foremost among the defenders of the doctrine of Chalcedon, which, owing to the controversy generated in its aftermath, brought on a permanent schism between adherents of Chalcedon and those of Monophysitism, the faith of the Jacobites and the Nestorians. In the battles that ensued with the Monophysites, Maronites lost 350 monks. Many of their monasteries were destroyed by the Monophysites. Saint Maron's monastery, however, continued to serve until the middle of the seventh century as the stronghold of the Chalcedonians as well as the center of their missionary activities in northern Syria.

In the eighth century John Maron advocated the Monothelite theory that attributed one will to Jesus, a compromise among those who stressed one or the other of the two natures of Christ, a dualism that was unacceptable to the early fathers of Christianity. Maron and his followers found themselves in opposition not only to their Christian neighbors among the Syrians, but also to the Muslim imperium that upheld the churches that had maintained detachment from Byzantium.

Muslims had conquered Syria in the seventh century and dominated most of the known civilized world from China to France by the middle of the eighth. Maronites at this time were dubbed *maradah* (rebels). But the attempts of civilian authorities to suppress the Maronite monks only served to strengthen the bond between them and their lay followers, as did their use of Syriac, a derivative of Aramaic and the spoken vernacular of the region.

Heads of monasteries were invested with an episcopal character, and the people in the surrounding areas came under their direct jurisdiction. Over a period of time, the monks shaped the people's religious life and imparted a peculiar character to them, which bore the stamp of the monks' customs and traditions. This legacy has remained until today an important and enduring characteristic of the Maronite church and people, their canon law and church governance. This monastic origin explains also the persistently strong influence of the patriarch in civil and religious matters among Maronites at present. Indeed, Maronites regard their patriarch as the actual leader of their "nation."

Patriarch Anastasius II was the last Chalcedonian to reside in Antioch. He was killed in 721. Only titular heads were appointed after 721, by Constantinople, the capital of Christendom. The vacancy persisted until 742, when the Umayyad caliph, Hisham, allowed the Maronites to elect their own patriarch. In electing Stephen III, Maronites acquired control over their own destiny. An independent Maronite patriarchate evolved in consequence thereof. Historians claim that it was in 685 that Maronites acquired their first elected patriarch.

From the very beginning, their bishops took the title "of Antioch." Maronite authors dispute the argument of Eutyches (Saʿīd ibn Batriq), the Monophysite patriarch of Alexandria, who claimed that the Maronites renounced their Monothelite heresy when the Crusaders showed up, early in the twelfth century. They allege that Eutyches's writings misled the Latin writer William of Tyre—the standard Latin authority on the Crusades—who wrote that the Maronites entered the Catholic church after contacts with Latin kingdoms and after renouncing Monothelitism. Although this assertion may be disputed, there is no disputing that the Maronite connection with the Latin West came via the Latin kingdom of Jerusalem. The connection might have been hastened by the pressures of their Monophysite neighbors—who enjoyed influence among the Muslim caliphs of Damascus and, later, those of Baghdad—especially after the Maronites were forced to abandon their Syrian habitat for the northern mountain fastness of Lebanon, in order to escape the attacks of both Melchites (adherents of Constantinople) and Monophysites at a time when they had no contacts directly with Rome.

The first church in Mount Lebanon was established (according to Maronite writings) around 749 and was protected by a feudal system of government, which the monks organized to that end. Accordingly, the patriarch headed the "nation," assisted by bishops who served as his vicars. When Crusaders, heading to conquer Jerusalem, appeared on the coastal strip below their mountain strongholds, Maronites greeted and befriended them. Latin writers allege that Maronite contacts with Rome were broken after Pope Hormisdas responded a letter of 518 and that they were reestablished only after the visit of Jeremias al-ʿAmshiti (1199–1230), the first Maronite patriarch to visit Rome and attend the Lateran Council, in 1215. Following this visit, he received a bull and a pallium from Pope Innocent III, signaling his integration with the Latin church. Relations with Rome were interrupted once again during the rule of the Mamluk sultans, who had completely ended the presence of Crusaders in Syria by 1298.

The canonical legislation that gives the Maronite rite its ecclesiastical church discipline and hierarchical structure is distinct from other canonical rites of the Eastern Uniate churches. What came down from the Middle Ages is enshrined in the only surviving copy of the *Kitāb al-Huda* (Book of Guidance), which is written in Karshuni (Arabic in Syriac script). The priest-monk Yūsuf (Joseph) Elias, the Nestorian metropolitan of Nisibis (1058–1059), and ʿAbdullah ibn al-Tajīb (d. 1043) both assert that the Byzantine-rite Melchites and Maronites share the same doctrine on the nature of Christ, the difference being that Maronites admit one will in Christ, instead of two.

When they were cut off from the Holy See in Rome during the Mamluk era (1291–1517), and when they found that the *Kitāb al-Huda* no longer provided sufficient guidance, Maronites adopted the canons of the Coptic ibn al-ʿAssāl. Avoiding such contacts was prudent even after the Mongol invasions and the subsequent attempts by their khans to elicit Latin Europe's support against the Muslim Mamluks. Contacts were reestablished during the patriarchate of John Jaʿjaʿ (1404–1445), before the Maronite prelates were recognized formally as patriarchs of Antioch. Pope Paul III (1534–1549) sent Franciscans to teach the Maronite clergy Latin and to instruct them in the Latin rite for administering the sacraments.When the Mamluks were ousted by the Ottomans in 1517, Sultan Selim I (1512–1520) introduced the *millet* system (a transformation of the *dhimmi* status that was enjoyed by Christian sects during the Arabian caliphates). The Maronites were able to govern their own internal affairs even though they themselves were not officially accorded the millet status, which status was first granted in 1453 to the Greek Orthodox patriarch, following the conquest of Constantinople by Mehmet II in 1453 and, later, in 1461, to the Armenian patriarch. Uniate churches received such recognition only after the Ottomans were compelled to grant it by French and papal pressures in the seventeenth century, in consequence of serious Ottoman military reverses in Europe.

In 1584 Pope Gregory XIII founded a Maronite college in Rome to train their clergy, and among the brilliant scholars it produced, many years later, were the Assemani (al-Simʿāni) brothers, one of whom (Yūsuf), served as custodian of the Vatican library. They were among the principal informants of the West about Eastern Christianity. Before the creation of the college, the Maronite church had maintained its essential character, that of a monastic institution. Indeed, the patriarch still resides in the monastery of Qannubin in the sacred valley of Kadisiya (al-Qādisīyah) when he is not at the official residence in Bakırköy.

Three synods (1580, 1596, 1598) were convened by the Maronite patriarch at the urging of the papal legates for the purpose of introducing the legislation of Trent and the Latin liturgy, which called for relaxing their fasting rules during Lent and other changes in liturgical customs. Patriarch Yūsuf al-Rizzi had already introduced the Gregorian calendar. In the atmosphere of tolerance that prevailed late in the seventeenth century, new monasteries and a number of European missions were established in the East. Patriarch al-Duwayhi in 1700 organized the Maronite order of Saint Anthony, to further buttress the monastic attributes of the church.

Following the Council of Trent, in 1562, efforts were made to Latinize the Eastern churches. Survivors of the Latin kingdom of Jerusalem, which had been ended by Saladin, took refuge among the Maronites and were allegedly responsible for preparing the way for the Latinization of their church. Latinization efforts took on a decisive character in the seventeenth and eighteenth centuries, when the advent of Latin missions helped speed up the process. An added impetus followed the establishment of Maronite orders in the aftermath of the Lebanese synod of 1736.

In 1734 Yūsuf al-Khāzin and his bishops requested the Holy See to send them an apostolic visitor to help them reform their church. The pope sent al-Simʿāni as his personal legate to call a synod of the Maronite hierarchy and to preside over it. The synod was held in Rayfun in upper Kisrawān (present-day north-central Lebanon), on 14 September 1736. Customs that were first introduced by the Crusaders were codified, and the synod ended with the Latinization of church liturgical procedures and the administration of the sacraments.

This Mount Lebanon Synod (as it came to be known) split the Maronites. Its enactments generated a five-year crisis that drew in even the Druze ruler of Mount Lebanon (Emir Milḥim Shihāb). A battle was fought between the "Integrists" and the "Reformists," and peace was restored only after the pope took into account Maronite attachment to their time-honored traditions and decreed that they could keep their old customs and liturgy. Maronites were content now to return to their old disciplines. They were permitted to conduct in Syriac their "Mass of Saint James." Their clergy were allowed to marry, elect their own patriarch, and keep the hereditary title "of Antioch." In 1744 Pope Benedict XIV formally confirmed on the current patriarch the title of "Maronite Patriarch of Antioch."

In spite of the controversy it generated, the Synod of Mount Lebanon is remembered as a landmark in Maronite history, in that it led to the formal establishment of the present Maronite diocese. Only Aleppo, however, and sometimes Nicosia and Damascus, had resident bishops—a surviving memory of numerous pre-Islamic eparchies of the Maronites in the Near East.

The austere life they led was noted by a visiting French diplomat, Chevalier Laurent d'Avrieux, who described Maronite life-style as being influenced by monastic institutions (1735). For centuries, they had abided by spiritual and social ways that had been shaped by their monastic environment. Churches were erected in northern Lebanon by private families and were largely the mortmains of these families, which dated back to the twelfth century, in Batrun, Jubayl, and Jubbat Bsharrī.

Seminaries were established for the purpose of training priests—the earliest in 1624, in Hawga, followed by another in Aleppo in the second half of the seventeenth century. They attracted scholars and novices, and more were to follow in Mount Lebanon. The 1818 synod made new efforts to regenerate clerical studies. A major central seminary was established at ʿAyn Waraga. After returning to Lebanon in 1831, the Jesuits opened an interritual seminary in Ghazir in 1844, which was converted in 1875 to the University of Saint Joseph and relocated in East Beirut. In 1881 it became the first pontifical university in the East.

Bibliography

Avrieux, Chevalier Laurent d' (1735). *Mémoires du Chevalier d'Avrieux*. 6 vols. Paris.

Blaybil, Lewis (1924). *History of the Lebanese Maronite Order* (in Arabic). Cairo.

Gibbon, Edward (1776–1788). *The History of the Decline and Fall of the Roman Empire*. 6 vols. London.

El-Hayek, Elias (1967). "Maronite Rite." In *The New Catholic Encyclopedia*. Vol. 9, 247–253. New York: McGraw-Hill.

Joseph, John (1983). *Muslim-Christian Relations and Inter-Christian Rivalries in the Middle East*. Albany: State University of New York Press.

Mahfoud, George Joseph (1967). *L'organisation monastique dans l'Église Maronite*. Jounieh, Lebanon: Université Saint-Esprit de Kaslik.

Mahfoud, Pierre (1965). *Joseph Simon Assémani*. Rome.

Naaman, Paul (1971). *Théodoret de Cyr et le Monastère de Saint Maron: Les origines des Maronites. Essai d'histoire et de géographie*. Jounieh, Lebanon: Université Saint-Esprit de Kaslik.

Ristelheuber, René (1925). *Les traditions françaises au Liban*. Paris.

Salibi, Kamal (1959). *Maronite Historians of Medieval Lebanon*. Beirut: American University of Beirut Press.

Vailhé, S. (1906). "L'Église Maronite du Vè au IXè siècle." In *Échos d'Orient*. Paris.

CAESAR E. FARAH

Mbeere

ETHNONYMS: Embu, Mbere

Orientation

Identification. The Mbeere live in Embu District in the Eastern Province of Kenya, East Africa. The name "Mbeere" means "first," referring to their belief that they were the initial occupants of their territory. The earlier literature sometimes referred to them as "Embu," who are distinct but culturally close neighbors. Other accounts have described both the Mbeere and Embu as "subgroups" of the Kikuyu.

Location. Mbeere territory, comprising more than 1,500 square kilometers in the southeastern part of Embu District, is an area of variable rainfall, soil types, and vegetation. It is divided into three ecological zones that fall away from Mount Kenya along a northwest-to-southeast gradient. The zone above 1,000 meters supports banana and maize cultivation. The middle zone, between 750 and 1,000 meters, sustains millet, sorghum, beans, and drought-resistant maize. The zone below 750 meters, suitable for herding, is a desiccated area of cactus and acacia.

Demography. According to the 1989 national census, the Mbeere inhabitants of Embu District numbered 88,092. Population densities reflect sharp differences in the economic potential of the three ecological zones and range from 10 to over 200 people per square kilometer. The ratio of males to females is 100 to 111, indicating the tendency of men to seek employment outside the territory.

Linguistic Affiliation. The language is known as Kimbeere. It belongs to the Bantu Subfamily, which in turn is a subdivision of the Banue-Congo Group of Niger-Congo languages. Kimbeere is closely related to the other Bantu languages of the Mount Kenya periphery.

History and Cultural Relations

Numerous legends recount how various clans migrated to the present territory. Much remains unclear about when and how the migrations occurred. By the mid-nineteenth century, the current ethnographic map of east-central Kenya had taken shape. The Mbeere maintained a variety of shifting relationships with neighboring groups, particularly the Embu, Kamba, Kikuyu, and Chuka. Periodic raids for livestock or grain occurred in times of economic distress. Peaceful trading sometimes took place. The European penetration of East Africa reached Mbeere in 1851, when the German missionary Johann Ludwig Krapf crossed the Tana River. The British established a protectorate in Kenya in 1895 and secured control over Embu District in 1906. Catholic and Anglican missionaries soon followed and established the first schools. Travel and social connections to towns and cities have been facilitated by great improvements in roads. Increasing rates of literacy and the availability of telecommunications further enhance awareness of national and international events affecting local communities.

Settlements

The Mbeere customarily live in small, circular, thatched houses made of wooden poles and mud. A group of houses comprises a homestead, which includes families related to each other, usually through patrilineal kinship ties. In physical terms, a homestead may include a cattle kraal, goat and sheep shelters built like thatched houses, and granaries. Homesteads range in size from newly formed units composed of a married pair and their young children to long-established settlements of more than forty people. A homestead is bounded by its gardens, fallow lands, and bush areas.

Economy

Subsistence and Commercial Activities. Horticulture is central to the economy. The most important crops are maize, millet, sorghum, beans, cassava, sugarcane, bananas, and mangoes. Tobacco and cotton are the most important cash crops. The distribution and relative importance of these cultigens vary according to soil type, elevation, and amount of rainfall. The Mbeere value livestock, particularly cattle, sheep, and goats, as markers of wealth and prestige. Their distribution varies by ecological zone. Herd sizes tend to increase in the low-lying areas. Chickens and ducks are ubiquitous, but owning them carries no prestige. The Mbeere also exploit a number of wild-food resources such as fruits. The most important and valued wild food is honey. It is eaten raw and used in the preparation of beer.

Industrial Arts. Among Mbeere crafts are pottery and woven basketry, both practiced by women. Leather is worked by men. Blacksmiths, always men, manufacture decorative rings, spear and adze blades, knives, arrow points, razors, and the like. Decorative gourds are fashioned by women, and various carved wooden items, including bows, arrows, and spear handles, by men. Production of these items had steadily diminished given the growing cash economy; substitute consumer goods are available in rural shops. Manufacture of metal weaponry has also diminished with the cessation of warfare, reduction of wild game, and the official hunting ban on large animals.

Trade. Trading relationships were an essential feature of traditional society and helped even out the effects of shortages or famines. The Mbeere traded various goods, livestock, and foodstuffs with their neighbors. In the colonial era, formal markets were established throughout Embu District, including the largest one, begun in 1927, at Ishiara in lower Mbeere. The markets included shops and a weekly open-air bazaar for the sale of livestock, produce, processed foods, locally manufactured crafts, and inexpensive imported consumer items.

Division of Labor. A sexual division of labor sharply defines many activities. Men control livestock and gather honey. They hunt and clear fields. Both men and women cultivate, harvest, and gather other wild foods without restriction. Likewise, marketing activities are unrestricted. Craft production is clearly delineated by sex: only men forge metal, and only women produce pottery and basketry. Women perform most domestic tasks such as grinding grains, gathering firewood, drawing water, and cooking.

Land Tenure. Land was traditionally a plentiful resource. Individuals or family groups could claim pieces of uncultivated bush and begin clearing it for cultivation. Pasturage was also freely available. Once land was claimed, it remained inalienable within the founding patrilineal segment, although an individual could pledge his piece of lineage land in exchange for livestock or some other value. The pledge was redeemable because an individual could regain his land on repayment of what he had received in exchange. Lineage land was heritable by male descendants. A woman did not inherit lineage land but was allocated gardens by her husband from his own lineage property. This pattern has been altered dramatically since the end of World War II as land has become a commodity, convertible into cash and controlled increasingly by individuals rather than groups. Beginning in the 1950s and continuing with the independent government, this pattern has gained legal sanction, as individual ownership has become the centerpiece of a land-reform program. Contemporary land tenure thus emphasizes individual ownership of registered plots of land. The constraints previously exercised by one's lineage on the use or disposition of land are now greatly diminished.

Kinship

Kin Groups and Descent. Patrilineal descent organized lineage of varying depth. The *mũcii*, or home, constitutes a shallow lineage, which sometimes embraces four generations. It holds land collectively. Lineages in turn are embedded in dispersed noncorporate exogamous clans. These form nonexogamous moieties. In the 1960s, when land became scarce, larger lineages grew more important. They mobilize to press claims for very large parcels of land. These parcels could then be divided among the membership, according to government directive. Descent coalitions consisting of several lineages of the same clan also emerged to establish their interests in sizable blocks of land.

Kinship Terminology. Terms of address and reference are distinguished for several categories of kin. Bifurcate-merging terminology marks Ego's parental generation. In Ego's generation, a variant of the Iroquois system occurs. Parallel cousins and siblings are equated, but both are collectively differentiated from cross cousins. Patrilateral and matrilateral cross cousins may be categorized together or separated by descriptive terms. Grandparents and grandchildren use reciprocal designations. Various classificatory usages and other extensions of primary kin terms are utilized. All men of father's generation and clan are classed as fathers. Members of father's age set or generation set are similarly classified.

Marriage and Family

Marriage. Bride-wealth paid out over a number of years legitimates marriage. Clan mates and second-degree cross cousins are ineligible to marry. Polygyny is valued but occurs infrequently. The number of wives is not limited by any cultural rule, although sororal polygyny is prohibited. At marriage, a woman takes up residence in her own dwelling at the homestead of her husband. He maintains his own sleeping quarters, where he can also entertain his age mates. If he marries a second wife, she will have her own residence, where she will cook and support her children separately from her cowife. Traditionally, divorce was infrequent. Secondary patterns of marriage include the true levirate and the fictive marriage of women. These forms of marriage can occur when a union has failed to produce male heirs. Numerous changes in marriage patterns include increasing numbers of Christian unions and growing resistance to bride-wealth payment.

Domestic Unit. Each homestead is comprised of several types of domestic units, including elementary, polygynous, and extended families. Each married woman in the homestead normally has her own house, where she cooks, maintains her children, and is visited by her husband. Following initiation, a son moves out of his mother's house. The coresident patrilineal kinsmen of the homestead founder constitute the core of a shallow lineage. The founder exercises considerable, but not exclusive, authority in economic matters concerning the group.

Inheritance. Inheritance follows patrilineal principles. In polygynous marriages, the rules of the house-property complex operate. A man's allocation of land and livestock to his wife will pass to her sons. Daughters inherit only minor property such as household implements because they will receive allocations of land and livestock from their husbands at marriage. An elder son often inherits more than his brothers and is entrusted with the responsibility of managing the corporate property.

Socialization. Prolonged nursing and indulgent child rearing are the norm. Large homesteads and nearby female kin, both matrilateral and patrilateral, provide an extensive number of care givers besides the biological mother. Older women of the homestead, either grandmothers or classificatory equivalents, take an active role in nurturing children. Older siblings frequently act as nurses for the very young.

Sociopolitical Organization

Traditional society lacked chiefs. The political system was diffuse and unorganized beyond the local level of the homestead or neighborhood, where principles of kinship and age organized social and political relations. The imposition of colonial rule led to the appointment of chiefs, the centralization of authority, and the creation of political hierarchy.

Social Organization. Shallow patrilineages and complementary affinal and uterine relationships lay at the center of kinship organization. Classificatory extensions of lineage relations encompassed people of the patriclan. Male age sets and generation classes also organized social relations. Exclusively male groups, determined by age and generation, formalized the influence of male elderhood, both in political and ritual matters. The age and generational systems proved very fragile under colonial influence and have not been viable institutions since the early 1950s. Lineage affiliation remains important, but its value has been turned toward protecting one's interest in land under the government program of land reform.

Political Organization. Male elders were invested with considerable influence, exercised formally in councils. The councils were not standing bodies. They were situationally activated by each dispute within the neighborhood. Elderhood, marked by membership in one or another senior age set, defined eligibility for participation in a council. Especially able elders, eloquent in speech and skilled at mediation, regularly were called by disputants to help settle their cases. Resolution emphasized arbitration and compromise rather than adjudication. Elder men enjoyed special powers of cursing, which insured that the effected compromise would be honored. A disputant violating the terms of settlement might fall ill through the effects of a curse. Councils continue to meet, but their functions and range of action have greatly diminished owing to imposed court systems and chiefs.

Social Control. Informal mechanisms of social control, including ridicule and songs of mockery, are effective in limiting deviant behavior. Curses and the threat of sorcery also function to insure conformity by threatening illness, infertility, or death against people who might otherwise ignore the force of collective opinion.

Conflict. Cattle raids ended at the close of the nineteenth century, when Kamba and Mbeere warriors fought skirmishes on either side of the Tana River. Until that time, the Mbeere engaged in intermittent warfare against their Bantu neighbors and, occasionally, against the Maasai. Internal raids among Mbeere also ended at the same time. Food shortages usually prompted the warrior forays.

Religion and Expressive Culture

Religious Beliefs. The Mbeere believe in a High God, Ngai, said to live atop Mount Kenya. Ngai created humanity and all else in the world. Little mythological elaboration about the activities or manifestations of Ngai has developed. He stays at a distance from the lives of people, although they periodically offer sacrifices to secure his blessing for rain and abundant livestock. More intrusive and less welcome in human affairs are ancestral spirits bringing illness and death. They may act for an understandable reason, or they may punish capriciously. The spirits inhabit hilltops, the bush, or other areas beyond human habitation. People try to keep them at bay by right conduct and by not disturbing areas where they are believed to dwell. Christian churches, particularly Catholic and Anglican, have won numerous converts. The churches have shown little tolerance for traditional beliefs and actions regarding ancestral spirits.

Religious Practitioners. Diviners, medicinal specialists, and healers who treat illness induced by magical means are collectively known as medicine men (*andũ ago;* sing. *mundũ mũgo*). Women may also practice these specialities, but they do so infrequently. Each specialty is learned through apprenticeship or instruction. Sorcerers (*arogi;* sing. *mũrogi*) cause mayhem and illness through their curses or magical actions and are generally feared. Occasionally, a prophet (*mũrathi*) emerges with the power to foretell events.

Ceremonies. The major ceremonies celebrate seasonal and life-cycle transitions. Rites of sacrifice were the province of two generation classes; these rites sought to insure adequate rain for good crops and the health of livestock. Sacrifices occurred at the onset of the rainy season and the dry season. The life-cycle transition most elaborated ritually is initiation of young men and women into adulthood. At about age 15, young men are circumcised. Young women, prior to the onset of first menstruation, traditionally would undergo circumcision, or clitoridectomy. They were then eligible to marry. Missionaries unsparingly attacked female circumcision on religious and medical grounds. There have also been official government efforts to ban it. Many Christian women reject the custom. The practice continues amid strong feelings on both sides of the issue. Its frequency is certainly much less under these various pressures. Male circumcision remains universal. It is increasingly performed in hospitals without traditional ritual accoutrements. Missionaries have also criticized the beer consumption and the erotic songs and dances accompanying both the male and female rite.

Arts. Mbeere aesthetics center on the verbal arts, song, and dance. Riddles, folktales, and proverbs are popular forms of creative expression that also contain strongly didactic messages. The rite of circumcision was an important occasion for song and dance performance, which emphasized collective participation rather than solo virtuosity.

Medicine. The Kimbeere term for medicine, *mũthege*, is broader than its English rendering. It includes ingested substances prepared from plants. These derivatives combat malaria, coughing, stomach distress, and the like. Additionally, mũthege comprises various objects such as gourds, animal horns, or other organs manipulated by a medicine man or woman seeking to cure. The theory of disease accounts for illness in terms of naturalistic and mystical, or supernatural, causation. The latter includes sorcery, cursing, or affliction by ancestors.

Death and Afterlife. A concept of the afterlife is little developed, and death ritual is traditionally very austere. Corpses were set out in the bush for hyenas to carry off. Burial became the norm under colonial rule. If a person dies within the home, it should be destroyed by fire to remove the taint of death. The dead person joins other spirits in the wilderness, where they may make their presence known by nocturnal singing. A spirit, by itself, or with other ancestors, can afflict the living, who remain very fearful of ghostly actions. People claim that the spirits sing much less frequently than in the past and that they have been driven off by Christians. Accordingly, attribution of illness or suffering to the ancestors has declined.

Bibliography

Glazier, Jack (1976). "Generation Classes among the Mbeere of Central Kenya." *Africa* 46(4): 313–326.

Glazier, Jack (1984). "Mbeere Ancestors and the Domestication of Death." *Man* 19(1): 133–147.

Glazier, Jack (1985). *Land and the Uses of Tradition among the Mbeere of Kenya*. Lanham, Md., New York, and London: University Press of America.

Middleton, John, and Greet Kershaw (1965). *The Kikuyu and Kamba of Kenya*. London: International African Institute.

Riley, Bernard W., and David Brokensha (1988). *The Mbeere in Kenya*. Vol. 1, *Changing Rural Ecology*. Lanham, Md., New York, and London: Unversity Press of America.

JACK GLAZIER

Mende

ETHNONYMS: Boumpe, Hulo, Kossa, Kosso

The Mende are a group of people who live primarily within the southern third of Sierre Leone. Historically, they are rather recent arrivals to this area, appearing no earlier than the sixteenth century as invading forces advancing from the south. Linguistically, the Mende are related to Niger-Kordofanian and Niger-Congo groupings; they have at least two major dialects—Kpa and Ko—and two less prominent dialects—Waanjama and Sewawa. In 1987 the Mende numbered about one million, of whom 75 to 80 percent were Kpa Mende and most of the remaining portion, Ko Mende. The Mende comprise about 30 percent of Sierre Leone's total population.

The small country of Sierre Leone, of which the Mende occupy the southern portion, lies very close to the equator on the western coast of Africa. The climate is distinguished by a dry season from October to May and a wet season from June to October. There is much variation in humidity, sunshine, and rainfall, depending on the terrain, the distance from the coast, and the time of year. Until the twentieth century, much of the terrain consisted of forests, which have since been greatly reduced by clearing for farming. Farm-bush is the dominant vegetation type of the southern part of the country, where the Mende reside.

The Mende live primarily in villages of 70 to 250 residents, which are situated from 1.5 to 5 kilometers apart. There is little or no mechanization over the greater part of rural Mende country. Mende farmers use hoes and machetes, but few other tools. Coffee, cocoa, and ginger are grown as cash crops, whereas rice, pepper, groundnuts, beniseed, and palm oil are grown for local consumption. Rice cooperatives have been formed in some rural areas.

Work is divided by gender: men attend to the heavy work of clearing the land for planting rice while women are occupied with cleaning and pounding rice, fishing, and weeding the planted crops. This routine is followed during ten months of every year, with a couple of months left around the New Year, when they can spend more time in the village engaging in domestic pursuits like house building.

The household unit is represented by at least one man and perhaps several of his brothers, with all of their wives and children. One or more brothers and married sisters usually leave sooner or later and are incorporated into other residential units. The senior male has moral authority—the right to respect and obedience—over the family as a whole, especially with regard to the negotiation of debts, damages, and bridewealth.

Because of their recent origins, their contact with other peoples in the area, their involvement in the slave trade, and the strong influence of Islam and later colonial powers, as well as missionary contact, it is difficult and perhaps misleading to speak of the traditional culture of the Mende. Mende culture is an eclectic blend that has resulted from all of these different influences. Mende religion, likewise, has native elements—a Supreme Being, ancestral spirits, secret societies, and witch finders—that coexist with and are sometimes interspersed with adherence to Christian or Islamic beliefs.

Bibliography

Gittins, Anthony J. (1987). *Mende Religion: Aspects of Belief and Thought in Sierra Leone*. Wort und Werk. Nettetal: Steyler Verlag.

Harris, W. T., and H. Sawyerr (1968). *The Springs of Mende Belief and Conduct*. Freetown: Sierra Leone University Press; Oxford University Press.

Jedrej, M. C. (1974). "An Analytic Note on the Land and Spirits of the Sewa Mende." *Africa* 44:38–45.

Mijikenda

ETHNONYMS: Chonyi, Digo, Duruma, Giriama, Jibana, Kambe, Kauma, Nyika, Rabai, Ribe

Orientation

The group known as the Mijikenda is made up of nine closely related but distinct peoples—the Kauma, Chonyi, Jibana, Giriama, Kamabe, Ribe, Rabai, Duruma, and Digo—who live along the coast of Kenya and share a common linguistic and cultural heritage. Traditionally, each group lived within its own hilltop village (*kaya*) on the ridge along the Kenya coast, between the towns of Kilili and Vanga.

The members of each of the nine Mijikenda groups speak a separate dialect of the same language. That language, Mijikenda, is one of the Northeast Coastal Bantu Group of languages and is closely related linguistically and historically to other languages along the Kenyan and Tanzanian coasts. There were an estimated 730,000 Mijikenda speakers in 1980. The largest groups of Mijikenda are the Giriama, who numbered about 350,000 in 1987, and the Duruma, with a population of approximately 190,000 in 1986. Some of the dialects are mutually intelligible; some are not.

While change has come to the Mijikenda, they have maintained many of the beliefs and practices of their traditional culture. They have resisted the conversion attempts of Muslim and Christian missionaries to a much greater extent than many of their neighbors, and they adhere to many beliefs that were derived from their traditional religion, which was a form of ancestor worship. They have incorporated the myth of their origins, as well as a description of their kaya-based, stratified social structure, into a written record of their culture, which is passed on to their children.

According to a Mijikenda myth, the Mijikenda orginated in Singwaya (or Shungwaya), which was to the north of the Somali coast. They were driven south by the Oromo until they reached their present locations along the ridge, where they built their kayas within a protective setting. The historical accuracy of this myth is a point of controversy between those who believe that the Mijikenda originated from a single point in the north and those who believe that they do not have a single origin, but migrated primarily from the south.

Economy

The most fertile area in Mijikenda is the kaya ridge. It receives 89 to 127 centimeters of rain annually, in two rainy seasons (from March through May and from September through October). In the past, this area was densely forested, but now much of the land is planted with fruit trees: mango, cashew, orange, and coconut palms. Along the narrow band next to the coast are planted annual crops, such as sorghum, maize, and rice, as well as groves of fruit trees. The interior plateau is a drier and less fertile area that borders the Taru Desert to the west. At a distance of 40 to 48 kilometers inland, precipitation drops below 64 centimeters annually, and cultivation becomes nearly impossible.

When everyone still lived within the hilltop villages, people cultivated the lower slopes of the hills and the adjacent plateau. Fields were used for a few years and then allowed to lie fallow for a longer period. By the mid-nineteenth century, people began to move away from the hilltop villages to vacant land. They burned away the virgin woodlands of the plateau, settling there for a few years and then moving on. The traditional staple crops of the Mijikenda were sorghum and millet, but these two cultigens were largely replaced during the nineteenth century by maize. Additional food crops were beans, cassava, sweet potatoes, and yams. Coconuts and castor seeds were grown for oil, and coconuts, sesame, sorghum, millet, and maize were traded.

The most important crop of the Mijikenda is the coconut palm. The major products of the coconut palm are the oil that is extracted from the meat, the palm wine tapped from the shoots, and the fronds, which are woven into baskets, mats, and roofing shingles. In the eastern areas, each homestead also keeps a few goats, sheep, chickens, and ducks for domestic consumption. Galla and Kwavi raids restricted cattle keeping until late in the nineteenth century, but today cattle are kept in the marginal areas to the west.

Kinship, Marriage, and Family

Prior to the mid-nineteenth century, each Mijikenda group lived together in or near its own kaya. Each kaya was located in a cleared, circular glade on a hilltop, surrounded by dense forest. At the center of the kaya were the meeting houses of the different clans. Surrounding each clan house were the individual residences of its members. The clans were unilineal-descent groups that were primarily patrilineal, and this pattern varied from kaya to kaya. The number of clans remained constant, but each clan was further divided into subclans, which increased in number as new members were born into the group and as alien groups were adopted. Each subclan was further divided into local lineage groups that lived together in homesteads. The homestead averaged three generations, but its membership was not fixed. The ideal homestead included a man, his sons, and his grandsons, but sons could form their own separate homesteads.

The clans played a central role in kaya affairs. Each clan had its own area within the kaya and its own specialized function. The subclans were not important political units, but they played an important role in the social life of the Mijikenda, particularly with regard to the organization of major social evevts, such as weddings and funerals. The local lineage was the local residential group that farmed the land corporately held by the homestead head.

Each kaya was divided by age as well as by descent. The men of the kaya were formed into age sets (sing. *rika*), and the members of a given age set progressed together from childhood through adolescence to adulthood. The age sets existed on two levels. Every four years, the uninitiated boys were circumcised and initiated into a sub-rika. When thirteen such sub-rikas had been initiated, all were then corporately initiated as the next rika. The senior three sub-rikas ruled for twelve years and were succeeded by the following two sub-rikas, which ruled for eight years. This pattern continued by pairs until all thirteen sub-rikas had ruled as senior elders, at which time the succeeding thirteen sub-rikas were initiated as the next rika.

Sociopolitical Organization

Traditional Mijikenda society was primarily a gerontocracy: old men had authority over young men, and both old and young men had authority over women. If members objected to their positions in the hierarchy, they could leave and find other sources of power or support. Rabai women, for example, created their own sacred friction drum, which was used to extract fees from any outsiders who inadvertently saw it. Similarly, spirit possession by women, who could become mediums for messages from the ancestors, has been used to extract material goods from men. These female mediums sometimes formed tactical alliances with kaya elders.

The power of the elders was sometimes challenged in disputes over rain magic. Given that insufficient rains often led to famines, control over the rain was a highly valued skill. Such control was a source of ritual power for kaya elders because it was their duty to take corrective actions, usually in the form of organizing rain-making ceremonies, if the rains stopped. Sanctions for not fulfilling their duties included physical attacks and accusations of witchcraft, which could result in murder.

The Mijikenda were not directly involved in the slave trade, but they did buy, sell, and kidnap people for their labor. These people were not classified as slaves, but as resources of a clan. As such, they could be used as a form of exchange between homesteads or between an individual family and a nonkin patron, especially in times of need (e.g., during famines). Dependents could be moved between homesteads of their own accord or transferred to another homestead by the homestead head. The person handed over occupied a generally low position, but his or her transfer still served to strengthen the family that acquired the dependent and was not regarded as slavery. This kind of arrangement also occurred between distantly related or nonkin groups: individuals could sell themselves or their dependents to a patron who could provide them with the immediate needs for their survival. This practice was known as "pawning"; there was always the possibility that the pawns could be sold if the original loan was not repaid.

Because young men and, especially, young women were the least powerful people in the homesteads, it was they who bore the brunt of any shortage of food. Also, the wealthier families could call in their debts in time of famine and rely on the support of those networks that their wealth had created. The dependents of lesser patrons, without such support, often tried to place themselves in new networks by leaving the homesteads of their paternal kin in search of new patrons before their seniors sold them or pawned them for food. Such migration was not always in response to famines; sometimes it was prompted by arguments between the generations.

Bibliography

Champion, Arthur M. (1967). *The Agiryama of Kenya*. London: Royal Anthropological Institute of Great Britain and Ireland.

Eastman, C. (1971). "Who Are the Waswahile?" *Africa* 41:228–236.

Gallagher, J. T., ed. (1976). *East African Culture History*. Syracuse: Syracuse University, Maxwell School of Citizenship and Public Affairs.

Grimes, Barbara F., ed. (1988). *Ethnologue: Languages of the World*. Dallas: Summer Institute of Linguistics.

Mutoro, Henry W. (1985). "Spatial Distribution of the Mijikenda Kaya Settlements on the Hinterland Kenya Coast." *Trans-African Journal of History* 14:78–100.

Spear, Thomas T. (1978). *The Kaya Complex: A History of the Mijikenda Peoples of the Kenya Coast to 1900*. Nairobi: Kenya Literature Bureau.

Spear, Thomas T. (1981). *Traditions of Origin and Their Interpretation*. Papers in International Studies. Africa Series, 42. Athens: Ohio University Center for International Studies.

Willis, Justin (1993). *Mombasa, the Swahili, and the Making of the Mijikenda*. Oxford Studies in African Affairs. Oxford: Clarendon Press.

Mongo

ETHNONYM: Lomongo

Orientation

The Mongo inhabit the Congo Basin of central Zaire. They speak a dialect or language within a larger group of Mongo languages, which are themselves within, or related to, the Niger-Kordofanian, Niger-Congo, Benue-Congo, Bantoid, and Bantu groups. There are 216,000 speakers of the Mongo dialect (Welmers 1971) and 3,200,000 speakers of the entire group of Mongo languages (Hayes, Ornstein, and Gage 1977).

The climate of the Congo Basin is noted for its high temperatures, abundant rainfall, and high humidity. Equatorial forests cover more than 1,040,000 square kilometers of the 3.9 million square kilometers of the basin. The distribution of flora and fauna is uneven, however, creating local habitats that have led to variations in human life-styles.

The Mongo began to enter the central part of the Congo Basin around the first century A.D. The first migrants probably settled in the most favorable ecological niches, mainly along rivers, where fishing became a major productive activity. Other groups moved inland to engage in hunting and yam farming. The banana, which produced larger food harvests than the yam, became a staple crop around A.D. 1000.

The colonial experience and the independence that followed drastically changed Mongo culture, as well as the cultures of all of the other indigenous peoples of Zaire. Many traditional Mongo beliefs and practices have survived, and they continue to be prevalent within the wider Zairean society today, despite the pressures to assimilate to the Zairean national culture. Clearly, the Mongo participate in the Zairean economy and work within a national labor force. They attend private or nationalized schools, and they have converted to Christianity in large numbers. It also seems clear that the Mongo have retained their tribal or ethnic identity, which implies the survival of key aspects of their traditional culture.

Economy

Gathering natural resources and foodstuffs was and still is an important subsistence activity. The Mongo harvest a wide range of products from the equatorial forest: wild fruits, vegetables, palm kernels, mushrooms, snails, and edible insects (e.g., caterpillars, termites), as well as roots and vegetation used for beverages, spices, and medicines. Products harvested from the *Elaeis* oil palm are especially important.

Traditionally, small animals were trapped using ropes with nooses. Larger animals, such as antelopes, boars, and elephants, were tracked and hunted by groups of men with nets, bows and arrows, and long stabbing spears. Small hunting expeditions were mounted year-round by groups of young men, and special celebrations or feasts were often marked by villagewide hunts.

By the nineteenth century, agriculture had become an important part of Mongo subsistence activities. Maize, groundnuts, and beans were introduced to Central Africa by the Portuguese in the sixteenth century, augmenting the established staples of yams, bananas, oil palms, and other crops. Some foodstuffs and medicinal plants, such as sweet bananas, hot peppers, and indigenous greens, were grown in small homesite gardens established near residences. Major crops, such as yams and bananas, were cultivated in larger fields, farther away from the homestead. The Mongo practiced shifting agriculture by rotating fields. After three to five years of cultivation, new fields were cleared, and the old fields were left to be reclaimed by tropical vegetation.

Kinship, Marriage, and Family

The household, village, and district were the three principal territoral units of Mongo society. The household compound (*etuka*) was the primary residence and the main unit of economic production and socialization. The average size of an etuka was generally between twenty and forty members. Each compound was largely autonomous in its internal affairs and was led by a senior elder, who was commonly referred to as "Tata," or "Father." Several compounds in the same area generally formed a village.

Sociopolitical Organization

Villages usually ranged in size from 100 to 300 people. As a cohesive unit, the village undertook certain large tasks, such as clearing the forest, and formed a defensive unit against outside attacks. Community affairs were administered by a council of compound elders and the *bokulaka* (village chief), an elder who had received the council's recognition as group leader. In times of war and instability, dispersed Mongo villages often formed districts, which were essentially territiorial alliances intended to provide for a stronger common defense. In contrast to the situation in the villages, decisions at the district level were made by a loose collection of village chiefs, other prominent male seniors, and medicine men, who were respected for their war magic and divination skills.

The Mongo distinguished gradations in social status in three broad categories: those with authority, those with inferior status, and those with no voice at all in local matters. At the top of village society were the leaders of compounds, who were the dominant "big-men" of the Mongo. They administered the internal affairs of their compounds, delegated tasks and managed food production, acted as arbitrators of disputes, and represented the compounds to the outside world. Within the villages, they formed the councils of elders that governed according to ancestral laws and regulated external relations. These village leaders held special signs of office, consumed the best portions of the hunt, had the most wives, and received respect and deference from the entire community.

There were several categories of people with inferior status in Mongo society. The largest group with low status were the women, who clearly occupied a lower social rung than the men. Although economically incorporated into her husband's family, a wife remained a member of her own family politically, and she had little say in the larger issues concerning the community. Women were given the monotonous task of gathering foods and forest products; men gathered only the items that were considered more prestigious. With few exceptions, women did not possess individual property and could not dispose of the fruits of their labor without the consent of their husbands. They also received harsher penalties than men for social infractions such as adultery.

Refugees, maternal kin, and slaves were other groups with low status in Mongo society. They were all considered inferior to the resident kin group and were dependent upon the reigning big-men. The refugees were groups of people, usually comprising one or two household compounds, who had fled their homes because of war, famine, or epidemics. Groups or individuals sometimes left their own household compounds to find refuge with their maternal kin for personal reasons (such as being denied bride-price or being obliged to leave following serious offenses, such as murder).

Most slaves were captured as a consequence of small-scale warfare. Separated from the protection of their kin, slaves had no rights. They were completely dependent on their patrons—politically, economically, and socially. In most cases, slaves were well treated even though they remained socially inferior. Their loyalty was ensured through controlled assimilation by their masters, who provided the slaves with wives and land. Masters also protected their slaves from the abuse and exploitation of others.

Kinship and seniority were both important in Mongo society. Political authority was based on wealth, but it was legitimized according to genealogical descent. Once established, big-men maintained or increased their power through land allocation, matrimonial exchange, and rights of appropriation, which were all expressed in terms of kinship and seniority. Young men were expected to follow the direction of their elders because they, too, would eventually inherit positions of power and prestige.

Religion and Expressive Culture

Ideological and moral principles and social reality are mirrored in the culture of the Mongo, particularly in their oral literature, which includes histories, folktales, proverbs, poems, songs, and greetings. Traditional folktales, which were usually centered on a moral or a piece of wisdom, were an essential part of a child's education, and proverbs dealt with all aspects of life, although the ideals of mutual obligation, respect for authority, and the importance of the family were particularly stressed.

The worship of ancestors played a central part in the traditional religion of the Mongo. People believed in a number of different deities and spirits, including a Supreme Being, but these were approachable only through the intervention of deceased elders and relatives. Prayers for healthy children, success in battle, or safe journeys were therefore addressed to the ancestors. The practice of witchcraft was also a part of Mongo culture. Villagers attributed most types of misfortune—including illness, infertility, bad luck, or extreme poverty—to spells or charms in operation against them. These, in turn, were most often attributed to a competitor's greed, ambition, or hatred. At the same time, significant good fortune or success was perceived to be linked to the possession of beneficial charms and amulets, of which the witch doctor possessed more than anyone else in the village.

Bibliography

Birmingham, David, and Phyllis M. Martin, eds. (1983). *History of Central Africa*. Vol. 2. New York: Longman.

Fetter, Bruce (1983). *Colonial Rule and Regional Imbalances in Central Africa*. Boulder, Colo.: Westview Press.

Hayes, Curtis W., Jacob Ornstein, and William W. Gage (1977). "Appendix: Languages of the World." In *ABC's of Languages and Linguistics*. Silver Springs, Md.: Institute of Modern Languages.

Jewsiewicki, Bogumil (1981). "Lineage Modes of Production: Social Inequalities in Equatorial Central Africa." In *Modes of Production in Africa: The Precolonial Era*, edited by Donald E. Crummy and Charles C. Stewart, 93–113. Beverly Hills, Calif.: Sage Publications.

Miracle, Marvin (1967). *Agriculture in the Congo Basin: Tradition and Change in African Rural Economies*. Madison: University of Wisconsin Press.

Nelson, Samuel H. (1994). *Colonialism in the Congo Basin, 1880–1940*. Monographs in International Studies. Africa Series, no. 64. Oslo: Oslo University Center for International Studies.

Reid, Rev. Alexander James (1979). *The Roots of Lomomba: Mongo Land*. Hicksville, N.Y.: Exposition Press.

Vansina, Jan (1979). "Finding Food and the History of Pre-Colonial Equatorial Africa: A Plea." *African Economic History* 7:9–20.

Welmers, William E. (1971). "Checklist of Language and Dialect Names." In *Linguistics in Sub-Saharan Africa*, edited by Thomas A. Sebeok, 759–900. Current Trends in Linguistics Series, 7. The Hague: Mouton.

RONALD JOHNSON

Mossi

ETHNONYMS: "Moose" is the currently favored form according to the nationally adopted orthography. It is traditionally written "Mossi"; "Moshi" formerly appeared frequently in British and Ghanaian writing. "Mosi" also occurs. One contemporary scholar who employs the officially favored spelling notes for his Anglophone readers that the pronunciation is "MOH-say" (Fiske 1991, 24).

Orientation

Identification. The Mossi are the most prominent ethnic group in the modern nation of Burkina Faso (formerly Upper Volta). They are also well known in the anthropological literature as a society with an especially high rate of labor migration to neighboring countries. They are noted historically for their resistance to the regionally dominant Islamic states and missionaries, although their culture shows numerous Islamic influences.

Location. The traditionally Mossi areas expanded at the moment of French conquest (1896–1897) from the central core, or so-called Mossi plateau, of Burkina Faso. There are also significant numbers of Mossi in Ivory Coast (where they are the second-largest ethnic group) and in Ghana. The core area, however, is approximately 11°30′ to 14°00′ N and 0°00′ to 3°00′ E. Names and boundaries of local government units have changed repeatedly in the modern era; Mossi country can be defined generally as the area of Burkina containing the cities of Ouahigouya, Kongoussi, Kaya, Koudougou, Ouagadougou, Manga, Tenkodogo, Koupela, and Boulsa.

The Mossi states were well placed for trade; they were "inland" from the great bend of the Niger River, where the empires of Ghana, Mali, and Songhay rose and fell. At the same time, they were north of Asante and the other Akan states that come to prominence as trade shifted from trans-Saharan toward European outposts on the coast.

Because of the proximity of Mossi country to the more prosperous (at times) economies of Ghana and Ivory Coast, the relatively dense Mossi population, and the poverty (in colonial and postcolonial economic terms) of Burkina Faso, very substantial numbers of Mossi have drawn upon their precolonial trade and frontier traditions of movement, working and even settling in neighboring countries.

Demography. The Mossi make up approximately half of the population of Burkina Faso. The national censuses of 1975 and 1985 did not report national statistics for ethnicity. The 1961 sample survey reported 49 percent of the population of the then Upper Volta to be Mossi. If that figure is carried forward to the 1985 population of 7,964,705, there would then be some 3.9 million Mossi. The 49-percent figure, apart from deriving from a 10-percent sample, was often suspected of having been politically manipulated to deny the dominant ethnic group in the new country formal majority status. Therefore, a figure of 4 million or so Mossi should be considered the minimum. The 1994 CIA *World Factbook* estimates the population of Burkina Faso as 10,134,661 in July of 1994; that same source estimates the Mossi population as 2.5 million, lower than the 4.96 million that is 49 percent of the 1994 estimated population. Given that estimates of the Mossi population of Burkina Faso residing outside the country as labor migrants at any one time range as high as 20 percent, a higher figure is plausible.

Linguistic Affiliation. The name of the Mossi language was usually written as Moré, although the 1976 national standards stipulate "Moore." It is also encountered as "Molé" or, in more recent works, "Mooré." Labeled "Mossi" in Greenberg's classification (1963), it is a member of the Voltaic of Niger-Congo; "Molé-Dagbané" is also found as a label for the grouping. In recent scholarship, "Moore" is placed in the Oti-Volta Subgroup of the Gur languages; a recent summary notes that "Gur" is common in English and German writing, whereas French scholars more often use "langues voltaïques."

History and Cultural Relations

The Mossi states have existed for at least 500 years; the exact dates and origins of the states and their ruling clans are still debated by scholars. The Mossi were in conflict with the Songhay Empire in the period from 1328 to 1333, and again between 1477 and 1498. In general terms, the Mossi were strong enough that they were never conquered until the French arrived in 1896–1897, but they were not strong enough to do more than raid the kingdoms along the Niger. Their expansion was by annexing other, often stateless, peoples at the edges of Mossi polities, peoples whose general culture was the same and whose languages were related. Within one generation of the French conquest, French writers had already employed the term *mossification* to describe the assimilationist expansion of the Mossi states into surrounding communities.

Settlements

Rural communities are dispersed: each extended-family compound is surrounded by fields; households are therefore 75 to 100 meters apart. When millet is fully grown (with stalks up to 4 meters), each compound is invisible to others. Boundaries may be based upon natural features like streams, but the dispersed settlement pattern forces recognition that communities are social and political—not geographic—units. It is often impossible to assign a compound to one village or another on a basis of location. Households are compounds of adobe, usually circular, houses with thatched roofs and surrounded by adobe walls. Although metal roofs are hotter and noisier and hence less comfortable than thatch, their prestige value and lessened maintenance has made them common, if not yet dominant, in the countryside.

District chiefs tended to live in noticeably larger compounds, but in villages that otherwise resembled ordinary ones. Kings, however, lived in larger towns or cities—places with artisans, sizable markets, and links to long-distance trade.

In the colonial and postcolonial periods, there has been an increase in movement to towns, but also an increase in ease of communication for rural villages and in capital available to them from their migrant members.

The modern ease of communications—better roads and motor transport, railroads, and telecommunications—has greatly expanded the social field within which individuals and families live and move while still remaining participating members of their home social and ritual communities. The still-high rate of labor migration nowadays takes place within a network of relatives and neighbors already in a several-country region, who can house and sponsor, if not directly employ, the new migrant.

Economy

Subsistence and Commercial Activities. The basis for life throughout the region was (and is) the cultivation of millet and sorghum. Millet flour is made into porridge, eaten with a sauce of meat and/or leaves and condiments. Sorghum is made into beer. Because of the lack of substantial agricultural surpluses, together with a cultural expectation that each household head grow his own millet for subsistence, almost everyone was a farmer. Many cultivators also engaged in local market trading; indeed, sale of beer on market days was the main source of independent income for women. As is usual for West Africa, markets are on a regional rotation; for the Mossi, that cycle is seven days. When a market falls on a Friday, it is especially large and well attended. Formally non-Muslim, this is one of the several ways in which Mossi culture is affected by the Sahelwide presence of Islam.

Industrial Arts. In common with inhabitants of their larger region, Mossi blacksmiths and potters are distinct, castelike, descent groups living in specially named villages or neighborhoods.

Trade. Besides the local markets, which involved much of the population, there are also, among the Mossi, long-distance traders, the Yarsé. Of Mandé origin, from what is now Mali, they settled among the Mossi. They were not unusual in their assimilation of Mossi culture and language, but are distinct from other Mossi in their retention of Islam, a necessary affiliation for Sahelian traders. Mossi exported cattle, donkeys, and cotton cloth (in large, strip-woven "wheels") and imported salt, kola nuts, and luxury goods.

Division of Labor. Work in household fields is done by all family members. When a cooperative work group is held, women in the host household prepare beer and porridge for the participants. Women are generally responsible for food preparation, including collecting water and firewood. Spinning cotton is done by women, whereas weaving the thread into cloth and sewing the strips into panels and clothing is done by men. Precolonial iron smelting and contemporary smithing were/are the preserve of specific lineages, which in some but not all Mossi societies are endogamous; throughout West Africa, iron is associated with the earth, and smiths are held in spiritual awe and frequently segregated from the rest of society. Pottery is likewise made by specialist lineages, which also provide drummers who set the rhythm for large cultivating and threshing parties.

Land Tenure. Land is held by virtue of membership in one's patrilineage, although, in cases where sufficient land is available, it may also be let by the lineage to affinal kin or outright strangers. As heritage from the ancestors to the living lineage members, land is not alienable, but is rather held in trust for future descendants. The lineage allocates fields to households on the basis of need, dividing at intervals both the fields within the settlement that surround the houses, and those further away.

Kinship

Kin Groups and Descent. The formal organization of Mossi society is by patrilineal descent groups. Lineages are grouped into larger clans, which share a presumed common ancestor and a totemic animal whose avoidance as food is explained by the clan origin myth. Individual lineages within a clan may not be able to trace any genealogical links beyond their apical ancestor. In general, with the exception of chiefly lineages whose members have claims to power to maintain, genealogies are shallow and mutable. For most cultivators, all that is necessary is enough depth of genealogy (perhaps three generations) to clearly validate one's rights to a house plot and fields. Whereas formal authority in a lineage is assigned by genealogical seniority, in day-to-day life other elders, with perhaps less seniority but more wisdom, function as leaders. Indeed, a man might be represented in marriage negotiations by an elder not of his lineage, if circumstances of local knowledge and standing made that desirable.

Kinship Terminology. A consequence of the relative weakness (or, in positive terms, the adaptive flexibility) of the patrilineages is that there is only one word—*buudu*—for "clan" and "lineage"; it spans all descent-based groups above the immediate household compound. Members of a clan share a surname, although the formalities and mutability of this practice are not well studied.

Marriage and Family

Marriage. Marriages are arranged by lineage heads. Lineages are exogamous within the local community, with clear genealogical connections. People could and did move from village to village, making it possible for nearby members of one's clan to be genealogically distinct enough to allow intermarriage. Indeed, there is a continuum ranging from those close kin with whom marriage is forbidden, to complete strangers (even non-Mossi) as spouses. In between are clan members who are eligible marriage partners, and closer still to oneself are clan members too close genealogically to marry, but too far away genealogically to remarry widows from one's own lineage. Mossi marriage includes levirate and sororate. Polygyny was practiced, within the economic limits of a man's need for additional household labor and the prestige of multiple wives, against his ability to pay the compensating goods and services required by his wives' lineages.

In addition to marriages arranged (or accepted) by local lineages, members of chiefly lineages or prominent commoners might be granted a wife by a chief or king. Such a marriage obligated the recipient to betroth a daughter or sister to the king or chief in return. The chief might then marry that woman, but would be more likely to award her to another man, expanding the web of marriage ties and obligations centered on the chief. This practice, *pugsiure,* was not often a factor in the lives of ordinary cultivators, but it was not unknown for a man of renown to be rewarded with a wife by his political superiors.

Polygyny is not an option for Christian Mossi; some villages are predominantly Christian, but the overall Mossi population is only 10 percent Christian.

Domestic Unit. The classic Mossi household was comprised of a man, his younger brothers and any married sons, their wives, and children. This household unit, the *zaka*, in turn contained residential areas for each husband and his family. Houses were usually round adobe structures with conical thatched roofs; each adult had his or her own house, and others served as kitchens and animal pens. Adobe walls surrounded the entire compound and subdivided it into households. A cleared "patio" area, to the west of the compound, was conceptually part of the living unit; it contained granaries and sunshades under which guests were entertained; only close kin or close friends would enter the compound itself.

Inheritance. Goods and livestock were inherited by patrilineal descendants—in principle by sons, but in practice by children of both genders. Land, houses, and granaries were the property of the lineage, not of the individual, and were inherited within the descent group as much on the basis of need as on that of seniority.

Socialization. Children were raised within the extended-family compound. Muslim boys (as in Yarsé communities) might receive religious instruction from the local *maalam* and, in unusual cases, travel for advanced instruction. Similarly, within the Mossi religion, an occasional individual might travel to gain education as a seer or healer.

In modern Burkina Faso, even after large increases in the number of schools relative to the period of French rule (which ended in 1961), formal education still does not reach most children, including the Mossi. The 1990 estimate for literacy of those older than age 15 nationwide was 18 percent, with men estimated at 28 percent and women 9 percent. The increase in Islam has increased the number of children, chiefly boys, receiving instruction in basic Arabic and the Quran.

Sociopolitical Organization

Social Organization. The Mossi, in common with other Voltaic peoples, state and stateless, were organized in patrilineally defined lineages within clans. Membership in such units, however, was only rigidly constrained for those of royal and chiefly descent. Ordinary cultivators could and did incorporate new members into their lineages, whether affinal kin (sisters' sons seeking better opportunities matrilaterally) or outright strangers, even non-Mossi.

Political Organization. Survey literature often refers to the Mossi Empire. In fact, there were three independent kingdoms and around fifteen dependencies and interstitial buffers. The three kingdoms, in order of seniority, but not power, were Tenkodogo (Tankudugo), Ouagadougou (Wogodogo), and Yatenga. An easterly fourth kingdom, Fada N'Gurma, is sometimes counted as a Mossi state. The polities, as in most of Africa, were based on control of trade, whether of sources or routes. The burden of the state on the ordinary cultivators, then, was not great. Kings and chiefs possessed *naam*, the supernatural power required to rule others, which was conferred in consequence of a ruler having been properly chosen and installed. It is this intertwining of political power and religious legitimization that accounted for the well-known Mossi resistance to Islam. An occasional king or chief might convert, as several Ouagadougou kings did in the 1700s, but the system as a whole could not separate a ruler from the religion that conferred his power.

Kings had court officials who were each responsible for a sector of the kingdom; district chiefs in turn had twenty or more village chiefs reporting to them. Proper selection and validation indicated the possession of naam, without which one could not validly rule, but the officeholders were picked from their predecessor's patrilineage. Kings, district chiefs, and village chiefs all bore the title *naba,* with a geographic qualifier (e.g., Tenkdogo Naba, Koupela Naba). Only the king of Ouagadougou, the Mogho Naba, had a title (chief of Mossi country) that was not tied to a place-name; he was by far the most powerful of the various Mossi kings and chiefs.

Since Burkina Faso became independent in 1961, traditional kings and chiefs are not formally recognized by the government and its colonially derived administrative structure. They remain locally important, however, and have served as deputies during periods when there has been an elected legislature.

Social Control. Lineages, and village elders generally, exerted a good deal of influence upon people and their behavior. A society in which several crucial tasks (cultivating, weeding, harvesting, threshing, and, not least, roof replacement) depended on cooperative work groups allows effective ostracism for nonparticipation. The complex of Mossi chiefdoms and states and the expanding Mossi frontier at their edges allowed resettlement as a means of improving one's opportunities or escape from a difficult community, even before the French colonial regime intentionally stimulated massive labor migration by imposing a head tax payable in francs. Village chiefs represented the state and resolved differences brought to them.

In independent Burkina Faso, courts and police exist as well, although their impact on the countryside is variable. The avowedly revolutionary government of Thomas Sankara in the 1980s created "revolutionary defense committees" in every community, including rural villages, but their impact during that period and since the overthrow of that government in 1987 has not been reported.

Conflict. Military power was cavalry based. As was true across the Sahel, the absence of wheeled transport and semiarid conditions made garrisons impossible owing to the inability to feed a concentration of horses. In consequence, the power of a political center depended on its ability to mobilize local chiefs, with their horses and dependents.

The Mossi states were, however, strong enough to survive wars with the Muslim empires of the great bend of the Niger River, to their north. The Mossi are noted as the major—if not the only—Sahelian states to withstand the spread of Islam in the region. Mossi forces, like those of the other states around them, raided the stateless peoples around their perimeters for slaves. As a result of the loose nature of Mossi states and their weak military basis, there was also conflict between them. At the time of the French conquest, the oldest—but smallest and weakest—Mossi state, Tenkodogo, was engaged in a war of mutual raids with a chiefdom to its north, which in turn was a dependency of a buffer state on the edge of the largest Mossi kingdom, Ouagadougou.

Religion and Expressive Culture

Religious Beliefs. There are three major components to Mossi religion. One is the general African belief in an otiose "High God," who created the universe but has no role in its daily life. There are lesser, but more relevant, supernatural powers that govern the two major elements of life: soil fertility and rainfall. They are worshiped by conducting rituals at specific sites, often trees (or sites where one grew) or rock outcrops. Lastly, and most immediately, are the ancestors in one's patrilineage, who play an active role in regulating the behavior and success of their descendants. In the interests of the lineage, the ancestors link the past, present, and future.

Because of the close ties between Mossi religion and political organization, most Mossi—apart from the Yarsé long-distance traders—did not become Muslims. The French conquest in 1896–1897 undermined the traditional religion by implying that it was no longer effective in the face of superior outside forces. The French sent Catholic missionaries, and, very reluctantly, admitted U.S. Protestant missionaries in 1921, but cultural differences and the demands of Christianity have limited its impact. The first African cardinal in the Catholic church is a Mossi, however. Islam has a long-standing presence in the region, and, because its proselytizers are Africans, Mossi have been converting to Islam at an increasing rate. The lack of ethnic statistics at the national level makes numbers imprecise, and the more traditionally Muslim areas (west of the Mossi) would affect the totals, but the current estimate that Burkina is 50 percent Muslim suggests a clear trend toward conversion.

Religious Practitioners. The Mossi are known ethnographically for a formal dichotomy between political and spiritual power: the political power of the chiefs, signified by the naam, is offset by the religious power of the *tengsoba,* or "earth-owner." In much of West Africa, an important distinction is drawn between wild land and animals, and domesticated animals and farmland. Ownership of land is not merely vested in an ongoing descent group, but is validated by the presumption that the family in question "domesticated" unsettled land, thereby gaining both title to it and access to the supernatural forces controlling its fertility. Since the Mossi political system is founded upon an origin myth of immigrant cavalry, the political rulers cannot claim spiritual power over the land. That power is retained by the lineage of the tengsoba, presumed to be the descendants of the autochtonous people, the original settlers who antedated the Mossi military. This dichotomy, and its ability to check royal abuse with refusal to perform vital fertility rituals, was so well known ethnographically that James G. Frazer had swept it into *The Golden Bough* by 1919, barely twenty-two years after the Mossi had been conquered. Whereas the dichotomy is fundamental to a number of Voltaic societies as well as the Mossi states of Yatenga and Ouagadougou, it is not found in the original Mossi state of Tenkodogo. There, the autochtonous people, the Bisa, were not assimilated into Mossi society, which instead relies upon sisters' sons to perform fertility rituals; the dichotomy in this case is between the lineage and its nonmember relative.

Lineage rituals, propitiating ancestors rather than earth spirits, are performed by the eldest male; lineage members from even scores of kilometers away may send chickens to be sacrificed by the lineage head on the ancestral graves. Finally, funerals are performed by the household head of the deceased, who may be the heir of the latter.

Ceremonies. Sacrifices for the sake of fertility or to call down rain are performed when conditions demand, by "earth-owners" or, in the case of Tenkodogo, a "sister's son" of the local lineage. Ancestor-oriented rituals, even at the kingdom level, are lineage or clan based; that is, even a king's harvest thanksgiving, although it is immense in scale and takes precedence over everyone else's, is, strictly speaking, offered to his ancestors for the sake of his harvest, rather than to those of the collective inhabitants of his realm. Inhabitants of a given district are not able to perform sacrifices to thank their ancestors until their district chief has performed his.

This harvest festival, which occurs after the millet has been harvested in late autumn, but before it is threshed in midwinter, is the *basega;* the chief's or king's is the *na'basega.*

Arts. Mossi men weave cotton cloth, using the strip looms common in West Africa. Pottery, made by specialist lineages, is decorated with inscribed and painted designs. The western Mossi share the traditions of wood sculpture and masked dancing with the societies to their west, but these practices are not found in Tenkodogo. Unlike some other Voltaic peoples, the Mossi do not paint designs on their adobe walls and houses. Until banned by the modern government, facial scarification in locally distinctive patterns was practiced.

Medicine. Traditionally, curing was in the hands of one's family and individuals locally renowned as healers. Modern medicine is now available to the Mossi, within the limitations imposed by the fact that Burkina Faso is among the poorest nations in both Africa and the world.

Death and Afterlife. Men were buried to the west of the cleared area west of their compounds. Women were buried in household fields; the funeral was performed by members of their own patrilineages. As is common in Africa, elders are venerated because their accumulated knowledge and experiences form the collective information in societies without written records. They are also considered "almost ancestors"; upon death, they become part of the generalized community of ancestors who watch over their living descendants and intervene to reward or punish behavior. Because of the shallowness of commoner genealogies, the ancestors one addresses in rituals like the basega are a collectivity, not named spirits whose individual intercession might be requested.

Bibliography

Fiske, Alan Page (1991). *Structures of Social Life: The Four Elementary Forms of Human Relations*. New York: Free Press.

Greenberg, Joseph H. (1963). *The Languages of Africa*. Indiana University Research Center in Anthropology, Folklore, and Linguistics, Publication no. 25. The Hague: Mouton.

Hammond, Peter B. (1966). *Yatenga: Technology in the Culture of a West African Kingdom*. New York: Free Press.

McMillan, Della E. (1995). *Sahel Visions: Planned Settlement and River Blindness Control in Burkina Faso*. Tucson: University of Arizona Press.

Schildkrout, Enid (1978). *People of the Zongo: The Transformation of Ethnic Identities in Ghana*. Cambridge: Cambridge University Press.

Skinner, Elliott P. (1964). *The Mossi of the Upper Volta: The Political Development of a Sudanese People*. Stanford, Calif.: Stanford University Press. Reprint, with supplementary chapter. 1989. *The Mossi of Burkina Faso: Chiefs, Politicians, and Soldiers*. Prospect Heights, Ill.: Waveland Press.

Skinner, Elliott P. (1974). *African Urban Life: The Transformation of Ouagadougou*. Princeton, N.J.: Princeton University Press.

GREGORY A. FINNEGAN

Nandi and Other Kalenjin Peoples

ETHNONYMS: Endo: Chebleng'. Keiyo: Elgeyo. Kipsigis: Lumbwa, Sotek. Kony: Bong'om, Bok, Elgon Maasai, Elgonyi, Sabaot. Marakwet: Cherang'any, Maragweta, Sengwer. Nandi: Chemwal, Teng'wal. Okiek: Akiy, Dorobo, Ogiek. Pokot: Pakot, Suk. Sebei: Kipsorai, Mbai, Sabaot, Saping', Sor. Terik: Nilotic Tiriki, Nyang'ori. Tugen: Cherangani, Kamasia.

Orientation

Identification. The Kalenjin are related East African peoples (Kipsigis, Nandi, Keiyo, Tugen, Marakwet, Endo, Sabaot, Terik, Okiek) who form one branch of the Highland Nilotes, formerly referred to as "Southern Nilo-Hamites" or sometimes "Nandi-speaking peoples." This description focuses on the Nandi; about one-third of all Kalenjin and second-largest of the Kalenjin subgroups, they are geographically the most centrally located.

Location. The Kalenjin live mainly in the highland of western Kenya, although the Sebei and some Pokot are located in eastern Uganda. Physical environment and ecological adaptation vary throughout Kalenjin country. The Nandi and Kipsigis live primarily on high plateaus with good agricultural potential: average elevation of 1,800 to 2,000 meters, thick topsoil, and 150 to 200 centimeters of rain annually distributed over the entire year. Many of the Kalenjin groups (Keiyo, Tugen, Marakwet/Endo) live along escarpments in the Rift Valley system, and the Sabaot on Mount Elgon. In these cases, most cultivation occurs between 1,350 and 2,000 meters, animals are herded in low-lying plains, and some communities may be situated at elevations of over 2,700 meters. The pastoral Pokot, the northernmost Kalenjin, live in arid lowlands where little cultivation is possible. The Okiek, mountain-forest-dwelling Kalenjin speakers, historically are foragers.

Demography. There are probably just over 2 million Kalenjin, at least 95 percent of whom live in Kenya. The Kipsigis were 32 percent of all the Kenya Kalenjin in the 1969 census, followed by the Nandi (27 percent), Pokot (13 percent), Tugen (8.6 percent), Keiyo (8.5 percent), Marakwet (6 percent), Sabaot (4.2 percent), and Okiek (less than 1 percent by official census figures, but perhaps undercounted). The number of Uganda Sabaot (Sebei) is close to their number in Kenya. In the 1979 census, there were 1,652,243 Kalenjin in Kenya. They were the fifth-largest ethnic group—10.8 percent of the population. The vast majority of Kalenjin are rural, and population density differs greatly throughout Kalenjin country owing to highly varied ecological conditions.

Linguistic Affiliation. Although the Kalenjin are regarded as a unit on the basis of speaking a common language, there are numerous dialects. All of them, it seems, are mutually intelligible with practice, although not necessarily immediately. Nandi and Kipsigis are distinguished by small sound and terminology differences, similar to the difference between English as spoken in Britain and the United States. Speakers of these dialects cannot immediately understand Pokot, Sabaot, and regional variants of Marakwet. Greenberg (1963) classifies Kalenjin as a Southern Nilotic language (Eastern Section, Nilotic Branch, Eastern Sudanic Language Family). Aside from Tatoga, which is spoken by a few small peoples of northern Tanzania, the nearest language to Kalenjin is Maasai.

History and Cultural Relations

The oral traditions of all the Nilotic peoples of East Africa refer to northern origins. There is a consensus among historians and linguists that the Plains and Highland Nilotes migrated from a region near the southern border of Ethiopia and Sudan shortly before the beginning of the Christian Era and diverged into separate communities shortly thereafter. Ehret (1971) believes that pre-Kalenjin who already were cattle keepers and had age sets lived in the western Kenya highlands 2,000 years ago. Presumably, these people absorbed other populations already living in the region. From some time after A.D. 500 to about A.D. 1600, there seems to have been a series of migrations eastward and southward from near Mount Elgon. Migrations were complex, and there are competing theories about their details.

The Nandi and Kipsigis, in response to Maasai expansion, borrowed from the Maasai some of the traits that distinguish them from other Kalenjin: large-scale economic dependence on herding, military organization and aggressive cattle raiding, and centralized religious-political leadership. The family that established the office of *orkoiyot* (warlord/diviner) among both the Nandi and Kipsigis were nineteenth-century Maasai immigrants. By 1800, both the Nandi and Kipsigis were expanding at the expense of the Maasai. This process was halted in 1905 by the imposition of British colonial rule.

Introduced during the colonial era were new crops/techniques and a cash economy (Kalenjin men were paid wages for their military service as early as World War I); conversions to Christianity began (Kalenjin was the first East African vernacular to have a translation of the Bible). Consciousness of a common Kalenjin identity emerged to facilitate action as a political-interest group during and after World War II—historically, the Nandi and Kipsigis raided other Kalenjin as well as the Maasai, Gusii, Luyia, and Luo. The name "Kalenjin" is said to derive from a radio broadcaster who often used the phrase (meaning "I tell you"). Similarly, "Sabaot" is a modern term used to mean those Kalenjin subgroups who use "Subai" as a greeting. Nandi and Kipsigis were early recipients of individual land titles (1954), with large holdings by African standards because of their historically low population density. Economic development schemes were promoted as independence (1964) approached, and afterward many Kalenjin from more crowded areas resettled on farms in the former White Highlands near Kitale. Today's Kalenjin are among the most prosperous of Kenya's ethnic groups. Kenya's second president, Daniel arap Moi, is a Tugen.

Settlements

The typical settlement pattern is scattered. Groups of family homesteads make up a neighborhood (Nandi: *koret*), and today (in Kenya) several neighborhoods are combined into a sublocation, the smallest unit of government administration. Neighborhood size varies, but twenty to fifty or sixty households is typical. Among the Nandi, Kipsigis, pastoral Pokot, and Sebei, local communities historically were not, or were only to a limited extent, kin-based; among some other Kalenjin, they were based on patrilineal clans. Most Kalenjin combined neighborhoods to form a *pororiet*, a unit with mutual-defense functions. Old-style houses are round, of wattle and daub, thatched, and divided internally into two rooms; the back room traditionally sheltered sheep and goats. Modern houses (still the minority) are usually square and of permanent material, with iron-sheet roofs. A typical household consists of a small extended family, or a nuclear family with some attached nonnuclear kin, living in a compound composed of several individual houses facing each other.

Economy

Subsistence and Commercial Activities. The Kalenjin are essentially semipastoralists. Cattle herding is thought to be ancient among them. Although the real economic importance of herding is slight compared to that of cultivation among many Kalenjin groups, they almost all display a cultural emphasis on and an emotional commitment to pastoralism. Cattle numbers have waxed and waned; however, cattle/people ratios of 5:1 or greater (typical of peoples among whom herding is economically dominant) have been recorded only for the pastoral Pokot. In their late-nineteenth-century heyday of pastoralism, the Nandi and the Kipsigis approached this ratio; 1–3:1 is more typical of the Kalenjin, and in some communities the ratio is even lower than 1:1.

The staple crop was eleusine, but maize replaced it during the colonial era. Other subsistence crops include beans, pumpkins, cabbages, and other vegetables as well as sweet and European potatoes and small amounts of sorghum. Sheep, goats, and chickens are kept. Iron hoes were traditionally used to till; today plows pulled by oxen or rented tractors are more common. The importance of cash crops varies with land availability, soil type, and other factors; among the Nandi and the Kipsigis, it is considerable. Surplus maize, milk, and tea are the major cash crops. Kalenjin farms on the Uasin Gishu plateau also grow wheat and pyrethrum.

In most communities there are a few wage workers and full-time business persons (shopkeepers, tailors, carpenters, bicycle repairmen, tractor owners) with local clienteles. It is common for young married men to be part-time entrepreneurs. Historically, women could brew and sell beer; this became illegal in the early 1980s. Some men work outside their communities, but labor migration is less common than elsewhere in western Kenya.

Industrial Arts. Traditionally, there were no full-time craft specialists. Most objects were manufactured by their users. The blacksmith's art was passed down in families in particular localities, and some women specialized in pottery.

Trade. Traditionally, women conducted a trade of small stock for grain between pastoral-emphasis and cultivation-emphasis (often non-Kalenjin) communities. Regular local markets were rare prior to the colonial era. Today large towns and district centers have regular markets, and women occasionally sell vegetables in sublocation centers.

Division of Labor. There was little traditional division of labor except by age and sex. Men cleared land for cultivation, and there is evidence that married men and women cooperated in the rest of the cultivation process. Husbands and wives did not (except during a limited historical period)—and do not—typically cultivate separately, other than the wife's vegetable garden. Today women do more cultivation if their husbands are engaged in small-scale business activities. Children herded cattle close to the homestead, as well as sheep and goats; warriors (young initiated men) herded cattle in distant pastures. Women and girls milked, cooked, and supplied water and firewood. Today boys are the main cowherds, and girls are largely responsible for infant care. The children's role in domestic labor is extremely important, even though most children now attend school.

Land Tenure. In Nandi, individual title to land replaced a system in which land was plentiful, all who lived in a community had the right to cultivate it, and a man could move with his family to any locality in which he had a sponsor. Land prepared for cultivation, and used regularly, was viewed as belonging to the family that used it, and inherited from mother to son. The tenure systems of other Kalenjin were mainly similar. The Kerio Valley groups cultivated on ridges and at the foot of ridges, using irrigation furrows that required collective labor to maintain. This labor was provided by clan segments, which cleared and held land collectively, although cultivation rights in developed fields were held by individual families.

Kinship

All Kalenjin have patrilineal clans, but clans do not universally have strong cooperative functions other than regulating marriage (with various rules). Specific patrilineal links are traced for only three to four generations.

Kin terminology is basically Omaha. The most common sibling terms do not differentiate gender. There are a large number of specific terms for types of affines.

Marriage and Family

Marriage. Traditionally, marriage took place in two stages: *ratet*, a small ceremony after which the couple lived together, and *tunisiet*, a large public feast held only at the completion of bride-wealth payment. Among the Nandi, these stages have typically occurred in rapid succession since about the turn of the twentieth century; among some other Kalenjin, at least during certain periods, a separation of many years has been customary, probably depending on availability of cattle or other livestock. Most Kalenjin—with some exceptions, notably the Okiek—pay bride-wealth in cattle. Once payment is complete, marriage is theoretically irrevocable. Traditional divorce grounds and proceedings exist, but divorce is in fact extremely rare, even in modern times. Permanent separations occur but do not technically negate marriage.

Polygyny is prestigious and, in the 1970s, was practiced by about 25 percent of ever-married Nandi men. Christians were monogamous slightly more frequently than non-Christians. Woman-woman marriage, found among Nandi, Kipsigis, and, since about the mid-twentieth century, among Keiyo, is not customary among other Kalenjin. Both women and men are active in negotiating marriages and reconciling separated couples. Husbands are jurally dominant, with the right to beat wives for certain offenses. Wives are publicly deferential; private relations are more nearly egalitarian. Leisure is spent with same-gender companions more than with one's spouse.

Domestic Unit. Each wife has her own field, cattle, and house within the family compound. A separate farm for each wife is the ideal. Compounds may include the husband's parents or mother, and other kin, depending on circumstances. Brothers and their wives may share a compound, although this is rare.

Inheritance. Traditional norms of cattle inheritance have been extended to land, money, and other property. Each wife's house-property consists of cattle given to her at marriage, acquired by her on her own, or given as bride-wealth for her daughters. These may be inherited only by her own sons (or, in Nandi and Kipsigis, the sons of her wife). A man's other property is inherited in equal shares by each wife's house. Failing lineal heirs, a man's property reverts to his brothers or their sons, a woman's to her co-wives' sons.

Socialization. Infants are treated indulgently, but strict obedience (enforced by corporal punishment) is expected from children by about the age of 6. Routine care of infants and toddlers is largely the responsibility of girls between ages 8 and 10. Children are economically important and have heavy responsibilities. It is common to spend a part of childhood fostered by a relative, helping with domestic work in exchange for board and school fees.

Adolescent initiation (circumcision for boys and clitoridectomy for girls, and instruction for both) is a key feature of Kalenjin life and ethnic identity. These are sex-segregated rituals for most, but not all, Kalenjin groups. Adolescents are allowed a period of license to indulge in courtship and sexual play—before initiation for girls and afterward for boys. Girls marry directly following initiation; boys become warriors. Today some (mostly highly educated) girls refuse initiation.

Sociopolitical Organization

Social Organization. Rotating age sets formerly existed among all Kalenjin, with the same or nearly the same names in all groups. There were eight sets among the Tugen, Marakwet, and Sabaot and seven among the Keiyo, Nandi, and Kipsigis (with some evidence that there may have been eight formerly). The Marakwet, Tugen, and Sabaot have formalized age sets for women, and other Kalenjin probably once had them. Members of younger age sets defer to members of older age sets. Men initiated together have a very high level of solidarity: they spend much time together, form work teams, try to live in the same neighborhood and marry sisters (wife's sister's husband is an important reciprocal kin type), and may not marry each other's daughters. Aside from territorial units and clans, there were no other formal associations.

Political Organization. Most political action took place in the *kokwet*, or council of the locality (today, sublocation council). Theoretically, any married man could be an active participant; in fact, a small group of influential elders formed the core. Women could observe—but not speak unless invited. Local councils sent representatives to occasional meetings of pororiet councils. Such councils continue to be important under the leadership of a government-appointed sublocation chief.

Traditionally, there were no central authorities, although the Nandi and Kipsigis came close to having chiefs in the head orkoiyot. All the Kalenjin had men called orkoiyot, believed to have power to control weather and foretell events. The nineteenth-century Nandi and Kipsigis came to rely on one central authority to coordinate warfare (through representatives on pororiet councils) and predict the success of raids. The orkoiyot was rewarded with a share of the booty of successful raids, and his family became wealthy and powerful. For its short existence, this office was passed from father to son.

Social Control. Internal conflicts and norm violations are brought before neighborhood elders' courts. In modern Kenya, serious offenses are automatically matters for the police and government courts; other disputes can become police matters if someone files charges, but the elders' court is still the main arena for litigation. Offending parties would normally comply with fines imposed by elders; elders could also order punishments (e.g., beating) to be administered by offenders' age sets. People convicted of witchcraft were ordered to be put to death by their own kin. Traditionally, local groups of women could sanction men deemed guilty of "crimes against women."

Conflict. Cattle raiding was extremely important in the social life of the pastoral Kalenjin. The warrior age grade (youngest initiated age set) was responsible for defending cattle, and acquiring their own fortunes in captured cattle. War was not specifically for territory, but the Nandi and the Kipsigis did expand territorially at the expense of the Maasai. Whereas the Nandi and the Kipsigis did not raid each other, they did at times raid other Kalenjin.

Religion and Expressive Culture

Religious Beliefs. The statistical majority of Kalenjin are nominally Christian, but many still follow traditional beliefs and practices. They believed in one god, with many names, identified with the sun and now believed to be identical to the Christian God. Prayers were addressed primarily to God. The *oiik* (sing. *olindet*), or spirits of dead ancestors, were also believed able to intervene in human life. They were occasionally, but not systematically, propitiated. Thunder was another named supernatural being. Inchoate evil spirits were believed to lurk on pathways, especially at night, and cause harm.

Religious Practitioners. Every neighborhood has elders who serve as ritual experts. Diviners foretell events by patterns of pebbles poured from a calabash. The Kalenjin also believe in an array of different named types of sorcerers and witches.

Ceremonies. Formerly, there was an important communitywide festival, *kipsunde*, after the harvest. The major ceremonies now are the life-cycle rituals, many (e.g., those for for newborns) restricted to the family. The most important larger ritual is initiation.

Arts. The most highly developed visual art is decorative beadwork. Expressive culture and leisure activities include storytelling, singing and dancing, beer drinking (for men), and games of strategy. A lyrelike stringed instrument traditionally accompanied singing but is now becoming rare.

Medicine. Traditionally, "doctors" (male), with primarily supernaturally based skills, could ascertain the cause of bad luck or illness and treat it. These practitioners still treat patients, particularly for mental illness. Female herbalists' and midwives' skills are more technical than supernatural.

Death and Afterlife. Death customs varied. The Nandi buried only infants and elders. Corpses of adults were left to be consumed by hyenas. In some Kalenjin groups (e.g., Marakwet), only barren people were left for scavengers. Death was polluting, and corpse handlers (sons or other close kin) had to be ritually purified and compensated from the estate. Many stories refer to an afterlife that is an idealized version of precolonial Kalenjin life. In a family ceremony, elders decided which ancestral spirit has been reincarnated in a newborn infant.

Bibliography

Ehret, Christopher (1971). *Southern Nilotic History: Linguistic Approaches to the Study of the Past*. Evanston, Ill.: Northwestern University Press.

Goldschmidt, Walter (1976). *The Culture and Behavior of the Sebei*. Berkeley and Los Angeles: University of California Press.

Greenberg, Joseph H. (1963). Indiana University Research Center in Anthropology, Folklore, and Linguistics, Publication 25. *The Languages of Africa*. The Hague: Mouton.

Huntingford, G. W. B. (1953). *The Nandi of Kenya: Tribal Control in a Pastoral Society*. London: Routledge & Kegan Paul.

Kipkorir, B. E., with F. B. Welbourn (1973). *The Marakwet of Kenya*. Nairobi: East African Literature Bureau.

Oboler, Regina Smith (1985). *Women, Power, and Economic Change: The Nandi of Kenya*. Stanford, Calif.: Stanford University Press.

Orchardson, Ian (1961). *The Kipsigis*. Nairobi: East African Literature Bureau.

Peristiany, J. G. (1939). *The Social Institutions of the Kipsigis*. London: Routledge & Kegan Paul.

REGINA SMITH OBOLER

Ndebele

ETHNONYMS: Amandebele, Mapoggers, Ndzundza, Ndzundza-Ndebele or Manala-Ndebele, Southern Ndebele

Orientation

Identification. The people refer to themselves as "Amandebele," or "Ndzundza" or "Manala," denoting the two main tribal groupings. Early writers used the term "Transvaal Ndebele" to distinguish them from the Zimbabwean Ndebele (or Matebele). On geographical grounds, the Transvaal Ndebele were subdivided into the Northern (Transvaal) and Southern (Transvaal) Ndebele sections. Oral tradition points to a possible common origin for both the northern and southern sections, although the former, as the numerically smaller group, became absorbed into their Northern-Sotho-speaking neighbors. The Southern Ndebele are comprised of the Ndzundza and the Manala ethnic groups or tribes. During the colonial era, White settlers derogatively referred to the Ndzundza-Ndebele as "Mapoggers" or "Mapoêrs," after their ruler Mabhoko, called "Mapog" or "Mapoch" by Whites. Early ethnographies identified a third Southern Ndebele tribe, the Mhwaduba, which also became completely integrated with neighboring Sotho-speaking communities.

Location. The majority of Ndebele live in the former Bantustans or "homelands" of KwaNdebele and Lebowa, between 24°53′ to 25°43′ S and 28°22′ to 29°50′ E, approximately 60 to 130 kilometers northeast of Pretoria, South Africa. The total area amounts to 350,000 hectares, including the Moutse and Nebo areas, which were previously part of the former Lebowa homeland. Temperatures range from a maximum of 36° C in the northern parts to a minimum of –5° C in the south; rainfall averages 50 centimeters per annum in the north and 80 centimeters per annum in the south. Almost two-thirds of the entire former KwaNdebele lies within a vegetational zone known as Mixed Bushveld (Savanna type), in the north. The southern parts fall within a zone known as Bankenveld (False Grassland type).

Demography. Population figures are based on the 1991 sensus figures for the former KwaNdebele homeland (now part of Eastern Transvaal Province) and updated for the April 1994 general elections. The total for the area was estimated at 403,700. A minority of labor tenants and farmworkers outside the former homeland were not included.

Linguistic Affiliation. IsiNdebele is a Southern Bantu language, part of the Nguni Language Group. Mother-tongue speakers seldom distinguish between the dialects IsiNdzundza and IsiNala. A written orthography was published only in 1982. Most Ndebele are fluent in the neighboring Northern Sotho language called Sepedi, as well as Afrikaans (elderly people) and English (the younger generation).

History and Cultural Relations

It is still unclear when and how the Ndebele parted from the main Nguni-speaking migration along the eastern part of southern Africa. Oral history suggests an early (c. late 1500) settlement in the interior, to the immediate north of present-day Pretoria, under a founder ruler called Musi. A succession struggle among Musi's sons is a probable explanation for the twofold split in clans and the resultant two main tribal categories, Ndzundza and Manala. The twofold split resulted in clans associating themselves with one of the two groups. The majority of clans followed Ndzundza, who migrated to KwaSimkhulu, approximately 200 kilometers east of present-day Pretoria. The numerically smaller Manala occupied the areas called Ezotshaneni, KoNonduna, and Embilaneni, which include what are today the eastern suburbs of Pretoria.

The Ndzundza chieftaincy is believed to have extended its boundaries along the Steelpoort (Indubazi) River catchment area between the 1600s and early 1800s. Several of these settlement sites (KwaSimkhulu, KwaMaza, and Esikhunjini) are known through oral history and are currently under archaeological investigation.

Both the Ndzundza and Manala chiefdoms were almost annihilated by the armies of Mzilikzazi's Matebele (Zimbabwean Ndebele) around 1820. The Manala in particular suffered serious losses, but the Ndzundza recovered significantly under the legendary Mabhoko, during the 1840s. He revolutionized the Ndzundza settlement pattern by building a number of impenetrable stone fortresses and renamed the tribal capital KoNomtjharhelo (later popularly known as Mapoch's Caves). During the middle 1800s, the Ndzundza developed into a significant regional political and military force.

They soon had to face the threat of White colonial settlers, with whom they fought in 1849, 1863, and, finally, in 1883, during the lengthy Mapoch War against the ZAR forces. The latter's tactic of besiegement forced the famine-stricken Ndzundza to capitulate. They lost their independence, their land was expropriated, the leaders were imprisoned (Chief Nyabela to life imprisonment), and all the Ndebele were scattered as indentured laborers for a five-year (1883–1888) period among White farmers. The Manala chiefdom was not involved in the war and had previously (1873) settled on land provided by the Berlin Mission, some 30 kilometers north of Pretoria, at a place the Manala named KoMjekejeke (Wallmannsthal).

Chief Nyabela Mahlangu was released after the Anglo-Boer War (1899–1902) in 1903 and died soon afterward. His successor tried fruitlessly in 1916 and 1918 to regain their tribal land. Instead, the royal house and a growing number of followers privately bought land in 1922, around which the Ndzundza-Ndebele reassembled. Within the framework of the bantustan or homeland system in South Africa, the Ndebele (both Manala and Ndzundza) were only allowed to settle in a homeland called KwaNdebele in 1979. This specific land, climate, and soil was entirely alien to them.

Settlements

Precolonial Ndebele homesteads (*imizi*) were organized along three-generational patrilinear agnatic lines. It seems that these might have extended into large localized lineages (*iikoro*) under the social and ritual leadership of the senior male member. During and after the indentured period, the three-generational homestead remained popular despite restrictions in size and number imposed by White landlords. The homestead consists of a number of houses (*izindlu*) representing various households and centered around a cattle enclosure (*isibaya*). Other structures in the homestead include the boys' hut (*ilawu*), various smaller huts for girls behind each house (*indlu*), and granaries. Each house complex was separated from the other by an enclosure called the *isirhodlo*. This enclosure was subdivided along gender lines into a men's section in the front and a domestic (cooking) area (*isibuya*) at the back.

Precolonial Ndebele structures were of the thatched beehive-dome type. Since the late 1800s, Ndebele have adopted a cone-on-cylinder type, consisting of mud walls and a thatched roof, while simultaneously reverting to a linear outlay, replacing the circular-center cattle pattern. In the current rural settlement pattern, the nuclear-family single house built on a square stand predominates, occasionally with provision for two or more extra buildings. A wide range of modern building material and designs have been introduced, including modern services and infrastructure.

Economy

Subsistence and Commercial Activities. The precolonial Ndebele were a cattle-centred society, but they also kept goats. The most important crops, even today, are maize, sorghum, pumpkins, and at least three types of domesticated green vegetables (*umroho*). Since farm-laborer days, crops such as beans and potatoes have been grown and the tractor has substituted for the cattle-drawn plow, although the latter is still commonly used. Pumpkins and other vegetables are planted around the house and tilled with hoes. Cattle (now in limited numbers), goats, pigs, and chickens (the most prevalent) are still common.

Industrial Arts. Present crafts include weaving of sleeping mats, sieves, and grain mats; woodcarving of spoons and wooden pieces used in necklaces; and the manufacturing of a variety of brass anklets and neck rings. Since precolonial times, Ndebele are believed to have obtained all pottery from trading with Sotho-speaking neighbors. The Tshabangu clan reportedly introduced the Ndebele to blacksmithing.

Trade. Archaeologists believe that societies such as that of the Ndebele formed part of the wider pre-nineteenth century trade industry on the African east coast and had been introduced to consumer goods such as tobacco, cloth, and glass beads. Historians such as Delius (1989) believe that a large number of firearms reached the Ndzundza-Ndebele during the middle 1800s.

Division of Labor. In a pastoral society such as that of the Ndebele, men attended to animal husbandry and women to horticultural and agricultural activities except when new fields (*amasimu*) are cleared with the help of men who join in a communal working party called an *ijima*. Even male social age status is defined in terms of husbandry activities: a boy who herds goats (*umsana wembuzana*), a boy who herds calves (*umsana wamakhonyana*), and so forth. Men are responsible for the construction and thatching of houses, women for plastering and painting of walls. Teenage girls are trained by their mothers in the art of smearing and painting. Even today girls from an early age (approximately 5 or 6) assist their mothers in the fetching of water and wood, making fire, and cooking. Female responsibilities have arduously increased in recent years with the increase in permanent and temporary male and female labor migrants to urban areas. It is calculated that some 80 percent of rural KwaNdebele residents are labor migrants.

Land Tenure. Land was tribal property; portions were allocated to individual families by the chief and headmen as custodians, under a system called *ukulotjha*, with the one-time payment of a fee that also implied allegiance to the political ruler of the area. Grazing land was entirely communal. The system of traditional tenure still applies in the former KwaNdebele, except in certain urban areas where private ownership has been introduced. In South Africa, Black people could never own land; the Ndzunzda-Ndebele's land was expropriated in 1883, when they became labor tenants on White-owned farms. Most Ndzunzda-Ndebele exchanged free labor for the right to build, plant, and keep a minimum of cattle. Since the formation of the KwaNdebele homeland, traditional tenure, controlled by the chief, has been reintroduced.

The lastborn son inherits the land, but married sons often build adjacent to their natal homesteads, if space allows it. In certain rural areas (e.g., Nebo), this form of extended three-generational settlement is still intact.

Kinship

Kin Groups and Descent. On the macro level, Ndebele society is structured into approximately eighty patrilineal exogamous clans (*izibongo*), each subdivided into a variety of subclans or patrilineages (*iinanzelo* or *iikoro*). Totems of animals and objects are associated with each clan. The three- to four-generational lineage segment (*i oro*) is of functional value in daily life (e.g., ritual and religion, socioeconomic reciprocity); it is composed of various residential units (homesteads) (imizi).

Kinship Terminology. Classificatory kinship applies, and with similar terms in every alternate generation—for example, grandfathers and grandsons (*obaba omkhulu*). Smaller distinctions are drawn between own father (*ubaba*), father's elder brothers (*abasongwane*), and his younger brothers (*obaba omncane*), although all these men on the same generation level may be called *ubaba*.

Marriage and Family

Marriage. Polygyny has almost disappeared. Bride-wealth consists of cattle and/or money (*ikhazi*). Marital negotiations between the two sets of families are an extended process that includes the stadial presentation of six to eight cattle and may not be finally contracted until long after the birth of the first child. Marital residence is virilocal, and new brides (*omakhothi*) are involved in cooking, beadwork, and even the rearing of other small children of various households in the homestead. Brides have a lifelong obligation to observe the custom of *ukuhlonipha* or "respect" for their fathers-in-law (e.g., physical avoidance, first-name taboo). A substitute wife (*umngenandlu* or *ihlanzi*), in case of infertility, was still common in the 1960s. In case of divorce, witchcraft accusation, and even infidelity, a woman is forced to return to her natal homestead. Currently, wealthy women with children often marry very late or stay single. Fathers demand more bride-wealth for educated women. Both urban and rural Ndebele weddings nowadays involve a customary ceremony (*ngesikhethu*) as well as a Christian ceremony.

Domestic Unit. The traditional Ndebele homestead (*umuzi*), based on agnatic kinship and intergenerational ties, consists of several households. Apart from the nuclear household, the three-generational household along agnatic lines still seems to be the prevalent one among rural Ndebele. Married sons of the founder household head still prefer to settle adjacent to the original homestead, provided that building space is available. A single household may be composed of a man, his wife and children (including children of an unmarried daughter), wives and children of his sons, and a father's widowed sister.

Inheritance. Although the inheritance of land and other movable and immovable household assets are negotiated within the homestead as a whole, Ndebele seem to subscribe to the custom of inheritance by the youngest son (the *upetjhana*).

Socialization. The three-generational household enhances intergenerational contact; the absence of migrant mothers and fathers necessitates that grandparents care for children. Contemporary Ndebele households are essentially matrifocal, and children interact with their fathers and elder male siblings only over weekends.

Sociopolitical Organization

Social Organization. In precolonial times, Ndebele clan organization seemed to have been hierarchical in terms of duration of alliance to the ruling clans, Mahlangu for Ndzundza and Mabhena for the Manala. This pattern pervaded the entire political system.

Political Organization. Tribal political power is in the hands of the ruling clan and royal lineage, Mgwezane Mahlangu (among the Ndzundza) and Somlokothwa Mabhena (among the Manala). In the case of the Ndzundza, the paramount (called Ingewenyama), the royal family, and the tribal council (*ibandla*) together make political decisions to be implemented by regional headmen (*amaduna* or *amakosana*) over a wide area, including the former KwaNdebele, rural areas outside KwaNdebele, and urban (township) areas. The headmen system includes more than one hundred such men of whom the greater portion are *amakosana*, or men of royal (clan) origin. Certain of these headmen were elevated to the status of subchiefs (*amakosi*).

There is currently a national political debate as to whether headmen, chiefs, paramounts, and kings like these will in future be stipended by local or central government.

Social Control. Traditionally, criminal and civil jurisdiction were vested in the tribal court. The latter still presides over regional disputes (i.e., those relating to land, cattle and grazing, and bride-wealth). All other disputes are forwarded to local magistrates in three districts in the former KwaNdebele.

Conflict. Except for the 1800s, the Ndebele as a political entity were not involved in any major regional conflicts, especially after 1883, when they lost their independence and had their land expropriated. Almost a century later, in 1986, they experienced violent internal (regional) conflict when a minority vigilante movement called Imbokodo (Grinding Stone) took over the local police and security system and terrorized the entire former homeland. In a surprising move, the whole population called on the royal house of Paramount Mabhoko for moral support, and, within weeks, the youth rid the area of that infamous organization. Royal leaders emerged as local heroes of the struggle.

Religion and Expressive Culture

Religious Beliefs. Nineteenth-century evangelizing activities by the Berlin Mission did little to change traditional Ndebele religion, especially that of the Ndzundza. Although the Manala lived on the Wallmannsthal mission station from 1873, they were in frequent conflict with local missionaries. Recent Christian and African Christian church influences spread rapidly, however, and most Ndebele are now members of the Zion Christian Church (ZCC), one of a variety of (African) Apostolic churches, or the Catholic church. Traditional beliefs were centered on a creator god, Zimu, and ancestral spirits (*abezimu*).

Religious Practitioners. Disgruntled ancestral spirits cause illness, misfortune, and death. Traditional practitioners (*iinyanga* and *izangoma*) act as mediators between the past and present world and are still frequently consulted. Sorcerers (abathakathi or abaloyi) are believe to use familiars like the well-known "baboon" midget (*utikoloshe*), especially in cases of jealousy toward achievers in the community in general. Both women and men become healers after a prolonged period of internship with existing practitioners.

Ceremonies. Initiation at puberty dominates ritual life in Ndebele society. Girls' initiation (*iqhude* or *ukuthombisa*) is organized on an individual basis, within the homestead. It entails the isolation of a girl after her second or third menstruation in an existing house in the homestead, which is prepared by her mother. The weeklong period of isolation ends over the weekend, when as many as two hundred relatives, friends, and neighbors attend the coming-out ritual. The occasion is marked by the slaughtering of cows and goats, cooking and drinking of traditional beer (*unotlhabalala*), song and dance, and the large-scale presentation of gifts (clothing and toiletries) to the initiate's mother and father. In return, the initiate's mother presents large quantities of bread and jam to attendants. The notion of reciprocity is prominent. During the iqhude, women sing, dance, and display traditional costumes as the men remain spatially isolated from the courtyard in front of the homestead.

Male initiation (*ingoma* or *ukuwela*), which includes circumcision, is a collective and quadrennial ritual that lasts two months during the winter (April to June). The notion of cyclical regimentation is prominent: initiates in the postliminal stage receive a regimental name from the paramount, and it is this name with which an Ndebele man identifies himself for life. The Ndzundza-Ndebele have a system of fifteen such names that are used over a period of approximately sixty years. The cycle repeats itself in strict chronological order. The Manala-Ndebele have thirteen names.

The numerical dimension of Ndebele male initiation is unparalleled in southern Africa. During the 1985 initiation, some 10,000 young men were initiated and, during 1993, more than 12,000. The ritual is controlled, installed, officiated, and administered by the royal house. It is decentralized over a wide area within the former KwaNdebele, in rural as well as urban (township) areas. Regional headmen (see "Political Organization") are assigned to supervise the entire ritual process over the two-month period, which involves nine sectional rituals at *emphadwini* (lodges in the field) and *emzini* (lodges at the homestead).

Arts. Ndebele aesthetic expression in the form of mural art and beadwork has won international fame for that society during the latter half of the twentieth century. Mural painting (*ukugwala*) is done by women and their daughters and entails the multicolor application of acrylic paint on entire outer and inner courtyard and house walls. Earlier paints were manufactured and mixed from natural material such as clay, plant pulp, ash, and cow dung. Since the 1950s, mural patterns have shown clear urban and Western influences. Consumer goods (e.g., razor blades), urban architecture (e.g., gables, lampposts), and symbols of modern transportation (e.g., airplanes, number plates) acted as inspiration for women artists.

Beadwork (*ukupothela*) also proliferated during the 1950s; it shows similarity in color and design to murals. Ndebele beadwork is essentially part of female ceremonial costume. Beads are sown on goat skins, canvas, and even hard board nowadays, and worn as aprons. Beaded necklaces and arm and neck rings form part of the outfit that is worn during rituals such as initiation and weddings. As Ndebele beadwork became one of the most popular curio art commodities in the period from the mid-1960s to the mid-1990s, women also beaded glass bottles, gourds, and animal horns. The recent prolific trading in Ndebele beadwork concentrates on "antique" garments as pieces of art. Some women are privately commissioned to apply their painting on canvas, shopping center walls, and even cars.

The recent discourse on Ndebele art suggests that the phenomenon should be interpreted in terms of the conscious establishment of a distinctive ethnic Ndebele niche at a time in South African history when the Ndebele struggled to regain their land and were not regarded as a society with its own identity.

Medicine. Current medical assistance includes the simultaneous use and application of traditional cures and medicines and visits to local hospitals and clinics. Children are born with or without the assistance of modern maternity care.

Death and Afterlife. Death is attributed to both natural and supernatural causes. A period of night watch over the body precedes the funeral. Funerals reunite the homestead and family members and involve the recital of clan praises (*iibongo*) at the grave and the slaughtering of animals at the deceased's homestead afterward. Today many Ndebele receive church burials. Widows are regarded as unclean; they may be ritually cleansed after many months or even a year. Traditionally, the deceased are buried at family grave sites, which are usually at the ruins of previous settlements and often far away from their homes. Nowadays, however, people are mostly buried at nearby cemeteries.

Bibliography

Courtney-Clarke, Margaret (1986). *Ndebele: The Art of an African Tribe*. Cape Town: Struik.

Delius, Peter (1989). "The Ndzundza-Ndebele: Indenture and the Making of Ethnic Identity." In *Holding Their Ground*, edited by P. Bonner, I. Hofmeyr, D. James, and T. Lodge. Johannesburg: Ravan Press.

James, Deborah A. (1990). "A Question of Ethnicity: Ndzundza Ndebele in a Lebowa Village." *Journal of Southern African Studies* 16(1).

Kuper, Adam (1976). "Fourie and the Southern Transvaal Ndebele." *African Studies* 37(1).

Levy, D. (1989). "Ndebele Beadwork." In *Catalogue: Ten Years of Collecting (1979–1989)*, edited by W. D. Hammond-Tooke and A. Nettleton. Johannesburg: Witwatersrand University Press.

McCaul, Colleen (1987). *Satellite in Revolt: KwaNdebele—An Economic and Political Profile*. Johannesburg: South African Institute of Race Relations.

Schneider, Elizabeth A. (1885). "Ndebele Mural Art." *African Arts* 18(3).

Van Vuuren, Chris J. (1991). "Historical Land and Contemporary Ritual: The Innovation of Oral Tradition in Understanding Ndzundza-Ndebele Ethnicity." In *Oral Tradition and Innovation. New Wine in Old Bottles*, edited by E. Sienaert, N. Bell, and M. Lewis. Durban: University of Natal Oral Documentation and Research Centre.

Van Warmelo, N. J. (1930). *Transvaal Ndebele Texts*. Ethnological Publications, vol. 1. Pretoria: Government Printer.

CHRIS J. VAN VUUREN

Ndembu

ETHNONYMS: Lunda, Southern Lunda

Orientation

Identification. The Ndembu constitute the southern arm of the ancient empire of the Lunda in the Congo. Their domain was trisected in 1905 by the territorial boundaries created by the European nations that annexed central southern Africa. These territories were named, until independence, Northern Rhodesia (now Zambia), the Belgian Congo (now Zaire), and Portuguese Angola (now Angola). Despite of their peripheral and rural position, the Ndembu have experienced considerable economic change. They have been closely studied, particularly with regard to their complex ritual.

Location. The Ndembu inhabit the western portion of Mwinilunga District in Zambia's Northwestern Province, (approximately 11° to 12° S and 24° E), in territory roughly 560 kilometers from the nearest sizable city. The land forms part of the plateau region of northwestern Zambia, consisting of mostly poor laterite soils. It was formerly under high savanna forest with evergreen gallery forest along the rivers but has undergone considerable deforestation around settled areas. Owing to its situation close to the Zambezi-Congo divide, it is a source area for many rivers. Precipitation, which begins each year in November and ends in April, varies from about 100 to about 150 centimeters. The average low temperature is 7° C in June; during the "second winter" of the tropics (January through February), the temperature briefly dips to around 15° C. In September and October the average high temperature is 32° C.

Demography. The Ndembu, numbering about 40,000 in Zambia, constitute about 1 percent of the total population.

The average population density is around 2.8 per square kilometer, increasing to 18 in settled areas beside the roads and a much higher figure in townships. The infant mortality rate is about 140 per thousand.

Linguistic Affiliation. The Ndembu language, which is part of the West Central Bantu Language Zone, is agglutinative with ten noun classes.

History and Cultural Relations

Between 1750 and 1800 the Ndembu, led by their chief, Kanongesha, migrated from the large Northern Lunda (or Luunda) Empire of the paramount chief Mwantiamvwa in the Kapanga District of the southern Congo. In their new home, they abandoned their former patrilineal descent system in favor of the local matrilineal pattern and also lost their centralized organization. In the second half of the nineteenth century, Ovimbundu slave traders and Chokwe and Lwena raiders took many slaves from among the Ndembu and sold them to the Portuguese for guns and cloth. The British South Africa Company began to administer Mwinilunga District in 1906, and missionaries soon arrived. In 1913 many Ndembu fled over the border to Angola to avoid taxation.

In the 1930s the Ndembu began to travel for work to the new copper-producing cities in central Zambia and the Katanga region of the Congo. A money economy took root. It was not until 1964 that Zambia won independence from the British. From 1964 to 1970, because of high copper prices, the gross national product of Zambia rose to two thousand times its value in the early 1960s. That prosperity also reached the Ndembu. In the early 1970s prices slumped, however, and an endemic depression developed. The Ndembu population had risen sharply during the copper boom but did not fall when hard times arrived. Maize production in Mwinilunga fell lamentably below government targets, and the people have been hard put to feed themselves on dwindling crops of cassava (manioc).

The Ndembu tend to hold themselves politically apart from their neighbors. Formerly, they traded cassava to the copper towns; nowadays they supply pineapples to a government canning factory. In the 1970s and 1980s they peacefully absorbed a number of refugees from war-torn Angola. Their present cultural relations occur mainly in the religious sphere. There is much interaction and visiting in the form of conference meetings of the Christian Fellowship, the Apostles of John Maranke, and Baha'i adherents.

Settlements

Ndembu villages are changing from a pattern of discrete circles of houses inhabited by matrilineal kin to a conglomeration of groups of two or three mud-brick houses that face inward to a small courtyard. Such conglomerations themselves seem to be villages, although they are not regarded as such. The tiny groups are spinoffs from larger matrilineally based parent villages, and an Ndembu's immediate neighbor is still likely to be a matrilineal relative. The small groups are called "farms." Circular villages still exist and are referred to by the Ndembu term for village (*mukala*). A typical mukala has eight to ten houses with 30 to 50 inhabitants. The conglomerations, built-up areas, vary greatly in population—from 100 to 800 to 2,000 people. Their larger size is a response to the government's policy of centralization for the sake of the schools and of branch-committee control.

Almost all the houses are rectangular, mud-brick structures with thatched roofs, wooden doors and window frames, and hard mud floors; usually a dwelling has two rooms and a veranda. A round meeting shelter is sometimes added.

Economy

Subsistence and Commercial Activities. The Ndembu practice hoe cultivation in small garden plots. Cassava is the Ndembu staple crop. It is grown on cleared upland and left in the ground for more than a year, then harvested during the following year or two. Owing to shortage of forest land near the now permanent villages, rotations of thirty years have given way to very brief ones of a year or two, resulting in lighter yields. Some rice is grown in wetlands. Pineapples are raised in the more fertile upland gardens, as are some peanuts, potatoes, and cucurbits. Beans and maize are grown in streamside gardens, along with tomatoes, onions, and cabbages. Bananas and mango trees grow in the villages. Very occasionally, hunters obtain game. Fishing contributes a small amount of protein. Mushrooms, white ants, fruits, and medicinal plants are gathered. The main cash crops are pineapples and some maize and rice. A type of gin is produced, which accounts for much trade locally. Cattle raising is spreading; herds number up to fifty head. Some goats, pigs, and chickens are also raised. Most cash is acquired from jobs at the district center or from labor migration. There is a high rate of unemployment.

Industrial Arts. At the district center, tailors, carpenters, and blacksmiths operate small businesses, and others are engaged in the modern occupations of mechanic or electrician. In the villages, most men are builders and some are mechanics. Mats are made locally.

Trade. There are markets at the district center and chiefs' courts. Local stores have given way to the centralizing tendency encouraged by government policy. The missions also run trading trucks through the villages, selling South African maize meal to the many who cannot produce sufficient cassava. There is informal local trade in beef and gin.

Division of Labor. Because of their traditional role as hunters, Ndembu men still do not engage in agriculture except to clear the ground for a new garden. They weave mats and make children's wire toys. Women plant and tend their own gardens and those of their husbands, sometimes traveling with a baby as far as 16 kilometers away from their homes to garden sites with less exhausted soil. They also cook, fish, and fetch water. Owing to unemployment, a man often has no role.

Land Tenure. Traditionally, the first to settle in an area was named "owner of the cultivation." He would allow all comers to cultivate also. There is no buying and selling of land, although owing to pressure on land near the nucleated settlements, there have begun to be disputes about rights to the land when the head of a family dies.

Kinship

Kin Groups and Descent. Matriliny governs immediate residence patterns, although the direct offspring of a headman will be more likely than in the past to stay in their father's village. Surnames have been universally adopted, these being the name of the father. Headmanship descends from mother's brother to sister's son.

Kinship Terminology. A classificatory naming system follows the matrilineal principle.

Marriage and Family

Marriage. Monogamy has been adopted by the Christians, whereas traditionalists practice polygyny. Marriage payments are made by the family of the bridegroom to that of the bride. The common pattern of virilocal postmarital residence creates difficulties in keeping a matrilineage together; therefore, divorce, a means to return to the matrilineage, was very common in the past. Because divorce is now discouraged by the churches, matrilineal residence is becoming less clearly defined. The age of marriage for women has risen to 17 or so, thus dissociating marriage from a girl's initiation, which still takes place at puberty. Other than Christian weddings, there are no traditional marriage customs distinct from initiation.

Domestic Unit. In the polygynous family, each wife has her own house, runs her own gardens, and controls her own budget. If her husband is a labor migrant, she usually resides with her matrilineage. Children often sleep separately from their parents, along with others of the same generation or with their grandparents.

Inheritance. At death, a close matrilineal senior relative is appointed as executor. He divides the property, first between uterine siblings of the elder generation, then sisters' children, and wives and children of the deceased, according to the executor's good will. Wives will return to their matrilineages once a payment has been made to the relatives of the dead man. Formerly, a ritual of name inheritance was sometimes performed in response to the call of the spirit of the dead.

Socialization. Children's growth is stunted because the land is not producing enough food. Small children are breastfed until 3 years of age and are not left to cry. Older children play at grown-ups' roles. They are assigned domestic duties, which they usually fulfill after a special word of authority from an elder. Laughter is the main sanction against faults, although theft is punished with beating. Older girls delight in caring for baby siblings, but boys play at hunting or at being soldiers. Conflict between mothers and daughters is common as the latter approach puberty. With the exception of fundamentalist Christians, most 12-year-old girls are initiated, one or two at a time, in a ritual involving seclusion for perhaps a week. Boys are circumcised in larger groups between the ages of 7 and 12 and are secluded in the bush until the wounds are healed. Formerly, complex initiations with much symbolism prevailed, with milk symbolism predominating for the girls, ending with a highly aesthetic "breast" dance, whereas masked spirit figures appeared at boys' circumcisions. Both rituals followed the form of a rite of passage. School authorities and missions now require the curtailment of initiation. Celebration rather than ritual has become the style.

Sociopolitical Organization

Social Organization. Neighborhoods join informally at healing rituals and initiations, and friends join in informal groups to use or borrow a vehicle, molds for brick making, or the like. Women share pounding mortars. The churches, schools, and branch committees of government have replaced most of the crosscutting functions of the old cult associations, which were based on spirit manifestations in the form of illness.

Political Organization. A paramount chief, Kanongesha, heads a local law court and promulgates edicts concerning local safety or housing measures. He ideally attends the finale of the circumcisions. Subchiefs visit villages and harangue the inhabitants on local issues, thus creating a sense of self-identity among the Ndembu people. Village headmen, although they are becoming less important, are now chosen by election. The numerous farms give a strongly individualistic character to rural life. Modern elections are held to choose political branch heads and the rural council. Certain chiefs are nominated for the rural council by the minister of provincial and local government and culture in Lusaka.

Social Control. Very revered elders eventually become judges. They meet to hear civil cases in a village meeting shelter. More serious cases go to the district court.

Conflict. Bandits occasionally enter the region and ransack isolated villages. Local violence is mainly owing to alcoholism or jealousy, the latter being expressed in deeds of witchcraft. These are countered by antiwitchcraft rituals. Overt conflicts are resolved in the village courts.

Religion and Expressive Culture

Religious Beliefs. Some 40 percent of Ndembu are now Christians. The old religion was imbued with a strong moral character: people would be afflicted by the spirits of deceased relatives wishing to remind them (or their relatives) of their social and religious duties. This spirit would "come out" in a certain mode, the mode of the appropriate cult association. Patient, doctors, and spirit belonged to a single sacred community, which initiated the patient as a new member. When honored in a ritual, the spirit would bestow hunting prowess and healing upon on the living members.

An otiose god, Nzambi, has been co-opted into Christianity, and spirit practioners invoke this god on behalf of the sick. Cult associations have disappeared. Today dynasties of doctors exist who work through their doctor ancestor spirits or some foreign tutelary spirit. Male sorcerers possess familiars, which they deliberately raise and induce to do harm, or they use mystic poisons. Evil women—witches—contain a substance inside them that impels them to harm others. Witches are also the involuntary hosts of familiar spirits.

Religious Practitioners. A doctor (*chimbuki, chiyang'a*) is first and foremost a spirit ritualist. Most doctors are men. Some come to their vocation through a call in the shape of a spirit-induced illness necessitating a ritual, by means of which the budding doctor develops his sense of spirit matters. He also learns medicines and ritual from a teacher, for whom he acts as assistant and apprentice. The office is usually inherited from some bilateral ancestor, with or without a major vocational episode. The doctors treat what are defined as "African diseases"—those that the hospital cannot cure but that are well understood by the healers. Diviners have become rare. Herbalists, men or women, treat minor ailments, and a traditional midwife, briefly trained by the hospital, attends births.

Ceremonies. Ritual (*ng'oma,* meaning "drum") is performed by a skilled doctor with the help of the community (formerly led by the cult association concerned) in order to reveal the spirit, previously as figurine, effigy, or voice, and still today as hunter's tooth. "Revealing" was—and continues to be—the basic principle of Ndembu religion and curing. It is mainly through sickness that an individual begins to sense the existence of spirits or witchcraft powers. Thus, it is the irregularities of life that develop the sense of nonempirical powers. Some of the curative rituals still follow the form of the rite of passage, with a preliminary rite of separation, a seclusion phase, and a ritual of reintegration. Some show a marked point when the afflicting spirit leaves the body of the sufferer. Important elements in ritual are drumming, singing, dancing, medicines, shrines, symbolic objects, revealing and removing a spirit form, the power of the doctor, the participation of the community, and the cooperation of the patient. Healing rituals are on the increase, partly because the central medical authorities are unable to control what goes on in rural areas. Thus, traditional ritual skills have been developed and adapted, often with many successes.

Arts. Mask making is almost obsolete, but drum making persists. In the past there were highly gifted wood carvers. The principal Ndembu art today is music, both in drum rituals and in churches; harmonizing and choral skill have reached a high level.

Medicine. A great number of herbal medicines are used for healing, childbirth, madness, and even as poisons. Curative medicines used in rituals have both herbal and spiritual effects. White and red clay and the horns, blood, and other parts of animals give power to ritual.

Death and Afterlife. Death used to be celebrated by the appearance of a masked dancer or stilt walkers drawn from the funerary association, followed by the burning down of the deceased's house. Medicines were used to expel the ghost. The dead existed in a number of spirit forms, some of them being able to reincarnate in a patrilateral descendant, some as matrilineal ancestral guides, and some as dangerous ghosts; the latter are still feared today. Present-day funerals are greatly simplified because knowledge of ancestor spirits is disappearing.

Bibliography

McCulloch, Merran (1951). *The Southern Lunda and Related Peoples*. Ethnographic Survey of Africa. London: International African Institute.

Turner, Edith (1992). *Experiencing Ritual: A New Interpretation of African Healing*. Philadelphia: Pennsylvania University Press.

Turner, Edith, with William Blodgett (1987). "The Carnivalization of Initiation in Zambia." *Play and Culture* 1(3): 191–204.

Turner, Victor (1957). *Schism and Continuity in an African Society: A Study of Ndembu Village Life*. Manchester: Manchester University Press.

Turner, Victor (1968). *The Drums of Affliction: A Study of Religious Processes among the Ndembu of Zambia*. Oxford: Clarendon.

White, C. M. N. (1948). "Material Culture of the Lunda-Luvale." Occasional Papers of the Rhodes-Livingstone Museum, Livingstone, Zambia, no. 3.

EDITH L. B. TURNER

Nestorians

ETHNONYMS: none

Orientation

The designation "Nestorian" connotes both a religious rite and a linguistic minority, a phenomenon that is often misunderstood, especially by scholars but by many outsiders as well. This misunderstanding was dramatically illustrated in the aftermath of World War I, in the general lack of concern for the welfare of the Nestorians, both as an ethnic and as a religious entity.

Nestorians derive their name from Nestorius, who was bishop of Constantinople from 428 to 431, following the major controversy that split the early Christians over the nature of Christ: dual (human or divine) or singular (two in one, inseparable and closely bound together). They were influenced by the Antiochan writers of the preceding century, who emphasized Jesus' humanity with its inherent imperfections. But the real shaper of Nestorianism was Theodore (d. 428), bishop of Mopsuestia in Cilicia, who was a pupil of Diodorus, bishop of Tarsus. Theodore affirmed the true humanity of Jesus, arguing that he acquired his perfect sinlessness in union with the Person of the Divine Word, which he had received as a reward for his foreseen sinlessness. The Word, accordingly, dwelt in the man Christ (Hastings n.d.). Nestorians thus rejected the union of God and man in Christ. Mary was regarded as the mother of the man, not of God. It was not until Nestorius came to Constantinople that his teachings became popular and thus were named after him. Theodore's doctrine was formally condemned at the Fifth Ecumenical Council of Constantinople in 553.

Nestorians today, some 100,000 of them, have found a lasting home in the mountains of Kurdistan, the neighboring plains of Azerbaijan, in northwestern Iran, and in the mountainous region of eastern Turkey, in what is commonly referred to as Kurdistan. They are concentrated around Lake Urmia and in the low-lying plain of Mosul in northern Iraq, generally in close proximity to the Kurds, with whom they have had an on-and-off relationship throughout the centuries. Their great school was once located in Edessa (contemporary Urfa, in south-central Turkey).

Of complex ethnicity, Nestorians list in their ancestry Aramaeans, Assyrians, Kurds, Persians, and Arabs. After being Christianized, they came to be known as "East Syrians," to distinguish them from the "West Syrian" Monophysites or the Jacobites.

History and Cultural Relations

A Syriac tradition describes Nestorius as being of Persian origin, perhaps to connect him with the later Nestorians of the Persian Empire. He became a monk and dwelt in the monastery of Euprepius, near Antioch, where he acquired fame for his eloquent preaching and was appointed bishop, through the influence of Emperor Theodosius II, on 10 April 428. (The rivalries of the ecclesiastics of the city had necessitated the selection of an outsider.) It was but a few days later that he launched a fierce attack on heresy, promising the emperor a future in heaven if he would purge the earth of heretics. Arians and Novatians were both purged from Constantinople, and the womanhood of Mary was affirmed through the Antiochan presbyter Anastasius.

His bold policies angered both Bishop Cyril of Alexandria and Bishop Coelestine of Rome, who, at a synod held in Rome in 430, declared Nestorius a heretic; however, the Antiochans supported Nestorius rather than the Alexandrine's teachings. It was at the Council of Ephesus in 449 (known as the "Robber Synod") that the Nestorian "heresy" was ended, to create an unbridgeable schism between Antiochans and the rest of the early Christians. Two years later, the Orthodox creed that contained the expression "Theotokos" (mother of God) was adopted by the Antiochans. Henceforth Antiochans were to be divided from Nestorians on doctrinal grounds. Bishops who stuck by Nestorius lost their sees. Several traveled to the east, taking their priests and deacons with them, thus reinforcing what was to become known as the "Syrian" or "Suryâni" church.

In the Persian Empire, the "East Syrian church" had existed from the Apostolic age. Persian authorities fostered it for political purposes: it was a buttress against the Greco-Roman Empire to the west. The "emigrants" had nothing good to say about Cyril, but the final separation from the Orthodox church took place only after the Muslim conquest (637–640). Extensive missions were launched in Asia, India, Ceylon, Socotra, southwestern Arabia, Turkestan, and farther east in China and Mongolia. A monument at Sian dates their presence to 781. They converted the sister-in-law of Kublai Khan, wife of Hülegü, who conquered Baghdad in 1258. Syriac burial inscriptions in Mongolia bear testimony to their evangelistic zeal, which even gave rise to the story of Prester John. Wherever they went, they retained Syriac as their liturgical language. According to Gibbon (p. 50), there were more Nestorians and Jacobites than there were Latins and Greeks combined. Tamerlane and his Turco-Tartar invaders almost wiped them out, however, after they had survived all the Islamic caliphates up through the fourteenth century.

After they were driven out of Edessa by Emperor Zeno in 489, the Nestorians went to Nisibis to reestablish their school. By the time Baghdad was built in 763, to serve as the capital of the ʿAbbāsid Muslim caliphate, the Nestorian patriarch was a welcome figure in the city, to which he had moved from Seleucia-Ctesiphon.

Caught in the titanic struggle of the two empires, Persia and Rome, the Nestorians found it necessary to build up their own ecclesiastical organization and to maintain a distance from their brethren in the enemy camp. They were abetted in the process by the insistence of the Persian emperor, Khosrow Anūshīrvan, who, while battling the Byzantine Christian Heraclius, demanded that they choose between the Nestorian and the Jacobite rite if they wished to stay in their native country (Joseph 1961, 25–26). Sāssānian emperors generally tolerated their Christian subjects, especially the Nestorians. In this way the Persian church became a sort of national church for the Nestorians. Their bishop, of Seleucia-Ctesiphon, came to wield unlimited power, in contrast to that of the metropolitan of Edessa. This power was further consolidated under Islam because the caliphs wanted the continued existence of native churches, in order to separate themselves from the Byzantines. Nestorian patriarchs were very much respected as important Christian dignitaries under the caliphs. Their centers of learning at Nisibis, Jundishapur, and Merv became important cultural landmarks and contributed scholars who abetted the development of an Arabo-Islamic cultural heritage. These scholars served in numerous offices of trust, and their patriarch was regarded most highly under the Islamic imperium, except during the caliphates of ʿUmar II (717–720) and al-Mutawakkil (847–861), who were responsible for reducing Nestorians to the level of other sects.

The Mongol conquests revived hope: more than one emperor espoused Christianity, as did some Turco-Tartar tribes of Central Asia (Joseph 1961, 28). On his march westward, Hülegü spared Christians because his wife was "a believing and true Christian queen" (Mingana 1927). The metropolitan of Cathay in 1280 was a Mongol Nestorian. Another church father of Tartar origin was Rabban Bar Sawma (d. 1317). He was sent by the Mongol emperor, Arghun, to the West in 1287 to gain the support of the Christian monarchs of Europe to conquer Muslim Palestine and Syria.

Hierarchical struggle for the top positions led to controversy, especially after the elected patriarch in 1450 enacted a law that restricted his office to members of his own family. Because the patriarch had to be a celibate, it meant that a nephew or an uncle would succeed him. Hereditary succession was against the canons of the Nestorian church. The process was challenged in 1551, following the advent of Catholic missionaries from the Latin West. With the aid of Franciscan missionaries of Mosul, a monk, Ḥanna Sulāqa, from the monastery of Rabban-Hormizd, was elected and sent to Rome via Jerusalem, where he was received as a Catholic and ordained as the first Uniate patriarch. His successor in 1692, however, renounced Catholicism, but the line from Sulāqa has persisted until today, bearing the title "Mār Shamʿūn" (Saint Simeon). Other successors, who bore the title "Mār Ilīya" (Saint Elias), attempted reconciliation with Rome, in order to put an end to the rival branch of Sulāqa.

Hakkâri Nestorians sought to separate themselves from the Armenian patriarch's tutelage in the late nineteenth century by petitioning for direct Ottoman supervision, but without success. Their legal status remained vague at the turn of the twentieth century. Hakkâri Nestorians were nominally under the jurisdiction of the Hakkâri tribe and were protected by their mountain fastness, which accounted for their independence.

The advent of Protestant missionaries in the nineteenth century impacted rather negatively on Nestorian communities. The "evangelical awakening" of the eighteenth century in Great Britain had quickened religious life in Protestant circles, and the Church Mission Society was established in London in 1799, to be followed in 1804 by the British and Foreign Bible Society. In the United States, the American Board of Commissioners for Foreign Missions was organized in 1810; the Catholic "foreign Gospel conquest" preceded them by a few centuries. With the rise of economic imperialism in Europe, the road was paved for the missionaries, who had both financial resources and personnel, to make a global assault on "barbarian heathen nations."

The American Board dispatched two missionaries, who established a station in Smyrna (İzmir, Turkey) in 1828, followed by stations in Beirut and İstanbul in 1831. By the end of the nineteenth century, there was "scarcely a village, except in the mountains of Kurdistan and some parts of Mesopotamia and Syria bordering on Arabia" that did not have occasion to "hear the Gospel" (Dwight et al. 1904, 755).

H. O. Dwight and Eli Smith were sent to investigate the more than 100,000 Nestorians who were subject to the hereditary patriarch in the land of the Kurds (*Missionary Herald* 1830, 75). Reaching Urmia in 1831, Smith was jubilant over the prospects of "rekindling their [the Nestorians'] ancient missionary spirit" so that they might exert a commanding influence on "the spiritual regeneration of Asia" (Smith 1833, 2:234; Perkins 1843, 28–31).

Needless to say, the presence of such missionaries had a negative impact on the villages. The missionaries excited the hatred of the Muslims, with harmful repercussions for the Nestorians who were living under the nominal jurisdiction of the emir of Hakkâri (who served as administrator under the Ottoman *vali,* or governor, of Erzurum). The vali of Mosul was against the presence of "Franks" (foreigners) in Nestorian country, and the American missionary Asahel Grant had to call on the British vice-consul to restrain the vali. George Percy Badger, as representative of the British missionaries, then commenced his feud with Grant, who represented the (Protestant) Society for the Propagation of the Gospel. Badger tried to convince the patriarch that his true enemies were the Catholic missionaries. Consequently, Grant was held indirectly responsible for the massacre of Nestorians in 1843, owing to his "inspiring fallacious hopes and exciting dangerous prejudices" (Joseph 1961, 65). The Kurds and the Ottomans saw Grant's mission as political. Both the Anglican and the American missions were injudiciously conceived. Badger excited the patriarch's fears when he alleged that the American missionaries would destroy his temporal as well as his spiritual authority by cultivating the Hakkâri chief, Nurallah. Grant's death from typhus led the Board to shift its work from the Nestorians of Kurdistan to the Nestorians of Urmia, in Persia, "which country was more peaceful." Their work was tolerated when they first arrived in Azerbaijan, where they started, with the help of Orientalists, to reduce the vernacular Syriac, a language of direct communion with God for the public, to a literary written language. Given that the literacy rate of the Nestorians was low, literary Syriac had become the preserve of only the clergy and the missionaries.

By 1855, the missionaries had lured 158 Nestorians to embrace Protestantism, and in 1862 a native presbytery was organized within the Nestorian church. No separation had taken place, but the intolerance and uncompromising attitude of the missionaries did lead to a rift. Perkins dubbed the fasts of the Nestorians "little more than a senseless routine of forms" and called the sound of their prayers "a chattering noise," which he claimed was a contrivance of Satan (*Missionary Herald* 1837; Perkins 1843, 253). The "Reformed Nestorian Church" was born at last, an evangelical church that only served to galvanize the resistance of Rome's Sacra Congregatione della Propaganda Fide (Sacred Society for the Propagation of the Faith). Although poorer than the Americans, the Lazarists fought back to protect their flock, after receiving French missionary reinforcements in 1838 with the backing of France's minister in Tehran (Louvet n.d.). The Persian government issued a decree against conversions, on penalty of criminal prosecution for those who did convert. The Americans concluded that "Catholic malevolence is unparalleled in corrupt Persia" (American Board of Commisioners 1868, 60).

England next stepped in, to "render assistance"; Rev. Edward L. Cutts was sent out by the Church of England to help "improve and extend the education of the Nestorian people" (Cutts 1877, 178). The archbishop of Canterbury endorsed the mission to the "Assyrian Christians" (as they were to be known in England), but with the caveat that the end was to reform, not to proselytize, the church. The mission was to defend, rather than to change, the Assyrians' religion, as the Americans were attempting to do (Joseph 1961, 82). Like the Catholics, they, too, emphasized the use of classical Syriac in their school, and students were taught to take pride in their culture. American Presbyterians, after having given the Bible to the people, now faced stiff competition from the English "ritualists." Ensuing feuds excited the anxieties of the authorities, who feared a repeat of the English takeover of India, where missionaries had preceded the army (Thompson 1858, 384).

Russia was already pressuring from the north, and when England declared war on Persia in 1856, Muslim landlords incited their tenants against the Christians, who were perceived as allies of the English. American missionaries begged for Christian Russia's protection of the Nestorians as the only alternative to the Muslims' hostility (Joseph 1961, 87). Once again, the Eastern Christians found themselves caught in the rivalries of the great European powers and the targets of local resentment.

In 1869 the Church Missionary Society of Great Britain commenced work in Eşfahān and in the following year renamed the undertaking among Nestorians the "Mission to Persia." The Presbyterian Board of Foreign Mission now took over the stations already founded in Tehran, Tabrīz, Hamadān, and Rasht. Meanwhile, the Nestorian Evangelical church established itself as a separate organization. By 1880, the Protestant community had a civil head representing the community before the government. Then, in 1877, the Anglicans, who had been absent for thirty-five years owing to the ill-fated mission of Badger, were back at work among the Nestorians. This time, they were better received by Persian officials. Even American missionaries fared better after acquiring a fuller knowledge and appreciation of Nestorian culture (Shedd 1895, 746).

Support for the Nestorians was boosted with the archaeological discoveries of Nineveh and Assyria and with the growing belief that the Nestorians were descendants of the warrior race that had lived there. British interest in them was aroused at the highest level of government, and the Ottoman government was urged to safeguard the Nestorians' interests and heritage in the face of increased Kurdish aggressiveness (1866–1868). When British efforts failed them, the Nestorians did not hesitate to turn to the Russians for protection after the latter had expanded southward into the Caucasus (Joseph 1961, 99). To gain this support, the bishop of Urmia promised to renounce "error" and return to Christian orthodoxy. The Saint Petersburg church authorities dispatched priests and monks to Azerbaijan in 1897 to aid in the process. When Japan defeated Russia in 1905, however, one Nestorian congregation joined the United Lutheran church, demonstrating the political nature of the Nestorians' move. Meanwhile, the Anglicans moved their headquarters to Van. The German Orient Mission established an orphanage in Urmia, and various denominations of Baptists followed.

The Ottomans were growing suspicious of all these Western missions and began to refer to the Armenians as the "Americans," which only aroused opposition to the American missionaries. The American missionary Benjamin Labaree was killed by a Kurd near Urmia in 1904. World War I brought the retreat of the Russians, and American missionaries found themselves caring for refugees of all denominations, Muslim and Christian alike. The Nestorians held out in their mountain fastness, and, by 1917, Allied forces dispatched a unit to Tbilisi, which aroused Muslim opposition. The Hakkâri Christians held them off until outside help could arrive, but the patriarch and forty-five of his followers were assassinated, and the region lapsed into a state of anarchy. With Lionel Charles Dunsterville in 1918 leading an expeditionary force north to occupy Persia, thousands of Kurds, Nestorians, and Persians fled south to British lines, driven by starvation. Many perished en route, but many more were saved (Joseph 1961, 142–144).

When the dust had settled on World War I and the ensuing peace process, the Nestorians, like the Kurds and Armenians, found themselves without the benefit of self-determination or a state of their own. The Nestorian patriarch sought permanent British protection for his communicants. The "Assyrians" of America pressed not only for security but also for an independent state for Nestorians, Jacobites, Chaldeans, and even for "Islamic Assyrians" under the protection of the European mandatory regimes, independent of the Kurds.

Four "Assyrian Evangelical churches" resulted from the reopening by the Presbyterian Board of their missions and schools around Urmia after 1923. The British, under Winston Churchill as colonial secretary, recruited able-bodied Nestorian Christians for service in a newly formed Iraqi army consisting of Arabs, Turkomans, and Kurds. Nestorians had been included in the gendarmerie in order to protect their own refugees and defend the Mosul frontier. With the establishment of Kemal Atatürk's Turkey in the 1920s, the Nestorians were resettled in the Mosul area, ostensibly so that they could be under the protective umbrella of the British. When the British announced the end of their mandate over Iraq in 1930, however, the Assyrians voiced concerns about the safeguarding of their rights, and, after the Kurdish uprising that year, the British insisted on using Assyrian levies against them to give proof of their loyalty to the government—"with the same faithfulness they have served His Britannic Majesty" (Joseph 1961, citing *Iraq Report* 1930, 24–28, 31).

The Mosul Commission met in 1925 to find some means to ensure the security of minorities in Iraq and some autonomy for the "Assyrians" (Nestorians), but to no avail. The patriarch and his followers had voted for Iraq's establishment when a plebescite was held in Mosul at the end of the war, but they gained no autonomy for themselves. They had cast their lot with the British, and the British could not deliver on their promise to the Nestorians. The Mār Shamʿūn was warmly received by King Faisal of Iraq and his prime minister, Nuri al-Saʿid, but the message he received from them was that religion and state were to be henceforth separated. Nestorians were to mind their churches—and the king, the state. The *millet* system, with its stress on autonomy for ethnoreligious entities during the Ottoman era, had now given way to the national state. Appeal to the Council of the League of Nations yielded a negative reply on the issue of autonomy.

The faction of Nestorians that supported the patriarch sought refuge in Syria after coming to blows with their opponents, but when some 700 decided to recross the border into Iraq, troops barred them entry; some 20 Assyrians were killed. General Bakr Ṣidqi followed up with the massacre of some 300 men and boys at their village of Simail, two days after they had surrendered their arms. The British did not stand by their protégés; their policy now was to buttress the Arab government in place at Baghdad, not to support minority issues. Eventually Hakkâri Nestorians were settled in the Mosul and Erbil districts of upper Iraq.

At the end of World War II, the Nestorians of Urmia were dislocated; most of them resettled among relatives and friends in the major cities of Iran. All but four of the fifty Protestant missions that had aroused the hopes of the Nestorians were asked to leave the country. With their departure, the native Christians (Nestorians, Chaldeans, and Jacobites) were placed in relatively favorable positions in both Iraq and Iran (Joseph 1961, 225).

See also Chaldeans; Jacobites; Syriacs

Bibliography

American Board of Commissioners for Foreign Missions (1868). *Annual Report*. Boston: ABC-FM.

Baynes, Norman H. (1949). *History of the Byzantine Empire*. Oxford: Oxford University Press.

Browne, L. E. (1933). *The Eclipse of Christianity in Asia from the Time of Muhammad till the Fourteenth Century*. Cambridge: Cambridge University Press.

Budge, E. A. T. Wallis, trans. (1928). *The Monks of Kublai Khan: The History of the Life and Travels of Rabban Sâwma*. London.

Cutts, Edward L. (1877). *Christians under the Crescent in Asia*. London.

Dwight, Henry Otis, Rev. H. Allen Tupper, Jr., and Rev. Edwin Munsell Bliss (1904). *The Encyclopedia of Missions*. New York.

Gibbon, Edward (1776–1788). *Decline and Fall of the Roman Empire*. Vol. 6. London.

Great Britain (1931). *Special Report . . . to the Council of the League of Nations on the Progress of Iraq . . . 1920–1931*. Colonial no. 58. London: His Majesty's Government.

Hastings, James (n.d.) "Nestorians." *Encyclopedia of Religion and Ethics*. Vol. 9, 323–332. New York: Charles Scribner's Sons.

Joseph, John (1961). *The Nestorians and Their Muslim Neighbors*. Princeton, N.J.: Princeton University Press.

Louvet, Louise-Eugene (n.d.). *Les missions catholiques au XIXme siècle*. Lyon: Desclée de Brouwer.

Mingana, Alfonso (1927). "The Early Spread of Christianity in Central Asia and the Far East." *John Rylands Library Bulletin* 11:77–98.

Missionary Herald 26 (1830); 33 (1837).

Montgomery, J. A., trans. (1927). *The History of Yaballaha III . . . and of Bar Sauma*. New York.

Perkins, Justin (1843). *A Residence of Eight Years in Persia, among the Nestorian Christians, with Notices of the Muhammedans*. New York.

Shedd, W. A. (1895). "Relation of the Protestant Missionary Effort to the Nestorian Church." *Missionary Review of the World* 8 (October): 741ff.

Smith, Eli (1833). *Researches of . . . and the Rev. H. G. O. Dwight in Armenia*. 2 vols. Boston.

Stewart, John (1928). *Nestorian Missionary Enterprise: The Story of a Church on Fire*. Madras.

Thompson, J. P. (1858). *Memoirs of Rev. David Tappan Stoddard, Missionary to the Nestorians*. New York.

CAESAR E. FARAH

Nubians

ETHNONYMS: Egyptian Nubians, Halfans, Lower Nubians, Sudanese Nubians.

Orientation

Identification. The Nubians are a non-Arab Muslim population who lived in the geographical region known as Nubia in southern Egypt and northern Sudan. One hundred and twenty thousand Nubians were relocated beginning in 1964 because their villages were inundated by the Aswan High Dam Lake. Some argue that the name "Nubians" derives from a word in the Nubian language meaning "slaves," but others say that the ancient Egyptian word *nab* meant "gold" and that the Ancient Egyptians used that term to refer to the Nubian Valley because of the gold mines that were nearby. Another source mentions that the word *nebed* appeared in an inscription of Thotmes I (1450 B.C.) to designate people with curly hair who were invaded by the Pharoe.

Location. The Nubians lived until 1964 in a boundaryless geographical region known as Nubia, the southern edge of which lay along latitude 19° N, in village clusters along the banks of the Nile. The river, south of Aswan, is broken by five stony passages known as "cataracts." Nubia stretched from Aswan in Upper Egypt in the north, at the Nile's First Cataract, to the Republic of Sudan in the south, for some 300 kilometers, midway between the Third and Fourth cataracts. After 1964, and before the Aswan High Dam Lake inundated a large portion of their land, the Egyptian Nubians were relocated to reclaimed land in Komombo in the governorate of Aswan, 50 kilometers north of the city of Aswan. The Sudanese Nubians were resettled at Khashm al-Girba in what was eventually known as the New Halfa Project, 800 kilometers away from their original homeland.

Demography. The Nubian community, both in Sudan and Egypt, barely reproduced itself prior to resettlement. At a time when the larger society was experiencing an annual population increase ranging from 2.5 to 3.0 percent, Nubia was experiencing a population decline. Ever decreasing land availability owing to the construction of the Aswan Dam earlier in the twentieth century led to the emigration of males to cities. An imbalance existed in the sex ratio, especially in the middle-range age. Such an imbalance further led to natural decrease in the population. Among the Egyptian Nubians this population pattern was maintained after relocation. Among the Sudanese Nubians, population has increased since relocation. Many emigrants came back after relocation to settle, because the land acreage they were granted by the government was generous. Today the Sudanese Nubians have almost doubled their population in certain villages and have even tripled their population in New Wadi Halfa.

Linguistic Affiliation. According to Rouchdy (1991, 4) the Nubian languages, excluding Arabic, are classified as Eastern Sudanic languages, a branch of the Nilo-Saharan Group. The Nubians generally can be divided into four groups, each inhabiting a separate part of the Nubian Valley and speaking a different language. The groups, according to Fahim (1983, 10–11), are the Kenuz, the Arabs, the Nubians (Fadija), and the Halfans. The Kenuz, who prior to resettlement occupied the territory from Aswan south along the Nile for a distance of 150 kilometers, spoke a dialect called Metouki. Today the Kenuz still live in the northernmost region in relation to the rest of the Nubians, northeast of Komombo. The Arabs, who lived before resettlement in the next 40 kilometers south of the Kenuz, spoke Arabic. Today this group lives east of Komombo in Aswan. The Nubians (who are often referred to as "Fadija," a derogatory term the northern groups use to connote alien status) who live in the southern extremity of Egypt and north of Sudan speak Mahas. Today the Nubians live southeast of Komombo in Aswan. The Sudanese Nubians, Halfans, who originally resided in Wadi Halfa south of the Egyptian border, have their own dialect known as "Sukkot."

History and Cultural Relations

Few facts are available regarding Nubian history and culture prior to the sixth century. The primary archaeological survey of Nubia was conducted between 1907 and 1910 (Reisner 1910); it revealed that Nubia has possessed an advanced culture since the Predynastic period. The Nubian culture prior to 3200 B.C. was exactly the same as that of Egypt. During the period from the fourth to the eighteenth dynasty, tribes from the south and the west of the continent infiltrated the Nubian Valley and sometimes controlled it. This infiltration reduced the ethnic homogeneity between Nubian and Egyptian populations; the Nubian population eventually came to resemble tribes from Central Africa. Skeletal remains from the eighteenth dynasty to the thirtieth suggest a return to Egyptian population characteristics and material culture. Infiltration from Nilotic stock into the Nubian Valley during the Roman era is evidenced by skeletal remains that are taller, with more protruding jaws and flatter noses. After the sixth century A.D., Nubia was Christianized and remained Christian until the fourteenth century A.D., when the Nubian king converted to

Islam. At the time of the Islamic conquest of Nubia in 641 A.D., the Nubians opted to pay a poll tax and tribute instead of converting. The poll tax was referred to as *baqt*, probably an Arabization of the word pact. The Nubian church was a branch of the Coptic Monophysite church centered in Cairo. With the advent of the Ottomans into the region, Nubia was subjugated and troops from all over the empire intermingled with the local population, but intermarriages remained rare. In 1848 Muhammad Ali declared Egypt and Sudan independent from the Ottoman Empire and Nubia during that time became a passageway for trade in gold, slaves, and ivory between Africa and the Mediterranean. In 1882 the British occupied Egypt; their major plan was to increase cotton production. More water was required to implement such a plan, however, and, therefore, in 1902 a dam known as the Aswan Dam/reservoir across the Nile, a few kilometers south of Aswan, was built. The dam was heightened in 1912, and again in 1933. The elevation of the dam first affected only the northern region of Nubia, but as the height of the dam increased most of the Nubian Valley was affected. Many homes were moved to elevated land and cultivable land became scarce. In 1952 and 1956 Egypt and Sudan, respectively, gained their independence from the British. Whereas during the 1940s there were ideas of developing a huge reservoir at Lake Victoria to provide enough water for prosperity, Egypt's Revolutionary Council in 1952 adopted the idea of erecting a high dam in Aswan, as proposed by the Greek-Egyptian agronomist Adrien Daminos. In 1959 Egypt and Sudan signed a water agreement. The Nubian Valley was to be covered by the lake that would be formed by the Aswan High Dam. Hence, the Nubians had to be moved. The Nubians in Egypt were moved to newly reclaimed land in the Komombo area between October 1963 and June 1964. The Nubians in Sudan were relocated to Khashm el-Girba (later called the New Halfa Project) between January 1964 and February 1967. A few Nubians who refused to leave stayed behind, relocating to higher elevations.

Settlements

The inhabitants of old Nubia formed riverine communities clustered in villages along the banks of the Nile. Prior to relocation, Nubia was located between Aswan in Egypt and 150 kilometers into Sudan. The Kenuz occupied the northern area, the Arabs resided in the middle, and the Nubians were located in the south of Egypt and the north of Sudan. About 50,000 Sudanese Nubians and 70,000 Egyptian Nubians were relocated. There were attempts in the relocation plans to maintain the location of the villages in relation to each other.

The villages are further divided into hamlets. The size of the village, the number of its hamlets, and the density of its population are directly related to the width of the agricultural land. The villages with wider agricultural land were smaller, had higher population density and contained fewer hamlets. The hamlet is both a regional and kinship unit of settlement. The inhabitants are related to each other by marriage and descent. Three types of hamlet existed in old Nubia. In a patrilineal hamlet, all inhabitants were descended from the same patriarch, and the hamlet was named after this common ancestor. A second type of hamlet includes members of various patrilineal clans who are related through matrilineal descent and is usually named after the male founder of the settlement. In some hamlets, inhabitants are not related at all.

The hamlet is further divided into dwelling quarters. In patrilineal hamlets, each family is connected to the dwelling quarter by patrilineal descent. In other types of hamlets, the dwelling quarters reflect patrilineal clan/tribal affiliations. In all types of hamlets, dwelling quarters were separated from each other by natural divisions, including small hills and barren land. Inside the dwelling quarters, closeness of patrilineal relationship determines the spatial location of housing. Each hamlet had a mosque and a *modiafah* or a *mandara*, visiting quarters. The relocation of the Nubians presented new experiences to which they had to adapt. In Egypt, Nubian villages were given their old names, but, rather than being located along the banks of the Nile, were 3 to 10 kilometers away. The palm trees that were characteristic of the old Nubian environment did not exist in the new villages. The rocky hills that separated the villages and hamlets from each other also did not exist. The previous widely separated hamlets were brought together, thus increasing the density of the settlements. In old Nubia, a hamlet often represented a clan or kinship unit. In New Nubia, the dwelling patterns were built in four blocks to the size of the living quarters, and during resettlement houses were allocated on the basis of family size. As a result, the dwelling patterns that were based on kinship disappeared. In Sudan, the Nubian villages were no longer located at the banks of the Nile. Instead they were located at the Atbara River, which is narrower than the Nile. Their agricultural land, unlike that in old Nubia, was broad, and they had to cope with rotational crops.

Economy

Subsistence and Commercial Activities. Agriculture was and still is the basis of the Nubian economy. The scarcity of cultivable land was an outstanding feature of old Nubia. As a result, men migrated to cities to find work, and women were left to do the agricultural work. The Nubians in Egypt had two cultivation seasons, winter crops, *shitwi*, and summer crops, *sifi*. The Nubians in Wadi Halfa had, in addition, the flood cultivation, *dameira*. The Nubians depended on the rise and fall of the Nile water to irrigate winter crops. In summer cultivation, the Nubians used the *shadof* (water wheel) or buckets. Winter-crop season started in mid-October and ended in April. Some of the winter subsistence crops included millet, wheat, and barley. Peas and lentils were cash crops sold by the Sudanese Nubians at the Halfa market. Summer crops were the least important to the Nubian economy. Most crops were used for household consumption, and they included a variety of beans, okra, and some greens. The summer-crop cycle started in July and ended in September. The flood cultivations started in September and ended in December or January. Some of the dameira crops included lupines and tomatoes. In old Nubia, palm dates were an important subsistence crop. Transplanting palm shoots was governed by the Coptic calendar. There were two seasons for this activity. The first started around March and the second started around July. Dates were harvested from late August to late October, depending on the owner's desire for the texture of the date. The harvest of dates was a celebrated occasion in Nubia. In reality, dates and palm trees, writes Dafalla, "have affected many sides of the inhabitants' lives, and its traces could be observed everywhere. Its uses were varied and considerable and nothing was ever wasted" (1975). Today the Egyptian Nubians use their land to cultivate sugarcane as a cash crop sold at a government-regulated price. They use chemical fertilizers and modern modes of irrigation (perennial vs. basin). Other crops such as fruits and vegetables are rare, cultivated only by the well-to-do landowners. The Sudanese Nubians also use their land to cultivate a cash crop, namely cotton. They have had to cope with the requirements of cultivating vast lands, a practice that they were not used to in old Nubia. Dates are no longer part of the subsistence economy, either among Egyptian or Sudanese Nubians, owing to the environment of the resettlements. Women and men engage in different crafts. Women used to make utilitarian items—plates, mats, clothes, and so forth. Today Nubian women no longer engage in craftwork because household needs are readily available to them in the market. Nubian men leave blacksmithing, clay making, carpentry, weaving, and hair shaving to non-Nubians. They prefer to engage in crafts that are related directly to agriculture (e.g., making water wheels). After resettlement, many Nubian men worked as grocery-store owners and cab drivers.

Trade. The location of old Nubia made it difficult to navigate the Nile. After relocation, both the more accessible roads and integration into the cash economy contributed to an increase in trade activities in Egyptian and Sudanese Nubia.

Division of Labor. Prior to relocation, the scarcity of cultivable land forced Nubian men to emigrate to Cairo in search for jobs. Nubian women farmed the land, cared for animals and poultry, and performed domestic tasks. Since relocation, men have been cultivating the land because it is at quite a distance from the home. In cases where there is no able-bodied male to tend the land, a relative or hired helper from one of the surrounding Saidi villages does the work. Among the Sudanese Nubians, generous tenancies enabled many of the labor migrants to come back home after relocation and tend their land all year long. Labor in the home is still a woman's domain, but Nubian women also work outside the home as schoolteachers, government-center workers, and seamstresses.

Land Tenure. Prior to relocation four types of land tenure existed, each reflecting land use. These types were individual tenure, land inundated by the first Aswan dam, land on which the home was built, and clan land. Individual tenure included land used for cultivating winter crops and land on which irrigation projects were built; it was acquired by purchase. Land inundated by the building of the initial dam was inherited patrilineally by men only and had symbolic value. The home land was inside the hamlet and was usually located near the home. This type of land was not very common in Nubia and was inherited patrilineally by men only. Clan land was dispersed around the village and was passed on to leaders of the clan. Only men inherited this type of land, although prior to 1927 there were records of women inheriting. In New Nubia, as part of the relocation plan, Nubian families were allocated land individually in relation to size of family.

Kinship

Kin Groups and Descent. Kinship in Nubia is organized around the tribe. Because of the isolation of the old settlement and the double-descent rule, however, the village and the hamlet are more important units. Both father's and mother's relatives are important in organizing mutual obligations.

Kinship Terminology. Nubians use three terms that classify kinship and descent. These are, from closest to farthest: asi (children), *bayt* (home), and *qabiila* (clan). Only the first term is an indigenous Nubian term; the rest are borrowed from Arabic. Among contemporary Nubians, the Nubian languages are evolving toward Arabic, and some Arabic kinship terms are being used.

Marriage and Family

Marriage. Cross-cousin marriage is the preferred marriage type. Intermarriage among the various Nubian groups was and is still rare. Only women are bound by endogamous marriage rules. A dowry is exchanged as a sign of public declaration of marriage. The dowry then becomes the possession of the bride, and it may not be returned even if the marriage is not consummated. The age of marriage among the Nubians after relocation has risen because of economic conditions and the legal establishment of a minimum marital age. Divorce is frowned upon by tradition, and the demographics as well as the marriage rule of (Egyptian) Nubians leaves divorced women scant opportunity for remarriage.

Domestic Unit. Before relocation, the extended family (bayt) constituted the domestic unit in Nubia. This was a unit of at least four generations of double descent. The able-bodied men worked in cities and sent remittances. Owing to the pattern of land and dwelling redistribution that occurred after relocation, the domestic unit became smaller, encompassing only two or three generations of relatives.

Inheritance. The Nubians in some cases follow the Sunni Islamic rules of inheritance, which grant males double the share of the females. This share is passed on both from the father and the mother, if there is a male heir. In cases of land, however, such rules do not hold true (see "Land Tenure").

Socialization. The family in old Nubia was the primary agent of socialization. The mother and other womenfolk did most of the child rearing. Fathers played a minimal role in socialization, given that they mainly worked in cities. Older men presented the male image in the process of socialization. Today, with universal education policies, the introduction of electricity, and the integration of the Nubians into their respective states of Egypt and Sudan, the school, the radio, and the television provide additional socialization agencies.

Sociopolitical Organization

Political Organization. Prior to resettlement, Nubia was relatively isolated from the Egyptian and Sudanese governments. In Egypt, Nubia was divided into thirty-nine districts, each headed by a government-appointed headman (*ʿomda*), who acted as the liaison between the district and the government. The town of Eneba was the seat or center of the Nubian government. In Sudan, there were six districts that served the same political function. The districts in Sudan did not exist before Muhamad Ali's conquest of Egypt and Sudan. The ʿomda also appointed the town heads and the police officers, whose responsibilities included aiding citizens to register births and deaths, dealing with the rare instances of crime, and distributing government aid sent to the Nubian Valley. After resettlement, all of the Nubian groups acquired the new political organization of their respective states, which were in the process of postcolonial nation building.

Social Control and Conflict. Disputes and crime were originally handled by the elders of the hamlet, and rarely was a police officer or headman involved. Arab councils—tribunals based on tribal or clan affiliation—intervened to mediate any conflict that escalated (usually conflict over land).

Today traditional social-control mechanisms are used to resolve some conflicts, but, increasingly since 1965, conflict resolution has required more modern mechanisms, for example courts and state-trained police officers.

Religion and Expressive Culture

Religious Beliefs and Practitioners. The Nubians are Sunni Muslims who believe in one God and his Prophet Mohammed, in the angels created by God, in the prophets through whom his revelations were brought to humankind, in the Day of Judgment and individual accountability for actions, in God's complete authority over human destiny, and in life after death. They also follow the Ibadat, or practicing framework of the Muslim's life: the Five Pillars. In Islam there is no hierarchal authority, no priest or shaman. Islam also permits its intermingling with local tradition. In Nubia this process of intermingling is expressed in the animism that is predominant along the Nile and in the activities of the local *shuyukh* (sing. *shaykh*), who regulate daily concerns about health, fertility, and marriage.

Ceremonies. Nubian ceremonies can be divided into three kinds: the rite de passage, the religious ceremonies, and the agricultural rituals. The latter have completely disappeared from the Nubian culture given that the crop that was celebrated, palm dates, is no longer cultivated because of environmental changes in the new settlements. The rite-de-passage celebrations include the naming ceremony (Subu), birth, circumcision for males and females, marriage, and death. The religious ceremonies include the seven main Islamic celebrations: al-Fitr, the feast that clebrates the end of the fasting month; prepilgrimage celebrations; al-Adha, the feast that follows the pilgrimage to Mecca; Lilat al-Qadar, celebrating the night of the first revelations of the first Quranic verse; Isra' Wal Mirag, commemorating the night the Prophet Mohammed flew to Jerusalem, and from there to the seventh sky, to establish the Five Pillars of Islam; al Sana al-Higriah, the Islamic New Year; and Mulid al-Nabi, the Prophet's birthday. In all these celebrations drums and religious songs are recited for the duration of the feast, which may extend up to fourteen days. After relocation, ceremonies in general have become limited to the village because the homes were built so close to each other. Also, owing to increasing costs, the length of celebrations (but not their conspicuousness) has decreased.

Arts. The art forms in old Nubia are divided into three categories: utilitarian, decorative, and symbolic. The utilitarian arts included the making of plates, mats, fans, and jars from material available in the environment, such as straw and clay. Women practiced this art form. Bright colors distinguished the Nubian form from other Egyptian or Sudanese plates or jars. After resettlement, this art form disappeared because the utensils are available in the market. The decorative art included mainly bead necklaces and bracelets. Grooms and brides used these ornaments to decorate themselves. Since resettlement, modern decorative jewelry, including silver and gold, has replaced these items. Women traditionally made the bead necklaces, and today a commercial version of these necklaces is sold in the market. The symbolic arts included wall and door decoration. Relief decoration was typical of Nubian houses. Icons of animals were made to protect houses from the evil eye. After resettlement, relief decorations were replaced by painting. Most paintings have religious motifs, and some of the decorations indicate that someone in the house recently completed the holy duty of pilgrimage to Mecca.

Medicine. Prior to resettlement, government medical care was almost nonexistant in old Nubia. Today, in Egyptian Nubia, there are small clinics and health units that provide both in-patient and out-patient services. In Nasr town, in Aswan, there is a hospital. In New Halfa, the government provides basic services including sanitation facilities, piped water, and medical care. Health units provide out-patient services, and an in-patient hospital is available in Halfa town. In the late twentieth century infectious disease is on the rise among Sudanese Nubians, largely owing to population increase and lack of maintenance of water filters. On the other hand, change in the water supply in the Nile has decreased the prevalence of schistomosomiasis (a debilitating parasitic disease caused by a blood worm that inhabits the water). A more severe strain of schistosomiasis, however, has developed.

Death and Afterlife. Nubian traditions with regard to death follow Islamic teaching. At death, a Muslim's body must be washed, dressed, wrapped in white cloth, and buried appropriately (the face pointing toward Mecca) before the first sunset. For women, the mat on which the deceased was carried to the grave was "shaded with arches of palm branches over which a red silk cloth worn by women at weddings was laid" (Dafalla 1975, 54).

The picture of life after death in Islam both serves to comfort the bereaved and challenge the community to live lives of integrity and responsibility with the sure knowledge that the labor of today will be enjoyed in the hereafter and that both justice and mercy will prevail in the life to come. Islamic teachings emphasize two levels of judgment. The lower—often referred to as the "tomb judgement" or *barzakh*—takes place before Judgment Day; it is directed to the individual soul only. The higher judgment in Islam is reserved for Judgment Day, a day when humanity (Muslims and non-Muslims) will meet their creator.

Bibliography

Ammar, Hamed (1973). *Growing up in an Egyptian Village: Silwa, the Province of Aswan*. New York: Octagon Books.

Ammar, Nawal H. (1988). "An Egyptian Village Growing Up: Silwa, the Governorate of Aswan." Ph.D. dissertation, University of Florida.

Dafalla, Hassan (1975). *The Nubian Exodus*. London: C. Hurst & Co.

Fahim, Hussein M. (1981). *Dams, People, and Development: The Aswan High Dam Case*. New York: Pergamon Press.

Fahim, Hussein M. (1983). *Egyptian Nubians: Resettlement and Years of Coping*. Salt Lake City: University of Utah.

Geiser, Peter (1986). *The Egyptian Nubian: A Study in Social Symbiosis*. Cairo: American University in Cairo Press.

Hamed, Sayyed (1994). *Al-Nuba Al-Gadida: Dirasah anthro-*

pologia fi al-Mugtama' Al-Misri (The New Nubia: An anthropological study of Egyptian society). Cairo: Ein for Human and Social Studies.

Reisner, George (1910). *Archaeological Survey of Nubia, Reports for 1907, 1908, 1908–1909, and 1909–1910*. Cairo: National Printing Department.

Rouchdy, Aleya (1991). *Nubians and Nubian Language in Contemporary Egypt: A Case of Cultural and Linguistic Contact*. Leiden: E. J. Brill.

Wenzel, Marian (1972). *House Decoration in Nubia*. Toronto: Toronto University Press.

NAWAL H. AMMAR

Nuer

ETHNONYM: Naath

Orientation

Identification and Location. The Nuer speak of themselves as "Naath," or "human beings." Nuerland is located in the southern Sudan between 7° and 10° N and 29° and 34° E. The main channel of the Nile River divides their country into western and eastern regions. Most of Nuerland consists of open savanna and is subject to considerable flooding during the two rainy seasons (April to June and July through October). In 1956 the Nuer were estimated to number in the range of 450,000 persons, with an average population density of approximately 2.8 persons per square kilometer, a figure that varies considerably in the wet and dry seasons.

Linguistic Affiliation. The Nuer speak a Nilotic dialect most closely related to Atuot. Nuer, Dinka, and Atuot have been conventionally defined as a distinct subgroup. There are no significant subdialects of Nuer.

History and Cultural Relations

Nuer living to the east of the Nile speak of their western relatives as "homeland Nuer" and have a consistent oral tradition indicating that their expansion across the Nile, as far as the Ethiopian border, has a 200-year legacy. In the process of this expansion, they forced the Anuak to migrate farther east into Ethiopia, and incorporated many Dinka into Nuer communities. Nuer versed in such matters suggest that at one time three "brothers"—Nuer, Dinka, and Atuot—once lived in a neighboring territory. Legends suggest that they parted company to go their own ways following a dispute about the rightful ownership of a number of cattle. Both Atuot and Nuer traditions indicate that this separation and initial migration originated in a cattle camp in what is now termed western "Nuerland." These legends of migration sometimes have mythical properties, but it is prudent to appreciate them also for their historical character. It is certain that the Nuer, Dinka, and Atuot have a common "origin," and archaeological research may indicate that the spread of domesticated cattle in this region of Africa was contemporaneous with the origin of distinct ethnic identities. An especially active period of Nuer eastward migration began in the middle of the nineteenth century. Beginning at the turn of the twentieth century, British colonial policy in Nuerland was aimed at fixing boundaries between the Nuer and the Dinka, thus effectively halting a dynamic process of cultural change that had been unfolding for centuries.

Settlements

Traditional Nuer settlements take radically different form as a consequence of ecological changes throughout the year. In the rainy season, floods force Nuer to seek narrow strips of land above the flood line. During this period, women are engaged in the cultivation of millet and maize, the staple horticultural resources, and men pasture their large herds nearby. With the coming of the dry season, able-bodied men move their herds away from the elevated ridges, following, with their herds, the course of lowering riverbeds and channels. Thus, at the height of the dry season, the human population is most dispersed. At this time, agnatically conscripted groups live in cattle camps. With the coming of the new season's rains, herders commence a gradual process of transhumance back toward the elevated ridges, away from the rising rivers. Here, wet-season settlements form once again, and horticulture follows the regularity of the rains. Nuer huts in wet-season settlements consist of circular mud walls with thatched roofs. Temporary scaffoldings are made to dry the millet and maize as it is harvested. In the dry-season cattle camp, shelters are made from local grasses, as the need for protection from the elements is less pressing.

Economy

Nuer technology is simple in manufacture and sophisticated in suitability to the local environment. Like the Dinka and Stuot, Nuer carry out their economic life in a manner that highlights cultural conceptions of gender and the division of labor by sex. Wet-season homesteads, horticultural produce, and huts themselves have strongly feminine associations, whereas masculine images are associated with tending cattle and manufacturing the corresponding technological items. Staple crops consist of millet, maize, and introduced vegetables and groundnuts where soil conditions allow. Cattle are centrally important domesticates, and Nuer also pasture large flocks of sheep and goats. Nuer men enjoy occasional success in taking game animals such as antelopes, hippopotamuses, and elephants. No crops are produced for commercial or market purposes.

Kinship

Nuer domestic groups are based on the ideal of patrilateral descent. Kith should in some way be recognized as agnatic relatives. This principle is often confounded by the actual composition of local groups, but the ideal configuration persists across time. Nuer imagine that all adult males can claim ancestry to all other adult males, although in actuality neither domestic settlement patterns nor territorial segments conform to this ideal. Anthropologists continue to disagree about the significance of kinship and patrilineal descent in the organization of Nuer political and domestic life.

Marriage and Family

Marriage. All legal marital unions are recognized through the exchange of bride-wealth, in the form of cattle, between the husband's kin and the rightful claimants of these goods among the family of the bride. A standard ideal of forty head of cattle comprises the expected number of cattle to be received by the bride's family. In Nuer eyes, however, a marriage has not been finalized until the bride has given birth to at least two children. The actual exchange of bride-wealth cattle is thus a lengthy process and can be stalled or broken off by a number of phenomena. Once a third child has been born of the union, Nuer consider the marriage to be "tied." The woman has become a full member of her husband's agnatic lineage, along with her children. Through marriage, the continuity of the husband's lineage has been assured, and, following the birth of two or three children, the wife's role in expanding relationships of kinship has been realized.

Domestic Unit. As among neighboring peoples, commensality is the most consistent measure of moral solidarity at the domestic level. With luck, a woman may give birth to six children during her childbearing years. Co-wives do not necessarily reside in near proximity. When they do, the domestic unit can easily number more than a dozen individuals. Normally the bride is relocated in the husband's natal family following her marriage. Patrilateral residence thus further solidifies the patrilineal structure of Nuer communities.

Sociopolitical Organization

In a classic study by the late E. E. Evans-Pritchard (1940), Nuer political life was characterized as a system of fission and fusion. Lineage groups would bind together in some instances, and, in principle, the Nuer could conceive of all distinct descent groups uniting in this fashion. When disputes were localized, segmentation between smaller patrilineal groups would occur. Localized disputes, theft, or homicide were mediated by individuals called *kwar* (chiefs), whose words were effective because of their authority rather than their overt power. Chiefs could settle a dispute only once those in conflict agreed to a settlement. The introduction of secular chiefs and courts irrevocably changed traditional custom and usage.

Religion

As among the neighboring Dinka, religious thought and practice is a dialogue with a creator divinity the Nuer call "Kowth." This term has a variety of meanings, depending on the context. Indeed, understanding the contextual usage of the term "Kowth" is central to an appreciation of the complexity of Nuer religion. Evans-Pritchard wrote that although the Nuer lacked a tradition of embellished plastic arts, their intellectual life was complex. The Nuer believe that all life comes from Kowth and returns to the same divinity at death. The Nuer pray for health and well-being to Kowth, offering sacrifices of cattle in hopeful expectation that their sentiments may be realized. Whereas many individuals become diviners and healers (*tiet*), there is no organized cult or hierarchy of religious functionaries. This fact is fully consistent with the aggressively egalitarian Nuer social ethics. Nuer religion is decidedly "this-worldly" in orientation; they do not imagine a heavenly abode awaiting them upon death. Like other Nilotic peoples, the Nuer regard long-deceased ancestors with respect and veneration, but are concerned in their earthly lives with the power of the recently deceased to cause misfortune. In sum, Nuer "religion" attends virtually every aspect of individual and social experience.

Bibliography

Evans-Pritchard, E. E. (1940). *The Nuer*. Oxford: Clarendon Press.

Evans-Pritchard, E. E. (1951). *Kinship and Marriage among the Nuer*. Oxford: Clarendon Press.

Evans-Pritchard, E. E. (1956). *Nuer Religion*. Oxford: Clarendon Press.

JOHN W. BURTON

Nuristanis

ETHNONYMS: none

The area known as Nuristan is located at the southern end of the Hindu Kush mountain range in Afghanistan. Historically, this area was known as Kafiristan and the inhabitants as Kafirs. Nuristan has a temperate climate with enough precipitation to provide plenty of water for irrigated agriculture. There are limited amounts of arable land in the Hindu Kush, but there are abundant amounts of pastureland well suited for transhumance. Subsistence is based on the production of cereal grains and of dairy products from goats and cattle.

Nuristan is an ethnically and linguistically diverse region in which six mutually unintelligible and unwritten languages are spoken. The Nuristani Group of languages, a branch of the Indo-Iranian Subfamily of Indo-European languages, contains five of these languages. The sixth language, Pashai, is spoken in the far western part of Nuristan by groups of Pashai peoples who are considered to be a culturally distinct group and who live mostly outside Nuristan.

On the basis of linguistic and cultural affinities Nuristanis may be divided into three different groupings: those calling themselves Kalasha; the Kati, Mumo, Kshto, and Kom peoples; and the Vasi. The Kalasha groups live in the southern part of Nuristan and constitute three of the five Nuristani linguistic communities. The Ashkunu, Gramsana, and Kalasha all speak dialects of a single language. The Kalasha speak an independent language called Kalasha-ala, which is further divided into two dialects. The Tregami speak an independent language that is distinct from, but related to, Kalasha-ala.

The Kati are the most numerous of Nuristani peoples. The Mumo, Kshto, and Kom all speak different dialects of the same language and are separated into different villages, primarily within central Nuristan. The Vasi, who are considered the most culturally and linguistically distinct of the Nuristani peoples, speak a language that is divided into dialects according to village.

Even though each Nuristani group often regards itself as being as distinct from the others as it is from neighboring non-Nuristani groups, features of their languages and cultures suggest a common origin. The Nuristani languages are believed to share a common phylogeny. Oral traditions indicate a long history of interaction, and there is a common belief that Nuristanis formerly inhabited the Kunar Basin.

The Nuristanis once shared a common religion. They believed that the world was divided into pure and impure, corresponding to the division between gods and people. The gods controlled the destiny of people, which was determined by the generosity of sacrifices to the gods and the purity of individuals and their families. Shamans acted as intermediaries for the people. Sacrifices and purification rites were performed by other specialists. Feasts were seen as acts of generosity in sacrifice, bestowing on the giver(s) both purity and formal social rank.

The basic sociopolitical unit in Nuristan is the village. Villages are surrounded by agricultural land and by mountain and valley grazing areas. The land is owned by male heads of households, and access to grazing areas is a hereditary right of male residents.

Men who are seen as promoting cohesiveness tend to gain leadership within the village. Open conferences are held whenever decisions affecting the entire community are needed. At these conferences, skilled leaders are given the authority to resolve a community crisis. Leaders maintain their authority only as long as they have the consensus of other political leaders or until the crisis is resolved.

The role of mediator is crucial to the maintenance of social cohesion. Political leaders emerge largely because of their abilities to resolve conflicts within the community. Conflict resolution takes the form of determining, through mediation, an appropriate compensation. In disputes involving bloodshed, blood money is demanded and expected. Blood disputes are particularly dangerous for the community because the aggrieved, or his agnatic kin, may seek blood vengeance. Avoiding bloodshed is a major motivation prompting men to become mediators.

Cooperation within Nuristani culture is based on kinship ties. Agnatic kin are expected to support each other in times of crisis or need. Because agnatic ties are so central, Nuristani men who have frequent interpersonal relations with Nuristanis from other villages will adopt them as brothers. Those adoptive ties, along with the ties of intermarriages, are the primary links between different Nuristani groups.

Traditionally, only men could own property, and grazing rights were inherited through the male line only. Today, under Islamic law, women are also entitled to a share of the patrimony, but in practice their share usually reverts to their brothers or close male agnates.

Nuristanis are divided into two endogamous castes—a lower caste of artisans and a landowning upper caste. The former were slaves until the twentieth century, and they are still predominantly disenfranchised. The lower caste produces the woodworking, blacksmithing, pottery, weaving, and basketry products used by all Nuristanis.

In addition to caste specialization, there is also a division of labor based on gender. Traditionally, males and females were expected to contribute to the production of a meal. The women provided the bread, which meant they were responsible for all agricultural production and the gathering of firewood. The men provided a dairy product, which meant they cared for the goats and cattle.

Some of the cultural divergences among Nuristani groups arise from differences in the environment and the availability of land; others are based on variations in kinship organization. For example, the Kalasha and Kati recognize formalized groupings of close agnates that are lacking in the descent model of the Kom and Kshto. Other cultural differences, such as variations in dress, house construction, and music, coincide with the three major Nuristani ethnic divisions.

Nuristanis have generally considered themselves dominated by an oppressive regime ever since their incorporation into Afghanistan in 1896. They saw no advantage in a Soviet-led Communist government after the coup of 1978, and therefore launched an attack that led to a nationwide uprising against that regime. Since the Soviet invasion of Afghanistan in 1979, there have been few reports on the Nuristani culture.

Bibliography

Edelberg, Lennart, and Schuyler Jones (1979). *Nuristan*. Graz: Akademische Drucku.

Katz, David J. (1982). "Kafir to Afghan: Religious Conversion, Political Incorporation, and Ethnicity in the Waygal Valley, Nuristan." Ph.D. dissertation, University of California, Los Angeles.

Strand, Richard F. (1973). "Notes on the Nuristani and Dardic Languages." *Journal of the American Oriental Society* 93(3): 297–305.

Strand, Richard F. (1974). "Principles of Kinship Organization among the Kom Nuristani." In *Cultures of the Hindu-Kush: Selected Papers from the Hindu-Kush Cultural Conference Held at Moesgaord, 1970*, edited by Karl Jettmar in collaboration with Lenaart Edelberg. Wiesbaden: Franz Steiner.

Strand, Richard F. (1975). "The Changing Herding Economy of the Kom Nuristani." *Afghanistan Journal* 2(4): 123–134.

Strand, Richard F. (1984). "Nuristanis." In *Muslim Peoples: A World Ethnographic Survey*, edited by Richard V. Weekes, 569–574. Westport, Conn.: Greenwood Press.

Nyakyusa and Ngonde

ETHNONYMS: none

Orientation

Identification. The Nyakyusa of southwestern Tanzania have been ethnographically studied since 1934 and are known from missionary and traveler's records since the beginning of

European contact with the East African interior in the 1870s. The Nyakyusa are especially noted for their system of "age villages," a residential segregation of generations in adjoining communities, and both the Nyakyusa and the Ngonde, a closely related people of northern Malawi, are known for the "divine" powers of their former chiefs.

Location. The Nyakyusa inhabit the coastal plain at the north end of Lake Malawi and the section of the East African Rift Valley extending northward up the southern flank of Mount Rungwe, an extinct volcano; the Ngonde are found on the northwestern coastal plain immediately across the border in Malawi, separated from Tanzania by the Songwe River. Rainfall is distributed throughout much of the year, with a concentration in March and April; it exceeds 250 centimeters per year on the slopes of Mount Rungwe and is around 100 centimeters per year on the lake plain in Ngonde country. BuNyakyusa (the country of the Nyakyusa) is dissected by rivers, which contributed to its relative isolation and political fragmentation in precolonial times. The lakeside locale of the Ngonde, which was accessible to trade routes, allowed the rise of a centralized chieftaincy in the nineteenth century but also increased their exposure to slave raiding.

Demography. In 1931 the Nyakyusa population was approximately 195,000, and by 1966 it was about 360,000. In 1967 its estimated natural rate of increase was 2.4 percent. The Ngonde in the same period had grown by at least an equivalent amount, from 83,000 in 1945 to 137,000 in 1966. There is a preponderance of women over men, largely brought about by wage migration. Increasing pressure on the land and the absence of men has obliged many women to fend for themselves because of diminishing agricultural resources.

Linguistic Affiliation. The Nyakyusa and Ngonde speak closely related Bantu languages. The Nyakyusa of the Mount Rungwe uplands and those of the lake plain exhibit minor dialectal differences.

History and Cultural Relations

Tradition recalls that Nyakyusa/Ngonde chiefs and commoners were of different stock. The ancestors of the "commoners" are remembered as hunters and honey gatherers who came from the mountains surrounding the Rift Valley or from the vicinity of Lake Rukwa to the north. The ancestors of the "chiefs" were related to the aristocracy of the Kinga, a neighboring (although otherwise unrelated) people in the mountains east of the lake. The chiefs came "ten generations ago," bringing cattle, cultigens, fire, and iron, and found the commoners eating their food "raw." The chiefs arrived not as conquerors, but as culture bringers with power over rain and fertility. They are remembered as being "pale" and the commoners as "black," but there has been intermarriage for as long as anyone remembers, and no physical difference is discernible in their descendants. This myth of migration and settlement resembles many others from Africa concerning the origins of the complementary relationship between rulers and the ruled.

Whereas the Nyakyusa were relatively isolated because of their geographical situation, the Ngonde were incorporated into an extensive precolonial ivory-centered trade network. English and German missionaries, traders, and explorers arrived in the 1870s. The initial phase of contact was soon followed by elimination of the slave trade and the establishment of European colonial regimes; the Ngonde ended up in the British Protectorate of Nyasaland (called Malawi upon independence), and the Nyakyusa were incorporated in the German colony of Tanganyika. With the defeat of the Germans in World War I, control of Tanganyika passed to the British, who assumed the territory under a League of Nations mandate and administered it until independence.

Scots missionaries established themselves in Ngonde territory, and Lutherans and Moravians, followed by Catholics, settled in BuNyakyusa. The missionary presence resulted in challenges to the values of precolonial society (e.g., polygyny), a division of the population along religious lines, and a withdrawal of Christians from participation in traditional communal ceremonials. Wage migration has taken many men out of the country to work for various periods in the mines of the Rhodesian (now Zambian) Copper Belt or in South Africa. The introduction of cash cropping and private land has further enhanced these individualistic tendencies. The overall effect of such changes has been a transition from a society based on kinship to one based on the nuclear family and voluntary association.

Settlements

The Nyakyusa have preferred to live in nucleated settlements and are best known for their system of "age villages," whereby new generations of young men set themselves up in residential communities separate from those of their fathers. This separation is not strictly an "age set" system composed of named grades (as among many East African herding societies), but rather an outgrowth of the idea that the sexual activities of the generations should be kept separate and that contemporaries make the best neighbors—that they provide "good company" for one another. There was a powerful avoidance between fathers-in-law and daughters-in-law. The germ of a new village would form as boys reaching adolescence set up huts on the edge of a parent village; this new village recruited for perhaps five years, and then closed its membership. The fundamental principle of residential affiliation was therefore not kinship but age (kin often lived in the same village, however, or at least in the same "side" of the chiefdom).

Although there were no named age sets, each generation had a corporate identity in that it went through a collective transition ritual called a "coming out." Seniors were supposed to "move aside" in a comprehensive redistribution of land within the chiefdom. At this time new chiefs were also brought out, as were commoner headmen, the headmen of the villages newly elevated to senior status. Ideally, the chiefdom would also split, dividing between the two senior sons of the old chief. The system can be seen as an institutional way of handling a natural process of growth and fission, but the way in which it actually worked remains somewhat obscure. In any event these arrangements were dependent on an ample supply of vacant land; with the onset of colonial rule and an increasing population, it began to fall apart. The last recorded "coming out" in Ngonde occurring in 1913, the last in BuNyakyusa in 1953. By 1969, the establishment of age villages had also ceased, and the system itself was scarcely remembered.

Economy

Subsistence and Commercial Activities. The ample rainfall of the region makes possible a stable mixed economy of banana, plaintain, and grain cultivation, accompanied by cattle herding. Shifting cultivation is not practiced; the land is kept in condition by fallowing and green manuring. The cash cropping of rice, coffee, and tea has had a profound effect on the local economy and, because land has now acquired commercial value, contributed greatly to the demise of communal land tenure and the institution of the age village. Subsistence cultivation, however, remains the norm. With the exception of the marketing of cash crops, there is slight commercial activity.

Industrial Arts. Blacksmiths were present in precolonial society, but the iron was smelted by the Kinga (from whom the Nyakyusa chiefs were thought to be derived). Pottery making was in the hands of a non-Nyakyusa specialist group residing on the northeastern lakeshore.

Trade. In precolonial times there was regional traffic in iron, cloth, pottery, and salt and, among the Ngonde, participation in the ivory trade to the coast, an activity that enhanced the power of the Ngonde chief through the extraction of tribute. The giving and receiving of salt and iron (in the form of hoes) were important markers of social relationships. Salt came in from the Tanganyika plateau to the north. Rice from the lowlands near the lake is currently exchanged for highland produce such as groundnuts.

Division of Labor. There is ideally a gender-based division of labor: men and boys hoe and herd; women cook and attend the household. A son was expected to hoe for his father. Likewise, a son-in-law was expected to hoe for his father-in-law; in the absence of cattle for bride-wealth, this service was the only way a poor man could acquire a wife. Skill at hoeing was once a primary masculine virtue. Now, because of the absence of the many men who are pursuing outside employment, women have increasingly been obliged to hoe and tend the home fires.

Land Tenure. The age village was the landholding unit, and allotment of land was determined at the coming-out ceremony. The allocation of land within the village was its own concern, and there was much flexibility in practice. Villages of fathers and sons were usually close to one another, and, before the general redistribution, sons would often take over plots tilled by their fathers. With the collapse of the age-village system, land tenure became the affair of the nuclear family; even as early as the 1930s private ownership had been established over valuable plots in old volcanic craters. By the late 1960s, a substantial landless class had emerged.

Kinship

Kin Groups and Descent. A person was both a member of an agnatic kin group and an age village. With the exception of the chiefly lines, lineage groups were unnamed, genealogically shallow, and residentially dispersed because of the age-village system. The corporate political significance of lineages was therefore limited. Their main relevance emerged in judicial proceedings, inheritance, and ritual; kin had greater legal responsibility for one another's behavior than did age mates. Marriage between descendants of a common great-grandfather was frowned upon, but marriage between descendants of a common grandfather was considered "impossible." Unlike many peoples of the region, cross-cousin marriage was not considered permissible, although in other respects cross cousins behaved familiarly and had mutual obligations in the ritual of kinship.

Kinship Terminology. Father, father's brothers, and their structural equivalents were terminologically equated, as were mother, mother's sisters, and so forth. Father's sister and mother's brother were distinguished. Parallel cousins and cross cousins were distinguished in Iroquois fashion. Grandparents and grandchildren used a self-reciprocal term for one another. Wife's sister and husband's brother were addressed by the same term as one's spouse. Lineal features in the terminological system are relatively undeveloped.

Marriage and Family

Marriage. Marriage ages once differed markedly for men and women, the former marrying at an average age of 25, and the latter near puberty, having been betrothed by their fathers even earlier. In the 1930s as many as 70 percent of married women lived in polygynous households, but as many as 70 percent of adult men were either unmarried or monogamous. There was "a premise of inequality" between men and women. Marriage was virilocal except in cases where a husband without cattle was incorporated into the household of his father-in-law by virtue of bride-service; children from such a match became part of the father-in-law's lineage. Transfer of cattle was therefore an essential part of contracting an honorable marriage; "kinship is cattle," it was said. Men with such resources translated them into polygynous marriage. Even so, in the interval between the 1930s and the present, women began marrying at a later age, and polygyny underwent a relative decline, particularly among Christians. Tanzanian national family law has promoted the autonomy of women with respect to marriage and property rights.

Domestic Unit. The basic unit is the nuclear family. In polygynous households each wife has her own house, or in former times a separate room in a long house; each household is allotted its own land, which the husband helps cultivate.

Inheritance. A brother traditionally inherited the farms and wives of a deceased sibling and raised children in the latter's name. Failing this, an elder son was the legitimate heir. Presently, father-to-son inheritance is the norm, another function of the privatization of economic life and the breakup of wider kinship units. Widows, rather than being inherited, now are likely to live in the household of a son unless they remarry.

Socialization. Young boys were expected mainly to socialize with age mates and eventually to live with them in age villages. Sharing within the group was a paramount value, and those who did not incurred much animosity, culminating in witchcraft accusations. Girls were taught the virtues of deference.

Sociopolitical Organization

Social Organization. The social organization of contemporary Nyakyusa and Ngonde society is oriented around the family, individual agricultural production, national politics, and the churches. In former times the age village was the center of social life; the wider community came into play via war, the power of chieftaincies, and the enactment of collective ritual.

Political Organization. In the 1930s there were at least a hundred chiefdoms in Nyakyusa country, each with a chief descended from the original Kinga immigrants. The commoners, for their part, had powers of witchcraft as well as of defense against it, and provided wives for the immigrants. Commoners also played an essential role in the installation rituals for the chiefs and were symbolically associated with the chief as woman is to man; the exercise of the complementary powers of chiefs and commoners ensured fertility and protection against evil. There were several Nyakyusa figures who transcended ordinary chiefs to the point that they have been labeled "divine kings." It was widely believed that formerly, when their powers began to wane, they were killed lest they take their powers into the grave with them; however, these "kings" had no political power as such, whereas an equivalent figure among the Ngonde, the *kyungu*, became paramount administrative chief of his domain. Tanzania deprived all such chiefs of their powers, and replaced them with elected local authorities.

Social Control. Social control is, for the most part, exercised informally, often through witchcraft accusations or fear of them, and by threat of the mystical powers of senior relatives to discipline wayward kin. Village headmen had the responsibility to arbitrate disputes. The obstinate were subject to banishment, and were also susceptible to "the breath of men," a mystical projection of dislike or dissatisfaction resulting in illness. Headmen had innate powers to combat witches by engaging in dream combat with them at night, but might be accused of witchcraft themselves if they misused their offices. In extreme cases of suspected witchcraft, a poison ordeal could be administered as a kind of lie-detector test.

Conflict. Small-scale warfare and cattle raiding were once endemic between adjoining chiefdoms; occasionally a chiefdom would be subsumed by another because of defeat in war. The most violent period in local history occurred in the late nineteenth century, when a coastal slaver set himself up in Ngonde country—an activity brought to an end by British intervention in 1895.

Religion and Expressive Culture

Religious Beliefs. The precolonial Nyakyusa/Ngonde cosmology was nontheistic. It focused on the powers of the founding heroes and their chiefly descendants, on the powers of commoner headmen to combat witches, and on the ability of deceased relatives to affect the fortunes of the living. Since then Christianity has made very substantial progress, although not equally in all areas. In 1955 Moravians, Lutherans, and Catholics comprised some 14 percent of the total population, with significant numbers in other sects such as the Pentecostal Holiness, Assemblies of God, Watch Tower (Jehovah's Witnesses), Seventh Day Adventists, and a number of indigenous sectarian groups.

Religious Practitioners. Descendants of the "divine kings" (the Lwembe of Nyakyusa, the Kyungu of Ngonde) performed important rituals for the well-being of the country at large, such as ceremonies of national purification. There were also commoner priests and diviners, who worked together with the chiefs to avert misfortune, officiate at communal ceremonials, and preside over the grave sites of dead chiefs.

Ceremonies. The "coming out" was the most impressive and important of the collective ceremonials. Sacrifices at the burial groves of chiefs were important in times of misfortune. Kinship rituals, particularly the elaborate burial service, were the most common type of ceremony; there were also rituals accompanying puberty and marriage, and normal and abnormal birth (e.g., the birth of twins).

Medicine. "Medicines" were used to enhance the powers of chiefs and village headmen; they were administered to nourish the "python in the belly," the source of mystical power. The actual content of the medicines is uncertain, although some were composed of ground stone and others of vegetable substances, the latter type being of particular importance in strengthening a pubescent girl.

Death and Afterlife. The shades of the dead were of great importance. Neglect of the proper form in funeral services could lead to illness. The main function of funeral ceremonial was to produce a certain distance between the living and the dead. The shades of past kings and agnatic ancestors were frequently consulted when interpreting or attempting to avert misfortune.

Bibliography

Charsley, Simon R. (1969). *The Princes of Nyakyusa*. Nairobi: East African Publishing House.

Gulliver, Phillip H. (1958). *Land Tenure and Social Change among the Nyakyusa*. East African Studies, no. 11. Kampala: East African Institute of Social Research.

McKenny, Michael G. (1973). "The Social Structure of the Nyakyusa: A Re-Evaluation." *Africa* 63:91–107.

Wilson, Godfrey (1968). *The Constitution of Ngonde*. Manchester: Manchester University Press.

Wilson, Monica (1950). "Nyakyusa Kinship." In *African Systems of Kinship and Marriage*, edited by A. R. Radcliffe-Brown and D. Forde, 111–139. London: Oxford University Press.

Wilson, Monica (1951). *Good Company*. London: Oxford University Press.

Wilson, Monica (1957). *Rituals of Kinship among the Nyakyusa*. London: Oxford University Press.

Wilson, Monica (1959). *Communal Rituals of the Nyakyusa*. London: Oxford University Press.

Wilson, Monica (1977). *For Men and Elders: Change in the Relations of Generations and of Men and Women among the Nyakyusa-Ngonde People, 1875–1971*. London: International African Institute.

MICHAEL G. KENNY
(with thanks to Donna Robertson)

Nyamwezi and Sukuma

ETHNONYMS: Banyamwezi, Basukuma

Orientation

Identification. The Nyamwezi and Sukuma are two closely related ethnic groups that live principally in the region to the south of Lake Victoria in west-central Tanzania. When using ethnic names, they describe themselves as "Banyamwezi" (sing. Munyamwezi) and "Basukuma" (sing. Musukuma) respectively; they refer to their home areas as "Bunyamwezi" or "Unyamwezi," and as "Busukuma." The term "Sukumaland" is sometimes used for the Sukuma area. The name "Sukuma" literally means "north," but it has become a term of ethnic identification.

Location. The Nyamwezi and Sukuma region lies between 2°10′ and 6°20′ S and 31°00′ and 35°00′ E. The Nyamwezi "home" area is in Tabora Region and western Shinyanga Region, and Sukumaland lies to the north and east, covering eastern Shinyanga Region and also Mwanza Region. There has been much population movement in and beyond these areas, and members of both groups have also settled on the coast and elsewhere. Sukuma and members of other groups, such as the Tusi and the Sumbwa, are often found in Nyamwezi villages, but Sukuma villages are ethnically more homogeneous. Sukuma took over the Geita area of Mwanza Region during the colonial period, and they have expanded farther west since then. They have also moved down into Nzega and the neighboring Igunga District, and some have migrated into the southern highland areas of Tanzania, and even into Zambia. These Sukuma movements have stemmed from political factors, such as colonial cattle-culling policies, and from local overcrowding and deteriorating soil conditions. The two areas form a large and undulating tableland, most of it at elevations between 1,150 and 1,275 meters. There are several rivers in the region, but most of them do not flow during the drier months. The year can be broadly divided into a rainy season, from about November until April, and a dry season the rest of the year. Average annual rainfall is about 75 centimeters for most of the Sukuma area, and about 90 centimeters for Unyamwezi, but there is much variation from year to year and from place to place. Across the region, there is a regular sequence of soil and vegetation zones. The upper levels are dry woodland typified by trees of the Brachystegia-Isoberlinia association; these areas are often called *miombo* country, after one of these trees. Lower areas of grass and thornbush steppe are also common, and in Sukumaland there are large tracts of park steppe interspersed with baobabs.

Demography. Estimates of the modern population are difficult to make because Tanzanian censuses no longer record the ethnic affiliation of enumerated local populations. According to Tanzanian newspaper reports based on official estimates, there were 1 to 1.5 million Nyamwezi and between 3 and 3.5 million Sukuma in 1989. Census figures for 1978 show a wide range of population densities, from 73.3 per square kilometer in the Mwanza Region to 10.7 per square kilometer in the Tabora Region. Since then, population growth in Tanzania generally has been about 2.8 percent per annum, but densities have also been influenced by population movement.

Linguistic Affiliation. Although sometimes classed as two closely related languages, Nyamwezi and Sukuma are probably best considered as a single Bantu language with several mutually intelligible dialects. These features include a seven-vowel system, use of tone, true negative tenses, class prefixes to indicate size, and the restriction of double prefixes to determined situations. In addition to their own dialect, most people today also speak Swahili.

History and Cultural Relations

It is not known how long the people have inhabited the area. The first clear written references to Nyamwezi occur in the early nineteenth century. According to local traditions, most of the region was uninhabited until the seventeenth century, when chiefly families began to arrive from various directions. Some are said to have come as hunters. As the population grew, new chiefdoms were formed by expansion and division. Trading visits to the coast and other areas were common in the nineteenth century, and Indian and Arab traders visited the area from the coast. Tabora was established as an Arab settlement, probably in the 1840s. John Hanning Speke and Richard Francis Burton were the first European visitors, in 1857. During the next thirty years, foreign traders, explorers, and missionaries made frequent visits, and local traders continued to travel to the coast. Exports included ivory and slaves, and imports included cloth and, later, guns. Secular aspects of chieftainship seem to have developed strongly at this time, and Arab intervention in local politics brought them into conflict with a rising chief, Mirambo, whom Henry Morton Stanley described as the Napoleon of Central Africa. Mirambo established his influence over many other chiefdoms in the Nyamwezi and southern Sukuma areas, but this "empire" broke up shortly after his death in 1884. The colony of German East Africa was established in 1890, and the area was brought under control by 1893. The Germans ruled through local chiefs who were expected to keep order and collect taxes. Several chiefdoms that had formerly had matrilineal succession to the chieftainship changed to patrilineal succession under German rule. The British formally took over the administration of the country in 1919, three years after the expulsion of the Germans from Tabora during World War I. British rule continued until Tanzanian independence in 1961. Several changes were made in the number and internal organization of the chiefdoms in this period, and communications were extended and improved. Many people were moved from areas where sleeping sickness was prevalent into new settlements. Cotton was developed as a cash crop in Sukumaland. Since independence, chieftainship, as a political office, has been abolished, and the development of collective forms of village organization has been encouraged, albeit without much success.

Settlements

In the nineteenth century large compact villages were common, especially among the Nyamwezi. As the country became peaceful, people moved out to build in their own fields. The dispersal of settlement continued until the first years of independence, and villages passed through phases of expansion and decline as soils became worn out and the age structure of their populations changed. In the mid-1970s new compact villages, ideally of 250 households, were established by decree throughout this and other parts of Tanzania. Each household had a 0.4-hectare plot within the village on which to build and cultivate, and families also had access to fields in surrounding land. The 0.4-hectare plots were commonly arranged in blocks of ten between new village streets. This policy has since been relaxed, and some settlements are said to be disbanding.

Economy

Subsistence and Commercial Activities. Agriculture and cattle keeping are the chief economic activities. Most families grow food for themselves and attempt to produce some surplus for the market. Maize, sorghum, and rice are the main food crops sold, and cotton and tobacco are produced in substantial quantities. Other crops include groundnuts, beans, cassava, and some vegetables and fruits. The main cattle owners are Sukuma. Some families own very large herds of a thousand head or more, but smaller herds are more usual. Small stock are also raised. Most families still use hoes, but plows pulled by oxen are quite common. Some richer people own tractors that they hire out to others, in addition to using them to cultivate large areas for themselves.

Industrial Arts. Traditional crafts include building, ironwork, pottery, basketry, drum making, and stool carving. These crafts are usually part-time occupations, and some have declined as foreign goods have been imported. Bow and arrow making has enjoyed a resurgence with the rise of Sungusungu (see "Sociopolitical Organization"). Some carpenters make Western-type chairs and other furniture, and some men work as sewing-machine operators in local shops.

Trade. Local caravans down to the coast ceased in colonial times, but people continued to go as porters and migrant laborers. Shops were largely owned by Asians and Arabs, but after independence local shopkeepers became common in the villages and towns. Private trade was discouraged by the state for many years, and cooperative shops and state trading agencies were established. The private sector has persisted, however, and there are many successful businesses, especially among the Sukuma.

Division of Labor. There is a strong sexual division of labor. In general, men do shorter, heavy tasks, and women do more repetitive chores. Cattle are mainly men's concern, as are ironworking and machine sewing. Only men hunt. Pottery is women's work. Some urgent tasks, such as harvesting, are done by both sexes. Most diviners are men. The state has been keen to draw women into politics, but only moderate progress has been made.

Land Tenure. Under the chiefs, land could be acquired in several ways. A villager might clear new land or obtain cleared land from a village headman. He might also inherit land with agreement from the headman. The chief was said to be "owner" of the land; this meant that those who held it were his subjects, and that the prosperity of the chiefdom depended on him and his ancestors. There was some variation in the degree of control that chiefs and headmen exercised over land. Fields could not customarily be sold, but those who had cleared land could often lend it to others and pass it on to heirs. In the 1960s, once chieftainship was abolished, land started to be sold, but this was stemmed by government. Later, land was defined as belonging to a village as the agent of the state. Villagers were allocated land for their own use, and some land was retained for communal production. Some villagers are now returning to live on their former holdings.

Kinship

Kin Groups and Descent. The main kin groups in the area were those vested with political office. Since independence, their importance has diminished, although they still provide valuable personal networks for their members. The groups were mainly based on descent from former chiefs and other officeholders. Officeholders were also a focus for sets of relatives who clustered around them. Some Sukuma classify themselves into "clans" defined in terms of their members' chiefdom of origin. For most people, kinship is important mainly for interpersonal relations. A person's kin are widely dispersed, and villages are not typically kinship units. The main structural elements of the kinship system are oppositions between male and female, senior and junior, and proximal and alternate generations. One notable feature of behavior between kin is the division between those with whom one is familiar or jokes, and those whom one "respects" or avoids. This runs partly along generation lines and is at its strongest between affines. Sexual difference is also a factor. Thus, brothers-in-law joke with each other, and there is avoidance between a man and his daughter-in-law and mother-in-law. Known kin should not marry. A main determinant of people's status vis-à-vis their kin is the form of their parents' marriage (see "Marriage").

Kinship Terminology. Some features of the kinship system are reflected in the Iroquoian kinship terminology used by the Nyamwezi, which distinguishes kin from affines, mother's kin from father's kin in proximal generations, cross cousins from siblings and ortho-cousins, and proximal from alternate generations. Parental and great-grandparental generations are merged, as are those of grandparents and great-great-grandparents. Similar patterns are followed in the terms for junior generations. Some puzzling Crow features (father's sister's son = father) have been reported for the traditional Sukuma terminology.

Marriage and Family

Marriage. Local forms of marriage fall into two main classes, marriage with bride-wealth and marriage without bride-wealth. In bride-wealth marriage, a husband customarily acquires full rights over the children his wife bears. He should receive bride-wealth for his daughters and provide it for his sons, and his children should inherit from him. He also has customary rights to compensation for his wife's adultery. Adultery is still an offense if no bride-wealth has been given, but compensation is not customarily paid. Rights over children of non-bride-wealth unions are mainly vested in maternal kin, unless the father makes redemption payments for them. These payments are larger for a daughter than for a son. The verb *kukwa* is used for these payments and also for paying bride-wealth. Bride-wealth marriage is more common in prosperous areas and times. The verb *kutola* is commonly used for both forms of marriage. A man "marries," and a woman "is married." Residence at marriage varies but is increasingly neolocal. Patrivirilocal residence is most common when bride-wealth is paid, but sons often move away eventually. Bride-service with initial uxorilocal residence is reported to have existed formerly among the Sukuma. Polygyny is a common male ambition, but polygynous marriages are relatively unstable. Many men have been polygynous, but, with the main exception of chiefs in the past, older men are less polygynous than those in their forties. More generally, divorce is frequent. Women's first marriages in which bride-wealth has been paid are the most stable.

Domestic Unit. Before the 1970s, homesteads sometimes contained a dozen or more people, although most were smaller. They commonly consisted of a man and his wife or wives, their resident children, and perhaps the spouse and the children of one or more of the resident children. Other close relatives of the head of the homestead might also be present. Homesteads were the largest units in which members of one sex regularly ate together. They contained one or more households that were distinct food-producing and child-rearing units. The household was the basic economic unit and the husband-wife relation was its key element. This has been reinforced in new compact village where each 0.4-hectare plot is assigned to a *familia* (modern Swahili) based on a couple and their children. Neighboring households collaborate in a wide range of activities.

Inheritance. Questions of inheritance are usually resolved within the families concerned. Customarily only sons of bride-wealth marriages, or redeemed sons, inherit the main forms of wealth. Such heirs should look after the needs of daughters. Sometimes one son looks after an inheritance for all his siblings. Unredeemed children are in a weak position; they may fail to inherit either from their father or from their mother's kin, whose own children may take precedence.

Socialization. Socialization takes place largely within the family and village. Ceremonies within a few days of birth symbolize a baby's future as a male or female member of society. Girls especially learn their gender roles quite early, through participation in household tasks. Boys help in herding and other work but have more free time than do girls during their teens. There are no formal age groups or ceremonies of initiation into adulthood. Primary schooling is now compulsory, but parents sometimes keep children from school if their labor is required. Training in citizenship is part of the school curriculum.

Sociopolitical Organization

Before independence the main forms of political organization were the chiefdoms and the villages. Neighbors, and also kin, collaborate in many activities, and there are several ritual and secular associations and societies. Since independence, as part of the Republic of Tanzania, the area inhabited by the Nyamwezi and the Sukuma has been subject to its laws and constitution. It falls administratively within Mwanza, Shinyanga, and Tabora regions, which contain several administrative districts. These districts are segmented into divisions, which, in turn, contain wards, within which there are officially constituted villages. There are governmental and party officials at each level, and a series of elected committees. Since 1973, villages have been the basic unit of organization, although, within them, ten-house groups are recognized. In the early 1980s a new grass-roots village-security organization—Sungusungu or Busalama—emerged, and it has spread to all parts of the area. All able-bodied village men belong to the local Sungusungu group, and there is sometimes a women's wing.

Conflicts have occurred between the Revolutionary party (CCM) and Sungusungu, but there has also been some cooperation between them, and the groups are now legally recognized. Each village has its own group, but there is also some intervillage collaboration. Single-party rule is due to end, and multiparty elections are planned in the mid-1990s.

Social Control. There are official district-level courts, and below these there are primary courts. These administer national and some customary law. Neighbors' courts dealt with many disputes in the past, but nowadays Sungusungu groups hear cases. Their function is to maintain village security against cattle thieves and other enemies, including witches in some areas. Members are armed with bows and arrows, which have proved to be effective weapons for them, and with whistles for sounding alarms.

Conflict. Since World War I, the area has been relatively peaceful. The independence struggle was active but mainly nonviolent. Class conflict is not yet strongly developed, although there are substantial differences in wealth in some areas. Initial official reactions to Sungusungu were mainly negative, but the groups received qualified support from Julius Nyerere and some other leading Tanzanian figures. Government has since tried to control the groups and encourage their development elsewhere, but there are signs that enthusiasm for the system is declining among villagers themselves.

Religion and Expressive Culture

Religious Beliefs. With the main exceptions of the villages around Tabora and of areas around some Christian missions, neither Islam nor Christianity has flourished strongly among villagers. Religion in the area, like society itself, is accretive rather than exclusive.

Beliefs in a High God are widely held but involve no special cult. Ancestor worship is the main element in the religious complex. Chiefs' ancestors are thought to influence the lives of the inhabitants of their domains, but ordinary ancestors only affect their own descendants. Belief in witchcraft is widespread and strong.

Religious Practitioners. In addition to the High God and the ancestors, some nonancestral spirits are believed to influence some people's lives. Spirit-possession societies, such as the Baswezi, deal with such attacks and recruit the victims into membership. As a link between belief and action, the diviner (*mfumu*) is a key figure in religious life; diviners interpret the belief system for individuals and groups. They decide which forces are active and help people to deal with them. Although it is not strictly an hereditary art, people often take up divination when a misfortune is diagnosed as having been induced by a diviner ancestor who wishes them to do so. There are often several diviners in a village, but only one or two are likely to attract a wide clientele. All diviners, like their neighbors, engage in farming and participate fully in village life.

Ceremonies. Divination takes many forms, the most common being chicken divination, in which a young fowl is killed and readings are taken from its wings and other features. Sacrifices and libations, along with initiation into a spirit-possession or other society, may result from a divinatory séance. Divination and subsequent rituals may divide people, especially if witchcraft is diagnosed, but in many contexts the system allows villagers to express their solidarity with each other without loss of individual identity. In addition to ritual focused upon individuals and attended by their kin and neighbors, there is some public ceremonial at village and wider levels. Chiefly rituals are still sometimes performed, and there are ceremonies to cleanse a village of pollution when a member dies.

Arts. Representational art is not strongly developed; it has mainly ritual functions. Music and dancing are the main art forms, and drums are the main instruments, although the nail-piano (a box with metal prongs that twang at different pitches) and other instruments are also found. Traditional songs are sung at weddings and at dances, but new songs are also composed by dance leaders. Male dance teams are the most common, but some female and mixed teams perform. Ritual and other societies have their own dance styles. Transistor radios are now widespread. Local and visiting jazz and other bands play in the towns.

Medicine. Diviners and other local experts provide herbal and other forms of treatment for illness. Shops sell some Western medicines, including aspirin and liniments. Village dispensaries and state and mission hospitals also provide Western medicine. People commonly use both Western and indigenous treatments rather than trusting wholly in either.

Death and Afterlife. Funerals are important rituals for bereaved families and their kin and neighbors. Neighbors dig the grave and take news of the death to relatives of the deceased who live outside the village. The dead become ancestors who may continue to affect the lives of their descendants and demand appeasement. The idea that the dead live on in their descendants is expressed in terms of shared identity between alternate generations.

Bibliography

Abrahams, Ray G. (1967). *The Peoples of Greater Unyamwezi.* Ethnographic Survey of Africa. London: International African Institute.

Abrahams, Ray G. (1981). *The Nyamwezi Today.* Cambridge: Cambridge University Press.

Abrahams, Ray G. (1987). "Sungusungu: Village Vigilante Groups in Tanzania." *African Affairs,* April, 179–196.

Abrahams, Ray G., and Sufian Bukurura (1993). "Party Bureaucracy and Grass-Roots Initiatives in a Socialist State: The Case of Sungusungu Vigilantes in Tanzania." In *Socialism: Ideals, Ideologies, and Local Practices,* edited by Chris Hann, 92–101. London: Routledge.

Malcom, D. W. (1953). *Sukumaland: An African People and Their Country.* London: Oxford University Press.

RAY G. ABRAHAMS

Okiek

ETHNONYMS: Athi, Dorobo, Ndorobo, Torobbo, Wandorobo

Orientation

Identification. "Okiek" is the name of a Kenyan people who formerly lived by hunting game, making beehives, and gathering and trading honey; it is also the name of their language. The collective name "Okiek" includes over two dozen local groups, each with more specific names (e.g., Kapchepkendi, Piik aap Oom, Kaplelach). Okiek are usually called "Il Torobbo" by Maasai speakers, a derogatory reference they apply to all hunters—and even to impoverished Maasai who have no cattle; other names for the Okiek—"Athi," "Dorobo," "Ndorobo," "Torobbo," and "Wandorobo"—are derived from the Maasai term. These names have long been a source of confusion because they refer to more peoples than the Okiek. For example, the term "Torobbo" combines Okiek together with Maa-speaking hunting peoples living in northern Kenya around the Mathews Range, Mount Ny'iru, the Ndoto Mountains, and the Leroghi plateau. There is no clear historical relation between these Torobbo and Okiek living in highlands farther west and south. Other Torobbo-based names have the same ambiguity. Okiek call themselves "Okiek" in their own language.

Location. With the exception of the Akie, who live in the Maasai Steppe region of Tanzania, most Okiek groups live in the highlands of west-central Kenya (e.g., the Mau Escarpment, the Tindiret forest area, and the highlands north of Nakuru). The majority of these areas are located within Rift Valley Province. Digiri and Omotik Okiek groups live on savanna plains rather than in areas of highland forest. Until the late 1800s, Kalenjin-speaking hunters (who may have been Okiek and who were known to Kikuyu speakers as "Athi") lived around Mount Kenya and the Aberdares as well; they were largely absorbed or displaced by Kikuyu adoption, intermarriage, and "land sales."

Demography. The Okiek are one of Kenya's smaller ethnic groups. Because they live in dispersed groups, it is difficult to estimate accurately the total number of Okiek living in Kenya today. This uncertainty is magnified because of the use of the term "Dorobo," rather than "Okiek," in the national census. The Kaplelach and Kipchornwonek Okiek groups include approximately 600 people each. If other groups are roughly the same size, the total Okiek population in Kenya would be around 15,000. Including the Tanzanian Akie group would increase this estimate slightly. Okiek settlement patterns and population density in Okiek areas have changed significantly since about the mid-twentieth century (see "Land Tenure," "Settlements," and "Subsistence and Commercial Activities").

Linguistic Affiliation. Okiek is part of the Kalenjin Branch of Southern Nilotic languages. In addition to Okiek, the Kalenjin ethnolinguistic group (formerly called "Nandi-speaking tribes") also includes Kipsigis, Nandi, Marakwet, Pokot (Suk), Sebei, Keiyo, and Tugen. Kalenjin languages are more distantly related to Eastern Nilotic languages (e.g., Maa, Teso, Turkana, Karamojong) and Western Nilotic languages (e.g., Luo, Nuer, Dinka). The Okiek spoken by different groups can vary lexically, morphologically, and tonally, but Okiek dialects are mutually understandable. Okiek are usually multilingual, speaking the language of their nearest neighbors in addition to Okiek. Many contemporary Okiek also speak Kiswahili, a national language in Kenya and Tanzania alike; those who have attended school know some English as well.

History and Cultural Relations

Living in different locations, each Okiek group has had distinctive histories of interaction with neighbors of other, more populous ethnic groups (e.g., Maasai, Kipsigis, Nandi, and Kikuyu). Their experiences with colonial and national administrations have also differed. To suggest this variability, this article will describe Kaplelach and Kipchornwonek Okiek as examples, briefly noting how they contrast with other Okiek groups. Kaplelach and Kipchornwonek live adjacent to one another on the southern part of the Western Mau Escarpment in Narok District, Kenya.

Like other Okiek groups, Kaplelach and Kipchornwonek interact regularly with their pastoral or agropastoral neighbors. Cattle-keeping Maasai live on the savanna to their south, and Kalenjin-speaking Kipsigis are their nearest western neighbors. Other Okiek groups live to their north, elsewhere on the escarpment. Okiek are a minority group in the area, considered low-status and inferior by their neighbors. This attitude is based in part on their neighbors' negative evaluations of the Okiek hunting-and-gathering economy and of the forest environment where Okiek live.

Despite these stereotypes, Okiek have interacted regularly with both neighbors. They have traded, intermarried, and, at times, formed long-term friendships with both Maasai and Kipsigis. Kipchornwonek-Kipsigis interaction has historically been more intensive than that of Kaplelach with Kipsigis because Kipchornwonek live farther west, closer to Kipsigis areas. In the late twentieth century, however, Kipsigis have been buying land from Kaplelach and settling in their midst (see "Land Tenure").

Okiek have diversified their economic pursuits over the mid- and late twentieth century, a complex process that different Okiek groups began at different times and in different ways. They began by supplementing hunting and honey gathering with small-scale gardening and started to keep small herds of domestic animals at about that same time. Gradually, the balance between hunting, honey gathering, farming, and herding has shifted. Most contemporary Okiek rely on maize and other crops, supplementing agriculture with trading, hunting, and honey gathering. Many keep cattle, sheep, or goats as well; a relatively small number of Kipchornwonek and Kaplelach have taken long-term wage labor in towns.

Settlements

Okiek settlements have changed over time in conjunction with shifts in economy and mode of subsistence. When hunting and honey gathering were major sources of subsistence for Kaplelach and Kipchornwonek, they lived in small settlements composed of extended-family groups. For example, one residence group might include the households of a man and his adult sons or of a group of brothers. At times, they might also include households linked by affinal relations. People moved several times a year, with households sometimes regrouping, going to live in forests at different elevations according to honey seasons.

As agriculture became more important, Okiek began to settle more permanently in middle-altitude forest. These settlements provided a home base where gardens were located and from which men traveled to more distant forests to hunt and check their hives. As lineages owned land (see "Land Tenure"), the lineage basis of smaller settlement groups remained the same. Some larger communities with multiple crosscutting ties based on patrilineal, matrilateral, and affinal relations formed as well, especially in Kipchornwonek areas.

Settlement patterns began to change again in the late 1970s and 1980s in response to government changes in land tenure. As government-demarcated group ranches in Narok District began to be subdivided into individual holdings (see "Land Tenure"), Okiek families moved onto the tracts that would be theirs. They were also able to sell portions of their land for the first time. The result of this has been a large influx of people from farther west, where population densities are higher and land is scarcer and more costly. Most immigrants into Kipchornwonek and Kaplelach areas are Kipsigis, although some people from Kisii and Kikuyu ethnic groups have also bought land. Kikuyu are the main settlers in areas on the Mau Escarpment between Narok and Nakuru.

Economy

Subsistence and Commercial Activities. Okiek have a long history of hunting wild game and collecting honey. Whereas most Okiek groups continue these activities, they have diversified their economy to include farming and herding (see "History and Cultural Relations"). Hunting weapons consist of bows and arrows, spears, and clubs, along with traps. Animals hunted include bushbuck, buffalo, duikers, hyraxes, bongo, and giant forest hogs (probably the most common quarries); in the past, Okiek also hunted elephants with poison spears and arrows. Maize is the staple crop, supplemented by millet, beans, greens, pumpkins, and other vegetables. Some Kipchornwonek Okiek plant pyrethrum as a cash crop; Okiek of other areas (e.g., Piik aap Oom), have smallholdings of tea and sell milk from crossbreed cattle.

Industrial Arts. Okiek crafts include the making of pottery, baskets, leather bags and clothing, and beaded personal ornaments by women. Men produce their weapons (bows, clubs, and various kinds of spears and arrows) and fashion snuff and tobacco containers from horn, ivory, and wood. Okiek do not smelt the iron for arrows, swords, and spears, but obtain it from blacksmiths among the Maasai. They do, however, file them to shape.

Trade. Okiek have long traded a variety of products with their neighbors, honey being the most important trade item. Honey is important as food, but is especially sought for brewing into honey wine for ceremonial uses and drinking. With Maasai, Okiek men exchanged buffalo hides for shields and hyrax hides for ritual capes; Okiek also could offer herbal medicines from the forest and various finished articles such as sheaths, necklaces, and tobacco containers of ivory or buffalo horn in trade. Okiek would get livestock from Maasai; before they were keeping herds, they ate the animals received. Early in the twentieth century, the price for a large container of honey was a cow, but money later became the medium of exchange. Okiek also performed certain services for Maasai in exchange for livestock, including circumcising boys and, sometimes, herding cattle.

Trade with Kipsigis brought hunting dogs and grain to Okiek, also in exchange for forest products. Okiek women also made and traded pottery with Kipsigis. Before prices began to be reckoned in monetary terms, a pot would fetch the amount of grain that it could hold. More recently Okiek men have begun to participate in other small-scale commerce, opening small shops and teahouses in village centers, managing public transportation vehicles, or participating in long-range cattle trade. Okiek women now also sell agricultural produce, shop goods, tobacco, beads, or secondhand clothing in markets and at home.

Division of Labor. Gender is the major principle of Okiek labor division, although age is also relevant. Women's work includes processing and cooking food, keeping the household supplied with water and firewood, most child care, and making animal hides into leather bags, straps, and, formerly, into clothing. Hunting, making hives, and gathering honey are all forest-based work that is done by men. Agricultural work is shared by men and women, with men responsible for heavy garden clearing. Households vary in how farmwork is divided between husband and wife. Women are responsible for milking livestock, and herding is often done by children. Men are considered managers of the herd and might take them grazing when children are not available. Children are also expected to help with farmwork, and girls assist in housework (e.g., getting water and firewood, cooking).

Land Tenure. Until recent land reforms, Kaplelach and Kipchornwonek divided land into lineage-owned tracts that stretched along the slope of the escarpment. Each crossed four or five of the escarpment's altitudinally defined ecological zones, giving every family access to each zone during each honey season throughout the year. Each lineage tract was subdivided into named places. Some lineages allocated honey rights by place to particular families; others used the entire tract cooperatively.

Legislation for general land demarcation was passed in Kenya in 1969. Prior to that, a group-owned-ranch division policy was developed for two Maasai-dominated districts (Narok and Kajiado). Although their high- or medium-potential highlands are very different from semiarid Maasai savanna country, Kaplelach and Kipchornwonek land was included because they live in Narok District. Group-ranch demarcation began in the mid-1970s, consolidating and crossing previous lineage land boundaries, incorporating non-Okiek neighbors into some groups, and registering some Okiek land to influential individuals who had never lived there. The highest Okiek forests were declared forest reserve. These changes initially had little effect on Okiek land use, although they were extremely consequential and became the basis for later developments. Beginning in the 1980s, Okiek began to subdivide their joint group ranches into individually held plots. Accordingly, families moved to claim and live on their own land, perhaps settling with a few close relatives. Subdivision also gave individuals the right to sell or lease land; almost all have done so, resulting in a large influx of settlers from other parts of Kenya (see "Settlements").

Kinship

Kin Groups and Descent. Okiek groups vary in the relative importance they place on lineages and clans as kinship groups (see "Social Organization"). For Kaplelach and Kipchornwonek, patrilineally defined lineages are most important: they figure in landholding and residence, the arrangement of marriages, and legal matters. Matrilateral and affinal relations are important emotionally, in the recruitment of work groups, and on ceremonial occasions; they can also affect residential and legal decisions. For some Okiek groups farther north, such as Kapchepkendi and Piik aap Oom, the patriclan is far more important as a social unit and is central in defining land rights.

Kinship Terminology. Kipchornwonek and Kaplelach Okiek reckon kinship in a way that resembles an Omaha system, but their cousin terminology is not the same as the canonical Omaha model. Mother's brothers, all their children, and all children of one's father's sisters are called *maama*. The children of one's mother's sisters are regarded as siblings (*tuupca*), but are called *lianashe*, a term related to the Maasai word for "sister," *enkanashe*.

Marriage and Family

Marriage. Until the late 1980s, Kaplelach and Kipchornwonek Okiek lineages arranged most marriages. Young men usually married while in their twenties, whereas young women married at about sixteen, soon after initiation to womanhood. Arrangements were made through a series of four or more visits from the groom's family to the bride's. Discussion during later visits centered on bride-wealth property, which today averages six or seven cows (or their equivalent). In the past, engagements could begin when the couple were still young children, but such early engagements became rare after the 1970s. Between formal meetings, the groom was expected to visit, bring small gifts, and help his future affines in various ways. Alternatives to arranged marriage were also possible through various kinds of elopement, although these attempts to circumvent family plans were not always successful. Marriages are usually patrilocal.

With the multiple demographic and economic changes related to land sales, increasing education, and economic diversification, far more young Okiek have been eloping, refusing arranged marriages, or delaying marriage since about the mid-1980s. These shifts have also contributed to an increase in plural marriage, relatively rare among Okiek in the past. The pattern of plural marriage has also changed: it is now possible for young men to an extent never before feasible. Many plural marriages in this new trend are between Okiek men and women from other, settler ethnic groups.

Domestic Unit. Husband, wife, and their children form the core of a typical Okiek household, but other relatives (e.g., an aged parent of the husband or children of the couple's siblings) might also be part of it on a permanent or temporary basis. If a man has more than one wife, each woman has her own house. Parents do not sleep in the same house with adolescent children of the opposite sex. A separate sleeping house might be built for an adolescent son or adolescent children might sleep in another house with friends.

Inheritance. Land, hives, livestock, and other property are inherited patrilineally. In some cases, daughters might receive an animal or some other particular item. A man's widow does not inherit his property, but should be cared for by his siblings after his death if her sons are still young. Some contemporary Okiek argue that daughters should have inheritance rights as well, a national issue that the Kenyan parliament is also considering.

Socialization. Okiek mark the growth and maturation of children through a series of life-cycle ceremonies (see "Ceremonies"). These are the same for boys and girls until initiation into adulthood, which occurs at 14 to 16 years of age. There are important gender differences, however, in the way that children are socialized, ranging from the games they play to the tasks they are given. These correspond to and help to teach them the work they will do as adult men and women; they also teach children that men and women have different rights, responsibilities, and abilities.

Sociopolitical Organization

Social Organization. Lineage, clan, local group, and age set are the main units of Okiek social organization above the household level. Lineages are the most important large-scale social grouping for some Okiek groups; for others, clans play a similar role (see "Kin Groups and Descent"). For Kaplelach and Kipchornwonek Okiek, clans are invoked as a more diffuse mode of relation, for instance to establish a link with a stranger. Clan membership is defined patrilineally. These Okiek lineages often share clan names with Maasai; in some cases, people can also equate the Okiek clans with those of Kipsigis.

The local group is a significant social unit for Okiek in terms of cultural identity and history. Local groups have specific names, such as Kaplelach or Maresionik, but local-group membership is not associated with particular rights or responsibilities. A local group is constituted of six to ten lineages that traditionally held adjacent tracts of land (see "Land Tenure").

Age sets (sing. *ipinta*) define relations that crosscut those of lineage, uniting men of different lineages into a cohort of equals. An age set is a named group that includes all men who undergo initiation into adulthood within a specified period of time, usually about fourteen years (although each age set is further divided into two shorter periods, the "right" and "left" sides). Kaplelach and Kipchornwonek age sets share names with those of nearby Maasai, and they can also relate these names to the different age-set names used by Kipsigis. Men of a single age set should treat one another in a brotherly way; they should respect and honor men of senior age sets. Women have no separate, parallel age sets, but they are integrated into male age sets in terms of their male relations. For instance, a woman is known as a wife of her husband's age, a daughter of her father's age, and so forth.

Political Organization. Local political organization parallels social organization for Kipchornwonek and Kaplelach Okiek. Until recently, when a few Okiek individuals became administrative government chiefs, Okiek had no ranked overall offices. When there were political or legal issues to discuss, men from the appropriate groups were called together to meet. These could be meetings of men from one lineage, from several lineages, or men from a large neighborhood area (*latyet*). Women were not part of these meetings. Whereas all adult men have the right to attend and speak at meetings, older men often address the gathering more fully, and they are able to relate precedents and other experience to the issues at hand. When contemporary meetings about national, district, or development matters are held, adult women sometimes attend as well.

Conflict and Social Control. Meetings (see "Political Organization") are also forums in which legal disputes can be heard and resolved. These might concern theft, assault, murder, serious arguments, or (rarely) accusations of witchcraft. Those at the meeting decide cases, fining the person(s) found at fault. Before calling such a large meeting, however, attempts are usually made to settle matters with smaller meetings, within or between the families involved. Late in the 1800s, some quarrels led to lineage feuds and raids; these conflicts usually arose over issues related to land and women. Contemporary Okiek continue to resolve some disputes in local council meetings, but they take others to be heard at governmental offices and courts.

Religion and Expressive Culture

Religious Beliefs and Practitioners. Okiek believe in one god, called Torooret or Asiista, who is thought to be beneficent and is invoked in blessings. Ancestor spirits, on the other hand, can cause illness and misfortune for the living if they are forgotten or in retribution for wrongs committed among their relatives (see "Medicine" and "Death and Afterlife"). Okiek visit a variety of healing specialists and diviners who can identify ancestor spirits responsible for such difficulties (see "Medicine"). Kaplelach and Kipchornwonek Okiek know about Christian churches, but Christian missionary activity is relatively recent in their areas, taking hold only after 1980 and largely in conjunction with the settlers who have moved in (see "Land Tenure"). Other Okiek groups, such as Maresionik, have a longer history of involvement with Christian churches.

Ceremonies. Life-cycle ceremonies marking stages of maturation are the major rites celebrated by Kaplelach and Kipchornwonek Okiek. The first is a one-day ceremony that includes shaving the heads of child and mother and giving the child a new name. In the second, rarely practiced now, the ear lobes are pierced; this takes place when a child is 12 to 14 years old. The final and most important ceremony is initiation into adulthood. Performed at about age 15, initiation itself consists of four ceremonies. During a seclusion period, children are taught about gender-appropriate adult behavior and rights and learn sex-specific ritual secrets from a pair of ritual leaders. Girls and boys both go through this ceremonial sequence. Other Okiek ceremonies have to do with marriage, peacemaking, and pouring libations to ancestor spirits.

Arts. Okiek artistry has material expression in a range of products, including tightly woven baskets, a range of rouletted ceramic forms, and other material culture. Beaded personal ornaments, worn in various combinations, are one of the most aesthetically striking Okiek creations. Okiek also decorate containers and other objects with beads or incised patterns and in the late twentieth century have begun to paint houses with designs for special occasions. Okiek verbal art is rich and varied as well, including many genres of song, skilled oratory, proverbs, and stories.

Medicine. Okiek use a variety of treatments for health problems, which can have physical and social causes alike. They have substantial knowledge of herbal medicines made from forest plants and trees and also consult a range of traditional healers. For Kaplelach and Kipchornwonek Okiek, these include Okiek diviners (who use the fruit of the *lowisto* tree), Maasai diviners, and Kipsigis or Nandi diviners. Other Okiek groups probably avail themselves of healing specialists from other neighboring ethnic groups. Health clinics and hospitals make biomedical treatments available, although they may not be nearby or well provided.

Death and Afterlife. Death is not an occasion for elaborate ritual observance among Okiek. For several days, mourning families observe certain restrictions in dress, on visiting other houses, and on sharing food. In the past, corpses were laid to rest in the forest or bush; now they are buried. Upon death, adults become ancestor spirits and can continue to affect the living in some ways. If angered, for instance, they can bring disease or bad luck to their living relatives.

Bibliography

Blackburn, Roderic (1974). "The Okiek and Their History." Azania 9:139–157.

Blackburn, Roderic (1982a). *Okiek*. London: Evans Brothers.

Blackburn, Roderic (1982b). "In the Land of Milk and Honey." In *Politics and History in Band Societies*, edited by Eleanor Leacock and Richard Lee, 283–305. Cambridge: Cambridge University Press.

Huntingford, G. W. B. (1951). "Social Institutions of the Dorobo." *Anthropos* 46:1–46.

Huntingford, G. W. B. (1954). "The Political Organization of the Dorobo." *Anthropos* 49:123–148.

Huntingford, G. W. B. (1955). "The Economic Life of the Dorobo." *Anthropos* 50:602–634.

Kenny, Michael (1981). "Mirror in the Forest: The Dorobo Hunter-Gatherers as an Image of the Other." *Africa* 51(1): 477–496.

Klumpp, Donna, and Corinne A. Kratz (1993). "Aesthetics, Expertise, and Ethnicity: Okiek and Maasai Perspectives on Personal Ornament." In *Being Maasai*, edited by T. Spear and R. Waller, 195–222. London: James Currey.

Kratz, Corinne A. (1981). "Are the Okiek Really Maasai? or Kipsigis? or Kikuyu?" *Cahiers d'Études Africaines* 79(20): 355–368.

Kratz, Corinne A. (1986). "Ethnic Interaction, Economic Diversification, and Language Use." *SUGIA* 7(2): 189–226.

Kratz, Corinne A. (1991). "Amusement and Absolution: Transforming Narratives during Confession of Social Debts." *American Anthropologist* 93(4): 826–851.

Kratz, Corinne A. (1993). *Affecting Performance: Meaning, Movement, and Experience in Okiek Women's Initiation*. Washington, D.C.: Smithsonian Institution Press.

Rottland, Franz, and R. Vossen (1977). "Grundlagen fur eine Klarung des Dorobo-Problems." In *Zur Sprachgeschichte und Ethnohistorie in Afrika*, edited by W. J. G. Mohlig, F. Rottland, and B. Heine. Berlin: Dietrich Verlagen.

CORINNE A. KRATZ

Palestinians

ETHNONYM: Filastinyoun

Orientation

Identification. Palestinians inhabit an area east of the Mediterranean Sea and south of Lebanon. The Jordan River, Lakes Huleh and Tiberias, and the Dead Sea separate Palestine from Jordan. Palestinian territory stretches as far south as the Gulf of ʿAqaba. Palestinians refer to their land as "Filastin," the name of an Aegean population (Philistines) who inhabited coastal Palestine before the Israelites. Christians refer to Palestine as "the Holy Land." Today Palestine is divided among Israel and the Palestine National Authority. Palestinian territory falls into two major geographic zones: the coastal area, and the northern extension of the Great Rift Valley.

Location. Palestine is located between 30° and 33° N and 34° and 36° E. Its total land area is 27,128 square kilometers, divided between Israel and the two towns (Gaza and Jericho) administered by the Palestine National Authority. The total area under direct Palestinian control since 1993 is 135 square kilometers. Palestine lies at the southern tip of the fertile eastern Mediterranean region, and almost half of its total area is arid or semiarid. Only parts of the narrow coastal plain, the Jordan Valley, and the Galilee region in the north receive adequate rainfall. Palestine, on the whole, enjoys typical Mediterranean weather. The Great Rift Valley, or the Jordan Valley, has a semitropical climate. The main city in the Jordan valley, Jericho, is the lowest spot on earth—250 meters below sea level. The arid and semiarid areas to the south enjoy a desertlike dry and hot climate.

Demography. Between 5.8 million and 6 million Palestinians live in Israel, on the West Bank, in the Gaza Strip, and dispersed all over the world. As of 1989, there were 900,000 living in the West Bank, 550,000 to 770,000 in the Gaza Strip, and 800,000 in Israel proper. East Jerusalem, annexed to Israel since 1967, is the home of 155,000 Palestinians. Those living under the Palestine National Authority since 1993 number 775,000 in Gaza and 20,000 in Jericho. There are also 1.7 million Palestinians living in Jordan, 350,000 in Lebanon, 225,000 in Syria, 70,000 in Iraq, 60,000 in Egypt, 25,000 in Libya, and 250,000 in Saudi Arabia. Until the Gulf War, there were 400,000 in Kuwait. There are other, smaller Palestinian communities in the Persian Gulf area, amounting to 113,543 people. It is estimated that 104,856 Palestinians live in the United States and another 140,000 around the globe. The highest ratio people to land is in Gaza, where there are 3,577 people per square kilometer. Many Palestinians live as refugees in camps: 248,000 in the Gaza Strip, 100,000 on the West Bank, 187,000 in Jordan, 143,300 in Lebanon, and 67,000 in Syria. Palestinians speak Arabic, but most are bilingual, their second language depending on their place of residence.

Linguistic Affiliation. Arabic is a member of the Hamito-Semitic Family of languages. Modern Arabic is a South Semitic language. Palestinians speak a distinct dialect of Arabic but write classical Arabic, like the rest of the Arab world.

History and Cultural Relations

The Palestinians are a racial amalgam of the indigenous pre-Israelite population and later groups that settled in Palestine. Even though the Canaanite and Philistine city-states were defeated by the Israelites under King David in 1,000 B.C., their populations were not exterminated. The Muslim Arab conquest of A.D. 638 did not result in a large transfusion of Arabs, but the local inhabitants' culture became increasingly Arabized, and large numbers converted to Islam. The Peninsular Arab conquerors took great interest in Palestine because of the Prophet Mohammed's association with Jerusalem: his nocturnal journey there in A.D. 621 and his ascension to heaven from the spot where the Jewish Temple once stood bestowed a holy status on the city. When Muslims conquered Jerusalem, Caliph Omar came to receive the keys to the city from the Byzantine patriarch, Sophronius, and issued the Pledge of Omar: he vowed to protect the holy sites and freedom of worship of all religious communities. During the Umayyad dynasty (A.D. 661–750), Caliph ʿAbd al-Malik ibn Marwān built a magnificent mosque (691–692) over the ruins of Solomon's Temple to commemorate Mohammed's ascension to heaven. Known as the Dome of the Rock, it is the oldest example of early Islamic architecture in the world. The Western Wall (the Wailing Wall), which is the only remaining portion of Solomon's Temple, was consecrated as a Muslim charitable trust in later years on the grounds that Mohammed tethered his steed, al-Buraq, at the wall. In view of its holy status, Jerusalem was never made into an Arab capital. Muslims also permitted the return of Jews to Jerusalem, from which they had been barred since the Roman period. Under the ʿAbbasīd Emperor, Harun al-Rashīd (786–809), the number of hostels for European pilgrims increased. Jerusalem's religious status attracted foreign invaders, including the Christian Crusaders, who took over the city in 1099. Frankish invaders established the Latin Kingdom of Jerusalem, which lasted until 1187. Disputes between the Arabized eastern Christians, who coexisted peacefully with Muslims, and the European Crusaders cemented a lasting bond between Palestine's two religious communities. During the Latin Kingdom, the Dome of the Rock was converted into a Christian site known as Templum Domini. Jerusalem was liberated by Saladin (Ṣalāḥ al-Dīn) the Ayyūbid sultan of Egypt and Syria in 1187. Muslim families were restored as the guardians of the holy sites, and Jews were permitted to return in large numbers. The Crusaders repossessed the city from 1229 to 1244. The Egyptian Mamlūk dynasty liberated the city again, but in 1516 Jerusalem and Palestine fell to the Ottoman Turks. Under their rule, Palestine was divided into districts and attached to the province of Syria. In the nineteenth century European Jews began to settle in Ottoman-controlled Palestine. Jewish efforts to purchase the Wailing Wall and large areas of land with the help of foreign consuls were met with stiff resistance. With the financial support of European banking families, Jews fleeing Russian pogroms during the second half of the nineteenth century were able to establish collective farms. There was also significant Arab economic development. Following the Crimean War (1854–1856), Gaza emerged as a major grain-producing area. Cotton production expanded during the 1860s. Palestinians also became successful citrus growers, producing 33 million oranges in 1873. Jewish colonists who settled at Petach Tikva, near Jaffa, were exporting 15 percent of Palestine's total orange crop by 1913. Arab economic activity expanded around Nablus, an area specializing in olive oil and soap production. Jewish purchase of Arab land had a detrimental effect on Palestinian prosperity. Once bought, land became the perpetual property of Jews, and Arab laborers were thrown off. The land problem continued to bedevil Arab-Jewish relations after Britain took over Palestine. British interest in Palestine was the result of the strategic significance of the Suez Canal. During World War I, the British concluded several secret agreements regarding the future of Ottoman-held territories. One of these agreements, the Balfour Declaration, granted Jews the right to establish a national homeland in Palestine. In 1920, when the British acquired control over Palestine as a mandate under the League of Nations, they made the Balfour Declaration official policy, which was at variance with their responsibility under the mandate: to prepare the native population for eventual independence and majority rule. As a result, Palestinian demographics changed drastically. According to the 1922 census, the total population of Palestine was 752,000, of whom 660,000 were Arabs and 84,000 were Jews. The Arab population included 71,000 indigenous Christians who shared most of the sociocultural traits of the Muslim Palestinian population. By the end of World War II, the Palestinian population grew to two million. By 1946, there were 1,269,000 Arabs, as opposed to 608,000 Jews. Around 70,000 of the Jews were unauthorized immigrants who entered Palestine in the immediate postwar period. Throughout the mandate era (1920–1948), Arab despair over Jewish immigration fostered a policy of noncooperation with the mandate government. A proposed constitution offered in 1922 by the high commissioner, Sir Herbert Samuel, was rejected by both Muslim and Christian Palestinians. The only body that continued to represent the Palestinians was the Supreme Muslim Council, which supervised the Islamic charitable trusts and the court system. The appointed head of this institution, Amin Husseini, was the highest religious authority and emerged as the sole leader of the Palestinian community. He became the head of the Arab Higher Committee, representing both Christians and Muslims, following the 1936 Arab Revolt. The first major outbreak of Arab-Jewish violence was a result of attempts by Revisionist Zionists, led by Vladimir Jabotinsky, to expand Jewish rights over the Wailing Wall. This violence was investigated by British parliamentary commissions, which concluded that unrestricted Zionist immigration and land purchases led to the impoverishment and anger of the Palestinian peasantry. A general Arab strike and uprising in 1936 led the British to convene the Peel Commission, the first such commission to recommend the partitioning of Palestine into an Arab and a Jewish state. The Peel Commission allotted 20 percent of the most fertile land to the Jews, and 80 percent to the Arabs. The Commission also recommended the internationalization of Jerusalem and Bethlehem. Both the Higher Arab Committee and Arab governments rejected this plan. By 1942, Zionist lobbying efforts shifted from Britain to the United States. A Zionist conference in 1942, which was held at the Biltmore Hotel in New York City, called openly for the establishment of a Jewish commonwealth in Palestine, and efforts were made to obtain the endorsement of major U.S. political parties and members of Congress. The Nazi Holocaust against European Jews succeeded in winning powerful world leaders, including U.S. president Truman, over to the cause of Israeli statehood. Once the British Government made the decision in 1947 to end its mandate over Palestine, the latter became the responsibility of the United Nations. A special eleven-member committee, known as UNSCOP, was organized to make recommendations to the General Assembly regarding the future of Palestine. These recommendations were made in the form of majority (8 votes) and minority (3 votes) reports. The majority report, which was adopted by the General Assembly on 29 November 1947, stipulated that Palestine be partitioned into a Jewish state and an Arab state, with Jerusalem and Bethlehem brought under a UN regime as a *corpus separatum*. Both the United States and the Soviet Union voted for General Assembly Resolution 181, the majority plan. Palestinians were outraged over the decision by an outside agency to give away half of their land without consulting them. Arab states in the United Nations did not oppose the Vatican-sponsored resolution on Jerusalem. During the following year, a U.S. State Department report by George F. Kennan predicted that the partition resolution could not be enforced without war. Clashes between Jewish armed forces and Palestinian and other Arab armies quickly followed. Jewish forces moved not only to consolidate their UN lands but to acquire additional areas in the Galilee and Negev areas. The UN partition plan granted one-third of the population—namely, the Jewish community—one-half of the total land area of Palestine. The Jewish community at the time owned 20 percent of all cultivable areas, amounting to 6 percent of the total land area of Palestine. At the end of this conflict, the Egyptian army remained in control of the Gaza Strip and the Jordanian Arab Legion maintained control over eastern Palestine and eastern Jerusalem. The Arab states signed separate armistice agreements with newly founded Israel. Soon thereafter, Transjordan changed its name to the Hashemite Kingdom of Jordan, naming the area east of the Jordan River the "East Bank" and the area west of the river the "West Bank." The 1947–1948 Arab-Jewish War produced one of the Middle East's major refugee problems. Palestinians who fled their homes or were driven out by Jewish forces numbered between 500,000 and 750,000 people. Some placed the percentage of Palestinians who became refugees at 80 percent of the total Arab population. Between 125,000 and 150,000 of the Palestinian peasantry retained their homes but lost their agricultural lands. The state of Israel continuously rejected UN resolutions calling for the return of the refugees or providing them with financial compensation. The only Arab country that granted citizenship rights to the Palestinians was Jordan. The rest of the Arab countries declined to extend citizenship rights for fear of jeopardizing the refugees' right of return. The League of Arab States created a seat for Palestine, which was occupied by the Gaza-based government of All Palestine until 1957. The Gaza government was a rump Palestinian authority that was directed by Amin Husseini's deputy, Ahmad Hilmi Abd al-Baqi; it existed under the watchful eye of the Egyptian military governor. By 1964, a new Palestinian authority—the Palestine Liberation Organization, headed by Ahmad Shuqairy—was created at the behest of President Gamal Abdel Nasser of Egypt. Conflicts with the Egyptians forced Shuqairy's resignation in 1968. Another PLO emerged during that year and was soon headed by Yasser Arafat, the leader of Fatah, a militant underground organization. The new PLO rejected the need to rely on Arab governments and promoted the principle of the armed struggle. After a brief stay in Jordan, armed conflict with the Jordanian army drove the PLO to Lebanon, where it established itself inside Palestinian refugee camps. The launching of attacks against Israel from Lebanon's southern borders eventually resulted in a massive retaliation by the Israeli Defense Forces in 1982. The PLO was forced to evacuate its militias out of Lebanon under U.S. protection and relocate to Tunisia. The Israeli invasion of Beirut during the latter days of that war resulted in a Lebanese-led massacre of Palestinian refugees in the Sabra and Shatilla camps. The PLO's rehabilitation by the world community was a slow process, which began in 1974. During that year, the Arab summit meeting at Rabat, Morocco, recognized the PLO as the sole representative of the Palestinian people. Also in 1974, the United Nations confirmed this designation by granting the PLO observer status. The United Nations also recognized the inalienable rights of the Palestinian people, a gesture of enormous symbolic significance because it was the United Nations that divided the Palestinian homeland in the first place. The outbreak of the *intifada* (uprising) in 1987, in the West Bank and Gaza, provided the PLO with another opportunity to integrate itself with the international community. The PLO declared itself a state and sought recognition by the Uniited States. This was granted upon the PLO's unilateral recognition of Israel and of Security Council Resolution 242. Following the Gulf War in 1991, the PLO agreed to participate in a U.S.-sponsored Middle East peace conference. During these talks, a secret channel to the Israelis was opened with the mediation of the Norwegian government. In 1993 Israel and the PLO signed a "declaration of principles" that provided a framework for settling all issues pertaining to the Palestinian-Israeli conflict and granted the newly created Palestine National Authority autonomous rule over Gaza and Jericho. Negotiations over the future of the rest of the West Bank, as well as that of Jerusalem, were to follow.

Settlements

Until the establishment of Israel in 1948, the Palestinian coastline was dotted with Arab villages. The Galilee area in the north was also heavily settled. The Bedouin (nomadic) population was concentrated in the Negev Desert area. After the division of Palestine into Israel and the West Bank, the coastal area became heavily Jewish. The Jordan Valley was less settled than the Mediterranean coast. After Israel's occupation of the West Bank and Gaza following the 1967 Arab-Israeli War, Israeli settlements were built on Palestinian lands, using up to 50 percent of these territories. Around 125,000 Israeli settlers began to live within the Arab area. Under international law, these settlements are considered illegal and may be dismantled as the price of a lasting peace settlement. There are also ancient cities in Palestine: Jerusalem (built by the Jebusites), Jericho (the oldest city in the world), Bethlehem, Beershiba, Gaza, and Nablus (ancient Samaria). Most of these urban centers have an old city surrounded by walls and modern suburbs in the nearby hills. Typical village dwellings are built of local building material, stone in the hills and mud and straw in the villages. Jerusalem's old city and ancient walls are built exclusively of Jerusalem limestone. Wood, which has always been in short supply, is rarely used.

Economy

Subsistence and Commercial Activities. Until the creation of Israel and the dispersal of the Palestinians, 60 percent of the population was engaged in agricultural activities and food processing. Village crafts included the rich and ancient tradition of embroidery. Mother-of-pearl and olive-wood artifacts were common in the cities. After 1948, Palestinians who became refugees subsisted on daily rations supplied by the United Nations Relief and Works Agency (UNRWA). Skilled and educated refugees became professional and white-collar workers in the Persian Gulf oil countries.

Industrial Arts. Along with food processing and tourist-related arts and crafts, Palestinians were engaged in oil refining, a British-run industry, in Haifa. After 1948, Palestinians lost access to this industry and turned to phosphate mining in the Dead Sea area. There was also a thriving glass industry in Hebron.

Trade. Before 1948, Palestinians exported citrus fruits to Egypt and other parts of the Middle East. Fruits, vegetables, hand soap, and olive oil were the mainstay of trade with Arab markets after the West Bank was taken over by Jordan. Since 1967, this area has become a captive market for Israeli goods.

Division of Labor. Palestinian village women and Bedouin women always participated in agricultural work. In towns and cities, women have been increasingly integrated in gender-specific occupations such as teaching, nursing, and clerical positions. Palestinian women are also employed as teachers in the Persian Gulf area. Since 1967, many West Bank women have been proletarianized and work as migratory laborers within Israel proper, employed in food processing and the garment industry. Women have also become heads of households as a result of the imprisonment or exiling of Palestinian men.

Land Tenure. Until the British period, there were three types of landholding: public lands (*miri*), privately owned land (*mulk*), and state and private lands cultivated by peasants as communal lands (*musha*). The cultivation of land by the peasants of an entire village was abolished by the British in the 1940s in order to facilitate the purchase and sale of land held by individuals. Jewish efforts to buy land were facilitated by the existence of absentee landlords in the Galilee region, such as the Lebanese Sursuq family. After 1967, public lands previously considered the property of the Ottoman, British, and Jordanian governments were transferred to Israeli settlers.

Kinship

Kin Groups and Descent. The basic unit in society is the family, with the village unit quite often being an extended family. Political upheaval over a long period of time strengthened the traditional family structure. Kin groups, as exemplified by the family or the clan (*hamula*), survived despite increased mobility and urbanization. Entire families and clans from the same village relocated together to the same refugee camps after 1948. Descent, as in all Muslim societies, is traced patrilineally.

Kinship Terminology. Palestinians follow the Sudanese kinship terminology commonly found in patrilineal societies such as those in North Africa. Kinship terms referring to the mother's side of the family are distinguished from those referring to the father's side of the family.

Marriage and Family

Marriage. Palestinians are, generally speaking, monogamous, although polygyny is sanctioned by Islam. Marriages are normally determined by families, but, increasingly, individual choice is accepted. Statistics for the 1931 census indicate that early marriages were rare. The average age of marriage within the Muslim community was 20 years for women and 25 for men. Until around the mid-twentieth century, the preferred match, in both the Christian and Muslim communities, was between first cousins.

Domestic Unit. Postmarital residence is patrilocal. A woman returns to her natal unit only in the event of divorce or widowhood. The authority of the male head of the family is exercised over matters of marital, educational, and occupational choice despite frequent geographic separation of members of the nuclear family. Grandparents and unmarried aunts and uncles frequently share the domestic unit. Women rarely establish independent places of residence.

Inheritance. Muslim law regulates division of the estate and does not ignore female members of the family. Land is divided equally among surviving males, but females inherit half of the male's share because they are not expected to support the family. Among the indigenous Christian population, inheritance customs are not regulated by church law and often mirror Muslim customs.

Socialization. Children are socialized by various generations within the household, commonly along gender lines. The socialization of Palestinian children encourages a commitment to education and to family solidarity.

Sociopolitical Organization

Palestinians inhabiting the West Bank are under Israeli rule, but in Gaza and Jericho they live under the Palestine National Authority. In Jordan, where they constitute 60 to 70 percent of the population, they are full citizens. In other Arab countries, Palestinians are resident aliens, carrying temporary UN travel document. Palestinians in the West Bank and Jerusalem are still Jordanian nationals. In Gaza they are stateless, and within Israel they are citizens of the Jewish state.

Social Organization. Before 1948, Palestinians were divided along class lines determined by private wealth. In the Christian community, class differentiation accorded more to educational level than to wealth. The Muslim and Christian communities were always allied in the national struggle. The Palestinian diaspora after 1948 had a great leveling impact. The massive loss of land weakened the landowning class. Education is highly valued as a movable form of wealth and the determinant of status. Today there is a large professional class that prospered as a result of employment in the Persian Gulf countries.

Political Organization. In the West Bank and Gaza, Palestinians have been living under Israeli military rule since 1967. Those living in Arab Jerusalem, annexed to Israel in 1967, are allowed to participate in municipal elections but are barred from national elections. Because Jerusalem's Arabs are Jordanian citizens, they do not enjoy Israeli civil liberties. The Israelis permitted one round of municipal elections in the West Bank and Gaza in 1976, but since then most town councils have been headed by Israeli military officers. The Islamic religious institutions of Jerusalem and the West Bank, which are linked to Jordan, are still under the jurisdiction of the Supreme Muslim Council. Within Israel proper, Palestinians are full citizens, but they suffer from frequent land confiscations and exclusion from military service and from higher political office. The PLO, on the other hand, functions as a nonterritorial state, with a parliament in exile, an executive committee, and militia units.

Social Control. Social control is exercised by the family, females being subjected to greater restrictions than males. In some refugee camps, social control was dictated by the PLO, which attempted to influence the patterns of female education and female morality.

Conflict. Palestinians suffer from harsh military rule in the West Bank and from constant police surveillance in Arab countries. Clashes with the Israeli military and with Israeli settlers are frequent. The mythology of the popular uprising of 1987, the intifada, still exercises a powerful influence on the popular imagination.

Religion and Expressive Culture

Religious Beliefs. Muslims make up two-thirds of the population. The majority are Sunni, but there is also a small Druze community. Christians are almost one-third of the population. The largest denomination is Greek Orthodox, followed by the Greek Melkite Catholic, the Roman Catholic, the Episcopal, and the Lutheran. Muslim-Christian harmony was always the norm. The rise of militant Islamic groups like Hamas is a new phenomenon among people who have a powerful ecumenical tradition.

Religious Practitioners. Palestinian Muslims view themselves as guardians of the Muslim holy sites, especially the Dome of the Rock, considered the third holiest in Islam. Christian Palestinians maintain a similar view of their role as guardians of the holiest places of Christendom, such as the Church of the Holy Sepulchre and the Church of the Nativity.

Arts. Palestinian arts center around village group dances, such as *dabka.* Village music is performed on traditional instruments such as the flute (*nay*), drums (*tabla*), and the lute (oud). Since the rise of the PLO, Palestinian music and song have for the most part reflected patriotic themes. Art flourished after 1948, with several artists depicting the Palestinian refugee experience. The PLO has fostered political poster art and holds exhibits in many parts of the world.

Medicine. Modern medical facilities are badly lacking in the West Bank and Gaza. Most medical institutions are supported by Arab donations from outside and private donations from within the country.

Death and Afterlife. Funerals are conducted by the family and the entire neighborhood. Long periods of mourning are observed by the Muslim and Christian communities. Cemeteries are public lands. Both communities believe strongly in an afterlife. Muslims, who believe Jerusalem will be the site of the Day of Judgment, consider burial there to be greatly desirable.

Bibliography

Abu-Lughod, Ibrahim, ed. (1971). *The Transformation of Palestine.* Evanston, Ill.: Northwestern University Press.

Beatty, Ilene (1971). "The Land of Canaan." In *From Haven to Conquest,* edited by Walid Khalidi, 3–19. Beirut: Institute for Palestine Studies.

Boullata, Isa (1989). "Modern Palestinian Literature." In *Palestine and the Palestinians: A Handbook,* 72–76. Toronto: Near East Cultural and Educational Foundation of Canada.

Graham-Brown, Sarah (1980). *Palestinians and Their Society, 1880–1946.* London: Quartet Books.

Khalidi, Walid (1984). *Before Their Diaspora: A Photographic History of the Palestinians, 1876–1948.* Washington, D.C., Institute for Palestine Studies.

Nassar, Jamal, and Roger Heacock, eds. (1990). *Intifada: Palestine at the Crossroads.* New York: Praeger.

Near East Cultural and Educational Foundation of Canada (1989). *Palestine and the Palestinians: A Handbook.* Toronto: Near East Cultural and Educational Foundation of Canada.

Polk, William R., David M. Stamler, and Edmund Asfour (1957). *Backdrop to Tragedy: The Struggle for Palestine.* Boston: Beacon Press.

Said, Edward (1980). *The Question of Palestine.* New York: Vintage.

Smith, Charles D. (1988). *Palestine and the Arab-Israeli Conflict.* New York: St. Martin's Press.

Talhami, Ghada (1986). "From Palestinian Nationhood to Palestinian Nationalism." *Arab Studies Quarterly* 8:346–357.

Talhami, Ghada (1994). "The History of Jerusalem: A Muslim Perspective." In *The Spiritual Significance of Jerusalem for Jews, Christians, and Muslims*, edited by Hans Ucko, 21–31. Geneva: World Council of Churches.

GHADA HASHEM TALHAMI

Pashai

ETHNONYMS: Kohistanis, Korashi, Safi, Sare, Tajik

The Pashai are an ethnic group located in the northeast corner of Afghanistan. They are estimated to number about 108,000 (1982). "Pashai" is the term used to refer to a specific language, to the speakers of that language, and to the area that some of the Pashai speakers inhabit. Pashai is classified as a Dardic language by some linguists, but that categorization is not clear nor universally accepted. Dardic languages are spoken in a wide-ranging area, but Pashai is spoken only in Afghanistan. Pashai speakers live in the area north of the Kabul River, extending about 160 kilometers from Gulbahar on the Panjshir River in the northwest to Chaga Serai in the east. "Pashai" is used by the inhabitants of this area to refer only to the language spoken in the western section of the area.

Speakers of Farsi, Pashto, Ashkun, Kati, Parachi, and Shumashti languages live in areas surrounding Pashai, and there is evidence indicating that they have influenced the Pashai language and suggesting that there has been a great deal of interaction with the speakers of these other languages for generations.

There are two conflicting theories on the origin of the Pashai. One theory suggests that the Pashai were members of the classic Gandhara culture and that they were pushed out of their original homeland in the lowlands by an invasion of Pashto-speaking Afghans from the Sulaiman Mountains. The Pashai then found refuge in the high mountain valleys of the Hindu Kush, where their descendants live today. Another theory, based on ethnographic evidence, does not support a link to the Gandharan culture. Because the social structure and culture of all mountain people in the area are similar, it is probable, according to this theory, that all these groups, including the Pashai, share common historical roots that predate the rise of the Gandharan civilization.

The Pashai economy is one of mixed herding and agriculture. In the lower elevations, agriculture is more important than herding. The major crops cultivated are rice in the lower elevations and wheat and maize in the high valleys. Other crops include walnuts, mulberries, and poppies. Goats are the primary domesticated animals; some sheep and cattle are also herded. In the remote villages at high elevations, men are responsible for herding activities, whereas women tend to the agricultural work. In contrast, in villages at lower elevations, the men are involved in all aspects of crop cultivation.

Some Pashai groups are divided hierarchically into categories based on occupation. The highest-ranking group, the *siyal*, consists of men and related women who own property. A lower-ranked group is the *peishawar*, or artisans, and the *rayat* are the landless tenants. These groups form a castelike system in which endogamy is the norm, although it is not the officially sanctioned policy.

Social relationships based on patrilineal descent are found in all Pashai-speaking communities, but the political importance of patrilineal descent relationships varies across villages. In some villages, patrilineal-group membership is not a factor in political ties, but it does influence the structure of village councils. Taking sides in fights and feuds is more directly related to kinship reckoned through both males and females. In other villages, patrilineal descent group membership more directly influences political allegiances.

Criteria for judging leadership skills include age, ability to mediate disputes, generosity, and reputation for being honorable. Political leaders have more influence than authority. For example, in previous times the village *maliks*, or headmen, lacked political authority and acted, instead, as intermediaries between villagers and government officials.

Authority is shared among a group of people—the village council—and is usually limited to agricultural matters, such as the distribution of irrigation water. In some cases, village councils have set regulations regarding bride-wealth, betrothal, weddings, and funerals and set rates for the work of carpenters, blacksmiths, and barbers. With regard to individual rights and wrongs, however, each person is responsible for enforcing his own rights and avenging wrongs committed against him. Kinship, marriage, and friendship relations may also influence the outcome of disputes between individuals. Sometimes disputes may be settled with the help of mediators; at other times, bloodshed occurs.

Feuds are an important part of Pashai culture, and many cultural values are reflected in the feud. For example, masculinity and honor are strong values, and provide themes for many stories and songs. Men strive to be fierce warriors who are loyal to their kin, dangerous to their enemies, and ready to fight whenever necessary. Men carry knives, and wielding a knife in a fight is an important skill learned early in life. Some men own rifles and handguns. Negative sanctions are applied to men who fail to adhere to these values. For example, they are called men without honor, and people belittle what they say, make jokes at their expense, and may pour ashes on their heads as a form of humiliation.

The Pashai are Sunni Muslims similar to the Nuristanis and Pashtun who are their closest neighbors. Especially in the more remote villages, saints do not play a very important role in local politics, as they do in some other ethnic groups. Another contrast with non-Pashai villages relates to the status of women. In many Pashai villages, women are not secluded, may interact freely with men, and possess a degree of sexual freedom uncommon in most areas of Afghanistan.

Bibliography

Jettmar, Karl (1980). "Urgent Tasks of Research among the Dardic Peoples of Eastern Afghanistan and Northern Pakistan." *International Union of Anthropological and Ethnological*

Sciences, Bulletin of the International Committee on Urgent Anthropological and Ethnological Research 2:85–96.

Keiser, R. Lincoln (1971). "Social Structure and Social Control in Two Afghan Mountain Societies." Ph.D. dissertation, University of Rochester.

Keiser, R. Lincoln (1974). "Social Structure in the Southeastern Hindu-Kush: Some Implications for Pashai Ethno-History." *Anthropos* 69:445–456.

Keiser, R. Lincoln (1984). "Pashai." In *Muslim Peoples: A World Ethnographic Survey*, edited by Richard V. Weekes, 600–604. Westport, Conn.: Greenwood Press.

Morgenstierne, Georg (1967). *Indo-Iranian Frontier Languages*. Vol. 3, *The Pashai Language*, Part 2, *Grammar*. Instituttet for Sammenlignende Kulturfokrskning. Oslo: Universitetsforlaget.

Ovesen, Jan (1981). "The Continuity of Pashai Society." *Folk* 23:221–234.

Pedi

ETHNONYMS: Bamaroteng, Bapedi, Basotho, Marota, Northern Sotho

Orientation

Identification. "Pedi," in its broadest sense, has been a cultural/linguistic term. It was previously used to describe the entire set of people speaking various dialects of the Sotho language who live in the northern Transvaal of South Africa. More recently, the term "Northern Sotho" has replaced "Pedi" to characterize this loose collectivity of groups. The Northern Sotho have been subdivided into the high-veld Sotho, which are comparatively recent immigrants mostly from the west and southwest, and the low-veld Sotho, who combine immigrants from the north with inhabitants of longer standing. The high-veld Sotho include the Pedi (in the narrower sense), Tau, Kone, Roka, Ntwane, Mphahlele, Th wene, Mathabathe, Kone (Matlala), Dikgale, Batlokwa, Gananwa (Mmalebogo), Mmamabolo, and Molet e. The low-veld Sotho include the Lobedu, Narene, Phalaborwa, Mogoboya, Kone, Kgakga, Pulana, Pai, Kutswe. Groups are named by using the names of totemic animals and, sometimes, by alternating or combining these with the names of famous chiefs.

"Pedi," in the narrowest sense, refers more to a political unit than to a cultural or linguistic one: the Pedi polity included the people living within the area over which the Maroteng dynasty established dominance during the eighteenth and nineteenth centuries. Even this narrower usage should not be understood in a rigid sense because many fluctuations occurred in the extent of this polity's domination during the eighteenth and nineteenth centuries, and processes of relocation and labor migration have occasioned the widespread scattering of its former subjects during the twentieth century. The present entry will consider the Pedi in this narrower sense.

Location. The present-day Pedi area, Sekhukhuneland, is situated between the Olifants River (Lepelle) and its tributary, the Steelpoort River (Tubatse). It is bordered on the east by the Transvaal Drakensberg range and crossed by the Leolo Mountains. At the height of its power, however, the Pedi polity under Thulare (about 1790 to 1820) launched raids on an area stretching from the site of present-day Rustenburg, in the east, to the low veld, in the west, and ranging as far south as the Vaal River.

The area in which Pedi could reside was severely limited when the polity was defeated by British troops in 1879. A reserve called Geluks Location—roughly coinciding with the core area of the Pedi heartland and including the village of Mohlaletse, where the paramountcy had been based—was created for them, and reserves were created for other Northern Sotho groups that had been subjugated with less effort, by the Transvaal Republic's Native Location Commission. Over the next hundred years or so, these reserves were then variously combined and separated by a succession of government planners. By 1972, this planning had culminated in the creation of an allegedly independent national unit, or "homeland," named Lebowa. Part of the government's plans to accommodate ethnic groups separately from each other, it was designed as a place of residence for all Northern Sotho speakers. Many Pedi had never resided in the reserve. During the period since the polity's defeat, they had become involved in a series of labor-tenancy or sharecropping arrangements with White farmers, lived as tenants on Crown land, or purchased farms communally as freeholders. Many had moved to live in the townships adjoining Pretoria and Johannesburg, on a permanent or semipermanent basis.

Demography. Given the changing extent of Maroteng domination, the fluidity of these subsequent residential arrangements, and the ambiguities about who the Pedi really are, it is difficult to make statements about population with any certainty. The 1961 census put the total population of Sekhukhuneland at 118,743. What can be stated incontrovertibly, however, is that the population of the Lebowa homeland increased rapidly after the mid-1950s, owing both to the forced relocations from rural areas and cities undertaken by apartheid's planners and to voluntary relocations by which former labor tenants sought independence from the restrictive and deprived conditions under which they had lived on the White farms.

Linguistic Affiliation. Sepedi, also known as "Sesotho sa Leboa" (Northern Sotho) is a southern Bantu language. The term "Sesotho" is used locally to describe not only a language but also a set of customary practices and moral codes conceived of as traditional. Whatever cultural and linguistic uniformity came to exist between the diverse peoples living in the northern Transvaal area was blurred at its geographical edges, through a variety of dialects and practices, into other languages and customs. Northern Sotho is thus closely related both to dialects not officially recognized, such as *setlokwa*, and to the officially recognized tongues of Setswana and Sesotho sa Borwa (Southern Sotho), with both of which it shares common origins.

History and Cultural Relations

The complex multiplicity of groups described under "Identification" was already coexisting in the northern and northeastern Transvaal by the end of the eighteenth century, and some concentration of political authority was already in place. In the course of their migrations into and around this area, clusters of people from diverse origins had come to center themselves around a series of *dikgoro* (sing. *kgoro*), or ruling nuclear groups. The people clustered together in this way identified themselves through their shared symbolic allegiance to an animal, sometimes called a totem in the literature—*tau* (lion), *kolobe* (pig), *kwena* (porcupine), and others. The Maroteng or Pedi, with their symbolic animal *noko* (porcupine), were an offshoot of the Tswana-speaking Kgatla. By about 1650, they had settled in an area to the south of the Steelpoort River and of their present heartland. Here, over several generations of interaction, a degree of linguistic and cultural homogeneity developed. It was only in the latter half of the eighteenth century that they extended control over the region, establishing the Pedi paramountcy by bringing powerful neighboring chiefdoms under their sway.

Pedi power, at its height during Thulare's reign (about 1790–1820), was undermined during the period of the *difaqane* by Ndwandwe invaders from the southeast. A period of dislocation followed, after which the polity was reestablished under Thulare's son Sekwati, who engaged in numerous negotiations and struggles for control over land and labor with the Boers who had subsequently settled in the region. Sekwati's success in these struggles, and later that of his heir, Sekhukhune I, owed in part to the firepower enjoyed by the polity, purchased with the proceeds of early labor migration to the diamond fields of Kimberley. During this period, the power of the Pedi paramountcy was entrenched through the insistence that the chiefs of groups subordinate to the Pedi take their principal wives from the ruling dynasty. A system of cousin marriage resulted, which perpetuated hierarchical marriage links between ruler and ruled, and which involved the paying of inflated bridewealth to the Maroteng house.

By the 1870s, the Pedi represented one of three alternative sources of regional authority, alongside the Swazi and the ZAR (Zuid-Afrikaansche Republiek) that the Boers had established. Intensifying struggles between Boers and Pedi over land and labor resulted in the war of 1876, in which the Boer aggressors suffered a resounding defeat. British annexation of the Transvaal followed in 1877, partly spurred by the Boers' failure to subjugate the Pedi. The defeat of the Pedi was finally accomplished by British troops under the command of Sir Garnet Wolsley in 1879.

The Berlin Missionary Society established the first mission to the Pedi, west of the Leolo Mountains, in 1861. Resistance from Sekhukhune led a missionary named Merensky to establish a village for converts, Botshabelo ("the place of refuge"), to the southwest of the polity, from which several groups of independent Christians later left to purchase land and found their own communities, independent of both paramount and missionaries. Here Christian Pedi continued living until they were forcibly removed into the Pedi reserve during the 1960s and 1970s, in the interests of "ethnic consolidation." In more recent times, Catholic, Anglican, and Dutch Reformed missionaries have been active.

Settlements

In preconquest times, people settled on elevated sites in relatively large villages, divided into dikgoro, groups centered around agnatic family clusters. Each consisted of a group of households dwelling in huts built around a central area that served as a meeting place, a cattle byre, a graveyard, and an ancestral shrine. Households' huts were ranked in order of seniority. Each wife of a polygynous marriage had her own round thatched hut, joined to other huts by a series of open-air enclosures encircled by mud walls. Separate huts housed the older boys and the older girls. Practical demands, and aspirations to live in a more modern style, have led many families to abandon the round hut for rectangular houses with flat tin roofs. In addition, as a result of forced and semivoluntary relocation, as well as of a government planning scheme implemented in the name of "betterment," many newer settlements and the outskirts of many older ones consist of houses built in grid formation, occupied by individual families unrelated to their neighbors.

Economy

Subsistence and Commercial Activities. Preconquest Pedi combined cattle keeping with hoe cultivation. The principal crops were sorghum, pumpkins, and legumes, which were grown by women on fields allocated to them when they married. Most major tasks were done by communal work parties. The chief was entrusted with, and was depended upon to perform, rainmaking for his subjects. The introduction of the animal-drawn plow and of maize was later to transform the labor division involved in cultivation in significant ways, especially when combined with the effects of labor migration. Men's leaving home to work for wages was initially undertaken by regimental groups of youths in order to satisfy the paramount's firepower requirements, but later became increasingly necessary to individual households as population increase within the reserve and land degradation made it impossible to subsist from cultivation alone. Despite increasingly long absences, male migrants nonetheless retained a keen commitment to the maintenance of their fields: plowing now had to be carried out during periods of leave or entrusted to professional plowmen or tractor owners. Women were left to manage and carry out all other agricultural tasks. Men, although subjected to spiraling controls in their lives as wage laborers, fiercely resisted all direct attempts to interfere with the sphere of cattle keeping and agriculture. Their resistance erupted in open rebellion—ultimately subdued—during the 1950s. In subsequent decades, some families have continued to practice cultivation and to keep stock, but these activities are a long-term commitment to the rural social system in order to gain security in retirement, not a viable form of household subsistence.

Division of Labor. In preconquest times, women hoed and weeded; made pottery, sleeping mats, and baskets; built and decorated huts with mud; ground grain; cooked; brewed; and collected water and wood. Men did some work in fields at peak times, hunted and herded animals, did woodwork, prepared hides, and were metal workers and smiths. In the early 1960s it was estimated that about 48 percent of the male population was absent as wage earners at any given time. Between the 1930s and the 1960s, most Pedi men spent a short period working on nearby White farms, moved to employment in the mines or in domestic service, and later—especially in more recent times—to factories or industry. Female wage employment began more recently, and is rarer and more sporadic. Some women work for short periods on farms; others have begun, since the 1960s, to work in domestic service in the towns of the Witwatersrand. But in the late twentieth century there has been a rise in levels of education and of expectation, combined with a sharp drop in employment rates. Many youths, better educated than their parents and hoping for jobs as civil servants or teachers, stand little chance of getting employment of any kind.

Land Tenure. The precolonial system of communal or tribal tenure was retained by the colonial administration. In this system, a man would be granted land by the chief for each of his wives. Unused land was reallocated by the chief and was not inherited within families. Massive overpopulation resulting from the government's relocation policies has led to a modification of this system. A household's fields, together with its residential plot, are now inheritable, ideally by the youngest married son. Christian Pedi communities that owned freehold farms were removed to the reserve without compensation, but, since the advent of the postapartheid era in South Africa, many have reoccupied their land or are preparing to do so. The few Pedi who still live as labor tenants on White farms have been promised some security by a 1995 law passed by the government of national unity elected in 1994.

Kinship

Kin Groups and Descent. The kgoro—a loose collection of kin with an agnatic cluster at its core—was as much a jural as a kinship unit, given that membership was primarily defined by acceptance of the head of the kgoro's authority, rather than by descent. Royal or chiefly dikgoro sometimes underwent rapid subdivision as sons contended for positions of authority.

Kinship Terminology. Pedi use a bifurcate merging system of classificatory terminology. Agnatic kin are distinguished from maternal kin. Within both groups, there is some distinguishing of relatives by age and sex. In the agnatic group, relatives of the parental generation are distinguished thus: father's older and younger brothers are *ramogolo* (big father) and *rangwane* (small father), respectively; and father's sisters, who are called *rakgadi* (female father), are treated with immense respect. In the maternal kin group, relatives of the paternal generation are distinguished thus: mother's older and younger sisters are *mmamogolo* and *mmangwane* (big mother and small mother); mother's brother is *malome* (male mother) and is treated with familiarity. Cousins within the agnatic group are distinguished by sex and given the same term as siblings: *mogolle* (for boys) and *kgaet edi* (for girls), whereas cousins outside the agnatic group are referred to as *motswala* and are undistinguished by sex. The use of this terminology appears to be for the most part unchanged, although terms deriving from Afrikaans are sometimes substituted (e.g., *buti* [brother]; *sisi* [sister]).

Marriage and Family

Marriage and Domestic Unit. Residence after marriage was traditionally patrilocal. Polygyny was practiced mostly by people of higher, especially chiefly, status. The preferred marriage partner was a close or classificatory cousin (especially, for a man, a mother's brother's daughter), but this preference was most often realized in the case of ruling or chiefly families: practiced by the ruling dynasty, during its period of dominance, it represented a system of political integration and control (see "History and Cultural Relations"). The preference for cousin marriage was based on an idea that the two sets of prospective in-laws were closely connected even before the event of marriage, and with an ideology of sibling linkage—the *bohadi* (bride-wealth) procured for a daughter's marriage would in turn procure her brother's bride, and he would repay his sister by offering a daughter to her son in marriage. Cousin marriage is still practiced, but is far less frequent than before. Polygyny is infrequent, many marriages end in divorce or separation, and a large number of young women remain single and raise their children in small (and often very poor) female-headed households. But new forms of domestic cooperation have come into being, often between brothers and sisters, or matrilineally linked relatives.

Inheritance. Previously, the oldest son of a household within a polygynous family would inherit the house and property of his mother, including its cattle, and was supposed to act as custodian of these goods for the benefit of the household's other children. With the decline of cattle keeping and the sharp decrease in the availability of land, there has been a switch to a system of lastborn inheritance, primarily of land (see "Land Tenure").

Socialization. The stages of the life cycle for both sexes were differentiated by important rituals. Boys spent their youth looking after cattle at remote outposts, in the company of peers and older youths. Circumcision and initiation at *koma* (initiation school), which was held about once every five years, socialized youths into groups of cohorts or regiments bearing the leader's name, whose members then maintained lifelong loyalty to each other and often traveled together to find work on the farms or in the mines. Girls attended their own koma and were initiated into their own regiments, usually two years after the boys' koma. Initiation is still practiced; it provides a considerable income to the chiefs, who license it for a fee or, in the late twentieth century, to private entrepreneurs who have established initiation schools beyond the chiefs' jurisdictions.

Religion and Expressive Culture

Religious Beliefs and Practitioners. Ancestral worship (*phasa*) involved animal sacrifice or the presenting of beer to the shades, on both the mother's and father's side. A key figure in family ritual was the *kgadi* (father's older sister). The position of *ngaka* (diviner) was formerly inherited in the patriline but is now commonly inherited by a woman from her paternal grandfather or great-grandfather. This is often manifested through illness and violent possession of the body by spirits, the only cure for which is to train as a diviner. There is a proliferation of diviners at present, and many are said to be motivated only by the desire for material gain.

Arts. Important crafts included pottery, house building and painting, woodworking (especially the making of drums), metalsmithing, beadwork. Pedi music (*mmino wa setso*: traditional music; lit., music of origin) has a six-note scale. Formerly played on a plucked reed instrument called a *dipela*, its musicians now make use of trade-store instruments such as the Jew's harp, and the German autoharp (*harepa*), which have come to be regarded as typically Pedi. The peak of Pedi (and Northern Sotho) musical expression is arguably the *kiba* genre, which has transcended its rural roots to become a migrant style. In its men's version it features an ensemble of players, each playing an aluminum end-blown pipe of a different pitch (*naka*; pl. *dinaka*); together they produce a descending melody with richly harmonized qualities. In the women's version, a development of earlier female genres that has recently been included within the definition of *kiba*, a group of women sings songs (*diko a*; sing. *ko a*) in which individuals improvise on older lyrics. Both are accompanied by an ensemble of drums, previously wooden but now made of oil drums and milk urns.

Bibliography

Delius, P. (1980). "The Pedi Polity under Sekwati and Sekhukhune, 1828–1889." Ph.D. thesis, University of London.

Delius, P. (1983). *The Land Belongs to Us: The Pedi Polity, the Boers, and the British in the Nineteenth-Century Transvaal.* Johannesburg: Ravan Press.

Delius, P. (1989). "Sebatakgomo: Migrant Organisation, the ANC, and the Sekhukhuneland Revolt." *Journal of Southern African Studies* 15(4).

Delius, P. (1990). "Migrants, Comrades, and Rural Revolt: Sekhukhuneland 1950–1987." *Transformation* 13.

James, D. (1983). *The Road from Doornkop: A Case Study of Removals and Resistance*. Johannesburg: South African Institute of Race Relations.

James, D. (1985). "Family and Household in a Lebowa Village." *African Studies* 44(2): 159–187.

James, D. (1987). "Kinship and Land in an Inter-Ethnic Community." M.A. dissertation, Witwatersrand University.

James, D. (1988). "Land Shortage and Inheritance in a Lebowa Village." *Social Dynamics* 14(2): 36–51.

Kuper, A. (1975). *The Pedi*. Pretoria: J. L. van Schaik.

Preston-Whyte, E. (1974). "Kinship and Marriage." In *The Bantu-Speaking Peoples of Southern Africa*, edited by W. D. Hammon-Tooke. London: Routledge & Kegan Paul.

Sansome, B. (1970). "Leadership and Authority in a Pedi Chiefdom." Ph.D. dissertation, University of Manchester.

DEBORAH JAMES

Pende

ETHNONYMS: none

Orientation

Identification and Location. The Pende occupy a territory that extends from the banks of the Lutshima, a tributary of the Kwilu, to the Kasai. The Kwilu crosses this territory, as does another large stream, the Loange, forming a boundary between the Zairean provinces of Bandundu (formerly, Léopoldville) and Kasai and separating administratively the western Pende from the eastern Pende (or Pende-Kasai). The latter differ markedly in language, certain customs, artistic styles, and economic development from the western group, which is the focus of this article. They have as neighbors, to the south, the Sonde, Lunda, and Cokwe; and, to the east, along the Kasai, the Luluwa and Luba-Kasai. Along the Loange, the western Pende adjoin the Wongo and Lele; to the north, they share a border with the Mbun (Mbunda) and Mbala. The Mbala and Kwese inhabit areas to the west of the western Pende; the Kwese language resembles that of the Pende, but the Kwese lack their artistic gifts. Torday (1913) describes as Kwese three districts that he visited in 1906: Moshinga, Ndala, and Samba. The district heads who reviewed this text affirmed that they always called one another "Pende." He describes as "Pindi" the remainder of Pende territory.

Demography. The last colonial census (1959) indicated that there were 200,000 western Pende and another 40,000 Pende in Kasai, the whole divided into about fifty districts of varying population—from a few hundred (e.g., Niegenene, with 420) to more than 20,000 (e.g., Moshinga, with 23,000). According to figures released prior to the 1988 elections, the Pende may have numbered 450,000 at that time. The high birthrate made double that number probable. But the Mulele rebellion produced a good many victims (except in Kasai, which was not involved). With the disappearance of medical service, and the increase in dietary deficiencies (in proteins and salt), infant mortality has become higher than ever. Emigration to the cities of Kikwit, Leverville, and Bandundu is also occurring.

History and Cultural Relations

There is no memory of being led solely by one great chief of the Pende in Angola, where they were subjects of sovereigns such as Ngola and Kasanji. Fleeing from slave raids carried out by Lunda chiefs like Mwata Kombana, their neighbor, who claimed to be their suzerain, the Pende emigrated from the area of the Cuanza and upper Kwango. They did not recognize the suzerainty of Mwata Kombana because he could not defend them from Cokwe invaders. At first retreating from the Cokwe, the Pende became refugees among the Mbun; in 1892 the Pende, with the help of the Mbun, defeated the Cokwe and took back their original territory. The arrival of European colonists ended hostilities and any Lunda claim of suzerainty. Certain elements of precolonial relations remain, however, as evidenced by Lunda-Pende marriages, Pende who were retained as slaves among the Cokwe, and mixed Pende-Mbun villages in the north.

Settlements

The Pende used to live in hamlets scattered along or close to streams, but the sanitary authorities regrouped them into big villages on the plateau and imposed a clearing of 50 meters around the village. Villagers were thus less exposed to tsetse flies and mosquitoes. Some Pende divided themselves up again, however, into traditional hamlets formed from lineage segments.

Pende keep goats, pigs, chickens, and a few dogs. Millet, maize, manioc, and peanuts are cultivated. At Kilembe, some sorghum plants were still being grown near a few huts, intended solely to be prepared for offerings of their customary food to the dead. Sorghum had been part of the traditional diet, but a disease (possibly ergot) made it too dangerous to eat: "Sorghum has killed many men," they say. The basic food is now a flour—half manioc, half millet or maize—accompanied sometimes by meat or, most often, by a vegetable, such as manioc leaves.

Economy

Western Pende territory is a plateau with an average elevation of 800 meters, incised by seagoing rivers and smaller streams. The plateau forest has disappeared; the last original forest among the western Pende, the forest of Mulwa, was razed by an agent full of zeal for the war effort (1940–1945) and the planting of fibers (*Urena*). The humus rapidly disappeared, replaced by sterile white sand. Forested corridors remain in the valleys, along watercourses. On the plateau, thickets of small trees that are resistant to bush fires—particularly *mikhoso* (*Erythrophleum africanus*) thickets, which nourish edible caterpillars—and numerous palm trees and natural oil-palm groves of *Elaeis guineensis*, which, until 1960, fed many oil works, are important sources of jobs and wages. Among the Pende of Kasai, the forest has likewise disappeared, and there are no more oil palms. The western Pende traditionally went as far as Tshikapa to sell their oil. Since 1960, the oil works have no longer operated except for local needs (including those of the Pende-Kasai and neighboring tribes). The efforts that were first made before 1960 to get the western Pende accustomed to cattle raising are being continued, and herds of cattle are now given to some Pende farmers. The colonial authorities also pushed for the creation of pools or fish ponds along the brooks. The western Pende energetically undertook the job of digging out pools and making dikes, work that was foreign to them. In 1956 they were ahead of all the other territories in the number and area covered by ponds, and they are still maintaining them. None of these initiatives was proposed to the Pende-Kasai, who have remained less prosperous and less developed. Although they live in a mining region, they have refused mine work. They have not yet been touched by the most elementary economic initiatives.

Founded in 1901, the Kasai Company, with a view to harvesting rubber from *Landolphia thollonii* plants, established three processing posts, at Kandale, Bienge, and Dumba. A man named O. Bombeek, who directed them and who provided both Hilton-Simpson (1911) and Torday (1913) with information, related that 2 to 3 tons of rubber were produced per month at Dumba, compared with 6 to 7 tons at Bienge and Kandale. The Cokwe came to the latter post to trade rubber for palm oil (a 2-liter calabash of oil for 1 kilogram of rubber), which Bombeek used to buy from the Pende. The collapse of the price of rubber in 1913 put an end to this commerce. The local economy then turned to exploiting palm oil, an activity that was more suited to the tastes and aptitudes of the Pende, who are good climbers and fruit cutters; they were recruited in large numbers to work on plantations. This activity probably insured some decades of prosperity (prior to independence) for the Pende and the oil works.

Kinship

The Pende live in matrilineal clans and lineages. In the district, the top clan, or *manda* (which is generally divided into three lineages, each furnishing the chief in turn) is the first to have arrived in a territory, hence the first to have buried its dead there. The earth belongs to the dead and therefore to those who represent them, their descendants. The area that is occupied in each district is hunting territory and is thus vast. Lineages who arrive later are authorized to settle there and farm, but each one owes a tribute from the hunt and one or two wives to the top clan, which thus becomes "father" of the whole group of subjects. It decides about arranging for bush fires and collective hunts. Marriage being virilocal, the clans are dispersed, with a top lineage in one district and others as "subjects" in other districts. Thus, one can ask a man, "Where do you have your hat [*cheffal*]?"—that is to say, "Where is your clan chief?"

Because virilocal postmarital residence is the usual pattern, a son could either choose to live with his father or join his uterine uncle; a girl lives with her parents until she marries and leaves for her husband's home. Women are either regularly "traveling" or "married," but never "in the village," and therefore one should, in theory, expect to find in a village only the men of the lineage and their families. Occasionally, however, divorced women or widows who have come back to their brothers' homes are among the villagers. The reality is in fact more complicated. Most of the lineages and villages and all of the top lineages have their own slaves, who are called "children" or "grandchildren" and are bound to their purchasers by a fictive relationship. This relationship is transmitted by the women. Ancient slave stocks enjoy the prestige of being associated with the owning lineage. The lineage that furnishes the top wife and the chief's minister is guardian of the regalia (*kifumu*) and the only lineage able to manipulate them (for certain ones have a magic power, and the chief is dissociated from all magic). The top wife is superintendent of the cultivation of crops, and the women must effectively choose lands for this or that crop and decide on the duration of fallow periods. The transmission of the Pende agricultural tradition from mother to daughter is theoretically impossible under a discordant regime, in which the women are perpetually going to and fro, never "at home, in the village," and the fields are cultivated by outsiders. As a matter of fact, except for the top wife, many other women contract a "union on the premises," the slaves ensuring a matrilocal as well as a matrilineal society. It is difficult to know who is a slave, for any allusion to such status in conversation is prohibited and constitutes a grave offense, especially its revelation to an outsider. De Sousberghe succeeded in ascertaining that in two villages at Totshi at least half of the villagers were slaves. The colonial authority had prohibited all sales, but had authorized clans to buy back any slave member. This authorization permitted sales to take place, disguised as "buying back," with the evocation of fictive genealogy in the palaver. In 1956 de Sousberghe recorded at Gungu the palaver, or the so-called buying back, of a woman called Kienda and her descendants. Subsequently, de Sousberghe learned that she had been "bought back" twice: the second palaver denounced the "errors" in the genealogy that had previously been invoked.

Marriage and Family

Traditionally, polygyny was practiced on a limited basis (three or four wives), and men generally added an inherited wife as they grew older. Marriage was concluded without the remittance of assets, but the prospective groom did bring a calabash of palm wine to the father of the girl, whereupon the marriage was concluded on the spot. When outside influences changed this practice to the extent that Pende women could relocate to distant places and be lost to their families, payment of assets was introduced. At the same time, the missionaries, convinced that the payment of assets was an essential element and a factor of stability in Bantu marriage, required evidence of such payment before any celebration could be held. The Pende say, therefore, that the payment of assets was introduced by the missionaries, although in fact several factors played a part.

For the Pende, the child comes entirely from the father; the mother receives from him the seed that she carries and nourishes, just as the earth nourishes the seeds that it receives. The child's gratitude accrues to her only because of "the weight of the belly and the birth pains." It would be a grave offense to say that a child resembles his or her uterine uncle, an allusion that implies incest between the mother and her brother; the child necessarily resembles its father. At present, great importance is attached to the education of children, including girls, and fathers are inclined to consent to the heavy sacrifices that are involved. Having invested thus in educating their children, the fathers have the final say about everything the children do. Their authority increases, and, reciprocally, so does the attachment of their children to them. Land rights are always inherited from the maternal side, however.

Preferential union (i.e., union between relatives) is traditionally called marriage "at home," *gu mujiba,* contrasted with marriage "abroad," *gu balakaji.* A father has the right to order his son to take a wife from his own lineage "to give back his face to his lineage." A father's sister often wants her brother's son to marry one of her daughters, whom she has presented to him from his youngest age on as "your little wife." A boy finds it still more dangerous to displease her than to displease his father. Her authority is as great and her curse more to be feared than that of his own father. Refusal brings imminent penalty. From another point of view, the father and the uterine uncle have the duty of procuring a wife for their son or nephew. A young man has first to make application to his father: "Father, give me a wife from behind your back," that is, a wife of your lineage. Or he might address his uterine uncle, asking him for one of his descendants. A widower grandfather could require that he be given one of his granddaughters—not only a classificatory granddaughter but even his own granddaughter.

Sociopolitical Organization

Those who possess authority possess it in the name of the ancestors. They must be faithful to the rules that were left by them and be exemplary in conduct, especially in sexual matters. They are responsible for the transmission of the life that was received from them. Around the middle of the twentieth century, a chief was dismissed because he had seen his sister's nudity, which amounts to incest. It is those in authority who speak in public and who practice nearly all of the trades (smith, sculptor, weaver, tanner, healer, diviner, musician or singer, hunter, and public orator). The women's jobs are raising crops and preparing food, making pottery, and freshwater fishing. It is said of the local lineage chief (there is no chief of the whole clan), an old man, that "he holds, controls, the seed" (*wakwata mbuto*); he is the guardian of the fecundity of the lineage. Of the chief of the district, they say that "he holds, controls the earth" (*wakwata mavu*). The earth is considerd to be the source of fecundity or life, in the widest sense, of the universe and the stars. Yongo, a Moshinga chief, said that he had to sleep alone "in the entry [*ha khukhe*] when the moon is in its last quarter so that it might come back to its full brightness," whereas to abstain from sexual relations in the light of day would be an offense against the sun. He must also sleep alone when several women of the district are pregnant, so that they may be able to bring their pregnancy to term. For the whole group, continence is to be observed from sowing time, especially of millet (millet is the chief of the seed and has its own storehouse), until the first shoots appear. The top wife gathers some of the shoots, prepares them, and presents them to the chief. When he has eaten them, he can resume sexual relations. People announce that the chief has slept (with his wife), and the next day the lineage chiefs follow his example, then all of the people. Similarly, the hunters, several days before the hunts, and the chief with them, even if he does not take part, are expected to abstain from sexual relations. Artists or artisans—the smith, the sculptor of masks, dressers of these masks for dancing, the dancers themselves, and the player of the big drum—often have to observe continence before undertaking their activities. Continence is imposed on the *ngambi* (lawyer-judge) for eight days before he can pick up the sculptured can that he handles at the palaver, and for as many more before putting it back in its compartment. But it is on the chief that such periods of continence and other prohibitions are imposed in large numbers. In certain districts, as at Niegenene, complete continence with the wearing of a condom was imposed from the time of a chief's investiture. The chief was obliged to send back his wife or wives, and a brother's wife brought him his meals.

Religion

The Pende refer to God by three names: Nzambi, Kalunga, and Mawese. "Nzambi" is probably the most recent. "Kalunga" is also the name of the abode of the dead, but western Pende say, "Our dead have left for Mawese; it is he who showed our ancestors the customs and the *hamba* [the object or rite bequeathed by the ancestors through which one enters into communication with the guardian spirits and renders them favorable], which they have transmitted to us."

God made everything. To the Pende, he is the great chief, but a faraway chief. The ancestors who are their immediate masters, implicated in all acts of life, for everything belongs to them. One does not share a kola nut or a calabash of palm wine without reserving a small part for them, either thrown or poured on the ground while saying, "This is for you."

The Pende individual believes that by mastering genetic power, which enables him to conquer time and death, he can also master his environment. In the person of the chief, this environment stretches to the stars. It is the universe conceived, it is true, as a living whole. The chief is a cosmocrator, but a cosmocrator who may initially be humiliated. The chief is chosen from the district lineage, a fearsome choice. The man thus designated often refuses and flees. He is seized and severely beaten, so severely that, if the chief designated is aged or is judged to be too feeble to undergo such treatment without endangering his life, a brother who is younger or more robust is chosen to undergo it in his place. The western Pende used to hasten the end of a moribund chief by wringing his neck, but such practices were prohibited by the colonial authorities. One aspect remains mysterious: the chief may not go near the masks that are considered to be a manifestation of circumcision. He, like the women and children, may see them only from afar. The Pende say that "the chief is like a woman" or that "he has become a woman by the investiture." Nevertheless, the dance area is situated near the chief's hut—but it remains empty, and the door has to stay open lest the women be threatened with sterility. This prohibition appears to betray an antagonism between a chief's power and the rite of circumcision. The first embodies fecundity, parental values, and diachronic bonds. The second is the expression of a solidarity that is synchronous with age classes. Modesty, with which the Pende child was impregnated in the family surroundings, is attacked during the circumcision rites by repeated allusions to the sexual organs of the father and mother of each candidate, allusions judged to be intolerable in everyday life. The Christian missionaries decreed that the Pende could not subject their children to such rites, and, given that most Pende had become Christian, circumcision ceremonies have not been held in the region since well before the mid-twentieth century.

Bibliography

Delaere, J. (1950). "À propos de cousins croisés." *Bulletin des Jurisdictions Indigènes* (Elisabethville), no. 7.

Delaere, J. (1942). "Nzambi-Maweze." *Anthropos* 37(11): 620–628.

Hilton-Simpson, M. W. (1911). *Land and Peoples of the Kasai*. London.

Nicolaï, H. (1963) *Le kwilu*. Cemubac-Université Libre de Bruxelles.

Sousberghe, Léon de (1954). "Étuis péniens ou gaines de chasteté chez les pende." *Africa* (London), July.

Sousberghe, Léon de (1955). *Structures de parenté et d'alliance d'après les formules pende*. Brussels: Académie Royale des Sciences Coloniales.

Sousberghe, Léon de (1961). *Deux palabres d'esclave chez les pende*. Brussels: Académie Royale des Sciences d'Outre-Mer.

Sousberghe, Léon de (1963). *Les pende: Aspect des structures sociales et politiques*. Annales du Musée Royal de l'Afrique Centrale. Sciences Humaines, no. 46. Tervueren.

Torday, E. (1913). *Camp and Tramp in African Wilds*. London.

LÉON DE SOUSBERGHE
(Translated by Jean H. Winchell)

Peripatetics of Afghanistan, Iran, and Turkey

ETHNONYMS: *Afghanistan*: Badyanesin, Balatumani, Baluch, Chalu, Changar, Chighalbf, Ghalbelbaf, Ghorbat (Qurbat), Herati, Jalali, Jat (Jaṭṭ), Jat-Baluch, Jogi, Jola, Kouli, Kuṭaṇa, Lawani, Luli Mogat, Maskurahi, Musalli, Nausar, Pikraj, Qawal, Sabzaki, Sadu, Shadibaz (Shadiwan), Sheikh Mohammadi, Siyahpayak, Vangawala (Bangṛiwal/Churifrosh). *Iran:* Asheq, Challi, Changi, Chareshmal (Krishmal), Dumi, Feuj, Ghajar, Ghorbati (Ghorbat, Gurbat, Qurbati), Gurani, Haddad (Ahangar, Hasanpur), Howihar, Juki, Karachi, Kenchli, Kowli (Kuli), Luli, Luti, Mehtar, Ojuli, Qarbalband, Sazandeh, Suzmani, Tat, Toshmal. *Turkey:* Abdal, Arabci, Bosha, Çingene, Gäwändi, Ghorbati, Qeraçi, Susmani, Tahtacı, Tsigan.

Orientation

Identification. The data concerning Afghanistan and Iran refer to the period prior to the Saur and Islamic revolutions, respectively. It is not known whether such communities still exist in these two countries.

Each of these ethnonyms does not probably correspond to one community; many are locally or regionally used (sometimes as occupational names), others are used only by group members, and still others are used pejoratively only by outsiders. Thus, in Afghanistan, "Jat" is a pejorative term used generically by nonperipatetics to designate peripatetics belonging to at least six different communities. In Iran and Turkey, the terms "Ghorbati" and "Çingene" appear to be used in a similar fashion. Some of these ethnonyms are also encountered in other neighboring areas of the Middle East, the Balkans, or South Asia. Each existing community is primarily endogamous, and subsists traditionally on a variety of commercial and/or service activities. Formerly, all or a majority of their members were itinerant, and this largely holds true today. Migration generally takes place within the political boundaries of each state. These communities have often been termed "Gypsies" or "Gypsylike"; this comparison is relevant only in so far as their traditional subsistence activities, migration patterns, and generally low status are similar to those of some of the Roma/Sinti groups in Europe or North America.

Linguistic Affiliation. Each of the peripatetic communities is multilingual; it speaks one or more of the languages spoken by the local sedentary populations, and, additionally, within each group, a separate dialect or language is spoken. The latter are either of Indic or Iranian origin, and many are structured somewhat like an argot or secret language, with vocabularies drawn from various languages. The languages recorded in Afghanistan do not contain elements of Romani, but some—such as Adurgari (spoken by the Sheikh Mohammadi), Mogatibey (spoken by the Jogi), or Qazulagi, spoken by the Ghorbat—have affinities with languages spoken by similar communities in parts of Iran and also in parts of Central Asia. Their vocabularies also contain Arabic words, but a large percentage of words are of an as yet unknown origin. There are indications that in northern Iran at least one community does speak Romani, and some groups in Turkey certainly do speak Romani.

Demography. In 1975 the Nausar of northern Afghanistan claimed to count roughly 700 households. In 1976–1977 the Ghorbat of Afghanistan consisted of roughly 1,000 nuclear families, each with an average of 5.0 individuals. During the same period in Afghanistan, the Baluch (also known as Chalu, Herati, or Jat-Baluch) estimated their own population at some 2,500 individuals; estimates for the Jalali, the Pikraj, the Shadibaz and the Vangawala are 500, 2,000, 1,500, and 3,000 persons, respectively. In 1939 the Gurbat of the Fārs region of Iran were reported as numbering 1,000 families, and in 1965 the Haddad estimated themselves at roughly 1,500 families. In the 1970s the entire peripatetic population in Iran was estimated at between 20,000 and 30,000 individuals, between 2,000 and 3,000 of whom were Luti and Toshmal.

History

Little is known for certain about the past of these communities; the history of each is almost entirely contained in their oral traditions. Although some groups—such as the Vangawala—are of Indian origin, some—like the Sheikh Mohammadi—are most probably of local origin; still others probably migrated from adjoining areas. The Ghorbat and the Shadibaz claim to have originally come from Iran and Multan, respectively, and Tahtacı traditional accounts mention either Baghdad or Khorāsān as their original home. The Baluch say they were attached as a service community to the Jamshedi, after they fled Baluchistan because of feuds. The earliest author mentioning peripatetic communities in this broad region is the Persian Ḥamzah al-Isfahani (d. A.D. 972). He refers to the fifth-century A.D. Sāssānian king Bahrām-i-Gor as having requested of the king of India that he send him 12,000 Kowli as musicians. These, wrote Ḥamzah, were the forefathers of the Zott, who were still to be found in Persia in his day. Ottoman documents mention one such community, the Tahtacı, from the sixteenth century onward; the Tahtacı consider themselves to be Turkmen.

Settlements

In Afghanistan in the mid-1970s, all these communities were more or less nomadic; they migrated twice a year between summer and winter camps. Their migration patterns were at least partly linked to harvest cycles of various types of agricultural produce. Whereas Ghorbat families could be found in various parts of the country, the Jalali, the Jogi, the Nausar and the Pikraj lived and migrated predominantly in northern Afghanistan. The Kuṭaṇa and Sheikh Mohammadi restricted themselves to the eastern parts of the country; the Shadibaz and the Vangawala were predominantly in the east, the southeast, and parts of central Afghanistan. The Baluch had villages and migrated mainly in northern and western Afghanistan. In Iran, as in eastern Anatolia, there have always been some families of peripatetics who have lived and worked attached to each of the region's nomadic pastoral populations. Around 1960, among the Basseri pastoralists, the Ghorbat thus constituted a guest population of some fifty to sixty elementary families. They spent part of the year with their patrons, but also partly migrated independently in search of additional subsistence. In the Ottoman period, many of the communities in Turkey had a wide-ranging pattern of migration that extended over large parts of the empire. Today some of these communities have become more sedentary and have their own villages, or part-villages, or even urban localities. Many, however, still continue to migrate along traditionally fixed itineraries.

Economy

In Afghanistan, the Nausar worked as tinkers and animal dealers. Ghorbat men mainly made sieves, drums, and bird cages, and the women peddled these as well as other items of household and personal use; they also worked as moneylenders to rural women. Peddling and the sale of various goods was also practiced by men and women of various groups, such as the Jalali, the Pikraj, the Shadibaz, the Sheikh Mohammadi, and the Vangawala. The latter and the Pikraj also worked as animal dealers. Some men among the Shadibaz and the Vangawala entertained as monkey or bear handlers and snake charmers; men and women among the Baluch were musicians and dancers, and Baluch women also practiced prostitution. Jogi men and women had diverse subsistence activities, such as dealing in horses, harvesting, fortune-telling, bloodletting, and begging.

In Iran, the following groups worked as professional musicians in the 1970s: the Asheq of Azerbaijan; the Challi of Baluchistan; the Luti of Kurdistan, Kermānshāh, Īlām, and Lorestān; the Mehtar in the Mamasani district; the Sazandeh of Band-i Amir and Marv-dasht; and the Toshmal among the Bakhtyari pastoral groups. The men among the Kowli worked as tinkers, smiths, musicians, and monkey and bear handlers; they also made baskets, sieves, and brooms and dealt in donkeys. Their women made a living from peddling, begging, and fortune-telling. The Ghorbat among the Basseri were smiths and tinkers, traded in pack animals, and made sieves, reed mats, and small wooden implements. In the Fārs region, the Qarbalband, the Kuli, and Luli were reported to work as smiths and to make baskets and sieves; they also dealt in pack animals, and their women peddled various goods among pastoral nomads. In the same region, the Changi and Luti were musicians and balladeers, and their children learned these professions from the age of 7 or 8 years.

The nomadic groups in Turkey make and sell cradles, deal in animals, and play music. The men of the sedentary groups work in towns as scavengers and hangmen; elsewhere they are fishermen, smiths, basket makers, and singers; their women dance at feasts and tell fortunes. Abdal men played music and made sieves, brooms, and wooden spoons for a living. The Tahtacı traditionally worked as lumberers; with increased sedentarization, however, they have taken to agriculture and horticulture.

Marriage and Family

In Afghanistan, among all these communities, patrilateral-parallel-cousin marriages as well as exchange marriages among siblings were preferred. In such marriages, bride-price was lower than usual. Among the Ghorbat, polygyny was very rare, but among the Baluch, polygyny was common, and additionally many of the wealthier men had concubines. In Iran, Kowli women were reportedly married from the age of 10 upward, whereas the men married around age 16. Polygyny was not infrequent. In Turkey, the basic domestic unit of the Tahtacı is the nuclear family, and the youngest son is considered responsible for the welfare of the elderly parents.

Sociopolitical Organization

Sociopolitical organization varied greatly among communities. Thus, for example, among the Ghorbat of Afghanistan, there was no superordinate political structure, nor were there any permanent positions of leadership; the community was, in principle, egalitarian. Among the Baluch, on the other hand, each of the eight segmentary lineages had a chief (*arbab*), whose power was absolute. Each lineage had a strict hierarchical structure and the organization of economic resources was entirely in the hands of the lineage chief. The Vangawala were split into five descent groups, which considered one another equal. Within each descent group, there was an institutionalized form of chiefship, which was hereditary in the fraternal and filial line. The Pikraj, however, were divided into three regional subdivisions, each of which had a fluid structure, and a person or family could change his subdivisional affiliation. The Luti of Iran were also divided into lineages, the structure of which appears fairly fluid. Among the Kowli of Iran, authority was in the hands of men with a fairly large clientele; these men directed migration and settled disputes. Given the marginal political and social position of each of these communities within their respective greater societies, continuous attempts had to be made to avoid conflicts with nongroup members. This was achieved by most communities in Afghanistan and Iran by acquiring locally influential sedentary or nomadic pastoral patrons; on the economic level, these patrons were, in fact, their clients.

Religion and Expressive Culture

All the concerned communities are Muslim. Although none of the groups in Afghanistan or Iran were considered good Muslims, and some—such as the Luti of Iran—were considered polluting, their beliefs and practices did not diverge basically from local Islamic patterns in the perspective areas. In Afghanistan, the majority are Sunni, but most Ghorbat are imami Shia. In Turkey, the Tahtacı are also imami Shia, but they call themselves "Alevis" and are attached to the Anatolian mystical order of the Bektashi. They still practiced certain pre-Islamic traditions well into the twentieth century.

Bibliography

Amanolahi, S. (1978). *Cultural Variations among the Gypsies of Iran*.

Amanolahi, S., and E. Norbeck (1975). "The Luti, an Outcaste Group of Iran." *Rice University of Studies in Cultural Anthropology* 61(2): 1–12.

Brepohl, F. W. (1913). *Die Zigeuner im alten Orient*. Berlin-Lichterfelde: Paul Zillmann.

"Çingane." (1960). In *Encyclopaedia of Islam*. New ed. Leiden: E. J. Brill.

Kehl, K. (1988). *Die Tahtacı: Vorläufiger Bericht über eine ethnisch-religiöse Gruppe traditioneller Holzarbeiter in Anatolien*. Occasional Papers, no. 16, F.U. Berlin: Verlag Das Arbische Buch.

Le Coq, A. von (1912). "Die Abdal." *Baessler Archiv* 2(5–6): 221–233.

Olesen, A. (1987). "Peddling in East Afghanistan: Adaptive Strategies of the Peripatetic Sheikh Mohammadi." In *The Other Nomads: Peripatetic Minorities in Cross-Cultural Perspective*, edited by Aparna Rao. Cologne: Böhlau Verlag.

Rao, Aparna (1982). *Les gorbat d'Afghanistan: Aspects économiques d'un groupe itinérant Jat*. Paris: Éditions ADPF and Institut Français d'Iranologie de Téhéran.

Rao, Aparna (1986). "Peripatetic Minorities in Afghanistan—Image and Identity." In *Die ethnischen Gruppen Afghanistan*, edited by E. Orywal. Wiesbaden: L. Reichert.

Rao, Aparna (Forthcoming)."Notes on the Languages Spoken by some Peripatetic Communities in Afghanistan." In *Die Sprachen Afghanistans*, edited by C. M. Kieffer. Wiesbaden: L. Reichert.

Roux, J-P. (1970). *Les traditions des nomades de la Turquie méridionale*. Paris: A. Maisonneuve.

Svanberg, Ingvar (1989). "Marginal Groups and Itinerants." In *Ethnic Groups in the Republic of Turkey*, edited by P. A. Andrews. Wiesbaden: L. Reichert.

Windfuhr, G. L. (1970). "European Gypsy in Iran: A First Report." *Anthropological Linguistics* 12(8): 271–292.

APARNA RAO

Peripatetics of Iraq, Syria, Lebanon, Jordan, Israel, Egypt, Sudan, and Yemen

ETHNONYMS: *Iraq:* Duman, Guˤaidiyah, Janganah, Karaj, Kauli(a), Zutt. *Syria:* Ghurbat (Karbat, Kurbat), Guˤaidiyah, Juki (Aspasheshti), Kauli(a), Nawar, Ṣuleyb, Zutt. *Lebanon:* Juki. *Jordan:* Nawar. *Israel:* Nawar. *Egypt:* Aˀwwadat, Baḍˀḍˀaaˀh, Bahlawan, Banu Sasan, Barmaki, Batatiyeh, Chingana, Fehemi, Ghajar, Ghawazi, Ghurbat (Kurbat), Ghurradin, Hajala, Ḥalabi (Mahlebash), Ḥawee, Ḥemmeli, el Heweidat, Masalib, Mashaˀiliyyah, Meddaḥin, Muaˀmeratijjeh, Nawar (Nuri), Qarrad, Ramadiya, Rifaˤiyya, Romani, Ṣaˤideh, Samaˤina, Ṣaniˤa, Shahˀaini, Shoeiha, Surutiyeh, Ṭahwağiya, Tˀatˀar, Ṭawayifa, Waled Abu Tenna. *Sudan:* Bahalawan, Besuni, Fehemi, Gewhassi, Ghajar, Ghuraba (Ghurabi), Halab, Shahaini. *Yemen:* Ahl al-Muzaiyad, Ahl al-Nawwaḥ, Dawashin, Maˤn (Shaḥath).

Orientation

Identification. All these ethnonyms are probably not in use today, and even formerly, each of them did not necessarily correspond to one community; there is a certain degree of duplication or overlapping, according to self-designation, locality, gender, and profession. Further, it could well be that some of these communities have been and still are confused with other nonperipatetic but nomadic communities, or else with sedentary communities having similar low-status subsistence activities. Some of these ethnonyms may be encountered elsewhere in the Middle East. Each existing community is primarily endogamous and subsists traditionally on a variety of commercial and/or service activities. All or a majority of their members were formerly itinerant, and, in the late twentieth century, some still are. They have often been termed "Gypsies", or "Gypsylike"; this comparison is relevant only in so far as the traditional subsistence activities, migration patterns, and generally low status of these communities were similar to those of some of the Roma/Sinti groups in Europe or North America. A few, but by no means all, of these communities had linguistic affinities with the Roma/Sinti.

Linguistic Affiliation. Each of these groups speaks a different language. In Egypt, the language of the Ghajar is a dialect of Romani; that of the Halab (Ḥalabi) is a mixture of Romani, Arabic as spoken in Yemen, and some other languages; Nuri is also a mixed language in which Arabic predominates. The language of the Halab in Sudan is also a mixture of Arabic and other elements. It has been suggested that some of these languages originated in part as protective secret languages.

Demography. In Iraq in 1976, the total estimated peripatetic population was 8,138 individuals. At the beginning of the twentieth century, the entire population of the Kauli of Iraq and Syria was estimated at 1,500 tent-households. The same source gives the following estimates: Zutt in Basra, about 70 households; Karbat in Aleppo, about 150 households. The Samaʿina, one of the Egyptian communities, was estimated at 300 individuals in the late 1970s. For another community—the sedentary Ghajar of Sett Guiranʿha—an estimate of just under 900 individuals has been advanced. For the Sudan as a whole, an estimate of 100,000 to 200,000 is available.

History

It is thought that many of these groups originally came from the east, probably from some part of the Indian subcontinent, and entered Persia between the fifth and seventh centuries A.D. Further migration probably took place from Persia toward Turkey on the one hand and Syria on the other, after the Arabian conquest of Persia in the seventh century. The Juki are supposed to have migrated into the Latakia region of Syria and thence into Lebanon from the area of the Nur Mountains of Turkish Anatolia. The earliest Arabic reference to "peripatetic" is probably to be found in a thirteenth-century shadow play written by the ophthalmologist Idn Daniyal (1248–1310) in Cairo, in which a woman named Ṣaniʿa appears. It is likely that similar figures were known to the public much earlier. The various communities have their own legends of origin, some of which are connected with well-known regional epic heroes, such as Zir Salem.

Settlements

Most of these groups are now sedentary or semisedentary, and only a few are still nomadic.

Economy

Men and women of the different groups have different occupations. In Syria and Lebanon, the Juki used to work as fruit pickers. In Syria, the Suleyb worked as metalcrafters and as traders. In Iraq, the Karaj make sieves and baskets; the men work as bricklayers, smiths, grocers, and dentists. Many Nawar in Jordan work as professional musicians. In Egypt today, tinkering, the manufacture of rough iron implements for household or agricultural use, dealing in hides, the capture of snakes and scorpions, and music are male activities; women work as peddlers, selling cloth, shoes, and kitchen utensils. Both men and women work seasonally as sheep shearers, and women and older men also spin wool. Formerly, fortune-telling, acrobatics, tattooing, circumcising, and medicating were important sources of subsistence, but these are no longer practiced. Also on the wane is female dancing. In Sudan, the various communities engage in the following activities: men work as smiths, tinkers, grooms, farriers, and contractors for horse and donkey carts; they shear sheep and trade in horses, donkeys, and other farm animals. Both men and women peddle, tell fortunes, and circumcise and tattoo men and women, respectively; they also wash the dead and arrange for funerals. Women and children go begging, and women are also called in to pierce ears and noses. The communities mentioned in Yemen are minstrels and professionals musicians.

Kinship, Marriage, Family, and Residence

Among the Ghajar of Egypt, marriages are overwhelming endogamous. They take place at an early age—if possible before puberty—and are preferentially between parallel and/or cross cousins. Among the Ghajar community of Sett Guiranʿha, polygynous marriages are not unknown. Dowry payment is compulsory and may consist of cash or household furniture. This expenditure is, however, balanced by the payment of the dower or bride-wealth (*mahr*) by the groom; this dower, which is compulsory in Islam, is not paid to the bride, but to her father. In addition, the groom's father meets the entire expense of the wedding day. After marriage, residence is virilocal. Extended families are the rule and can be very large. Divorce is common and its initiation a male prerogative.

Sociopolitical Organization

There is no overall system of political organization within any of these communities, but cohesion within each community is strong. In Egypt, members of the communities are treated as citizens and are expected to comply with all the laws of the land. In Iraq, however, they are not considered nationals and have few political or economic rights.

To prevent inequitable accumulation of wealth, the Ghajar of Sett Guiranʿha have a system of mutual financial help and gift giving (*nuqut/nokoot*). Gifts are given at various festive and ceremonial occasions, such as weddings and circumcisions; gift giving also takes place at specially organized parties hosted by men who have financial problems. This is an obligatory form of financial support, even among families hostile to each other, but the amounts offered must be repaid on an appropriate occasion. Grave disputes were formerly settled by contests, at which either money or slaughtered animals were pledged. Nowadays conflicts are resolved with the help of group elders and, to some extent, even with the help of people outside the group.

Religion and Expressive Culture

All the above-mentioned communities largely share the beliefs and practices of the local Muslim populations. Some of the music played by these groups has been recorded.

Bibliography

Canova, Giovanni (1981). "Note sulle tradizioni aingare in Egitto attraverso la testimonianza di un cap Nawar." *Lacio Drom* 17(6): 4–25.

Elfret, Pia (1985). "Zigeuner in Ägypten: Eine kritische Auswertung des aktuellen Forschungsstandes." M.A. thesis, Hamburg.

al-Hadithy, M. T. Hamadi Obeid (1979). *Gypsies and Karaj in Iraq* (in Arabic). Mosul: University of Mosul, Department of Social Sciences.

Hanna, Nabil Sobhi (1982). *Ghagar of Sett Guiran ʿha: A Study of a Gypsy Community in Egypt*. Cairo Papers in Social Science, vol. 5, monograph 1. Cairo: American University.

Littmann, Enno (1920). *Zigeuner-Arabisch: Wortschatz und Grammatik der arabischen Bestandteile in den morgenländischen Zigeunersprachen*. Bonn and Leipzig: K. Schroeder Verlag.

Macalister, R. A. S. (1914). *The Language of the Nawar or Zutt, the Nomad Smiths of Palestine*. London: T. & A. Constable.

Pott, A. F. (1846). "Über die Sprache der Zigeuner in Syrien." *Zeitschrift für die Wissenschaft der Sprache* (Berlin) 1(2): 175–186.

Rao, Aparna (1983). "Zigeunerähnliche Gruppen in West-, Zentral- und Südasien." In *Zigeuner: Roma, Sinti, Gitanos, Gypsies zwischen Verfolgung und Romantisierung*, edited by R. Vossen. Berlin: Ullstein Sachbuch.

Streck, Bernhard (1989). *Di Halab im Sudan: Herkunft, Gewerbe und Eigenart der Zigeunergruppen am mittleren Nil*. Habilitationsschrift, University of Mainz.

Weber, Alain (1989). "Les tsiganes d'Egypte." *Études Tsiganes* 35(3–4): 47–59.

Westphal-Hellbusch, Sigrid, and Heinz Westphal (1968). *Zur Geschichte und Kultur der Jat*. Berlin: Dunker & Humbolt.

APARNA RAO

Peripatetics of the Maghreb

ETHNONYMS: *Mauritania:* Maalemin (Sánʾa), Tatari. *Morocco:* Beni Bacchar, Beni Hami, Bez-Carne, Ghenanema, Romani, Susi, Zigani. *Algeria:* Beni ʿAdes, ʾAmer.

Very little is known of peripatetic communities in the Maghreb. In the early twentieth century certain communities such as the Ghenanema of Morocco and the Beni ʿAdes and the ʾAmer of Algeria had already become largely sedentary. The above list of ethnonyms is neither exhaustive nor up to date. It is known, however, that in Morocco the Bez Carne were known to others as Beni Bacchar and consisted of four subgroups. The community that called itself Romani was known to others as Zigani. Each of the communities in Morocco and Algeria spoke its own language, in addition to Arabic. The Bez Carne and the Romani of Morocco claimed that their ancestors hailed from the Canary Islands and Sudan, respectively. In Mauritania, the Maalemin (Sánʾa) work as smiths and are attached to the pastoral nomads of the area, known as Beidane. There are similarly attached communities of itinerant minstrels. The Tatari reportedly worked as acrobats. In Morocco in the late nineteenth century, among the Bez Carne, the men worked as caravan guides and tinkers; the women told fortunes and, in one subgroup, were prostitutes. The Beni Hami also told fortunes and performed magic, whereas the Ghenanema were petty traders and beggars. In Algeria, the men of the Beni ʿAdes dealt in animals, circumcised, and tattooed, and their women told fortunes. Among the ʾAmer the men and women were animal dealers and tattooers, respectively. All the above-mentioned communities are Muslims. In Morocco, the common patron saint was Didi Hassan O Moussa, whose shrine is in Sus. Similarly, in Algeria, the patron saint common to all communities was Dis Ahmend Ben Youssef of Miliana.

Bibliography

Burton, R. (Bu Bacchar) (1980). "Gypsy Acrobats in Ancient Africa." *Journal of the The Gypsy Lore Society* 2(4): 193–291.

Hames, C. (1969). "La société mure ou le système des castes hors de l'Inde." *Cahiers internationaux de dociologie* 46:163–177.

Toupet, C. (1963). "L'évolution de la nomadisation en Mauritanie sahélienne." *Nomades et nomadisme au Sahara* (Paris: UNESCO) 1(4).

Van Gennep, A. (1911–1912). "North African Gypsies." *Journal of the Gypsy Lore Society* 5(3): 192–198.

APARNA RAO

Persians

ETHNONYM: Iranians

Orientation

Persians are an ethnic group defined primarily by language and location. The Persian language, also known as Farsi, which linguists classify in the Indo-Iranian Branch of the Indo-European Language Family, had about 23 million speakers in Iran in 1986 and 6 million in Afghanistan the same year (Grimes 1988). It is the official language of Iran, and also the language of Iran's government bureaucracy, educational institutions, mass media, and literature. A dialect of modern Persian is used as the language of elites in Afghanistan. Standard Persian, or Farsi, followed Middle Persian, or Pahlavi, which was the language of the Sāssānian period of Iranian history (A.D. 224 to 642). In the centuries that followed the Arab conquest of Iran, Pahlavi absorbed numerous Arabic elements. The addition of Arabic words into Persian is the primary difference between the language spoken today and that spoken thirteen centuries ago.

History and Cultural Relations

The Iranian plateau was inhabited by a hunting and gathering group by 10,000 B.C. Around 3000 B.C., waves of pastoralists from Eurasia drifted into the area searching for new pastures. Some of these pastoralists were warriors on horseback who supplanted the indigenous populations of the Iranian plateau. The first Iranians (Aryans) arrived about 1,000 B.C. They also penetrated the Iranian plateau in waves lasting several centuries, and, like their predecessors, they were pastoralists who also relied on agriculture to some extent.

The Iranians consisted of several tribal groups, including the Medes, Persians (Pars), Parthians, Bactrians, Soghdians, Sacians, and Scythians. For several centuries they absorbed the cultural influences of existing civilizations. In the seventh century B.C. they began to take over the known world. Between 625 and 585 B.C., the Medes developed a powerful civilization, with its capital at Ecbatana, modern day Hamadān. They defeated the powerful Assyrians and sacked their capital, Nineveh, in 612 B.C. Those tribes that had settled near Lake Urmia moved south and occupied Persis (Parsa), the modern province of Fārs, from which they obtained their name. These loosely federated Persian tribes became a more cohesive political unit under the Achaemenian dynasty. In 553 B.C., Cyrus, the ruler of Persis, overthrew the Median dynasty and consolidated the Medes and Persians into the mighty Achaemenid Empire.

For 1,200 years Persia maintained a culture that grew increasingly complex and rigid. The social structure supported rulers, priests, warriors, artisans, scribes, pastoralists, agriculturists, and other producers. By the seventh century A.D., a small privileged class dominated a large mass of people who were blocked from attaining any upward social mobility; this was an important factor in setting the stage for a successful Arab conquest.

In the thirteen centuries since the Arab invasion, there has been a steady Persianization of the society. Persians have been able to maintain their independence from invaders and their dominance over non-Persian minorities. An intense nationalistic movement began in 1925, which included the official adoption of the name "Iran," the use of Farsi as a national language, and government encouragement to produce the best in Persian culture.

Economy

Persians are a sedentary people who have traditionally relied on agriculture as a means of subsistence. Much of the agriculture in Iran is based on dry farming. Farming methods and implements are primitive by Western standards, but well adapted to the steep and rocky terrain and shallow topsoil of much of the country. Important crops include wheat, barley, legumes, and a few cash crops such as tobacco, sugar beets, and sesame. Few villages have a substantial surplus.

The production of oil has added immensely to the economic base of Iran in the twentieth century. The role of oil in providing jobs for the labor market is clear, and Persians have certainly benefited from an expanded job market. The proportion of Persians involved in oil production and the effects of huge oil revenues on the daily lives of the Persian population are not clear at this point.

Kinship, Marriage, and Family

The basic social and economic unit in Persian society is the nuclear family. Some families combine into larger units comprised of a man, his wife or wives, and their married sons and their families. The Persian family is patriarchal, patrilineal, and patrilocal. Women defer to their husbands in public but may wield considerable decision-making power in private. The father is usually aloof and a disciplinarian, whereas the mother is permissive and affectionate, often acting as an intermediary between the children and their father. Men are the guardians and defenders of the family honor; they are responsible for protecting the chastity of their daughters and sisters. This obligation has sometimes led to the sequestering of women in the more traditional segments of society.

Marriages are arranged only after negotiation and approval by both sets of kin. Husband and wife usually have similar educational and socioeconomic backgrounds. Endogamy is the traditional practice, although it is avoided by the urban, educated people. There is a preference for marrying cousins.

Sociopolitical Organization

Persians are concentrated in and near several cities on the Iranian plateau—Kermān, Shirāz, Yazd, Eṣfahān, Kāshān, and Tehran—and in Herāt in Afghanistan. Each city is the economic and political center of dozens of towns, and each town integrates hundreds of villages into a regional economic network. Urban Persians can be grouped into distinct occupational and social classes based on their degree of control over economic and political resources. At the top of the hierarchy are real-estate investors and speculators and other industrial and commercial entrepreneurs. This class includes many deputies, senators, ministers, ambassadors, and governors. On the next rung of the hierarchy are high-ranking administrators, who derive their power from above. Merchants and shopkeepers, the Bazaaris, constitute the third level of the social system and are perhaps the most cohesive segment of Iranian society. The Bazaaris have been closely allied with the *ulama* (clergy), who comprise another step on the hierarchical ladder. They are the interpreters and practitioners of Islam and in the past have led successful protest movements against unpopular rulers. The fifth urban category might be considered the middle class. It includes a large proportion of the educated white-collar workers, civil-service employees, doctors, teachers, engineers, and other specialists, including the military. In the 1970s the middle class was growing rapidly in size and political importance. Below the middle class is the urban proletariat. They comprise more than a third of the urban population, including factory and construction workers, municipal employees, and menial laborers. On the bottom rung is the subproletariat—the unskilled and often unemployed. Primarily Persian, this group consists primarily of poor nomads and landless villagers who come to the city in search of wage labor.

Persian towns are far more homogeneous than are the cities. Religious observances are practiced more regularly and fervently than in the city. Townspeople criticize urban dwellers because of their religious laxity and decadent Western behavior and values. At the same time, however, many townspeople, especially the more affluent, try to emulate the city life-style.

A large proportion of the Persian population still lives in thousands of villages and hamlets. Village populations vary between a few households and a thousand inhabitants. The size of a village depends on two critical factors, arable land and availability of water, both of which can be privately owned.

Like the Persian family, the social system is hierarchical, paternalistic, and authoritarian. Initiatives originate and decisions are almost always handed down from the top; subordinates seldom assume responsibility. This vertical system of social relations sometimes produces friendships between people of equal status that are very close and intimate but difficult to maintain over time.

Religion and Expressive Culture

The Islamization of Iran after the Arab conquest was possibly more far-reaching in its effects than were the linguistic changes. The Iranian religion prior to that time was Zoroastrianism, which was based on the belief that there was an eternal struggle between the forces of good and evil. Shiism became the national religion of Iran during the sixteenth century, at which time the ulama began to play an important role in the social and political life of the society. When Ayatollah Khomeini led the revolution that toppled the shah in 1979, he declared that the ulama were needed to purify Islam and apply its laws. As an Islamic republic, Iran is guided by the tenets of Islam as interpreted by the ulama. Most Persians today are Shia Muslims of the Ithna Ashari sect and adhere to Islamic laws and principles.

Persian art is found in a variety of forms ranging from intricately patterned tiles and Quranic inscriptions on the walls of mosques to handicrafts, miniature painting, and calligraphy. Poetry with well-defined meter and rhyme is a popular Persian art form. Persian poetry often deals with subjective interpretations of the past and sometimes satirizes social problems such as inequality, injustice, and repression.

A popular religious or philosophical theme that is expressed in Persian literature is *qesmet,* or fate. Persians believe that all unexplainable occurrences are the will of God, and that most things in life are controlled by fate rather than by humans. The unpredictable nature of life is sometimes used to justify the pursuit of pleasure.

Bibliography

Arasteh, A. Reza (1969). *Education and Social Awakening in Iran, 1850–1968*. Rev. ed. Leiden: E. J. Brill.

Beeman, William O. (1986). *Language, Status, and Power in Iran*. Bloomington: Indiana University Press.

Critchfield, Richard (1973). *The Golden Bowl Be Broken: Peasant Life in Four Cultures*. Bloomington: Indiana University Press.

English, Paul Ward (1966). *City and Village in Iran: Settlement and Economy in the Kirman Basin*. Madison: University of Wisconsin Press.

Fazel, Golamreza (1984). "Persians." *Muslim Peoples: A World Ethnographic Survey*, edited by Richard V. Weekes, 604–612. Westport, Conn.: Greenwood Press.

Grimes, Barbara F. (1988). *Ethnologue: Languages of the World*. Dallas: Summer Institute of Linguistic.

Keddie, Nikki R. (1971). "The Iranian Power Structure and Social Change, 1800-1969: An Overview." *International Journal of Middle East Studies* 2(1): 3–20.

Keddie, Nikki R., ed. (1982). *Religion and Politics in Iran: Shi'ism from Quietism to Revolution*. New Haven: Yale University Press.

Lambton, Ann K. S. (1969). *The Persian Land Reform, 1962–1966*. London: Oxford University Press.

Lambton, Ann K. S. (1984). "Dilemma of Government in Islamic Persia: The Siyasat-nma of Nizam al-Mulk." *Iran* 22:55–66.

Pierce, Joe E. (1971). *Understanding the Middle East*. Rutland, Vt.: Charles E. Tuttle.

Smith, Harvey H., et. al. (1971). *Area Handbook for Iran*. American University FAS, DA Pam 550–568. Washington, D.C.: Government Printing Office.

Szliowicz, Joseph S. (1973). *Education and Modernization in the Middle East*. Ithaca, N.Y.: Cornell University Press.

RONALD JOHNSON

Pokot

ETHNONYM: Suk

Orientation

Identification. During the colonial period, the Pokot were called "Suk" by Europeans. To some Pokot, the older designation is a reminder of an era in which Africans lacked the power to name themselves; to others, it represents the clever ruse of a forebear who outwitted powerful strangers by disguising his identity. In the first perspective, "Suk" is an ethnic slur that Europeans borrowed from the Maasai, who denigrated nonpastoral pursuits; the name is said to derive from *chok*, a short sword or staff used by Pokot cultivators to till the soil. In the second perspective, a Pokot elder, when questioned by Europeans, referred to himself as "Musuk," a term for the nearby tree stumps; his reply is said to exemplify ingenuity and cunning, two highly valued but morally ambiguous traits.

Location. The Pokot live in an ecologically complex region that extends from the plains of eastern Uganda across the highlands of northwestern Kenya to the plains of Lake Baringo. Most Pokot reside in Kenya's West Pokot District, a pestle-shaped administrative unit of approximately 9,135 square kilometers stretching from 1°07′ N to 2°40′ N and from 34°37′ E to 35°49′ E. West Pokot is the northernmost district in the Rift Valley Province. Situated alongside the Uganda border, West Pokot abuts the districts of Turkana to the north and the east, Baringo and Elgeyo Marakwet to the southeast, and Trans Nzoia to the southwest. Cool, rugged highlands that form part of the western wall of the Rift Valley run through the center of the district, separating the dry, hot plains. The highlands—the Cherangani Hills, the Sekerr Mountains, and the Chemerongit range—rise to over 3,000 meters; the eastern plains have an average elevation of 900 meters, whereas the western plains vary from 1,200 to 1,800 meters. Four perennial rivers, all of which feed Lake Turkana, flow northward through West Pokot: the Suam/Turkwel, the Kerio, the Weiwei, and the Morun. There are two rainy seasons—the long rains, from March to June, and the short rains, from mid-October to mid-November. Rainfall varies from less than 40 centimeters per year in the lowland areas to more than 150 centimeters in the highland areas, with deviations of up to 40 percent from these long-term averages. Mean annual temperatures range from less than 10° C in the highlands to more than 30° C in the lowlands. Vegetation includes moist forest, dry woodland, bush land, and desert scrub. The soils, derived primarily from metamorphic rocks of the Precambrian Basement System, are shallow, rocky, and prone to erosion in some areas; deep, fertile, and well drained in others. The highland areas are covered by forests, but deforestation owing to population pressure outpaces the designation of forest reserves; to increase forest cover, which is critical to water retention, the government operates a number of tree nurseries in West Pokot.

Demography. Vital statistics for the Pokot region date from the onset of British rule, but demographic data have not been collected systematically, and administrative boundaries have undergone extensive revision. Estimates for West Pokot, based on colonial tax rolls and national censuses, indicate that the district's total population has grown from less than 20,000 in 1927 to an estimated 233,000 in 1988. Natural increase accounts only partly for this dramatic growth: the number of children born per Pokot woman does not seem to be higher than the Kenyan average, estimated at 6.7 in 1984, and epidemiological surveys suggest that infant mortality may be higher among the Pokot than among other Kenyan groups. Immigration has fueled population growth since independence in 1963, especially in the southern highlands, where the principal administrative and commercial centers are located and where the land supports sedentary cultivation. Population density per square kilometer ranges from 64 persons in the southern highlands to less than 8 persons in the northwestern and eastern lowlands. The age structure of the population forms a classic pyramid shape.

Linguistic Affiliation. The Pokot are a Kalenjin-speaking people whose language (ng'ala Pokot, "tongue or language of Pokot") incorporates words from the neighboring Karamojong and Turkana. The term "Kalenjin" dates from World War II; it is a self-chosen label that has replaced various colloquial, scholarly, and administrative designations, including "Nandi-speaking peoples," "Nilo-Hamites," "Southern Nilotes," and "Paranilotes." The Kalenjin consist of eight principal groups: the Keiyo, Kipsigis, Marakwet, Nandi, Pokot, Saboat, Terik, and Tugen.

History and Cultural Relations

Linguistic and archaeological evidence suggests that Kalenjin-speaking peoples have occupied Kenya's western highlands for the past 900 years, expanding and contracting their territories and altering their grazing and cultivation patterns in response to environmental and political pressures. Such pressures were especially pronounced during the last two decades of the nineteenth century: drought, rinderpest, and famines destroyed cattle herds and undermined human populations within and beyond the region, causing massive shifts in population. Great Britain began to establish its sphere of influence by defining and, later, enforcing political boundaries that cut through ecological zones and local and long-distance trade networks. During this period, the Pokot moved into areas that were previously occupied by the Karamojong, but they lost grazing grounds to the Turkana, who were pushing down from the north and the west. A decade after the onset of British administrative activity in 1910, the southern grazing grounds of the Pokot were alienated for European farms.

Throughout the colonial period, West Pokot was a "closed" district, a status consistent with its role as a buffer between the northernmost reaches of the "White highlands," the name given to Kenya's European-settled areas, and the shifting frontiers of Turkana. With the exception of a handful of colonial civil servants and Protestant and Catholic missionaries (the London-based Bible Churchmen's Missionary Society, which opened a station in West Pokot in 1931, and the Irish Catholic Kiltegan Fathers, who opened a school for catechumens in 1942), few Europeans ventured into the district. Government- and missionary-sponsored projects for economic and social betterment expanded after World War II, in conjunction with the rise of a grass-roots religious movement called "Dini ya Yomöt" that sought to drive Europeans out of the region. These projects focused on soil conservation, education, and health care; the latter was pioneered largely by the Catholic church, which opened the first hospital in the heart of the district in 1956 under the care of the Holy Rosary Sisters, an order of Irish nuns.

Owing to its social and political-economic isolation during the colonial period, West Pokot was the least-developed district in Rift Valley Province at the time of independence. The onset of modern infrastructure and transport, commercial townships, and land adjudication dates from the 1970s. So, too, does the expansion of primary- and secondary-school education, health-care services, religious denominations, and government involvement in the organization of women's cooperatives.

Settlements

The Pokot have divided their countryside into named and bounded "neighborhoods" or settlements. As physical units, these neighborhoods vary in size, topography, ecological potential, and population density. As social units, they are organized around local councils, which are composed of household heads who meet periodically to discuss community affairs, resolve disputes, and coordinate productive activities such as the clearing and sowing of fields, the digging of dry-season wells, and the repairing of irrigation furrows. The centrality of these councils to the maintenance of peace and prosperity is marked linguistically: the month of Pokokwö (lit., "of council"), which corresponds to March, heralds the onset of the long rains.

The social, economic, and ritual ties that link people within and between neighborhoods derive from proximity and kinship; highland neighborhoods are more likely than lowland neighborhoods to be populated by a small range of clans. Exchange relationships between settlements in different ecological zones help reduce economic risk, which is especially important in periods of environmental adversity.

Economy

Subsistence and Commercial Activities. Cattle keeping and grain growing (traditionally, sorghum and finger millet; more recently, maize) are at the center of Pokot subsistence and commercial activities, but their relative importance varies regionally. In general, cattle are more essential to subsistence in the lowlands than they are in the highlands. To ensure an adequate food supply, Pokot herding and cultivating practices take advantage of the region's complex ecology: herds are moved seasonally, and crops are planted in different ecological zones in order to stagger harvests and maximize yields; furrow irrigation is practiced in the highlands.

Surplus maize is sold to a government-operated marketing board, along with sunflowers, pyrethrum, coffee, and cotton, the other major field crops that were introduced in the colonial and postcolonial periods. Surplus vegetables and fruits (potatoes, beans, cabbages, onions, kale, bananas, and oranges) are sold locally. Livestock marketing has been less successful than grain marketing.

Industrial Arts. Women weave baskets, work leather, and make milk gourds and unglazed pots for cooking and water storage. Men specialize in woodworking, making beehives, headrests, and the handles for spears, knives, and hoes. Blacksmiths forge metal tools, but the art of smelting seems to have died out in the precolonial era with the growth of the iron trade.

Trade. The most important forms of exchange are the marriage prestation and *tilia*, a stock partnership based on the exchange of a cow for an ox. The bartering and selling of grain, vegetables, cattle, and forest products (primarily honey) takes place between highland and lowland neighborhoods and in local markets.

Division of Labor. Productive activities are organized by homestead and by neighborhood, with women performing the greatest part of the homestead work, from milking cows to cultivating the fields to cooking. Children assist with herding, cultivation, and miscellaneous tasks.

Land Tenure. Rights to land are obtained through local land committees, inheritance, gift, contract, and purchase. Beginning in 1973, highland regions have been adjudicated as smallholdings and lowland regions as group ranches, in which land and animal management and liability for credit are collective.

Kinship

Kin Groups and Descent. There are some thirty-six named, exogamous patrilineal clans. Many of these clans are found among other Kalenjin groups; a few originated among the Turkana. Clan histories recount the movements of people from one locale to another, emphasizing the vulnerability of humans and their dependence upon supernatural benefactors to help them overcome hunger, thirst, and, ultimately, death itself; the attributes of these benefactors are praised in poetry and song. Clans are conceptualized as "pathways" and fellow clan members as children of the same "father" or "grandfather." Although members of the same clan are dispersed geographically and are differentiated internally, they are said to hold their herds in common. Unlike some East African cattle-keeping groups, the Pokot retain their clan affiliations throughout their lives; there is no ceremony to sever clanship in the event of marriage. Genealogical reckoning tends to be shallow, reaching back three to four generations (see "Marriage").

Kinship Terminology. Relatives are differentiated according to the logic of clanship, generation, and gender. Relatives are categorized as "father's people" (*kapapo*), "mother's people" (*kamama*), and "spouse's people" (*kapikoi*). Father's people are fellow clan members and hence the source of fathers, brothers, sisters, and "aunts" (father's sisters). Mother's people are differentiated according to their relationship to "uncle" (mother's brother). Terms for spouse's people often are derived from the names of the livestock that have been exchanged to establish affinal ties. In addition, people who share the same name, marry into the same family, establish stock partnerships, or are cut by the same circumcision knife also are considered relatives.

Marriage and Family

Marriage. Marriage is underwritten by gift giving, with the flow of gifts moving from the groom and his family to the bride and her family, often over a period of years. The amount and the types of gifts are agreed upon before the bride moves to her husband's home. The bride's family often receives a combination of livestock, goods, and cash, and the bride receives milk cows and rights to land.

Divorce owing to incompatibility or to lack of children is not uncommon in the early years of a marriage, but, after the birth of children, divorce is rare. The bond between a husband and wife and their respective families and clans endures for three to four generations, after which time the relationship is said to "disappear," and marriages may again take place between the two groups. A man may have more than one wife, but polygyny is uncommon among men under 40 years of age.

Domestic Unit. A homestead is composed of one or more buildings that provide housing, cooking, and storage for a man and his wife (or wives) and children; co-wives have separate houses. Where cultivable land is inherited (primarily in the highlands), married sons tend to live near their fathers.

Inheritance. A young adult woman is promised stock by her family after her initiation and at the time of her marriage, but generally she asks for and receives only one gift of stock from her family. A woman acquires additional stock, along with rights to land, from her husband and her mother-in-law; she transmits this property to her children and her daughters-in-law. Young men usually receive stock from their fathers and close agnates after initiation, but a man does not obtain full ownership of the stock he inherits until he marries and establishes his own homestead. In the highlands, a man receives full control of a portion of the family's land after he marries.

Socialization. Families are responsible for supporting their children, but socialization per se is a communitywide affair. The role of the community in teaching children ethical rules and responsible behavior is emphasized during initiation, the most important rite of passage for most Pokot. Initiation consists of a series of neighborhood-based ceremonies organized by adult men and women who, by turns, teach, encourage, remonstrate, cook for, and laud the initiates during and after their ordeals (circumcision for boys; clitoridectomy for girls). The work of initiation is organized by gender, with women taking primary responsibility for girls' initiations, and men for boys' initiations.

Sociopolitical Organization

Social Organization. Distinctions based on gender and generation are essential to the etiquette of everyday life within homesteads and neighborhoods, the two principal social groupings. When boys are circumcised, they acquire membership in one of eight age sets, the names of which rotate cyclically through time; the opening and closing of each set is determined by elderly men. A second age-based system for men, called *sapana*, has two divisions. Adopted from the neighboring Karamojong in the second half of the nineteenth century, sapana may take the place of circumcision in the lowlands, but in the highlands the ceremony, if undertaken at all, follows circumcision. Women do not have age-sets.

Political Organization. Neighborhood councils (see "Settlements") were the only formal political arenas prior to colonial rule. The British imposed a system of local headmen, district courts, legislative councils, and a national assembly.

Social Control and Conflict. Disputes may be aired in neighborhood councils and in government courts. Other sanctions include shaming, cursing, and bewitching.

Religion and Expressive Culture

Religious Beliefs. In Pokot cosmology, the universe has two realms, the above and the below. The above, remote and unknowable, is the abode of the most powerful deities—Tororot, Asis (sun), and Ilat (rain); the below is the abode of humans, animals, and plants. Men and women are considered responsible for the peace and prosperity of the realm that they inhabit, but they must rely upon divine vitality and knowledge to achieve and maintain these conditions. The Pokot communicate with their deities through prayer and sacrifice: Tororot is said to listen to his creatures below, Asis to witness their activities, and Ilat to serve as a messenger between the two realms. Deities, in turn, communicate with humans, warning and rebuking them about their misconduct. Christianity has reshaped Pokot cosmology, primarily by reducing the number of deities, while augmenting their attributes.

Religious Practitioners. The divine messenger Ilat has a human counterpart called a *werkoyon* (prophet), who foresees disaster and recommends expiation, usually animal sacrifice, to alleviate it. A werkoyon may be either male or female; his or her ability to foresee and to advise is considered a divinely given gift, to be used on behalf of all Pokot.

Ceremonies. The main ceremonies mark transitions in the social lives of individuals and communities. Especially notable among these are the cleansing of a couple expecting their first child; the cleansing of newborn infants and their mothers; the cleansing of twins and other children who are born under unusual circumstances; male and female initiation; marriage; sapana, a coming-of-age ceremony for men; and summer-solstice, harvest, and healing ceremonies.

Arts. Singing, storytelling, and decorative arts, especially bodily adornment, are highly valued. Singing accompanies ceremonies, dances, and beer parties; folktales often incorporate songs. Bodily adornment consists of beadwork, hairstyling, scarification, and the removal of the lower central incisors.

Medicine. Most Pokot have some knowledge of herbal remedies and convalescent cookery, and Pokot women specialize in the diagnosis and treatment of disease and in midwifery. Ritual specialists may be called upon to treat the mentally disturbed. The Pokot use their own healing and preventive methods, along with those provided by hospital- and clinic-based practitioners.

Death and Afterlife. A death is signaled by the mourning of close kin, but the Pokot have no funeral ceremony per se, and no singing accompanies the burial of the body or the subsequent distribution of the deceased's effects. Ancestral spirits anticipate reincarnation in their living descendants; an infant is said to resemble physically and temperamentally one of his or her agnatic ancestors, after whom the infant should be named.

See also Nandi and Other Kalenjin Peoples

Bibliography

Bianco, Barbara A. (1991). "Women and Things: Pokot Motherhood as Political Destiny." *American Ethnologist* 18: 770–785.

Bianco, Barbara A. (1992). *The Historical Anthropology of a Mission Hospital in Northwestern Kenya*. Ann Arbor, Mich.: University Microfilms International.

Conant, Francis P. (1965). "Korok: A Variable Unit of Physical and Social Space among the Pokot of East Africa." *American Anthropologist* 67:429–434.

Crazzolara, J. P. (1973). *A Study of the Suk (Pokot) Language*. Bologna: Editrice Missionaria Italiana.

Dietz, Ton (1987). *Pastoralists in Dire Straits: Survival Strategies and External Interventions in a Semi-Arid Region at the Kenya/Uganda Border: Western Pokot, 1900–1986*. Netherlands Geographical Studies, 49. Amsterdam: University of Amsterdam.

Edgerton, Robert B., and Francis P. Conant (1964). "Kilipat: The Shaming Party among the Pokot of East Africa." *Southwest Journal of Anthropology* 20:404–418.

Hasthrope, Elizabeth (1983). "A Study of Pokot Songs." Ph.D. dissertation, School of Oriental and African Studies (London).

Hendrix, Hubert, ed. (1985). *District Atlas West Pokot*. Nairobi: General Printers.

Huntingford, G. W. B. (1953). *The Southern Nilo-Hamites*. London: International African Institute.

Meyerhoff, Elizabeth (1981). "The Socio-Economic and Ritual Roles of Pokot Women." Ph.D. dissertation, Cambridge University.

Meyerhoff, Elizabeth (1982). "The Threatened Ways of Kenya's Pokot People." *National Geographic* 161:120–140.

Nyamwaya, David (1982). "The Management of Illness in an East African Society: A Study of Choice and Constraint in Health Care among the Pokot." Ph.D. dissertation, Cambridge University.

Nyamwaya, David (1983). "Coping with Illness among the Pokot of Kenya." *Curare* 6:181–196.

Peristiany, John G. (1951). "The Age-Set System of the Pastoral Pokot." *Africa* 21:188–206; 279–302.

Peristiany, John G. (1975). "The Ideal and the Actual: The Role of Prophets in the Pokot Political System." In *Studies in Social Anthropology: Essays in Memory of E. E. Evans-Pritchard by his Former Oxford Colleagues*, edited by J. H. M. Beattie and R. G. Lienhardt, 166–212. Oxford: Clarendon Press.

Reynolds, John Eric (1982). *Community Underdevelopment, Ethnicity, and Stratification in a Rural Destination: Mnagei, Kenya*. Ann Arbor, Mich.: University Microfilms International.

Schneider, Harold (1956). "The Interpretation of Pokot Visual Art." *Man* 56:103–106.

Schneider, Harold (1958). "Pokot Resistance to Change." In *Continuity and Change in African Cultures*, edited by William R. Bascom and Melville J. Herskovits, 144–167. Chicago: Phoenix Books.

Schneider, Harold (1967). "Pokot Folktales, Humor, and Values." *Journal of the Folklore Institute* 4:265–318.

Tully, Durene E. (1985). *Human Ecology and Political Process: The Context of Market Incorporation in West Pokot District, Kenya*. Ann Arbor, Mich.: University Microfilms International.

BARBARA A. BIANCO

Qashqa'i

ETHNONYM: Turk

Orientation

Identification. The Qashqa'i are tribally organized, Turkic-speaking, nomadic pastoralists and agriculturists who live in southwestern Iran. They possess a strong sense of ethnic identity and are one of Iran's many national minorities. They are Shia Muslims, unlike most of Iran's other minorities, who are either Sunni Muslims, Christians, Jews, Zoroastrians, or Baha'is.

Location. The Qashqa'i are located in the Zagros Mountains, in the province of Fārs. Their territory extends from the Persian Gulf-coast littoral in the east to the Shīrāz-Eşfahān highway in the west, and from the Persian Gulf-coast littoral in the south to the Bakhtiyari border south of the city of Eşfahān in the north. Shīrāz, the major urban center of southwestern Iran, is located in the middle of Qashqa'i territory. Qashqa'i nomads migrate between their low-elevation winter pastures near the Gulf and their high-elevation summer pastures to the north or northeast—a distance as great as 560 kilometers—and en route they pass by Shīrāz and through settled agricultural zones. Their winter pastures are hot and dry in late spring, summer, and early autumn, and their summer pastures have a deep snow cover all winter, both features necessitating seasonal occupation and migration.

Demography. The Qashqa'i number approximately 500,000 people. Although the Iranian government has never taken a census of the Qashqa'i, their tribal leaders give quite accurate estimates of the people under their authority. Until the national land reforms of the 1960s, the vast majority of Qashqa'i were nomadic pastoralists, but, since then, many Qashqa'i have settled in villages, sometimes creating new ones, in and near the territory through which they had migrated as nomads. Qashqa'i people are also found in Shīrāz and Eşfahān and in the region's towns.

Linguistic Affiliation. The first language for the majority of Qashqa'i is Turkish, a southwestern Oghuz Turkic language. Qashqa'i Turkish is not a written language. The Qashqa'i tribal confederacy was formed over several centuries by diverse peoples, and, as a consequence, the first language of some Qashqa'i—Luri, Kurdish, Persian, Arabic, Baluchi, or Rom (Gypsy)—reflects this diversity. Almost all Qashqa'i men also speak Persian, the official language of Iran and the medium of communication with markets, government agents, and the surrounding dominant, Persian-speaking society. Since 1955, Qashqa'i schoolchildren have been taught to read and write in Persian. Most Qashqa'i nomad women know enough Persian to negotiate with itinerant peddlers and other outsiders, but the settled Qashqa'i women speak Persian more fluently than the nomad women.

History and Cultural Relations

The Qashqa'i trace their origins to the steppes of Central Asia, east of the Caspian Sea, and they state that their ancestors resided for a while in the Caucasus Mountains, between the Caspian and Black seas, before they came to Fārs Province. It is likely that the originating and ruling dynasty of the Qashqa'i tribal confederacy, the Janikhani family, did have such a history, but the majority of the Qashqa'i of the mid-twentieth century consisted of diverse peoples—Turks primarily, but also Lurs, Kurds, Arabs, Persians, Baluch, Gypsies, and others—who joined together for the first time in southwestern Iran. No historical evidence exists of a Qashqa'i group anywhere outside of Fārs. The ruling family and the many components of the confederacy have origins in what are today Central Asia, Afghanistan, Turkey, Iraq, Syria, and the vast Iranian territory. The Qashqa'i tribal confederacy was formed in the late eighteenth century during or just following the rule of Karim Khan Zand in Shīrāz. It grew in power under the Qajar dynasty in the nineteenth and early twentieth centuries and played a military and political role during World War I, when the British and Germans competed for influence in Iran. Reza Shah Pahlavi, ruler of Iran from 1925 to 1941, imprisoned and executed Qashqa'i leaders, forcibly stopped Qashqa'i migrations and ordered the nomads to settle, disarmed the tribespeople, and assigned military governors. When Reza Shah abdicated, Qashqa'i leaders resumed power and kept it until Reza Shah's son, Mohammed Reza Shah Pahlavi, exiled them from Iran to punish them for their opposition. They remained in exile until the Iranian Revolution of 1978–1979, when they returned to Iran to resume rule. After an initially good relationship with the Ayatollah Ruhollah Khomeini, they fell into disfavor with other members of the ruling clergy. The Islamic Republic's Revolutionary Guards arrested an important Qashqa'i leader, who, with others, had mounted an insurgency in 1980. Revolutionary Guards succeeded in stopping the insurgents and capturing the principal leaders in 1982. (See "Political Organization.") The Qashqa'i people—the vast majority of whom played no role in the insurgency—have devised various ways to cope with and adapt to the new Islamic regime.

Settlements

Qashqa'i nomads live in small tent encampments in both their winter and their summer pastures. Most of the Qashqa'i nomads who have settled in villages since the 1930s have chosen locations in or near their summer or winter pastures, and most have continued to practice pastoralism. In 1992 many Qashqa'i lived in small houses in one seasonal pasture for part of the year and migrated to the other seasonal pasture for the other part. Some Qashqa'i people also live in towns and cities in southwestern Iran.

Economy

Subsistence and Commercial Activities. The vast majority of Qashqa'i subsist on a mixed pastoral-agricultural economy. The nomads are more dependent on their sheep and goats, whereas the villagers place a greater reliance on agriculture. They sell surplus live animals once a year, usually in cities, and dairy products (fresh and clarified butter, dried curds) in villages and town markets. The animals provide meat for the Qashqa'i on ceremonial occasions and also whenever one is slaughtered because of injury or illness. The people consume diverse dairy products, primarily yogurt, sour milk, butter, cheese, and dried curds. The nomads rely heavily on their wide territories for meat from game animals and for gathered foods of many kinds. Their staple food is bread baked both from the wheat that they cultivate in winter and summer pastures and from wheat that they purchase. Women weave many items from the yarn they spin from the raw wool of their sheep and from the raw hair of their goats—including knotted pile carpets (for which the Qashqa'i have been internationally famous since the nineteenth century), various flat weaves, saddlebags, horse covers, and tent fabric. Most of these items are used in Qashqa'i tents or given as gifts within the group, but some are sold in villages and urban bazaars.

Division of Labor. Men, women, and children share the tasks of nomadic pastoralism and agriculture. Men and boys tend the sheep and goats, herd the camels, care for the pack animals (camels, mules, donkeys), pitch the tents, lead the seasonal migrations, cultivate the crops, trade in markets, and hunt. Women and children perform most of the chores connected with the home. Women care for children, cook, bake bread, weave, tend animals near the tent, collect water and fuel, and gather wild fruits and vegetables. Boys assist their fathers, and girls help their mothers. During the migration and in any kind of crisis, all of the people help with whatever work is necessary. Among the Qashqa'i who live in villages, men cultivate fields and negotiate economic affairs, and women and children are responsible for domestic tasks. For the nomads in particular, a fairly equitable social and economic relationship exists between men and women.

Land Tenure. Until the national land reforms of the 1960s, the Qashqa'i derived their rights to use pastures and agricultural land through membership in their tribal groups. Tribal leaders held control over territory and distributed land rights. In the 1960s, when the government nationalized Iran's pastures and confiscated much of the cultivable land, most Qashqa'i lost their customary rights. The shah's government had not yet adequately formulated a new system of land tenure for the pastoralists when the 1979 Revolution occurred. Despite much talk about land reform, the Islamic Republic has continued to avoid any systematic reorganization of land tenure. It does, for the moment, recognize the private rights of individual users of pastoral and agricultural land, especially if they can demonstrate and prove past occupancy and use of the land.

Kinship

The Qashqa'i people follow notions of patrilineal descent in forming social categories and in defining personal rights. Each Qashqa'i person is a member of a named patrilineage and derives status and reputation from this group. Bilateral ties are also important, especially because of the high rates of lineage endogamy and intermarriage between lineages. Every person is bound by multiple ties to others of the local and wider sociopolitical groups to which he or she belongs.

Marriage and Family

Marriage. Until the 1980s, men married in their late teens or early twenties, whereas women often married soon after puberty. In the 1980s, however, political and socioeconomic changes—particularly the impact of the Iran-Iraq War (when many Qashqa'i were killed or wounded), the expansion of formal education for both sexes, and the rise of job training and employment outside the camps and villages—have led to a rising marriage age for both sexes. The preferred form of marriage, in the past as well as in the early 1990s, has been between patrilateral relatives, especially patrilateral parallel cousins. Patrilineages are highly endogamous. When a Qashqa'i man marries, he brings his bride to live in his parents' household. After they have produced children and are prepared economically to form their own independent household, they set up a new tent or build a new house nearby and move out of the home of the husband's parents.

Domestic Unit. A son brings his bride to live in his natal household, and many domestic units consist, therefore, of three generations. The youngest son, the "son of the hearth," remains in the parental home and cares for his parents in their old age.

Inheritance. The Qashqa'i practice anticipatory inheritance, a system by which married children receive their portions of the parental wealth when—in the cases of sons—they form independent households or when—in the case of daughters—they marry and leave their natal homes. The youngest son shares with his parents the last portion of the parental wealth. The Qashqa'i do not observe Islamic inheritance rules.

Socialization. Qashqa'i boys and girls learn their roles from an early age, as they follow their elder brothers or sisters and their fathers or mothers in the many tasks that sustain the livelihood. Children perform tasks as soon as they are physically able to do so. Aunts and uncles on both the father's and the mother's side play important roles in caring for and instructing their nephews and nieces.

Sociopolitical Organization

Social Organization. Qashqa'i nomads live in small tent encampments in winter and summer pastures; during the long seasonal migrations, they travel in larger groups for purposes of defense and security. Their social groups at the local level are based primarily on patrilineal ties, but ties of economics, social compatibility, and politics are also considered relevant. Qashqa'i villagers live in similar social groups, although larger, and they lose the flexibility and the seasonal social changes that the nomads appreciate.

Political Organization. The Qashqa'i confederacy consists of a ruling dynasty (the Janikhani [var. Shahliu] family), five large tribes (Amaleh, Darrehshuri, Kashkuli Bozorg, Farsi Madan, and Shesh Boluki), and some smaller tribes. Different tribally organized people in Fārs Province have allied with the confederacy and its component tribes during certain historical periods, and thus both confederacy and tribal forms of membership have varied. The leader of the confederacy is the *ilkhani*, or paramount khan, a member of the Janikhani family and a direct descendant of the first Qashqa'i ilkhani. He is assisted by the *ilbegi*, the deputy khan, also a Janikhani. Each Qashqa'i tribe except the Amaleh has its own ruling family of khans. The ilkhani appoints one khan from each tribe as *kalantar*, or leading khan; he is responsible for liaison with the ilkhani. The last functioning ilkhani, Khosrow Khan Janikhani, was captured and executed by the Islamic Republic's Revolutionary Guards in 1982, at the end of the insurgency that he had formed and led. All of the other members of the Janikhani family who could possibly succeed Khosrow Khan are either under house arrest in Iran or in involuntary exile abroad. Despite these restrictions, the Janikhanis and other Qashqa'i still animatedly discuss the possible successors, in case the political situation in Iran should change and they could return to Qashqa'i territory. Most of the khans of the component Qashqa'i tribes were still living in Qashqa'i territory in 1992, but the current regime restricts their political activities, and they are no longer the mediators and brokers they once were.

Each Qashqa'i tribe consists of many subtribes, each of which is headed by a *kadkhoda*, or headman. Until the late 1960s, these men were appointed by the khans of their tribes, who usually recognized the men whom the tribal people themselves desired as their headmen. Since the late 1960s, the government has recognized headmen by following the same practice. Headmen rely on and respect the advice and wishes of the "gray beards," the elders of the community. Throughout the 1980s, the Islamic Republic encouraged local Qashqa'i groups to form councils and to rely on them instead of relying on individual headmen, who, by 1992, had greatly diminished power and authority.

Social Control. The nomads regulate among themselves their relationships to others and may also seek assistance from elders, headmen, and—since the 1980s—from councils, when necessary. The small groups in which the nomads live are formed on a voluntary basis and can easily be disbanded when problems arise. The elders, both men and women, exercise influence and some control over others, and men exercise some control over women. Until the 1980s, Qashqa'i people sought help from their tribal khans, but, since then, the regime has discouraged them from doing so.

Conflict. Traditionally, conflicts were regulated by representatives of a progressive order of authority: nuclear families, extended families, lineages, subtribes, tribes, and the confederacy. Since the late 1960s, government agents—the rural police, the army, and various government agencies—have become involved when problems reach the higher levels.

Religion and Expressive Culture

Religious Beliefs. The Qashqa'i are Shia Muslims, members of the dominant religious group in Iran. Until the revolution of 1979 and the establishment of the Islamic Republic, few Qashqa'i expressed any interest in the formal institutions and learned practitioners of Shia Islam, but, since 1979, they have had to adjust to the presence and power of the new Islamic state and the many agents who are connected with Islamic and Islamic/state institutions. Before 1979, few Qashqa'i said daily prayers or fasted during the month of Ramadan, and few observed other Islamic rites or ceremonies except for the Feast of Sacrifice (Id-e Qorban). They considered themselves good Muslims, and they often compared the sincerity of their basic religious beliefs with those of the men who held power over them—such as the ostentatiously pious merchants and moneylenders who, although praying and fasting as Muslims are required to do, also routinely violated Islamic law by engaging in usury and theft.

Religious Practitioners. Throughout their history, the Qashqa'i have had had no formal religious practitioners of their own. Most groups had one or two men who could recite Quranic passages at funerals and write marriage contracts. The nomads and villagers relied on itinerant dervishes and others (all non-Qashqa'i) who dispensed prayers and fulfilled vows. Their only contact with Muslim clerics was in the city, when they sought to have their marriage contracts certified. With the establishment of the Islamic Republic, a few young Qashqa'i men have entered theological schools, and most of them intend eventually to provide services to their own groups. The ritual specialists and the musicians and circumcisors who were once associated with each Qashqa'i tribe have been curtailed in their activities since 1979.

Ceremonies. Wedding celebrations are the ceremonial highlights of Qashqa'i life and are virtually the only occasions for large gatherings of Qashqa'i people. Usually three days long, they are festive affairs hosted by the groom's parents at their camp or village. On the third day, a delegation collects the bride from her parents' home. Since 1979, the ceremonial center of these rites—the public dancing of men and women, the traditional music played on oboes and skin drums, and the stick-fighting game performed to music—has been declared immoral and anti-Islamic by the new regime. In the early 1990s some Qashqa'i groups took advantage of loosened restrictions and again invited oboe players to perform at their weddings. When a young married couple decides to form an independent household, they invite their closest kin and their group elders to participate in a small celebration to commemorate the event. Group elders oversee the transference of property from the husband's parents to the new household. The birth of a child, especially a son, is marked by a small celebration of close kin. The circumcision of young boys, usually around the age of 3 or 4, is also accompanied by a small celebration.

Arts. The Qashqa'i say that they receive aesthetic pleasure from their freedom of movement, the sight of the surrounding mountains and the vast expanse of uninhabited territory, the process of weaving and the beauty of their woven goods, and their music and storytelling. Two Qashqa'i artists, Bijan Kashkuli and his son, Siroos, are well known in Iran for the watercolor depictions of "traditional" Qashqa'i life, and several Qashqa'i men are beginning to experiment with writing and publishing the short stories that customarily had only oral expression. Because Qashqa'i Turkish is not a written language, they are forced to write in Persian.

Medicine. Until the 1980s, the Qashqa'i relied mainly on their own forms of medical treatment, a system based primarily on the plants and minerals that they collected in the vast territories through which they traveled. Certain individuals had special interests and abilities and were sought out for help, but every household had its own collection of curative substances. The nomads' intimate understanding of natural causes, derived from their reliance on nature, has given them confidence in their own treatments. With the expansion from the 1970s of what passes in Iran as "modern" medicine, Qashqa'i people have come to rely more heavily on urban doctors, hospitals, and pharmacists.

Death and Afterlife. When a person dies, close relatives wash and prepare the body for burial. Men carry the body, wrapped in cloth, to a graveyard or other secluded place. The body is placed in the grave so that it faces Mecca, and, after the grave is filled with dirt, someone in the group recites passages from the Quran. On the seventh and fortieth days after the death, family members gather at the tent or house of the deceased to mourn and to visit the grave site. Beginning in the 1980s, many Qashqa'i have added a ceremony at the nearest mosque, at which a clergyman recites from the Quran. The Qashqa'i believe in heaven as they have heard it described by villagers and urbanites.

Bibliography

Beck, Lois (1986). *The Qashqa'i of Iran*. New Haven: Yale University Press.

Beck, Lois (1990). "Tribes and the State in Nineteenth- and Twentieth-Century Iran." In *Tribes and State Formation in the Middle East*, edited by Philip Khoury and J. Kostiner. Berkeley and Los Angeles: University of California Press.

Beck, Lois (1991). *Nomad: A Year in the Life of a Qashqa'i Tribesman in Iran*. Berkeley and Los Angeles: University of California Press.

Cronin, Vincent (1957). *The Last Migration*. London: Rupert Hart-Davis.

Oberling, Pierre (1974). *The Qashqa'i Nomads of Fars*. The Hague: Mouton.

LOIS BECK

Qizilbash

ETHNONYMS: none

The Qizilbash have been defined to a large extent by historical circumstances. The Qizilbash were formed out of several Turkish Shia groups that were living in northwest Persia (Azerbaijan) in the fifteenth century. These groups were oppressed by the Osmanli Turks in the early years of the Ottoman Empire. Shaykh Ḥeydar, a charismatic Sunni religious leader, attracted a large following of Shia from Azerbaijan. He called his most loyal Turkic followers "Qizilbash" and created a special hat for them to wear. The Ḥeydar hat was red, and "Qizilbash" came to mean "red hats," "red heads," or "red beards."

Shaykh Ḥeydar was killed in 1488 in a battle between his Qizilbash and other Turks. Civil war in Azerbaijan ensued. In 1501 Ḥeydar's son, Esmāʿīl, founded the Ṣafavid dynasty and conquered most of what is Iran today. Shāh Esmāʿīl spread Ithna Ashari Shiism throughout Persia, the religion that is still dominant in Iran today.

The Qizilbash became known as skilled warriors. They could put 70,000 armed horsemen in the field at one time.

Some became mercenaries, but most of them supported the Ṣafavid shahs who were fighting against the Sunni Ottoman and Sunni Uzbek Turks.

The Qizilbash, though not always aligned with the shahs in power, seemed always to have a central role in the power struggles that were constantly in play over the centuries. Their formidable military organization was utilized by various shahs and played a prominent role in the expansion of empires, particularly the Durrani Empire (1747–1793), which extended through Afghanistan and into India. When not at war, the Qizilbash served as personal bodyguards of the shahs and as household troops. Such forces were used to quell rebellions within the empire.

In the course of expansion, groups of Qizilbash (and others) were left at various places to protect communication and supply routes, to maintain law and order, and to collect tribute from conquered peoples.

The Qizilbash became better situated (if not more numerous) in what is now Afghanistan and Pakistan than they had been in Iran. In Afghanistan, the Qizilbash gradually accepted Dari (Afghan Farsi or Persian) as their primary language. Because they remained Shia and maintained a strong influence in the Afghan court, the predominant Sunni population resented their presence, and the Qizilbash felt the discrimination. Nevertheless, the Qizilbash became an entrenched part of the Afghan population, particularly in urban areas, where they became administrators, clerks, traders, and artisans.

By the end of the nineteenth century, the Qizilbash influence in the Afghan court had diminished. The Qizilbash supported, or were thought to be supporters of, the Hazarajat, who fought unsuccessfully against the ruling emir. For these reasons, and others, the emir tried forcibly to convert the Qizilbash to Sunni Islam. Those who refused were forced to wear red turbans. Because of the threat of persecution, many Qizilbash claimed to be Sunni, but secretly remained Shia.

This adoption of a dual religious identity, known as *taqiyya,* still occurs today. Obtaining accurate population figures for the Shia Qizilbash in Afghanistan and Pakistan is virtually impossible because they claim to be Sunni, Tajik, Farsiwan, or Pashtun, or they identify themselves according to their place of origin in India. Population estimates for Afghanistan range from 30,000 to 200,000, but some suggest the figure is closer to one million. The story is similar in Pakistan. Few influential Qizilbash live in Iran, their original home.

The Qizilbash are no longer considered a warrior class, but they are still thought to be within the upper strata of power and among the intelligentsia. They also tend to be predominantly urban professionals—doctors, teachers, engineers, and lawyers. Because of physical dispersal and taqiyya, they are no longer a cohesive group; nevertheless, they have maintained their strong ethnic pride.

Bibliography

Dupree, Louis (1979). "Further Notes on *Taqiyya:* Afghanistan." *Journal of American Oriental Society* 99(4): 680–682.

Dupree, Louis (1980). *Afghanistan.* Princeton, N.J.: Princeton University Press.

Dupree, Louis (1984). "Qizilbash." In *Muslim Peoples: A World Ethnographic Survey,* edited by Richard V. Weekes, 637–642. Westport, Conn.: Greenwood Press.

Tapper, Richard (1979). *Pasture and Politics.* London: Academic Press.

Watkins, Mary Bradley (1963). *Afghanistan: Land in Transition.* Princeton, N.J.: Van Nostrand.

Rukuba

ETHNONYM: Bache (sing. Unache; self-denomination)

Orientation

Identification. The Rukuba live in central Nigeria, on the High Plateau at some 30 kilometers west of the town of Jos, capital of Plateau State. They are one among the numerous small groups inhabiting the region. These groups are, by African standards, demographically small.

Location. The Rukuba inhabit a rugged country and, until the mid-1950s, when some of them descended to the foothills, lived on the hilltops, where many still remain. The geography is Northern Guinea zone characterized by thickets on the hills and "orchard bush" (cultivated land on which useful trees have been retained). Elevation is about 1,200 meters; annual rainfall averages 150 centimeters and falls mainly from April to September, with a peak in July–August. The average temperature in the early dry season (December–January), when the northern wind blows, is 20.5° C; it rises to 25° C in March–April, the hottest months, and goes down again in the wet season.

Demography. The Rukuba number around 12,000 people who occupy a territory of about 440 square kilometers with a population density of nearly 27 people per square kilometer. Most of the Rukuba are farmers, and only a few Western-educated civil servants live in Jos township.

Linguistic Affiliation. The Rukuba language is classified in the Niger-Congo Family, Subfamily Benue-Congo, Group Plateau A, Subgroup 4. None of their immediate neighbors understand this language.

History and Cultural Relations

The Rukuba claim to have migrated to their present territory from Ugba, a locality about 64 kilometers northward. Their historical tradition connects them closely with neighboring peoples of different linguistic subgroups, the Jere, the Buji, the Ribina, the Amo and, some say, the Chara. This migration is difficult to date, but the eighteenth century seems the best estimate, although it might have taken place earlier. Linguistically isolated, the Rukuba nevertheless have various formal links of a ritual nature with thirteen neighboring populations that are also small by African standards. In spite of the language barrier, these peoples formally invite representatives of other groups to communal hunting, to initiation ceremonies, to certain funerals, and so on. The British, while searching for tin on the High Plateau, subdued the Rukuba in 1905. Tin extraction by soil washing began in mining camps, providing an opportunity for the local peoples to pay a newly introduced personal tax without migrating away for long periods. This explains the relative conservatism of these Plateau ethnic groups, which met the monetary needs of the British administration by getting hired in mining camps for only a few weeks a year or by growing foodstuffs for the foreign permanent residents in the same mining camps. The town of Jos also offers some opportunities to work without going far away from home.

Settlements

Rukuba villages are generally comprised of a core nucleus densely populated with outlying settlements, which were originally dispersed on rocky eminences around the core nucleus. This pattern slowly changed in the 1950s, when people started migrating to their farms situated in the plains and valleys at the bottom of the rocky outcrops. Village populations range between seventy residents in the smallest ones to more than a thousand in the largest. Manured gardens, often fenced with high euphorbias, are close to the houses. A belt of small fields, usually cultivated by women, surrounds the village; the small fields are less manured, and some remain fallow for several years. Bush farms constitute another field category, sometimes at a distance of several kilometers from the village. People with faraway fields spend several weeks there in the rainy season. Such fields are never manured, except nowadays by an occasional Fulani cattle camp.

Economy

Subsistence and Commercial Activities. The staple crops of the Rukuba are *fonio* (*Digitaria exilis* and *D. iburua*), sorghum, and late millet, the proportion varying from village to village, according to the quality of soils. Eleusine millet and sesame are also grown in far lesser quantities. Several species of yam, sweet potatoes, and cocoyams (*Colocasia*) are important crops. Crop rotation is complicated. The main cereals are grown on bush farms; sorghum is planted first, for a year or two, followed by late millet for a year, and by fonio. The land lies fallow the third and fourth years, but this period may last longer. In manured fields and gardens, everything can be grown according to household needs. The Rukuba also plant peppers, okra, cucurbits, Kaffir potatoes, spinach, red sorrel, beans, climbing beans, groundnuts, Bambara nuts—all told about twenty-five species. Groundnuts were introduced in the 1920s and cassava in the 1950s. The former is mainly a cash crop; however, any of these crops can be sold to feed the permanent population of the urban and mining camps. Every compound has several goats (needed for ritual slaughter), dogs (for hunting), and chickens (for sacrifices); sheep are not widely kept. Some of these animals are also sold. Horses were numerous in the 1920s; every compound owned one stallion for hunting purposes. The prevalence of horses has now drastically diminished. The Rukuba do not keep cattle, nor do they cultivate textile fibers, given that they formerly went entirely naked, except for a raffia penis sheath for the men and two bundles of leaves for the women. Hunting, which is culturally important, does not add significantly to the diet. Only those living along rivers fish; it is an occasional activity with no economic importance. Milk is not consumed, and eggs are almost never eaten.

Industrial Arts. Formerly, the Rukuba were noted iron smelters, but smelting disappeared relatively soon after the arrival of the British. A number of blacksmiths are still operating. Female potters make domestic utensils, which are sometimes sold to neighboring ethnic groups.

Trade. There was a small amount of trade with neighboring peoples. Imports were not necessary, except for salt, which came from Zaria Emirate through the intermediary of adjacent ethnic groups. Markets were unknown until the British introduced them. Eastern Rukuba go directly to the Jos main market to trade but attend the local markets to drink sorghum beer.

Division of Labor. Men and women both perform agricultural work, but the men do the heaviest part of the hoeing. Both sexes cultivate the same plants, but women specialize in groundnuts, Bambara nuts, sweet potatoes, sesame, eleusine millet, and most pulses. Men cut firewood, but women carry it home. All meals, except ritual ones, are prepared by women. Men do all husbandry and hunting. Women fish with small nets; men trap fish. Women do all basketry; men plait sleeping mats and beer filters and craft all leatherwork, such as baby carriers and sheaths for swords and knives. Mortars, pestles, wooden seats, and wooden spoons are carved by part-time specialists, of which there are only few. Blacksmithing, in spite of its high prestige, was—and still is—a part-time occupation. Soothsayers and local medicine men also practice agriculture.

Land Tenure. Land passes from father to son(s), women being excluded from land inheritance because they work on farms allotted to them by their husbands. Patrilineal people tend to remain together at the same location generation after generation; if a man has too many sons, land will be sought from remote patrilateral kin whose family is depleted. Land can also be borrowed on a short- or long-term basis—or even bought, from neighbors who have enough farms.

Kinship

Kin Groups and Descent. Although descent is patrilineal, genealogies are not remembered after three or four generations. Patrilocality is very strong, however, and people are believed to have remained patrilineally grouped since the time of their arrival in the country. Thus, most villages consider themselves ultimately to be agnates and abide by the law of exogamy.

Kinship Terminology. The Rukuba use Hawaiian cousin terminology with bifurcate-merging terms for maternal uncles.

Marriage and Family

Marriage. For the purposes of marriage, the Rukuba population, as a whole, is divided into two exogamous moieties. According to the ideational model, each village may belong to either moiety, and there are approximately the same number of villages in each exogamous moiety. Each village is also exogamous, and every girl from one moiety must, by definition, marry into the other. For premarital relations, however, each village was endogamous; every young girl had, prior to marriage, premarital relations with young men from other patrilines of the same village. No offspring could be borne of such unions; unwanted pregnancies were terminated by abortion. A girl could have premarital relations with only one man at a time, following the payment of a sort of "lover price." The relationship had to last at least six months, but it could continue for a longer period. A girl could have several of these unions in succession before she married out, around the age of 20. This system of premarital relations led, until its termination in the 1950s, to a unique form of preferential marriage: the eldest girl of a set of uterine sisters was betrothed to the son of her mother's last lover. Subsequent sisters were also engaged to boys from their mother's natal village, the whole operation being a delayed exchange: all the daughters of a woman had to be married in their mother's natal village. This practice occurred in conjunction with another type of marriage. As soon as a girl was betrothed to her preferential mate, any man from other villages of the girl's opposite moiety could court her and she could choose one among them to become her first husband. Only 9 percent of the women had their preferential suitor as future husband. The remaining majority married first the man they had selected by free choice. The woman stayed with him for a month or two and was then escorted to the preferential suitor. The stay with him of one month was compulsory, after which the girl, now a spouse, could either remain with him or go back to the first, deserted husband. After a year, a woman could choose to remain with the husband with whom she stayed, to join the husband she previously deserted (preferential or free choice), or to select a new husband from the right moiety. All these marriages remained valid and a woman had the right to return to any of her husbands. Nowadays the woman spends the whole year with her free-choice husband and can remain with him if she likes or marry another husband. The minimal stay with a husband is a year, but a woman can stay as long as she wishes. There is no bride-wealth refund because the woman is still considered married to all her husbands, although she cohabits with only one at a time. In case of contested paternity rights, the child belongs to the husband the woman names as the father. When a woman with one child under 5 years of age moves from one husband to another, the new husband has to take care of the child, who will be sent back to his or her true father after the age of 5 to 6 years. A husband can have several wives living elsewhere, but he can also have several living with him at the same time. The proportion of men having two wives or more living together with him is only 28 percent of married men, the rest having only one. Many husbands remain wifeless while waiting for one of their wives to come back or trying to marry a new one.

Domestic Unit. The typical family household consists of a walled compound of round mud huts. The entrance, which is the kitchen and/or pounding house, is used by all the women of the compound. The owner of the house has his own room; each wife has hers as well, as do the nubile daughters. Married sons establish similar compounds very close to the parental house, one married son remaining very often within the paternal enclosure. Square huts are also to be found, but corrugated iron roofs are exceptional.

Inheritance. Inheritance passes from father to sons and is divided equally. If there are no sons, the next agnate in line—brother or paternal cousin—will inherit the most important property: land, goats, hoes, and debts, if any.

Socialization. Boys undergo a compulsory three-stage initiation following a complex calendar encompassing all the villages in turn. The first stage is normally *kugo,* a ritual that initiates and terminates an entire ten to twelve years' initiation cycle. The second state is *izaru,* the circumcision ceremony that every boy attends before he is 7. Nowadays, however, the actual circumcision is practiced soon after birth. The third state, *aso,* makes the boy ritually adult before he is 12. He is then taught the principal rules regarding marriage and adultery. No initiation pertains to girls, although they play a symbolic role in boys' initiation ceremonies.

Sociopolitical Organization

Social Organization. Each village is divided into patrilineal clans, which have complementary duties at the village level. One clan provides the chief, and another is responsible for both the control of witchcraft and for calling big communal or intertribal hunts. Yet another clan is in charge of the well-being of all the uterine nephews and nieces of the village. Lesser offices such as rainmaker, rain appeaser, or master of the village drum can be the prerogatives of other clan chiefs or are simply vested in houses of clans that already have a more important office. Each clan chief hears intraclan civil disputes; if not successful, the case may be brought to the village chief. Interclan civil disputes are dealt with by the clan chiefs, assisted by the village chief. Criminal cases are investigated by the clan chief or, more often, the village chief.

Political Organization. The Rukuba constitute a federation of villages, each village being a chiefdom. Several villages form a section comprised of villages that ultimately claim to have originated from the section head village. There are five such sections. The section head village has important ritual duties; its chief reckons the dates of all important panethnic rituals. Politically speaking, this chief can arbitrate conflicts between villages of his section if the involved parties ask him to do so. Two head villages have a more prominent ritual role in organizing, in turn, the kugo initiation ritual. Interethnic relations were rather particularistic, some villages or even clans being either "brothers" or enemies of other neighboring ethnic groups.

The Rukuba never acted as a coordinated unit against foreign enemies. After numerous administrative experiments carried out by the British, the Rukuba were finally united in a single district in 1936, and in the early 1950s they elected a single administrative chief, assisted by the village chiefs in council, section chiefs being the more prominent among them.

Social Control. During initiation, rules of proper behavior are taught regarding marriage prohibitions and injunctions, as well as the respect of chiefs. Witchcraft is controlled through meetings attended by clan representatives. Difficult cases were submitted to a panethnic ordeal, which has now lapsed. Civil cases are still settled by clans or village chiefs, but, since 1936, they may as well be brought to the Rukuba Central Court. Petty criminal cases are tried in this court; major ones are sent to the Divisional Court in Jos.

Conflict. Most intraethnic conflicts erupted during communal hunts, over the sharing of game. They were followed by retaliatory raids, but such outbreaks were usually quieted quickly. Interethnic conflicts flared up on the same occasions; there were mechanisms to make a truce, and relations rarely remained strained for long. The Rukuba victoriously repelled attacks from the Zaria Emirate's armies until the colonial era.

Religion and Expressive Culture

Religious Beliefs. The Rukuba believe that the prosperity and the well-being of the land and people rests in the physical person of the village chief, who is a scapegoat. If prosperity fails, or if drought, locust invasions, plagues, defeats in war, or deep dissensions between the villagers occur, the chief is deposed and replaced to remedy the situation. The village chief is a variation of James G. Frazer's "divine king"; he is forced to commit a transgression, which makes him good and bad at the same time. Like any of the other divine kings, his bad part is sacrificed by proxy at regular times and one of his alter egos is also killed in the two prominent ritual villages, the beneficial effect being shared by the other villages as well. An individual's well-being also depends on his "double" residing in his mother's natal village, under the care of a clan chief. The High God is beyond reach, and ancestors play almost no role. No more than 4 to 5 percent of the Rukuba are Christians (Evangelical Church of West Africa), but they constitute the most politically active and "modernist" group. Islam has made no inroad.

Religious Practitioners. The Rukuba have two kinds of local doctors: those curing with herbs and plants, and diviners. No special power is vested in the first type, whereas the second is credited with spiritual powers. The most sought-after diviners, however, come from neighboring tribes, and Rukuba diviners are, conversely, more known across the ethnic border. Some specialize in treating illnesses coming from the maternal side of the patient.

Ceremonies. The most important ceremonies are connected with initiations during which numerous goats are slaughtered. Agricultural rites are not spectacular, although each clan chief has to undertake them. The most secret rituals are those connected with the person of the chief, but most Rukuba men know them. Ritual knowledge can be shared by all men, but women are supposed to know nothing about it.

Arts. There is no art in the Western sense of the word. The Rukuba decorate their village ritual hut, their village sacred pots and drums, and, in one village only, there is a septennial private display of decorated objects for the benefit of people organizing the ritual.

Medicine. Traditional curing goes side by side with other methods of treating disease. Western medicines are eagerly sought from the missionaries and a dispensary that is well attended. Hospitals in the nearby town of Jos are frequently visited, especially by Christians.

Death and Afterlife. Chiefs, clan chiefs, blacksmiths, diviners, and witches reincarnate. Their souls stay in a shooting star, or somewhere else, before reentering a pregnant woman's womb. Other people's souls simply disappear; their influence may remain, temporarily, through their bones or through curses uttered when they were alive. Burial ceremonies and mourning practices are aimed at getting rid of the dead as completely and as soon as possible.

Bibliography

Muller, Jean-Claude (1973). "On Preferential/Prescriptive Marriage and the Function of Kinship Systems: The Rukuba Case (Benue-Plateau State, Nigeria)." *American Anthropologist* 75(5): 1563–1576.

Muller, Jean-Claude (1976a). *Parenté et mariage chez les rukuba (État Benue-Plateau, Nigéria)*. Paris and The Hague: Mouton.

Muller, Jean-Claude (1976b). "Of Souls and Bones: The Living and the Dead among the Rukuba, Benue-Plateau State, Nigeria." *Africa* 46(3): 255–270.

Muller, Jean-Claude (1976c). "Replication, Scission, and Territory among the Rukuba (Nigeria)." *Anthropos* 71:738–767.

Muller, Jean-Claude (1980). *Le roi bouc émissaire: Pouvoir et rituel chez les rukuba du Nigéria central*. Paris: L'Harmattan.

Muller, Jean-Claude (1989). *La calebasse sacrée: Initiations rukuba*. Grenoble and Montreal: La Pensée Sauvage; Presses de l'Université de Montréal.

JEAN-CLAUDE MULLER

Sakalava

ETHNONYMS: Alternative spellings, especially in French: Saclave, Sakalave, Séclave (archaic); on Mayotte (Comoro Islands): Kibushy

Orientation

Identification. The Sakalava inhabit an expansive region of Madagascar; their territory today encompasses nearly all of the west coast of this large Indian Ocean island. "Sakalava" is a compound term meaning "the long valleys" or "rivers." A noun as well as an adjective, it refers both to a specific ethnic group and its affiliated language. Its origin is obscure, although one argument is that Andriamisara, an early southern ruler, settled on the banks of the Sakalava River, which subsequently gave its name to his settlement and followers. "Sakalava," as a collective ethnic term, encompasses a diverse array of communities that are united by their common respect for a host of related royal dynasties. Other important markers of ethnic affiliation include regional dress, such as the waist wrap (*kitamby*) for men and the two-piece body and head wrap (*salovaña* and *kisaly*, respectively) for women; dietary preferences; the observance of local food and behavioral taboos; and dialect. Censuses conducted among the Sakalava during the colonial period and following independence in 1960 have periodically included such groups as the Vezo, who are fishers of southern Madagascar, and the Makoa, people of African slave descent found along the west coast. Sakalava draw sharp distinctions between local "insiders," referred to as *tera-tany* or *tompontany* (meaning "masters of the soil"), and *vahiny* or "guests." Nevertheless, intermarriage with non-Sakalava occurs frequently, involving unions with other Malagasy speakers (such as the Tsimihety), as well as immigrants of foreign origin (including French, Chinese, Indians, Comoreans, and Yemenis). The quintessential mark of Sakalava identity is that one respects, honors, and works for living and dead royalty.

Location. Over the course of several centuries, Madagascar's history has been marked by the formation and expansion of royal kingdoms, and here the Sakalava are no exception. Today the Sakalava form the island's fifth-largest subgroup of Malagasy speakers, who, as a whole, comprise the majority of Madagascar's population. Sakalava are also found on the Comoro Islands, especially on Moyotte, where they are referred to as Kibushy speakers; these are the descendants of Sakalava who followed Andriantsoly, a ruler who fled from western Madagascar to Mayotte in the 1820s when threatened by Merina armies from the central highlands.

The Sakalava of Madagascar (who will be the focus of this article) are organized into a string of kingdoms located along the entire western coast, extending from the south, at the Bay of Augustin near Toliary at 23°35′ S, to as far north as the offshore island of Nosy Be, the Bay of Ampasindava, and the Mahavavy River, all of which lie at approximately 13° S. Sakalava territory is bordered to the south by the island's arid region; to the east by the central highlands; and in the far north by mountainous terrain, where the highest peak is Mount Tsaratanana at 2,876 meters. The Sakalava inhabit a variety of ecological zones: the far north, in particular, is forested; as one moves south, the terrain turns into grassy savanna and then sandy (and, at times, arid) areas, with palm and baobab trees. The Antakarana are the Sakalava's northern neighbors; to the west are the Tsimihety, and to the south is territory occupied by such pastoral groups as the Bara and the Mahafaly.

Within their own territory, the Sakalava draw distinctions between "southern" and "northern" Sakalava, each exhibiting local variations in dialect as well as ritual activities that focus primarily on their respective royal dynasties and associated tombs. Menabe, encompassing the territory surrounding the city of Morondava, is the seat of the southern Sakalava, and also that of the original Maroseraña dynasty, which was founded in the 1600s by the ruler Andriandahifotsy, his classificatory father Andriamisara, and his grandfather Andriamandazoala. In the northwest is Boeny (or Boina), centered around Marovoay near the city of Majunga. Boeny was founded by the ruler Andriamandisoarivo in the early 1700s. All Sakalava dynasties trace their origins to the Maroseraña rulers of the far south, each having moved progressively north following disputes over royal succession. The Bemazava dynasty, based today in the town of Ambanja, is located in the far north and is the youngest of all, having been established in the nineteenth century. Sakalava dynasties are also further categorized as being of one of two dynastic groups: the Zafinibolamena (also abbreviated to Zafin'i'mena and meaning "Grandchildren of Gold"), of Maroseraña origin, and the more recent Zafinibolafotsy (or Zafin'i'fotsy, "Grandchildren of Silver"). Today each is represented throughout Sakalava territory.

Demography. Census information for Madagascar has been collected sporadically throughout the twentieth century. The reliability of census data is hampered by political agendas (such as election preparations) that can affect their outcome; furthermore, data for different ethnic groups are not always available, or may be defined differently from one census to the next. Thus, the label "Sakalava" has at times encompassed the Vezo and Makoa, for example, whereas at other times these groups have been recognized as distinct categories. With these qualifications in mind, the 1987 census recorded that Sakalava comprised 5.8 percent of Madagascar's total population of approximately 9.9 million (or of 12.6 million in 1992).

Linguistic Affiliation. Sakalava is a dialect of Malagasy, the dominant language of Madagascar. As a Western Austronesian language, Malagasy reveals the cultural and historical roots of the Malagasy people as a whole, who trace their origins in part to southeast Asia, Melanesia, and Austronesia. Linguistically, the Sakalava dialect reflects the impact of worldwide trade networks, with loanwords drawn from Arabic, kiSwahili, numerous Bantu languages, and, mostly recently, French. There is also a smattering of loanwords from Portuguese, German, English, and several Chinese and Indian languages. When compared to Merina, the island's dominant dialect (which is spoken in the central highlands), Sakalava offers striking differences in pronunciation, vocabulary, and grammar. Among the most significant of these is the nasal ñ sound (which approximates the "ng" in "sing") and a preference for the active over the passive voice. In bureaucratic and educational settings, Sakalava speakers also make use of Madagascar's two official languages: French and Official Malagasy (*malagasy officiel*).

History and Cultural Relations

The earliest references to Sakalava kingdoms appear in the writings of traders, most notably Portuguese sailors, as well as the prolific Jesuit Father Luis Mariano, all of whom either visited or settled on Madagascar's coast in the early 1600s. For centuries, the Sakalava have actively plied trade routes that have extended to the Persian Gulf, India, and the Far East; the African continent (especially the north, along the east coast, and the central interior); neighboring islands such as Mauritius and Réunion; and the Americas. Sakalava ports supplied oceangoing merchants with such foods as beef, fruit, and rice; Sakalava were also actively engaged as both buyers and suppliers of spices and slaves. Goods acquired from abroad included guns, ammunition, rum, and European manufactured items. Sakalava hegemony in the arena of Indian Ocean trade was particularly pronounced during the seventeenth and eighteenth centuries.

Early European contact in the 1600s involved trade as well as relatively unsuccessful missionary attempts by Portuguese and French Catholic fathers. Over a century later, French priests (as well as planters) had greater success in the northwest, especially on the offshore island of Nosy Be. Throughout the nineteenth century, Sakalava formed alliances with the French and with sultans of Zanzibar and Muscat as they sought to fend off invasions by the Merina ruler Radama I (r. 1810–1828), who sought to unite the entire island under his rule. Although Radama I took a daughter of a Maroseraña ruler as a wife, the Sakalava of the northwest proved difficult to conquer. In the late nineteenth century, the Sakalava found themselves subjugated by their former allies: under the leadership of General J. S. Gallieni, the French conquered the Merina kingdom and, subsequently, the rest of the island. In 1886 Madagascar was declared a colony of France, and remained so until independence in 1960. Sakalava have nevertheless guarded their royal traditions, even when faced with censure, imprisonment, and exile under French rule; when necessary, royal activities were conducted clandestinely. In the decades following independence, the Sakalava have continued to emphasize their political alienation—and independence—from the highland Merina and Betsileo, describing themselves as *côtiers*, or "coastal dwellers," whose concerns and customs (*fomba*) vary radically from those that characterize the inhabitants of the island's metropole of Antananarivo.

Settlements

The size of Sakalava communities ranges from small-scale homesteads or villages of perhaps only a dozen to several hundred inhabitants, to large towns and cities (e.g., Morondava, Majunga, Analalava, Ambanja, and the island of Nosy Be). Urbanization is not a new phenomenon: Portuguese accounts from the 1600s describe the southern town of Sadia as having as many as 10,000 inhabitants. Nevertheless, the more recent economic demands of a colonial administration certainly encouraged rapid urbanization in numerous locations.

Sakalava settlements, often regardless of size, follow common patterns. Dwellings are typically lined up along a main path or road in parallel formation, reflecting an older pattern found throughout Madagascar, whereby houses are oriented according to compass directions (northeast being a sacred and thus auspicious point of reference). A common design is a square structure with a peaked roof, elevated a foot or two off the ground. Houses are built of ravinala palm or other locally available plant materials, corrugated tin, or concrete or earthen bricks. Houses generally have one or two rooms, each of which will then have a separate door leading out onto a small veranda where perhaps up to half a dozen people may sit comfortably under the roof's shade during the hotter afternoon hours. Such houses may have windows as well, made with hinged wooden shutters that can be locked from the inside. There may also be granaries, which are higher off the ground, or shaded platforms under which people sit, work, visit, or hold ceremonies. Cooking is generally done outdoors over a wood or charcoal fire on a three-stone hearth, a three-legged iron support, or a small brazier.

In villages, the occupants of any given household are usually expanded or extended family; household membership can vary radically from day to day in response to the demands of labor migration and child fostering and because of short- and long-term visits from kin. In precolonial times, royal households were often polygynous. Furthermore, village affiliation, especially in the past, was generally clan based.

Economy

Subsistence and Commercial Activities. Sakalava territory is vast, encompassing four diverse ecological zones: the west coast and the adjoining sea, riverine areas, savanna pasturelands, and forests. The local ecology shapes a highly diversified subsistence economy. Sakalava are avid fishers, who use outrigger canoes of the same design as those used by proto-Malagasy when they made their voyages across the Indian Ocean. Canoes are propelled using paddles; some also deploy a rectangular sail when there are winds. Sakalava consume fish of all sizes as well as shellfish and turtles; since about the 1970s, fishing for sea cucumbers for Asian markets abroad has become a highly lucrative commercial activity. Sakalava also catch freshwater fish; settlements are found along all major rivers and many lakes in western Madagascar. Seafood is prepared in a variety of ways: cooked in stews, fried, smoked, or salted. Hunting and occasional gathering of wild foods further supplement local diets. Crickets and other insects, which are available seasonally, are rich sources of protein, as are hunted animals, including birds, fruit bats, lemurs, and wild boars. Wild honey is also gathered.

When the French arrived in northern Madagascar, they were struck by the quality and quantity of cattle raised in the region. Although herd sizes diminished during the colonial period, Sakalava continue to raise humpbacked zebu cattle for meat and for ceremonial purposes and to pull two-wheeled wooden carts. Cattle were owned collectively by clan members, and large herds were a mark of wealth and prestige. Within the last generation or two, private ownership of cattle has become more common. Cattle of particular colors and markings continue to be reserved exclusively for royal herds or ceremonial use. Other animals raised for food consumption include goats, chickens, guinea hens, ducks, geese, and turkeys. Meat and eggs are consumed sporadically.

Sakalava are also horticulturists who practice primarily swidden agriculture. Local diets are supplemented by what is available during the two primary seasons: the wet (November to April) and dry (May to October). The two main staples of the Sakalava diet are rice (dry and paddy, depending on the terrain) and, especially in the dry regions of the south, manioc. Accounts from the early 1600s also report millet as a staple. In some regions, Sakalava cook with coconut milk, which is used either as an ingredient in stews or is added to rice as it cooks. Vegetables consumed include an assortment of leafy greens that are boiled in a copious amount of water. Other fruits and vegetables vary according to the terrain, temperature, and fertility of the soil: these include mangoes, green and sweet bananas, papayas, oranges, cashews, maize, beans, and other garden vegetables. Participation in cash cropping varies considerably from one region to another. The city of Majunga, for example, is a major source for cashews, whereas, in the north, cocoa, coffee, and, to a lesser extent, spices (such as vanilla, pepper, and cinnamon) are grown on plots ranging from large-scale private and state-owned plantations to the smallest of village and individual gardens. Madagascar also has a copious pharmacopoeia of wild and domestic plants from which teas and medicines are derived.

Arts and Industrial Arts. Knowledge of indigenous textile arts has declined considerably within the last generation or two; earlier in the twentieth century, Sakalava textiles exhibited complex weaving techniques. Single *ikat* designs, with colors derived from plant dyes, were woven in cotton and raffia on a horizontal loom with a fixed heddle. Today mats and storage containers are plaited by hand into a basket-weave design from palm and other plant leaves. This, like weaving, is the occupation of women. Fishing nets, on the other hand, can be made by either men or women, depending on the region. Men are responsible for boat building, woodworking, and carpentry, depending on local economic needs; items produced include ox carts and outrigger canoes as well as furniture made of palasander, ebony, and other tropical woods. Today embroidery, lacework, and *riche-lieu* cutout work decorate even the most modest homes and provide supplementary income for many women. Both men and women are actively engaged as tailors and seamstresses, making use of electric and hand-driven sewing machines.

Trade. From the tenth century onward, accounts written by Muslim traders describe the Sakalava as being active participants in Indian Ocean commerce. From the fifteenth through the nineteenth centuries, Sakalava ports were central to the success of the slave trade that linked Madagascar to the African continent, the Middle East, Europe, Asia, and the Americas. As the British and French developed sugarcane plantations on Mauritius and Réunion, they created a large-scale and regular demand for slaves; by the eighteenth century, Sakalava were among the more important slave traders for the region. Sakalava themselves raided East African ports and the Comoro Islands for captives, although most slaves were brought to Madagascar by Muslim traders sailing from Kilwa, Zanzibar, and the coast of what is now Mozambique. These captives were exchanged for cattle and rice, supplies that were generally taken to Mauritius and Réunion to feed the inhabitants there. Slaves purchased by the Sakalava were generally resold for guns, ammunition, or rum. Sakalava kept slaves of their own to work, for example, in the royal rice fields; slaves were also sold to neighboring Malagasy groups or were marched across Madagascar and resold from eastern ports. Defiance of local and international decrees that outlawed slavery was rampant throughout the nineteenth century: Sakalava cooperated with Muslim and European traders in clandestine slaving activities, and the trade continued to flourish well into the 1870s (and, along the northwest coast, as late as 1900). In Sakalava territory, the term "Makoa" (derived from the ethnic label "Makua" in Mozambique) denotes slave ancestry, and today it is applied to people whom Sakalava assume to be of "African" origin. Some continue to work for royalty as their ancestors once did, set off as a loosely defined group of royal laborers.

Small-scale commerce is also very much a part of Sakalava economic activity today. Even the smallest villages often have a local *epicerie*, where such essential items as kerosene, salt, sugar, cooking oil, soap, and matches are sold. Larger stores sell items varying from freshly baked cakes to fabrics and brightly colored body wraps manufactured in Madagascar and abroad. Marketing activities are widespread throughout Sakalava territory. Larger towns and cities have daily markets; there are also regional rotating markets that occur in specific villages or towns on a weekly basis. Both Sakalava men and women engage in market activities, selling goods they themselves have produced or that they have either bought at a larger market in the region or in the nation's capital of Antananarivo. Individual sellers may also develop personal networks, selling items to favored clients in the privacy of one another's homes. Many children become involved in commerce at an early age, assisting adults with clients, running errands, or setting up their own small market or roadside stands; their clients include adults as well as other children. Commercial specialization by age and gender is quickly evident in any large market: for example, young and middle-aged women sell dried fish; grandmothers specialize in woven mats and leafy green vegetables; and older men sell a host of medicinal herbs.

Division of Labor. For Sakalava, "to labor" or "work" (*miasa*) is an action that includes subsistence activities, household chores, ritual affairs, and national development. The most essential agricultural activity is rice farming: men, women, and children are involved at all stages of its production. Until the late twentieth century, work was taboo on Tuesday (Talata), providing a respite from the arduous work in the rice fields. Among fishing communities, the division of labor along gender and age lines varies radically from one region to another: in some areas, only men and boys fish; in others, men and women of all ages as well as children fish. Men and boys hunt, using rifles, slingshots, and hunting dogs. Women and children are most often responsible for water retrieval and cooking. Daily housework is shared by all; chores are often divided between boys and girls. Girls, however, often do the more time-consuming work, such as polishing floors, washing dishes, and doing the laundry.

As noted, the act of honoring royalty is a central defining principle of Sakalava identity. Such loyalty is demonstrated by periodically performing royal work that honors both living and dead rulers. Among the most important ceremonies is the "royal bath" (called *fitampoha* in Menabe and *fanompoa-be* in Boeny), the annual purification of a dynasty's sacred relics (and sometimes the reigning ruler). Other forms of royal work include entombing royalty, building a new royal residence, celebrating royal circumcisions, and instating new rulers. The division of labor for royal work was determined by birthright, each clan having its particular duties. Although clan-based labor is being forgotten in many areas, a special caste, called the Sambarivo, continues to be actively involved in royal work. Sambarivo live in special villages; both men and women help orchestrate royal events and perform a multitude of duties during royal ceremonies.

Colonialism has had a major impact on the division of labor throughout Madagascar. Household, head, and cattle taxes drove Sakalava men in particular into wage labor and cash cropping early in the twentieth century. A French bureaucratic system that favored the nuclear family has given rise to a patriarchal bias within many Sakalava households. Adolescent boys and men were affected in other ways as well: they were conscripted into the army, police, and civil service. Men, more so than women, were saddled with the much-despised annual labor quotas that were designed to build up the colony's infrastructure. In the plantation areas of the north, Sakalava refused to work on plantations, and Malagasy from other areas were brought in to work the fields. The French instituted primary schooling throughout much of Sakalava territory; boys, in particular, however, received more advanced training at centers for teachers and civil servants. In postindependence Madagascar, both Sakalava men and women have made their way into these professions as well as medicine, government, and other high-status work.

Land Tenure and Inheritance. Sakalava typically practice virilocality, and inheritance patterns exhibit a patrilineal bias; hence, land most often passes from fathers to one or more of their sons. Nevertheless, women often inherit land from their brothers, fathers, and maternal kin, exhibiting the bilineal (or, more recently, bilateral) quality of Sakalava commoner kinship. The point at which men and women inherit land can best be understood by examining the life cycle: young married men (particularly those who do not relocate or migrate out) generally assume the care of their aging parents' fields, whereas older women (who are often widows) will return to their natal villages upon inheriting fields, homesteads, or houses from maternal or paternal kin. Women also buy land for their personal use. In regions where the soil is fertile and large-scale plantations exist, it is essential that small-scale peasant farmers have land deeds in their possession. Although the concept is not as strongly held as it was prior to the colonial period, land continues to be considered collectively owned as well: the Sakalava of a given region are the rightful tera-tany or tompontany, the "masters of the soil," of a region the boundaries of which coincide with those of the local kingdom.

Kinship

Kin Groups and Descent. At the time of French conquest, Sakalava were organized into a loosely defined caste system composed of royalty, commoners, royal workers (Sambarivo), and slaves. Royal descent assumes the form of truncated patrilineages that preserve primarily the names of former rulers. Today royalty maintain with care written records of genealogies that extend back several centuries.

Several principles guide commoner kinship, although they are being forgotten in some areas, particularly where there is pronounced urbanization and the in-migration of non-Sakalava. The first is the village-based clan (*firazaña* or *firazanana*), the membership of which is often sentimental. That is, individual affiliation depends upon choices made in response to where one has spent much of one's life. Clans are organized hierarchically in reference to their royal-work responsibilities, their names reflecting as well the nature of such work. Commoner kinship tends to be bilineally conceived. The second guiding principle of Sakalava commoner affiliation is the *tariky*, or kindred, composed of an individual's matri- and patrikin. Again, personal residence patterns typically determine tariky affiliation. A third principle distinguishes paternal and maternal kin, respectively, as the "children of men" (*zanakan'lahy*) and the "children of women" (*zanakan'vavy*); these are particularly important categories of reference in ritual settings because both must be represented at circumcisions and other important rites to be performed. Sakalava also distinguish the children "of one belly" (*kibo araiky*) from others because they are united by their common links to maternal kin. In the past, this final principle placed restrictions on the children of sisters and excluded fostered and adopted children from full participation in their adoptive clan's royal-work activities.

Kinship Terminology. Sakalava use classificatory kinship terminology. As with other Malagasy groups, kinship terms distinguish between the age and gender of the speaker relative to other kin. Thus, for a male Ego, "brother" is *rahalahy* and "sister" is *anabavy*. For a female ego, "brother" is *anadahy* and "sister" is *rahavavy*. *Zoky* serves as an additional term of reference and address for older siblings, *zandry* for younger ones. Parallel and cross cousins are labeled and addressed as siblings. Ego's parents' siblings are also differentiated by age and sex. Thus, the terms used for the father's kin are: *baba* (father), *bababe* ("big father," or father's older brother), *babakely/babahely* ("little father," or father's younger brother), and *angovavy* (father's sister). For the mother's kin: *nindry* or *mama* (mother), *nindrihely/mamahely* ("little mother," or mother's older sister), and *zama* (mother's brother). The spouse of one's angovavy is referred to as zama (and vice versa); the spouses of Ego's parents' same-sex siblings are addressed as nindry and baba. Ego's spouse's siblings are *rañao;* and, in turn, their spouses are referred to structurally as Ego's siblings. The relationship with one's rañao is restrained. A joking relationship exists between agnates of the opposite sex; for a female Ego, this individual is called the *rokilahy;* for a male Ego, the *rokivavy*. The classificatory term for "child" is *zanaka*, although the children of Ego's opposite sex sibling are referred to *as asidy*. The classificatory term for "grandchild" is *zafy*. As a result of the impact of colonialism, in some regions these kin terms have been replaced by others, of French origin.

Fictive kinship is also common, the most elaborate form being *fatridra*, a ritual that links nonkin as blood brothers and blood sisters (between men and women as well as between the sexes).

Marriage and Family

Marriage. Indigenous marriage patterns reflect differences between individuals of royal and nonroyal descent. A generation or two ago, royalty exhibited a preference for caste endogamy; some marriages, deemed incestuous, are recorded as occurring between classificatory siblings who shared parents that were kibo araiky. Although outlawed by the French, royal polygyny is still practiced in some areas. The marriages of Sakalava rulers often operate as forms of political alliance.

A generation ago, commoner marriages exhibited a pattern of clan endogamy: particular clans were grouped hierarchically as appropriate marriage partners, based on the royal services they performed. Endogamous unions could occur if purification rituals were performed. Virilocality continues to be the norm for commoners; the derogatory term *jaloky* is used to describe a man who takes up residence with his wife's kin and farms her father's fields. Only high-status commoner groups practiced uxorilocality.

Sambarivo continue to practice endogamy as well as virilocality. Until slavery was outlawed at the turn of the twentieth century, slave marriages were endogamous. Although slave origin continues to be an important marker of low status in other regions of Madagascar, this factor is not as relevant in Sakalava territory: the label "Makoa" more closely resembles an ethnic rather than a caste distinction.

Today Sakalava marriage is a flexible institution, whereby one may have a series of partners over the course of one's lifetime. Married men and women also take lovers. Literature by Christian authors in particular identifies such behavior as a sign of sexual laxity that has sprung from Western contact, an opinion that runs contrary to the evidence found in historic documents. Most often, cohabitation signifies marriage, its permanence confirmed by the subsequent births of healthy children. In the past, bride-price was paid in the form of cattle. Some Sakalava also opt for Muslim or Catholic weddings, or they obtain a marriage license through the state. When marriages are troubled, typically it is the wife who leaves her husband and returns—with or without her children—to her parents, hoping to be cared for by her mother and protected by her father. Ideally, parents in such circumstances serve as advocates for the wronged wife, and the husband may be required to pay stiff penalties (in the past, in the form of cattle) to win his wife back. A father, however, may insist that his daughter return to her husband, and, if so, she has little recourse but to obey.

Domestic Unit. A marriage blessing heard throughout Madagascar is "may you have seven sons and seven daughters." A generation ago, peasant households of this size were not uncommon; today, however, one of this size would struggle to survive. Sakalava households assume a variety of forms, the most common being the nuclear family, extended family, and female-headed household. Household membership size is extremely flexible, particularly where children are involved. Short- and long-term fostering is common: children sometimes move on a daily basis among the houses of their parents, parents' siblings, and grandparents. A woman may bear and give a child to a sister who is having difficulty conceiving; one or more children may be sent to assist grandparents in the fields; and either boys or girls may be offered to siblings who require assistance in commercial activities. If the siblings live in a town, they may take in the children of village kin so that they may continue their schooling. Single and married adults likewise move in and out of different households, especially if they are involved in labor migration or commerce. The rice-harvest season leads to the migration back and forth of individuals or even entire households from their permanent dwellings to temporary structures near their fields, if they are more than a few kilometers away. Sakalava prefer to live near kin (*havaña*), which is thought to ensure social and economic security. In both towns and villages, a house occupied by aging parents will be surrounded by separate dwellings, which are occupied most often by married sons with children. If a daughter lives close by, she will try to visit on a regular basis, and she will send her own children to visit, acquire agricultural produce, and provide her parents short-term labor in the home or in the fields.

Socialization. Many persons are actively involved in the socialization of children. Infants remain in close proximity to their mothers throughout the first year of their lives. They are often breast-fed for two years or so, with solid foods being introduced when their first teeth appear. The ingestion of rice is an important first meal. Fathers play an active role on a daily basis in caring for children, as well as teaching them proper behavior; they return an infant to its mother when it needs to breast-feed. Even men who do not cook often assume the responsibility of feeding solid food to toddlers. Children learn at an early age (before they are 10 years old) how to care for their younger siblings, and, by the time they can walk and talk, they are allowed to roam freely with their playmates. By this age, they are also assigned household tasks, and they run errands for adults. As boys and girls grow older, their duties shift: girls assist female kin in food preparation; boys hunt or fish with older male kin. Boys and girls are equally likely to be sent to the market or local epicerie to buy food and other supplies or to the well to fetch water. Although both are assigned daily domestic chores, in towns, girls are more likely to be hired out to do part-time housework or child care, assisting households where the parents work and the children are in school full-time.

Several rites of passage mark the progress of a child's life. During a forty-day postpartum period, a Sakalava mother and her child are secluded. Throughout this time, the mother and infant must be bathed several times a day with either warm or cold water, depending on whether the mother follows "hot" (*mifana* or *mafana*) or "cold" (*ranginalo*) restrictions. The day that the child emerges is one of celebration: it is coddled and played with by all who come to visit. The eating of the first mouthful of rice and the first hair cutting are also important events in an infant's life. Circumcision is an important ceremony for boys; preferably, it is performed during the cooler months of the year (June to August). A healthy child is generally circumcised at about the age of 5, although some boys may wait until they are 10 or older. If a child is a member of a Muslim household, the ceremony will reflect this affiliation. Circumcision celebrations are more elaborate for royal children than those for commoners: they involve special public dances, such as the *rebiky*, and spirit mediums will be invited so that the royal ancestors (*tromba*) can give their blessing. There is no equivalent rite of passage for girls. Other ceremonies that mark the progress of a child's life may include baptism and first communion, if the family is Christian. To mark changes in status, an individual's name may change throughout the course of his or her life: children often are not named until after the postpartum period, and, once they are baptized, they may take on another name.

Marriage is another important transition in an individual's life, although it is the birth of the first child that truly marks the passage to adult status and that often cements the relationship between two adults. Upon the birth of the first child, parents change their names and assume teknonyms, such as "Maman'i'Soa" and "Baban'i'Soa" ("Mother" and "Father" "of Soa"). They bear these names until their own children are adults and have offspring. If this child should die, the parents are quickly assigned another name, either taking the name of another child or reverting to nicknames or terms that designate that they are the aunt or uncle of a sibling's child. Once adults attain elder status (most often marked by the birth of grandchildren), their names change again, either to a name they had when young, or to a nickname that makes note of their abilities, temperament, or physical appearance. This name will often be preceded by the honorary "Mama" or "Baba" (without the possessive i). Elders are also typically addressed by kin and nonkin alike by the honorary forms "Dady" and "Dadilahy," or "Grandmother" and "Grandfather."

Special naming rules apply to rulers. At the onset of his or her reign, a ruler is given a new name; when the ruler dies, this name becomes taboo and is replaced with a praise name (*fitahina*) that makes note of events or achievements during the ruler's lifetime. This name is usually preceded with the prefix *Andrian-* or the variant *Ndram-*, meaning "royalty," and ends with the suffix *-arivo*, meaning "thousands" or "many." Thus, Andriamandentarivo means "the king who slit the throats of many," whereas Andriamarofalinarivo is "the king who has many taboos." Praise names are also used when addressing the tromba spirits of dead Sakalava royalty.

Sociopolitical Organization

Social Organization. Sakalava are organized into clans, each with separate duties that they perform periodically for royalty. Sakalava social organization is hierarchical, consisting of royalty (*ampanjaka*); the "people" (*vahoaka*) or "commoners" (*vohitry*), who may also simply be called "Sakalava"; those who serve royalty at ceremonial occasions (most notably the Sambarivo); and slaves (*andevo*), many of whom are of more recent African descent (such as the Makoa). Although Sambarivo status is low with respect to the state hierarchy, they are considered to be the closest to royalty because of the nature of their work.

Political Organization. There are few steadfast rules that govern royal succession: although a first son might be preferred by a living ruler as his successor, Sakalava dynasties reveal a history of disputes over succession. A ruler's successor is as likely to be the son of a first or later wife, the child of a sibling, or, at least since colonial times, either male or female. New dynasties are typically established in response to dissent over succession.

Political leadership is a complex process in any Sakalava kingdom: the ruler, or *ampanjakabe*, is the head of the state, but he or she cannot work successfully without the assistance of a host of advisers. Among these are the *manatany*, an older man appointed as the ruler's primary counselor and spokesman; the *fahatelo*, or "third" in command; and a collection of other male elders, composed of the hereditary *rañitry* and nonheredity *rangahy*. Although women do not serve as royal advisers, they occupy other primary roles in royal ritual contexts. Historical accounts of several rulers also identify the diviner-herbalist (*moasy*) as an essential adviser; some who held this office even appear to have become rulers themselves. One may not address a ruler except through these advisers. They serve as interpreters, sitting beside the ruler when he or she receives visitors. Male and female royalty are also actively involved in counseling and directing a ruler's affairs. The amount of influence they wield depends upon the temperament and political abilities of the ruler. No major decisions can be made without first consulting—and receiving the blessing of—the most powerful of the tromba, or spirits of royal dead, who are the ruler's ancestors and, thus, his or her grandparents (*dadibe*). These spirits possess mediums, who live full-time at the royal tombs. Throughout Sakalava territory the French sought to undermine royal power; as a result, possession and other royal activities were often conducted in secret. Royal power continues to hold sway in much of western Madagascar today.

Social Control. Rulers serve as judges in major disputes; in daily affairs, elders as well as village chiefs (a position created under the French colonial administration) may hear cases and pass judgments. Serious crimes—such as theft, assault, and murder—as well as land disputes and child-support cases are handled by the court of the local county seat (Fivondronana). Social ostracism, gossip, and, in extreme cases, accusations of the use of harmful magic (*fanafody raty*) are effective methods of social control. In response, the accused party is forced to change his or her behavior; otherwise, there may be no other recourse than to move away and settle elsewhere. The latter is a serious decision, however, given that it often requires moving away from close kin.

Conflict. Sakalava dynastic power is thought to have originated in what is now Mahafaly territory, in southern Madagascar. The first "Sakalava" were those who willingly submitted themselves to (i.e., were most likely conquered by) the earliest Maroseraña rulers. At the time of European contact, the Sakalava were considered fierce warriors, a reputation that kept early French missionaries and planters out of much of their territory. Disputes over royal succession often led to armed conflict, a fact that is recorded ritually in the rebiky dance (see "Religious Beliefs"). The wars against the Merina also figure prominently in the historical memory of Sakalava. In the early nineteenth century the Merina ruler Radama I sought to conquer and, subsequently, unify the entire island into one kingdom. His efforts proved futile, however, throughout much of Sakalava territory. The memories of related events are preserved in the tales surrounding several Zafin'i'fotsy tromba spirits who committed suicide by drowning rather than submit to Merina rule. Hostility toward Merina remains pronounced, and, in some ceremonial contexts, taboos (*fady*) exist that prevent Merina participation.

Religion and Expressive Culture

Religious Beliefs. Religious practices and beliefs are closely linked to royal affairs. Today the term "tromba" is used throughout Madagascar to describe a host of forms of spirit possession; strictly speaking, however, it is a Sakalava term. At the heart of Sakalava religion are the royal ancestors, or tromba, who are the spirits of dead royalty. Tromba spirits are arranged hierarchically into generations that correspond to dynastic lineages of the northern and southern Sakalava. They are then further differentiated by the two broad categories, the Zafin'i'mena and Zafin'i'fotsy. When mediums are possessed by tromba spirits, they don clothing that is indicative of their rank, lineage, and the time period in which they reigned or lived. The oldest and most powerful of these spirits possess select mediums (called *saha*), commoners who are usually single women living full-time in villages located next to royal tombs (*mahabo*). These spirits are the *dady*, and they guide living rulers in all major decisions that affect the kingdom as a whole.

Other less powerful and younger spirits are a pervasive force in the everyday lives of commoners living in villages and towns. A given spirit may have many mediums, but can only be present in one medium at any one time. Women constitute the majority of mediums for these lesser tromba spirits, although men can be possessed as well. Other possessing spirits include *tsiñy* (nature spirits that are associated with sacred trees) and *kalanoro* (small, impish forest spirits). There are also numerous kinds of malevolent spirits that cause misery and suffering. These go by a host of names, including *jiny, Njarinintsy, troma hely* (or "little tromba"), *bilo*, and *kokolampo*.

Expressive culture takes form in drumming, song, and dance, all of which are essential components of royal celebrations. Specialized drums, called *hazolahy*, are played when royalty are present, particularly at such ritual events as circumcisions, during the instatement of a new ruler, or at the village of the royal tombs on days when royal work is performed. Men are the exclusive players of these drums. Dances reserved for royal festivities are performed to the accompaniment of the hazolahy, the most frequent being the graceful and slow-paced rebiky (which depicts battles among rival dynastic branches) and, far less often, the animated *maganja*, which is said to be of more recent African origin.

Many Sakalava are simultaneously followers of other faiths. Catholicism has made significant inroads into Sakalava communities. It is not uncommon to find women who are spirit mediums during the week attending Mass on Sunday. Royalty, especially in the north, are more likely to be Muslim, their forebears having been converted to Islam in the nineteenth century as they sought to win allies against the French. Sakalava royal tombs also bear evidence of Islamic influence: they are often decorated with stars and crescent moons.

Religious Practitioners. Religious practitioners fall into several categories. Among the most common are those whose religious duties overlap with (and are often indistinguishable from) those of practitioners of the healing arts. Important healers include mediums for tromba, *tsiñy*, and kalanoro spirits, the first category being the most widespread today. Other healers include moasy, who are particularly skilled in the use of local pharmacopoeias, and *mpisikidy*, or diviners. An individual who uses magic (*fanafody*) to harm others is considered dangerous and is labeled a "witch" or "sorcerer" (*mpamosavy*). Other religious practitioners include those individuals who serve royalty throughout the course of their lifetimes. These include the Sambarivo, as well as male and female tomb guardians (*antimahabo*), who oversee the care of royal tombs.

Ceremonies. Sakalava ceremonies are guided by auspicious and inauspicious or taboo (fady) days of the week, months of the year, and phases of the moon. For example, Friday (Zoma) is the most auspicious time to perform a royal ceremony; restrictions on other days and on certain months depend on the regular flow of activities that occur at various locations where royal tombs are found. Possession ceremonies, as well as all other royal events, can only take place during the phases of an ascension to full moon. For example, if a ruler dies during the phase of no moon, his or her body can not be moved to the tombs until the moon enters the new phase. In general, Sakalava describe royal practices as "difficult" (*sarotra ny fomba ny ampanjaka*) because of the complex set of taboos associated with royal events. Thus, the observance of royal ritual rules is a sign of love for and devotion to the ruler. Spirit mediums, diviners (mpisikidy), and healers such as moasy also often play an active part in determining the appropriate time and location for a ceremony.

Much of Sakalava ritual life is complementary along gender lines; many ceremonies can not be performed unless both men and women participate. Circumcisions, for example, require the participation of the zanakan'lahy and zanakan'vavy (represented by the boy's mother and mother's brother) and both matri- and patrikin, represented by the boy's mother and father.

Various ritual items figure prominently in Sakalava ceremonies. As noted, the hazolahy drums appear at royal festivities; other sacred items that symbolize sacred power and that are employed for purification and healing purposes include gold (*vola mena*) and silver (*vola fotsy*) and, most often, the *tsanganolo* (an archaic French coin), precious metals that symbolize the two major dynastic categories of "Gold" and "Silver." Other items include honey mead (*tô mainty*) and rum (*toaka*).

Medicine. Madagascar has a rich pharmacopoeia of plant and animal products acquired from the land and sea. These medicines are applied to the skin, boiled to make medicinal teas, mixed into bath water, or added to amulets. Both men and women—particularly elders—are well versed in the use of many plants that can be used to treat such common ailments as headaches, fatigue, and malaria. More difficult or persistent ailments are handled by a variety of healers whose knowledge is rooted in Sakalava religious practice (see "Religious Practitioners"). They draw from the power of ancestors and other spirits to diagnose and heal as they simultaneously apply plant remedies. Sakalava turn as well to cosmopolitan clinical medicine at state and privately run hospitals and/or to healers associated with Islam or Christianity. These sorts of decisions are dependent on the forms of health care available, the perceived etiology of the illness, and personal choice. Dream interpretation is also a specialization of numerous categories of healers.

Death and Afterlife. Sakalava do not practice the *famadihana*, or reburial ceremony, which characterizes Betsileo and Merina cultures of the central highlands. Another factor that separates Sakalava from other Malagasy speakers is that personal ancestors do not figure prominently in the lives of commoners; rather, royal ancestors are the focus for collective identity. Tales of cultural origin likewise focus on royal events. The Zanahary created the world and human society, but they are remote deities who rarely participate in daily human affairs (although they must be honored at the opening of any ceremony). Tromba spirits are far more prominent in thoughts of the afterlife. Descriptions of death focus on the discomfort of tombs, which *troma* spirits describe as cold and lonely. It is for this reason that these spirits appear regularly in mediums—they wish to continue to participate in the daily affairs of the living.

As with all Malagasy, it is essential that the bodies of Sakalava be entombed properly and in their rightful place. Commoners are entombed with the kin (havaña) with whom they had the strongest sentimental ties. Thus, an adult is as likely to be entombed with one or both parents as with a spouse. Commoners' tombs are simple structures generally void of decoration, and they can be found in the forest, in rock grottos by the sea, or in Catholic or Muslim cemeteries. A body that is lost and thus unable to be placed in the tomb is a terrifying image; it means that the person's ties to kin have been severed. These individuals become *lolo*, troubled spirits that haunt the locations where they died, causing sickness, accidents, and deaths among those who cross their paths. The dead may also appear in the dreams of close relatives in order to let them know that they are troubled and are in need of care. In the past, some individuals, including those who had committed serious crimes (such as murder) or who suffered from leprosy or serious physical disfigurement, were not entombed but left in taboo areas.

Royal funerals are elaborate and may extend over a period of several months or even years before being completed. A specialized vocabulary and body of taboos (fady) surround all royal rituals, and this is especially pronounced in the context of royal funerals. For example, rulers do not die, as do commoners; rather, the verb *mihilaña* ("to turn around," or do an about face) is used. It is forbidden for a ruler's body to enter the royal residence: if a ruler dies in the palace it is forever polluted and cannot be inhabited by future rulers. Throughout the funerary period, Sakalava (royal and commoner alike) may not bathe, comb their hair, or wear shoes, and they must wear Sakalava body wraps. The ruler's body is taken to a special location and placed in a temporary structure, where it is attended by different categories of Sambarivo, each with particular duties to perform. The body is allowed to rot away, the effluvia collected with care in special earthenware pots and discarded at night in a sacred location. Relics—including occiput bone and patellae, teeth, hair, and nails—are retained for future ceremonial occasions, and the remains are placed in a temporary stone structure within the wall that surrounds the royal tombs. Eventually, a permanent structure is built to house the remains of this particular ruler. Once the remains have been placed within the tomb walls, the formal public discussion and debate may begin regarding the instatement of a successor.

Bibliography

Baré, Jean-François (1980). *Sable Rouge: Une monarchie du nord-ouest malgache dans l'histoire*. Paris: Éditions l'Harmattan.

Bissoondoyal, U., and S. B. Servansing, eds. (1989). *Slavery in South West Indian Ocean* [sic]. Moka (Mauritius): Mahatma Gandhi Institute.

Covell, Maureen (1987). *Madagascar: Politics, Economics, and Society*. London: Frances Pinter Publishers.

Dandouau, André (1911). "Coutumes funéraires dans le nord-ouest de Madagascar." *Bulletin de l'Académie Malgache* 9:147–172.

De Foort, (Captain) E. (1907). *Étude historique et ethnologique sur le secteur d'Ambato-Boéni*. Tananarive: Imprimerie Officiel, Colonie de Madagascar et Dépendances.

Estrade, Jean-Marie (1977). *Un culte de possession ä Madagascar: Le tromba*. Paris: Éditions Anthropos.

Feeley-Harnik, Gillian (1988). "Dancing Battles: Representations of Conflict in Sakalava Royal Service." *Anthropos* 83:65–85.

Feeley-Harnik, Gillian (1991). *A Green Estate: Restoring Independence in Madagascar*. Washington, D.C.: Smithsonian Institution Press.

Guillain, C. (1845). *Documents sur l'histoire, la géographie et le commerce de la partie occidentale de Madagascar*. Paris: Imprimerie Royale.

Jaovelo-Dzao, Robert (1982). *Anthropologie religieuse sakalava: Essai sur l'inculturation du christianisme à Madagascar*. Thèse de Troisième Cycle en Ethno-Théologie. Université des Sciences Humaines de Strasbourg, Faculté de Théologie Catholique.

Kent, Raymond K. (1968). "Madagascar and Africa: Part II. The Sakalava, Maroserana, Dady, and Tromba before 1700." *Journal of African History* 9(4): 517–576.

Kent, Raymond K. (1979). "Religion and the State: The Antanosy and the Sakalava in the 1600s." *Madagascar in History: Essays from the 1970s*, edited by R. K. Kent, 80–101. Berkeley and Los Angeles: Foundation for Malagasy Studies.

Lambek, Michael (1981). *Human Spirits: A Cultural Account of Trance in Mayotte*. Cambridge: Cambridge University Press.

Lambek, Michael (1993). *Knowledge and Practice in Mayotte: Local Discourses of Islam, Sorcery, and Spirit Possession*. Toronto: University of Toronto Press.

Lombard, Jacques (1988). *Le royaume sakalava du Menabe: Essai d'analyse d'un système politique à Madagascar. 17è-20è*. Paris: Éditions de l'ORSTOM.

Mellis, J. V. (1938). *Nord et nord-ouest de Madagascar: Volamena et volafotsy*. Tananarive: Imprimerie Moderne de l'Emyrne.

Ottino, Paul (1965). "Le tromba (Madagascar)." *L'Homme* 5(1): 84–94.

Picton, John, and John Mack (1979). *African Textiles: Looms, Weaving, and Design*. London: British Museum Publications.

Raison-Jourde, Françoise (1983). *Les souverains de Madagascar: L'histoire royale et ses résurgences contemporaines*. Paris: Éditions Karthala.

Rason, R. (1968). "Le tromba chez les sakalava." *Civilisation Malgache* 2:207–214.

Russillon, H. (1908). *Un culte dynastique avec evocation des morts chez les sakalava: Le tromba*. Paris: Picard.

Sharp, Lesley A. (1993). *The Possessed and the Dispossessed: Spirits, Identity, and Power in a Madagascar Migrant Town*. Berkeley and Los Angeles: University of California Press.

Tegnaeus, Harry (1952). *Blood-Brothers: An Ethno-Sociological Study of the Institutions of Blood Brotherhood with Special Reference to Africa*. New Series, Publication no. 10. Stockholm: Ethnographic Museum of Sweden.

Valette, J. (1958). "1700–1840: Histoire du Boina." *Bulletin de Madagascar* 149:851–858.

LESLIE A. SHARP

Samaritans

ETHNONYMS: Benei Yisrael, Shamerim, Shomeronim

The Samaritans are a sect numbering about 500 who currently reside in Nablus, on the west bank of the Jordan River in Israeli-occupied Jordan, and in Holon, south of Tel Aviv, on the Mediterranean coast of Israel. The Samaritans call themselves "Benei Yisrael," Hebrew for the "Children of Israel," or "Shamerim," Hebrew for "Observant Ones." The name "Samaritans" is based on the belief that the modern population is descended from the people who occupied Samaria about 2,700 years ago.

Modern-day Samaritans live in Samaritan neighborhoods or quarters in Nabulus and Holon, with about 250 people in each settlement, a significant population increase from a low of about 150 in the 1930s. There is an ongoing debate as to whether the Samaritans are Jews or Arabs or Jordanians or Israelis (those in Holon are considered citizens of Israel), but Samaritans prefer to see themselves as a distinct people. In Nablus, Samaritans are culturally similar to the Arab population, whereas those in Holon more closely resemble their Israeli neighbors; both populations are now politically aligned with Israel.

Depending on who they are communicating with and whether the subject matter is secular or religious, Samaritans use the English, Hebrew, Arabic, Samaritan, and Samaritan Aramaic languages, although Hebrew is now the primary domestic language.

According to Jewish tradition and the Bible, the modern-day Samaritans are descendants of foreign peoples who were brought into ancient Israel after the Assyrians conquered and drove the Judeans out in 701 B.C. The Samaritans, however, trace their ancestry to remnants of the Judean population who remained in Samaria following the conquest. Recent scholarship tends to support the Samaritan view. With the return of the Judean exiles from Babylonia in the fifth century B.C., a break developed between the Judeans and the Samaritans, resulting, in part, from the Samaritans' refusal to accept new religious texts and interpretations. At about this time, the Samaritans began calling themselves "Shomeronim" (Hebrew for "to conserve") in reference to their adherence to traditional religious beliefs and practices. Barred by the Jews from participating in the rebuilding of the Jewish Temple, the Samaritans, in the fourth century B.C., built their own temple on Mount Gerizim, overlooking Nablus. The temple was destroyed in 128 B.C.; a new one was built, and it too was destroyed, in A.D. 486. Since the building of the first temple, Mount Gerizim has been the destination for Samaritan pilgrimages, and continued access to the site is a major concern to contemporary Samaritans.

At about the time of Jesus, the Samaritans numbered several hundred thousand and were spread in settlements across the Fertile Crescent. Both before and since that time, Samaritan numbers and settlements steadily decreased at the hands of the Jews, Persians, Greeks, Romans, Byzantines, and Arabs.

Relatively few in number, the Samaritans have been easily absorbed into the Israeli and Jordanian economic systems, with many employed as civil servants in the Israeli government. Samaritans in Holon serve in the Israeli military. Again, because of their small population and because of their ambiguous identity, Samaritans occupy an uneasy position within the Israeli nation and enjoy no formal political or religious representation nor designation as a distinct ethnic minority. Their situation vis-à-vis Jordan was much the same prior to the Israeli occupation of the West Bank.

Endogamous marriage is the rule; only Jews are allowed to marry in, and those who do (virtually all women) are expected to follow Samaritan religious beliefs and practices. Family relationships are now more egalitarian than in the past, when men dominated the family. Arranged marriages have given way to freedom of choice in selecting a spouse. Families are generally nuclear and small and provide the major arena for socialization into the Samaritan religion.

The Samaritan religion resembles the Karaite Jewish tradition in that Samaritans and Karaites are both outside the mainstream of Israeli Judaism, which mostly follows the Rabbinite tradition. Samaritans believe in one God, that Moses is the only Prophet, that only the first books of the Bible (the Torah) are authoritative, that Mount Gerizim is sacred, and that there will be a future time of messianic revival. They celebrate most major Jewish Holy Days and festivals, although their practices, such as the ritual slaughter of a lamb at Passover (Pesach) and kneeling in prayer, do not conform to those of modern Judaism. In short, Samaritan religion resembles contemporary Judaism in many ways, but also includes various beliefs and practices characteristic of early Judaism. There is a priestly class among the Samaritans, which consists of only a few priests and one high priest.

Bibliography

"Samaritans" (1972). In *Encyclopaedia Judaica*. Vol. 14, 726–758. Jerusalem: Keter.

San-Speaking Peoples

ETHNONYMS: G|wi, G||ana, Hai||om, Kxoe (Makwengo), Nharo (Naro); !Koõ (!Xoõ); !Xu; Zhu|õasi (!Kung)

Orientation

Identification. The term "San" has replaced "Buchman" as an ethnographic term designating both the contemporary and the precolonial southern African peoples who speak, or spoke, languages containing click consonants and who have been described as hunter-gatherers or foragers. Thus, San-speaking peoples do not constitute an ethnic group in the usual sense. The most widely known are those who call themselves "Zhu|õasi" (!Kung or Juwasi in most ethnographies), although the other peoples mentioned above have also been extensively described; about ten other groups have been well studied by linguists. In Botswana, all these peoples are called collectively "Basarwa," and this term is often seen in recent ethnographic literature.

Location. The Zhu | õasi live in the semiarid *savdveld* (savanna) of northwestern Botswana (Ngamiland) and in adjacent parts of Namibia. The !Xu, whose anglicized ethnonym is the source of the name "!Kung," live in the better-watered tropical open woodlands of southern Angola. The Axoe live along the Okavango River, in the Caprivi Strip of Namibia; the Hai | | om occupy a large part of north-central Namibia, between the Cunene River and the Etosha Pan. The Nharo live in the limestone karst zone of the Ghansi District of Botswana. The G | wi, G | | ana, and !Koõ live throughout the poorly watered central sand zone of Botswana, extending into Namibia, in conditions most closely approximating true desert. The | | Anikhoe, the so-called Swamp Bushmen, live in the Okavango Delta floodplain; the Deti live along the Botletli River. Several other peoples who are called San in the ethnographic literature speak Khoe languages and live in the hill, *mopane*-forest, and salt-pan environments of eastern Botswana. These highly diverse geophysical regions share a number of features: seasonal rains, falling mainly as localized thunderstorms during the hot months, October to May; high variation in average annual rainfall—around 45 centimeters in Ngamiland, some 50 percent higher in Angola, and 50 percent lower in central Botswana; summer temperatures that often exceed 37° C; and cool winters, with night temperatures as low as –4° C in Botswana and Namibia.

Demography. In 1980 the most reliable sources estimated that about 30,000 San-speaking peoples lived in Botswana, about 12,000 in Namibia, and about 8,000 in Angola—representing about 3 percent of the population of Botswana, 1.2 percent of that of Namibia, and 0.1 percent of Angola's people. The Zhu | õasi, who previously had wide birth spacing and a low birthrate, now have one of the highest recorded birthrates in the world, according to 1980 statistics, with 6.7 live births per 1,000 women of childbearing age. Zhu | õasi infant mortality, at 85 per 1,000 births, is comparatively low by African standards, as is child mortality. Life expectancy at birth was 45 years for Zhu | õasi in the 1960s, but improved nutrition and health care have probably lengthened life spans; survivors to age 5 have good prospects of living into their 70s. There are no comparable statistics for other San speakers, but health-ministry surveys suggest that similar demographic profiles may be found in Botswana.

Linguistic Affiliation. San languages are usually classified as being in the Khoisan Family; there are three sets of these languages, each with its own history. Zhu | õasi, !Xu, and Au | | ei (formerly spoken around Lake Ngami, now with few living speakers) are mutually intelligible and together constitute the Northern Khoisan Group; they are grammatically, syntactically, and lexically distinct from other Khoisan languages. G | wi, G | | ana, Kxoe, Nharo, and | | Anikhoe, plus Deti, Buga, Tshukhoe, Kwa, and several others, form the Khoe Group, formerly Central Khoisan, which is closely related to the Nama that is spoken by Khoi peoples (often called Hottentots in the past); Hai | | om is a dialect of Nama. In general, the geographically adjacent Khoe languages (e.g., G | wi and G | | ana) are very similar and are mutually intelligible, whereas those farther apart (e.g., Nharo and Deti) are structurally alike but become progressively less interintelligible. The principal extant Southern Khoisan languages are !Koõ and Tsassi, spoken across a long, narrow band of the southern Kalahari. All Khoisan languages are predominantly mono- and bisyllabic and tonal, and they contain click consonants (which are conventionally represented by | , !, and | |—although Bantu orthography, which uses *c* for | and, *q* for !, and *x* for | | , is preferable in nonlinguistic contexts). The replacement of click by nonclick consonants is common in the Khoe languages of eastern Botswana, where some of these languages are being completely replaced by Setswana.

History and Cultural Relations

Accumulating archaeological and archival evidence provides the basis for a more comprehensive reconstruction of the later prehistory of southern Africa than was possible as recently as 1970, when it was generally thought that Bantu-speaking peoples arrived only two or three centuries ago, bringing with them grain horticulture and cattle-sheep-goat pastoralism. It is now known that cattle and sheep were widely kept, almost certainly by Khoisan-speaking peoples, beginning about 2,000 years ago; both the Khoe languages and Zhu | õasi contain indigenous vocabularies for stock keeping, indicating that some of these pastoralist-foragers must have been San speakers. About 500 years later, Bantu-speaking agro-pastoralists spread into many parts of the region, introducing sorghum, millet, and probably goats, as well as metallurgy; linguistic evidence suggests that speakers of Nguni and Sotho-Tswana Bantu languages obtained cattle from Khoisan peoples. Since that time, mixed economies that combine foraging, herding, and farming in varying proportions have been predominant. Nevertheless, it has not been uncommon for local groups of both Bantu and Khoisan speakers to rely exclusively on foraging when drought, disease, raiding, or political subjugation have made herding and farming impossible; San peoples in this condition have been the subjects of most ethnographic studies. Interregional and transcontinental trade is archaeologically documented from the ninth century, when iron and copper jewelry, glass beads from Asia, and cowrie shells from the Indian Ocean were widely distributed and reached even into the Kalahari and Ngamiland. The Portuguese Atlantic-coast trade penetrated from the Congo through Angola into Namibia and Botswana in the seventeenth century and was recorded a hundred years later by the first Europeans to enter those areas; these observers noted that many different groups of San speakers engaged with Bantu and Nama speakers in such trade, which followed ancient routes of communication and exchange. European hunter-merchants accelerated this trade, beginning in the 1840s. Throughout the 1880s, until the market collapsed, San speakers were major providers of ivory and ostrich feathers, for which the merchants paid with European goods. Horses and donkeys were introduced by these merchants; donkeys, especially, became important economic assets. Most of the San-speaking peoples became impoverished during the period from 1850 to 1920, but some of them (the Deti and a few Zhu | õasi, for example) retained modest herds. Many, especially in southern and eastern Botswana, became serfs of Twsana patrons; a few became marginal foragers, partially dependent on their serf and client kin. Labor migration to South African gold mines, which began in the 1890s, increased dramatically for San speakers in the 1950s, when efforts to recruit them were intensified in order to augment insufficient Bantu labor. Different groups were variably affected: as many as 50 percent of Kwa men were absent from their villages at any given time, but only 10 percent of Zhu | õasi men ever went to the mines. Opportunities to work in the mines are no longer available to San speakers.

Settlements

San settlements are composed of one to a dozen or more homesteads, each containing a set of separate households, the heads of which are ideally related as parent and child or as descendants of common grandparents, that is, as siblings and first cousins. Larger settlements may contain 200 or 300 persons. Many homesteads, as well as individual households today—and probably all of them in precolonial times—also set up temporary encampments near seasonal rain pools, from which their members hunt and collect wild-plant products; livestock are usually kept there as well, and fields may be cultivated nearby. In Botswana, settlements rarely contain only persons of a single language group; in Ngamiland, for example, Zhu | õasi, ǂAu | | ei, Nharo, Nama, Mbanderu, Mbukushu, and Tswana homesteads may all be found in the same settlement. Houses within a homestead are normally built close together and usually face a common open area, but homesteads within a settlement may be 2 to 3 kilometers apart; clients and persons employed as herders tend to live adjacent to their patrons and employers. Conical grass huts are frequently used, especially at temporary encampments, but round, one-room, wattle-and-daub houses with thatched roofs are more common among most groups.

Economy

Subsistence and Commercial Activities. Although famed as foragers, fewer than 5 percent of San-speaking peoples have relied on foraging for the bulk of their subsistence during the twentieth century; even these few have depended on herding-farming relatives and on neighbors for dietary supplements of meat, milk, and grains, as well as for supplies of such desired goods as iron for arrow points and spears, metal containers, glass beads, tobacco, and, when obtainable, sugar, coffee, and tea. Herding-farming San speakers also forage, as do rural Bantu speakers (the poorer of whom obtain 25 percent of their livelihood from foraging). It has been reported that during the 1970s hunting provided 11 percent of the diet of the Zhu | õasi, whereas gathered plants contributed 85 percent of the calories that were consumed by those who owned no livestock and 10 percent to 68 percent of the caloric intake of stock owners. Large antelope—eland, kudu, gemsboks—and giraffes still provide the bulk of the dietary meat, but small antelope, birds, and reptiles are also important. Seasonal and annual variation is great; the proportion of the diet that is obtained by hunting may rise to 30 percent during the dry winter months (May to August) but falls to less than 1 percent during the wet summer (December to February). Those Khoe speakers who live along rivers and in the delta rely heavily upon fish, the abundance of which is also highly seasonal. The contribution of gathered plants, about 100 species, is subject to similar fluctuation. For example, in September and October *mongongo* nuts may supply as much as 90 percent of the calories of Zhu | õasi who own no livestock, but these nuts are seldom available from November to March. Mongongo groves are restricted to narrow ecological zones; most San-speaking groups rely on more widely distributed wild nuts and legumes (mainly *marula* nuts and species of *Bauhinia* beans). Goats are kept by individuals in all San-speaking groups, but fewer than one-third of households own any of these animals; cattle ownership is even more restricted, but the Deti are wealthy in these animals, as are small proportions of families in several other groups. Goats are readily slaughtered for home consumption and are sold locally for slaughter by others. Cattle are milked and are eaten when they die; when available, surplus oxen and old bulls are slaughtered for important ritual occasions and may also be sold. The few owners of large herds fatten oxen for commercial sale. Crops are grown by most homesteads and, where conditions are favorable (i.e., in Angola and eastern-southern Botswana), contribute substantially to subsistence. Mixed fields are usual; these are planted with some combination of sorghum, millet, maize, sweet-reed (a type of sugarcane), cowpeas, and melons. Women sell home-brewed beer. The cash purchase of maize meal, sugar, coffee and tea, soap, cosmetics, clothing, and utilitarian household items has increased since the late 1970s.

Industrial Arts. Leatherworking was important in the past, as was blacksmithing, but no longer. A few women in the riverine-delta area still weave baskets for local use and for sale.

Trade. The majority of San speakers live in or near villages, in which one or more small shops are located. Those who live in the central Kalahari, in western Ngamiland, and on many cattle posts rely primarily on itinerant traders and on informal arrangements with periodic visitors. Fairly often they travel on foot, donkey, or horseback to the nearest shop, which may be 100 kilometers away.

Division of Labor. Women bear the major responsibility for child care, but men play important supporting roles. Adolescents learn their adult roles mainly from older members of their respective sexes. Men hunt the larger animals, but women collect smaller species, such as tortoises, and may assist in the monitoring of snare lines. Women gather the greater quantity of plant foods, but men bring in smaller amounts as well, especially after successful hunts. Men of all groups do the heavier work of cattle management (well digging, corral building, branding, slaughtering). In some groups, women may participate in herding and be responsible for milking (as among the Zhu | õasi). Elsewhere, these may be considered inappropriate activities for women (as among most Khoe speakers). Among the Zhu | õasi, relative age modifies the division of labor, in that older cohorts and siblings have some directional control over their juniors. Leadership positions—which may be held by either men or women in a related set of families—do not relieve the leaders from obligations of work, but they do provide avenues for disproportionate long-term gains; the terms for "leader" in the Zhu | õasi and Khoe languages are derived from words that designate "wealth." Diviners and curers, who also may be women as well as men, are generally held in high esteem.

Land Tenure. Land tenure is vested in a set of related families whose claim to generationally inherited rights to a particular area is considered legitimate. Generally, individuals acquire two such rights bilaterally through their parents. Residence in one of these tenure areas and regular participation with relatives in the other are essential if a person wishes to retain these rights. Seasonal movement within tenures is common, as is vesting among relatives in different tenures. The current leader of a landholding group is in most cases also the nominal "owner" of the land. Nonresidents must obtain permission from this person to use the land; such permission is rarely refused to kin and rarely given to others.

Kinship

Kin Groups and Descent. All San speakers reckon kinship bilaterally; membership in Zhu | õasi and Khoe local descent groups is determined by rights that are inherited through either father or mother or through both. The Hai | | om, who in the past lived in patrilineal local groups, reckon descent unilineally.

Kinship Terminology. Zhu | õasi terminology is of the Eskimo type, with older siblings and cousins distinguished by sex; all Khoe and !Koõ terminologies are Iroquois, with bifurcate-merging avuncular terms.

Marriage and Family

Marriage. The majority of marriages are monogamous, with polygyny being restricted to the wealthier men. Marriages are ideally arranged by parents, in consultation with senior members of the kinship group. The Zhu | õasi prefer bilateral-cousin marriages, excluding first cousins; Khoe speakers prescribe cross-cousin marriage, including first cousins. The !Koõ permit marriage only to more distant relatives. The Zhu | õasi prefer virilocal postmarital residence for couples who are related matrilaterally and vice versa; the other groups prefer uxorilocal residence. Bride-service was once required, but today it is often replaced by marriage payments in livestock. Divorce is common until a child is born to a couple, after which time it is rare.

Domestic Unit. Each family has its own hut; adolescent children often build small huts for themselves next to those of their parents. Each wife in a polygynous family has her own hut. Families prefer to live in homesteads that include other members of their extended family.

Inheritance. Land-tenure rights are inherited at birth. Personal property and partnerships devolve from parent to child during the lifetimes of both.

Socialization. Children are instructed from infancy in proper forms of etiquette, especially toward kin. Corporal punishment is applied and ridicule is used, but threats are very rare. In the past, groups of adolescent boys were initiated in seclusion, but this is no longer done; circumcision is reported only for the Tshukhoe. Zhu | õasi, Nharo, and G | wi girls still go through a brief initiation at first menstruation. No female genital mutilation has been recorded for any group. Scarification of the face, back, chest (for men,) and thighs (for women) was commonly applied to mark important life events, but is seldom done now.

Sociopolitical Organization

Social Organization. Residence is based on bilateral kinship. Nonresident associations are also important. Among the Zhu | õasi, *hxaro* networks link persons who are related through common great-grandparents over distances of 200 kilometers or more; the Nharo and a few other Khoe groups have similar exchange networks. Hxaro (the Zhu | õasi term) is a system of delayed reciprocity, with obligations attached to partners; important partnerships are frequently inherited from parents, and marriages are often arranged through these channels. To celebrate marriages, childbirth, and girls' puberty initiations, gifts—called *kamasi* in Zhu | õasi and *kamane* in Nharo—are given in a separate series of exchanges. Zhu | õasi age sets, *| arakwe*, are composed of persons who are not necessarily kin; these age sets now have few functions, but they appear to have been important in the past, when they probably were central to the hxaro framework for long-distance trade. Zhu | õasi name groups, which once may have functioned as clans, are now almost entirely forgotten; the Kxoe and some eastern Khoe have analogous residual forms.

Political Organization. All San-speaking groups have positions of hereditary leadership; the term *| | xaiha*, derived from a root designating "wealth," is usually translated as "chief." These leaders now have limited authority of a traditional kind, but among the Zhu | õasi they are usually elected to state-created posts such as chairman of the village-development committee.

Social Control. Ridicule, verbal abuse, dispersal, and divination are the usual means of maintaining social order, but consensually sanctioned executions and murders were not uncommon in the past. Minor disputes are adjudicated in informal hearings in which all interested parties participate. Nowadays village headmen appointed by district councils hear minor civil cases; more serious cases are referred to local and district courts.

Conflict. For many years, all San speakers have engaged in small-scale fighting among themselves and their neighbors, but there are no special war officers, and no particular prestige follows success in battle.

Religion and Expressive Culture

Religious Beliefs. The Zhu | õasi and the !Koõ each divide their chief deity into a creator, who now plays little active role in earthly affairs, and an administrator, whom they hold responsible for all that happens on earth. Some Khoe speakers incorporate these roles in one being. All believe in lesser spirits, who are ancestors. Ecumenism is characteristic of southern African peoples, who share numerous mythic themes: many ideas have been transferred among the different cosmologies of the region, including the various Christian forms that were added during the nineteenth century.

Religious Practitioners. There are no religious practitioners other than the diviners and curers (see "Medicine").

Ceremonies. The main ceremonies among San speakers are dance performances; these are usually attended by members of an extended family, but may include other relatives. The girls' initiation dance is restricted to relatives of the initiate—one adult-male relative plays a central ritual role. Male initiation, which was important in the past, is no longer performed.

Arts. San-speaking peoples have long been famed for beadwork, both of ostrich-eggshell beads, which they manufacture, and of glass beads, which they purchase or obtain in trade. They are widely believed to be responsible for the fine rock paintings of southern Africa. Recently three men (two Zhu | õasi and one Nharo) have gained recognition as watercolorists; in 1980 one of them received a prize at the Botswana National Art Show.

Medicine. Both men and women may be curers, but most diviners are men; often both roles are combined in a single person. Divination is directed toward the analysis of problems, such as the source of misfortune, the location of stray livestock, or the cause of illness. Divination takes two forms: in one, a set of bones or disks is thrown, and the resultant patterns are interpreted; in the other, a dance is performed, during which one or more practitioners may go into a trance. Cures are almost exclusively attained through the dance performances, usually involving trance, which are directed toward physical and psychological healing as well as social well-being.

Death and Afterlife. Death is a passing into a spiritual realm that is distinct from the material realm. To the Zhu | õasi, human death is senseless because people are not properly earthly food; it can be explained, however, by the belief that the administrator deity feeds on the people he causes to die. Recently dead relatives are dangerous because their spirits yearn for their kin and may attempt to bring about their early deaths in order to be reunited; this danger recedes as memory of the deceased dims with time.

Bibliography

Barnard, Alan (1991). *Hunters and Herders: A Comparative Ethnography of the Khoisan Peoples*. Cambridge: Cambridge University Press.

Denbow, James (1984). "Prehistoric Herders and Foragers of the Kalahari: The Evidence for 1500 Years of Interaction." In *Past and Present in Hunter Gatherer Studies*, edited by Carmel Schrire, 175–193. Orlando, Fla.: Academic Press.

Lee, Richard (1979). *The !Kung San: Men, Women, and Work in a Foraging Society*. Cambridge: Cambridge University Press.

Silberbauer, George (1981). *Hunter and Habitat in the Central Kalahari Desert*. Cambridge: Cambridge University Press.

Vossen, Rainer, and Klaus Keuthmann, eds. (1986). *Contemporary Studies on Khoisan: In Honor of Oswin Köhler on the Occasion of his 75th Birthday*. Hamburg: Helmut Buske.

Wilmsen, Edwin (1989). *Land Filled with Flies: A Political Economy of the Kalahari*. Chicago: University of Chicago Press.

Wilmsen, Edwin, and James Denbow (1990). "Almost Outcasts: Paradigmatic History of San-Speaking Peoples and Current Attempts at Reconstruction." *Current Anthropology* 31:489–524.

EDWIN N. WILMSEN

Sara

ETHNONYM: Kirdi

Orientation

Identification. "Sara" is the term employed by outsiders to refer to a group of non-Muslim tribes in southern Chad, all of whom speak mutually intelligible dialects. Each tribe is a distinct geographic, political, and endogamous entity. Major tribes are the Kaba, Sar, Nar, Gulay, Ngambay, and Mbay.

Location. Most Sara are now, and have been for centuries, located between Lake Iro in the east and the Logone River in the west.

Linguistic Affiliation. The Sara language Group belongs to the Central Sudanic Branch of the Nilo-Saharan Language Family and is related to languages spoken by the Barma, the Kenga, and the Bulala in Chad, as well as to those spoken by the Bongo and the Krech in Sudan. There are Eastern Sara (Sar, Nar, and Gulay) and Western Sara (Ngambay and Mbay) dialects.

Demography. There appear to have been approximately 1,045,000 Sara in 1977. This was the largest single ethnic group in Chad, roughly 23 percent of the total population. The Ngambay at this time were the largest subgroup (425,000), followed by the Gulay (112,000), and the Sar (92,000). Sara fertility is higher than that of more northerly Muslim peoples, and the area in which they reside is considerably smaller. This means that, in places, previously low population densities have begun to increase.

History and Cultural Relations

Most Central Sudanic speakers reside in Chad. The Bulala—who live near Lake Fitri—are the northernmost of the Central Sudanic speakers, and the Sara are the southernmost; the Barma—who are found near the Bahr Erguig—are intermediate. From approximately A.D. 1000 to 1900, Central Sudanic history was characterized by a regional political economy consisting of different types of societies performing different roles in the trans-Saharan trade, which was largely in slaves. In the north were desert specialists, societies like that of the Tubu that assured the travel of caravans across the desert. In the center were states—Muslim emirates like that of the Bagirmi (in which the Barma were preeminent)—that warred to acquire and sell slaves. In the south were cereal producers, societies like that of the Sara that were the major reservoirs of slaves.

People in the precolonial states called those they raided "Kirdi," which generally meant any non-Muslim, and hence enslavable, person. The Bagirmi specialized in raiding Kirdi Sara during the nineteenth century. In the early twentieth century the Sara were incorporated into French Equatorial Africa. The southern portion of Chad was considered by the French "le Tchad utile," and it was here that administrators concentrated their efforts. The impact of colonization thus fell squarely upon the Sara. Their society was transformed by the introduction of taxes, paid in cash; of forced labor, especially on the Congo-Ocean Railroad; of obligatory cotton production; and of service in the French military, especially during World War II. By independence in 1960, the Sara were better educated and had greater experience with French political institutions than did the northern populations that had formerly raided them.

Settlements

Most Sara who are Nar (hereafter reference will be to the Nar unless otherwise mentioned) reside in small villages located near streams or along roads. In precolonial times, in principle, a hamlet (*gir be*) was a distinct area in which members of a patriclan (*gir ka*) lived with their wives, children, other kin, and followers. Villages (*gir begi* [the *gi* suffix is a plural marker]) were divided into a number of such tracts of different clans. Households in these villages tended to be dispersed, with their circular thatched huts standing in the midst of family members' fields, but colonial and postcolonial officials have obliged the relocation and concentration of households along more easily administered roads. In the 1970s most villages had 200 to 300 inhabitants.

Economy

Subsistence and Commercial Activities. The Sara, who live in a moderately well-watered Sudano-Guinean ecological zone, specialize in the slash-and-burn cultivation of cereals, especially sorghums and millets. They fish and raise chickens, dwarf goats, and a few horses. Plow oxen, introduced during the 1960s and still rare, are the only cattle kept, owing to a high incidence of sleeping sickness. The French, in search of a stable supply of cotton fiber for their textile industry, introduced cotton as a cash crop in 1928. Postindependence governments have continued to emphasize the crop because its sale has brought 80 percent of the country's foreign exchange. Because of cotton's importance, its production has been mandatory throughout the colonial and immediate postcolonial periods. Most cotton is produced by the Sara, who have added this work to their normal subsistence activities. Raising cotton is more labor intensive than growing food crops. Its farm-gate price has usually been kept low. It has a tendency to exhaust soils.

Increasingly, manioc is substituted for cereals in areas where cotton production is high. Manioc requires less labor than do cereals but has less nutritional value. One reason for its popularity may be that it allows labor that would have been allocated to the growth of cereals to be directed instead to the maintenance or expansion of cotton cultivation. Studies suggest that areas of considerable manioc production are those with lower nutritional levels.

Industrial Arts. Precolonial crafts included metalworking, pottery, cloth and basket weaving, calabash carving, and different forms of woodworking. All of these are in decline as their products are increasingly being replaced by manufactured imports.

Trade. There do not appear to have been indigenous markets among the precolonial Sara. Merchants from Bagirmi, and to a lesser extent from other Muslim states, circulated in the area, usually exchanging sumptuary goods for slaves. Lack of commercial experience has meant that many small stores and other enterprises in Sara towns are owned by members of northern ethnic groups.

Division of Labor. Little is known of the precolonial division of labor. The contemporary ideal, however, is that a wife should work for her husband in farming and domestic activities. In exchange, he should provide her and her children with food and other necessities. In principle, the husband owns the fields and their harvest, which he doles out. As women grow older, however, they clear and plant their own fields, and therefore they own these fields' crops and can dispose of them as they see fit. Both men and women derive labor for their fields from kin, especially children. Gender alone does not seem to confer advantage in securing labor. Rather, what counts is the ability to be generous with grain, alcohol, and cooked food. Women, it appears, can be just as generous as men. Thus, men and women effectively possess the same access to land and labor. This division of labor was reported for a Sara group with abundant land. It is possible that such abundance allows for a more egalitarian access to agricultural resources.

Land Tenure. Perhaps the most important aspect of past and present Sara land tenure, at least in regions of low population density, is the absence of cultural notions producing differential access to land. In the past each clan had its area that it farmed to the exclusion of all other clans. The main rule regulating access was that clan members could acquire land by farming it. Those who were not members of clans could acquire fields simply by asking any clan member for permission to farm. Land inheritance was of little importance. Most fields were on virgin bush or long fallows over which no one exercised rights. The French were convinced that all Sara had *chefs de terre* who, by virtue of supernatural association with land, might at least partially regulate access to it. Although there may have been some Sara with chefs de terre in this sense, they were rare. The founders of villages, and their descendants, called *kwa begi,* were sometimes said to "own" the land. Such persons had only a hazy, moral prestige, however, almost indistinct from that resulting from age, which was irrelevant to land apportionment. Today there is a person, known as the *chef de carré,* who, following consultation with members of his carré (lit., "plot") selects where its cotton fields will be located.

Kinship

Kin Groups and Descent. The Sara combine a cognatic, ancestor-focused, system of kinship with patriclans. The term "gir ka" can, depending on the context, mean either "ancestor" or "patriclan." A gir ka is any ancestor from which a person is descended in any way. Descendants of a person's ancestors are that person's cognates. Cultural notions specify that such kin should join in each other's work groups, share food, welcome each other as members of their residential group, and in general provide mutual support. Persons who stipulate that they share agnatic descent from an ancestor belong to a "gir ka," with the term here used in the sense of a patriclan that has its place of residence, its gir be. Clans were in principle exogamous. Clan members should participate in its funeral ceremonies and other clan affairs, such as the taking of vengeance and sacrifices to the spirit (*besi;* pl. *besigi*) associated with the clan. There was absolutely no belief that the different clans in a village were part of a common organization based upon agnatic descent. Similarly, neither the village itself, nor other villages, were conceived of as descent groups bound in a single, pyramidal structure, as was found among the Nuer.

Kinship Terminology. Sara kinship terminology is of the Hawaiian type.

Marriage and Family

Marriage. The Sara verb *tar* means "to love," but the notion of "tar" carries with it an additional connotation of "giving things." The idea that "giving" is intrinsically linked to "deep affection" is a basis of Sara marriage, which tends to be ideally viewed as a reciprocal relationship in which a husband gives grain and a wife provides services in exchange. It was believed that kin, especially mother's brother's offspring, were more likely than others to love each other. Payment of bridewealth was a condition for creating marriages; it gave men rights to their wives' sexuality and children. Polygyny and widow inheritance were practiced. Divorce was possible, although wives, rather than going through the bother of divorce, simply opened their own fields, thereby gaining considerable independence.

Domestic Unit. A married man ideally builds his wife or wives houses adjacent to those of his father's household and thus resides patrilocally with his extended family. In fact, such households appear to occur in less than half the cases studied.

Inheritance. Traditionally, there was rarely much to be inherited. Although there were rules guiding inheritance of fields, these were rarely applied because land was abundant. In general, movable property went to younger agnates of the deceased. Some supernatural property—such as knowledge of how to turn into an animal, how to perform sorcery, and how to control besi spirits—was inherited from father to son or mother to daughter. A change has occurred with respect to the inheritance of certain new forms of movable property that require prior investment, such as plows or carts. These tend to be inherited by children rather than siblings.

Socialization. Child-rearing practices tended to be exacting. Children were expected to learn to behave. They were punished if they did not. The male initiation ceremony was important for inculcating gender roles (see "Ceremonies"). Today formal education is very much appreciated.

Sociopolitical Organization

Social Organization. There was no differential access to the major productive resource, land. Recruitment to the few ritual positions that conferred distinction was restricted to those satisfying the rules of their inheritance. There was no ranking, even within descent groups. Hence, precolonial Sara society appears to have been rather egalitarian, with some ranking. Cultural notions pertaining to age, gender, and kinship influenced most social activities. The Sara lacked the age grades and sets found in Nilotic populations. Nevertheless, they strongly believed that juniors should defer to elders. They also generally felt that women involved in social relations with men should defer to the men, although the capacity of this attitude to affect action may have been restrained by attitudes pertaining to appropriate kin behavior. All kin—especially close agnates—owed each other assistance. A husband might therefore refrain from exercising excessive authority over his wife for fear of losing support from her relatives.

Political Organization. Most precolonial Sara tribes were highly acephalous; however, incessant raiding by the more northerly states had transformed nineteenth-century Sara lands into a laboratory of incipient centralization. Chiefdoms had begun to emerge among certain Sar, Nar, and Gulay. The most highly elaborated of these, organized around a person called the *mbang* (the Barma postindependence term for "sovereign"), was that of the Sar near the town of Bedaya.

The Sara have been extremely important in postindependence Chad. The first president, François Tombalbaye, was a Sar, and he and other Sara completely dominated the government, a reality that non-Sara—especially northerners—bitterly resented. Civil war began in 1966. In 1973 an increasingly hard-pressed and authoritarian Tombalbaye, in a bid to strengthen his legitimacy by reinstating certain, "traditional" Sara institutions, created the Mouvement National pour la Révolution Culturelle et Sociale. For example, officials were supposed to participate in male initiation. Tombalbaye was assassinated in 1975 in a southern coup. By 1978, power had passed from the south to the north. The 1980s were a time of difficulty for the Sara: famine was exacerbated by oppression.

Social Control. No courts existed among precolonial Sara at any level. Family disputes were not settled by elders, or the village "owners" (kwa begi). In fact, there appear to have been no peaceable conflict-resolution mechanisms in either the clan village or tribe. Disputes tended to be settled by some form of self-help. Divination may be performed at the death of a person to discover the cause. Should the divination indicate that a particular individual was responsible for the death, then a vengeance party—largely composed of the deceased's agnates—might be formed.

Conflict. Two major types of extrasocietal conflict dominate Sara history. Both have north-south dimensions. Precolonial wars were fought between Muslim emirates and the Sara as the former sought slaves among the latter. Since Chadian independence, the Sara and more northerly peoples have contested for control over the central government. An important form of contemporary intrasocietal conflict pits government officials against traditional religious specialists in local communities.

Religion and Expressive Culture

Religious Beliefs. Precolonial religion was based on notions that different religious specialists could, by performance of appropriate ritual, influence different supernaturals to restore or maintain natural and social well-being. Many Sara in contemporary times have converted to Christianity, often opting for some form of Protestantism.

There appear to have been three major forms of the supernatural. Nuba was a sort of otiose god who had created the world. A besi was a sort of "spirit" that was immanent in, symbolized by, and named after natural objects—especially trees—or social activities, such as initiation. Besigi interfere in peoples' lives by bringing misfortune. Some besigi were not powerful; others had the ability to influence entire clans or villages. *Badigi* (sing. *badi*), the dead conceived of in their afterlife, were the third form of the supernatural. A badi, usually a deceased father or mother, can attack people and, like a besi, bring misfortune.

Religious Practitioners. There appear to have been four main varieties of religious specialists in precolonial times:

those who owned a besi; those who presided over initiations, who were called *mohgi;* those in charge of harvest festivals; and rainmakers. In general, practitioners were not organized into a hierarchical priesthood, except around the mbang at Bedaya.

Ceremonies. Much ceremonial activity was ritual to propitiate besigi or badigi, thereby creating or restoring beneficent natural and social worlds. The most important ceremonies were initiations, funerals, and those following the harvest. Initiations were important for a number of reasons, one of which was that they helped define gender relations. Men became initiated (*ndo*), whereas women and young boys remained uninitiated (*koy*). As a result, men were thought to have learned how to act, a knowledge denied to women.

Arts. Singing and dancing have been and remain an important part of Sara life. Visual arts such as sculpture were little developed.

Medicine. In precolonial times, and still largely today, illness was believed to be the result of supernatural actions—either those of a besi, a badi, or a practitioner of sorcery (*kuma*). Divination was performed to identify the attacking supernatural and to suggest a manner of diagnosis.

Death and Afterlife. Many Sara conceived of death not so much as a biological event as a modification in social status. Each person was believed to have something like a soul (*ndil*). At death, this separated from the body. Provided the proper rituals were performed, however, the deceased did not perish but became a badi. Participation in mortuary ceremonies was important as a way of validating a person's membership in a clan.

Bibliography

Brown, E. P. (1983). *Nourrir les gens, nourrir les haines*. Paris: Société d'Ethnographie.

Fortier, J. (1982). *Le couteau de jet sacré: Histoire des sar et de leurs rois au sud du Tchad*. Paris: l'Harmattan.

Jaulin, R. (1967). *La mort sara*. Paris: Plon.

Magnant, J.-P. (1987). *La terre sara, terre tchadiene*. Paris: l'Harmattan.

Pairault, C. (1966). *Boum-le-Grand: Village d'Iro*. Paris: Institut d'Ethnologie.

S. P. REYNA

Shahsevan

ETHNONYMS: none

Orientation

In various parts of Iran live the remnants of several tribal groups called "Shahsevan," numbering perhaps 300,000 people. Most are now settled villagers or town dwellers who preserve little of their former tribal organization or pastoral nomadic culture, but some 50,000 Shahsevan still live a nomadic or seminomadic life in the province of East Azerbaijan, close to the former Soviet frontier. They winter near sea level on the Moghan steppe and spend the summer months 160 kilometers or so to the south in the high pastures of the Savalan range, in the districts of Ardabīl, Meshkin, and Sarab. Shahsevan nomads form a minority of the population in this region, although, like the settled majority, whom they know as "Tat," they are Shia Muslims and speak Azerbaijani Turkish. A century ago, Shahsevan identity in this region implied membership in any one of a number of recognized tribes, through political allegiance to its chief (*beg*); most tribespeople were pastoral nomads, but large numbers were settled farmers. Today, after decades of government suppression of the tribal political structure, "Shahsevan" signifies nomadic, tent-dwelling pastoralists, and most settled nomads soon lose their tribal identity.

History and Cultural Relations

Shahsevan means "those who love the Shah." Shahsevan ancestors are said to have been formed into a special tribe in about A.D. 1600 by Shah ʾAbbas of the Safavid dynasty. There is no historical evidence to support this story, however, and it is unlikely that there was a single unified tribal group of this name until the early eighteenth century, when Shahsevan tribal warriors are recorded as resisting invading Ottoman forces in the Ardabīl-Moghan region. Soon afterward, several Shahsevan groups were moved to other parts of northern and western Iran, leaving the ancestors of the present Shahsevan tribes of Ardabīl and Moghan unified under a paramount chief who was appointed by the famous Iranian conqueror Nader Shah Afshar. The constituent tribes are mainly of Turkish descent, tracing their origins to Central Asia, although the ancestors of several were probably Kurdish. In the last 250 years, Azerbaijan has often been a battleground between Iran and her neighbors, and the Shahsevan figured prominently in the history of the period. Early in the nineteenth century, Russian invaders established their present frontier with Iran. The Shahsevan, deprived of the greater part of their traditional winter quarters in the Moghan steppe, became increasingly lawless. The raids sometimes disrupted trade and settlement far into both Russia and Iran and caused friction between the two countries, although neither government hesitated to exaggerate the extent of Shahsevan raiding. In 1909, after the constitutional revolution in Iran, most Shahsevan chiefs and their followers joined a Tribal Union with the neighboring tribes of Waradagh and Khalkhal, sacked the city of Ardabīl, and threatened, with secret Russian encouragement, to march on Tehran in the name of Islam to restore the deposed Mohammed ʾAli Shah. In 1910 Tehran government forces defeated them, but from 1911 until they were disarmed by Reza Shah in 1923, they maintained their independence of the government. Old men today preserve vivid memories of those times and of their victories over the Cossacks sent against them by Russia. From 1923 to 1978, they remained loyal to the rulers in Tehran, in conformity with their name. Soon after the Islamic Revolution, their name, with its Royalist connotation, was changed to "Elsevan" (lit., "those who love the people or tribe"). During the

1960s and 1970s, massive government-backed irrigation schemes were put into effect in Moghan, removing much of the remaining winter pastureland and forcing many more nomads to settle. After the Revolution, there was a brief revival of tribalism and pastoral nomadism, but it seems likely that the direction of change is irreversible. (The "ethnographic present" in this article, except where indicated, is the 1960s.)

Settlements

Shahsevan nomads commonly join forces in cooperative herding and camping groups of three to five households. Such a herding unit usually camps on its own in the mountain pastures between June and early September but joins with one or two others to form a winter camp of ten to fifteen households during the period from November to April. Two to three such winter camps comprise the basic nomadic community (*tireh*), which moves and camps as a unit during the autumn migration in October and the spring migration in May. Apart from their distinctive frontier location and history, the most obvious distinguishing characteristic of the Shahsevan with respect to other nomads is the type of tent they erect. Most nomads in Iran live in rectangular goat-hair tents, similar to those of Arab Bedouin. The Shahsevan tent (*alaçigh*) resembles an upturned saucer and is related to the Central Asian yurt. A wooden framework of curved struts, held together by long girths, radiates out and down to the ground from a central roof ring, which is itself anchored to the ground by a massive peg. A covering of thick felt mats keeps out both heat and cold. The hearth, focus of all domestic life, lies between the doorway and the central peg. The wooden parts, which are bought in the bazaar, are expected to last two years, and the felts, which need replacing every three years, are made in camp from the wool of the flocks. Such a tent or hut, heavier and sturdier than other types, is very expensive to maintain, and only two out of three families can afford one: poorer families use a much smaller, simpler, and cheaper construction (*kümeh*).

Economy

Subsistence, Commercial Activities, and Trade. Shahsevan nomads raise flocks of sheep and goats—the former for milk and milk products, wool, and meat, the latter only in small numbers, mainly as flock leaders. Camels, donkeys, and horses are used for transport. Most families raise chickens for eggs and meat, and a few keep cows. Every family has several fierce dogs to guard the home and the animals against thieves and predators. Bread is the staple food. Some nomads have relatives in villages, with whom they cooperate in a dual economy, sharing or exchanging pastoral for agricultural produce. Most, however, must sell milk, wool, and surplus animals to traders in order to obtain wheat flour and other supplies. Some work as hired shepherds and are paid with 5 percent of the animals they tend for every six-month contract period. Others go to towns and villages seasonally for casual wage labor. Every camp is visited almost every day by itinerant peddlers, but householders go on shopping expeditions to town at least twice a year (e.g., during the seasonal migrations). Most purchases are made on credit, against the next season's pastoral produce. The wealthiest nomads raise flocks of sheep commercially and may own shares in village lands as absentee landlords.

Industrial Arts. Shahsevan women produce a variety of colorful and intricate flat-woven rugs, storage bags, and blankets, and some produce knotted pile carpets, but these are all for domestic use and figure prominently in girls' trousseaux. Since about 1970, however, these Shahsevan artifacts have been recognized by the international Oriental-carpet trade, and hard times and escalating prices have forced many nomads to sell items that were never intended for the market.

Division of Labor. Herding, milking, shearing, and the marketing of produce are the work of men, who also see to the erection and maintenance of tents. The household head is rarely at home during the day unless he has guests. Younger men and boys help with the herding and fetch fuel. Women and girls may fetch water, but they normally stay in camp to run their households. Their main regular chore, at least once a day, is baking flat bread over the hearth; for home consumption, they also turn milk into cheese, yogurt, and butter, as well as cooking both regular and ceremonial meals, weaving, and keeping the insides of the tents clean.

Land Tenure. Although the pasturelands are legally owned by the state, each tireh has rights to defined areas in summer and winter quarters. Each full member usually has rights to a specific share of these pastures, rights that, with consent of fellow members, may be rented or sold for cash. Similarly, nomads who have sold or lost their grazing rights, as well as outsiders from the villages or towns, may rent grazing land for their animals from owners who have surplus land to dispose of. They may join the camp of the owner as "client" members of the community or set up separate camps of their own.

Kinship

Kin Groups and Descent. The male householders of a herding camp are usually brothers or paternal cousins, but often they also include hired shepherds and clients, who may be related to "core" members by marriage. Men of the twenty to thirty households of a community are most often from a single lineage, tracing their descent patrilineally from an ancestor some four generations back, whose name they usually bear. A woman married out of the community never loses her original lineage identity, although jurally and morally she is strongly assimilated into the community of her husband and children.

Kinship Terminology. Like that of most people in the region, Shahsevan kinship terminology is "Sudanese": paternal and maternal uncles and aunts are differentiated, as are all four types of first cousin, who are distinguished again from siblings. All members of the lineage regard each other as father's brother's cousins, whereas members of one's mother's community (if she is an outsider) are all mother's brothers or mother's brother's cousins. There is considerable depth in the terminology, with separate terms existing for father's father's father and sister's sister's sister's sister's sister, as well as for all generations between.

Marriage and Family

Marriage. About four marriages in ten involve couples from the same community, but, unlike many Muslims, Shahsevan rarely marry their first paternal cousins; mother's brother's daughter/father's sister's son is a more common link. Marriages are most often made between distant relatives of the same community, or between members of neighboring communities. Many boys and girls are able to choose their own partners, and many say that they marry for love. The ceremonies associated with marriage provide the most elaborate and colorful occasions among the Shahsevan. Several years of visits, exchanges, and several large feasts culminate in a week or more of festivities, leading to the fetching of the bride to join her husband's family. There is virtually no divorce or separation. Perhaps three men in a community have second wives, who are usually remarried widows.

Domestic Unit. In each tent lives a household of seven or eight people, on average. The Shahsevan prefer larger households, and often brothers and their wives and children, or an older couple and their married sons, all stay together. There are no partitions in the tent, with the exception of the curtain behind which a son and his bride sleep during the first years of their marriage.

Inheritance. Livestock and other movable property are usually inherited by males only. Following Islamic law, a daughter nominally inherits half a son's share in pastures or farmland, although in practice she almost always transfers her inheritance to one or all of her brothers. Women do own certain items of household property, however, and may be able to accumulate cash and valuables, the existence of which is often kept secret until they die.

Socialization. A father participates indulgently in the socializing of his daughters and young sons, often leaving normal discipline to their mother. As a boy approaches the age when he can help with the herding, however, he is liable to severe discipline by his father. Boys are taught the qualities of bravery and stamina that are associated with their warrior tradition, as well as moderation, respect for elders, and jealousy of community honor. Girls should be modest but also responsible, strong, and hardy. Many stories are told of women managing nomadic households of their own or berating warriors who returned home defeated.

Sociopolitical Organization

No trace is left of the eighteenth-century organization of the Moghan Shahsevan as a centralized tribal confederacy of some ten thousand families under a single family of paramount chiefs. The family split in two before 1800, dividing the confederacy into the Ardabīl branch and the Meshkin branch. The former branch soon settled and dispersed in and around the city of Ardabīl and in some other parts of Iran. In the mid-nineteenth century, the Meshkin branch of the chiefly family also settled, and the powerful tribes of the region, mostly of the Meshkin branch, were organized into a shifting series of clusters and coalitions under rival chiefs. The chiefs were very much weakened under the Pahlavi dynasty (1925–1978), and the tribes they led lost much of their cohesion. The authorities now attempt to deal directly with the communities and their elders. The thirty-odd Shahsevan tribes today vary in size from two to three communities (fifty families) to twenty-five or more (nearly a thousand). Few contacts, and less than one in ten marriages, are made between tribes, each of which feels itself different in subtle ways from the others. The chiefs no longer have the arbitrary power over their followers that they once enjoyed, but several of them and their families remain a privileged class, distinct from ordinary nomad society.

Social Organization. Community activities are directed by the elder, who has the difficult job of dealing with the authorities. Either he or his son is expected to be literate. Members of the community look to his life-style as a source and symbol of their honor, and he should be wealthy enough not only to entertain important visitors but also to provide lavish entertainment at feasts. There are wide differences of wealth among the Shahsevan. An elder may own several hundred sheep, five to ten camels, and some donkeys and horses, whereas a poor kinsman may own only fifteen sheep and two camels and have to work as a shepherd or supplement his income by casual labor or petty trading. The elder will ensure that all members contribute to the welfare of a family that has fallen on particularly hard times.

Political Organization, Social Control, and Conflict. An elder rarely displays his authority. Instead, with most members of the community, he uses skillful persuasion. Disputes, especially those involving women, are not discussed openly but are resolved if possible by private communications between elders and participants. Women have their own leaders, who act somewhat differently. Shahsevan women do not wear veils; they do, however, cover the lower part of the face in the presence of unrelated men. This rule is strictly observed by newly married women; young girls and older women are more casual. Women past childbearing age may reach positions of considerable respect, and a few become influential leaders, comparable to the male elders. Women leaders are consulted privately by the male elders, but among the women they exercise their influence in public, at feasts attended by guests from a wide range of communities. At feasts, men and women are segregated. While the men are enjoying music and other entertainment, the leaders in the women's tent are likely to be discussing matters of importance both to men and women, such as marriage arrangements, disputes, irregular behavior among community members, or broader subjects bearing on economic and political affairs. Opinions are formed and decisions made, which are then disseminated as the women return home and tell their menfolk and friends. This information network among the women serves a most important function for the society as a whole.

Religion and Expressive Culture

Religious Beliefs, Religious Practitioners, and Ceremonies. Shahsevan are Shia Muslims, who believe in Allah, respect Mohammed his Prophet, and regard Mohammed's cousin and son-in-law ʿAli as God's deputy. They are strongly attached to ʿAli's family, especially his son Hoseyn, who was martyred at the battle of Karbala in A.D. 680. This martyrdom is commemorated in the first ten days of the Islamic month of Moharram, the most important event of the Shahsevan religious calendar. Ceremonies in Moharram and during the fasting month of Ramazan are a community affair, directed by the elder, but with everybody contributing to the expenses of feasting and the hire of a mullah, who is brought from a nearby village or town to officiate. Every family observes the feast of Sacrifice, coinciding with annual pilgrimages to Mecca. Great respect is paid to those who have made pilgrimages to Mecca and to the Shiite shrines at Karbala and An Najaf in Iraq and at Mashhad in northeastern Iran. The departure and return of Mecca pilgrims are occasions for large gatherings of friends and relatives.

Circumcision for boys is seen as a religious duty, but religion plays little part in the ceremonies, which resemble weddings. Guests at major life-cycle ceremonies—weddings, circumcisions, pilgrimage departures, funeral feasts—are from the sponsor's circle of *kheyrüshärr* (lit., "good-and-bad"), those whose feasts he (or she) attends and who attend his (or hers); such guests contribute money toward the expenses of the feasting and often bring food or lend equipment.

Medicine. Shahsevan women and some men believe in the malicious power of spirits of various kinds to harm the weak, especially childbearing women, children, and animals. Beliefs in the evil eye are also common, but vague. Such beliefs are invoked only on the occasion of some malignant or unexpected illness or sudden death. In both summer and winter quarters, nomads are within a day's travel from towns and cities with modern medical facilities. These facilities are basic, however. They can be costly, and they are resorted to only in severe emergencies. Each community has at least one man and one woman with a knowledge of charms and countermeasures against evil forces and of traditional herbal and magico-religious remedies for common ailments. More powerful experts are found in the towns and villages.

Arts. In addition to the artistic textiles that are produced by the women, there is a lively tradition among both men and women of storytelling and of performing tribal songs and dances; most music at festivities today, however, is rendered by hired musicians from the villages and cities. Favorites are the minstrels who travel throughout the region to perform at wedding and circumcision feasts.

Death and Afterlife. After a death, the body is washed and buried in a nearby village graveyard, under the supervision of a mullah. Commemorative feasts follow on the third, seventh, and fortieth days, and on the anniversary of the death. As with other Shiites, there are few elaborations of standard conceptions, based on Quranic and Islamic traditions, concerning the nature of paradise and hell.

Bibliography

Housego, Jenny (1978). *Tribal Rugs: An Introduction to the Weaving of the Tribes of Iran*. London: Scorpion Publications.

Parviz, Tanvoli (1985). *Shahsevan: Iranian Rugs and Textiles*. New York: Rizzoli.

Safizadeh, Fereydoun (1984). "Shahsevan in the Grip of Development." *Cultural Survival Quarterly* 8(1): 14–18.

Siyawosch, Azadi, and Peter Andrews (1985). *Mafrash*. Berlin: Reimer.

Tapper, Nancy (1978). "The Women's Sub-Society among the Shahsevan Nomads." In *Women in the Muslim World*, edited by Lois Beck and Nikki Keddie. Cambridge: Harvard University Press.

Tapper, Richard (1979). *Pasture and Politics: Economics, Conflict, and Ritual among Shahsevan Nomads of Northwestern Iran*. London: Academic Press.

RICHARD TAPPER

Shilluk

ETHNONYM: Collo

Orientation

The Shilluk are the most northern Nilotic-speaking people in modern Africa. Shilluk country covers approximately 320 kilometers on the west bank of the White Nile, from 10° to 12° N and from 30° to 33° E. Shilluk oral traditions, however, indicate that at some time in the past their country reached to the confluence of the Blue and White Niles, the site of the modern city of Khartoum. At the time of the last official census (1956), the Shilluk were estimated to number 120,000 individuals. Most of Shilluk country is open savanna and free from the annual floods of the White Nile. The Shilluk language is most closely related to Anuak. Together, the two languages comprise a subfamily of the larger classification of Nilotic, which is spoken by different cultural groups throughout eastern Africa.

History and Cultural Relations

Considerable controversy surrounds the topic of the history and origins of the Shilluk. Indeed, the "origin" and history of all of the Nilotic peoples of the southern Sudan remains an enigma in the field of African prehistory. According to Shilluk oral traditions, the early descendants of these people began to migrate into their present country some three to four hundred years before the present. The quasi-mythical or epic leader of the first settlement is known as Nyikang, an individual with both divine and secular powers. At one time, Nyikang and his brother Gilo had a disagreement, and, as a result, Gilo and his supporters separated to migrate south and east. Like Nyikang for the Shilluk, Gilo is now cited as the culture hero and founder of the Anuak. Anthropologists posit that, before they arrived in their present country, the Shilluk practiced a nomadic form of pastoralism. As they eventually spread out and settled in more permanent communities, a horticultural mode of livelihood eventually replaced their primary dependence on cattle.

Settlements

The distribution of Shilluk communities has been likened to beads on a string, spread out on the banks of the White Nile, the one separated from the next by a distance of from 180 meters to 1.5 kilometers. Settlements range in size from hamlets made up of the mud and thatched-roof huts of a few families to villages of some one hundred families. At roughly the center of Shilluk country is the village of Pachoda, the residence of each succeeding Shilluk "king" (see "Sociopolitical Organization"). Population densities in Shilluk country exceed all others among the Nilotic-speaking peoples of the southern Sudan. Each hamlet is formed around a cluster of patrilineal kin who claim membership in a common clan. Individual clans are dispersed widely throughout Shilluk country. Postmarital residence is patrilocal, and each homestead within a hamlet consists of a hut for each adult man as well as a separate dwelling for each of his wives.

Economy

The Shilluk keep small herds of cattle, in addition to larger flocks of sheep and goats. Cattle are normally used for food only in the context of ritual and ceremonial occasions. In the evening, the cattle are tethered around dung fires in an effort to lessen the adverse effects of biting flies and insects. Shilluk aggressively and successfully exploit the rich resources of the White Nile and regularly catch many species of fish with fishing nets and spears. They also hunt hippopotamuses. Less frequently, small hunting parties are organized to pursue antelope, buffalo, and giraffes. Hamlets are surrounded by gardens of millet, maize, and sesame, as well as other species introduced during the twentieth century. The Shilluk also cultivate tobacco for personal use and for sale. Herding, hunting, and spearfishing are primarily male activities; women traditionally have manufactured cooking utensils, cultivated gardens, and prepared food.

Kinship

The Shilluk are divided into some one hundred patrilineal and exogamous clans. Clans are not localized and have no specific territorial referents. Instead, clans are scattered widely through different hamlets. Conversely, the lineages that comprise clans are conceived of as localized groups. As Wall (1976, 155) notes, the family homesteads (*gol*) or those of individual lineage members are grouped together to form hamlets of agnatically related kin. A hamlet of this type may include as many as fifty homesteads. Ultimately, these scattered hamlets may form a larger settlement with a clearly defined territory. In each hamlet there is an original or "owner" lineage, called a *diel*. The Shilluk, like the other Nilotic-speaking peoples of southern Sudan, have a system of relationship terminology that is commonly known as "descriptive." Legal marital unions are established by the exchange of bride-wealth cattle, which pass from the agnatic kin of the groom to the adult members of the bride's family. A man is commonly 25 years old before his first marriage, whereas it is customary for a young woman marry before she reaches the end of her teen years. A wedding feast in the bride's father's homestead follows the exchange of bride-wealth cattle. At the end of these festivities, the bride and groom return to establish their own homestead in the hamlet of the groom's father. It is reported that a mock battle is enacted between the groom's and the bride's kin, once the last of the promised bride-wealth cattle are given. The ideal number of bride-wealth cattle should amount to at least ten animals, including cows, oxen, and a bull. In addition, the bride's family expects to receive *diek nom*, a number of sheep, as well as *jam nom*, gifts of spears and other goods. The latter gifts belong to the parents of the bride, but the sheep are distributed among the bride's agnatic kin. When a wife is pregnant for the first time, it is customary for her to return to her natal village to give birth.

Sociopolitical Organization

At the hamlet level, the primary political figures of traditional life were settlement "chiefs," who, ideally, were nominated from the diel, or founding lineage. The position of village "chief" is subject to the approval of the *reth*, or "king," of the Shilluk. All Shilluk settlements collectively comprise a dual division of Shillukland, between Luak in the south and Ger in the north. The reth of the Shilluk is a living symbol of the unity of Shilluk history, culture, and polity, and each succeeding reth is thought to be possessed by the spirit of Nyikang, the Shilluk culture hero and first king. Nyikang is intimately associated with the spirit the Shilluk call "Juok," and, in consequence, each reth is though to be an incarnation of the past within the world of the present. Because of this association between a spiritual power and a mortal human being, the Shilluk reth has sometimes been referred to as a "divine king." The selection and the installation of a new reth are woven in a complex web of ritual and symbolism. Modern anthropologists still do not agree on the process through which a reth was selected in precolonial days. It is certain that the final candidate to become a new reth had to be approved by both northern and southern Shilluk. Civil war would erupt unless unanimous agreement was achieved. Evans-Pritchard (1948) suggested that the reth of the Shilluk reigned but did not rule. What he meant was that the reth was the incarnation of a sacred order of an ideal Shilluk society. His "kingly" status derived from sacred authority rather than secular power. The present reth of the Shilluk is the thirty-first in succession since the origin of Shilluk polity. His status and authority have been transformed in the twentieth century, first by British colonial policy in Sudan and second by the strictures created by the independent government of Sudan.

Religion

Shilluk religious concepts are drawn into relief by an emphasis on the creator-god or divinity known as Juok (a common Nilotic term for a spiritual power), the veneration of Nyikang through the persons who become kings, and the recognition of the ways in which the spirits of the deceased can affect those who survive them. Juok is a ubiquitous spirit, a phenomenon manifest in all places and at all times. Juok can be addressed through sacrifice of cattle, goats, and sheep. Juok is also strongly associated in Shilluk thought with the river spirit that first gave birth to Nyikang. Most Western depictions of Shilluk religion have been colored by nineteenth-century visions of "primitive religion." The Shilluk figured prominently in evolutionary schemes put forward to depict the course of religious evolution. Ironically, although the Shilluk have become well known in the anthropological literature, no prolonged research has been carried out by a trained observer in their settlements. Thus, much of what has been written about the Shilluk relies upon data that were collected in an inconsistent manner in the early twentieth century.

Bibliography

Arens, W. (1979). "The Divine Kingship of the Shilluk: A Contemporary Reevaluation." *Ethnos* 44:167–181.

Evans-Pritchard, E. E. (1948). *The Divine Kingship of the Shilluk*. Cambridge: Cambridge University Press.

Lienhardt, R. G. (1954). "The Shilluk of the Upper Nile." In *African Worlds*, edited by D. Forde, 138–163. London: Oxford University Press.

Seligman, C. G., and B. Z. Seligman (1932). *Pagan Tribes of the Nilotic Sudan*. London: Routledge & Kegan Paul.

Wall, L. (1976). "Anuak Politics, Ecology, and the Origins of Shilluk Kingship." *Ethnology* 15:151–162.

Westerman, D. (1912). *The Shilluk People*. Philadelphia: United Presbyterian Church.

JOHN W. BURTON

Shona

ETHNONYM: Karanga (historical)

Orientation

Identification. The Shona-speaking peoples comprise about 80 percent of the population of Zimbabwe, with significant groups in Mozambique. Most of what follows applies to the Shona in Zimbabwe, who have been extensively studied.

There are a number of linguistic subgroups of Shona: the Zezuru, who inhabit the central plateau of Zimbabwe; the Karanga, to the south; the Korekore, to the north and dropping into the Zambezi Valley; the Manyika, to the east; the Tavara, in the Zambezi Valley in Mozambique and in the extreme northeast of Zimbabwe; the Ndau, in the southeast of Zimbabwe and stretching down to the coast in Mozambique; and the Kalanga, in the southwest of Zimbabwe and overflowing into Botswana.

These linguistic classifications led to the formation of distinct ethnic classifications in colonial times. Historically, however, neither the subgroups nor the Shona as a whole comprised distinct political or ethnic units. The Kalanga and the Ndau, in particular, have been considerably influenced by neighboring Nguni peoples.

Location. Central Shona country is the high plateau of Zimbabwe, with an elevation of 1,200 meters or more, a temperate climate, and an annual rainfall of 70 to 100 centimeters. The Zambezi Valley, in the north, is hotter and drier, as is the southwest. Few Shona now inhabit the eastern highlands, which are cool and wet. Generally, the colonial administration moved the majority of Shona away from the best farmland, into areas where the soils are sandy and thin and where the amount of rainfall is less favorable for agriculture.

Demography. The Shona population is estimated to have been slightly more than half a million early in the twentieth century. There has been rapid population increase in Zimbabwe throughout the twentieth century: there are now around 8,000,000 Shona in Zimbabwe and perhaps half a million outside. Approximately 26 percent of the population now reside in urban areas. Life expectancy at birth is 57, and the population growth rate is estimated at 3 percent.

Linguistic Affiliation. The Shona language is tonal and is one of the Bantu Group. There is relative ease of communication with neighboring peoples. A kind of pidgin Bantu, *chilapalapa*, based largely on Zulu and Afrikaans, is widely spoken in the region, especially in the towns.

History and Cultural Relations

The ancestors of the Shona settled in their region in the first millennium A.D., introducing settled agriculture, cattle, and iron mining to the area. Although the Shona have been organized, for the most part, into small, independent chiefdoms, from time to time during the course of their history, conglomerations of chiefdoms have been united into larger states. Control of trade in gold and ivory with Arabs and Portuguese on the coast constituted both a motive and a support for political rulers to expand their spheres of influence. From the twelfth century onward, techniques of drystone walling were developed by the Karanga in the south, who, with the formation of large states, constructed a number of large stone buildings.

In the nineteenth century, the Shona were disturbed by Nguni migrations from the south, particularly by the Ndebele who, possessing superior military techniques, settled in and dominated the southeast of what is now Zimbabwe. Colonial settlement came at the end of the century. An uprising against the settlers was defeated. Independence came after further wars in Rhodesia and Mozambique in the 1960s and 1970s.

From the nineteenth century onward, the Shona have migrated to work in the mines of South Africa. After the colonial settlement of southern Rhodesia, employment became available within the country, on farms and mines, and particularly in the growing industrial cities. Some groups were moved off their land to make way for settlers who wanted to farm it.

Widespread education was introduced by various groups of missionaries, who also established hospitals and diverse forms of technical training, including training in improved agriculture. These services were subsequently taken over and expanded by government. Plow agriculture is now prevalent.

Settlements

There were some large stockaded villages prior to colonial settlement, but in some areas people lived in scattered family hamlets. The dominant settlement pattern is one of villages with homesteads spread out in lines next to agricultural land. The traditional homestead included a number of round, pole-and-mud huts with conical thatched roofs. These huts have largely been replaced by brick houses, roofed with zinc, sometimes in the traditional style of round huts.

Economy

Subsistence and Commercial Activities. In precolonial times the main crops were various types of millet. Now, except in the drier areas, maize is predominant. Groundnuts and various vegetables are also grown for relish. Early in the colonial period, farmers grew surpluses for sale. Cash crops such as tobacco and cotton are also grown. Today, shortages of land are acute in many areas, and few Shona are able to make much of an income from farming. Agriculture is largely supported by salaried or wage labor in the towns. A cash income in the family allows for expenditure on implements and on quality seed and fertilizers, which increase agricultural output.

Except in the low-lying, tsetse-fly–infested areas, cattle are widely kept. Traditionally, cattle comprised the main indicator of wealth. They retain importance in this respect in the rural areas and have the added utility of providing draft power. Other domestic animals include goats, sheep, pigs, donkeys, and various types of poultry.

Industrial Arts. In the rural areas everyone is involved in agriculture and there are no full-time specialists. In the past there was extensive iron and gold smelting, but all the surface gold has now been mined, and superior iron is now obtained from modern plants. One still finds blacksmiths in many villages, however. Traditional crafts of basketwork and pottery are still widespread. One now finds carpenters, builders, tailors, and other semiskilled specialists in many rural areas. Women engage in sewing and knitting, now often on a cooperative basis.

Trade. Although there is a long history of trade both between Shona groups and with outsiders, there were traditionally no markets in Shona settlements. These are now well established in cities, towns, and many rural centers of administration and trade. Even the remotest areas have access to some stores in which basic consumer goods are sold.

Division of Labor. The division of labor in Shona society is primarily based on sex. Women make pottery, do all the domestic work, and perform many of the less strenuous agricultural tasks. Men are responsible for more strenuous (but less time-consuming) agricultural work, raising cattle, hunting, and ironwork. They are also involved in politics, which requires much sitting around and talking.

Certain men, such as a chief or a man with many daughters, can expect to have dependents do chores for them. People with good incomes from wages or salaries are now able to employ others to do some of their agricultural work.

Land Tenure. Traditionally, every adult man was given land by his father or village headman. Land could not be bought or sold; it was returned to the community for redistribution when no longer in use. Now there is a scarcity of agricultural land in most communities, and land rights are carefully guarded and inherited. Land has acquired a commercial value. Grazing land, however, remains communal and, except in freehold commercial-farming areas, is habitually overused.

Kinship

Kin Groups and Descent. Patrilineal groups are the basic unit of economic cooperation and, usually, of residence: extended families traditionally shared a homestead or lived in adjacent homesteads. Except in chiefly families, such a group is rarely more than three or four generations in depth, and it is easy for an individual to attach instead to matrilateral relatives. The descendants of a deceased woman may occasionally gather for ritual purposes.

Kinship Terminology. Patrilineal kin are classified according to sex, generation, and seniority by age. Parallel matrilateral kin are accorded the same terms as patrilineal kin. Other matrilateral kin are classified simply by sex.

Marriage and Family

Marriage. Polygyny was traditionally preferred, but the cost of living, and especially of education, has made monogamy more common. The preferred form of marriage is virilocal, with the payment of bride-price, traditionally in cattle but now in cash and kind. Bride-service was formerly an alternative; in the remoter low-lying areas where cattle are not kept, it remains a prominent part of marriage transactions. Occasionally, a young girl may be pledged to a wealthy man against help in time of extreme hardship. Divorce, although discouraged, is common and usually involves the return of a proportion of the bride-price, depending on the duration of the marriage and the number of children born.

Traditionally, the sexual activities of women were strictly controlled, and girls were inspected for virginity at marriage. Such controls have largely broken down.

Domestic Unit. In a polygynous marriage, the domestic unit was usually a wife and her children. Such a unit was usually allocated its own fields for subsistence purposes. A nuclear family is now the most common domestic unit.

Inheritance. A man's status, wives, and possessions may be inherited by his brother or by his adult child. The inheritor takes responsibility for the family of the deceased. Adelphic succession results in the position of chieftainship rotating between houses descended from different wives of the founder of the dynasty. Adelphic inheritance sometimes poses problems in a modern family, when the deceased husband's kin take all the family property, leaving the wife destitute. A woman's personal property is inherited by her daughters.

Socialization. Infants are pampered and receive much personal attention until the age of 3 or 4, resulting in rapid development of motor and cognitive skills. Thereafter, they are strictly disciplined. Children receive much personal attention from peers and a number of adults in the extended family. Although importance is attached to authority structures, including authority based on age among siblings, this authority is diffused among a number of older persons. Now, with more emphasis on the elementary family, authority often rests entirely with the family head and is more open to abuse.

Sociopolitical Organization

Social Organization. Shona societies are primarily organized around kinship. Relations between nonkin may be formalized in bond friendship, which imposes mutual obligations of hospitality, material assistance, and certain ritual services. Heavy tasks, such as thatching a house, clearing or plowing a field or reaping the harvest, may be performed by work parties, at which neighbors work and are rewarded with supplies of millet beer. Attendance at such parties imposes obligations of reciprocation.

Political Organization. The principal Shona political unit was the chiefdom. A hereditary chief was ultimately responsible for the distribution of land, for appeasing the territorial spirit guardians, and for settling disputes. Larger chiefdoms were sometimes subdivided into wards, each with its ward headman. The details of distributing land and settling minor disputes were left to the village headmen, but in the colonial era his main function became keeping a tax register.

Although the traditional political authorities are still recognized in order to maintain Shona culture and values, they now have little power. Dispute settlement is now in the hands of elected presiding officers, and land distribution is controlled by government administrators.

Social Control. Serious crimes, such as incest and homicide, used to be in the control of the guardian spirits, through their mediums. All other offenses were dealt with by a hierarchy of courts from the village level to the chiefly level. Now offenses are dealt with by a hierarchy of government-controlled courts, from the community level to the High Court.

Conflict. Warfare between the scattered Shona chiefdoms was rare. A number of Shona groups suffered from raids by Ndebele armies during the nineteenth century. Tensions between the Shona and the Ndebele have not yet been totally resolved.

Religion and Expressive Culture

Religious Beliefs. The ancestor cult is the dominant feature of Shona religion. Ancestors are largely benign; they protect their descendants from malign influences, both human and spiritual. Ancestors make their wishes known through the mediums they possess and often through causing their descendants to suffer mild but persistent illness. They dislike dissension among their descendants and are therefore a force for keeping groups together. Ancestors can be extremely dangerous; when they become angry, they can cause multiple deaths.

Ancestors of chiefly lineages often have a political function. They support and control the chiefly office and are often involved in the selection of a new chief. These spirit guardians are believed to care for all who live in their territory. They are responsible for rain and fertility. In some parts of Shona country, remote hero spirits can take on these territorial and political functions.

Most Shona have a vague idea of a remote High God but no traditional cult in his honor. Among the Karanga and the Kalanga, however, there is a cult of the High God Mwari, with a complex organization, which overshadows local chiefly or territorial cults. Partly through use of the name by missionaries, knowledge of Mwari has now spread throughout Shona country.

There are a variety of lesser spirits that may provide individuals with particular skills or protection. Belief in witchcraft and sorcery is widespread and can become obsessive, particularly under the strain of survival in urban environments.

Around 25 percent of the Shona belong to a variety of Christian denominations, and many ideas from Christianity have penetrated the thought of non-Christians. Among the denominations Shona have embraced are a number of independent churches that emphasize prophecy and healing through possession by the Holy Spirit.

Religious Practitioners. The most important practitioners are spirit mediums, men or women who have been chosen by particular spirits to be their hosts. From time to time, a medium becomes possessed by the spirit, and the spirit is believed to act and speak through the host. Hosts may have relatively unimportant spirits and have little function other than providing entertainment at possession dances. They may have healing spirits and thus be primarily concerned with divination and healing, or they may have ancestral spirits or politically important territorial spirits.

In the south, the cult of Mwari has a specialized priesthood that cares for a number of hill shrines and performs ceremonies at them. Otherwise, any adult male, and occasionally an adult female, may perform routine ceremonies in honor of deceased ancestors.

Ceremonies. Most important ceremonies involve offerings of millet beer to the spirits concerned. Small libations are poured, and the remainder is consumed by the gathering, amid singing and dancing. Sacrifices may occasionally be offered to ancestors and territorial spirits but are regularly offered to Mwari. Spirits may also be honored with gifts of cloth or money, handed over to the medium.

Arts. The most important musical instrument is the *mbira*, consisting of up to thirty finely tuned metal reeds, set on a wooden base and played inside a gourd resonator. The reeds are plucked with fingers and thumbs. The Shona also have a variety of drums, and in different parts of the country one finds horns, friction bows, gongs, panpipes, and xylophones.

Visual arts were relatively undeveloped in precolonial times. More recently, fine wood and stone carving have become widespread.

Medicine. Western medicine is widely available in Shona country and is widely accepted for most ailments. A wide range of herbs and charms are available for ordinary ailments or protection against them. When illness is persistent or when it is accompanied by tension in the community, spiritual causes are suspected and traditional healers are consulted. These divine the cause by dice or through spirit possession and prescribe both ritual and herbal remedies. Such healers may also prescribe charms for good fortune in various domains. A common result of divination is that a spirit wants the sick person to become its host; in such cases, healing may be achieved through possession trances. Traditional healing is particularly effective in dealing with psychological tensions: responsibility is transferred to spirits, and the whole community is involved in sorting out the problem.

Death and Afterlife. Although the ancestral cult is important, traditional Shona rarely speak about an afterlife; a person's future after death is vaguely thought to depend on having descendants who will remember the deceased and hold rituals in his or her honor. Funeral ceremonies are performed to take a dead person away from the community and to keep him or her away. For an adult with descendants, an additional ceremony a year or more later welcomes the deceased into the company of benign ancestors and back into the homestead.

Bibliography

Beach, David N. (1980). *The Shona and Zimbabwe, 900–1850*. Gweru: Mambo Press.

Bourdillon, M. F. C. (1987). *The Shona Peoples*. 3rd ed. Gweru: Mambo Press.

Ellert, Henrik (1984). *The Material Culture of Zimbabwe*. Harare: Longman.

Gelfand, Michael (1979). *Growing Up in Shona Society*. Gweru: Mambo Press.

M. F. C. BOURDILLON

Sleb

ETHNONYMS: Salīb, Slavey, Ṣlêb, Sleyb, Solubba, Ṣulaib, Suleib, Ṣulubba, Szleb

Orientation

Identification. These ethnonyms are applied to a little-known, endogamous, and traditionally itinerant community practicing a variety of low-status occupations and living in large parts of the Arab Middle East. It is not clear to what extent the term "Sleb" is a generic one, but it does embrace distinct and preferentially endogamous groups. Although they perform many needful services for the pastoral population of the area, the Sleb are held in great contempt. Owing to the combination of an itinerant life-style and low status, they have often been termed "Gypsies" and have been mentioned by a host of travelers and researchers in different parts of Arabia.

Location. A peripatetic people, the Sleb live and migrate in the Syrian desert, in Jordan, Iraq, Kuwait, and Saudi Arabia. In the late twentieth century, however, many have become sedentary.

Linguistic Affiliation. The Sleb do not appear to speak any language other than Arabic.

Demography. Around 1898, the entire Sleb population was estimated at about 3,000 individuals; another estimate, made a few years later for a part of the Syrian desert (between Palmyra and Suchne) was 1,700 individuals. Ottoman records indicate that there were about 500 Sleb in the region of Mosul.

History

Next to nothing is known about the history of the Sleb. It has been suggested that Sleb populations are descended from those referred to in Middle and Late Assyrian texts as the "Selappayu," or from the Banu Saluba, who inhabited the area of Hira and Kalwadha, as well as certain villages on the Euphrates, during the Arab conquest. Anthropological data indicate that the Sleb are of Proto-Mediterranean origin, and it is thought that they formerly drew subsistence almost exclusively from hunting.

Settlements

Sleb camps are currently small and scattered, sometimes even consisting of a single family, with one or two tents. In the nineteenth century, however, camps of fifteen to twenty-five tents, with twenty to thirty families per tent, were observed.

Economy

In addition to hunting (mainly gazelles, but also ostriches and Arabian oryx), which in the nineteenth century was the mainstay of the economy of the itinerant parts of the community throughout the area, the following activities have been reported by various authors: collection of salt from salines in the southern Jezira, breeding asses and camels, smithery and tinkering, tracking water, guiding caravans, healing animals, carpentry, fortune-telling, tattooing, music, poetry, and prostitution. The pastoral peoples of the area rely upon these services, and every group of Sleb is attached to a local tribe. In recent years many families have sedentarized in Jordan as traders, but, even in the nineteenth century, many itinerant families marketed the salt they collected in towns such as Baghdad or Mosul.

Kinship, Marriage, and Family

Everywhere, the Sleb divided into several preferentially endogamous subgroups. Marriages take place shortly after puberty and with the consent of all. The remarriage of widows and divorcées is allowed, and in such cases the bride-price is lower than that for a virgin. A woman divorcing for the first time may keep half the bride-price for herself, whereas in subsequent divorces she must return in its entirety. The bride-price may consist of hunting reserves or grazing lands. It is reported that until the middle of the nineteenth century, when polygyny was introduced, marriages were monogamous.

Sociopolitical Organization

The Sleb are integrated into the *khuwa* system prevalent in their area, whereby pastoral communities, which act as patrons toward politically weaker groups, exact tribute from them in return for shelter and protection.

Religion and Expressive Culture

Formally, all Sleb are Muslims. Various authors, however, have observed numerous pre-Islamic traditions among them, and some have speculated about Christian influences.

Traditionally, the Sleb had a distinctive hooded dress or shirt made from several gazelle skins; it was open at the neck and had long sleeves gathered at the wrist but extending to and covering the hands.

Bibliography

Dostal, W. (1956). "Die Ṣulubba und ihre Bedeutung für die Kulturgeschichte Arabiens." *Archiv für Völkerkunde* 9:15–42.

Henninger, J. (1939). "Pariastämme in Arabien." *Sankt Gabrieler Studien* 8:503–539.

Pieper, W. (1923). "Der Pariastamm der Ṣlêb." *Le monde oriental* 17(1): 1–75.

APARNA RAO

Somalis

ETHNONYMS: Samaale, Soomaali

Orientation

Identification. The Muslim Somalis of the Horn of Africa speak the Somali language and live in the Somali Democratic Republic (Somalia). There are also substantial numbers of Somalis in neighboring countries: the southern half of Djibouti, the eastern part of Ethiopia, and the northeastern part of Kenya. There are large stable settlements of Somalis in the north of Tanzania and in the Yemeni city of Aden. Although Somalis regard themselves as ethnically one people, there are several subgroups based on patrilineal descent. The term "Somali" is popularly held to derive from the expression *so maal*, or "come and milk," an expression used among nomads, which alludes to the pastoral subsistence and the Somali ideal of hospitality.

Location. Somalia is located between 1°30′ S and 11°30′ N and 41°00′ and 51°25′ E; it extends over an area of 638,000 square kilometers. Somalia has a warm climate: daytime temperatures range from 25° C to 35° C. There is high humidity along the coastal plains. The country is traversed by two perennial rivers, the Jabba and the Shabelle. Average annual rainfall is less than 60 centimeters. There are two rainy seasons, *gu'* (April to June) and *dayr* (October to November).

Demography. In 1994 the population of Somalia was officially estimated to be 6.67 million. The average population density varies between 9.4 and 13.3 persons per square kilometer; however, density is substantially higher along the riverbanks. A rapid urbanization rate has brought 20 percent of the population to urban centers, with the bulk of this population living in the capital, Mogadishu. With an average life expectancy of about 46 years (1975), more than 58 percent of Somalis are below 20 years of age.

Linguistic Affiliation. The Somali language, Af-Soomaali, belongs to the East Cushitic Branch of Afroasiatic languages. It is closely related to languages of some of the neighboring peoples: the Oromo, the Rendille, and the Boni. These languages are sometimes referred to as the "Sam" languages. The Afar language, too, has many similarities with Somali. The Somali people also share many important cultural traits with these linguistically related groups. Somali has adopted a substantial amount of vocabulary from Arabic, but, since 1972, the Latin alphabet has been used for writing. The language has a number of different dialects, most of which are mutually intelligible. The dialects that standard Somali speakers find most difficult to comprehend are the Af-May dialects that are spoken in the south.

History and Cultural Relations

There are two major versions of how the Somali people came into possession of their current territory. Some oral-historical evidence suggests that Somalis gradually spread from the north of the country toward the west and, pushing Oromo and Bantu peoples ahead of them, appeared in the south only during the last millennium. According to another version that possibly relates to movements of a much earlier date, the "Sam"-language speakers first emerged east of Lake Turkana in Kenya. Proto-Somali speakers spread to the northeast from the Tana River and into the Somali Peninsula. Neither of the versions can draw support from archaeological finds. There is evidence that two northern port towns, Zeila and Berbera, were already flourishing in 100 B.C. During the first half of the current millennium, the coastal settlements along the southern shore, in the Benadir region, became established as important commercial centers, with trade networks extending along substantial parts of the East African coast and into the interior of the Horn. During the nineteenth century, Benadir ports came under the dominion of the Omani sultanate, and southern Somali agriculture received an influx of imported slave labor. In the late nineteenth century southern Somalia became an Italian colony; the northern part of country was colonized by the British. After the Italians were defeated during World War II, they were granted their former colony in United Nations trusteeship from 1950 until the independence and unification of the two former colonies in 1960. The frail parliamentary democracy that was installed was overthrown in a 1969 coup d'état that brought Major General Mohammed Siad Barre to power. During some two decades of military rule, the Soviet Union and the United States succeeded one another as Somalia's chief ally. In 1977–1978 Somalia sought unsuccessfully to take from Ethiopia the Ogaden region, which is inhabited primarily by ethnic Somalis. The final resolution of that conflict was not reached until the spring of 1988. In the late 1980s a bloody civil war between Somali government troops and several resistance groups led to a mass exodus of at least 400,000 northern Somalis to Ethiopia.

Settlements

There are two major types of Somali villages. One is the densely clustered nomadic encampment, with portable huts (sing. *aqal*) occupied by five to ten families that stay in the vicinity of the pastures of their herds. Another type of village is found among sedentary cultivators and agro-pastoralists. These are permanent settlements, with an average of five hundred inhabitants and about one hundred mud huts (sing. *mundul*) with thatched roofs. An increasingly common type of building is the tin-roofed mud house (*baraako*). Settlement in these villages may be more dispersed than in the nomadic encampments and may also seasonally include some of the villagers' nomadic kin. The permanent villages are surrounded by farms, and in the center of each village a mosque and a market can often be found. In the grazing areas, small groups of young herders often reside in the open.

Economy

Subsistence and Commercial Activities. Animal husbandry is traditionally the major subsistence activity, and the only one in large parts of northern and central Somalia. A wealthy household in the north may have several hundred camels and also considerable numbers of cattle, sheep, and goats. The commercialization of the livestock sector has made livestock and livestock products into the single most important contributor to the gross national product. The total number of camels in Somalia was estimated to be 6.4 million in 1987. Herd management continues to be carried on according to traditional methods, with transhumance between water holes and suitable pastures. In the south, nomadic pastoralism is often mixed with rain-fed agriculture, primarily of sorghum and maize. Other crops include vegetables, fruits, and sesame. With the exception of large foreign-owned banana plantations, agriculture is largely unmechanized, and most crops are planted, weeded, and harvested with hoes and knives. The consumption of fish is increasing, but the 3,300 kilometers of seashore remain little exploited. Hunting is generally seen as defiling and is left to groups that most other Somalis see as inferior.

Industrial Arts. Every one of the larger Somali villages has inhabitants who specialize in the manufacture of iron goods, pottery, and leatherwork. Often such artisans belong to groups that are considered inferior. Larger villages may also host some tailors and, in the riverine zones, sesame-mill operators.

Trade. Although the bulk of agricultural production is for family consumption, the sale of surplus in small-scale markets provides important income for most families. Both crops and animal produce are traded. Women have come to play increasingly important roles in commercial activities.

Division of Labor. Polygynously formed households assume specialized functions within the larger family economy. One wife and her children may be chiefly responsible for the camels, whereas another such sibling group is assigned the agricultural work. The herding and milking of camels is the exclusive domain of men, but women and children usually tend the small stock. Both men and women engage in farm work. Child rearing and household chores are the tasks of women and their elder daughters. Somali men often express embarrassment if they stay for a long period in the home.

Land Tenure. Pastoral territorial control of rangelands is primarily centered on the water sources that are available within an area. Thus, although there exists some association between a clan group and a certain tract of land, more definite property rights are articulated regarding wells and other water points. Pastoral territorial feuding is most marked where routes of migration conflict with the interests of cultivators. Agricultural territory belongs to the person who has cleared or inherited the land, and, theoretically, it may be sold or rented as that person sees fit. In colonial times, a form of community control was exercised; members of the same village or kin group were given the first option to buy farmland. The military regime has since introduced a system of centralized farm registration, and there have been reports that wealthy urban settlers use the system to appropriate rural estates from small-scale farmers.

Kinship

Kin Groups and Descent. The Somali system of patrilineal descent embraces the whole nation in a genealogical grid and claims ultimate descent from the Qurayshitic lineage of the prophet Mohammed. At the level of residential groupings, a set of patrilineally related kinsmen will form the nucleus of a kin group, to which other people are joined by ties of affinity or matrilaterality. For practical purposes, the genealogical depth of a residential kin group rarely goes beyond four or five generations; however, in matters such as feuding and payment of blood-wealth, the range of agnatically related kinsmen who are involved is greatly expanded.

Kinship Terminology. Parental siblings are referred to by bifurcate-collateral terms. Cousin terms are either Sudanese or Hawaiian. Where the latter prevails, it is usually for reasons of politeness, just as any stranger of approximately the same age as Ego may be addressed as "brother/sister." Seniority is emphasized in the use of intragenerational terms. Many intergenerational terms are used self-reciprocally, so that, for instance, a man addresses his son as "father."

Marriage and Family

Marriage. In northern Somalia, marriages were traditionally contracted between previously nonrelated families, explicitly to enable the establishment of new alliances. In the south, the favorite spouse is a patrilateral parallel cousin, real or classificatory. As a Muslim, each Somali man has the right to be married to four women. Although viri-patrilocal and neolocal residence are characteristic of both endogamous and exogamous marriages, several clans practice an initial period of uxorilocal residence that, lasting as it occasionally does for many years, may develop into a permanent residence. The divorce rate is high. In one southern study, half of all rural women in their fifties had been married more than once.

Domestic Unit. The principal domestic unit is the uterine-sibling group (*bah*), but it is not a closely bounded unit; many such groups have more distant relatives living with them, sometimes for extended periods. The descendants of a man, divided into several uterine-sibling groups, are collectively called a *reer*. This term means "people" and is, in principle, applicable to any level of agnatic grouping.

Inheritance. Sons generally receive an equal share of the father's property, whereas the rights of the daughters are less secure. Although daughters theoretically should inherit half the share that is allotted to each of their brothers, they have in several areas traditionally been allowed to inherit neither camels nor landed property. The ambitious 1975 family-law reform, stipulating that daughters should have equal rights to inheritance, has had little impact in either rural or urban areas.

Socialization. The duties of child rearing are essentially the mother's, although the father will take part in Quranic and religious education. The mother is usually aided in her task by both her sisters and her elder daughters. The values of respect for both seniority and the integrity of others are constantly emphasized. Small children are rapidly taught their position within the age hierarchy, but it is noteworthy how often parents will treat seriously even the most inchoate statement of a younger child.

Sociopolitical Organization

Somalia, constitutionally a socialist republic, is divided into regions, districts, and subdistricts. At each of these administrative levels, there is an elected body of officials and a parallel assembly of members of the Socialist party. The traditional form of sociopolitical organization, based on clan membership, was formally abolished and condemned as "tribalism" in 1971, yet clans and agnatic groupings remain the focus of articulation of all important societal matters. The modern administrative system is in many parts of the country only superimposed upon the old system of segmentary lineages, and it has by no means replaced that system.

Social Organization. The Somali people are divided into six major clusters of patrilineal clans, usually labeled clan-families, that are internally segmented. For most purposes, the largest social unit is a clan (*qabiil*) or a subclan that may vary in size between a few thousand and a hundred thousand members. Based on the reckoning of agnatic descent, clans are internally divided into lineages and sublineages, the size of which rarely exceeds a few hundred to a thousand members. In the north, there are additional small scattered groups of despised artisans and serfs that are collectively known as *sab*. In the south, there are large numbers of such small groups of people—some of whom are descendants of former slaves—who are frequently called in as farm labor. Known collectively as *boon* (inferior), they are regarded and treated as second-class citizens. Marriage with members of these groups is not permitted. In the southern regions of Somalia, it is possible to be "adopted"—given full membership—in a clan, even though one is the descendant of another clan. The sedentary villages in the south often have a leadership that is independent from that of the clan.

Political Organization. Interclan and interlineage affairs are handled by committees of clan elders, supervised by the clan chief, the *suldaan* or *ugas*. In the north, there exists a system of contractual agreements between different agnatic groupings, and the fines that are to be exacted for different breaches of customary law are specified. These agreements also specify the range of solidarity within the different contracting segmentary lineages. In the south, the lineages that constitute a clan are less likely to contract such agreements on their own, but the clan as a whole will agree on blood-wealth size, grazing rights, and other arrangements with other clans. Political life in rural Somali society has always been marked by negotiation, counseling, and free debate—features that inspired Ioan M. Lewis to title his major work on the northern Somali "A Pastoral Democracy" (1961).

Social Control. The traditional means of social control are closely linked with the clanship system. Lineage elders and chiefs are expected to ensure that the conduct of lineage members conforms to customary law, both in internal dealings and in affairs with other agnatic groups. Traditional cooperatives and associations, such as water-hole (war) maintenance groups, have their own sets of rules to guide their internal affairs, and they elect headmen to be responsible for doing so. Nowadays the police force is involved in most rural affairs and will often act together with local leaders. The *guulwada*, or "victory-carriers," a paramilitary militia, are frequently relied upon to implement government decisions. Another government agency, the National Security Service (NSS), has also had a high degree of presence, even in remote rural settings.

Conflict. Feuding and armed conflicts over grazing and water rights are not uncommon. In the past, conflicts often emerged following cattle or camel raids. In the war zones in the north of the country and along the Ethiopian border, a considerable supply of submachine guns and other light weaponry exists.

Religion and Expressive Culture

Religious Beliefs. Somalis are Sunni Muslims, the vast majority of whom follow the Shafi rite. Islam probably dates as far back as the thirteenth century in Somalia. In the nineteenth century Islam was revitalized, and popular versions of it developed following the proselytizing of *shuyukh* (sing. *shaykh*) belonging to different Sufi orders.

The Muslim faith forms an integral part of daily social life. The activities of Catholic and Protestant missionaries have never been successful. Somali scholars debate the extent to which Somali Muslims may have incorporated elements of a pre-Islamic religion. Some of the terms for "God" (e.g., Wag) are also found among the neighboring non-Muslim peoples. In urban areas, groups have appeared that, inspired by the Egyptian Muslim Brotherhood (Akhiwaan Muslimin), propagate a more orthodox Islam and criticize the government on moral grounds.

A variety of spiritual beings are believed to inhabit the world. The *jinny*, the only category of spirits that Islam recognizes, are generally harmless if they are left undisturbed. Other categories of spirits, such as *ayaamo*, *mingis*, and *rohaan*, are more capricious and may bring illness by possessing their victims. Groups of those who are possessed often form cults seeking to soothe the possessing spirit.

Religious Practitioners. The Somali culture distinguishes between a religious expert (*wadaad*) and a person who is preoccupied with worldly matters. There is no formal hierarchy of clergy, but a wadaad may enjoy considerable respect and may assemble a small party of followers with whom to settle in a rural community. The five standard Muslim prayers are generally observed, but Somali women have never worn the prescribed veils. Villagers and urban settlers frequently turn to the wadaad for blessings, charms, and advice in worldly matters.

Ceremonies. Somalis do not worship the dead, but they do perform annual commemorative services at their graves. Pilgrimages (sing. *siyaaro*) to the tombs of saints are also prominent events in ritual life. The Muslim calendar includes the celebration of 'Iid al Fidr (the end of Ramadan), Araafo (the pilgrimage to Mecca), and Mawliid (the birthday of the Prophet). Among the non-Muslim ceremonies, the *dab-shiid* (the lighting of the fire), at which all household members jump across the family hearth, is most widely performed.

Arts. Somalis enjoy a broad variety of alliterated oral poetry and songs. Famous poets may come to enjoy nationwide prestige.

Medicine. Illnesses are attributed both to abstract entities and emotions and to tangible causes. Somali nomads discovered the role of mosquitoes in the spread of malaria long before this connection was scientifically proven. The medical system is a plural one: patients have a free choice between herbal, religious, and Western medicines.

Death and Afterlife. Although graves are insignificant looking, the symbolic dimensions of funerals are considerable. The corpse is seen as harmful and must be disposed of rapidly. Within the local community, relations with the deceased must be cleared of grievances, and his or her passage from "this world" (*addunnyo*) to the "next world" (*aakhiro*) ensured. Funerals serve as a reminder to the living of the return of the Prophet and the approaching day of judgment (*qiyaame*), when the faithful will have nothing to fear, but sinners will be sent to hell.

Bibliography

Cassanelli, Lee V. (1982). *The Shaping of Somali Society: Reconstructing the History of a Pastoral People, 1600–1900.* Philadelphia: University of Pennsylvania Press.

Helander, Bernhard (1990). *The Slaughtered Camel: Coping with Fictitious Descent among the Hubeer of Southern Somalia.* Uppsala: Acta Universitatis Upsaliensis.

Lewis, Ioan M. (1961). *A Pastoral Democracy: A Study of Pastoralism and Politics among the Northern Somali of the Horn of Africa.* London: Oxford University Press.

BERNHARD HELANDER

Songhay

ETHNONYMS: Gao borey, Kado, Kwaara borey, Songhoi, Songhrai

Orientation

The Songhay are the fourth-largest ethnic group in Niger, West Africa. There are also considerable Songhay populations in Mali and Benin. They are closely related culturally to the Zarma. The Songhay are spread over a large area of eastern Mali, western Niger, and northern Benin. The largest concentrations are in eastern Mali and western Niger. In eastern Mali, the Songhay population lives along the Niger River from east of Lake Debo to south of Ansongo. In Niger, Songhay live along the Niger River from Firgoun to Sansane-Hausa, as well as west of the Niger north of Niamey in the region of Tera. In regions far from the Niger, the geography consists of laterite plateaus broken by occasional mesas. The vegetation in Songhay country, which is by and large scrub desert, is sparse. Water is deep and in short supply, except in the land along the Niger River, which is lush with wild vegetation as well as vegetable and fruit gardens. The climate of Songhay country, like that of Zarma country, consists of a single rainy season that begins in June and ends in September. Average rainfall varies from 20 centimeters in the north of Songhay country to roughly 40 centimeters in the south. The average high temperature, as in Zarma country, is 36° C, but temperatures reach the mid-40s at the peak of the hot season in mid-May. The average low temperature is 22° C.

History and Cultural Relations

The Songhay trace their origins to the coming of Aliman Za (or Dia) to the Niger River (near Koukya) in the latter part of the eighth century. With the help of iron weapons, Za conquered the indigenous populations of Gabibi (hunters and farmers) and Sorko (fishers). Aliman Za, probably a Lemta Berber from southern Libya, founded the Za dynasty of Songhay that endured from the latter part of the eighth century to 1491 and the death of Sonni Ali Ber, who was succeeded by Askia Mohammed Toure (founder of the Askiad, the second and last dynasty of Songhay). During the reigns of Sonni Ali Ber and Askia Mohammed, the Songhay Empire reached the zenith of its imperial power. The weaknesses and avarice of most of Askia Mohammed's successors—his sons—sapped Songhay of its strength. In 1591 a small Moroccan force sent to Songhay by El Mansur routed a much larger Songhay army, marking the end of the Songhay Empire. Descendants of Askia Mohammed continued to rule a unified southern state of Songhay until 1660, in what is today Niger. Rivalries among the ruling princes, however, precipitated the balkanization of the south into five principalities: Garuol, Tera, Dargol, Kokoro, and Anzuru. These principalities remained independent until the coming of the French military in 1898.

Settlements

Like Zarma villages, Songhay villages are usually nucleated settlements of round mud or thatched dwellings with straw roofs. In these villages, one also finds an increasing number of rectangular mud-brick houses with either thatch or corrugated-tin roofs. Villages far from the Niger River are surrounded by cultivated fields (mostly of millet) and by bush areas. There are substantial rice fields and garden plots around the riverine villages.

Economy

Nonriverine Songhay are dryland farmers who cultivate millet as a principal subsistence crop. Most farmers do not sell their grain after the harvest. Millet is cultivated along with cowpeas, sorrel, and groundnuts. Sorghum and manioc are also cultivated in regions with heavy soils. In riverine areas, rice is cultivated. In both riverine and nonriverine areas, dry-season gardens are also cultivated. Gardeners harvest mangoes, guavas, citrus fruits, papayas, dates, and bananas, as well as tomatoes, carrots, peppers, lettuce, cabbages, squashes, sorrel, and okra. The Songhay, like the Zarma, rely heavily upon the household for agricultural labor, but rice cultivators often hire nonkin to harvest their crops.

Like the Zarma, the Songhay are well-known migrants. During the colonial period, both Songhay and Zarma migrated in droves to the colonial Gold Coast, where they were known collectively as either "Zabrama" or "Gao." In Ghana, Nigeria, Togo, and Ivory Coast, Songhay today are cloth merchants as well as *nyama-nyama ize* ("the children of disorder"), who sell a variety of goods. In Niger, Songhay men sell surplus millet and rice and engage in transport and commerce; women sell cooked foods and condiments.

Kinship

As with the Zarma, the patrilineage and lineage segments are the most significant kinship groupings. Descent is also patrilineal. Unlike their Zarma cousins, however, the Songhay also recognize noble lineages, principally those whose apical ancestor is Askia Mohammed Toure (*maiga*), Sonni Ali Ber (*sohanci*), or Faran Maka Bote (*sorko*). The Songhay employ Iroquois cousin terminology, using bifurcate-merging terms.

Marriage and Family

Polygyny is highly valued among the Songhay, as it is among the Zarma, but the great percentage of Songhay households are monogamous—primarily for economic reasons. Among Songhay nobles, firstborn sons are pressured to marry their parallel cousins (father's brother's daughters), in order to maintain the purity of the noble lineage.

Sociopolitical Organization

The household is the fundamental unit of Songhay social organization. Beyond the household is the village quarter (*kurey*), which elects a quarter chief (*kurey koy*). The neighborhood chiefs constitute a village council, which elects the village chief (*kwaara koy*). Whereas the Zarma profess a rather egalitarian ideology, the Songhay do not. Village chiefs are accorded deference, especially if they are of noble descent, which is usually the case in major towns.

In precolonial times, Songhay social organization consisted of nobles, other free Songhay, and captives. The latter were originally prisoners taken in precolonial raids. Captives could be sold, but their offspring were considered members—albeit stigmatized—of noble families. Captives became weavers, smiths, and bards.

The most important political authorities in Songhay country are various paramount chiefs. These men are appointed in Songhay villages of historical consequence (Dargol, Tera, Kokoro, Ayoru, Yatakala). Such chiefs are always of noble descent, and they have at least symbolic authority over the village chiefs in their jurisdiction.

Religion and Expressive Culture

Religious Beliefs. According to Songhay religious beliefs, there are a number of paths that situate Songhay in the cosmos. These paths are magic, possession, ancestor worship, witchcraft, and Islam. Islam is superficially important, in that every town has a mosque, and larger towns have Friday mosques. Possession, magic (and sorcery), ancestor worship, and witchcraft, however, are the vital components of Songhay belief. Most Songhay towns have possession troupes and magician-healers, as well as suspected witches.

Religious Practitioners. For Muslims, there are marabouts, Islamic clerics who either heal the sick or lead the community in prayer. Some Songhay communities have imams, who teach Islamic philosophy to lesser clerics. There are also healers as well as priests who are associated with the possession cults and are also healers in their own right.

Ceremonies. Muslim ceremonial activities are the most frequent rituals practiced among the Songhay (daily prayers, weekly prayer, the Ramadan fast, and the Tabaski). There are also spirit-possession ceremonies, which in some Songhay towns occur at least once a week. The most important spirit-possession ceremonies are the *genji bi hori,* a festival in which Songhay make offerings to the black spirits that control pestilence, and the *yenaandi,* or rain dance. Both of these ceremonies are held in the hot season.

See also Zarma

Bibliography

Boulnois, J., and B. Hama (1953). *Empire de Gao: Histoire, coutumes et magi des Songhai.* Paris: Maisonneuve.

Gabbal, Jean-Marie (1988). *Les génies du fleuve.* Paris: Presses de la Renaissance.

Kati, Mahmoud (1912). *Tarikh al-Fattach.* Translated by M. Delafosse. Paris: Maisonneuve.

Olivier de Sardan, J-P. (1982). *Concepts et conceptions songhay-zarma: Histoire, culture, société.* Paris: Nubia.

Olivier de Sardan, J-P. (1984). *Sociétés songhay-zarma.* Paris: Karthala.

Rouch, Jean ([1960] 1989). *La religion et la magie songhay.* Brussels: Éditions de l'Université de Bruxelles.

es-Saadi, Mohammed (1900). *Tarikh es-Soudan.* Translated by O. Houdas. Paris: Leroux.

Stoller, Paul (1989). *Fusion of the Worlds: An Ethnography of Possession among the Songhay of Niger.* Chicago: University of Chicago Press.

Stoller, Paul, and Cheryl Olkes (1987). *In Sorcery's Shadow.* Chicago: University of Chicago Press.

PAUL STOLLER

Suku

ETHNONYMS: Basuku, Bayaka, Yaka

Orientation

Identification. "Suku" is the term now accepted by the Suku themselves and in Zaire and in the ethnographic literature. Just before and after 1900, they were often referred to as "Yaka" or, more specifically, "Yaka of MiniKongo" (the title of the Suku king)—in contrast with their neighbors, the Yaka proper, who are ruled by the king titled *kasongo lunda.*

Location. The Suku occupy an irregularly shaped, roughly rectangular area, approximately 60 to 80 kilometers east to west and 180 kilometers north to south, between 5° and 7° N and 17°30′ and 18°15′ E, in the Kwango subregion of the Bandundu region. Located at an elevation of about 750 meters, the area consists of rolling savannas and savanna-woodland, cut by swift rivers and streams. A May-to-September dry, cool season alternates with a rainy season.

Demography. At the mid-twentieth century, the Suku numbered about 80,000, with a population density of 5 to 6 persons per square kilometer. At present, the population may be approaching 150,000, about one-third of it residing more or less permanently in urban centers, particularly Kinshasa.

Linguistic Affiliation. The Suku language is part of the Kongo Cluster within Central Bantu, closely related to Yaka and the various Kongo dialects.

History and Cultural Relations

The Suku polity was founded by refugees from the middle Kwango River area, which was being conquered by Lunda invaders in the seventeenth century. Although the Suku are culturally akin to the Kongo peoples, their political organization and nomenclature carry a distinct Lunda imprint. After shallow and sporadic contacts with the Portuguese in the nineteenth century, in the 1890s the Suku came under the control of the Congo Free State (eventually the Belgian Congo). European traders appeared early in the twentieth century; serious missionary (Catholic and Protestant) and government presence commenced in the late 1920s. From the 1930s, the Suku economy, lacking local resources, became progressively dependent on labor migration to plantations and urban centers.

Settlements

Traditionally, settlements were small (rarely with more than fifty inhabitants) and scattered. Colonial authorities regrouped them into larger clusters of several hundred inhabitants. Traditional houses are rectangular (2.4 to 3.0 meters by 4.5 to 6.0 meters), usually of two rooms, and consist of a wooden framework covered with grass. The colonial period introduced the typical pan-African modern house of wattle-and-daub or clay-brick walls and a tin roof.

Economy

Subsistence and Commercial Activities. Swidden gardens supply manioc, the staple food, supplemented by sweet potatoes, yams, pumpkins, beans, peas, maize, and peanuts, with occasional bananas and "European" vegetables. Several varieties of palm are tapped for "wine." Grubs and caterpillars are collected, and there is fishing and hunting and trapping of antelopes, monkeys, rodents, and birds. Dogs, goats, pigs, and chickens are the main domestic animals. Owing to the distance from markets, there are no food exports of any commercial importance. Cash to pay for imports has come from local employment, mainly at the missions and with the government, and the savings and remittances of migrant labor.

Industrial Arts. Houses, furniture, bows, and simple utensils are usually made by the users. Artisans supply the more specialized objects, such as baskets, mats, fishing nets and weirs, mortars, drums, hoes, knives, arrows, axes, adzes, and ritual objects. Pottery is made by women. These items are (and were traditionally) sold for shell money by the artisans. Importation of many largely nonutilitarian items began with the colonial period.

Trade. In the nineteenth century the Suku profited from a trade that channeled oil and raffia from the forested areas to the north in exchange for cloth, beads, guns and gunpowder, and shell money from the Angolan coast. With the imposition of colonial boundaries, this trading network lapsed, and Sukuland became an economic backwater, with only migrant labor as its main resource.

Division of Labor. Traditionally, except for miniscule tobacco and medicinal gardens and the tapping of palm wine, cultivation was entirely in the hands of women, who also made pottery. All the other crafts were men's, as were such professions as diviner, judge, kingroup and political chief, and the majority of ritual specialists. Men also hunted the larger animals, did most of the fishing and trapping, and kept dogs, pigs, and goats. All specializations were part-time, and every Suku was engaged in a range of activities. The modern economy expanded men's choices primarily; it brought laboring jobs, mostly in distant towns and plantations, and some new occupations, such as domestic servant for expatriates, clerk, driver, policeman, medical assistant, and teacher, and, since independence, higher political, bureaucratic, and professional positions.

Land Tenure. Traditionally, ownership rights in land (as in everything) belonged to kin groups. The open bush was subdivided into large sections bounded by streams, usually of a score or more square kilometers. Control over such a section had primarily to do with hunting: a leg of any large game caught in it was owed to its owner's lineage, and only the owners were entitled to fire the bush for the large collective hunts of the dry season. Installing a new village also required the permission and ritual sanction of the owner's lineage. Land was free for cultivation, involving only a very minor ritual tribute. Separate usufruct rights were held over palm trees (tapped for wine), fishing sites, and small patches of rich soil used for peanut planting. This system had remained intact during the colonial period and has undergone no fundamental changes since Zairean independence.

Kinship

Kin Groups and Descent. The basic unit of social life is the autonomous matrilineage, seldom of more than forty members, which functions as a very strongly corporate, property-holding, marriage-arranging, and bride-wealth-collecting unit. Traditionally, it was jurally responsible for all its members' actions, and it held life-and-death and selling rights over its members. It is also the unit of all mystical and ritual functions. The lineage is localized within an area of convenient communication (some twenty kilometers across), its membership dispersed among the villages of this neighborhood; the lineage owns one of the villages, which serves as its headquarters, and in which its head (its oldest male) resides. Lineage dispersal results from Suku residence rules. Upon marriage, a woman joins her husband. A man resides near his father at least until the father's death and usually with the father's brothers after that. As they grow older, the men trickle into the lineage headquarters. Several such autonomous but related matrilineages recognized their common identity through occasional actions such as a symbolic sharing of bride-wealth receipts. They regard themselves as chapters of a larger kin group: thus, a member of one lineage, moving into the neighborhood of another, will be incorporated into the latter. In addition to the matrilineage, the Suku also recognize what might be called a patrikindred or a truncated patrilineage that includes all patridescendants of one's father and his patribrothers.

Kinship Terminology. The pattern of the kinship terminological system is Iroquois. It is skewed in a Crow manner in that upon the demise of the father's generation in the father's lineage, the father's sisters' sons succeed to its social and terminological position and all the linked relatives are reclassified accordingly. Beyond the active core of the kin network (including mainly those in one's matrilineage, father's matrilineage, and patrikindred and their spouses, and one's wife's matrilineage), the kin terms are infinitely extendable through successive recognizable links.

Marriage and Family

Marriage. Traditionally, about a fifth of married men were polygynous. Postmarital residence is virilocal. Traditional marriage involves a transfer of rights from a woman's lineage to the groom's, in exchange for money and a sacrificial goat. Included are rights of sexual possession and exclusion; rights to her domestic and agricultural labor; and eventually, rights to a son's lifetime assistance and to a portion of a daughter's bride-wealth as compensation for rearing her. Lineage filiation rights remain with the wife's lineage. Divorce (which is not infrequent) and a wife's death reverse these transfers, but the amount of returned bride-wealth is discounted for each child and the length of the wife's services. No reimbursement is due if the widow remarries within the husband's lineage. A slight preference is expressed for a man to marry his father's sister's daughter.

Domestic Unit. Newlyweds set up in a separate compound near the man's father. In terms of lineage affiliation (and therefore economic, jural, and ritual interests), the domestic unit is divided between the husband and the wife-and-her-children cluster. Polygyny simply adds more such independent clusters to the compound.

Inheritance. The property-owning unit being the matrilineage, all the wealth of a deceased person reverts to his or her lineage's control, being effectively allocated to its elders. The one exception is the inheritance by the sons of the father's hunting paraphernalia. Since the mid-twentieth century, there has been a tendency to expand the portion of goods inherited by sons.

Socialization. Personhood is achieved a few weeks after birth at a coming-out and naming ceremony. Breast-feeding, eventually supplemented with food, lasts until the age of 2 or 3, during which there is a taboo on sexual intercourse. Children continually experience casual close body contact with adults and other children. Boys are left very free until late adolescence, learning routine skills by participation and imitation; by contrast, girls from an early age are an indispensable part of the household's labor force. Groups of adolescent boys are taken into adulthood through circumcision rites, lasting for weeks and involving the acquisition of new adult names. No comparable rites of passage exist for girls. All these patterns have had to accommodate to the ever-growing presence of schools from the 1930s on.

Sociopolitical Organization

Social Organization. The primary groups of loyalty are one's own matrilineage and the village, which involves the patrikindred and the father's matrilineage. Given male patrilocality and household virilocality, one's everyday life tends to focus on the village, whereas one's economic, jural, and ritual obligations focus on the dispersed matrilineage. Although this sometimes leads to conflicts of loyalty, it also provides a certain relief from the near-totalistic demands of one's lineage. Status achievement was traditionally a matter of aging: for both males and females, eldership (from middle-age on) brings with it an ever-increasing involvement in the affairs of one's lineage, surrounding community, and region. Nowadays status is also bolstered by education, position in the larger Zairean society, and wealth. Traditionally, there was little wealth differentiation among lineages; the main variable in social power lay in the size of the lineage.

Political Organization. The political organization of the Suku kingdom was pyramidal. The royal lineage (whose current head was the king) stood at the apex and also ruled directly its own immediate region. The rest of Sukuland was divided into about a dozen regional chieftaincies (of unequal size and occasionally subject to fission), each controlled by a specific lineage holding the right to its chiefship. The larger of these were subdivided into several smaller subordinate chieftaincies; the smaller ones were not. Below this, the political organization was coterminous with relations among the local matrilineages. The main concerns of the formal political system were prestige and tribute. Tribute flowed upward through each successive level to the king. The political system was also formally concerned with ensuring public order, but it lacked effective institutionalized means (such as police or standing troops) for doing so, and the chiefs' order-keeping roles were played out capriciously, sporadically, and often reluctantly.

Social Control. Traditionally, social control depended primarily on mechanisms usually characteristic of acephalous societies. Lineages were totally autonomous in their internal affairs, and the elders' control rested on their formal power to curse and their suspected witchcraft, a control tempered by fear of witchcraft accusations. Between lineages, most conflicts were conditioned by the need of every corporate lineage to redress any imbalance in its relationship with every other lineage. Any lasting indebtedness upset this balance. Most conflicts arose from theft, property destruction, homicide, marriage-payment obligations, and infringement of sexual rights. The aggrieved party frequently resorted to violent self-help or to an attack on a third party, forcibly involving it in the settlement process. Conflicts between lineages could also be taken to independently practicing arbitrators who relied on argument or divination. Since the colonial period, customary courts, with powers of enforcing decisions, have been dealing with civil and minor criminal cases, and government courts have been dealing with serious crimes.

Conflict. The only armed conflict with a neighboring group in Suku history lay at the foundation of the Suku polity, with the defeat of the Lunda-Yaka attempt to subdue the fleeing Suku king. Since then, conflicts with neighboring groups occurred locally at the level of lineages, the methods of settlement being the same as those between Suku lineages.

Religion and Expressive Culture

Religious Beliefs. The key traditional elements were the Creator, medicines, the powers of eldership, witchcraft, and divination. The Creator was akin to a logical postulate of a first cause, with no direct impact on everyday activities. A variety of individually held medicines allowed for magical action, beneficent or nefarious, or both. A lineage-held medicine was one that had brought misfortunes to the lineage and had to be ritually taken in and nurtured to prevent further depredations. Lineage elders had the power to curse their juniors, withdrawing from them the mystical protection of the lineage against misfortunes. Witches (whose power was acquired at birth from other witches) were regarded ambivalently: they could promote lineage interests but had occasionally to "consume" lineage members. Thus, a misfortune, such as a sickness, could arise from one or several of these sources. It was the diviner's role to sort them out and indicate the necessary countermeasures. This conceptual system of dealing with misfortunes was not always satisfactory in practice, resulting in periodic revitalization-type movements that predate colonial control. These movements and Christianization have gradually undermined the integrity of the traditional system. At present, what is left are discrete bits and pieces of it, operating in conjunction with various Western Christian (Catholic and Protestant) and modern Afro-Christian beliefs.

Religious Practitioners. Traditionally, aside from diviners, there were no fully engaged religious specialists. All lineage heads performed the basic lineage rituals (such as marriages, burials, appeals to dead elders, curses), and all political chiefs performed the basic chiefly rituals (harvest, hunts, installation of chiefs and villages). Circumcision rituals were conducted by part-time ritual entrepreneurs. Lineage medicines were maintained by lineage members initiated for that purpose. At present, religious specialists are found in the Christian churches and in Afro-Christian movements.

Ceremonies. In addition to circumcision, the outstanding public rite was Kita, a periodic rite of revitalization of the society as a whole involving all men and women not previously initiated. Other public rituals included the founding of a new village, the chiefly first-fruits ritual, and the initiation and installation of new lineage and regional chiefs and the king. The most frequent rituals were those having to do with medicines: acquiring them for a lineage, curing their victims, or renovating their force, but these were private lineage rituals.

Arts. The outstanding nonspecialist performing arts included singing, dancing, telling of parables and tales, and playing drums and thumb pianos. Decorative artistry finds expression in hairstyling and in mat, basket, and gourd making. More specialized artistic elaboration appears in the manufacture of pottery, tobacco mortars, drinking cups, bowls, axes, adzes, knives, bracelets, and stools and in the carving of ritual figures and dance masks.

Medicine. Herbalism, which is the basis for treatment of minor diseases, is a part-time specialty. Other methods of curing by ritual specialists are inextricably bound with "mystical" notions of "medicines" (see "Religious Beliefs," "Religious Practitioners," and "Ceremonies") that bring misfortunes and provide the ritual means of curing them. Misfortunes as a class incorporate both disease and unfortunate events (such as bad luck or poor hunting), and both could also be brought about by witchcraft and magic. Western medicine has been widely accepted as a way of dealing with physical systems, but not the deeper causes of disease.

Death and Afterlife. Burial takes place within a day of death. Traditionally, the corpse is placed in a small subterranean niche; nowadays caskets are also used. The grave site is marked with objects such as glasses, plates, and chairs. There is a firm recognition (coupled with a profound agnosticism about the details) of life after death and of the influence of the dead on the living. Occasionally, one has contact with the dead, in the form of ghosts, but the dead with whom one has a persistent relationship are the dead of one's own lineage. The power of one's dead elders (ancestors) is an enhanced version of their power while alive, and one communicates with them at the grave sites, cajoling them for help in everyday events. As with the living elders in formal matters, the dead elders are treated as a collectivity. These notions have continued among Christian Suku, who find some measure of support for them in Christian and, especially, Catholic beliefs.

Bibliography

Kopytoff, Igor (1964). "Family and Lineage among the Suku of the Congo." In *The Family Estate in Africa,* edited by Robert F. Gray and P. H. Gulliver, 83–116. London: Routledge & Kegan Paul.

Kopytoff, Igor ([1965] 1988). "The Suku of Southwestern Congo." In *The Peoples of Africa,* edited by James L. Gibbs, Jr., 441–478. New York: Holt, Rinehart & Winston.

Kopytoff, Igor (1977). "Matrilineality, Residence, and Residential Zones." *American Ethnologist* 4:539–558.

Kopytoff, Igor (1981). "Knowledge and Belief in Suku Thought." *Africa* 51:709–723.

Lamal, F. (1965). "Basuku et bayaka des districts Kwango et Kwilu au Congo." *Annales, Musée Royal de l'Afrique Centrale,* Sciences Humaines, no. 56.

Torday, E., and T. A. Joyce (1906). "Notes on the Ethnography of the Ba-Yaka." *Journal of the Royal Anthropological Institute* 36:39–58.

IGOR KOPYTOFF

Suri

ETHNONYMS: Bale, Chai, Nyikoròma, Surma, Tirma

Orientation

Identification. "Suri" is the self-name of a little-known group of agro-pastoralists/cultivators straddling the borderland of southwestern Ethiopia and Sudan. They show some historical and cultural affinities with the Nilotic peoples in neighboring Sudan; they are also related to the Ethiopian Mursi and especially the Me'en, other "tribal" groups in this area. The Suri are composed of three subgroups; the Chai and Tirma (very closely related) and the Bale.

Location. The Suri live in a remote, inaccessible part of Maji and Bero-Shasha provinces in the Kefa region of Ethiopia. Some Bale live in Ethiopia but most are in Sudan, on the eastern side of the Boma plateau. Whereas the Bale group lives at a higher elevation (mostly above 1,500 meters), the Tirma and Chai are typical lowland dwellers whose settlements are all below 1,000 meters, in a semiarid area along one perennial river, the Kibish. Their present habitat lies between 5°10′ and 6°00 N and 35°20′ and 34°10′ E. During the 1980s, the Suri moved about 50 kilometers to the north, owing to drought, famine, and war with their southern neighbors, the Nyangatom. They now live closer to the Dizi and other highlanders, who are found in the agricultural zone to their north and east. Average temperatures in the lowlands are about 33° C in the dry season (October to April) and about 25° C in the rainy season (April to late September), with only minor cooling off during the nights. The Dizi highland area is notably colder and has more rain. The lowland area is vulnerable to droughts and occasional livestock epidemics. The last serious drought and famine period, in 1984–1985, claimed several thousands of Suri lives. Their area has no roads and no transport facilities. Even mule transport is absent, because highlanders fear that lowland flies (e.g., tsetse) will kill off their animals.

Linguistic Affiliation. Like the Me'en and the adjoining Murle, the Suri speak a "Surmic" (formerly called "Surma") language. It is classified (together with Mursi, which is very similar) as South-East Surmic. The virtually unknown Bale language, however, is probably South-West Surmic (like Murle, Didinga and Narim). These clusters both fall within the East Sudanic Group of the Nilo-Saharan Phylum. The

Suri are mostly monolingual: Amharic or languages of the neighboring Dizi and Nyangatom are spoken only by a very small minority. Most of the Bale, however, also speak Murle.

Demography. Official census figures on the Ethiopian Suri (Tirma and Chai) for 1984 indicate a total of 8,194 people. Abbink estimated in 1992 that there were about 37,000 (8,000 Bale, 13,000 Tirma, 16,000 Chai).

History and Cultural Relations

The Suri, a nonliterate group, have no written history, but they do have an oral tradition that contains many historical referents. This oral tradition—reconstructed partly through comparison of genealogies and stories about the movement of clan groups—refers to a migration history of Suri constituent groups, starting in the lower Omo River area (i.e., north of Lake Turkana). No clues have been found as yet in their tradition to point to a historical base in, for example, southern Sudan, from where they—as their linguistic profile suggests—might have originated. They claim that in former times their name was "Nagos," not Suri. They have substantial cultural similarities with the Mursi but deny the idea of an original unity with this group. Both groups place their "core area" in the same region, in the lower Omo Valley. In the early nineteenth century the Suri started to move to the west, toward Naita Mountain (which they call "Shulugui"), on the Sudan-Ethiopian border. Subsequently they migrated toward the highland ridge north of Naita (the "Tirma" range). They had their pastures well into Sudan. In general, their oral tradition is dominated by the theme of conflict with their southern neighbors, the Para-Nilotic Nyangatom (an offshoot of the Karamojong cluster, who speak a language very close to Turkana). There is, nevertheless, an oral tradition shared by the Dizi and the Suri, about a kind of historical pact or alliance between them: when the Suri entered the lowland area where they are now settled and which belonged to the Dizi people, their leading families established a ritual bond associated with the control of rain. The Dizi chiefs were acknowledged to have the ultimate mastery over the rain: when the Suri rain chiefs failed to produce rain in times of extreme drought, they would bring sacrificial animals to the Dizi and ask them to perform the rain ceremony. This pact has broken down, especially since the 1980s, owing to the changing balance of power between the groups. The Suri have regained their cattle wealth and have all acquired automatic rifles. They do not feel obliged to respect the Dizi any longer out of deference to any "historical agreement." Regular contacts between the leading families of the Suri and the Dizi have also diminished. Before the early years of the twentieth century, the Suri never belonged to any overarching state structure—neither colonial nor indigenous. Their area of Shulugui and the Tirma range was penetrated by the imperial troops of the Ethiopian emperor Menilek II (r. 1889–1913) in 1897. The region was formally incorporated into Ethiopia, but the Suri were not really conquered, in the sense of being brought under political and administrative control. They were able to maintain their relatively autonomous way of life in this frontier area between the Ethiopian Empire and the British-controlled territories of Kenya and Sudan. The activities of soldier forces, northern traders, and hunters and adventurers in the new encampment villages such as Maji, Bero, and Jeba led to frequent raiding of the native groups, including the Suri, for cattle and slaves. The Suri, however, suffered less from massive slave-raiding than the "Gimira" or "Dizi" peoples, who were also made subservient as a kind of serf class. Few European travelers visited the Suri—the first were probably the British consuls in Maji, among them A. Hodson. Italians entered Suri territory in 1932; they established three posts—two on the border mountains of Shulugui and Tamudir and one in Zilmamo, near the Bale area. These small settlements of soldiers only endured for about three years. Compared with the relations between northern Ethiopian settlers and Suri, relations between Italians and Suri were less tense and violent. There was barter and trade for livestock and foodstuffs, and peace generally prevailed. Intergroup raiding was suppressed. In the war of liberation of Ethiopia in 1940–1941, British forces crossed the Suri area in the south, toward Maji, to drive out the Italians (in 1940). The new administration established upon Emperor Haile Selassie's restoration included some soldier posts in the Suri area, and, in the first decade of the Haile Selassie era, part of the Suri paid taxes. In the last year of the revolutionary Marxist era in Ethiopia (1974–1991), the soldiers left the area, having become redundant and/or frightened because of the massive purchase of automatic weapons by the Suri from Sudan (through the Sudan People's Liberation Army, a guerrilla organization, or through Anuak gunrunners). The Suri effectively have "law and order" in their own hands and now form a kind of virtually autonomous enclave in the Kefa region. The struggle with the Nyangatom, their "archenemies," has continued unabated. Violent raids and counterraids, during which livestock are robbed and dozens of people are killed, remain one of the constants in Suri history.

The cultural affinity of the Suri is with other Surmic groups like the Me'en, Mursi, and Murle, with which they share certain core ideas and ritual practices (e.g., pertaining to marriage, burial, initiation, and purification). Also, many aspects of their material culture and their customs concerning cattle (which are central in their economy, culture, and worldview) are similar. They have undergone little influence from Ethiopian Highland or other cultures.

Settlements

The Suri have always lived in closely settled and named villages of 25 to 80 domestic units, averaging from 250 to 350 people per village. Young men have their own "cattle-camp" settlements, near the pasture areas for livestock (which are usually kept together in very large herds). A village is part of a territorial unit called a *b'uran,* a term derived from the name of the (traditional) place where Suri cattle were herded. Villages are clusters of family units, each with their own small gardens and compounds. Most men have more than one wife, and each wife has her own hut, cooking place, and garden. Young men of herding age live in the cattle camps, which are from six to eight hours' walk from the permanent settlements.

Economy

Subsistence and Commercial Activities. The Suri are predominantly cattle-pastoralists, certainly in outlook: they see themselves as free and independent herders. Cattle—and, in addition, goats and sheep—are their most prized possessions and their repository of wealth. Women also have their own cattle, but always in much smaller numbers than their husbands. The permanent villages, however, are the centers of maize and sorghum cultivation. These two products provide the mainstay of the Suri diet, but the Suri absolutely do not consider themselves "peasants" or "cultivators." Another subsistence activity is hunting: of antelope and virtually all other animals (e.g., buffalo, elephants, giraffes, leopards, lions, and ostriches), if they find them. The meat of some animals is eaten; skins, ivory, feathers, tail hair, and so forth formerly were sold to highland dealers. Suri hunting also occurs in the Ethiopian national parks. Berries and fruits are gathered. In the gardens, the women cultivate cabbages, peppers, pumpkins, cassava, and gourds. A very important commercial activity is the sale of gold, which the Suri pan and/or dig near the southern tributaries of the Akobo River, at the northern fringe of their territory. The gold is sold in the local towns. They probably took over this practice from the Anuak people to their north, or may have been inspired by Dizi people employed by the Italians in the search for minerals and metals in South Kefa in the late 1930s. Since the 1980s, the Suri have bought cattle and guns with the proceeds of the gold. This gold commerce is a wholly "indigenous" affair; only the traders taking it out to Addis Ababa are outsiders.

Industrial Arts. Crafts are virtually absent among the Suri. They make their own sparse household utensils of wood, leather, and gourds, but the only product sold to non-Suri are clay cooking pots and plates (bought by Dizi people). Some ritual objects like clan drums and ivory horns (only very few of which still exist) are old possessions of only a handful of leading families.

Trade. Apart from gold, livestock, and pottery, the Suri only occasionally sell surplus sorghum or maize to highlanders, in the harvest season. They take this produce to the local markets. In return, they acquire cash, iron or iron tools, coffee, bananas, and small items from the trade shops: razor blades, soap, clothes, or white cloth. On the illegal market, they acquire ammunition for their rifles.

Division of Labor. Boys and men of the two lower age grades are economically active: they herd, build houses, hunt, clear and burn the fields, and go to war or on raiding expeditions. Members of the two senior age grades are "retired." They are the debaters and formal decision makers (in public meetings). Women and girls are continuously active in the economic sphere, more than men: they cultivate the fields (weeding, planting, and caring for garden crops), engage in small trade and barter, and take care of all domestic tasks such as grinding grain, getting water and firewood, and preparing food and beer. They also produce and sell the pottery and do much of the leatherwork (cleaning, cutting, drying, and decorating the skins). Iron tools are made by certain male "smiths" (they do not forge iron but buy it from Dizi or in the towns); bracelets or necklaces are produced by either male or female experts. No Suri work as traders, government employees, or domestic servants in the towns, nor as plantation wage laborers.

Land Tenure. The Suri area as a whole is formally "government land," but, as there is no state administration or taxation, the Suri know only that the land they live on has been theirs since time immemorial. Land for cultivation is found around the permanent villages. There is no land scarcity in the Suri area, although crowding of many people in villages close to each other occasionally causes problems about the choice and division of fields. Pasture is sufficient except that there is always a threat of raiding from the Nyangatom in the far south.

Kinship, Marriage, and Family

Kinship. Suri always say they belong to a unit called a keno, a word that means "branch" or "stem" and could be translated with the traditional concept of "clan," patrilineally defined. Strict descent is, however, only a loose condition for membership. These "clans" are not territorial units, as their members are found in all the territorial divisions and villages. Within the clans, the Suri see themselves as belonging to lineage groups, with a named, known (great-) grandfather. Their relationship terminology is of the Omaha type: on the mother's side, Ego's male agnates—for example, mother's brothers and their sons—are denoted with the same term; mother's sister is called with the term for "mother." There is strong solidarity among lineage and clan members—at least when they live together in one village; it is manifest at occasions such as marriages, reconciliation ceremonies, and burials.

Marriage. Marriages are possible across keno (clan) lines only. This stricture is carefully observed, although sexual liaisons between members of nominally the same clan (some of them have fissioned in two named halves) do occur. Marriages are usually arranged after the rainy-season dueling contests have ended. At that time, a girl, having watched the contests and selected her favorite duelist, tries to approach the chosen one by indirect messages sent through friends and relatives. In traffic between the two families, the possibility for a marriage alliance is tested. Decisive are, first, the preference of the girl and, second, the amount of bride-wealth (in cattle, small stock, and/or bullets and a rifle) to be paid by the groom's family. After negotiations start, it may take months before agreement is reached. When a deal is clinched, the real wedding ceremony is organized, with beer, song and dance, and the ritual entrance of the girl into the new hut and into the family of the groom. Among the Suri, a marriage implies a multistranded alliance between two kin groups. Divorce is rare.

Domestic Unit. The domestic unit is basically that of a married wife and her children. She has her own hut, garden, economic activities, and social network. The husband is part of the unit as an added member, so to speak; he usually has to spend his time among various wives. He has no personal hut. He is marginal to most of the activities of this unit: he sleeps and eats in the hut of a wife, keeps personal belongings there, and meets and cares for his children there, but his main responsibilities are herding, guarding, occasionally gold mining, agricultural work, participation in raiding, and public discussions and meetings, all done outside the domestic sphere, and often outside the village. Domestic units are independent. There are no systematic patterns of cooperation between extended kin groups.

Inheritance. As the basic wealth of the Suri is livestock (but now also rifles), the rules and debates around inheritance of the herds is the main preoccupation of kin when an adult person dies, especially when it is a man. There is proportional division of the animals, according to seniority of age of the sons and brothers. Personal property (such as tools, milk containers, decorations, and a dueling outfit) is divided among sons—but not without arguments. The favorite rifle (usually a Kalashnikov or an M-16) goes to the eldest responsible son.

Older, nonautomatic rifles go to younger sons, or to brothers or brothers' sons. There is no inheritance of fields. Agricultural implements and other small items are divided among the children who need it. Some livestock and cash are also inherited by wives. Livestock property of deceased women is distributed among her sons and daughters.

Socialization. The Suri push their children—both boys and girls—to be independent and assertive: this is very evident from the games young children play. There is no physical punishment, such as beating or pinching, but much verbal discussion, encouragement, and reprimanding. Children of both sexes learn their respective gender activities by following their parents, older relatives, and peers. From the ages of 6 to 7, children start collective activities (play, gathering of fruits, some herding, drawing water, fetching firewood, grinding) in groups of their own sex. Adolescent males organize ceremonial stick-dueling fights, which are big, all-Suri events. Participation is a must for all maturing males. Suri elders form an age set that the younger people respect. In the domestic sphere, parents are much respected by their children. There is virtually no intergenerational violence, as there is among the Me'en, a closely related Surmic people. Although in the past the Suri had two primary schools, there is now no state school among the Suri, and Suri children do not frequent schools outside their own area. Thus, they are not exposed to much interethnic or out-group social contact. They develop a strong group consciousness and pride, which often results in disdain of all non-Suri groups.

Sociopolitical Organization

The Suri can be seen as a virtually independent ethno-political unit: they live in their own area (although the land is formally owned by the Ethiopian government), where there is no administration and where members of non-Suri-speaking groups do not live. They do not pay taxes to the state, no state agency has offices in their area, and they receive no agricultural and/or veterinary services. In the later Haile Selassie years and also in the first decade of the Dergue regime, there were such services in rudimentary form, but they have been crumbling because of security problems and the absence of transport facilities.

Suri political organization is not centralized. The formal war leaders and ritual mediators that are the figures of moral authority inherit their offices along three lines, within three clans. These men are much respected, not primarily for personal reasons, but because they are the incumbents of the ancient lines. These leaders have no executive authority and cannot force their will on any member of the society. They express and synthesize common opinion—that is, they are always the last to speak and summarize matters during public debates. They also initiate fields and perform protective rituals. Suri society is divided into age sets, of which the senior one (*rora*) is the most important. The Suri have been able to maintain their basically acephalous structure without much interference from the Ethiopian state. There was a brief encounter between the Suri and Ethiopian revolutionary cadres in 1976, but this was not successful in bringing about change.

Conflict. On the interethnic level, there has always been tension and violent conflict between the Suri and the Nyangatom and Toposa. The Bale Suri see as their traditional enemies the Murle and the Anuak peoples, who live to their northwest. When the Suri area (including the Boma plateau) was nominally incorporated into the Ethiopian Empire, the level of intergroup fighting, stimulated by slave and cattle raiders in the wake of the conquest by Ethiopian imperial troops, intensified. Since the 1980s, the Suri (having been pushed to the north by the heavily armed Nyangatom and Toposa) have encroached on Dizi lands. This infringement has led to frequent—almost monthly—violent incidents. Armed robbery on the roads to the market towns has been on the increase since the mid-1980s.

Religion and Expressive Culture

Religious Beliefs and Practices. The supreme deity, Tumu, is a vaguely defined source of power in, and of, the sky. There is no "cult" for Tumu, who is seldom addressed in prayer and ritual incantations. The ritual mediator is seen as having contact with the powers (presumably Tumu) that bring rain and growth of crops, livestock, and people, and he traditionally has the task of performing all rituals for the protection of crops, for bringing rain, and to avert epidemics and locusts. Certain ancestors of the clan line are seen as having powers influencing people's wealth and health. There are, however, no sacrifices or offerings made to them. Among Suri divination techniques are the interpretation of bird song and flight, the throwing of small wooden sticks, sandal throwing, and the reading of (cattle) entrails. Some older men and women also prepare amulets, made from secret roots and used for a variety of purposes ("love medicine," protection when traveling, and so on). Suri have no interest whatsoever in orthodox Christianity or Islam, if they have even heard of these beliefs.

Arts. Suri material culture is simple and unspectacular. The one expressive art in which they excel is body painting, for both males and females. They create intricate multicolored patterns, covering the entire body. These decorations have no symbolic or ritual value but are simply done for aesthetic reasons and on certain occasions. The Suri are a people who take great pride in beautiful physique (especially that of adolescents). No other "art" forms are well developed. Decorative talents also also come into play in beadwork, geometric designs on women's leather frocks, earrings, bracelets of carved copper, and clay ear and lip plates. Men make decorative iron and leather neck- or headbands for their favorite cattle.

Medicine. The Suri have their own elaborate traditional herbal medicine. Dozens of plants yield treatment for afflictions ranging from headaches to skin infections. Some treatments (e.g., the remedy for cut wounds) are known to all; experts are consulted for other maladies, (e.g., snakebite poisoning). They also have their own native "surgeons," who operate on people wounded in raids or during stick duels. For serious intestinal and stomach infections and for malaria, no effective treatments are known. No modern medical facilities exist in the Suri area. Occasionally the Suri visit the primary health care center in Maji, the main market town.

Death and Afterlife. A dead person is impure, taboo to touch for all Suri except members of the specified clan that sees to the actual funeral, after which they have to be washed with sheep's blood. Men who fall on the battlefield are not interred but are left there and covered with branches. Every deceased person is mourned in his or her homestead for five days. Cattle are sacrificed; the entrails are read, and the meat is distributed among the visitors. With the blood and certain other parts of the killed cow or ox, the compound is ritually purified. For the Suri, life is absolutely finished with physical death—there is no concept of an afterlife on earth or in heaven.

Bibliography

Abbink, J. (1992a). "Settling the Surma: Notes on an Ethiopian Relief Experiment." *Human Organization* 51(3): 174–180.

Abbink, J. (1992b). "Gold and Famine: The Suri Effort at Self-Rehabilitation, 1985–1991." In *Preproceedings of the Sixth MSU Conference on Northeast Africa, April 23–25, 1992*, edited by J. T. Hinnant and B. Finne, 12–28. East Lansing: Michigan State University, African Studies Center.

Klausberger, F. (1985). "Notizen zur Kultur und Sozialordnung der Boma-Suri im Süd-Sudan." *Wiener Völkerkundliche Mitteilungen* 27:49–79.

Lyth, R. (1947). "The Suri Tribe." *Sudan Notes and Records* 28:106–115.

Rizetto, F. (1941). "Alcune notizie sui Tirma." *Annali dell' Africa Italiana* 4(4): 1203–1211.

J. ABBINK

Swahili

ETHNONYMS: none

Orientation

The people known as Swahili (sing. Mswahili, pl. Wa Swahili) live along the narrow East African coastline and the adjacent islands (Zanzibar, Pemba, and Mafia) between southern Somalia and northern Mozambique; they also live in the Aomoro Islands and northwestern Madagascar, and there are Swahili settlements in the far African interior near Lake Tanganyika. On the coast, they live in distinct settlements within approximately 2 kilometers of the seas, placed on creeks and on the leeward sides of the many small islets that are protected from the Indian Ocean. Their language, KiSwahili, with its many dialects, belongs to the Sam Family of Northeastern Bantu and has many loanwords from Arabic. It has long been used in a debased form as a lingua franca throughout eastern Africa. It was traditionally written in Arabic script but today Roman script is mostly used. The name "Swahili" comes from the Arabic *swahili* ("coast" or "margin"). The term was first used to refer to the eighteenth-century coast dwellers by the colonial rulers of the time, the Omani of the sultanate of Zanzibar; they prefer to use the names of their local settlements, such as Mvita (Mombasa), Unguja Zanzibar, or Amu (Lamu). "Swahili" is essentially the name others have given them. They number between 200,000 and 400,000, censuses being unreliable because self-designations have varied from one period to another.

History and Cultural Relations

Pre-Swahili settlements are reported from the first century onward, mainly in Arabic and Chinese medieval records, and later in those of the Portuguese and other Europeans. Many Swahili claim Arabic and other Asian origins, but these claims, rather than having a historical basis, reflect ambitions to deny African origins (i.e., those of their slaves). They suffered under Portuguese rule from 1498 until 1729, when they were forcibly incorporated into the sultanate of Zanzibar. In the nineteenth century they came under the rule of Britain and Germany, and in the 1960s they were incorporated into the independent states of Kenya and Tanzania, not always with their approval. As Muslims, the Swahili have felt themselves distinct from the non-Muslim majorities of these countries, which have rarely supported the social and political wishes of the Swahili, who are remembered as slave traders and owners.

Economy

The basis of Swahili economy has been the long-distance commerce between the interior of Africa and the countries of the northern Indian Ocean, in which they played the role of middlemen merchants. Their settlements, strung along the coastline, have been urban—some closely built-up places and others more like large villages—but all are known by the same Swahili term, *mji*. The commerce, now virtually extinguished, lasted for almost two thousand years. Raw and unprocessed items from Africa (e.g., ivory, slaves, gold, grain, mangrove poles) were exchanged for processed commodities from Asia (e.g., textiles, beads, weapons, porcelain). The oceangoing sailing vessels from Asia and the foot caravans from the interior met at the coast, where the Swahili merchants provided safe harbors and the many complex skills and facilities needed for mercantile exchange.

"Stone-towns"—permanent houses built with "stone" (coral block), set in narrow streets, and often surrounded by walls—provided these services. Interspersed with these are the "Country-towns," large villagelike places of impermanent housing that have provided the Stone-towns with foodstuffs and labor but have not themselves taken direct part in the long-distance commerce. The whole has formed a single *oikumene*, never a single polity, but a congeries of towns with a single underlying structure. Country-towns grow foodstuffs in gardens and fields; Stone-towns once had large plantations worked by slave labor for the growing of export grains, their own food coming mainly from the Country-towns.

The staple foods are rice and sorghums; the most important of the many other crops and trees are the coconut, banana, tamarind, mango, and clove (the last grown mainly in large plantations formerly owned by Omani Arabs). Fishing is important everywhere, and few livestock are kept.

Labor has been provided from three sources: the family and kin group, slaves, and hired laborers. In the Country-towns, men and women are, in most respects, considered equal and their respective labor as being complementary: men have the heavier work—as contract laborers on clove plantations and in the largest towns such as Mombasa, Zanzibar

City, and Dar es Salaam. In the Stone-towns, domestic and agricultural work was carried out by slaves until the beginning of the twentieth century. Since then, it has been done in most towns by hired and "squatter" labor from the Country-towns and by non-Swahili immigrants. Shortage of seasonal labor has always been a serious problem in all the Swahili settlements; this remains true today.

Kinship, Marriage, and Family

There is a wide variation in forms of descent and kin group among the Swahili settlements. Country-towns are divided into moieties, and these into wards or quarters. The wards, composed of clusters of cognatically related kin, are the corporate and landholding units. Marriage is preferred between cross and parallel cousins; it is seen largely as a way to retain rights over land within the small kin group. Authority is held by senior men and women, and all local groups are regarded as equal in rank.

Within the Stone-towns, the main social groups are in most cases patrilineal subclans and lineages. The clans are distributed among the coastal towns and even in southern Arabia, from which immigrant origin is often claimed. These towns are likewise divided into moieties and constituent wards, the former once providing indigenous forms of government; their structural opposition is expressed in fighting at certain rituals, football matches, and poetry competitions. The corporate groups are the lineages, segments of subclans, that, in the past, acted as business houses and owned the large permanent houses that are so marked a feature of these towns. The subclans are ranked, position depending largely on antiquity of claimed immigration and settlement, as well as on commercial wealth and standing. Members of these mercantile lineages are known as "patricians."

Marriages are centrally important and weddings the most elaborate rituals. In the Stone-towns, the preferred marriage forms vary. For firstborn daughters, they should be between close paternal parallel cousins. Bride-wealth and dowry are both transferred, as are residential rights (not full ownership, which is vested in the lineage) for the daughter in her lineage house, marriage thus being uxorilocal. Marriages of later-born daughters are more usually with cross cousins, often in neighboring Stone-towns so as to make and retain useful commercial ties. Stone-town weddings are traditionally elaborate and costly, the bride needing to show her virginity and so her purity, which reflects upon the honor and reputation of her husband. Country-town weddings are basically similar but less elaborate and less ritualized.

Divorce is permitted under Islamic law: it is easy for husbands but extremely difficult for wives. The marriages of firstborn patrician daughters are monogamous (although concubinage was frequent), and divorce has been rare; all other marriages have often been polygynous, and divorce has been and is extremely common, as high as 90 percent in some areas.

Today Swahili women undergo initiation (without physical operation) at puberty, in order to be permitted to marry. Boys nowadays are not initiated but are circumcised in infancy; in the past there was more elaborate male initiation. Both boys' and girls' socialization after infancy takes the form of Islamic education in the Quranic schools attached to mosques, and consists largely of moral and theological learning based on knowledge of the Quran, although instruction in poetry and music has been an important part of their training to become pious Muslims. Today most children also attend nonreligious schools in order to acquire "Western" education, but religious education retains its central place, and overtly Christian schools are totally avoided.

Sociopolitical Organization

Swahili towns have traditionally been autonomous, many at one time being ruled by kings and queens. (Lamu Town, ruled by an oligarchy, was an exception.) Country-town local government remains largely in the hands of small, indigenous government organs, known as "the Four Men" and similar titles, representing constituent wards.

The Swahili patricians kept and traded in slaves; the Country-towns did neither. Slaves, numbering between 25 percent and 50 percent of the total population, were obtained from the interior from indigenous rulers and used as trade commodities, for house- and fieldwork, and as concubines. Slavery was abolished under the British in 1897 in Zanzibar and Tanganyika and in 1907 in Kenya. Its abolition brought the traditional mercantile economy largely to an end.

Open conflict has been—and remains—unusual among the Swahili, and institutions such as the feud are not known; however, *fitina,* intrigue and backbiting, is a well-recognized aspect of Swahili domestic and social life. Nevertheless, the towns have frequently waged war against one another, as part of wider processes of colonial subordination. The Omani sultanate of Zanzibar extended its sway along the coast during the eighteenth and nineteenth centuries by attacking towns in turn, using other towns as allies; local opposition to Zanzibar hegemony was soon put down by the sultans' forces of mercenary troops from outside eastern Africa. The Swahili also revolted against German rule in Tanganyika in the early years of the twentieth century and were put down with great brutality by German-led troops. The Zanzibar Revolution of 1964 removed the Omani colonial administration, and there have since been many small clashes, often couched in religious terms, with the forces of independent Kenya.

Religion and Expressive Culture

The Swahili are Sunni Muslims; even though their former Omani rulers of the sultanate of Zanzibar were Ibadhi, the Swahili were shown religious tolerance. The first mosques on the coast date from about the mid-tenth century, the identity of Swahili as Muslims dating also from that period. The central building of every town is its mosque, typically placed in a space between the two moieties; the male population assembles there on Fridays (women are not permitted to attend). In most towns, a Muslim school is built next to the mosque. There may be many mosques in a large town, built and administered privately and entailed for charitable purposes. Swahili religion is comprised of two aspects: orthodox Islam, or *dini,* and the set of local beliefs and practices known as *mila,* which are perhaps almost always originally pre-Islamic. It is often held that the dini is Arabian and associated with men, whereas the mila is African and associated with women. Both men and women, however, see themselves as orthodox Muslims, and in fact almost all observe the practices of the mila. An important part of the mila is spirit possession, which is largely practiced and controlled by women, even though they stress their Islamic purity. Women who are possessed typically join associations, even though these are in most case controlled by men, and most such associations have members of both free and of slave ancestry.

The Swahili recognize as crucial to the maintenance of their identity the concepts of *ustaarabu* ("civilization") and *utamaduni* ("urbanity"), both linked to Islam and contrasted to what they see as the *ushenzi* ("barbarism") of the other, non-Muslim peoples of eastern Africa. Important rites that maintain these concepts include the originally pre-Islamic "New Year," Mwaka or Nauroz, at which the towns are symbolically purified, and the regular Islamic ceremonies of Id-al-Fitr and other occasions, along with the regular public reading known as *maulidi*, that deal with the life and deeds of the Prophet.

Closely linked to religious beliefs and practice are forms of medical healing. Herbal medicines and possession by "doctors" are employed, as well as prayer and ritual purification. In the latter, the main practitioners are members of the clans known as Sharifu, composed of people who claim to be direct descendants of the Prophet and who live scattered in the coastal towns. All Swahili believe in the existence of many categories of both evil and good spirits, and also in that of witches and sorcerers, whose activities can be controlled by recourse to "doctors" who use both pre-Islamic and Islamic means.

The Swahili practice certain forms of visual art—the carving of elaborate wooden doors and furniture, the making of gold and silver jewelry—but the art most highly regarded is poetry. Swahili poetry is complex and of many kinds; like Islamic scholarship and knowledge, it is open to both women and men (and formerly, also to slaves). Poetry is used for both devotional and historical writings, the latter taking the form of the "chronicles" that relate the founding of the various towns and other key historical events. Today poetry is composed for both domestic and town occasions, such as weddings and competitions at New Year, and also for political purposes on radio and television.

Bibliography

Cooper, Frederick (1977). *Plantation Slavery on the East Coast of Africa*. New Haven: Yale University Press.

Middleton, John (1992). *The World of the Swahili: An African Mercantile Civilization*. New Haven: Yale University Press.

Pouwels, Randall L. (1987). *Horn and Crescent: Cultural Change and Traditional Islam on the East African Coast, 800–1900*. Cambridge: Cambridge University Press.

Sheriff, A. M. H. (1987). *Slaves, Spices, and Ivory in Zanzibar*. Athens: Ohio University Press.

JOHN MIDDLETON

Swazi

ETHNONYMS: Ebantfu ba kwa Ngwane (the people of Ngwane), emaSwati, emaSwazi, Swati

Orientation

Identification. "Swazi" refers to the nation, tribe, or ethnic group, or an individual, "siSwati" to the language. SiSwati speakers are found in Swaziland, South Africa, and Mozambique.

Location. The Swazi reside in Swaziland, a small, landlocked country of 17,363 square kilometers, which is perched on the edge of the southern African escarpment. It is bounded on three sides by South Africa and on the fourth by Mozambique, both countries in which many ethnic Swazis reside. Four distinctive topographic steps largely determine the characteristics of Swaziland's natural environment: the high veld, averaging 1,219 meters in elevation, with forests and grassy hills; the middle veld, averaging 610 meters in elevation, with hills and palatable grasses suited for livestock and rich soils good for agriculture; the low veld, averaging 274 meters in elevation, with tall grasses suited for grazing but usually not for dry-land agriculture; and the Lubombo mountain range, a narrow plateau averaging about 610 meters in elevation, with a warm, subhumid climate and basaltic soils suited for arable agriculture. Several rivers—the Mbeluzi, Ngwavuma, Great Usutu, Komati, and Lomati—cut through the high veld, middle veld, and Lubombo Mountains.

Demography. Swazi identity is based on allegiance to a dual monarchy, headed by a hereditary king, titled by his people *ingwenyama* (lion), and a queen mother, *indlovukati* (Lady Elephant). Ethnic Swazis living in the Republic of South Africa and in Mozambique are not under their effective political control, however. Within Swaziland, the population (the great majority of which is Swazi) was estimated at 860,000 in 1992, with an annual growth rate of about 3.4 percent. Most Swazis live in rural homesteads, but, in the middle veld, where nearly one-half of the Swazi population resides, rural homesteads are interspersed with densely populated settlements around employment centers. The two major cities are Mbabane and Manzini.

Linguistic Affiliation. SiSwati is a tonal Bantu language of the Nguni Group, closely related to Zulu and, more distantly, to Xhosa. It is spoken in Swaziland and in the Eastern Transvaal Province of the Republic of South Africa. Little has been published in siSwati.

History and Cultural Relations

Swazi history dates back to the late sixteenth century, when the first Swazi King, Ngwane II, settled southeast of modern-day Swaziland. His grandson Sobhuza I established a permanent capital and drew within a centralized political system the resident Nguni and Sotho people. During the mid-nineteenth century, Sobhuza's heir, Mswati II, from whom the Swazis derive their name, expanded the Swazi nation to an area much larger than modern Swaziland. Mswati established contact with the British. By the late nineteenth century, Mswati's successor, Mbandzeni, granted Europeans land concessions for grazing and prospecting, thus unwittingly giving rise to serious, prolonged conflicts regarding land-usage rights. In 1894 the Boer and British powers granted the South African Boer Republic of the Transvaal control over Swaziland. After the Anglo-Boer War (1899–1902), Britain made Swaziland a protectorate. The Partitions Proclamation of 1907 confirmed the concessionaires control of two-thirds of the land, which was contested in 1922 by King Sobhuza II. Today the Swazi nation controls about two-thirds of the land area (see "Land Tenure"). Swaziland became independent in 1968.

Settlements

The ordinary Swazi derives rights to land access and use by virtue of his/her residence or membership in a particular homestead (*umuti*). According to Hilda Kuper and Brian Marwick, the homestead is patriarchal, with a male homestead head (*umnumzana*) assuming primary powers, but the position of the main wife is important in family life. The homestead head determines resource allocation such as land distribution, makes major decisions regarding both production (plowing and types of crops grown) and economic expenditures, and mobilizes homestead labor.

The traditional Swazi homestead was circular in shape; the dwelling huts and cooking huts were built around the circumference of a circle, forming two "horns" embracing the courtyard and partially enclosing the cattle byre. Homestead residents have access as individuals to arable land and as members of the larger community to communal pasturage. Following the arrival of Europeans in Swaziland, homesteads changed; customarily tenured land was reduced in area, fragmented, and taxed. New agricultural methods, new hybrid seeds and fertilizers, and new technologies were introduced. At the same time, men migrated within Swaziland and to South Africa in search of income, thereby reducing labor power, altering sex roles, and changing the locus of decision making within homesteads. When homestead production activities changed, the social composition and physical organization of homesteads also changed.

Economy

Subsistence and Commercial Activities. Swazi homesteads focus on subsistence agricultural activities—primarily the cultivation of maize, sorghum, beans, groundnuts, and sweet potatoes. Maize had been essentially unknown until the mid-nineteenth century, at which time it was introduced and gradually replaced sorghum as the staple crop. Despite the importance of agriculture to the homestead economy, cattle are the basis of wealth and status. Swazi have the "cattle complex" typical of many eastern African tribes: cattle provide for individual food and clothing needs as well as serving wider economic and ritual purposes.

Industrial Arts. Smithing, a hereditary occupation for men that requires long apprenticeship, is surrounded by taboos. It was, at one time, the most exacting and remunerative of the industrial arts. The iron hoes, knives, and various kinds of spears (weapons of war) produced by smiths were in great demand. The smithy was built at a distance from the homestead and put off limits to women. In the past, the Swazi also had specialists in copper and brass. Today wood carving is important but is mainly limited to functional objects, such as meat dishes and spoons. Wood carvers are not required to enter a restricted apprenticeship and do not receive the status accorded healers, or even smiths. Pottery making lies within the domain of women, who, using the coil technique, produce different sizes and shapes of drinking and cooking vessels. Swazi specialists do not have at their disposal markets comparable to those found in West Africa.

Trade. Swaziland's main export crop is sugar, based on irrigated cane. Several other cash crops, including maize, rice, vegetables, cotton, tobacco, citrus fruits, and pineapples, are traded both within and outside the country. Its mineral wealth, which consists of iron ore, coal, diamonds, and asbestos, is mined for export. Meat and meat products are also exported. The industrial estate at Matsapha produces processed agricultural and forestry products, garments, textiles, and many light manufactures. The main imports are motor vehicles, heavy machinery, fuel and lubricants, foodstuffs, and clothing.

Division of Labor. Swazi division of labor proceeds according to sex, age, and pedigree. Most men know how to construct house frames and cattle kraals, plow, tend and milk cattle, sew skins, and cut shields. Some men are (or were in the past) particularly accomplished at warfare, animal husbandry, hunting, and governing. Most women know how to hoe, tend small livestock, thatch, plait ropes, weave mats/baskets, grind grain, brew beer, cook foods, and care for children; some women specialize in pot- and mat making. Age determines who will perform tasks associated with ritual performances. Rank determines who will summon people for work parties in district and national enterprises and who will supervise the workers. Work parties, sometimes consisting of hundreds or thousands of workers, compete in separate groups of men and women and receive customary rewards of thanks from the host according to rank, age, sex, and locality.

Land Tenure. Land-access rights in Swazi areas (as opposed to freehold areas established by the colonial land partition of 1907) are held by the community as a whole, and the king, representing the entire Swazi nation, is responsible for its allotment to chiefs. The chiefs, in their turn, distribute land to homestead heads. Swazi citizens can pledge allegiance to a chief and rulers and thereby obtain rights to land according to four acquisition methods: *kukhonta* (direct grant by the chief), *kubekwa* (direct grant by another individual), inheritance, and *kuboleka umhlaba* (being "lent" land by another individual). Rose (1992) has maintained that land disputes commonly center around problems of use rights, boundaries, cattle trespass, inheritance, natural-resource ownership and management, or chiefly legitimacy and territorial jurisdiction. In the late twentieth century land disputes have intensified or become more frequent, as populations have expanded or migrated toward employment centers. New varieties of disputes, often in association with development projects (e.g., construction of buildings, roads, or dams) have arisen.

Kinship

Kin Groups and Descent. At the center of each Swazi homestead is the biological family, extended through classificatory kinship to maternal and paternal groups, the largest of which is the clan. The clan, as the farthest extension of kinship, contains a number of lineages in which direct descent can be genealogically traced over three to eight generations. The exogamous patrilineal clan (*sibongo*), with members usually residing in the same locality (*sifundza*), is the fundamental unit of Swazi social organization.

Kinship Terminology. One's father is called *ubabe*, whereas father's older brother is *ubabe lomkhulu*, and father's younger brother is *ubabe lomncane*. One's father's sister is *ubabe lomsikati* (female father). One's own mother, the other wives of his/her father, and his/her mother's sisters are called *umake*. One's father's brother's wife is also umake, and one's mother's sister's husband is also ubabe. One's mother's brother and his wife are called *umalume*. Grandfathers are called *ubabemkhulu*, and grandmothers *ugogo*, but the kinship terms can be specified by the addition of explanatory words (e.g., the paternal grandfather may be called *ubabemkhulu lotala babe* to distinguish him from the maternal grandfather). All grandchildren are *umtukulu*.

Marriage and Family

Marriage. Clan membership is important in regulating marriage and succession. Marriage with a person of one's own paternal clan is prohibited (although permissible for the king) but allowed with a woman of the maternal clan. At one time, a preferred form of marriage was the sororate, in which a man married his wife's sister, who became the subsidiary wife (*inhlanti*). A woman retains her paternal clan name upon marriage, but her children acquire at birth their father's clan name. Paternal rights are acquired by the man's family through the transfer to the woman's family of bride-wealth (*lobola*)—valuables such as cattle (and, in modern times, possibly cash). Bride-wealth varies with the rank and education of the bride. Marital residence is virilocal; the bride goes to live with her husband and in-laws. In contemporary Swaziland, several forms of marriage are found: traditional marriages—"love" matches, arranged marriages, and marriage by capture, the latter being uncommon and not always involving the exchange of bride-wealth—as well as Christian marriages. More individuals are eloping or remaining single. The marriage ceremony, particularly for high-ranking couples, involves numerous and sometimes protracted ritualized exchanges between the families of the man and the woman, including singing, dancing, wailing, gift exchange, and feasting. Divorce, which is discouraged in association with traditional marriages, although permissible in situations of adultery, witchcraft, and sterility, proceeds according to a variety of arrangements.

Domestic Unit. Within a complex homestead are households, each household (*indlu*) generally consists of one nuclear family (a man, his wife and their children) whose members share agricultural tasks and eat from one kitchen. When there are several households on the homestead, each consists of a simple polygynous family, an extended agnatic family, or a complex family grouping. Sometimes a wife has an attached co-wife (*inhlanti*), who, along with her children, forms part of the same "house." A married son and his wife and dependents occasionally form another house within the wider "house" of his mother.

Inheritance. Upon the death of a homestead head (umnumzana), the family council of agnates (including full and half-brothers of the head, his own and brothers' senior sons, etc.) meet to discuss the disposal of his estate. The council primarily considers the household divisions prevailing within the homestead group during the life of the head as well as the land allocations made by him during his life. In monogamous families, the largest land allocation and administrative responsibilities usually go to the oldest son, whereas in large polygynous families, the largest land allocation and administrative responsibilities usually go to the oldest son of the senior wife who is named the general heir (*inkosana*) and acts as guardian over the special heirs of each wife's house's estate. When a woman dies, her property (e.g., her pots, mats, and implements) goes, by tradition, to the wife of her eldest son, who resides in the same homestead or village, unlike her married daughters. In contemporary Swaziland, traditional rules of inheritance are not applicable when a Christian marriage, which disallows polygyny and which is governed by Roman-Dutch law, is contracted.

Socialization. Preadolescent girls play and help their mothers with minor domestic chores and child care, whereas preadolescent boys play and run errands around the homestead until they are old enough to accompany their age mates to the fields with the herds. Fathers sometimes play a small role in child rearing, particularly if they are employed at distant locations within Swaziland or in South Africa. The Swazi have not circumcised males since King Mswati's reign in the mid-nineteenth century, but both boys and girls traditionally had their ears cut (*ukusika tindlebe*). By custom, a boy who has reached puberty is tended by a traditional healer, and a girl who has had her first menstruation is isolated in a hut for several days and instructed by her mother about observances and taboos. A boy learns about manhood and service to the king when he joins his age (warrior) regiment (*libutfo*).

Sociopolitical Organization

Social Organization. During the seventeenth and eighteenth centuries, the dominant Dlamini clan created a hierarchy of control by amalgamating and ranking through conquest, treaty, and peaceful incorporation over seventy disparate, equal clans under a hereditary monarchy. The Swazi hierarchical ranking system came to consist of several units: the polygynous patriarchal family, the hierarchy of clans and lineages, the dual monarchy, the age grades, and the groups of specialists. The stability of the ruling elite's control was achieved through a balance of power among the king, his mother, princes, and commoners, as well as between the dual monarchy and the chiefs. Moreover, Swazi hierarchy harmoniously blended authoritarian political privileges of birth with egalitarian participation in age classes and councils. With the coming of Europeans in the late nineteenth century, the traditional hierarchy was forced to compete with a new, colonial administrative hierarchy that was based upon race and oriented toward the accumulation of wealth. After Swaziland achieved independence in 1968, a complex administrative system was fused together from parts of the dual hierarchy (see "Political Organization"). Currently, traditional hierarchical arrangements are most threatened by the developing class system that found root in the economic and social changes of the colonial period.

Political Organization. Swaziland's government is a monarchy. Its political organization is characterized by dualism: the parallel political structures consist of a "traditional" and a "modern" (postcolonial) hierarchy. At the apex of the traditional hierarchy is the Swazi monarch, who as a member of the Dlamini clan, holds supreme executive, legislative, and judicial power. He governs with the assistance of his traditional advisers. At the middle level of the traditional hierarchy are chiefs who consult with their council of elders (*bandlancane*), and at the lowest level are homestead heads who consult with their *lusendvo* (lineage council). The modern structure, through which the monarch's power is also delegated, consists of modern, statutory bodies, such as a cabinet and a parliament that passes legislation (subject to approval by the king), which is administered in four regions, and less formal governmental structures, consisting of Swazi Courts and forty subregional districts in which the traditional chiefs are grouped.

Social Control. The colonial powers altered some Swazi customary legal rules and procedures and imposed Roman-Dutch law as the general law. As a result, Swaziland developed a dual system of law and courts consisting of traditional councils, in which procedures are not controlled by legislative enactments or by codified legal rules, and modern courts, which have been formalized by national legislation. Traditional councils consist of the clan/lineage council (lusendvo), the chief's council (bandlancane), and the king's council. Modern courts consist of both Swazi and European-influenced courts at lower levels, including the Swazi Courts, two Courts of Appeal, the Higher Swazi Court of Appeal, and the king on the Swazi-influenced side, and the Subordinate Courts, the High Court, and the Court of Appeal on the European-influenced side. The Swazi Courts Act of 1950 provided for the formal composition of customary courts, the type of law they may apply (customary law), the procedure to be followed, and the limits of the courts' jurisdiction over persons. Swazis may exercise some discretion, depending upon individual circumstances, in choosing which legal forum to pursue a case.

Conflict. Swazis were engaged in tribal warfare until the imposition of European control in the late nineteenth century. Following the arrival of European concessionaires, severe conflicts developed between Swazis and Europeans regarding alienated land (see "History and Cultural Relations"). Throughout history, conflicts arose between Swazi clan and lineage members (commonly co-wives and half-brothers) in association with daily interactions and were often attributed to suspected acts of witchcraft and sorcery. In modern-day Swaziland, interpersonal conflicts are influenced by many social and economic changes, including altered sex roles, increased job competition, labor migration, and the growth of an educated elite. Some Swazis believe that the legal prohibition of "witch finding" exacerbates conflicts by protecting evildoers who promote themselves at the workplace and in personal affairs through the use of magic. New or intensified pressures upon status relationships in stratified Swazi society are also producing conflicts.

Religion and Expressive Culture

Religious Beliefs. Adherents of traditional religion believe(d) in an aloof Supreme Being known as Mkhulumnqande, who fashioned the earth but who demands no sacrifices and is neither worshiped nor associated with the ancestral spirits. Swazi men play important roles in Swazi traditional religious life, offering sacrifices for the ancestral spirits, who are ranked, as are humans. Despite the important role of men in religious matters, female diviners also communicate with spirits, and the queen mother acts as custodian of rain medicines. Swazi ancestral spirits take many forms, sometimes possessing people and influencing their welfare, primarily their health (see "Religious Practitioners" and "Medicine").

Methodists established the first mission in Swaziland. Currently, many Christian sects exist in Swaziland, ranging from the more eclectic Catholics to the more rigid Afrikaner Calvinists. A majority of Swazis are registered as "Christian." Many converts belong to nationalistic Separatist "Zionist" churches, which practice a flexible dogma and great tolerance of custom. Christianity as practiced by Swazis has been influenced by existing traditions, including beliefs in ancestral spirits, and traditional religion has been influenced by Christianity.

Religious Practitioners. Swazi practitioners of traditional religious beliefs articulate belief systems and link the spirit and human worlds. Their primary role, as healers, is to identify and correct the imbalances between these worlds, imbalances that lead to human misfortunes and illnesses. Swazi healers are of three types: herbalist (about 50 percent), diviner-medium (about 40 percent), and Christian faith healers (about 10 percent). Diviners are usually accorded more prestige than herbalists because ancestral spirits are believed to work through them directly. They are called to their profession through spirit possession and may become novices-in-training in a ritual school run by a master diviner. Although the healer categories overlap, in general, herbalists work primarily with natural materia medica (e.g., roots, bark, leaves), whereas diviner-mediums diagnose the "mystical" causes of illness, rely on spirit possession, and perform the femba ceremony, through which agents of illness are removed. Since the late colonial period (1960s), most healers (more than 80 percent) have been officially registered and are thus subject to taxation. Many belong to healers' organizations.

Ceremonies. The annual ritual of kingship, the Incwala, a ceremony rich in Swazi symbolism and only understandable in terms of the social organization and major values of Swazi life, has been described in numerous writings by Hilda Kuper. According to her, the central figure is the king, who alone can authorize its performance. The Incwala reflects the growth of the king, and his subjects play parts determined by their status, primarily rank and sex. Before this ceremony (which is sometimes described as a first-fruits ceremony or a ritual of rebellion) can be performed during a three-week period each year, considerable organizational and preparatory activities must be undertaken. For example, water and sacred plants are collected at distant points to strengthen and purify the king. Thereafter, the oldest warrior regiment opens the Incwala. Sacred songs that are concerned with the important events of kingship (a king's marriage to his main ritual wife, the return of ancestral cattle from the royal grave, and the burial of kings) as well as dances are performed. Themes of fertility and potency predominate. Celebrants are adorned in striking clothing, including feathers of special birds and skins of wild animals. Kuper maintains that the Incwala symbolizes the unity of the state and attempts to reinforce it; therefore, it dramatizes power struggles between the king and the princes, or between the aristocrats and commoners, with the Swazi king ultimately triumphing. Kuper, Beidelman, and other scholars have discussed other Swazi royal rituals, including the reed dance and rainmaking rites, as well as ceremonies that involve Swazis as individuals or groups, including funerals, marriages, and initiations.

Arts. Swazi implements and utensils, such as clay pots and baskets, are unornamented, serving mainly a utilitarian purpose. Wood carvers did not traditionally produce masks or sculptured figures, although in the late twentieth century schools have encouraged woodcraft for the tourist trade. Musical instruments are crafted to accompany popular singing and dancing activities; among those instruments used either in the past or present are the *luvene* (hunting horn), *impalampala* (kudu bull horn), *ligubu* (calabash attached to a wooden bow), and *livenge* (wind instrument made from a plant). Drums and European instruments have been introduced.

Medicine. Swazis resort to various medical practitioners, primarily biomedical or traditional practitioners. Traditional practitioners retain their high standing among the Swazi, as indicated by their relatively high ratio within the general population: currently, about one person in 110. About half of traditional healers are female, and the vast majority are diviner-mediums (see "Religious Practitioners"). Swazis believe that most serious diseases do not simply happen: they are created and sent by a person of ill will. Furthermore, Swazis differentiate between diseases or conditions regarded as "African" or "Swazi" and those that are foreign, emphasizing that the former, such as madness caused by sorcery, is a Swazi disease best treated by traditional medicine and practitioners, and that the latter, such as cholera, is a foreign disease best treated by Western orthodox medicine and biomedical practitioners. According to Green (1987), Swazi healers claim to be most effective in healing sexually transmitted diseases, sorcery and bewitchment types of ailments, children's illnesses, and migraines. By tradition, a recognized Swazi healer-diviner would commonly receive an initial gift of a goat, spear, or other articles, an intermediary gift of meat from a beast that was slaughtered during treatment, and a cow given in thanks for effecting a successful cure. The diviner's fee did not constitute a regular stipulated payment but did depend on her or his technique and the seriousness of the situation. Nowadays a healer may demand set fees for particular medicines and services.

Death and Afterlife. Swazi mortuary ritual varies with both the status of the deceased and his or her relationship with different categories of mourners. The more important the deceased, the more elaborate the rites given the corpse (particularly so for the king). The closer the relationship through blood or marriage of the deceased and a mourner, the greater the stereotyped performance demanded by the spirit from the mourner. A headman is traditionally buried at the entrance of the cattle enclosure, and his widows, children, siblings, and other relatives are expected to grieve dissimilarly and for different lengths of time. Widows grieve longer than do widowers. A widow may be expected to continue her husband's lineage through the levirate (*ngena*), in which she is taken over by a brother of her deceased husband. The spirit of the deceased may manifest itself in illness and in various omens; sometimes it materializes in the form of a snake. Ancestral spirits, acting as custodians of correct behavior and moral standards, inflict suffering on their descendants only as just punishment, not out of malice. The head of the family appeals to the ancestors and directs offerings to them at specific domestic events such as births, marriages, and deaths and during hut-building activities.

Bibliography

Beidelman, T. O. (1966). "Swazi Royal Ritual." *Africa* 36(4): 373–405.

Bowen, Paul N. (1993). *A Longing for Land: Tradition and Change in a Swazi Agricultural Community*. Aldershot: Avebury, Ashgate.

Gailey, Charles R. (1968). "Changes in the Social Stratification of the Swazi, 1936–1967." Ph.D. dissertation, University of South Africa.

Gort, Enid (1987). *Changing Traditional Medicine in Rural Swaziland: A World Systems Analysis*. Ann Arbor: University Microfilms International.

Green, E. C. (1987). "The Integration of Modern and Traditional Health Sectors in Swaziland." In *Anthropological Praxis*, edited by R. Wulff and S. Fiske, 87–97. Boulder, Colo.: Westview Press.

Holleman, J. F. (1964a). "The Land Use Survey." In *Experiment in Swaziland*, edited by J. F. Holleman, 52–57. Cape Town: Oxford University Press.

Hughes, A. J. B. (1962). "Some Swazi Views on Land Tenure." *Africa* 32(3): 253–278.

Hughes, A. J. B. (1972). *Land Tenure, Land Rights, and Land Communities on Swazi Nation Land: A Discussion of Some Interrelationships between the Traditional Tenurial System and Problems of Agrarian Development*. Monographs of the Institute for Social Research, no. 7.

Kuby, David Joseph (1980). *Elitism and Holiness in Swazi Conversion*. Ann Arbor: University Microfilms International.

Kuper, Hilda (1947a). *An African Aristocracy: Rank among the Swazi*. London: Oxford University Press for the International African Institute.

Kuper, Hilda (1947b). *The Uniform of Color in Swaziland: A Study of White-Black Relationships in Swaziland*. Johannesburg: Witwatersrand University Press.

Kuper, Hilda (1963). *The Swazi: A South African Kingdom*. New York: Holt, Rinehart & Winston.

Kuper, Hilda (1978). *Sobhuza II: Ngwenyama and King of Swaziland*. London: Gerald Duckworth & Co.

Marwick, Brian Allan (1940). *The Swazi: An Ethnographic Account of the Swaziland Protectorate*. Cambridge: Cambridge University Press.

Ngubane, Harriet (1983). "The Swazi Homestead." In *The Swazi Rural Homestead*, edited by Fion de Vletter, 95–122. Mbabane: University of Swaziland, Social Science Research Unit.

Nhlapo, Ronald Thandabantu (1992). *Marriage and Divorce in Swazi Law and Custom*. Mbabane: Websters.

Rose, Laurel L. (1991). "Swaziland: Witchcraft and Deviance." In *Deviance: Anthropological Perspectives*, edited by Morris Freilich, Douglas Raybeck, and Joel Savishinsky. New York: Bergin & Garvey.

Rose, Laurel L. (1992). *The Politics of Harmony: Land Dispute Strategies in Swaziland*. Cambridge: Cambridge University Press.

Rosen-Prinz, Beth (1976). "Urbanization and Political Change: A Study of Urban Local Government in Swaziland." Ph.D. dissertation, University of California, Los Angeles.

Russell, Margo (1983). "Boundaries and Structures in the Swaziland Homestead." Research paper no. 6. University of Swaziland, Social Science Research Unit.

Sibisi, Harriet (1980). "Sociological Observations on Some Aspects of Rural Development in Swaziland." Traditional Securities and the Response to "Modern" Economic Opportunities, Paper no. 3. Ministry of Agriculture and Cooperatives. Mbabane.

LAUREL L. ROSE

Syriacs

ETHNONYMS: East Syrians, Nestorians, Suryânê, Suryâyê, Syrian Jacobites

"Syriac" is both a lingual and a group designation. It applies to East Syrians or Nestorians, who are known also as "Suryâyê," and to Syrian Jacobites, or "Suryânê." The term "Syrian Christians" refers not to residents of the land of Syria, but rather to those Christians who employ the Syriac language in their church liturgies or speak it in its vernacular form. Broadly speaking, those who had recourse to Syriac historically are the Jacobites of Mesopotamia and Turkey, the Nestorians of Mesopotamia and Iran, the Maronites of Lebanon, and the Chaldean Uniates, as well as the converts of Saint Thomas in the Malabar region of southwestern India today.

Syriac is a branch of the Aramaic family of languages and was the lingua franca of the eastern Roman Empire at the beginning of the Christian era. It is also spoken extensively in the regions farther east. It became the language of liturgies and patristic literature after serving for over a millennium as the vernacular at Edessa (present-day Urfa, in southern Turkey) with very slight variation from the Aramaic or "Chaldee," as it was once called. Syriac eventually gave way vernacularly and, to some extent, liturgically, to Arabic, following the absorption of these communities into the Arabo-Islamic Empire from the eighth century onward.

Aramaic, from which Syriac derived, was the spoken language of peoples who came from a variety of ethnic backgrounds, in the same manner that Arabic, which displaced it, molded together peoples inhabiting the land in which Aramaic was popularly spoken. After being Christianized, Aramaeans called themselves "Syrians," which explains why the churches they constituted were referred to by others as the "Syrian" churches. The early constituents were Jews and Gentiles of all ethnic origins. The original Aramaic is still spoken today by the much-diminished community of Maʿlūla near Damascus.

Bardesanes of Edessa is credited with founding Syriac literature in the third century and of referring to the church it molded as a "universal church." This designation reportedly gave rise to a "new race" of Christians without reference to geographical boundaries, from Gaul eastward to Parthia, Mesopotamia, and India. The term also referred to any group that made use of the language, without distinction as to race or location (original sources cited in Joseph 1961, 19).

The Syriac spoken in the various rites of the Syrian church was a vernacular form that differed from village to village. The highest and most renowned form was the dialect of Edessa, which eventually was adopted as the language of the church, even though it was not well understood by Christians in next-door Iraq and Persia. The Edessan and the locally spoken dialects existed side by side for centuries, with the former constituting the classical standard of measure from which the vernacular borrowed.

Syriac became a "new language" when evangelical Protestant missionaries from the United States and orientalists combined efforts in the early nineteenth century to study the language scientifically and to reduce it to a comprehensible and standardized written form. Once they had completed their scientific study and had remolded the language into its modern form, missionaries H. O. Dwight and Eli Smith proceeded to translate the Bible into Syriac. Until then, there was no complete Bible in the language, only the Psalter, Gospels, and Epistles, which were in the possession of the Nestorian church. The only books in the vernacular that were discovered by the missionaries in 1831 were some translations of a Catholic catechism and a few prayers. To teach the "new Syriac," missionaries produced primers, grammars, textbooks, philological treatises, and dictionaries. By the end of the nineteenth century, modern Syriac had become a literary medium among Nestorians in the Urmia region of northwestern Persia. Indeed, the popularization of Syriac literature at this time served to reinforce the spirituality of its churches.

The popular forms of the vernacular are still spoken by those termed East Syrians (i.e., the Nestorians and Uniate Chaldeans in the Mosul region of Iraq and the Jacobites around Jabal Ṭūr. The rest of the Syrian Christians, including the Maronites, use Arabic for their vernacular. All of them, however, still use Syriac as their liturgical language. Maronites use the Syriac script to record their Arabic prayers in what is known as "Karshūni," a form of writing that is not intelligible to the common people. Bishops are ordained in Syriac, and they conduct services in Syriac only. All Syrian Christians were expected at one time or another to read, write, and understand classical Syriac.

Historically, Syriac was first and foremost a literary term, the language of the Eastern churches. There was considerable activity in Syriac during the early Christian centuries. The Gospels at first were written in Syriac, before the doctrinal controversies of the fifth century split the Christian community. The Four "Gospels Separate," known as the "old Syriac," were discovered in Egypt in 1842 (Cureton 1858). The so-called Sinaitic palimpsest, discovered in 1893 in the holdings of the Monastery of Saint Catherine, at the foot of Mount Sinai, is housed today in the British Museum. Both of these manuscripts probably date from the fourth century.

The second-century *Diatessaron* of Tatian, also known as the "Mixed Gospels," is a "harmony" of the Four Gospels Separate handed down through a commentary by Ephraim in an Armenian translation, by quotations in Aphraates, and by an eleventh-century Arabic translation of the *Harmony* by the Nestorian monk Ibn al-Ṭayyib. The *Pshîttâ* or "simple" version is the one still used by Syrian Christians. That version, also called the "Syriac Vulgate," contains the whole Bible, Old and New Testaments, plus the Old Testament Apochryphal less 2 Peter, 2 and 3 John, Jude, and Revelation. There are also the recensions of the *Pshîttâ* made by Philoxenus, bishop of Mabug (Hierapolis) near the Euphrates in 508 and by Thomas of Harqel in 614. Both writers were Monophysites (Jacobites), who, more than the Nestorians, were dissatisfied with the *Pshîttâ*.

Other noted pre-fifth-century Syriac works include the third-century *Disputation with Manes*, by Archelaus, bishop of Kashkar in Mesopotamia, which survives only in Greek fragments and in a Latin translation; the *Doctrine of Addai* (Phillips 1876), written around the beginning of the fourth century; the voluminous works of Ephraim, which include commentaries, homilies, letters, and hymns (for details, see Burkitt 1904b, 113); *On the Holy Spirit*, which was translated into Greek before Jerome's time; the *Homilies* of Aphraates, the Persian martyr and sage, written c. 337–345; and the *Syriac Doctrine Apostolorum*, known also as the *Edessene Canons*, written c. 350 and constituting some form of "church order." The *Canons* are important because they reveal a great deal about the customs of the Edessa church of that time, including the extent of its activity—a strong missionary proclivity is indicated. Addai emerges in them as the apostle of Edessa, Aggai, a "maker of silks" known in Persia, Assyria, Armenia, Media, and in the countries around Babylon, to the Huzites and the Gelae, and all the way to the border of India and the land of Gog and Magog. *Syriac Martyrology* was probably written in the middle of the fourth century. A commentary on the Gospels by Abba, a disciple of Ephraim, survives in a few fragments. The poems of Syrillona were composed around 396. Also among pre-fifth-century literature are the *Martyrdom of Barsamya* and the *Martyrdom of Habbîb; Acts or Hypomnemata of Sharbil* (the Maronite saint), accounts of the deaths of three Edessene heroes; *de Fato of Bardaisân;* the early-fifth-century *Book of Martyrs* of Mârûtha, which commemorates those who suffered under the Persian king Shapur II; the *Life of Rabbulâ*, written after his death in 435; and the *Acts of Judas Thomas* (the apostle), a highly interesting religious novel, probably written by an unorthodox third-century pioneer missionary in eastern Mesopotamia. The popular *Hymn of the Soul* (translated in Burkitt 1904a, 218ff.) is contained in the *Acts*. The *Clementine Homilies and Recognitions* of around the third century may also have been written in Syriac.

Bibliography

Baumstark, Anton (1922). *Geschichte der Syrischen Literatur*. Bonn.

Burkitt, Francis C. (1904a). *Early Eastern Christianity*. London.

Burkitt, Francis C. (1904b). *Evangelion da-Mepharreshe*. Vol. 2. Cambridge.

Cureton, William, ed. (1858). *The Four Gospels Separate*. London.

Hastings, James (n.d.). *Encyclopedia of Religion and Ethics*. Vol. 9. New York: Charles Scribner's Sons.

Joseph, John (1961). *The Nestorians and Their Muslim Neighbors*. Princeton, N.J.: Princeton University Press.

al-Khūri, Tūma (1963). "Dawr al-Lughah al-Suryânîyah fi al-Adab wa 'l-Falsafah, wa 'l-Dîn." al-Majallah al-Batriyarkîyah 1:458–462.

Phillips, George, ed. (1876). *Doctrine of Addai*. London.

CAESAR E. FARAH

Tandroy

ETHNONYM: Antandroy

Orientation

Identification. The Tandroy live in the far south of Madagascar and speak a Malagasy dialect. Their land is known as "the Androy," literally, "where the *roy* (*Mimosa delicatula*) is," but more commonly rendered as "land of the thorny bush" or "spiny desert," both of which are allusions to the highly adapted vegetation of this semiarid region. "Tandroy," the name of the people, translates as "those of the thorny bush." In the vernacular, the prefix "An-" is normally dropped.

Location. The Androy is located south of the Tropic of Capricorn between 24° and 26° S and 44° and 47° E, in an area approximately bounded by the Mandrare and Menarandra rivers. Its climate is semiarid or even subarid, with average annual rainfall varying from 35 centimeters on the southwestern coast to 70 centimeters toward the north. There is no clear-cut wet season, although the months of December, January, and February generally receive more than 5 centimeters of rain. Irregular precipitation makes the Androy subject to periodic drought, and, save for the Mandrare in the east, the riverbeds are often dry. South of the savanna, the xerophilous bush, with its Didiereaceae and Euphorbiaceae families of plants, is the most specialized of all Malagasy habitats. An estimated 48 percent of its plant genera and 95 percent of its species are endemic to Madagascar.

Demography. In 1980 the population of Madagascar was estimated at around 9 million. Numbering more than 400,000, the Tandroy are of an average size among the twenty officially recognized ethnicities; the census, however, included other groups, such as the Karembola in the southwest. The average population density has been reckoned at 10 per square kilometer, and annual population growth at between 2.8 percent and 3 percent. The southeastern coastal strip is the most densely populated; once described as "the Tandroy cradle," it has been the area from which clans set out to colonize the north.

Linguistic Affiliation. Although Madagascar lies only 382 kilometers from the East African mainland, its native languages are considered to belong to the Indonesian subgroup of the Malayo-Polynesian Family. When and how this designation came about is as uncertain as is the question of the peopling of Madagascar itself. Even though it is often said that the languages spoken in Madagascar are relatively homogeneous, preliminary glottochronological studies have established shared cognate rates of between 61 percent and 69 percent for Tandroy—considered to belong to a dialect family with Vezo, Bara, and Mahafale—and Merina, a dialect of the highlands and now the official language of Madagascar. More extensive research on Tandroy syntax and phonology, as well as on diversification between so-called Tandroy speech communities, is required. The existence of dual vocabularies to indicate a person's status in the social hierarchy also merits attention. The transcription of Tandroy, which is taught nowadays in school, is based on the official orthography of the Merina dialect, which has four vowels and twenty-seven consonants, to which the velar *n* was added by official decree in 1962.

History and Cultural Relations

It is generally accepted that Tandroy is a composite ethnicity and that its many clans, which are of diverse origins (including Sakalave, Bara, Mahafale, and Tanosy), arrived in the Androy no more than several centuries ago. Sites of the "pre-Tandroy" habitats dating to the eleventh and twelfth centuries have been reported, the first at Talaky, on the coast. Prior to the eighteenth century, the southwestern Androy was known as the *pays de Caremboules*, which has led some authors wrongly to suppose that the clans that are known today as "Karembola" are autochthons. In fact, all the evidence shows that the whole of the Androy has been settled and resettled by never-ending waves of migrants. Although this evidence would seem to imply that cultural boundaries must be rather fluid, most authors have represented Tandroy culture as remarkably homogeneous. According to tradition, this mosaic of clans was dominated from the late fifteenth or early sixteenth century onward by the Andriamañare (Zafimanara) dynasty. The origins of this dynasty and the extent and nature of its dominion are uncertain, but by the late nineteenth century its power had declined, as the southwestern Androy had been annexed in the early eighteenth century by the Maroseraña dynasty on the Menarandra. Throughout the nineteenth century, the Androy remained independent of the Merina military installations at Fort-Dauphin, but it was conquered by the French between 1901 and 1903. Resistance, however, kept the Androy in a state of emergency until 1917. The year 1928 was notable in the Androy for the destruction of the cactus by the cochineal beetle. Madagascar became independent in 1960. A popular uprising erupted in the Androy in 1971 against the power of Tananarive (currently spelled "Antananarivo"). Harshly repressed, the uprising was followed by various administrative reforms.

Settlements

The average population of rural settlements varies from a few persons to a few hundred. Settlements are divided between two contrasting types: those with a recognizable center, in which the closely juxtaposed houses and cattle pens are aligned to the cardinal points, according to the seniority and relative ranks of the village members, and those in which the houses and cattle pens of individual families, each enclosed by cactus or agave, are widely dispersed. At the same time, the mobility for which the Tandroy are renowned is reflected in a shifting pattern of settlement. Human settlement in the Androy involves both centripetal and centrifugal processes, although the exact nature of the environmental and sociopolitical factors that determine these processes is not yet known. The villages are connected by footpaths, some of which are accessible by cart. The Tandroy house is rectangular, its walls between 2.5 and 3.5 meters long, constructed mostly of timber planks but sometimes of thatch, and with a gabled roof of thatch. Oriented to the cardinal points, it generally has two doors and little furniture, save for the bed. The interior is usually furnished with mats. In the towns, one finds houses of cement with corrugated iron roofs.

Economy

Subsistence and Commercial Activities. The Tandroy economy is based upon a mixture of pastoralism and horticulture, supplemented by gathering. The transhumant herding of zebu cattle has been described as the basis of Tandroy religious and social life. As well as supplying milk, meat, and leather, their herds are an important determinant of status and wealth. The Tandroy are renowned, moreover, for their hecatombs. Sheep, goats, and chickens are also kept. Crops include maize, manioc, sorghum, sweet potatoes, legumes, groundnuts, and cucurbits; the dry climate of Madagascar prohibits rice agriculture. Although most villages now possess at least one plow, the triangular spade remains in extensive use, particularly in districts such as the southwest, which are least touched by socioeconomic change. Cultivation is mostly for subsistence: besides extensive sisal plantations in the lower Mandrare region, only groundnut production is commercialized on any large scale; the decline in traditional export crops, such as cotton, has been accompanied by an increasing dependence upon imported rice. What remains of the forest is a source of charcoal and house timbers, as well as supplies to pharmaceutical companies, and there are some localized fishing industries. Despite the provision of government wells, the shortage of rain remains a serious problem, and the periodic famines, which in the past led to migrations within the Androy and into the neighboring regions, now fuel the rural exodus to Toliary and the north. Between 16 percent and 30 percent of the Tandroy are reckoned to live outside the Androy. Nearer at hand, many work as agricultural laborers in the sisal concessions.

Industrial Arts. Part-time or seasonal silversmiths, sewing-machinists, and cobblers and carpenters who specialize in the manufacture of carts and coffins are found among the Tandroy; blacksmiths nowadays are few. In the villages, basketry and raffia work are still common, but the weaving of dyed cottons is now more or less restricted to the production of loincloths and shawls for ceremonial use. Most other traditional crafts, such as silk weaving and pottery making, have fallen into disuse. The weaving of goat's wool, which was introduced in the colonial era, particularly in the southwest, was not an indigenous craft and has since declined.

Trade. Stores, mostly under the control of Indo-Pakistanis, Chinese, and Malagasy from the highlands, are found in the urban centers, which also have weekly markets at which rural Tandroy sell homegrown produce in small quantities and purchase soap, pots, material, and other goods. Traders on foot hawk tobacco and other contraband in the villages.

Division of Labor. In addition to the important dual symbolic classification of religious activities, manual labor, too, is organized by age and gender. Collecting water and firewood, preparing and cooking food, raising poultry, child care and household duties, sowing, weeding, harvesting, mat making, weaving, and spinning are all classed as female activities, whereas herding, milking, slaughtering and butchering, collecting honey, constructing houses, burning the forest, and preparing the fields are classed as male. This classification is modified somewhat in ritual activities and also by demographic factors, status, and wealth.

Land Tenure. The greater part of the land is still unregistered. Although it is conceptualized as clan territory, in which individuals enjoy customary rights, the settlement of people is subject to local government controls. Reports differ as to whether tenant farming and sharecropping are known in the Androy; this lack of agreement may reflect political and demographic variation. Individuals work variable combinations of shifting and permanent fields, but only a very small part of the land is cultivated (estimated at less than 5 percent), the rest being pasture. Land use today is in a critical state, with deforestation, population pressure, overgrazing, and the accelerating stabilization of the south. Conflicts, which previously led Tandroy either to extend their territory or to migrate, are not infrequent, particularly over cultivable fields, transhumance, and grazing rights. If a conflict cannot be settled by the communities concerned, then government officials intervene.

Kinship

Kin Groups and Descent. Ancestry is very important to the Tandroy. Scholars have distinguished three types of group: named clans (*firazana, kopabe*), whose numerical strength and territorial importance vary considerably but whose members (between 100 and 10,000 in each clan) claim a common origin and share transhumant pasture and cattle earmarks; the patrilineage (*famosora*), which may or may not have a residential component but whose several hundred members share a known ancestor and a sacrificial cult; and the sublineage (*tarira, tarike*), which, either as a hamlet or a village quarter, is the localized residential group, whose members, under the authority of an elder, are close kin who share cattle pens. The divisions at each level are normally ranked. All authors stress the importance of agnation in the composition of these groups; patrilateral parallel-cousin marriage ensures that the children of female agnates are often group members. Matrilateral kinship also involves extensive ties. The mother's brother/sister's son relationship is particularly important. Among some groups, it is the idiom in which relationships between dominant and vassal groups are expressed.

Kinship Terminology. Tandroy terms reflect the importance that is attached to both lineality and generation as indicators of either hierarchical or equivalent status. How they are used is determined partly by the political context.

Marriage and Family

Marriage. The literature differs on the question of marriage preference. In the southwest, marriage is a group concern, and an ideology of patrilateral parallel-cousin marriage is pronounced, whereas for northern Androy it has been reported that all types of marriage are practiced indifferently. Nonetheless, all accounts agree that agnatic and village endogamy are common, but that they coexist with intergroup alliances. Tandroy marriage is often polygynous, and divorce and serial marriage are common. Ideally, perhaps, marriage is patrilocal for both parties; otherwise virilocality is preferred. A negative political value attaches to a man who contracts an uxorilocal union. Marriage involves a series of gifts between both parties, including agricultural assistance and mortuary duties on the part of the son(s)-in-law.

Domestic Unit. The house (*traño*), in which a married couple and their unmarried children reside and to which fields and granary attach, is the basic unit of agricultural cooperation and consumption. The same term, however, extends to all coresident agnates, emphasizing the fact that the boundary between the domestic unit and the local descent group is at best unclear; this lack of distinction is also true of arrangements of the ownership and herding of cattle.

Inheritance. In principle, a man's cattle are distributed among his children before his death, while he retains ritual ownership. Although the oldest son often receives the most, he is obliged in turn to give cattle to his brothers. Married couples do not normally inherit from one another, save in the case of the first or chief wife. Outmarrying women and their offspring receive livestock, money, and household goods, with the amount of each generally depending on the standing of the parties and the sociopolitical importance that is attached to their alliance. Cultivable land stays in the ownership of the local descent group. In the past, personal and household effects were sent to the grave or burned with the house of the deceased, but this custom is changing, particularly in the urban centers.

Socialization. Infants and children are raised by members of the household and the village. The main emphasis in their training is upon observing ancestral custom and developing honor and fortitude; admonition is normally verbal, although physical punishment may be employed. Although education is provided by the state, many Tandroy children are unschooled.

Sociopolitical Organization

Social Organization. An independent republic since 1960, Madagascar has a president and an elected assembly. Tandroy society, in contrast with those of other Malagasy groups, has been described as markedly egalitarian. Permanent social hierarchy has been absent since the decline of the Andriamañare and Maroseraña. Nonetheless, traditional sociopolitical organization in the Androy is based on the clan, and the size, territory, wealth, and ritual importance of the clans vary considerably. Moreover, hierarchical values order many of the relationships within and between clans. Social differentiation based on ancestry, residence, and wealth is therefore important but unstable, owing to several environmental and sociopolitical factors. The development of markets and new local power structures, together with a reported decline in cattle raising, are said to have brought changes in ceremonial and group structure.

Political Organization. Madagascar is divided into six provinces (*faritany*). The provinces are divided into prefectures, and the prefectures into *fivondronam-pokontany* (subprefectures). The Androy is in the prefecture of Faradofay in the province of Toliary, with five fivondronam-pokontany (Ambovombe, Amboasary, Bekily, Tsihombe, and Beloha). Each fivondronam-pokontany is composed of several *firaisam-pokontany* (equivalent to cantons), each of which is composed in turn of smaller *fokonolona* (village communities). Little is known of the relationship of indigenous political organization to the colonial and postcolonial local administrative structures.

Social Control. Social control is maintained largely by respect for "ancestral custom" (*lilin-drazañe*) and for the traditional authority that is vested in the elders, on the one hand, and by highly developed values of honor and shame, on the other. Extensive exchange networks also act as mechanisms of social control, as do gossip and the threat of prison. Local councils of elders deal with village and intervillage affairs; wherever possible, external intervention is avoided.

Conflict. In the past, raiding of neighboring groups was common. The endless wars over cattle, land, women, tribute, and succession, in which military alliances were forever changing, have been linked to the political fragmentation of Tandroy groups. Some authors have suggested that segmentary organization developed as an adaptive response to attack. The colonial administration put an end to war, although disputes remain.

Religion and Expressive Culture

Religious Beliefs. Each clan has its own *hazomanga* ("blue" or "sacred wood") and its own type of funerary cults. There are relatively few Christians outside the towns and the southeastern coastal strip. The Tandroy believe in a sacred efficacy (*hasy*) and in moral blame (*hakeo*), which are conceived as largely determining prosperity and power. "Indigenous" spirits (*kokolampoñe*) and "foreigner" spirits (*doany*), both maleficent and benign, are, together with dwarfs, all important.

Religious Practitioners. The priest (*mpisoro*), who is the spiritual and moral head of the group and who officiates at its sacrifices, is the senior male of the senior generation; various adjuncts assist him in his offices. Funerary ritual among certain groups is directed by a priest drawn from uterine nephews or a vassal group. Diviners, exorcists, and spirit doctors, employing incantations, charms, and possession, are also found throughout the Androy.

Ceremonies. Marriage, pregnancy, birth, circumcision, naming, harvests, death, and the inauguration of the priest are all occasions for ritual. In addition, the Tandroy hold incest and curing rites. Most ceremonies involve extensive gift exchange among kin and allies, as well as ritual performances.

Arts. The most notable work of art among the Tandroy is the tomb, which, in its size and construction (often between 12 and 15 meters long and built of stone), contrasts sharply with the Tandroy house. Quadrilateral and oriented to the cardinal points, the traditional tomb (*valavato*) has walls of flat stones (which can be decorated with cut stones and can also incorporate standing stones) and a stone-filled interior, sometimes surmounted by wooden carvings (*aloalo*) and a central edifice. Since World War II, tombs with cement-finished sides and painted designs have become prevalent, but the expense involved in their construction has prompted a traditional revival.

Tandroy musical instruments include the conch shell, fiddle, calabash-resonated cordophone, rattle, and drums of various styles, together with the accordion and *marovane*, a type of zither, both more recent arrivals. Singing, dancing, wrestling, and cattle stampeding are common pastimes; the Androy is known for its semiprofessional traveling entertainers. The arts of skin tattooing and plaiting of men's hair have declined.

Medicine. Illness is attributed to various combinations of the following: intervention of the ancestors, spirit possession, infringement of a prohibition, witchcraft, or an imbalance of elements in the body. The services of diviners and healers are sought, and remedies include herbal medicines, sacrifice, exorcism, possession, and curing rites.

Death and Afterlife. The funeral is the most important of all Tandroy ceremonies. Before burial, the corpse remains in the house for a period of several weeks to several months. The tomb, which can take the community over a year to complete, is built upon the grave; stages in its construction are marked by cattle sacrifice and ceremonial exchange, culminating in the placing of cattle horns upon the completed tomb. The more prestigious and senior the deceased, the more elaborate the tomb and the mortuary rites, and the more extensive the slaughter and the ceremonial exchange. Among certain groups today, but probably at one time throughout the Androy, the services of a funerary priest are employed. Relatively little is said of the afterlife, other than that cattle accompany the deceased's soul.

Bibliography

Decary, Raymond (1930–1933). *L'Androy*. 2 vols. Paris: Société d'Éditions Géographiques, Maritimes et Coloniales.

Heurtebize, Georges (1986). *Histoire des Afomarolahy (Clan Tandroy—extrême-sud de Madagascar)*. Paris: Centre National de la Recherche Scientifique (CNRS).

Middleton, Karen (In press). *Lord of the Funeral: Hierarchy and Gender in Southern Madagascar.* Oxford: Oxford University Press.

KAREN MIDDLETON

Teda

ETHNONYMS: Tebou, Tebu, Tibbu, Toda, Todaga, Todga, Toubou, Tubu, Tuda, Tudaga

Orientation

The Teda inhabit the Tibesti Massif, in northern Chad. They are generally considered to be part of a larger grouping of people known as "Tebu," "Tebou," "Tibbu," or "Toubou." Patterns of growth, intraethnic differentiation, and migration among the more widespread Tebu have left the Tibesti mainly to the Teda and to smaller numbers of Daza. Most of the Teda are isolated in the mountainous plateaus of the Tibesti.

The modern European occupation of the Tibesti put new pressures on old patterns. The Europeans arrived with different technology and objectives that were totally foreign to the Teda. There were three primary European objectives: pacification, sedentarization, and the abolition of slavery. Apart from these essentially political pressures, there is also evidence of climatic pressure, particularly the progressive desiccation of the area over a period of more than fifty years. The emancipation of the people upon whom the Teda relied for agricultural labor compelled the Teda to abandon cultivation rather than to sedentarize and take up a despised occupation. The slaves who were freed did not continue in their traditional line of work, that is, in agriculture, because they too shared the values of their culture, which gave little prestige to agricultural work. They, in fact, tended to become increasingly nomadic. The pacification achieved under European colonization also increased the attraction to travel by rendering it safer. Some of the traditional lifeways of the Teda, particularly a reluctance to rely on cultivation and a preference for migratory activities, have withstood the pressure to change, a demonstration of the tenacity of Teda culture.

In sum, important features of the Teda culture include their reliance on flexible subsistence strategies, a pattern of social stratification that discourages the accumulation of dependents and encourages flexible alliances, a property system that favors movable property over land and that fostered an ethos favoring mobility and military prowess over secure land tenure and intensive production, and a traditional history of small-group (clan) migration and predatory relations with adjacent communities. These features are common to groups that seek to avoid—at almost any cost—their own subjugation or taxation by wealthier predatory peoples.

The massif is centered in the southwestern corner of the Sahara. The people of the massif inhabit an area roughly between 15° and 22° E and 16° and 24° N. The population of the area was an estimated 12,000 to 15,000 in the early 1980s. There are 10,000 to 13,000 Teda in the Tibesti and another 3,000 in the southernmost oases of Libya. Others are scattered in Niger and Chad.

The Teda language includes dialects of the Tebu (Tubu, Tibbu, Toubou, Daza) and Teda or Tedaga (Tuda, Toda, Tugada, Tegada) languages, which belong to the Nilo-Saharan Language Group. The only people who speak Tedaga are the Teda of Tibesti. Daza or Dazaga is the language of the Tebu, and the language in which poetry and songs are composed even by the Teda, whose knowledge of Dazaga is often imperfect.

The climate of the Tibesti region is one of abrupt daily temperature fluctuations, long rainless seasons, and considerable variation according to elevation. Generally, however, it is extremely arid and follows a specific pattern of seasonal variation. December through February are cold and dry months, with violent northeast winds; March and April are hot and dry, but overcast; May and June are hot and dry, with maximum temperatures; July is humid with rainstorms and tornadoes; August and September are rainy and increasingly hot; and October and November are hot and dry, with extreme daily fluctuations in temperature. The greatest extremes for the region at different seasons and elevations are around 46° C. and –26° C, but a 17° daily fluctuation is not unusual.

Most of the massif is made up of steep plateaus dissected by many drainage channels. The west has narrower and more precipitous valleys, whereas the east has broader plateaus with more rounded peaks. Several summits are more than 3,000 meters high, and there are volcanoes on a sandstone plateau with elevations averaging 1,800 meters. The major mineral resource of Teda country is salt, which has long been exploited as a principal trade commodity. In addition, there are deposits of natron, sulphur, amazonite, and superficial deposits of hematite that have yielded sufficient iron ore for native use.

Apart from domesticated dogs, sheep, goats, camels, horses, and donkeys, the fauna includes gazelles, antelope, addaxes, oryx, wild sheep, ostriches, jackals, lizards, and even small numbers of fish and water fowl. There are also poisonous varieties of snakes and scorpions and seasonal swarms of locusts and beetles. Of the uncultivated plants, various shrubs—especially acacias—and grasses grow where and when moisture is sufficient. Doom and date palms are found at sites with permanent water.

History and Cultural Relations

Teda traditional history consists mainly of accounts of the migration of various clan groups into and around the Tibesti. They reveal a good deal about the nature of the Teda clan as a social unit, the formation process of the Teda as an ethnic group, and the character of power and status in Teda society. The recorded history of the Teda territory begins with a seventh-century Arab chronicle, but it is not until around 1300 that solid evidence of the Teda presence is found.

A critical feature of the Tibesti is its remoteness. For the Teda this remoteness is a refuge; others passing through the region are charged a fee. Because of the strategic location of the Tibesti relative to the major caravan routes, the Turks, Arabs, Italians, and French vied to control it, but political control did not always result in significant cultural influence. The most significant effect of contact with other cultures was a stricter adherence to Islamic doctrine. Thus, while the Teda clans immigrated to Tibesti from areas that were already Muslim, their practice of the faith had been extremely unorthodox. Between 1850 and 1930, the Senusi brotherhood a rather puritanical Islamic sect emphasizing scriptural education, established its mission among the Teda and made some headway in eliminating nonstandard and pre-Islamic features.

The Teda are considered solitary, rather tough mountain and desert people. They were on quite hostile terms with their Arab and Tuareg neighbors throughout the colonial period. Their style of social interaction tends to be oriented more toward independence than cooperation. Their character has been described as Spartan, softened by an Islamic emphasis on giving over receiving.

Economy

The Teda are, by numerical majority and by cultural preference, nomadic pastoralists. They have herds of goats and, in some areas, camels. As is the case throughout North Africa and the Middle East, the actual degree to which any sector of the population relies on migratory herding for its subsistence, however, varies regionally with social conditions, climate, and terrain. Most of the Tibesti is so barren as to require migration for pasture, and since herding is not a self-sufficient subsistence mode, seasonal migration is also necessary for date harvesting. Even in the best years, however, these two activities do not produce an adequate diet. In the north-central and northeastern Tibesti, there are areas of arable land where sedentary and semisedentary sectors of the population cultivate vegetable gardens, cereals, groves of palm and fruit trees, grapes, and some cotton. Trade between the pastoral and agricultural sectors is essential to the diets of both, whether it be carried out between social units that are almost exclusively migratory or entirely sedentary, or accomplished by division of labor within a social unit whose members exploit both pastures and arable lands. Thus, there is a continuum of patterns of community land use, mobility, and subsistence strategies, with a stated preference and higher status for the end of the continuum that is most exclusively nomadic pastoralism.

Kinship, Marriage, and Family

The Teda are divided into as many as forty patrilineal clans. In some instances, these clans are clustered in certain areas, but they cannot be considered territorial units. Each member traces descent to a common ancestor, who may have been forced to flee from some other area into the Tibesti. Most Teda clans cannot trace descent beyond about ten generations.

The dominant rule governing actual social organization is one of bilateral kindred and relationship rather than patrilineality. Marriage is kindred exogamous and ideally virilocal. Years of drought and revolution have reduced the economic viability of the Tibesti to the point that men sometimes remain absent most of the year, and residence has become more commonly uxorilocal, as the women stay with the children to care for the herds. The basic unit of social organization is the nuclear family. Friendship plays at least as large a part in determining cooperation as does kinship.

Sociopolitical Organization

The patriclans vary in rank and status according to traditions of length of residence in the Tibesti, conditions under which they settled there, or reputations in war. One clan usually claims the right to the office of paramount chief, or *derdai*, but it appears that this right has at times been held by other high-ranking clans. There is some suggestion that the transfer of the office from one clan to another has been the result of some strategic interclan marriages, which may explain the assertion by some authors that certain clans (presumably high-ranking ones) are preferentially endogamous. Apart from access to the office of chief, distinctions among clans seem to be matters of prestige rather than of power.

The office of derdai itself is almost exclusively that of chief arbitrator in disputes. No power of coercion accompanied the position under precolonial conditions, and relatively little income could be accrued from it. Taxes for the derdai's support were not levied until the Turkish occupation. Traditionally, the derdai derived his income as any other Teda man, with the additional rights to shares from passing caravans and war booty, one-tenth of the blood money paid to the family of a homicide victim, one-tenth of inherited wealth, all property of anyone who died without heirs, and a fine paid the new husband if a divorced woman should remarry before the prescribed period. Clearly, only a powerful and energetic leader could enforce these claims in so dispersed a society, and then only the first item is likely to have been lucrative.

In addition to the mainstream Teda clans, there are two Teda subgroups that are usually described as inferior castes. The Azza intermarry only occasionally and only with extremely impoverished Teda. Generally referred to as blacksmiths and hunters, these people seem to be the artisans of the population; they practice metalwork, leatherwork, pottery making, and hairdressing and perform as musicians and singers at Teda celebrations. In the past, their customary leather garments set them apart, and they tended to travel from one community to another, either singly or in small family groups.

The second caste group, the Kamaya, is comprised of freed slaves or their descendants. The French outlawed slavery during their occupation of the Tibesti, but until that time the Teda kept slaves, acquired either by purchase or capture, and employed them chiefly for the sedentary agricultural labor they themselves so despise. The term of bondage was limited to the individual's lifetime and did not extend to enslave his or her offspring. The Teda are reported in most sources to have treated their slaves reasonably well, given the constraints of their own poverty. Slaves were frequently permitted to accrue wealth with which to purchase their freedom and acquire means of independent livelihood, and it was not uncommon for a master to free a slave and make an additional present of income-producing property. Nevertheless, it has always been considered a great disgrace for a Teda to marry even a descendant of a slave.

Religion and Expressive Culture

It is thought that all the Teda are Muslims. Their Islamization dates very probably to early in the Arab conquest, although most education in the Quran and in the intricacies of the legal system was a result of the establishment of Senusi schools in Libya and Chad within the last century. Although there are some traces of pre-Islamic belief, most of these have been incorporated into the Muslim system. The Islamic calendar is followed. Prayer is regularly practiced by both men and women, as is the Ramadan fast and *zakat*. Inheritance is Islamic. Although the Tibesti does not shelter many men educated in the Quran because few return to live permanently in the mountains, there are families boasting five generations of religiously learned men. In the late twentieth century more and more Teda, both men and women, have been able to perform the hajj.

The health status of the Teda as a group has generally been good. The principal problems are seasonal caloric deficiencies and periodic protein deficiency. In years when nutritional stress has been prolonged, susceptibility to respiratory infections has been a serious health problem. In the late twentieth century rheumatism, dental deterioration, and syphilis have become common.

Bibliography

Bremaud, O., and J. Pagot (1962). "Grazing Lands, Nomadism, and Transhumance in the Sahel." In *The Problems of the Arid Zone*. UNESCO Proceedings in the Paris Symposium. Arid Zone Research, no. 18. Paris: UNESCO.

Briggs, Lloyd Cabot (1960). *Tribes of the Sahara*. Cambridge: Harvard University Press.

Cline, Walter (1950). *The Teda of Tibesti, Borkou, and Kawar in the Eastern Sahara*. General Series in Anthropology, no. 12 Menasha, Wisc.: George Banta.

Haseltine, N. (1953). "Toubbou and Gorane: Nomads of Chad Territory, Notes on Their Origins." *South African Archaeological Bulletin* 14:21–27.

Johnson, Douglas L. (1969). *The Nature of Nomadism: A Comparative Study of Pastoral Migration in Southwestern Asia and North Africa*. Chicago: University of Chicago, Department of Geography.

Kramer, Kim St. Clair (1975). "The Effects of the Drought on the Teda of the Libyan Tibesti." *Proceedings of the First Conference on the Geography of Libya*. University of Benghazi.

Nelson, Harold D., et al. (1972). *Area Handbook for Chad*. American University FAS, DA Pam 550–159. Washington, D.C.: Government Printing Office.

Nyrop, Richard V., et al. (1973). *Area Handbook for Libya*. 2nd ed. American University FAS, DA Pam 550–85. Washington, D.C.: Government Printing Office.

Temne

ETHNONYM: Timmannee

Orientation

Location. The Temne occupy some 29,000 square kilometers of Sierra Leone's Northern Province, specifically in the districts of Bombali, Karene, Kambia, Port Loko, and Tonkolili. They are bounded on the west by the nearly absorbed Bullom; on the north by the Susu, Limba, and Loko; on the east by the Kuranko and Kono; and on the south by the Sherbro and Mende. The area occupied predominantly by Temne thus stretches roughly west from 11°20′ E, to the Atlantic and from 8°20′ to 9°20′ N. In elevation most of the Temne area is below 150 meters, excluding only isolated hills and the extreme eastern portion. Rainfall averages between 254 and 305 centimeters annually, with higher averages of 305 to 356 centimeters along the Atlantic beaches and the extreme eastern portion. Ninety to 95 percent of the annual rainfall is received during the period from May through November, the rainy season. Much of Sierra Leone was once covered by forest, but it has been almost completely cleared; the only primary forest remaining is in the remote reserves. Most of the area is farmed using the slash-and-burn technique, whether it is secondary forest, savanna, or mixed trees on grassland. Small stock are kept, but comparatively few cattle—and these only of the dwarf Ndama strain.

Demography. Of Sierra Leone's 4.5 million people, about one-third are Temne. Population density is highest in the west, in the Kambia and Port Loko districts (57 to 96 persons per square kilometer), and lower in the east (20 to 58 persons per square kilometer). Both fertility and mortality estimates are high for Temne in particular and for Sierra Leone as a whole.

Linguistic Affiliation. The Temne language is included in Greenberg's West Atlantic category and in Dalby's MEL category (with Bullom, Gola, and Kissi in Sierra Leone and others to the north), which is a subdivision of West Atlantic. Dalby found at least five Temne dialects: Western (with variations in the Sanda area), Yoni, Bonbali, Western Kunike, and Eastern or Deep Kunike. The major cleavage is between a grouping of the first four and the Eastern or Deep Kunike, which is nearly unintelligible to speakers of the other dialects. There is no lingua franca in use, although the pidgin English of the Freetown area, known as Krio, has come close to serving as such since the early twentieth century.

History and Cultural Relations

There is no archaeological record for the present-day Temne area that covers the precontact era. Oral traditions, however, are fairly consistent in citing a Temne migration from the northeast, from the Fouta Djallon plateau area in the Republic of Guinea. Subsequent movements of small groups crisscrossed the Temne area in all directions.

There were Temne speakers along the coast when the first Portuguese ships arrived, probably in the 1460s. Temne were indicated on subsequent Portuguese maps, and references to them and brief vocabularies appear in the texts. Trade began, albeit on a small scale, in the fifteenth century with the Portuguese and expanded in the late sixteenth century with the arrival of British traders, and later traders of other nations. Slaves, gold, ivory and local foodstuffs were exchanged for European trade goods—mostly cloth, firearms, and hardware.

As Temne traders were in contact with the permanent European factories in the river mouths, so did they establish and maintain relations with the settlement at Freetown after its founding in the late eighteenth century. This settlement, inspired by philanthropic abolitionists, was regarded ambivalently by Temne traders, who had long been involved in the profitable export slave trade. In the nineteenth century, following abolition, Freetown became the primate trade entrepôt, attracting trade caravans from Temne and beyond. Creoles from Freetown moved progressively up-county to trade in the second half of the nineteenth century, and relations with the Temne and other were not always amicable. The British colonial government at Freetown followed a policy of "stipendiary bribery" punctuated by threats to use armed force in an attempt to prevent Temne and other chiefs from hindering trade from and with areas farther inland. When diplomacy failed, British expeditions invaded the Temne area of Yoni (1889) and then at Tambi (1891).

The Protectorate of Sierra Leone was proclaimed in 1896, and, subsequently, a colonial overadministration was instituted. The traditional Temne chiefdoms became units of local government, and a house tax was levied to support the colonial administration. Armed rebellion broke out in 1898, first in Mende country and later in the western Temne area, where a Temne chief, Bai Bureh, led successful campaigns and became a folk hero. The colonial era began again after 1898, with a more effective administration and increased penetration of the hinterland. Railway construction and, later, feeder roads were pushed in an effort to increase exports. Towns developed to meet the needs of government and increased trade, and expatriate firms and Lebanese and Creole traders expanded their activities throughout Temne and adjacent areas. Schools developed slowly under Christian missions and, later, under government aegis. For the Temne, culture change accelerated.

Portuguese Christian missionary efforts began before the Protestant Reformation but had no lasting effects on the Temne. The Protestant presence accompanied the founding of Freetown in the late eighteenth century; Church Missionary Society representatives were active up the Rokel River and elsewhere in Temne country through the nineteenth century. In the 1890s the Soudna Mission was the first American mission in the Temne area; American Wesleyans and the Evangelical United Brethren subsequently joined the field.

Muslim contacts probably go back several centuries, and fifteenth-century Portuguese were cognizant of Muslim peoples. Early traders, holy men, and warriors brought Islam into the Temne area from the north (Susu) and northeast (Fula, Mandinka, and so on). Through the nineteenth century, as the volume of trade grew, Muslim influences increased; in the late twentieth century a significant proportion of Temne claim to be Muslim converts.

Settlements

Traditionally, Temne resided in villages that varied in size and plan. During the nineteenth century, the village of a chief was larger and included people from several patriclans; often it was either palisaded or had a walled fortress/redoubt built nearby, where the population could reside in times of emergency. Other villages in a chiefdom were built by those given land-use rights by the chief; subsequently, other patrikin groups settled if they were given land-use rights by the initial grantee. If a household farmed land at some distance, people would build a hamlet (*tagbom;* Krio: *fakai*) to reduce travel. Paths connecting villages were often paralleled by secret paths used only by local people. During the colonial era, public paths were cleared and secret paths fell into disuse; village palisades and mud walls were left to deteriorate. When the motor road system developed, villages cut paths to the roads, and some villages, in whole or in part, relocated along them. The compact village plan gave way to a linear pattern along the roads, where larger garden areas separated houses.

The traditional Temne house was round, of varying diameter, with walls of mud plastered over a stick frame; the roof frame, of wooden poles connected by stringers, was conical and covered with bunches of grass thatching. Rectangular houses with a gabled roof became more commonplace during the colonial era. Houses became larger—and also fewer—after the "Hut Tax" was instituted. Chiefs and some subchiefs had rectangular, open-sided structures with thatch roofs, which they used for hearing court cases and for various ceremonies. Some associations, (e.g., Poro, Wunde) had small buildings for regalia. Adobe-brick and cement-block structures were introduced during the colonial era, along with iron-pan and tile roofs.

Economy

Subsistence and Commercial Activities. The Temne have long been predominantly farmers of upland/dry rice, intercropped with a variety of secondary crops. Some swamp/wet rice was grown from at least the nineteenth century in inland swamps and seasonal ponds and in cleared overflow areas along the lower Scarcies River, a development pushed by the colonial administration from the 1930s. Rice surplus to household needs was exchanged. Peanuts, cassava, and other crops were planted on the previous year's rice farm, and around and behind the house were gardens. Oil palms and fruit and other trees provided additional foodstuffs. Through most of the nineteenth century, wooden farming tools (hoes, digging sticks, and knives) continued to be used, although they were progressively being replaced by iron hoes, cutlasses, and knives made by local blacksmiths and, subsequently, imported. Most village households keep chickens; some also keep ducks, sheep and/or goats, dogs, and cats. A few maintain cattle, at least part of the time. Nearly all of the cattle are bred outside the Temne area. Hunting, formerly of some significance, has decreased as the human population has increased. Fishing in the interior rivers and permanent ponds is more important, and a wide variety of techniques is used; off the coast, the western Temne engage in fairly intensive fishing activity, dry the catch, and trade much of it inland.

Industrial Arts. Other than a few long-distance traders, itinerant Poro and Ragbenle society officials, traditional diviners/healers and Mori men, and mercenary warriors, almost no Temne made a living by specializing in an economic activity other than farming. Some farmers, male and female, possessed one or more specialized skills and made some supplementary income from them. For men, the main specialized skills were those related to iron smelting and working, weaving, woodworking, leatherworking, fishing, hunting and trapping, and drumming. The twentieth century brought new forms of specialized knowledge (e.g., carpentry, stonemasonry, sewing, tailoring, literacy) and imported manufactured goods that precipitated the loss of some traditional craft skills.

Trade. Some western Temne were involved in export trade from the late fifteenth century on, whereas many eastern Temne were little involved before the late nineteenth century. Trade, the exchange of goods and services by bartering and/or selling, operated on basically three levels in the nineteenth century: first, horizontal exchanges between households in a village or a group of neighboring villages; second, interchiefdom/regional trade; and third, long-distance trade. The latter two were usually bulking and break-bulking marketing chains. Spatially, long-distance trade patterns were usually dendritic in form. Nineteenth-century trade depended upon canoes and porters head-loading goods over footpaths. The colonial administration brought changes to facilitate a growing volume of trade goods. The construction of a narrow-gauge railway (the SLGRR) brought the establishment of towns along the route, which served as bulking and break-bulking centers and locations for marketplaces. The building of feeder roads extended the areas served by the SLGRR; the completion of an integrated, nationwide road system subsequently led to the closing of the railway. Government programs to increase agricultural productivity were begun; the rice research station at Rokupr and government-run oil-palm plantations and oil mills were the most important of these efforts. The establishment of the Sierra Leone Produce Marketing Board (SLPMB) was of pivotal importance for exports and for income possibilities for the government. Gold, most of it produced further inland than the Temne are, had been traded from Sierra Leone since the fifteenth century but had its last peak in the 1930s; iron was first exported in 1933, from the mine at Marampa, by the Sierra Leone Development Company (SLDC/DELCO); and diamonds were exported after the formation of the Sierra Leone Selection Trust in 1935. Although the diamond areas were outside Temne country, large numbers of Temne migrated as wage laborers in this initially illegal business.

Division of Labor. In farming, the traditional gender division of tasks, which never held for domestic slaves, has substantially broken down in the twentieth century, although men still do most of the clearing and hoeing, and women do most of the weeding. Basically, Temne have always had—and have today—a household mode of production: most farmwork is done by members of the household on its own farmland. At times of peak labor input, cooperative work groups are utilized when possible, for hoeing (Kabotho) harvesting (Ambira), and so on. Domestic slavery in Sierra Leone ended in 1926, but, before then, wealthier Temne used slave workers as well. A household's food and income production is augmented by selling or bartering surplus products locally, in the marketplaces of provincial towns, or to builders. Remittances from household members who have migrated also help. Little wage labor is used in agriculture.

Land Tenure. The chief of each chiefdom is said to "own" the land comprising it, given that he "bought it" and the people on it during that part of his installation ceremonies usually called "Makane." The land/chiefdom was originally secured by the chiefly kin group by occupation of vacant land or by conquest. According to tradition, chiefs "gave" portions of land to immigrants to farm, and the receivers reciprocated with a *lambe*, a return gift, to the grantor-chief as seal on the agreement. The receivers, in turn, could reallocate portions of their land to others, receiving a lambe from them. Such transfers were regarded as permanent. After 1900, as the best farmland became shorter in supply, temporary land-use rights were negotiated with a lambe to seal the deal. Land-use rights became temporary and lambe, now of real economic and not merely symbolic value, had to be given annually; lambe thus increasingly resembled "rent," in our terms. Outright, permanent sale of farmland does not occur.

Kinship

Each individual's second name indicates the patriclan (s. *abuna*) with which she or he is affiliated. There are twenty-five to thirty such patriclans. The names are mostly of Mande origin and are also found among several neighboring ethnic groups. Most patriclans have alternative names, and each is usually geographically concentrated, resulting from isolation during migration. In general, however, Temne patriclans are dispersed and are neither ranked nor exogamous. Each patriclan has several totems—usually of animals, birds, fish, or plants—and prohibitions on seeing, touching, eating, or using that vary considerably from one area to another. Penalties for violating a prohibition are mild, and many adults do not know what the prohibitions are until a diviner diagnoses the cause of a misfortune. Early sources and some contemporary Temne indicate that a common patriclan bond was formerly of significant social importance, but that is not the case today. Each patriclan consists of smaller, localized segments or patrilineages, each of which is comprised of a number of (usually extended) families, each of which in turn usually forms the core of a household. Temne kinship terminology is the type that Murdock calls "Eskimo," in which mother's brothers and sisters are not differentiated terminologically from father's brothers and sisters. In discourse, seniority is indicated more often than laterality. A person is usually closest to and receives most assistance from his or her own (father's) patrilineage, but often ties with the mother's patrilineage are nearly as important; Temne speak of their mother's patrilineage as their "second line of help and protection."

Marriage and Family

Marriage. To be married is strongly desired by adult Temne, especially in the rural agrarian context, where subsistence is very difficult for a single adult, especially if that adult has children. In the traditional Temne marriage system, bride-wealth, comprised of consumer goods and/or money, passes from the groom's kin group to the bride's and/or to guardians and is subsequently distributed more widely. The exchange of bride-wealth and dowry or counterpayment seals the transfer of rights and obligations from the bride's father/guardian; this transfer marks a true marriage from other forms, which may be equally permanent but not as acceptable to the kin groups concerned. The rights transferred are those with respect to domestic service, labor and the income from that labor, children, and sexual services. All subsequent major decisions are made by the husband, who may or may not consult with his wife. Marriage ceremonies differ between Muslim and non-Muslim Temne; both differ from Christian rites.

Although the incidence of polygynous marriages has declined since the 1950s, especially in urban areas, nearly four of every ten married men still had two or more wives in 1976, and six of every ten married women were part of a polygynous family. A polygynously married man's first wife becomes the head wife/manager. Co-wife tensions can lead to discord but usually do not.

Since the 1950s, divorce rates have increased in both rural and urban areas; urban rates are higher than rural rates at any given time. There are generally accepted grounds for a husband, and also for a wife, to secure a divorce. If a wife initiates proceedings, the bride-wealth must be returned; if a husband, it is usually forfeit. Previous divorce(s) are a barrier to remarriage only in rare instances.

Domestic Unit. The male- or female-headed household is the primary residential unit. There are various types of households, but most have a family (husband, wife or wives, and their children) as the core. Some are complex (two or more married men, either father and son or two brothers), often with other, more-distant kin or even strangers in residence. The household head resolves disputes by mediation and moot proceedings and represents the household in village affairs.

Inheritance. Land-use rights and most portable forms of wealth are inherited patrilineally; womens' jewelry, clothing, and rare other items pass from mother to daughter. Disputes occur between the deceased's brothers, between his sons, and between his brothers and his sons.

Socialization. A child is socialized by a comparatively large number of people including parents, older siblings and elders in the household where he or she grows up. For a variety of reasons, fosterage is common; many children are raised outside the parental household. Significant socialization formerly took place during a girl's initiation into the Bundu society and a boy's initiation into Poro. Since about the 1940s, however, initiates into both societies have been younger and have spent little time receiving training in seclusion. Both societies helped prepare adolescents for their roles in adult life. Socialization continued intermittently throughout adult life as people learned from new experiences and patterned their behavior on role models who came to be widely respected and even revered.

Sociopolitical Organization

Social Organization. Traditionally, chiefly kin groups enjoyed superior status, as did big-men, such as wealthier farmers and traders, successful subchiefs or village headmen, society officials, Muslim "holy men," prominent warriors, and the heads of large households. There were wealth differentials between households, based on size, access to farmland, numbers of domestic slaves, and people with specialized skills; the head's prestige was largely determined by his household's relative wealth. As the colonial era progressed and the urban population grew, a social-class system developed, based on wealth as traditionally defined, on money, on nontraditional occupations, and on literacy in English. Elderly males dominated traditional society, and there was a marked "upward flow of wealth" to such men. Slaves, children, junior males, and most females were largely powerless.

Political Organization. The Temne were traditionally organized into fifty-odd chiefdoms, each under a titled chief (*ɔ bai*), whom the British would later call a "paramount chief." Some of the larger chiefdoms were sectioned, but usually each large village or group of smaller villages had its own untitled subchief (*ɔ kapr*). Each village also had an elected headman. In the chief's village there usually resided four to six titled subchiefs, who served their chief as advisors and facilitators. One of these, usually titled *kapr mə sə m*, served as interim ruler after his chief's demise. A chief selected his subchiefs, and they were installed with him. Each subchief, titled or not, selected a sister's daughter as his helper (*mankapr*), and each chief selected one or more sister's daughters to help him. These "female subchiefs" had only ritual—not administrative—duties.

In the western and northern Temne chiefdoms, the chiefs and subchiefs are installed and buried with Muslim ceremonies and bear titles such as *alkali*, *alimany*, and *santigi*. Elsewhere, the Ramena, Ragbenle, or Poro societies perform these rites; there is considerable variation. In the "society chiefdoms," the chief is divine; he has a mystical connection with the chiefdom and the line of previous chiefs. These chiefs have prohibitions—some on their own behavior, and others on the behavior of people toward them.

Chiefly succession systems are either alternating between two patriclans or two lineages within one patriclan, or rotating among three or more lineages of one chiefly patriclan. The fixed rotational patterns were often abrogated. In the nineteenth century it was not unknown for a man who didn't want the job to be selected.

The intrachiefdom power game was primarily a struggle between the chief and those big-men who supported him and those big-men who opposed him. In some instances, the chief and his supporters ruled tyrannically; in others, the chief became a manipulated figurehead. Some chiefs were well liked and had a broad base of popular support; others were disliked, distrusted, and generally opposed.

With the proclamation of the Protectorate in 1896, the chiefdoms became units of local government, and the chiefs, on stipend, became low-level administrative bureaucrats. Some small chiefdoms were amalgamated to make fewer, economically more viable units. Each British district commissioner worked with and through the paramount chiefs of the chiefdoms comprising his district. As chiefly administrative responsibilities widened, nonliterate chiefs had to hire literate assistants, chiefdom clerks. After the Native Administration (N.A.) system was implemented, the chiefs' courts were more closely regulated, and, in the larger chiefdoms, N.A. messengers/police were hired. In 1951 a district council was created in each district, comprised initially of the paramount chiefs and an equal number of elected members and chaired by the district commisioner. When political parties were first formed in the 1950s, they dealt with the chiefs and depended upon them as "ward healers" to turn out their voters for elections.

Social Control. Among nineteenth-century Temne, the law did not have the preeminent place in the resolution of disagreements and conflicts in the way court systems do in twentieth-century democracies. There was no separate, largely independent judiciary; sociopolitical leaders tried certain cases as a prerogative of their positions. Rather than applying abstract ideals of justice, equity, and good conscience, these leaders made decisions in light of the particular political and social settings in each specific instance. Disagreements and conflicts between individuals and groups were adjudicated at, first, the kin-group and residence-group level; second, at the association level (especially the Poro and Bundu societies); and third, at the chiefdom and subchiefdom level (in a chief's court). The first level used primarily moot proceedings, the second usually inquisitory techniques, and the third, a kind of adversarial contest. In the colonial court system, only courts of those chiefs recognized as paramounts served as local courts. Somewhat modified, the system continues today.

Conflict. Raiding and warfare among Temne and between Temne and people of other groups were long-standing. In the eighteenth and nineteenth centuries raids were carried out to steal foodstuffs and people, both disposed of in domestic and foreign trade. People on and near the coast tried to prevent inland traders from having direct contacts and thus preserve middleman profits for themselves. A period of "trade wars" occurred in the second half of the nineteenth century, and a body of professional warriors developed then. These were full-time, itinerant mercenaries, known for their cruelty and fearlessness, who inspired terror and specialized in quick, surprise raids. For defense, Temne surrounded larger villages with walls of tree trunks and mud and built separate fortresses, to which people from several smaller villages could retire in times of emergency. The establishment of the colonial overgovernment put an end to Temne raiding and warfare.

Religion and Expressive Culture

Religious Beliefs. The traditional Temne creator-High God is Kurumasaba, who, in judging the Temne, is thought to be kind, generous, just, and infallible. Kurumasaba is never approached directly, only through patrilineal ancestors as intermediaries. These ancestors also judge their descendants. Sacrifices are offered to them to obtain help for the living. Various nonancestral spirits, some regarded as good and helpful, others as mischievous and even vicious, also receive sacrifices and make agreements to help or—at least not to harm—the living. Temne also believe in witches (*rashir*), individuals, both male and female, who can make victims fall idle, have an accident, or even die. The identity of a witch may be determined by several divinatory techniques and, once identified, can be countered by magical medicines. Especially useful are "swearing medicines," which bring illness and death to an identified witch, thief, or other target. Borrowings from Islam and Christianity have altered many traditional beliefs during the twentieth century.

Religious Practitioners. Traditional diviners used various methods and made protective charms for individuals to protect farms from thieves and to protect a house or farm from witches. These specialists paid for the necessary knowledge from established practitioners during an apprenticeship. Morimen, itinerant Muslims, provided the same range of services with different methods. Officials of the major associations (Poro, Ragbenle, Bundu, and so on) used techniques particular to their group. Confidence in particular practitioners and particular techniques varies over time.

Ceremonies. Ceremonies are held for most life-stage transitions for both sexes. For women, circumcision, coming of age, initiation into the Bundu society, marriage, and giving birth are paramount. For men, circumcision, initiation into the Poro society, marriage, and fathering children are most important. The primary public ceremonies are those that mark the end of initiation of groups into Bundu and Poro, both for ordinary initiates and the rarer initiation of officials, and those that are part of the installation or burial of a chief. The principal Christian and Muslim holidays are also marked by ceremonies (e.g., Christmas and the end of Ramadan).

Arts. Graphic and plastic arts are essentially limited to the adornment of utilitarian objects and the masks and other items used by the various societies. In the past, the Ragbenle masks, especially, were many and varied. The verbal arts are stressed, and Temne use riddles and proverbs in instruction, engage in storytelling that verges on dramatic performance, and employ vocal music and drumming on various occasions. Jewelry is becoming more popular.

Medicine. Disease and ill health are viewed in terms of obvious surface "symptoms" (e.g., fever, rash, swelling) and the "underlying causes" of those symptoms (e.g., witchcraft, being caught by a swearing medicine). Symptoms can be relieved by traditional and/or Western medicine, but these have no effect on the underlying cause(s), which require divination and the proper supernatural response.

Death and Afterlife. Relatives assemble after a death, and the corpse is washed, oiled, and dressed in good clothing. Burial usually occurs in or near the deceased's house. Mourning periods and the number and form of sacrifices vary with the status of the deceased. Divination of the cause of death was usual in the past. Witches require special burial procedures, and society officials and chiefs are also prepared and buried in special ways. One common thread in all is the attempt to appease the spirit of the deceased and prevent disturbance of the living in the future.

Bibliography

Biji, Esu (1913). "Temne Land Tenure." *Journal of the African Society* 12:407–420.

Dalby, David (1962). "Language Distribution in Sierra Leone." *Sierra Leone Language Review* 1:62–67.

Dalby, David (1965). "The MEL Languages: A Reclassification of Southern 'West Atlantic.'" *African Language Studies* 6:2–17.

Dorjahn, Vernon R. (1959). "The Organization and Functions of the *Ragbenle* Society of the Temne." *Africa* 29:156–170.

Dorjahn, Vernon R. (1960). "The Changing Political System of the Temne." *Africa* 30:110–139.

Dorjahn, Vernon R. (1962a). "African Traders in Central Sierra Leone." In *Markets in Africa,* edited by Paul Bohannan and George Dalton, 61–98. Evanston, Ill.: Northwestern University Press.

Dorjahn, Vernon R. (1962b). "Some Aspects of Temne Divination." *Sierra Leone Bulletin of Religion* 4:1–9.

Dorjahn, Vernon R. (1975). "Migration in Central Sierra Leone: The Temne Chiefdom of Kolifa Mayoso." *Africa* 45:28–47.

Dorjahn, Vernon R. (1977). "Temne Household Size and Composition: Rural Changes Over Time and Rural-Urban Differences." *Ethnology* 16:105–127.

Dorjahn, Vernon R. (1982). "The Initiation and Training of Temne *Poro* Members." In *African Religious Groups and Beliefs*, edited by Simon Ottenberg, 35–62. Sadar: Archana Publications.

Dorjahn, Vernon R. (1988). "Changes in Temne Fertility." *Ethnology* 37:376–390.

Dorjahn, Vernon R. (1990). "The Marital Game, Divorce, and Divorce Frequency among the Temne of Sierra Leone." *Anthropological Quarterly* 63:169–182.

Fyfe, Christopher H. (1956). "European and Creole Influence in the Hinterland of Sierra Leone before 1896." *Sierra Leone Studies*, n.s. 6:113–123.

Fyfe, Christopher H. (1962). *A History of Sierra Leone*. London: Oxford University Press.

Gamble, David P. (1963). "The Rokel River and the Development of Inland Trade in Sierra Leone." *Odu*, n.s. 3:45–70.

Greenberg, Joseph H. (1963). *The Languages of Africa*. Indiana University Research Center in Anthropology, Folklore, and Linguistics, Publication no. 25. The Hague: Mouton.

Ijagbemi, E. Ade (1973). *Gbanka of Yoni*. Freetown: Sierra Leone University Press.

Laing, Alexander G. (1825). *Travels in the Timanee, Kooranko, and Sulima Countries of Western Africa*. London: John Murray.

Littlejohn, James (1960). "The Temne *Ansasa*." *Sierra Leone Studies* 13:32–35.

Loveridge, A. J. (1957). "The Present Position of the Temne Chiefs of Sierra Leone." *Journal of African Administration* 9:115–120.

McCulloch, M. (1950). *Peoples of Sierra Leone*. International African Institute. Ethnographic Survey of Africa, Western Africa, Part 2. London: International African Institute.

Sayers, E. F. (1927). "Notes on the Clan or Family Names Common in the Area Inhabited by Temne-Speaking Peoples." *Sierra Leone Studies* 10:14–108.

Sisay, O. (1939). "Funeral Ceremonies among the Temne." *Sierra Leone Studies* 21:94–100.

Skinner, David E. (1978). "Mande Settlement and the Development of Islamic Institutions in Sierra Leone." *International Journal of African Historical Studies* 11:32–62.

Thomas, Northcote W. (1916). *Anthropological Report on Sierra Leone*. Part 1. London: Harrison & Sons.

Wylie, Kenneth C. (1977). *The Political Kingdoms of the Temne: Temne Government in Sierra Leone, 1825–1910*. New York: Africana Publishing Co.

VERNON R. DORJAHN

Tigray

ETHNONYM: Tigre

Orientation

Identification. The Tigray are the largest ethnic group in the Ethiopian province of Tigray and in the Eritrean nation. The Tigray have not been as thoroughly studied as their culturally similar neighbors, the Amhara, with whom they share an "imperial" heritage. The Aksumite Kingdom had its seat in Tigray territory.

Location. In addition to Tigray Province and the southern highland portions of Eritrea, the Tigray occupy parts of Ethiopia's Gonder and Welo provinces. The terrain is high plateau, cut through by deep ravines. Nearly all the land is either under cultivation or in pasturage, although reserved areas that surround churches suggest that the climax growth of much of Tigray is cedar forest. The average annual rainfall hovers around the 50 centimeters required for cereal agriculture. Droughts are frequent. Rainfall concentrates in two periods: the "large rains" fall for three months beginning in mid-June and the "small rains"—if they come—fall in January or February. Most Tigray live in the highlands, where daytime high temperatures are relatively cool (21° to 27° C); nighttime temperatures occasionally plunge below freezing in December.

Demography. There are approximately 2,000,000 Tigray, primarily divided between Tigray and Eritrea. Drought, civil war, and resettlement make precise estimates impossible. Since the mid-1970s, severe droughts have resulted in extremely high rates of infant mortality. Prior to the droughts and civil war, the population density had reached the carrying capacity of the land, requiring pasturage to be converted to cultivation.

Linguistic Affiliation. Tigreñña is Semitic and more closely related to the liturgical language Ge'ez than is Amhara. All three languages are written using a common script. The language should not be confused with Tigre, a language spoken by a nearby group.

History and Cultural Relations

The Tigray have been in their present location since before the time of Christ and began converting to Christianity in the fourth century. Some of the population may have migrated from the Arabian peninsula. There seems to be a long-term process of migration south, with Tigray imperceptibly "becoming" Amhara as they marry into Amhara communities. The

Tigray, with the Amhara, are the coinheritors of the Aksumite Kingdom, which later become the Ethiopian Empire. Tigray as well as Amhara were eligible for the emperorship, the last Tigray emperor being Yohannes (1872–1889).

The Tigray living in Tigray Province experienced a relatively short colonial period (1936–1942) compared to that of their Eritrean neighbors, who were dominated by the Italians from the 1890s until 1942. The heavily Tigray-influenced Eritrean Liberation Front (ELF, now the EPLF) led a separatist revolt through the 1960s until it was joined by the now-stronger Tigray People's Liberation Front (TPLF) after the 1974 overthrow of Haile Selassie. Most Tigray are rural; Asmara in Eritrea and Maqelle in Tigray are the only urban centers. War, drought, and international relief agencies have played a major role in this region since the mid-1970s.

Settlements

Tigray "parishes" equate with local communities and are the smallest units of administration for both the state and the Ethiopian Orthodox church, having a chief appointed from above. Priests and deacons are responsible to church authorities. Parishes range in population from 500 to 4,000 people. There is regional variation in settlement pattern: climatic conditions favor dispersed settlement of small hamlets across parishes where rainfall is relatively constant from year to year, and nucleated villages, one per parish, where rainfall is less predictable. Villages go through a process of dividing into quarters, which reunite when new, more powerful quarters try to dominate them. Depending on the phase of their life cycle, villages have two or three quarters. Houses range from wattle-and-daub huts to impressive masonry lime-domed or zinc-corrugated roofed edifices, depending on the family's economic success.

Economy

Subsistence and Commercial Activity. The Tigray practice plow cultivation of primarily cereal crops: wheat, barley, *t'af* (Amharic: *ṭyeff; Eragrostis abyssinica*), and sorghum. A second crop per year is risky or impossible in most areas. Legumes, primarily garbanzos, are included in the crop-rotation cycle. After several years, weeds become too strong for competition, and the field is fallowed until grasses choke out the weeds and the turf can be removed again, bringing the field into cultivation. Flax is grown for linseed oil. In some zones, frankincense figures prominently. For those living near the eastern escarpment, transportation of salt from the Danakil Depression for sale in the highland markets is an important source of income. In addition to the salt trade, individuals earn some cash by purchasing cattle and small animals in the lowlands and selling them further into the highlands. Cattle are important as plow animals. When population density is high and pasturage is in short supply, plow animals are the most critical variable in the agricultural process.

Industrial Arts. Crafts are associated with pariah "castes" of artisans who are believed to be witches. Blacksmithing, pottery making, tanning, weaving, and music making fall under this stigma. A person with a physical disability, however, can engage in weaving without being regarded as a witch.

Trade. Markets, shops, and mills are associated with towns. Shops are often run by Arab merchants. Products of artisanry (pottery, hides, metal tools), herbs and spices, coffee, salt, and bread are sold. Towns, especially those associated with administrative offices, have mead houses; each quarter of a village has at least one beer house.

Division of Labor. For nonartisans, sex and age account for most of the division of labor. Men are responsible for nearly all agriculture and husbandry. The sole exception is weeding, which is done by women. Once the grain has left the threshing floor, its storage and processing into *injera* (the crepelike staple) and bread is also the province of women. Boys, after the age of about 12, begin herding and helping with plowing and planting. Girls help with food preparation and child care. At least one herd boy is needed if a household is to be independent. If there are more herd boys than necessary, some may go off to study the Bible to prepare for careers as deacons, with the eventual possibility of joining the priesthood. Priests, like other male heads of households, are farmers. As many as 10 percent of a parish's households may be headed by priests. Most curing, which depends heavily on ecclesiastical training, is done by defrocked priests and deacons; most treatment of spirit possession is done by women. Artisans sometimes form their own villages, where they also practice agriculture; however, in other villages, they are found interspersed in individual households with nonartisans. Elders and powerful men are designated as "recognized men" and "big-men."

Land Tenure. Land tenure is complex and governed on a parish-by-parish basis. Each parish chooses from permutations of two basic forms: *ristî* (hereditary) and *ĉigurafgotet* (communal). To make a claim under ristî, a person must trace descent from a parish founder through any combination of males and females. The system has inherent contradictions: all plots of land potentially have multiple claimants, giving rise to a political as well as a genealogical component to land claims. Ĉigurafgotet land tenure, unlike ristî—which can be used to restrict the inflow of new farmers—encourages newcomers and becomes salient after a drought depopulates an area. Because the choice of land-tenure systems affects the size of the holdings of many people, parishes switch from one system to the other only under extreme ecological and demographic conditions. The two land-tenure systems are not associated with settlement patterns; nucleated and dispersed forms of settlement are found with both types.

Kinship

Kin Groups and Descent. Descent is omnilineal or ambilineal. Descent groups form and disperse depending upon the particular land claim that is being prosecuted. Persons who are allies for one purpose are enemies for another. This does not follow the familiar pattern of "fission and fusion" described by Evans-Pritchard for the Nuer (1940), in that groups are not segments of larger groups but are based on a particular individual's genealogical relations in a particular parish. He or she will be brought together with a distinct collection of people in each parish and at each genealogical level. These associations do not achieve the kind of solidarity that would make them useful for purposes other than land claims. Kinship is bilateral and, like descent, is traced through any combination of males and females. The importance to each household of having at least one herd boy leads to boys often being brought up in the household of a father's or mother's brother or sister, as adjustments to household work forces require.

Kinship Terminology. Tigray kin terms reflect their bilateral kinship and omnilineal descent. Generation and lineality are distinguished. Sex is distinguished only in Ego's generation and for parents. Kin types are grouped as follows: son and daughter, brother, sister, father, mother, father's and mother's brother, father's and mother's sister, and father's and and mother's father and mother. All eight great-grandparents are referred to by a single term.

Marriage and Family

Marriage. Marriages are monogamous and "contractual." First marriages involve a dowry, usually of animals, given by the bride's family to the couple. Second marriages usually require equal contributions from both parties. Should the potential wife not have capital comparable to her potential husband's, an arrangement is made in which she is "paid" and her accumulated shares are eventually converted into community property. Only older couples and deacons intending to become priests are married before the church. The "life expectancy" of a marriage at the time it is contracted is between seven and twelve years. Marriage contracts incorporate the potential of divorce. At marriage, a guardian is selected to help reconcile difficulties and to aid in division of property in case of divorce. Elders are called in to oversee the process. After the wedding, for a first marriage, there is a period of bride-service during which the couple goes back and forth between the two parental households, spending time in each. Once bride-service has been completed, there is no formal rule of postmarital residence. Practical considerations of joint herding often lead to a period of viripatrilocal residence.

Domestic Unit. The nuclear family is the most common domestic unit. Youngest children may remain with the family homestead to take care of aging parents. A small number of economically successful households retain their own sons and daughters and draw in their mates, thus forming large multifamily households. Partition takes place in stages: separation of hearths, separation of grain bins, and final separation.

Inheritance. Inheritance rules distinguish between land and household property. If the parish is ristî, each child, regardless of gender or marital status, inherits an equal share of the land of his or her dead parent. Domestic equipment tends to remain with the child who took care of the aging parent. Other property (principally livestock), if not consumed in the funeral commemoration a year after death, may be divided.

Socialization. Small children are indulged, particularly boys. Girls begin helping their mothers earlier than boys begin helping their fathers. Girls gradually take on domestic chores. At about age 7, boys must begin to learn to obey, which involves a period of apparent trauma. Children are baptized. A series of vertical scars to the outside of either eye, found on most adults, is regarded as "medicinal" rather than "ritual" and is done on the occasion of eye infections. A cross is often made by tattoo or scarification in the middle of the forehead. Movement from minority to adulthood is not dramatic. Boys move to the adult part of the parish meeting when they become married or when they become deacons. Women tend to act in political contexts only in the absence of their husbands but have the rights of jural majors after marriage.

Sociopolitical Organization

Social Organization. The most significant unit beyond the household is the *h'agareseb* (lit., "farm people"), which is the parish or local community. It is at the parish meeting, held on Sunday mornings after church services, that all important community decisions are made, whether they be religious or civil, whether to add a new saint to the local church calendar or to repair a path. Parish meetings are presided over by a secular community leader, or "manager." In nucleated parishes, village wards are significant and have informal leaders. Neighbors participate in one another's life-cycle ceremonies and have the legal duty to respond when a neighbor raises a hue and cry. Descent groups have little relevance outside of land-tenure issues. Most adults belong to "twelve apostle" eating clubs, consisting of men or women or couples who meet once a month for feasting and discussion.

Political Organization. When the Ethiopian state was functioning well, the Tigray of Tigray Province were full participants in politcal life and on several occasions provided emperors. This relationship was interrupted in Eritrea by the long Italian colonization. After the 1974 Revolution, many of the Tigray in both areas rose in rebellion. Nowadays the state organization involves provincial, district, and subdistrict governors. Each parish has an official, appointed from above, who owes loyalty to the subdistrict governor. The official at each level of government owes loyalty to the official immediately above him, not to the central government. Parish priests are responsible to the bishops.

Social Control. In native theory, people are "good" because they fear what their neighbors will think, what the courts will do, and what God will do. Beyond this, the parish chief is an officer of the court and has the responsibility to handle minor cases and to carry more serious ones to higher courts. The institution of *awuĉhaĉh* requires all members of the community to assemble for three days or until someone confesses knowledge of a crime.

Conflict. The Tigray see conflict as a natural consequence of weak authority. Conflicts occasionally transpire, ranging from those at the the intervillage level to rebellions against the state, as happened in the 1940s and again since the Revolution. Outlaws with a large following are sometimes later made part of the state, and state officials sometimes become outlaws.

Religion and Expressive Culture

Religious Beliefs. Christianity is said to have come to Tigray with the shipwrecked Syrian Fromentius, in the third century. Each parish is associated with a church, which in most regions is built of masonry and, in some others, carved into cliffs. It is through Bible study that most young men gain literacy. The Ethiopian Orthodox church was formally affiliated with the Coptic church in Alexandria, to which, until 1954, it was obliged to turn for archbishops. The Tigray recognized three categories of belief as "religion" (*haymanot*): Christianity, Islam, and Judaism. A number of the saints are indigenous and not shared by the Roman or Greek churches. Spirit possession, in the form of the *zar* cult, is prominent, but many Tigray regard it as illegitimate. Zar has special significance in empowering women.

Religious Practitioners. Priests and deacons, many monastery trained, celebrate the Mass. Diviners are defrocked deacons or priests. Spirit mediums are typically women, as are the vast majority of those afflicted with possession. Priests and deacons receive a special allotment of land for their services, plus honoraria from their penitents. Diviners charge for their services, as do spirit mediums.

Ceremonies. The most frequent ceremony is the celebration of Mass, which occurs a number of times per week, depending on the local church calendar and parish patron saints. Other important rituals are baptism and funerals. Ordinary weddings are more ceremonial than ritual. Divination and curing have a ritual character, as do ward or neighborhood dances intended to affect the weather.

Arts. Arts, crafts, and secular music are primarily the domain of the pariah castes of artisans. The exceptions are sacred music, which is led by monastically trained (but not necessarily ordained) men, and icon painting, biblical illumination, and scroll making, which are undertaken by a few deacons.

Medicine. Most affliction (including illness) is treated by diviners rather than by priests or spirit mediums. Affliction is attributed to transgressions against God, sorcery motivated by envy, or witchcraft unconsciously executed by artisans or others possessed by Satan. Diviners both diagnose and treat. Spirit possession by entities other than Satan and his minions primarily affects women and is regarded as outside the realm of Christian belief. Such possession may be brought under control but not cured.

Death and Afterlife. After death, people are judged, in what is popularly thought of as a setting much like a secular court, and proceed to heaven or hell.

Bibliography

Bauer, Dan F. (1978). *Household and Society in Ethiopia*. 2nd ed. East Lansing: Michigan State University, African Studies Center.

Bauer, Dan F. (1990). "The Sacred and the Secret: Order and Chaos in Tigray Medical Practice and Politics." In *Creativity of Power*, edited by William Arens and Ivan Karp. Washington, D.C.: Smithsonian Institution Press.

Bruce, John (1975). "Land Reform Planning and Indigenous Communal Tenures: A Case Study of the Chigurafgwoses in Tigray, Ethiopia." Ph.D. dissertation, University of Wisconsin, Madison.

Evans-Pritchard, E. E. (1940). *The Nuer*. London: Oxford University Press.

Hoben, Allan (1973). *Land Tenure among the Amhara of Ethiopia*. Chicago: University of Chicago Press.

Levine, Donald (1965). *Wax and Gold*. Chicago: University of Chicago Press.

Nadel, S. F. (1946). "Land Tenure on the Eritrean Plateau." *Africa* 16(1): 1–21.

DAN F. BAUER

Tiv

ETHNONYMS: Munchi, Munshi, Tivi

Orientation

Identification. The Tiv (sing. Or-Tiv) are a group of about a million people who live on both sides of the Benue River, 220 kilometers from its confluence with the Niger, in Nigeria. "Tiv" is the name of the common ancestor from whom all are descended. In Hausa they are called "Munshi" or "Munchi."

Location. The heartland of Tivland stretches from about 6°30′ to 8°00′ N and from 8°00′ E to 10°00′ E, although Tiv settlements are also found north and east of that area. In the southeast, Tivland borders the foothills of the Cameroons, from whence the Tiv say they originally came. Some hills, especially in southern Tivland, are as high as 1,200 meters. The undulating plains of tall grasses (as much as 3 meters high), dotted with savanna trees, lose elevation until they reach the Benue, at about 100 to 120 meters. The Tiv, who are an expanding people, are well along in their occuptaion of the similar plain that extends northward from the river toward the Jos Plateau.

Demography. The earliest estimate of the Tiv population, in 1933, was 600,000. In 1950 the count was about 800,000. By 1990, the figure had climbed to more than a million. The density of population in Tivland in 1950 was about 166 per square kilometer, but that figure is misleading. In the southern area, where the Tiv reside adjacently with the small groups of peoples they know collectively as the Udam, the density rises to at least 1,430 per square kilometer.

Linguistic Affiliation. There is a single Tiv language intelligible to all, although regional dialects allow one to distinguish the area from which a person comes. The language is classified as the only example of its subdivision (on the same level as Bantu languages) of the Niger-Congo Language Family.

History and Cultural Relations

The Tiv say they emerged into their present location from the southeast. "Coming down," as they put it, they met the Fulani, with whom they still recognize a joking relationship. The earliest recorded European contact was in 1852, when Tiv were found on the banks of the Benue. In 1879 their occupation of the riverbanks was about the same as in 1950. British occupying forces entered Tivland from the east in 1906, when they were called in to protect a Hausa and Jukun enclave that Tiv had attacked. The Tiv said in 1950 that they had defeated this British force, then later invited the British in. The southern area was penetrated from the south; what southern Tiv call "the eruption" of the British there occurred in 1911.

Dutch Reformed missionaries from South Africa entered Tivland in 1911; they were joined, and then succeeded, by U.S. Protestants in the 1940s and 1950s. Catholic missions arrived in the 1920s.

The early administration, coming as it did from the east where Tiv had come under the influence (but not the hegemony) of Jukun and Hausa kingdoms, established "District

Heads," who were influential men to whom the British gave authority in which other Tiv did not concur. That system was extended beyond the area of Jukun influence to other Tiv, causing disturbances. Beginning in 1934, the administration created Tiv experts—men who learned the Tiv language and stayed for far longer periods of time than most colonial officers stayed with any given people. Their reports provided a firm basis for administrative reform.

Settlements

The Tiv say—and archaeological sites confirm—that before the British "eruption" they lived in stockaded villages of perhaps 500 to 600 people. After the Pax Britannica became effective, they "went to the farm," establishing smaller compounds spread more or less evenly over the land. In 1950 these compounds contained from 12 to 120 people. Eighty-three percent of the males in each compound were members of the patrilineage associated with the area; the other 17 percent were descendants of daughters of the lineage living temporarily with their maternal patrilineages.

Reception huts, each identified by the name of a mature male member of the compound, are arranged in a circle or an oval, their entrances facing in toward the center. Behind each reception hut is a sleeping hut for each of that man's wives. A recently married son may build his wife a sleeping hut behind his mother's hut before he has a reception hut of his own. Reception huts are circular, with conical thatched roofs supported on posts. They are open on the sides and as much as 9 meters in diameter. Sleeping huts have solid walls and are usually no more than 4.5 meters in diameter; each contains a cooking fireplace with a storage platform built above it. Granaries of several sorts are associated with sleeping huts.

Economy

Subsistence and Commercial Activities. The Tiv are subsistence farmers. Their main crops—like those of peoples to their south—are yams, cassava, and sweet potatoes; they have in common with the peoples to their north grain crops, particularly sorghum, millet, and maize. Peanuts, peppers, several types of cucurbit, tomatoes, okra, and cotton are grown. Mango trees abound, although the fruit is eaten only by children; oranges were introduced by British agricultural officers. The Tiv gather greens, mushrooms, seeds, leaves, and plants to be used in sauces. They keep goats, sheep, chickens, ducks, and guinea hens; sleeping sickness prevented the keeping of cattle or horses. Tiv men set great store by hunting, but in most areas all game has been hunted out.

Industrial Arts. Pottery is made by women; weaving of cotton cloth is done by young men; baskets are woven by men and boys. Chairs, both indigenous chairs and deck chairs, are made by mature men, as are beds, stools, mortars, and grinding stones. The Tiv share the general West African respect for blacksmiths; they made and hafted hoes, digging sticks, and spearheads as recently as the 1950s. All specialists is such crafts are farmers.

Trade. Although markets were indigenous, their importance and number increased vastly with the Pax Britannica. Markets meet every five days except in areas associated with mission compounds, where they are held on Fridays or Saturdays. Every area in Tivland maintains a calendar built on five-day market cycles. Goods move from smaller markets to large central markets, from which they are exported, particular in the south.

Division of Labor. Tiv gender ideas are expressed primarily in terms of the division of labor, although the ideas penetrate every aspect of their culture. Men do the hard labor of clearing land and making mounds for planting yams; they also run the legal, political, and religious systems. Women do the rest of the farm work: weeding (which is often done by parties of women), harvesting, and carrying the crops to the granaries and storehouses in the compound. Women cook and are in charge of child rearing but traditionally had help from older children, either their own or those they "borrowed" from kin.

Land Tenure. Tiv land tenure, closely associated with residence, is an integral part of political and social organization (see "Sociopolitical Organization").

Kinship

Kin Groups and Descent. All Tiv reckon patrilineal descent from their earliest ancestor. They see themselves—all one million of them—as a single patrilineage. Tiv had two sons, the ancestors of the major division of the group. They divide themselves at every generation, thus forming an immense lineage system. The genealogies collected in the early 1950s were from fourteen to eighteen generations from Tiv, the original ancestor, to living elders. Obviously, to get that number of people in that number of generations, there has to be a "correction factor." The eight senior, hence largest, levels of lineage form the core of the political organization; they are probably resistant to change. The most recent four or five generations are relevant to exogamy and land tenure; their genealogy is generally known. Where the political and domestic systems overlap, there is likely to be a dispute about ancestral names.

The Tiv see their large-scale patrilineal genealogy as the basis of their land-tenure system. Every Tiv male has a right to a farm beside that of his full brother; their collective farms belong beside those of their half-brothers. The sons of their common father have farms beside the farms of their father's brothers' sons. So it continues, through the generations. All geographical locations that do not accord with the genealogy are given special explanations.

A lineage is called a *nongo* ("line"). The Tiv call their own patrilineal lineage, at all levels, their *ityo*. Their mother's patrilineal lineage is their *igba*. The more distant in the genealogy their ityo and their igba, the greater number of people each contains; this factor can be important in computing political influence.

Kinship Terminology. The major distinctions made by kinship terms are between lineals and collaterals. *Ter* means father, both grandfathers, and all male ascendants. If Tiv want to distinguish the generations, they say "great ter" for the older generation and "little ter" for the junior one. *Ngo* means mother, both grandmothers, and all female ascendants. *Wan* means child and all of one's descendants. The word is also used for all male members of one's agnatic lineage (ityo) younger than oneself and all female members of any age. "Child of my mother" (*wanngo*) is anyone with whom I share a female ascendant. "Child of my father" (*wanter*) is anyone with whom I share a male ascendant. People who share both a father and a mother at any level are called *wangban*—as is anyone with whom a kinship relationship can be traced by two paths. There is one word for all affines—it means "outside." The words for husband and wife are the words for male and female; a co-wife is a *wuhe*.

Marriage and Family

Marriage. The Tiv, at first European contact, used an involved form of exchange marriage. The ideal was that two men exchanged full sisters. The children were then double cousins. Seldom, however, could that be arranged. Therefore, one of the lineages (usually three or four generations deep) was called a "ward-sharing group." Each woman in the group was assigned to one of the men of the group—her "guardian"—who then exchanged her for a wife. Nevertheless, the Tiv usually "followed their own hearts" in matters of marriage and eloped. That meant that the exchange system was a network of long-term debts between lineages. The debts sometimes took several generations to straighten out. The British administration outlawed exchange on the stated principle that they could never administer justice under so complex a system. They and the Dutch Reformed missionaries pressed for a form of bride-wealth marriage, which the Tiv saw in terms of their own system of *kem* marriage. "Kem" means "to accumulate." By 1950, bride-wealth was paid, a little at a time, more or less over the life of the marriage.

Tiv marriage is brittle. Divorce is inaugurated by women, never by men (although men may behave badly enough that they know their wives will leave them). Children of nursing age go with the mother, of course; a boy returns to his father's compound when he is about 8 years old, a girl in time to be married from her father's compound.

Domestic Unit. Every married woman has her own hut, at least after the birth of her first child. The husband's reception hut is surrounded by the huts of his wives. Each married woman has her own store of food; she cooks and takes food to her husband every day, and he shares it with all the children present. The children also eat with their mothers. Several such polygynous families, linked by the agnatic links of the husband/fathers, live in the same compound. Their compound is next to those of his agnatically close kinsmen (see "Kin Groups and Descent").

Inheritance. Land is not, properly speaking, inherited. It is a right of lineage membership. Ritual positions are not inherited. A man's personal property is taken over by his sons and grandsons, a woman's personal property by her daughters-in-law.

Sociopolitical Organization

Social Organization. Tiv social organization is based on the lineage system (see "Kin Groups and Descent"). Market courts are secondary. Age-sets were important in some ritual situations.

Political Organization. Tiv political organization was traditionally based solely on the lineage principle. That principle was recognized by the colonial government, which nevertheless added a hierarchy of offices, one for each lineage level recognized by the government. Market organizations were often used for political purposes.

Social Control. Social control was achieved through the lineage system.

Conflict. Traditionally, there were struggles and wars between lineages (which were limited by the lineage system) and conflicts between the Tiv and their neighbors (in which case all Tiv were "against" all the neighbors). The usual means of settling conflict within the lineage was by a moot of elders who met, heard the cases, and made decisions. They did not have—and by and large did not need—the right to enforce their decisions.

Religion and Expressive Culture

Religious Beliefs. The Tiv recognize an otiose god called Aondo (Sky) who created the universe, but they do not postulate that he has any current interest in them. They acknowledge ancestral spirits and, sometimes, make offerings to them—but do not pray to them or regard them as either good or evil. Evil is to be found in the hearts of human beings—it is called *tsav*. Tsav, set in motion by evil men using forces that the Tiv call *akombo*, caused misfortune. Each akombo is a disease or symptom, as well as being a set of special symbols. The ritual task is, by sacrifice and medicines, to keep the akombo repaired.

Religious Practitioners. The Tiv utilize diviners. Most Tiv men also come to be masters of at least some akombo, a few of many akombo. A man who has mastered an akombo carries out rites when that akombo is implicated in a curing ceremony.

Ceremonies. Akombo ceremonies are performed in order that individual people (and, very occasionally, communities) can recover from illness already manifest or else may prosper in general.

Arts. The Tiv decorate almost everything. They produce some sculpture, little of it of the high quality that is known in much West African art.

Medicine. Herbal medicines are known to most Tiv elders. The masters of specific akombo specialize in the medicines associated with that akombo. Only after the akombo ceremony is carried out can the medicine be effective.

Death and Afterlife. The Tiv say that they do not know whether there is an afterlife and that a funeral ceremony is like calling down the path to a person who is departing—one cannot be sure how much of the message the person heard.

Bibliography

Bohannan, Laura, and Paul Bohannan (1953). *The Tiv of Central Nigeria*. London: International African Institute.

Bohannan, Paul (1954). *Tiv Land Tenure*. London: Her Majesty's Stationery Office.

Bohannan, Paul (1957). *Justice and Judgment among the Tiv*. London: Oxford University Press for International African Institute.

Bohannan, Paul, and Laura Bohannan (1968). *Tiv Economy*. Evanston, Ill.: Northwestern University Press.

Keil, Charles (1979). *Tiv Song*. Chicago: University of Chicago Press.

PAUL BOHANNAN

Tonga

ETHNONYMS: Balumbila, Batoka, Batonga, Bawe, Toka

Orientation

Identification. The Tonga occupy much of Southern Province in Zambia (formerly Northern Rhodesia), spilling over on the east into Zimbabwe (once Southern Rhodesia or Rhodesia). Tonga in Kalomo and Livingstone districts are known as Toka; to the north are Plateau Tonga; Gwembe Tonga live in Gwembe District and in nearby Zimbabwe. The Tonga never formed a single political unit. Today they are an ethnic group united by common language and in opposition to other Zambian ethnic groups, with whom they compete.

Location. Tonga country, Butonga, lies between 16° and 18° S and 26° and 29° E, bounded on the north by the Kafue and Sanyati rivers, in Zambia and Zimbabwe, respectively. Its southern boundary follows the Zambezi and Gwai rivers. It includes the southern Zambian plateau, which rises to more than 1,000 meters, the escarpment hills facing the Middle Zambezi Valley, the Zambezi plain lying some 600 meters below the plateau, and the escarpment hills within Zimbabwe. The Middle Zambezi Valley is knows as Gwembe Valley. Average annual rainfall varies from nearly 80 centimeters at the escarpment edges to 40 centimeters in northern Gwembe Valley. Drought years are frequent. Rains are expected by mid-November and taper off through March and April, when the cold dry season begins. June and July may bring light frost. In late August the hot dry season begins abruptly. Temperatures in northern Gwembe may reach 45° C. The Zambian Railway and a highway paralleling it cross the plateau south to north, giving access to markets for agricultural produce first created when copper mines were opened in Zaire and Zambia in the 1920s. This led to European farming settlement, the building of small townships dominated by Indian shopkeepers, and cash cropping by Plateau Tonga. Since the completion of Kriba Hydroelectric Dam in 1958, much of the Zambezi plain and the lower reaches of its tributary rivers have been flooded by Kariba Lake. Over 54,000 Gwembe Tonga were displaced from the river plain to new habitats in the hills above Kariba Lake or in more arid country below Kariba Dam. They also became more accessible.

Demography. In 1980 Southern Province had an estimated population of 791,296, at an average density of 7.9 per square kilometer, some of whom were non-Tonga immigrants. Many Tonga have emigrated to Central Province since the 1940s in search of agricultural land or urban jobs. In 1969 Tonga speakers comprised slightly over 10 percent of the Zambian population; in the 1980s they probably numbered over 800,000. There were approximately 40,000 Tonga settled in Zimbabwe in the 1950s. Birthrates are high; the rate of population increase is around 2.8 percent per annum.

Linguistic Affiliation. The Tonga speak dialects of ciTonga, a Central Bantu language, along with other languages of central and northern Zambia and adjacent regions in Zaire. It was committed to writing by missionaries in the early twentieth century and today has a minute literature, but Tonga writers prefer to write in English, the official language of Zambia. The Central Plateau dialect is becoming the standard used in schools and for broadcasting.

History and Cultural Relations

Tonga oral history is local history of no great time depth. Archaeological sites on the southern plateau associated with the arrival of the Tonga from the northwest date from the twelfth century A.D. Although they were shifting cultivators who had cattle, they also relied on game and fish. Their crafts included pottery and ironwork; a few scraps of copper remain. There is little evidence of differences in status or of long-distance trade. Sites in northern Gwembe from much the same period have richer assemblages and may not have been Tonga sites. Finds from Ingombe Ilede indicate trade contacts with the Indian Ocean. Some fourteenth- and fifteenth-century graves contained trade beads and worked gold, copper, and bronze. Ingombe Ilede may have been an outpost of one of the Shona kingdoms. Shona speakers still live nearby. In the eighteenth and nineteenth centuries northern Gwembe was visited by Portuguese and Chikunda from Mozambique, who first sought ivory and slaves, and then settled. In general, the nineteenth century was a time of turmoil: Toka country was occupied for a few years by Makololo from southern Africa; in the last half of the century, Lozi raiders from the Upper Zambezi and Ndebele raiders from Zimbabwe harassed all of Tonga country, and the Lozi established hegemony among the Toka. In the 1890s the British South Africa Company had little difficulty in annexing Tonga country and administering it as part of the newly created Northern Rhodesia that, in 1923, was handed over to the British Colonial Office. Early administrators organized the country into districts and created a skeletal administration based on appointed village headmen. These headmen were grouped into chieftaincies under appointed chiefs, who were responsible to a district administrator. Much land was taken for European settlement. After 1923, native reserves were set aside and allocated to the three divisions into which Tonga were by then grouped, under councils called the Plateau Tonga, the Toka-Leya, and the Gwembe Tonga native authorities. Missions arrived at the beginning of the twentieth century. They established schools and, on the plateau, provided instruction in plow agriculture. The Plateau Tonga developed a cash-crop economy by the 1930s; the Toka, with poorer soils, and the Gwembe Tonga, cut off by the escarpment, continued to work as labor migrants, usually in Zimbabwe, until after Zambian independence in 1964. Independence removed restrictions on African access to employment and the use of lands reserved for European development.

Settlements

Plateau villages in the late nineteenth century were small clusters of round pole-and-mud huts with associated granaries and cattle pens, frequently housing a single extended family or a small number of kinsmen with their dependents, including slaves. Shifting cultivation encouraged the relocation of villages; these occasions provided the opportunity for dissidents to hive off. In the west, the placement of homesteads along long ridges to avoid floods led to larger aggregates. On the Zambezi plain, where alluvial soils permitted long-term cultivation, villages were stable and could contain up to 400 or 500 people. Early colonial administrators amalgamated small villages and required each village to have a minimum of 10 able-bodied male taxpayers, who had to build near their appointed headman. When these rules were relaxed in the 1950s, plateau villages were already somewhat stabilized by the placement of schools, by the planting of fruit trees, and by the construction of more permanent housing; nevertheless, villages rarely contained more than 300 people. Gwembe villages began to fragment after their relocation to the hills in 1958. Many Tonga now live in cities or in the small towns of the province, which are commercial and service centers for rural people.

Economy

Subsistence and Commercial Activities. The Tonga were hoe cultivators whose staple crops were sorghums and millets until well into the twentieth century. Maize, cucurbits, groundnuts, ground peas, sweet potatoes, tobacco, and cannabis were additional crops. Livestock included cattle (in areas where tsetse flies were absent), goats, sheep, dogs, and chickens. Hunting, fishing, and gathering wild produce were important. Plow agriculture, using oxen, is now universal. Many Plateau Tonga have substantial farms of more than a hundred hectares, as well as large herds of cattle. Some own small tractors that they hire to neighbors. Maize has been the primary plateau crop since the 1930s, but farmers have also experimented with beans, cotton, and sunflowers. They began to keep pigs in the 1930s. The shift to plowing in much of Gwembe came in the late 1950s. Gwembe farmers raise maize, sorghums, bulrush millet, and, since the 1970s, cotton, now the main cash crop, which, like maize, is sold to governments depots. Income is also derived through the sale of cattle, goats, chickens, and out-of-season vegetables. Tobacco is no longer an important crop. Pigs were recently introduced. Hunting is now important only in some sections of Gwembe and on the western plateau. Commercial fisheries exist on the Kafue River and on Kariba Lake, where most fishers are immigrants. Rural diets continue to rely upon plants collected in the bush.

Industrial Arts. Crafts were part-time occupations despite being practiced by specialists, among them blacksmiths, woodworkers, potters, and basket makers. Work at a craft was validated by the belief that an ancestor required a given person to carry on the skill. Other specialists were diviners, herbalists, song makers, and hunters. Old crafts, in abeyance because of a preference for factory-made imports, were revived after the 1970s when the difficulty of transportation and the high cost of foreign goods made imports difficult to obtain. Production is now for the tourist trade as well as local use. New crafts include carpentry, brick making, auto repair, tailoring, and needlework.

Trade. Marketplaces and shops are twentieth-century phenomena; earlier, trade took the form of direct exchange based on equivalences. Marketplaces are located in townships, where women are prominent as traders. Shops exist both in townships and villages and usually have male owners. In the townships, shop owners are frequently Indians.

Division of Labor. Building houses, clearing fields, taking care of cattle, woodworking, blacksmithing, hunting, and most fishing are the responsibilities of men. They work in their own fields and usually do the plowing. They are hawkers and shop owners and work in a wide variety of paid jobs. Women are potters and basket makers. They do much of the agricultural work, gather wild produce, fish with baskets, process food, brew beer, care for small stock, do much transport, plaster huts, and provide most care of children. Increasingly, they plow. Some also work for wages, as shop assistants or house servants, but also in professional positions. Both men and women are ritual experts and both are politically active.

Land Tenure. Alluvial fields along the Zambezi were lineage property but were allocated to individual men and women. In general, rights in a field belonged to the person who cleared it and were transferable. Where shifting cultivation prevailed, land was not inherited. A man was expected to clear fields for himself and for each wife. Wives controlled the produce from their own fields, which they stored in their own granaries. The crop from the husband's field was his. Uncleared land is now scarce, and fields are kept in permanent cultivation. Sale of land in former reserve areas is prohibited, and land is obtained through loan, gift, or inheritance. Grazing areas are held in common. Claims to fishing and hunting grounds are now unimportant, except on Kariba Lake, where the government licenses *kapenta* (*Limnothrissa miodon*) fishing outfits and assigns them sites along the lake. Land pressure has led to emigration. The emergence of a landless rural class is imminent. Already, smallholders hire themselves to farmers who need additional labor. Cultivators are also being dispossessed as government allocates large tracts to multinational agribusinesses in hopes of spurring production.

Kinship

Tonga belong to the clans and matrilineal descent groups of their mothers, although children also identify with their fathers and the descent groups of the latter. Residence is usually virilocal. The residential group, or homestead, usually consists of a man, his wife or wives, and their children. Sons may settle initially with their father but are likely to join other kin or establish their own homestead on the death or divorce of their parents. Descent groups disperse, but matrilineal kin assemble for funerals as long as common descent is remembered, and those living in proximity consult frequently. They inherit from each other and, in the past, formed a mutual defense and vengeance group. Residential units based on multilateral linkages, however important at any one time, are ephemeral. Continuity is created by the ties of matrilineal descent. Some fourteen clans exist. People with the same clan name are assumed to be related. Clanship provides a means of legitimating associations, which over time can be converted into kinship. The system of clan joking links clans for the provision of essential services at funerals and in some other tense situations.

Alternate generations are merged. Within-generation speakers refer to each other as senior or junior. On the plateau and in the Gwembe hills, Iroquois cousin terms are used. Plain dwellers use Crow cousin terms.

Marriage and Family

Marriage. Polygyny is common and may be increasing as farmers marry additional wives to obtain labor for expanded operations. Christians divide on whether monogamy is necessary. Childhood betrothal was abandoned by Plateau Tonga in the 1920s and by Gwembe Tonga in the 1950s. Cross cousins of both types were preferred spouses among Plateau

Tonga and in the Gwembe hills, whereas Plains Tonga preferred marriage into the descent groups of their grandfathers. Most marriages linked people of the same village or neighborhood. Marriage today is usually initiated by elopement or when the woman is pregnant. Both damages and marriage payments are required, even in Christian marriages, and their value is steadily inflating. Young couples are initially attached to a relative's homestead; formerly, they did not have the right to their own cooking fire or to make beer for ancestral offerings until several years after marriage. A second wife may be attached to the household of the first wife for the probationary period; thereafter each wife is independent. Couples who begin married life in urban areas usually establish an independent household immediately. Divorce was and is common. Households headed by a single woman are increasingly common, although even early in the twentieth century some women chose to have children by lovers rather then accept a husband's domination. Couples do not hold property in common; upon divorce, each spouse retains his or her assets. Once equitable, this practice now places women at a disadvantage because the property they helped earn can be claimed by the husband. They also lose when widowed because the husband's assets are taken by his kin. Therefore, women try to build up their own assets, which they safeguard by sending to their own kin. Widows are ideally inherited by someone in the husband's descent group, but this practice is increasingly controversial, especially among Christians.

Domestic Unit. Each established wife or senior single woman is expected to cook for herself, her children, and other dependents and to send food to her husband. Women, girls, and very young boys of the homestead eat either together, sharing food, or separately, each woman eating alone with her children. Men and boys of the homestead eat together, sharing the food contributed by all the women. Each woman has her own dwelling. Monogamous women share the dwelling with their husbands; polygynous men move from wife to wife. Only unmarried men have their own houses. Co-wives have separate fields and separate granaries.

Inheritance. As the inheritance council held when the funeral ends, claims are canvassed. The father of the deceased, or his heir, can claim a share in stock and, today, money, but the bulk of the estate goes to matrilineal kin who appoint someone to become the guardian of the new spirit. This person is the primary heir, but stock and other possessions are distributed among a large number of claimants. The heir becomes the ritual parent of any children of the deceased and has claims upon their services and property, including marriage payments for daughters. In the past the preferred heir was of the same or alternate generation. Sons and daughters do not have the right to inherit, but in rural areas they may be given one or more head of cattle, and courts increasingly argue that those who work to increase the wealth of their father should benefit from that labor. Widows may be permitted to retain their fields but can be driven away if they refuse to be inherited.

Socialization. Infants and children are raised by parents and siblings, and frequently by other kin. Grandparents often care for children after divorce. Today children are exchanged between urban and rural areas to work for relatives or to attend school. Training in the past was oriented toward ensuring that children acquired skills essential to rural life; now families urge children to succeed at school so they can get good jobs and provide support to parents and siblings.

Sociopolitical Organization

Social Organization. Tonga society was once strongly egalitarian despite differences in wealth and the existence of slavery. Slaves were incorporated into the descent group of the owner, and they or their descendants might then be chosen as spirit guardians. The colonial administration abolished slavery. Today few know whose ancestors were or were not slaves. Lineages claiming priority of settlement within a neighborhood were said to hold *katongo* in that area, which amounted to a right to provide custodians for local shrines and sometimes a right to receive a portion of game killed. In southern Gwembe, status differences were more apparent. Today status reflects success in exploiting new economic opportunities, including education. Teachers and others with technical training, along with shop owners and wealthier farmers, form an emerging rural elite.

Political Organization. The Republic of Zambia is a single-party state organized into provinces and districts with their own administrations. Districts are divided into wards, and these into branches and sections. Elected councillors provide the effective grassroots political organization and have replaced the chieftaincy/village hierarchy that was the backbone of the colonial administration. Chiefs and village headmen still exist, but headmen have few functions, and chiefs act primarily as land allocators and ceremonial heads. Political initiative flows from the central government. As much as possible, the Tonga maintain their independence by avoiding contact with authority except when it might work to their advantage. Prior to the colonial era, and even much later, political leadership was usually provided by "big-men," whose exercise of power did not create a permanent office. Hereditary political office was the exception. Usually the political community was the neighborhood, of perhaps a thousand people, whose name derived from a geographical feature. Political authority was shared by senior men and women who assembled to settle disputes and organize communal rituals. Neighborhood residents were expected to attend each other's funerals. They had to observe ritual restrictions associated with "the work of the neighborhood," which centered on the agricultural cycle. They came together at local shrines to appeal for rain. Neighborhoods are still important under the party organization. Branch and section councillors summon people for communal labor: repairing roads, building additions to the local school, and other community work. Gwembe neighborhoods also have drum teams that perform at local funerals and represent the neighborhood on ceremonial occasions.

Social Control. Homestead members were expected to settle their own differences. Neighborhood moots dealt with quarrels between descent groups or general issues. Direct action to enforce rights or redress injury was common, but cross-cutting ties of kinship damped down the possibility for prolonged feuding. Gossip and the fear of sorcery were important mechanisms of social control. The colonial administration instituted chief's courts and delegated to headmen the right to settle village disputes. Messengers attached to the chief's court provided an embryonic police force, reinforced by district messengers under the authority of the district commissioner. In 1964 elected party officers took over adjudication at the neighborhood level, and local courts are no longer under the jurisdiction of chiefs. Courts are responsible to the Ministry of Justice, which appoints their members and regulates procedures. Courts are still expected to operate within customary law unless it clashes with national legislation. Police units, party vigilantes, and other representatives of the central government are constant reminders of the centralization of authority.

Conflict. In years of hunger, neighborhood once raided neighborhood to obtain food, and neighbor stole from neighbor. In the Zambezi plain, lineage members quarreled over the allocation of alluvial fields, and adjacent cultivators accused each other of moving boundary marks. When cattle or other stock invaded fields, damages were demanded. There were quarrels over adultery, the flight of wives, and failure to meet marriage payments. Deaths, illnesses, and other misfortune led to accusations of sorcery. Many of these grounds for conflict still exist, and theft of livestock has increased vastly, as has armed banditry along the roads. The availability of alcohol, since beer has become commercialized, has increased the amount of physical violence.

Religion and Expressive Culture

Religious Beliefs. Tonga have been exposed to Christian missions of many denominations since the beginning of the twentieth century. More recently, they have been evangelized by Pentecostal and Apostolic groups originating in the towns. Churches exist in many neighborhoods. Many people consider themselves Christians, but they may also adhere to some aspects of earlier Tonga belief and practice.

The Tonga recognized the existence of a creator god, Leza, now identified with the Christian God but formerly not responsive to human appeals. *Basangu* are spirits concerned with the fate of neighborhood communities and sometimes with larger regions. *Mizimo* are the spirits of the dead, concerned with the affairs of their own kin. Adult men and women become mizimo after death. Mizimo of parents are the most important, but offerings are also made to any former member of the descent group, to siblings of the father, and to grandparents. Invading spirits, *masabe*, attack individuals, as do ghosts, *zelo*. In the twentieth century new masabe are frequently recognized; recent ones have been Angels, Negroes, and the Regiment. Many Christians say these, along with the spirits of the dead and the community spirits, are demons.

The world is basically good. Evil exists through the malice of human beings who try to obtain power to maximize their own interests by use of medicines. Suffering may also occur because of failure to deal correctly with spiritual forces.

Religious Practitioners. Adult men and women serve as officiants at offerings to their ancestors. Spirit guardians are appointed to make such offerings on behalf of the children and grandchildren of the deceased. Shrine custodians perform rituals at neighborhood shrines and first-fruit rituals at their homes. Spirit mediums and diviners discover the will of spirits. Many women and some men are subject to possession by masabe and, when treatment is completed, may treat others similarly afflicted. Since the 1970s, some Tonga have become heads of evolving cults. Witch finders, today based in the towns, provide a means of controlling sorcerers. Evangelists, pastors, and other Christian leaders are other religious figures.

Ceremonies. Christians attend church services, and Christmas and Easter are now days of feasting. Appeals for rain and community protection are held at local shrines, but such rites are now rare among Plateau Tonga. Mediums are consulted by neighborhood delegations to learn why communal spirits are angry and how to renegotiate relationships with them. The spirits may demand an offering of beer or the sacrifice of a chicken, goat, or cow, after which those attending share a communion meal. Men and women pour an offering of beer at the doorway of a dwelling or at a special spirit shrine in the doorway. The beer should be made from grain grown in the field of the supplicant. Possession by invading spirits is treated by holding the appropriate dance and drama, through which the demands of the spirit are enacted.

Arts. Wood carving, pottery, basketry and metalwork are utilitarian, although fine pieces are made. Beadwork was formerly elaborate, but beads are now scarce and styles have changed. Music is important: Gwembe Tonga pride themselves on their drum teams; musical instruments include several types of drums, antelope-horn flutes, rattles, hand pianos, musical bows, and crude xylophones. Guitars, homemade banjos or ukeleles, and accordions cater to new musical interests. Men compose elaborate songs describing personal adventures or embodying insulting comments toward others. Women compose lullabies, dirges, and other songs. Beer drinking is enlivened by dramatic dancing.

Medicine. Illness is attributed to the anger of ancestral spirits, sorcery, the misuse of medicines acquired for success, the use of a tabooed substance, or spirit invasion. Minor illnesses are considered normal. Treatment may involve driving out an invading ghost through fumigation, sucking out the intrusive object, cupping (drawing blood by suction), pacifying an indignant ancestor, or taming an invading alien spirit through a dance, as well as the use of medicines. Herbalists supplement the widespread knowledge of home remedies. Medicines are infused and drunk, rubbed into cuts, or used in fumigation. People also use Western medicine, dispensed by hospitals, local health centers, private doctors, and herbalists.

Death and Afterlife. Infants and small children are given abbreviated funerals, and their spirits return to their mother's womb to be reborn. Adults receive elaborate funerals in preparation for their return as ancestral spirits at the end of the funeral, when the chosen guardian is pointed out to the spirit. If possible, beer is poured in its honor, to which it summons fellow spirits, thereby becoming acceptable to them. Burial is immediate, and usually close to the dwelling of the deceased; some villages have established cemeteries. Formerly, bodies were buried in the fetal position; today they are laid at full length and, if possible, in a coffin. Christians attend and pray over the grave even if the deceased was not a Christian.

Bibliography

Colson, Elizabeth (1958). *Marriage and the Family among the Plateau Tonga*. Manchester: Manchester University Press.

Colson, Elizabeth (1960). *Social Organization of the Gwembe Tonga*. Manchester: Manchester University Press.

Colson, Elizabeth, and Thayer Scudder (1988). *For Prayer and Profit: The Ritual, Economic, and Social Importance of Beer in*

Gwembe District, Zambia, 1950–1982. Stanford, Calif.: Stanford University Press.

Holy, Ladislas (1986). *Strategies and Norms in a Changing Matrilineal Society: Descent, Succession, and Inheritance among the Toka of Zambia*. Cambridge: Cambridge University Press.

Reynolds, Barry (1968). *The Material Culture of the Peoples of the Gwembe Valley*. Manchester: Manchester University Press.

Scudder, Thayer (1962). *The Ecology of the Gwembe Tonga*. Manchester: Manchester University Press.

Vickery, Kenneth (1986). *Black and White in Southern Zambia: The Tonga Plateau Economy and British Imperialism, 1890–1939*. New York: Greenwood Press.

ELIZABETH COLSON

Tropical-Forest Foragers

ETHNONYMS: Aka: Babinga, Bayaka, Biaka, Mbenzele. Asua: Aka, Bambuti. Baka: Bangombe. Bofi: Babinga. Bongo: Akoa, Bazimba. Efe: Bambuti. Kasia Twa. Kola: Bagyeli. Mbuti: Basua, Kango. Medzan: Tikar. Ntomba Twa. Rwanda and Burundi Twa.

Orientation

Identification. The term "tropical-forest foragers," or "pygmies," refers to ethnolinguistically diverse peoples distributed across the forested regions of Central Africa who are particularly short in stature and who traditionally have lived by specializing in hunting and gathering wild forest resources, which they consume themselves or trade to neighboring farmers in exchange for cultivated foods. There are exceptions to these generalizations: some "pygmies" are tall, independent from farmers, and live in the savanna. There is so much diversity among these groups that it is impossible to describe a "pygmy" culture. That there is no generic term other than the European word "pygmy" (derived from the Greek *pyme*, meaning a unit of measure equivalent to the distance from the elbow to a knuckle) bears testimony to the absence of any pan-"pygmy" awareness or culture. Forest foragers in most areas are unaware of the existence of "pygmies" in other regions, and there is currently no sense of solidarity among the different populations. Unfortunately, no term has been developed to replace the derogatory term "pygmy."

Multinational logging, the establishment of conservation parks and reserves in the tropical forest, gold and diamond mining, central-government programs and policies to sedentarize "pygmies," and more farmers moving into the forest because of population increases outside the forest areas are just some of the forces dramatically influencing forest foragers today. Traditional forager-farmer relations are breaking down, and most forest foragers today also farm, although it may only amount to planting a field in the middle of the forest or near a village and then abandoning it to hunt and gather until it is close to harvesttime. Few forest foragers receive health or education services from national governments.

Location, Linguistic Affiliation, and Demography. Forest foragers are distributed discontinuously across nine different African countries (Rwanda, Burundi, Uganda, Zaire, the Central African Republic, Cameroon, Equatorial Guinea, Gabon, and Congo). Most forest foragers live in the Congo Basin and are usually found within 5° N or S of the equator and between 10° and 30° E. There is enormous diversity in the natural environments occupied by forest foragers of the Congo Basin—from upland dense tropical rain forest to lowland swamps to mixed savanna-forest environments. Ethnolinguistic diversity is also evident. The estimated 30,000 to 35,000 Aka, who live in southeastern Central African Republic, speak a Bantu language, whereas the 3,000 or so Asua of the Ituri Forest of northeastern Zaire speak a Sudanic language. About 10,000 Efe also reside in the Ituri Forest and speak a related Sudanic language. The Baka of southwestern Cameroon, who number about 30,000 to 40,000 individuals, speak a language classified as Oubanguian, as do the roughly 3,000 Bofi of the forest-savanna areas of southeastern Central African Republic. Other Bantu-language speakers among forest foragers are the estimated 2,000 Bongo of western Gabon, the 3,500 Kola of the southeastern coast of Cameroon, the 7,500 Mbuti of the Ituri Forest of northeastern Zaire, the 250 Medzan of the forest-wet savanna region of central Cameroon, the 14,000 Ntomba Twa of the Lake Tumba area of central Zaire, an unknown number of Kasai Twa inhabiting the forest-wet savanna areas of southern Zaire, and 10,000 Rwanda and Burundi Twa living in the western portions of those two nations.

Settlements

The Aka, Asua, Baka, Efe, and Mbuti are relatively mobile; they live in temporary spherical huts. The Bongo, Kola, and Twa tend to be more sedentary; they build rectangular, mud-thatch village houses. Average camp sizes of the Aka, Baka, Efe, and Mbuti are relatively small, ranging from 17.8 inhabitants among the Efe to 37.4 among the Mbuti. Baka and Efe camps tend to be closer to villages than are Aka and Mbuti camps (4 to 8 kilometers versus 5 to 40 kilometers).

Economy

In the late twentieth century most forest foragers are specialized in extracting resources from the forest (e.g., game meat, honey, caterpillars) and thus are often nomadic. Some of these resources are traded to farmers for such foods as manioc, maize, and plantains and for iron implements, salt, tobacco, and clothes. In many areas of Central Africa, specific clans of forest foragers have traditional relations with specific clans of farmers, and these relationships are transmitted from one generation to the next, creating a complex web of economic and social exchange that leads to high levels of cooperation and support. Today most forest foragers live in association with farmers, but the nature and extent of the association varies substantially.

Among the Aka, Bofi, Bongo, and Kola, a type of cooperative net hunting is practiced, in which men, women, and children all participate; other groups utilize some combination of bows and arrows, spears, and snares.

Kinship, Descent, and Marriage

Aka, Baka, Efe, and Mbuti utilize Hawaiian kinship terminologies and reckon descent patrilineally. The Efe and Mbuti practice sister exchange, and the Aka and Baka require bride-service. Postmarital residence is very flexible in each of these four groups, but there is a tendency toward patrilocality in all of them. Polygyny rates vary from 3 percent among the Efe to 20 percent among the Baka. Efe also have one of the highest intermarriage rates with farmers: 13 percent of Efe women have married a neighboring farmer.

The Aka, Efe, and Mbuti have relatively high levels of multiple care giving; Aka and Mbuti fathers are especially active care givers. Infants are indulged: they are held virtually all the time and attended immediately when they fuss or cry, and they nurse on demand. Children grow up in multiage play groups, and autonomy is greatly encouraged. Male circumcision and adolescent tooth pointing are practiced by all three groups.

Sociopolitical Organization

Patriclans are common to all forager groups, but their function tends to be less pronounced by comparison to clan organization among farmers. Forest foragers are often members of the same patriclans as those of their traditional farming trading partners. Patrilineage ideology is not strong: mother's relatives are recognized, often with specific terms. Patriclans are "shallow," in that most foragers recall two or three generations in the clan, whereas farmers frequently can cite five or six generations.

Most forest foragers are known for their relatively egalitarian social systems. They maintain this egalitarianism through prestige avoidance, rough joking, and pervasive sharing.

Religion and Expressive Culture

Religious Beliefs. Origin stories often make reference to a god who created the world, the forest, and the first humans, after which she or he withdrew to the sky and paid no more attention to the affairs of the world. A certain powerful forest spirit influences the "living dead" (i.e., the souls of dead forest foragers).

Religious Practitioners. All the forager groups have traditional healers, and several of them (e.g., the Aka, Baka, and Mbuti) recognize the supernatural abilities of great hunters, who can communicate with the supernatural world, make themselves invisible, and take the forms of various animals.

Ceremonies. Each of the forager groups has several hunting rituals; their nature, occurrence, frequency, and intensity depend on hunting success, failure, and uncertainty. Among the Aka and Baka, the most important hunting rituals are linked to elephant hunting. Honey is symbolic of life substance, and gathering of the first honey is preceded by collective ceremonies, music, and dance.

The most important ceremonies follow death. The forest spirit participates in these, either through the sound of a trumpet (among the Efe and Mbuti) or dancing under a raffia mask (among the Aka and Baka).

Music. Forest-forager music is distinct from that of farmers of Central Africa. It exhibits complex vocal polyphony; yodeling is incorporated, but there is a relative lack of musical instruments. Varying by region, the latter include whistles, two-stringed bows, and drums. Unison singing is seldom realized. Collective songs have superimposed parts. The lyrics are usually not important; they may consist of meaningless vowels and syllables.

Bibliography

Bahuchet, Serge (1993). *Dans la forêt d'Afrique Centrale: Les pygmées aka et baka*. Paris: Peeters-SELAF.

Bailey, Robert C., Serge Bahuchet, and Barry S. Hewlett (1992). "Development in the Central African Rainforest: Concern for Forest Peoples." In *Conservation of West and Central African Rainforests*, edited by K. Cleaver, M. Munasinghe, M. Dyson, N. Egli, A. Peuker, and F. Wencélius, 260–269. Washington, D.C.: World Bank.

Cavalli-Sforza, L. L., ed. (1986). *African Pygmies*. Orlando, Fla.: Academic Press.

Kent, Susan, ed. (Forthcoming 1996). *Cultural Diversity among Twentieth-Century African Foragers*. Cambridge: Cambridge University Press. [Chapters on tropical-forest foragers by B. Hewlett, M. Ichikawa, and D. Joiris.]

Turnbull, Colin (1965). *The Mbuti Pygmies: An Ethnographic Survey*. Anthropological Papers of the American Museum of Natural History. New York: Museum of Natural History.

BARRY S. HEWLETT

Tsimihety

ETHNONYMS: none

Orientation

Identification. The term "Tsimihety" usually refers to one of the eighteen or twenty tribes or ethnic groups of the Republic of Madagascar; however, Tsimihety possess neither political unity nor an ideology of unity. They are best described as an association of people who have a similar history of avoiding domination and of observing various traditions (*fombandrazana*) that maintain their independence. The name means "those who do not cut their hair," a sign of refusal to recognize a monarch. More generally, it can be taken to identify all those people who refuse to recognize the authority of external powers presented as a hierarchy. Sizable minorities of other Malagasy groups live among Tsimihety.

Location. Tsimihety are located between 13°50′ and 16°10′ N and between 47°10′ and 50°00′ E, in the central part of northeastern Madagascar. Because they are seminomadic, however, their boundaries change constantly. Tsimihety territory is bounded on the east by that of the Betsimisaraka, on the south by that of the Sihanaka, on the west by that of the Sakalava, and on the north by that of the Antankarana (but with forest between the people to the east and south and with the Massif de Tsaratanana between Tsimihety and the Antanakrana). The northern uplands of the Massif are uninhabited, but vanilla is grown on the lower slopes, around Andapa. Otherwise, Tsimihety country comprises well-watered narrow valleys separated by low ridges. Temperatures range between 19° C and 23° C, except in the highlands. The hottest months are between November and March; the rainy season lasts from October to March, and there are dry southeast winds from April to July.

Demography. Population statistics are hopelessly inaccurate, but Tsimihety have been estimated to number between 340,000 and 700,000.

Linguistic Affiliation. Tsimihety is a dialect of Malagasy, which is a Malayo-Polynesian language. The nearest related language to Malagasy is Maanjan of Borneo.

History and Cultural Relations

Tsimihety are immigrants, or the descendants of immigrants from Betsimisaraka villages of the east coast. A small autochthonous population, the Vohilava, received Betsimisaraka immigrants who were fleeing from Merina oppression in the early nineteenth century. Before that, the Vohilava had allied with Zafinfotsy Sakalava fleeing from Zafinmena Sakalava coming from the west. Radama I, the Merina king, conquered the Tsimihety in 1823. The Merina put down numerous small rebellions, but were themselves conquered by the French in 1896. Some Tsimihety rebelled unsuccessfully against the French. Tension between Tsimihety and Merina is never far below the surface, even though Tsimihety avoid all outsiders as far as possible. Tsiranana, a Tsimihety from near Mandritsara, was the first president of the Malagasy Republic, which gained independence in 1960.

Settlements

Traditionally, Tsimihety prefer to live in small villages of about a dozen houses. There are a few larger villages, however, which are relics of the French policy of amalgamation. These villages have survived because they are located near particularly rich soils. Although their houses are built of semipermanent materials (mud, dung), Tsimihety are highly mobile; consequently, villages grow and decline constantly. Homesteading is not uncommon. Rice fields surround the villages, and pastures rise above them, on the lower hill slopes. All houses are built in parallel rows, oriented on a northeast/southwest axis. Granaries are on the perimeter.

Economy

Subsistence and Commercial Activities. Dry rice, interspersed with occasional wet-rice paddies, is the subsistence base; it is supplemented by male gardens (maize, yams, plantain) and female gardens (vegetables, herbs). Wild fruits are gathered, and occasional small game (lemurs, civets, guinea fowl, fruit bats) is hunted. Large numbers of cattle (*Bos indicus*) are kept, but meat is eaten only ceremonially, and milk is rarely drunk. Chickens are kept in all villages and are eaten regularly. Few villages keep pigs. Tsimihety avoid commercial activity, but they are sometimes forced by circumstances to buy and sell rice, raffia, kapok, and meat. Near the small towns, Tsimihety cater to European demands and sell food in the markets. A barter economy is maintained between villagers and forest dwellers (rice in exchange for tobacco, honey, and vegetable salt). Around Andapa, vanilla is grown as a cash crop.

Industrial Arts. Women weave raffia into cloth, hats, and baskets. Blacksmithing, using piston bellows, is traditional. Some individuals make their own furniture, knife handles, and sandals, but this is rare. The making of musical instruments is almost a lost art.

Division of Labor. Young boys and adolescent males herd cattle. Males prepare the rice fields and tend male gardens. Men build houses and cattle byres; they hunt and work wood and metal (occasionally). Women weed the rice fields, winnow and store rice, tend female gardens, prepare rice, and cook; they also do laundry. Both sexes fish and gather fruit. Men divine and cure; women monopolize the possession trance (*tromba*). The division of labor is not hard and fast, but generally holds true.

Land Tenure. Land is held by the ancestors who are buried in the family tomb (*fasana*) and by their largely patrilineal descendants (*zafintany*), who are understood to be an indivisible group. Individuals are allocated rights of use, according to need, on an annual basis. Land cannot be bought or sold but can be loaned to "guests" (*vahiny*). Land left unused reverts back to the common pool.

Kinship

Several grades of bilateral kinship are recognized: *havana* are kin in general, *havana lavidavitra* are distant kin, and *havana akaiky* are close kin. *Fianakaviana* are close kin who are intimate and in constant contact; *tokontrano* refers to a group of kin living as neighbors; *ankohonana* is a household, the intimate family group. Especially close relations are also recognized, for example, *mianaka*, parents/children; *mianadafy*, siblings; and *miafy*, grandparents/grandchildren. The term for the relationship is also used by the two parties to refer to each other. For jural purposes—such as title to burial in the tomb, right to the use of land, and claim to "ownership" of land and living sites—patrilinal ascent (*fokondray*) is dominant. Primary claimants to a particular tomb are united by patrilineal ascent into a named association (*foko*). As associations of people with proprietary rights to land, they are known as zafintany. To describe the situation in which one is living as part of a zafintany, a person is said to live *ambenilahy* (in the father's line).

Marriage and Family

Marriage. The dominant form of marriage that is followed today is virilocal, often patrilocal. A bride-price (*miletry*) of up to five head of cattle and money is usually paid. This custom has been modified, however, by the popularity of trial marriage (*diajofa*), in which a couple lives together for a year before the miletry is paid. The woman brings a dowry (*meomeo*), which furnishes the house and remains her property. Probably a large percentage of couples now settle without ceremony or miletry. Divorce is informal and immediate. Although polygamy and polyandry are permitted, instances are rare. Levirate is practiced according to circumstance.

Domestic Unit. Villages are small and cooperative. Households (ankohonana, *fehitry*) are based on—but not limited to—the nuclear family. Neighboring households whose heads are close kin (brothers, father/sons) formerly worked and ate together as a unit (*jao*), but this custom is less frequently observed nowadays. Larger villages are divided into sections (*fizarana*) that are loosely based on the common foko identity of male heads of households. Work groups (*asareky*) are loosely based on these sections.

Inheritance. Land is generally the common property of ancestors and their descendants and is not owned individually. The right to use land that is continuously worked may be claimed by patrilineal descendants (*zazalava*), but this right lapses if the land is left idle. Cattle are owned individually; most are sacrificed in a commemorative feast at the owner's death. Personal items (clothes, tools, plate, cutlery) are buried or disposed of. Inheritance is negligible.

Socialization. Except for blows struck in anger, corporal punishment is seldom seen. Relative age—hence, respect for elders—and male precedence are the principal practices and instruments of socialization. Males and females are generally separated.

Sociopolitical Organization

Political Organization. Madagascar is an independent republic. Mosst Tsimihety live in the province of Majunga, principally in the districts of Marotandrano, Mandritsara, Befandriana, Bealanana, and Andapa. The administration is further divided into cantons, *quartiers*, and villages. Tsimihety may become *chefs de quartier* and *chefs de village*, but they do their utmost to avoid participation in central, or imposed government. Elders (*rayamandreny;* lit., "mothers and fathers"), under the leadership of the senior male of the senior generation (*soja*), manage village affairs. A chef de village may formally convene the whole village for discussions (*fokon'olona*). Tsimihety shun large political gatherings or amalgamations; tricky situations are best resolved by disbanding a settlement and migrating to another location.

Social Control. The central government maintains police stations in the district and provincial centers. The Parti Sociale Democratique (PSD) is dominant in the region and maintains a network of agents throughout the villages. Effective social control is maintained through family and kinship solidarity, public meetings (*kabary*), divination (*sikidy*), and the strong but covert influence of diviners and general advisers (*ombiasa*). Many difficulties are blamed on various types of spirits (*zanahary, zanambatrotraka, kalinoro*) and ancestors (*razana*), but are resolved through taboos (*fady*), offerings, and promises.

Conflict. Tsimihety have made themselves past masters at avoiding open conflict with outsiders, preferring evasion, stonewalling, dissembling, and other tactics of frustration. Alcohol is not widely available, and people are not aggressive. Open discussion of disagreements is the preferred way of finding solutions to domestic problems. Historically, Tsimihety have been defeated whenever they resisted invasion, and this has led them to hide in the hills from any outside threats. Resentment of outsiders—in particular, of Merina—suggests constant tension.

Religion and Expressive Culture

Religious Beliefs and Practitioners. As is the case throughout Madagascar, Tsimihety have a vague belief in a Supreme Being (Andriamanitra) who presides over a spirit world in which the most important inhabitants are the ancestors. Ancestors occupy the world in general but retain a specific presence and influence in the area (*tanindrazana*) that surrounds their particular tombs. So strong is the sense of the presence of ancestors that it would be accurate to suggest that the living are a part of the world of the ancestors and that life is just the pathway to death. Tsimihety tombs are undecorated natural caves in the hills. Although Christian missionaries (Protestant and Catholic, English and French) have been present among Tsimihety for more than a century, only a small percentage of Tsimihety are Christians. These are found mostly in the small towns, where the missionaries have educated children in church schools.

Arts. Tsimihety are extraordinarily nonaesthetic, and their crafts are entirely functional. Little if any decoration is applied, music is rarely played, stories are hardly ever told, cooking is plain boiling with only salt added, special costumes are absent, and dancing is occasional and no more than a shuffle. Cattle are the entire focus of aesthetic attention. Sometimes they are branded; otherwise, each clan designates its cattle with a special earmark. Cattle are admired for the shape of their horns, the size of their humps, and the combinations of colors in their coats.

Medicine. Traditional medicine, utilizing plants and prophylactic amulets, is predominant and is prescribed and administered by specialists (ombiasa). Healing by shamans (tromba) is common but less sought after. Most adults have some knowledge of medicinal plants and treatments and treat themselves and their children for minor ailments. Mandritsara has a hospital, and other district towns have medical centers and private pharmacies owned by Merina or other *vazaha* (outsiders, including Europeans) who sell Western medicines. These are used widely by the town dwellers, including Tsimihety.

Death and Afterlife. Life is measured as a progress toward death and ancestorship, but this concept does not prevent death from being treated with apprehension. First burial is usually beneath a large rock. The corpse is bathed and dressed, attended constantly by close kin; other mourners grieve or put on a show of grief in a special construction, *fondra ratsy* ("bad place"). A large feast for all kin, friends, and neighbors is held, at which most of the deceased's cattle may be slaughtered. Some years later (the government decrees a minimum of three years), there is a secondary burial (*famadihana*): the bones are exhumed, wrapped in a special winding cloth (*lamba mena*), and placed in the ancestral tomb. Famadihana is usually the occasion for a feast, but Tsimihety engage in very little ritual during such observances.

Bibliography

Magnes, Bernard (1953). "Essai sur les institutions et la coutume des tsimihety." *Bulletin de Madagascar* 89:1–52.

Molet, Louis (1959). "L'expansion tsimihety: Modalités et motivations des migrations intérieures d'un groupe ethnique du nord du Madagascar." *Institut Scientifique de Madagascar, Mémoires*, Série C, 5:1–196.

Tanngasolo, Patrice (1985). *Fomban-dRazana Tsimihety* (Tsimihety ancestral customs). Ambozontany: Fianarantsoa.

Wilson, Peter J. (1967). "Tsimihety Kinship and Descent." *Africa* 37:133–154.

Wilson, Peter J. (1971). "Sentimental Structure: Migration and Descent among the Tsimihety." *American Anthropologist* 73:199–208.

Wilson, Peter J. (1992) *Freedom by a Hair's Breadth: Tsimihety of Madagascar.* Ann Arbor: University of Michigan Press.

PETER J. WILSON

Tswana

ETHNONYMS: Batswana, Bechuana (colonial appellation)

Orientation

Identification. Batswana are divided into a number of subgroups or "tribes": Bahurutshe, Bakaa, Bakgatla, Bakwena, Bamalete, Bangwaketse, Bangwato, Barolong (Seleka and Tshidi), Batawana, Batlhaping, Batlharo, and Batlokwa. There are approximately twenty-five totems (sing. *seanô* or *serêtô*), which crosscut "tribal" boundaries.

Location. The Batswana region extends from approximately the Okavango River in the northwest, running southeast to the upper reaches of the Limpopo and southwest to the Kuruman area, northeast of the Orange River. In South Africa the majority of Batswana are in the north, in the region that was British Bechuanaland in colonial times, subsequently included the disconnected blocks that constituted nominally independent Bophuthatswana under the apartheid regime, and is now in the Northwest District. Although many Batswana were forced into the overcrowded homeland of Bophuthatswana after 1960, many others remained throughout South Africa, particularly in the urban areas around Johannesburg, in what is now the province of Guateng. There are also Batswana in Namibia and Zimbabwe. Batswana live in all parts of Botswana but are concentrated most heavily in the eastern part of the country, along a strip running east and west of the rail line that extends from South Africa north into Zimbabwe. This is also the region of Botswana that receives the greatest amount of rainfall and has the best agricultural potential. West of this region is the Kalahari (Kgalagadi) Desert (which is not considered a true desert but has sandy soils and is characterized by a lack of permanent surface water), where Batswana reside along with other ethnic groups, predominantly Bakgalagadi and Basarwa (Bushmen). Agriculture is practiced in the Kalahari but is extremely risky. Livestock (particularly cattle) raising has become widespread in the Kalahari since the 1960s, when numerous boreholes were drilled, and this, along with drought and overhunting, has led to the diminution of game (most of the large mammals of Africa are found in Botswana) in the region. The Central Kalahari and Chobe Game reserves are protected from livestock grazing and are still rich in game. The climate is semiarid subtropical; average daily maximum temperature reaches 33° C in summer and 22° C in winter. Average rainfall ranges from 65 centimeters in the northeast to 25 centimeters in the southwest.

Demography. The population of Botswana is approximately 1.4 million. Ethnic affiliation has not been recorded in the census since 1946; whether ethnic Batswana ("Batswana" can also refer to all citizens of Botswana, regardless of ethnic affiliation) make up the majority in the country remains a contentious issue. Most Batswana live in rural areas, but Botswana has the highest urbanization rate in Africa. There are over 2 million Batswana in South Africa. In Botswana, the population growth rate is 3.5 percent.

Linguistic Affiliation. Setswana is a Bantu language of the western Sotho group. (The prefix "Se*f*" refers to "language/culture of," "Bo*f*" refers to "land of," and "Ba*f*" refers to "people," whereas "Mo*f*" is the singular.) There are a number of dialects within Setswana, all of which are mutually intelligible. Sekgalagadi (which is spoken by the Bakgalagadi) and the languages of many other neighboring groups are sufficiently similar to Setswana to be classified by some scholars as dialects, although this is debated by others. Setswana and English are official languages of Botswana and Setswana is one of eleven official languages in South Africa. Many Batswana also speak English, Afrikaans, or other Southern African Bantu languages; many adult men speak Fanagalo, the language of the mines.

History and Cultural Relations

New archaeological evidence continues to push the arrival of Bantu speakers into the Batswana area further back in time; it is now assumed that they arrived in southeastern Botswana around A.D. 600 or 700, displacing, absorbing, and/or living among Khoisan foragers and pastoralists. Ancestors of Sotho speakers are believed to have been in the area by about A.D. 1200, and by 1500 the major Batswana tribes/chiefdoms/nations began to form, through a process of fission and amalgamation of agnatic groupings, as they spread northward and westward from the Transvaal, in search of better watered pastureland.

A period of warfare, political disruption, and migration commonly termed the *difiqane* (Zulu: *mfecane*) characterized the first quarter of the nineteenth century. These wars have conventionally been attributed to the rise of the Zulu state and to the innovative forms of political and military organization of its leader, Shaka. The causes of the difiqane have become a subject of late twentieth-century debate; it is now argued that European trade and slaving initially precipitated the period of warfare. The difiqane engendered a period of chaos, during which Batswana polities experienced varying degrees of suffering, impoverishment, political disintegration, death, and forced movement. At the same time, however, some groups, particularly the western Batswana chiefdoms, eventually prospered and strengthened to the extent that they incorporated refugees and livestock. Batswana polities are noted for their capacity to absorb foreign peoples, to turn strangers into tribespeople, and to do so without compromising the integrity of their own institutions. Socioeconomic mechanisms such as *mafisa* (which provided for the lending of cattle) and the ward system of tribal administration (see "Political Organization") facilitated the integration of foreigners.

Not all peoples were welcomed into the Tswana fold; some remained foreigners, and some became subjects. The latter category includes peoples of the desert (Bakgalagadi and Bushmen) who are accorded a servile status termed "Batlhanka" or "Bolata."

European traders and missionaries (of the British nonconformist sects) began to arrive in the Batswana region in the first two decades of the nineteenth century. Trade (ivory, furs, and feathers being the most valued items) escalated after this period, and control over this trade dramatically empowered some Batswana chiefs, who were able to consolidate their control over extensive areas. By the mid-nineteenth century, Afrikaners, newly settled in the Transvaal, posed a threat to Batswana; Batswana chiefdoms acquired firearms to protect themselves, and many Batsana moved westward, into the area that is now Botswana. Christian missions were established throughout the region in the nineteenth century; today most Batswana profess to be Christian.

The discovery of diamonds and gold in the 1860s and 1870s in southern Africa led to the industrialization of South Africa and the introduction of the migrant-labor system, which continues to draw thousands of Batswana men to the mines (although recruitment from Botswana has been restricted since 1979). In 1885 the Bechuanaland Protectorate was established in the north of the region, and, in the south, British Bechuanaland was established as a Crown colony; ten years later it was annexed to the Cape. In 1966 Botswana achieved independence. In 1910 British Bechuanaland was incorporated into the Union of South Africa; in 1977, under the apartheid regime, the Tswana ethnic "homeland" of Bophutatswana was granted nominal independence by South Africa, but no other nation recognized it; in 1994, in conjunction with the first all-race elections in South Africa and the dismantling of apartheid, Bophutatswana was reincorporated into South Africa.

Settlements

Batswana are noted for their large, nucleated villages, which can comprise as many as 30,000 people. Large compact villages or towns are associated with the aridity of the areas and the necessity of settling near reliable water sources and under chiefly power. In the past, chiefs were able to control the movements of people, the allocation of land, and the timing of agricultural activity through their centrality in rituals performed to ensure agricultural fertility. Town or village residence is the norm, but Batswana disperse their economic activities and typically have temporary residences at their agricultural fields (as far as 40 kilometers from the village) and near their grazing lands. Grazing lands are less demarcated than agricultural lands and can be hundreds of kilometers from the village. This settlement pattern can be envisioned as a series of concentric circles, with the main village residence in the center, agricultural fields surrounding the inner circle, grazing lands comprising the outer circle, and the bush beyond. There is a social dimension to this model, in that (with the exception of the temporary residences) those of highest rank tend to reside in the center, whereas those of lowest rank, especially members of servile groups such as Bushmen, reside on the periphery. Most Batswana continue to maintain a rural residence, even as urbanization increases. With the decline of chiefly power, more Batswana have established their primary residence at smaller centers, often near their agricultural fields.

Villages are organized into wards, each with its own headman, who is ideally closely related to the chief—or appointed by him—and is responsible to him. Wards are based on the patrilineal model, but many have absorbed nonagnates or nonrelatives. Within wards, compounds, which tend to be close to one another, are surrounded by perimeter bush or stone fences. Internal low mud walls separate living from cooking and other spaces. Each married couple has a house (traditionally, a round mud hut with a thatch roof, although rectangular concrete block houses with tin roofs are becoming popular) in which they and some younger children may sleep; there are additional huts for sleeping and storage. Raised granaries are less common now than in the past. Kitchen areas are usually inside the perimeter fence and enclosed by a bush-fence firebreak.

Economy

Subsistence and Commercial Activities. Batswana have been called a peasant-proletariat to reflect the fact that they have been migrating to the mines, and to a lesser extent, to the White commercial farms of South Africa, for over a century and that wages constitute their single largest source of revenue. Mine contacts were temporary, often enabling the migrant to return home for the plowing season; until the late twentieth century, migrants were prevented by South African law from establishing permanent residence at their place of employment. New forms of employment have been emerging, especially in Botswana, where diamond mining has led to dramatic economic growth. State-sponsored welfare is important in both countries.

Local economic activities center on agro-pastoralism. Batswana rely on ox-drawn iron plows (but tractors are becoming increasingly common); the principal crop is sorghum. They also grow maize, beans, sweet-cane, and some millet. Some farmers engage in commercial agriculture. Batswana husband goats, sheep, and most importantly, cattle. Cattle are valuable for local exchange, for ritual purposes, for their milk, and less so for their meat; their sale provides an important source of revenue for rural peoples. Most households also keep chickens, and, in the east, some keep pigs. Hunting is far less important than it was in the past, when game was plentiful.

Industrial Arts. Batswana have long been tied to the South African industrial economy and have purchased items that formerly were made locally; these include most metal goods. In the past, men worked in metal, bone, and wood; women made pots, and both sexes did basketwork. These skills were often passed from parents to children. Some men still specialize in skin preparation and sewing, usually for trade, and men still make some wooden items, such as yokes for livestock. In northern Botswana, women make baskets, many of which are exported. Women build "traditional" Tswana huts, whereas men specialize in European-style thatch and "modern"-style houses. The latter are highly specialized skills. As in much of Africa, children fashion toys out of fence wire, tin cans, old tires, and almost anything they can acquire.

Trade. Archaeological evidence points to the great antiquity of local and long-distance trade. Marketplaces were not common in the region; most trade occurred among neighbors or with itinerant peddlers; in the early nineteenth century

Griqua traders from the south traveled into the region; they were followed by Europeans. Trade increased with the arrival of missionaries during the nineteenth century, many of whom encouraged such commerce as a means of bringing "civilization" to the area. Europeans and, later, Asians established shops over the course of the colonial period. Virtually all villages now have trading stores, and many individuals—especially women—are "hawkers" who engage in trade from their compounds. Botswana is part of the South African Customs Union, and virtually every commodity is available in both countries.

Division of Labor. In pre-European times, men tended livestock, hunted, prepared fields, engaged in warfare, and participated in the formal public political arena. Women tended fields, gathered wild foods, and were responsible for the domestic arena, including looking after domestic fowl. With the introduction of the ox-drawn plow in the nineteenth century, men assumed the task of plowing, but women continued to perform most other agricultural work. The division of labor became less strict as more men migrated for wage labor and women increasingly engaged in livestock activities, especially plowing and milking. Boys worked extensively with livestock and spent long periods away from home at cattle posts. All children helped in the fields, and girls helped their mothers, especially with looking after younger siblings. Although wage labor has been available for men for over a century, until about the 1970s, women had little opportunity for wage employment; those jobs available were largely as domestics and on White-owned farms. In the late twentieth century greater opportunity exists for both men and women, but men still have an advantage over women.

Land Tenure. Traditionally, the right to use (but not to sell) agricultural land was inherited patrilineally by sons; women received access to agricultural lands as wives. Closely related agnatic kin tended to have fields in the same general area, which facilitated cooperation. Pastureland was in theory communal, but often areas were associated with particular groups. Since the advent of boreholes, the land surrounding them has become increasingly associated with (but not formally owned by) the borehole owners.

In Botswana, the majority of people live in the districts (former tribal reserves), where most land is held in common. Some areas, as provided under the Tribal Grazing Land Policy established in 1975, have been demarcated as commercial ranch land, and wealthy Batswana who are willing to invest in infrastructure (fences, boreholes, etc.) may take out long-term leases. Other land has been reserved as wildlife-management areas. Permission to use land in the communal areas is obtained from land boards. The land cannot be sold. Unlike in Botswana, where very little land was given over to Europeans, in South Africa Blacks were given only 13 percent of the land after 1913.

Kinship

Kin Groups and Descent. Agnation is emphasized in Batswana kinship: along with primogeniture, it traditionally had the greatest influence on inheritance of property and succession to office. Individuals were identified with and came under the jural authority of their agnatic group (*kgotla*, or the diminutive *kgotlana*); however, the formation of discrete agnatic units was and continues to be inhibited by the marriage system, which permits cousin marriages of all kinds. Patrilineal parallel-cousin marriages of near kin, although practiced mainly by the elite but permitted to all, serve to complicate the principle of unilineality and create ambiguous and overlapping links. Thus, there is a cognatic element to the system, which places emphasis upon kindreds (sing. *losika*) and gives greater license to individuals to "construct" their social networks than is found in many patrilineal societies.

Kinship Terminology. With the exceptions of the term for cross cousin (*ntsala*) and the term for sibling of the opposite sex (*kgaitsadi*), virtually all Batswana kinship terms imply relative seniority and thus, relative authority. It is a classificatory system that distinguishes cross from parallel cousins (parallel cousin terms are the same as sibling terms), siblings of the same sex (these are distinguished by seniority) from those of the opposite sex, father's sister (*rrakgadi*) from mother's sister (*mmangwane* ["small mother"]), and mother's brother (*malome*) from father's brother (*rrangwane* ["small father"]). Parents' older siblings are referred to by grandparental terms (*rremogolo* ["great-father"], *mmemogolo* [great-mother]). There is considerable variation in the use of affinal terms.

Marriage and Family

Marriage. Traditionally, Batswana marriage was a process marked by a number of rituals and exchanges between the two families. No single ritual or exchange was definitive in confirming the existence of a marriage. Bride-wealth (*bogadi*—typically eight head of cattle) exchange was the most elaborate materially and ritually but it often occurred several years after the couple had been cohabitating, after children had been born, and occasionally after the death of the wife. Church and civil marriage have begun to replace traditional marriage, which has removed some of the ambiguity in marital status, but many people who observe "modern" marriage procedures still conduct traditional rituals and pay bride-wealth. Some tribes have prohibited bride-wealth.

Polygyny, although not absent, is no longer common; serial monogamy and "concubinage" have, in some instances, replaced polygyny. Arranged marriages have largely ceased; however, despite the fact that spouses now choose each other, family approval is usually still sought and not always granted. Decisions are based less on the identity of the new spouse than on his or her family, the assumption being that families, not just spouses, are being joined together and that the right family will produce the right spouse. Family members (and sometimes even the chief) intervene if there are marital problems. The consequences of conjugal separation vary with the type of marriage and the stage of the marriage process. Civil marriages require formal divorce if the parties wish to remarry in the same way. If a "traditional" marriage dissolves, the wife usually returns to her natal home, taking some household property if she is the aggrieved party. Bride-wealth is almost never returned, attesting to the fact that its primary function is to affiliate children. The affiliation of children born before marriage or after divorce or widowhood is ambiguous and a subject of negotiation.

Batswana postmarital residence is ideally patrilocal; in some areas, overcrowding prevents this ideal from being realized. In addition, neolocal residence is common in urban areas, although most urban households maintain a rural residence.

Domestic Unit. A compound (*lolwapa*) typically houses a family or multifamily unit, including foster children and, occasionally, nonkin dependents or servants. It is headed by the senior male—or female, if she is single. The eldest (sometimes the youngest) married son often resides with his wife and children in his parents' compound and eventually assumes headship of it. Younger married sons build their compounds near those of their parents, and co-wives maintain their own compounds adjacent to one another or separated by those of married sons or unmarried daughters. Grandparents may live with their children or occupy a nearby compound. If the latter is the case, they usually maintain close links with their children and "eat from the same pot." Over 40 percent of rural households in Botswana are now headed by single mothers.

Inheritance. Primogeniture and agnation are the most critical factors influencing inheritance. A man's eldest son inherits most of his cattle, other property, and political office, although the latter can be contested. Younger sons receive fewer numbers of cattle from their fathers. Daughters are occasionally given livestock, although a daughter's cattle may remain with her brothers upon marriage or be transferred to her husband. Daughters inherit their mother's household utensils. A deceased person's personal effects are inherited by his linked maternal uncle or the uncle's survivor. Boys and, sometimes, girls inherit an ox from their maternal uncle after they have given him a specified gift—usually a bull, first animal hunted, or first paycheck. (See "Land Tenure" for rules of inheritance regarding land.)

Socialization. Both sexes nurture children, but their care and upbringing are largely the responsibility of women and other children, particularly girls. Grandmothers devote much time to child rearing. It is often believed that a young mother is not ready to entirely care for her own children, and elder female kin take on the responsibility—either keeping children with them or regularly intervening and training the young mother. As young women increasingly pursue employment or education, infants and children are sent to live with their grandmothers. The conventional two-year breast-feeding period is being reduced. In the past initiation ceremonies existed for boys (*bogwêra*) and girls (*bojale*). During the confinement away from the village, the children were subjected to hardships and tutored in adult responsibilities and knowledge. These ceremonies were made illegal by the British and are now undergoing somewhat of a revival, although their functions in terms of education have been largely replaced by formal education.

Sociopolitical Organization

Social Organization. The Batswana developed powerful chiefdoms in the nineteenth century; members were internally ranked into royals (*dikgosana*), commoners (*badintlha*), immigrants absorbed into the tribe (*bafaladi*), and non-Batswana clients (*bolata*). High rank brought both privilege and responsibility; for instance the chief (*kgosi*) could command stray cattle (*matimela*), labor, and first fruits from the harvest, but was also expected to display largesse to his followers. The system of rank, privilege, and responsibility has been much eroded but not eradicated. Now rank, patron-client relations, and class coexist as forms of stratification. Many Batswana own vast amounts of property and have highly remunerative employment, but far greater numbers are welfare recipients.

Political Organization. In the precolonial period the most powerful Batswana chiefs presided over large tributary states. Subchiefs and headmen who presided over wards and villages outside the capital were responsible to the chief. Chiefly power and succession were open to challenge, resulting at times in dynastic contests and tribal secession. Chiefs controlled the timing of initiation ceremonies and, thus, the creation of new regiments; these regiments provided chiefs with a labor and military force. In Botswana, the House of Chiefs was established at independence; the House advises but cannot make law. Chiefs and headmen have been incorporated into the civil service and preside over customary courts in Botswana. Traditional leaders have also played a role in South Africa, and the postapartheid government elected in 1994 is developing a policy toward them.

Social Control. Socialization, positive and negative social sanction, and fear of illness or other misfortune are powerful means of social control; however, when behavior violates custom or law, means of redress exist. Although not systematically codified, customary law (*maloa*) and legal protocol are highly developed among the Batswana. Less serious crimes can be dealt with by the families of the parties involved. If a problem cannot be resolved at that level, it is taken to the kgotla. "Kgotla" refers both to a group of people and the place where they meet. Each ward has a kgotla, over which a headman presides. Villages have a central kgotla, and the central kgotla of the tribal capital is presided over by the chief. All men, and, in the late twentieth century, women, may speak at the kgotla and advise the chief. If a case cannot be resolved at a minor kgotla, it moves up the system and may eventually be tried at the chief's kgotla, which, in Botswana, is sanctioned by government. Certain offenses, such as murder, are addressed by the civil court system.

Conflict. In precolonial times Batswana groups fought among themselves and with others over territory, trade routes, and control over subject peoples. They raided for livestock and other property. British control and the demarcation of tribal boundaries in the late nineteenth century significantly diminished intergroup conflict. In the early twentieth century chiefs began to employ lawyers in their disputes with other chiefs. Ethnic tension is minimal but not absent and appears to be on the rise in the 1990s. Many Batswana were involved and some lost their lives in the antiapartheid struggle. Violence accompanied the dismantling of Bophutatswana in 1994, as some leaders were reluctant to relinquish their power.

Religion and Expressive Culture

Religious Beliefs. Although Batswana received Christian missionaries in the early nineteenth century (see "History and Cultural Relations") and most belong to a church today, precolonial beliefs retain strength among many Batswana. Missionaries brought literacy, schools, and Western values, all of which facilitated the transition to migrant wage labor. In precolonial times Batswana believed in a Supreme Being, Modimo, a creator and director, but nonetheless distant and remote. More immediate and having a greater influence in daily affairs were the ancestors, Badimo. Ancestor worship was reflected in the respect given to the elders and their capacity to influence the young; after death, their spirits left their bodies to join others. Badimo were venerated and invoked; appeals were addressed to them, and they were placated with sacrifices, prayers, and appropriate behavior. Badimo intervened actively in daily life and they could withdraw their support, rendering their descendants vulnerable to disease and misfortune. Most Batswana today belong to African Independent churches that incorporate Christian and non-Christian practices, beliefs, and symbols.

Religious Practitioners. Most people have some knowledge of medicinal plants; *dingaka* (doctors; sing. *ngaka*), however, are specialists in healing and magic. "Dingaka" is a collective term referring to many different types of specialties, which among others include rainmaking, compound protection, avenging sorcery, and women's reproductive health. Formerly, dingaka presided over rituals and aided the chief in protecting and controlling the village and tribe. Dingaka apprentice with others, often paying them a cow. Many divine using a set of bones: the interpretation of how they fall determines the source of a patient's problem. *Baloi* (sorcerers; sing. *moloi*) manipulate substances for malevolent purposes. Baloi are believed to work by day or by night; in the latter case, they meet together, often transform into animals, and may cause their victims to do the same. Much illness and misfortune is attributed to their powers. Practitioners of the African Independent churches (e.g., a *baporafota* [prophet] or a *baruti* [minister or teacher]) also engage in healing. Their training is considered less rigorous than that of the dingaka.

Ceremonies. There are many ceremonies to mark life-cycle events: these include birth, the end of the three-month postpartum confinement, several marriage ceremonies, bridewealth payment, and death. Increasingly, funerals have become the most elaborate life-cycle rituals. Funerals used to be conducted shortly after death but now the use of mortuaries has enabled funerals to be postponed. Thus, the expectations in terms of attendance, quality of coffin, and level of hospitality have escalated, and many more people can be notified and material resources assembled. Funerals have become one of the main venues for the expression of cultural, time, and resource commitment, both on the part of the aggrieved family and those attending, who are expected to work at the funeral and who expect to be fed. In the past initiations into adulthood were elaborate ceremonies lasting a few months, in which girls and boys were taken separately to the bush in the winter. The boys were circumcised. Other ceremonies tied to the agricultural cycle, such as those to initiate planting, to make rain, and first-fruits rituals, are no longer regularly practiced.

Arts. There are few specialized arts. Beadwork is practiced by some, and children are often adorned (sometimes for protection from malevolent forces) with beads and other decorations. Compounds and houses are often beautifully designed and painted. Song (*pina*) and dance (*pino*) are highly developed forms of artistic expression. Choirs perform and compete with each other on official and ritual occasions. They compose lyrics that offer narratives and critiques of the past and present. (See also "Industrial Arts.)

Medicine. Batswana have an extensive local pharmacopoeia. Medicines (*ditlhare* ["trees"] or *melemò*) are used for treating ailments in humans and animals, for fortification, protection, fertility, injury, making rain, and so on. Batswana seek medical help from a number of sources, including clinics and hospitals, traditional practitioners, and Christian healers. Western medicine is more or less universally acknowledged for its ability to treat symptoms, but other healers are frequently sought in order to address the causes of illness and misfortune. (See "Religious Practitioners.")

Death and Afterlife. Death is usually considered to have both natural and supernatural causes. Traditionally, men were buried in their cattle kraals and women in the compounds. Small children were buried under houses. Many people are still buried in this fashion, although cemeteries are increasingly used. Funerals are highly elaborated, expensive, and can last up to a week (see "Ceremonies"). Livestock are slaughtered during the funeral to feed guests. Priests and, often, traditional healers preside over funerals, administering rites to the bereaved that are directed toward exorcising thoughts of the dead from the living so that they will not "go mad" from their grief. After death, elders become ancestors (Badimo) (see "Religious Beliefs"). People who die with regrets are believed to become ghosts (*dipoko*); their souls remain in the grave by day but rise at night to haunt the living.

Bibliography

Alverson, Hoyt (1978). *Mind in the Heart of Darkness: Value and Self-Identity among the Tswana of Southern Africa*. New Haven: Yale University Press.

Comaroff, Jean (1985). *Body of Power, Spirit of Resistance: The Culture and History of a South African People*. Chicago: University of Chicago Press.

Comaroff, Jean, and John Comaroff (1991). *Of Revelation and Revolution: Christianity, Colonialism, and Consciousness in South Africa*. Chicago: University of Chicago Press.

Comaroff, John L. (1978). "Rules and Rulers: Political Processes in a Tswana Chiefdom." *Man* 13:1–20.

Comaroff, John L. (1980). "Bridewealth and the Control of Ambiguity in a Tswana Chiefdom." In *The Meaning of Marriage Payments*, edited by John L. Comaroff, 29–49. London and New York: Academic Press.

Comaroff, John L., and Jean Comaroff (1992). *Ethnography and the Historical Imagination*. Boulder, Colo.: Westview Press.

Comaroff, John L., and S. A. Roberts (1981). *Rules and Processes: The Cultural Logic of Dispute in an African Context*. Chicago: University of Chicago Press.

Good, Kenneth (1992). "Interpreting the Exceptionality of Botswana." *Journal of Modern African Studies* 30(1): 69–95.

Gulbrandsen, Ornulf (1986). "To Marry—or Not to Marry: Marital Strategies and Sexual Relations in a Tswana Society." *Ethnos* 51:7–28.

Gulbrandsen, Ornulf (1993). "The Rise of the North-Western Tswana Kingdoms." *Africa* 63:550–582.

Hitchcock, Robert (1980). "Tradition, Social Justice, and Land Reform in Central Botswana." *Journal of African Law* 24:1–34.

Holm, J., and P. Molutsi, eds. (1989). *Democracy in Botswana*. Gaborone: Macmillan.

Kerven, Carol, and Pamela Simmons (1981). *Bibliography on the Society, Culture, and Political Economy of Post-Independence Botswana*. National Migration Study. Gaborone.

Kinsman, Margaret (1983). "Beasts of Burden: The Subordination of Southern Tswana Women." *Journal of Southern African Studies* 10:39–54.

Kuper, Adam (1970). *Kalahari Village Politics: An African Democracy*. London: Cambridge University Press.

Kuper, Adam (1978). "Determinants of Form in Seven Tswana Kinship Terminologies." *Ethnology* 17:239–286.

Kuper, Adam (1982). *Wives for Cattle: Bridewealth and Marriage in Southern Africa*. London and Boston: Routledge & Kegan Paul.

Lagassick, Martin (1969). "The Sotho-Tswana Peoples before 1800." In *African Societies in Southern Africa*, edited by L. Thompson. London: Heinemann.

Lye, W. F., and C. Murray (1980). *Transformations on the Highveld: The Tswana and Southern Sotho*. Cape Town and London: David Philip.

Molutsi, P., and J. Holm (1990). "Developing Democracy When Civil Society Is Weak: The Case of Botswana." *African Affairs* 89:323–340.

Parson, J., ed. (1990). *Succession to High Office in Botswana*. Ohio University Monographs in International Studies, Africa Series, no. 54. Athens: Ohio University Press.

Parsons, N. Q. (1977). "The Economic History of Khama's Country in Botswana." In *Roots of Rural Poverty in Central and Southern Africa*, edited by R. Palmer and N. Q. Parsons, 113–142. Berkeley and Los Angeles: University of California Press.

Peters, Pauline (1983). "Gender, Developmental Cycles, and Historical Process: A Critique of Recent Research on Women in Botswana." *Journal of Southern African Studies* 10:101–122.

Peters, Pauline (1994). *Dividing the Commons: Politics, Policy, and Culture in Botswana*. Charlottesville and London: University of Virginia Press.

Roberts, Simon (1972). *Tswana Family Law*. London: Sweet & Maxwell.

Roberts, Simon (1986). "The Tswana Polity" and "Tswana Law and Custom." *Journal of Southern African Studies* 12:75–87.

Schapera, Isaac (1938). *A Handbook of Tswana Law and Custom*. London: Oxford University Press for the International African Institute.

Schapera, Isaac (1940a). *Married Life in an African Tribe*. London: Faber.

Schapera, Isaac (1940b). "The Political Organization of Ngwato in the Bechuanaland Protectorate." In *African Political Systems*, edited by M. Fortes and E. E. Evans-Pritchard, 56–82. London: Oxford University Press for the International African Institute.

Schapera, Isaac (1943a). *Native Land Tenure in the Bechuanaland Protectorate*. Alice: Lovedale Press.

Schapera, Isaac (1943b). *Tribal Legislation among the Tswana of the Bechuanaland Protectorate*. Monographs on Social Anthropology, no. 9. London: London School of Economics.

Schapera, Isaac (1947). *Migrant Labour and Tribal Life: A Study of Conditions in the Bechuanaland Protectorate*. London: Oxford University Press.

Schapera, Isaac (1950). "Kinship and Marriage among the Tswana." In *African Systems of Kinship and Marriage*, edited by A. R. Radcliffe-Brown and C. D. Forde, 140–165. London: Oxford University Press for the International African Institute.

Schapera, Isaac (1952). *The Ethnic Composition of Tswana Tribes*. Monographs on Social Anthropology, no. 11. London: London School of Economics.

Schapera, Isaac (1965). *Praise-Poems of Tswana Chiefs*. Oxford: Oxford University Press.

Schapera, Isaac (1970). *Tribal Innovators: Tswana Chiefs and Social Change*. London: Athlone Press.

Schapera, Isaac, and John Comaroff (1991). *The Tswana*. Rev. ed. London: Kegan Paul International in Association with the International African Institute.

Solway, Jacqueline (1994). "From Shame to Pride: Politicized Ethnicity in the Kalahari, Botswana." *Canadian Journal of African Studies* 24(2): 254–274.

Werbner, Richard (1971). "Local Adaptation and the Transformation of an Imperial Concession in Northeastern Botswana." *Africa* 41:32–41.

Werbner, Richard, ed. (1982). *Land Reform in the Making: Tradition, Public Policy, and Ideology in Botswana*. London: Rex Collings.

Wylie, Diana (1990). *A Little God: The Twilight of Patriarchy in a Southern African Chiefdom*. Hanover, N.H.: University Press of New England for Wesleyan University Press.

JACQUELINE S. SOLWAY

Tuareg

ETHNONYMS: Kel Tagelmust, Kel Tamacheq, Tamacheq, Targui. There are also numerous names designating the different political confederations and descent groups. These latter are ofter preceded by "Kel," which denotes "people of."

Orientation

Identification. The Tuareg, a seminomadic, Islamic people who speak a Berber language, Tamacheq, live in the contemporary nation-states of Niger, Mali, Algeria, and Libya. They are believed to be descendants of the North African Berbers and to have originated in the Fezzan region of Libya but later to have expanded into areas bordering the Sahara, assimilating into their traditionally stratified society the sedentary farming peoples from regions south of the Sahara. Tuareg traded with these populations and also raided them for slaves. Thus, Tuareg display diverse physical and cultural traits ranging from Arabic influences to influences stemming from south of the Sahara. "Tuareg," the term by which they are most commonly known today, is actually a term of outside, possibly Arabic origin. It was imposed as a gloss, or cover-term, to designate the ethnicity and culture of a people who, although unified by their common language and culture, belong to diverse social strata based on descent, have different geographic origins, and practice varied subsistence patterns of stockbreeding, oasis gardening, caravanning, professional Quranic scholarship, and smithing. There are also names for numerous subdivisions of Tuareg, based upon precolonial descent groups and confederations. Many Tuareg call themselves "Kel Tamacheq" (people of the Tamacheq language), "Kel Tagelmust" (people of the veil, a reference to the distinctive practice of men's face veiling), and other more specific terms. There are names referring to the precolonial social categories based on descent, still ideologically important in rural communities: *imajeghen*, denoting nobility, refers to those Tuareg of aristocratic origin; *imghad* refers to those of the tributary social stratum; *inaden* refers to smith/artisans; and *iklan* and *ighawalen* denote, respectively, peoples of various degrees of servile and client status. Currently, there is disagreement regarding which term to use to refer to these peoples as a group. "Tuareg" still predominates in most English-language historical and ethnographic literature. "Touareg" and "Targui" are often found in French-language sources. Many contemporary local intellectuals of Niger and Mali refer to themselves as "Tuareg," but some have expressed a preference for "Kel Tamacheq." For purposes of standardization, the term "Tuareg" is used in this article.

Location. The Saharan regions where Tuareg originated—southern Algeria, western Libya, eastern Mali, and northern Niger—are still the regions where they predominate today. During the late twentieth century, many Tuareg have migrated to rural and urban areas farther south—into Sahelian and coastal regions of West Africa—because of drought, famine, and political tensions with the central governments of Mali and Niger. Since the early 1990s, some Tuareg have joined an armed insurrection against those governments (Bourgeot 1990, 129–162). A few Tuareg have emigrated to France. The Saharan and Sahelian regions of Mali and Niger, where most Tuareg still live are the principal biomes to which the culture is adapted (Baier and Lovejoy 1977; Bernus 1981). The topography includes volcanic mountains, flat desert plains, rugged savanna, and desert-edge borderlands where agriculture is possible only with daily irrigation. The major ranges are the Ahaggar Mountains in Algeria and the Aïr Mountains in Niger. Temperatures range from 4° C at night in the brief cold season, from December to March, upward to 54° C during the day in the hot season. There is a short and unreliable rainy season between June and September; annual precipitation often amounts to less than 25 centimeters. Pasturelands have been diminishing, and, consequently, livestock herds are shrinking. Many herds were decimated in the droughts of 1967–1973 and 1984–1985. During the brief cold season, there are high winds and sandstorms.

Demography. Tuareg constitute about 8 percent of the population of Niger (U.S. Department of State 1987). The total population of Tamacheq speakers who identify themselves culturally as Tuareg has been estimated at about 1 million (Childs and Chelala 1994, 16).

Linguistic Affiliation. There are numerous dialects of Tamacheq, a language of the Berber Family. French sources (Fraternité Charles de Foucauld 1968, 1) list the three major dialects as "Tamaheq" (in the Ahaggar Mountains of Algeria and in the Tassili mountain range in the Ajjer region of Mali), "Tamacheq" (in the desert-edge region along the River Niger and in the Adrar des Iforas of Mali), and "Temajeq" (in the Aïr Mountains of Niger). In many other sources (Rodd 1926; Nicolaisen 1963; Bernus 1981), the major language is called "Tamacheq," without specifying dialectal distinctions, a usage also adopted in this article. Tuareg also use a written script known as Tifinagh. Many contemporary Tamacheq speakers also speak Songhay, Hausa, or French.

History and Cultural Relations

Early origins and migrations of the various confederations of Tuareg are related in oral traditions and have been documented by Rodd (1926), Nicolaisen (1963), and Bernus (1981). Early events are also recorded in Tifinagh inscriptions on Saharan rocks and in Arabic manuscripts such as the Agadez Chronicle. Many of these written records were lost when the central Sahara was plundered by French colonial patrols after the unsuccessful 1917 Tuareg revolt against France.

The Tuareg came to prominence as stockbreeders and caravanners in the Saharan and Sahelian regions at the beginning of the fourteenth century, when trade routes to the lucrative salt, gold, ivory, and slave markets in North Africa, Europe, and the Middle East sprang up across Tuareg territory. Nicolaisen (1963, 411) suggests that the first Tuareg to come to the Aïr region were caravan traders who were attracted by the area's excellent grazing grounds. As early as the seventh century A.D., there were extensive migrations of pastoral Berbers, including the two important groups related to contemporary Tuareg: the Lemta and the Zarawa. Invasions of Beni Hilal and Beni Sulaym Arabs into Tuareg Tripolitania and Fezzan pushed Tuareg southward to Aïr (Nicolaisen 1963, 411). Among these was a group of seven clans, allegedly descended from daughters of the same mother, a matrilineal myth widespread among many Tuareg groups, with cultural vestiges today in the high social prestige and economic independence of women. These matrilineally based social institutions, manifested in inheritance and descent, mythology and ritual, counterbalance more recent Islamic elements in the culture. In the late nineteenth century European exploration and military expeditions in the Sahara and along the Niger River led to incorporation of the region into French West Africa. By the early twentieth century, the French had brought the Tuareg under their colonial domination. As a result, Tuareg forfeited their rights to tariff collection and protection services for trans-Saharan camel caravans. Ocean routes had diverted most of the trade to the coast of Africa. Laws against raiding and slavery were strictly enforced.

After independence and the establishment of nation-states in the region in the early 1960s, the Tuareg continued to lose economic strength and political power. They had resisted, first, French, and later, central-state schools and taxes, suspicious of them as strategies to forcibly sedentarize them and gain control over their destiny. As a result, Tuareg tend to be underrepresented today in jobs in the new infrastructure of the towns, as well as in central governments in the region. These governments imposed restrictions on trade with neighboring countries, in order to protect national economic interests. Droughts and decreasing value of livestock and salt—the last remaining export commodity of the Tuareg—have weakened a once strong and diverse local economy (Childs and Chelala 1994, 17). Development programs involving the Tuareg from the 1940s to the 1970s failed miserably because they worked against the traditional pastoral production systems. During the 1984–1985 drought, some Tuareg men, calling themselves *ishumar* (a Tamacheq variant of the French verb *chomer,* denoting "to be unemployed"), left for Libya, where they received military training and weapons. In the early 1990s they returned to their homes and demanded autonomy. Since that time, there has been continuous guerrilla warfare in some regions of Mali and Niger. Some Tuareg have been forced into refugee camps in neighboring countries (e.g., Mauritania).

Settlements

Precolonial Tuareg communities were predominantly rural and nomadic, with a few urban settlers. Today most Tuareg are seminomadic and remain in rural areas. Rural communities range from clusters of six to ten nomadic tents, temporarily camped to follow herds in search of pasture, to semisedentarized hamlets with compounds of tents and adobe houses reflecting the mixed subsistence of herding and gardening, to fully sedentarized hamlets, the inhabitants of which engage primarily in irrigated gardening. In all communities, each tent or compound corresponds to the nuclear household. Each compound is named for the married woman, who owns the nomadic tent, made by elderly female relatives and provided as a dowry, from which she may eject her husband upon divorce. Within compounds in more sedentarized areas, residential structures are diverse: there may be several tents, a few conical grass buildings, and sometimes, among the more well-to-do, an adobe house, built and owned by men. There are thus significant changes taking place in the property balance between men and women as a result of sedentarization.

Economy

Subsistence and Commercial Activities. Traditionally, occupations corresponded to social-stratum affiliation, determined by descent. Nobles controlled the caravan trade, owned most camels, and remained more nomadic, coming into oases only to collect a proportion of the harvest from their client and servile peoples. Tributary groups raided and traded for nobles and also herded smaller livestock, such as goats, in usufruct relationships with nobles. Peoples of varying degrees of client and servile status performed domestic and herding labor for nobles. Smiths manufactured jewelry and household tools and performed praise songs for noble patron families, serving as important oral historians and political intermediaries. Owing to natural disasters and political tensions, it is now increasingly difficult to make a living solely from nomadic stockbreeding. Thus, social stratum, occupation, and socioeconomic status tend to be less coincident. Most rural Tareg today combine subsistence methods, practicing herding, oasis gardening, caravan trading, and migrant labor. Nomadic stockbreeding still confers great prestige, however, and gardening remains stigmatized as a servile occupation. Other careers being pursued in the late twentieth century include creating art for tourists, at which smiths are particularly active, as artisans in towns, and guarding houses, also in the towns. On oases, crops include millet, barley, wheat, maize, onions, tomatoes, and dates.

Trade. The caravan trade, although today less important than formerly, persists in the region between the Aïr Mountains and Kano, Nigeria. Men from the Aïr spend five to seven months each year on camel caravans, traveling to Bilma for dates and salt, and then to Kano to trade them for millet and other foodstuffs, household tools, and luxury items such as spices, perfume, and cloth.

Division of Labor. Most camel herding is still done by men; although women may inherit and own camels, they tend to own and herd more goats, sheep, and donkeys. Caravan trade is exclusively conducted by men. A woman may, however, indirectly participate in the caravan trade by sending her camels with a male relative, who returns with goods for her. Men plant and irrigate gardens, and women harvest the crops. Whereas women may own gardens and date palms, they leave the work of tending them to male relatives.

Kinship

Kin Groups and Descent. The introduction of Islam in the seventh century A.D. had the long-term effect of superimposing patrilineal institutions upon traditional matriliny. Formerly, each matrilineal clan was linked to a part of an animal, over which that clan had rights (Casajus 1987; Lhote 1953; Nicolaisen 1963; Norris 1975, 30). Matrilineal clans were traditionally important as corporate groups, and they still exert varying degrees of influence among the different Tuareg confederations. Most Tuareg today are bilateral in descent and inheritance systems (Murphy 1964; 1967). Descent-group allegience is through the mother, social-stratum affiliation is through the father, and political office, in most groups, passes from father to son.

Kinship Terminology. Tuareg personal names are used most frequently in addressing all descendants and kin of one's own generation, although cousins frequently address one another by their respective classificatory kinship terms. Kin of the second ascending generation may be addressed using the classificatory terms *anna* (mother) and *abba* (father), as may brothers and sisters of parents, although this is variable. Most ascendants, particularly those who are considerably older and on the paternal side, are usually addressed with the respectful term *amghar* (masc.) or *tamghart* (fem.). The most frequently heard kinship term is *abobaz*, denoting "cousin," used in a classificatory sense. Tuareg enjoy more relaxed, familiar relationships with the maternal side, which is known as *tedis*, or "stomach" and associated with emotional and affective support, and more reserved, distant relations with the paternal side, which is known as *aruru*, or "back" and associated with material suport and authority over Ego. There are joking relationships with cousins; relationships with affines are characterized by extreme reserve. Youths should not pronounce the names of deceased ancestors.

Marriage and Family

Marriage. Cultural ideals are social-stratum endogamy and close-cousin marriage. In the towns, both these patterns are breaking down. In rural areas, class endogamy remains strong, but many individuals marry close relatives only to please their mothers; they subsequently divorce and marry nonrelatives. Some prosperous gardeners, chiefs, and Islamic scholars practice polygyny, contrary to the nomadic Tuareg monogamous tradition and contrary to many women's wishes; intolerant of co-wives, many women initiate divorces.

Domestic Unit. Tuareg groups vary in postmarital-residence rules. Some groups practice virilocal residence, others uxorilocal residence. The latter is more common among caravanning groups in the Aïr, such as the Kel Ewey, who adhere to uxorilocal residence for the first two to three years of marriage, during which time the husband meets the bride-wealth payments, fulfills obligations of groom-service, and offers gifts to his parents-in-law. Upon fulfillment of these obligations, the couple may choose where to live, and the young married woman may disengage her animals from her herds and build a separate kitchen, apart from her mother's.

Inheritance. Patrilineal inheritance, arising from Islamic influence, prevails, unless the deceased indicated otherwise, before death, in writing, in the presence of a witness: two-thirds of the property goes to the sons, one-third to the daughters. Alternative inheritance forms, stemming from ancient matriliny, include "living milk herds" (animals reserved for sisters, daughters, and nieces) and various preinheritance gifts.

Socialization. Fathers are considered disciplinarians, yet other men, particularly maternal uncles, often play and joke with small children. Women who lack their own daughters often adopt nieces to assist in housework. Although many men are often absent (while traveling), Tuareg children are nonetheless socialized into distinct, culturally defined masculine and feminine gender roles because male authority figures—chiefs, Islamic scholars, and wealthy gardeners—remain at home rather than departing on caravans or engaging in migrant labor, and these men exert considerable influence on young boys, who attend Quranic schools and assist in male tasks such as gardening and herding. Young girls tend to remain nearer home, assisting their mothers with household chores, although women and girls also herd animals.

Sociopolitical Organization

Precolonial Tuareg society was characterized by servility in a multiethnic setting (Baier and Lovejoy 1977, 393). This pattern arose partly as an adaptation to cycles of drought in the Sahara. In the core area of Tuareg operations, the desert, outsiders were acquired as domestic servants, herders, and farmers. Formerly, persons could belong to individuals, tribal sections, or to offices. Those persons who were in areas beyond direct control, particularly the herders, were more like clients than slaves. Still further away, in the savanna, some were settled on agricultural estates administered by resident agents and occupied a position somewhat between that of tenant farmers and serfs. The former clients and slaves now simply owe hospitality to their former masters. Traditionally, Tuareg social stratification guaranteed that power to make economic decisions remained in the hands of a few. Yet political power in the pastoral nomadic society was fragmented. At the lowest level was the camp (*eghiwan*) of five or six families of four or five members each, with dependents (including slaves). There were half as many dependents as free Tuareg. Two to twenty camps formed a descent-group section (*tawsit*). The male noble heads of the noble clan of the descent-group section traditionally have chosen chiefs from members of their own clan, but election usually is confirmed by all components of the section. Officeholders keep their positions for life, but traditional powers have been curtailed by colonial and postcolonial governments. Tenure of office has depended on the willingness of all nobles of the section to pay a small tribute to the chief each year (Briggs 1960, 146; Jean 1909, 175–176; Baier and Lovejoy 1977, 397). These traditional chiefs, called *chefs de tribus*, now serve as government links in collecting taxes and registering children for school. A group of sections recognizing a common leader constitutes the next level, the drum group, or confederation. Together, the noble clans of the confederations elect the *ămenokal*, or sultan. His precolonial function was to conduct peaceful relations with outsiders or to lead expeditions against enemies; today he acts as a liaison with the central government.

Social Control. In the traditional segmentary system, no leader had power over his followers solely by virtue of a position in a political hierarchy. Wealth was traditionally enough to guarantee influence. Nobles acted as managers of large firms and controlled most resources, although they constituted less than 10 percent of the population. Even traditionally, however, there were no cut-and-dry free or slave statuses. Below the aristocracy were various dependents whose status derived from their position in the larger system (e.g., whether attached to a specific noble or noble section); they had varying degrees of freedom. Tuareg assimilated outsiders, who formed the servile strata, on a model of fictive kinship: a noble owner was expected to be "like a father" to his slave. Vestiges of former tribute and client-patron systems persist today, but also encounter some resistance. On some oases, nobles still theoretically have rights to dates from date palms within gardens of former slaves, but nowadays the former slaves refuse to fetch them, obliging nobles to climb the trees and collect the dates themselves.

Conflict. In principle, members of the same confederation are not supposed to raid each other's livestock, but such raids do occur (Casajus 1987). In rural areas today, many local-level disputes are arbitrated by a council of elders and Islamic scholars who apply Quranic law, but individuals have the option of taking cases to secular courts in the towns.

Religion and Expressive Culture

Religious Beliefs. The local belief system, with its own cosmology and ritual, interweaves and overlaps with Islam rather than standing in opposition to it. In Islamic observances, men are more consistent about saying all the prescribed prayers, and they employ more Arabic loanwords, whereas women tend to use Tamacheq terms. There is general agreement that Islam came from the West and spread into Aïr with the migration of Sufi mystics in the seventh century (Norris 1975). Tuareg initially resisted Islam and earned a reputation among North African Arabs for being lax about Islamic practices. For example, local tradition did not require female chastity before marriage. In Tuareg groups more influenced by Quranic scholars, female chastity is becoming more important, but even these groups do not seclude women, and relations between the sexes are characterized by freedom of social interaction.

Religious Practitioners. In official religion, Quranic scholars, popularly called *ineslemen,* or marabouts, predominate in some clans, but anyone may become one through mastery of the Quran and exemplary practice of Islam. Marabouts are considered "people of God" and have obligations of generosity and hospitality. Marabouts are believed to possess special powers of benediction, *al baraka*. Quranic scholars are important in rites of passage and Islamic rituals, but smiths often act in these rituals, in roles complementary to those of the Quranic scholars. For example, at babies' namedays, held one week following a birth, the Quranic scholar pronounces the child's name as he cuts the throat of a ram, but smiths grill its meat, announce the nameday, and organize important evening festivals following it, at which they sing praise songs. With regard to weddings, a marabout marries a couple at the mosque, but smiths negotiate bride-wealth and preside over the evening festivals.

Ceremonies. Important rituals among Tuareg are rites of passage—namedays, weddings, and memorial/funeral feasts—as well as Islamic holidays and secular state holidays. In addition, there is male circumcision and the initial men's face-veil wrapping that takes place around the age of 18 years and that is central to the male gender role and the cultural values of reserve and modesty. There are also spirit-possession exorcism rituals (Rasmussen 1995). Many rituals integrate Islamic and pre-Islamic elements in their symbolism, which incorporates references to matrilineal ancestresses, pre-Islamic spirits, the earth, fertility, and menstruation.

Arts. In Tuareg culture, there is great appreciation of visual and aural arts. There is a large body of music, poetry, and song that is of central importance during courtship, rites of passage, and secular festivals. Men and women of diverse social origins dance, perform vocal and instrumental music, and are admired for their musical creativity; however, different genres of music and distinct dances and instruments are associated with the various social strata. There is also the sacred liturgical music of Islam, performed on Muslim holidays by marabouts, men, and older women.

Visual arts consist primarily of metalwork (silver jewelry), some woodwork (delicately decorated spoons and ladles and carved camel saddles), and dyed and embroidered leatherwork, all of which are specialties of smiths, who formerly manufactured these products solely for their noble patrons. In rural areas, nobles still commission smiths to make these items, but in urban areas many smiths now sell jewelry and leather to tourists.

Medicine. Health care among Tuareg today includes traditional herbal, Quranic, and ritual therapies, as well as Western medicine. Traditional medicine is more prevalent in rural communities because of geographic barriers and political tensions. Although local residents desire Western medicines, most Western-trained personnel tend to be non-Tuareg, and many Tuareg are suspicious or shy of outside medical practioners (Rasmussen 1994). Therefore rural peoples tend to rely most upon traditional practitioners and remedies. For example, Quranic scholars cure predominantly men with verses from the Quran and some psychological counseling techniques. Female herbalists cure predominantly women and children with leaves, roots, barks, and some holisitic techniques such as verbal incantations and laying on of hands. Practitioners called *bokawa* (a Hausa term; sing. *boka*) cure with perfumes and other non-Quranic methods. In addition, spirit possession is cured by drummers.

Death and Afterlife. In the Tuareg worldview, the soul (*iman*) is more personalized than are spirits. It is seen as residing within the living individual, except during sleep, when it may rise and travel about. The souls of the deceased are free to roam, but usually do so in the vicinity of graves. A dead soul sometimes brings news and, in return, demands a temporary wedding with its client. It is believed that the future may be foretold by sleeping on graves. Tuareg offer libations of dates to tombs of important marabouts and saints in order to obtain the al-baraka benediction. Beliefs about the afterlife (e.g., paradise) conform closely to those of official Islam.

Bibliography

Baier, Stephen, and Paul Lovejoy (1977). "The Desert-Side Economy of the Central Sudan." In *The Politics of Natural Disaster: The Case of the Sahel Drought*, edited by M. H. Glantz, 144–175. New York: Praeger.

Bernus, Edmond (1981). *Touaregs nigeriens: Unité culturelle d'un peuple pasteur.* Paris: Éditions de l'Office de la Recherche Scientifique et Technique d'Outre-Mer (ORSTOM).

Bourgeot, André (1990). "Identité touraegue: De l'aristocracie à la révolution." *Études Rurales* 120:129–162.

Briggs, Lloyd Cabot (1960). *Tribes of the Sahara*. Cambridge: Harvard University Press.

Casajus, Dominique (1987). *La tente dans l'essuf*. Paris and London: Cambridge University Press.

Childs, Larry, and Celina Chelala (1994). "Drought, Rebellion, and Social Change in Northern Mali: The Challenges Facing Tamacheq Herders." *Cultural Survival Quarterly*, Winter, 16–20.

Fraternité Charles de Foucauld (1968). *Initiation a la langue des touaregs de l'Aïr.* Niamey and Agadez, Niger: Petites Soeurs de Charles de Foucauld; Service Culturel de l'Ambassade de France.

Jean, C. (1909). *Les touareg de sud-est: L'Aïr.* Paris: Émile Larose Librairie–Éditeur.

Lhote, Henri (1953). *Touareg du Hoggar.* Paris: Payot.

Murphy, Robert (1964). "Social Distance and the Veil." *American Anthropologist* 66:1257–1274.

Murphy, Robert (1967). "Tuareg Kinship." *American Anthropologist* 69:163–170.

Nicolaisen, Johannes (1963). *Ecology and Culture of the Pastoral Tuareg.* Copenhagen: National Museum of Copenhagen.

Norris, H. T. (1975). *The Tuareg: Their Islamic Legacy and Its Diffusion into the Sahel.* Wilts, Eng.: Aris & Phillips.

Rasmussen, Susan J. (1994). "Female Sexuality, Sexual Reproduction, and the Politics of Medical Intervention in Niger: Kel Ewey Tuareg Perspectives." *Culture, Medicine, and Psychiatry* 18:433–464.

Rasmussen, Susan J. (1995). *Spirit Possession and Personhood among the Kel Ewey Tuareg.* Cambridge: Cambridge University Press.

Rodd, Lord of Renell (1926). *The People of the Veil.* London: Anthropological Publications.

United States Department of State (1987). "Niger." *Background Notes,* 1–8. Washington, D.C.: Bureau of Public Affairs.

SUSAN J. RASMUSSEN

Turkana

ETHNONYM: Ngiturkan

Orientation

Identification. "Turkana" is the name given to the pastoral and formerly pastoral people living in the arid and semiarid rangelands of northwestern Kenya. The Turkana refer to themselves as "Ngiturkan" and their land as "Eturkan." The Turkana ethnic group as a whole is composed of two major divisions, and each division composed of territorial sections. The major divisions are the Ngimonia and the Ngichoro; Ngimonia are divided into Ngissir and non-Ngissir sections. The sections of the Ngichuro division are: Ngilukumong, Ngiwoyakwara, Ngigamatak, Ngibelai, and Ngibotok. The sections of the Ngimonia division are Ngikwatela, Ngiyapakuno, Ngissiger, Ngijie, Ngissir, Ngibocheros, Ngiseto, Ngisonyoka, Ngimazuk, Ngatunyo, Nganyagatauk, Ngikuniye, Ngikajik, and Ngimamong. Each section is identified with an area in Eturkan, but the extent to which the sectional territory is occupied exclusively by members of the section varies according to the rules governing natural-resource use of that particular section.

Location. The area occupied by the Turkana people corresponds closely with the current boundaries of Turkana District in Kenya. It lies between 1°30′ and 5°00′ N and encompasses approximately 67,000 square kilometers. Eturkan lies entirely within the Gregory Rift Valley and is bordered to the west by the Rift Valley wall, to the north by the mountains and plains occupied by the Taposa of southern Sudan, to the east by the western shoreline of Lake Turkana, and to the south by the plains inhabited by the pastoral Pokot.

Eturkan is a broad low-lying plain, broken by lava hills and mountains. The plains are arid and lie at an elevation of 300 to 800 meters, whereas the mountain receive more precipitation and rise to an elevation of 2,200 meters. The climate of Eturkan is hot, dry, and highly variable. Precipitation is most likely during the months of April through June and, to a lesser extent, during the month of November. The mean annual rainfall at Lodwar, the district capital (elevation 506 meters), is 16.5 centimeters, with a high of 49.8 centimeters and a low of 1.9 centimeters.

The vegetation of the area is characterized by annual grasses and shrubs in the plains, and perennial grasses and large tress in the highlands. The lowlands are crosscut with many temporary stream and river courses. The larger of the river courses, the Kerio and the Turkwell, support a dense gallery forest, and acacia trees grow along the banks of most smaller stream and river beds.

The Turkana people have adapted to the aridity and the spatial and temporal variability in climate by herding five different species of livestock and by moving frequently. Although arid, Eturkan is blessed with numerous springs and areas where water can be obtained by digging wells. Early travelers' accounts report an abundance of wild animals in Turkanaland, but today most wildlife is restricted to the forested areas and the unoccupied areas that serve as a buffer between the Turkana and the tribal groups on their borders.

Demography. Gulliver estimated the Turkana population as approximately 80,000 in 1950, based on government tax roles. More recent census information suggests that the Turkana population has increased to about 200,000. Demographic information among pastoral people has always been difficult to collect, and the harshness and vast expanses of Turkana District, combined with the high degree of mobility of the people, has added to the problems associated with collecting census data; demographic information, therefore, has to be weighed with caution.

Population densities are low and settlements few and scattered. Following the introduction of a famine-relief program in the 1980s, the settlement areas experienced rapid growth.

Linguistic Affiliation. According to Lamphere (1992), the Turkana belong to the Ateker Group of the Eastern Nilotic Language Family. The Ateker Group, referred to in the past as the "Karamojong Cluster," "Central Paranilotes," or the "Iteso-Turkana Group," consists of the Iteso, Karamojong, Dodoth, Ngijie, Taposa, Jiye, and Donyiro or Ngiyengatom languages, as well as that of the Turkana. Their speech is mutually intelligible, and all are pastoral or agro-pastoral peoples. Although all the groups are linguistically related and live in close proximity to one another, their relations with the

Turkana have generally been based on conflict, characterized by raids and counterraids.

History and Cultural Relations

The Turkana people emerged as a distinct ethnic group sometime during the early to middle decades of the nineteenth century. Oral history and archaeological evidence suggest that, prior to A.D. 1500, the ancestors of the Ateker Language Group lived somewhere in the southern Sudan and most likely subsisted as hunting and gathering peoples. After beginning their southern migration, these ancestral peoples incorporated both agricultural and pastoral pursuits, and eventually split into groups that emphasized one subsistence strategy or the other.

The period from 1500 to 1800 appears to have been characterized by frequent splitting and fusing of ethnic groups, and shifting alliances among the groups. During this time, the Karamojong established a distinct identity with a subsistence system based on the raising of livestock, principally cattle, combined with small-scale agriculture.

Oral histories suggest that the Jie seceded from the Karamojong, and that a group split off from the Jie and established themselves in the region near the headwaters of the Tarach River, in what is now Turkana District, sometime during the early part of the eighteenth century. By the beginning of the nineteenth century, Turkana cattle camps began to push down the Tarach in search of new pastures upon which to graze their animals. As they moved westward, the Turkana encountered other pastoral groups, some of which herded camels (most likely the Rendille and Borana). As the Turkana expanded eastward, they began both to assimilate and disperse other groups. They first pushed to the north and east to Lake Turkana, and then to the south, crossing the Turkwell River. It appears that by 1850 the Turkana occupied much of the territory they use today.

The first European to enter into the land of the Turkana was Count Samuel Teleki von Szek, whose expedition reached Turkana in June of 1888. He was preceded by Swahili caravans in search of ivory, which first arrived in 1884. About the same time that the Swahili arrived in the south of Turkanaland, Ethiopian ivory hunters began arriving in the north. Within a few years, there ensued a period of conflict and contestation between the British and the Ethiopians over the colonial domination of the Turkana, which lasted until 1918.

The Turkana resisted British domination of their homeland throughout the early part of the twentieth century. Turkana raiding on their pastoral neighbors, especially against the Pokot to the south, caused large-scale social disruption and influenced the British decision to launch one of the largest military expeditions they ever mounted against an indigenous people. In 1918 a combined force of over 5,000 well-armed men, consisting of Sudanese troops, troops of the Kings African Rifles, and levies composed of warriors from groups antagonistic to the Turkana, launched what came to be known as the Labur Patrol.

The Labur Patrol broke the military might of the Turkana; in 1926 civil administration was reintroduced, and in 1928 taxes were reinstated. The period from 1929 until World War II appears to have been peaceful. Beginning in the 1950s, the Turkana again began to resist British domination, and the British launched a series of military expeditions against the Turkana. The use of occasional military forays against the Turkana was continued by the Kenyan government following independence in 1963.

Development in Turkana District was slow. Only two primary schools operated in the district at the time of independence. During the 1970s major efforts were made to help the Turkana integrate into the larger Kenyan economy; however, antagonistic relations among the Turkana and their neighbors continued, and by the early 1980s the entire district was considered highly insecure. Insecurity combined with two severe droughts in the early 1980s to inhibit development efforts. Despite the growth of settlements, the area remains remote, insecure, and relatively underdeveloped.

Settlements

The Turkana are one of the most mobile populations in the world. Traditionally, there were no permanent settlements occupied by them. Small settlements were built during the colonial period, but very few Turkana were attracted to them. Following the droughts of the 1980s, approximately one-half of the Turkana population settled in, or adjacent to, large famine-relief camps. Today it is estimated that about one-third to one-half of the Turkana population remains settled. The fastest-growing settlements are the district capital, Lodwar, and the villages located along the Turkwell River that depend upon irrigated agriculture.

Economy

Subsistence. The Turkana are primarily a pastoral people; they depend on five species of livestock for their subsistence. Camels, cattle, sheep, and goats provide most of their subsistence needs; donkeys are used to transport household goods during migrations. The Turkana who live along the major water courses also engage in small-scale agriculture, and one section of the Turkana, the Ngibocheros, live along the shore of Lake Turkana and depend on fishing and aquatic hunting, as well as herding for subsistence.

Trade. The Turkana remain one of the more isolated ethnic groups in Kenya, and trade is still small in scale. The Turkana sell livestock to buy grains and household needs. The Turkana traditionally traded livestock for iron with ethnic groups in the highlands of Uganda.

Division of Labor. Most aspects of the Turkana economy are strongly influenced by the needs of the livestock and by the migratory pattern. During the rainy season, when all people and animals are together, men are responsible for the daily herding operation, and women are responsible for watering and milking the livestock, feeding the family, and other domestic chores. During the dry season, the livestock are often separated into milking and nonmilking herds. The nonmilking herds are usually herded by young men, who may be separated from the rest of the family for six months or more. During this time, all work related to the livestock is performed by the men.

Land Tenure. The land-tenure system is similar to that of many pastoral peoples. Grazing resources are open to all members of a territorial section; water resources, however, may be open to all or owned. In general, water in rivers and streams when they are flowing, open pools, and shallow wells are not owned. Deep wells dug through sand, clay, or rock are owned by the individual who dug them, and can be used by close male relatives and friends. In northern Turkana, the rules governing access to grazing do not appear to be as strict as those found among the sections living in the south.

Kinship

Kin Groups and Descent. One of the fundamental units in Turkana social organization is the exogamous patrilineal clan (*ateker* or *amachar*). There are twenty-eight clans among the Turkana, and, in general, they crosscut the sectional boundaries; some of the smaller clans, however, are quite localized. Each clan is associated with a particular brand for its livestock, and an individual can identify a relative in a new location in this way. Clan members call upon each other for help in times of need, but clan membership implies more of an opportunity for an individual to seek assistance than an obligation on the part of the person from whom it is requested.

Kinship Terminology. Kinship terminology is classificatory, but does not form a uniform system with respect to clan members. Terms such as those for "mother," "father," "brother," and "sister" are sometimes extended to clan members, but, to a large extent, this usage is based on the strength of individual relationships.

Marriage and Family

Turkana marriage is polygynous and often patrilocal. Bridewealth is unusually high among the Turkana; a typical bridewealth payment might include 30 to 50 cattle, 30 to 50 camels, and 100 to 200 small stock. This high bride-wealth often means that a man cannot marry until his father has died and he has inherited livestock. The high bride-wealth also requires that the prospective groom collect livestock from all his relatives and friends, thus reinforcing social ties through the transfer of livestock.

A Turkana homestead (*awi*) is composed of a man, his wives and their children, and often his mother and other dependent women. Each wife and her children build a daytime sitting hut (*ekol*) and, in the rainy season, a nighttime sleeping hut (*aki*). When a new wife comes into the homestead, she stays in the ekol of the mother or first wife of the household head until she has borne her first child.

Wives are often inherited by a brother or the son of a co-wife upon the death of a husband. A woman has the right to refuse to be inherited and can live with one of her sons, if she chooses. As each wife comes into the household, the head of the family allocates milking livestock to her. Although she has no ownership rights to these livestock, they will form the basis of the herds that will be inherited by her sons. Most of a woman's livestock will be inherited by her firstborn son.

Sociopolitical Organization

The Turkana, like many pastoral populations in East Africa, have no formal political hierarchy based on chiefs and subchiefs. Political influence is gained through age, wealth, wisdom, and oratorical skill. Turkana social organization can be seen as two systems of social relationships operating simultaneously. One system is based on territory and rights in pasture and water; the other is based on kinship, relationships among individuals, and rights in livestock and labor.

The basic unit of Turkana social organization is the awi. Most herd owners live and travel with two to five other herd owners and their families, forming what is referred to as an *awi apolon*, or large awi. The composition of this unit changes frequently, as individuals and families leave to join other homesteads, or others come to join the awi apolon. During the wet season, many homesteads congregate into temporary associations (sing. *adakar*); these associations break up as resources become scarce with the progression of the dry season.

Above the awi, the next level of territorial organization is the section; above that, the tribe. Sectional membership confers upon the individual rights to grazing. It appears that in the past there were a number of ceremonial occasions in which tribal identity was reinforced. Today tribal identity is reified by rules of appropriate behavior concerning raiding and banditry among the sections.

Nonterritorial aspects of social organization are primarily related to clan and kinship relations. A critical feature of Turkana social organization, however, is the network of personal relationships, based on the exchange of livestock, which is built up by each herd owner over the course of his lifetime. It is to individuals in this network that a herd owner turns in times of need. From the perspective of an individual herd owner, most members of this association will be agnatic or affinal kinsmen, but there may also be many people in this network who are simply his friends.

Finally, each man is a member of alternating generation sets. If a man is a Leopard, his son will be a Stone; thus there are approximately equal numbers of Stones and Leopards at any one time. These groups will be formed when there is a need to organize large groups quickly. Some authors refer to a functioning age-set system, but almost all of the Turkana with whom McCabe worked had never heard of such a system, and a few others had only a vague recollection that an age-set system existed at some time in the past.

Conflict is usually resolved by the men living in proximity to one another. Men discuss such issues at "the tree of the men," and special attention is paid to men of influence. The decisions of the men will be enforced by the younger men of the area.

Religion and Expressive Culture

Religious Beliefs and Practitioners. The Turkana believe in a single God, Akuj, who is thought to be omnipotent but who rarely intervenes in the lives of people. Contact between Akuj and the people is channeled though a diviner, or *emeron*. All diviners come from a particular clan and are thought to have the power to interpret dreams, predict the future, heal the sick, and make rain. There are a number of gradations in the power of diviners—from those who predict the future by throwing sandals or reading intestines, to those who can make rain. Although the Turkana believe in the power of the emeron, they are also skeptical of those from the Emeron clan who say they have mystical powers, but fail to demonstrate that power in everyday life.

Ceremonies. The ceremonial life of the Turkana is less important than that of many neighboring tribes. There are no large corporate ceremonies and no physical initiations. The *asapan* ceremony signifies the transition from youth to adulthood, and every man is supposed to perform this ceremony before marriage.

Arts. The Turkana produce finely crafted carved wooden implements used in daily life. Another striking aspect of Turkana culture is the beautiful and intricate singing that is heard on moonlit nights during the rainy season. Men and women sing in groups; those with particularly good voices take the lead. Songs are often about cattle or the land, but the subject can also be improvised and pertain to immediate events. Turkana now weave baskets that are sold in all the tourist shops in Nairobi.

Medicine. The Turkana have an intimate knowledge of plants and their medicinal properties, both for humans and for livestock. Animal fat is considered to have medicinal qualities, and the fat-tailed sheep is often referred to as "the hospital for the Turkana."

Death and Afterlife. Although witchcraft and sorcery are found among the Turkana, it is important to note that the Turkana do not dwell on the magical or religious aspects of life. The corpse of a woman who has raised many children and a that of a man who has been successful will be buried; others are left in the bush. Some people feel that after death a person will join Akuj, and others say that they do not know what happens after death.

Bibliography

Barber, James (1968). *The Imperial Frontier*. Nairobi: East Africa Publishing House.

Dyson-Hudson, R. (1989). "Ecological Influences on Systems of Food Production and Social Organization of South Turkana Pastoralists." In *Comparative Socioecology: The Behavioral Ecology of Humans and Other Mammals*, edited by V. Standen and R. Foley. Oxford: Blackwell.

Dyson-Hudson, R., and J. Terrence McCabe (1985). *South Turkana Nomadism: Coping with an Unpredictably Varying Environment*. Ethnography Series, FL17–001. New Haven: HRAFlex Books.

Ellis James, and David Swift (1988). "Stability of African Pastoral Ecosystems: Alternate Paradigms and Implications for Development. *Journal of Range Management* 41:450–459.

Galvin, K. (1985). "Diet and Nutrition of Turkana Pastoralists in a Social and Ecological Context. Ph.D. dissertation, State University of New York at Binghamton.

Gulliver, Philip (1951). *A Preliminary Survey of the Turkana*. New Series, no. 26. Cape Town: Commonwealth School of African Studies.

Gulliver, Philip (1955). *The Family Herds: A Study of Two Pastoral Tribes*. London: Routledge & Kegan Paul.

Lamphere, John (1992). *The Scattering Time: Turkana Responses to Colonial Rule*. Oxford: Clarendon Press.

McCabe, J. Terrence (1985). "Livestock Management among the Turkana: A Social and Ecological Analysis of Herding in an East African Pastoral Population." Ph.D. dissertation, State University of New York at Binghamton.

McCabe, J. Terrence (1990). "Turkana Pastoralism: A Case against the Tragedy of the Commons." *Human Ecology* 18(1): 81–103.

Sobania, Neal (1991). "Feasts, Famines, and Friends: Nineteenth Century Exchange and Ethnicity in Eastern Lake Turkana Region." In *Herders, Warriors, and Traders: Pastoralism in Africa*, edited by John Galaty and Piere Bonte. Boulder, Colo.: Westview Press.

von Hohnel, L. (1891). *Discovery of Lakes Rudolf and Stefanie: A Narrative of Samuel Teleki's Exploring and Hunting Expedition in Eastern Equatorial Africa in 1887 and 1888*. Translated by N. Bell. 1968. London: Frank Cass & Co.

J. TERRENCE McCABE

Turks

ETHNONYMS: Türken (German), Türkler (Turkish)

Orientation

Identification. Ethnically, the Turks are a cultural group united by a common language, but the term "Turk" has no clearly defined racial significance; it can be properly applied to those communities historically and linguistically connected to the nomadic people whom the Chinese identified as the "Tu-Kiu." Some scholars consider that the name "Hiungnu," which appears in Chinese sources of the second millennium B.C.E., refers to the Turks; however, it was probably a generic term that included both Turks and Mongols, and perhaps other peoples.

Today ethnic Turks constitute approximately 80 percent of the population of the Republic of Turkey. Turkish-speaking peoples can be found in Iran, Azerbaijan, Kazakhstan, Uzbekistan, Turkmenistan, Afghanistan, and China. Turks are linked by their common history and language, which are strong and persistent; additionally they are linked by their religion—Islam; with the exception of the Turkish tribe called the Yakut, who live in eastern Siberia and the Altai region, almost all Turks are Muslims.

Location. Turkey is located in southwestern Asia and fits roughly between 36° and 42° N and 25° and 45° E. It is bounded on the west by the Aegean Sea and Greece; on the north by Bulgaria and the Black Sea; on the northeast by Georgia, Armenia, and Azerbaijan; on the east by Iran, and on the south by Iraq, Syria, and the Mediterranean Sea. The total area of the country is 780,580 square kilometers. The greater part of the country lies in Asia, specifically Asia Minor or Anatolia. About 8 percent of Turkey—called Turkish Thrace—is in Europe. Because of the mountainous terrain and the maritime influence, climates vary greatly. The country has three main temperate climates: Mediterranean on the south and southwestern coasts, Black Sea in the north, and steppe throughout most of Anatolia.

Demography. The population of Turkey in 1994 was estimated as 62,154,000. More than half the population lives in urban areas. Turkey has one of the highest rates of population increase in the world, as the result of a high birthrate, estimated in 1994 to be 25.98 births per thousand and an average death rate of 5.8 deaths per thousand. The current annual rate of growth is 2.02 percent. From 1923 to 1994, the population multiplied by approximately five. Large-scale migration to the cities since the middle of the century has led to overcrowding. In 1990, 65 percent of the population was urban. İstanbul is the cultural, industrial, and commercial center. Ankara is the capital. Other major cities are: Adana, Antalya, Bursa, Diyarbakır, Gaziantep, Izmir, Kayseri, Konya, and Samsun.

Linguistic Affiliation. Turkish is the language of more than 90 percent of the population of Turkey. Until recently, some scholars contended that Turkish is part of the Ural-Altaic Language Group. Philologists today, however, consider Turkish an Eastern Turkic language. Turkish is an agglutinating language; words are made by adding strings of suffixes to a root that does not change. Perhaps the most striking characteristic of the Turkish language is vowel harmony. The vowels in a Turkish word are either all back vowels (a, ı, o, u) or all front vowels (e, i, ö, ü). Turkish is totally unrelated to Arabic or Persian, but it has borrowed many words from these two languages. In 1928 the Arabic script that had been used to write Ottoman Turkish was abandoned in favor of a twenty-nine letter Latin script. After the establishment of the modern Republic of Turkey in 1923, attempts were made to purify the Turkish language by creating new words to replace many Arab, Persian, and some French words. These attempts met with only limited success, and borrowed words are still very common.

History and Cultural Relations

The origins of the Turkish peoples are among the nomadic and pastoral peoples who lived east of the Eurasian steppes from the borders of China across Turkestan. Their earliest appearance in history was in what would be today Outer Mongolia, south of Lake Baikal and north of the Gobi Desert. The Turks were once part of a group of Altaic peoples, which includes the Mongols, the Manchu, the Bulgars, probably the Huns, and others. The first group known to be called Turks emerged in the sixth century C.E. The Tu-Kiu founded an empire stretching from Mongolia and the northern frontier of China to the Black Sea. In the seventh century the Arab conquest of Persia carried Islam to the Turkish fringes of Central Asia. In the ninth century and later, many Turks were recruited as slaves for the ʿAbbāsid armies and converted to Islam. Some rose to important administrative positions. The larger portion of Turks, however, still being essentially nomadic in Central Asia east of the Aral Sea, did not accept Islam until the tenth century. Bands of Turks joined in the gradual war of attrition that was being waged by Muslim warriors along the frontiers with the declining Byzantine Empire. A tribe of Turks called the Oghuz (Oğuz) wrested control of Persia from the Ghaznavids and founded the Seljuk Turkish Empire in 1037. The Seljuks took control of Baghdad from the Buyids in 1055. The Seljuk Turkish victory in 1071 over the forces of the Byzantines at Manzikert, northwest of Lake Van, led to the migration of Turkoman tribes into Anatolia. Within a very short time, the Seljuks had penetrated as far as Nicaea (present-day İznik), only 80 kilometers from Constantinople. Although driven away from this city in 1097, their hold on eastern and central Asia Minor was firmly established. By the early twelfth century, most of the Anatolian plateau was a Seljuk principality, which came to be called Rum. The capital of Seljuk Rum was Konya, and in this city there developed a hybrid Islamic culture that combined elements of Arab Sunni Islam with Persian Shia Islam and Turkish mystical humanism. The invasion of the Mongols in the thirteenth century ended the dominance of the Seljuks in Anatolia.

The Ottoman principality of Sogut was one among ten successor-states that survived from the Seljuk Empire and the Mongol protectorate. In the 1290s the ruler of this principality was Osman, from whose name comes that of the dynasty: Osmanlı in Turkish. Sogut was located on the Byzantine frontier, closest to Constantinople. As Osman's emirate expanded, it created both the territorial basis and the administrative organization for an empire. Osman's grandson, Murad I, crossed the Hellespont to extend the young empire into the Christian Balkan states. He applied the principle of toleration to allow non-Muslims to become full citizens and rise to the highest offices of state, and thus, at this very early stage, established the character of the vast multilingual and multiethnic Ottoman Empire. In 1453 Sultan Mehmed II conquered Constantinople, and the city's name was changed to İstanbul. In its first two centuries, most of the Ottoman Empire's energies had been directed toward Christian Europe; however, Selim I (r. 1512–1520), called "the Grim" by Westerners, turned his attention toward Asia. He transformed the Ottoman Empire from a Ghazi state on the western fringe of the Muslim world into the greatest empire since the early caliphate. Selim defeated the Ṣafavids and moved fierce Kurdish tribes to eastern Anatolia to seal that border with the Persians. He defeated the Mamluks and took over their vast empire. The Ottomans became the rulers of Syria, Egypt and the Hejaz—the heartland of Arab Islam. At its peak, the Ottoman Empire stretched from the Persian Gulf to Algeria. The empire reached its cultural zenith under the son of Selim I, Süleyman I, "the Magnificent" (r. 1520–1566). His reign also marked an Ottoman cultural renaissance. A considerable poet in his own right, Süleyman encouraged the arts at his court. Like all great civilizations, the Ottoman absorbed and transformed various external cultural influences. The first sultans took from the Byzantines. Selim and Süleyman brought artisans from Tabrīz, in western Persia, to beautify İstanbul. Under Süleyman, with the help of Sinan (the son of a Christian from Anatolia and one of the finest architects of all time), İstanbul became a city of true magnificence, at the point of confluence of Eastern and Western civilization. Immediately after Süleyman's death, the Ottoman Empire began to suffer a decline. In the eighteenth and nineteenth centuries it lost several wars to the expanding Russian Empire. It did enjoy another period of cultural renaissance during the reign of Sultan Ahmed III (r. 1703–1730), which is called the Tulip Period. Some reform of the government was accomplished at this time. Nevertheless, the empire lost territory around the Black Sea and in the Balkans during the last part of the eighteenth century and first half of the nineteenth. Russian ambitions were checked by Great Britain and France in the Crimean War (1854–1856), but the Russo-Turkish War liberated Bulgaria, Romania, and Serbia from the control of the sultan. The Ottoman Empire was drawn into World War I, on the side of the Central Powers. With its defeat and the abdication of its last sultan, Mehmed VI, the empire finally collapsed. The Allies sought to divide Turkey among themselves after their victory, but the country saved itself by waging a war of liberation directed by the empire's most successful general, Mustafa Kemal (who would later take the surname "Atatürk"). Turkey made a remarkable recovery under Atatürk's leadership. He abolished the sultanate and the caliphate, and Turkey became a republic on 29 October 1923. It was declared a secular state, and religious toleration was guaranteed by the new constitution. Many other reforms were set in motion to modernize Turkey along Western lines. Turkey remained neutral during World War II, until it joined the Allies in February 1945. It joined the North Atlantic Treaty Organization (NATO) in 1952. Turkey suffered political instability that led to military takeovers in 1960, 1970, and 1980. In 1982 a new constitution was promulgated that provided the reestablishment of democratic government.

Settlements

Although there are many large cities and towns in Turkey, Turkish Thrace and Anatolia are essentially rural. About 45 percent of the population lives in rural settlements. There are about 36,000 villages in Turkey. The houses in the villages vary from region to region. In Eastern Anatolia, the Aegean region, and in the Taurus Mountains, they are made of stone. In the Black Sea region, village houses are made of wood, and, on the Anatolian plateau, they are made of sun-dried bricks. A typical village house is two stories high and has a flat roof. The lower floor is used to shelter animals and for storage. Many villages in eastern Turkey lack running water, and some do not have electricity. The number of villagers who are migrating to urban areas continues to grow.

Economy

Industry and Trade. Modern industry dates from the beginning of the republic. The government has played an important role in the development of industry from that time and in the late twentieth century owned 47 percent of the industries. Manufacturing accounts for about 20 percent of the nation's gross national product but employs only about 10 percent of the labor force. Turkish industries include textiles, food processing, mining, steel, construction, lumber, and paper. Antimony, borate, copper, and chrome are mined in sufficient quantities to be exported. Tourism is a growing industry and has become an important source of national income. Turkey has close economic ties with Western Europe and applied for full membership in the European Economic Community in 1987. At the same time, it has sought trading partners in the Middle East. Turkey controls the headwaters of the Tigris and Euphrates rivers and has had disputes with Syria and Iraq in this regard. In 1993 it was estimated that there were 1,800,000 Turks working outside of Turkey, mostly in Germany.

Agriculture and Land Tenure. About 30 percent of Turkey's land area is considered arable. More than one-half of the land is devoted to cereals. Agriculture accounts for nearly one quarter of the gross national product and employs 48 percent of the population. The main cash crops include tobacco, cereals, cotton, olives, mohair, wool, silk, figs, grapes, nuts, citrus fruits, and sugar beets. Turkey is self-sufficient in food production, and it exports its surplus. Forests cover about 25 percent of the land and are protected by the state. Much of the wood that is harvested from these forests is used for fuel.

Division of Labor. The mechanization of agriculture has relieved the burden of women's agricultural chores, but the harvest continues to be a time of hard physical labor for all of the members of families who make their living from agriculture. Women continue to do much of the hoeing of vegetables and the digging for potatoes. Girls and young women are involved in the weaving of rugs.

Kinship, Marriage, and Family

Marriage and Domestic Unit. Marriage continues to be a very important institution in Turkey. From the time parents have their first children, thought is given to their eventual marriage. Some of the marriages that take place are "love matches," but most of them are still being "arranged." In villages, girls are still usually married at a young age. In rural areas, large transfers of wealth are often involved in the marriage arrangement. Turks often marry their first cousins and other close kin, under the incest laws of Islam, to keep control of wealth within the extended family; however, many marriages in Turkey today involve completely unrelated persons. Households in rural areas consist of a man, his wife, his adult sons and their wives, and his young children and grandchildren. In the city, households are usually smaller, being limited to the immediate family and paternal grandparents.

Socialization. Parents assume primary responsibility for raising children, and they are assisted by members of the extended family. The educational system of Turkey was modernized after the founding of the republic as part of an effort to Westernize the country. Today education is compulsory for children ages 6 to 14, and in 1991 it was estimated that 78 percent of this age group do attend school. Instruction is coeducational, and, in state schools, free. The literacy rate among persons 15 years of age and older was estimated in 1990 to be 81 percent. Religious instruction in state schools, having been prohibited when the republic was established and then later made optional, is now compulsory. There are not sufficient numbers of elementary or secondary schoolteachers or school buildings. Many schools have a morning and an afternoon session, and often the number of students in a class is greater than forty. Approximately 35 percent of high school graduates go on to higher education. In 1992 there were twenty-nine universities in Turkey.

Sociopolitical Organization

Social Organization. Strong class prejudice does not seem to be a part of the structure of modern Turkish society, which does, however, show very marked social divisions. This apparent paradox is explained by the fact that although there are very real differences between various social groups, the Turks do not usually think of themselves in terms of class. Political parties are not organized along class lines. The ideology of the republic has avoided class distinctions, and there is increasing social mobility. There is an educated elite in Turkey, which is basically located in the cities. It has been the ruling element in the country in both Ottoman and republican times.

Political Organization. Atatürk established the ideological basis for the modern Republic of Turkey. It has a republican form of government and a democratic, multiparty system. His reforms included the disestablishment of the role of Islam in government and the adoption of the Swiss civil code. The voting franchise includes men and women aged 21 or older. Women were given the vote in national elections in 1934. The 1982 constitution provides for a democratic, parliamentary form of government. The president is elected for a seven-year term and is not eligible for reelection. The prime minister and his or her council of ministers hold executive power, although the president can veto legislation. Turkey is divided into seventy-three provinces (*iller;* sing. *il*), administered by governors (*valiler;* sing. *vali*).

Social Control. Turkey has long been familiar with military power. This is evident not only in the Seljuk, Ottoman, and republican governments, but in the prestige patterns of Anatolian village societies. Early nomadic existence on the Central Asian steppe, where boundaries were not stable, created within those Turkish tribes a closer reliance on military force than was generally the case in more settled communities. A strong militaristic attitude continues to permeate Turkish society. The military is respected and, generally, trusted. Conscription, which is fifteen months for males at the age of 20, is viewed as a necessary duty.

Although Turkey is a secular state and has adopted the Swiss civil code, civic morality is still governed to a large degree by the laws and traditions of Islam.

Religion and Expressive Culture

Religious Beliefs and Practices. More than 99 percent of the population is Muslim, and most of them are Sunnites. Estimates of the number of Shiites fall between 5 percent and 35 percent of the population. There are approximately 50,000 Christians and 20,000 Jews in Turkey today. Villagers, although they are for the most part Muslims, continue to believe in superstitions like the evil eye, which is the ancient belief in the power of certain persons to harm or damage someone else with merely a glance. Beliefs in the power of jinn and *efrit,* as well as other supernatural phenomena, also persist in rural Turkey.

Ceremonies. Most Turks celebrate the two most important Islamic holidays. Ramazan is the ninth month of the Islamic calendar; it is the holy month of fasting. Muslims celebrate the end of the fast with Çeker Bayramı (the Candy Holiday), during which visits of friends and relatives take place, and boxes of candy are taken as presents. Kadir Gecesi (the Night of Power) is the eve of the 26th of Ramazan. This is the night on which Mohammed was given the power of prophecy, and it is celebrated in the mosques by prayers and a nightlong service. Kurban Bayramı (the Festival of Sacrifice) comes during the month of Muharrem. If Muslims make a pilgrimage to Mecca, they must arrive there ten days before Kurban Bayramı. The pilgrimage ends when a sheep or a goat is sacrificed, and the meat is given to the poor. The sacrifice is performed whether the person goes to Mecca or stays at home. The Muslim calendar is based on twelve lunar months and is therefore ten or twelve days shorter than the solar year. This means that the months and the religious holidays fall a bit earlier each year. The Mevlevi dervishes, better known in the West as the Whirling Dervishes, are an order of Sufis that was established by the son of the great mystical thinker, Jalāl ad-Dīn ar-Rūmī, in the thirteenth century. Every year the Mevlevi dervishes have a ceremony in which they whirl for fifteen days before and on the anniversary day of Rūmī's death, which is 17 December.

Clothing. The Western style of clothing has been adopted by most Turks in large urban areas; however, in the rural regions men and women wear baggy pants. Village women enjoy wearing bright colors and flowered prints. The wearing of a turban or a fez by any man in Turkey was outlawed during Atatürk's administration. Many conservative Muslim women wear long coats and white head scarves. Wearing a veil is not against the law, but it is not a usual practice except in some areas of eastern Turkey. Nevertheless, women in villages anywhere will often make an effort to cover their faces in front of strange men, using a corner of their scarf or handkerchief.

Arts. Seljuk and Ottoman Turkish culture is rich—and well represented in museums like the ethnographic museums in İstanbul and Ankara. They include fine examples of calligraphy, rug weaving, ceramics, metalwork, and miniature painting. The weaving of carpets is an industry that dates among the Turks from Seljuk times. Much of the symbolism in the design of Turkish rugs and kilims is pre-Islamic and shares its origins with the Turkish people in Central Asia. Nevertheless, these rugs have become an important part of the prayer ritual in Islam. Turkish culture, since the establishment of the republic, has been dominated by nationalism. Writers, authors, and musicians have left the tradition of Islam. Turkish folk music and dancing are popular. The ministry of culture was established in 1971, and the government extensively supports a national network of the arts, encompassing theater, opera, ballet, music, and fine arts, as well as popular art forms.

Medicine. Medical services provided by the government are free to the poor. Although health services are improving, rural areas suffer shortages of physicians and facilities. In 1992 there were 126,611 beds in 928 hospitals and health centers in Turkey.

Death and Afterlife. Death in Quranic terms is the beginning of a new life, which will be eternal. Muslims believe that it is a phenomenon like the phenomenon of life and is created by Allah (God). When an individual dies, according to Islamic teachings, the dead person begins a long wait that lasts until the day of resurrection. The grave becomes a garden in the garden of heaven or a well in the well of hell, depending on the life that the deceased has led. When Turkish Muslims die, they are buried the next day at the noontime *namaz,* or call to prayer. There are several rituals that are performed, including washing the body and covering it in a white cotton cloth. Then the body is taken to a nearby mosque and the funeral namaz is performed, after which it is taken to the cemetery and placed in a grave. The body must be attended to as quickly as possible, and people must abstain from exorbitant expenses.

Bibliography

Davidson, Roderic H. (1981). *Turkey: A Short History.* Walkington, Beverly, Eng.: Eothen Press.

Halman, Talat, et al. (1983). *Mevlana Celaleddin Rumi and the Whirling Dervishes.* Istanbul: Dost.

Kinross, Lord (1971). *Atatürk: The Rebirth of a Nation.* 5th ed. London: Wiedenfeld & Nicholson.

Kinross, Lord (1977). *Ottoman Centuries*. New York: Morrow.

Lewis, Bernard (1968). *The Emergence of Modern Turkey*. London: Oxford University Press.

Lewis, Geoffrey (1974). *Modern Turkey*. 4th ed. New York: Praeger.

Shaw, Stanford J., and Ezel Kural Shaw (1977). *History of the Ottoman Empire and Modern Turkey*. 2 vols. New York: Cambridge University Press.

Stirling, Paul (1965). *Turkish Village*. New York: John Wiley & Sons.

ALAN A. BARTHOLOMEW

Wolof

ETHNONYMS: Chelofes, Galofes, Guiolof, Gyloffes, Ialofes, Iolof, Jalof, Jolof, Olof, Ouoloff, Valaf, Volof, Wollufs, Yaloffs, Yolof

Orientation

Identification. The Wolof constitute a large ethnic group inhabiting the West African country of Senegal, a former French colony, and Gambia, a former British colony. "Wolof" is the name by which the people refer to themselves, and it is also the name of their indigenous language. They manifest a highly conscious sense of ethnic identity and ethnic pride.

Location. The great majority of the Wolof are concentrated in northwestern Senegambia, between the Senegal and Gambia rivers (16°10′ to 13°30′ N); the Atlantic Ocean lies to the west, and Wolof territory extends inland to about 14° 30′ W. This entire area has a tropical climate and a fairly flat landscape. Whereas the northern section has a predominantly semidesert environment called the Sahel, to the south, a grassy savanna gradually emerges with increasing numbers of shrubs and trees. This shift in vegetation coincides with an increase in the average annual rainfall, which ranges from 38 centimeters or less in the north to around 100 centimeters in the south. The rainy season lasts from June into October, and the rest of the year is distinctly dry. Because there is very little or no surface water through most of the area, villages generally depend on wells for all of their water needs except agriculture.

Demography. The Wolof are the dominant ethnic group in Senegal, both politically and numerically. Rapid population increase since the early 1960s, in combination with the Wolofization of members of other ethnic groups, resulted in a 1976 census estimate of about 2,000,000 Senegalese Wolof, around 41 percent of the total population. It must be noted, however, that these figures are crude approximations.

Linguistic Affiliation. The Wolof language has been classified within the Northern Branch of the West Atlantic Subfamily of the Niger-Congo Language Family. The most closely related languages are Serer and Fula. The Lébu, a separate ethnic group, speak a distinct Wolof dialect. Although French remains the official language of Senegal, Wolof has become the de facto national vernacular.

History and Cultural Relations

The first substantial documentary information on the Wolof dates from the travels of Ca da Mosto from 1455 to 1457. According to oral traditions, however, it was probably during the preceding century that the Wolof were unified into a loose political federation known as the Dyolof Empire, centered in northwestern Senegal. Around the middle of the sixteenth century, this empire fragmented into its component parts, giving rise to the four major Wolof kingdoms of Baol, Kayor, Dyolof proper, and Walo. The subsequent history of these kingdoms is rife with political intrigue, rebellions, exploitation, and warfare, both against one another and against the Moors. European contacts did not become of major significance, except for the slave trade, until the nineteenth century. Gradually, a few commercial centers were established along the coast, the principal ones being the key slave ports of Saint Louis and Gorée. Peanut growing was introduced into Senegal around 1840, and peanuts soon became the main export. In the 1850s, primarily to protect their economic interests, the French launched their first serious attempts to conquer the Wolof kingdoms. The Wolof put up a bitter resistance, but, by the end of the century, they were completely subjugated; French colonial rule lasted until the independence of Senegal in 1960. During this same period, the Wolof, who had a long and ambivalent (often hostile) involvement with Islam, became rapidly and thoroughly Islamicized. The French stimulated the development of urban centers, which became the major sources of Westernization during the twentieth century.

Settlements

The bulk of the Wolof, about 70 to 75 percent, are rural villagers; the remainder constitute an important element in many of the larger urban centers of Senegal and in the Gambian capital of Banjul. The average size of Wolof villages tends to be quite small, with a mean population range of about 50 to 150, but up to 1,000 or 2,000 people inhabit some political centers. Most Wolof villages have one of two types of settlement plan: a village consisting of two or three separate groups of residential compounds with no central focus, or a nucleated village with the residential compounds grouped around a central plaza, where a mosque is usually located. In either type of village, compounds generally consist of square huts (traditionally round, as is still true in Gambia) with walls made of millet stalks or *banco* (an adobelike material), and conical, thatched roofs. In addition, there are several small cooking huts, storehouses, and animal shelters, all enclosed by a millet-stalk fence. More affluent villagers may have one or more modern, multiroom, rectangular houses constructed of cement blocks with tile or corrugated tin roofs. Many Wolof villages have an attached hamlet or encampment of Fulbe who "belong" to the village and herd their cattle.

Economy

Subsistence and Commercial Activities. The subsistence economy is based on agriculture, which in turn depends on rainfall. Wide annual variations in rainfall may result in poor harvests, causing widespread hunger and deprivation. The basic subsistence crop and staple food is millet (mainly *Pennisetum gambicum*); the main cash crop is peanuts (*Arachis hypogaea*). The second major foodstuff is rice, but it is not grown by most villagers and must be purchased. Manioc (cassava) is often a cash crop. The main domestic animals that serve as sources of meat are chickens, goats, and sheep. Fish, another important source of protein, is usually purchased in dried or smoked form. In each village a few people own cattle, but these are considered more as a sort of wealth reserve than a food resource. Beef tends to be eaten only when cattle are killed for a ceremonial feast. There are agricultural cooperatives, centered in the larger villages, that help farmers obtain loans and agricultural machinery and coordinate the marketing of the peanut harvest to the government.

Industrial Arts. In addition to agriculture, many villagers engage in a wide variety of specialized crafts, among them metalworking, leatherworking, weaving, the dyeing of cloth, tailoring, pottery and basketry making, hairdressing, house building, and thatching. There are two types of smiths: blacksmiths, who mostly make agricultural tools, and jewelers, who work in gold or silver. Much less weaving is done than formerly because bolts of manufactured cloth are available for purchase. Some village men are employed outside the villages in modern industries such as phosphate mining.

Trade. Regional and urban marketplaces are the principal centers for the sale and purchase of foodstuffs and other types of goods. Some bartering occurs, but most transactions make use of the national currency, the CFA franc.

Division of Labor. Two major factors structure the division of labor: social status and sex. Certain occupations—smith, leatherworker, and praise singer and drummer—are the prerogatives of males in several hierarchically ranked, castelike social groups; a separate status group formerly did the weaving, but now it is done by descendants of slaves. The making of mortars, pestles, and the like is done by a specialized Fula-speaking group that wanders from village to village. Other male occupations include clearing fields, harvesting, house building, thatching, fishing, herding, and butchering. Men also fulfill most religious and political roles. Female occupations include caring for children; managing the household; planting, weeding, and harvesting crops; gathering wild plants; drawing water; collecting firewood; engaging in petty trade; and practicing midwifery. Women of the castelike groups also make pottery. Both sexes may make basketry.

Land Tenure. Traditionally, agricultural land has been "owned" by patrilineages. Land is inherited patrilineally within a lineage and controlled by the head of the patrilineage, to whom the users pay a tithe or rent (*waref*). This system has been changing since Senegal passed its Domaine Nationale law in 1964. This law attempts to do away with the traditional form of land control, which the government viewed as exploitative, by transferring the ownership of all land to the state. The state then grants parcels to the farmers currently working them, thereby eliminating all types of land rents and tribute. The full implementation of this law could have a major effect on Wolof society.

Kinship

Kin Groups and Descent. The basic social units in a village are the residential groups, which usually occupy a single compound. These groups generally have at their core a patrilocal extended family but may also include unrelated members. Each such corporate group has as its head the senior male of the dominant family unit. Groups of contiguous residential groups usually consist of patrilineages. The larger and more important patrilineages may have segments in several villages. Traditionally, the patrilineages have been the pivotal kin groups at the political-legal level, especially with respect to the control of land and political offices. The senior male of a patrilineage becomes its official head, the *laman*. The Wolof also recognize the *meen*, a matrilineal descent line. There is a good deal of controversy in the literature as to whether or not the meen truly constitutes a matrilineage, and thus whether or not the Wolof have a double descent system (cf. Diop 1985 and Irvine 1973 for opposing viewpoints—pro and con, respectively—on this issue). In modern times the meen does not constitute a corporate group, nor does it have any politico-jural functions. The meen is important because it is believed to be the main source of one's moral character and because it includes those maternal relatives to whom one turns for help in times of trouble such as illness or economic problems.

Kinship Terminology. The Wolof have bifurcate-merging kin terms in the first ascending (parental) generation (i.e., father's brother and mother's sister are called by the same terms as father and mother, respectively, whereas father's sister and mother's brother are called by separate terms). The cousin terminology does not fit any of the standard classifications. Parallel cousins are called by the same terms as one's siblings; cross cousins are differentiated both from parallel cousins and from one another, but they are not called by distinct terms. Rather, they are called "child of the father's sister" and "child of the mother's brother," respectively. There is a joking relationship between cross cousins: one's matrilateral cross cousins are called "master," and one's patrilateral cross cousins are called "slave."

Marriage and Family

Marriage. Social status and kinship are the two factors most influential in regulating marriage. The castelike groups form two pairs of endogamous units: the smiths and leatherworkers constitute one unit, the praise singers and former weavers the other. In addition, the higher-ranking "nobles" and the lower-ranking "slaves" each form endogamous groups. But a "noble" man may marry a "slave" woman under special circumstances. Bilateral cross-cousin marriage is the preferred form, with priority given to marriage between a man and his mother's brother's daughter. Parallel-cousin marriage was once forbidden, but this prohibition is no longer in force. According to Islamic law, a man may have up to four legal wives, and in fact about 45 percent of Wolof men have at least two wives. Sororate and levirate are still practiced. The basic marital residence pattern is patrilocal, although there are some cases of temporary avunculocal residence. Divorce is rather frequent.

Domestic Unit. The main residential group may or may not constitute an integrated household. It is often composed of more than one family unit. Family units that form a single cooking unit and eat together constitute a single domestic unit. Separate domestic units tend to be established within a residential group when there have been disputes between family units or when one of the family units is of a lower social rank and unrelated to the others.

Inheritance. Both inheritance of material goods and succession to important kinship and political roles are determined patrilineally. The Wolof divide these goods and roles into two categories, *nombo* and *alal*. The former term is associated with land, wives, and social positions such as the headship of a residential group, of a patrilineage, or of a village, each of which passes first to a man's brother, secondly to his father's brother's sister, and only when none of these are left do they pass to his son (all but the wives). The term "alal" applies to money, cattle, and houses, which are inherited directly by a man's sons. (Formerly, slaves were also "alal.") As for matrilineal inheritance, it is believed that if the mother is a witch, the children will be witches. If only the father is a witch, the children will be able to see into the witches' world but will not actually be witches.

Socialization. Children are weaned at about 1.5 to 2 years of age, and are carried on the mother's back until that time. Boys live in their mother's hut until they are circumcised at about 8 to 12 years of age. Physical punishment of children is strongly disapproved of and rarely inflicted. Some children attend primary schools, which are available in the larger villages.

Sociopolitical Organization

Social Organization. Wolof society is characterized by a relatively rigid, complex system of social stratification. This system consists of a series of hierarchically ranked social groups in which membership is ascribed by bilateral descent, except when one parent (usually the mother) is of a lower-ranking group, in which case the children are always ranked in the lower group. In the literature, these groups are usually called "castes" or, less frequently, "social classes." The application of these concepts to the Wolof data has created analytical problems rather than increasing understanding of the system; thus, the component groups will be referred to here as status groups. These status groups are organized into three major hierarchical levels. First, there is an upper level that in preconquest times was divided into several status groups including royalty and nobility; the socially prominent commoners (i.e., village and regional chiefs, large landowners, and religious leaders); peasants; and slaves of the Crown, who were ranked equivalent with the prominent commoners, and from whom were drawn the king's warriors. In modern times, these groups have essentially merged into a single status group, the nobility. Second is the level of the occupationally defined status groups—smiths, leatherworkers, and *griots* (praise singers and musicians), together with the former weavers. The third level is composed of the descendants of slaves. The latter are differentiated into status groups that are named and ranked according to the status groups of their former masters (e.g., slave–praise singer). This stratification system is a crucial aspect of village social life and remains significant in the urban areas.

Political Organization. Wolof politics have been characterized by authoritarianism, manipulation, exploitation, intrigue, and factionalism. The four traditional kingdoms had basically similar political systems: a complex hierarchy of political officials and territorial commands headed by a ruler whose power depended to an important extent upon his slave warriors. These political structures were destroyed by the French conquest and replaced by the system of French colonial administration. The latter, in turn, was replaced by the current Senegalese national state. Political organization at the village level has retained many traditional features, but there is much local and regional variation. The top political officials in most villages are of noble status. The office of village chief, the *borom dekk*, is hereditary within the patrilineage of the village founder, but the village notables (who include the patrilineage heads) also have a voice in his selection, and the official appointment must be made by a government official. The chief is officially responsible for administering village affairs, collecting taxes, maintaining order in the village, and acting as an intermediary between villagers and higher-level officials. The chief is usually also a Muslim religious leader, a *seriñ* (marabout). To assist him, the chief may appoint a council selected from the most important village notables. The chief also appoints the *yélimaan* (imam) and the *saltigé*. The imam is the religious leader of the village and leads the prayers in the mosque. The saltigé, whose position is hereditary within a particular patrilineage, was traditionally the leader of the village warriors and of hunting parties. Nowadays he directs the public works in the village and acts as an intermediary between the young men of the village and the chief. The heads of the major patrilineages are politically very influential, especially the ones who are also *chefs de quartier* (i.e., heads of the sectors into which some villages are divided for particular activities or situations). Finally, there are the heads of the residential compounds.

Social Control. The system of social control is characterized by hierarchy, reciprocity, suppression of overt hostility, and the use of intermediaries to settle disputes. Gossip and ridicule, or fear of them, are effective means of social control because of the importance of maintaining one's status and prestige. Formal controls are exercised by the courts and by political officials—especially the village chief and regional officials. People readily resort to the courts to settle important differences. Muslim tribunals are headed by a *qadi*, who judges cases on the basis of Malikite law or traditional customs (*ada*), depending on the matter at issue; civil courts administer a legal system derived from French law.

Conflict. In modern times, land, marital disputes, and political factionalism are the major sources of conflict in the villages. Physical violence rarely occurs except in the political arena.

Religion and Expressive Culture

Religious Beliefs. Nearly all Wolof are Muslims; they are mainly organized into two Sufi orders or brotherhoods, the Tijaniyya and the Muridiyya. Men become members of an order upon circumcision, whereas women become members upon marriage, joining the same order as their husbands. The main tenets of Islam are generally adhered to, but the Wolof version of Islam clearly shows an emphasis on social relations rather than on abstract theology. Along with Islam, there is continuing adherence to many traditional (i.e., pre-Islamic) magicoreligious beliefs and practices. This traditional system emphasizes belief in malevolent spirits (jinn) and witches and the need to protect oneself from them.

Religious Practitioners. Among Muslims, the basic complementary religious roles are those of *taalibé*, a disciple, and marabout (seriñ), a religious leader. There is a hierarchy of marabouts ranging from those who have only an elementary knowledge of the Quran and little influence, up to the powerful heads of the Sufi orders. There is also the *muqaddam*, who has authority to induct new members into a order, and the imam (yélimaan). Within the traditional magico-religious system, there are a variety of ritual specialists, including the *jabarkat*, who is a combination shaman and sorcerer; the *lugakat*, who magically cures victims of snakebite; the *ndëpukat*, usually a female, who performs the *ndëp* ceremony to cure the mentally ill; and the *botal mbar*, who is in charge of newly circumcised boys.

Ceremonies. The Wolof observe the major Muslim festivals, the most important for them being Korité, the feast at the end of Ramadan, and Tabaski, the feast of the sacrifice of sheep. The principal life-cycle ceremonies include the naming ceremony (*nggentée*), and the circumcision ceremony for boys. It is likely that circumcision was a pre-Islamic Wolof custom, given that the key ritual specialists and practices are non-Islamic.

Arts. There is a striking lack of emphasis on art. Most notably, the Wolof do not carve wooden sculptures or masks as many other West African peoples do. Dancing is performed mostly by women of the praise-singer group. Several musical instruments are played, especially drums and a type of guitar called *xalam*. Wandering actors occasionally perform in the villages at night, singing and dancing satirical skits that become more and more lewd as the night deepens. Smiths make filigree jewelry.

Medicine. The Wolof make use of most available medication and medical practitioners—modern, Muslim, or traditional. Nearly all Wolof wear numerous amulets that are believed to have the power to protect the wearer from illness, evil spirits, witchcraft, or other harm. The most common function of marabouts at the village level is to make these amulets, which consist of passages from the Quran written on slips of paper encased in leather packets. The shaman (jabarkat) may also be hired to make amulets, in which case the leather casings contain pieces of magical roots or leaves.

Death and Afterlife. After the death of a person, the usual Muslim funeral ceremonies are followed. Burial is within a few hours unless the death occurs at night. Formerly, members of the praise-singer group were "buried" in hollow baobab trees, so as not to contaminate the earth. Suicide is rare, and it is believed that the soul of a suicide goes straight to hell.

Bibliography

Diop, Abdoulaye-Bara (1981). *La société wolof: Tradition et changement*. Paris: Éditions Karthala.

Diop, Abdoulaye-Bara (1985). *La famille wolof: Tradition et changement*. Paris: Éditions Karthala.

Gamble, David P. (1957). *The Wolof of Senegambia*. Ethnographic Survey of Africa, Western Africa, Part 14. London: International African Institute.

Irvine, Judith T. (1973). "Caste and Communication in a Wolof Village." Ph.D. dissertation, University of Pennsylvania.

Lagacé, Robert O. (1963–1964). "Ethnographic Fieldnotes." Manuscript.

ROBERT O. LAGACÉ

Xhosa

ETHNONYMS: Caffre, Cafre, Isixhosa, Kaffer, Kaffir, Koosa, Southern Nguni, Xosa

"Xhosa" is the generic name used for a number of related cultural groups in South Africa. Xhosa groups include the Mpondo, Bomvana, Bhaca, Thembu, Mpondomise, Xesibe, Mfengu, Hlubi, and the Xhosa proper. These Southern Nguni peoples, as they are sometimes called, share a common language, Isixhosa, and are culturally similar to one another. Because of their contact with other peoples in the area over the centuries and the strong influence of colonial powers, as well as missionary contact, it is difficult speak of the traditional culture of the Xhosa. Rather, Xhosa culture today is a blend that has resulted from these influences and others. The Xhosa today are much involved in South African political affairs and play a major role in the postapartheid government.

The traditional homeland of the Xhosa was located on the southeastern seaboard of the Republic of South Africa in an area that is currently divided politically into two independent states, Transkei and Ciskei. In 1989 the estimated number of Xhosa living in Transkei was 3,500,000 and in Ciskei, 1,000,000. Xhosa also live in South African cities—especially Cape Town, Port Elizabeth, and East London—and on farms outside Transkei and Ciskei. In 1986 the total population of Xhosa in South Africa was estimated at approximately six million.

The Xhosa-speaking peoples originally consisted of three main groups: the Pondo, the Tembu, and the Xhosa proper. They all spoke the same language and shared the same belief that their culture originated at the headwaters of the Dedesi River. Their customs and beliefs were similar, generally centering around the herding of cattle. They were linked to one another through intermarriage as well as by the diplomatic, military, and political alliances they formed. Through the centuries, internal dissension and further subdivision, contact with San and Khoi-speaking peoples whose territories they overran and conquered, and the arrival of refugees from wars in Natal broke the original Xhosa-speaking nations into diversified chiefdoms and peoples. Nevertheless, the basic division of the Xhosa speakers into Pondo, Tembu, and Xhosa still remains.

In the sixteenth and seventeenth centuries the Nguni herded cattle, hunted game, and cultivated sorghum. They lived in beehive-shaped huts in scattered homesteads and were ruled by chiefs. One of the main reasons for Xhosa expansion was the splitting off of the sons of reigning chiefs to found new chiefdoms of their own, which relieved the political pressure at the center of the kingdom. Movement was also precipitated by the need to find new hunting grounds and fresh pastures. This was a slow process because of the need to burn down the forest to provide grazing prior to occupation.

The Xhosa traditionally were not a nomadic people, although the need for large pastures to accommodate expanding herds of cattle encouraged steady movement. Xhosa kraals, or cattle enclosures, were surrounded by huts. The kraals formed family clusters tied by allegiance to the Great Place, the principle kraal, that of the chief. The Great Place was usually only a modest grouping of huts.

A Xhosa family homestead was known as an *umzi* (pl. *imizi*), and several adjoining imizi formed a village. An umzi generally housed an extended family, including the head of the family; his wives, children, and aging parents; his married sons and their families; and his unmarried daughters. The huts faced east, toward the sun, and stood in a semicircle around the main focus of their communal existence, the kraal. In the case of a man rich in cattle, who had more than than one wife, each wife had a household of perhaps three huts: a main hut for living and cooking, a second hut for children and visitors, and a third as a storeroom. Close to these huts and never too far from the stream from which they were watered were the gardens in which were cultivated the limited number of crops the Xhosa raised seasonally: cereals such as sorghum, as well as maize, pumpkins, and melons.

Apart from its gardens, a village or group of villages would be surrounded by a substantial territory that represented the hunting grounds and pastures that were common to all.

Villages could contain from fifteen to fifty huts and could be as close as 0.4 kilometers from one another or as far as four to five hours' away by footpath. The inhabitants of a village, or group of villages, could be members of a chiefdom, the many and complex lineages of which could be traced back to a common ancestor. There was generally a local chief, or headman, who ruled over the kraals and who was subordinate to a great chief of a whole district.

Cattle were the focal point of Xhosa existence. Life literally circled around them. Cattle intricately bound together the material realm with the sacred. They were the medium of sacrifice to the ancestral spirits, linking the living with the dead. They represented the future, because they sealed the marriage bond. They also represented wealth and stability. In ordinary daily life, they supplied the principal item of the diet, milk, as well as meat for occassional feasting and leather for clothing. Cattle were viewed as individually as the members of the family itself. The Xhosa language was profuse with varieties of descriptive terms for cattle, mainly based on color combinations and the shapes of the horns.

The Xhosa were bound in their daily lives and actions by reverence for and fear of their ancestors, whose spirits were believed to be omnipresent. If these spirits were offended, they would express their displeasure by inflicting illness, accident, or some other disorder. They were appeased through sacrifice. The sacrificial beasts had to be the best of the herd. During the sacrifice, the slaughterer cut open the belly, thrust his arm up to the heart, and wrenched out the arteries. These ceremonies took place in the cattle kraal and the skulls of the sacrificial animals were placed at the gate posts.

An important traditional value of Xhosa culture is *ubuntu*, or humanness. At the core of ubuntu is the preservation and stability of the whole. An example of its application is that, in times of war, women and children were never killed. During their anticolonial wars, Xhosa were known to kill White men and their grown sons ruthlessly, at the feet of their wives and sisters; they spared women and children, however, despite the fact that the same kindness was not reciprocated by their enemies.

Bibliography

Costello, Dawn (1990). *Not Only for Its Beauty: Beadwork and Its Cultural Significnce among the Xhosa-Speaking Peoples*. Pretoria: University of South Africa.

Hodgson, Janet (1982). *The God of the Xhosa*. Cape Town: Oxford University Press.

Mostert, Noel (1992). *Frontiers: The Epic of South Africa's Creation and the Tragedy of the Xhosa People*. New York: Albert A. Knopf.

Yakö

ETHNONYM: Yakurr (the official Nigerian spelling)

Orientation

Identification. The Yakö numbered 38,204 people at the last published census (1953) that listed their settlements separately. They have for the most part been administered from Obubra Town, but have variously been included in Ogoja Province (under British and early Nigerian administration), in Cross River State (in the 1970s) and, in Akwa Ibom State of southeastern Nigeria, West Africa.

Location. The territory of the Yakö, just over 150 square kilometers in area, centers on 5°50′ N and 8°15′ E and lies south and west of the middle Cross River. By road, the area is about 110 kilometers north of Calabar. The valleys are prone to flooding in the wet season; movement along the ridges is easier. The wet season begins with moderate rain in April and May, and heavier rains commence in June. In July there may be a break in the rains, but by August heavy rains return and normally continue until November, when there is a sharp drop in precipitation, followed by a drought that lasts from December to March. The drought of the dry season is exaggerated by the geology. As the population is concentrated into five very large settlements, the problem of obtaining a good water supply in the dry season has long been of concern to the people.

The natural vegetation of the area is that of dense tropical forest, transitional between the evergreen equatorial forest and the mixed deciduous forest of the area farther north. Much of this forest remains, or did until the latter half of the twentieth century, in the wettest, low-lying areas that present the greatest problem both for farming and for timber extraction. The drier, upland areas have, however, been farmed to the extent that few trees of any size remain. In consequence of this deforestation and because of the activities of hunters, few large mammals remain: elephants were extinct by the beginning of the twentieth century; buffalo were disappearing by the 1960s; leopards have long been rare; hippopotamuses, which were not uncommon on the Cross River while the "Dane gun" was the usual weapon of the hunter, have diminished in numbers owing to the increase in sophisticated weaponry since the Biafran war. Bush pigs, antelope, monkeys, lemurs, civets, porcupines, and pangolins, all formerly common animals, are now suffering severely, both from direct attack by humans and, more indirectly, from the loss of habitat.

Demography. The population of the Yakö has increased markedly throughout the twentieth century. By the mid-1930s, the population was reported to have increased "rapidly" over the previous two generations. That this increase has certainly continued may be judged from the fact that a careful estimate of the population of the main town, Ugep, in 1935 placed it at 11,000, but that in 1953 this figure had risen to 17,567, despite the absence of any significant immigration.

Linguistic Affiliation. The main language, Kö, is of the Eastern Subgroup of the Delta-Cross Division (Cook 1969) of the Cross River Subbranch (Greenberg 1963) of the Benue-Congo Language Division. Its links are thus to languages to the south and east of Nigeria. Among four of the five main Yakö towns, only minor dialectal differences exist; the language of the town of Ekuri, in which no social research has been done but which is claimed to be Yakö, is classified by linguists as a markedly different dialect.

History and Cultural Relations

For the history of the Yakö prior to the twentieth century, one is dependent on oral tradition, first collected in the mid-1930s. It has been related that the ancestors of the Yakö migrated northward, relatively recently and perhaps as late as the early nineteenth century, from the area of the Oban Hills, which lie to the southeast. These traditions sometimes suggest that various non-Yakö groups, as well as the proto-Yakö, dispersed from this area; however, the only other people known to share this tradition with the Yakö are the Olulumo of Okuni, who live separated from them, much farther up the Cross River, near Ikom. According to Yakö traditional accounts, the dispersal took place as a consequence of quarrels; their ancestors came overland, not by the river, in various groups over a number of years. According to these accounts, the migrants settled first at the present-day agro-towns of Idomi, Nko and Umor (present-day Ugep). Discontent at Umor led to the founding of Ekuri and Nkpani by dissidents. According to other traditional accounts, however, the residents of small, matrilineally based hamlets in the vicinity of these towns moved for safety into the security of the larger settlements because of warfare. These two sets of traditions are not ultimately incompatible. Traditions do not elaborate the nature of the "warfare," and there does not appear to have been either one major enemy or a particular fear of raids by external slave traders. There are, nevertheless, stories of sporadic conflict between the major Yakö towns, and also between Nko and the Mbembe-speaking village-group of Adun. Indeed, both the Adun and the Nko agree that the Igbo speakers now living in the border area between them are settlers who were invited in to form a buffer zone between their two societies. A further factor may have been that the members of some Yakö men's societies were particularly noted as headhunters. This activity was common to most local groups, but it is agreed, both by the Yakö themselves and by their neighbors, that they were outstanding for their success in this field. The fact that head-hunting was ritually forbidden only between fellow townsfolk, not between members of the different Yakö towns, may be a major factor in accounting for the striking size of the Yakö settlements (which were much larger than those of the neighboring Mbembe, for example, who ritually prohibited head-hunting between linked but separated villages). European influence began to have an effect only in the last years of the nineteenth century. In 1895 the British were engaged in extending their influence up the Cross River, particularly with a view to breaking the power of certain (non-Yakö) river trading settlements that were seeking to control all traffic on the river. That year, a small expedition of 200 members of the Constabulary and their indigenous allies attacked the Ekumuru town of Ediba, from which some traders regularly went to deal with the Yakö. Serious clashes took place the following year at the Yakö settlement of Ekuri, near the river. According to Adun traditions, influential traders had organized a resistance force consisting of groups from the Adun as well as the Yakö. This force was defeated, however, and Ekuri was burned by the British, apparently ending concerted opposition, although it was reported in 1905 that the Ekuri themselves were still defiant. By this time, however, a rudimentary administrative system had been established over the Yakö area, and warfare, although not at first including head-hunting, was effectively stopped. Prior to the establishment of British control, the main outsiders to visit the Yakö areas regularly were a few traders based in villages farther down the Cross River, especially from the area of Agwa Aguna. Individual traders established personal links with a particular town and enjoyed protected passage between that town and the river. In addition, associated with the traders, there came also cult experts, who seem to have organized profitable group trips to consult certain well-known oracles (especially the "Long Juju," in the Agwa Aguna area). Thus, although travel was not easy for anyone prior to the establishment of peaceful conditions by the British government, trade goods and new cults were able to circulate. Moreover, there was a considerable degree of cultural borrowing, so that, for example, men's associations with the same name have long been established not only in the different Yakö settlements but also in neighboring non-Yakö villages. Best-known of these associations was the Ekpe Society of Calabar, which many traders joined, probably because it provided them with useful links to local influential men, who considered membership prestigious. Local branches of Ekpe were certainly established in the nineteenth century: they are recorded by the first district officers in 1902. Christian missions and schools had also been established by the early 1930s, and by that time the district officers were making efforts to involve younger local men in new forms of administration. By the 1960s, the area had a high rate of literacy and political sophistication. By then, too, a few Yakö men who had gone on to higher and technical education were pursuing prominent careers outside the district. There was also some temporary migration of unskilled workers to the towns; this migration owed less to dire necessity than to the fact that young men were reluctant to earn money as hired laborers at home, perhaps because hired labor had become associated with work done by the somewhat despised, Igbo laborers who had immigrated temporarily from the Abakaliki area. The construction in the late 1960s and 1970s of a road—ultimately stretching from Enugu to Calabar through the western end of the Yakö area, with a bridge over the Cross River (replacing a somewhat problematic ferry crossing)—has greatly increased contacts with, and movement toward, the outside world. The district, although not entirely unscathed, was less damaged than most of eastern Nigeria by the events of the Biafran war, and it is still a predominantly agricultural district. No detailed study has been undertaken in this area since that war and since the road was built.

Settlements

The Yakö live in large, compact, agro-towns that rank in size with many Yoruba towns. These towns have been referred to in the anthropological literature as "villages" only because most of their inhabitants farm. Each of the five Yakö towns was, prior to British rule, a politically independent unit, and the people began to refer to themselves as "Yakurr," instead of identifying themselves by the name of their town, only in the postindependence years. Each town except Idomi is divided into three or four small residential areas, or wards—*yekpatu* (sing. *kekpatu*). Only exceptionally do such groups have any tradition of ultimate common descent; rather they are/were purely residential groups whose inhabitants farmed in the same general area. They were the main secular political units of the town, but they formed important ritual units only insofar as the rites were concerned with the defense of the area from external dangers. Until the post-1945 period, when questions of public health began to be seriously considered, a Yakö village seemed to be a continuous spread of compounds separated only by narrow alleyways. Each ward, however, had its own central assembly place, where certain shrines were located, where ward leaders and ward-based men's associations met, and where the men of an age set, organized on a ward rather than on a townwide basis, might also be called to meet. From the assembly place of each ward, a path led to the approximate center of the village, where a rather larger assembly place was located, close to the substantial compound of the town head. The compounds that composed the wards were normally approached through narrow alleyways leading into enclosed spaces that focused on the house of the compound head, which was flanked on both sides by the houses of his wives, each of whom was entitled to her own house. So far as possible, sons built within their father's compound. The houses were built of wood or, more usually, of mud daubed with wattle, and were roofed with a palm-frond thatch. This material decayed rapidly, and, because the houses of the dead were not repaired, there was usually room in the traditional compound for new houses or new occupants as they were needed.

Economy

Subsistence and Commercial Activities. The Yakö are primarily agriculturists. Their main crop, except where the soil is exhausted, is the yam, and traditionally all other cultivation was subordinated to its requirements; however, subsidiary crops such as cocoyams, maize, okra, and pumpkins are also grown. Where the soil is poor, cassava, which is less demanding, may be grown instead of yams. In very wet areas, rice is a relatively recent introduction. Tree crops—bananas, plantains, kola nuts, papaws, and coconuts—are grown within the village and along farm paths. The most important tree, however, is the oil palm, which is planted in groves and is protected when found growing wild in the bush. The Yakö acquire palm wine by climbing the tree and tapping the inflorescence; they can therefore satisfy their desire for wine without destroying the tree. The traditional social and ritual activities of the Yakö did not preclude their active involvement in palm-nut collection. Indeed, it seems to have been palm oil that particularly brought traders to the Yakö areas, and trade in palm oil long supplied Yakö men with their only important cash income.

Small domestic animals have long been of some significance: cats (as catchers of vermin), dogs (as scavengers), and chickens were found in almost every household. Sheep and dwarf goats were quite common. There were a few pigs and ducks, the latter valued particularly for ritual because of their association with water and "coolness." Originally, dwarf cattle were kept primarily as status symbols by a few wealthy men, but during the colonial period some of these animals were sold to Igbo, who came to buy them for reasons that were also related to prestige. In the 1950s an attempt was made by the veterinary service to make such animals of economic significance, and, to this end, bulls of a larger breed were lent to the Yakö towns.

Industrial Arts. There were very few specialist artisans among the Yakö. Exceptions were those who carved wooden ritual and ceremonial objects and other woodworkers. Blacksmiths were itinerant non-Yakö. There was no strong tradition of pottery or basket making—pots and baskets have long been supplied by traders. On the other hand, new skills have rapidly appeared: bicycle repairer, tailor, photographer, and lorry mechanic have become quite common occupations for young men.

Trade. Most local traders operated on a very small scale. The most common form of trading was carried on by men who, usually while also pursuing farming activities, bought up small quantities of palm oil from local households and transported it to the trading depots on the Cross River. Women were also petty traders, in palm kernels. Trade at the end of the nineteenth century seems to have centered on the exportation of palm oil and the importation of cloth, gunpowder, and salt. Fom then on, and right up through to the 1950s, trade experienced a steady growth, but one that was limited by the restrictions on the availability of products for sale. Four of the five Yakö towns lack easy access by water to the Cross River, and, for that reason, although the traders from downriver were, in general, keen to buy yams (and the Yakö had plenty of them), yams did not fetch a price high enough to warrant the cost of hiring people to carry them on their heads to collection points. Thus, until the road network was substantially improved, palm oil continued to be the main export. Each Yakö town had a biweekly market, but, until the 1940s and 1950s, these remained essentially places for the exchange of household surpluses and local food specialties. Non-Yakö women brought to market dried fish and various vegetable produce, and hunters brought dried meat from the forests to the east. To some extent, non-Yakö male traders seem to have entertained exaggerated fears of Yakö headhunting and to have been discouraged from making casual expeditions into Yakö territory, although a few who had good contacts visited regularly. The building of the bridge over the Cross River and of the road linking Calabar and Enugu has obviously transformed this situation.

Division of Labor. Traditionally, there was a complex formula for determining who did what aspect of farm work. At its simplest, men, at the beginning of the farming year, cleared the bush from the land to be farmed in that season. This is usually heavy work, and traditionally it was done by working parties of patrikinsmen, the size of which was related to the prestige of the farmer concerned. Clearing parties did the basic work, but the farmer, either on his own or with a small group of kinsmen, had to dig out most of the smaller roots and collect and burn the rubbish. Women then hoed the yam hills, and men planted the yams. Women weeded the crop and later put in plants other than yams on the sides of the mounds; men trained the yam vines so that they grew up the supports placed between every few yam hills. Women continued to weed throughout the growing season. At harvest time, the farmer dug up his yams and, if he had a substantial farm, carefully organized women and younger men so that they washed and carried the yams to his storehouse, where they were checked and tied separately to racks in big "barns." The main point at which labor constrained farming was in the hoeing of yam mounds: the Yakö, like the Mbembe, regarded it as beneath the dignity of a mature farmer to hoe his own yam mounds. Therefore, from the 1920s onward, working parties from northeastern Igbo groups on the right bank of the Cross River have been hired to do this work, at which they are particularly skilled. They work with hoes far larger than those used by Yakö women.

Land Tenure. Government legislation has made most Nigerian land, in principle, alienable, which must be effecting great changes in Yakö society. Until this legislation was passed, Yakö land had been considered inalienable. Land was claimed by the five agro-towns, each of which had its own exclusive territory. Beneath this level, the land was divided into great blocks extending outward from the town itself, with each block claimed by one of the wards of the town. The ward head had ultimate secular responsibility for the ward land, both on ordinary occasions (e.g., choosing the day the paths from the ward to the farmland were to be cleared at the beginning of the farming season), and in the event of serious disputes. These disputes, in practice, were likely to occur between the members of different patrikin groups because each ward was divided up territorially into patrilineal kin groups, within which most rights to land were inherited. Between these groups, there was no assertion of ultimate common descent; therefore, disputes could not be settled by senior kinsmen. It was the ward head and the prominent men within the ward, recognized formally as the leaders of the ward as a spatial unit, who had to ensure that quarrels over land did not disrupt the community. The lands of the different patrikin groups within a ward were often intermingled, thus occasioning fairly frequent disputes. In general, however, the men of one such kin group would, in any one year, make their farms along the same minor farm path. A senior man of the kin group, acting as the "Farm-Path Elder," sought to resolve any problems over land between men of the kin group. A young man, when he married, was allocated some of his father's land by his father; initially his farm would almost certainly be small, restricted by the limited number of essential seed yams that he and his wife could initially amass. When his yams grew in number, so that his father could no longer be expected to provide for him directly, the father was expected to go to the Farm-Path Elder to ask for land on the son's behalf. Thus plots of land were not necessarily passed directly from father to son; most land was controlled by the patrilineage, which retained authority over the plots once they had been initially cleared from forest, even though they were normally left fallow after one season's crops had been harvested. The normal expectation was that a man could claim sufficient land to plant all his seed yams, and in the mid-1930s it was commonplace for men of the same lineage to have farms of different sizes, depending upon their resources in yams and on the skill and dedication of the work force that they were able to command. As a consequence, old men seldom had the largest farms. Until the land of the ward as a whole came to be perceived as scarce, a man who came from a lineage that for some reason was short of land found it a relatively cheap and simple matter to obtain temporary rights to land in the area of a different lineage. Matrilineal kin groups claimed certain residuary rights to particular tracts of land. By the 1930s, these rights normally had been restricted to that of matrikin to enter such tracts on the death of an elder and freely to take palm wine from any suitable tree, even one already prepared for tapping by a man with a patrilineal claim to the land. The Forestry Department then paid a royalty to the town for felling certain particularly valuable timber in these areas, and the matrikin groups immediately and successfully claimed a share. Matrikin groups have ritual associations with water; accordingly, it was the matrikin and not the patrikin who could claim the right to any groves of the valuable raffia palm, which must be planted in swamps.

Kinship

Kin Groups and Descent. The Yakö were the first group with double unilineal descent to be well described. The lowest-level patrilineal group was the *eponama* (pl. *yeponama*), which traced descent to a common ancestry, three to five generations back. The men of this group normally lived with their wives in a cluster of several adjacent compounds and recognized a senior man as their head, although the position was not formally recognized. These patrilineages were aggregated into patriclans (*yepun;* sing. *kepun*) that were also territorially compact. Each had a name that referred both to the group and to its dwelling area. In some contexts, the men would imply that they shared common descent from a patrilineal ancestor, but, when they were quarreling, they would assert distinct origins. Nevertheless, they all recognized the relevance of a common shrine (*e-pund-det;* lit. "shrine of the patriclan"), at which the dead of the patriclan were supplicated by the *obot kepun*, a formal, primarily secular, official. This man was, ex officio, one of the leaders of the ward, although the majority of ward leaders were not heads of patriclans. All those born within the patriclan were bound by rules of exogamy. Matriclans (*yajima;* sing. *lejima*) were complementary to the patrilineal kin groups. Because residence was patrilocal for men whereas women moved out, the members of any matrilineal group were necessarily dispersed within a town and, to a limited extent (limited because most marriages were endogamous within a town), between towns. Formally, the rights and duties of the two sets of kin groups did not conflict. Patrikin were concerned with land, residence, and work. Matrikin groups were concerned with the transmission of property that could be physically moved and with claims over individuals. At death, an individual's wealth went to the matrikin, and responsibility for debts was borne by them. If an individual injured or killed another, recompense was paid between matrikin. A sorcerer was thought to be able to attack only a junior matrilineal relative, just as, in the past, only a senior matrikinsman could sell a junior into slavery. The ties of matrikinship were deeply ambivalent.

Kinship Terminology. Kinship terminology is complicated by the necessity, in formal contexts, of expressing relationships to Ego's own matrilineage and own patrilineage, as well as relationships to Ego's father's matrilineage and mother's patrilineage. In practice, most kin are addressed by name most of the time, and kinship terms are used primarily as terms of reference, except where particular deference—usually because of a marked difference in age—needs to be expressed, or where groups of kin gather for rites and ceremonies and have specific rights and duties—particularly at funerals. The mother's brother and all senior male matrikin are referred to by the same term as the one used for sons of Ego's own mother and her sisters: it is most simply translated as "brother"; however, the mother's brother may be addressed by a respectful term that is also used when speaking of one's own father. The father's brother is referred to and addressed by the term used for one's own father, and his children are, literally, "children of the father." A single reciprocal term (*okpan;* pl. *yakpay*) is used between Ego and the mother's patrikin and between Ego and children of the father's matrikin (and, thus, between Ego and the children of the mother's brother).

Marriage and Family

Marriage. The nuclear family is the nucleus of the Yakö household, but the majority of middle-aged men have more than one wife; older men, however, tend not to be notably polygamous. Sororal polygamy was not approved. Men very seldom divorced their wives, but wives, certainly since at least the early twentieth century, have had considerable liberty to leave marriages they disliked and remarry, provided only that they did not remarry within the same patriclan. The patriclan that supplicates at the same e-pun-det shrine is an exogamous unit (despite any gossip about what may have been different ultimate origins). The matrilineage (but not the matriclan) is also exogamous. Kin are, of course, involved in marriage: the patrikin of the groom are concerned with the bride who is coming to live in their midst; her matrikin, who will be replenished through her offspring, are concerned ritually with her fertility, and, traditionally, they organized, for a girl's first marriage, both visits to matrilineal shrines and a clitoridectomy rite (female circumcision was common throughout much of the middle Cross River area). Other groups are, however, involved in marriages even more than the kin. For a first marriage, the age mates of the bride's mother and those of the groom's father play very important roles; a married couple turn for help in any marital difficulty mainly to their age mates, not to their kin. Ultimately, the town as a whole is concerned with the marriage of its women, given that the great majority of marriages are endogamous within the town.

Domestic Unit. Traditionally, a girl did not take up residence with her husband's people until the birth of their first child. In her husband's compound, she had her own house and was not subservient to the wives who were already in residence. In the event of divorce, the wife had the right to take her younger children with her. Her daughters stayed with her and her new husband until they themselves married. Her sons were supposed to return to their father's compound, at least when they were old enough to farm; however, in practice, it seems to have been quite common for them to become effective adoptees into the patrikin groups of the stepfather.

Inheritance. The fact that houses and land have traditionally gone to patrikin and movable goods to matrikin is crucial to the distinct existence of patrikin and matrikin groups. By the mid-1930s, however, it was being reported that sons resented the transmission of the father's wealth to the matrikin. Whether inheritance is now effectively patrilineal is doubtful because debts are also inherited by the matrilineal heir. The Yakö have not been a heavily indebted people, but the outstanding men who had the most property to leave were likely to join various men's societies and omit to pay their full fees, which consequently became charges on their heirs; inheritance was not an unmixed blessing. There was no strict rule about inheritance in relation to particular children. Houses of the dead were allowed to fall into ruin, and the sites were then claimed by sons about to marry. Fallow land passed within the patrilineage, but not by strict division to brothers or sons. The main matrilineal heir was the person who was prepared to take responsibility for debts and the general cost of the funeral; this person then allocated the deceased's personal possessions to the kin, taking the main share for himself or herself.

Socialization. In Yakö society, as in others in the area, great emphasis was placed on a child becoming a well-behaved member of his or her age set. Children were taught from the age of 6 or 7 that they must not quarrel with their age mates; rather, they must cultivate the self-discipline to meet obligations toward them and settle any disputes in an amicable manner. It is preferable to accept decisions counter to one's interests than to alienate one's age mates.

Sociopolitical Organization

Although indigenous political integration did not extend beyond each agro-town, it is clear that so many people were resident in these settlements that their organization and the maintenance of relatively peaceful and orderly conditions within these towns depended on a high level of social and political skill.

Social Organization. Each town was divided into wards, which in turn were subdivided into smaller territorial units claimed by patriclans. Within each ward, age sets cut across these smaller units and united men and women of the same age, regardless of kin affiliation. The political significance of this arrangement was, of course, particularly salient for men because they were residentially more restricted to patrikin areas than were the women. Each man was in many respects ultimately dependent on his age mates rather than on his kin. Since adjacent age sets were traditionally hostile to each other, rather like rival groups of football supporters, each set developed a strong esprit de corps that was an important counter to kin rivalries and provided a firm basis for work groups to be mobilized for communal activities on behalf of the ward. The many societies provided additional territorial rather than kinship links; the most important of them were solely for men and operated on a townwide basis. These societies imposed sanctions, sometimes as severe as death, on those who flouted their rules. They therefore became targets for action by the colonial administration in the very early years of the twentieth century. By the mid-1930s, it was already difficult to determine their precise political significance in the indigenous system. It seems probable, however, given the fact that their entrance fees were high, that they were to some extent vehicles for the exercise of power by the more wealthy members of the community.

Social Control. Problems of social control, when they involved fellow group members, were dealt with by the leaders of those groups; however, because the Yakö lived in such large settlements, other control mechanisms were also utilized, notably the granting of rights to important men's societies to punish particular categories of offenders by seizing and eating their matrikin's livestock. It was then in the interest of these kin to bring the recalcitrant members into line. As male matrikin were dispersed, this system had the advantage that such a sanction did not antagonize territorial groups.

Conflict. There was a specific war society (*eblembe*) for each town. The most meritorious way of entry into such a society was by payment of a fee and proof of success as a warrior, especially the presentation of an enemy's head. Officeholders had titles indicating their military functions (e.g., Leader on the Path and Leader of the Rear Guard). Upon the death of a member, it was the duty of his patrilineage to supply a successor and pay a joining fee.

Religion and Expressive Culture

Religious Beliefs. The Yakö recognized a creator, Obasi, who was invoked as the ultimate power in many rituals and at many shrines, but their beliefs about Obasi were not elaborated. More immediately significant were the Dead, the Yabö (who were not necessarily direct ancestors) and the various spirit agencies that might act independently (but more commonly were intermediaries with the Dead, who were the source of blessings and of all the information revealed to diviners). The Yakö borrowed and incorporated a wide range of cults from neighboring peoples, fitting any that seemed powerful into the appropriate category of spirit agency, hoping that they would be an effective defense against witches, sorcerers, and other malign influences. Each territorial and kin-based group had at least one associated cult. The Yakö were unusual as compared with the neighboring Mbembe (who were also people with double unilineal descent) in that they ascribed mystical powers to matrilineal priests. The head of a matriclan was a male priest who was believed through his induction rite to gain fellowship with the Dead: this enabled his spirit, or *kidom*, to mingle with them. By ritual, he could make fertile both women and the earth itself. Jointly, the matrilineal priests within each town performed the seasonal rituals that were considered essential for the well-being of all its people. These rituals, because they united people across the great secular divisions between wards and patrikin, seem to have been politically crucial in that they created a sense of town unity that transcended these divisions. The leader of the village, the *obot lopon*, was the ritually senior matriclan priest; as such, no matter what his patrilineal affiliation, he took up residence in a particular compound that was adjacent to the ritual center of the matrilineal cult. The obot lopon was in close contact with, and in some sense dominant over, the town's corporation of diviners. The final induction of a new diviner into the corporation depended on formal acceptance by the obot lopon. Matriclan priests and diviners each wore on one finger a ring given to them in the ritual of induction. It was this ring that enabled them to "see" and move among the Dead and the water-traveling sorcerers, who included sorcerers from the Dead among their number. Some believed that the wearer, however sick, could not die until this ring was removed. Priests and diviners were linked in ritual; in the absence of formal dogma, much of what people believed, the essential ideology, depended on what they were told by diviners when these were consulted about illness and misfortune. Matriclan priests seem generally to have denied that they used their powers for nefarious purposes, but the diviners so commonly ascribed death and illness to the sorcery activities of the priests that their clients must have doubted their innocence. The strength of the people's beliefs in the mystical powers of the matriclan priests seems to account for the politically significant role of the matriclan priests in uniting each town through matrilineal rituals, although effective secular power seems to have rested with the leaders of the wards. The balance was achieved not by some Machiavellian conspiracy but by the very potent beliefs about the mystic powers for good and ill that were controlled by these "Lords of the Rings"—beliefs in some ways reminiscent of those ascribed to the chiefs of the Bangwa of southern Cameroon.

Religious Practitioners. A new matriclan priest, usually a middle-aged rather than an old man, was chosen by the elders of the clan—in consultation with the other matriclan priests of the town because, in principle, the latter could veto the elders' choice. The rituals of induction then gave him his mystic powers. A new diviner, who might be male or female, first manifested signs of a kind of possession by a deceased diviner, always related, and only subsequently underwent a final induction by the senior diviner, in the presence of the other diviners and the matriclan priests. A new diviner, once possessed by a former diviner, could "see" the Dead and was driven/taken to the bush by them to be shown "medicines" and small objects of mystical power, which were then collected to form the core of a shrine through which the Dead could subsequently be contacted in séances. Public sign of the new vocation was given by the diviner when he or she brought uprooted "trees" back to the town and tossed leaves from the trees onto the veranda of each of the other diviners. Between this announcement and the final induction, the diviner could see and hear the Dead and those with mystic powers—but not ordinary people; he or she necessarily passed them in silence, without returning any greeting. At the final induction, the head of the diviners put medicines in the eye of the novice, who, looking at the sun, claimed to see certain stereotyped indications of blessing. The ring was put on the diviner's finger and, afterward, contact with the Dead was in the diviner's control. Effectively, the novice had returned, for most purposes, to the mundane world. Diviners were consulted when people had serious problems. Ailments believed to be minor were treated by men or women who used various leaves and roots as nonmystical cures.

Ceremonies. The principal Yakö ceremonies are linked to agriculture, to the life cycle of the individual, to the induction of diviners, to the induction and burial of priests, and to the induction and burial of members of important societies. The burial and funeral ceremonies for adults involved presentations of gifts between the different kin groups and social organizations to which the dead person belonged, and thus made manifest the complexity of each individual's social ties; naturally the funerals of the politically and ritually important were the most elaborate. The ceremonies of greatest general significance, however, both ritual and political, were the agricultural ceremonies, of which the main ones were those of First Planting, First Fruits, and Harvest. The rites were conducted by the matriclan priests, and the First Fruits and Harvest rites were highly elaborated and necessitated the collaboration of the most significant social groups in each town: the wards; the important men's societies and women's societies, with their masked dancers; and the corporation of diviners. The core rituals included processions lasting several days to all of the matriclan shrines and to other important shrines of the town. At least in formal terms, the Yakö acknowledged the dominant ritual position of the matriclan priests. The themes of the rites stressed the appeal to spiritual forces for the well-being of the town as a whole and for its defense against mystical enemies. In addition, especially through the parading of the men's societies, the ceremonies asserted the power of the town against secular external foes. During the First Fruits rites, which persisted into the 1950s, it was dangerous for a stranger from another place to travel within the territory of the celebrating town or wander through its streets at night.

Medicine. The Yakö regarded almost all but minor illnesses as the result of attacks or errors made by humans. They could be caused by witches; by water-traveling sorcerers; by vengeful people who covertly placed small objects in powerful shrines and later removed them to wreak harm on some particular enemy; by ghosts of the recently dead; or by the spirits that were associated with shrines if, through some carelessness or greed, an individual trespassed on the places that they guarded. The early illnesses of infants were usually attributed to the desire for recognition by the reincarnating ancestor. It is possible to make certain generalizations about diagnosis—for example, that the conditions that involved pneumonia were likely to be ascribed to water-traveling sorcerers. The Yakö were, however, essentially pragmatic: if the treatment prescribed by the diviner who had made a particular diagnosis failed to result in a speedy cure, the patient could have recourse to another diviner who, finding out about the first failure, might diagnose not only a different treatment but a different cause.

Death and Afterlife. A person's spirit (kidom), which in the case of a matriclan priest, diviner, water sorcerer, or witch can travel separately from the living body, journeyed at the death of each individual to the linked town of the Dead (located beneath each town of the living), where behavior, involving farming and going to market, was much the same as in the town of the living. In the normal case, the proper burial rites insured a swift journey for the kidom; if, because of some unclean sickness, the rites were abnormal and the body were buried outside the town, then the transition was delayed. Until this transition had been effected, the dead person could not indwell a child. A dead person was not restricted to being reincarnated within a single child (diviners who had to name the reincarnating ancestor were quite likely to associate the name of a well-known person with several children). There were also some beliefs about Bad Dead: if the Bad Dead indwelt a child, he or she quickly died; a woman who lost a succession of children was assumed to be the victim of the Bad Dead and had to make special sacrifices. Except in this sense, however, no moral distinction was made between the different Dead. In dealing with the affairs of the living, the Dead were motivated by their own interests; they were not believed to make value judgments between the living based on the behavior of the living toward one another.

Bibliography

Cook, T. L. (1969). *Benue-Congo Newsletter* 6 (December). Cyclostyled.

Forde, Daryll (1951). *Marriage and the Family among the Yakö in South-eastern Nigeria*. London: Percy Lund Humphries & Co. for the International African Institute.

Forde, Daryll (1962). "Death and Succession: An Analysis of Yakö Mortuary Ritual." In *Essays on the Ritual of Social Rela-*

tions, edited by Max Gluckman. Manchester: Manchester University Press.

Forde, Daryll (1964). *Yakö Studies*. London, New York, and Ibadan: Oxford University Press for the International African Institute.

Greenberg, Joseph H. (1963). *The Languages of Africa*. Indiana University Research Center in Anthropology, Folklore, and Linguistics, Publication no. 25. The Hague: Mouton.

Harris, Rosemary (1957). Field notes.

Partridge, Charles (1905). *Cross River Natives*. London: Hutchinson & Co.

ROSEMARY HARRIS

Yemenis

ETHNONYMS: none

Orientation

Identification. The Yemenis are a Muslim and Arabic-speaking people who are mainly Arabs, although a small percentage of the population has African and Asian ancestry. Yemeni values have traditionally relied on a hierarchical, tribally organized, and sex-segregated society. In 1962, following the overthrow of a conservative monarchy that had been supported by members of the Zaydi Islamic sect, the Republic was established, marking Yemen's entry into the modern world.

Location. Yemen occupies the southern shore and the southwestern corner of the Arabian peninsula. Its western boundary is the Red Sea. The country has a mountainous interior with a temperate or subtropical climate. The central highlands divide Yemen into a coastal plain called the Tihama, which has a tropical climate with sparse rainfall, and a desert region that stretches into the Empty Quarter. A midlands area consists of valleys (wadis) and foothills that slope down to the lowlands. Southwest monsoons influence Yemen's climate. The southern highlands receive the most rainfall, particularly where mountains provide less of a barrier to precipitation.

Demography. In the first national census that was conducted in 1975, the population of over 5 million included male laborers temporarily employed outside the country but excluded many Yemenis in the lowest servant groups. Population figures taken from various census reports between 1985 and 1989 range from more than 6 million to more than nine million. In the early 1990s the population of Yemen surpassed 10 million.

Linguistic Affiliation. Yemenis speak the dialect of Arabic spoken in the region or urban center from which they originate. Regional variations in the pronunciation of certain Arabic phonemes (especially the phoneme /q/) differentiates the speech of northerners from southerners, for example. The speech pattern of Tihama residents is marked not only by dialectal variations but by characteristic accents, intonations, and inflections.

History and Cultural Relations

Yemen is an ancient country. In the millennia before Christianity, the two Yemens, known as South Arabia and Arabia Felix ("Happy Arabia"), were important points along the incense trade routes. South Arabian kingdoms dating from 1000 B.C. included the land from which the Queen of Sheba made her visit to King Solomon. Prior to the coming of Islam in the sixth century A.D., the South Arabian kingdoms declined, the conquests of Persian and Ethiopian rulers failed, and the famous dam at Maʿrib was destroyed. Remnants of the dam and pillars, reputedly from the queen's temple, are still to be found in the eastern desert of Yemen. Leadership under the Zaydi imams began in the ninth century. Between the eleventh and fourteenth centuries, various external and local dynasties struggled for power in different parts of Yemen. Among these were the Sulayhid (including the noted queen, Arwa), Ayyubid, and Tehirid dynasties. Yemen resisted foreign rule, but two occupations by the Ottoman Turks occurred—between the mid-sixteenth to early seventeenth centuries and from the 1870s to 1918. The imams then sought to reassert their political authority over the tribes of Yemen and against Saudi Arabia. The assassination of Iman Yahya in 1948 was eventually followed by a successful revolt of dissident army officers, intellectuals, and businessmen in 1962. Civil warfare lasted into the 1970s and reerupted in the 1990s.

Settlements

Most Yemenis live in small, widely dispersed farming villages and towns. Three-quarters of the population lives in roughly 50,000 settlements with less than 500 inhabitants. The cities of Aden, Abyan, Al-Houta, Al-Hudaydah (a port), Sanʿa, and Taʿizz have more than 100,000 residents each. Many foreign countries have assisted in the building of roads, hospitals, and schools, but improvements such as sanitary water facilities and power supply typically remain local development projects.

Economy

Subsistence and Commercial Activities. In the rapid transition from a subsistence to a cash economy, most families can no longer support themselves exclusively by farming. Yemen, once a chief exporter of Mocha coffee (from the port of the same name) now has a highly inflated economy that is dependent on imports. Yemenis who continue to plow their fields manually or with the aid of oxen do so not only because traditional methods are more efficient on narrow traces, but also because farmers are far too poor to own or even to rent the services of a tractor. Radical changes in the subsistence economy began in the 1970s with the export of male labor to Saudi Arabia. By the mid-1980s, remittances from abroad, including U.S. earnings, amounted to a billion dollars and resulted in a sharp rises in bride-price and the cost of land, food, modern consumer items, and professional services. Yemeni dependence on the oil-producing economies now means that staple grains (such as drought-resistant maize, sorghum, wheat, and barley), livestock (including goats, sheep, cattle, and chickens) and even cash crops (cotton and sesame, for example) cannot compete with high-yield commodities from the industrialized world. Oil was discovered in 1984 by the U.S. Hunt Oil Company. By fulfilling its potential to become a modest oil producer, Yemen would reduce its economic dependence on Saudi Arabia. Presently, the most important cash crop for local consumption is *qāt* (*Cathe edulis*), the mild leaf stimulant that Yemenis chew for its euphoric effects and which is an essential component of daily social and business gatherings. One measure of increasing affluence is the affordability of qāt, especially among town dwellers.

Industrial Arts. Yemenis are applying new skills to old trades or entering new occupations that were formerly reserved only for members of despised groups. Operating a sewing machine is an example of a new skill; women do the sewing at home, or, more often, men do the work in shops. Prior to their exodus from Yemen in the mid-twentieth century, Jews were the silversmiths. Now jewelry trades have been taken up by Yemeni Arabs. Returning migrant laborers apply the metal crafts they learned abroad in the making of steel doors, which are much desired by Yemeni homeowners and shopkeepers. Certain regional crafts and services must compete with imports and modernity: weaving, pottery, and charcoal selling fall into this category. Selling goods in the market was formerly an occupation considered too lowly for individuals of tribal status, but now shopkeeping offers men one of the few opportunities to invest their foreign earnings. On the other hand, greater spending on meat consumption and the resultant increase in the demand for butchers has not meant an elevation in the social status of butchers despite their upgraded economic position.

Division of Labor. Various tasks in the cultivation of crops are divided according to sex. Men, women, and children share responsibility for the care of livestock. Women gather firewood and water; in some regions, they now receive assistance from the men, who have acquired Japanese trucks. The family's livelihood may also depend on women selling homemade goods and produce in the marketplace.

Land Tenure. Farmers either own their plots, which tend to be small, or they work as shareholders. No stigma is attached to nonlandowners unless one is a member of a group that, in the past, was not permitted to buy land.

Kinship

Kin Groups and Descent. In the northern highlands, tribal lineages are based on claims of descent from a named male (patronymic) ancestor. More characteristic of social organization in the southern and coastal regions are smaller alliances and/or greater association with others residing in the same vicinity.

Kinship Terminology. Yemenis recognize the concept of "closeness" to describe desired relationships through marriage.

Marriage and Family

Marriage. Islamic law and custom guide contemporary Yemeni marriages, although government regulations establishing ceilings on bride-price are often ignored. The legal marriage age of 16 for girls is also difficult to regulate because births are not routinely recorded. Arranged marriages prevail, but women do have veto power over a prospective groom. Fewer than 5 percent of Yemeni males exercise their option as Muslims to have up to four wives. The difficulty of supporting multiple wives equitably, as Islamic law requires, as well as the high cost of getting married, probably discourages polygyny. Divorce can be accomplished by men with far fewer restrictions than are imposed on women. Customarily, wives (through fathers or brothers) must remunerate their husbands if they wish to terminate the marriage. Legally, fathers' rights to the children after divorce supersede those of mothers.

Domestic Unit. Women preside over the work of the household, which may be comprised of blood relatives, neighbors, and members of client or servant groups in families of high social status. Women are valued members of the household unit as agricultural producers and are also crucial to the maintenance of the Yemeni ideal of domestic hospitality.

Inheritance. Landownership is concentrated within the dominant patrilineages, the result both of inheritance practices and marital strategies. Under Islamic rules, a woman's inheritance is only half that of her brother. In Yemen, women often do not renounce their claims of ownership. Thus the ideal marriage between patrilateral cousins would ensure that land remains within the patrilineage. Similarly, marriage to an outsider encourages the renunciation of claims to land that is too far away to farm.

Socialization. In Yemeni society, the responsibilities of child care are willingly assumed by many others besides the mother, including older children and grandmothers. Once children are able to walk, they freely roam their village, observing the activities of any household. Physical punishment is reserved for more severe infractions, but mothers have ingenious ways of getting their children's attention.

Sociopolitical Organization

Social Organization. Yemeni society is hierarchically organized on the basis of birth status and occupation. Until relative political stability was achieved in the late 1970s, birth and occupational statuses were legitimized as ascribed social categories. The elimination of practical barriers that restrict power and privilege—especially through marriage and education—to certain members of the society has only just begun. Under the system of ranked social categories, members of respectable groupings recognized their own noble descent and considered themselves the protectors of servants, former slaves, artisans, and certain farmers, all of whom were thought of as "deficient," either because they provided a service or craft—such as bloodletting, butchery, or barbering—that involved contact with polluting substances, or because their origins were discredited as ignoble. The tribal code of protection was also extended to elites at the top of the social scale, especially to sayyids, the reputed descendants of the Prophet, who originally came to Yemen to serve as mediators between tribes and who are respected for their religious expertise. Another social category, that of legal scholars, also inherits high status in the ranking order. Scholars, along with *shuyukh* (sing. *shaykh*), who are tribal leaders, typically serve as village administrators. The majority of Yemenis use various equivalent or substitute terms to identify themselves within the social hierarchy, including *qabaʿil* in the northern highlands to connote tribal membership, *raʾiyah* in the south to mean "cultivators," and *ʿarab* along the coast to signify respectable ancestry. Former slaves continue to act as agents and domestics in the households of former masters, but the most menial jobs (e.g., removing human waste from the street) are reserved for Yemenis who are alleged descendants of Ethiopians of the pre-Islamic era. In addition, Yemen relies on a range of foreigners from the East and West for professional, technical, and custodial services.

Political Organization. It is a continuing challenge of governmental strategies to achieve a stable balance between relatively autonomous tribes and the state. Alliance with dominant tribal confederation therefore may still be influential in the distribution of development projects by central authorities.

Social Control. A strict and complex code of honor based on tribal values governs behavior among groups and proper decorum between the sexes, including veiling of women in urban or northern areas.

Conflict. The cultural concept of honor also regulates the handling of disputes, which depends on confirming significant kinship ties.

Religion and Expressive Culture

Islam is the major force that unifies Yemenis across social, sexual, and regional boundaries. Yet most adherents of the different schools of Islam reside in distinct sections of the country, and this fact has certain political implications. Zaydis, who belong to the Shia subsect of Islam, are located in the northern and eastern parts of Yemen, whereas Shafis, orthodox Sunnis, live in the southern and coastal regions. Location in the highlands apparently enables Zaydis more successfully to repel invasions than Shafis in the lower lying areas. A smaller Shia subsect, the Ismaili, and also the remnants of an ancient Jewish community, may still be found in certain parts of Yemen.

Religious Beliefs. As Muslims, Yemenis aspire to fulfill the five tenets of Islam: affirmation of the Islamic creed, prayer, fasting, charity, and pilgrimage.

In the Shafi areas of Yemen, the tombs of certain holy men are visited by believers for their special healing and other powers.

Religious Practitioners. Being of sayyid status, even in contemporary Yemeni society, still validates (but does not necessarily guarantee) one's access to religious learning. Men gather at the mosque for prayers and sermons on the Sabbath, which in Yemen occurs on Friday. Strict segregation of the sexes usually does not permit women to worship in public.

Ceremonies. Yemenis observe the major holidays, such as Ramadan, the holy month of fasting, as well as lesser festivals in the Arabian calendar.

Arts. Despite the imposition of modernity, Yemenis remain proud of their architectural and oral-poetry traditions. Houses and mosques found in different regions of the country reflect unique stylistic and functional variations. Highlanders construct multistoried buildings from smooth, layered mud, mud brick, or cut stone. Dwellings in Sanʿa are particularly impressive with their decorative colored-glass windows. In the rural highlands, houses constructed atop terraced embankments were fortresses against enemy tribes. In cities along the coastal plain, the former elegance of houses and mosques can be seen in their elaborate doors and facades. Rural towns in the Tihama usually include a walled compound that contains mud and thatched-roof huts identical to those found in Africa, on the other side of the Red Sea. The interiors of Tihama houses may be highly ornamented. Buildings constructed of cinder blocks are routinely replacing the huts. Competitive poetry duels performed at weddings by men of tribal status are highly valued. In the past, celebrations for circumcision (required of all Muslim males) were particularly elaborate, but now government officials discourage postinfancy circumcisions, thereby undermining the importance of ceremonial specialists.

Medicine. Yemenis often continue to rely on traditional healers and midwives while simultaneously taking advantage of modern medical technologies. Illness is thought to be caused by such factors as fright—which many believe can be cured by branding (*misam*)—and possession by malevolent spirits (jinn), which requires the performance of the *zar* exorcism ceremony.

Death and Afterlife. On the occasion of a death, most households receive visits from those with whom they have social bonds. Such visits to the bereaved are part of the formal visiting networks that have been established, especially among women in towns and cities. Yemeni views regarding the Day of Judgment are far from simplistic, even though a fatalistic belief system is implicit in Quranic teachings of an all-powerful Allah. Yemenis also believe that whether one's soul spends eternity in heaven or hell is ultimately the responsibility of the individual Muslim.

Bibliography

Nyrop, Richard F. (1986). *The Yemens: Country Studies*. Washington, D.C.: U.S. Government Printing Office.

Swanson, Jon C. (1979). *Emigration and Economic Development: The Case of the Yemen Arab Republic*. Boulder, Colo.: Westview Press.

Weir, Shelagh (1985). *Qat in Yemen: Consumption and Social Change*. London: British Museum Publications.

DELORES M. WALTERS

Yoruba

ETHNONYMS: Anago, Awori, Egba, Egbado, Ekiti, Ibadan, Ife, Ifonyin, Igbomina, Ijebu, Ijesha, Ketu, Kwara, Ondo, Owo, Oyo, Shabe

Orientation

Identification. The name "Yoruba" appears to have been applied by neighbors to the Kingdom of Oyo and adopted by missionaries in the mid-nineteenth century to describe a wider, language-sharing family of peoples. These peoples have gradually accepted the term to designate their language and ethnicity in relation to other major ethnic groups, but among themselves they tend to use the subgroup ethnonyms listed above.

Location. The Yoruba peoples reside in West Africa between approximately 2° and 5° E and between the seacoast and 8° N. Today this area occupies most of southwestern Nigeria and spills into the People's Republic of Benin (formerly Dahomey) and Togo. Yoruba homelands, roughly the size of England, straddle a diverse terrain ranging from tropical rain forest to open savanna countryside. The climate is marked by wet and dry seasons.

Linguistic Affiliation. Yoruba belongs to the Kwa Group of the Niger-Congo Language Family. Linguists believe it separated from neighboring languages 2,000 to 6,000 years ago. Despite its divergent dialects, efforts are being made to standardize the language for use in the media and primary schools.

Demography. The Yoruba-speaking population of Nigeria was estimated to be 20 million in the early 1990s.

History

The movement of populations into present Yorubaland appears to have been a slow process that began in the northeast, where the Niger and Benue rivers meet, and spread south and southwest. Archaeological evidence indicates Stone Age inhabitants were in this area between the tenth and second centuries B.C. By the ninth century A.D., blacksmithing and agriculture had emerged at Ife, a settlement that reached an artistic and political zenith between the twelfth and fourteenth centuries and is mythologized as the cradle of Yoruba peoples. Political development also appears to have been slow and incremental. Never unified politically, the Yoruba at contact were organized in hundreds of minor polities ranging from villages to city-states to large kingdoms, of which there were about twenty. Expansion took place through the federation of small communities and, later, through aggressive conquest. The famed Kingdom of Oyo, which emerged in the fourteenth century, relied heavily on trade and conquest to make it West Africa's largest coastal empire. At its peak in the late seventeenth century, seventy war chiefs lived in the capital city.

For many Yoruba, urbanism was a way of life. Europeans learned of the city of Ijebu Ode early in the sixteenth century, when they exchanged brass bracelets for slaves and ivory. The Ijebu Yoruba were, and continue to be, known for their business acumen. Commerce with Europe expanded in the seventeenth and eighteenth centuries as the New World demand for slaves increased. This lucrative trade stimulated competition, a thirst for increased power, and a rise in internal warfare that laid waste to the countryside and depopulated vast areas. Oyo declined in the late eighteenth and early nineteenth centuries, but urban populations expanded, and two new states emerged, Ibadan and Egba, founded by wartime refugees.

Following the abolition of the slave trade, missionaries arrived in the 1840s, and Great Britain annexed a small strip of the Yoruba-dominated coastland—the Settlement of Lagos—in 1861. Gradually, British forces and traders worked their way inland; by the dawn of the twentieth century, all Yoruba were brought into the empire. Early exposure to Christian education and economic opportunities gave the Yoruba an advantage in penetrating European institutions. By the time of Nigerian independence (1960), they had taken over most high administrative positions in their region, making theirs a relatively smooth transition to a Westernized bureaucratic government.

Cultural Relations

Neighboring groups are the Bariba, Nupe, Hausa, Igala, and Idoma to the north; the Edo (Benin), Ijo, Urhobo, and Igbo to the east; and the Fon, Ewe, and Egun to the west. Since precolonial times, there has been extensive contact among population groups and, consequently, much cultural blending in the borderlands.

Settlements

From early times, Yoruba settlements varied in size from hunting and farming camps to cities, the largest of which had 20,000 to more than 60,000 inhabitants by the 1850s. Most indigenous capitals were circular, densely settled, and protected by earthen walls. Typically, a royal compound measuring around a hectare and a market occupied the centers. Clustered around them in pie-shaped wedges were the residences of chiefly and commoner families. Agricultural lands lay outside the walls, and farmers commuted from town to farm. The usual in-town residence was a rectangular compound, the outer walls consisting of contiguous rows of rooms that surrounded an inner courtyard used for cooking, domestic work, and social life. Buildings were constructed of mud bricks and covered with thatch. Today they are of concrete blocks or concrete-washed walls roofed with tin or zinc. Compounds are being replaced by large multistoried, freestanding structures, arranged in two long rows of rooms bisected by a central corridor.

Economy

Subsistence and Commercial Activities. The precolonial economy was primarily based on agriculture and trade, although fishing, hunting, and crafts were significant. As recently as 1950, two-thirds of the men were farmers. Depending on the ecological zone, the main food crops included beans, yams, and, later, cassava and maize. The main cash crops have been kola and cocoa in the forest belt and cotton and, more recently, tobacco elsewhere. Intercropping and swidden methods have been practiced, with fallow periods ranging from three to ten years following a typical three-year cultivation period. Until around the mid-twentieth century, mechanization and draught animals were lacking; the main tools are still the hoe, ax, and machete. Yoruba women seldom farm, although they may assist with harvesting or transporting produce. Farmers have suffered in the late twentieth century from fluctuating world prices for cash crops, civil war, and an oil boom, all of which have driven many into urban employment in commercial, governmental, and service sectors.

Industrial Arts. Men traditionally practiced metalworking, wood carving, and weaving. Since the mid-nineteenth century, they have also taken up carpentry, tailoring, and shoemaking. Artisans often belonged to guilds. Women's crafts included pottery making, spinning, dyeing, weaving, and basketry; dressmaking was added in the nineteenth century.

Trade. An extensive system of marketing and long-distance trade is a hallmark of Yoruba history. Precontact overland commerce emphasized kola, woven cloth, and salt; coastal trade with Europeans involved slaves, cloth, ivory, and, by the nineteenth century, palm products. Both men and women conducted long-distance commerce. Women organized local trade networks and markets and, as a consequence, were given official roles in public affairs. Markets still meet daily, at night, and in periodic cycles of four or eight days. Their revenues still help to support local government.

Division of Labor. There is a division of labor according to sex (see "Industrial Arts" and "Trade") and a clear division of finances. Husbands and wives keep their work and accounts separately, each taking responsibility for some household and child-care expenses. Labor also is divided according to age: heavy work is reserved for the young; the load lightens with age. The goal is to gain sufficient wealth to control the labor of others and thereby free oneself from physical work and from being accountable to a superior.

Land Tenure. Most land is held corporately by descent groups and allocated to members according to need. Rights to use farmland and housing are primarily patrilateral in the north (although rights can be acquired through female agnates) and cognatic in the south. Tenant farming, sharecropping, and leasing were introduced by the British. The land-tenure system was changed in 1978 when the Nigerian government took control of all unoccupied or unused land and rights to allocate it.

Kinship

Kin Groups and Descent. Descent groups are important in marking status, providing security, and regulating inheritance. There are strong bilateral tendencies, but agnatic ties are emphasized among northern Yoruba, among whom descent groups once were largely coterminus with residence, but not among southern Yoruba, who tend to have more dispersed residences and stress cognatic ties. Descent groups have names and founding ancestors, and in some cases they own chieftaincy titles. Women rarely succeed to the titles, although their sons can. Descent groups formerly regulated marriage, agriculture, and family ceremonies and maintained internal discipline. Elder male members still act as decision makers, adjudicators, and administrators; formerly, they served as representatives in civic affairs. Extended-family relationships are individually cultivated and are important for mobilizing various types of support.

Kinship Terminology. The few basic kinship terms are applied in a classificatory manner. Except for mother/father, grandmother/grandfather, and wife/husband, there are no gender-specific terms; senior siblings are distinguished from junior siblings; no cousin distinctions are made; and all children are addressed by the same term regardless of sex or age. To indicate more precise relationships, descriptive phrases must be used.

Marriage and Family

Marriage. Marriage is prohibited among people who can trace a biological relationship. There are no ideal partners. First marriages still may be arranged by elders, who assess the suitability of spouses in terms of mental and physical health, character, or propitiousness of the union. Some marriage alliances were arranged for political or economic reasons. The type of ritual and amount of bride-wealth depended on the status of the partners. Marital residence was patrilocal but in the late twentieth century has become neolocal. Men traditionally married, and some continue to marry, polygynously. Increasingly since the mid-twentieth century, marriages between educated men and women reflect personal choice. Divorce is now common, although it is said to have been rare in precolonial times.

Domestic Unit. Agnatically related men often shared the same large compound, taking separate sections for their wives and children. Each wife had a separate room but cooked for and made conjugal visits to her husband in rotation. Until the age of puberty, children slept in their mothers' rooms; youths moved to a common room, and girls soon moved to the compounds of their husbands.

Inheritance. Landed property is inherited corporately following descent-group lines; other property such as money or personal belongings is divided among direct heirs, with equal shares going to the set of children born to each wife. Nothing is passed to a senior relative or wife unless there is a will. Wives and slaves were once inherited by junior siblings.

Socialization. The closest ties are between mother and child. Mothers indulge their children, whereas fathers are more remote and strict. A child is treated permissively until about age 2, after which physical punishment and ridicule are used to regulate behavior. Pre-Western and pre-Islamic education stressed economic and psychological independence, but not social independence. Children learned occupations from parents of the same sex by participating from age 5 or 6 in their work. Imitation and games played a large part in socialization.

Sociopolitical Organization

Social Organization. Social status was and still is determined according to sex, age, descent group, and wealth. These features determine seniority in social relationships and govern each actor's rights, obligations, and comportment vis-à-vis others. In the past, elder males ideally held most positions of civic authority, although senior women were known to do so. Emerging class distinctions are calculated according to wealth, education, and occupation. High prestige also goes to people who are generous, hospitable, and helpful to others.

Political Organization. The indigenous political system consisted of a ruler and an advisory council of chiefs who represented the significant sectors of a society: descent groups, the military, religious cults, age grades, markets, and secret societies. Such representatives advised, adjudicated, administered, and set rules. The ruler performed rituals, conducted external affairs, kept peace, and wielded general powers of life and death over his subjects. Palace officials acted as intermediaries between the king and chiefs of outlying towns and tributary holdings. The political structure of each village or town replicated, in smaller scale, the structure of the capital. Kingship and some chiefships were hereditary. Primogeniture was not practiced; rather, branches of a ruling house were allowed to choose, in turn, from among competitor-members. Other titles could be achieved or bestowed as an honor. Today the ancient political systems survive with new functions as arms of local government.

Social Control. Depending on gravity and scale, disputes or crimes were judged by descent group leaders, chiefs, rulers, or secret societies. Order was maintained by these same authorities and their aides. Deterrents included fear of harsh punishment, supernatural retribution, curses, ostracism, and gossip.

Conflict. Internal struggles for power were strongest between the monarch and town or warrior chiefs. External conflict involved raiding for slaves and booty and large-scale warfare. From 1967 to 1970, a civil war pitted Yoruba and northern peoples against their eastern neighbors; the battle ravaged the nation and depleted its resources. Hostility, precipitated by the quest for power and national resources, persists along ethnic and subgroup lines.

Religion and Expressive Culture

Religious Beliefs. The ancient Yoruba religious system has a pantheon of deities who underpin an extensive system of cults. Rituals are focused on the explanation, prediction, and control of mystical power. Formerly, religious beliefs were diffused widely by itinerant priests whose divinations, in the form of verses, myths, and morality tales, were sufficiently standardized to constitute a kind of oral scripture. In addition to hundreds of anthropomorphic deities, the cosmos contains a host of other supernatural forces. Mystical power of a positive nature is associated with ancestors, the earth, deities of place (especially hills, trees, and rivers), and medicines and charms. Power of an unpredictable, negative nature is associated with a trickster deity; with witches, sorcerers, and their medicines and charms; and with personified powers in the form of Death, Disease, Infirmity, and Loss. Individuals inherit or acquire deities, through divination or inspiration.

Christianity was introduced from the south in the mid-nineteenth century; Islam came from the north in the seventeenth or eighteenth century. Today Yoruba allegiances are divided between the two global faiths, yet many simultaneously uphold aspects of the ancient religious legacy. Syncretistic groups also blend Islam or Christianity with Yoruba practices.

Religious Practitioners. Priests and priestesses exercised considerable influence in precolonial times. They were responsible for divining, curing, maintaining peace and harmony, administering war magic, and organizing extensive rites and festivals. Many duties of political and religious authorities overlapped.

Ceremonies. Rituals are performed largely to appease or gain favor. They take place at every level, from individuals to groups, families, or whole communities. In addition to rites of passage, elaborate masquerades or civic festivals are performed for important ancestors, to celebrate harvest, or, formerly, to bring victory in war.

Arts. The Yoruba are known for their contributions to the arts. Life-size bronze heads and terracottas, sculpted in a classical style between A.D. 1000 and 1400 and found at the ancient city of Ife, have been widely exhibited. Other art forms are poetry, myth, dance, music, body decoration, weaving, dyeing, embroidery, pottery, calabash carving, leather- and beadworking, jewelry making, and metalworking.

Medicine. Yoruba medicine involves a full spectrum of ritual, psychological, and herbal treatments. Rarely practiced in isolation, curing is as dependent on possession, sacrifices, or incantations as medicinal preparations. Curing is learned through an apprenticeship and revealed slowly, because treatments are closely guarded secrets.

Death and Afterlife. Each individual is endowed with an inner force that determines his or her destiny. It is part of one's "multiple soul," which after death either resides in the sky with other mystical powers or is reincarnated. As ancestors, the dead influence the living, and sacrifices are made to gain their favor. Funeral rites are commensurate with one's importance in life—simple for children but elaborate for authority figures.

Bibliography

Bascom, William (1969). *The Yoruba of Southwestern Nigeria*. New York: Holt, Rinehart & Winston.

Eades, J. S. (1980). *The Yoruba Today*. Cambridge: Cambridge University Press.

Fadipe, N. A. (1970). *The Sociology of the Yoruba*. Ibadan: University of Ibadan Press.

Lloyd, P. C. (1965). "The Yoruba of Nigeria." In *Peoples of Africa*, edited by James L. Gibbs, Jr., 549–582. New York: Holt, Rinehart & Winston.

Smith, Robert S. (1988). *Kingdoms of the Yoruba*. 3rd ed. Madison: University of Wisconsin Press.

SANDRA T. BARNES

Yörük

ETHNONYMS: Turkish nomadic pastoralists, Yürük

Orientation

Identification. The Yörük are an ethnic-tribal grouping found widely throughout Turkey but primarily along the Aegean and Mediterranean coasts. The Yörük are not linguistically distinct from most of the rural populations among whom they live. They speak the Western Turkish dialect of Anatolia. The term "Yörük," an ethnic designation encompassing perhaps as many as eighty-eight tribal entities, is first encountered in Ottoman accounts dating to the twelfth century, and is generally thought to be derived from the verb *yürümek*, "to walk." Regardless of the merits of this etymology, which is contested by some Turkish historians, it is fitting for a nomadic people moving seasonally with their flocks of sheep and goats. It should be noted that in some usages "Yörük" is synonymous with "nomad" and consequently encompasses a number of ethnic groups, most notably the Tahtacilar and the Turkmen tribes of Anatolia, from whom the Yörük have always considered themselves distinct.

Location. Historically, Yörük tribes followed the Ottoman conquests of the Balkans, Greece, Cyprus, and Crete. Today they are found almost exclusively in villages along the Aegean and Mediterranean coastal plains and the adjacent Taurus mountain range, in the southeast (where pastoralism remains important), and in scattered communities around Konya, in central Anatolia. As a nomadic people, they traditionally followed a transhumant pattern, which involved camping during the winter months along the coast (*kishlak*), and moving upland into high pastures in the Taurus range during the summer (*yayla*). Yayla pastures are snowbound during winter and kishlak grazing too desiccated during summer. Thus, by seasonal nomadism, they keep their herds on good grazing throughout the year, utilizing very distinct ecological zones. Those who still practice animal husbandry, mainly in Gaziantep and Maraş provinces, use trucks and tractors to move animals between pastures.

Demography. It is difficult to estimate accurately the numbers of those claiming Yörük descent in Turkey; no census has recorded such information, and estimates vary widely. The most recent estimate (1925) is 300,000. The Yörük constitute about 0.5 percent of the Turkish population. On the basis of field surveys, the Yörük population is increasing at an annual rate of around 2.6 percent.

Linguistic Affiliation. The Yörük speak the standard Anatolian dialect of Western Turkish. Turkish is one of many Ural Altaic languages: the Turkic Group of closely related modern languages—spoken by over 110 million people—includes Western Turkish, Azeri, Turkmen, Kazakh, Tartar, and Uzbek. Mongolian is much more distantly related via common descent from a "proto-Turkic" common ancestral language. Korean, Japanese, Yukagir, and (some would say) Finnish and Hungarian are even more distantly related.

History and Cultural Relations

The Yörük, according to their own accounts, which are substantiated by some documentation, were among the Turkic tribes that moved into Anatolia from Iran during the eleventh century A.D. As with similar groups, their original homeland was Central Asia. Most historians regard the Yörük as closely related to the Turkmen tribes who came in large numbers after the battle of Manzikert in 1071, but it is also likely that indigenous nomadic pastoral populations along the coast became Turkified and acquired Yörük identity during the early period of Turkish rule in Anatolia. The Yörük, like other Anatolian populations—but unlike the Turkmen and related populations of Iran and Central Asia—have predominantly Caucasian features. As early as the reign of Bayezid I (1389–1402), there are accounts of Yörük tribes in Macedonia, Thrace, and elsewhere in the Balkans. Following the conquest of Cyprus by Selim II (1564–1574), Yörük groups moved to that island, where they may be found today as settled villagers. The Yörük tribes followed early conquests as sappers, transport corps, and soldiers. Even as late as the eighteenth century, Yörük tribal leaders supplied the Ottoman government 52,000 troops. During the late nineteenth century, substantial numbers of Yörük moved to southeastern Turkey, the ethnic makeup of which is otherwise predominantly Kurdish and Arabic. Today the Yörük, while retaining strong pride in their identity, clearly consider themselves part of the mainstream of Turkish history and sharply distinguish themselves from other ethnic groups among whom they may live, for example, Alevi, Tahtacilar, Gypsies, Kurds, Circassians, Arabs, and Turkmen.

Settlements

The Yörük were traditionally tent-dwelling, nomadic pastoralists who moved on a fairly regular schedule between highland (yayla) and lowland (kishlak) pastures. The settlement system comprised camp groups of families, usually close agnates, the size of which varied according to available grazing, social relations, and, in some cases, defense. It was rare for a household to camp alone. In the southeast, where the last significant populations of pastoralists were migrating with flocks of sheep and camels (for transport) as recently as 1979, winter camp groups ranged from two to six households and summer camps from five to twenty-five. The tents are of goat hair woven into rectangular panels that are stitched together to form a cover, which is supported by three poles, one at either end and one in the middle. To this structure, side panels of the same material are added and the entire tent is held in place by woven guy ropes and stakes. Internally, the tent is organized around the central division marked by the hearth. One side is primarily used to receive guests, for male socializing, and eating; the other, primarily the domain of women, is where food is prepared. Village-dwelling Yörük, like other Anatolian peoples, usually organize their houses in a somewhat similar fashion: certain areas are reserved for guests, ceremonial occasions, and male visitors, and other areas are reserved for the women of the household. The patrilocally organized household is the primary unit of social and economic organization. Each household is a unit of shared production and consumption. Separate domiciles almost always indicate separate households with separate sources of income.

Economy

Subsistence and Commercial Activities. Economic activities vary regionally. Historically, the Yörük were nomadic pastoralists specializing in goat and sheep production. In the mid-nineteenth century, agricultural development meant the restriction of grazing throughout most of their nomadic range. Many settled, taking up agriculture—in particular dry farming of mixed grains and vegetables. Yörük farmers along the fertile coastal plain have ventured into citrus production, irrigated agriculture, and commercial horticulture using greenhouses. In the Maraş-Gaziantep region, cotton is a principal cash crop, but pastoralism has also remained a very profitable endeavor, and sheep are raised in large numbers. Sheep and products such as milk, wool, and cheese are sold in the national marketplace and increasingly exported to Arab states. Sheep production had become so profitable by 1987 that some Yörük were renting land that was formerly farmed to use as pasturage.

Industrial Arts. Apart from those who have settled in urban areas or found factory employment in industry, there is little industrial specialization. Some families weave rugs and textiles for sale, but the practice of this craft is not at present particularly common.

Trade. In many rural communities, Yörük specialize in running small business concerns and shops. In some areas, they are among the more prosperous rural dwellers. Almost all pastoral or agricultural production is market oriented—little is used for home consumption. Historically, too, much animal production was for market sale. Prior to the development of the modern grid of railroads and highways, Yörük were active in providing overland transport by camel.

Division of Labor. The Yörük are similar to other rural Muslims in Turkey in that they maintain a fairly strong sense of what is appropriate male and female behavior. Women are not encouraged to work outside of the household, to seek commercial employment or to engage in herding or working in the fields. Nevertheless, the female members of very poor families may be forced to do so. Men tend to dominate public life and to conduct the public activities of the household, as is common throughout the Middle East. Girls increasingly are being sent to public school but rarely beyond middle school. Men are not expected to be active in child care, washing, cooking, or domestic work.

Land Tenure. Arable land is privately owned. Generally, Yörük pasture their animals either on fields owned by others or on grazing tracts held as village commons; in either case, herd owners pay rent for access to grazing. Between the 1920s and 1950s, a number of Yörük villages were established on state-owned lands that were divided up and deeded to Yörük settlers. Yörük are not large landowners in the southeast (where absentee landlordism is common); their holdings range from 2 to 70 hectares.

Kinship

Kin Groups and Descent. The term "Yörük" denotes membership by patrilineal descent in an *ashiret* or a *kabile*, usually glossed as "tribe" or "clan," according to context. Descent ideology refers to the common descent of all Yörük tribes without specifying a single ancestral figure nor the linkages among various tribes. Most Yörük agree that there were twelve core or original tribes; there are many more tribes today, and Yörük differ greatly as to which of these are among the original twelve. What is termed a "tribe" has little or no political significance today but is important as a social referent and as a source of personal identity. *Mahale*, or *sulale*, designates subdivisions within the tribe (lineages); at this level, genealogical reckoning is much more precise, and economic and social interaction among members is more significant. The term *aile* refers to family within the context of patrilineal descent and is often coterminous with the household. There is a strong sense of family honor; one important but unnamed grouping is that circle of close patrilineal relatives who are expected to rally to the defense of—or exact vengeance for—a wronged kinsperson. Economic and social interaction is most intense among patrikin. It includes arrangements for selling milk and producing cheese, processing and marketing wool, and the like.

Kinship Terminology. Normal Sudanese terminology is used, as is the case throughout Turkey. The relative ages of siblings are indicated in terms of address; kin terms are widely employed as terms of address to signify age and/or status differentials.

Marriage and Family

Marriage. Although prohibited by Turkish law, polygynous marriage is not uncommon among the Yörük; however it is generally restricted to older, wealthier males. In a 1969 study, 6 percent of presently married women were found living in polygynous matches. Marriages are arranged by parents. Formerly, a relatively high bride-price was paid prior to nuptials. Nowadays it is more common for both households to contribute to purchases of household items and gold for the newlyweds. Elopement and bride-theft or -kidnapping are common (about 30 percent of all marriages) and contribute to interfamily conflict. Such marriages usually entail a higher bride-price if peace between the families is to be even nominally restored. Marriage preference is for closely endogamous matches: marriages to father's brother's daughter or father's brother's son accounted for 21 percent of all marriages in a survey of 360 households; marriages between first cousins, for 39 percent. There were virtually no marriages with non-Yörük. Postmarital residence is almost always with the husband's household; 35 percent of households surveyed were extended-family households. Divorce is initiated by males and approximately 7 percent of those ever married had at least one marriage terminated by divorce.

Domestic Unit. People who share production and eat together are considered a household. Nomadic households are somewhat larger than sedentary ones, and average household size is somewhat larger than the rural national average for both nomadic and sedentary households. One 1971 sample of 360 households found mean nomadic household size to be 7.4 persons for village-dwelling Yörük and 8.3 for nomadic tent dwellers.

Inheritance. Property is generally divided equally among sons, to the exclusion of wives or daughters. Among the nomadic Yörük, anticipatory inheritance is common; that is, a son may claim his share of the family herds and establish a separate household during his father's lifetime. He will have no further claim on the estate. Usually a younger son takes responsibility for caring for parents or surviving parent and will also inherit the domicile and household possessions.

Socialization. Sex-role distinctions are inculcated from an early age; girls are put to productive tasks earlier than boys and are trained to pay close attention to sexual modesty. Respect for elders is also emphasized.

Sociopolitical Organization

The Yörük are not recognized as part of the formal political structure of Turkey, although, historically, tribal entities and leaders were used for purposes of taxation, conscription, and administration. Each person is registered as a resident of a designated town or village.

Social Organization Yörük social organization is closely focused on ties of kinship, with an emphasis on patrilineal descent. Because the Yörük practice close-cousin endogamy, their matrilateral relatives are apt to be members of their own lineage. Egalitarian ideology is strong; there are no hereditary leaders or elite families, although, in practice, wealth differentials are important in determining relative influence.

Political Organization. Traditional political organization stresses consensual decision making by adult male heads of household. Each tribal segment usually has an informal leader, called an *aga*, who acts as a spokesman and often mediates disputes but has no jural authority. Alliances and factions are strongly correlated with lines of descent, even within tribes and lineages. Superimposed on the tribal, kin-based system is the highly centralized Turkish national administration. Thus, each Yörük, villager or nomad, is a member of a settlement or neighborhood headed by a *muhtar* (headman), who reports to a *kaymakam* (district officer), who is appointed, as are provincial governors, by the state.

Social Control. The state maintains effective control through a nationwide gendarmerie and police. Within the Yörük communities, the practice of *intekam* (vengeance) is a powerful means of controlling violence; assaults of any kind on the person or character of another may bring retribution from a circle of male kin responsible for collective honor. The fear of gossip is also a powerful force for social control.

Conflict. Vengeance disputes, confrontations among youths over family honor, and conflicts over marriages (or arising from elopement and bride-theft) support the impression of a fairly high level of violence, even homicide.

Religion and Expressive Culture

Religious Beliefs. Sunni Islam (Hanefi school) is a major force in Yörük society. Most adults tithe, males attend mosque services once a week or when possible, and children are trained by privately or communally engaged tutors.

Yörük beliefs conform to those common among rural-dwelling Sunni Muslims of Turkey. Like many rural dwellers, they frequent local shrines and consult soothsayers and faith healers. Some participate in Sufi or Dervish brotherhood rites, among them those of the Kaderli sect.

Religious Practitioners. Although devout, very few Yörük males train for the Muslim clergy; most leaders of congregations and itinerant clergymen, healers, soothsayers, and teachers are thus non-Yörük. Like many rural Muslims, they believe in the "evil eye" and take steps to ward off its effects, which are particularly threatening to young children, livestock, and women.

Ceremonies. The religious calendar follows that of Sunni Islam. The fast of Ramazan is closely observed. Wealthy men will likely attempt to make the hajj to Mecca, and Sunni ceremonies commemorating the dead are important. Boys are circumcised, although this is not as major a ritual ceremony as it is among some other Muslim groups. The most secular ceremony is the wedding; weddings frequently last three days and involve significant expenditures for entertainment on the part of the groom's family. These are major occasions for widely dispersed households to meet and socialize.

Arts. Yörük musical arts, which have been under pressure from religious leaders, have languished, and most music for weddings is now provided by Gypsies. Young men often compose love poems, and women may sing and dance at weddings, but separately from men; women weave flat-woven textiles and rugs and make felt rugs of elaborate design.

Medicine. Clinics and modern health-care facilities are available to the Yörük; in addition, they frequently rely on folk remedies and healers.

Death and Afterlife. In accord with standard Sunni belief, burial takes place on the day of death, if possible. Bodies are washed, shrouded, and buried; commemorative rites held at designated dates after death are more important than the actual burial ceremony.

Bibliography

Bates, Daniel G. (1971). *The Yörük of Southeastern Turkey: A Study of Social Organization and Land Use*. Ann Arbor: University Microfilms.

Bates, Daniel, G. (1972). "Differential Access to Pasture in a Nomadic Pastoral Society: The Yörük of Southeastern Turkey." *Journal of Asian and African Studies* 7:(1–2): 48–59. Reprinted in *Perspectives on Nomadism*, edited by William Irons and Neville Dyson-Hudson. Leiden: E. J. Brill.

Bates, Daniel G. (1973). *Nomads and Farmers: The Yörük of Southeastern Turkey*. University of Michigan Museum of Anthropology Monograph no. 52. Ann Arbor: University of Michigan.

Bates, Daniel G. (1974). "Sheperd Become Farmer: A Study of Sedentarization and Change in Southeastern Turkey." In *Turkey: Geographic and Social Perspectives*, edited by Peter Benedict, Erol Tumertekin, and Fata Mansur. Leiden: E. J. Brill.

Bates, Daniel G. (1974). "Normative and Alternative Systems of Marriage among the Yörük of Southeastern Turkey." *Anthropological Quarterly* 47(3): 270–287.

Bates, Daniel G. (1980). "Nomadic Settlement in Turkey." In *When Nomads Settle: Processes of Sedentarization as Adaptation and Response*, edited by Philip K. Salzman, 124–139. New York: J. Bergin; Praeger.

Bates, Daniel G. (1984). "The Yörük of Turkey." In *Muslim Peoples: A World Ethnographic Survey*, edited by Richard V. Weekes, 876–879. Westport, Conn.: Greenwood Press.

Dömez, Usuf (1963–1964). "A Yörük (Nomadic) Settlement West of Karasu." *Review of the Geographical Institute of the University of Turkey*, nos. 9–10, 161–179.

Eberhard, Wolfram. "Nomads and Farmers in Southeastern Turkey: Problems of Settlement." *Oriens* 6:32–49.

Johansen, Ulla (1965). "Die Nomadenzelte Sudostenanatoliens." *Zeitschrift für Kultur, Politik und Wirtschaft der Islamischen Lädern*, Nr. Y: 33–37.

Kolars, John (1963). *Season, Tradition, and Change in a Turkish Village*. Department of Geography Research Paper no. 82. University of Chicago, Department of Geography.

Planhol, Xavier de (1958). *De la plaine pamphylienne aux lacs pisidiends: Nomadisme et vie paysanne*. Bibliothèque Archéologique et Historique de l'Institut Français d'Archéologie d'Istanbul, vol. 3. Paris.

DANIEL G. BATES

Zande

ETHNONYMS: Much of the literature uses "Azande." Some early writers refer to the "Niam-Niam," but this term is now regarded as inaccurate. The westernmost groups call themselves "Nzakara" and are so termed in the literature.

Orientation

Identification. The Zande, whose homelands lie within three modern African states (Republic of the Sudan, Zaire, Central African Republic), constitute a large and complex amalgam of originally distinct ethnic groups, united by culture and, to a considerable extent, by political institutions and by language. Because they originated in kingdoms founded by conquest, however, some scattered enclaves of earlier peoples still speak their original languages.

Location. The Zande homeland extends for some 800 kilometers from west to east (13° to 30° E, i.e., from the Kotto River, a tributary of the Ubangi, to the foothills of the Bahr-al-Ghazal watershed) and about 400 kilometers from north to south (from 6° to 3° N, most of their land lying north of the Uele River). Most, therefore, live in sparsely wooded savanna country—a vast plain crossed by many small, tree-fringed streams—but the Zande of the Congo Basin live on the threshold of tropical rain forest, which grows denser with proximity to the equator. The habitat, climate, rainfall, and vegetation are thus quite divergent; in general, the rains fall from April to October, but the pattern varies not only geographically but also over time.

Demography and Linguistic Affiliation. There are said to be approximately a million Zande (about 300,000 of them Nzakara speakers). Of these, about 400,000 live in Zaire, 300,000 in Sudan, and 300,000 in the Central African Republic—where the population is said to be decreasing. In terms of Greenberg's categories (1963), the Zande language belongs to the Eastern Branch of the Adamawa-Eastern Language Family in the Niger-Congo Group; a newer classification places Zande within the Ubangi Branch of the Adamawa-Ubangi Group. Zande and Nzakara speech forms are mutually comprehensible, although these languages differ in some 30 percent of their lexicon.

History and Cultural Relations

The Zande were formed by military conquest, beginning probably in the first half of the eighteenth century; they were led by two different dynasties that were similar in organization yet differed in origin and political strategy. The Vungara clan, starting out from near present-day Rafai, in the south of the Central African Republic, overran a large number of small preexisting peoples, whom they incorporated—politically, but also, in varying degrees, culturally and linguistically—into the main body of the Zande people. Their kingdoms—from Zemio eastward—remained both fissiparous and expansionist until the era of European colonization. Over the same period, a non-Zande dynasty, the Bandia, starting out from southwest of Bangassou in northern Zaire, expanded first east and then north; their territorial expansion seems to have ended around 1855, to be followed by in-depth consolidation. In contrast to the Vungara, the Bandia, although they remained a distinct "foreign" dynasty, adopted the Nzakara/Zande language and customs of their subjects. Both dynasties apparently owe their success to superior political and military organization; they seem to have possessed no determining technological superiority. Both still constitute a recognizable aristocracy in the areas of their former domination.

A number of important cultural features are said to have been derived from the Mangbetu, a similarly organized people living to the south of the Uele River who were never subdued by the Zande. Contact and sporadic conflict with Arabs seem to date from the second half of the eighteenth century but resulted in neither Arab domination nor any profound cultural influence—except for the acquisition of guns, which helped safeguard continued Zande autonomy and reinforced the existing political system.

The first European travelers arrived in the 1860s. Toward the end of the nineteenth century, the Zande came under three different colonial administrations—Belgian, French, and Anglo-Egyptian, the frontiers of which have been inherited by their respective successor states.

The main impact of colonial rule was, at first, the end of the wars that had up to then been both culturally and structurally endemic between the Vungara-led kingdoms. Colonial administrations also imposed changes in the settlement pattern (away from the traditional scattered homesteads along the banks of streams, toward settlement along newly built or widened roads). In addition, they introduced labor recruitment for government or concessionary-company projects, particularly road building and cotton growing. In other respects the Azande were—except near the towns—shielded by colonial officials from Arab and other outside influences. Since independence, British officials in Sudan have been replaced largely by northern, Islamic Sudanese; many Zande are said to have trickled across the border into Zaire.

Settlements

The traditional settlement pattern, later revived with some variations toward the end of the colonial period, was in scattered homesteads, often widely separated from each other by cultivations and forest. Each was home to one man, his wife or wives, his children, and other unmarried dependents. His nearest neighbors were, in precolonial times, usually his closest male relatives and their households. A chief or his deputy would settle near a stream, with kinsmen and clients nearby, connected by radial paths; a king's court was a more elaborate version of the same plan: it was connected by narrow but well-maintained roads to the homesteads of chiefs. More recent settlements range from towns with modern health and educational facilities to hamlets comprising three or four homesteads, still sited in traditional fashion near a stream. Homesteads include two main types of traditional thatched huts: an older, round type with conical roof and a newer, square, gable-roofed type. Also traditional are round clay granaries, usually with access through a movable roof or lid, which are often used as temporary shelters during periods of intensive cultivation. In towns, new houses are usually square; a corrugated-iron or sheet-metal roof is a sign of relative wealth.

Economy

Subsistence and Commercial Activities. In western Zande country, cassava has displaced the former main food staple, eleusine millet. Maize, rice, sorghum, sweet potatoes, peanuts, squashes, okra, legumes, greens, and bananas are grown in fields and gardens. Goats have now been added to the traditional domestic animals, dogs and chickens. The diet is supplemented by the game men hunt and the fish women catch. In the dry season, termites are eaten as a delicacy.

In colonial times, traditional patterns of shifting cultivation were disrupted by cotton growing and other economic schemes and consequent resettlement. Hunting became less important, but it is still practiced away from the main roads. A number of new activities generated cash income. Some men worked for wages on government projects; tobacco was grown as well as cotton, and some craft products were sold.

Since independence, coffee has become an important cash crop in western Zandeland, and in many areas some cotton is still grown. Roads have everywhere deteriorated, however, making it more difficult to market crops. Some villages off the main road remain virtually self-sufficient, buying "luxury items" such as manufactured soap, cloth, and kitchen utensils with money from the sale of subsistence-crop surpluses, any local cash crop, game, craft work, palm wine, or cassava spirits.

Industrial Arts. The Zande have long been known as expert blacksmiths, potters, and wood carvers; many of their techniques were borrowed from the Mangbetu. A few smiths still operate as nearly full-time specialists, but most of their work consists of repairing blades and tools; iron smelting has ceased. Zande still make pots, carve wooden utensils, and weave baskets and mats.

Trade. Markets are a comparatively recent introduction but are increasingly relied upon as more Zande live in or near towns, and self-sufficiency decreases.

Division of Labor. Subsistence cultivation was and remains the province of women, who also prepare and cook food and make palm wine and cassava spirits. Men build and maintain traditional homesteads, hunt, and practice the various crafts; they are also, where applicable, the wage earners. Commoners formerly provided labor in the extensive eleusine plantations that enabled kings to feed large numbers of retainers and visitors at court.

Land Tenure. The homestead and its surrounding gardens and fields long remained the main landholding unit; homesteads were separated from each other by considerable stretches of bush, which made it easy for them to shift their locations and for a younger kinsman to set up his own near that of the lineage head. Modern resettlement has disrupted this pattern. Cultivable areas are, in Sudan at least, subject to artificial limitation: married sons often have to reside some distance from the paternal homestead.

Kinship

Kin Groups and Descent. The society as a whole exhibits a strong patrilineal bias, but relationships are not traced back for more than a couple of generations; local ties have long been based on cognatic, political, and personal criteria rather than on unilineal descent. Accordingly, there is very little interest in tracing the interrelationships of the widely dispersed named patriclans, many of which undoubtedly represent remnants of Zande-conquered peoples.

Kinship Terminology. Simple terms exist for mother and parallel kin (except mother's brother) of her lineage and generation, for father and parallel kin of his lineage and generation, for mother's brother and matrilateral cross cousins, for own-generation same-sex parallel elder kin, and for own-generation same-sex parallel younger kin; there are two terms (male/female Ego) for same-generation opposite-sex parallel kin and for child and parallel members of child's generation, and there is a mutual term for grandparent/grandchild. All other terms are compound.

Marriage and Family

Marriage. Marriage is normally contracted by payment of bride-wealth. It is virilocal and ideally polygynous, although, in practice, not many men are able to afford more than one wife. Kings and nobles had more wives than other men, many of them of commoner origin; they would occasionally give wives "for nothing" to reward retainers and warriors. Traditional bride-wealth took the form of iron spears; Zande rulers formerly provided their pages and courtiers with spears to enable them to marry, but the Bandia dynasty of the Nzakara seems to have provided wives directly instead. In the 1920s it became easier for young men to marry; they were no longer dependent on their elders for bride-wealth spears but could buy their own with money earned in the service of the European administration. Nowadays most bride-wealth is in cash, although it may also include goats, cloth, sacks of cassava, and so forth. A young man's family usually contributes, but he often scrapes together some of the money himself, and thus has some say in the matter.

Domestic Unit. Within the traditional homestead, each wife had her own sleeping hut for herself and her young children, but the hut of a man's senior wife might be rather better built. Such homesteads are still the rule in villages off the main road. In towns and large villages, administrative and mission influence has resulted in second and subsequent wives often living alone, with only occasional visits from the husband.

Inheritance. The property of commoners, their wives, and any debts or vengeance obligations are inherited by their patrilineal male kin. Competition often arises between representatives of the senior and junior branches of a lineage. It is important to the Zande that organic witchcraft, *mangu,* may be transmitted by a man to some of his sons and by a woman to some of her daughters.

Socialization. Small children share their mother's life, and girls may do so until marriage, thus learning women's occupations. In precolonial days, many boys served as pages at royal or noble courts. When these courts disappeared, ritual circumcision of pubescent boys in the forest (almost certainly borrowed from neighboring tribes) replaced such service as an initiation into manhood. This tradition has also fallen into disuse.

Sociopolitical Organization

Political Organization. In precolonial times, the vast Zande homeland consisted of a number of tribal kingdoms, separated from each other by wide fringes of unpopulated bush. Among Zande speakers, most of these kingdoms, the number and sizes of which varied over time, were ruled by members of the Vungara dynasty, except for the westernmost kingdom, Rafai. In Rafai the ruler was, like those of the similarly organized Nzakara kingdoms, a member of the Bandia dynasty, which was recognized by the Vungara as its equal. These kingdoms, born of conquest, were sustained by more or less continual warfare.

Each kingdom was divided into provinces, which were administered mainly by the king's younger agnates, although in some eastern Vungara kingdoms Bandia governors were also at times appointed. In each kingdom, the central province was under the monarch's personal rule. Governors, although bound to pay tribute and assist the king in war, had considerable autonomy and ruled over deputies of their own. In each kingdom and each province, the ruler's court was centrally situated, and roads radiated out from it to the courts or homesteads of subordinates.

Under colonial rule, and even where the British preference for "indirect rule" held sway, this political system inevitably decayed. Western-style education produced new leaders; in Sudan, in 1954, an educated commoner defeated the son of the ruling prince in a local election. In the Central African Republic, mayors and village chiefs are still often of Vungara or Bandia descent, but national-level officials, usually non-Zande, are appointed from the capital.

Social Organization. The homestead remains the common unit for most day-to-day activities, although men congregate in larger numbers for activities such as hunting. In colonial times, closed associations, open to both sexes, were important for the collective performance of magical rites. These associations, probably of non-Zande origin, remain popular in present-day Zaire. They have been described as quite elaborately organized, but individual associations seem to have been short-lived. Kings and princes, as well as both colonial and postcolonial governments, have generally regarded them with disfavor.

Social Control. Day-to-day behavior is largely governed by the universal belief that most misfortunes are caused by witchcraft and that a witch will only attack those against whom he has a grudge. In precolonial days, serious accusations (e.g., of adultery or of murder by witchcraft) were brought to a ruler's court and resolved by oracle consultations in the ruler's presence. For adultery with a nonroyal wife, fines were exacted; witchcraft resulting in death was generally settled by magical vengeance. The adulterous lover of a royal wife, or a persistently murderous witch, might be put to death. Nowadays serious accusations (e.g., of witchcraft in connection with deaths by drowning or other accidents) can be handled by consulting a Nagidi prophetess and may, if her verdict is confirmed by local-government courts, result in prison sentences.

Conflict. Within the Vungara dynasty, conflict normally resulted in war, especially over succession to a recently dead king, but also in cases of rebellion against a reigning one. Changes in the number and size of kingdoms ensued. Among commoners, conflict, when not resolved amicably, was usually carried on by magical means directed against a suspected witch by the opposing party.

Religion and Expressive Culture

Religious Beliefs. Zande tend to attribute a soul, *mbisimo* (under certain circumstances separable from the body), to both animate and inanimate beings; in traditional belief, the souls of people became ghosts after death. Ghosts were believed to inhabit earth caverns in the bush, as did the Supreme Being, Mbori, who partook in their ghostly nature. In Nzakara-speaking areas, where the word "Mbori" did not exist, "Zagi" referred not only to the Supreme Being, but also to the outside universe in general, and ancestor spirits had concomitantly greater importance. Mission influence has ensured that Mbori is today almost universally associated with the Christian God and that the ghosts, once regarded as potentially benevolent, propitiable ancestors, are more and more associated with evil. Catholic and Protestant congregations are well established and numerous, and have, widely if superficially, affected traditional beliefs and other cultural features. Belief in witchcraft remains important, however, and both belief in and the practice of magic seem to be on the increase.

Witchcraft, mangu, is seen as an organic phenomenon, hereditary in the male line for men, and in the female for women. It need not be conscious; its action is understood as psychic. A witch sends out his or her "witch soul," *mbisimo mangu*, said to be visible at night, to consume the *mbisimo pasio*, "flesh soul," of the victim's organs. Witches are also believed to cause other kinds of misfortune by less clearly defined means. Although their mode of action is mysterious, witches are not seen as in any way supernatural, but as part of the normal order of things. They are believed not to be able to operate at any great distance; commoners are usually unable to bewitch nobles or vice versa. Witchcraft is assumed to be at least a factor in all misfortune; for remedial action, it is thus important to identify the witch. Identification was formerly achieved through divination by witch doctors or by means of various oracles, especially one in which a poison, *benge*, was administered to chickens, the outcome depending on whether or not the fowl survived. The use of benge was already severely discouraged in colonial times, and such oracles are now used very rarely, and never officially. Witch doctors are largely a phenomenon of the past, as are the closed associations through which people formerly sought both offensive and defensive magic. For consultations, including the identification of witches, recourse is now often to (generally female) diviners, who are prophetesses of the "native" Zande Christian church (Nzapa Zande), which now shares the people's allegiance with the European and American missions.

Religious Practitioners. The traditional cult of domestic ancestor shrines required no specialized priesthood. Matters of witchcraft and magic have always been determined by part-time specialists/practitioners. Witch doctors, who were trained in the use of magical medicines, operated at public séances; Nagidi are believed to derive their power directly from God and are, for day-to-day purposes, consulted in private.

Ceremonies. The most important ceremonies were formerly witch doctors' séances. One or more witch doctors, in colorful ceremonial dress, would dance and sing to musical accompaniment before commencing their divination. The circumcision of pubescent boys also forms part of an elaborate series of ceremonies; others were associated with initiation into the (now defunct) magical-medicine associations.

Arts. Music, both instrumental and vocal, is very important in Zande culture; traditional instruments—wooden gongs, skin drums, whistles, xylophones, and large bow harps—also accompany singing and dancing. Harps are occasionally decorated with carved human heads; otherwise, nonutilitarian carving is poorly developed.

Medicine. Zande apply generally known common-sense cures to minor ailments. All serious diseases are attributed to witchcraft and are accordingly combated by magical medicine. The general term *ngua,* which originally meant simply "plant" or "tree," once covered both good and bad "medicines" of every sort. Nowadays Zande distinguish between protective or curative "medicine," which is increasingly becoming known by the Arabic term *dawa,* and ngua used as vengeance "medicine." Magical "medicines" are used, not only to ward off (or avenge) misfortune, but to obtain successful harvests, human fertility, good hunting, and other benefits, including job promotions and success in examinations. Such "medicines" are bought from people believed to have the requisite knowledge; payment is held indispensable if they are to be efficacious.

Death and Afterlife. All deaths, except those of very small children, are attributed to witchcraft or magic and call for magical vengeance. Upon death, the soul (mbisimo) becomes a ghost, which in some sense may be present in the homestead ghost shrine, but also dwells with other ghosts and with the Supreme Being, Mbori, in earth caves in the forest.

Bibliography

Baxter, P. T. W., and A. Butt (1953). *The Azande and Related Peoples of the Anglo-Egyptian Sudan and the Belgian Congo.* London: International African Institute.

Calonne-Beaufaict, A. de (1921). *Azande.* Brussels: Lamertin.

Dampierre, E. de (1967). *Un ancien royaume bandia du Haut-Oubangui.* Paris: Plon.

Evans-Pritchard, E. E. (1937). *Witchcraft, Oracles, and Magic among the Azande.* Oxford: Clarendon Press.

Evans-Pritchard, E. E. (1971). *The Azande.* Oxford: Clarendon Press.

Greenberg, Joseph H. (1963). *The Languages of Africa.* Indiana University Research Center in Anthropology, Folklore, and Linguistics, Publication no. 25. The Hague: Mouton.

Lagae, C. R. (1926). *Les azande ou niam-niam.* Brussels: Vromant.

EVA GILLIES

Zaramo

ETHNONYMS: Zalamo, Zalamu, Zaramu

Orientation

Identification. "Wazaramo" is the preferred name for the people who live in the coastal area of Tanzania, in the vicinity of the capital city, Dar es Salaam. "Wazaramo" refers to the ethnic group, "Mzaramo" to an individual, and "Kizaramo" to the language.

Location. The Zaramo occupy the area roughly between 6°20′ S and 7°25′ S. The area extends from Kisiju to the northern coast along the Indian Ocean at the mouth of the Ruvu River near Bagamoyo and west from the irregular Indian Ocean coastline inland approximately 150 kilometers. The coastal area, 15 to 50 kilometers inland, and the Ruvu River Valley are low in elevation and flat. A series of rugged hills rising to a plateau begins near the coast and extends southwest to Pugu, Kisarawe, Maneromango, and Kisangire. These 100-kilometer ranges extend to a width of 65 kilometers and reach an elevation of 450 meters at Maneromango. Five major ethnic groups—the Kwere, Kutu, Kami, Ndengereko, and Rufiji—live in close proximity to the Zaramo today. Various small settlements of Doe, Kamba, and Kyamwezi also live within Zaramo country and are considered to be clans within the Zaramo ethnic group.

Linguistic Affiliation. The Zaramo as they are known today are made up of clans that migrated from the Kutu and the Luguru around 1700. The common ancestry with the Luguru is substantiated, in that they have the same common language with only slight dialectal variations. The language of the Zaramo is mutually intelligible with those of the Jutu, the Luguru, the Kwere, and the Kami. Most Zaramo, however, speak Swahili, which is the lingua franca of Tanzania.

History and Cultural Relations

The Zaramo were not living in their present territory 200 years ago. They moved into this area later, at the time when there were raids by the Ngoni from the south and the Kamba from the north. The Shomvi, who have resided in this region much longer, called on Pazi Kilama of the Kutu for help. Pazi Kilama was known to be a brave hunter of elephants and lions. He helped to chase the Kamba away from the area, and most of them fled back to Kenya. Kamba place-names are still in evidence, however, and pockets of Kamba are still found among the Zaramo. After the war was over, Pazi Kilama sent his people to the Shomvi for payment. The Shomvi could not fulfill their promise, and they were then subjected to paying yearly tribute to Pazi Kilama. This payment was to continue forever and was eventually paid by the sultan of Zanzibar to the Zaramo.

Similarities in social structure, religious beliefs, and political organization are all indications that the Zaramo originated from the Luguru. The Luguru, the Kutu, and the Zaramo are not tribes in the organizational sense, because there is no political control over all the people. The various local clans or village groups were essentially independent politically, economically, and religiously. The binding factor was habitation within a clearly defined area of land, which was regarded as the property of a particular matrilineal lineage. As Iliffe (1979) observed, groups and identities in Tanzania in the early nineteenth century were categorized by adaptation to a specific environment. The Luguru comprise an ethnic group that lives in the Uluguru Mountains, about 200 kilometers west of Dar es Salaam. The name "Luguru" simply means "people of the mountains." The group expanded or moved down the mountains onto the plains south of the mountain area and formed the group known as the Kutu. The Kutu in turn moved farther east when they were called upon to help fight the Kamba from Kenya. Beidelman (1967), who studied the matrilineal peoples of eastern Tanzania, took matrilineality as the common denominator of these groups of people. He noted a great number of social features that were shared by the Zaramo, Kwere, Luguru, Kutu, Kaguru, Sagara, Vidunda, Ngulu, and Zigua. Besides the similarity in language, their material culture and the basis of their subsistence were practically the same.

Pazi Kilama may have been looked upon as the protector of the Zaramo for some time, but that protection did not develop into any political or organizational structure. Each village with a headman had autonomy and ruled its own affairs. There was much quarreling between headmen and clans, and no political unity developed. In 1875, however, the Zaramo mustered a large fighting force of 4,000 to 5,000 men, which marched to Bagamoyo when the sultan failed to pay his tribute. Although the sultan of Zanzibar had begun to extend his power on the mainland, he did not rule the inland tribes to any great extent. The sultan had dispatched an administrative officer, known in Swahili as the *liwali*, and under him lower officers, to collect taxes from trade caravans passing through the coastal towns; however, these officers did not have authority over the Zaramo. In 1879 Lieut. Henry O'Neill wrote, "Relations between the Sultan's authority of Dar es Salaam and the Wazaramo, with whom they came into contact during the late war, flavor somewhat of an armed neutrality and the soldiers are even now afraid of proceeding through the country thirty miles in the interior . . ." (quoted in L. W. Swantz 1965, 19–20). Swantz further notes that there is no mention in any written reference that the Zaramo were ever under the authority of the sultan.

Settlements

When the first explorers came to Zaramo country, they found it sparsely populated. In some areas, villages were few, and there were vast open plains with abundant wildlife. Early explorers described the Zaramo houses as haycock shaped and made of grass. Today all houses are rectangular, made with a framework of poles tied into place and plastered over with mud. The roof is thatched with grass or reeds or woven from coconut-palm leaves. The more prosperous Zaramo today have concrete floors, plastered walls, and corrugated iron roofs. Where people live has always depended largely on the water supply; vast areas are uninhabited because of water scarcity. Zaramo villages are small and do not give the appearance of developing into towns.

Economy

Plant life has more central significance than animal life to the Zaramo, given that their food is obtained primarily from agricultural activities. The Zaramo cultivate more fruit trees than other inland tribes do, and they transport large quantities of oranges and mangoes to Dar es Salaam markets, which brings them a considerable cash income. Coconut trees also produce fruit that is both consumed and sold. After cashew-nut processing plants were built in Dar es Salaam, cashew-nut trees became of considerable value to the Zaramo economy. During the early days of British colonial administration, the Zaramo were encouraged to raise cotton as a cash crop. Agricultural officers failed to give good instructions, however, and cotton raising failed. Instead, the Zaramo began to grow rice, which became a successful crop that is now being sold to the city.

Early explorers passing through Zaramo country mentioned the fertility of the soil. Traveling through the Ruvu River Valley, they noticed that the land was well watered. Rice, tobacco, maize, beans, sweet potatoes, pineapples, jackfruits, plantains, limes, kapok, mangoes, sugarcane, cassava, curry spices, eggplants, and cucumbers were grown in the area. Tsetse flies were prevalent, and consequently the Zaramo did not have cattle. Nevertheless, they raised sheep, goats, and chickens.

The Zaramo were involved in long-distance trade and slave trade in the nineteenth century. They demanded payment from all caravans that passed through their land, and they were themselves expert slave hunters. The Zaramo leaders not only sold slaves to Arab and Swahili traders on the coast but also kept some slaves for their own use. They also traded in ivory, salt, fish, gum copal, and rhinoceros hides.

Kinship

Kin Groups and Descent. The Zaramo lineage system is based on two principles. On the one hand, there is biological descent, following the line of the mother, and, on the other hand, there is spiritual descent, following the line of the father. The Zaramo are divided into several clans, which for them encompass the concepts of kinship, ancestry, and descent family. A Zaramo clan represents those people who acknowledge common descent, tracing their lineage through the female line. These individuals possess a common clan name, which they inherit matrilineally. The clan of the mother is also that of the children. The children always belong to their mother's clan, never to that of their father. The terms for the father's clan name (*mtala* in Kizaramo and *mtaa* in Swahili) mean "a division of a town or district" and also "the residence of a wife in a polygamous household." The father's mtala derives from his mother's clan name. His children will never belong to his clan, for they can only belong to their mother's clan. The children will use their father's clan name, or mtala, only to show from which father they were born. For instance, when a child is born, he or she is given a personal name and also the father's mtala. The mother's clan name is always understood to be the child's clan name, but it is not used in a child's name. Thus, a child knows to which clan he or she belongs, that of the mother; however, he or she is called by a personal name plus the father's clan name.

Swantz found fifty-nine Zaramo clan names (L. W. Swantz 1965, 26–28). The clans are not totemic: the Zaramo do not observe common prohibitions or taboos. There are taboos and sacrifices, but these practices are transmitted through the father's line. There is no sign of common worship or sacrifice within the clan. Religion among the Zaramo has long been a family or household affair. No religious leader, chief, or headman could grow in importance or leadership because each family had different spirits, ways of sacrifice, and prohibitions.

The Zaramo lineage system may have stemmed from the time when there was clan land, when all from the same clan lived in close proximity to one another. Despite the fact that the children belonged to their mother's clan, they used their father's clan name. If all children from several sisters living in the same area used only their given names, plus their mothers' clan name, it would be very difficult to tell from which father they really were born. The mtala of the father was therefore used to make that distinction.

Marriage and Family

The traditional Zaramo marriage is exogamous, with preference given to cross cousins. Although this pattern is still recognized as the original ideal, it is no longer the preferred model. Zaramo marriage is also polygamous. Traditionally, all wives and children belonged to one man, but the mtala defined his various households. This system, however, is changing because of strong Muslim influence, which stresses the father's authority and patrilineal customs. The Zaramo allow cross-cousin marriages, providing that the spouses do not have the same taboos. This is possible because the taboos are not carried through the mother's clan, but through the father's line. For several reasons, marriages are not lasting. The marital situation is often irregular, and the children do not always live with their biological parents. Kin togetherness and support have always been characteristic of traditional Zaramo society. Even a distant kin member is part of the family and must thus be cared for.

The safe birth of a child is a great event for the family and clan concerned. The Zaramo consider it a special blessing if a girl is born because she will bring bride-wealth to the family and secure continuation of the line. The important phases of a child's life are the first cutting of hair, the giving of a name, and the appearance of the first teeth. The mother is expected to breast-feed her child for at least two years, and she is supposed to abstain from sexual intercourse for six months after the birth of the child. The Zaramo give their children the names of their grandparents. The firstborn girl is named after her grandmother, and the first boy is given the name of the grandfather, following the mother's line. This custom is not only a gesture of respect but also indicates that the newborn child somehow represents the grandparent. Bearing the grandparent's name will bestow that relative's qualities on the child.

Children in Zaramo society normally remain close to their mothers, accompanying them to communal events and festivals. This practice can be seen as a way of educating them on the matters of life around them. Girls, in particular, stay close to their mothers and to other women in the household and soon begin to imitate them. They follow their mothers to the well and balance small tins until they learn to carry large water pots on their heads. The girls learn cooking, start taking their share in hoeing, and try their skill in making hats and braiding their hair. A certain secrecy is maintained with regard to everyday realities, increasing the atmosphere of magic and belief in powers beyond the visible.

Religion and Expressive Culture

Religious Beliefs. The Zaramo, Luguru, and Kutu traditionally made pilgrimages to honor a spirit called Kolelo. When Sir Richard Burton passed through the Uluguru Mountains in 1857, he heard that the Zaramo came there to offer sacrifices to "Kurero or Bokero." According to Burton's account, the place was a cave where a spirit produced a terrible subterranean sound. Women came to bathe in a pool in this cave in order to obtain success in bearing children. The pilgrims had to dress in black, and what they offered had to be black—for instance, a black goat. The social use of black may have many connotations. Black is seen as the color of death, but death is seen as a way to another life. Black is also a color of blessing when associated with the rain and the spirits that are believed to bring rain, success, and fertility. In 1935 Herman Krelle wrote a detailed account on the Zaramo and mentioned a woman called Mlamlali as the priest of Kolelo, who performed sacrifices at the cave of Kolelo. There was also another woman called Kambangwa. She was Kolelo's servant, who made journeys to the cave to pray for rain.

After harvesting the crops, the Zaramo performed harvest purification to cleanse the food. Without this rite, it was believed that the people who ate the food would become ill. The Zaramo also had a special combination of medicines to protect the harvest from thieves. This powerful charm was capable of causing disease and even death.

Among the Zaramo, the number seven is sacred and plays a part in much of their religious and social life. For example, seven knots are pulled on a rope if there is sudden throat pain, a woman is confined for seven days after the delivery of a child, and the relatives of a dead person sleep for seven days on bare ground. It is widely believed that the Zaramo concept of the number seven was influenced by the Arabs, Indians, Persians, and Portuguese.

According to Zaramo conceptions, a gust of wind or the rustling of leaves indicates that the spirits are going past; an eclipse of the moon is a war between the sun and the moon. The Zaramo also once believed in magic water that was supposed to stop bullets; thus persuaded, they participated in the Maji Maji rising against the German colonial administration. The Zaramo fear poison and witchcraft, which they hold to be the cause of practically all deaths.

The medicine man, or *mganga*, in his role of diviner, has the authority and position to function as the preserver of the traditional Zaramo social and religious patterns. His diagnosis and practice uphold the concepts of spirit forces, witches, powers of sorcery, and clan taboos, and also the need to keep the traditional Zaramo rituals. No other public figure in Zaramo society today represents Zaramo traditional concepts and life as does the medicine man. Despite changes in their belief system, the Zaramo basically affirm the powers of sorcerers and spirits and thus continue to consult the mganga.

Before 1890, boys' circumcision—or *jando*, in Swahili—was not practiced among the Zaramo; however, the Zaramo used to put their young boys through an initiation period called *kukula* in Kizaramo. During this time, the boys were taught about the customs of the clan. Today, owing to Islamic influence, jando is also included in the boys' initiation rites. Following a period of seclusion and training, the boys return to their homes, and there is celebration and dancing (L. W. Swantz 1965, 39). The most significant celebrations, however, are held when the girls come out of the seclusion that accompanies their initiation into womanhood. The onset of menstruation is an important period in a Zaramo woman's life, entailing the transformation from girlhood to womanhood; she becomes a new member of society, one who can fully partake in its rites and ceremonies. While the girl is secluded, her father's sister brings the family heirlooms: a chain of pearl or iron, which is hung around the girl's neck, and a little wooden doll, called an *mwananyang'hiti* in Kizaramo, or a gourd doll, called an *mwanasesere* in Kizaramo. When not in use, these much-treasured dolls are kept in the father's family. The girl remains secluded in the house; she is not supposed to see the sun or to see any man, especially her father. She is allowed to do ordinary chores in the house. The two guardians chosen for the girl are called the *kungwi* and the *nandi*. The kungwi can be chosen from the mother's side, and the nandi comes from the father's side. Traditionally, the girl was given instruction under an *mkole* tree, a tree that bears small, red, edible fruits. A Zaramo girl's instructor would sing of it: "It is the tree from which you have gotten your growth." The girl then hugged the tree and was imbued with its powers of fertility (L. W. Swantz 1965, 46). Nowadays girls do not normally go to be instructed under the mkole tree. Instead, they are instructed near their homes, holding a branch of the mkole tree. At the end of the seclusion period, there is much celebration and dancing.

Today the Zaramo are predominantly Muslims, but they have not been Muslims for very long. In the period between 1857 and 1881, when explorers passed through Zaramo area, nowhere was it mentioned that the Zaramo were Muslims. Instead, they went to worship at the cave of Kolelo. The big movement toward Islam came during two periods, from around 1890 to 1900 and from 1910 to 1925. Islam accommodated itself very well to Zaramo traditional religious and social structure. Very little in the way of theology and practice had to be altered. In some respects, the Muslim teacher, called *mwalimu* in Swahili, simply took over the role of the mganga. Islamic amulets, medicines, and special charms took the place of the traditional ones without difficulty. Islamic magic, sorcery, power to curse, and divination all fell within traditional usage. Instead of the diviner, the Muslim teacher conducted the ordeals, using the traditional ones and introducing others. The traditional initiation rites for boys were accepted completely as they were, except for the addition of circumcision.

Although the Christian church has been established and at work among the Zaramo for the past century, its influence on and acceptance by the Zaramo have been limited.

In August 1863 Father Antoine Horner crossed over from Zanzibar to Bagamoyo with letters from the sultan giving him permission to erect a mission station there. The center was intended to be an orphanage and a settlement for former slaves that incorporated an agricultural training school. A community of over 1,000 Christians grew, mainly of former slaves. In 1888 the Benedictines of Saint Ottilien, Germany, started mission work at Pugu, 19 kilometers west of Dar es Salaam. They built the largest Catholic secondary school in the country. A congregation of the Zaramo, however, never developed as such. Through the school and through medical work, the Catholics established contact with the Zaramo, but the number of converts has been insignificant.

In 1887 a Lutheran missionary called Greiner arrived in Dar es Salaam to open a settlement for freed slaves. A 400-hectare parcel of land in Magogoni, on the southeastern side of Dar es Salaam harbor, was set aside for the settlement. On the northern side of the harbor entrance, headquarters of the Lutheran Berlin Mission III and a hospital were built. In 1892 Greiner moved his work to Kisarawe, 32 kilometers inland, and in 1895 a church, a school, and a hospital were established at Maneromango, 80 kilometers inland, in the heart of Zaramo country. From three centers, about thirty-eight churches and preaching places were established, as well as two upper-primary schools, seven primary schools, and twelve bush schools. In spite of the good beginnings, the Lutheran church is comparatively weak among the Zaramo and is quite small compared to its presence in other areas of Tanzania. The Christian minority in an overwhelmingly Muslim community does not encounter enthusiastic hospitality, but Zaramo Muslims and Christians live and work together in relative peace.

There may be several factors that have contributed to the conversion of the Zaramo to Islam and not to Christianity; chief among them is the fact that Islam accommodated many of the traditional Zaramo practices whereas Christianity did not.

Bibliography

Beidelman, Thomas O. (1967). *The Matrilineal People of Eastern Tanzania*.

Forssen, A. (1979). *Roots of Traditional Personality Development among the Zaramo in Costal Tanzania*. Finland.

Iliffe, John (1979). *A Modern History of Tanganyika*. Cambridge: Cambridge University Press.

Koponen, J. (1988). *People and Production in Late Pre-Colonial Tanzania: History and Structures*. Helsinki.

Swantz, Lloyd W. (1965). "The Zaramo of Tanzania: An Ethnographic Study." M.A. thesis, Graduate School of Syracuse University.

Swantz, Lloyd W. (1974). "The Role of the Medicine Man among the Zaramo of Dar es Salaam." Ph.D. thesis, University of Dar es Salaam.

Swantz, M-L. (1985). *Women in Development: A Creative Role Denied?* London: C. Hurst & Co.

Swantz, M-L. (1986). *Ritual and Symbol in Transitional Zaramo Society*. Uppsala: Scandinavian Institute of African Studies.

Vuorela, U. (1987). *The Women's Question and the Modes of Human Reproduction: An Analysis of a Tanzanian Village*. Finland.

S. G. MJEMA

Zarma

ETHNONYMS: Djerma, Djermis, Dyabarma, Dyarma, Dyerma, Zabarmas, Zabermas, Zabirmawa, Zabramas, Zabrima, Zerma

Orientation

Identification. The Zarma are, after the Hausa, the second-largest ethnic group in the Niger Republic, in West Africa, and they have close cultural affinities with the Songhay.

Location. Zarma country covers an area of about 60,000 square kilometers in western Niger between the Niger River and the Dallol Mawri, a dry river valley in Dosso Department. The geography consists primarily of plateaus of sandy and poor lateritic soils, covered with Sudanian vegetation. Water is deep beneath the surface and scarce on the plateaus, which are traversed in a north-south direction by two wide valleys (the Dallol Bosso and the Dallol Mawri) of what were once tributaries of the Niger River. The valleys have heavier soils, shallower groundwater tables, widespread thickets of Doum palm (*Hyphaene thebaica*), and large populations of winter-thorn (*Acacia albida*), interspersed with semipermanent ponds. During the long dry-season months, these valleys provide an oasislike contrast with the plateaus. The climate is Western Sahelian, with a single rainy season beginning in June and ending in August or September. Average rainfall varies from 50 centimeters in the north to 80 centimeters in the south. The average high temperature is 36° C, with temperatures reaching the mid-40s shortly before the rainy season; the average low temperature is 22° C.

Demography. The Zarma number more than 800,000, and, together with the related Songhay to the west (see "History and Cultural Relations"), they account for about one-fifth of Niger's population of 8.05 million. The Zarma are largely rural village dwellers, but some also live in larger towns in western Niger (e.g., Dosso, Koygolo, Loga, Say, Simiri, Ouallam, Tondikwindi, Tillaberi) and in the capital, Niamey. Population densities in Zarma country range from an average of 14 persons per square kilometer in Niamey Department to 23 persons per square kilometer in adjoining Dosso Department, whereas rural densities in the northern Dallol Bosso may exceed 100 persons per square kilometer. Life expectancy at birth is about 45 years (as of 1988), but an estimated 13 percent of newborn children die before attaining their first year (per 1987 reports).

Linguistic Affiliation. Zarma is a tonal dialect of the Songhay dialect cluster (with Songhay and Dendi) and is generally considered to be unrelated to any other known language or language group. Greenberg (1963) considers it to be a part of the Nilo-Sahelian language family; it has also been classified as Congo-Kordofanian.

History and Cultural Relations

The Zarma are widely believed to have originated in the Lake Debo area of the Niger River's "interior delta," between Mopti and Gundam, in the western margin of the former Songhay Empire, in what is now Mali. Their historical proximity accounts for the high degree of linguistic continuity between Zarma and Songhay and for similarities in religious belief and political institutions. The Zarma and the Songhay treat each other as cousins, have a joking relationship, and intermarry.

Following repeated raids on the Lake Debo area by Tuareg, Fulbe, Mossi, and Soninke as early as the fifteenth century, the Zarma left for the area around Gao, and then moved into southeastern Mali. They continued to move southward during the mid- to late sixteenth century, settling in Anzourou and Zarmaganda, north of Niamey. During the seventeenth and eigthteenth centuries, some Zarma moved from Zarmaganda into the dry river-valley areas east of Niamey and into the Fakara and Zigui plateaus of Zarmatarey to the southeast.

At each stage, the Zarma settlers encountered indigenous groups, which they displaced or assimilated: Ki, Lafar, Kalle, Goole, and Sije in the dallols and plateaus of Zarmatarey. The Zarma, in turn, suffered intrusions by Mawri and Kurfeyawa from the east, but these outsiders are now assimilated. Strife between ethnic groups subsided until the early nineteenth century, when Zarmatarey was subjected to frequent raids by Lissawan and Kel Nan Tuareg from Tagazzar and Imanan in the north, and by Fulbe, who had migrated into Dallol Bosso from Say. The situation became so difficult by the late nineteenth century that the Zarma chief of Dosso, Zarmakoy Attikou, requested assistance in 1898 from French military troops stationed in Karimama (Benin). The French quickly responded, but, to the great dismay of Zarmakoy and his followers, they occupied Dosso and refused to leave, intitiating a period of nearly sixty years of French colonialism in Niger.

Settlements

Zarma villages are typically nucleated settlements made up of round mud or thatched dwellings with straw roofs and and also of occasional rectangular houses built of dried-mud bricks.

Economy

Subsistence and Commercial Activities. The Zarma are dryland farmers who cultivate varieties of millet as their principal subsistence crop. Only small amounts of the grain are sold following the harvest, but poorer families may have to sell grain at low prices shortly after the harvest to obtain needed cash. Typically, millet is intercropped with cowpeas, sorrel, and Bambara and other groundnuts. Sorghum and manioc are also widely cultivated in areas with heavier soils. Some dry-season gardening is also practiced in low-lying areas where the groundwater table is sufficiently shallow. Garden production is varied and includes a range of tree crops (such as mangoes, guavas, citrus fruits, papayas, dates, bananas, and nitta trees [*Parkia africana*]), together with vegetables, (tomatoes, carrots, peppers, lettuce, cabbages, squashes, sorrel, and okra), root crops (manioc, sweet potatoes), and some grains and pulses (rice and cowpeas).

Zarma agriculture is characterized by its heavy reliance on household labor, its widespread use of simple hand tools and very limited use of animal traction, and a production system that combines extensive annual cultivation of crops in nearby infields (which are fertilized with animal manure and domestic refuse) with cultivation for periods of from three to five years of unfertilized distant bush fields, which are then fallowed.

Household fields are divided between those fields that are managed by the household head (*windi koy*), in which all household members are required to do some communal work, and the fields that are allocated by the household head to family members to farm individually. Women cultivate sesame, tiger nuts, Bambara and other groundnuts, sorrel, and okra on their plots and often sell some of their produce.

The Zarma frequently raise small ruminants and poultry; they raise cattle less frequently. Livestock are left to multiply and are occasionally sold to raise cash; they are slaughtered but rarely, to provide meat for religious ceremonies, baptisms, and the like.

Industrial Arts. Women make both plain and brightly colored mats and round covers and hangers for storage containers from Doum-palm leaves; men use the leaves to make rope. Blacksmithing, leatherwork, and some woodworking (manufacture of mortars, pestles, and tool handles) is done by descendants of the servile Tuareg caste. Blanket weaving is done by descendants of domestic captives and, occasionally, by Fulbe (Rimaibe). The Zarma also make pottery.

Trade. Zarma men are well known throughout Sudano-Sahelian West Africa for their practice of migrating south each year to distant towns and cities in the forest areas along the Guinea Coast, where they engage in ambulant petty trade and where "Zarma" has become synonymous with "cloth trader." The Zarma refer to these migrants as "children of the forest" or "children of the south." Women are also active in trade, largely within Niger, where they often specialize in sale of condiments and palm-leaf mats.

Division of Labor. In the household fields, men have the primary responsibility for clearing, sowing, weeding, guarding against pests, and harvesting. In addition to shouldering a full range of demanding domestic tasks, women participate in the sowing and harvesting of the household fields, and they often cultivate small dry-season gardens in river-valley areas. In Zarmaganda, women work alongside their husbands in cultivating millet; in Zarmatarey, they do not.

Land Tenure. Almost all of the rural land in Zarma country is owned and managed by a corporate body consisting of the males who claim descent from the first settlers in the area. Household members gain usufruct rights to lineage land by virtue of their consanguineal or affinal ties with the patrilineage. Outsiders obtain access to community land through long-term loans, occasional rental, gifts, pawning, or, more rarely, purchase. The Zarma are adamant that, unlike their Hausa neighbors to the east, they do not sell their land. Whereas land sales in the countryside are scarce, some do occur in areas where shallow water tables make commercial gardening possible or in areas adjoining the main feeder roads and highways that connect with larger towns.

Kinship

The patrilineage and lineage segments are the most significant kinship groupings. Descent is patrilineal. Iroquois cousin terminology, with bifurcate-merging terms, is used.

Marriage and Family

Marriage. Polygyny is highly valued among Zarma men, but monogamy is more common statistically, accounting for 70 to 80 percent of all households. The incidence of polygyny is higher among older and wealthier men; it is considered evidence of social success. Residence is patrilocal.

Domestic Unit. The basic domestic social unit is the household (*windi*), which combines the functions of coresidence, production and consumption, and reproduction. It is headed by a male, who also heads one or more of the conjugal families within the household. Wives in polygynous households have individual dwellings within the household compound for themselves and their children. Households clustered together within larger compounds may embrace as many as three generations: the household head, his father's family, and his son's families.

Inheritance. Inheritance is patrilineal among the Zarma. Fathers bequeath their land to their male children, but the absence of primogeniture and the influence of Islamic law contribute to a parceling up of land across generations. A woman inherits land only if she is the sole survivor of a deceased husband or older brother.

Socialization. Zarma parents indulge their children through early childhood, although they do discipline them occasionally. Relations between firstborns and their parents are tempered by a degree of avoidance, an expression of a sense of shame or timidity (*hawi*), which is also expected of the young in their relations with their elders and superiors. This expression is manifest in social interaction as a looking away or down on the part of the younger person who is being addressed. From about 6 years of age, when their potential for using reason and good judgment (*lakkal*) begins to show itself, children are initiated through play and light work into their future gender roles as adults. Children accompany their parents to the fields at sowing time to watch, and they follow along, learn the movements, and help carry seed. Boys are assigned to watch after goats and sheep and to cut grass and branches for fodder. Girls care for younger children, often carrying them on their backs as older women do; they play at pounding millet and sell cola nuts or prepared foods in the village for their mothers. Boys are circumcised at an early age, but circumcision is not a rite of passage, and little is made of it. Girls do not undergo clitoridectomy.

Sociopolitical Organization

Social Organization. Significant social units beyond the household include the village quarter (*kurey*), whose households are headed by members of a lineage segment and who elect a quarter chief (*kurey koy*), and the village (*kwara*) itself, whose chief (*kwara koy*) is elected by the council of quarter chiefs. Village chiefs are accorded deference, but they occupy a status of first among equals and have little power to enforce decisions for the community. Age classes are not significant social categories among the Zarma, owing to the lack of emphasis given to coming-of-age. Cooperative endeavors are most frequently but not exclusively organized on the basis of agnatic or affinal ties. The most common form of community cooperation is the *boogu*, a short-lived collective-labor group that is organized to assist kin or neighbors with a variety of tasks ranging from clearing, planting, or weeding fields to building houses.

Precolonial Zarma society was divided into two classes: freemen, consisting of nobles (who were members of ruling families) and commoners, and captives. Captives were of two kinds: domestic captives, who were considered semikin, and captives who were seized in war and could be sold or traded. Slavery has been legally abolished in Niger, but the social distinction between the descendants of freemen and captives persists. Descendants of freemen and captives do not marry; some artisanal activities are practiced solely by descendants of captives or servile castes.

Political Organization. The most important chief in Zarma country is the Dosso Zarmakoy. The second level of authority comprises the canton chiefs, who are elected by councils of village chiefs. Village chiefs have tertiary authority; quarter chiefs report to them, and so on.

Social Control. Enculturation and the social pressure that comes from the transparency of personal life are quite effective as social-control mechanisms (see "Religious Beliefs"). Significant deviations and conflicts are handled initially by the village assembly or village elders, and then by the canton chief, who may, if the case warrants, call in government representatives.

Conflict. An essential part of Zarma history and ideology consists of the exploits of Zarma warriors in the precolonial period. Conflict, particularly with the pastoral Fulbe and Tuareg, is an essential element of the Zarma past. Despite the presence of indigenous mechanisms and a civil-court system for adjudicating disputes, conflict with the pastoral Fulbe, and occasionally with other Zarma from nearby villages, remains a part of the Zarma present. Disputes between Zarma villagers over land and with Fulbe over incursions by cattle and crop damage caused by livestock can be violent and occasionally fatal.

Religion and Expressive Culture

Religious Beliefs. Zarma religious beliefs are syncretic, combining some elements of Islam, which are most manifest in public life (in prayers, fasting, sacrifices, the hajj), with pre-Islamic beliefs that have strong ties to nature (e.g., earth and sky, thunder and lightning, water, and the bush). Among the latter, spirits, spirit cults, and spirit worship, as well as healing, magic, and sorcery, figure prominently. The major spirit "families" consist of those that control the sky and the forces of the Niger River; "cold" spirits, which are often ghosts; white, pure spirits; those that are responsible for misfortune and illness; those that control the forces of the soil; and the spirits of colonization and modernization. They manifest themselves through trances and the possession of individuals who thus become spirit priests and healers.

Religious Practitioners. Marabouts, Islamic leaders who have studied the Quran, lead Islamic observances. The priests of spirit-possession cults are often individuals who have been possessed by particular spirits and given healing powers thereby.

Ceremonies. Most Zarma participate both in Muslim ceremonies (daily and weekly prayer, Ramadan fast and prayer, and Tabaski) and in spirit-cult ceremonies, the most important of which is *yenendi* ("cooling off"), held toward the end of the long hot season (May/June). This a time of dancing and music, when the spirits are asked to provide good rains and ample harvests.

Arts. The most notable arts among the Zarma are their basketry (particularly the colorful, hand-dyed mats, covers, and hangers of storage containers, which are made by women from Doum-palm leaves); their pottery; and their woven blankets.

Medicine. Sickness can be somatic or behavioral. The former is treated by traditional and/or modern remedies. The latter has spiritual causes and must be treated by a healer or a marabout.

Death and Afterlife. The living person consists of three elements: the body (*ga*); the invisible double (*biya*), which gives each person his or her singularity; and the life force (*fundi*). These elements break up at death, which may be looked upon as having "natural" causes, or as having been caused by the actions of "cold" spirits.

See also Songhay

Bibliography

Diarra, Fatoumata-Agnes (1971). *Les femmes zarma du Niger. Femmes Africaines en Devenir.* Paris: Éditions Anthropos.

Greenberg, Joseph H. (1963). *The Languages of Africa.* Indiana University Research Center in Anthropology, Folklore, and Linguistics, Publication no. 25. The Hague: Mouton.

Olivier de Sardan, Jean-Pierre (1982). *Concepts et conceptions songhay-zarma: Histoire, culture, société.* Paris: Nubia.

Olivier de Sardan, Jean-Pierre (1984). *Les sociétés songhay-zarma (Niger-Mali).* Paris: Karthala.

Painter, Thomas M. (In preparation). "The Political Economy of Social Change and Peasant Response in West Africa: The Zarma of Niger, 1875 to 1985."

Rothiot, Jean-Paul (1984). "Zarmakoy Aouta: Les débuts de la domination coloniale dans le cercle de Dosso, 1898–1913." Thèse de dotorat de 3e cycle, Université de Paris VII.

Stoller, Paul (1989). *Fusion of the Worlds: An Ethnography of Possession among the Songhay.* Chicago: University of Chicago Press.

Tersis-Surugue, Nicole (1981). *Économie d'un système: Unités et relations syntaxiques en Zarma (Niger).* Bibliothèque de la SELAF, 87–88. Paris: Société d'Études Linguistiques et Anthropologiques de France/ACCT.

THOMAS M. PAINTER

Zoroastrians

ETHNONYMS: Gabar, Gabr, Guebre, Zardoshti

Orientation

Identification. The ethnic identity of this Iranian minority group is derived from their religion, Zoroastrianism. They constitute only 0.18 percent of the Iranian population. The term "Zoroastrian" is taken from the name of their prophet Zarathushtra (Greek: Zoroaster). The majority Muslims of Iran considered them to be "infidels," hence the Zoroastrians were known as "Guebres" (Gabrs, Gabars).

Location. The Zoroastrians are spread throughout Iran, which has an area of 1,648,000 square kilometers. It is bordered in the north by the Caspian Sea and in the south by the Persian Gulf. Fifty percent of the land is desert, mostly concentrated in the center of the country. Annual rainfall in Iran is 127 centimeters in the mountains of the west and southwest and 6 centimeters in the Central Plateau. Temperature varies from −28° C in the mountains to 55° C in the desert. The province of Yazd, in the Central Plateau, is considered to be their religious center.

Demography. According to the Iranian censuses of 1956 and 1966, the Zoroastrians were concentrated in villages, provincial towns, and the capital city of Tehran. In 1956, 42 percent and in 1986, 15 percent of the Zoroastrian population were living in villages. Today, because of favorable economic opportunities, the majority are residing in cities, especially in Tehran. As a result, a number of villages have been abandoned. In 1971 Fischer recorded that the population of the village of Sharifabad, the most traditional Zoroastrian village, was declining. The village has since been entirely abandoned, and most of the inhabitants have established themselves in Tehran. Other villages, such as Astarabad (Gorgān) and Sadrabad, have also been vacated. In 1969 there were an estimated 20,000 to 25,000 Zoroastrians in Iran; the 1986 census placed the figure at 90,891. There were 200 to 300 Zoroastrians residing in Tehran at the beginning of the twentieth century, 10,000 in 1971, and 24,240 in 1986. Early in the nineteenth century 7,000 to 8,000 were living in Yazd; their numbers had shrunk to 5,000 in 1971, and to 4,685 by 1986. According to the 1986 census data, there were 3,882 Zoroastrians in Kermān Province, 1,417 in Māzanderān, 5,794 in Eṣfahān, 5,008 in Gilān, 10,575 in Khorāsān, and 1,007 in Kurdistan. There have also been rumors of traditional villages existing in the valleys of the Alborz (Elborz) Mountains, but this has not been confirmed to date. In 1990 it was reported that some 20,000 Zoroastrians were residing in Tajikistan. The Zoroastrian population is relatively young. In 1986, 70 percent of the population was below the age of 30.

Linguistic Affiliation. Farsi, (Parsi, Persian) is the official language of Iran. This language belongs to the Indo-European Family of languages. The Iranian Branch of this family is spoken in an area ranging from the Pamir region on the east to the eastern border of Iraq on the west. The modern Persian language is derived from Dari, which was spoken in eastern parts of Iran. The transformation to the modern version occurred between the third and ninth centuries A.D. (Ahsan 1976). The Zoroastrians speak their own special dialect in addition to Farsi. Some scholars have classified it as Dari, but this has been a matter of debate. The Zoroastrian religious text is written in Avestan, the language spoken by early Zoroastrians. This language is also a member of the Indo-European Family and is closely related to Sanskrit (Wilber 1948, 23). The Avestan language was developed during the fifth century A.D. for the specific purpose of recording religious material; the existing languages were considered inadequate for the correct pronunciation of their holy words.

History and Cultural Relations

It is believed that the roots of the Zoroastrians are embedded in a tribal/pastoral ancestry. They resided in an area between the mountain ranges of the Hindu Kush and Seistan, a territory now divided between Iran and Afghanistan. Zoroaster, their prophet, is assumed to have been born between 2,600 and 3,500 years ago. His philosophy, which also set the foundations for Judaism, Christianity, and Islam, originated in the northeast of Iran and spread throughout the south and west during the Achaemenid dynasty (sixth to fourth centuries B.C.). After Alexander's conquest, Greek and Semitic elements penetrated the religion during the rule of the Graeco-Persian satraps (250 B.C. to A.D. 226). The Sāsānid dynasty (A.D. 224 to A.D. 651) adopted Zoroastrianism as the official religion. In the seventh century, after the Arab invasion, Islam replaced Zoroastrianism as the state religion, and the Zoroastrians were subjected to persecution and forced conversion. There ensued a migration of Zoroastrians to India, where today they are known as "Parsis." Many also moved to China, but that community was suppressed during the eleventh century. The Zoroastrians remaining in Iran were able to survive in conditions of extreme poverty and discrimination. By the thirteenth century, their numbers were extremely low, and thereafter they disappear from the historical record. It was during the seventeenth century, when Europeans began to travel in Iran, that other countries learned about their continued existence in Iran.

Settlements

The Zoroastrian population is distributed between the cities and the villages. For centuries their stronghold was in the provinces of Yazd, Kermān and Fārs, but nowadays the largest populations are in Tehran, Shīrāz, and Eṣfahān. The architecture of their houses has been heavily influenced by European styles, and there are no features distinguishing between the modern houses of Zoroastrians and Muslims. This was not the case in the past, however; until 1880, there were restrictions imposed on Zoroastrian architecture. Over the centuries, they had to develop architectural features that would satisfy their religious requirements while providing the security they needed against raids by fanatic Muslims. Most of the architecture that has been studied is located in the province of Yazd. Compared to Muslim houses, those of Zoroastrians used to be much smaller, and they lacked double doors, open courtyards, and wind towers—that is, tall chimneys with vents used to cool houses by creating a system of updrafts (Bonine 1980; Beazley 1977). To compensate for the lack of wind towers, they had to increase the number of air vents and holes in the roof. Roofs were restricted in height; Zoroastrians therefore built the main level of houses below ground level. Until the last two decades of the nineteenth century, two types of house were found among the Zoroastrians of Yazd, the *do-pesgami* and *cor-pesgami,* which differed in the manner in which their internal space was divided. Both types of dwellings featured a *pesgam-i mas* (great hall) and a *pesgam-i vrok* (small hall). These rooms were set aside for religious activities. (Muslim houses do not contain a room designated for religious observance.) The pesgam-i mas was never built facing the main door, in order to protect it from the eyes of those considered to be unclean according to the Zoroastrian religion. The cor-pesgami was much larger in size and was built in a cruciform shape (Boyce 1971a). The main characteristic found in a traditional Zoroastrian house is an open hearth in the kitchen, in which to maintain the sacred fire (the principal symbol of their religion). Clay boxes in the yard are used to sow herbs during festivals. Distinguishing features of every Zoroastrian community are the fire temples in which the holy fire is kept and members attend prayers and other religious activities. For centuries, communities concealed the location of the fire temples for fear of attacks by Muslims; fire temples were built to look like humble Zoroastrian dwellings (Boyce 1966). The restrictions imposed on Zoroastrian architecture were eliminated during the late 1920s, after the Pahlavi dynasty guaranteed Zoroastrian security. Today it is very difficult to differentiate their dwelling places from those of other ethnic and religious groups.

Economy

Subsistence and Commercial Activities. Until the nineteenth century, Zoroastrians were forbidden to follow any skilled trade or craft that could bring them into close contact with Muslims. The elder generation of contemporary Zoroastrians consists mostly of farmers, especially among those living in the villages. Because of educational opportunities made available during the Pahlavi dynasty, however, most Zoroastrians occupy various positions as teachers, doctors, engineers, bank clerks, private entrepreneurs, and the like. Owing to their improved economic status, Zoroastrians began to donate part of their wealth toward the construction of schools, hospitals, cultural centers, and places of worship. As in India, most Zoroastrians enjoy good reputations, owing to their honesty. Because many of Iran's professionals are Zoroastrians, their per capita income is above that of the rest of the Iranian population.

Industrial Arts. There are no specific industrial activities associcated with Zoroastrians.

Trade. Until the 1860s, Zoroastrians were not allowed to trade; they were thus forced to hide various goods in their cellars and sell them secretly. In the early 1900s they were given permission to trade in hostelries. These restrictions have been lifted, and many Zoroastrians are participating in various forms of trade.

Division of Labor. The women are mainly responsible for performing domestic duties and bringing up the children. The degree to which a woman contributes to the family income depends on the level of education of the head of the household. If the husband has had a college education, he is usually more tolerant of a woman finding a job and contributing to the finances of the household. Under the Islamic Republic of Iran, however, different means have been developed to force women to remain at home. Family-protection laws have been abolished, and abortion has been outlawed; women have been dismissed from high positions in the government and in the private sector; coeducation and coed sports have been banned; women have been prevented from participating in public tournaments; and an Islamic code of dress has been imposed on women, regardless of their religious orientation (Nashat 1980).

Land Tenure. Following the Islamic Revolution of 1979–1980, there was widespread confiscation of land, especially from those who were associated with the previous government of the Pahlavi dynasty. Private lands were seized and were to be transferred to villagers. In October 1986 the Iranian Majlis (the lower house of Parliament) approved the Temporary Cultivation Bill. This bill provides for the transfer of lands that had been seized immediately after the Revolution from owners to cultivators; however, the transfers have not been completed (Bakhash 1989).

Kinship

Kin Groups and Descent. The relationship between kin is much stronger than other social connections. A "family" consists of parents, offspring, and near and distant relatives. Relatives are expected to be financially responsible for each other. It is through their individual acts that near and distant kin influence each other's status in society. For example, when an individual reaches a high social standing, a number of relatives will surround him and create a new sociopolitical group. Marriage is still considered to be a system uniting two families rather than two individuals. This is the reason for the high percentage of marriages within the kinship group. The kinship group is also a system of protection. In times of crisis, it is to the family that one goes for security and protection.

Kinship Terminology. The Farsi terminology used for designating various relatives is very specific. The terms used to address uncles or aunts are determined by whether they are paternal or maternal: the maternal uncle is called *daye*, whereas the paternal uncle is *ammu;* the term for maternal aunt is *khala* and that for paternal aunt is *ama*. The terminology for cousins is also influenced by male or female parentage. The words "daughter" (*dokhtar*) or "son" (*pessar*) are added to the above terms; thus the daughter of the maternal aunt is addressed as *dokhtar khala*, the son of the paternal uncle is known as *pessar ammu*, and so on. The terms for members of the immediate family are *madar* (mother; Avestan: *matar*), *pidar* (father; Avestan: *patar*), *khahar* (sister; Avestan: *qanhar*), and *baradar* (brother; Avestan: *bratar*).

Marriage and Family

Marriage. The preferred system of marriage is next-of-kin or cousin marriage. The cousin-marriage system differs little from that of the Muslims. Zoroastrians insist more on marriage within one's religious group than on marriage with someone of equal status. One way for a Zoroastrian to perform social responsibilities is for a rich individual to marry a poor one. The problem that has emerged is the excess of inbreeding: this has resulted in a high recurrence of physiological defects such as diabetes, heart disease, and mental illness. These developments have led many among the younger generation to oppose cousin marriage. Because of the increase in the number of young individuals moving to Europe and the United States and marriage with non-Zoroastrians, there is a possibility of the extinction of the group. This has led to the acceptance of conversions to Zoroastrianism. According to the Zoroastrian *anjoman* of Iran, the marriage of a Zoroastrian to a non-Zoroastrian must be performed in compliance with Zoroastrian rituals. The marriage must be registered with the Registrar of Zoroastrian Marriages. The individual interested in marrying a Zoroastrian must make application to the anjoman and must submit various documents. The non-Zoroastrian party must certify that he believes in the Zoroastrian faith and will become part of the Zoroastrian community. The authorized *mobed* (priest) must certify that the person has learned the essential principles and prayers of the religion. A certificate signed by seven Zoroastrians testifying that the individual is of good character and integrity also is required. By Iranian law, a Zoroastrian girl who marries a Muslim boy must become a Muslim. One is not allowed to marry within one's primary and secondary kin. The prohibited group includes grandparents, parents, brothers, sisters, daughters, sons, uncles, aunts, nieces, nephews, and grandchildren. The best choice for marriage is with the children of paternal or maternal siblings and more distant cousins. The various steps that must be taken in order to marry are *xastegari* (expressing the desire for the girl's hand), *namzad* (engagement), and *nikah* (marriage) (Fischer 1973, 199–204). It is only during the twentieth century that divorce has been recognized.

Domestic Unit. The head of the household is the father or husband. The members of the family must respect him and submit to his will. In return, he must satisfy their financial, social, and material needs. The wife is expected to perform her wifely duties, which include the care of the home and children. Many women have become educated and have entered the work force. They are thus contributing also to the financial security of the family. In the traditional family, dominance is determined by age and sex. The older dominates the younger, the male dominates the female. The reputation and honor of the family, which are influenced by the accomplishments of the head of the household as well as its individual members, are strictly protected. Households are either conjugal or extended. An extended household includes parents, unmarried children, a married child with a spouse, and grandchildren. The conjugal family simply includes the parents and children.

Inheritance. If a husband dies without a will, a settlement has traditionally been made to the widow after all debts have been paid. Brothers and sisters are technically supposed to receive equal shares; however, a division similar to the Islamic rule of two parts for a son and one part for a daughter has been practiced (Fischer 1973, 196). The rule for division applies only if a husband dies without a will; otherwise, he may pass on his inheritance as he likes.

Socialization. It is the duty of a Zoroastrian to marry and have children. At birth, the child's lips are steeped in haoma (Sanskrit: *soma*), which is the juice of an intoxicating plant. The child becomes a full Zoroastrian at the age of 7. The initiation ceremony, *sedre-pushun*, lasts nine days and requires the learning of a few of the important prayers in Avestan. The child is also given the sacred shirt of cotton (*sudre sedre*) and the sacred girdle (*kusti*) of fine lamb's wool, which is formed of 72 threads, wound three times around the waist, and tied with three knots. The knots symbolize the three rules of Zoroastrianism, which are "good words, good deeds, and good thoughts." The kusti is tied over the sudra, which has a little purse sewn into the throat. The pocket is to be filled with the results of complying with the three rules. It is to assist the wearer in concentrating on the practice of the faith.

It was not until after the 1870s that Zoroastrians were given permission to establish schools for their children. In the villages, the schools were funded and supported by wealthy Parsis in India. Relative to the entire Iranian population, the level of education of Zoroastrians is high.

Sociopolitical Organization

Social Organization. The community is divided into two groups, the hereditary priests and the laity. As among the Muslims, the influential families are those that have members strategically distributed throughout the most important sectors of society, each prepared to support the other in order to ensure family prestige and status.

Political Organization. There is no supreme head of the Zoroastrians in Iran. In each city, there is a Zoroastrian association known as the "Anjoman Zardoshtian." Its governing members are elected by the community. Today the anjoman in Tehran, owing to its location, has developed a position of leadership; however, local affairs are handled by the local anjoman. In addition to these associations, each city has a youth club, which is mainly involved with sports and cultural activities. In Tehran, a Zoroastrian Women's Association has also been established. Government officials do recognize minority groups such as the Jews, Christians, and Zoroastrians. They are permitted to sustain organizations, elect a representative to the Majlis (lower house of Parliament), maintain religious schools, and publish periodicals; however, they are restricted in political activities. Non-Muslims cannot reach command positions in the armed forces and cannot achieve policy-making positions in government. The Zoroastrian community was formerly organized through priest rotation; now it is through appointments and by the influence of the anjoman structure. Formerly there was a *katkhoda*, a local political leader, and, at the highest level, the *kalantar* (magistrate) of the entire Zoroastrian community.

Social Control. Of concern to the Zoroastrian community are the ritual calendar, the upkeep of the priesthood, and conversion. There is also a conflict between the younger generation and the older one, which is more orthodox. The community is in transition, and the population is attempting to become Westernized.

Conflict. Boundaries have always been maintained between the various religious groups such as the Muslims, Jews, Christians, Zoroastrians, and Baha'is, especially under the Islamic government. One of the ways to alleviate intercommunal tension is to allow non-Zoroastrians to enter the fire temples. Muslims have been seen participating in the funerals of Zoroastrian friends. In the past, because of strict Zoroastrian observance of the laws of purity, this was not permitted. Until 1885, the Zoroastrians were subject to various forms of persecution. They were not allowed to wear rings, and their girdles were made of rough canvas. Until 1895, they were not permitted to carry umbrellas or wear glasses or spectacles. Until 1896, they were forced to twist their turbans instead of folding them (Malcolm 1905, 45).

Religion and Expressive Culture

Religious Beliefs. In Zoroastrianism, moderation, truthfulness, honest dealing, and charity are stressed. Having to capacity to select between good (Ohrmazd) and evil (Ahriman), individuals bear responsibility for their own souls. The *Zend-Avesta* is the Zoroastrian sacred book. Only a small portion of it, the *Gathas*, is considered to be the work of the Prophet. Their chief cult objects are fire and water. Water made life possible, and fire was the source of warmth and the means of cooking meat. Zoroaster saw divinity in its flames and called it Atar. Fire thus became the symbol of the religion and of righteousness. The holy fire is kept in their place of worship, which is a fire temple (*atesh kadeh*). Five times a day the mobed (priest) sprinkles perfumes on the fire. The lower part of his face is covered with a veil to keep his breath from polluting the sacred fire. Every Zoroastrian has a sacred fire in his own house. Today not many followers participate in temple-centered ceremonies. They usually participate twice yearly at festivals during early spring and autumn. Other ceremonies related to initiation, marriage, death, and the seasons are conducted at home.

Religious Practitioners. The priesthood is hereditary. Any male descendant of a priest (mobed/*dastur*) to the fifth generation may take up the profession. In the 1970s there were only fifteen active priests in all of Iran. Offerings are part of the required daily priestly activities (see "Ceremonies"). *Pav*, or "the pure place," is where all the high rituals are performed. This area consists of a small piece of ground, rectangular in shape, its boundaries marked off by prayers to exclude all evil influences. It is also purified with water and prayers. The primary duty of the priest is to keep himself in a state of purity and to pray and perform daily prayers. The rituals must be performed and attended only by those who are spiritually and physically clean. Non-Zoroastrians are usually not allowed to enter the temple because they do not observe the rules of cleanliness prescribed by the religion. The minimum age for the initiation of the priests is 12. The life of the priest is strongly linked with that of the temple. Major ceremonies are performed by a group of priests, the *dastur-nishin*, who reside near the fire temple.

Ceremonies. The chief ritual is the Yasna, or sacrifice, which includes the offering of haoma, the intoxicating juice of a plant, together with water and milk, presented before the fire and drunk by the priest in honor of Ahura Mazda and lesser deities and for the benefit of the dead and the living. The Yasna, a life rite, strengthens the forces of good against those of evil. In former days, the slaughtering of animals was part of the ritual; this practice survived into medieval times but is now extinct. The two main principles that form the basis of Zoroastrian ethics are the maintenance of life and the struggle against evil. There is a devotion to purity, physical as well as spiritual. The chief feasts are New Year (Nouroz); the equinox between seasons, which is consecrated to Mithra; the days of the dead at the end of the year; and the days of the full moon and new moon. Three offerings, which involve two elements from the plant world and one element from the animal world, are made to the fire. The offering usually consists of dried leaves of herbs and animal fat.

Medicine. Many Zoroastrians have access to modern medical facilities. (It is required that Iranian medical students serve four years as residents in the provinces.) Among the elderly, herbal medicines are used. Some of the traditional medical practices are accompanied with prayers.

Death and Afterlife. The traditional system of disposing of the corpse is the use of the towers of silence, which are technically cemeteries. Three main reasons have been given for their use. First, the corpse is considered to be the most polluting element in the world. The stone platform where the body is placed used to be built away from the area of habitation and the corpse was exposed to sun and vultures. Second, the body was given as a gift of nourishment to the birds. Third was the sub rosa, which is the speed with which a body is disposed of. This is taken as a symbol of the progress of the soul into the other world, and it is a signal for intensification of death ceremonies among the living. Because they live among Muslims, the Zoroastrians were forced to make certain adjustments. The towers of silence are no longer used. The body is now placed on a metal stretcher, the legs of which keep the body away from the ground. The bed of the stretcher is made of strips of metal so that a body, while supported, is also open to surrounding elements. The metal is nonporous, so as not to conduct pollution or disease-bearing microbes. The sides of the grave are cemented and a cement cover is placed on top so that dirt does not fall on the body (Fischer 1973, 63–65). It is believed that for three days the soul haunts the home. On the morning following the third night, the soul is taken by the angel Sorush, who has been protecting it on earth for three nights, to the judgment tribunal (*aka*). The soul is judged by using a balance and must cross the Chinvat bridge. If the soul is righteous, the bridge will be wide and will lead the individual to paradise. Good deeds are personified by a beautiful young woman or a handsome man, depending on the gender of the deceased, who will accompany the soul. If the soul was sinful, the bridge will narrow to a razor-sharp edge; the soul will eventually fall into hell and be accompanied by an old and unattractive individual. During the Farvardegan, which is the time to remember the dead, seven kinds of greens (wheat, barley, beans, etc.) are sown, to welcome the spirits with freshness. Most believe that the world of the souls coexists with the world of the living, and dreaming is a method of communication between the two worlds. It is also strongly believed that the soul wanders from the body during the dream state. The sites of visions of saints and angels and of communication from God are often made into shrines. Memorials are held on the tenth day, the thirtieth day, and each month thereafter until the anniversary, and each year until the thirtieth. The ritual setting of these memorials is in the *ja-pak* (clean place) of the pesgam. It must include four items: wine, milk, pomegranate, and quince. The cult of the ancestral spirit remains very strong among the Zoroastrians.

See also Parsi in Volume 3, South Asia

Bibliography

Ahsan, Shakoor A. (1976). *Modern Trends in the Persian Language*. N.p.: Iran-Pakistan Institute of Persian Studies.

Bakhash, Shaul (1989). "The Politics of Land, Law, and Social Justice in *Iran*." *Middle East Journal* 43:186–201.

Beazley, Elizabeth (1977). "Some Vernacular Buildings of the Iranian Plateau." *Iran* 15:89–102.

Bonine, Michael E. (1980). "Aridity and Structures: Adaptations of Indigenous Housing in Central Iran." In *Desert Housing: Balancing Experience and Technology for Dwelling in Hot Arid Zones*, edited by Kenneth N. Clark and Patricia Paylore, 193–219. Tucson: University of Arizona Press.

Boyce, Mary (1966). "The Fire Temples of Kerman." *Acta Orientalia* 30:51–72.

Boyce, Mary (1971a). "The Zoroastrian Houses of Yazd." In *Iran and Islam*, edited by C. E. Bosworth, 125–147. Edinburgh: Edinburgh University Press.

Boyce, Mary (1971b). "Zoroastrianism." In *Historia Religionum: Handbook for the History of Religions*, edited by C. Jouco Bleeker and George Widengren, vol. 2, 211–236. Leiden: E. J. Brill.

Fischer, Michael M. J. (1973). "Zoroastrian Iran between Myth and Praxis." Ph.D. dissertation, University of Chicago.

Malcolm, Napier (1905). *Five Years in a Persian Town*. London: Edinburgh Press.

Ministry of Planning and Budget (1986). *National Iranian Census of 1986*. Tehran: Center of Iranian Statistics.

Nashat, Guity (1980). "Women in the Islamic Republic of Iran." *Iranian Studies* 13:165–194.

Wilber, Donald N. (1948). *Iran: Past and Present*. Princeton, N.J.: Princeton University Press.

SABINA SHAHROKHIZADEH

Zulu

ETHNONYMS: Kaffir, KwaZulu

Orientation

The Zulu are located primarily in Zululand (28° S, 32° E), which is part of the province of Natal of the Republic of South Africa. The Zulu language is classified as a dialect of Nguni, a Zone S language of the South Eastern Area of Bantu proper. Before the days of Shaka, the early nineteenth-century king who consolidated the North Nguni tribes, the term *abakwaZulu* referred to members of the Zulu "clan," descendants of a man named Zulu. With Shaka's political conquests, the term "Zulu" came to include some hundreds of Nguni "clans," all of whom paid allegiance to the Zulu king. Many South African peoples, including the Zulu, are also called "Kaffirs," meaning "infidels," a name which was bestowed on them by early Arab traders.

Gluckman (1972) quotes a population estimate of 100,000 for the early nineteenth century, but he feels that this estimate is too low. According to the 1967 census, the Zulu population was 3,340,000. Berglund (1976) gives the population as 4,130,000. The population in 1986 was estimated at 5,960,000, distributed thus: 5,700,00 in South Africa, 37,500 in Malawi, 15,000 in Swaziland, and 228,000 in Lesotho.

History and Cultural Relations

The Zulu have a reputation as "a proud, fierce, recklessly brave though barbaric warrior race" (Ngubane 1977, viii). In 1815 Shaka, a descendant of the Zulu "clan" originator, came to power. Shaka, who is often referred to as the "Black Napoleon," organized a standing army and proceeded to conquer many of the surrounding Nguni "clans." The results of this turbulent period were widespread; tribes such as the Matabele, Shangana, and Ngoni were formed by people fleeing in Shaka's wake. During Shaka's reign, the first European trading company was established in Port Natal (later Durban). Up to that point, there had been only sporadic contact with Whites. In 1828 Shaka was assassinated by his brother Dingane. In 1835 the missionary Gardner established himself among the Zulu. Piet Retief and a number of Boer Trekkers were massacred by Dingane in 1838. After Dingane's defeat at the Battle of Blood River, his brother Mpande made an alliance with the Boers and forced Dingane into exile. In 1843 Natal became a Crown colony. Mpande was succeeded in 1872 by his son Cetshwayo, during whose reign the Zulu war of 1879–1880 took place. Britain established a magistracy in 1887, and in 1910 Natal became a part of the Union of South Africa. The end of the era of effective Zulu monarchs came with the death of Cetshwayo's son, Dinzulu, in 1913. As with the other indigenous South Africans, the Zulu were outcastes in White-controlled South Africa. Establishment of indigenous control in the 1990s brought conflict with the Xhosa and then accommodation. Zulu social, political, and economic interests have been represented since 1975 by the Zulu National Cultural Liberation Movement (Inkatha Ye Sizwe), commonly known as Inkatha or the Inkatha party.

Economy

Traditionally, the Zulu economy depended upon cattle and a considerable amount of agriculture. Villages were economically self-sufficient. Agriculture was the sphere of women, whereas cattle were tended by the men. Crops grown were mealies, Kaffir maize, pumpkins, watermelons, calabashes, native sugar reeds, and various kinds of tubers and beans. Although there was considerable ritual and magic associated with agriculture, the most impressive agricultural ceremonial was the First Fruits ceremony. This was held late in December, and in it the king partook of the new crops. The ceremony also included a magical strengthening of the king and a general military review.

A man's wealth was counted in cattle. Cattle provided the mainstays of the diet (meat and *amasi,* a form of soured milk), hides for clothing and shields, as well as the means of acquiring wives through *lobola,* or bride-price. In addition, cattle had enormous ritual value. Sacrifice of cattle was the principal means of propitiating the ancestors.

The modern Zulu are poor, with agricultural yield below subsistence level. Women still till the fields, but most men travel to the towns seeking work. Cattle are still a symbol of wealth, although the holdings are low. Cattle are seldom slaughtered for meat—usually only for ritual occasions. According to Clarke and Ngobese (1975), poverty and malnutrition were so severe that the traditional robust Zulu physique is changing and the Zulu are "becoming a puny, stunted and mentally enfeebled people."

Kinship and Sociopolitical Organization

Traditional Zulu political organization was hierarchical, with the king at the apex. Authority was delegated to chiefs of districts and from them to homestead heads. The lowest level of political and kinship organization was the *umuzi,* variously translated as "village," "kraal," or "homestead." These settlements were patrilocal extended-family or clan barrios. Polygyny was the norm and was often sororal. Each kraal was the homestead of a male, which included a separate hut for each of his wives. The huts were arranged, according to the status of the wives, around the central cattle kraal. Villages were moved every few years. The kraal head had the responsibility of keeping law and order and settling disputes. Disputes that could not be settled in the kraal or cases of a special nature were dealt with by the district head.

Zulu society was organized into patrilineal sibs. Through a process of growth, subdivision, and incorporation of aliens, the sib developed into a "tribe," which, however, was still known by the name of the ancestor of the dominant sib. The sibs were divided into lineages, which were composed of descendants of a common ancestor in the near past.

The king, the head of the Zulu "tribe" or "clan," had judicial and legislative power. The legislation, formed by consultation with old men or the council, was not of enormous significance, consisting of orders for the regiments to marry or announcements about campaigns. The council of the king consisted of headmen or the heads of important families who were required to live at the royal kraal for certain periods to advise the king.

Shaka made a number of military innovations, not the least of which was a reorganization of the regimental system. An *intanga* consisted of a group of men of roughly the same age who lived at the royal kraal, tended to the king's cattle, and formed the standing army. According to Reader (1966), the regimental system, although not organized for war, is still an active institution in Zulu society.

Religion

Despite some belief in spirits, there was no real worship of them. Religion was primarily concerned with ancestor worship. Divination was the means of discovering the wishes of the ancestors, and sacrifice of cattle was the means of propitiation. Sorcery and witchcraft were quite common. Missionaries have been in Zululand since 1835, and apparently have been quite successful: more than half the population is reckoned as Christian. According to Ngubane (1977) and others, Christianity does not conflict with ancestor worship or belief in witchcraft.

Bibliography

Berglund, Axel-Ivar (1976). *Zulu Thought-Patterns and Symbolism*. Uppsala: Swedish Institute of Missionary Research.

Bryant, A. T. (1970). *Zulu Medicine and Medicine-Men*. Cape Town: C. Struik.

Clarke, Liz, and Jane Ngobese (1975). *Women without Men: A Study of 150 Families in the Ngutu District of Kwazulu*. Durban: Institute for Black Research.

Gluckman, Max (1972). "Moral Crisis: Magical and Secular Solutions." In *The Allocation of Responsibility*, edited by Max Gluckman. Manchester: Manchester University Press.

Klopper, Sandra (1989). *Mobilizing Cultural Symbols in Twentieth Century Zululand*. Cape Town: Centre for African Studies.

Krige, E. J. (1968). "Girl's Puberty Songs and Their Relation to Fertility, Health, Morality, and Religion among the Zulu." *Africa* 38:173–198.

Ngubane, Harriet (1977). *Body and Mind in Zulu Medicine*. London: Academic Press.

Raum, O. F. (1967). "The Interpretation of the Nguni First Fruit Ceremony." *Paideuma* 13:148–163.

Reader, D. H. (1966). *Zulu Tribe in Transition: The Makhanya of Southern Natal*. Manchester: Manchester University Press.

Vilakazi, A. (1962). *Zulu Transformation*. Pietermaritzburg: University of Natal Press.

Appendix

Additional African Cultures

This is a listing of some 500 African cultures not already covered in the body of the encyclopedia. Estimates of the number of distinct cultures in Africa range from several hundred to several thousand. For Nigeria alone, the most ethnically diverse nation on the continent, estimates range from 250 to 800. These estimates vary so widely because cultures are neither fixed in time nor place. Centuries of social, political, and economic change in Africa have produced a broad mix of religious, ethnic, linguistic, political, occupational, and territorial groups that, depending on one's definition of a culture group, might be classified as a distinct group. Thus, it is impossible to list all the culture groups of Africa, and this appendix focuses on the larger groups or subgroups within broad groupings or clusters of related groups.

The culture groups that are entry titles in this appendix are in boldface. Cross-references are included for named subgroups that are covered in the main entries in the body of the encyclopedia. Population figures are mainly from the 1980s and are mostly estimates.

Abbe (Abé) A people of the Ivory Coast, numbering about 73,900.

Abidji (Ari) Farming people of the Ivory Coast, who number about 26,700.

Abron (Brong, Doma) An Akan people, of whom about 494,000 live in Ghana and another 78,000 in Ivory Coast.

Abuan A people of the southernmost part of Nigeria, who number about 24,000.

Abu Sharib A Muslim group, numbering about 25,000, who raise cattle, camels and goats in Chad.

Adioukrou (Ajukru) A people of Ivory Coast, numbering about 54,700. They are involved in the commercial exploitation of palm trees.

Adja (Aja-Gbe) A people of northern Benin numbering about 250,000.

Agni (Anyin) One of the Akan peoples, with a population of about 332,000 in southeast Ivory Coast and another 100,000 in Ghana.

Aizo A people of northern Benin.

Alaba (Halaba) An agricultural people of Ethiopia, numbering about 50,000.

Alladian (Alagia) A people of Ivory Coast, composed of three groups: Aware, Agrou (Akouri), and Kovou. They number about 12,600.

Amba (Bulebule, Hamba, Kibera, Kukamba) An agricultural people who live south of Lake Albert Nyanza (also known as Lake Mobutu Sese Seko), in Uganda, along the Zaire border, and number about 73,500. There are some also in Zaire.

Americo-Liberians One of the nontribal groups in Liberia, composed of descendants of early settlers from the United States and some of the indigenous peoples. They live primarily along the coast.

Anaang A people of southeastern Nigeria, who number about 246,000.

Anglophones of Cameroon (Westerners) A group of about 2 million to 2.5 million, the majority of whom speak one of the indigenous dialects.

Ankole A subgroup of the Sashi people of Tanzania.

Ankwe A people of central Nigeria.

ǁ Anikhoe. *See* San-Speaking Peoples

Annakaza. *See* Teda

Argobba (Argobbinya) An agricultural Muslim people of Ethiopia, numbering about 2,500-3,000.

Arna. *See* Teda

Attie A group of about 221,400 living in Ivory Coast, who are coffee and cocoa growers.

Avikam (Brignan, Gbanda, Kwaka, Lahu) A people of Ivory Coast who live at the mouth of the Bandama River. They number about 8,500.

Awi (Awngi, Agaw, Damot, Falasha, Yihudi) The largest of the Agew-speaking groups of Ethiopia, they number about 50,000.

Baboute (Bute, Nbule, Voutere, Vute) A people of the southern forest region of Cameroon, numbering about 30,000.

Bacongo. *See* Kongo

Badondo. *See* Kongo

Badyaranke (Gola, Pajade) One of the Tenda peoples who live along the Guinea-Senegal border and number between 5,000 and 12,000.

Baga (Baga-Binari, Baga-Koga, Barka, Kalum) A coastal people of Lower Guinea.

Baka (Tara-Baaka, Mbaka) A group numbering about 23,000 in Sudan and 1,300 in Zaire.

Bakhayo. *See* Luyia

Balante (Alante, Bulanda, Brassa, Frase) A people numbering about 255,000 in Guinea Bissau and about 50,000 in Senegal.

Baloundou-Mbo A people of the southern forest region of Cameroon.

Bambara (Bamana) A primarily Muslim people, closely identified with their system of village-based, cooperative farming, who number about 1.5 million. They are found primarily in Mali, with the rest distributed among Ivory Coast, Gambia, Guinea, Mauritania, and Senegal.

Bamileke A sedentary farming people of southern Cameroon, numbering about 600,000.

Bamoun A people of the western highlands of Cameroon, numbering about 215,000.

Banda The largest ethnic group in the Central African Republic, they number about 1,074,000.

Bandi (Gbunde) A group of people numbering 59,400 in northwestern Liberia and 66,000 in Guinea.

Banyala. *See* Luyia

Banyore. *See* Luyia

Banziri (Gbandere) A people who number about 3,000 in Zaire, with a few also along the Ubangi River in the Central African Republic.

Baoule One of the Akan peoples, and the largest ethnic group in Ivory Coast. Numbering about 1,500,000, they live in the forest region and the savanna woodlands.

Bariba (Bargu, Batonu, Berba) Muslim agriculturists, numbering about 195,000 in northern Benin and 55,000 in Nigeria.

Barma. *See* Bagirmi

Basonga. *See* Luyia

Bassa (Bikyek, Koko, Mvele, Northern Mbene, Tupen) A hunter-gatherer people of the southern forests of Cameroon, numbering about 230,000. A few are also found in Liberia.

Bassari (Ayan, Onian, Tenda, Wo) One of the Tenda peoples, who live along the Guinea-Senegal border. They number about 14,000, with a few also in Gambia.

Basundi. *See* Kongo

Batsotso. *See* Luyia

Baya A people of the eastern border of Cameroon.

Beja (Bedawiye, Beni-Amer) A cattle- and camel-herding Muslim people, with a total population of about 980,000 in eastern Sudan, Eritrea, Ethiopia, and southern Egypt.

Bemba (Chibemba, Wemba) A cluster of slash-and-burn agricultural peoples who live at the conjunction of Zambia, Tanzania, and Zaire and numbering in total about 1,850,000.

Bembe. *See* Kongo

Bena (Ekibena) One of the Shirazi peoples of Tanzania, they number about 490,000.

Beni-Amer One of the pastoralist Beja groups of the semi-arid regions of Sudan and Ethiopia.

Beri (Bai, Bari, Bideyat) A cattle-raising, camel-herding, Muslim people, numbering about 340,000, most of whom live in Sudan, with others in Uganda, Zaire, and Chad.

Berta (Beni Shangul, Wetawit) An agricultural people of Ethiopia, numbering between 28,000 and 50,000.

Berti (Zaghawa) A nominally Muslim people of northern Sudan, who are primarily cultivators.

Bete One of the Krou Complex peoples, they are farmers in the southwestern region of Ivory Coast and number about 600,000.

Bilen (Bogos) A primarily Muslim group of sedentary farmers in the northern highlands of Ethiopia, numbering between 90,000 and 120,000.

Binga A people of the northeastern forest region of Congo.

Birom (Afango, Gbang, Kibo) A people who live in central Nigeria and number about 200,000.

Black Maures A people, largely descendents of slaves, who identify themselves culturally with the White Maures of Mauritania, Senegal, and Mali.

Bngala A group of the Mboshi Cluster of Congo.

Bobo (Bobo Dioula, Bobo Fing, Zara) A farming people of Burkina Faso, with a population of about 170,000; a few also live in Mali.

Bolewa (Bole, Ampika) A Muslim people of northeastern Nigeria, who number about 32,000.

Boma-Sakata (Boma-Kasai, Kiboma) A cluster of peoples who live in the area of the lower Kasai River, in Zaire, and number about 8,000.

Bondei One of the Shirazi peoples of Tanzania, they number about 80,000.

Bongo (Bungu, Dor) A group numbering between 5,000 and 10,000, who live in Sudan.

Boran A farming and fishing people of the lower Omo Valley in Ethiopia.

Bororodjis (Bororo Fulani) Nomadic herders of the Dakoro-Tanout region of Niger.

Bubis (Bube Ediya) A mainly Catholic people of the island of Bioko in Equatorial Guinea, who number about 21,000.

Buduma (Yedina) A group of Muslim farmer-fishers, who inhabit the islands of Lake Chad; they number between 20,000 and 25,000.

Bukusu. *See* Luyia

Bulibuzi A subgroup of the Amba peoples of Uganda.

Busa (Boko, Bokobaru, Zugweya) A people found in eastern Benin and western Nigeria, with a total population of about 100,000.

Central Togo A cluster of groups in the mountain region of Ethiopia, who cultivate rice and cocoa.

Chamba A people who live on both sides of the border between Nigeria and Cameroon, with a total population of about 112,000.

Charfarda. *See* Teda

Chewa A people of central Malawi, who are closely related to the Nyanja.

Chokwe (Djok, Shioko) A people of Angola, Zaire, and Zambia, with about 500,000 distributed between Angola and Zaire and another 504,000 in Zaire.

Chopi A people of the southern coast of Mozambique, numbering about 400,000.

Congo. *See* Kongo

Coniagui (Duka, Tenda) One of the Tenda peoples, who live along the Guinea-Sengal border, numbering about 10,000.

Creoles (Crioulo, Krio) A group of Christian descendants of freed slaves from the West Indies, who live in Sierra Leone, the Cape Verde Islands, Gambia, Equatorial Guinea, Guinea, Guinea-Bissau, and Senegal.

Cussu A very small group of Bantu-speaking people of southeastern Angola.

Daba A people of northern Cameroon, numbering about 35,700.

Dagomba (Dagbamba, Dagbani) Muslim farmers of northern Ghana, with a population of about 400,000.

Daju (Bokoruge) A sedentary Muslim farming people of eastern Chad and western Sudan, numbering about 110,000.

Dakarkari (Kolela, Lalawa, Lela) A people of western and northwestern Nigeria, numbering about 69,000.

Dan (Diafouba, Yacouba) A Mande people, who live at the southern edge of the savanna woodland of Ivory Coast. They number about 346,900.

Dasanec (Dama, Geleba, Merile) A pastoralist and agricultural people, numbering about 30,000 in Ethiopia and another 2,500 or so in Kenya.

Dendi (Dandawa) A people of northern Benin, numbering about 21,000, with a few also in Nigeria and Niger.

Deti. *See* San-Speaking Peoples

Dey (Dewoi, Dewoin) A people of Montserrado County and Monrovia, in Liberia, numbering about 8,000.

Dghwede (Hude, Wa'a, Zaghvana) A people of northeastern Nigeria, who number about 30,000.

Dialonke (Jallonke, Yalunka) An agricultural people, of whom about 30,000 live in Sierra Leone and a few also in Guinea.

Dian. *See* Lobi-Dagarti Peoples

Diankhanke (Janhanka) A small group of Muslim people in Senegal, who are cultivators, stock raisers, and traders.

Dida One of the Krou Complex peoples of Ivory Coast.

Didinga (Lango, Toi, Xaroxa) A group of people who live in southern Sudan, numbering about 58,000.

Digo (Kidigo) One of the Mijikenda groups, they are agriculturists and fishers, numbering about 176,000 in Kenya and 88,000 in Tanzania.

Diola (Dyamate, Kudumata) A Muslim farming people numbering about 390,000, most of whom live in Senegal, Gambia, and Guinea-Bissau.

Djagada. *See* Teda

Djoheina A pastoralist people of Arab descent, who live in Chad.

Dodoth A pastoralist people of Uganda, who belong to the Karamojong Cluster.

Dombe A pastoralist people in Angola, who are related to the Ovimbundu.

Dondo. *See* Kongo

Dorossié. *See* Lobi-Dagarti Peoples

Dourou (Dui, Duru, Nyag Dii, Zaa) A people who live between the towns of Garoua and Ngaoundéré, in Cameroon, and number about 47,000.

Doza. *See* Teda

Dukawa (Duka, Ethun, Hune) A people of northwestern Nigeria, numbering about 30,000.

Ebrie The indigenous people of Abidjan, the capital of Ivory Coast, they are fishers and number about 52,900.

Edo-Speaking Peoples (Addo, Bini, Ovoiba) A grouping of peoples numbering about 1 million, who live in the state of Bendel, in southern Nigeria.

Efik (Calabar) A group numbering about 2 million in southeastern Nigeria and neighboring Cameroon, who speak dialects of the Ibibio language. The Efik were established as a separate group within the population of Ibibio speakers by their early and continuing contact with Westerners as slavers, traders, and converts to Christianity and as professionals and administrators in postcolonial Nigeria.

Eggon (Mada Eggoni, Megong) A people of central Nigeria, numbering about 80,000.

Ejagham (Ekoi) A people distributed throughout Nigeria (about 45,000) and Cameroon (about 35,000).

Eket A people numbering about 22,000, who live in southeastern Nigeria.

Endo. *See* Nandi and Other Kalenjin Peoples

Erdiha. *See* Teda

Etsako (Afenmai, Yekhee) A name that includes eight groups of people who live in southern Nigeria and number about 150,000.

Fang (Pahouin, Pangwe, Panue) A farming people numbering about 525,000, the majority of whom live in Equatorial Guinea, Gabon, and Cameroon.

Fante (Mfantse) One of the Akan peoples living in Ghana, they number about 1,170,000, of whom the majority are Christian and the rest Muslim.

Fongoro A very small and fast-disappearing group of Muslim hunter-gatherers who live along the border of Chad and Sudan.

Funj In modern times, a name that refers solely to the hereditary nobility of the former kingdom of Sinnér and applies to a small group of Muslims in Sudan.

Fur (Fora, Fordunga, Konjara) A Muslim farming people, numbering about 500,000 in Sudan with another 1,000 or so in Chad.

Furiiru (Kifuliiru, Fulero) A people who live in the eastern highlands of Zaire and number about 266,000.

Ga-Adandme-Krobo (Acra, Amina, Gain) A people who live in the coastal areas of Ghana and Togo, numbering about 1,020,000.

Gaeda. *See* Teda

Gagou (G'ban) A Mande people of the west-central region of Ivory Coast, numbering about 42,300.

Gallinas A subgroup of the Vai people of Sierra Leone.

Gamo-Gofa One of many groups of Omotic-language speakers of southern Ethiopia, they are sedentary agriculturists.

G||ana. *See* San-Speaking Peoples

Ganda (Luganda) An agricultural people, numbering about 2,352,000 along the northwest shore of Lake Victoria in southern Uganda and about 9,500 in Tanzania.

Gbagyi (Gwari Matai) A farming people of Nigeria, who number about 250,000.

Gbari (Gwari Yamma) A people who live in western Nigeria.

Gbaya Mandjia A largely Christian group of slash-and-burn agriculturists, of whom about 730,000 live in the Central African Republic and 132,000 in Cameroon.

Giriama (Agiryama, Kinyika, Nika) An agricultural people of the coastal region of Kenya, they number about 450,000 and are one of the Mijikenda groups.

Gisu A sedentary agricultural people of southern Uganda.

Glavda A people who live in the southernmost part of Nigeria (about 20,000) and in Cameroon (about 2,800).

Gogo (Chigogo) An agricultural people of Tanzania, numbering about 1 million.

Gola (Gula) A people linguistically related to the Kissi of Sierra Leone. There are about 84,000 in Liberia and about 6,400 in Sierra Leone.

Gonja (Ngbanyito) A farming people of Ghana, who number about 125,000.

Goun (Gun-Gbe, Alada, Egun) A people of Benin, numbering about 173,000.

Gourous. *See* Teda

Gouru (Kweni, Lo) A Mande people of the central and west-central regions of Ivory Coast, numbering about 206,500.

Gourounsi A people of the savanna region of Ivory Coast.

Grebo A name for a nine-group cluster of agricultural peoples of southeastern Liberia, numbering together about 2 million.

Grusi A subgrouping of the Gur peoples of Ghana.

Gu (Gun-Gbe, Kagu) A people who number about 173,000 in Benin with a few also in southwestern Nigeria.

Guan A number of groups connected by a shared language (Guan), who live in northern Ghana.

Gude (Cheke, Mubi, Mapuda) A group numbering about 40,000 in eastern Nigeria and about 18,000 in Cameroon.

Guere (Wee) One of the Krou Complex peoples of western Ivory Coast, they number about 197,100.

Guidar (Kada, Baynawa) A farming people of the northern savanna of Cameroon, they number about 65,600.

Guiziga (Dogba, Mi Marva, Tchere) A farming people of the northern savanna of Cameroon, numbering about 20,000.

Gurage (Silti) A sedentary agricultural people of Ethiopia with a population of about 742,000, of whom about one-third are Muslim.

Gurma A subgrouping of the Gur peoples of Ghana.

Gwe An agricultural Bantu people of Uganda.

Gwere (Olugwere) An agricultural people of Uganda, numbering about 250,000.

G|wi. *See* San-Speaking Peoples

Ha (Giha, Ikiha) A people of northwestern Tanzania, numbering about 725,000.

Haddad A people of Chad, Nigeria, and Sudan, numbering about 270,000.

Hadiyya (Adiye, Gudeilla) An agricultural people of Ethiopia, numbering about 2 million.

Haillom. *See* San-Speaking Peoples

Hamer (Amar, Gudella, Hadiya, Haner-Banna) A pastoralist Muslim people of Ethiopia, numbering about 15,000.

Hangaza A people of northwestern Tanzania, numbering about 150,000.

Harari (Adare, Gesinan, Hareri) A group of Muslim farmers and merchants, numbering about 84,000, who are found almost exclusively in the city of Harar in Ethiopia.

Hassouna A pastoralist people of Arab descent who live in Chad.

Haut-Katanga A people of the savanna region of southeastern Zaire.

Haya (Ekihaya, Ruhaya, Ziba) A sedentary farming people, numbering about 1 million, who live to the west of Lake Victoria in Tanzania.

Hehe A Bantu-speaking people of Tanzania, who number about 630,000.

Hemba (Eastern Luba, Emba, Kiemba) A cluster of peoples who live in the savanna region of southeastern Zaire.

Hima (Urohima) A small group of Nilotic nomads, who live in Rwanda and number about 4,000.

Holli A people of northern Benin.

Hororo A subgroup of the Kiga people of Uganda.

Hunde A subgroup of the Kiga people of Uganda.

Hutu A farming and cattle-raising people, comprising the largest ethnic group in Burundi. They are also found in Rwanda.

Idakho. *See* Luyia

Idoma A group numbering about 300,000 in southern Nigeria.

Igala A people of southern Nigeria, with a population of about 800,000.

Igbira (Ebira, Kotokori) An agricultural group living in western Nigeria and numbering about 500,000.

Ijaw (Ijo) A people of eastern Nigeria, with a population of about 420,000.

Ik (Teuso) A subgroup of the Teuso people of Uganda.

Ikwere A group that lives in the southernmost part of Nigeria and numbers about 200,000.

Ineme One of the Edo-speaking peoples of southwestern Nigeria.

Ingessana A people who live in the mountains along the Sudan-Ethiopian border.

Iramba (Nilamba) A people who live in northwestern Tanzania and number about 440,000.

Irigwe (Idafan, Kwoll, Miango) A group numbering about 40,000 in central Nigeria.

Isekiri (Jekri, Selemo, Sherkeri) A people of southwestern Nigeria, who number about 500,000.

Ishan (Esa, Isa) A group numbering about 185,000, that speaks a Kwa language and lives mainly in southern Nigeria. Major subgroups, including chiefdoms, villages, or village clusters include the Ekpoma, Irua, Ugun, Emu, Urhu, and Ewatto.

Isoko (Sobo, Biotu) A group found in southwestern Nigeria, who number about 300,000.

Isukha. *See* Luyia

Iyala (Yala) A people who live in southeastern Nigeria and number about 50,000.

Jabarti A Muslim farming people of Ethiopia, numbering about 207,000.

Jahanka (Diakkane) Not strictly an ethnic group, this collection of Soninké clans are Muslim farmers, most of whom live in Senegal and Gambia. They number about 50,000.

Jarawa (Jar) A cluster of peoples that includes the Bankal and Gingwak who live in eastern and central Nigeria, with a total population of about 150,000.

Jerawa A cluster of peoples including the Amo, Buji, Chokobo, Gussum, Gurum, Jere, and Limoro groups, who live throughout central Nigeria.

Jie A pastoralist people of Uganda, who belong to the Karamojong Cluster.

Jita (Echijita) A people who live on the southeast shore of Lake Victoria, in Tanzania. They number about 217,000.

Jiye A people of eastern Sudan.

Jonam A people who live near the Nile River, in northwestern Uganda, whose economy is based primarily on fishing and cotton cultivation.

Jukun (Wakaki, Wapa) Benue-Congo-language speakers of Nigeria, numbering about 60,000.

Kabras. *See* Luyia

Kaguru (Kagulu, Northern Kiningo, Sagala) A group in Tanzania that numbers about 217,000.

Kaje (Jju, Kache) A group found in Kaduna State, in north-central Nigeria, that numbers about 200,000 to 300,000.

Kakwa (Kwakwak) A farming people, closely related to the Beri, who live in Uganda (about 88,200), Sudan (about 40,000), and Zaire (about 20,000).

Kamadja. *See* Teda

Kamaku (Jindu) A people who live in western Nigeria and number about 20,000.

Kamba (Kekamba) A farming people of central Kenya, related to the Kikuyu. They number about 2,500,000, with some also in Congo.

Kambari A cluster of peoples who live in western and northwestern Nigeria, with a total population of about 100,000.

Kanembu A farming and cattle-raising Muslim people, who live in Chad (about 190,000), Nigeria (about 135,000), and Niger (about 6,000).

Kaonde (Kawonde, Luba Kaonde) A people of northwestern Zambia and Zaire, with populations of about 197,200 and 20,000, respectively.

Kapsiki A group of hill people who live near Mokolo, in Cameroon, and others also in Nigeria.

Katab A cluster of groups found in north-central Nigeria, who number about 32,400.

Kebu (Okebo) A small group that lives along the Uganda-Zaire border.

Kecherda. *See* Teda

Kefa-Mocha (Kafficho, Keffa) One of many groups of Omotic-language speakers of southern Ethiopia, they are sedentary agriculturists, numbering about 211,000.

Keiyo. *See* Nandi and Other Kalenjin Peoples

Kembats (Kambatta, Kemata) An agricultural people of Ethiopia, numbering about 1 million.

Kenyi A Bantu people of Uganda, who make their living as fishers in Lake Kyoga.

Kiga A farming people of Uganda, numbering about 500,000.

Kilba (Huba, Ndirma, Xibba) A people numbering about 100,000, who live in southeastern Nigeria.

Kimbundu A farming people of western and central Angola.

Kinga A people of the Livingstone Mountains and the northeastern shore of Lake Malawi, in Tanzania. They number about 65,000.

Kisa. *See* Luyia

Kissi (Gizi, Kissien) The Kissi are primarily rice cultivators, who live at the conjunction of Guinea, Liberia, and Sierra Leone and number about 441,000.

Kofyar A people of central Nigeria, who number about 40,000.

Kokorda. *See* Teda

Kongo (Bacongo, Badondo, Basundi, Bembe, Congo, Dondo, Kikongo, Kougni, Lali, Sundi) A collective name for a number of ethnic groups who live in the coastal, western region of Congo, with a total population of about 1,200,000 in Congo, 1 million in Zaire, and 1,027,000 in Angola.

Konjo (Konzo, Rukonjo) A Bantu people of Uganda, numbering about 250,000.

Kono A people of Eastern Province in Sierra Leone, numbering about 125,000.

!Koõ. *See* San-Speaking Peoples

Koranko A people who are distantly related to the Mandingo. There are about 200,000 in Sierra Leone and about 50,000 in Guinea.

Koro The name for a cluster of groups numbering about 35,000 in total, who live in north-central Nigeria.

Kotoko (Kuseri, Logone, Mser) A farming and fishing people of northeastern Cameroon, who number about 40,600.

Kougni. *See* Kongo.

Koulango A people of the northeastern region of Ivory Coast, numbering about 165,000. There are also about 10,000 in Ghana.

Kpe A people of the southern forests of Cameroon.

Krahn A Kruan-speaking people, numbering about 40,000 in Liberia and 27,500 in Ivory Coast.

Kreda. *See* Teda

Krim (Kimi, Kittim) A cultivating and fishing people of coastal Sierra Leone, related to the Sherbro. They number about 12,800.

Krou of Bas Cavally A group of people of Ivory Coast that includes the Bapo, Oubi, Ourouboue, Tabou, Tahou, Tepo, Touyo, Trepo, and Tribuoe.

Kru (Kroo, Krumen) A people of Liberia; inland dwellers are slash-and-burn agriculturists, whereas those on the coast are dock workers and fishers. There are also about 27,000 in Ivory Coast and an undetermined number in Liberia.

Kuba (Luna, Inkongo) A cluster of peoples who live in the lower Kasai River region of Zaire and number about 50,000.

Kuku A farming people of the highlands of Sudan, related to the Beri.

Kuman (Akum, Akokolemu, Ikokolemu, Kumam) An agricultural and cattle-raising people of Uganda, numbering about 147,000.

Kunema (Baden, Baza, Diila) An agricultural people of northern Ethiopia, numbering between 40,500 and 70,000.

!Kung. *See* San-Speaking Peoples

Kuria (Ikikuria, Tende) A people who live in Tanzania (about 213,000) and Kenya (about 132,000).

Kwangali-Gcikuru A very small group, living in southeastern Angola, Namibia, and Botswana.

Kxoe. *See* San-Speaking Peoples

Labwor A small group of people of the Karamoja District of Uganda, who are mainly traders.

Lagoon Cluster This term includes several groups of people of the coastal lagoons of Ivory Coast, who are fishers and farmers.

Lali. *See* Kongo.

Lamang (Gbuhwe, Kuvoko) A cluster of peoples who live in northeastern Nigeria (about 40,000) and Cameroon (about 9,000).

Lamba (Ichilamba) A people of the Copperbelt (central and northwestern provinces of Zambia), numbering about 170,000.

Landouma (Landouman, Tyapi) A group, related to the Baga peoples, who live in Guinea-Bissau and number 8,000 to 10,000.

Langi (Lango) A people of central Uganda, whose economy is largely dependent on cotton growing.

Lebou A Muslim people, who live on the Cape Verde Peninsula of Senegal and make their living primarily as fishers.

Lega (Kilega, Mwenga, Rega) A people of the plains, highlands, and forests of eastern Zaire, numbering about 400,000.

Lele (Bashilele, Usilele) One of the Kuba Cluster peoples, who live in the lower Kasai River region of Zaire and number about 26,000.

Lendu (Bale, Bbadha, Kilendu) A people of Zaire numbering about 490,000, with some also across the border in northwestern Uganda.

Lengola A people who live in the plains, highlands, and forests west of the Lualaba River, in eastern Zaire.

Limba (Yimbe) An agricultural people of Northern Province, in Sierra Leone, numbering about 269,000.

Liyuwa A very small group living in southeastern Angola, Zambia, and Namibia.

Lobirifor. *See* Lobi-Dagarti Peoples

Logoli. *See* Luyia

Lokko (Landogo) A people of the Bombali District, in Sierra Leone, who number about 76,000, with a few also in Guinea.

Lomwe (Ngulu, Mihavane, Nguru, Lolo) An agricultural people most of whom (about 40,000) live in Tanzania, with about another 19,000 in southern Malawi.

Longarim (Boya, Larim) A people who live in southern Sudan and number about 6,000.

Lotilla Murle An agricultural people of eastern Sudan.

Lovalle (Luena, Chiluvale) A people of Angola, Zaire, and Zambia, who are related to the Lwena and number about 600,000.

Lower Zambezi A cluster of peoples of the lower Zambezi Valley area and coastal Mozambique, at the mouth of the Zambezi River.

Lwena (Lovale, Lubale) A people of Angola, Zaire, and Zambia, numbering about 600,000.

Maba An agricultural Muslim people of eastern Chad who number about 200,000, with some others also in Sudan.

Maconde A sedentary farming people numbering about 840,000 in Tanzania, with others also in Mozambique.

Macua-Lomue (Alomwe, Lolo, Mato, Mihavane, Ngulu) A cluster of people combining two subgroups, the Lomue (with 1 million in Mozambique and 480,000 in Malawi) and the Macua (with 1,200,000 in Mozambique and 308,000 in Tanzania).

Mada A Hausa people of central Nigeria.

Madi (Ma'diti) A primarily agricultural people of the West Nile District of Uganda, numbering about 215,000. There are also about 18,000 in Sudan.

Madingo (Mandinka) A Muslim people found in Senegal (about 402,000), Gambia (about 290,000), and Sierra Leone (about 75,000).

Mahi (Maxi-Gbe) A group numbering about 20,700 in Togo, with a few also in northern Benin.

Makonde (Chimakonde, Konde, Matambwe) A largely Muslim people of the southeastern part of mainland Tanzania, numbering about 835,000.

Makua (Kimakua, Mato) A people found in Mozambique (about 1,200,000) and Tanzania (308,000).

Malinke A primarily Muslim people of Upper Guinea, who belong to the Manding Cluster.

Mama (Kantana, Kwarra) The name for a cluster of four subgroups—the Arum, Barrku, Burruza and Upie—who live in central Nigeria and number together about 20,000.

Mambila (Bang, Mambere, Nor Tagrbo) A group of people numbering about 60,000, who live in southeastern Nigeria.

Mancagne (Bola, Brame) A people numbering about 25,000 in Guinea-Bissau and about 15,000 in Senegal.

Mandara (Montagnard, Ndara, Wandala) An agricultural, Muslim people of northern Cameroon, numbering about 23,500. There are also about 19,300 in Nigeria.

Mandari (Shir, Kir) A people of southern Sudan, related to the Beri. They number about 36,000.

Mande-Speaking Peoples A cluster of Mande-speaking agricultural people of West Africa that includes the Bambara, Dyula, Malinke, Mende, and Soninké.

Manding (Mandingo, Malinke) An agricultural people who are distributed among the West African countries of Senegal (about 402,000), Gambia (about 290,000), and Sierra Leone (about 767,000).

Mandingo (Manya, Manya Kan) An indigenous Muslim people of Liberia numbering about 38,000.

Mandinka-Mory (Mande) A Malinke subgroup centered in the Kankan area of Guinea, numbering about 1,525,000. There are also about 96,000 in Guinea-Bissau and 30,000 in Liberia.

Mandjaque (Kanyop, Ndyak) A people numbering about 119,000 in Guinea-Bissau and 44,200 in Senegal.

Manga A people of northeastern Nigeria, who number about 180.

Marachi. *See* Luyia

Marakwet. *See* Nandi and Other Kalenjin Peoples

Marama. *See* Luyia

Maravi A grouping of peoples found largely in Malawi and Zambia and in smaller numbers in Mozambique, that combines Chewa, Nyanja, and Nsenga.

Masalit (Kaana Masala) Sedentary agriculturists, who live on the border of Sudan and Chad and number about 200,000.

Mashi A small group that lives in southeastern Angola, Zambia, and Namibia.

Massa (Banana, Walia) A farming and fishing people, numbering about 103,000 in Cameroon and 80,000 in Chad.

Matakam (Mafa, Mofa) A people of the Mandara Hills of Cameroon, numbering about 136,000. There are another 2,000 or so in Nigeria.

Matengo (Chimatengo) A people of southwestern Tanzania, numbering about 150,000.

Matumbi (Kimatumbi) A people who live on the Tanzania-Mozambique border; they number about 72,000.

Maures (Hassaniya, Moors, Sulaka) A Muslim people of Arab-Berber descent, most of whom live in Mauritania, others in Niger, Senegal, and Mali, with a combined population of 1,300,000 to 2,300,000. They are traditionally agriculturists, but the urban Maures of Senegal are largely engaged in various trades.

Mawia (Mabiha, Chimaviha) A people of Tanzania and Mozambique, who number about 70,000.

Mbanja A Banda-speaking group of northern Zaire.

Mbato A small group that lives along the coast of Ivory Coast.

Mbembe (Ekokoma, Okam, Wakande) A cluster of peoples numbering about 100,000, who live in southeastern Nigeria.

M'Bororo. *See* Teda

Mboshi (Boubangui) The name for a group of people in Congo that includes the Bngala, Bonga, Kouyou, Likoala, Makoua, and Mboshi. Primarily fishers and traders, they also engage in farming. They number about 169,400.

Mboum (Mboumtiba, Nzak Mbay, Wuna) A people of the northern savanna of Cameroon, they are farmers and fishers and number about 38,600.

Mbui A people of Angola, related to the Ovimbundu.

Mbundu (Benguella, Lunda, Ovimbundu) A farming people of southern Angola, numbering about 3,002,000.

Meidob (Tiddi) A pastoralist Muslim people who live in the Meidob Hills of western Sudan, they number about 45,000.

Mekyibo (Eotile, Vetere) A people of Ivory Coast, numbering about 2,000, who are predominantly fishers.

Mening A very small group that lives on the Sudan-Uganda border.

Meru (Kirwo, Rwo) A people who live along the northeastern border of Tanzania; they number about 90,000.

Mesticos A largely urban, mixed-race people of western Angola.

Metoko A people who live in the plains, highlands, and forests west of the Lualaba River, in eastern Zaire.

Mikhifore A small group in Guinea, linguistically related to the Malinke in Upper Guinea.

Mima-Mimi A group of Muslim peoples, composed of the Mima and the Mimi, who live in Chad and Sudan and number about 50,000. The Mimi are largely sedentary agriculturists, whereas the Mima are pastoralists.

Mmani (Mandenyi) A farming people, who live between the Kolente and Forecariah rivers in Guinea.

Mofou (Douvangar) A people of the hills of northern Diamare, in Cameroon, they number about 27,500.

Mole-Dagbane A collection of groups of Gur speakers of northern Ghana, numbering about 400,000.

Moundang (Kaele, Marhay, Musembani, Nda) A people who live in Cameroon, near the Chad border, and number about 100,000.

Mourdia. *See* Teda

Mousgoum (Mulwi, Munjuk, Musuk) A fishing and farming people of northeastern Cameroon and Chad, numbering about 61,500.

Murle (Ajibba, Beir, Boma-Murle, Merule) Seminomadic pastoralists, who originated in southern Ethiopia. Some 6,000 still live in Ethiopia, but the majority—about 60,000—are now located in Sudan.

Mursi (Merdu, Meritu) A farming and fishing people of the lower Omo Valley in Ethiopia, they number about 5,000.

Mvuba A very small group that lives among the Amba, in Uganda.

Mwera (Chimwera, Mwela) A people of southeastern Tanzania, numbering about 345,000.

Nagot (Ede Nago) A people of central and southeastern Benin.

Nalou (Nalu) A people who live near the lower Rio Nunez, Kogan Rover, and Tristão Islands in Guinea and in Guinea-Bissau, they are cultivators and artisans, with a total population of about 10,000.

Nangia-Napore An agricultural and trading people who live in the Nyangea and Rom mountains of Uganda.

Nara (Barea) A Muslim, agriculturalist people of Ethiopia, numbering about 25,000.

Ndali A people of Tanzania, numbering about 150,000.

Ndengereko (Kingengereko) A people of Tanzania, numbering about 110,000.

Nderobo A cattle-herding people of Kenya.

Ngabaka (Gbaya, Limba, Ma'ba, Minangende) A people of northern Zaire (about 761,000), and Central African Republic and Congo (about 3,000).

Ngbandi (Baza, Mbati, Mongwandi, Ngwandi) A people of northern Zaire, who number about 210,000.

Ngoni (Angoni, Kingoni, Kisutu) A cattle-raising people who live in Tanzania and Malawi, numbering about 170,000 in Tanzania.

Ngoni Cluster A name for several relatively small groups in Mozambique with a common origin among Nguni speakers of South Africa.

Nguu (Kingulu, Ngulu) A people of Tanzania, numbering about 132,000.

Nharo. *See* San-Speaking Peoples

Njembe One of the Kuba Cluster peoples, who live in the lower Kasai River region of Zaire.

Nkore (Hima, Iru, Nyankore, Nykole) A group of cultivators and pastoralists, who live in the Western Province of Uganda and number about 1,500,000.

Noarma. *See* Teda

North Mbukushu A small group living in southeastern Angola, Zambia, and Namibia.

Nuba An agricultural people of the Nuba Hills of western Sudan.

Nubi A small group of Arabic-speaking Muslims of Sudanese descent, who live among the Kisii people of Kenya.

Nupe (Nufawa, Nupenchi) A largely Muslim cluster of peoples of western Nigeria, they number about 1 million.

Nyakwai (Akwa, Jo Akwa) A small pastoralist group in Uganda, who are culturally similar to the Karamojong.

Nyamwezi An agricultural people of central Tanzania, who number about 904,000.

Nyaneka A people of southwestern Angola, numbering about 40,000.

Nyangatom A primarily pastoralist group of the lower Omo Valley of Ethiopia, who belong to the Kariamojong Cluster. They number about 5,000.

Nyanja (Chinyanja) A cluster of Bantu-speaking peoples, who live in Malawi, Zambia, and Zimbabwe, with a total population of about 2,500,000. They are known as Chewa in Malawi.

Nyaruanda (Banyaruanda, Hutu, Tutsi) This name includes both indigenous people of Bufumbira County, in Uganda, as well as a larger number of people who have emigrated from Rwanda since 1959.

Nyasa (Kimanda, Kinyasa, Manda) A people of the northeastern shore of Lake Malawi and western Ruvuma Province, in Tanzania, numbering about 18,000.

Nyiha (Shinyiha, Nyixa) A people numbering about 306,000 in Tanzania, with a few also in Zambia.

Nyika. *See* Mijikenda

Nyoro (Lunyole, Nyoole, Nyuli) A primarily agricultural people of Uganda, numbering about 205,800.

Nyuli (Lunyole, Olunyole, Nyole, Nyore) An agricultural Bantu group, numbering about 206,000 in Uganda and 120,000 in Kenya.

Nzima An Akan people with a population of about 210,000 in Ghana and 31,700 in Ivory Coast. They make their living as fishers, farmers, and traders.

Omo-Murle A farming and fishing people of the lower Omo Valley in Ethiopia.

Oromo (Arusi-Guji, Borana, Galla) A primarily Muslim group of pastoral and sedentary agriculturists numbering about 4,850,000, most of whom live in Ethiopia and Kenya. The name "Galla" is considered pejorative.

Oron (Oro) A people who live in southeastern Nigeria and number about 49,000.

Oropom (Oropoi) A people who originally lived near Mount Moroto in Uganda and are now scattered among the Ik, Karamojong, and Tesio groups.

Orri (Koring, Orringorrin) A people of Benue State, in southern Nigeria, they number about 25,000.

Ouassoulounke (Wasulunka) A people who live on both sides of the Guinea-Mali border, who are culturally related to the Malinke.

Ouled Sliman A pastoralist group of Arab descent that lives in Chad.

Ounia. *See* Teda

Ouobe (Wobe) One of the Krou Complex peoples of Ivory Coast, they number about 150,000.

Ovambo (Ambo, Humba, Kwanyama) A farming and cattle-raising people of Angola and Namibia, with a total population of about 240,000.

Ovimbundu (Mbundu) A people of the highlands of Angola. Originally farmers, many now work on coffee plantations and in industrial plants.

Padhola (Adhola, Dhopadhola) A cattle-raising people of Uganda, who number about 234,000.

Pahouin A people of the southern forests of Cameroon.

Paluo A cattle-raising people of Uganda.

Pila-Pila (Kpilakpila, Yom) A people of northern Benin, numbering about 50,000.

Pogoro (Chipolgolo, Pogolu) A people of Tanzania, numbering about 185,000.

Pondo A group of people in Transkei, South Africa, who are related to the Xhosa.

Rangi (Langi, Irangi, Kelangi) A people of Tanzania, who number about 275,000.

Rendille A cattle-herding people of the Marsabit District of Kenya, numbering about 22,000.

Reshawa (Gungawa, Reshe) A group that lives on the banks and islands of the Niger River in Nigeria. They are fishers and farmers and number about 30,000.

Rundi A people who number about 4,600,000 in Burundi, 294,000 in Uganda, and 106,000 in Tanzania.

Sabaot. *See* Nandi and Other Kalenjin Peoples

Sadama (Sidamo) An agricultural people of Ethiopia.

Safwa (Guruku, Mbila, Songwe) A people of Tanzania, numbering about 158,000.

Saho (Shiho, Shoho) A linguistic rather than an ethnic category, composed of Afar, Tigray, Tigre speakers, Arabs, and others. They are largely Muslim and pastoralist peoples, who live in southern Eritrea and number about 120,000.

Samburu (Burkeneji, Lokop, Nytuk, Sampur) A pastoralist people, who live in Kenya and number about 81,200.

Samia. *See* Luyia

Sangha A people of the forest region of northeastern Congo.

Sango A people of the Central African Republic numbering about 200,000, including some in Zaire, Chad, and Cameroon.

Sayawa (Seiyara, Seya) A group numbering about 50,000, who live in northeastern Nigeria.

Sebei (Sapei) An agricultural people who live on the northern slopes of Mount Elgon in Uganda.

Sena (Chisena) A name referring to several groups of people that live in the border area between Malawi and Mozambique and number about 200,000.

Senoufo A farming people of north-central Ivory Coast, numbering about 614,000.

Serer (Seex, Sine-Saloum, Sine-Sine) A sedentary farming people of Senegal numbering about 420,000, with a few also in Gambia.

Shanbaa (Kishambala, Sambara) A people of Tanzania, numbering about 485,000.

Shangawa (Kyenga, Shonga) A people who live in and around the Nigerian city of Shanga. They are farmers, fishers, and traders and number about 10,000.

Shashi (Sizaki, Sasi) A Tanzanian people numbering about 82,000.

Sherbro (Mampa, Shiba, Southern Bullom) A people who live along the Atlantic coast of Sierra Leone, numbering about 175,000.

Shirazi A name for a cluster of three subgroups—the Hadimu, Tumbatu, and Pemba—that live in Tanzania. The Shirazi are a mixture of Africans and people said to have originated in the Shīrāz area of Iran.

Sinyar (Shamya) A Muslim agricultural people living on the border of Chad and Sudan, who number between 5,000 and 10,000.

Soga (Lugosa, Lukenyi) A people of southern Uganda who are primarily agriculturists, although some also raise cattle. They number about 1,200,000.

Somba A people of northern Benin.

Soninké (Marka, Sarakole, Toubakai, Wakore) A sedentary farming people of West Africa, with about 600,000 in Mali, 200,000 in Burkina Faso and Ivory Coast, 130,000 in Senegal, 10,000 in Gambia, 30,000 in Mauritania, and 2,000 in Guinea-Bissau.

Sotho A large group of Bantu-speaking peoples of South Africa, who number about 5,307,000.

South Mbukushu A very small group who live in Angola, Namibia, and Botswana.

Sundi. *See* Kongo.

Sura (Mwaghavul, Mupun) A people of Plateau State, in central Nigeria, who number about 40,000.

Susu (Soussou) A group of cultivators, traders, and fishers, with a population of about 610,000 in Guinea, 96,000 in Sierra Leone, and 2,000 in Guinea-Bissau.

Suto (Sesotho) A people of southern Africa, primarily in Lesotho, with a total population of about 2,960,000.

Tachoni. *See* Luyia

Tama-Speaking Peoples A cluster of seven groups—the Abu Sharib, Asungor, Erenga, Gimr, Mararit, Mileri, and Tama—that live along the Chad-Sudan border. They are primarily agriculturists and together number about 104,600.

Tanaka A people of northern Benin.

Tangale A people of Bauchi State, in northeastern Nigeria, who number about 100,000.

Taturu (Datog, Mangati, Tatoga) A people of Tanzania who number about 104,000.

Teda-Tou. *See* Teda

Teguessie. *See* Lobi-Dagarti Peoples

Teke (Ibali, Iteghe, Kiteke, Ngungwel) Sedentary farmers of the plateau region north of Brazzaville, in Congo.

Tenik. *See* Nandi and Other Kalenjin Peoples

Tepeth (Tepes) A mountain people of the Karamojong territory of Uganda, who number about 5,000.

Tera A people of Bauchi State, in northeastern Nigeria, who number about 46,000.

Teso (Ateso, Bakedi, Wamia) A cluster of peoples largely dependent on cotton cultivation, who live in Uganda (about 1,221,000) and Kenya (about 133,000).

Teuso A people who live in the northeastern corner of Uganda and make their living through agriculture, hunting, and gathering.

Tikar A people of the western highlands of Cameroon, numbering about 20,000.

Timbaro An agricultural people of Ethiopia.

Tio A cluster of people who live in the region of the lower Kasai River in Zaire.

Tiriki. *See* Luyia

Tocouleur (Halpularen, Tukolor) A Muslim, sedentary farming people of West Africa, with about 603,000 in Senegal, 150,000 in Mauritania, and 50,000 in Gambia and others in Guinea, Mali, Burkina Faso, and Nigeria.

Toposa (Abo, Akeroa, Huma, Kare) A seminomadic people who live in Sudan (about 95,000) and in Ethiopia (about 10,000).

Toro A sedentary agricultural group that lives in Uganda.

Toubou. *See* Teda

Toubouri A group of farmers and fishers in northeastern Cameroon.

Tsonga (Gwamba) A major ethnic cluster found in Mozambique (1,500,000) and South Africa (2,496,000).

Tugen. *See* Nandi and Other Kalenjin Peoples

Tuku (Batuku) A pastoralist people who live in the lowlands south of Lake Albert Nyanza (also known as Lake Mobutu Sese Seko), in Uganda.

Tumbuka (Tombucas, Tew) A cluster of several peoples, including the Henga and Kamanga, who raise cattle in Malawi and Zambia and have a total population of about 1,500,000.

Tunjur An agricultural Muslim people who live in Chad and Sudan and number about 10,000.

Tutsi A pastoralist people of Burundi and Rwanda, where they are a minority ethnic group.

Twa A hunter-gatherer people of Benin, they are a subgroup of the Twide pygmies.

Uduk (Burun, Korara, Kwanim Pa, Othan) A group that lives in the mountains along the Sudan-Ethiopia border, they number about 11,000.

Urhobo (Biotu, Sobo) A people of Bendel State, in southeastern Nigeria, who number about 340,000.

Vai (Gallinas) A people related to the Kono, who live in northern Liberia and Sierra Leone, numbering about 75,000 and 13,000, respectively.

Venda A people of the South African Transvaal (about 513,000) and Zimbabwe (37,800).

Vere (Were) A people who live in eastern Nigeria (about 16,000) and in Cameroon (about 6,000).

Vonoma A very small group that lives among the Amba people of Uganda.

Waja (Wagga, Wuya) A people who live in Bauchi State, in northeastern Nigeria, and number about 30,000.

Wala. *See* Lobi-Dagarti Peoples

Wanga. *See* Luyia

Wanji (Kivwanji) A group numbering about 60,000 that lives in Tanzania.

Warjawa (Warji, Sar) A people who live in Bauchi State, in northeastern Nigeria, and number about 70,000.

Widekum A people of the western highlands of Cameroon.

Wolayta (Borodda, Ometo, Ualamo, Uba, Welamo) One of many groups of Omotic-language speakers of southern Ethiopia, they are sedentary farmers and number about 2 million.

Wurkum (Piya) A people of Gongola State, in eastern Nigeria, who number about 2,500.

Yakoma A people of the Central African Republic, who live along the Ubangi River.

Yans-Mbun (Yanzi, Kiyanzi) A cluster of peoples who live in the area of the lower Kasai River, in Zaire.

Yao (Achawa, Ayo, Djao, Veiao) A largely Muslim people of Malawi, Tanzania, and Mozambique, with a combined population of about 1,200,000.

Yergam (Tarok, Appa) A people numbering about 140,000, who live in central Nigeria.

Yombe (Mayombe, Kiyombe) A people of Angola, Congo, and Zaire.

Yungur (Binna, Ebuna) A people who live in eastern Nigeria and number about 45,000.

Zigua (Zigula, Zegua) A Muslim people of Tanzania, numbering about 340,000.

Bibliography

Bender, M. Lionel, ed. (1981). *Peoples and Cultures of the Ethio-Sudan Borderlands.* East Lansing: Michigan State University, African Studies Center.

Countries of the World on CD–ROM. (1991). Parsippany, N.J.: Bureau Development.

Grimes, Barbara F., ed. (1988). *Ethnologue: Languages of the World.* Dallas: Summer Institute of Linguistics.

Langlands, B. W. (1975). *Notes on the Geography of Ethnicity in Uganda.* Kampala: Makerere University, Department of Geography.

Murdock, George P. (1959). *Africa: Its Peoples and Their Culture History.* New York: McGraw-Hill.

Oliver, Roland, and Michael Crowder, eds. (1981). *The Cambridge Encyclopedia of Africa.* Cambridge: Cambridge University Press.

Shack, William A. (1974). *The Central Ethiopians: Amhara, Tigriña, and Related Peoples.* London: International African Institute.

Weekes, Richard W., ed. (1984). *Muslim Peoples: A World Ethnographic Survey.* 2nd ed. Westport, Conn.: Greenwood Press.

Wente-Lukas, Renate (1985). *Handbook of Ethnic Units in Nigeria.* Stuttgart: Franz Steiner Verlag Wiesbaden.

Ethnonym Index to Appendix

Glossary

affine A relative by marriage.

age grade A social category composed of persons who fall within a culturally defined age range.

agnatic descent. *See* patrilineal descent

ambilineal descent The practice of tracing kinship affiliation through either the male or the female line.

animal husbandry. *See* pastoralism

animism A type of religious belief in which the world is made to move and becomes alive because of spiritual (soul) forces in beings and things.

autochthones The indigenous inhabitants of a region. Often used to refer to the native inhabitants encountered by European explorers or settlers.

avunculocal residence The practice of a newly married couple residing in the community or household of the husband's mother's brother.

bilateral descent The practice of tracing kinship affiliation more or less equally through both the male and the female line.

bride-price The practice of a groom or his kin giving substantial property or wealth to the bride's kin before, at the time of, or after marriage.

bride-service The practice of a groom performing work for his wife's kin for a set period of time either before or after marriage.

bride-wealth. *See* bride-price

cassava A plant of the genus *Manihot* (also known as manihot, manioc, tapioca, and yuca), cultivated for its nutritious starchy roots.

clan A unilineal descent group in which people claim descent from a common ancestor but cannot demonstrate this descent.

cognates Words that belong to different languages but have similar sounds and meanings.

collaterals A person's relatives, not related to him or her as ascendants or descendants; one's uncle, aunt, cousin, brother, sister, nephew, niece.

consanguine A relative by descent from a common ancestor.

cousin, cross Children of one's parent's siblings of the opposite sex—one's father's sisters' and mother's brothers' children.

cousin, parallel Children of one's parent's siblings of the same sex—one's father's brothers' and mother's sisters' children.

cross cousin. *See* cousin, cross

cult The beliefs, ideas, and activities associated with the worship of a supernatural force or its representations, such as an ancestor cult or a bear cult.

double descent Kinship affiliation by both matrilineal and patrilineal descent.

dowry The practice of a bride's kin giving substantial property or wealth to the groom or to his kin before or at the time of marriage.

Ego In kinship studies, a male or female whom the anthropologist arbitrarily designates as the reference point for a particular kinship diagram or discussion of kinship terminology.

endogamy Marriage within a specific group or social category of which the person is a member, such as one's caste or community.

exogamy Marriage outside a specific group or social category of which the person is a member, such as one's clan or community.

fictive kinship A social relationship, such as blood brotherhood or godparenthood, between individuals who are neither affines nor consanguines but who are referred to or addressed with kin terms and treated as kin.

horticulture Plant cultivation carried out by relatively simple means, usually without permanent fields, artificial fertilizers, or plowing.

initiation rites Ceremonies and related activities that mark the transition from childhood to adulthood or from secular status to being a cult member.

kindred The bilateral kin group of near kin who may be expected to be present and participant on important ceremonial occasions, usually in the absence of unilineal descent.

kinship Family relationship, whether traced through marital ties or through "blood" descent.

kin terms, bifurcate-collateral A system of kinship terminology in which all collaterals in the parental generation are referred to by different kin terms.

kin terms, bifurcate-merging A system of kinship terminology in which members of the two descent groups in the parental generation are referred to by different kin terms.

kin terms, classificatory Kinship terms such as "aunt" that designate several categories of distinct relatives, such as mother's sister and father's sister.

kin terms, Crow A system of kinship terminology in which matrilateral cross cousins are distinguished from each other and and from parallel cousins and siblings, but patrilateral cross cousins are referred to by the same terms used for father or father's sister.

kin terms, descriptive Kinship terms that are used to distinguish different categories of relatives, such as "mother" or "father."

kin terms, Dravidian. *See* kin terms, Iroquois

kin terms, Eskimo A system of kinship terminology in which cousins are distinguished from brothers and sisters, but no distinction is made between cross and parallel cousins.

kin terms, generational A system of kinship terminology in which all kin of the same sex in the parental generation are referred to by the same term.

kin terms, Hawaiian A system of kinship terminology in which all male cousins are referred to by the same term used for "brother," and all female cousins are referred to by the same term used for "sister."

kin terms, Iroquois A system of kinship terminology in which parallel cousins are referred to by the same terms used for brothers and sisters, but cross cousins are identified by different terms.

kin terms, lineal A system of kinship terminology in which direct descendants or ascendants are distinguished from collateral kin.

kin terms, Omaha A system of kinship terminology in which female matrilateral cross cousins are referred to by the same term used for one's mother, and female patrilateral cross cousins are referred to by the same term used for one's sister's daughter.

kin terms, Sudanese A system of kinship terminology in which there are distinct terms for each category of cousin and sibling, and for aunts, uncles, nieces, and nephews.

levirate The practice of requiring a man to marry his brother's widow.

lineage A unilineal descent group in which all members can reckon their descent from a common ancestor either through males (patrilineage) or females (matrilineage).

magic Beliefs and ritual practices designed to harness supernatural forces to achieve the goals of the magician.

matrilineal descent The practice of tracing kinship affiliation only through the female line.

matrilocal residence The practice of a newly married couple residing with the wife's kin.

messianic movement A form of social movement in which adherents believe that a particular individual—a messiah—will lead them to a more prosperous and better life.

moiety A form of social organization in which an entire cultural group is made up of two social groups. Each moiety is often composed of a number of interrelated clans, sibs, or phratries.

monogamy Marriage between one man and one woman at a time.

neolocal residence The practice of a newly married couple living apart from the immediate kin of either party.

pacification The cessation of warfare by indigenous peoples enforced by colonial nations or their agents.

parallel cousin. *See* cousin, parallel

pastoralism A type of subsistence economy based on the herding of domesticated grazing animals, such as sheep or cattle.

patrilineal descent The practice of tracing kinship affiliation only through the male line.

patrilocal residence The practice of a newly married couple residing with the husband's kin.

peasants/peasantry Small-scale agriculturists producing only subsistence crops, perhaps in combination with some fishing, animal husbandry, or hunting. They live in villages in a larger state but participate little in the state's commerce or cultural activities. Today many peasants rely on mechanized farming and are involved in the national economy and are called "postpeasants" by anthropologists.

pidgin A second language, very often composed of words and grammatical features from several languages and used as the medium of communication between speakers of different languages.

polyandry The marriage of one woman to more than one man at a time.

polygyny The marriage of one man to more than one woman at a time.

puberty rites. *See* initiation rites

shaman A religious practitioner who receives his or her power directly from supernatural forces.

shifting cultivation A form of horticulture in which plots of land are cleared and planted for a few years and then left to fallow for a number of years while other plots are used. Also called swidden, extensive, or slash-and-burn cultivation.

sib. *See* clan

sister exchange A form of arranged marriage in which two men exchange their sisters as wives.

slash-and-burn cultivation A system of food production that involves burning trees and brush to clear and fertilize a garden plot, and then planting crops. The plot is used for a few years and then left to fallow while other plots are similarly used.

sorcery Magic practiced for evil and antisocial ends.

sororal polygyny The marriage of one man to two or more sisters at the same time.

sororate The practice of marrying one's sister's widower.

swidden The field or garden plot resulting from slash-and-burn field preparation.

teknonymy The practice of addressing a person after the name of his wife or his or her child rather than by the individual name. For example, "Bill" is called "Father of John."

transhumance Seasonal movement of a society or community. It may involve seasonal shifts in food production between hunting and gathering and horticulture or the movement of herds to more favorable locations.

tribe Although there is some variation in use, the term "tribe" usually applies to a distinct people who view themselves and are recognized by outsiders as a distinct culture. The tribal society has its own name, territory, customs, subsistence activities, and often its own language.

unilineal descent The practice of tracing kinship affiliation through only one line, either the matriline or the patriline.

unilocal residence The general term for matrilocal, patrilocal, or avunculocal postmarital residence.

usufruct The right to use land or property without actually owning it.

uterine descent. *See* matrilineal descent

uxorilocal residence The practice of a newly married couple living at or near the former residence of the wife.

virilocal residence The practice of a newly married couple living at or near the former residence of the husband.

wattle-and-daub A method of house construction whereby a framework (wattle) of poles and twigs is covered (daubed) with mud and plaster.

witchcraft The use of innate supernatural forces to control or harm another person. Unlike sorcery, witchcraft does not require the use of magical rituals.

Filmography

The following is a list of films and videos on African and Middle Eastern nations and cultures. The list is not meant to be complete; rather, it is a sampling of documentary films available from distributors in North America. Listing a film or video does not constitute an endorsement by the volume editors or any of the contributors, nor does the absence of a film represent any sort of nonendorsement. Abbreviations for names of distributors are provided at the end of each citation and full distributor names are provided in the distributor list following the index to the filmography. Some of the films and videos listed here are also available through the Extension Media Center of the University of California at Berkeley (2176 Shattuck Ave., Berkeley, CA 94704) and/or the Penn State Audio-Visual Services (Special Services Building, Pennsylvania State University, University Park, PA 16802), as indicated by (EMC) or (PS) at the end of the citation.

1. *A Luta Continua (The Struggle Continues)*. (Mozambique) 1971. Directed by Robert Van Lierop. Color, 36 minutes, 16mm. (PS).
2. *Africa Calls: Its Drums and Musical Instruments*. (Africa) 1971. Produced by WCAU. Color, 23 minutes, 16mm. CAROUF (PS).
3. *African Art and Culture*. (Africa) 1971. Produced by WCAU. Color, 21 minutes, 16mm. CAROUF (PS).
4. *African Carving: A Dogon Kanaga Mask*. (Dogon) 1974. Produced by the Film Study Center of Harvard University, E. Elisofon and T.D. Blakely. Color, 17 minutes, 16mm. PHENIX (PS).
5. *African Community: The Masai*. (Maasai) 1969. Color, 16 minutes, 16mm. BFA (EMC).
6. *African Drought!: Changing Nomadic Cultures*. (Niger) 1974. Color, 26 minutes, 16mm. XEROX (EMC).
7. *African Religions and Ritual Dances*. (Yoruba) 1971. Produced by WCAU. Color, 19 minutes, 16mm. CAROUF (PS).
8. *African Soul: Music, Past and Present*. (Africa) 1971. Produced by WCAU. Color, 17 minutes, 16mm. CAROUF (PS).
9. *The Africans: 1—The Nature of a Continent*. (Africa) 1986. Writer/host: Ali A. Mazrui. Produced by WETA, Washington, and the BBC. An Annenberg/CPB project. Color, 60 minutes, VHS. FI (PS).
10. *The Africans: 2—A Legacy of Lifestyles*. (Africa) 1986. Writer/host: Ali A. Mazrui. Produced by WETA, Washington, and the BBC. An Annenberg/CPB project. Color, 60 minutes, VHS. FI (PS).
11. *The Africans: 3—New Gods*. (Africa; Christianity, Islam) 1986. Writer/host: Ali A. Mazrui. Produced by WETA, Washington, and the BBC. An Annenberg/CPB project. Color, 60 minutes, VHS. FI (PS).
12. *The Africans: 4—Tools of Exploitation*. (Africa) 1986. Writer/host: Ali A. Mazrui. Produced by WETA, Washington, and the BBC. An Annenberg/CPB project. Color, 60 minutes, VHS. FI (PS).
13. *The Africans: 5—New Conflicts*. (Africa; Islam) 1986. Writer/host: Ali A. Mazrui. Produced by WETA, Washington, and the BBC. An Annenberg/CPB project. Color, 60 minutes, VHS. FI (PS).
14. *The Africans: 6—In Search of Stability*. (Africa) 1986. Writer/host: Ali A. Mazrui. Produced by WETA, Washington, and the BBC. An Annenberg/CPB project. Color, 60 minutes, VHS. FI (PS).
15. *The Africans: 7—A Garden of Eden in Decay*. (Africa) 1986. Writer/host: Ali A. Mazrui. Produced by WETA, Washington, and the BBC. An Annenberg/CPB project. Color, 60 minutes, VHS. FI (PS).
16. *The Africans: 8—A Clash of Cultures*. (Africa) 1986. Writer/host: Ali A. Mazrui. Produced by WETA, Washington, and the BBC. An Annenberg/CPB project. Color, 60 minutes, VHS. FI (PS).
17. *The Africans: 9—Global Africa*. (Africa) 1986. Writer/host: Ali A. Mazrui. Produced by WETA, Washington, and the BBC. An Annenberg/CPB project. Color, 60 minutes, VHS. FI (PS).
18. *The Afrikaner Experience: Politics of Exclusion*. (Afrikaner) 1978. Color, 35 minutes, 16mm. LCA (PS) (EMC).
19. *Anansi the Spider. (Africa) 1969*. Produced by Gerald McDermott. Color, 10 minutes, 16mm. TEXFLM (PS).
20. *The Ancient Africans*. (Africa) 1969. Produced by Julien Bryan. Color, 29 minutes, 16mm. IFF (PS).
21. *The Ancient Egyptians*. (Egyptians) 1964. Animation by Philip Stapp. Produced by Julien Bryan. Color, 27 minutes, 16mm. IFF (PS).
22. *Annual Festival of the Dead*. (Dogon) 1967. Color, 14 minutes, 16mm. IFF (EMC).
23. *Arabs Now, The*. The Arabs: A Living History Series. (Arabs) 1987. Color, 50 minutes, VHS. LANDMK (EMC).
24. *Argument about a Marriage*. (San) 1966. Color, 19 minutes, 16mm. DER (EMC).
25. *Art of Islam*. (Islam) 1970. Color, 10 minutes, 16mm. (PS).

26. *Asante Market Women*. (Asante) 1981. Directed by Claudia Milne. Produced by Andre Singer for Granada Television. Color, 52 minutes, VHS. (PS).
27. *Bakhtiari Migration: The Sheep Must Live*. (Bakhtiari) 1973. Produced by Anthony Howard and David Koff. Color, 51 minutes, 16mm. FI (PS).
28. *Bekoidintu—Any House is Better Than Mine*. (Africa) 1979. Color, 34 minutes, U-matic. PSUPCR (PS).
29. *Between Two Worlds*. In the series: The Arabs: A Living History Series. (Arabs) 1987. Color, 50 minutes, VHS. LANDMK (EMC).
30. *Bitter Melons*. (San) 1966. Color, 30 minutes, 16mm. DER (PS) (EMC).
31. *Boran Herdsman*. (Boran) 1974. Directed by David MacDougall. Produced by the American Universities Field Staff. Color, 17 minutes, 16mm. (PS).
32. *Boran Women*. (Boran) 1974. Directed by David MacDougall. Produced by the American Universities Field Staff. Color, 18 minutes, 16mm. (PS).
33. *Building A Nation*. The Arabs: A Living History Series. (Arabs) 1987. Color, 50 minutes, VHS. LANDMK (EMC).
34. *Bushmen of the Kalahari*. (San) 1975. Produced by the National Geographic Society. Color, 50 minutes, 16mm. NGS (PS).
35. *City Victorious?* The Arabs: A Living History Series. (Arabs) 1987. Color, 50 minutes, VHS. LANDMK (EMC).
36. *Coroh (Bone)*. (Mandingo) 1986. Directed and produced by Mohammed S. Kamara. Color, 26 minutes, VHS. (PS).
37. *The Cows of Dolo Ken Paye: Resolving Conflict among the Kpelle*. (Kpelle) 1970. Directed by Marvin Silverman. Color, 32 minutes, 16mm. PHENIX (PS).
38. *Cry, Ethiopia, Cry*. (Ethiopians) 1984. Produced for PBS Frontline series. Color, 60 minutes, VHS. PUBTEL (PS).
39. *A Curing Ceremony*. (San) 1966. Directed by John Marshall. B&W, 8 minutes, 16mm. DER (PS).
40. *Dances of Southern Africa*. (South Africa) 1973. Directed and produced by Gei Zantzinger. Color, 55 minutes, 16mm, U-matic. PSUPCR (PS).
41. *Debe's Tantrum*. (San) 1966. Directed by John Marshall. Color, 9 minutes, 16mm. DER (PS).
42. *Deep Hearts*. (Fulani) 1980. Color, 53 minutes, 16mm. PHENIX (EMC).
43. *Discovering the Music of Africa*. (Africa) 1967. Color, 22 minutes, 16mm. PHENIX (PS).
44. *Discovering the Music of the Middle East*. (Middle East) 1968. Color, 21 minutes, 16mm. PHENIX (PS).
45. *Falasha: Agony of the Black Jews*. (Africa) 1983. Directed by Peter Raymont. Produced by Simcha Jacobovici and Jamie Boyd. Color, 27 minutes, 16mm. (PS).
46. *Family Matters: The Role of the Family in the Middle East*. (Family; Middle East) 1984. Color, 25 minutes, VHS. EBEC (EMC).
47. *Family Ties*. The Arabs: A Living History Series. (Arabs) 1987. Color, 50 minutes, VHS. LANDMK (EMC).
48. *Fear Woman*. (Ghana) 1971. Color, 29 minutes, 16mm. UN (EMC).
49. *The Five Pillars of Islam*. (Islam) 1983. Color, 30 minutes, VHS. (PS).
50. *Grass*. (Bakhtiari) 1925. Produced by Merian C. Cooper and Ernest B. Schoedsack for Paramount. B&W, silent, 66 minutes, 16mm. FCE (EMC).
51. *Great Tree Has Fallen*. (Asante) 1973. Color, 22 minutes, 16mm. IU (EMC).
52. *Harambee ("Pull Together")*. (Kenya) 1975. Color, 19 minutes, 16mm. FIELDF (EMC).
53. *Heritage: Civilization and the Jews, 9—Into the Future*. (Israel) 1984. Produced by WNET. Color, 58 minutes, 16mm. FI (PS).
54. *Holy Land: Judaism, Christianity, and Islam in the Middle East*. (Christianity; Islam; Judaism; Middle East) 1984. Color, 25 minutes, VHS. EBEC (EMC).
55. *Homeland: Israel and Palestine*. (Palestinians) 1984. Color, 25 minutes, VHS. EBEC (EMC).
56. *The Hunters*. (San) 1957. Produced by the Peabody Museum, Harvard University. J. Marshall and R. Gordon. Color, 73 minutes, 16mm. FI (PM).
57. *In and Out of Africa*. (Africa) 1993. Color, 59 minutes, VHS. CMIL (EMC).
58. *Islam*. (Islam) 1962. B&W, 22 minutes, 16mm. NFBC (PS).
59. *Islam*. (Islam) 1972. Produced by the Ontario Educational Communications Authority. Color, 28 minutes, 16mm. (PS).
60. *Islamic Art*. (Islam) 1983. Color, 30 minutes, VHS. (PS).
61. *The Islamic City*. (Islam) 1983. Color, 30 minutes, VHS. (PS).
62. *Islamic Knowledge*. (Islam) 1983. Color, 30 minutes, VHS. (PS).
63. *Israel*. (Israel) 1979 (rev. ed.). Animation by Philip Stapp. Color, 28 minutes, 16mm. IFF (PS).
64. *A Joking Relationship*. (San) 1966. Directed by John Marshall. B&W, 13 minutes, 16mm. DER (PS).
65. *Kenya Boran I*. (Boran) 1975. Color, 33 minutes, 16mm. FIELDF (EMC).
66. *Kenya Boran II*. (Boran) 1975. Color, 33 minutes, 16mm. FIELDF (EMC).
67. *!Kung Bushmen Hunting Equipment*. (San) 1966. Directed by John Marshall. Color, 37 minutes, 16mm. DER (PS).
68. *Liebalala (Sweetheart)*. (Lozi) 1972. B&W, 58 minutes, 16mm. CMIL (EMC).
69. *Lion Hunters*. (Niger) 1970. Color, 68 minutes, 16mm. DER (EMC).
70. *The Long Search: 5—Islam: There is No God but God*. (Islam) 1977. Produced by the BBC. Color, 52 minutes, 16mm. AMBVP (PS).
71. *The Long Search: 7—Judaism: The Chosen People*. (Judaism) 1977. Produced by the BBC. Color, 51 minutes, 16mm. AMBVP (PS).
72. *The Long Search: 10—African Religions: Zulu Zion*. (Islam) 1977. Produced by the BBC. Color, 51 minutes, 16mm. AMBVP (PS).
73. *Lorang's Way*. (Turkana) 1980. Produced by David and Judith MacDougall. Color, 70 minutes, VHS, U-matic. CMIL (EMC).
74. *Magic Rites: Chicken Sacrifice*. (Dogon) 1967. Produced by Julien Bryan. Color, 8 minutes, 16mm. IFF (PS).
75. *Magic Rites: Divination by Animal Tracks*. (Dogon) 1967. Produced by Julien Bryan. Color, 7 minutes, 16mm. IFF (PS).

76. *The Magic Tree*. (Kongo) 1971. Animation by Gerald McDermott. Color, 11 minutes, 16mm. TEXFLM (PS).
77. *Making of the Arabs, The*. The Arabs: A Living History Series. (Arabs) 1987. Color, 50 minutes, VHS. LANDMK (EMC).
78. *Mammy Water: In Search of the Water Spirits in Nigeria*. (Ibibio) 1991. Color, 59 minutes, VHS, U-matic. CMIL (EMC).
79. *Maragoli*. (Maragoli) 1978. Color, 58 minutes, 16mm. NICHOLS (EMC).
80. *Man of the Serengeti*. (Maasai) 1972. Produced by the National Geographic Society. Color, 50 minutes, 16mm. NGS (PS).
81. *The Market's Edge: Glimpses of the Hausa World*. (Hausa) 1971. Color, 28 minutes, 16mm. (PS).
82. *Masai in Tanzania*. (Maasai) 1969. Color, 13 minutes, 16mm. FI (PS).
83. *Mau Mau*. (Kenya) 1973 (edited version). Directed by Anthony Howarth and David Koff. Color 27 minutes, 16mm. FI (PS).
84. *Mbambin: A Lineage Head in Ayikpere, North Togo*. (Togo) 1973. Directed by Dr. E.A.B. van Rouveroy van Nieuwaal. B&W, 23 minutes, 16mm. SFW (PS).
85. *The Meat Flight*. (San) 1975. Directed by John Marshall. Color, 14 minutes, 16mm. DER (PS).
86. *Men Bathing*. (San) 1966. Directed by John Marshall. Color, 14 minutes, 16mm. DER (PS).
87. *Moving On: The Hunger for Land in Zimbabwe*. (Zimbabwe) 1982. Color, 52 minutes, 16mm. NEWSC (EMC).
88. *N!owa T'ama: The Melon Tossing*. (San) 1966. Directed by John Marshall. Color, 15 minutes, 16mm. DER (PS).
89. *N/um Tchai: The Ceremonial Dance of the !Kung Bushmen*. (San) 1966. Directed by John Marshall. B&W, 20 minutes, 16mm. DER (PS).
90. *Nai, the Story of a !Kung Woman*. (San) 1980. Directed by John Marshall. Color, 59 minutes, 16mm. DER (PS).
91. *Nawi*. (Jie) 1969. Directed by David and Judith MacDougall. Color, 22 minutes, 16mm. CF (PS).
92. *Ndando Yawusiwana (Song of Sadness)*. (Chopi) 1981. Directed and produced by Gei Zantzinger. Color, 18 minutes, 16mm. PSUPCR (PS).
93. *New Knowledge for Old*. The Arabs: A Living History Series. (Arabs) 1987. Color, 50 minutes, VHS. LANDMK (EMC).
94. *The 1973 Mgodo wa Mbanguzi*. (Chopi) 1974. Directed by Gei Zantzinger and Andrew Tracey. Color, 53 minutes, 16mm. PSUPCR (PS).
95. *The 1973 Mgodo wa Mkandeni*. (Chopi) 1974. Directed by Gei Zantzinger and Andrew Tracey. Color, 48 minutes, 16mm. PSUPCR (PS).
96. *The Nuer*. (Nuer) 1970. Produced by Robert Gardner and Hilary Harris for the Peabody Museum, Harvard University. Color, 74 minutes, 16mm. (PS).
97. *The Palestinian People Do Have Rights*. (Palestinians) 1979. Produced by the United Nations. Color, 53 minutes, 16mm. UN (PS) (EMC).
98. *Palestinian Portraits*. (Palestinians) 1987. Color, 22 minutes, VHS. UN (EMC).
99. *Palestinians of '83*. (Palestinians) 1983. Produced by the U.N. Color, 26 minutes, 16mm. ICARUS (EMC).
100. *Power of the Word*. The Arabs: A Living History Series. (Arabs) 1987. Color, 50 minutes, VHS. LANDMK (EMC).
101. *Pygmies of Africa*. (Forest Peoples) 1939. B&W, 20 minutes, 16mm. EBEC (PS).
102. *The Pygmies of the Ituri Forest*. (Forest Peoples) 1975. Produced by Jean-Pierre Hallet. Color, 19 minûtes, 16mm. EBEC (PS).
103. *Pygmies of the Rain Forest*. (Forest Peoples) 1975. Produced by Kevin Duffy. Color, 51 minutes, 16mm. (PS).
104. *Rise Up and Walk*. (African Christian churches) 1982. Color, 28 minutes, 16 mm, VHS, U-matic. CMIL (EMC).
105. *Rivers of Sand*. (Hamar) 1974. Color, 83 minutes, 16mm. PHENIX (EMC).
106. *Saints and Spirits*. (Islam) 1979. Color, 26 minutes, VHS. ICARUS (EMC).
107. *Saudi Arabia: Oil, Money, Politics*. (Saudi Arabia) 1982. Written and produced by Jo Franklin-Trout for Pacific Productions and the Pacific Mountain Network. Color, 59 minutes, U-matic. (PS).
108. *Saudi Arabia: The Kingdom*. (Saudi Arabia) 1982. Written and produced by Jo Franklin-Trout for Pacific Productions and the Pacific Mountain Network. Color, 59 minutes, U-matic. (PS).
109. *Saudi Arabia: The Race with Time*. (Saudi Arabia) 1982. Written and produced by Jo Franklin-Trout for Pacific Productions and the Pacific Mountain Network. Color, 59 minutes, U-matic. (PS).
110. *Sects and Violence: Fragmentation within Religions*. (Islam) 1984. Color, 25 minutes, VHS. EBEC (EMC).
111. *Shadow of the West*. The Arabs: A Living History Series. (Arabs) 1987. Color, 50 minutes, VHS. LANDMK (EMC).
112. *Sherea: Dispute Settlement at the Court of the Paramount Chief N'zara, North Togo*. (Anufo) 1975. Directed by Dr. E. A. B. van Rouveroy van Nieuwaal. B&W, 22 minutes, 16mm. (PS).
113. *Soro*. (Fulani) 1968. Color, 25 minutes, 16mm. (PS).
114. *Souls in the Sun*. (Senegal) 1982. Color, 27 minutes, 16mm.
115. *South Africa Belongs to Us*. (South Africa) 1980. Color, 57 minutes, 16mm. ICARUS (PS) (EMC).
116. *South Africa: The White Laager*. (Afrikaners; South Africa) 1978. Produced by Peter Davis for the U.N. Color, 58 minutes, 16mm. LCA (EMC).
117. *South African Essay: Part 1—Fruit of Fear*. (South Africa) 1965. Produced by NET. B&W, 60 minutes, 16mm. IU (PS).
118. *South African Essay: Part 2—One Nation, Two Nationalisms*. (South Africa) 1965. Produced by NET. B&W, 60 minutes, 16mm. IU (PS).
119. *Strange Beliefs: Sir Edward Evans-Pritchard (1902–1973)*. (Azande, Nuer) 1991. Color, 52 minutes, VHS. FLMHUM (EMC).
120. *Traditional World of Islam: Knowledge of the World*. (Islam) 1977. Color, 28 minutes, 16mm. (PS).
121. *Traditional World of Islam: Man and Nature*. (Islam) 1977. Color, 28 minutes, 16mm. (PS).
122. *Traditional World of Islam: Nomad and the City*. (Islam) 1977. Color, 28 minutes, 16mm. (PS).
123. *Traditional World of Islam: The Inner Life*. (Islam) 1977. Color, 28 minutes, 16mm. (PS).

124. *Traditional World of Islam: The Pattern of Beauty*. (Islam) 1977. Color, 28 minutes, 16mm. (PS).
125. *Traditional World of Islam: Unity*. (Islam) 1977. Color, 28 minutes, 16mm. (PS).
126. *Tribal Dances of West Africa*. (Africa) 1969. Produced by R. A. Piper. Color, 28 minutes, 16mm. (PS).
127. *Tuareg*. (Tuareg) 1974. Directed by Bruce Parsons and produced for the BBC. Color, 48 minutes, 16mm. ICARUS (PS).
128. *The Two Rivers*. (Venda) 1985. Directed by Mark Newman and produced by Edwin Wes. Color, 60 minutes, 16mm. ICARUS (PS).
129. *A Veiled Revolution*. (Egypt) 1982. Directed by Marilyn Gaunt and Produced by Elizabeth Fernea. Color, 27 minutes, 16mm. ICARUS (PS).
130. *Ways of Faith*. The Arabs: A Living History Series. (Arabs) 1987. Color, 50 minutes, VHS. LANDMK (EMC).
131. *The Wedding Camels*. (Turkana) 1976. Directed and produced by David and Judith MacDougall. Color, 7 minutes, 16mm. (PS) (EMC).
132. *Wife among Wives, A*. (Turkana) 1982. Color, 72 minutes, VHS, U-matic. CMIL (EMC).
133. *White Man's Country*. (Kenya) 1973 (edited version). Directed by Anthony Howarth and David Koff. Color, 28 minutes 16mm. FI (PS).
134. *Yemenite Dancers*. (Yemeni Jews) 1976. Color, 27 minutes, 16mm. BLOLAND (EMC).
135. *Zulu Christian Dances: Part 1—The Church of Shembe*. (Zulu) 1968. Color, 21 minutes, 16mm. (PS).
136. *Zulu Country Dances*. (Zulu) 1968. Color, 16 minutes, 16mm. (PS).

Index to Filmography

Directory of Distributors

Please consult the National Information Center for Educational Media (NICEM) or the *Educational Film and Video Locator* for current addresses.

AMBVP	Ambrose Video Publishing
BFA	BFA Educational Media
BLOLAND	Sunni Bloland
CAROUF	Carousel Films, Inc.
CF	Churchill Films
CMIL	University of California Extension Center for Media and Independent Learning
DER	Documentary Educational Resources
EBEC	Encyclopedia Brittanica Educational Corporation
EMC	University of California, Extension Media Center
FCE	Film Classic Exchange
FI	Films, Incorporated
FIELDF	Fieldstaff Films
ICARUS	FirstRun/Icarus Films
IFF	International Film Foundation
IU	Indiana University
LANDMK	Landmark Films, Inc.
LCA	Learning Corporation of America
MCI	Mass Communications, Inc.
NEWSC	California Newsreel
NFBC	National Film Board of Canada
NGS	National Geographic Society
NICHOLS	Sandra Nichols
PHENIX	Phoenix Films
PS	Pennsylvania State University
PSUPCR	Pennsylvania State University Psych Cinema Register
PUBTEL	National Public Television
SFW	Stitching Film en Wetenschap
TEXFLM	Texture Films
UN	United Nations
XEROX	Xerox Films

Ethnonym Index

This index provides some of the alternative names and the names of major subgroups for cultures covered in this volume. The culture names that are entry titles are in boldface.

The Editors

Editor in Chief
David Levinson (Ph.D., State University of New York at Buffalo) is vice president of the Human Relations Area Files, in New Haven, Connecticut. He is a cultural anthropologist whose primary research interests are in social issues, worldwide comparative research, and social theory. He has conducted research on homelessness, alcohol abuse, aggression, family relations, and ethnicity. Among his dozens of publications are the award-winning *Toward Human Culture* (with Martin J. Malone), *The Tribal Living Book* (with David Sherwood), and *Family Violence in Cross-Cultural Perspective*. Dr. Levinson also teaches anthropology at Albertus Magnus College, in New Haven, Connecticut.

Volume Editors
John Middleton (D.Phil., Oxford University) is professor emeritus of anthropology at Yale University, in New Haven, Connecticut. His areas of interest include religious studies, social and economic change, and urbanization. His field research has been among the Lugbara of Uganda (1949–1952); the Swahili of Zanzibar (1958); the Igbo of Lagos, Nigeria (1964); the Akan of Ghana (1966–1967); and the Swahili of Kenya (at various times between 1986 and 1993). He has taught social anthropology at the University of London, the University of Cape Town, Northwestern University, New York University, and the School of Oriental and African Studies (London). His publications include *Black Africa: Its People and Their Cultures Today; Lugbara Religion; Spirit Mediumship and Society in Africa* (with John Beattie); *Witchcraft and Sorcery in East Africa* (with E. H. Winter); and *The World of the Swahili: An African Mercantile Civilization*. He is at present writing a book on early Indian Ocean trade.

Amal Rassam (Ph.D., University of Michigan) is a cultural anthropologist and professor of anthropology at Queens College and the Graduate Center of the City University of New York. She has conducted research in a number of Middle Eastern communities, especially in Iraq and North Africa, with a focus on ethnicity and social and political organization. She is the author of numerous articles, including "French Colonialism as Reflected in Male-Female Interaction in Morocco" in the *Transactions of the New York Academy of Sciences* (1974) and "Ethnicity, Cultural Discontinuity, and Power Brokers in Northern Iraq: The Case of the Shabak" in *American Ethnologist* (1974). She is also the coauthor, with Daniel G. Bates, of the textbook *Peoples and Cultures of the Middle East*.

Associate Volume Editors
Candice Bradley (Ph.D., University of California, Irvine) is a cultural anthropologist and assistant professor of anthropology at Lawrence University, in Appleton, Wisconsin. She is also a senior research fellow at the Population Studies and Research Institute, University of Nairobi. Her doctoral dissertation was a cross-cultural study of children's work in ninety-seven cultures. Her recent research focuses on women, power, and fertility in Western Province, Kenya. Her publications center on these and related topics and include, most recently, the articles on demography and division of labor in the forthcoming *Encyclopedia of Cultural Anthropology*.

Laurel L. Rose (Ph.D., University of California, Berkeley) specializes in sub-Saharan African customary law—particularly land law—and local-level conflict management, which is the subject of her book *The Politics of Harmony: Land Dispute Strategies in Swaziland*. Over the past seventeen years she has done fieldwork in Germany, Swaziland, Malawi, and Somalia. She currently divides her time between teaching at Carnegie-Mellon University and consulting/researching in Africa.